ad usum
Michael P. Joyce, ...

SAINT VINCENT DE PAUL

INDEX

VOLUME XIV

SAINT
VINCENT DE PAUL

CORRESPONDENCE

CONFERENCES, DOCUMENTS

INDEX

VOLUME XIV

NEWLY TRANSLATED, EDITED, AND ANNOTATED

FROM THE 1925 EDITION

OF

PIERRE COSTE, C.M.

Edited by:
SR. MARIE POOLE, D.C. *Editor-in-Chief*
SR. ANN MARY DOUGHERTY, D.C., *Editorial Assistant*

Translated by:
SR. MARIE POOLE, D.C.

Annotated by:
REV. JOHN W. CARVEN, C.M.

NIHIL OBSTAT
Very Rev. Michael J. Carroll, C.M.
President of the National Conference of Vincentian Visitors

Published in the United States by New City Press
202 Comforter Blvd., Hyde Park, New York 12538

Cover by: Tommaso Giannotta

Printed in the United States of America

Library of Congress Cataloging-in -Publication Data:

Vincent de Paul, Saint, 1581-1660
Correspondence, Conferences, Documents.

Translation from the French of *Saint Vincent de Paul, Correspondance, entretiens, documents.*
Includes bibliographical references and index.
Contents: I. Correspondence V. 1. 1607-1639.—v. 14.
1. Vincent de Paul, Saint, 1581-1661—Correspondence
2. Christian saints—France—Correspondance. I. Coste, Pierre, 1873-1935. II. Title.
BX4700.V6A4 1985 271'.77'024[B] 83-63559
ISBN 0-911782-50-8 (v. 1)
ISBN 978-1-56548-498-6 (v. 14)

TABLE OF CONTENTS

Introduction 7

Index 9

Appendix 1: Biblical References 629

Appendix 2: Errata 644

Introduction

After more than 40 years devoted to the preparation of the English edition of the correspondence, conferences, and documents pertaining to Saint Vincent de Paul, the present volume, the cumulative Index, marks the culmination of the entire series. This collection is translated from the French and is based on the work of Pierre Coste.

To facilitate research, each entry in the alphabetical index is accompanied by a brief annotation of how it is used on the page or pages given. Place names are printed in italics, and cross references are supplied, where judged appropriate. Many variations in spelling occur.

Following the Index are two Appendixes: Biblical References and Errata.

Index

PLACE NAMES ARE IN ITALICS

A

A Rosta (Fr.) - V, 296.

Aaron, brother of Moses - Priests stand between God and His people as Aaron did, XI, 194.

Abain (Mlle d'), foundress of Visitation in Poitiers - Asked Saint-Cyran to negotiate with Paris Visitation for foundation in Poitiers, XIIIa, 122.

Abancour (M. d'), Chancellor in Saint-Quentin - Informs Saint Vincent of plots of Huguenots in that town, VIII, 457; other mention, VIII, 541.

Abandonment [**Interior state**] - Saint Vincent encourages Saint Louise to honor it in Our Lord and the saints, I, 157.

Abbas (Nicolas de Tudeschis, also known as Panormitanus) - Thoughts on vows of religion, XIIIa, 404.

Abbess - On bad terms with her nuns, I, 339; Saint Vincent asks Abbess to take back a nun, IV, 129.

Abbeville, town in Somme - Visitation nuns, VI, 163; XIIIa, 157, 189; coaches, III, 529; XIIIb, 273; other mentions, V, 82; VI, 564.

Abbeys - See ***Longchamp***, ***Saint-Césaire d'Arles***, ***Saint-Méen***, ***Sainte-Geneviève***, etc.

Abeille (Jean) - In Marseilles, V, 163; VII, 134.

Abelly [**Abeline**] (Louis), Vicar-General of Bishop of Bayonne, Pastor of Saint-Josse in Paris - Biographical data, I, 466–67; II, 3; III, 72; IV, 17; V, 56; VI, 11; VIII, 22; quotes from Saint

Vincent's writings in his biography of latter, I, *xl–xlii*; XI, *xxv*; his *Défense de la hiérarchie de l'Église,* VII, 499; VIII, 22, 58, 155; letters from Saint Vincent, II, 3, 52; mention of letter to Saint Vincent, VIII, 23; his book *De l'obéissance et soumission qui est due à N. S. P. le Pape en ce qui concerne les choses de la foi*, VI, 374; book presented to Pope, VI, 552; gives missions, I, 466–68, 470, 476; Saint Vincent expresses opinion concerning administrative difficulties, II, 4, 53; would be happy to be replaced by Abelly as Superior of Visitation nuns of Paris, III, 72; asks service of Abelly, V, 226; Abelly sends money to slave, V, 325; Pastor of Saint-Josse in Paris, III, 329; confessor of Carmelites, VIII, 496.

Aberdeen, town in Scotland - Fr. Francis White [François Le Blanc] imprisoned there, V, 368, 389; XI, 176.

Abiram, Jewish Levite in Old Testament - Rebellion against Moses, X, 349; XIIIb, 351.

Abraham, Patriarch of Old Law - Sacrifice of Isaac, III, 188; XI, 339; XII, 117–18, 196; according to Ombiasses of Madagascar, V, 525; great faith, III, 279; obedience, XI, 156; XII, 178, 196; God could raise up children of Abraham from stones, V, 216; VII, 251; VIII, 103; XI, 254; other mentions, I, 314; III, 186; IX, 105; XIIIa, 275.

Absalom, son of King David - Revolts against father, I, 314.

Absolution - Not to be given without knowledge of penitent, XIIIa, 387.

Abstinence - Difficulty in Madagascar, III, 578–579; Rule of Daughters of Charity, X, 505.

Abuses - Do not use severe measures to get rid of them if greater harm would result, II, 6–7; IV, 126–27.

Acarie (Mme), Bl. Marie de l'Incarnation, Carmelite - Biographical data, I, 192; gave account of prayer to her maid, IX, 4.

Accar (M.), administrator of residence for galley convicts in Paris - II, 218; V, 337.

Accounts - Saint Vincent recommends exact keeping of accounts, I, 519; II, 75; X, 165; suggests change of duty for one who has difficulty keeping accounts, III, 508; difficult for Missionaries to keep accounts, IV, 75; rendering accounts necessary for good order, IV, 80; refuses to render accounts to Bishops, VIII, 539; Congregation not required to provide financial accountability, XIIIa, 198.

Achmet I, son and successor of Sultan Mohammed III - I, 7.

Acqs - See ***Dax***.

Acts [Official Documents] - Saint Vincent writes to Superior in Genoa that official proceedings for Community are not undertaken in name of Procurator but in that of Superior, VII, 439.

Actions - Do one's actions well, XII, 431; with proper spirit, XII, 408; esteem and practice "little things," XII, 410; 422. See also **Purity of Intention**.

Actors - Saint Vincent proposes them as models for preachers, VI, 399; transformed actress, II, 185.

Ad Sacram, Apostolic Constitution of Alexander VII - Renews predecessor's condemnation of Jansenists' Five Propositions, VI, 132, 152, 290.

Adam, father of human race - His history according to Ombiasses of Madagascar, III, 557; sin, contrition, repentance, punishment, IX, 40; X, 2, 14, 45, 65–66, 189, 359, 373, 558; XI, 44, 202; XII, 176; disorder brought on us by his sin, XI, 97, 202; XIIIb, 398; results of his sin on us, XII, 128–29; was simple when in state of grace, XII, 143; had grace of willing and not willing, XIIIa, 171.

Adaucte (Saint) - Martyrdom, XI, 374.

Admirault (Charles), Priest of the Mission - Biographical data, IV, 469; VI, 272; VII, 75; XI, 177; Superior at Bons-Enfants, IV, 469; very ill; Procurator at Bons-Enfants, IV, 558–59; health, VI, 272, 274; VII, 75, 515, 583; in charge of ceremonies at Saint-Lazare; XI, 177, 197; XII, 237; Sub-Assistant, XI, 299, 325.

Admirault (Claude), Priest of the Mission, brother of Charles - Biographical data, III, 521; VI, 9; VII, 5; VIII, 52; in Richelieu, III, 521; named for Marseilles, VI, 99; in Agen, VI, 369; VII, 516; VIII, 52, 63; requested for Notre-Dame de Lorm, VII, 5.

Admonitions - Conferences, IX, 288–95, 295–305; 448–55; explanation of Rule on admonitions, X, 334–40, 423; XI, 304; mention of other conferences, XII, 406, 407, 423; reports to Superiors concerning faults of others: text of Rule of Daughters of Charity, X, 334, 339; of Missionaries, XII, 289–90; usefulness of these reports, IX, 16, 167–68, 253, 445; X, 266, 334–37; those who do not inform Superiors of faults of others are guilty of consequences of those faults, XI, 86; XII, 289–97; example of Visitandines, X, 266; objections that may be raised, XII, 295; limit reports to certain, specific cases; conditions required, XII, 64, 296; fault must be serious, or important by reason of consequences, X, 334, 339; XI, 93; better to say nothing if one feels jealousy or antipathy, X, 337; if fault is secret, begin by informing individual, IX, 37; how to make these reports, X, 337–40; accept reproaches humbly,

III, 339; each should be glad that Superiors know her faults, I, 555; IX, 16, 89, 91, 253–54, 453; X, 339; beautiful example of Sister, IX, 254; Saint Louise indicates to Saint Vincent shortcomings of Sisters, IX, 298, 300.

Advice for those who give admonitions: they must be given if necessary, I, 555; X, 335, 369; XI, 304; XII, 65; in the right way, X, 339; after prayer, IX, 433; without exaggeration, X, 337; in spirit of humility and charity, IV, 58; VI, 623; IX, 178, 180–81; X, 337–38; XI, 93, 95, 126; while kneeling, IX, 433; how to give admonitions, X, 354; with kindness, without passion, making excuses, I, 110; V, 63; XII, 155–56; for serious faults only, IX, 433; even Sister Servants must be admonished, IX, 451; exclude those we foresee would not profit from them, IX, 178; Sister whom another Sister asks charity of admonition should not excuse self because of youth, IX, 304; remedy for general failings, VIII, 401.

Reproofs Superior gives are of two kinds: general and particular, IX, 451; duty to admonish, VII, 606; speak as father, not as judge, XII, 296; give admonitions gradually, XI, 126; back admonition with good example, V, 583; inform Major Superiors if admonition is not accepted, X, 292; inform Community in certain cases of fault of one of its members, IV, 55; at times, take no notice that admonition will be taken badly, VI, 623; VII, 534; IX, 452; sometimes Superiors exaggerate to test people, XI, 305; how they should advise men of faults committed, IV, 56; how Saint Vincent gave admonitions: by letter, III, 501; IV, 58–59, 599; VI, 406–08; VII, 79. See also **Codoing**, **Escart**; at Repetition of Prayer, XI, *xx–xxii*; XIIIb, 301; spoke of good and bad things he noted, XII, 32; particular examples, XI, 96–97, 105, 135, 175, 181, 182, 186–88, 195, 199, 203, 271, 294–96, 296–300, 321, 325–26, 387; XII, 58, 63–65; how Saint Louise gave admonitions, X, 578, 583; Saint Vincent asks Daughters of Charity not to reprove one another any longer; example of Jesuits, IX, 234; asks Sisters who make visitations of Paris houses never to reprimand Sisters, IX, 205.

Dispositions for those who receive them: consider ourselves fortunate to receive admonition, IX, 91, 178, 208, 253–55, 288–89, 294–95, 296–97, 299–300, 448–50, 452, 454; even to ask for it, IX, 253–54, 453; even if person is Superior, VII, 610–11; better still, acknowledge, to person reproving us, fault of which he or she was unaware, IX, 178, 299–300, 453–54; misfortune of those who do not accept admonitions, IX, 293; receive admonitions in spirit of humility and charity, X, 339–40; XII, 296; without making excuses, even if accusations are false or exaggerated, IX, 289–92; XI, 304; XII, 296; benefit derived from false accusation, XI, 304–05; example of Jesus and Saint Vincent, XI, 304–05; first reaction is involuntary, XI, 305; pride keeps us from accepting reproofs, IX, 292, 293; XI, 305; faults that may be committed by those admonished, IX, 297–98; means for accepting admonitions and profiting well from them, IX, 295, 449; what to do when correction has not been well received, IX, 297; example of monk, IX, 299.

Sister Servant asks Saint Vincent to order companion to admonish her, IX, 433; letter of Sister to companion asking for same charity, IX, 254; Sister accuses self of not accepting admonition well, IX, 296; two Sisters ask pardon of one another, one for not having taken reproof well, other for not having given it properly, IX, 300; Saint Louise declares that some Sisters become angry when reminded of faults, IX, 299; example of first Christians, IX, 304; example of two Kings, IX, 305.

Admonitions given at Chapter: mention of conference, XII, 406; good sign when admonitions are given at Chapter; contentious persons never give admonitions for fear of being admonished in turn; danger of giving too many admonitions; same person should not be reproved more than twice, XI, 96; things for which admonitions should not be given, XI, 97; reprove about things good in themselves only if there has been excess, XI, 100–01; never admonish from antipathy, self-interest, or vengeance, XI, 96; practice at Saint-Lazare of admonishing at Chapter, XII, 291; how Sisters should admonish one another at Friday conference, IX, 292. See also **Admonitors**, **Correction**.

Admonitors - Admonitor of Superior General; Visitors have right to give Superiors admonitors, II, 673; duties of Superior toward admonitor and vice-versa, VII, 611; Saint Vincent complains that his admonitor does not remind him of faults, IX, 293; Fr. Dehorgny was his admonitor in 1641, IX, 37; 1642 Assembly gives him Fr. Portail as admonitor, XIIIa, 331; Saint Louise asks for admonitor, IX, 292; blames self for not yet having designated admonitor, IX, 297; Julienne Loret, named admonitor, feels unworthy of duty, XIIIb, 302; other mention, II, 636.

Adrienne, Daughter of Charity - See **Plouvier** (Adrienne).

Advent - Practices to sanctify Advent, VI, 641; mention of conferences during Advent, XII, 415, 420, 434.

Advice - See **Counsel**.

Affability [**Approachability**] - Soul of good conversation, perfection of union begun by charity, XI, 57; wins hearts, XII, 156; especially necessary for Missionaries because of functions,

XI, 57–58; XII, 156–57, 394; example of Jesus, XII, 157. See also **Gentleness** [Meekness].

Affairs (Secular) - Missionaries should not get involved in secular affairs, but concern themselves with spiritual, II, 38–39, 45, 362, 470, 493; III, 515; IV, 11.

Afflictions - See **Trials**, **Sufferings**.

Africa - XIIIa, 394. See also ***Algiers, Barbary, Bizerte, Madagascar, Morocco, Salé, Tunis.***

Agan (Jean d') - Vicar-General of Bishop of Montauban; zeal for diocesan seminary, IV, 559; VII, 505; VIII, 257; mention of letter from Saint Vincent, IV, 559; letter addressed to him for Fr. Bajoue, V, 234.

Agapyt (M.), slave in Algiers - V, 354.

Agde, town in Hérault - Unhealthful climate, VII, 282; Bishops: François **Fouquet**, Louis **Fouquet**; François Fouquet invites Daughters of Charity to Agde, V, 629; X, 533; XI, 327–28; XIIIb, 338, 342–43, 371; slave native to Agde diocese, V, 36; mention of letter to Saint Vincent from Vicar General, V, 226; Missionaries in Agde: foundation contract, V, 101; letters of Saint Vincent to Agde Missionaries, V, 166, 399; VIII, 112; see also **Durand** (Antoine); diocesan seminary, V, 136, 147; integration of parish with diocesan seminary, VI, 634; VIII, 478; François Fouquet has seminary erected, to be placed under direction of Congregation of the Mission, VIII, 114, 369; Saint Vincent judges foundation contract unclear; requests new agreement indicating union in perpetuity, VIII, 114; plan for internal seminary, V, 136; epidemics, V, 219, 226, 244, 248, 251, 374; VIII, 161; Saint Vincent withdraws Missionaries, V, 399; visit of Fr. Berthe to Agde, VI, 638; advice to Fr. Durand, named Superior of Agde house, XI, 310.

Assignments and changes: V, 190, 212, 535; VIII, 144, 212; list of Superiors, historical synopsis of house, VIII, 618; personnel: see **Brisjonc**, **du Chesne** (Jean), **du Chesne** (Pierre), **Durand** (Antoine), **Férot**, **Lebas**, **Lemerer**, **Mugnier**, **Tanguy**; other mentions, V, 170, 247; VII, 554.

Agen, town in Lot-et-Garonne - Epidemics, V, 28, 31; Bishop: see Barthélemy d'**Elbène**; plan for foundation of house for missions, IV, 50, 51; seminary before arrival of Priests of the Mission; causes of decline, II, 172, 462, 506; Dominicans of Agen, III, 386; other mentions, I, 404, 430, 487; IV, 467; VII, 354; X, 467; Missionaries from La Rose to serve in this region, II, 318; Missionaries in Agen: imminent arrival of first Priests of the Mission, III, 372; letters of Saint Vincent to Agen Missionaries, V, 607: see **Delattre**, **Fournier**, **Leclerc**,

Menestrier; endowments, IV, 539; proceedings for union of priory to seminary, IV, 539; V, 126; litigation concerning chapels whose revenue for seminary is contested, VI, 441, 472; inadequacy of revenues, III, 499; IV, 279; Bishop fails to give seminary what is necessary for subsistence, VI, 441, 562; VII, 5, 350; VIII, 17, 222–23; Saint Vincent speaks of recalling priests if Bishop is not more generous, VI, 368–69, 442, 473; refuses to authorize purchase of house adjoining seminary, VI, 613.

Number of diocesan seminarians on December 17, 1659, VIII, 222; canonical visit by Fr. Berthe, VI, 504, 613; by Fr. Dehorgny, VIII, 222; assignments and changes, lack of personnel, V, 607; "quarrels" provoked by change of Brothers, III, 522; question of placing Fr. Le Vazeux in Agen or Montauban, IV, 521; list of Superiors, historical synopsis of house, VIII, 616; personnel: see **Admirault** (Claude), **Delattre**, **Didolet**, **Dupuich** (Antoine), **Fournier** (François), **Grimal**, **Julles** [**Jullie**] (Pierre), **Leclerc** (Pierre), **Menestrier**, **Rivet** (Jacques), **Robin** (Jacques).

Agenais, former Province in France - Duchesse d'Aiguillon was also Comtesse d'Agenais, XIIIa, 335.

Agès - See **Saint-Martin d'Agès**.

Agibirabi (Mustafa), in Algiers - VIII, 532.

Agulhas - Cape at tip of South Africa; III, 542; V, 304.

Aides - Taxes levied on commodities and merchandise, III, 394; IV, 328; V, 486, 503–04; XIIIa, 261. See also **Angers**, **Melun**.

Aigle (Marquis de l') - XIIIb, 379.

Aigue - Prior, I, 229.

Aigues-Mortes, town in Gard - Saint Vincent lands there after captivity, I, 9.

Aiguillon, town in Lot-et-Garonne - Missions given here, I, 404, 412; 582; III, 125; other mentions, I, 430–31; XII, 240.

Aiguillon, duchy - VIII, 17.

Aiguillon (Marie de Vignerod, Marquise de Combalet, Duchesse d') - Biographical data, I, 321; II, 8; III, 4; IV, 9; V, 2; VI, 9; VII, 109; VIII, 8; X, 185; letters from Saint Vincent, II, 54; III, 267; IV, 113, 415, 506, 507, 548, 560, 605; V, 53, 364; VI, 268, 275; VIII, 239; to Saint Vincent, III, 410; V, 393, 482; VI, 125, 326; VIII, 51; reference to letter from Saint Vincent, II, 182.

Matters Saint Vincent is asked to recommend to her, II, 220; VIII, 418; promises to ask her, II, 65; III, 121; asks her, II, 297; IV, 548; shares letters from Missionaries or encourages them to write her, I, 431; II, 267, 272, 358–59; III, 4; VI, 326;

VII, 488, 522–23, 556; visits her, II, 48, 126; IV, 35; offers her gift, IV, 354, 411; proposes candidate to her for canonry, III, 605; for priory, IV, 508; concern of Duchess for health of saint, III, 431; IV, 561; proposes appointment to canonry in Champigny-sur-Veude, III, 605; then changes her mind, IV, 10, 12, 69, 70.

Duchess stopped approaching Queen before 1657, VI, 609; her chaplain, I, 436; XIIIa, 106; her great charity, VI, 47, 50; fears smallpox, VI, 202; welcomes coadjutor Brother to her table, XIIIa, 392; endowment for Our Lady of Loreto, VII, 569, 595, 635; VIII, 7–8, 21, 39, 70, 109, 133, 148, 239; renders service to Cardinal Antonio Barberini, V, 2; Saint Louise consults her about marriage of son Michel, III, 472; meetings of Ladies of Hôtel-Dieu, which she attends or to which she is invited, II, 8, 328; III, 149, 268, 384; VI, 202; VIII, 52, 239; resigns as president of Ladies of Hôtel-Dieu; resignation not accepted, V, 365.

Generosity toward Daughters of Charity, II, 601–02; III, 61; XIIIb, 231, 325; receives as deposit in trust money designated for purchase of Motherhouse for them, XIIIb, 120–22; approves investment of another sum given for same purpose, II, 208–09; asks for Sisters for Le Havre (Havre de Grace), XII, 19–20; for Nantes Hospital, I, 600; for self, I, 321–23; X, 515; helps Daughters in Richelieu find place to live, I, 500.

Funds establishment of Missionaries in Marseilles for galley convicts and for slaves in Barbary, XIIIa, 335–37; resolutions taken together with her concerning establishment, XIIIa, 365–67; copies of foundation made by Duchess, VII, 539, 556; sends Mass stipends to Superior of house, III, 465; assistance for hospital for galley convicts, II, 511; III, 271, 273; V, 145; VI, 304, 392, 431, 617; VII, 109–10, 168, 263, 289, 302, 392, 403, 467; VIII, 462, 485; XIIIa, 336, 365; thoughts about wages of chaplains, VI, 99; plans to get money owed them and subsidies necessary for hospital, VI, 195, 207, 260–61, 279, 301, 328, 383; Saint Vincent and others keep her informed of interests of Marseilles house, hospital, chaplains, III, 267, 468; VI, 99.

Funds Marseilles house for ministry to slaves in Barbary, XIIIa, 336; thanks to her, Congregation of the Mission obtains consulates of Tunis and Algiers, III, 395; V, 90; consulted by Saint Vincent about resale, VI, 322, 338; VII, 245, 262; VIII, 321; Saint Vincent sends her M. Husson, named Consul in Tunis, IV, 560; obtains from Privy Council decree confirming M. Husson in rights of office, VI, 120–21; steps taken to reinstate him in consulate, VI, 314; asks her advice on how to extricate M. Barreau from difficulties, VI, 359, 466, 479; offers a thousand livres to help M. Barreau pay his debts, VI,

372; distressed by bad news from Algiers and Tunis, V, 482; sends five hundred écus to Tunis, V, 191; gift for construction of hospital in Algiers, V, 398, 407, 408; VI, 9; sees to ransom of slaves, III, 223; V, 353, 379, 398, 408; VII, 195, 222; and to release of Turks from Tunis who are slaves in France, VII, 392; tries to convince Chevalier Paul to lead ships against Algiers, VII, 145; VIII, 32; and, in lieu of him, M. de Beaufort, VII, 154.

Interest taken in Sisters at Saint-Sulpice, I, 557; II, 187–88, 291; in inhabitants of duchy of Aiguillon: see ***Aiguillon***; in ministry for ordinands, II, 585–86; for galley convicts in Paris, IV, 417; for General Hospital, V, 53; VI, 126, 269, 275; for foundlings, I, 432, 434, 436; II, 151–52, 292, 299; III, 254, 404, 410, 420, 468; for ravaged Lorraine, II, 54–55, 68, 260–61; III, 201, 202; XIIIb, 407; for other devastated provinces, IV, 519; V, 60; VI, 503; VIII, 29; for Charity of Richelieu, I, 402; for Missionaries' house in Richelieu, II, 96, 416; III, 412, 515; IV, 8–11, 114; for Saint-Méen, II, 666; for La Rose, II, 318; III, 267; for Rome, II, 170, 267, 272, 304, 305, 318, 349, 358, 359, 362, 406, 416, 426, 430, 432, 436, 438, 449, 465, 469, 542; for Levant missions, V, 394; for China and Indochina, IV, 605; for Madagascar, V, 286; VIII, 201, 576; for Daughters of Providence, VI, 550; contacts with Visitation nuns, II, 201, 535; present at funeral of Saint Vincent, XIIIa, 209; other mentions, II, 259, 355, 424, 537; III, 414; V, 282; VII, 350, 523; VIII, 441, 514; X, 185.

Aimée, Daughter of Charity - Departure from Company, II, 194.

Aire, town in Landes - Indulgence requested and obtained for Pastor in Aire diocese, VI, 483; VII, 37.

Aix, island in Charente-Maritime - VIII, 562.

Aix, town in Bouches-du-Rhône - Archbishop: see Paul Hurault de **L'Hospital**; scandalous processions on feast of Corpus Christi, II, 576; other mentions, VII, 134; XIIIa, 488.

Alain (Jean), Priest of the Mission - Biographical data; in Sedan, II, 541; III, 29; in Le Mans, II, 676; III, 104; at Saint-Lazare, III, 29, 419; death, III, 422, 423.

Alais (Louis-Emmanuel de Valois, Comte d') - II, 575.

Alan (François) - IV, 249.

Albano, diocese in Italy - Bishop: see Bernardino **Spada**.

Albergati-Ludovisi (Niccolò), Cardinal-Archbishop of Bologna - Biographical data, III, 65; VII, 39; VIII, 515; contacts with Fr. Dehorgny, III, 65; urges ailing Saint Vincent to take care of self, VIII, 515; Nuncio's reply to *Propaganda Fide*, XIIIa, 239.

Alberici (Marius), Secretary of *Propaganda Fide* - VII, 435.

Albiac, seminary - VIII, 488.

Albigensians, heretics from south of France - I, 526; XI, 273.

Albon (Gilbert-Antoine, Comte d') - V, 17; member of association against dueling, V, 617.

Albret (César-Phoebus de Miossens (Miossanx), Chevalier d' - Biographical data, V, 612; VI, 398; refuses to pay tithes to Superior of Saintes Seminary, V, 612; VI, 398, 445.

Alcalay (Messrs.) - Safe conduct for brothers Jacob and Isaac, VII, 523.

Alchemy - Saint Vincent learns it from master in Tunis, I, 6; VIII, 600; discloses secrets to Pietro Montorio, I, 9.

Alençon, town in Orne - Nearby property owned by Le Mans Seminary, VI, 36; VII, 338; postulant from there, VII, 55.

Aleppo, town in Syria - French Consul in Aleppo: see **Picquet** (François).

Alet, town in Aude - Bishop: see Nicolas **Pavillon**; Saint Vincent plans to go there, I, 520, 526, 544; retreat for clergy, II, 543; poverty of Alet diocese, II, 220; Sister Carcireux prepares there to teach young people, VIII, 379; X, 587; Saint Vincent seeks authorization for resignation of Pastor in diocese, IV, 65; Michel Le Gras could not be of service there without experience, I, 427–428; other mentions, IV, 190.

Missionaries in Alet: sending of four Missionaries, I, 582; Fr. Duhamel invited to join them, if he wishes, II, 114, 117; letters sent by Saint Vincent, II, 146, 211, 338; mission given, II, 310; recall of Missionaries, II, 339; Pavillon regrets recall, II, 340; M. Féret is lent there, III, 100, 329; Missionaries stationed in Alet: see **Blatiron**, **Brunet**, **Lucas** (Antoine); history of house, VIII, 608.

Alet Seminary: beginnings under Priests of the Mission, II, 221, 256; search for residence; Pavillon intends to unite Alet parish to seminary, II, 221; reopening of seminary at end of 1645; number of seminarians, II, 614; number of seminarians in 1660, VIII, 283.

Alex (Jean d'Aranthon d'), Bishop of Geneva - Biographical data, VI, 404; VII, 209; VIII, 307; letters from Saint Vincent, VI, 404; VII, 209, 398; VIII, 307; mention of letters to Saint Vincent, VII, 209, 398; kindness to Annecy Missionaries, VI, 405; praise from Saint Vincent, VI, 405; VIII, 308; saint hopes for episcopate for him, VI, 405; VII, 398; congratulates him on elevation to See of Geneva, VIII, 307; opposition to election, VIII, 487, 491.

Alexandre (Bro.) - See **Véronne** (Alexandre).

Alexander VII, Pope - Before nomination to sovereign pontificate: see **Chigi** (Fabio); Saint Vincent announces election of Pope to Saint-Lazare community, XI, 171; writes to congratulate him, V, 370–71; requests, on behalf of Missionaries, faculty to absolve from reserved cases, V, 548; seeks beatification of Francis de Sales, VII, 600–01; Pope condemns Jansenism, VI, 132, 152–153, 290–291; approves vows of Missionaries and exemption from jurisdiction of Ordinaries, XIIIa, 417; explains their vow of poverty, XIIIa, 480–82; reading of Brief on vow, XII, 311; joins Saint-Lazare Priory to Congregation of the Mission, XIIIa, 409; and conventual income of Saint-Méen Abbey, XIIIa, 423; entrusts to Missionaries in Rome spiritual direction of College of *Propaganda Fide*, V, 606; permits them to carry out ministries in Rome, VII, 229; obliges ordinands of Rome to make retreat in house of Congregation of the Mission, VIII, 238, 254; petition regarding foundation of Loreto, VIII, 239; decision regarding Carmelites, VIII, 474; 496, 506; wants Congregation of the Mission to continue ordination retreats in Rome, XIIIa, 192; Bull of 1656 Jubilee, XI, 301; other mentions, VIII, 70, 176; XIIIa, 420, 423, 472–73, 479, 486–87.

Alexander the Great, King of Greece - Sends money to Diogenes, XI, 156.

Alexandria, city in Egypt - XIIIa, 346; Consul of France there: see Christophe de **Bermond**; Archbishop: see Jean **l'Aumonier** [**John the Almsgiver**] (Saint).

Alexis (Saint) - Feast day, VIII, 580.

Alexis I, Tsar of Russia - Has no designs on Poland, V, 143; attacked Sweden, VI, 128.

Algiers, city in Africa - Mention of letters sent from Algiers, VI, 326, 359; letters sent to Algiers, V, 530; VI, 384; VII, 115; rumor of return to France of several renegades, VII, 191; plague, III, 218–23, 304–10, 349; V, 90; change of Pashas, V, 404; VI, 10; contacts between Marseilles and Algiers, VI, 353, 480; sale of slaves to Tunis by ships from Algiers, V, 131; dispatch of ten ships from Algiers to Sultan's army, V, 132; they are not going to Levant, V, 405; naval strength of Turks in Algiers; they fear only the English, V, 392; acts of piracy, V, 35, 390–91; plan for expedition against Algiers. See also **Paul** (Chevalier).

Missionaries in Algiers: several sent to give mission to Christian slaves (1642); get no farther than Marseilles, II, 355, 394, 407; arrival of first Missionaries (1646), II, 677; III, 6,

24; advice of Saint Vincent, XIIIa, 344–45; plans to send Pierre du Chesne to visit Barbary Missionaries, V, 147; letters of Saint Vincent to Missionaries: see **Nouelly**, **Barreau**, **Le Vacher** (Philippe); from Missionaries in Algiers to Saint Vincent. See also **Barreau**. Worries about them, VII, 403; XI, 291; Fr. Get has no news from there, VII, 456; Saint Vincent urges him to look out for them, VIII, 376, 396, 485; revenues of Algiers mission: VI, 54; benefactors. See also **Aiguillon** (Duchesse d'); list of Superiors and historical synopsis, VIII, 615; ordeals of Missionaries, VIII, 537; zeal, III, 192, 194; faculties requested of Rome for Missionaries, III, 40; IV, 25; VI, 526, 636; VII, 28–29; money sent for needs, V, 247–48, 325; VI, 153, 188, 289, 304, 466, 487; VII, 7, 123, 458; personnel in Algiers: see **Barreau**, **Dieppe**, **Lesage**, **Le Vacher** (Philippe), **Nouelly**; Jean Le Vacher willing to go there after temporary expulsion from Tunis, XI, 277; meeting at Saint-Lazare regarding Algiers business, VII, 174; other mentions, VII, 289; VIII, 600. See also ***Barbary***. Consulate of France in Algiers: acquisition of consulate for Congregation of the Mission, II, 678; V, 90; letters of appointment to consulate on behalf of Fr. Lambert, XIIIa, 346–47; imprudent actions and ordeals of M. Barreau the Consul: see also **Barreau**; letter of Louis XIV to Pasha of Algiers, asking protection for Consul, V, 644.

Vain attempts by Rome to have consulate run by priests, VI, 386, 401, 461–62, 629, 636; VII, 39, 46; Saint Vincent disposed to resell consulate, V, 367; VI, 322, 328, 372; reasons against sale, VII, 245; opposition of Duchesse d'Aiguillon, VI, 338; VII, 262; small return from consulate, V, 328, 392; gifts for new Pasha, V, 404; Fr. Dieppe dies there, III, 451; Saint Vincent considers replacing M. Barreau the Consul. See also **Huguier**, **Aiguillon** (Duchesse), ***Barbary***, **Barreau.**

Slaves in Algiers: slaves being sold in Algiers, I, 4; approximate number of slaves in Algiers in 1642 and 1658, II, 355; XII, 62; servants of Cardinal Antonio Barberini captured at sea and taken into slavery to Algiers, V, 2, 23, 35–36, 55, 325, 355; hospital for sick slaves, II, 407; V, 398, 407, 408; VI, 9, 187, 392; Cheleby Hospital, III, 307; ransom of slaves, III, 25; V, 35, 119, 141, 145, 146–47, 150, 163, 170, 216, 227, 247, 259, 325, 327–28, 353–55, 379–80, 380–81, 390–93, 405–08; VI, 187, 189, 273, 276, 279, 289, 302, 315, 320, 327, 328; VII, 134, 161, 170, 179, 186, 195, 196, 208, 228, 232, 234, 237, 250, 254; VIII, 309, 319, 401, 503, 532; XI, 192, 385; XIIIa, 421; other services rendered slaves by Missionaries and Consul, III, 51; VI, 11, 392, 441, 613; VIII, 319, 337, 387, 397; XI, 385, 393–94; Saint Vincent stops sending money to Algiers, lest it be seized by Turks or misused by M. Barreau; money deposited in Marseilles while awaiting opportunity, VI, 359, 431, 446; VII,

103, 123, 124, 149, 154, 187, 190–91, 195, 273, 303, 463, 555, 632; VIII, 4, 18–19, 137–38, 287, 309, 320, 327; Fr. Get's account of money, VIII, 319; martyrdom of slave: see **Borguñy**; conversion of heretic slaves, V, 355, 405; King's prisons, III, 222, 310; Cheleby, III, 223, 305, 307–08; Collorgli, III, 305; Customs Office prison, III, 307–08; other mentions, VII, 411, 555; VIII, 369, 373, 503; XI, 290; XII, 61. See also ***Barbary***.

Alias Nos, Papal Brief on vow of poverty taken in Congregation of the Mission - Saint Vincent asks that it be sent soon, VII, 401; receives draft, VIII, 71; receives final copy, VIII, 133; prepares to distribute it, VIII, 134; assistance of Fr. Hilarion Rancati in obtaining it, VIII, 142, 143; reading of it to confreres at Saint-Lazare, XII, 311; text of Brief, XIIIa, 480; other mentions, VIII, 37.

Alimondo (Lucas) - See **Arimondo**.

Alix (Bonet), of Châtillon-les-Dombes - XIIIa, 46, 50.

Alix (Michel), Pastor of Saint-Ouen-l'Aumône - Saint Vincent urges him to reconsider before resigning parish, I, 189; invites him to meeting of Pastors at Saint-Lazare, I, 201; urges him to postpone trip, I, 214; sympathetic to his sufferings, III, 120; promises help for foundation; reproaches him for dedication of book, III, 121; text of dedication, XIIIa, 152–54.

Alix (Sister) - I, 262.

Allegré (Philibert), Canon in Mâcon - XIIIb, 78.

Allet (Marie), Daughter of Charity - Departure from Company, VII, 158.

Allier (Raoul), author of *La Cabale des dévots* - Opinion about recipient of letter, II, 575; defends Saint-Cyran against accusation of Saint Vincent, III, 361; insinuations concerning gift of Queen of Poland, IV, 437; books on Company of Blessed Sacrament, IV, 520; other mention, II, 576.

Allot (Julienne), Daughter of Charity – VIII, 232; XIIIb, 228.

Allou (Toussainte), Daughter of Charity - XIIIb, 228.

All Saints' Day - Most abundant in graces because there is the greatest number of intercessors, XI, 382; mention of conferences, XII, 406, 414, 417, 421.

Alméras (Anne-Marie), sister of René Alméras the younger - Biographical data, VI, 163; founding Sister and Superior of Visitation Monastery in Amiens, II, 455.

Alméras (Hélène, Demoiselle), mother of Jean Duhamel - Executrix of his will, XIIIa, 333.

Alméras (M.), uncle of Jean Duhamel - Jean Duhamel leaves money for annual Mass for late uncle, XIIIa, 334.

Alméras (René the Elder), Master of Accounts, then seminarian in Congregation of the Mission - Biographical data, III, 30; V, 620; VI, 39; VII, 54; displeasure at son's departure without saying goodbye; Saint Vincent urges son to apologize to father, III, 30; sends father letter of excuse, III, 67–69; beautiful response of father, III, 88; father received at Saint-Lazare, V, 620, 624, 627; VI, 39; enters Internal Seminary, VI, 265, 267; admitted by exception, VII, 217–18, 307; anxiety at news of son's illness, VI, 540; Saint Vincent dares not tell him of son's relapse, VI, 571; father's illness and death, VII, 54, 55, 56, 58, 68, 75; mention of conference on his virtues, XII, 430; other mention, VI, 183.

Alméras (René the Younger), Priest of the Mission, son of preceding - Biographical data, I, 529; II, 344; III, 14; IV, 33; V, 9; VI, 82; VII, 26; VIII, 77; XI, *xxii*; letters to him in Rome from Saint Vincent, III, 192, 371, 385, 448, 459, 477, 491, 510, 537, 584, 613; IV, 42, 52, 61, 134, 139, 145; in Tours, VIII, 413; in Richelieu, VIII, 452, 463; reference to letter from Saint Vincent, III, 313; to letters to Vincent, III, 371; IV, 33; VIII, 413, 463; to Nicolas Duperroy in Saint Vincent's name, VII, 639; studies theology at Bons-Enfants, I, 529; member of first General Assembly, II, 344; XIIIa, 323, 331; Assembly names him alternate member of commission for preparing Rules, XIIIa, 326; presence at councils held for affairs of Daughters of Charity, XIIIb, 244, 250, 256–59, 318, 322, 345; "gift" for Élisabeth Martin, XIIIb, 260; "Rules of Alméras," XIIIb, 147, 148; mission in Clichy, II, 360; in Paris, II, 529; at meeting of Tuesday Conference, II, 534; in La Rose, III, 63, 64; Saint Vincent considers sending him for visitation of Rome house, II, 624, 631; and for houses in Marseilles, Annecy, and others, II, 631; III, 67–68; Fr. Alméras leaves Paris without saying good-bye to father, III, 31, 67–69, 88; journey from Paris to Rome, II, 666, 668; III, 14, 30, 89, 93, 103, 114, 116, 124, 154, 171, 190.

Named Superior of Rome house, III, 192; works on Rules for Company, III, 238; on getting approval of vows, III, 247; Saint Vincent asks Fr. Dehorgny to share his (Vincent's) letter to him with Alméras, III, 329; Alméras offers resignation, which is refused, III, 374; Saint Vincent encourages him, III, 374, 385, 448; IV, 145; refuses to send him "presentable men," III, 491; regrets recall of Fr. Dehorgny, III, 613; asks him to assist Fr. Vitet, IV, 47; to get faculties for Philippe Le Vacher, IV, 88; asks for qualified man to deal with Sacred Congregation, IV, 133; donates money to Company for purchase of house in Rome, IV, 134; health, IV, 139, 145–46; Superior in Rome, IV, 33, 47, 73, 133, 148, VIII, 609; upcoming return to Paris, IV, 166; presence at 1651 General Assembly, XIIIa, 369, 372, 374, 389; opinion on vows of Company, XIIIa, 379, 383; and on other questions, XIIIa, 384, 385, 389; named member of commission for examining Rules, XIIIa, 396; refuses to pay to advance process of approving vows; leaves outcome to Providence, III, 478; Saint Vincent's advice on how to deal with Bro. Doutrelet, III, 510–511; Alméras tells Saint Vincent of Authier's appointment as Bishop of Babylon, IV, 148; Superior of Saint-Charles Seminary in Paris, IV, 292, 335; VIII, 614; invasion of house by pillaging soldiers, IV, 409, 468; Director of Internal Seminary at Saint-Lazare, IV, 469, 474, 573; XI, 108; leaves for Poitou and Bretagne, IV, 602; visits Nantes houses, V, 9, 32–33; in Le Mans, V, 24–25; at neighboring houses, V, 38, 48; at Collège des Bons-Enfants, V, 76; assists inhabitants of Picardy, devastated by war, V, 79, 99, 101, 110, 120, 124; falls ill in Laon, V, 137; recalled to Paris, V, 148; convalesces at Saint-Lazare; V, 157; recuperates in Sedan, V, 184.

Assistant at Motherhouse, V, 208; journey to Troyes for canonical visitation of Missionaries, V, 261, 312; health, VI, 184, 272; goes to Bourbon-l'Archambault for thermal baths, VI, 309; returns to Paris, VI, 341; returns to Bourbon, VI, 424, 435, 440, 443, 445; XI, 369; falls ill in Bourbon, VI, 523–24, 527–28, 530, 535, 538, 540, 548, 554; health improves, VI, 556, 558, 560, 562, 564; convalesces in Moulins, VI, 570, 571; return to Paris, VI, 585; in Paris, V, 205, 492, 501; VI, 82, 378–79; VII, 68, 371, 528, 569; VIII, 77, 207–08, 550, 599; XI, 186, 301, 325; XIIIa, 195, 335, 337; health, VI, 498, 585, 589–90, 593–94, 603, 608, 612, 614, 621, 639; VII, 26, 73, 75; VIII, 207; XII, 238, 241.

Present for distribution of Common Rules, XII, 11, 242; Saint Vincent asks him to distribute *Entretiens* to seminarians and priests, XII, 242; writes circular letter to Superiors to accompany sending of Rules, VII, 296, 401; relapse, VII, 473; put on milk diet, VII, 515, 583; new health problems, VIII, 157, 211, 212, 254; condition improves, VIII, 301; sent to Richelieu at time when King and new Queen are passing through, VIII, 371, 385; illness in Tours, VIII, 413, 421, 423, 439; prepares to set out from Tours for Richelieu, VIII, 452; Saint Vincent expresses anxiety, VIII, 452; joy of Saint Vincent at his improvement, VIII, 463–64; returns to Paris on litter, VIII, 483, 536; Saint Vincent names him Vicar-General, XIIIa, 207; letter of nomination, XIIIa, 483; letter proposing him in first place as Superior General, XIIIa, 484; Superior General, VIII, 597; named by Pope as Visitor of Carmelites, VIII, 70; signs

Particular Rules for Daughters of Charity and Advices to Hospital Sisters, XIIIb, 177, 182, 185, 202, 204; gift of property to Company, VII, 339; has gone to see father only once since entrance into Company, IV, 352; V, 347; sees to appointment of monitor, XII, 56; Saint Vincent questions him during conferences to Missionaries, XI, 155, 266–68, 306; makes recommendations, XI, 136, 158–59, 161, 178, 299, 325, 326; XII, 56; comments on his gifts, XI, 253; other mentions, VIII, 439–40, 609, 614; XI, 135; XII, 405; XIIIa, 271, 344.

Alms - Free-will offerings may be accepted, but not as remuneration for expenses, VI, 170–171.

Almshouses - Reasons for obliging poor persons to remain in them, IV, 69–70.

Alorge (M. M.), Prioress of Madelonnettes - XIIIa, 101.

Alsace - VI, 534, 591; VII, 336. See also ***Trois-Épis*** (*Notre-Dame*).

Altieri (Giovanni Battista), Vicegerent of Rome - Biographical data, V, 1; Saint Vincent writes to him, V, 1; other mentions, II, 232; XIIIa, 313–14.

Alzan (M. d') - Member of association against dueling, V, 617.

Amat (M.), *Receveur Général* (Principal Tax Collector) - VII, 488; VIII, 266.

Amaury (Claire-Marie), Visitandine - Biographical data, I, 556; XI, 169; trials, XI, 169, 355; XIIIa, 78–79, 95.

Amaury (Mlle) - IV, 212, 213.

Ambition - Conference, XI, 51.

Amboise, town in Indre-et-Loire - I, 194.

Ambolo, valley in Madagascar - III, 565; VI, 220.

Ambrose (Saint) - Firmness with Emperor Theodosius, IX, 304; features of his life, XI, 134; XII, 47–48; other mentions, III, 310; XII, 326; XIIIa, 33.

Ameline (Fr.) - Quarrels with Protestants in Saint-Quentin, VIII, 457, 539.

Amelot (Charles), Seigneur de Gournay, Presiding Judge of Great Council - VIII, 472.

Amelote (Denis), Priest of the Oratory - Biographical data, V, 575; Lenten preacher in LeMans, V, 575; Prior of Champdolent, V, 626; begins, with Fr. Olier, seminary at Vaugirard and then at Saint-Sulpice, II, 308.

America - IV, 377: see ***Canada***.

Amfreville (M. and Mme d') - Gift to Visitation Nuns, VIII, 48–49.

Amiens, town in Somme - Bishop: see François Lefèvre de **Caumartin**; Visitation Monastery, I, 367; II, 454; VI, 163, XIIIa, 157, 189; mission in Amiens, I, 278; other mentions, I, 350, 490; II, 669; IV, 33; V, 217, 405; VI, 80, 103, 422, 437, 481; VIII, 382; X, 344; XI, 4; XIIIa, 222–23, 235; XIIIb, 47.

Ammerschwihr, town in Upper Rhine - Famous for pilgrimage of *Trois-Épis*, VII, 335.

Amour (Isidore), Abbot of Cuissy - IV, 330.

Amsterdam, town in Netherlands - VIII, 587, 593, 594, 596.

Amville (François-Christophe de Levis-Ventadour, Duc d'), Viceroy of Indies - IV, 359.

Ananias, personage in *Acts of the Apostles* - Sent to instruct Saul in Christian faith, X, 223.

Ananias, Jewish convert in *Acts of the Apostles* - Struck dead for lying to Saint Peter, X, 167–68, 170, 173; XI, 211; XIIIb, 351.

Andilly (Mme d') - Abbé de Saint-Cyran attends her on her death bed, I, 393; XIIIa, 112.

Andranahary, village in Madagascar - VI, 249.

Andrée, Daughter of Charity - Sent to Le Mans Hospital, II, 642; Saint Louise requests for her grace of Holy Vows, III, 301; reproaches self for having taken "too much pleasure in serving the poor," IX, 537.

Andrew (Saint), Apostle - First Apostle attracted to Jesus; preached from his cross, II, 385; XII, 157; patron of church in Châtillon, XIIIa, 57; XIIIb, 3, 18; feast day, XIIIb, 18.

Ange (Fr.), Franciscan - In Algiers, III, 223.

Ange de Clavasio (Bl.), Friar Minor of the Observance - Opinion on vows, XIIIa, 404.

Angels - Higher angels enlighten intellects of lower hierarchies, XI, 315; models in fulfilling God's Will, XI, 282; cooperate in extension of God's Kingdom, XII, 117; in song and praises, XII, 267; in practice of mutual respect, IX, 115; in indifference, X, 564–65; in manner of being inclined to good: proposing it without pressing others to do it, I, 351; III, 356; VIII, 224; services they render us, X, 54, 479–80; ministries of Daughters of Charity resemble those of Guardian Angels, IX, 125; God sends angels to enlighten Church and Holy See, VI, 293; Guardian Angel is guide for Sister who is alone, IX, 8; angels count all their steps, IX, 365; X, 4; Saint Vincent prays to Guardian Angels of others, IV, 66; tells Sisters to imagine they are visible Guardian Angels of the poor, IX, 5; thinking of Guardian Angel contributes to practice of mutual respect, IX, 115, 117, 121; to serve foundlings well, think of their Guardian Angels, IX, 125; devotion of Fr. Pillé and of Saint Frances to their Guardian Angels, II, 379–80.

Angelus - Explanation of this prayer, X, 458; not part of morning prayer at Saint-Lazare, V, 156.

Anger (Pierre), priest in Alet - Letter to Saint Vincent, VIII, 282.

Anger - Passion opposed to spirit of Daughters of Charity, IX, 363; blurs reason, XII, 155; should be detested, XI, 55; never get angry in public, XI, 92.

Angers, town in Maine-et-Loire - Climate of Paris disastrous for Sisters from Anjou, II, 151; Fronde in Angers, IV, 320; Bishops: see Henri **Arnauld**, Claude de **Rueil**; reform of Saint-Nicolas Abbey by Abbé de Saint-Cyran, XIIIa, 131; Carmel, VIII, 506; Visitation, I, 367, 369, 594; III, 409, 418; VI, 163; nuns of Sainte-Geneviève, II, 223, 224; hospital for prisoners, I, 195; V, 629; VI, 75, 139; taxes (*aides*) paid to Condé by Angers, II, 359, 662; IV, 320; V, 486, 503–04; Confraternity of Charity at Hôtel-Dieu, II, 25; administrators of Hôtel-Dieu, II, 2, 11, 81, 106–07, 223–24; administrators request more Sisters, III, 35–36; administrators of Nantes Hospital want Daughters under conditions as those of Angers, II, 644–45.

Journeys of Saint Vincent to Angers, his stays there, III, 397, 405, 409, 415; visitations, III, 420, 423, 424; visits of Saint Louise, I, 493–94, 599, 601; II, 1, 8–16, 23–26, 35; III, 8–10, 17; mission given in diocese; Bishop desires and funds establishment for Missionaries, VI, 410; other mentions, V, 277–78; VI, 409, 526, 553; VII, 78; IX, 195.

Daughters of Charity in Angers: Mme Goussault requests three Sisters for hospital, I, 469, 594; contract with Saint-Jean Hospital, XIIIb, 114; Act of Establishment of Daughters of Charity at hospital, XIIIb, 117–19; Saint Vincent hastens their departure for Angers, I, 572; arrival of first Sisters, I, 603; II, 654; Sisters who signed contract in Angers, XIIIb, 116; their title, II, 8, 9; Saint Vincent and Saint Louise judge it advisable to ask Bishop to approve establishment, II, 223, 224; Regulations for Sisters of hospital, IX, 17; XIIIb, 108–14; Sisters are doing well, III, 168, 431; self-sacrifice during plague, IX, 34; choice of Director, III, 277; kindness of Abbé de Vaux, I, 603; XIIIb, 262; Saint Vincent congratulates Cécile Angiboust, Sister Servant, on leadership, IV, 567; visit of house by Barbe Angiboust, I, 596; by Fr. Lambert, II, 81; by Fr. Portail, II, 643, 668; his recommendations to Sisters (1646), XIIIb, 127; visit by Jeanne Lepeintre, XIIIb, 272; by Fr. Alméras, V, 9; Daughters of Charity requested for prison hospital, V, 629; VI, 75, 139; Sister from Angers on retreat at

Motherhouse, II, 205; bad example of Sister, XIIIb, 283; assignments and changes, III, 208; XIIIb, 284, 340.

Sisters on mission in Angers: see **Angiboust** (Cécile-Agnes), **Caillou**, **Despinal**, **Étiennette**, **Ferre**, **François** (Marguerite), **Martin** (Élisabeth), **Matrilomeau**, **Mongert**, **Moreau** (Marguerite), **Perrette**, **Perrine**, **Toussaint** (Barbe), **Trumeau**, **Turgis** (Élisabeth); other mentions, II, 51, 185, 189, 601; III, 61; VII, 87; X, 263; XIIIb, 142, 231, 263–64, 269.

Angerville, commune in district of Étampes - Mme Goussault passes through there en route to Angers, I, 193.

Angibaut (M.), Beadle - XIIIa, 474.

Angiboust (Barbe), Daughter of Charity, daughter of Mathurin Angiboust and Perrine Blanne - Biographical data, I, 299; II, 3; III, 22; V, 61; VI, 424; VII, 386; IX, 8; conferences on her virtues, X, 511–523, 541–44; letters from Saint Vincent, V, 61; VI, 424; VII, 386; health, I, 299, 303; at Saint-Nicolas-du-Chardonnet, I, 323; placed in home of Duchesse d'Aiguillon but begs to be sent back to poor, I, 322; X, 515–16; question of sending her to Saint-Germain-en-Laye, I, 411, 423; in Saint-Germain-en-Laye, I, 457–58; recalled to Paris, again requested for Saint-Germain, I, 469; parishioners want to keep her despite Saint Vincent's need of her, I, 486.

Proposed for Richelieu, I, 402, 439, 448, 458, 493; goes to Richelieu, I, 499, 500, 504; Sister Servant, I, 502; in Richelieu, I, 592; II, 10; X, 522; Saint Vincent speaks of sending her to make visitation of Sisters in Angers, I, 596; Sister Servant, II, 24, 81; in Nantes, XIIIb, 248–49; plans to recall her from Richelieu, II, 128, 148; in Paris, II, 195; wishes to make her Jubilee, II, 225; devotion to galley convicts in Paris, II, 197, 291; X, 517; makes perpetual vows, V, 356; X, 511; many visits to foundlings out with wet-nurses, X, 520; XIIIb, 248; devotion to foundlings, X, 522; Sister Servant at Charity in Fontainebleau, III, 22, 316, 317, 379, 380; at Saint-Denis Hospital, X, 513, 520; in Brienne-le-Château, V, 62; at Châlons-sur-Marne Hospital, nursing wounded soldiers, V, 61; X, 519; at Châteaudun Hospital, VI, 424; X, 541–544; good leadership there, VII, 386; illness and death, VII, 436, 445; X, 511, 520–21, 541–42, 544; other mentions, I, 320, 359, 414, 485, 496, 497; II, 112, 194, 196, 225; III, 400; XIIIb, 227.

Angiboust (Cécile-Agnès), Daughter of Charity, sister of preceding - Biographical data, I, 486; IV, 257; V, 214; VI, 455; Saint Vincent admits her to Daughters of Charity, I, 486; she is sent to Angers Hospital, II, 12; XIIIb, 116, 118; Sister Servant there; words of praise for her, III, 416, 420; recall is requested, IV, 257; Saint Vincent is pleased with her leadership, IV, 567;

Saint Louise thinks she would do well in Poland, V, 214; sent to Richelieu, VI, 455; Saint Louise asks her to return to Paris, VI, 513; Bishop of Angers is informed of change, VI, 455, 513; proposed as Sister Servant of Petites-Maisons in Paris, VI, 583; other mention, XIIIb, 227.

Angiboust (Mathurin), father of Barbe and Cécile-Agnès Angiboust - X, 511.

Anglure (Charles-François d'), Abbé de la Crète, son of Claude d'Anglure - I, 459.

Anglure (Claude d') - See **Bourlemont** (Comte de).

Anglure (Louis d'), brother of Charles-François - I, 459.

Angoulême, town in Charente - Bishops: see Jacques **du Perron**, François de **Péricard**; clergy conference; they write to Saint Vincent, II, 488, 501; success of retreats for ordinands, II, 475; Missionaries are invited to diocese, II, 475, 490; offer of house; Saint Vincent does not accept, V, 436; missions given in Angoulême diocese, II, 488: see ***Blanzac, La Marguerie***; other mentions, I, 486, 488.

Angoumois, province - Elie Laisné provides Saint Vincent with revenue for missions there, I, 430.

Angran (Louis) - Sent by Jansenists to Rome to prevent condemnation, IV, 581, 594.

Anjalbert (Raymonde), of Cahors - IV, 284.

Anjou - Native place of M. Doublard, VI, 409.

Ann (Saint) - Mme de Gondi implores her help, XIIIa, 59.

Annat (François), Jesuit - Biographical data, V, 172; VI, 390; VII, 23; Alain de Solminihac seeks to interest him in choice of Solminihac's Coadjutor, V, 172; writings against Jansenists, VII, 23; King's confessor, VI, 390, 534.

Anne, Daughter of Charity - See **Gennes** (Anne), **Hardemont** (Anne), **Vaux** (Anne de), **Vallin** (Anne).

Anne, Daughter of Charity - In Fontenay house, II, 285–86, 287, 291.

Anne, called the Elder, Daughter of Charity - II, 16.

Anne, Daughter of Charity - At Motherhouse, IX, 255.

Anne of Austria, Queen of France, wife of Louis XIII - Letter from Saint Vincent to prevent loss of revenues, II, 469; to inform her of disorders of Longchamp Abbey, IV, 271; to thank her for favor, IV, 303; to ask her protection against predators, IV, 421; to ask her to take action against heretic Labadie, IV, 457; she writes to French Ambassador to Rome to support request of Congregation of the Mission for new privileges, XIIIa, 246; saint is asked to speak with Queen about Bicêtre, II, 444; about vacant diocese of Couserans, III, 241; requests canonry for Solminihac's Officialis, II, 451; action she should take at beginning of regency, II, 446–447; Nuncio will speak with her regarding diocese or abbey for Bishop of Babylon, II, 457; she gives Superior General lifetime title of Royal Chaplain to Galleys, VIII, 610; seeks information from Saint-Pardoux Priory, II, 489; Solminihac writes to her about Huguenots in Saint-Céré area, II, 503; she approves visitation of Saint-Pardoux Priory, II, 508; orders Solminihac to make visitation of Poor Clare Monastery, II, 489–490; appoints Saint Vincent to Council of Conscience, II, 495; Saint Vincent advises her regarding Saint-Geneviève Abbey, XII, 361; consults her about Sedan mission, II, 525; General of Dominicans seeks support, II, 561–562.

Mathieu Molé asks for bishopric of Bayeux for his son, II, 615; Queen approves transfer of Bishop of Maillezais to archbishopric of Bordeaux, III, 34; considers Bishops of Alet and Bologne good Bishops, III, 105; asked for help for poor regions in Bologne diocese, III, 105; reform of Saint-Césaire Abbey, III, 176; Saint Vincent plans to speak to her of coadjutorship of Babylon, III, 169; asked to grant patent to Prioress of Le Pouget, III, 240; wants Bishop of Condom named, III, 249; Solminihac urges her to appoint good Bishops, III, 293–295, 342, 348; IV, 27–28, 249; her position on Jansenism, III, 319; Council of Conscience advises her regarding Pope's orders against Arnauld's book, III, 323. Maupas du Tour asks Saint Vincent to inform her of incident in his diocese, III, 383; Queen is overwhelmed by petitioners, III, 391; saint considers asking her for general collection for Foundlings, III, 431; receives order from Queen to return to Paris, III, 429; she provides grain during Fronde, III, 410; Solminihac seeks help in legal matter, III, 516, 525; IV, 247–248; writes to her about his successor, IV, 475; her part in getting position for Michel Le Gras, III, 585; Fr. Nacquart hopes for commission from her for Captain Le Bourg, III, 599.

Saint Vincent advises Bishop to speak with her regarding appointment of Abbot, III, 618; advises Fr. Codoing on how to address her, IV, 44; she will be asked to assist Barreau, IV, 87; wishes to defer appointment of Bishop of Maçon, IV, 95; advises her son to grant safe-conduct to confreres serving in Picardy and Champagne, XIIIa, 368; Solminihac wants her informed of his health problems, IV, 153; Saint Vincent does so, IV, 162–63; he wonders if she should be informed about Cahors situation, IV, 191; she lets Solminihac choose his successor, IV, 222–23; contacts with her concerning union of

Saint-Corneille Abbey with Val-de-Grâce, IV, 244–45; promotes reform in abbeys, IV, 331; Saint Vincent has not visited her for six or seven months, IV, 379; is accustomed to go to see her once a year, VI, 148; Queen is in Reims for coronation of Louis XIV, V, 176; Solminihac wants her to work against laxism, VII, 628.

Saint Vincent plans to establish Confraternity of Charity at Court; Queen would be President, XIIIb, 441–42; her humility, XII, 391; her part in promoting Louis XIII's bequest for Sedan, XIIIa, 339–340; her fund in Sedan to promote good works, VIII, 204; possibility of her becoming protectress of Saint-Denis Hospital, II, 400; support for Rome seminary, II, 498; for ministry of ordinands, II, 552; meeting of benefactresses, including Queen, considered foundresses of Daughters of Providence, VI, 550; Duchesse d'Aiguillon no longer approaches her about helping the poor, VI, 609; revenue given to support Daughters of Charity, II, 601–602; provides Château de Bicêtre for their housing, XIIIb, 425; interest in Daughters in Chantilly, V, 332; contacts with Abbot of Saint-Germain, VIII, 405; proposal to have her confer abbey on Saint Vincent, VIII, 518; charity for poor nobility of Lorraine, II, 533; for foundlings, III, 404; has mission given in Fontainebleau, II, 534; in Metz, VI, 639; VII, 102, 108, 112; XII, 3–4; joy at success of mission in Metz, VII, 404; promises help for Missionaries' house in Spain, II, 502; benefactress of Metz house, VIII, 14, 16, 449.

Kindness toward Daughters of Charity, X, 134; asks Pope to make them dependent on Superior General of the Mission, XIIIb, 141; calls Daughters near her in various places, XIIIb, 369; asks them to nurse Mazarin's sister, X, 209; wounded soldiers in Sedan, X, 2, 233; in Montmédy, X, 381; asks for Sisters for Calais, X, 407; for Metz, X, 449; XII, 35; for Charity of Fontainebleau, III, 21.

Saint Vincent asks Fr. Lucas to pray and have prayers said for Queen's pregnancy, I, 422; Mazarin's judgment concerning people who have recourse to her, XIIIa, 154–55; his relationship with her, III, 356; Solminihac asks Queen for Fr. Sevin as Coadjutor, IV, 609; action to bring about union of Saint-Corneille de Compiègne Abbey with that of Val-de-Grace, IV, 244, 245; method of prayer, IX, 336; manner of making stations of Jubilee, IX, 488; her chaplain: see **Saint-Jean** (Nicolas de); other mentions, I, 432, 495; II, 542, 545, 566, 605, 615; III, 229; IV, 253, 585; VI, 534; XII, 391; XIIIa, 16.

Anne-Marie, Daughter of Charity - Unsuitable conduct, III, 470, 472.

Annecy, town in Haute-Savoie - Saint Vincent plans to go there, II, 67, 69; body of Louis de Chandenier is transported there and buried, VIII, 355; Visitation Monastery in Annecy, I, 362; II, 683, IV, 318, X, 266; other mentions, II, 160, 238; VI, 92; VII, 444; VIII, 488, 490.

Missionaries in Annecy: Foundation of house, I, 552, 565–68, 571; II, 61; benefactors: see **Chantal** (Saint Jane Frances de), **Cordon** (Jacques de), **Sillery** (Noël Brûlart de), **Trinité** (Mère de la); impending departure of Missionaries assigned to Annecy, I, 578, 582; departure, II, 18; letters of Saint Vincent to Annecy Missionaries: see **Codoing**, **Dufestel** (François), **Escart**, **Guérin** (Jean), **Le Vazeux**, **Sauvage**, **Tholard**; from Missionaries to Saint Vincent, IV, 532.

First accommodations of Missionaries, I, 566; new lodgings, II, 118; Saint Vincent presses for purchase of house, II, 235, 320; asks that they be satisfied with paying one thousand ducats for one, II, 255; Visitandines offer house to confreres, II, 333; evaluation by Saint Jane Frances of each of first Missionaries in Annecy, II, 31–33, 60; they are living the life of the seminary there, II, 118; mission in Annecy, II, 118, 405; great success of missions, II, 66, 225–26, 521; XI, 106; retreats for ordinands, XI, 106; Saint Vincent thinks ordinands should pay their expenses, II, 89.

Juste Guérin, Bishop of Geneva, plans to open seminary and to entrust it to Missionaries; Saint Vincent approves plan, except with regard to children, II, 171; agrees that future Annecy Seminary should accept only seminarians in Orders, not to teach them sciences, but only practice of their functions, II, 214; reprimands Fr. Codoing for not having sought advice before opening seminary and accepting contract entrusting it to Congregation of the Mission, II, 236; does not want professors to dictate in class, II, 240, 249, 262–67, 269–72; advises them to explain familiarly an author–Binsfeld or Toledo, for example, II, 266, 608; number of seminarians in 1647, III, 175; this seminary and the one in Alet are first two directed by Congregation of the Mission, II, 256; canonical visitation of house by Fr. Dehorgny, II, 214; by Fr. Portail, III, 267, 466; suggestion that Fr. Codoing make visitation, II, 532; visitation by Fr. Berthe, V, 598; VI, 638; VII, 25, 30, 512; Fr. Alméras, assigned to visit house, is unable to go, II, 631; III, 67–68, 93, 103, 116, 124; plan for uniting Saint-Sépulcre to Congregation of the Mission, VI, 331; VII, 40, 406, 411, 498.

Riot against Missionaries, IV, 294; VI, 517; problems of Fr. Le Vazeux, Superior, with lawyer; lawsuit, attempt at settlement, VII, 91, 95–97; Saint Vincent thanks two presidents of Senate of Chambéry, who protected Missionaries during lawsuit, VII, 98; Fr. Le Vazeux, Superior, is lent to Fr. Martin,

Superior in Genoa, for mission, VI, 523, 525; Saint Vincent permits Fr. Get, Superior in Marseilles, to go to rest in Annecy, VII, 282, 289; eccentricities of Fr. Cogley [Coglée], Superior, VII, 586; assignments and changes, II, 239, 240, 502; list of Superiors and historical synopsis of house, VIII, 608; personnel: see **Bourdet** (Étienne), **Boussordec**, **Charles** (François), **Codoing**, Cogley [Coglée], **Deheaume**, **Dufestel** (François), **Duhamel**, **Escart**, **François** (Bro.), **Guérin** (Jean), **Huitmille**, **Le Vazeux**, **Mugnier**, **Sauvage**, **Tholard**; other mentions, XIIIa, 327, 329.

Annemont (M. d'), Chaplain of Maréchal de la Meilleraye in Nantes - Advises administrators of Nantes Hospital to invite Daughters of Charity there, II, 644; concern for Sisters, III, 178, 181, 602; IV, 19; receives visit of Fr. Mousnier, Missionary, V, 278, 280; latter sends him from Madagascar recollections of Fr. Nacquart, V, 286.

Annonciades - Annonciades of Boulogne, XIIIa, 132; of Stenay, V, 473.

Anossi, region in Madagascar - III, 565; V, 519, 524; VI, 242.

Ansart (André-Joseph), priest - In citations: IV, 35; VIII, 175.

Anse [**Dans**] (Marie-Lambert, Demoiselle d'), Lady of Charity - Biographical data, III, 276; VI, 652; connection with Saint Louise, VI, 652; Mazarin's opinion of her, XIIIa, 155.

Antavares, village in Madagascar - III, 583.

Anthony (Saint), Abbot - Wished always to be kept busy, IX, 175; to be recollected was his prayer, X, 484; creatures lifted his mind to God, XI, 347; his temptation, XII, 282.

Antioch (Patriarch of), Ignatius - In Paris, V, 104.

Antoine (Bro.) - See **Flandin-Maillet** (Antoine).

Antoine (M.), Chaplain and organist in Amiens - I, 490.

Antoinette, Daughter of Charity - At Motherhouse; IX, 458, 480.

Antoinette, Daughter of Charity from Montreuil - See **Larcher** (Antoinette).

Antonines, religious Order of men - VII, 335.

Antonin de la Paix - See **La Paix** (Antonin de).

Antonio (Cardinal) - See **Barberini** (Antonio).

Antonio di Savoia [**Antoine de Savoie**], illegitimate son of Charles-Emmanuel [Carlo Emanuele], Duke of Savoy - VI, 331.

Antwerp, town in Belgium - VI, 392; VIII, 596.

***Apennines*,** mountains in Italy - V, 137.

Apocalypse - X, 373; XII, 49, 267.

Approachability - See **Affability**.

Apollonia (Saint) - IX, 470.

Apologie de Jansenius - Book lent to Saint Vincent by Comtesse de Maure, III, 168; *Apologie* to be condemned by Rome, IV, 584; condemned propositions contain teachings of Jansenius, IV, 600.

Apologie des Casuistes - Censure, VII, 499, 546–550, 627–28.

Apologetics - See **Controversy**.

Apostles - Had few temporal goods, XII, 120; carried weight of apostolate until death, IV, 54; had their differences, III, 462; IV, 442; V, 142; humbled and despised, XII, 168; abandoned Our Lord, V, 5; VI, 282–83; faults and ordeals, VIII, 401; X, 590; XI, 353; not forced to observe law of Moses, II, 158; Jesus treated them as friends, III, 319; did not want them to argue with Scribes and Pharisees, VII, 442; chose only twelve men, VIII, 183; God chose these simple men to convert the whole world, IX, 9; X, 408–409; trust in God caused them to undertake great works, X, 163; they lived the vows, XII, 300; Christ formed them to live poorly, XII, 307; meetings and councils, XIIIb, 386.

Apostles' Creed - How it was drawn up, X, 422; why, XII, 169.

Apostolic Datary, Office in Roman Curia - Comments on union of a benefice, II, 295.

Apostolic Visitation (Congregation) - Pope instructs Sacred Congregation to give confreres means of exercising functions in Rome, VII, 229; this Congregation authorizes them to have house in Rome, VII, 246; proposal to give Missionaries spiritual direction of new seminary being considered by *Propaganda*, VII, 285.

Apostolic Visitor - Question of naming one for Visitation nuns, I, 564–65, 567; need for Visitor, II, 161; Fr. Codoing should not interfere in this, II, 333.

Aquitaine - Province in France in which Dax is located - XIIIa, 297; Louis VII was Duc d'Aquitaine, XIIIa, 342.

Arabia - Saint Vincent is willing to send Missionaries there, III, 333; *Propaganda Fide* confides this mission to him, III, 372.

Arbiste (Mother) - I, 423.

Arcadius, Emperor of the East - XIIIa, 33.

Arcelin (Alexandre), Provost - Member of Charity of Mâcon, XIIIb, 74, 76, 77.

Arces, village in Charente-Maritime - VII, 575.

Archimedes, famous geometer of antiquity - I, 12.

Archives - Instructions for keeping archives in Missionaries' houses, VIII, 467–68.

Arcueil, town near Paris - Pastor is mistreated inhumanely, II, 446.

Ardilliers (***Notre-Dame***), in Saumur - Historical note, I, 512; pilgrimage of Mme Goussault, I, 193; other mentions, I, 522, 603: see ***Saumur***.

Argensolles (Mme d') - III, 513.

Argensolles Monastery - III, 513.

Argenson (Marc-René d'), son of René de Voyer d' - Biographical data, IV, 375; letter from Saint Vincent, IV, 375; other mention, I, 343.

Argenson (René de Voyer d'), Intendant in Picardy - Biographical data; his praise, I, 342; other mention, IV, 375.

Argenteuil, town in Val-d'Oise - Charity established there, XIIIb, 103; other mentions, I, 232, 239, 388, 469.

Aridity - See **Spiritual Dryness**.

Arimondo [**Alimondo**] (Luca), Priest of the Mission - Biographical data, VI, 53; XI, 333; volunteers to assist plague-stricken, VI, 53; XI, 333; assists them, VI, 157; Saint Vincent recommends him to prayers of Community, XI, 345; death, VI, 171–72, 177, 182.

Arisaig, village in Scotland - V, 121.

Ariste (Françoise-Madeleine), Visitandine - Biographical data; her praise, I, 556.

Aristotle, Greek philosopher - His philosophy, XII, 58; says nothing about humility, XII, 162; his maxim was *omnis mutatio morbus* (every change is a sickness), XIIIa, 382.

Arles, town in Bouches-du-Rhône - Bishops: see Jean Jaubert de **Barrault**, François-Adhémar de **Monteil**; Arles diocese, XIIIa, 222, 223; other mention, X, 263.

Armenians - Transported as slaves to place near Ispahan, II, 459; Armenian Bishops in Persia, III, 189; aid to Armenian priest, III, 273.

Armies - See **Soldiers**.

Arnaud (Guillaume) - Brother of the Mission - Biographical data, II, 347.

Arnaud (M.) - I, 559.

Arnaudin (M. d') - I, 10.

Arnauld (Antoine), Jansenist scholar - Biographical data, III, 322; V, 587; VI, 101; XI, 292; various works of Arnauld, III, 73, 168; IV, 182, 186; errors of Arnauld on universality of redemption, III, 324; grace and possibility of observing Commandments, III, 325; Arnauld teaches that public penance is necessary for mortal sins, even secret ones, and must precede absolution, III, 322, 358–63; teaching is opposed to that of Saint Charles Borromeo, III, 362; claims refraining from confession and Communion is act of penance, III, 358, 365; demands admirable dispositions for receiving Communion, yet says daily Mass himself, III, 363–64; Arnauld's book *De la fréquente communion,* III, 73, 321, 358–59; this work discourages faithful from receiving Communion, III, 321, 363–66; and priests from saying Mass, III, 364–65; Bishop approves it without having read it, IV, 567; Patriarch of Jansenists, IV, 593; Pope and Sorbonne censure writings, V, 587; VI, 60, 101, 132; XI, 292; Saint Vincent pleased that anyone not signing censure will lose title of Doctor, and may not take rank of Bachelor or teach theology, XI, 292; according to Arnauld, Mazarin claims Arnauld also won over Fr. Lambert, XIIIa, 155. Bro. Ducournau tells Saint Louise that Saint Vincent has not seen Arnauld's letter, V, 646; other mention, XIIIa, 171.

Arnauld (Henri), Bishop of Angers, brother of preceding - Biographical data, V, 575; VI, 75; summons Saint-Cyran to Saint-Nicolas Abbey in Angers to establish reform there, XIIIa, 131; desires Missionaries in his diocese, VI, 410; wants to entrust hospital for mentally ill to Daughters of Charity, V, 629; VI, 75, 139; Saint Vincent tells him he is sending Cécile Angiboust to Richelieu for rest, VI, 455; Saint Louise asks that he be informed of recall of this Sister to Paris, VI, 513; other mention, V, 575.

Arnauld (Marie-Angélique), sister of preceding - Abbess of Maubuisson, XIIIa, 125; misery occasioned by troubles of Fronde, IV, 396, 421; Queen of Poland sends money, asking her to see to its distribution; Queen's astonishment at seeing it being spent without consulting her, IV, 437, 612; funds Institute of Blessed Sacrament, XIIIa, 114; abbess goes several months without receiving absolution or Communion, XIIIa, 125.

Arnaut (M.) - Signed document by which Saint Vincent assumed lease of Saint-Léonard de Chaumes Abbey, XIIIa, 11.

Arnoul (Marand-Ignace), Priest of the Mission - Biographical data, VI, 210; VII, 101; Saint Vincent, who assigned him to Madagascar, requests usual faculties for him from *Propaganda*

Fide, VI, 210–11; departure for Madagascar, VII, 102, 104, 108; shipwreck and return, VII, 239, 257, 265, 282–83, 286, 287, 616; ship captured by Spaniards, VIII, 183.

Arras, town in Pas-de-Calais - Bishop: see Étienne **Moreau**; see also **Bridgettines** [**Brigittines**]; young women from Arras, II, 197; V, 13, 177; VI, 66, 80; X, 181, 183; postulants from Arras, VI, 80; Daughters of Charity, natives of Arras, III, 419; VIII, 350; clergy of Congregation of the Mission, natives of Arras diocese, V, 605; VI, 80, 161; VIII, 9, 122; Saint Vincent writes to Officialis to request two dimissorial letters, VIII, 121–22; missions, VI, 82; refuses Saint-Jean parish in Arras, which Fr. Delville offers him, VI, 634–35; Confraternity of Charity, VI, 162, 211; X, 182. See also **Delville**, **Hanotel**.

Daughters of Charity in Arras: Imminent departure of two Sisters for that town, VI, 79; permission for them to go, XIIIb, 228; exhortation of Saint Vincent before their departure, X, 181; death en route of young woman traveling with them; arrival in Arras, VI, 102; letters from Saint Vincent: see **Chétif** (Marguerite); opposition to establishment of Sisters, VI, 113; Saint Vincent unwilling to send third Sister, VI, 156; further talk of sending a third Sister, VI, 547, 589; condition for sending another Sister, VI, 609; unwilling for them to nurse sick soldiers at Hôtel-Dieu, VII, 80; withdraws prohibition, X, 594; Sisters are doing well, VI, 162, 211; X, 594; their health, VI, 211, 212, 307; other mention, X, 524; XIIIb, 428.

Arsaut (M.), notary in Paris - XIIIa, 341.

Ars-en-Ré, town in Île de Ré - François de Lanson, Prior of Saint-Étienne, XIIIa, 42

Artenay, town in Loiret - Mme Goussault spends night there, I, 193.

Arthur [**Water**] (Nicolas), Priest of the Mission - Biographical data, VI, 311; VIII, 58; sent to Montmirail, VI, 311; request for *extra tempora* for ordination, VIII, 58, 160; considered for Genoa, V, 205.

Arthur (Richard), Bishop of Limerick - III, 90.

Artois - Priests of the Mission born in Artois, VIII, 229; customary to present to King names of three monks for choice of Abbot of Saint-Éloy, V, 96. Other mention, VIII, 378.

Ascendente Domino - Bull concerning vows in approved religious Order, XIIIa, 380, 382, 405.

Asia - Capuchins request that no other Community be allowed to open houses in its towns, III, 40; Church almost entirely destroyed there, XI, 279; great diversity of languages, XII, 24.

Asnières, town near Paris - Confraternity of Charity, I, 173.

Assay, commune in Indre-et-Loire - IV, 166.

Asseline (Jacques), Priest of the Mission - Biographical data, VI, 99; VIII, 274; assigned to Marseilles house, VI, 99; in Crécy, VIII, 274, 363–64.

Assemblies of the Clergy - See **Clergy**.

Assemblies (General Assemblies of Congregation of the Mission) - Reasons for General Assemblies; purpose, members, time, place, object of deliberations, method, XIIIa, 324–25; different kinds of Assemblies, XIIIa, 374; deliberations not to be prolonged, XIIIa, 384; minutes of 1642 Assembly, XIIIa, 322–331; procedure to be followed, II, 344; examination of Rules, XIIIa, 325–27; decisions about election and deposition of Superior General, XIIIa, 327–28, 329–30; erection of provinces, XIIIa, 327, 329; means to prevent seeking of posts and benefices, XIIIa, 328; triennial assemblies, XIIIa, 329; seminary for renewal, XIIIa, 328; Saint Vincent tenders resignation, which is refused, XIIIa, 329; election of Assistants, XIIIa, 331.

Saint Vincent thinks about convoking new assembly, III, 414, 430; held in 1651, IV, 166, 226, 233, 255; minutes, XIIIa, 368–373; members, XIIIa, 369, 372, 374, 397; account of assembly, XIIIa, 374; discussion and decision about vows, XIIIa, 369, 375–83, 393–94; decisions taken about missions, XIIIa, 369–70, 383–84, 386–88; election of Superior General, XIIIa, 370, 385, 394–95; priests of Tuesday Conferences, XIIIa, 370, 386; means to prevent aspiring to posts and benefices, XIIIa, 371, 388; coadjutor Brothers, XIIIa, 371, 392–93; means to correct offenders, XIIIa, 371, 391; causes of disunion, means of maintaining charity, XIIIa, 371, 388; direction of Daughters of Charity, XIIIa, 389; obligations of poverty, XIIIa, 389–91; examination of Rules, XIIIa, 371, 395; petition to Archbishop of Paris for approval of Common and Particular Rules, XIIIa, 397; Saint Vincent's response to questions asked during assembly, XIIIa, 372–73.

Assistants, Local - IV, 448; VI, 475.

Assistants to Superior General of Congregation of the Mission - Office instituted, II, 344; its importance; required qualities; election of two Assistants by 1642 General Assembly, XIIIa, 330; what Superior General must do to replace Assistant, XIIIa, 331. See also **Superior General**.

Assistant to Superioress of Daughters of Charity - Assignments and duties, XIIIb, 124, 134, 324: see **Officers**; elections of 1651, XIIIb, 305; of 1655, V, 413; XIIIb, 226; of 1657, X, 210;

of 1660, X, 591; Saint Louise reminds Saint Vincent in 1658 and 1659 that election day is approaching, VII, 188, 597.

Assuerus [**Ahasuerus**], King of Persia - XIIIa, 41.

Assumption - Feast; confession and Communion day for Ladies of Confraternity of Charity of Châtillon, XIIIb, 18.

Assumption of Our Lady (Priests of) - I, 247.

Astronomy - Saint Vincent's knowledge of astronomy, V, 182–83; X, 475; XII, 103–04; interest in astronomic phenomena, V, 168; judges superstitious conjectures drawn by certain persons from eclipses, V, 168, 182–83; speaks with astronomer, Pierre Gassendi, V, 182; lunar eclipse after Fr. Gondrée's death, III, 443.

Athanasius (Saint) - Knowledge of principal mysteries necessary for salvation, XI, 344; shunned honors, V, 180; XII, 326; Creed bears his name, XIIIa, 32.

Atri (Geneviève Doni d'Attichy, Duchesse d'), wife of Duc d'Atri - I, 85, 336, 459; services rendered her by Antoine Le Gras, III, 518.

Atri (Marie-Angélique d'), daughter of Duc and Duchesse d'Atri - Biographical data, I, 409; Saint Vincent hears her confession, I, 409–10, 461; request for report on her condition, I, 459; judged to be possessed by demon and is exorcised, I, 459–63; cure, I, 461–63; enters Jacobins (Dominicans); ties with Port Royal, I, 462; contacts with Saint Louise, III, 518, 521.

Atri (Scipione d'Acquaviva d'Aragon, Duc d') - I, 459.

Attachments - Conference, XI, 71–72; on trials and attachments, XI, 103; mention of conference, XII, 406, 438; what is understood by attachments, IX, 198; X, 128–39; two kinds of attachments: one to what we have, another to what we desire, X, 129; permissible attachments, X, 130, 137; attachments to one's judgment, X, 134; to certain persons, IX, 198; X, 552; to relatives: see **Relatives**; to one's confessor: see **Confessors**; to women: see **Chastity**; to esteem of men: see **Vanity**; to convenience: see **Mortification**; to persons, places, and work: see **Indifference**; to worldly goods: see **Poverty**; to certain spiritual practices, X, 136–37; for frequent Communion, one must rid self of every immoderate attachment, IX, 269; lady's attachment to her dog, X, 135, 321; fearful effects of attachments, X, 132–35, 140–41, 144; this is idolatry, X, 137; adultery, X, 138; attachment to venial sin is obstacle to Communion, IX, 198; to gaining Jubilee, X, 193; attachments ensuing from too much tenderness for self, IX, 128–43; why fight against them, IX, 129–34, 136–39; how to do this, IX,

128–34, 140–43; faults they bring about, IX, 129–35. See also **Detachment**.

Attichy (Achille d'), Jesuit, son of Valence and Octavien d'Attichy - I, 336.

Attichy (Anne d'), sister of Achille d'Attichy, wife of Comte de Maure - See **Maure** (Comtesse de).

Attichy, town in Oise - I, 85.

Attichy (Geneviève d'), sister of Anne de Maure - See **Atri** (Duchesse d').

Attichy (Louis-Denis d'), Minim (Franciscan), Bishop of Riez, brother of Achille d'Attichy - Biographical data, I, 398; IV, 497; Saint Vincent writes to thank him, IV, 497.

Attichy (Octavien Doni, Sieur d'), Superintendent of Finance - I, 86.

Attichy (Valence de Marillac, Demoiselle d'), wife of Sieur d'Attichy - Her children, I, 86; contacts with Saint Louise, I, 163.

Attire [**Habit**] - Attire of Missionaries: worldly fashions must not be followed, I, 524; choir dress, I, 136; summer clothing, V, 156; cap to be worn in house, hat outdoors, II, 660; VII, 366; gloves and muffs, VII, 366; those who leave Company must give up collar, V, 128; special custom for Poland, V, 350; Saint Vincent refuses to permit Missionaries in Marseilles to wear short cassock in galleys, II, 500; hesitates to allow Missionaries in Rome to dress Italian style, II, 306–07; Jesuits in Poland wear dressing gowns in towns, V, 350; Saint Louise puts on habit of Daughter of Charity, II, 199; uniformity, II, 206–207; Saint Vincent urges Solminihac to send man to Rome without habit, III, 226; monk who alters habit is excommunicated, IV, 77, 79; men sent by Solminihac were at risk in Rome because of this, IV, 135; Sister Nicole wants to leave Company but continue to wear habit, V, 44; Sister asks to receive it, VII, 465.

Attire of coadjutor Brothers: black habit in house, grey outdoors, XII, 207–08; not given black habit easily, XIIIa, 371; short habit, even in Italy, II, 513; failings of Brothers in Genoa, XIIIa, 392; of Bro. Pintart, VII, 591; grey attire for guard duty and work on fortifications, IV, 284.

Attire of Daughters of Charity: may not make their own clothing, but take what is made for them, X, 252–55; wear dress of country women, XIIIb, 125; consequently, as lay women, IX, 165; in grey dress, IX, 530; and poor, IX, 139, 213, 248, 529; X, 299; same everywhere, II, 81, 151; VII, 477; IX, 139, 400; X, 253–54, 283–84, 299, 302–03; XIIIb, 125, 136; no vanity in clothing, X, 152, 230, 238–41, 298; no veil, II, 207, 675; IX, 545; X, 15, 282; beautiful robe of charity, X, 379, 401. See also **Headdress**.

Aubel (Nicolas), of Mâcon - XIIIb, 74.

Aubert (Charles), priest of Le Mans - Dedication to Saint Vincent of *Discours du respect et honneur des enfants envers leurs pères et mères* (*Discourse on Respect and Honor of Children for Their Parents*), III, 152.

Aubert (M.), chaplain of Mme de Longueville - Asks Saint Vincent to receive children of Duchesse de Longueville and give them his blessing, VIII, 498; letters from Saint Vincent regarding succession to throne of Poland, VI, 94–95, 98, 296.

Aubert (M.) - VIII, 499.

Aubert (Pierre), merchant in Le Mans - III, 237, 492; VII, 533.

Aubervilliers, town near Paris - See ***Vertus*** (*Notre-Dame*).

Aubin (Bro.) - See **Gontier** (Aubin).

Aubrai (Mlle d'), niece of Fr. Olier - Consulted by her, Saint Vincent gives wise advice concerning vocation, VIII, 400; she enters Daughters of the Holy Virgin, VIII, 400, 473.

Aubry (M.) - Priory of Chandenier, V, 505, 549–50.

Aubry de Vitry (Mlle) - Asks for indulgences for Confraternity of Charity, I, 246.

Auch, town in Gers - VIII, 602.

Auchy (Vincente), Daughter of Charity - Biographical data, II, 165; X, 493; requested by Ladies of Charity of Saint-Germain-l'Auxerrois, II, 176; questioned in course of conference; sentiments concerning Barbe Angiboust, X, 493, 522; other mention, XIIIb, 227.

Auclerc (Mme), sister of Jacques Tholard - Request refused for admission of self and daughter to Company of Daughters of Charity, XIIIb, 348.

Audiat (Louis) - XIIIa, 12.

Audibert (Honorat) - V, 326.

Auditors - Contacts with Saint Louise, I, 172.

Audoire (Antoine), Mercedarian Father - VIII, 309–10.

Augny (Philibert Estienne, Sieur d'), Lieutenant General in Metz - VII, 86.

Auguste - Titular Bishop: see Pierre **Bédacier**.

Augustine (Saint) - His Communities, IX, 194; X, 166; XIIIb, 351; Rule, III, 487; submission to Pope, VI, 292; writes catechism,

XIIIa, 33; *Confessions*, XI, 3, 44; XII, 291; did not find God until he sought Him within himself, XII, 111; Jansenius read his works several times, III, 323; but did not understand him as well as Council of Trent, III, 328; errors of Jansenius were different from those in Augustine's time, XIIIa, 166; comparison to explain Mystery of Trinity, XIIIa, 176; danger of venial sins, X, 206; counsels obedience to physicians, III, 301; authorizes measures in favor of sinners and prisoners, VII, 443; recommends that abuses not be attacked too soon, IV, 127; interpretation of Matthew 5:4, III, 498; began Rules of his Institute by stating its purpose, XII, 68.

Teachings of Saint Augustine: no salvation without explicit knowledge of Mysteries, X, 271; XI, 172–73, 343–44; XII, 72; grace is necessary to do good, XIIIa, 165; not that we lack grace, but that we fail to use it, XIIIa, 168–72; conversion should not be put off until hour of death, XIIIa, 112; anything that leads one to do good comes from God, X, 79; same for works that seem to come about by themselves, IX, 166, 247, 357, 359, 473, 537; XII, 6; misfortune not to have loving heart, XII, 317; truths of God never deceive, IX, 199; cautions about attacking straightaway vice that is rampant, IV, 127; fire of purgatory burns more than one imagines, IX, 482; in heaven parents see the good their children are doing on earth, XI, 363, 390–91; one who refuses penance, refuses forgiveness, IX, 444; quotations, XI, 130; XII, 263; XIIIa, 113; publicly admonished persons of faults, XII, 40; other mentions, XI, 117, 354.

Augustinian monks - Spirit of poverty of first Augustinians, X, 255; Augustinian monks of Paris; Forty Hours' Devotion in their church in 1656, V, 563; contacts of Assistant with Fr. Vitet; Chancelade affair, IV, 73, 96; rebellion against orders of Parlement and against armed violence, XII, 53; Augustinians of Bar-le-Duc, II, 29.

Augustinian nuns - Of Hotel-Dieu of Paris: Saint Vincent compares their vocation to that of Daughters of Charity, IX, 106, 114; sometimes considers vocation of those nuns more noble, IX, 32, 361; sometimes that of Daughters, X, 92, 93, 102, 117; Daughters should have virtues of those nuns, X, 118; nuns think Ladies of Charity tire sickest patients too much, III, 261–62; satisfaction with work of Ladies, XIIIb, 384, 387, 389; Saint Vincent recommends that Ladies not give advice to nuns, but rather notify their Officers, XIIIb, 389; nuns no longer sit up with sick at night, X, 548; ask for brass crosses to assist dying, XIIIb, 389; contacts of Saint Louise with Prioress, III, 209, 519, 520; remembered in Mme Goussault's will, XIIIb, 393. Other mention, I, 211.

Aulent (Charles), Priest of the Mission - Biographical data, I, 542; III, 226; forthcoming entrance to Saint-Lazare, I, 278–79; assists poor people of Lorraine, I, 542; Superior in Toul, III, 69; VIII, 605; death, III, 226.

Aumale, town in Seine-Maritime - Birthplace of Fr. Callon, I, 441; he becomes Pastor there, I, 445; mission in area, I, 584; vicariate of Aumale, III, 478; Abbot of Aumale, II, 419.

Aumône - Name given to Charity of Mâcon, XIIIb, 77.

Aumone Abbey - See **Blampignon**, **Chandenier** (Claude de).

Aunis, province of France - XIIIa, 20.

Auroy (Antoine), convict in Toulon - Money sent to him, VI, 487; VII, 101, 187, 274, 489, 539.

Auteuil, former village, today district of Paris - Daughters of Charity requested for Charity of Auteuil, VIII, 429, 465, 501; Saint Vincent fears that Jansenist Pastor might have bad influence on Sisters, VIII, 501.

Authority - Conference on responsibilities and positions of authority, XI, 124; do nothing against statutes of Princes, VI, 30.

Authier de Sisgau (Christophe d'), Bishop of Bethlehem, founder of Priests of Most Blessed Sacrament - Biographical data, I, 221; II, 276; IV, 61; recalls priest from Senlis to send to Rome, II, 281; letter from Saint Vincent, II, 281; Superiors of their Company would like him to be General's Coadjutor, II, 438; goes to Paris to bring about the union, II, 452; Saint Vincent has put off discussing union with him, II, 459; determined to get See of Babylon, II, 465; confidence in success of minor seminary, II, 506; his community first called Priests of the Clergy, VI, 517; Saint Vincent denies trying to harm him or his Community, IV, 145, 148; named Bishop of Babylon, IV, 148; other mentions, IV, 294, 295, 346. See also **Blessed Sacrament** (Congregation).

Autin (Marguerite), Daughter of Charity - Signs attestation after reading of Common and Particular Rules reviewed and arranged in order by Fr. Alméras, XIIIb, 206.

Autin (Nicolas), Pastor of la Madeleine in Paris - VIII, 507.

Auton (Louis), merchant in Rome - V, 272, 276.

Autun, town in Saône-et-Loire - Autun diocese, VI, 606; Bishop: see Louis d'**Attichy**.

Auvergne, province - I, 547; V, 442; VIII, 229, 479; IX, 308; Fr. Alméras cannot cross mountains of Auvergne, III, 124–125.

Auvergne (Émilie-Léonore de la Tour d'), Carmelite - Desires to make retreat with Visitation Nuns, VII, 419; habit taking, VIII, 481–82, 511.

Auvergne (Louise de la Tour d') - Asks Saint Vincent's permission for her sister Mauricette to go to habit taking of their sister Émilie, VIII, 511.

Auvergne (Mauricette-Fébronie de la Tour d') - Biographical data, VIII, 472; boarder at Second Monastery of Visitation in Paris, VIII, 472; asks permission of Saint Vincent to attend habit taking of her Carmelite sister, VIII, 481–82; Superioress of Monastery sees no difficulty in granting permission, VIII, 511.

Auvry - See **Savry**.

Aux Couteaux [**Lambert aux Couteaux**], Priest of the Mission - Biographical data, I, 207; II, 9; III, 103; IV, 113; V, 167; IX, 464; letters Saint Vincent writes to him: in Toul, I, 323; in Richelieu, I, 417, 437, 447, 452, 458, 500, 508; II, 78, 95, 112, 149, 237, 563; IV, 149, 166; at Saint-Lazare, III, 392, 405; in Warsaw, IV, 289, 315, 319, 326, 339, 347, 352, 370–71, 375, 382, 396, 410, 517, 527; Superior, VIII, 1651; reference to letter of Saint Vincent to him, II, 9; III, 431, 433; letters to Saint Vincent: from Richelieu, II, 294; from Nantes, III, 216; reference to letter from Saint Vincent to him at Saint-Lazare, III, 405; in Richelieu, IV, 113; in Warsaw, IV, 327, 340, 348, 354, 450; reference to letter from Fr. Codoing, III, 515; reference to letter to Duchesse d'Aiguillon, IV, 113; Saint Vincent uses him as an example, I, 277, 335; V, 167; cites him in letter to Blatiron, IV, 527; Superior at Saint-Charles, VIII, 614; his praises, II, 65, 237; III, 169, 340, 374; IV, 348, 538, 544; his nephew: see **Jouailly**.

On mission in Southwest, I, 183, 207; Superior in Toul, VIII, 605; military chaplain, I, 335, 342; at Saint-Lazare, I, 376–77; Superior and Pastor in Richelieu, I, 402, 404, 440, 442, 499, 504, 589, 591; II, 9, 24, 107, 130, 208, 343; VIII, 607; asked to make visitation of Sisters in Angers, II, 81; health, I, 500; other visitations: La Rose, II, 69, 78, 467; Saint-Lazare, II, 237; Lorraine, II, 322, 324; Annecy, II, 235, 331, 335; asked to take charge of Confraternities of Charity, II, 166; at 1642 General Assembly, II, 343–44; XIIIa, 323, 331, 396; member of commission for revision of Rules, II, 344; XIIIa, 326, 396; negotiates Sedan foundation, II, 524–25; contacts with Daughters of Charity, II, 189.

At Saint-Lazare, II, 335, 353, 461, 533, 537, 541, 624, 655, 656; III, 303, 316, 317, 331, 399–401, 439, 456, 470; Saint Vincent proposes him to Superiors as substitute for Fr. Portail, Assistant, in latter's absence, II, 585; Fr. Lambert acts as Assistant, III, 374; present at Council of Daughters of Charity,

XIIIb, 287, 289, 291–93, 299; replaces Saint Vincent in his absence, III, 392, 404–05, 408, 430–31; makes short renewal in Internal Seminary, II, 584; III, 297; Superior of Collège des Bons-Enfants, III, 103; VIII, 604; Saint Vincent thinks of him for coadjutorship of Babylon, III, 169, 189; visitation of Nantes Sisters, III, 185, 216; XIIIb, 143; of Missionaries in Saintes, Cahors, III, 239, 340–41; Luçon, IV, 149; Le Mans, IV, 275; Cahors seminary, III, 239; Superior in Richelieu, IV, 114; VIII, 607; Saint Vincent hesitates to send him to Marseilles, III, 267; Fr. Lambert asks to be sent to Madagascar, XI, 372; Mazarin thinks he has spoken ill of him, XIIIa, 154; and has been won over by ideas of Antoine Arnauld, XIIIa, 155; named Titular Consul of France to Algiers, XIIIa, 346–47; at 1651 Assembly, XIIIa, 369, 372, 374, 384, 396–97; opinion concerning vows, XIIIa, 380, 383.

Sent to Warsaw, IV, 251; XIIIa, 398; Superior, XIIIa, 398–99; arrival in Warsaw, IV, 273, 289; in Warsaw, IV, 335, 456, 541; VIII, 617; IX, 464; health, IV, 450, 452, 456; assists plague-stricken of Warsaw, IV, 472, 514; Queen has him live in her palace, IV, 472; death, IV, 536–39, 544, 558; mention of conference on his virtues, XII, 416; other mentions, I, 273; III, 340; XIIIa, 344. See also ***Poland, Warsaw***.

Auxerre, town in Yonne - Birthplace of Fr. Guillot, Priest of the Mission, IV, 573; V, 84, 93.

Availability - Disposition of good servants and apostolic men, sign of true children of God, VIII, 10; conference, XII, 44–47; means to put self in state of availability, XII, 47, 198, 223, 274. See also **Indifference**.

Avançon, village in Ardennes - Ruined church, VIII, 27, 29.

Avania - Definition, VI, 9; XI, 151, 334; XIIIa, 345; avania caused by Fr. Sérapion hindered construction of hospital in Algiers, VI, 9; suffering of Barreau from avania, VI, 466; VIII, 309, 327; XI, 334; could be used against Fr. Huguier because he is a priest, VII, 186; Jean Le Vacher subjected to avania, XI, 151; Husson and Jean LeVacher cautioned to avoid anything that could provoke it, XIIIa, 402.

Avaratra Malemy, village in Madagascar - VI, 242–43.

Avarice - Sin of Judas, IX, 362; to be avoided, IX, 390; vice of liberality, X, 392; Sisters going to Metz must combat it, X, 448; root of all evil, XI, 223–226.

Avaugour (Baron d'), French Ambassador to Sweden - Efforts to lure Fr. Guillot to Sweden, V, 180, 229, 249, 255, 352; Avaugour sends for three priests from France, V, 323; Saint Vincent entrusts to him Priests of the Mission and Daughters of Charity in Poland, V, 418, 424; his chaplains, V, 363; VIII, 193.

Aversa (Raffaello), Superior General of Theatines - Biographical data, V, 567; VI, 373; consulted by Saint Vincent, V, 567; death, VI, 373.

Aversion [**Antipathy**] - Text of Rule of Daughters of Charity, X, 368; involuntary aversion not a hindrance to charity, X, 371; aversions must be overcome, IX, 127; X, 369; XI, 92; by support and humility, VI, 51; IX, 198; do not dwell on them, IX, 99; causes and remedies, IX, 198; X, 369–73; tell Superiors about them, IX, 10, 88; their dangers, IX, 88; XIIIb, 126, 137; make no correction out of antipathy, X, 337; XI, 96; for election of Officers, Daughters of Charity must not allow themselves to be guided by likes and dislikes, X, 216.

Avignon, town in Vaucluse - Saint Vincent's time there, I, 9, 11; convent of Celestine Fathers, V, 380; Collège of Savoyards, IV, 294; VI, 517; other mentions, II, 262; V, 78; VII, 97.

Avignon (***Comtat d'***), area near Avignon - II, 64.

Ávila (Fr.), Spanish priest - XIIIa, 130.

Ávila (Bl. John), Apostle of Andalusia - I, 153.

Ávila (Teresa), Saint - See **Teresa**.

Avoie, Daughter of Charity - See **Vigneron** (Avoie).

Avoy (Antoine), galley convict in Toulon - VI, 338.

Avril (M.), in Angers - Saint Vincent writes him about sum of money, VI, 409.

Avrit (M.) d' - V, 503.

Ax-les-Thermes, town in Ariège - Dispute between Archpriest of Ax and other priests, III, 96.

Ay, town in Marne - Mission given, VII, 169.

Aymon (Jean) in Courboin - Reference to his wife; XIIIb, 93.

Azor (Jean), Jesuit theologian - V, 319.

B

Bab-Azoun, near Algiers - Christian cemetery; III, 222, 309.

Babel, tower - XII, 349.

Bab-el-Oued Gate, Algiers - III, 222.

Babylon, capital of ancient Chaldea - Jewish captives in Babylon, I, 8; Jean Duval named Titular Bishop; departure for Ispahan,

II, 65; returns to France, submits resignation on condition of having in France an abbey or another diocese, II, 457–58; bishopric offered to Congregation of the Mission, II, 457–58; difficulties preventing Saint Vincent from accepting bishopric and mission of Ispahan, II, 522; reasons inclining him to accept it, III, 164–65, 169, 187–89; offers it to Fr. Féret, III, 165; to Fr. Brandon, III, 165; considers Fr. Gilles, III, 165; Fr. Lambert aux Couteaux, III, 169, 189; Fr. Authier has his eye on bishopric, II, 465; takes steps in Rome, IV, 148; accuses Saint Vincent of thwarting his plans, IV, 145, 148; Fr. des Lions [Deslyons], in Senlis, has 'notion' about bishopric, IV, 145, 148. Placide-Louis Duchemin named Bishop, VIII, 192; other mentions, II, 470, 492; III, 372.

Bachelet (Mme), in Paris - VII, 313.

Bacourt (Françoise) - Member of Charity of Folleville, XIIIb, 48.

Badou (M.) - Saint Vincent thinks he has no vocation to priesthood, VI, 494.

Bagard (Catherine), Daughter of Charity - Biographical data, III, 178; sent to Nantes, III, 8; XIIIb, 249; faults, III, 208; question of replacing her, III, 178, 215; return to Paris, III, 216; other mention, I, 533.

Bagni (Paolo Nicolò di), Cardinal - VIII, 543.

Bagno (Giovanni Francesco Guidi di), Nuncio to France, then Cardinal - Biographical data, I, 165; II, 44; his praise; Saint Vincent keeps his portrait, I, 538, 586; benefactor of the Mission, I, 537–39, 585–86; II, 44–45, 170; reply to *Propaganda Fide* concerning suitability of Saint Vincent to direct Congregation of the Mission, XIIIa, 238; asked to inform Saint Vincent of papal approval, XIIIa, 240; letters to Cardinal Ludovisi, XIIIa, 242, 245; letters to Msgr. Francesco Ingoli, XIIIa, 244, 246, 251; from *Propaganda Fide* to Nuncio to France, XIIIa, 234, 250, 252.

Bagno (Nicolò Guidi di), Nuncio to France, then Cardinal - Biographical data, II, 550; III, 162–63; V, 45–46; VI, 22; VII, 12; VIII, 109; XI, 373; letters from Saint Vincent, IV, 268, 331; V, 45, 68; VI, 22, 322, 498; VIII, 139; mention of letter to Saint Vincent, VI, 498; detains Solminihac, II, 616; has written to Solminihac about Capuchin Provincial, III, 162; proposes mission of Persia to Saint Vincent, III, 165; also proposes Madagascar, VIII, 616; XI, 373; XIIIa, 358; baptizes native of that country, III, 282, 560; gives full authority to Missionaries sent to this mission, III, 282; Saint Vincent sends him names of other missionaries destined for Madagascar, IV, 109; Cardinal Sforza presents letters regarding Fr. Nacquart and Fr. Gondrée going to Madagascar, XIIIa, 361; Saint Vincent tells him what he has learned from Carmelite destined for mission of Memphis, IV, 269; asks to be excused from sending anyone to mission of Morocco since Recollects wish it for themselves, IV, 332; has spoken with Nuncio about bishopric of Babylon, IV, 145, 148; asks that Nuncio be requested to check on qualifications of abbé supposed to be in charge of seminary in Gentilly, IV, 296; asks *Propaganda* to grant faculties to priests for America, with Nuncio's approval, IV, 337; and for Madagascar, IV, 338; V, 175–176; proposes Fr. Berthe for mission of Mount Lebanon, VI, 22, 23, 28; goes to see Ambassador of Portugal, V, 46, 68; Nuncio and Jansenism, II, 550; III, 73; IV, 184, 584, 592; speaks to Saint Vincent about matters in Poland, V, 143; informs him of death of Archbishop of Myra, V, 103.

Saint Vincent congratulates him on elevation to cardinalate, VI, 322; Nuncio asks saint to send two priests to visit missions of Ireland and Scotland; saint asks if this invitation comes from *Propaganda Fide*, VI, 460–61; proposes Missionary to Cardinal di Bagno, VI, 499–500, 618; VII, 12; Cardinal invites Missionaries in Rome to give mission in his diocese, VI, 349, 429, 605; helps them find lodging, VII, 40; sells them his own palace at reduced price, VIII, 109, 117, 134, 147, 173, 610; receives thanks from Saint Vincent, VIII, 139; wants to see Missionaries established in his diocese, VII, 46–47; health, VII, 543, 561; authentic copy of Bull of Erection of Congregation of the Mission certified by Nuncio, IV, 398; Nuncio sent by Innocent X to remedy problems in France, IV, 446; his return to Italy, VI, 267. Other mentions, III, 289; VI, 553.

Bagot (Jean), Jesuit - Biographical data; praises Missionaries in Rome, II, 412; Saint Vincent questions him about practice of Jesuits, VI, 104.

Bahouache (Dian), chief in Madagascar - VI, 221.

Baignolz (Charles de), priest of Community of Saint-Nicolas-du-Chardonnet - VII, 504.

Baillé (Charlotte), Daughter of Charity - Signs attestation regarding Common and Particular Rules reviewed and arranged in order by Fr. Alméras, XIIIb, 206.

Bailleul (Élisabeth-Marie), Lady of Charity - I, 230.

Bailleul (Nicolas de), Provost of Tradesmen - I, 22, 230.

Baillon (M.) - VIII, 113.

Baillon (Marie-Cécile), Visitandine - II, 454.

Bailly (Barbe), Daughter of Charity, sister of Philippe - Biographical data, VII, 408; VIII, 214; Saint Louise asks permission for her to renew vows, VII, 408; VIII, 214–15; authorization to travel to Poland, XIIIb, 238–39; signs attestation regarding Common and Particular Rules reviewed and arranged in order by Fr. Alméras, XIIIb, 206; other mentions, XIIIb, 227, 375.

Bailly (Philippe), Daughter of Charity, sister of Barbe - Biographical data, V, 357; X, 595; Saint Louise asks permission for her to renew vows, V, 357; election to office of Bursar, VIII, 312; X, 595, 596; other mention, XIIIb, 227.

Bains (Lancry de), Prioress of Carmel on rue Saint-Jacques, Paris - VIII, 506–07.

Baius [**De Bay**] (Michel), Professor at University of Louvain - Biographical data, III, 320; XIIIa, 166; errors taken up by Jansenius and condemned by Popes and Sorbonne, III, 320, 323; IV, 607; XIIIa, 166.

Bajoteau (Claude), boarder at Le Mans Seminary - V, 101.

Bajoue (Emerand), Priest of the Mission - Biographical data, III, 29; IV, 333; V, 232; VI, 178; VII, 165; letters Saint Vincent writes to him in La Rose, IV, 333; in Notre-Dame-de-Lorm, IV, 557, 587; in Montauban, V, 232; letters Saint Vincent receives from him, VI, 626; VII, 165; reference to letters to Saint Vincent, IV, 467, 558, 588; V, 232; at Saint-Lazare, III, 29, 104, 381; XIIIa, 335, 337; Superior in La Rose, IV, 372, 467; VIII, 606; receives from Coadjutor of Montauban benefice of Notre-Dame-de-Lorm and Saint-Aignan parish, IV, 383, 588–89; Superior at Notre-Dame-de-Lorm, IV, 544, 587–88; VIII, 618; illness, V, 233; Saint Vincent urges him not to resign too quickly benefice of Notre-Dame-de-Lorm and Saint-Aignan parish, IV, 558, 588; rebukes him for accepting parish of Brial, since he already had one, IV, 588–89; recalled to Paris, V, 233; in Luçon, VI, 178; at Saint-Lazare, VI, 476; out giving missions, VI, 358; VII, 373, 430; mission in Sillery: see ***Sillery*** (village); in Fontaine, VII, 165; in Ay, VII, 169; present when Saint Vincent receives Last Sacraments, XIIIa, 203; other mentions, VI, 632; VII, 505; XIIIa, 344.

Balaam - II, 5; VI, 292.

Balaguier, priory - II, 417; income used to support establishment of Missionaries in Cahors diocese, VIII, 611.

Balan, village near Sedan - V, 63; VI, 624; VIII, 611.

Balar (M.), colonist in Madagascar - VI, 219.

Bâle [***Basel***], town in Switzerland - Bishop: see Johann Conrad **Roggenbach**.

Baliano (Pietro Paulo), Priest of the Mission - Biographical data, III, 332; V, 154; VI, 299; VII, 543; mention of letter to Saint Vincent, V, 154; in Genoa; health, III, 332; in Rome, V, 154; VI, 374, 525, 636; out giving missions, V, 275; VII, 543; Saint Vincent talks of sending him to Turin, VI, 299, 308; sends him to Genoa, VI, 630.

Ballagny (Charles), convict in Toulon - VII, 289, 392, 457; VIII, 138.

Bance (Jean), Brother of the Mission - Biographical data; desires to go to Madagascar, III, 287.

Bandini (Ottavio), Cardinal - Member of Congregation of *Propaganda Fide*, XIIIa, 229, 239.

Bandits - Great number in Italy; conversions obtained by Genoa Missionaries, III, 258, 385; IV, 406–08; VII, 484; XI, 245–46, 380.

Banquets - Saint Vincent forbids Missionaries to take part in them, V, 334, 346–48, 384, 592; VIII, 178; Rules of Daughters of Charity forbid them to eat outside their houses, X, 114. See also **Meals**.

Baptism - Oils to be taken to Madagascar, III, 282; Naquart's administration of Sacrament and his thoughts on it, III, 559–563, 566; question of validity of Huguenots' administration of Baptism, VIII, 21, 31; two Baptisms at Table Bay, VIII, 587; Church's practice of giving godparents, IX, 181; foundlings, IX, 112; lay persons may baptize in absence of priest, XI, 173; vows are new Baptism, XII, 302; mention of conference, XII, 437.

Barabbas, Jewish criminal, released in preference to Jesus - XI, 383, 388.

Baradat (François de), Seigneur de Damery - VIII, 518.

Baradat (Henri de), Bishop of Noyon - Takes interest in sanctuary of Notre-Dame-de-Paix, VIII, 26, 60, 71, 82, 93; death, VIII, 518.

Barat (Néméric), Master Alderman of Toul - Entrusted hospital he built there to Order of Saint-Esprit, I, 417; II, 40.

Barbadigo (Gregorio), Cardinal Bishop of Bergamo - VI, 541.

Barbara (Saint) - Mme de Gondi implores her help, XIIIa, 59.

Barbary, in North Africa - Conference on greatness of Barbary Mission, XI, 63; Ducoudray sent for release of slaves and mission to others, II, 355; Saint Vincent tells Codoing to be at peace about Barbary, II, 394; spiritual assistance to poor slaves, II, 398, 407; mission not handled at expense of

Congregation of the Mission, II, 427; plague, III, 481; V, 401; transport of contraband merchandise, V, 412; letters and packages sent from Barbary, IV, 521; V, 140; VII, 6, 323; letters and money sent to Barbary, V, 121, 227; Capuchins in Barbary, III, 308, 310, 311.

Missionaries in Barbary: Christ sent Apostles even there, XI, 264; detachment necessary for this mission, XII, 198; Jacques Le Soudier set out, but is still in Marseilles, III, 82; Recollect Father usurped his place there, III, 92; Jean Guérin's willingness to go there, IV, 535; martyrdom of priest from Calabria, XI, 167; letters from Saint Vincent, V, 495; VIII, 358; cautions about expenses, III, 394; letters to Saint Vincent, III, 445; V, 401; Fr. Get takes steps to prevent loss of letters from there, VI, 200; Bro. Nodo's desire to go there, III, 335; ministries, XIIIa, 350; income, V, 191; VI, 54, 486; VII, 115; XIIIa, 421; Saint Vincent considers sending Pierre du Chesne for canonical visit, V, 11, 147; their occupations, IV, 291, 335, 493; V, 72, 180, 339, 495, 573; VIII, 277; XI, 180, 191, 261; difficulties of their task, V, 316, 573, 603, 612; VIII, 528; XI, 63, 66, 191–192; doing well there, IV, 335, 372; conversions of Turks and renegade slaves, III, 445–46; V, 401–02; reports on ministries, VI, 199; services Marseilles house renders to Barbary mission: see ***Marseilles***; Jean Le Vacher advises against sending more men until disorders are remedied, VII, 522; Saint Vincent's captivity there, I, 1-11; VIII, 599; Marseilles house established to console captives, VIII, 610; other mentions, III, 372; IV, 107; XI, 184, 261–62, 302, 364; XII, 79, 81; XIIIa, 186. See also ***Algiers, Salé, Tunis***.

Barbe, Daughter of Charity - Considers entering religious Order, I, 390–91.

Barbe, Daughter of Charity - In Fréneville, III, 406.

Barbe, Daughter of Charity - In Saint-Leu, I, 371, 388, 391, 398.

Barbe, Daughter of Charity - In Hennebont, IV, 238.

Barbe, Daughter of Charity - In Metz, X, 447.

Barbe, Daughter of Charity - Saint Vincent advises Saint Louise to have her make retreat, XII, 358.

Barberini (Antonio), Cardinal, nephew of Francesco Antonio Barberini (Pope Urban VIII) - Biographical data, I, 584; II, 254; V, 2; VIII, 148; XII, 369; letters from Saint Vincent, IV, 369, 443, 483; V, 23, 77; XII, 369; letters to Saint Vincent, II, 556; V, 55; asks saint for Missionaries to Ireland, II, 557; VIII, 615; Saint Vincent proposes to him Missionaries for Madagascar, V, 78; objects to French priests seeking authorization from *Propaganda Fide* for new body of missionaries in France, XII, 369; reports on visit to Longchamp Abbey, IV, 484; writes concerning Bishops of Tonkin and departure for Madagascar, V, 78; Saint Vincent informs Fr. Codoing of letter from Mazarin to Cardinal Barberini, II, 254; has delivered letter from Cardinal to Archbishop of Trabzon [Trebizond], V, 176; capture by Turks of ship carrying servants and baggage of Cardinal; efforts for release of servants and return of baggage, V, 2, 23, 35, 36, 55, 325, 355; petition to impede multiplication of Congregations having same ministries, IV, 610; decision about foundation made in Loreto by Duchesse d'Aiguillon, VIII, 148, 239; other mention, IV, 611.

Barberini (Antonio Marcello), Cardinal, Capuchin, called Cardinal of Sant'Onofrio - Biographical data, II, 349; brother of Pope Urban VIII, II, 232; asks Saint Vincent to send Missionaries to Ireland, II, 556; requests Missionaries for his diocesan seminary, II, 515; other mentions, II, 232, 434; IV, 611; XIIIa, 250.

Barberini (Carlo) Cardinal, grand-nephew of Pope Urban VIII - Biographical data, VII, 329; XIIIa, 239.

Barberini (Francesco), Cardinal, brother of younger Cardinal Antonio - Biographical data, II, 434; IV, 43; letter from Saint Vincent, IV, 43; other mentions, II, 232, 434.

Barbezieux, town in Charente - Saint Vincent tells Fr. De Sergis to pass through there on his way to preach a mission in La Marguerie, I, 430.

Barbier (C.), Pastor in Maule - Letter to Saint Vincent, VIII, 548.

Barbier (Louis), Abbé de la Rivière - Biographical data, III, 411; chapels in Le Mans, III, 381. See also **Rivière** (Abbé).

Barbuise, village in Aube - Bishop of Troyes would like to unite parish to seminary, V, 82, 142, 312.

Barcelona, city in Spain - Project for establishment of Missionaries, II, 498–99, 502, 507, 520. See also ***Catalonia.***

Barcos (Martin de), nephew of Abbé de Saint-Cyran - Writings, I, 6, 7; III, 73–74; praise of his knowledge by Saint-Cyran, XIIIa, 114; other mentions, XIIIa, 107, 171.

Bardin (M.) - VII, 320.

Barillon (M.) - See **Morangis** (Antoine Barillon de).

Bar-le-Duc, town in Meuse - Missionaries distribute relief to inhabitants, I, 582; II, 26, 42, 73, 76–77, 93; Missionary dies there, II, 29, 42.

Barnabas (Saint), Apostle - Disagreement with Saint Paul, IV, 233; VII, 442; IX, 10; feast day, X, 475; other mention, III, 558.

Barnabites (Order) - In their collèges they entrust humanities to associates, VI, 338; other mention, V, 354; friar sends money for his brother's ransom, VII, 195; Jeanne Dalmagne entrusts future to decision of Dom Morice, IX, 156.

Barny (Georges), Superior General of Order of Grandmont - Saint Vincent writes to him about Fr. Frémont, IV, 308.

Baron, locality in district of Senlis (Oise) - Pastor awaits Sister, II, 390.

Baron (M.), merchant in Paris - V, 36.

Barra, island in Hebrides - V, 122.

Barrault (Jean Jaubert de), Bishop of Bazas, then Archbishop of Arles - Saint Vincent consults him on Pébrac affair, I, 208–09; sends him Missionaries, I, 332; tried to restore regularity in Saint-Césaire Monastery, III, 161; other mentions, I, 58; II, 452.

Barre (M.), settler in Madagascar - VI, 249.

Barreau (Jean), seminarian of the Mission, Consul of France in Algiers - Biographical data, II, 677; III, 6; IV, 86; V, 2; VI, 7–8; VII, 7; VIII, 261; XI, 192; letters from Saint Vincent, III, 24, 46, 242, 384; IV, 86, 146, 227, 360, 597; V, 34, 146; VI, 7, 153, 187, 344, 479; VII, 303, 462, 632; mention of letters from Saint Vincent, III, 51, V, 2, 23, 35, 145, 163, 324–25, 353, 530, 405; VI, 328, 384; VII, 114, 263; letters to Saint Vincent, III, 218, 304; V, 324, 353, 390, 403; mention of letters to Saint Vincent, III, 25, 243, 268, 349, 452; IV, 372; V, 34, 170, 326, 530; VI, 7, 133, 183–84, 187, 200; VII, 303, 462, 632; native place and family, V, 91; brothers, V, 35, 149, 327, 404; VI, 480, 487; VII, 303, 464; aunt, III, 25, 47.

Advice saint gives before Barreau's departure for Algiers, XIIIa, 344; arrival in Algiers, II, 677; will serve as Consul, II, 678; III, 6, 24; new recommendations of Saint Vincent, III, 46–48; IV, 360; difference of opinion with Boniface Nouelly, III, 50; advice from Saint Vincent, III, 51; Consul helps to ransom slaves, XI, 192; Portail urged to delay sending new personnel unless Barreau can bear expenses, III, 414; Philippe Le Vacher encouraged to defer to Barreau's opinions, IV, 128; Barreau takes upon self to pay 40,000 livres to free Father of Mercy, III, 94, and 7,000 *piastres* for other captives, III, 107–08; Saint Vincent works to get this sum, reprimands him, forbids him to get involved in ransom of slaves, III, 126; Barreau pays for his imprudence by imprisonment (June 26-July 20, 1647), III, 218–19; new imprisonment, slaves living in Consul's residence, III, 223, 311; V, 391; VIII, 503; Saint Vincent promises to intervene with King of France, IV, 147;

Louis XIV writes to Pasha on behalf of Barreau, V, 644; saint congratulates Barreau on his freedom, IV, 227.

Destitution of Consul, V, 248, 328, 404; debts, VI, 11, 154; XI, 334; Saint Vincent reproaches him for superfluous expenses, VI, 10, 153; urges him to decrease them and no longer get involved, V, 34; VI, 154; difficulty ransoming many slaves with little money, V, 379; his work for ransom of slaves, V, 380; sends money to Duchesse d'Aiguillon for ransom of slave, V, 408; is sent money from coach revenues, VI, 54; steps taken by Fathers of Mercy to compensate him for money spent for one of their men, VI, 9–10, 483; VII, 468; VIII, 309–310; goes deeper into debt; Saint Vincent laments this, V, 326, 385; VI, 64, 154, 188, 189, 200; VII, 122, 132–33; declares he can do nothing for him, VI, 154, 188; Consul acknowledges having spent money owed to slaves, V, 353–54.

Another imprisonment and ill treatment, following bankruptcy of Rappiot, Marseilles merchant: see **Rappiot**; King of France prefers to bear, without complaint, insult to Consul, VI, 401; Saint Vincent encourages Barreau, VI, 345, 479; Barreau takes on new commitments in order to get out of prison, VI, 359, 363, 371, 401, 418; freedom, VI, 394; owed money by Flemish man, VI, 392; writes Fr. Get very biting letter, VII, 122; uses money destined for slaves to free himself, VI, 418, 465; VII, 122, 468, 522; Saint Vincent verifies this from account book of Consul, VII, 197; remains in dire circumstances, VI, 431, 455, 461; requests money, VI, 485; Saint Vincent reminds him how scarce money is, VI, 486; Consul mistreated by Turks, VI, 461, 470, 472, 478, 489, 492, 636; VII, 95, 227; XI, 394; is in debt because of avanias and extortion of Turks, VI, 629; VII, 105–106.

To help pay debts, Philippe Le Vacher seeks funds in France: see **Le Vacher** (Philippe); Jean Le Vacher sends him money: see **Le Vacher** (Jean); Barreau must indicate that he has received it, VII, 8; against orders, draws bill of exchange on Fr. Get, VI, 599; Saint Vincent asks Ladies of Charity for money, VI, 479; consults M. de Lamoignon and other experienced persons on means of extricating Jean Barreau, VII, 174, 178–79; works to obtain reimbursement for money owed Consul, VII, 238, 288; VIII, 326–27; considers recalling him to France, VI, 401; VII, 122, 133, 179, 212, 228; sends Missionary to Algiers to discuss question with Pasha: see **Huguier**; money collected is deposited in Marseilles until it is prudent to take or send it to Algiers: see also ***Algiers***; work continues on his affairs, VII, 34, 90–91, 93, 115; he is at peace, VII, 237; requests money for clothing, etc., VII, 325. Saint Vincent wants him held accountable for money received from Mercedarians, VIII, 327; money sent to him or to Philippe Le

Vacher for captive, VIII, 337; letter for another is sent through him, VII, 411; VIII, 357; Saint Vincent wonders if collections are to free him or Jean Le Vacher in Tunis, VIII, 514.

Barreau continues to contract new debts and to divert money destined for slaves, VII, 458–59; VIII, 320; XI, 334; Saint Vincent forbids him to do this, VII, 463, 633–34; Consul again mistreated by Turks (1658), VII, 132; Turks try to force him to pay for ship they had lost, VII, 168; torching of Bastion of France gives reason to fear he may have to endure wrath of Turks, VII, 361–62; XII, 61; imprisonment, VII, 456; release, VII, 463; Saint Vincent rejoices that he did not suffer more, VII, 458; Barreau sends two "lions" to France, VIII, 261; difficulties with Chancellor Constans: see **Constans**; other mentions, III, 50, 445, 446; V, 91, 212, 398, 530.

Barreau (M.), Coadjutor of Bishop of Sarlat - I, 413–14.

Barreau (M.) - XIIIa, 271.

Barrême (René), Oratorian - Biographical data, I, 165.

Barrillon (Mme), Lady of Charity - VI, 203.

Barriot, convict on *Richelieu* - VIII, 244.

Barry (Edmund), Priest of the Mission - Biographical data, III, 93; IV, 291; VI, 357; VII, 166; VIII, 172; mention of letters to Saint Vincent, VIII, 255, 257; departure for Ireland, III, 93, 103; danger shortens stay, IV, 291, 341; stops in Richelieu on way back from Ireland, IV, 468; considered for Montech Seminary, later for Notre-Dame-de-Lorm, IV, 559; Superior there, VIII, 618; letters from Saint Vincent addressed to him at Notre-Dame-de-Lorm, VI, 357, 380, 475, 590; VII, 166, 372, 430, 505; VIII, 172, 255, 257; health, VI, 477; postulant sent by him to Internal Seminary of Richelieu, VIII, 306, 341.

Barry (M.) - VI, 518.

Barry (Paul de) - Author of two works known as the *Philagie* books, VI, 630; VIII, 580.

Barry (Robert), Bishop of Cork - Saint Vincent comes to his aid, V, 422; VI, 151, 270.

Barsabbas Justus (Joseph or Justus), figure in New Testament - XII, 45.

Bartet (Isaac), secretary of Prince Casimir, Cardinal of Poland - Biographical data, III, 243.

Bartholomew (Saint), Apostle - XII, 43; feast day, XIIIb, 4, 107.

Baschet de la Chassaigne (Françoise), Lady of Charity of Châtillon-les-Dombes - XIIIa, 55; XIIIb, 10, 21, 22.

Basil (Saint), Father of the Church - Made "type of" vow of poverty, XI, 211; in imitation of first Christians, XI, 211–12; Rule of Saint Basil, XII, 175; what he said about self-denial, XII, 181, 183; taught catechism, XIIIa, 32.

Bas-Poitou, region of France - Missions, III, 304.

Baspréau (M. de), of Nantes - V, 32, 33.

Basque Slaves - V, 36; VI, 11, 418, 446; VII, 30, 161, 179, 190, 196, 213, 233. See also **Celhay**, **Hirigoyen**, **Lissardy**.

Bassancourt (Balthazar Brandon de), Vicar-General of Périgueux - Biographical data, IV, 175; determined to put Périgueux Seminary under direction of Order priests; Alain de Solminihac urges him to confide it to Priests of the Mission; after one month, he no longer wants them, IV, 190; Saint Vincent writes to inform him of their recall, IV, 175; expresses sympathy at death of Philibert de Brandon, Bishop of Périgueux, IV, 429.

Bassancourt (Fr. de) - Begins, with Fr. Olier, seminary at Vaugirard, and then at Saint-Sulpice, II, 308.

Bassecole (Marie-Catherine), extern Sister of Visitation - II, 454.

Basseline (M.) - II, 515.

Bassompière (Louis de), Bishop of Saintes - Surrounded by Jansenists, IV, 161; contacts with Saintes Missionaries, IV, 389; V, 538; VI, 97, 355; VII, 214; other mention, VII, 374.

Bastia [***La Bastida***], town in Corsica - IV, 408.

Bastien or Sébastien (Bro.) - See **Nodo**.

Bastin (Fr.), Priest of the Mission - Departure from Company, II, 541.

Bastion of France, in Barbary - Historical note, VI, 371; VII, 115; VIII, 4; torching of stronghold and escape of Governor, VII, 361–62; XII, 61; Saint Vincent worries about consequences of this act, VII, 361, 403, 463; other mentions, VI, 371; VII, 249, 253, 464, 488; VIII, 4.

Batavia, town on island of Java - VIII, 577, 582, 583, 589, 590.

Baths, Thermal - Towns with thermal baths, see ***Bourbon-l'Archambault, Forges-les-Eaux***; medicinal purposes, see **Remedies**.

Baucher (Catherine), Daughter of Charity - Biographical data, VII, 465; recalled from Nantes, XIIIb, 312; departure for Poland, XIIIb, 239; other mentions, VII, 465; XIIIb, 228.

Baucher (Marin or Martin), Brother of the Mission - Biographical data, VI, 564; VII, 425; VIII, 64; Saint Vincent tells him to stay in Saintes until obedience places him elsewhere, VI, 564; consoles him on death of mother, VIII, 64; mention of letters to Saint Vincent, VI, 564; VIII, 64; other mention, VII, 425.

Baudelot (Nicolas) - Witness to Saint Vincent's will, XIIIa, 100, 101.

Baudoin (Marthe), Daughter of Charity - XIIIb, 228.

Baudouin (Daniel), seminarian of the Mission - Biographical data, V, 278; XI, 370; in Nantes, XI, 370, 371; his sister, V, 278.

Baudouyn [**Baudouin**] (Jean), secretary of Archbishop of Paris - I, 145; XIIIa, 73, 97, 218, 220, 221, 231, 233, 234, 235, 241, 280, 293, 317; XIIIb, 133, 138.

Bauduy (François), Priest of the Mission - Biographical data, V, 271; leaves Rome for Genoa, V, 271, 274; arrival in Marseilles, V, 380; asks permission to go to his family to recuperate; Saint Vincent sends him to La Rose, V, 441–42.

Bault (M.), nephew of Bishop of Troyes - Pleased with uncle's action for good of diocese, I, 444.

Baurème (Fr.) - VII, 631.

Bausset (Antoine de), Assistant Seneschal of Marseilles, nephew of Bausset brothers below - His praise, VII, 94; sister in Carmel, VII, 145; exiled to Issoudun, VIII, 429; other mentions, VII, 81, 93, 317.

Bausset - Prior in Marseilles; VIII, 137.

Bausset (M.), brother of Prior - At Saint-Sulpice Seminary, Paris, VIII, 137.

Bausset (Philippe de), Canon of Marseilles Cathedral - Exiled to Issoudun, VIII, 429.

Bausset (Pierre de), Provost of Marseilles, brother of Philippe - His praise, VII, 94; asks Saint Vincent to intervene to obtain pardon for brother and nephew, exiled in Issoudun, VIII, 429; contacts with Saint Vincent, V, 180; VI, 326; VII, 317; VIII, 250; duties at hospital for convicts in Marseilles, VII, 81, 93, 101, 109, 121, 289; XIIIa, 365–67.

Bautru (M. de), Comte de Serrant - Biographical data; Saint Vincent writes to him concerning tax, II, 661.

Bauvoy (Guillaume), painter, slave in Algiers - VIII, 503.

Bâville, hamlet in Saint-Chéron (Essonne) - Several sick Missionaries hospitalized in château of Guillaume de Lamoignon, IV, 473–74, 494; one dies there, IV, 495.

Bayard (Nicolas), municipal magistrate in Mâcon - XIIIb, 73.

Bayart (Charles), Priest of the Mission - Biographical data, IV, 31; Superior in Sedan, VIII, 611; Superior at Périgueux Seminary, IV, 137; VIII, 617; recalled to Paris, IV, 174, 175; Superior in Montmirail, VIII, 612; at Saint-Lazare; responsible for Daughters of Charity, IV, 354–55; garden for Daughters at Hôtel-Dieu in Montmirail, IV, 512; obligations of foundation of Missionaries in Montmirail, IV, 513.

Bayeux, town in Calvados - Coaches, III, 529: see also Bishop: Édouard **Molé**; Canon: Gilles **Buhot**.

Bayn (Joseph) - Biographical data, VIII, 372; visits to Saint-Lazare, VIII, 386; letters to Saint Vincent, VIII, 441, 480; visit to Duchesse d'Aiguillon, VIII, 441; thanks Saint Vincent for care during his illness, VIII, 372, 463, 480; unable to have him nursed at Saint-Lazare, VIII, 462; recovery, VIII, 485, 528.

Bayn (Thomas), brother of Joseph - Thanks Saint Vincent for care given sick brother, VIII, 463; other mentions, VIII, 441, 528.

Bayonne, town in Basses-Pyrénées - Saint Vincent advises against establishing convent of nuns there, II, 53; Visitation Monastery, III, 355; VIII, 427; seminary, II, 311; Bishops: see Jean **Dolce**, François **Fouquet**; Vicars-General: see Louis **Abelly**, Fr. **Perriquet**; nephew of Bishop of Condom aspires to diocese, III, 230; Daughters of Charity requested, X, 317; other mentions, I, 11; II, 57; IV, 467, 468; V, 147; VI, 258, 273; VII, 257, 287, 616.

Baytaz de Doucy (Nicolas), Seigneur de Château-Martin, Superior of Visitation Monasteries in Annecy - Biographical data, I, 564; opinion regarding Extraordinary Visitor for Visitation Nuns, I, 564.

Bazas, town in Gironde - Samuel Martineau, Bishop: see **Martineau**.

Bazoches, commune in district of Soissons - Letter to Bro. Goret there, IV, 286.

Béarn, region of France - I, 12; II, 141; VII, 460, 623; XIIIa, 21.

Beatitudes - Mention of conferences, XII, 417–18; during Tuesday Conferences, VII, 405.

Beaucaire, town in Gard - Its fair, I, 3; convent of Ursulines, VIII, 362.

Beaufils (Gilles), Priest of Chartres diocese - XIIIa, 24.

Beaufort (François de Vendôme, Duc de) - Biographical data, VII, 154.

Beaufort (Mme de), Lady of Charity - Promised to go to meeting of Ladies, I, 231; responsible for foundation of Charity in Saint-Étienne-du-Mont parish in Paris, I, 359; its president, I, 450; asks how to act with churchwardens, II, 293.

Beaugé (M. de), resident of Le Mans - III, 607–08.

Beaulac (Joseph), Priest of the Mission - Biographical data, V, 554; letter from Saint Vincent on occasion of his vows, V, 554.

Beaulieu (Jean de la Valette-Cornusson) - Abbot of Beaulieu, candidate for bishopric of Vabres, II, 555.

Beaulieu (M.), in Tunis - VII, 524.

Beaulieu (M. de), in Nantes - VIII, 557.

Beaumais (M.), haberdasher - Talent as controversialist, IV, 528–29.

Beaumont, county in France - Transactions conducted before notary regarding withdrawal from lease, XII, 377, 379.

Beaumont (Pierre de), Priest of the Mission - Biographical data, II, 585; III, 51; V, 75; VI, 51; VII, 176–77; VIII, 103; letters of Saint Vincent addressed to him in Richelieu, V, 443, 566, 601; VI, 468; VII, 176, 188, 224, 323, 451, 466, 511; VIII, 305, 329, 341, 347; mention of letter from Saint Vincent, VI, 468; mention of letters to Saint Vincent, VII, 324, 511; VIII, 305, 341; goes to Bons-Enfants "for courses," II, 585; at Saint-Méen, III, 51, 458; remains at seminary despite writ of arrest, III, 42; imprisoned, then released, III, 51–52, 53, 56, 65; Director of Internal Seminary in Richelieu, V, 75, 443; Superior and Pastor, V, 585; VI, 476, 538, 637; VII, 323, 331; VIII, 103, 158, 257, 607; Sisters in Richelieu complain about him, VI, 51; his praises, VI, 51, 468; VII, 451; reprimanded for not taking sufficient care to see that peace is maintained in parish, VI, 468; mission of Verteuil, VIII, 305; recalled to Paris, VIII, 371; at Saint-Lazare, VIII, 522; present at Saint Vincent's deathbed, XIIIa, 203.

Beaumont-Carra (Anne-Catherine de), Visitandine - Biographical data, I, 107; III, 196; Saint Vincent replies to two letters, III, 196.

Beaune, town in Côte-d'Or - XII, 236.

Beaupré [**Gilles Marguerin**], slave in Algiers - VI, 328; VII, 196: see also **Marguerin**.

Beaure (Jacques), Priest of the Mission - Biographical data, VI, 521; VII, 153; VIII, 136; in Turin, VI, 521, 525, 578, 579; in Genoa, VII, 153, 210, 230, 234, 236; Fr. Martin complains about his conduct, VII, 231, 242; in Marseilles, VII, 410; VIII,

136; goes with Gabriel Delespiney to open mission in Vins, VIII, 320; other mention, VII, 555.

Beauregard (M.), Dean of Alet Cathedral - II, 572.

Beauregard (M. de), slave in Algiers - V, 35.

Beausse (Abbé de), Canon of Évreux - VIII, 417.

Beauty (physical) - Not worthy of esteem, X, 113, 149.

Beauvais, town in Oise - Bishops: see Nicolas Choart de **Buzenval**, Augustin **Potier**; disagreement between Bishop and Chapter, V, 107; Saint Vincent directs retreats for ordinands in Beauvais, I, 56; returns to this town I, 90, 317, 531; II, 300, 303; convent of Ursulines, I, 94; II, 303; plan for mission in this diocese, I, 58, XI, 29; Daughters of Charity from Beauvais, II, 178; Daughters of Charity established there, XIIIb, 142; other mentions, I, 216, 339–40; III, 529; X, 533.

Confraternity of Charity: Establishment of Confraternity, I, 91; opposition of King's Lieutenant, I, 92; difficulties in establishing Charity, I, 281; Saint Vincent sends Saint Louise to Beauvais to complete organization of Charity; gives her instructions about role of Treasurer, presence of Ladies at funerals of the poor, and collections, I, 92–94; Saint Louise visits again, I, 281–83, 286; Saint Vincent advises her to return there, I, 283, 286, 287; then advises her to postpone trip and to return to work on regulations of Confraternity, I, 288; sends her regulations of Charity of Saint-Sauveur, asking her to adapt them to Beauvais, I, 281.

Union of Confraternity of Charity with Rosary Confraternity in diocese, I, 288; Saint Louise finds fault with certain arrangements and suggests modifications, I, 294–96; Saint Vincent wants her to go once more to Beauvais, I, 317; preferable for each parish to have its own Charity, X, 182; names of sectors served by Charities: Basse-Oeuvre, I, 93; Saint-Étienne, I, 93; Saint-Gilles, I, 93; Sainte-Marguerite, I, 282; Saint-Martin, I, 93; Saint-Sauveur, I, 93; decision made regarding Sainte-Geneviève affair, III, 586; other mentions, I, 86, 95, 295.

Beauvais (Denis), convict in Toulon - VIII, 402, 513.

Bécan (Martin), Jesuit - Writings, I, 57.

Becket (Thomas) - See **Thomas Becket**.

Bécu (Benoît), Priest of the Mission, brother of Hubert, Jean, Madeleine, Marie - Biographical data, I, 389; II, 57; IV, 11; letters Saint Vincent writes him in Richelieu, I, 589; IV, 11; at Saint-Lazare, I, 389, 391; sent to Richelieu, I, 419; knows how to intone psalms and teach catechism, I, 419; in Richelieu,

I, 442; sent to La Rose as Superior, I, 589; VIII, 606; in La Rose, II, 57; Saint Vincent reproves him for his conduct, II, 78; needs to be replaced, II, 79; saint speaks of sending him back to Richelieu, II, 80, 112; in Richelieu again, III, 521; IV, 11; Saint Vincent sends him to visit his sister Marie, Daughter of Charity, I, 389, 391.

Bécu (Hubert), Brother of the Mission, brother of Benoît, Jean, Madeleine, Marie - Biographical data, I, 475; his praises, I, 475, 590; question of sending him to Picardy, I, 561.

Bécu (Jean), Priest of the Mission, brother of Benoît, Hubert, Madeleine, Marie - Biographical data, I, 39; II, 343; III, 104; V, 258; VII, 73; VIII, 301; XII, 11; letters from Saint Vincent, sent to Bécu: in Saint-Victor, I, 454; in Champagne, I, 155; in Montmirail, I, 466, 470, 474, in Amiens, I, 489; at Saint-Lazare, I, 102, 434, 445; III, 104; V, 466; XIIIa, 235; giving mission near Montmirail, I, 177; I, 466, 470, 474; I, 454; I, 489; in Nancy, where he helps poor people of Lorraine, I, 541–42, 589; Superior in Toul, II, 343, 476; III, 69; VIII, 605; at 1642 General Assembly, II, 343; XIIIa, 323, 331, 396; at Saint-Lazare, II, 348; III, 104; XII, 11; XIIIa, 204, 205, 206; at 1651 General Assembly, XIIIa, 369, 372, 374, 396, 397; opinion on vows of Company, XIIIa, 380, 381; opinion on another topic, XIIIa, 383; health, I, 454, 474; II, 348; III, 133–34; V, 258, 580, 588; VII, 73, 75, 84, 515, 583; VIII, 301; XII, 241; praise for him, XII, 241; signs petition to Urban VIII requesting approval of Company, I, 39, 45, 47, 53; other mentions, I, 102; XIIIa, 259, 262.

Bécu (Madeleine), Daughter of Charity, sister of Benoît, Hubert, Jean, and Marie - Destined for Angers, XIIIb, 284.

Bécu (Marie), Daughter of Charity, sister of Benoît, Hubert, Jean, and Madeleine - Health, I, 389; Saint Vincent unable to visit her, I, 391; sends brother, Benoît, to visit her, I, 389, 391; death, III, 158; other mentions, I, 391, 561.

Bédacier (Pierre), Titular Bishop of Augusta, suffragan administrator of Bishop of Metz - Biographical data, VII, 63; kindly disposed toward mission in Metz, VII, 63, 77, 85, 100, 113, 132; other mention, VII, 384–85.

Bede the Venerable (Saint) - Stresses importance of priests celebrating Mass, III, 365; slave child is compared to him, II, 653.

Béga (Laurent), resident of Clichy - XIIIa, 24.

Begat (Félix), slave in Tunis - VI, 322; VII, 196.

Bègue (M.), slave in Algiers - Jean Barreau advances money for his release and is reimbursed, VI, 200, 206, 264, 273, 289.

Béguin [Bègue] (Jean), slave in Algiers - VIII, 319, 327.

Béguin (M.), administrator of Petites-Maisons in Paris - V, 400.

Béguin (M.) - Provides legacy for ministry of Daughters in Fontenay-aux-Roses, II, 285.

Béguines - In Amsterdam, VIII, 594; in Rotterdam, VIII, 596.

Bélart (Honoré), Priest of the Mission - Biographical data, VI, 406; Saint Vincent reproaches harsh way of acting, VI, 406–08; mention of letters to Saint Vincent, VI, 406.

Belin (Fr.), chaplain of house of Philippe-Emmanuel de Gondi in Villepreux - Letters from Saint Vincent, I, 269, 397; mention of his letters to saint, I, 76, 122, 126; what he is doing for Charity and school in Villepreux, I, 76, 87, 122, 126; Saint Vincent welcomes him at Bons-Enfants, I, 160; tells him Company owes him a great deal and invites him to participate in a mission, I, 269–70; other mentions, I, 77, 122, 126, 441.

Bellarmine (Robert) - See **Robert Bellarmine**.

Belle-Isle-en-Mer, island in gulf of Morbihan - Hospital entrusted to Daughters of Charity; Mathurine Guérin is sent there, VIII, 340; religious state of island; situation of Sisters, VIII, 459–61.

Bellebarbe (Fr. de), priest - In Madagascar, III, 287, 553, 570; on Île Sainte-Marie, III, 556, 561; referred to but not named as "not behaving properly," XI, 373; despite desire to return to France, consents to remain in Madagascar if Fr. Nacquart leaves, III, 595.

Bellefont (M.), French Consul in Nauplia - VI, 279.

Bellegarde, town in Ain - Birthplace of Fr. Vageot, IV, 591.

Bellegarde (Octave de Saint-Lary de), Archbishop of Sens - Biographical data, I, 563; II, 59; asked for advice on establishment of Visitors in Visitation Order, I, 563, 565; II, 59–60, 100, 162, 242; on book entitled *Traitez des Droits et libertez de l'Eglise gallicane*, III, 591; other mentions, II, 242, 539.

Bellegarde (Roger de Saint-Lary, Duc de) - Biographical data; lays claim to ownership of coaches of France, II, 469.

Belles (M. de) - Helped M. de Flacourt publish *Dictionnaire de la langue de Madagascar*, XIIIa, 187.

Belletia (President) - Kindness toward Missionaries in Turin, V, 485, 636.

Belleville (Mathurin de), Priest of the Mission - Biographical data, V, 425; VI, 13; VII, 17; VIII, 181; XI, 371; impending departure for Madagascar, V, 425; death, VI, 15–16, 214, 217, 227–28, 232, 447, 451, 452, 453, 455, 460, 463, 464, 469, 471,

475, 478, 481, 488, 491, 501, 528, 530, 535, 537, 567, 583, 586; VII, 15, 17; VIII, 180, 554; XI, 371; praise for him, VI, 15–18, 228–30; account of last illness and death, XI, 378; conference on his virtues, XI, 376–78; mention of other conferences, XII, 428; other mentions, VI, 13; VIII, 553; XII, 428. See also ***Madagascar***.

Belleville-sur-Sablon [***Sablons***], today part of Neuilly, near Paris - XIIIa, 479.

Belley, town in Ain - Bishop: see Jean de **Passelaigue**; seminary, II, 354; other mention, VIII, 541.

Bellièvre (Catherine de), Abbess of Longchamp - IV, 484.

Belot (Mme) - II, 196.

Belot (Maître) - Fears lawsuit to retain Daughter of Charity in Fontenay-aux-Roses, II, 285.

Belval-Bois-des-Dames, village in Ardennes - Belval Abbey, V, 224, 237, 240.

Bence (Fr.), Superior of Oratory in Lyons - Asks Cardinal de Bérulle for priest for Châtillon-les-Dombes parish, XIIIa, 50; intervenes to have Saint Vincent return to Paris, I, 20.

Benedict (Saint) - Foresees decline of his Order, XII, 80–81; XIIIb, 344; says that first step in humility is silence, XI, 199; began Rules of his Institute by defining it, XII, 68; other mentions, VII, 162; IX, 194, 359.

Benedicta [**Benoîte**] (Saint) - Biographical data, I, 180.

Benedictine Monks - Saint Benedict foresees decline of his Order, XII, 80–81; XIIIb, 344; unhappy effects of its laxness, XI, 183; reform of Saint-Maur, II, 307; III, 383; Benedictine Rule, XIIIa, 405; Benedictines profess only two vows: stability and conversion of manners, II, 142; their principal aim is recitation and chanting of Divine Office, XII, 267; Reformed monks have no right to enter any house of Saint Benedict if not called there, VII, 162; abbeys: see ***Monestier, Saint-Germain-des-Prés, Saint-Méen***; priory of same Order: see ***Champvent***; Benedictine slave in Algiers, III, 310; other mentions, VII, 141, 163; XIIIa, 131.

Benedictine Nuns - Diabolical possession of Benedictines of Cognac, VII, 138; letter of Benedictine to Saint Vincent, VIII, 416; Benedictines of Chanteloup, II, 142.

Benefactors - Saint Vincent's deep gratitude toward benefactors, I, 489; V, 19, 168, 475–76, 477; VI, 88; disposed to sell chalices in order to assist them, V, 397; supports them in their need, III, 37; V, 181; VI, 83; prefers to renounce endowments than to engage in lawsuit against them, VI, 88; XII, 199–200; accustomed to give them, or have others give them, news of works they have funded or in which they have an interest, II, 267, 349; III, 267; V, 482; VI, 326; the dying Saint Vincent blesses them, XIIIa, 205–206; 1651 Assembly stresses need to be grateful to them, XIIIa, 373. See also **Aiguillon** (Duchesse), **Callon** (Louis), **Chandenier** (Claude de), **Chandenier** (Louis de), **Fabert** (Marquis de), VI, 147; **Gondi** (Philippe-Emmanuel de), **Gondi** (Mme de), **Gondi** (Jean-François Paul de), **Le Bon** (Adrien), **Lorthon** (M. de); **Monchia** (Cristoforo), IV, 266, **Rancati** (Hilarion), VIII, 141.

Benefices (Ecclesiastical) - Conference, XII, 324–27; clergy began to possess benefices under Pope Telesphorus, XII, 324; priest ordained only if he had a benefice; no longer required later; patrimonial title sufficed; XI, 211; institution of benefices has greatly harmed virtue of priests, XII, 324; Saint Vincent justifies union of certain benefices to seminaries, III, 44, 111–12; VII, 163; procedure followed in France for union of benefices, VIII, 353; those who govern have aversion for union of benefices, II, 295; union of abbeys and conventual revenues is very difficult in France, VII, 219; benefices are not for children, II, 583–84; Saint Vincent defends man who had resigned benefice despite prohibition of parents, VII, 619; Queen of Poland wants to use benefice for upkeep of seminary, VIII, 88–89; Missionaries must not aspire to benefices, VII, 192, 442; XII, 323–27; XIIIa, 216, 328, 371, 388; Missionary may accept benefice in order to unite it to Company, V, 29–30, 125; must not have charge of several parishes at same time; only reluctantly has Company ever accepted a parish or permitted members to accept one, IV, 589; first Missionaries renounced benefices in order to serve rural poor better, I, 41, 49; Missionaries may not take lapsed benefice, VII, 394; other mention, VII, 376.

Bene Vagienna, town in Piedmont - Mission given, VIII, 355, 385.

Benjamin (Abbé de) - Visit to Visitandines, VIII, 430; participation in election of Ursulines in Melun, VIII, 516.

Benjamin, biblical personage - Jacob's love for him, IX, 373.

Benjamin (M. de), deacon - Saint Vincent asks Bishop of Alet to receive him into his house for a time, III, 260–61; Bishop refuses, III, 268.

Benoît (Jean), slave in Algiers - III, 223, 311.

Benoît (Fr.), Priest of the Mission - See **Bécu** (Benoît).

Benonier (Jean), priest in Châtillon-les-Dombes - XIIIb, 21.

Bentivoglio (Guido), Cardinal - Present at sessions for approval of Congregation of the Mission, XIIIa, 229, 239; gives unfavorable report, XIIIa, 250.

Benyer (Étienne), merchant, master shoemaker in Paris - Witness to Saint Vincent's will, XIIIa, 100, 101.

Béon, village in Yonne - Carthusian Monastery of Valprofonde, II, 124.

Bergamo, town in Italy - Bishop: see Cardinal Gregorio **Barbadigo**.

Bergen, town in Netherlands - VIII, 596.

Bergera (Giulio Cesare), Archbishop of Turin - Kindness toward Missionaries, V, 476; insists on mission in Racconigi, VI, 196; names, on his own authority, Superior of Visitation, VI, 522; asks Fr. Martin to be confessor of Visitandines, VI, 522; sends him to give mission in small market town, VI, 639; Saint Vincent suggests Martin try to get Archbishop to approve catechizing and confessing only in rural areas, VI, 111, 351; refuses Holy Orders to seminarian of the Mission, VIII, 87; other mentions, V, 493; VI, 308, 601–02, 639.

Bergerac, town in Dordogne - Dominicans, III, 386.

Bergeres-lès-Vertus, village in Marne - Letter of Saint Vincent to Pastor, I, 117; Saint Louise instructs girls and visits Charity there, I, 116, 117, 118, 125; mission, I, 125.

Bergh (Eléonore-Catherine de): see **Bouillon** (Duchesse de).

Bergier (Antoine), Canon in Mâcon - XIIIb, 78.

Bergues-sur-Sambre, village in Aisne - I, 421.

Bermond (Christophe de), French Consul in Alexandria - VII, 274.

Bernard (Bro.), Dominican - III, 383.

Bernard (Bro.) - Mentioned in letter of Fr. Vitet to Saint Vincent, IV, 67.

Bernard (Claude), priest - Founder of Trente-Trois Seminary, VIII, 203.

Bernard (de Sainte-Thérèse) - See **Jean Duval**, Bishop of Babylon.

Bernard (Gratien), Archdeacon of Mâcon diocese - XIIIb, 78.

Bernard (Joseph), of Mâcon - His charity, XIIIb, 73.

Bernard (Fr.), Carmelite, in the Hague - VIII, 596.

Bernard (Saint), Abbot of Clairvaux - Features of his life, IV, 566; VI, 252; IX, 387; X, 64, 104, 289; XI, *xvii*; did not institute Daughters of Charity, IX, 359; considered insensitivity sign of reprobation, XII, 260; cited: IX, 70; X, 110, 198, 204, 229; XI, 306; XII, 150, 274, 302; XIIIa, 127. See also **Cistercians**.

Bernardines - I, 388; XIIIa, 131; of Clermont Abbey, VIII, 518.

Bernusset (Vital), slave in Nauplia [Nafplion] (Greece) - VI, 278; VII, 410, 557; VIII, 377, 397, 444, 513.

Berny, town, today section of Fresnes (Val-de-Marne) - VIII, 466.

Berruyer (M.), of Company of the Indies - IV, 354.

Berry, province - VIII, 429.

Berry-au-Bac, village in Aisne - Mission here, I, 95.

Berthe (Thomas), Priest of the Mission - Biographical data, II, 583; III, 82; IV, 164; V, 29; VI, 23; VII, 6; VIII, 13–14; XI, 165; letters from Saint Vincent to Fr. Berthe: III, 127; in Laon, IV, 482; in Rome, IV, 554, 598; V, 29, 59, 65, 153, 157, 165, 175; in Toul, VIII, 13, 16; in Turin, VIII, 206; mention of other letters from Saint Vincent, V, 42; VII, 414; letters to Saint Vincent, V, 270, 273; VIII, 342; mention of other letters to Saint Vincent, V, 59, 153; VII, 49; VIII, 13; Saint Vincent has him in mind for Cahors, III, 82; Fr. Berthe goes back to parents' home, III, 97, 115; encouragement from Saint Vincent, III, 127; Superior at Bons-Enfants, III, 273; VIII, 604; visits Sedan house, IV, 188–89; Ladies of Charity appreciate his assistance to poor of Picardy and Champagne, VI, 28; XII, 367–68; falls ill in Laon, IV, 450, 452, 482.

Sent to Rome as Superior, IV, 520; VIII, 609; in Rome, V, 42, 55, 127, 151, 184, 222, 254, 355; deputed to negotiate approval of vows in Company: see **Vows**; looks for house for Missionaries: see ***Rome***; gives hospitality to Cardinal de Retz in Rome; Mazarin is enraged and orders his recall, V, 270–76, 334, 338–39; VI, 23–24; XI, 165; return to Paris, V, 334, 363, 369; XI, 165; replaced in Rome by Fr. Jolly, V, 377; well accepted in Rome, where they are hoping for his return, V, 384, 403, 472.

Sent to Poland to visit Missionaries' house; recalled before sailing, V, 264, 334, 403, 414, 419, 424; canonical visit of houses in Le Mans, Richelieu, Saint-Méen, Marseilles, Genoa, Turin, and others, V, 474, 476, 501–02, 547, 555, 574, 584, 594, 598, 611; Saint Vincent proposes him for mission in Lebanon, VI, 23, 28; return to Paris, VI, 26, 31, 55; Director of Internal Seminary, VI, 87, 158; XI, 326; question of sending him to Sedan during visit of Court, VI, 368; does not go, VI, 390.

Visit of houses in Le Mans, Richelieu, Saint-Méen, Tréguier, Luçon, Saintes, La Rose, Agen, Notre-Dame-de-Lorm, Agde, Marseilles, Annecy, Turin, VI, 381, 444, 504, 505, 537, 548, 563, 570, 590, 593, 600, 613, 638; VII, 6, 24,

28, 30, 49; returns to Annecy for delicate affair, then back to Paris, VII, 95–96; giving mission, VII, 222; new journeys to Marseilles, Turin, Genoa, and Rome, VII, 242, 289, 291, 307, 312, 316, 325, 363, 375, 377, 378, 388, 414, 429, 435, 436, 439; visits houses in Annecy, Toul, Sedan, Montmirail on his way back, VII, 366, 512, 536, 586, 606, 613; VIII, 13, 16, 54, 84; put in charge of negotiating purchase of new house in Metz for Missionaries, VIII, 14–15, 16; prepares to return to Italy, VIII, 99; falls ill in Turin; health, VIII, 157, 176, 191, 206, 210, 214; continues journey, VIII, 230; from Chambéry, announces to Saint Vincent death of Louis de Chandenier, VIII, 342, 360; returns to Paris, VIII, 354, 355.

In Paris, XIIIa, 195, 199; assists dying saint, XIIIa, 204, 205, 206; presides over Assembly that elects Fr. Alméras as Vicar-General, XIIIa, 207; his is second name Saint Vincent proposes in writing to future General Assembly as next Superior General, XIIIa, 484–85; his praise, VI, 23; other mentions, IV, 383; VII, 351, 367, 406; VIII, 84, 165, 535; XIIIb, 239.

Berthod (François), Franciscan Friar, *Chargé d'affaires* of Poland in Paris - Contacts with Saint Vincent, IV, 327, 354, 397, 411.

Bertier (Pierre de), Coadjutor, then Bishop, of Montauban - Biographical data, II, 556; III, 240; IV, 68; V, 224; VI, 476; VII, 167; VIII, 257; devotion to Saint Vincent, IV, 374; entrusts sanctuary of Notre-Dame-de-Lorm to Congregation of the Mission, IV, 383; VIII, 618; quarrels with Anne de Murviel, Bishop of Montauban, II, 555–56; XIIIa, 147; what he is doing for his seminary, IV, 383, 520; VI, 63, 476; VII, 430, 505; VIII, 447; XIIIa, 198; Saint Vincent writes to Queen for him, IV, 457–58; Prelate requests services of Bro. Sirven, V, 224; gathers information about matter concerning Belval Abbey: see ***Belval***; other mentions, III, 240; IV, 68, 373; V, 234; VII, 167, 373–74; VIII, 257.

Bertost (M.) - VIII, 450.

Bérulle (Pierre de), Cardinal - Biographical data, I, 19; II, 460; VIII, 224; IX, 48; XI, 51–52; sends Saint Vincent to Châtillon-les-Dombes, XIIIa, 50–51; recalls him to Paris, I, 19–20; XIIIa, 55–56; refuses to send back to Queen a page who had entered the Oratory, III, 476; would like to prevent foundation of Congregation of the Mission, II, 460; knowledge and holiness, XI, 116; considers office of Superior dangerous, XI, 52, 125; would raise his soul to God before making a decision, XI, 116; XIIIa, 385; to those seeking advice, he was accustomed to proposing, not imposing, his insights, III, 356; VIII, 224; other mention, IX, 48.

Bérulle (Pierre de), nephew of Cardinal - Named Apostolic Visitor of Carmelites, VIII, 70; in Rome on behalf of Carmelites, VIII, 191.

Berziau (Théodore de), Seigneur d'Arcueil - Mistreats Pastor of Arcueil, II, 446–47.

Besambo (Louis), native of Madagascar - VI, 222.

Besançon (M. de) - Pillaging and cruelties of his regiment of Navarre, IV, 204.

Besson (Jean), Brother of the Mission - Biographical data, I, 477; III, 467; Saint Vincent sends greetings, I, 479; at Saint-Lazare, III, 467.

Besson (Jean), Priest in Châtillon-les-Dombes - XIIIa, 48, 57; XIIIb, 21; other mention, I, 479.

Bétan (M.), friend of Saint Vincent in Pouy - I, 17.

Bétharram, shrine in Pyrénées-Atlantiques - Historical note, VII, 459; VIII, 54; this place of pilgrimage offered to Mission several times, VII, 459; difficulties Saint Vincent finds in union, VII, 460; proposes Fr. Cornuel as Superior, VII, 623; writes about this to Bishop of Lescar; awaits in vain Prelate's response, which is lost, VIII, 54, 84, 432; how union could take place, VIII, 433–36; other mention, VIII, 118, 434–35, 602.

Bethlehem, town in Palestine - Birthplace of Jesus, II, 343; X, 457; Mary's prompt obedience in going there, IX, 59; Titular Bishop: see Christophe d'**Authier de Sisgau**.

Béthune, town in Pas-de-Calais - VIII, 378.

Béthune (Comte de), French Ambassador to Holy See - Encouraged by King to support request for approval of Congregation of the Mission, XIIIa, 243–44; Queen Regent writes to him for same reason, XIIIa, 246.

Béthune (Henri de), Bishop of Maillezais, then Archbishop of Bordeaux - Becomes Archbishop of Bordeaux, II, 616; accepts See of Bordeaux when that of Maillezais is moved to La Rochelle, III, 20, 32; his trials, IV, 249; Alain de Solminihac thinks that, on advice of Henri de Béthune, Bishop of Maillezais will sign petition of Bishops against Jansenism, IV, 161.

Beurrier (Fr.), Augustinian - III, 352.

Beurrier (Paul), Pastor in Nanterre - I, 433.

Beuvardes, village in Aisne - Missions, II, 546; VII, 301, 334; why no mission has been given there for a long time, VII, 220; Saint Vincent looks for priest to say daily Mass there and to teach school, VII, 301.

Beynier (Denise) - Member of Charity of Châtillon, XIIIb, 4, 21.

Beynier (Jacques), son of Jean Beynier - XIIIa, 48, 50, 55.

Beynier (Jean), inhabitant of Châtillon, brother of Jacques Beynier - Uncle of Jean Garron, VI, 76; Huguenot, XIIIa, 48, 50–51; offers hospitality to Saint Vincent, VI, 76; bad conduct, XIIIa, 50; conversion, XIIIa, 52, 53, 55; Procurator of Charity, XIIIb, 21, 22; other mention, XIIIa, 48.

Beyrie (M.) - Service rendered him by Fr. Fonteneil, I, 481.

Bezay (M. de) - I, 502.

Bézé (M.) - VII, 457.

Bèze [**Besze**] (Théodore de), leader of French Protestantism - Saint Francis de Sales worked for his conversion, XIIIa, 88.

Béziers, town in Hérault - Clément de Bonzi, Bishop: see **Bonzi**.

Biaches, village in Somme - See Estourmel.

Biarritz, town in Pyrénées-Atlantiques - XIIIa, 21.

Biarrotte (Fr.), Dominican - III, 383, 386.

Biblical References - See **Appendix 1**.

Bicêtre, château near Paris - Historical data, IV, 5; II, 444; IV, 5; X, 585; Queen gives it as housing for Foundlings, XIIIb, 425; Ladies of Charity ask Saint Vincent to transfer foundlings there, II, 444; objections to transfer, II, 596–97; transfer, III, 212; complaints of Saint Louise about organization of work by Ladies, III, 211, 213; M. Le Roy demands spiritual direction of work, III, 228–29; Saint Louise organizes school, III, 231–33; bakery, sale of wine, III, 263, 266, 297; chapel, III, 266; death of foundlings, III, 232, 266; substantial donations given for this ministry, III, 254; concern about proximity of troops during Fronde, III, 400, 418; God protects the house, III, 419; Saint Vincent wants children housed elsewhere, III, 420, 431; Daughters of Charity who care for the children, III, 213, 397, 399, 400; IV, 380; X, 585. See also **Carcireux** (Françoise), **Poisson** (Geneviève); they prepare to return to Bicêtre, III, 422; Saint Vincent learns at Saint-Méen that children have left Bicêtre, III, 423; distress, III, 266, 403–04, 419, 431, 504–05, 507, 517, 519, 520; Attorney General promises protection, IV, 23–24; visits and sojourns of Saint Louise at Bicêtre, III, 228, 231, 263, 370; she complains about wet-nurses and that Ladies do not separate sufficiently boys from girls and nurses, IV, 5; fear that Ladies might send children back to Bicêtre, IV, 193; other mention, VII, 156.

Bichi (Alessandro), Nuncio to France, then Cardinal - Biographical data, I, 164; II, 36; VI, 387; offers to sell palace to Missionaries in Rome at price Saint Vincent finds too high, II, 36; other mentions, II, 141; VI, 387, 460.

Bichot (M.), ship's captain - V, 282, 302.

Bidache, town in Pyrénées-Atlantiques - Saint Vincent receives Tonsure and Minor Orders there, XIIIa, 1, 2.

Bidre (M.) - VII, 555.

Biecz, town in Poland - V, 152.

Bienvenu (Étienne), Priest of the Mission - Biographical data, VI, 123; VII, 331; in Le Mans, VI, 151, 277; ordination, VI, 123, 584; Saint Vincent writes to affirm him in vocation, VII, 331, 332, 387; laxity, VII, 370–71.

Bienvenu (M.), farmer of Gonesse - I, 476–77.

Bìète (M.) - IV, 24.

Bigeon (Gervais), Pastor in Arcueil - Mistreatment by seigneur of area, II, 446–47.

Bignon (Jérôme), Advocate General of Parlement - Biographical data, I, 242; Saint Vincent consults him on union of Saint-Lazare Priory, I, 242, 244; Abbé de Saint-Cyran dispels hesitations on this point, I, 395; XIIIa, 128.

Bildet (Nicole), Daughter of Charity - Signs attestation regarding Common and Particular Rules reviewed and arranged in order by Fr. Alméras, XIIIb, 206; entered before the Act of Establishment, XIIIb, 228.

Billain (François) - See **Villain** (François).

Billi (François), Bishop of Pavia - VI, 639.

Bimenet (Étienne), Priest of the Mission - Biographical data; concern of Saint Vincent about health of his mother, IV, 544.

Binet (Étienne), Provincial of Jesuits of France - Biographical data, I, 564; opinion concerning Extraordinary Visitor for Visitation Order, I, 564; inspection and certification of documents pertaining to Hospitaller Nuns of Charity of Notre-Dame, XIIIa, 102, 103; approval of their Constitutions, XIIIa, 103; other mention, I, 185.

Binsfeld (Pierre) - Biographical data, II, 266; author of manual of theology recommended by Saint Vincent, II, 266, 608; III, 282; VIII, 584.

Biot (M.), lawyer in Joigny - Member of Charity, XIIIb, 66.

Bishops - Letters of Saint Vincent to Bishops: II, 479, 480; III, 161, 176, 376, 528, 617, 618; IV, 36, 53, 110, 156, 173, 178, 202, 313, 335, 497; V, 56; VII, 184; VIII, 195. See also **Gondi** (Jean-

François de), **Pavillon**, **Perrochel**, **Solminihac**; Bishops write to Saint Vincent, IV, 285; VI, 59; letter to priest who did not want to be Bishop, IV, 83; Saint Vincent is consulted on nomination of Bishops, II, 427; does not want to be obliged to render accounts to Bishops, II, 507; IV, 75, 409; VIII, 539; considers instituting among Missionaries vow of obedience to Bishops, I, 554; obedience is owed to them, I, 125; II, 155; IX, 432; XII, 350–51; Missionaries are subject to them for external functions, not for spiritual direction and internal matters: see **Congregation of the Mission**; Bishop sends Missionaries to give mission, VI, 268; gives them faculties to hear confessions, V, 87; Missionaries owe obedience to Bishop, even in what is not their office, when he imposes his will, IV, 52, 69, 392; V, 576; VII, 592; exemption of Congregation of the Mission from Bishops, V, 459–60; discussion regarding accepting travel expenses from Bishops in whose diocese confreres are working, V, 490.

Sermon of Saint Vincent to parishioners, announcing upcoming visit of Bishop, XIIIa, 67; Bishop has right to visit his seminary, V, 538; how Missionaries should receive Prelate who comes to their house, VI, 314; Bishops plan to open seminary to prepare workers for non-Christian lands, VI, 541; if Bishop is in house, ask him to preside at Office, XI, 177; do not tell Bishops, without necessity, of shortcomings noted in parish during mission, VI, 420; Bishops bring people back to good more surely by kindness than by criticism, II, 5–6; people have greater esteem for poor Bishop than for pompous one, III, 106, 189; Bishop wanting to live as Carthusian would not be acting as God wanted, IX, 460; Saint Vincent tries not to visit any Bishop, V, 440; consecration of two Bishops at Saint-Lazare, VIII, 339; 344; Our Lord wants Bishops to be holy and to acquire holiness, XII, 300; good Missionary does everything Bishop does, XII, 325–26: see **Reserved Cases**, **Congregation of the Mission**.

Bishops and Regulars (Congregation) - Saint Vincent requests its approval of Congregation of the Mission, I, 140, 144.

Bisson (Jean-René), Brother of the Mission - Biographical data, I, 522; II, 519; other mention, I, 531.

Bisuel (M.), Vicar-General of Champfleur - VI, 151.

Bitault (M.), Councillor at Parlement - Delegate of Parlement at Reuil conference, III, 411.

***Bizerte* [*Bizerta*]**, town in Tunisia - Mission to slaves, III, 199; ransom of slave, III, 206; assistance for slaves, IV, 435; V, 130, 131; XI, 276–77, 393–95; Jean Le Vacher goes there from Tunis, V, 118; other mention, V, 89.

Blaise (Pierre), Pastor in Argenteuil - Requests erection of Charity in his parish, XIIIb, 103.

Blampignon (Claude de), member of Tuesday Conferences - Biographical data, IV, 320; V, 436; VIII, 258; preacher for ordinands at Saint-Lazare in 1652, IV, 320; Saint Vincent asks him to be confessor to First Monastery of Visitation in Paris, V, 496; Director of Sisters of Saint Thomas (Dominicans) and confessor of Visitation nuns, VII, 126; VIII, 425, 426–27, 430; one of preachers of 1658 mission in Metz, VII, 126, 136; Prior of Bussière-Badil, V, 496; VII, 239; Abbot of Aumône; one of witnesses heard before taking possession of Saint-Lazare, VII, 504; mission in Chartres diocese, VIII, 258; Visitor of Carmelites of France, VIII, 425, 427; intends to speak with Saint Vincent about affairs of Carmel, VIII, 507; other mentions, V, 436, 475; VII, 126, 170; XII, 391.

Blanchard (Antoine), notary in Châtillon-les-Dombes - Member of Charity of Châtillon, XIIIb, 21; other mentions, XIIIa, 47, 48, 49, 55, 57.

Blanchard (Claude), Daughter of Charity - XIIIb, 228.

Blanchart (François), Abbot of Sainte-Geneviève - Biographical data; Saint Vincent recommends him to M. de Saint-Paul, III, 487; recommends gentleman to M. Blanchart, III, 614.

Blanne (Perrine), mother of Angiboust sisters - X, 511.

Blanzac, town in Charente - Mission, II, 490; Confraternity of Charity, XIIIb, 5.

Blatiron (Étienne), Priest of the Mission - Biographical data, I, 580; II, 114; III, 1; IV, 75; V, 40–41; VI, 25; VII, 18; XI, 193; letters from Saint Vincent to him in Alet, II, 146, 211, 338; in Genoa, II, 625; III, 1, 26, 101, 107, 122, 150, 152, 166, 198, 206, 241, 257, 274, 335, 352, 367, 376, 388, 460, 467, 480, 523; IV, 75, 79, 102, 117, 120, 131, 142, 163, 255, 305, 322, 408, 439, 449, 492, 526, 529, 551; V, 41, 67, 135, 204, 252, 314 (2), 397, 399, 423, 458, 468, 473, 492, 497, 499, 506, 531, 564, 620; VI, 25, 52, 67, 84, 112, 118, 156, 396, 402, 436, 452, 462; letters to Saint Vincent, II, 664, 665; III, 85, 191, 258, 385, 494, 501; IV, 404, 565, 574; named consultor to Fr. Dehorgny, II, 542; devotion to Saint Joseph, V, 468; Superior in Alet, VIII, 608: see also ***Genoa.***

At Saint-Lazare, health, XI, 380; accompanies Nicolas Pavillon to Alet, I, 580; acts in a way that pleases Saint Vincent, II, 211; and Pavillon, II, 221; sent to Rome, II, 339, 340; journey delayed, II, 343; goes to seminary for renewal, II, 360; named for Saintes, II, 360, 395; receives orders in Richelieu to go to Rome, II, 426; journey to Rome, II, 432; in Rome, II,

467, 552; Consultor to Superior, II, 471, 542, 552; Superior in Genoa, II, 595, 620–21, 652; III, 41, 59, 137, 157, 159, 312, 313; IV, 253, 254, 266, 427, 439, 543; V, 208, 237, 244, 272, 275–76, 354, 485, 500, 502, 534, 535, 623, 637; VI, 57, 72, 83, 92, 99, 120, 127, 137, 154, 169, 172, 188, 361, 486; VIII, 614; XI, 265; Saint Vincent plans to send older man, III, 314; renders service to wife of Maréchal de Guébriant, III, 39, 48, 58, 66; concern for health of Fr. Blatiron, II, 625; III, 48, 58, 101, 107, 122, 167, 190, 194, 198, 200, 257, 460; IV, 417; V, 499; VI, 25; Saint Vincent urges him to moderation and prudence, III, 101–102; is consoled by his zeal and success, III, 26, 159, 167, 241, 275; IV, 133, 143, 305, 427, 438; V, 135–36; see ***Quarto al Mare, Lavagna, Niolo, Gavi, Bra***, where he gives missions.

Blatiron has left Genoa for Paris, IV, 207, 214, 220; in Paris, IV, 221, 226, 228, 229, 231, 237, 239; member of 1651 General Assembly, IV, 226; XIIIa, 369, 372, 374, 387, 397; gives opinion on vows, XIIIa, 377, 381; on other subjects, XIIIa, 383, 386, 387; returns to Genoa, IV, 246, 247, 256; entrusted with negotiations for foundation of Turin house, V, 252–54; Saint Vincent explains to him why vows are necessary in Company, V, 314–22; counts on him to obtain approval in Rome, V, 400; tells him how privilege of exemption was obtained, V, 460; urges him to trust God in temptation, V, 473; obliged to go to court to recover money owed by a slave, VI, 188.

In Rome, Fr. Blatiron obtains for all Missionaries plenary indulgence at hour of death, XI, 193; volunteers to assist plague-stricken; instructions of Saint Vincent, VI, 53, 68, 83, 85, 113, 156, 375, 396, 402; danger to which he is exposed, VI, 430, 432, 434, 437, 453, 462, 485, 486, 487, 488; death, VI, 504, 506, 507, 509, 510–11, 528, 530, 535, 537, 567, 583, 586; VII, 15, 18, 31; XI, 379; mention of conference on his virtues, VI, 552; XII, 430; eulogy, VII, 581; XI, 379–81; other mentions, VII, 374, 389, 568, 593. See also ***Alet, Genoa***.

Blavet (M.) - Advises leaving Verneuil, III, 529; money owed for coaches, IV, 506–07; VI, 125–26.

Blessed Sacrament, church in Turin - Confreres invited to staff it, V, 253.

Blessed Sacrament (Company) - Historical note, IV, 119–20, 520; founded by Duc de Ventadour, IV, 294; involved in ministry for galley convicts, I, 169; of General Hospital (Salpêtrière), V, 53; of house for girls in Montmorency, I, 424; fosters spread of Confraternities of Charity, V, 243; asks Saint Vincent to send Missionaries to Salé, II, 678; plenary assembly of Ladies of Charity wrongly taken for meeting of members of Company of Blessed Sacrament, IV, 391; members do wonders for needy in Paris, IV, 520.

Blessed Sacrament (Confraternity) - Its erection in Sedan, IV, 602; union with that of the Charity at Saint-Nicolas-du-Chardonnet in Paris, XIIIb, 99.

Blessed Sacrament (Congregation) - Founder: see **Authier de Sisgau**; attempts at approval from Rome and Paris, II, 466–67; IV, 296; proposal of union with Congregation of the Mission, II, 276–77, 281, 438, 452, 459, 465–66; III, 459; Saint Vincent is opposed to its taking name of Missionaries, I, 221–22; II, 466; IV, 61–62, 294–95; VI, 370–71, 516–17; sees no hope of union with them, II, 307; similarity of name brings on disturbance in Annecy against Priests of the Mission, IV, 294; VI, 517; runs risk of instigating lawsuit about legacy left in Marseilles to "Priests of the Mission," VI, 370–71, 517; Fr. Alméras' attempts to be established in Rome with confreres are opposed by priests of Fr. d'Authier, III, 459–60; missions given by priests of Fr. d'Authier to galley convicts in Marseilles, III, 265; establishment in Senlis, II, 281, 309, 506; in Valence, VI, 100, 496; in Marseilles, VIII, 136; Saint Vincent declares never having said or done anything against it, IV, 145, 148; priest leaves their Congregation and asks to work in missions in Piedmont, VII, 495–96.

Blessed Sacrament (Institute) - Historical note, XIIIa, 114; Abbé de Saint-Cyran is questioned about this Institute, XIIIa, 114, 124, 125.

Blessed Sacrament - Mention of conferences, XII, 427, 435, 438; Christ instituted Eucharist out of love, XI, 131–32; Saint Vincent sometimes reads letters on his knees before Blessed Sacrament, III, 174; Saint Vincent admonishes cleric who questions true presence of Our Lord in Blessed Sacrament, XI, 232; how to meditate on this feast, XI, 175; visit Blessed Sacrament before leaving house, XI, 326; pay respects to Blessed Sacrament at stops during journey, I, 504; XIIIb, 273; reverence before Blessed Sacrament, XI, 195; always keep lamp lit before Blessed Sacrament, II, 660; Exposition, I, 475; what to do when Blessed Sacrament passes in street during conference, X, 148.

Blessed Virgin - See **Mary**, **Mother of Jesus**.

Bliar (M.) - I, 71.

Blinvilliers (M. de) - Saint Vincent asks service of him, V, 603.

Blois, town in Loir-et-Cher - I, 193.

Blois (M. de), royal notary of Dax - Witness to contract by which Saint Vincent bought back family land that had been sold, XIIIa, 100.

Blonay (Marie-Aimée de), Superior of First Monastery of Visitation in Annecy - Biographical data, II, 213; other mentions, II, 238, 320.

Blondeau (Pierre), prisoner in Toulon - VIII, 250, 528.

Blondel (Fr.), Canon of Écouis - XIIIa, 29, 30.

Blondel (Pasquier), seminarian of the Mission - Sent to Rome, XIIIa, 359–60.

Blot (Jeanne), Daughter of Charity - XIIIb, 228.

Blotowski (Karol), seminarian of the Mission - Biographical data, VIII, 314.

Blotowski (Nicolas), seminarian of the Mission - Biographical data, VIII, 314.

Bloye (M. de) - Accompanies Frs. Nacquart and Gondrée to Madagascar; praise for him, III, 280, 289, 290.

Boarders - Conference on mentally ill or depraved boarders at Saint-Lazare, XI, 16; food to be given them, XI, 299–300; Saint Vincent recommends that Daughters of Charity not take boarders into their houses, VII, 65; XIIIb, 304, 348, 372; same for Priests of the Mission; exceptions, II, 427; V, 31, 597; VI, 316; VII, 306; in Richelieu, IV, 39; boarders with Visitandines, IV, 434; fees for boarders in Cahors, IV, 504; saint recommends that Fr. Get incline boarders toward interior life, VIII, 3; boarder in Crécy allowed to stay for a time, VIII, 294–95; Daughters' Council decides not to accept boarders, XIIIb, 288–91; Saint Vincent agrees, XIIIb, 304; Saint Francis de Sales allowed Visitandines to accept small number of boarders, XIIIb, 290; room and board for students, I, 106, 135; for ordinands in Paris, II, 89; for seminarians at Bons-Enfants, II, 658; III, 235; at Saint-Charles, VIII, 50; in Richelieu, III, 144; in Le Mans, IV, 59–60, 98; in Cahors, III, 153, 244; at Notre-Dame-de-Lorm, VIII, 257.

Boccone (Domenico), Priest of the Mission - Biographical data, VI, 411–12; VII, 18; assists plague-stricken of Genoa, VI, 411, 432, 491; death, VI, 504, 506, 528, 530, 535, 537, 567, 583, 586; VII, 18.

Bocheron (Anne), Daughter of Charity - In Châteaudun, VII, 437; other mention, XIIIb, 228.

Bochnia, town in Poland - V, 152.

Boice (M.) - II, 359.

Bois-Bouchard (fief) - Dependency of Richelieu house, III, 297, 408, 606.

Boislève (Louis), Councillor of King in Angers - Act of Establishment of Daughters of Charity at Saint-Jean Hospital in Angers, XIIIb, 117; other mention, XIIIb, 119.

Boissy (M. de), ship's captain - VIII, 583.

Boivin (Laurent), native of Mâcon - XIIIb, 74.

Bollain (Anne-Marie), Visitandine - Biographical data, II, 201; III, 302–03; VIII, 292; Superior at Sainte-Madeleine, II, 201; letters from Saint Vincent, III, 528; VIII, 292; she refuses to accept in this monastery a person presented by him, III, 303; Saint Vincent persuades her to remain in office, VIII, 292.

Bonacina (Martino), theologian - Biographical data, II, 263; VIII, 582; moral theology, II, 263, 270; V, 298.

Bonaflos (Jacques), Priest of the Mission - Biographical data, II, 327.

Bonaventure (Saint) - Writings, V, 297; knowledge not necessary to pray well, IX, 27; XII, 88; educated at foot of crucifix, IX, 172.

Bondy, forest - Site of Rougement farm, I, 250.

Bonhomme (Hélène), daughter of Noël Bonhomme - XIIIa, 352, 353, 354.

Bonhomme (Noël) - Proceedings regarding Nom-de-Jésus Hospice: see ***Nom-de-Jésus***.

Bonichon (Barthélemy), brother of Nicolas - Mother recommends him to Saint Vincent, VIII, 527.

Bonichon (Christophe), Brother of the Mission - Nephew of Jean Pillé, II, 376.

Bonichon (Nicolas), Priest of the Mission - Biographical data, II, 376; IV, 233; VIII, 271; nephew of Jean Pillé, II, 376; letters from Saint Vincent, IV, 233, 447, 451; mention of letters to saint, IV, 233, 451; in Cahors, IV, 482; VIII, 271, 527.

Boniface VIII, Pope - XIIIa, 316.

Bonnaud (M.), of Marseilles - VI, 173, 186.

Bonnefons (Amable), Jesuit - Author of *Le Chrétien charitable*, V, 297.

Bonner (Nicolas), convict in Toulon - VI, 638; VII, 187, 274, 403, 557; VIII, 250.

Bonnet (Jean), Priest of the Mission - Biographical data, VI, 429; in Rome; wants to go to Turin, VI, 429, 525; Saint Vincent hastens departure, VI, 521, 552, 557, 604; Fr. Jolly is waiting for passes to be open so he can send him, VI, 619.

Bonnet (Pierre), notary and royal tax collector - Signed sale of house in Luçon to Congregation of the Mission, XIIIa, 320.

Bonneville, priory - XIIIa, 119.

Bons-Enfants, collège in Paris - Historical data, III, 5; IV, 473; V, 32; VI, 128; VII, 28; VIII, 61; X, 184; XI, *xiii*; Saint Vincent, Principal, I, 22; XIIIa, 71, 75, 97, 98, 219, 222–23, 230, 241; XIIIb, 94; power of attorney for taking possession of collège, XIIIa, 70; act of taking possession in name of Vincent de Paul, XIIIa, 72; act of union of collège to Congregation of the Mission, XIIIa, 219, 230, 236; act of taking possession in name of Congregation of the Mission, XIIIa, 234, 236; letters patent approving union, XIIIa, 236; early days of Priests of the Mission at collège, XII, 7; buildings, I, 22–23; chapel is unhealthful, I, 315; plague, I, 316; bequest in Mme Goussault's will for chapel at Bons-Enfants, XIIIb, 396; collège ceases to be Motherhouse the day Saint Vincent moves to Saint-Lazare, I, 134; sometimes he would go there from Saint-Lazare and spend some time, I, 173, 202, 220, 231, 348, 451, 550; visited there occasionally, I, 262, 308, 375, 437; canonical visit by Fr. Portail, IV, 354; by Fr. Alméras, V, 76; Community retreat, I, 118; renewal of vows after Brief *Ex Commissa Nobis*, V, 501–02.

Meetings of priests at Bons-Enfants, I, 31; meetings of priests of Tuesday Conference, II, 616; VII, 405; XIIIa, 140; retreats for ordinands, I, 86, 103, 104, 516; XI, 200; XII, 56; laymen's retreats, I, 159, 293–94; opening of minor seminary around 1636; burse given by Richelieu in 1642 for twelve seminarians, II, 257; cleric from there sent to Rome, II, 499; few boys persevere; number of students on May 13, 1644, II, 506; on November 11, 1644, II, 541; transfer of humanities to Saint-Charles Seminary in 1645, II, 257, 585; Michel Le Gras is student there, I, 498, 577; Saint Louise asks Saint Vincent if Michel is there, II, 549.

In 1645 Bons-Enfants becomes seminary for priests, to be formed in duties of their state, II, 585; VI, 494; VII, 501, 623; VIII, 614; XII, 234; their number, II, 541; III, 5, 108, 175, 235; IV, 335, 573; V, 75; VI, 158, 257; VII, 28; mention of seminarians, VI, 128; VII, 284, 469; cost of boarding, II, 658; III, 235; how low cost is with respect to expenses, III, 235; students from Saint-Lazare go to Bons-Enfants to study theology, I, 528; IV, 499; classes there are less practical than at Saint-Nicolas Seminary, VII, 268–269; XIIIa, 200–01; Saint Vincent eliminates chair of scholastic theology, XIIIa, 200; public sessions on controversy, X, 502; Saint Vincent was sending young Priests of the Mission there to complete formation, VIII, 268; Rules of seminary, III, 154; Saint Vincent used to accept outsiders who were passing through, V, 32; VIII, 124; provided, however, they were willing to follow Rules, V, 597; VIII, 61; used to send seminary priests to give missions with confreres, III, 139, 250; or even placed them in houses as collaborators for relatively long time, III, 145, 147; offers several of them chaplaincies for galley convicts in Marseilles, III, 273; one of them is sent there, XIIIa, 360; priest-seminarians of Bons-Enfants go to Notre-Dame to say Mass, II, 585; IV, 328; lodging two priests in an irregular state, II, 582; Solminihac unable to attend Saint Vincent's conference, II, 616; Saint Vincent prefers to return there rather than render account of annual income of Saint-Lazare to Archbishop, IV, 427; Fr. Boussordec sent to study workings of seminary, VIII, 275; Saint Vincent unable to lodge Saint-Cyran, XIIIa, 122.

Assignments and changes, II, 499, 531; list of Superiors and history of house, VIII, 604–05; Missionaries stationed there: Admirault (Charles), Berthe, Champion, Cornuel, Cuissot (Gilbert), Damiens, Dehorgny, du Chesne (Pierre), Dufour (Antoine), Dufour (Claude), La Brière, Lambert aux Couteaux, Liébe, Pillé (Jean), Vincent de Paul, Watebled (Jean); guests at collège, I, 345; II, 582; III, 163; IV, 398; V, 32, 224; VII, 210; VIII, 124; other mentions, II, 549; III, 131, 409; IV, 342, 447; VIII, 415, 434; X, 184; XI, 327; XII, 234, 237; XIIIa, 49, 56, 110, 196, 260, 262–63, 272.

Bonseré (Barbe Le Juge, Dame) - Member of Charity of Montmirail, XIIIb, 32, 34.

Bonvilliers (Jeanne), Daughter of Charity - Biographical data, V, 439; entered Company before August 8, 1655, XIIIb, 228.

Bonzi (Clément de), Bishop of Béziers - Asks Saint Vincent for Missionaries, I, 304; letter of saint to Bishop, I, 297; unfortunate incident involving Priest of the Mission, IV, 295.

Books - Dedications to Saint Vincent, I, 152; II, 580; XIIIa, 148, 152, 185; saint reproaches M. Alix for having dedicated to him *Hortus pastorum*, III, 121; asks M. de Saint-Rémy not to dedicate theses in philosophy to him, IV, 219; fears practice of writing books: if introduced among Missionaries, might be obstacle to exercise of ministries, but admits exceptions, IV, 436; XI, *xxviii*; dissuades Fr. du Coudray from thought of translating Syriac Bible into Latin, I, 244–45; Brief permitting Missionaries to read forbidden books, VII, 123; Missionaries cannot have books for personal use, nor take them from house to house, VII, 293; XII, 321–22, 334; saint gives Fr. Tholard permission to keep his until his return to Paris, VIII, 74; books sent to Missionaries in Madagascar, III, 281–82; permission requested, for man preparing to go there, to read books on Index, VII, 571; Saint Vincent promises to send Fr. Gilles the books he wants, IV, 280; makes gift to M. Demyon of *Lives of the Saints*, IV, 165; has misplaced list of books Fr. Ozenne wanted in Poland, V, 366; sends Arabic books for Tunis to Fr. Delespiney, VIII, 321. See also **Reading**.

Boquit (Pierre), slave in Algiers - III, 220.

Bordeaux (Antoine de), president of Great Council, French Ambassador to London - V, 620, 624, 627.

Bordeaux, city in Gironde - Visit of Saint Vincent, I, 2; returns later to give mission to galley convicts, XII, 179; rumor about bishopric going to someone unworthy, II, 616; Saint Vincent writes to Mazarin about bishopric, III, 20; troubles of Fronde, III, 525; IV, 95, 102; Court is in Bordeaux, IV, 87; King is in Bordeaux, VIII, 77; Archbishops: see Cardinal François Escoubleau de **Sourdis**, Henri Escoubleau de **Sourdis**, Henri de **Béthune**; seminary, II, 172, 506; coach lines, II, 566; V, 233; VI, 125; VII, 258, 350, 352, 354; X, 467; Charities established in diocese, I, 487; other mentions, I, 271, 430, 482, 500, 520; II, 259; IV, 559; VI, 441; VIII, 240, 510, 524, 558–59, 564; XIIIa, 21. See also **Fonteneil**.

Boré (M.), colonist in Madagascar - VI, 249.

Borgia (Gaspar), Cardinal - XIIIa, 239, 249.

Borguñy (Pedro) [**Bourgoin** (Pierre)], Brother of the Mission, slave in Algiers - Martyrdom, V, 339–40; XI, 288–90.

Borja (Luís Crespi de), Bishop of Plasencia - VIII, 311, 326, 338.

Borrain (Mme) - I, 339.

Borray (Jean), slave in Algiers - V, 380–81.

Borrèze, village in Dordogne - IV, 563.

Borromeo (Charles) - See **Charles Borromeo**.

Bosius (Thomas) - Author of *De signis ecclesiae Dei*, V, 296.

Bosquet (François de), Intendant of Justice in Languedoc, then successively Bishop of Lodève and of Montpellier - Biographical data, III, 292; V, 384; VII, 547; VIII, 19; proceedings for elevation to See of Lodève, II, 605, 613, 617–18; visits Fr. Maurice in Paris, III, 292; Bishop and priests' association of Cahors diocese take him as arbitrator of differences, IV, 270; returns from Rome, V, 384; role in question of probabilism, VII, 547; entrusts seminary to Priests of the Mission, VII, 554; VIII, 260, 619; closes seminary: see ***Montpellier***; did not establish foundation to assure existence of establishment, VIII, 289; in praise of him, VII, 608; contacts with Saint Vincent, VII, 609; VIII, 19, 328, 330; health, VII, 631; other mentions, VIII, 69, 212, 303–04, 316, 320; XIIIa, 471.

Bosses (Alexandre-Gabriel de) - Referred to Saint Vincent by César de Saint-Bonaventure, but saint is unable to help him, IV, 453–54.

Bosside (Vincent), Dominican - II, 562.

Bossu (Marguerite), Daughter of Charity - IX, 437, 438.

Bossuet (Jacques-Bénigne), Archdeacon of Metz - Biographical data, VII, 62; VIII, 449; XI, *xvii-xviii*; letters to Saint Vincent, VII, 62, 85, 100, 112, 169; VIII, 449, 454, 455, 525; preparations for mission in Metz, VII, 62–63, 77, 85–86, 100, 112–13; his participation, VII, 132, 170; thanks Saint Vincent after this mission, VII, 169–70; negotiates establishment of Missionaries in Metz, VIII, 449, 454, 525; preaches retreat for ordinands at Saint-Lazare, VII, 498; other mention, V, 450.

Bouchard - See ***Bois-Bouchard***.

Boucher (Léonard), Priest of the Mission - Biographical data, I, 442; II, 28; III, 80; VIII, 99; letters of Saint Vincent to him in Montmirail, I, 442, 455, 467; in Toul, I, 528, 558; in Bar-le-Duc, II, 26, 42, 76; named for Barbary, II, 355, 398, 406–07; at Saint-Lazare, II, 539; in La Rose; attachment to ideas and person of Fr. du Coudray, III, 80, 81, 114, 133; at 1642 General Assembly, II, 344; XIIIa, 323, 331, 396; at 1651 General Assembly, XIIIa, 396; at Saint-Lazare; health, II, 228; VIII, 99, 129, 145; at Saint Vincent's deathbed, XIIIa, 204, 205; other mention, XIIIa, 206.

Boucher (Louise), Daughter of Charity - Stationed in Cahors, VII, 365; X, 464.

Boucher (Philippe-Ignace), Priest of the Mission - Biographical data, VI, 27; VIII, 9; XI, 294; Internal Seminary extended six months for disobedience, VI, 27, 80; XI, 294–96; Saint Vincent asks Rome for dispensation for his ordination, VIII, 9; dimissorial from Bishop of Arras, VIII, 122; departure from Company, XI, 296.

Bouchet (M.) - IV, 354, 373.

Bouchour (Claude), husband of Denyse Beynier - Member of Charity of Châtillon, XIIIb, 4, 21.

Boudet (Jacques), Priest of the Mission - Biographical data, I, 313–314; II, 258; Director of Internal Seminary, I, 313; pilgrimage to Chartres, I, 350; Saint Vincent plans to send him to Montmirail, I, 442; return to Paris, I, 474; goes from Brittany to Toulouse, passing through Bordeaux, I, 482, 487; becomes ill on arrival in Bordeaux, I, 500; in Fontaine-Essarts, II, 258–59, 273; in Crécy, II, 423; praise from Saint Vincent, I, 487; from Fr. Olier, I, 500; unable to genuflect, XI, 196; other mentions, I, 464, 542.

Boquet (Nicole-Colette), Daughter of Charity - XIIIb, 228.

Bouguenais (Commune) - See ***Saint-Pierre-de-Bouguenais***.

Bouhery (Françoise), Daughter of Charity - XIIIb, 228.

Bouhery (Perrine de), Daughter of Charity - Biographical data, VIII, 164; Saint Louise asks permission for her to take vows, V, 466; ill in Richelieu, VIII, 164–65, 170; other mention, XIIIb, 228.

Bouillon (Eléonore-Catherine de Bergh, Duchesse de), Lady of Charity, wife of Frédéric-Maurice de la Tour d'Auvergne - Biographical data, II, 181; IV, 419; VI, 339; conversion to Catholicism, II, 148; contacts with Saint Vincent, II, 181; with Saint Louise, II, 204; IV, 419; reference to letter from Saint Vincent, II, 182; requests removal of Sister, II, 667; sending of another, VI, 339; tries to turn Sister away from vocation, XIIIb, 349; other mentions, VIII, 97; XIIIb, 351.

Bouillon (Frédéric-Maurice de la Tour d'Auvergne, Duc de) - Conversion to Catholicism, II, 148; other mentions, IV, 409, 411.

Bouillon (Louise de la Tour d'Auvergne, Demoiselle de), daughter of preceding - Biographical data, VI, 283; proceedings in favor of Protestants of Saint-Céré, II, 503–04; Saint Vincent refuses entrance to Visitation Monastery, VI, 283–84; VII, 419; other mention, II, 667.

Bouillon (Mme) - Reference to letter to Saint Louise, VIII, 97.

Bouillon (Mauricette de) - See **Auvergne** (Mauricette-Fébronie de la Tour d').

Boulart (François), Augustinian - Biographical data, III, 352; IV, 245–46; V, 95–96; letters from Saint Vincent, III, 352; IV, 245, 307; V, 144, 358, 386, 415; placed on list of three, from which King will choose Abbot of Mont-Saint-Éloi, V, 95.

Boule (Jeanne-Marie), Daughter of Charity - X, 1; XIIIb, 228.

Bouleau (Abraham) - V, 17.

Boulier (Fr.), Priest of the Mission - In Rome, II, 395, 498.

Boulle (Dian), important person in Madagascar - V, 299.

Boulogne, town in Pas-de-Calais - Bishop: see François **Perrochel**; misfortunes of diocese, VII, 41–42; Convent of Annonciades, XIIIa, 132; slave from Boulogne, V, 36.

Boulon (Marie), midwife in Clichy - XIIIa, 74.

Bourbon [**Bourlon**] (Charles de), Coadjutor, then Bishop of Soissons - V, 438; VI, 616; VII, 301; VIII, 53; Saint Vincent informs him that Nicolas Guillot is being sent to Montmirail, XII, 373.

Bourbon (Henri de), Duc de Verneuil, Bishop of Metz - Biographical data, VI, 285; at request of Community of Jean-Jacques Olier, seeks Saint Vincent's assistance in electing successor to Olier, VI, 285; relationship with Saint Vincent, VIII, 405, 474.

Bourbon-l'Archambault, town in Allier - Saint Louise urges departure of Sister Anne Hardemont for this small town, V, 416–17; Fr. Alméras goes there for spa: see **Alméras** (René); Frs. Perraud, Watebled, Éveillard, VI, 423–24, 435, 440, 443, 445; Mme des Essarts, V, 356; Duc de Richelieu, VII, 289; Mme Potier de Lamoignon, VIII, 465, 501.

Bourbonnais, province - VIII, 494.

Bourchanin (Jean), Procurator in bailiwick of Mâcon - XIIIb, 74.

Bourdais (Marie), Daughter of Charity - Signs attestation of Common and Particular Rules reviewed and arranged in order by Fr. Alméras, XIIIb, 206.

Bourdaise (Toussaint), Priest of the Mission - Biographical data, V, 71; VI, 21; VII, 17–18; VIII, 104; XI, *xvi*; progresses so little in studies that dismissal is considered several times, XI, 391–92; named for Madagascar, V, 71, 76, 82; Nuncio promises to send his name to Rome, V, 175; Saint Vincent requests usual faculties for him, V, 551; voyage from France to Madagascar, V, 148, 278–86, 302–05; ministry, difficulties, and results achieved, V, 298–301, 305–12, 507–28; VI, 214–54; mention of letters to Saint Vincent, V, 637; VI, 21, 460, 464; what M. Flacourt says of Fr. Bourdaise, XIIIa, 186; what Fr. Mousnier says, V, 289, 290, 296; Fr. Étienne, VIII, 554–55, 577, 586, 589; Saint Vincent praises his zeal and devotion, VI, 447, 452, 453, 464, 469, 471, 475, 478, 481, 488, 492, 495, 501; VII, 17; VIII, 104; XI, 372; speaks of his plans, X, 96; prefers not to publish his reports; transmits copies of them: see ***Madagascar***; recommends him to confreres, XI, 214, 391; XII, 62; writes to encourage him, VIII, 180; proposes him to *Propaganda Fide* to be Prefect of Mission, VIII, 282; Fr. Bourdaise learns language of country, V, 525; Superior in Madagasacar, VIII, 616; death, VIII, 180; other mentions, V, 291, 431, 441; VI, 463; VII, 58, 61, 496; VIII, 199; XI, 263. See also ***Madagascar***.

Bourdeille(s) (François de), Bishop of Périgueux - Ordains Saint Vincent priest, XIIIa, 7; dies one month later, XIIIa, 8.

Bourdelet (Christophe), Vicar of Montmirail - XIIIb, 32.

Bourdet (Étienne), Priest of the Mission - Biographical data, I, 542; II, 32; VII, 515; XI, 106–07; not highly thought of in Paris, XI, 106–07; in Lorraine, I, 542; Superior in Toul, VIII, 605; in Annecy, II, 18, 88; XI, 106, 107; Saint Jane Frances de

Chantal's opinion of him, II, 32; on milk diet, VII, 515, 583; health, XII, 241.

Bourdet (Jean), Priest of the Mission - Biographical data, I, 542; II, 343; III, 12; letters Saint Vincent wrote to him in Saint Méen, II, 656, 670; III, 41; in Lorraine, I, 542; Superior in Troyes, II, 343, 657; VIII, 607; at 1642 General Assembly, II, 343; XIIIa, 323, 331; recalled from Troyes, II, 541; in Paris, II, 528, 541; Superior in Saint-Méen, II, 668; III, 12, 31; VIII, 613; Saint Vincent regrets his acceptance of Plancoët chapel, II, 656–57, 663; explains usefulness of canonical visitations, II, 657–58, 670–71, 673; Fr. Portail's advice about them, II, 668; tells him why Company cannot yield in lawsuit concerning Saint-Méen Seminary, III, 41–45; Fr. Bourdet regrets displeasure with Fr. Portail regarding visitation recommendations; apologizes to Saint Vincent, III, 84; escapes from Saint-Méen, III, 42; Saint Vincent considers sending him to Ireland as Superior, III, 82, 84, 93, 103, 107; Fr. Bourdet leaves Company, III, 97, 114.

Bourdet (M.), Director of Ursulines of Melun - Letter to Saint Vincent, VIII, 410; intimidates his successor, who resigns as confessor, VIII, 517.

Bourdin (M.), cousin of Nicolas Pavillon - II, 220.

Bourdin (M.), Vicar-General of Noyon - VIII, 28, 540.

Bourdin (Mme), of Villepreux - I, 357, 359.

Bourdoise (Adrien), Founder of Saint-Nicolas Seminary - Biographical data, I, 88; II, 174; XI, 6; letters from Saint Vincent, I, 535; II, 174; first to open seminary "to teach all the rubrics there," XII, 235; contacts with Saint Vincent, I, 88, 536; Saint Vincent persuades Mme de Liancourt to ask Fr. Bourdaise for priests for foundation she is proposing, I, 384, 385; illness and death, XI, 185; praise for him, XI, 6; other mention, I, 188. See also **Nicolaites.**

Bourdon (Michel), Pastor in Le Havre - VIII, 360.

Bourel (Étienne) - Enters Congregation, I, 304; dies during mission in Mesnil, I, 313.

Bourg (Roger), slave in Algiers - V, 405.

Bourg-en-Bresse, town in Ain - XIIIa, 55.

Bourg-sur-Gironde, town in Gironde - I, 487.

Bourgeois (Jean), Jansenist Doctor of Sorbonne - III, 73.

Bourgeois (Mme), Lady of Charity in Joigny - XIIIb, 28.

Bourgeois [**Bourgeoys**] (Marguerite) - See **Marguerite Bourgeois**.

Bourges - Bishop: see André **Frémiot**; revenues from parishes are among lowest in kingdom, II, 612; Saint Vincent thought Marquis de Châteauneuf was in Bourges, IV, 512.

Bourgneuf, hamlet in La Chapelle-Saint-Laud (Maine-et-Loire) - II, 2.

Bourgoin (Pierre) - See **Borguñy**.

Bourgoing (François), Superior General of Oratory - Resigns parish of Clichy in favor of Saint Vincent, XIIIa, 23; confessor of Gaston, Duc d'Orléans, II, 416; other mention, I, 165.

Bourlemont (Claude d'Anglure, Comte de) - State of health of Marie-Angélique d'Atri puts him in contact with Saint Vincent, I, 459–63; other mention, II, 219.

Bourlier (Françoise), wife of Eustache Collée - Lady of Charity of Folleville, XIIIb, 48.

Bourlon - See **Bourbon** (Charles de).

Bournay (Jean de) - XIIIa, 354.

Bourzeis (Amable de), member of French Academy - Biographical data, V, 36.

Boussordec (Charles), Priest of the Mission - Biographical data, V, 577; VI, 112; VIII, 76–77; XI, 336; mention of letters to Saint Vincent, VIII, 150; XI, 336; Saint Vincent, requests from Rome usual powers for him for Madagasacar, V, 577; in Nantes, VI, 112, 124, 128; shipwrecked on Loire, VI, 149–50, 159–60; VIII, 183, 554; XI, 336–37, 342; sent from Luçon to La Rose, VI, 611; volunteers again for Madagascar, XI, 374; Saint Vincent accepts his proposal, VIII, 103; asks him to go to Nantes, VIII, 115; in Nantes, VIII, 150, 160, 169; sent back to Richelieu, VIII, 169; effective speaker, VIII, 236; sent to Bons-Enfants to visit seminary, VIII, 275; mission in Vins, VIII, 276; Superior in Annecy, VIII, 608; other mentions, VI, 440; VIII, 76, 243, 262, 275, 287. See also ***Madagascar***.

Boust (M.), professor at Sorbonne - VIII, 150.

Bouthillier (François), Bishop of Troyes - Established seminary in Missionaries' house after Saint Vincent's death, VIII, 608.

Boutonnet (M.), passenger on *Maréchale* - Goes to Madagascar, VIII, 240, 557, 561–62; wears cassock; desires to be Missionary, VIII, 580–81; studies philosophy, VIII, 584; makes retreat, VIII, 587; will sail from Madagascar, VIII, 588.

Bouvant (Mme de), Foundress of Carmel of Reims - VIII, 506–07.

Bouvard (Charles) - King's physician, X, 276; physician of Saint Louise, I, 146–47.

Bouvard (Marie-Augustine), Visitation nun, daughter of Charles Bouvard - Biographical data, I, 146; III, 417; IV, 403; VI, 163; VIII, 189; Superior of Angers Monastery, III, 417; Superior of Second Monastery of Paris, IV, 403; VI, 163; illness, VIII, 189; death, VIII, 195.

Bouy (Catherine), Daughter of Charity - Sent to Poland, XIIIb, 239.

Bouzauct (Jacques), Commissioner of Roads of City and Faubourgs of Paris - III, 337.

Bouzon (Antoine), Archpriest of Cahors, *Procureur Fiscal* of Bishop - Episcopal synod, XIIIa, 309; appointed to committee to open seminary in Cahors, XIIIa, 309.

Bra, town in Piedmont - Mission, VI, 525, 557, 577, 582, 601, 639; VII, 59, 74, 89, 103, 118–19; XI, 380.

Bragelogne (Mme de), Lady of Charity, treasurer of work of Foundlings - XIIIb, 430.

Brancaccio (Francisco Maria), Cardinal, Bishop of Viterbo - Biographical data, V, 467; VI, 553; VII, 48; VIII, 134; missions in his diocese, V, 467, 487, 489; kindness toward Congregation of the Mission, VI, 553; VII, 595; Saint Vincent thanks him, VII, 139; VIII, 134, 140; sends him books, VII, 48; mention of letter to saint, VII, 412; other mention, VII, 360.

Branché - Member of Charity of Joigny - XIIIb, 66.

Brandon (Philibert de), Bishop of Périgueux - Biographical data, II, 38; III, 165; IV, 27; letters from Saint Vincent, IV, 48, 174; in Saint-Maur, II, 38; opens, with Fr. Olier, seminary at Vaugirard; follows Fr. Olier to Saint-Sulpice, II, 308; Saint Vincent considers proposing him for bishopric of Babylon, III, 165; Alain de Solminihac wants him for Périgueux diocese, II, 430; regrets that another may have been chosen, II, 679; happy to see him named, III, 342; people of Périgueux regret he is not named their Bishop, II, 681; entrusts Périgueux Seminary to Priests of the Mission; dismisses them shortly after: see ***Périgueux***; Solminihac sends him copy of establishment of Congregation of the Mission in Cahors, IV, 142; mention of letter to Bishop of Cahors, IV, 190; visit to Cahors, IV, 191; Brandon fully prepared to sign letter of Bishops to Pope against Jansenism, IV, 101; signs it, IV, 160; chosen as arbitrator in dispute between Alain de Solminihac and priests' association of Cahors diocese, IV, 270; death, IV, 429; other mentions, III, 473–74, 517; IV, 27.

Bray, region of France - VI, 310.

Brazil - V, 303; VIII, 568–69; XIIIa, 34.

Bréant (Louis), Priest of the Mission - Biographical data; in Tréguier, VI, 138; VII, 138; receives *extra tempora* from Rome for ordination, VI, 349; sent to Toul for ordination retreat, VI, 457; in Saintes, VII, 138; VIII, 324.

Bréauté (Marie de Fiesque, Marquise de) - Consults Saint Vincent, VIII, 547; other mention, VIII, 507.

Breda, town in Italy - V, 531.

Bredonique, small town in Scotland - VI, 546.

Brémont (M.), administrator of Châteaudun Hospital - VI, 575.

Brentel (Frédéric), artist - Portrait painted on commission from Saint Vincent, I, 332.

Bréquigny (Jean de), convict in Algiers - VIII, 462.

Breslay (René de), Bishop of Troyes - Establishes and partly funds house of Missionaries in Troyes, I, 415, 443–44; VIII, 608; kindness toward Missionaries, II, 249; concern for ordinands, I, 464–65; Paris houses, I, 415, 443–44, 530; Saint Vincent wants room reserved for Breslay in Missionaries' house, I, 570; his nephew, II, 168; illness and death, II, 230; other mentions, I, 521, 531, 571.

Bresse, region of France - VIII, 302; XII, 190; XIIIa, 49, 51, 54.

Bret (M.) - Saint Louise awaits him to give him answer from Saint Vincent, II, 137.

Bretonvillers, hamlet in Maisse (Essonne) - IV 236.

Bretonvilliers (Alexandre de Ragois de), Sulpician - Biographical data, VI, 295; VIII, 473; elected successor to Jean-Jacques Olier, VI, 285, 295; VIII, 473; keeps excerpt of allocution of Saint Vincent, VI, 295; XIIIa, 184; VIII, 473; begins Religious of Blessed Virgin, VIII, 473; goes to see Saint Vincent regarding this, VIII, 473, 476.

Brevedent (J. de) - Writes to Saint Vincent about Abbé de Saint-Cyran and about disagreement among Carmelites, VIII, 404–09.

Brèves (François-Savary, Marquis de), French Ambassador to Constantinople - Biographical data; journey to Barbary, I, 7.

Breviary - See **Divine Office**.

Brezé (Urbain de Maillé, Marquis de) - Biographical data, II, 220.

Brial, hamlet in Bressols (Tarn-et-Garonne) - IV, 588, 589; VI, 357; VII, 166.

Bricaud (Jacquemet), the widow Lévy, Lady of Charity in Châtillon - XIIIb, 22.

Bridget (Saint) - I, 560.

Bridgettines [**Brigittines**] in Arras - V, 13; VII, 198, 364; X, 183.

Bridoul (Mother Marie-Antoinette), Abbess of Bridgettines [Brigittines] in Arras - Biographical data, VI, 116; letter from Saint Vincent, VI, 116; encourages her in last agony, VI, 116–17.

Brie (André de), galley convict in Toulon - VII, 208.

Brie (Charlotte de), Lady of Charity in Châtillon - XIIIa, 55; XIIIb, 4, 11, 21, 22.

Brie-Comte-Robert, town in Seine-et-Marne - Historical note, I, 275; Commander de Sillery funds mission; Saint Vincent goes there, I, 465; VIII, 609; Confraternity of Charity, XIIIb, 5.

Brienne (Henri-Auguste de Loménie, Comte de), Secretary of State - Biographical data, II, 54; IV, 33; VI, 479; VII, 106; letter from Saint Vincent, II, 575; assistance for ruined nobles of Lorraine, II, 54; contacts with Saint Vincent, II, 462, 467, 472; IV, 33, 308; V, 414; VI, 479; other mentions, II, 416; IV, 87, 271; VI, 649, 650; VII, 106, 187, 523; XII, 382; XIIIa, 227, 253, 258, 283, 295, 338, 477, 478, 488; XIIIb, 235–36.

Brienne (Louise de Béon, Comtesse de), wife of Henri-Auguste - Biographical data, II, 444; III, 149, 404; IV, 34; V, 249; VI, 281; VII, 640; X, 5; Lady of Charity, III, 149, 404, 420, 506; Saint Vincent uses her influence with Comte de Brienne, IV, 34, 271; she asks that Missionaries be sent to Sweden, V, 249; takes an interest in Saint-Denis Hospital, V, 332, 484; in Saint-Fargeau Hospital, VI, 281; VII, 640; in Daughters of Providence, VI, 550; in Sisters sent to Sedan, X, 5; contacts with Anne of Austria, XIIIa, 155; other mention, VII, 641.

Brienne-le-Château, town in Aube - Daughters of Charity in Brienne, V, 61; VII, 465.

Brière, (M. de) - See **La Brière**.

Brigide [**Brigitte**] (Claude-), Daughter of Charity - Sent to Le Mans, II, 642.

Brigitte, Daughter of Charity - In Nantes, III, 216.

Brignole (Maria Emanuele), Genovese noble - Biographical data, VII, 558; VIII, 24; gratitude of Saint Vincent; Brignole asks to have mission preached in his marquisate, VII, 558; reduces considerably donation made by son to Genoa house, VIII, 24, 80–81; generosity toward Missionaries' house in Rome, VII, 559; VIII, 154; gratitude Missionaries owe him, VII, 585.

Brignole (Rodolfo Maria), son of preceding - Donation to Missionaries' house in Genoa, VII, 558, 560; Fr. Pesnelle's contacts with his father, VIII, 24; parents reduce most of his alms to Pesnelle, VIII, 80–81.

Brillehaut (Mathurine), Daughter of Charity - XIIIb, 228.

Brin (Gerard), Priest of the Mission - Biographical data, II, 642; III, 16–17; IV, 17; V, 158; VI, 39; VII, 27; VIII, 486; letters Saint Vincent sends him in Limerick, IV, 17; in Dax, IV, 466; in La Rose, IV, 543; in Meaux, VI, 458; VII, 353; mention of letters to Saint Vincent, IV, 466; VI, 458; VII, 353; in Le Mans, II, 642; at Saint-Lazare, II, 663, 669, 676; III, 16.

Goes to Ireland, III, 93, 103; Superior in Ireland; sends several confreres to France, III, 478; mission in Limerick, IV, 18; persecution and spread of disease, IV, 17–18, 291, 341, 373; return to France; gives mission near Dax, IV, 466; health, IV, 466; Superior in La Rose, IV, 543, 588; V, 159; VIII, 606; in Toul, VIII, 606; proposed to *Propaganda Fide* for mission of Scotland and Hebrides, IV, 478–479; chosen to visit Missionaries there, obliged to stop in London, V, 573, 620, 622, 624, 627; VI, 39, 112, 124, 429, 499; question of sending him to establishment planned for Spain, VI, 364; Superior in Troyes, VI, 381, 535, 570; VIII, 607; Superior in Meaux, VI, 458; VIII, 619; informs Saint Vincent of wishes of Bishop of Meaux, VIII, 486; at Saint-Lazare; health, VI, 639; VII, 27, 73; returns to Meaux as Superior, VII, 353, 369, 370; Superior in Toul, VIII, 606.

Brinvilliers (Mme de) - VIII, 418.

Briquet (Pierre de), notary in Paris - XIIIa, 20, 22.

Brisacier (Laurent de), entrusted with mission in Rome - Biographical data, II, 533; III, 375; VIII, 79; aversion for vows, III, 375; Saint Vincent tells Fr. Jolly how he should act with him, VIII, 79; foundation at Nom-de-Jésus, VIII, 344; other mentions, VIII, 131, 169.

Brisjonc (François), Priest of the Mission - Biographical data, VII, 316; VIII, 19; in Marseilles, VII, 316; Saint Vincent unsure if he is in Agde or in Marseilles, VII, 393; in Agde, VII, 410; desire to return to Marseilles, VIII, 19; sent to La Rose; departure; readmission, VIII, 35.

Brission (J.) - Member of Charity of Courboin, XIIIb, 93.

Brission (Louise) - Member of Charity of Courboin, XIIIb, 93.

Brission (Pierre) - Member of Charity of Courboin, XIIIb, 93.

Brittany, province - Saint Louise has high opinion of Breton women, VI, 75; Benedictines of Brittany, II, 307; Parlement supports them, III, 43; minor persecution results, III, 65; other mentions, I, 500; II, 343, 362, 416, 434; III, 76, 93, 107, 114,

393, 413, 451; IV, 269, 601–02; V, 9, 24, 76, 280, 350, 570, 617; VI, 229, 444, 495; VII, 120, 496; VIII, 129, 150, 170, 172, 185, 222, 306, 340, 519; X, 533; XI, 215; XII, 318, 365, 377, 379; XIIIa, 194, 332,-33; XIIIb, 267, 309.

Brocard (Élisabeth-Marie), Daughter of Charity - Biographical data, VI, 66; X, 160; sent to La Fère, VI, 66; X, 160; words of praise for her, X, 233.

Brochard (M.) - VIII, 130, 227.

Broille (Abbé) - VI, 263.

Broizot (Julienne) - Member of Charity of Montmirail, XIIIb, 32.

Brosses (Alexandre-Gabriel de) - IV, 453.

Brosses (M.) - See **Des Brosses**.

Brothers of Charity - VIII, 562; X, 442.

Brothers of the Mission - See **Coadjutor Brothers**.

Brou (Mlle), Lady of Charity - I, 261.

Brou (Mme de), Lady of Charity - I, 261, 485.

Brouard (Symphorien), "Father of the Poor" in Angers - XIIIb, 118–19.

Broully (M. de), Secretary of Archbishop of Sens - XIIIb, 27.

Brousse (Jacques), Pastor of Saint-Honoré in Paris - Sent to Rome by Jansenists to uphold their cause, IV, 581, 594.

Brousse (M. de) - Contacts with Alain de Solminihac, V, 172, 173, 590.

Brousse (M.) - VI, 349, 526.

Broussel (Pierre), Councillor of *Grand'Chambre* - Indignation aroused by his arrest, III, 356.

Broutel (Jean) - IV, 243, 244.

Broyer (François), Procurator General of Mâcon Chapter - XIIIb, 78.

Bruand (M.), clerk of Nicolas Fouquet - VII, 438, 455.

Brugière (Sébastien), Father of Mercy - Biographical data, III, 220; V, 391; charity toward slaves in Algiers, III, 220; toward Missionaries, III, 222, 223, 309, 310; in France, V, 391.

Brulart (M.) - See **Sillery** (Brulart de).

Bruneau (Pierre), slave in Algiers - V, 407.

Brunel (Mme), Lady of Charity - I, 83.

Brunet (Jean-Joseph), Priest of the Mission - Biographical data, I, 39; II, 141, 338; III, 313; signed letters to Urban VIII seeking approval of Congregation of the Mission, I, 39, 45, 47, 53; on mission in Bordeaux diocese, I, 268, 271, 279, 291; in Montpezat, I, 430; in duchy of Aiguillon, I, 442; returns via Bordeaux, I, 482; Saint Vincent reprimands him for leaving without his companion, Fr. de Sergis, I, 487; in La Rose, I, 589; sent to Rome from Alet, II, 339, 340; VIII, 608; departure for Rome delayed, II, 343, 359, 395; mission on galleys of Marseilles, II, 407; journey to Rome, II, 426, 432; in Rome, II, 467; in Genoa, III, 313; in Marseilles; zeal, III, 429; death, III, 464, 467, 468; words of praise for him, III, 494–98; XIIIa, 286; other mention, I, 198.

Bruno (Giovanni Antonio), Priest of the Mission - Biographical data; in Genoa, VII, 389; vows, VII, 540, 569.

Bruquedalle, ancient commune in Seine-Maritime - VI, 309.

Brussels, town in Belgium - VIII, 596–97.

Bruyères-le-Châtel, village in Essonne - Proposed union of priory to Congregation of the Mission, III, 234; mission, VII, 20–22.

Bruys (Pierre), Procurator Syndic of Mâcon - XIIIb, 73.

Bry (Marguerite du Tartre, Dame de), wife of Gabriel de Bry, Lieutenant-General of bailiwick of Étampes - V, 116.

Buade (Claude de), Abbess of Argensolles Monastery - III, 513.

Bucher (M.) - Conditions for daughter's entrance into Visitation Monastery, VII, 418–20.

Buchet (Benoît), King's attorney in bailiwick of Mâcon - XIIIb, 73, 76.

Bucy-les-Pierrepont, village in Aisne - Destroyed by fire, VI, 415.

Buenens, former village near Châtillon-les-Dombes - XIIIa, 44, 46, 47, 48, 57.

Buffier (M.) - Arrival from Poland, VII, 176; return there, VII, 180.

Buglose [***Burglosse***], shrine in Pouy (Landes) - Historical note, III, 245; proposed establishment of Missionaries, III, 245.

Buhot (Gilles), Canon of Bayeux - Biographical data, VI, 376–77; VIII, 295; mention of letters to Saint Vincent, VI, 376; offers Saint Vincent shrine of Notre-Dame-de-la-Délivrande, VI, 377; letter from Saint Vincent, VIII, 295.

Buire (Jeanne de), Daughter of Charity - Biographical data; wants assurance of her vocation for life, VIII, 350.

Buisson (François), surgeon, slave in Algiers - V, 36.

Buissot (Nicolas), Priest of the Mission - Biographical data, I, 419; II, 529; in Richelieu, I, 419, 442; good cantor, I, 419; on mission, I, 452; health, I, 500; leaves Company, II, 541.

Bulls - For newly-appointed Bishops, I, 526; for Prior of Bussière-Badil, VII, 239; for union of Saint-Pourçain Priory to Saint-Lazare, VII, 239, 252; for union of Saint-Méen Abbey to seminary, VII, 252; XIIIa, 423; for union of Saint-Lazare Priory to Mission, XIIIa, 409–16; for erection of Congregation of the Mission, XIIIa, 296–304: see ***Salvatoris Nostri***; concerning vows in approved religious Order, ***Ascendente Domini***, XIIIa, 380, 382, 405.

Bulles, village in Oise - Confraternity of Charity, I, 284; visit of Saint Louise, I, 284, 286.

Bullion (Claude de), judge - Biographical data, II, 92.

Bullion (Pierre), Abbot of Saint-Faron de Meaux, son of preceding - Death, bequeaths property for good works, VIII, 214.

Burdilliat (Eléonore) - Member of Charity of Châtillon, XIIIb, 21.

Bureau [**Beaure**] (Jean), Priest of the Mission - Biographical data; in Saint-Méen, III, 457.

Burgo (M. de) - IV, 468.

Burglosse - See ***Buglose.***

Burgundy, province of France - Missions in this province, V, 474, 475, 610; VI, 31; other mentions, I, 354; V, 98; VII, 127, 410.

Burlamacchy (Sauveur) - V, 17.

Bus (Blessed César de), Founder of Priests of Christian Doctrine - Biographical data, II, 459; VII, 484: see also **Christian Doctrine** (Priests).

Busée (Jean), Jesuit - Biographical data, VI, 120; VII, 81; author of *Enchiridion piarum meditationum,* I, 197; III, 282; VI, 120, 630; VII, 81, 289; VIII, 587.

Busquet (Pierre), Abbot of Mont-Saint-Éloy in Arras - V, 95.

Bussière-Badil, priory in Dordogne - Denis Laudin, Prior, VII, 239, 295; VIII, 524; Saint Vincent foresees that union of priory to his Congregation will be very difficult to obtain, VII, 344–45.

Busson (Simon), Brother of the Mission - Biographical data, III, 479; XI, 140; death, III, 478–79; conference on his virtues, XI, 140–41.

But (Jeanne de), Daughter of Charity - I, 341.

Butefer (Catherine), mother of Le Vacher brothers - Death and funeral service, XI, 392.

Butler (Peter), Priest of the Mission - Biographical data, IV, 468; VII, 329; VIII, 170; student at Saint-Charles Seminary, IV, 468; dismissorial letters, VII, 329, 345, 421, 541, 566; VIII, 170; in Tréguier, VIII, 170; does not want to be obliged to return to Ireland to get title needed for ordination, VII, 346; *extra tempora* for him, VII, 594.

Butler (Thomas), student at Saint-Charles Seminary - IV, 468.

Buy (M.), inhabitant of Châtillon - XIIIa, 57.

Buzay (Abbé de) - See **Gondi** (Jean François-Paul de).

Buzenval (Madeleine Potier, Dame Choart de) - II, 399–400.

Buzenval (Nicolas Choart de), Bishop of Beauvais, son of preceding - Biographical data, IV, 586; V, 107; Saint Vincent writes to him concerning hermit, IV, 586; favorable to Jansenists, V, 107; VIII, 407.

C

Cabals [**Factions**] - Avoiding factions, XI, 94.

Cabaret (Gabrielle), Daughter of Charity - Biographical data, IV, 311; VIII, 235; Saint Vincent sees no sign of vocation, IV, 311–12; Saint Louise asks permission for vows, VIII, 235; other mention, XIIIb, 227.

Cabart (Nicolas) - Recommends nephew to Saint Vincent for retreat at Saint-Lazare, VIII, 549.

Cabel (Pierre), Priest of the Mission - Biographical data, V, 73; VI, 367; VII, 3; VIII, 15; letters Saint Vincent sends him in Sedan, VI, 367, 390, 403, 487, 529, 595, 607, 622; VII, 3, 23, 151, 216, 296, 365, 393, 441, 537, 605; VIII, 177, 203, 223, 304; mention of letters to Saint Vincent, VI, 488, 529, 607, 608; VII, 365, 444, 537, 605; VIII, 178, 223; in Sedan, V, 73, 474; Assistant Superior, VI, 367; Superior, VI, 622; VIII, 15, 611; health, VII, 444; saint explains duties of Superiors, VI, 623; approves his conduct with Governor of Sedan, VIII, 224; lengthy sermons, VI, 623.

Cabo da Roca, cape near mouth of Tagus River, Portugal - VIII, 503.

Cabry (Françoise), Daughter of Charity - Sent to Sedan, X, 1; other mention, XIIIb, 227.

Cacquet (François), monk of Saint-Lazare Priory - I, 135; XIIIa, 263.

Caen, town in Calvados - Young man wants to join Congregation of the Mission, I, 479; young troublemakers, VIII, 296; Saint Vincent sends confessor for Visitation nuns, VIII, 505.

Caesar, name given to early Roman Emperors - Jesus says to render to Caesar what is Caesar's, VI, 30; XI, 120; XIIIa, 452; bloodstained garment of Julius Caesar, XII, 209.

Cahors, town in Lot - Character of people of Cahors, X, 465; Fronde in Cahors, IV, 505; plague, IV, 481–82, 498, 500–03, 506, 508; V, 28; Bishops: see Nicolas **Sevin**, Alain de **Solminihac**; Priests' Association of diocese, IV, 191, 540; Jesuits, VII, 550; Dominicans, II, 616, 681; Capuchins, III, 162; IV, 509; Ursulines, III, 463; Reformed Augustinians of Chancelade, III, 225; Poor Clares, II, 490; Canons Regular, VII, 754; no discussion of Jansenism in diocese, III, 345; Saint Vincent plans to go to Cahors, III, 429, 461; other mentions, IV, 557; VIII, 135; XIIIa, 382.

Missionaries in Cahors: Synod discusses opening seminary, XIIIa, 309; Priests of the Mission given direction of seminary; foundation contract, II, 417; beginnings, II, 427–30; letters of Saint Vincent to Cahors Missionaries, II, 631, 636; III, 123, 238; IV, 233, 283, 447, 451; VII, 337; VIII, 1; fire next to seminary, II, 452; good order, III, 461, 464; VII, 376; good being done, II, 489; III, 340; IV, 125, 252; ministry of Saint-Barthélemy parish in Cahors, IV, 480; VI, 634; union of priories in Gignac, VI, 606; VII, 12, 337; VIII, 135; of La Vaurette, II, 451; gift to seminary of Cayran farm: see ***Cayran***; financial situation, IV, 279; remuneration for room and board, III, 153, 244; Alain de Solminihac's concern for diocese, III, 163; not opposed to Cahors seminarians entering Congregation of the Mission under certain conditions, III, 340–41; diocesan seminarians spend year in seminary before sub-deaconate, six months before priesthood, IV, 125.

Number of seminarians: II, 452; III, 153, 175, 461; VI, 634; VIII, 89; assignments and changes, III, 81–82, 92, 522; V, 535; house has enough Brothers, VII, 514–15; list of Superiors and history of house, VIII, 610–11; Cahors Missionaries: see **Bonichon**, **Cuissot** (Gilbert), **Delattre**, **Dubourdieu**, **Dufestel**, **Fournier** (François), **Gazet**, **Gilles**, **Levasseur**, **Robin**, **Testacy**, **Thierry**, **Treffort**, **Vagré**, **Water** (Jacques), **Water** (Nicolas); canonical visitations by Fr. Du Coudray, III, 32; by Fr. Portail, III, 63, 81–82, 89, 102, 109, 114, 116, 124–25, 133, 137, 153; by Fr. Dehorgny, VIII, 270, 305; why Missionaries at seminary do not give missions, IV, 49; Missionaries in Cahors chant Divine Office, XII, 268, 270; other mentions: IV, 142, 342, 557, 559; V, 184; VII, 206; VIII, 479; XIIIa, 211.

Daughters of Charity in Cahors: Solminihac requests Daughters of Charity for foundling hospital, V, 629; X, 95; XIIIb, 338; for two hospitals, XI, 327; choice of Sisters, VI, 287; new request of Bishop for small hospital, XII, 20; Sisters sent to Cahors, VII, 157, 338, 350, 352–54, 365, 431–32; VIII, 144, 160, 187; instructions of Saint Vincent to Sisters, X, 464–65, 467, 533; Sisters in charge of orphanage, first one to be entrusted to Daughters of Charity, X, 464–65; Fr. Cuissot relieved of direction of Sisters, VIII, 270; Saint Louise plans to send Sister Carcireux to Cahors, VIII, 128; desire of Sister Hardemont to be assigned to Cahors, VII, 248, 256; personnel: see **Boucher** (Louise), **Plouvier**, **Trumeau**; other mentions, VIII, 1, 2; X, 263, 411, 524; XIIIa, 182.

Caiaphas - Saint Vincent calls him an evil man - VI, 292.

Caignet (Antoine), priest of Tuesday Conferences - Biographical data, I, 311; III, 250; V, 19; VI, 120; VII, 353; out giving missions, I, 441, 442; III, 250; confessor of Mme Goussault, I, 311; requests missions to be given by Crécy Missionaries, V, 19; Saint Vincent recommends that Superior of Meaux Seminary follow his advice, VII, 353; reply to letter, VII, 509–10; author of book of meditations, VI, 120.

Caignet (M.) - Reference to his death, II, 535.

Caillou (Geneviève), Daughter of Charity - Biographical data, VII, 465; in Angers, I, 601; II, 12; XIIIb, 118; desires to renew vows, VII, 465; signs attestation after reading Common and Particular Rules reviewed and arranged in order by Fr. Alméras, XIIIb, 206; other mention, XIIIb, 227.

Cairo, capital of Egypt - IV, 269.

Caithness, shire in Scotland - Religious situation of population, VI, 546.

Calabria - Priest from there desired martyrdom, XI, 167.

Calais, town in Pas-de-Calais - Coaches, III, 529; XIIIb, 273; Fr. Ozenne awaited there, V, 27; may return there, XII, 370; Visitandines sent to Poland disembark there, V, 48, 52; Daughters of Charity in Calais: Queen requests Sisters for care of sick, wounded soldiers; they go; two die, other two fall ill, VII, 200, 247; X, 407–09; XII, 35–36; Sisters volunteer to replace them, VII, 247–48; X, 469; XII, 36; Saint Vincent chooses four, gives instructions, X, 440; names of Sisters, VII, 200; other mention, VII, 299.

Calle [***La Calle***] - See ***El Kala***.

Callon (Louis), Priest of the Mission - Biographical data, I, 38; II, 418; III, 37; returns to Aumale, I, 441, 445; signs letter to

Urban VIII for approval of Congregation of the Mission, I, 38, 45, 47, 53; gives missions in vicinity of Aumale, I, 584; benefactor of Congregation, III, 37; XIIIa, 373; death, III, 274; other mentions, I, 342; II, 418; V, 233.

Calumny - Conference, XII, 225–32; text of Rule of Missionaries, XII, 225; servants of God graced with calumnies, VIII, 233; XII, 227; prepare to accept this, XII, 230; endure it patiently, XI, 304; as favor from God, IV, 301; without justifying self, VIII, 233; X, 3; XII, 231; rejoicing when it strikes Missionaries individually or Company in general, XII, 228–29; example of Jesus, II, 493; of Saint Vincent, XI, 305; advantages, I, 138; VI, 1; saint hopes Company may be calumniated, XII, 232; prayer for good use of calumny, XII, 232; advice to Fr. Jolly, VII, 517; saint refuses to defend himself against calumny, XII, 397.

Calvary, mount near Jerusalem - XII, 160.

Calvary (Sisters of) - Poitiers Monastery, XIIIa, 132.

Calvin (Jean), leader of French Protestantism - Author of method of preaching, XI, 267; heresy, III, 40; IV, 209, 213; XIIIa, 164; priests obliged to refute his teachings, III, 323–24; what Saint-Cyran says of him, III, 320; VIII, 405; Saint Vincent asks what Bishops of his day would have done if they lived in Calvin's time, IV, 186; refers to him as heretical priest, XII, 76; says Arnauld was imitating Calvin, III, 360; had fears of falling into heresy, XI, 150; recommends to Du Coudray popular author who wrote against Calvinism, I, 57; success of Missionaries in eliminating heresy in Montauban diocese, XIIIa, 282, 289; other mention, 30. See also **Huguenots**.

Camard (Guillaume) - Member of Charity of Joigny, XIIIb, 66.

Cambout (M. de), Councillor at Parlement of Brittany - VI, 598.

Cambrai, municipality in Nord - VIII, 597.

Campan (Dominique de), slave in Algiers - V, 35, 147, 355.

Campels (M. de) - II, 555.

Campion (Fr.), priest of Collège de Fortet - Saint Vincent will meet with him, II, 540.

Campou (M.) - VII, 634.

Camus (M.) - III, 587–89; IV, 481.

Cana, town in Galilee - III, 537.

Canada - Evangelization, II, 38; V, 362; VII, 448; X, 407–08; XI, 121; XIIIa, 34; Saint Vincent's admiration for ministry in Canada, IV, 365; IX, 121; cautions against desire for possessions, XII, 301; Jean Guerin's willingness to go there with Jesuits, IV, 535; other mentions, II, 407; III, 562; V, 54; XII, 24. See also **Bourgeoys**, **Jesuits**, **Montmagny**, ***Quebec***, **Vironceau de Saint-Joseph.**

Canalle (Jean-Marie), governor of Tabarka - VII, 522.

Canary Islands - VIII, 290, 564.

Candelou (Jean), Priest of the Mission - Biographical data, II, 407.

Candie, region in Scotland - VI, 546.

Canisius (Fr.), priest of Arras - Confessor of Daughters of Charity, VI, 114; X, 183; other mention, VI, 131.

Canna, island in Hebrides - Evangelized by Fr. Duggan, IV, 496; V, 121–22.

Cannes, town in Alpes-Maritimes - VIII, 478.

Canon Law - Imposes strict penances on priests, XI, 118.

Canos (Mme) - Asks permission to leave Visitation monastery to see Queen's entrance into Paris, VIII, 484.

Cantara [***El Kantara***], town in Tunisia - V, 118.

Cantelin (M.) - Saint Vincent approves Fr. Alméras' suggestion about him, II, 529.

Canterelle (M.) - I, 10.

Canto (Fr.), Recollect - IV, 332.

Cap Nègre, Cape on northern coast of Tunisia - V, 89.

Capbreton, village in Landes - I, 16; V, 35, 147.

Cape Verde (Archipelago) - Stopover of Missionaries en route to Madagascar; religious situation of islands, III, 330–31, 540, 542; V, 281–82, 302; VIII, 290, 565–68, 571; death of Fr. de Belleville, VI, 447, 452–53; XI, 371; Fr. Mousnier confirms need for Missionaries: Huguenots on islands, V, 282.

Capitain (M.), notary in Paris - XIIIa, 98, 101, 262.

Cappel (President), in Marseilles - VI, 592, 627.

Capponi (Luigi), Cardinal-Prefect of *Propaganda Fide* - Saint Vincent proposes Missionaries for Hebrides, IV, 99 (N.B. Letter 1271 should be addressed to Capponi); Apostolic Nuncio in Paris forwards Saint Vincent's letter of gratitude for help to Missionaries and request for faculties for two Irish confreres, IV, 100.

Capuchins - Founded to teach penance by example, IX, 17; in praise of them, XI, 121; forbidden to accept money; obliged to live on alms, III, 251; VI, 180; X, 250; spirit of poverty characteristic of Order, IX, 457, 469; X, 101, 167, 242; XI, 322; XII, 214; Rules are read every Friday, IX, 544; X, 82; monks do not feed visitors, X, 259; visitors received in church, not in parlor, XI, 161; Our Lord their only subject of prayer, X, 457; recite Office *media voce*, XII, 270; everywhere the same, IX, 173; preach in church of Oratorians, XI, 266; novices live apart, XII, 276; same habit everywhere, VI, 129; X, 253, 283; except when there is need for disguise, XII, 207; pretensions of some coadjutor Brothers, III, 319; Brother who thought he had no vocation, XIIIb, 283–84; saint dissuades confrere from entering Capuchins, IV, 569–70.

Capuchins in Annecy, II, 90; Barbary, III, 308, 310, 311; Cahors, III, 162; IV, 509; Cape Verde, V, 282, 303; Charleville, V, 447; Charmes, V, 618; Châtillon-les-Dombes, XIIIa, 55; Chinon, III, 412; Ispahan, II, 459; Joigny, XIIIa, 61; Marseilles, VII, 70; Meudon, XIIIa, 60; Nantes, V, 280; Saint-Honoré convent in Paris, XIIIa, 60; Saint-Jacques convent in Paris, XIIIa, 60, VIII, 404; Poland, V, 588; Rome, III, 486; Saint-Christophe Island, III, 594; Sedan, IV, 118, 194, 362; V, 155, 552; Sion, II, 122; question of sending them to Madagascar, VII, 37, 57; other mentions, I, 335, 444; III, 40, 515; IV, 520; VI, 151; VIII, 377; IX, 361; X, 104, 199; XI, 13, 146–47; XII, 274; XIIIa, 53, 109, 190–91, 376, 379. See also **Garron** (Jacques), **Joyeuse** (Henri), **Rougemont** (Comte de), **Sylvestre** (Fr.).

Carbon (Abbé de) - VI, 649.

Carcireux (Françoise), Daughter of Charity - Biographical data, II, 178; III, 430–31; IV, 193; VI, 51; VIII, 127–28; X, 533; letter from Saint Vincent, VIII, 379; to Saint Vincent, VIII, 470, 521; mention of her letter to Saint Louise, VII, 167; assigned to Saint-Germain-l'Auxerrois, II, 178; question of recall, IV, 193; in Richelieu, III, 430; VI, 51, 52; proposed for Cahors, VIII, 128; advice of Saint Vincent before her departure for Narbonne, X, 533; sent to Narbonne, VIII, 187; authorization to travel, XIIIb, 237; in Narbonne, VIII, 166, 379, 381, 470, 521; prepares for teaching youth in Alet diocese, VIII, 379; X, 587; signs attestation after reading Common and Particular Rules reviewed and arranged in order by Fr. Alméras, XIIIb, 205; father causes trouble, II, 613; entreats Saint Vincent to take brother back into Congregation of the Mission, VIII, 521; other mention, XIIIb, 227.

Carcireux (Paul), Priest of the Mission, brother of preceding - Biographical data, II, 492; III, 373; VIII, 521; requests dimissorial letters for ordination, II, 492; wants to leave to assist father in difficulty; saint urges him to stay, II, 610–13; ingratitude, III, 373; desires readmission; sister requests it for him, VIII, 521.

Caregré (Mme) - Contacts with Saint Vincent, II, 207, 216.

Carennac, village in Lot - Dean of Carennac, IV, 28, 125, 190.

Carignan (Marie de Bourbon, Princesse de) - Biographical data, VI, 284; VII, 220; Saint Vincent refuses entrance to Visitation Monastery, VI, 284; VIII, 154; she bears grudge for refusal, VII, 220.

Carlier (M.) - Mission to Notre-Dame-de-Liesse, VI, 415; at Saint-Lazare, VII, 562; delivery to Bro. Parre, VII, 574.

Carmelite Fathers - Spirit of poverty, X, 167; do not offer refreshments to visitors, X, 259; branches of Order, II, 518; declare themselves in chapter against Jansenism, III, 328; Saint Vincent dissuades Missionary from making retreat with them, IV, 103; examples of virtue, I, 525; V, 278; X, 50, 462; *Propaganda Fide* entrusts Madagascar Mission to them, III, 278; XIIIa, 361; Carmelites of Billettes in Paris, IV, 269; XIIIa, 131; in Barbary, III, 223; in Ispahan, II, 459; other mentions, IV, 520; VI, 591; VIII, 408, 596; XIIIa, 60, 109, 391; see also **Saint-Bonaventure** (César de).

Carmelite nuns - Principal purpose is spirit of prayer, X, 92, 299; great austerity, IX, 457; X, 49, 80, 102; Daughters of Charity have no reason to envy them, IX, 457, 516; X, 88–89, 117, 158, 286, 300; Daughters must have virtues of Carmelites, X, 118; one of holiest and most perfect Orders, VIII, 406; unrest over question of Visitors, VIII, 70, 191–92, 213, 408, 474, 496, 497, 506; Saint Vincent asks Rome for dispensation for person who made vow to enter Order, II, 281, 319, 358, 418–19, 431, 437; Jeanne Dalmagne, extern Sister at Carmel, IX, 144, 146, 149, 156, 158; Fr. de Blampignon named Visitor, VIII, 42–26, 430; Fr. Coqueret, one of three Superiors, II, 100; Carmel of Château-Thierry, VIII, 482, 511; Mâcon, XIIIb, 75–76; Marseilles, VII, 187; Neufchâteau, VI, 591; VII, 51–52; Paris, VI, 125; VIII, 189, 547; rue Chapon, XIIIa, 61, 65; Faubourg Saint-Jacques, XIIIa, 61, 65; Rouen, II, 228–29, VIII, 407; Troyes: see **Trinité** (Mother de la); other mentions, I, 336; VII, 145; IX, 458; X, 104, 286, 492.

Carnival - Penance done at Saint-Méen during carnival, V, 109; references to conferences on motives for sanctifying this time, XII, 410, 426.

Caron (Jean), Canon of Écouis - XIIIa, 26, 29, 30.

Caron (Fr.), Priest of the Mission - Biographical data, VI, 548; VII, 603; postulant, VI, 548; prepares to enter Internal Seminary, VI, 588; in Genoa; no intention of persevering, VII, 603; ordination, VII, 612; dismissal, VIII, 55, 81, 93, 100.

Caron (M.), of Arras - VII, 364.

Carpentier (Augustin or Auguste), seminarian of the Mission - Biographical data, VI, 547; in Le Mans, VII, 331.

Carré (Claude), Daughter of Charity - Biographical data, III, 216; in Nantes, III, 8, 216; entered before Act of Establishment was signed, XIIIb, 227.

Carré (M.) - XIIIa, 343.

Carriages - Saint Louise sometimes used carriage, I, 348, 374–75, 450, 468, 494, 505, 534, 569; II, 207, 410, 482, 571, 591; III, 523; IV, 6, 115; V, 643; VI, 66; VII, 280; Saint Vincent borrows Mme Goussault's carriage, I, 260; Saint Vincent's carriage, III, 431; IV, 259, 281; V, 480–81, 643; XII, 312; fall from carriage, VII, 75; XIIIa, 179; his "ignominy," his "infamy," XII, 19, 206; encourages Edme Jolly to use it, VIII, 101.

Carthage, city in Africa - Jean and Philippe Le Vacher, Vicars-General, IV, 126; V, 91; ruins of Carthage, X, 429.

Carthusians - Founded to honor God's solitude and to sing his praises, IX, 17; origin of name, IX, 457; characteristic virtue is spirit of solitude, I, 120; IX, 457; X, 101, 287; XII, 214; also chanting God's praises, IX, 469; XII, 267; Saint Vincent makes retreat with Carthusians, II, 123; they waited a century before formulating Constitutions, III, 272; make only vow of stability, II, 142; annual visitation to maintain them in original observance, II, 69, 670; each has his house, VIII, 594; Superior General rarely absents self, II, 552; local Superiors go each year to Motherhouse, X, 281; only Officers of house attend council, XII, 120; all letters pass through Superior, X, 326.

Monks prostrate to venerate Blessed Sacrament, XI, 195; Brothers do not serve priests, XIIIa, 392; they have servants, VI, 338; Carthusians, models of uniformity, XII, 211; Jesuits cannot enter any Order but Carthusians, XIIIa, 382; comparison between vocation of Missionaries and that of Carthusians, III, 344; XII, 384; Saint Vincent urges Carthusian not to leave Order, IV, 552–53; urges Missionary not to enter Carthusians, III, 172–74, 180, 204–05, 342–44; IV, 108–09, 364; many would like to go to Madagascar, IV, 109; if there were no Missionaries, Carthusians would have to leave solitude to go, IV, 364; Carthusian edified by retreats for ordinands, III, 204–05; some retreatants at Saint-Lazare become Carthusians, XI, 15, 377; XII, 257; Carthusians of Paris, XIIIa, 60, 105, 122; of Cahors, IV, 504; of Valprofonde, XIIIa, 61; other mentions, VII, 409; VIII, 581; IX, 361, 460; X, 104, 147, 286; XII, 303; XIIIa, 131. See also **Daudignier**.

Cases of conscience - Practice at Saint-Lazare with cases of conscience, II, 241, 664, 669; VIII, 259; Saint Vincent advises this for Missionaries between missions, VIII, 41; see also **Theology**.

Casenave (M. de), Secretary of Bishop of Tarbes - XIIIa, 4, 6.

Caset (Michel), Priest of the Mission - Biographical data, IV, 474; V, 360; VII, 22; VIII, 131; XII, 387; letters Saint Vincent writes to him in Toul, VII, 358; VIII, 322; in Bâville, IV, 474, 494; in Saint-Méen, V, 360; mission in Bruyères, VII, 22; in Toul; responsible for house in absence of Superior, VII, 322; mission in Charmes; Saint Vincent informs him of new Superior, VII, 359; Superior, VIII, 131, 606; complaints about him, VIII, 492; other mention, XII, 387.

Cashel, town in Ireland - Foundation of chair of theology, III, 315; ministries of Missionaries in Cashel archdiocese, III, 353–54; VIII, 615; seminarian native to diocese: see **Butler** (Peter); Vicar-General of Archbishop driven away by persecution, IV, 341; Thomas Walsh, Archbishop of Cashel: see **Walsh**; other mention, VII, 345.

Casimir (M.) - See **Zelazewski**.

Casimir (Jan) - See **Jan**.

Casimir (Saint) - V, 113.

Cassan (M.) - I, 297.

Cassandieux (M.) - See **Gassendi**.

Cassian (John), monk and ascetical writer - Cited, XI, 11.

Castelferrus, village in Tarn-et-Garrone - Local priests, VI, 476; VII, 430.

Castelnau (M. de) - I, 434, 435.

Castelnau-de-Montratier, village in Lot - II, 489.

Castelnuovo, town in Piedmont - Mission, VI, 282.

Castiglione, town near Genoa - Mission, IV, 123; Confraternity of Charity, IV, 124.

Castillon (André), Jesuit - Biographical data, VIII, 504.

Castillon (M. de) - I, 431.

Castres, town in Tarn - I, 2.

Castres (Jean), slave in Tripoli - VIII, 162.

Castruccio (Lorenzo), Bishop of Spoleto - IV, 52.

Casuists - Alain de Solminihac condemns *Apologie des Casuistes*, approves censure by other Bishops, VII, 546–50; attempt to have it approved in Rome, VII, 627–28; Saint Vincent wants confreres to avoid debates; prays for union of hearts, VIII, 100.

Catalonia, province of Spain - Project for establishment of Missionaries, II, 498–99, 502, 507: see also ***Barcelona***; youth ministry, II, 520; assignment of benefices, other ecclesiastical matters, XIIIa, 150; other mentions, II, 220; XIIIa, 382.

Catechism - Sermon of Saint Vincent on catechism, XIIIa, 31; teaches catechism to poor persons at Nom-de-Jésus, XIIIa, 173; conference on duty of Missionaries, even Brothers, to catechize the poor and others, XI, 342–45; XII, 425; mention of conference, XII, 425, 436; instruction in seminaries on teaching it, II, 264, 266, 271; regular and short catechism classes during missions: see also **Missions**; practice at Saint-Lazare on teaching catechism, VIII, 90–91, 93; XII, 234–42; Daughters of Charity must learn and teach catechism, I, 305; X, 382, 499, 501–04; XIIIb, 273, 365; book of catechetical instructions, VII, 271; Bellarmine's catechism, XIIIb, 299–300; *Catéchisme de la grace*, IV, 185; other mentions, I, 228–29, 275, 419, 439.

Catherine (Saint), martyr - Courage before Emperor Maxentius [Maximus], X, 495–96; other mentions, X, 488, 491.

Catherine, Daughter of Charity - At Saint-Sulpice; change of mission, II, 302–03.

Catherine, Daughter of Charity - Infirmities; deliberation on her dismissal, XIIIb, 245–46.

Catherine of Siena (Saint) - Respect for priests, VI, 69; abominable thoughts at moment of Communion, IX, 184, 188; model of forbearance, IX, 215; other mention, III, 370.

Cauchon (Seigneur de) - See **Trélon**.

Cauffry, village in Oise - I, 295.

Caudron (Jacques), slave in Algiers from Dieppe - V, 405.

Caulet (Catherine), Baronne de Mirepoix - See **Mirepoix** (Baronne de).

Caulet (François-Étienne de), Abbot of Saint-Volusien de Foix, then Bishop of Pamiers, brother of preceding - Biographical data, I, 210; II, 308; III, 95; IV, 101; VI, 43; VII, 27; VIII, 162; words of praise for him, VI, 597, 619; letters from Saint Vincent, IV, 209; VI, 389; VII, 205; reference to letter to Saint Vincent; enclosure of letter for Jean Des Lions [Deslyons], VI, 290; wants to reform abbey, I, 210; speaks to Saint Vincent about Saint-Cyran, XIIIa, 105–06; opens, with Fr. Olier, seminary at Vaugirard and then at Saint-Sulpice, II, 308; Governor of comté de Foix is urged to help reform abuses, III, 95; gives conferences for ordinands at Saint-Lazare 1656–57, VI, 389, 619; VII, 27, 36; influenced by Nicolas Pavillon, Bishop of Alet, IV, 101–02; Alain de Solminihac hopes he will sign collective letter of episcopate against Jansenism, IV, 160; Caulet does not respond to request, IV, 179; Saint Vincent invites him to sign, IV, 209; refusal of Caulet, IV, 268; tries to obtain submission of Des Lions [Deslyons] to Pope, VI, 44; condemns *Apologie des Casuistes*, VII, 499; renders service to Cahors Seminary, VII, 206; recommends slave to Saint Vincent, VIII, 162; note to Fr. Jolly, VI, 619; Saint Vincent helps his sister in legal proceeding, VI, 597; helps Caulet to obtain request from Rome, VII, 205, 498, 507, 570, 599; VIII, 198; other mentions, VI, 637; XIIIb, 366.

Caulier (Marguerite) - XIIIa, 354.

Cauly (M. de) - Contacts with Saint Vincent at Bons-Enfants, VI, 128; returns to Savoy, VI, 127, 138; VII, 284.

Cauly (Fr. de), Pastor in Savoy, brother of preceding - Contacts with Saint Vincent, VI, 127–128, 138; VII, 284.

Caumartin (François Lefèvre de), Bishop of Amiens - Contacts with Saint Vincent, II, 454; approval of Charity of Folleville, XIIIb, 47, 48, 53; other mentions, XIIIa, 158, 190.

Cauna, village in Landes - II, 145.

Caussade, town in Tarn-et-Garonne - Alain de Solminihac complains about Pastor of Caussade, IV, 503, 506, 540; Pastor complains about Cahors Seminary, VII, 338.

Cavaillon, town in Vaucluse - François Hallier, Bishop: see **Hallier**.

Cavallermaggiore, town in Piedmont - Mission, VII, 130, 147.

Cavelier (Nicolas) - XIIIa, 354.

Cayran, farm near Cahors - Given to seminary, III, 461; conditions of donation, IV, 283; Bishop proposes lodging seminarians there during plague epidemic, IV, 480–82.

Cazet (Sébastien), member of Society for Indies - Saint Vincent apologizes for not sending Missionaries to Madagascar on his ships, VIII, 199, 201; seeks to obtain union of Society with that of Maréchal de la Mailleraye, VII, 60; VIII, 205; see also ***East Indies***; other mention, VIII, 200.

Ceiling - Ceiling of assembly room collapses, II, 577; IX, 63.

Celestine I (Pope) - Extract from second letter to Bishops of France, III, 320.

Celestine Fathers - Convent in Avignon, V, 380.

Celhay (Martisans de) - Basque slave in Algeria taken to Levant, VII, 161, 179, 521.

Censure - Priests must know teachings with regard to censures, I, 527–28; Bishops censure *Traitez des droits et libertez de l'Église gallicane*, III, 591.

Ceranesi, town in Liguria - Mission, VII, 438.

Ceré (Jacques) - VIII, 475.

Ceremonies - Obligation to perform them well, III, 509; XI, 281–82; neglected in France at beginning of century, IV, 328; XII, 212; practice for them on eve of feasts, XI, 178; must be taught, IV, 570; perform them well in all houses as at Saint-Lazare; teach them in seminaries, II, 264, 266, 271; III, 509; reprimand of seminary professor who refused to teach them, VII, 524–25, 578; ceremonies during Mass in houses of great lords, I, 344; XI, 21; other mention, XI, 177. See also **Chant**, **Customs**, **Divine Office**.

Cerise, village in Orne - Mission, I, 515.

Cerisy (Abbé de) - See **Habert** (Germain).

Cervia, town in Italy - Giovanni Francesco Guidi di Bagno, Bishop: see **Bagno, (**Guidi).

César de Saint-Bonaventure (Fr.) - See **Saint-Bonaventure**.

Cévennes, mountainous region - Religious state of region, I, 245; missions, I, 289, 304; II, 449; other mentions, I, 28, 441.

Ceyffat (Jacques) - XIIIa, 44.

Chablais, duchy in Savoy - Evangelized by Saint Francis de Sales, XIIIa, 81, 87.

Chabre (Antoine), Lieutenant for Criminal Affairs in Seneschal's court of Auvergne - V, 398.

Chaduc (Fr.), Oratorian - Recommends slave, VII, 520, 521.

Chahu (Jeanne-Marguerite), Visitandine - Biographical data; Saint Vincent urges her departure for Meaux Monastery, of which she had just been elected Superior, III, 453.

Chahu (Mme), of Auteuil - VIII, 465.

Chailli (Abbot of) - See **Lorraine** (Charles-Louis de).

Chaillot, village, today section of Paris - Visitation Monastery, IV, 403; V, 345; VI, 426; VIII, 314; Minim Fathers live there, VIII, 501.

Châles (Paul Millet de), Bishop of Saint-Jean-de-Maurienne - Rumored to be succeeding Bishop of Annecy, II, 333.

Chalices - Sell them for care of sick confreres, I, 521; Saint Vincent tells Fr. Codoing to buy silver one, II, 310; tells Fr. Portail they will sell them to assist him, III, 466; inquiry whether Daughters of Charity should hold chalice for safe-keeping, IV, 455.

Challons (M.), notary in Paris - Witness to Jean Duhamel's will, XIIIa, 334.

Chalon-sur-Saône, town in Saône-et-Loire - Jean de Maupeou, Bishop: see **Maupeou** (Jean de); Fr. Grenu to travel there, I, 404; other mention, VII, 151.

Châlons-sur-Marne, town in Marne - Bishops: see Henri Clausse de **Fleury**, Félix **Vialart**; missions in diocese, VII, 166; Daughters of Charity at hospital, V, 61–62, 65; X, 5, 519; Congregation of the Mission present in diocese, XIIIa, 228; other mentions, I, 64, 481; VIII, 218.

Chamargou (M. de), assistant and ally of Duc de La Meilleraye - In Madagascar, VI, 249; rumor of his death; his praises, VIII, 589.

Chambelin (Mlle) - Member of Charity of Montmirail, XIIIb, 32, 33.

Chambéry, town in Savoy - Senate of Chambéry, II, 89; IV, 294; V, 253; VI, 517; VII, 96, 97; letter to judge in Chambéry, VII, 98; death of Louis de Chandenier, VIII, 342, 355, 358; advice from persons there about purchase of house for confreres in Annecy, II, 333; other mentions, VIII, 63, 475, 488. See also **Chamosset**.

Chamblon, hamlet in commune of Montlevon (Aisne) - Farm dependent on house of Montmirail Missionaries, II, 545; Confraternity of Charity, XIIIb, 93.

Chambon - See **Chandon**.

Chameson (M. de) - Goes to China, VIII, 595.

Chamesson (Mlle de Foissy de) - Leaves Institute of Blessed Sacrament, XIIIa, 124.

Chamillac (Mlle) - Near death, II, 212.

Chamosset (M.), Assistant Chief Justice of Chambéry Senate - Contacts with Saint Vincent, VIII, 490.

Champagne, slave in Algiers - VIII, 331, 337.

Champagne (Mlle), novice at Notre-Dame-de-Sézanne - Saint Vincent encourages perseverance, VII, 201.

Champagne, province of France - Missions in Champagne, II, 395; VII, 10; reference to area in Saint Vincent's letters to

Saint Louise, I, 118, 125–26, 128; other mentions, V, 98; X, 160; XI, 16; XIIIa, 63, 229, 329. See also **Simonnet** (M.), **Souyn**, (M.), ***Guise, Laon, Reims, Rethel, Sedan***; assistance to Champagne and Picardy by Ladies of Charity during and after Fronde: IV, 201, 482–83, 519, 521; V, 26, 47, 246; VI, 58, 389, 397, 414–15, 422–23, 437–38, 454, 467, 502–03, 531, 543, 561, 580, 624, 626; VII, 42, 348–49, 395, 421, 545, 562, 588, 597, 614; VIII, 13, 27–28, 60, 82–83, 94, 123, 304, 382, 384, 389–91, 398, 410, 445, 453; XI, 306; XII, 367; XIIIb, 427–29, 438; monthly expenditures, VI, 58, 624; alms of Ladies meant only for those who cannot earn living, IV, 188; Ladies prefer to provide means of working to earn living rather than giving money, VIII, 82–83; thanks and request of aldermen of Rethel, XIIIb, 448–50; periodical reports printed and distributed to get alms; *Relations*, IV, 94; VI, 58; Saint Vincent sends *Relations* to Comte de Chavigny, IV, 155; excerpts from *Relations*, IV, 138, 142, 151, 187, 218, 260, 301; V, 94–95, 102, 123; ministry of Daughters of Charity, IV, 157. See also ***Brienne-le-Château, Châlons-sur-Marne, Saint-Étienne-à-Arnes, Sainte-Menehould***; ministry of Priests and Brothers of the Mission: IV, 133, 157, 165, 181, 192, 263–64, 292, 339, 387, 411, 424, 428, 441, 450, 452, 482–83; V, 12, 77, 94–95, 101–02, 110, 120, 123–24, 137, 148, 386; VI, 28; VIII, 277–78; 123–24, 378–79, 386; XIIIa, 367–68; letters of Missionaries to Saint Vincent, IV, 138, 142, 150, 151, 187, 218, 260, 301; V, 102: see also **Alméras** (René the Younger), **Berthe**, **Cruoly**, **Deschamps**, **Ennery**, **Goret**, **Le Soudier** (Jacques), **Mousnier**, **Parre**; other mention, I, 422, VI, 187.

Champdolent, (Priory), in Charente-Maritime - Saint Vincent encourages Louis Rivet to write to Fr. Amelote about Assistant at Priory, V, 626.

Champfleur, village in Sarthe - VI, 151; VIII, 130.

Champigny (Antoine), clerk in Dax - Witness to Saint Vincent's will, XIIIa, 100–01.

Champigny-sur-Marne, town in Seine - Confraternity of Charity, I, 161; other mention, II, 327.

Champigny-sur-Veude, village near Richelieu - Fr. Romillon, hospital chaplain: see **Romillon**; canonry vacated or about to be vacated, III, 605; no changes to be made in chaplaincy, IV, 10, 12; plan for establishment of Daughters of Charity, III, 605; IV, 39; visit of Mlle d'Orléans, V, 443; other mentions, I, 404, 420, 440.

Champin (Omer de), Dean of Saint-Thomas du Louvre - VII, 62.

Champion (Louis), Priest of the Mission - Biographical data, III,

89; V, 20; letter Saint Vincent writes him in Montmirail, V, 49; mention of letter from Saint Vincent, V, 20; departure from Châlons, V, 61; writes to Saint Vincent of errors of Fr. du Coudray, III, 89; at Bons-Enfants; requests dimissorial letter for ordination, III, 611; Superior in Montmirail, V, 20, 65; VIII, 612; Saint Vincent obliges him to apologize to Bishop of Châlons, V, 64; changed to Marseilles, V, 170; in Marseilles, V, 192, 212, 217; journey to Agde, V, 227, 247; health, V, 259, 380.

Champion (René), Brother of the Mission - Sent to Rome, XIIIa, 359–60.

Champlan (M. de) - V, 186.

Champlan, village in Essonne - V, 186; VII, 279.

Champlin (Mlle), of Montmirail - I, 89.

Champmargou (M. de) - See **Chamargou**.

Champvallon (François de Harlay de), Archbishop of Rouen - Thanks Saint Vincent for Missionaries sent to give mission, V, 578; other mentions, I, 385; V, 118; VI, 342, 383, 386.

Champvant (Saint-Nicolas Priory) - Union with Richelieu house, to which Cardinal Richelieu had given priory, II, 467; Saint Vincent asks Fr. Blatiron, who is titular, to give it up, III, 150–51; Fr. Le Boysne becomes titular after death of Fr. Blatiron, VI, 510, 629; VII, 40.

Chancelade Abbey - Alain de Solminihac, Abbot of Chancelade, I, 206, 210; his visit there, III, 241; Prior of Chancelade, II, 489; III, 587; wants to resign, IV, 141, 160, 481; Jean Garat replaces him, IV, 523; V, 590; other mentions, II, 679; IV, 153, 223. See also **Garat**, **Solminihac**.

Chancelade (Augustinians of Reform) - Solminihac recommends monks to Saint Vincent, II, 451; separation from Augustinians of Sainte-Geneviève; lawsuit in progress before Great Council, III, 83, 163; Alain de Solminihac thinks Saint Vincent is not giving him enough help, III, 83; Saint Vincent tells him favorable results of lawsuit, but, for spiritual aspects, there must be recourse to Rome, III, 224–26; decision is appealed, lawsuit resumes, III, 461, 524–25, 586–92; IV, 26–27, 141, 159–160, 162, 248; proceedings in Rome, IV, 27, 46–47, 66–68, 73, 76–79, 96, 135–37; Saint Vincent intervenes in favor of Chancelade monks, III, 163, 340–41, 524, 586; IV, 26, 124, 162, 540; VII, 117, 318, 407; mention of letter monks write to Saint Vincent, IV, 224; they have right to give missions in Cahors, IV, 49; Sevin promises to write to Fr. Paulin's replacement about affair, IV, 563. See also Abbeys of

Chancelade, Foix, Sablonceaux; Monasteries of *Cahors* and *Saint-Girard*; see also **Parrot** (Fr.), **Solminihac** (Alain de) and **Vitet** (Fr.); other mention, XIIIa, 60.

Chandenier (Catherine de), Visitandine, daughter of Mme de Chandenier - II, 71; V, 369.

Chandenier (Charles de), brother of Catherine de Chandenier - IV, 64.

Chandenier (Claude-Charles de), Abbot of Moutiers-Saint-Jean, brother of preceding - Biographical data, IV, 64, 464–65; V, 31; VI, 38; VII, 126; VIII, 132; XII, 15; letter from Saint Vincent, V, 549; letters to Saint Vincent, VIII, 132, 176; mention of letter to Saint Vincent, V, 549; family, II, 71; IV, 64; praise for brothers Claude and Louis, IV, 64–65; who want to retire for a time near Bishop of Alet, IV, 64; Bishop remarks on edification received from them, IV, 325; Saint Vincent gives them hospitality at Saint-Lazare, V, 31; VII, 128, 375; VIII, 354–55, 358; one of brothers gives mission with Fr. Tholard, V, 208–09; disagreement with brother François, IV, 449, 464–65; V, 341, 369, 505, 550; arrangement of reconciliation, IV, 464–65; asks that confreres give missions in Burgundy, V, 610; mission of Metz, VII, 137; XII, 15; Abbot of l'Aumône, IV, 464; V, 370; of Moutiers, V, 497; Saint-Pourçain Priory, VI, 38; health, VII, 320, 404; XIIIa, 200; journey of brothers to Rome, VIII, 132, 176, 191–92, 210, 213, 254, 302–03, 339; sadness on death of Louis, VIII, 343, 349, 355; at Saint-Lazare, VIII, 454, 455, 462; XII, 242; contributes to ransom of Vital Bernusset, VIII, 377, 396, 444, 513; other mentions, V, 475, 476, 498, 596; VI, 38, 40, 94, 278, 279; VII, 126, 404, 504.

Chandenier (François, Marquis de), brother of preceding - Biographical data, IV, 448; V, 341, 369; letters from Saint Vincent, IV, 448; V, 504; mention of letters to Saint Vincent, IV, 449; V, 550; other reference, V, 369. See also **Chandenier** (Claude).

Chandenier (Henriette de), Visitandine, sister of preceding - II, 71; V, 369.

Chandenier (Louis de), Abbot of Tournus, brother of preceding - Biographical data, IV, 84; V, 31, 341; VI, 37; VII, 92; VIII, 132; XI, 157; letters from Saint Vincent, IV, 464; V, 341, 368, 475, 497, 596; VI, 37, 93; VII, 126, 136, 320, 404; VIII, 191, 213, 302; to Saint Vincent, VII, 132; VIII, 132, 176, 210; mention of letters from Saint Vincent, IV, 449; VIII, 210; to Saint Vincent, VII, 136, 404; praise for both brothers, IV, 65; they wish to retire for a time near Bishop of Alet, IV, 64–65; Bishop remarks on edification they gave him, IV, 325; they request that confreres give missions in Burgundy, V, 610; Louis proposed for

Mâcon diocese, IV, 84, 95; reluctant to accept diocese, V, 342, 369; resignation of Saint-Pourçain Abbey in favor of Saint-Lazare, V, 368; VI, 38, 402; VII, 314; giving missions, XI, 157; mission of Metz, VII, 92, 100, 102, 108, 116, 126, 128, 132, 136, 170, 384–85, 404; XII, 15; Visitor of Carmel, VIII, 70, 408; in Tournus, VII, 404; VIII, 132; in Rome, VIII, 254; returning from Rome, VIII, 339; family, VIII, 214; Saint Vincent gives brothers hospitality at Saint-Lazare, V, 31; VII, 128, 375; VIII, 354–55, 358; at Saint-Lazare, XI, 177; XII, 242; last illness and death; received into Congregation of the Mission, VIII, 302, 342–43, 349, 354, 358, 360, 363, 371; mention of conferences given on his virtues, VIII, 354–55, 361, 371, 375; XII, 438; praise for him, IV, 84; VIII, 354; XI, 177–78; other mentions, V, 550; VI, 278–79, 605; VII, 322, 410, 504; VIII, 377, 408; XII, 391. See also **Chandenier** (Claude).

Chandenier (Louise de Montberon, Mme de) - IV, 449, 464.

Chandenier (Marie de), sister of preceding - Biographical data, IV, 464; V, 369; VI, 38; VII, 126; VIII, 124; letter from Saint Vincent, VIII, 124; other mentions, V, 369, 498, 504–05, 549–50; VI, 38; VII, 126, 404, 410.

Chandenier (Marie-Louise de), Visitandine, sister of preceding - Biographical data, IV, 318; presence requested at meeting of Superiors of Visitation Monasteries, IV, 318; other mentions, II, 71; V, 369.

Chandenier (Priory) - V, 498, 504, 549.

Chandon, Abbé de - VII, 557.

Chandon (M.), former Lieutenant for Criminal Affairs in Mâcon - XIIIb, 73, 76.

Chandon [Chambon] (Nicolas), Dean of Mâcon Cathedral - XIIIb, 69, 71, 73, 76–79.

Chanevas (Mme) - Lady of Charity of Saint-Gervais parish in Paris, II, 590; XIIIb, 393.

Changes - Don't change what is working well, XIIIb, 279.

Channelain (Mlle) - III, 370.

Chanoine (Clément, known as **Deslauriers**), convict in Toulon - VI, 320.

Chant (Liturgical) - Every Missionary must learn chant, XI, 326; important in missions, I, 419; III, 90; and for Office, V, 195; VI, 277; XII, 276; teaching chant in seminaries, II, 264, 266, 271; IV, 570; VII, 138; at Saint Lazare, XII, 235; reprimand of seminary professor who refused to teach it, VII, 524–26, 577–78; recite and chant psalms devoutly, XI, 282; taught to candidate at Table Bay, near Cape Town, VIII, 581.

Chantal (Celse-Bénigne de), son of Saint Jane Frances - Biographical data, I, 35; concern he gives mother, III, 432; IV, 257.

Chantal - See Saint **Jane Frances** Frémiot de.

Chanteau (Suzanne), Daughter of Charity - Signs attestation after reading Common and Particular Rules reviewed and arranged in order by Fr. Alméras, XIIIb, 205.

Chanteloup, hamlet in Lagny - Benedictines, II, 142.

Chantereau (Claude), Daughter of Charity - XIIIb, 228.

Chantilly, small town in Oise - Daughters of Charity established here, III, 298; V, 242, 332, 438; problems for Daughters, III, 470–471; Saint Louise may pass there on way back from Liancourt, III, 471–72; Fr. Delahodde, chaplain of château of Chantilly; see **Delahodde**.

Chanvry (bailiwick and provost court) - XIIIb, 34.

Chapel - Daughters of Charity have no other chapel but parish church, X, 530–32.

Chaplains - Chaplain General of the Galleys: see **Vincent de Paul**; letter to one of King's chaplains, IV, 83; Queen's chaplains: see **Saint-Jean** (Nicolas de); chaplains of noblemen: conference on duties of office, XI, 20–22; advice to Fr. de Sergis, chaplain in home of Chancellor Pierre Séguier, I, 343–45; hospital chaplains: good that hospital chaplain can do, IV, 37, 91–92; duties, IV, 91; ministry suitable for Priests of the Mission, IV, 37; XII, 77; chaplains for Hôtel-Dieu of Paris: see ***Hôtel-Dieu***; chaplains of Galleys, III, 414–15; regulations for army chaplains, XIIIa, 307.

Chaplet - See **Rosary**.

Chappelle (Jean), weaver in Joigny - XIIIb, 67.

Chapter - Mention of conferences, XII, 420, 425, 435; text of Rule of Daughters of Charity, X, 489; chapter of faults among them, I, 550; IX, 292; X, 489–90; among Missionaries, I, 179; VIII, 572; XII, 291; manner of holding chapter, I, 555; secrecy regarding what is said and done there, XI, 97; advice given by saint during chapter, XI, 24, 25, 96, 100, 102, 108; dispensing with chapter on second class feast days, XII, 428; other mention, II, 37. See also **Admonitions**.

Chardon (Emmanuel), Priest of the Mission - Sent to Rome, XIIIa, 359–60.

Chardon (Philbert), Priest of the Mission - Biographical data, V, 141; VII, 243; sent to Troyes, V, 141; leaves Company, readmitted in Rome, sent to Genoa, V, 184; proposed for Turin, VII, 243.

Charenton, town near Paris - Royal army on verge of giving battle to Duc de Lorraine in 1652 near Charenton, IV, 399; mission, V, 144; François Véron, Pastor: see **Véron**; other mention, X, 198.

Charity - Love of God: see **God**; charity toward neighbor; conferences, XI, 66–67; XII, 213–25; mention of another conference, XII, 421; sign of predestination, XI, 67; text of Rule of Missionaries, XII, 213; of Daughters of Charity, X, 368; soul of virtues and paradise of Communities, XI, 67; God's cloister, IX, 231; essential for apostolic spirit, I, 390; charity and candor should always hold upper hand, I, 539; one grain of charity suffices to calm anxieties and ease differences, I, 572; patient, I, 577; perfect state, I, 598; charity is of precept, XII, 213; more meritorious to love neighbor for love of God than to love God with no thought of neighbor, XII, 214; having positive attitude, XII, 383; what is done for charity is done for God, XII, 391; duty of making good actions known, XII, 391; charity unites hearts, II, 413; absence of charity leads Communities to ruin, XI, 90; Company will last as long as charity remains in it, XI, 90; especially necessary for Daughters of Charity, X, 368, 378–80, 418, 422, 424–26, 431; and for Missionaries, XII, 214–15; example of Jesus, XII, 216; link between humility and charity, X, 425–26; match for temptation, XII, 392; in face of aversion, XII, 392; charity never permits violation of law of God and Rules, XII, 224; order of service in charity, XII, 383; having positive attitude about others, XII, 383; charity among members of same Confraternity of Charity, XIIIb, 19, 45, 52, 61, 91, 100–01, 106.

Give witness of charity by works and good results, XI, 68; principal acts, I, 597; XII, 213, 224; no act of charity that is not accompanied by justice, II, 68–69; do to others good we wish to be done to us, XII, 216–18; excuse one another, IX, 179, 221–37; XI, 68; yield the pulpit, V, 483; avoid contradicting another, XII, 218–19; show honor to one another, XII, 223; rejoice with those who rejoice, weep with those who weep, XII, 221–22; God considers the charity that accompanies good works, I, 205; in the kingdom of charity, one prefers to suffer inconvenience than to inconvenience the neighbor, II, 228; charity of Solminihac, I, 206–07; of Nouelly, III, 223; of Francis de Sales, XIIIa, 84–86. See also **Aversions**, **Calumnies**, **Condescension**, **Cordiality**, **Gentleness**, **Slander**, **Mockeries**, **Reconciliation**, **Support**, **Union**. Charity toward poor persons and the sick: see **Confraternity of Charity**, **Ladies of Charity**, **Daughters of Charity**, **Illness**, **Poor**.

Charity (Confraternity of) - See **Confraternity of Charity**.

Charity (Brothers of) - See **Brothers of Charity**.

Charity (Daughters of) - See **Daughters of Charity**.

Charity Hospital, Paris - Gift of Saint Vincent, XIIIa, 20.

Charlemagne, King of Franks - XIIIb, 432.

Charles, Brother of the Mission - Questioned during conference on retreats, XI, 146.

Charles (François), Priest of the Mission - Biographical data, II, 608; IV, 532; VII, 412, 537; sent to Annecy, II, 608; recounts illness and death of Fr. Guérin, IV, 532; letter to Saint Vincent, IV, 532; opposed to union of Saint-Sépulcre Abbey with Congregation of the Mission, VII, 412; temporary replacement for Mark Cogley in Annecy, VII, 537.

Charles (M.), notary in Paris - II, 432; XIIIa, 75, 77, 98, 101, 223, 262.

Charles (Prince) - See **Ferdinand-Charles**.

Charles Borromeo (Saint) - Differed from Jansenius on penance and Communion, III, 358, 362–63; taught that confessor must adapt penance to sin, V, 322; self-sacrifice during plague, IV, 501; meditated and made confession on horseback while traveling, X, 470; feared preaching, I, 83; had direction of seminaries entrusted to Communities, IV, 190–91; feast day, VIII, 176, 191, 585; XIIIa, 135; perfect clergyman, XI, 145; other mention, XIIIa, 189.

Charles III, King of France - IV, 461–62.

Charles V, King of France - IV, 462.

Charles V, Emperor of Austria and Holy Roman Emperor - Mortifications, X, 319.

Charles VI, King of France - IV, 461.

Charles X (Charles-Gustavus), King of Sweden - Declares war on Poland, V, 383; invades Poland, V, 418; rumored to have been captured by King of Poland, V, 454–55; continued war against Poland, VIII, 193.

Charles-Emmanuel II, Duke of Savoy - II, 325.

Charlet (Étienne), French Assistant of Jesuits - Saint Vincent takes his advice, II, 17, 37, 104, 142; III, 39–40; proposes foundation of Mme de Gondi, XI, 164; other mention, II, 436.

Charleville, town in Ardennes - Jesuits, IV, 471; Capuchins, V, 447; nuns, IV, 578; request for Daughters of Charity, IV, 577.

Charlotte, Daughter of Charity - See **Moreau** (Charlotte), **Poisson** (Charlotte), **Royer** (Charlotte).

Charmes-la-Côte, village near Toul - Missions, V, 618; VII, 358.

Charpentier (Hubert), Founder of Bétharramites - Biographical data, I, 461; VII, 459; praise for him, I, 461; clergy of his seminary aid unfortunates Fronde has multiplied in environs of Paris, IV, 520; founds Bétharram Community and restores pilgrimage, VII, 623; offers shrine to Saint Vincent, VII, 459.

Charpentier (M.), in Le Mans - III, 314.

Charpentier (Marie), Daughter of Charity - Signs attestation after reading Common and Particular Rules reviewed and arranged in order by Fr. Alméras, XIIIb, 206.

Charpentier (Mlle) - VI, 626.

Charpentier (Pierre), in Valpuiseaux - His widow, IV, 401.

Charreau (Comte de) - Saint Vincent writes to him in Calais, XII, 370–71.

Charrin (M.), of Lyons - Informs Saint Vincent of donation to fund Missionaries' house in Lyons; Saint Vincent thanks him, V, 194; but declines offer, V, 429–30; Fr. Martin handles affair, V, 457.

Chars, village in Val d'Oise - Jansenist tendencies of Fr. Pouvot, Pastor, III, 298; IV, 516–17; XIIIb, 310, 356; and of his Assistant, an Oratorian, XIIIb, 358; local Seigneurs, XIIIb, 310; Daughters of Charity in Chars: establishment founded by Mme de Herse, VI, 650; XIIIb, 310, 357; Saint Louise considers replacing Élisabeth Turgis, Sister Servant, with Jeanne-Christine, III, 298; Julienne Loret is sent there, XIIIb, 311; then recalled, IV, 516; question of sending Sister there, VI, 66; Sisters have much to suffer from Pastor, III, 298; IV, 516; VI, 651; XIIIb, 310, 356–59; and from his Assistant, XIIIb, 358; closing of house, XIIIb, 356–59; Saint Louise announces closing to Pastor and Mme de Herse, VI, 650–51.

"Charter" of Daughters of Charity - X, 530.

Charton (Jacques), Penitentiary of Paris - Biographical data, VIII, 474; opposed to Jansenists, III, 45, 319, 322; Saint Vincent consults him about vows, III, 247; about place to live, IV, 219; about underground noises in Saintes, VI, 96; Superior of Carmelites, he supports convents opposed to Brief of Pope, VIII, 70; his opinion on the matter, VIII, 496; writes to Saint Vincent about it, VIII, 474, 497.

Chartres, town in Eure-et-Loir - Devotion of Saint Vincent to Our Lady of Chartres, I, 211; II, 538; devotion of Saint Louise, I, 593; II, 526; Fr. Boudet makes pilgrimage there, I, 350; Bishops: see Léonor d'Estampes de **Valençay**, Jacques **Lescot**, Ferdinand de **Neufville de Villeroy**; letter to Vicar-

General of Chartres regarding meeting with Queen, IV, 567; Chartres coaches, II, 309; Visitation nuns, III, 70; mission in diocese, I, 279; VIII, 258; Confraternity of Charity, I, 65; place of refuge from plague in Paris, I, 222; Archdeacon receives Brief regarding differences between Sainte-Geneviève Abbey and Chancelade, IV, 68; other mentions, II, 13, 536; IV, 159; V, 536; VI, 429, 462, 499, 631; X, 511; XI, 29; XIIIa, 24, 228, 266; XIIIb, 118.

Chas (Mme de) - V, 240.

Chasnais, village in Vendée - Saint Vincent persuades Fr. Chiroye to place parish in hands of Bishop of Luçon and to dissuade him from giving it to Missionary, V, 120, 125, 409; VI, 178; and to Fr. Rasine, V, 469; plans to have permanent assistant priest for it, VI, 439; Fr. Chiroye relieved of parish, VI, 536; parish offered to Officialis of Luçon, who refuses it, VIII, 254–55.

Chastel (Simon), Brother of the Mission - Entrance into Congregation, I, 304.

Chastelain (Mme de) - VII, 327.

Chastellain (Fr. Eusèbe de), Director of Joigny Hospital - Saint Vincent writes to him about child, VIII, 364; other mention, VIII, 77.

Chastity - Conferences to Missionaries, XI, 159–62, 197–98; XII, 336–45; mention of conferences, XII, 420; conference to Daughters of Charity, X, 303–305; text of Rule of Missionaries, XII, 328–29, 336–37; of Daughters of Charity, X, 303; importance of practice of this virtue, XII, 337–39; XIIIb, 346; more necessary for Daughters of Charity than for nuns, X, 363–64; avoid carefully even deliberate venial sin in this area, XIIIb, 136; dispel even thoughts contrary to virtue, IX, 376; X, 303–04; in what this virtue consists, XII, 339–40; purity of body and mind, XII, 340; means to preserve chastity, X, 304; XI, 160–62, 197–98; XII, 340–45; prayer, IV, 566; XI, 198; humility, X, 304; XI, 162; sobriety, XI, 160, 198; XII, 341–42; avoid laziness, XII, 342; control over senses, XI, 198; XII, 340–41; modesty, X, 304–06; XIIIb, 126, 137; turning eyes away from harmful things, IV, 566; during temptation, place heart in wounds of Jesus, VIII, 516; make temptation known to Director, IV, 566; IX, 363; avoid being alone with men, IX, 71; never visit them in houses in parishes, VIII, 279; refrain from touching each other or allowing self to be touched, X, 123, 306, 392; do not take pulse of sick woman, II, 572; do not converse with persons of opposite sex except when necessary, briefly, and where people can see us, IX, 257, 362–63; X, 304, 333–34, 343–46, 553; XII, 19, 343; XIIIb, 126, 137, 314;

confreres should not maintain correspondence with women, even consecrated, XI, 161; XII, 343–44.

Daughters of Charity must not allow men in their rooms, except confessor in case of illness, VII, 466; IX, 464; X, 36–37, 262, 305, 331–34, 336, 344, 363, 513–14, 517–19, 543, 550, 553, 587–88; XI, 161; XIIIb, 314, 346–47; must not waste time talking to outsiders, X, 363; talk to confessors only in church, XIIIb, 347; Missionaries may not have women in their houses, IV, 312; nor allow them to enter, VI, 149; VIII, 254; precautions to take in parlor, XI, 161; XII, 19, 341; in relationships with confessors, IX, 363; X, 303, 528–29, 552–53: see also **Confession**; in confessional, XII, 342–43; in letters, XI, 161; XII, 344; by Sisters with convalescing soldiers, X, 165; not to blame climate for unruly inclinations, III, 345; faults contrary to chastity, X, 304; XI, 159; example of Jesus, XII, 336, 338, 340; of Fr. Pillé, II, 378; of Fr. Thibault, V, 359; of young slave, III, 18–19; of young country women, IX, 71; of Brother of the Mission who lived among savages, XI, 198; of Saint Francis de Sales, XIIIa, 88; chastity held in honor among Daughters of Charity, IX, 175, 363; XIIIb, 346.

Saint Vincent recommends vigilance to Missionary sent among heathen, corrupt people, III, 281; writes to Brother who wants to give up vocation in order to preserve chastity, IV, 566; reassures priests assailed by bad thoughts while hearing confessions, V, 613. See also **Tholard**; reproaches imprudent Missionaries, XII, 19, 341; to safeguard purity of Daughters of Charity, prohibits night duty, care of women in labor and those suffering from venereal disease, X, 547–48; how he himself acted in parlor, XII, 19, 341.

Château-de-Vins - Fr. Delespiney encouraged to give one or two missions there, VIII, 136.

Château-l'Éveque, village near Périgueux - Saint Vincent is ordained priest, XIIIa, 7.

Châteaudun, town in Eure-et-Loir - Mission, VIII, 366, 367; Missionary from this place, III, 611; Châteaudun coach, I, 593; Daughters of Charity in Châteaudun: Mme de Varize offers to send two Sisters in Varize to Châteaudun Hospital, IV, 416; missioning of first Sisters, XIIIb, 313–17; letter to Jeanne Lepeintre, Sister Servant, VI, 44; to Barbe Angiboust, Sister Servant, VI, 424; VII, 386; to Jeanne Delacroix, Sister Servant, VIII, 323, 362; letter of hospital administrators to Saint Vincent, VI, 575; mention of letter to them, VI, 575; missioning of Sister to Châteaudun, V, 452; recall of Jeanne Lepeintre, VI, 325; disobedient Sister, VI, 424–25; administrators neglect to observe certain clauses in foundation contract, VI, 325; promise to abide by them, VI, 575; illness and death of Barbe Angiboust: see **Angiboust** (Barbe)**;** personnel of establishment: see **Angiboust** (Barbe), **Bocheron**, **Delacroix**, **Lepeintre**, **Moreau** (Charlotte); other mentions, IV, 307; VII, 437.

Châteaufort (Mme de) - I, 103.

Châteauneuf (Charles de Laubespine, Marquis de) - Biographical data, IV, 61; Saint Vincent apologizes for not having visited him, IV, 512.

Châtelet (of Paris) - XII, 377; XIIIa, 14–15, 19–21, 42–43, 66, 74, 77, 213, 218, 220, 222–24, 230, 263, 281, 283–84, 289, 294, 334, 340, 476; XIIIb, 395.

Château-Thierry, town in Aisne - Carmel of Château-Thierry, VIII, 482; other mention, I, 456.

Châtillon (M.) - II, 214.

Châtillon-les-Dombes, village in Ain - Act of Resignation by Pastor in favor of Saint Vincent, XIIIa, 44; Act of Appointment of Saint Vincent, XIIIa, 45; Act of Taking Possession, XIIIa, 47; report on saint's stay in Châtillon, XIIIa, 49; measures taken by General of the Galleys and wife to bring Saint Vincent back to Paris, I, 19–21; Saint Vincent explains why he went to Châtillon, I, 18; consoles Mme de Gondi, I, 20; tells Charles du Fresne of approaching return, I, 21; returns to Paris, I, 21; Act of Taking Possession of parish by successor of Saint Vincent, XIIIa, 57; Capuchins of Châtillon, XIIIa, 55; beginnings of Confraternity of Charity, XIIIb, 3; Act of Establishment, XIIIb, 20–21; approval of Charity, XIIIb, 19–20; Regulations, XIIIb, 8–19; modification of regulations for Treasurer, XIIIb, 22; new admissions, XIIIb, 22; Saint Vincent recounts how Charity was founded, IX, 165- 66, 192-93; good that it did, XIIIa, 55; Jean Garron asks his advice, VI, 76; other mentions, I, 302; XIIIa, 46; XIIIb, 67.

Châtres, small town in Essonne - VII, 22.

Châtres, village in Dordogne - Châtres Abbey, IV, 174.

Chaudebonne (M. de) - Piety, IX, 174; other mention, VIII, 500.

Chaulnes (Honoré d'Albert, Duc de) - Biographical data, I, 219.

Chaumel (M.) - II, 536.

Chaumont (Marie de), Visitandine - Profession, II, 70–71.

Chaumont (Marie de Bailleul, Dame de) - Superior of Charity of Saint-Germain-en-Laye, I, 412; contacts with Daughters of Charity, I, 423, 469; with Saint Vincent, I, 486; II, 185; with Saint Louise, I, 494, 495; II, 186–87; other mention, I, 486.

Chaussée, hamlet in Montmirail - Farms dependent on house of Missionaries, II, 544, 547, 554; IV, 313; V, 49; VI, 312; priory and hospital, II, 547–48; III, 77; VIII, 612.

Chauteau (Madeleine), Daughter of Charity - Signs attestation after reading Common and Particular Rules reviewed and arranged in order by Fr. Alméras, XIIIb, 206.

Chauvel (M.) - II, 492.

Chavagnac, commune in Dordogne - Request for letter of provision from Rome for Pastor, VII, 285, 541, 569; resignation of Pastor, VIII, 135.

Chavigny (Léon Bouthillier, Comte de), Secretary of State - Biographical data, II, 238; IV, 154–55; Saint Vincent asks him to ensure that body of Saint Jane Frances de Chantal be returned to Annecy, II, 238; refuses giving benefice to his son, II, 584; sends report on devastated regions, IV, 154–55; contacts of Count with saint, II, 255, 297, 433, 438; contacts with Saint-Cyran, III, 322.

Cheerfulness - Saint Vincent encourages it, II, 153, 623; often recommends it to Saint Louise: see **Louise de Marillac** (Saint); cure for some illnesses, I, 523.

Chefdeville (Perrette), Daughter of Charity - Biographical data, II, 51; IV, 193; V, 61–62; native of Villers-sous-Saint-Leu, XIIIb, 249; not suited for teaching school, I, 495; praise for her, II, 51; in Saint-Germain-en-Laye, II, 207, 210, 292; named for Fontenay, II, 327–28; in Nantes, XIIIb, 249; recalled, IV, 193; proposed for Brienne, V, 61; other mention, XIIIb, 227.

Chehff (Messrs) - V, 326, 354.

Cheleby - See **Algiers**.

Chelles, commune in Seine-et-Marne - Mission given, I, 68, 69.

Chemerault (Mlle), Queen's maid of honor - I, 486.

Chémery, commune in Ardennes - IV, 578.

Cheneau (Fr.), priest of Nantes - III, 603.

Chenevis (M.) - I, 263; II, 55.

Cherasco, town in Piedmont - Mission, VII, 583; VIII, 29.

Chereau (M.) - Member of Charity of Joigny, XIIIb, 66.

Chéruby, son of Bey of Tunis - Biographical data, II, 677.

Chesnard (Salomon), King's customs official in Mâcon - XIIIb, 74, 77.

Chesneau (Guillemine), Daughter of Charity - Biographical data, XIIIb, 248; sent to Saint-Paul, II, 655; XIIIb, 248; withdrawn from Saint-Paul, XIIIb, 302; in Saint-Étienne-à-Arnes, IV, 168; XIIIb, 307–309.

Chesse (Marie), Daughter of Charity - Biographical data, VIII, 166; X, 533; sent to Narbonne, XIIIb, 187; advice received before departure, X, 533; arrival in Narbonne, VIII, 166.

Chétif (Marguerite), Daughter of Charity - Biographical data, V, 357; VI, 79; VII, 198; VIII, 122–23; IX, *xvii*; letters from Saint Vincent, VI, 113, 129, 212; VII, 198, 363; VIII, 350; mention of letters to him, VI, 113, 212; VII, 363; records conferences of Saint Vincent, X, 569, 582; Saint Louise asks permission for her to take perpetual vows, V, 357; considered for Poland, V, 414; awaits Saint Vincent's orders, V, 417; assigned to Arras, VI, 79; VI, 102–03; authorization to travel, XIIIb, 229; advice of Saint Vincent before her departure, X, 181; arrival in Arras, VI, 102–03; discouraged, VI, 113, 212; Saint Vincent asks her not to change headdress, even though style may be strange in Arras, VI, 129; health, VI, 211, 212, 547; in Arras, VI, 589; VIII, 122; proposed for Nantes, XIIIb, 335; for Angers, XIIIb, 340; replaces Saint Louise as head of Company, VIII, 312; X, 594, 596; XIIIa, 196; praise for her, X, 594; XIIIb, 335–36; other mention, XIIIb, 227.

Cheusse, seigneury - See **Lamet** (Gabriel de).

Chevalier (Paul), Canon of Saint-Aignan - See **Saint-Aignan**.

Chevallier (Marie-Agnès), Visitandine - Superior in Le Mans, II, 578; Superior in Saint-Denis, IV, 433; directions of Saint Vincent for moving nuns and boarders to First Monastery in Paris because of Fronde, IV, 433–34; Sisters of Compiègne Monastery ask to put her name on their list, VIII, 450.

Chevallier (Mathieu) - Proxy for last incumbent of Châtillon parish in resignation made of it to Saint Vincent, XIIIa, 46–48.

Chevitaines - I, 263.

Chevreuse (Claude de Lorraine, Duc de) - II, 247.

Chiavari, town in Italy - Seminarian, native of this place, VII, 581; VIII, 55.

Chieri, town in Piedmont - Mission, VI, 601.

Chigi (Flavius), Cardinal - Biographical data, VI, 374; Saint Vincent intends to write to him, VI, 374, 541.

Chigi (Fabio), Cardinal - Biographical data, IV, 580; VI, 29; XI, 171; adversary of Jansenism, XI, 171; Innocent X confers with him about Jansenism, IV, 580; Saint Vincent recommends his Congregation and cause of Saint Francis de Sales, V, 22–23. See also **Alexander VII**.

Children of Mary - Sodalities, VI, 605.

China - Departure of Bishops for China, VIII, 594, 595; Jean Guérin's willingness to go to China with Jesuits, IV, 535; other mention, VIII, 587.

Chinon, town in Indre-et-Loire - Possessed women, II, 80, 95, 112; Capuchins, III, 412; Daughter of Charity from Chinon, III, 118; other mentions, I, 596; II, 81.

Chiroye (Jacques), Priest of the Mission - Biographical data, I, 545; II, 79; III, 145; IV, 2; V, 100; VI, 177; VII, 182; VIII, 253–54; letters Saint Vincent writes to him in Luçon, II, 140, 279, 325, 353, 567; in Richelieu, III, 146; in Luçon, III, 490, 526; IV, 2, 95, 119; V, 100, 119, 125, 409, 469; VI, 177, 439, 536, 610; VII, 182; mention of letters to Saint Vincent, V, 120; VI, 178, 439; in Richelieu; sent to Joigny to care for Fr. Lucas, I, 545; proposed as Superior of Luçon house, II, 79, 112; named Superior in Luçon, II, 140; VIII, 607; praise for him, II, 276; health, II, 353; III, 285; mission in Luçon, II, 397, 405; return to Luçon, III, 144–47; returns to Richelieu after close of Luçon house, III, 145; Saint Vincent reproaches him for superfluous spending, IV, 2; for not being obedient to his orders, IV, 149; removes him from office, IV, 95; Superior again, V, 100; resignation of Chasnais parish, VI, 536: see also ***Chasnais***; saint advises him to refuse priory offered him, V, 120, 125; reprimands him for accepting donation and, in general, for acting too independently, without consulting anyone, VII, 182–83; claim concerning inheritance accepted by him, VIII, 412; recalled to Paris, VIII, 253; makes retreat in Paris, VIII, 306; Superior in Crécy, VIII, 609. See also ***Luçon***.

Chisé (Mlle de) - VII, 158.

Chives, village in Charente-Maritime - XIIIa, 242, 245.

Chocart (Nicolas), prisoner in Toulon - VII, 392–93; VIII, 373.

Choguillot (Nicolas), notary in Paris - XIIIa, 21.

Choiseul (Gilbert de), Bishop of Comminges - Jansenist sermons, III, 591.

Cholet (M.), Municipal Magistrate of Joigny - XIIIb, 65, 66.

Chomel (M.) - Bishop of Clermont dissatisfied with him, VII, 314.

Chomon (Louise), Daughter of Charity - XIIIb, 228.

Chouzé, village in Indre-et-Loire - I, 194.

Chrétien (Jean), Priest of the Mission - Biographical data, III, 7; IV, 506–07; V, 11; VI, 180; VII, 361; VIII, 36; XI, 158; letters Saint Vincent writes him in Marseilles, III, 252; in La Rose, V, 444; VI, 180; mention of letters from Saint Vincent, V, 35;

VI, 611; Superior in Marseilles, III, 7, 258–59, 273, 393, 414; IV, 332, 506; V, 35; VI, 473, 504; VII, 361, 514; VIII, 36, 52, 220, 232, 610; unsuccessful, III, 258–59; the saint encourages Fr. Nouelly to write to Fr. Chrétien, III, 51; he is to accompany Fr. Portail to Annecy, III, 466; remains in Marseilles to inform successor about matters, V, 11; arrival in Paris, V, 67; Sub-Assistant at Motherhouse, V, 208; XI, 158; Superior in La Rose, V, 233, 442, 444; VIII, 606; claim made against him by administrators of Marseilles hospital, VIII, 232, 249; Saint Vincent upbraids him for act of disobedience, VI, 180; thinks he does not preach enough, VIII, 254; suggests having one of his letters read in refectory, XII, 239. See also ***La Rose, Marseilles***.

Christian Doctrine (Congregation of Priests) - In praise of them, XI, 121; they take simple vows, as at Saint-Lazare, and give missions, VII, 484; want to enjoy same privileges as Congregation of the Mission, to be shared with them by communication, VII, 484; Saint Vincent cannot grant this, VII, 541; simplicity of their preaching in Toulouse, XII, 209; Archbishop of Narbonne has them minister in diocese, VIII, 478; division in Institute over vows, II, 459; union of Fathers of Christian Doctrine of Provence to Oratory, II, 465; Paris house, IV, 328; XIIIa, 131, 135; other mentions, V, 176; VIII, 172. See also **Bus** (César de), **Romillion** (Jean-Baptiste), **Vigier** (Antoine).

Christianity - Mention of conference, XII, 435.

Christine of France - See **Madame Royale**.

Christine, Daughter of Charity - See **Prévost** (Jeanne-Christine).

Christine, young daughter of Madagascar native - VIII, 587.

Christmas - Mention of conferences, XII, 406, 409, 420, 425; reflections of Saint Vincent, VI, 170; celebrated by Missionaries at Table Bay, VIII, 585.

Christophe (Bro.) - See **Delaunay** (Christophe), **Gautier** (Christophe).

Church - Saint Vincent's prediction of future of Church in Europe, III, 40–41, 164, 187; V, 425; XI, 279, 317–20; residence of Holy Spirit, XII, 387; its authority, II, 446; ignorance of many faithful, IV, 285; Church needs evangelical men, III, 204; principal enemies are bad priests, XI, 279; God refers us to it for enlightenment, VI, 293; God sustains it by destruction of all that seems to sustain it, XI, 367–68; duty to work for spread of faith: see **Zeal**; heresy of Two Heads: see **Barcos**; Saint-Cyran declared that true Church has not existed for five hundred years; would overturn Church of his day to restore ancient one: see **Saint-Cyran** (Abbé de).

Churches - Dirtiness and disorder of churches in France, IV, 328; money to repair ruined churches in Champagne and Picardy, VIII, 389, 391, 398, 409; XIIIb, 428–429; visiting certain churches is condition for Jubilee, IX, 41.

Chuza, Herod's steward - Mention of his wife, Joanna, IX, 18; X, 439; XIIIb, 437.

Cieurac, village in Lot - III, 461.

Cider - Use is common in Dax and environs, IV, 466; Jeanne Delacroix offers cider to Saint Vincent, V, 220.

Ciral (François), slave in Algiers - V, 36, 326.

Circulars - Circular letters to Congregation of the Mission, II, 363, 563, 567; III, 530; IV, 176; V, 571; VII, 163; VIII, 346, 375, 467.

Ciron (Abbé Gabriel de), Chancellor of University of Toulouse - Biographical data, IV, 119; V, 629; Pavillon recommends him to Saint Vincent, IV, 119–20; would like Daughters of Charity for Toulouse, V, 629.

Cistercians - Seigneur gives money to monks to allow them to hear Mass, IX, 35–36; Procurator General of Order judges that steps taken by Fr. Jolly to obtain approval of vows succeeded beyond all expectations, V, 467; Cistercian abbey (Saint-Léonard de Chaumes), XIIIa, 12–16. See also **Quincy**, (Abbot of).

Clair (Fr.), Jesuit - Work on Company of Blessed Sacrament, IV, 520.

Claire, Daughter of Charity - Proposed for Saint-Germain-en-Laye, II, 180.

Clanronald [**Clanranald**], laird - Conversion, IV, 496; conversion of inhabitants of his lands, V, 121.

Clare (Saint) - Saint Louise's birthday falls on her feast day, II, 204.

Claude (Bro.) - See **Le Gentil** (Claude).

Claude, Daughter of Charity - Assigned to Nantes, III, 8.

Claude, Daughter of Charity - Her suffering, V, 641.

Claude, Daughter of Charity from Chinon - III, 118.

Claude, Daughter of Charity - In Varize; recalled to Paris, VIII, 362.

Claude, Daughter of Charity - Anxiety about sin already confessed, II, 301.

Claude, Daughter of Charity - Saint Vincent does not want her to enter prisoners' quarters, where she had previously gone, V, 337.

Claude-Brigitte, Daughter of Charity - See **Brigide** (Claude).

Clauset (Fr.), priest - Asks to be admitted by Nicolaïtes; Saint Vincent recommends him, II, 174–75.

Clayes (Mme de) - II, 258.

Clayes [***Les Clayes***], Commune in Yvelines - Vincent mentions widow from there to Louise, I, 231; missions, I, 270; II, 258–59; suggests that Fr. Belin go there to teach catechism, I, 269–270; other mention, I, 231.

Clémence, Daughter of Charity - See **Ferré**.

Clément (Jacques) - Member of Charity of Courboin, XIIIb, 93.

Clément (Jean), cutler - Talent for debate, IV, 528.

Clement V, Pope - His *Glossa,* XIIIa, 404.

Clement VIII, Pope - Sanctity, IX, 9, 250, 368; X, 294; XI, 317; apprehensions about future of Church, XI, 318; XIIIa, 108; regret for having reconciled Henry IV to Church, V, 316–17; XII, 282–84; XIIIa, 377; forbids disputes about grace, III, 326; stipulates that all religious be given extraordinary confessor, XIIIb, 298; Saint Vincent saw him in Rome, IX, 250, 368; X, 294, 476; XII, 282; other mention, XIIIa, 381.

N.B.: St. Vincent erroneously attributed the following to Clement VIII instead of to Innocent VIII: *Ready to canonize any religious who has been faithful to Rules,* IX, 9, 250, 368; X, 285, 294, 329, 340, 434, 476, 541.

Clement IX (Giulio Rospigliosi), Pope - Papal Secretary of State under Alexander VII, whom he succeeded, VI, 132.

Clementia of Hungary, Queen of France - XIIIa, 27.

Clergy of France - Examples of ignorance, XI, 163; of incompetence, VI, 59; of neglect, II, 473; VIII, 168, 460; XI, 8; XIIIa, 50, 53; undisciplined, II, 316; extreme desolation, II, 411; "large and unaccountable number of ignorant and corrupt priests," II, 473; greed of great number of priests, XII, 304; priests hear confessions without faculties, VIII, 460; religion lost in many places because of bad lives of priests, XI, 279-80; dirtiness of churches, IV, 328; disorder in ceremonies, XII, 211–12, 235; assemblies of clergy of France, II, 561, 587; III, 113; IV, 67; V, 98; VI, 37, 101–02, 290, 295–96, 644, 647; instruction of ordinands could remedy state of clergy, XII, 383;

trust in Providence regarding retreat expenses, XII, 385; generosity in accepting retreatants, XII, 386.

Clerical promises - Renewal at Saint-Sulpice, XII, 335.

Clermont, abbey in Olivet (Mayenne) - VIII, 518.

Clermont (Collège de) - Famous Jesuit school in Paris, where Michel Le Gras was boarder, I, 99, 103, 106.

Clermont, town in Oise - I, 284; Saint Vincent suggests Sister Geneviève Poisson take Clermont cart for Liancourt, I, 353.

Clermont-Ferrand, town in Puy-de-Dôme - Bishops: see Joachim d'**Estaing**, Louis d' **Estaing**; seminary, IV, 141; journey of Fr. Gicquel to this town, VII, 252; Bishop wants confreres to give mission and teach theology there, VII, 314; other mentions, II, 79; VII, 319, 321.

Cléry, town in Loiret - I, 193, 396, 593.

Clichun (M.) - I, 172, 175.

Clichy, town near Paris - Saint Vincent takes possession of parish, XIIIa, 22; Pastor of Clichy, XIIIa, 66; canonical visitation by Archbishop Jean François de Gondi, XIIIa, 74; satisfaction inhabitants of Clichy give Saint Vincent, IX, 507; praise for their singing during worship, XII, 276; departure; receives pension from successor, XIIIa, 97; passes through Clichy during Fronde, III, 393; asks Captain to send soldiers from Clichy back home, I, 335; mission in Clichy, II, 360.

Clothing - See **Attire**.

Coaches - Saint Vincent inquires about revenues from Loudun coaches, I, 418; lawsuits between coach farmers and messengers, II, 406, 517; Saint Vincent gets nothing from Soissons coaches, II, 359; plans to sell them, II, 457; Duc de Bellegarde lays claim to ownership of coaches of France, II, 469; Soissons coach farmer goes bankrupt, II, 491; King uses at will revenue from coaches, II, 465, 514, 517; uncertainty of revenues, VI, 181; XIIIb, 325; Saint Vincent obtains ruling from King safeguarding rights on coaches, II, 522; Duchesse d'Aiguillon gives thousand livres from revenue of Orléans coaches to found establishment in La Rose, II, 318; five thousand livres income from Rouen coaches given to Rome house for retreats to ordinands, II, 430, 432, 438, 449, 472; advice of Saint Vincent about legal affair relative to coaches of Verneuil and of Dreux, III, 529; stoppage of coach service during Fronde deprives several houses of the Mission of part of revenues, III, 394; IV, 328–29, 366; settlement with coach farmers, IV, 506–07; revenue Barbary mission receives from coaches, VI, 54, 486; VIII, 337, 615; Rome house, II, 406, 430, 457, 472,

552; estimate of income from coaches for Saint Vincent and others, VI, 125; decrease of revenue from coaches, VII, 539; Daughters of Charity receive revenue, X, 552; Congregation of the Mission owns coaches and carriages between Paris and Rennes and towns of Brittany, XII, 377–381. See also ***Bordeaux, Orléans, Rouen, Soissons***.

Coadjutor Brothers of the Mission - Letters to Brothers, IV, 389, 440, 566; VI, 68, 165; VII, 482, 589; see also **Le Clerc** (Pierre), **Parre**, **Rivet** (Jacques), etc.; reference to letter received from one of them, VII, 589; exhortation to dying Brother, XI, 129–33; ministries of Brothers, I, 42, 50, 143; XI, 18; XII, 13, 84–85; not required to make Easter duty in parishes, V, 87; duties of Brothers toward priests, VI, 69; XII, 86–90; of priests toward Brothers, XII, 90–92; XIIIa, 371, 391–93; they are not to be kept in positions that are too lowly, III, 319; bear with their faults, III, 480; divisiveness among them, III, 499; as family members, they should be preferred to servants, IV, 3; Brother needed in Montmirail, II, 546; Saint Vincent, invited to eat with Duchesse d'Aiguillon, takes Brother with him, XIIIa, 392; life consistent with that of Our Lord, XI, 99, 287; find in Company what will sanctify them, XII, 87–89; Saint Vincent affirms Brothers, XII, 392; minister in Company for salvation of poor, XI, 123–24; XII, 84–86; efficacy of their prayers, XII, 14; edify by repetitions of prayer, IX, 175, 331; X, 60, 225–26; XIIIb, 301; exactness to particular examen, X, 485; learning to serve Mass, III, 29; promptness in giving, XII, 393

Uniformity of dress: see **Attire**; temptation to want to become priests, IV, 255, 306; VI, 166; daily account of expenditures to be given to Procurator, IV, 80; they do not read New Testament, VII, 222; no need of diversions, XI, 332; they catechize the servants, XI, 344; should not meddle in government of house, IV, 390; good Brother accepts duty Superior gives him, IV, 326; cooks must prepare best possible nourishment, XI, 299; postulants who withdraw from brotherhood are not to be kept in houses as servants, VII, 225; those who have begun studies and enter brotherhood do not usually do well, VII, 494.

Only one Brother in Company receives and is responsible for money, III, 318; Saint-Lazare uses servants for many duties, VI, 338; Company has enough Brothers; Saint Vincent asks that no more be accepted, VI, 547; VII, 501, 514, 559; VIII, 341; during Fronde, he authorizes Brother of Cahors house to be on guard duty and to work on fortifications, IV, 284; faults of certain Brothers, XI, 96, 284; illusions of others, IV, 440; VI, 166; Brothers commendable for virtue or service: see **Ducournau**, **Parre**, **Patte**, **Regnard**, **Robineau**, **Servin**, **Véronne**.

Coat of Arms - Fr. Codoing considers putting up Richelieu's coat of arms in Rome, II, 306.

Cochet (M.) - VII, 615.

Cochin China [***Indochina***] - Petition to Rome for nomination of Vicars Apostolic in Cochin China, IV, 595; V, 15; funds destined to assure their salary, IV, 605; V, 16, 78; Missionary about to depart for Tonkin and Cochin China makes retreat at Saint-Lazare, VI, 553.

Cochois (Fr.), Pastor of Brienne-le-Château - V, 62.

Cochouol (Jean) - Merchant in Macon, XIIIb, 74.

Cocquerel (M.) - III, 520.

Code - Saint Vincent suggests that Barreau use code in communicating with him, III, 47.

Codex Sarzana - See **Sarzana**.

Codoing (Bernard), Priest of the Mission - Biographical data, I, 402–03; II, 32; III, 1–2; IV, 8; XI, 127–28; letters to Fr. Codoing in Romans, I, 402; in Richelieu, I, 491, 514; in Annecy, II, 87, 117, 159, 213, 231, 235, 238, 240, 245, 248, 254; in Rome, II, 261, 268, 276, 280, 287, 295, 303, 314, 315, 318, 342, 349, 357, 393, 397, 404, 412, 415, 426, 430, 431, 437, 449, 453, 456, 461, 464, 469, 471, 498, 502, 505, 513, 514, 517, 520, 522, 551; in Saint-Méen, III, 141, 174, 195, 336; in Richelieu, III, 456, 462, 515, 521, 605; IV, 8, 38, 44, 69, 85; letter of Fr. Codoing to Saint Vincent, II, 356; mention of letter from Saint Vincent to him, II, 172; sent to Richelieu from Dauphiné, where he is giving missions, I, 402–06, 419; in Richelieu, I, 440, 442; reprimanded for dwelling too much on explanation of sixth Commandment, I, 453; health, I, 491, 500; II, 90, 471; III, 267; assigned to Luçon, I, 514; Saint Vincent proposes him as model for keeping accounts, I, 526; for organizing priests' meetings; at one time, considers sending his sermons to houses of Company, I, 527.

Named Superior in Annecy, I, 568; II, 18; Saint Jane Frances sings his praises, II, 32, 61; Bishop of Geneva does likewise, II, 66; his brother, II, 92; in Annecy, II, 99, 203, 171; Superior, VIII, 608; Fr. Escart's antipathy toward him, II, 157–59; desire to have Company established in Rome, II, 214; named for Rome, II, 232, 239; Saint Vincent urges him to hasten departure, II, 240, 245, 251; reproaches him for acting too quickly and not asking advice, II, 235–37, 249, 266–67, 278, 350–51, 520–21; for speaking to others about confidential matters, II, 304; for writing about affairs of state, II, 362; for trusting too much in human means, II, 310, 314–15, 350–51, 432; for holding too strongly to own ideas, II, 453; for encroaching on Providence, II, 499, 502; opposes his opinion on dictating lessons in class, II, 240, 262–66, 269–72; IV, 324; in Rome, II, 269, 321, 324, 491, 582; Superior, VIII, 609; urged to get Italian priest and Brother, II, 306; Saint Vincent does not want him to interfere regarding Visitor for Visitation nuns, II, 333; on a mission, II, 343; writes to Saint Vincent in Italian, II, 349; attacked by bandits, II, 358; wants Superior General to reside in Rome, II, 361, 434, 453; wants Saint Vincent to put up with incorrigibles instead of dismissing them from Company, II, 421; saint sends him power of attorney to buy house, II, 426, 432, 438; relieves him of duty of Superior at his request, II, 531, 537; III, 374; but asks him to remain in Rome to train successor, II, 531; suggests he make visitations of Marseilles house and Annecy, II, 531–32; named consultor to Fr. Dehorgny, II, 542; leaves Rome for Paris; en route, ministers in Genoa diocese, II, 595; doctrinal errors, II, 619; III, 2, 3, 108, 114; renounces them, III, 114; Superior at Saint-Charles, VIII, 614; in Paris, II, 663, 669; goes to Fontaine-Essarts, II, 674.

Superior in La Rose, VIII, 606; Superior in Saint-Méen, III, 83, 110, 115, 174; VIII, 613; Saint Vincent proposes him as companion to new Bishop of Tréguier for month or two, III, 195; forwards Guillaume Delville's letter to Codoing in Rouy, III, 76; Superior in Richelieu, III, 456; VIII, 607; Saint Vincent urges him to send back to Cahors Brother who had gone to help in Richelieu, III, 522; tells him not to be innovative in important matters, III, 606–07; IV, 39; not to become embroiled in secular affairs, III, 515; IV, 10, 69; difficulties with local leading citizens, III, 515; IV, 8–11, 69–70; chaplain in Champigny, IV, 69; confreres, III, 462–63; IV, 40, 85; instructions Saint Vincent gives him for Court's stay in Richelieu, IV, 44; Codoing receives orders to appear before Officialis of Poitiers, IV, 114; other mentions, I, *xxvi*; II, 119, 203. See also ***Annecy, Richelieu, Rome, Saint-Meen***.

Coëffort (Notre-Dame de), collegial church in Le Mans - II, 644; III, 28; VIII, 613.

Cogley [**Coglée**] (Gerard), Brother of the Mission, cousin of Laurence and Mark - Biographical data, V, 247; arrival in Paris, V, 261.

Cogley [**Coglée**] (Laurence), Brother of the Mission, brother of Mark and cousin of Gerard - Biographical data, V, 72; other mention, V, 156.

Cogley [**Coglée**] (Mark), Priest of the Mission, brother of Laurence and cousin of Gerard - Biographical data, II, 582; III, 99; IV, 31; V, 25–26; VI, 147; VII, 270; XI, 356; letters Saint Vincent writes him in Sedan, III, 504, 526; IV, 31, 38, 41, 54, 97, 117, 121, 164, 188, 194, 266, 333, 344, 362, 470, 479, 513, 521,

576, 601; V, 25, 46, 63, 72, 155, 269, 417, 445, 469, 473, 552, 591, 606; in Marseilles, II, 582; leaves Company, regrets it, makes short novitiate, sent to Sedan, II, 663, 669; III, 99; VII, 586–87; obtains permission to take vows, III, 504; Superior in Sedan, IV, 110, 195, 435, 483; VIII, 611; Saint Vincent encourages him to be excused from attending diocesan synod, IV, 165; Cogley deals tactfully with Governor of Sedan, so, despite complaints, saint does not remove him as Superior, IV, 264; contacts with Governor, IV, 470; saint urges him not to seek esteem of others, IV, 479–80; health, IV, 601; Fr. Cogley would like Sedan to be diocese, IV, 602; no longer Superior in Sedan, but remains in house, V, 198, 209, 222, 247; resumes direction of house after departure of Fr. Martin, V, 262; Superior again in Sedan, V, 417; VI, 147–48; VII, 611; Saint Vincent dissuades him from making retreat every Friday, V, 469; Fr. Cogley discontinues alms for Capuchins in Sedan, which Missionaries had been providing, V, 552; after consulting confreres, introduces custom of going out to eat in town, for which Saint Vincent rebukes him, V, 592; reprimands him for asking Missionary to divulge secret, V, 606; Cogley goes to thermal baths at Forges-les-Eaux, VI, 368, 390; returns to Paris feeling no improvement, VI, 404; in Paris, VI, 429, 488, 526; gets help for eye trouble, VII, 586; repetition of prayer, XI, 356; Superior in Annecy, VII, 270, 368, 395; VIII, 608, VII, 536; opposed to union of Saint-Sépulcre Abbey with Congregation of the Mission, VII, 412; vision problems, VII, 536–537, 586; mental problems, VII, 586–87; recalled to Paris, VII, 537; decides to leave Company; seeks position; VII, 586–87; at Motherhouse, VII, 605; mention of letters to Saint Vincent, IV, 576, 602; V, 25, 155, 445; VII, 536–537. See also ***Annecy, Sedan***; other mentions, I, *xxvi*; VII, 297.

Coglin (M.) - Captured Moor; seized merchandise of Jewish traders, V, 133.

Cognac, town in Charente - Benedictine nuns, VII, 138; Saint Vincent refuses direction of collège and parish, VI, 355.

Coignart (Jeanne), Daughter of Charity - XIIIb, 227.

Coignet (Jacques), Pastor of Saint-Roch - Recommends persons wishing to make retreat at Saint-Lazare, VIII, 496, 512.

Coimbra - Theologians, XIIIa, 382.

Cointerel [**Contarello**] (Mathieu), Cardinal - Prodatary, XIIIa, 405.

Colbert (M.) - Saint Vincent talks of sending him money for Algiers, VII, 273, 288; M. Colbert refuses to accept it, VII, 302.

Collection - Collection for Confraternities of Charity, I, 295–97; II, 630.

Colée (Antoine), Priest of the Mission - Biographical data, I, 378; Superior in Toul, I, 41, 544; VIII, 605; stinginess, I, 378; tries patience of Fr. du Coudray, II, 82; in Richelieu, II, 113; in Luçon; asked to return to Richelieu, II, 353; going to Paris, II, 529; health, II, 541; leaves Company, II, 669.

Colette (Mme) - Founding member of Charity of Châtillon-les-Dombes, XIIIb, 4.

Collée (Eustache, Antoinette, and Marie) - Members of Charity of Folleville, XIIIb, 48.

Collèges - Teaching in collèges inappropriate for Priests of the Mission, II, 272; VI, 355; VII, 161.

Colletot (Fr.), Prior of Forêt-le-Roi - I, 130.

Collier (M.), Bailiff of Neulhy - VI, 93.

Colin (Mathurin), slave in Algiers - Money left for him in Marseilles, VIII, 319.

Collin (M. et Mme) - Entrance of Madame to Visitation denied, VIII, 154.

Collorgli, convict prisons in Algiers - III, 305.

Colmoulin (M. de) - VI, 555.

Colombes, town near Paris - Postulants, I, 224, 296; other mention, IV, 24.

Colombet (Pierre), Pastor of Saint-Germain-l'Auxerrois - Letter to Saint Vincent, I, 365; reference to letter, I, 366; contacts with Saint Vincent, I, 364; II, 169, 177; with Saint Louise, II, 205; staffing Charity in his parish, I, 365; collection to help Fr. Hallier go to Rome for condemnation of Jansenism, IV, 394; other mentions, IV, 596; V, 17.

Combalet (Marquise de) - See **Aiguillon** (Duchesse d').

Combret (Michel), of Lyons - XIIIa, 46, 57.

Comet (Catherine de) - I, 1.

Comet [**Commet**] (M. de), Judge in Pouy - I, 2; patron of Saint Vincent, I, 6.

Comet [**Commet**] (M. de), brother of preceding - Saint Vincent writes him first two letters of correspondence, recounting captivity in Tunis, return, and sojourn in Rome, I, 1, 11; relationship with Saint Vincent's family, I, 16. See also **Saint-Martin**.

Commandment - Prudence in explaining sixth commandment, I, 439, 448, 453.

Commendatory Letters - Saint Vincent advises Fr. Alméras to admit no one to house without one, IV, 146.

Comminges (Town) - See **Choiseul**.

Communication, Spiritual - Conferences, X, 355–62; XII, 289–97; definition, XI, 200; mention of use of Conferences in Company, XII, 419–21, 435; in seminaries, XII, 235; reference to previous conference, XII, 415; text of Rule of Missionaries, XII, 289; of Daughters of Charity, VI, 341; X, 355, 508; Saint Vincent recommends practice, IV, 529; XIIIa, 159; Visitor should restore practice, VII, 444; advantages of spiritual direction, III, 603; necessary to tell troubles to Superiors, IX, 33; tell them temptations, IX, 504; communication to Superiors of anxieties, temptations, and grave faults allows them to govern Company better, XII, 292; to apply remedy to ills, X, 55, 362; XII, 292–94; example of saints and Communities, XII, 291–92; of Brother, VI, 68; X, 60; communication must be made to Superiors, not to others, IX, 33, 63; X, 56–57, 355–59; XII, 289–90; objections and responses, X, 58–59, 359–60; XII, 294–96; God directs souls deprived of spiritual directors, III, 603; how to make communication, X, 485–86; time of communication for Missionaries, II, 403; monthly communication of Daughters of Charity with Saint Louise, VIII, 279; IX, 11, 101, 177; X, 508, 554, 588; XIIIb, 126, 137; Saint Louise with Saint Vincent, II, 627–628. See also **Secretiveness**, **Illusions**, **Temptations**.

Communion - Conferences, IX, 182–90, 260–72; XI, 138–40; XIIIa, 36–38, 38–42; reference to other conferences, XII, 412, 416; mention of conference on spiritual Communion, XII, 420. Our Lord desired to give himself to us under beautiful name of Communion, IX, 81; importance of good Communion, XIIIa, 36–37, 38–42; happy effects of good Communion, IX, 235–36, 262–63, 398; XII, 390; those who make good Communion do all things well, IX, 261–263; capital virtue of Daughters of Charity is to receive Communion well, IX, 189; they imbibe spirit of their state, IX, 188–89; bad Communion is deplorable, IX, 185–87, 261–62, 263–64, 266–68; XIIIa, 38; signs to discern good Communion from bad, IX, 182–84, 188–89; means of making good Communion, IX, 183–184, 270–71; dispositions for good Communion, IX, 198, 265–69; for frequent Communion, IX, 268; disinclination should not keep us from Communion, IX, 235–36; nor should interior trials, I, 108; disunion with neighbor is hindrance, IX, 83; infrequent reception does not dispose us better for Communion, XI, 182; harmful influence of Jansenism regarding frequent Communion, III, 321, 358, 362; Saint Vincent counsels monthly Communion for pious layperson, VI, 595; days on which

Daughters of Charity have permission to receive Communion, V, 615; IX, 7, 95, 298, 422, 426, 532; X, 11, 164, 284, 506, 508; Saint Louise sometimes deprived Sister of Communion as penance, I, 234; Saint Vincent encourages Saint Louise to receive Communion, I, 507, 560; Communion recommended to members of Charities, XIIIb, 18, 45, 51, 83, 90; thanksgiving, IX, 266; prayer on eve of Communion, IX, 265; Saint Vincent sometimes recommended receiving Communion for special intentions, XI, 68, 158, 171, 198; XIIIb, 323, 328; First Communion, I, 324; III, 129–30; XI, 95.

Communities (Religious) - See **Religious Communities**.

Compaing (Guillaume), Curate at Saint-Nicolas-du-Chardonnet - Biographical data, I, 159; II, 411; letter to Saint Vincent, I, 536; contacts with Saint Louise, I, 218; II, 411, 474.

Company of the Indies - See **East Indies**.

Compans (Anne de), Abbess of Val-de-Grâce - Concerning union of benefice, IV, 243.

Compassion - Conference, XI, 69, 308–09; act of charity, XII, 221–22: see also **Mercy**; for Irish refugees, XII, 391.

Compiègne, town in Oise - Visitation, III, 355; VIII, 450, 530; Battle of Compiègne, IX, 233; other mentions, II, 554; V, 139; VII, 513.

Complaints - See **Murmuring**.

Compostela - See ***Santiago de Compostela***.

Conception (Sisters of) - Vincent tells Anne-Marguerite Guérin, Visitandine, that Pastor of Saint-Nicolas thinks she could render them service, IV, 319.

Conciergerie - Sisters serve prisoners, XIIIb, 231.

Concupiscence - Lust of eyes, concupiscence of flesh, and pride of life, IX, 348; XII, 17–18; XIIIb, 345.

Condé (Charlotte-Marguerite de Montmorency, Princesse), wife of Henri II de Bourbon - Biographical data, II, 8; III, 268; IX, 149; Lady of Charity, II, 8; III, 268, 404, 420, 506; her charity, III, 507; X, 320; other mentions, II, 560; IX, 149.

Condé (Henri II de Bourbon), Prince - Struggle against Jansenists, II, 550–51; other mention, V, 561.

Condé (Louis II de Bourbon), Prince, brother of Henri II de Bourbon - Biographical data, V, 53; III, 411; summoned for Rueil Conference, III, 411; rebellion against Court during Fronde, IV, 320, 343, 414, 460; V, 53.

Condé, town in Aisne - Saint Vincent refuses offer of house for Missionaries, VII, 220.

Condescension - Conferences, X, 383–90; XI, 58; Saint Vincent's rule of gracious condescension, XII, 398; mention of conference, XII, 406; text of Rule of Daughters of Charity, X, 383; exhortation to condescension, IX, 216; in what it consists, X, 386–87; form of obedience, XI, 68; sign of a Daughter of Charity, IX, 461; preserves union, IX, 519; gives consolation and tranquility, IX, 216; flows from gentleness and humility, XII, 259; recommended by Gospel, X, 386; Saint Francis de Sales, X, 389; XIIIb, 282; Saint Vincent Ferrer, I, 228; X, 387; XII, 175–76; example of deceased Sisters, X, 388; Superiors should be condescending, X, 387–88; but not always, even in what is good, X, 388; never condescend in something sinful, I, 304; X, 388; Saint Vincent urges Jean Le Vacher to practice it, IV, 127.

Condom, town in Gers - Bishops: see Antoine de **Cous**, Jean d'**Estrades**, Charles-Louis de **Lorraine**; Missionaries from La Rose to serve in diocese, II, 318; VIII, 606.

Condren (Charles de), Superior General of Oratory - Biographical data, I, 164; II, 346; IX, 413–14; XI, 119; Director of Gaston de Renty, II, 259; how he prepared for death gentleman condemned to deportation, IX, 413–15; according to him, Our Lord made vows, XII, 299; XIIIa, 375; disavows intrigues of one or several confreres against Mission, I, 164–66; esteem for Mission, XI, 119–20; for Antoine Lucas, II, 346; other mention, I, 461.

Condren (Gabrielle de), Carmelite, sister of preceding - I, 326.

Conduct - Never be discouraged in pursuit of something undertaken after mature reflection, IV, 139; V, 316; affairs succeed at time fixed by God, II, 470; IV, 139; property is evil when it is where God does not wish it, VIII, 175; we cannot please everyone, XIIIa, 381; change nothing of something that is not bad, XIIIb, 279. See also **Counsels**, **Constancy**, **Haste**, **Prudence**, **Secrecy**.

Condun (Seigneury) - See **Lamet** (Gabriel de).

Conference of faults - See **Chapter**.

Conferences (Clerical) - Assembling priests to discuss cases of conscience and duties of state is one of ministries of Congregation of the Mission, XI, 10; XIIIa, 299, 300; Bishops of Assembly of Estates of Languedoc decide to establish them in their dioceses, II, 614.

Conferences to Ordinands [***Entretiens des Ordinands***] - Author and usefulness of *Entretiens des ordinands*, XII, 236–37; Saint Vincent wants Saint-Lazare students and priests of seminary to have copy for study, XII, 242; material prepared for instruction of seminarians preparing for ordination, XII, 236–37, 242.

Conferences (Spiritual) - Mention of talks on value of conferences in Company, XII, 419, 421, 435; spiritual conferences date back to Jesus and Apostles, IX, 311; usefulness, II, 95; IX, 315; special benefit of conferences on virtues of deceased: see **Deceased**; spiritual conferences more useful than sermons, IX, 62; than Vespers, X, 556; God speaks through those questioned, IX, 306, 314–15; God will demand account of conferences at which one assists, IX, 309–10; dispositions for benefitting from them, IX, 312; means of profiting from them, IX, 316–19; how to prepare for them, IX, 186, 339, 404; make them topic of conversation in order to be edified; guard against criticizing what has been said, IX, 318; share with absent pious reflections heard, IX, 238; conferences common in seminaries, XII, 235.

Conferences at Saint-Lazare: List of conferences given 1650–60, XII, 405–38; conferences mentioned, I, 587; V, 232, 375, 376; VIII, 354, 371, 375; use of conferences gradually introduced at Saint-Lazare, with no plan beforehand, XII, 8; days for conferences, XI, *xiii*; no conference on All Souls' Day, feasts of Saints Matthew and Andrew, XII, 429; cancelled on second-class feast days, XII, 428–29; none on Conversion of Saint Paul because of devotion on that feast, XII, 430; nor when Saint Vincent did not feel well, XII, 435; conference not on usual day, XII, 434–35; time for conferences, XI, *xx*; XIIIa, 373; length, XI, *xiii*; topics, XI, *xiii-xiv*; same topic five times in succession, XII, 433–34; should not be held earlier without permission of Superior General, VI, 560; Saint Vincent thought it useful to note down what was said, XI, 152; XII, 434; simplicity, humility, earnestness, eloquence of Saint Vincent, XI, *xiv-xx*.

Action taken by Bro. Ducournau to copy and preserve conferences, XI, *xxii-xxiv, xxvii-xxxii*; records them himself, XI, *xxiii-xxiv*; what remains of his work, XI, *xxiv*; publications of conferences to Missionaries, XI, *xxv-xxvi*: see **Prayer** (Repetition).

Conferences to Daughters of Charity: on good use of instructions, IX, 305–20; conferences mentioned, I, 587; II, 77, 209, 292, 317, 444, 527, 539, 635; III, 28, 178, 256, 263; IV, 53, 519; V, 439, 465; VI, 136; VII, 381, 382; VIII, 105, 106; Saint Vincent encourages attendance at conferences, IX, *ix*,

23, 61–62, 101; X, 509; consolations he receives from them, I, 526, 576; IX, 85, 186; did not give Sisters conference for long time, IX, 16, 34; took resolution to be more faithful, IX, 11; led Sisters to hope for conference every two weeks, IX, 14; monthly, IX, 544; following month, IX, 48; when prevented by infirmities, gives conference at Saint-Lazare, VII, 382; X, 581; came to conference hall accompanied by priest, IX, *x*, 436, 445, 453; sometimes by two, X, 30; sometimes by Brother, IX, 487; sent replacement when unable to come, IX, 49, 337, 395, 448.

Topics for conferences, IX, *x*; Saint Louise sometimes suggested topics, IX, *xi*, 325, 365; notice sent to Sisters' houses to announce conference, IX, *xi*, 313, 353; audience, IX, *ix*, 182; method, IX, *xii-xv*; change in method; saint is happy with it, IX, 78, 82, 85, 191, 199; topics will have two points instead of three, IX, 186; prayer at beginning, IX, *xii*; blessing and prayer at end, IX, *xiv*; Saint Vincent kept head covered, X, 148; forgetfulness, IX, 453; tears, IX, 378; X, 441, 443, 577; kisses floor, IX, 260; kneels, IX, 449; declares he says nothing coming from self, IX, 192, 199, 271; eloquence, IX, *ix*; tells Sisters how to answer when questioned, IX, 78; X, 63; urges them to speak louder, IX, 491; to share thoughts humbly and simply, IX, 307; not to ask questions during the conference, X, 510–11; not to repeat what others have said, IX, 369; allows them to prepare response in writing and to read from notes, IX, *xiii*, 162, 230, 272, 309, 404, 494; X, 559, 561; Saint Louise herself wrote reflections, IX, 246, 269; congratulates Sisters who answered well, IX, *xii, xiii*, 261–62, 281–82, 285, 404–05, 416, 494; X, 559, 561; emotion prevents Sister from speaking, X, 577; Saint Vincent urges Sister who had not dared to speak to ask pardon, X, 75; Sisters question Saint Vincent, IX, 21–22, 24, 433; Saint Louise does likewise, X, 111; Sisters interrupt needlessly, IX, 43; accuse themselves of faults and, on their knees, ask pardon for them, IX, 62–63, 66, 87, 90–91, 142, 180, 260, 300–01, 325, 478; X, 62, 145, 159, 367, 390, 417, 432, 487, 523, 536, 596; collective expressions of good will, IX, 13, 16, 23, 66–67; what to do when Blessed Sacrament passes in street during conference, X, 148.

Editing of conferences, IX, *xv-xviii*; basis for editing, IX, 230, 246, 311; reflections of Sister who was editing, IX, 182; X, 511; Saint Louise mentions in her summaries what she said, without naming self, IX, 91; original notebooks, IX, *xv-xvi*; copies, IX, *xvii-xxi*; publications, IX, *xix-xxii*; conferences to Ladies of Charity: XIIIb, 378–389; to Visitandines of Paris, VI, 117; spiritual conferences in Missionaries' houses: every Friday evening on Rule or practice of virtues, I, 555; topics suggested by Saint Vincent to Superiors, II, 332; V, 235, 362.

Confession - Conference, IX, 440–48; text of Rules of Daughters of Charity, X, 506; good means of correcting faults, IX, 235; Priests of the Mission receive jurisdiction from Superior General for hearing confessions, X, 507, 525; hear confessions in dioceses only if authorized by Ordinaries, V, 87; Rule forbids hearing confessions in cities and of hearing religious: see **Congregation of the Mission**; Saint Vincent obtains from Rome faculty to absolve from cases reserved to Pope: see **Reserved Cases**.

Avoid tender words, IX, 443–44; X, 528; do not become attached to devout women, XII, 344; do not get too close to women, XI, 95, 161; XII, 342–43; disregard bad thoughts that come while hearing confessions, II, 20–23, 123; make act disclaiming them, II, 124; learn first words people use to confess most common sins, VIII, 173; ask only necessary questions, XII, 343; do not question upright persons, but be content with what they say, I, 344; keep matter of confession confidential, IX, 444; X, 36; speak of what was heard in confession only if no possibility of listeners recognizing penitent, XII, 249; virtues of penitent do not fall under seal of confession, IX, 157; always wear surplice when hearing confessions, IV, 598; gentleness and forbearance needed to hear confessions of poor persons, XII, 248; how to hear confessions of prisoners, II, 495; confreres may not hear confessions, during mission, of those outside diocese, or of anyone or anywhere without permission of Bishops or Pastors, VI, 445–46.

Preparing people for confession, II, 665; IX, 445; XIIIb, 381–82; confessions can be postponed to another day, III, 130; dispositions for good confession, IX, 440; necessity of contrition, IX, 442; do not refuse penance, IX, 444; do not communicate with confessor outside confession, III, 185; X, 587; XIIIb, 280, 296–99; do not be attached to confessor, IX, 363, 443, 526; X, 304, 414, 528–29, 552–53; confidentiality, IX, 444; X, 36; obey confessor, IX, 58; X, 412; unless contrary to Rules, IX, 58; what to do about confessor who is too tender or says offensive things, IX, 444; X, 36; for mortal sin, go to confession as soon as possible, X, 99; example of Cardinal de La Rochefoucauld, X, 99; Missionaries should go to confession on days set by Rule, XI, 182.

Saint Vincent reserves to himself designation of confessor for Daughters of Charity, X, 183; they should go to this confessor, IX, 443, 513; X, 412–14; because he alone has jurisdiction to absolve them, X, 412–14, 524–25; entire house should have same confessor, III, 603; X, 588; Sisters may have choice among several confessors, XIIIb, 296–99; confessor must not be chaplain of house, XIIIb, 280; nor religious, but rather priest of parish, XIIIb, 281; sometimes useful to change confessors, IX, 526; Motherhouse Sisters usually go to parish priests of Saint-Laurent, IV, 380; Saint Vincent sometimes hears their confessions, IX, 57; sends one of his priests monthly: see **Daughters of Charity**; for confession of young ladies, II, 77.

Saint thinks Sisters usually do not commit mortal sin; recommends accusing themselves of no more than three sins in ordinary confession, I, 550; IX, 57; add at least one from past life, IX, 442; X, 192; confess any scandals, specifying number of times, X, 41; request useful advice of confessor, IX, 392; no idle talking, VI, 51–52; do not speak in confessional of temptations against vocation, IX, 504; or of differences of opinion in community, or of sins of others, IX, 226, 234, 444; spiritual direction from Superior, not confessor, IX, 504.

Days for confession fixed by Rule of Daughters of Charity; Saint Vincent urges fidelity, I, 504; IX, 95; XIIIb, 110, 125, 136, 138; Pastor of Chars does not encourage this, IV, 516; XIIIb, 356; confession is proximate preparation for Communion, IX, 271; permissions confessors can give, IX, 515; X, 505; monthly confessions of Sisters to Priest of the Mission, VIII, 279; X, 508, 523–24, 554; annual confession, XIIIb, 125; extraordinary confessions, III, 401; XIIIb, 262; Jubilee confession; Saint Louise wants Sisters to have, on this occasion, greater liberty than usual in choosing confessor, V, 579; Saint Vincent puts self at disposal of Sisters, I, 328, 341; IX, 42; recommends to priests of Tuesday Conferences frequent confession to same confessor, XIIIa, 140; same advice to ordinands, XIIIa, 159; confessor may dispense from making Stations for Jubilee, IX, 488; general confessions, I, 271, 555, 582; II, 122, 664; XI, 2; XIIIa, 159; XIIIb, 382, 388; public confessions, XII, 291. See also **Congregation of the Mission**.

Confidence [**Trust**] **in God** - Conferences on trust in Providence, X, 403; XI, 31, 32; text of Rule of Daughters of Charity, X, 403; confidence in God explained, X, 403–05; exhortation to confidence, III, 206; IV, 346, 387; trust in God as infant to its mother, X, 403–04; reasons to trust in God, III, 385; VII, 171–72; X, 163, 404–09; XII, 117–21; example of Saint Vincent, II, 323; VII, 424; self-distrust must be accompanied by trust in God, III, 143, 207; V, 166; confidence and hope, X, 403; this confidence never disappoints, IX, 73; strength of weak and eye of blind, III, 159; God wants us to come to Him by love, I, 81, 150; three do more than ten when Our Lord puts His hand to things, IV, 122; what God guards is well guarded, IV, 381; if we do God's work, He will do ours, III, 398; IV, 284; XII, 117, 121; excellence of prayer and confidence in God, XII, 390; when all else fails, know how to trust in God, V, 442; better to depend on Providence than to be assured of having enough to live on, II, 517; see **Providence**.

Confidentiality - See **Secrecy**.

Conflans: Conflans-Sainte-Honorine, in district of Versailles, Yvelines - Mission there, VII, 21; visit of Saint Louise to Charity, XII, 356.

Confraternities - See **Confraternities of Charity, of Rosary, of Saint-Nom-de-Jésus, of Scapular**; Fr. Dufour starts one for salvation of people of Madagascar, VI, 19.

Confraternity of Charity [**Charity**] - Historical note, V, 243–44; IX, 3; XI, 94; foundation of first Charity in 1617: see ***Châtillon***; second is established in Villepreux, I, 79; spread of Charities; good being done, I, 246; XIIIb, 139; foundation of first Charity in Paris in 1629: see ***Saint-Sauveur***; obstacle to smooth operation of Charities in Paris; Saint Vincent remedies this by putting young country women at service of Ladies, I, 71, 111, 197; X, 82: see also **Daughters of Charity**; established in parishes by Congregation of the Mission, II, 600; III 59–60; Archbishop of Paris authorizes it to establish and visit Charities throughout diocese, XIIIa, 241; how to establish Charities in towns, II, 643; permission to be asked of Bishops and Pastors, I, 125, 131; XI, 95; Charities succeed better in villages than in towns, I, 347; better to establish Charity in each parish than one for entire town, X, 182; Priests of the Mission have rule of establishing Charities wherever they give missions, I, 41, 45, 49, 50, 53, 142, 246: see **Congregation of the Mission**; and of contributing to them, XII, 313–14; reestablish Charity, if it has fallen off, III, 332; general and particular rules: patron, purpose, members, reception, food, visit and assistance of sick; burial of dead, meetings, bequests and gifts; administration of temporal goods and rendering accounts, election, function and removal of officers; reciprocal duties of members; devotions; ceremonies customary on day of establishment; regulations, XIIIb, 1–67, 79–107, 441–42; other mention, I, 286.

Union of Charity of Montreuil to that of Saint-Nom-de-Jésus, I, 102; XIIIb, 94; attempt to unite Confraternities of Charity to that of Rosary, I, 288; II, 28; presentation of accounts, II, 571; better for curate not to be Treasurer, I, 70; agreement impossible where women are dependent on men for funds; nothing to criticize in administration of women, I, 70; IV, 76; duties of officers, I, 295; Ladies of Charity should cook meat themselves, I, 70; sick persons excluded from assistance of Charities, I, 130: see **Daughters of Charity**; Saint Vincent recommends that members designate someone to replace them after they die, I, 83; XIIIb, 439; precautions against plague, I, 130–31; visiting prisoners, XIIIb, 43; visit of Charities by **Louise de Marillac** (Saint), Mme **Goussault**, Bishop **Pavillon**, Mlle de **Pollalion**: see these names; by Saint Vincent, I, 280; by Missionaries, II, 337; assistance of Daughters of Charity to parish Charities, XI 173–74; relations between Sisters and Ladies of Charity: see **Daughters of Charity**; paintings of Lord of Charity, II, 14; III, 255; VI, 111; booklets on establishing Charity, II, 110; Saint Vincent considers giving Fr. Lambert overall direction of Charities, II, 166; God's protection on members of Charities, I, 186, 197; request for indulgences, I, 246–47; papal approval, VI, 63; VIII, 277; X, 82; XIIIa, 299–301; Saint Vincent wants papal approval for Regulations, VIII, 58; sends Regulations for Charities, I, 130; III, 381.

Charities in ***Angers, Argenteuil, Arras, Asnières, Auteuil, Beauvais, Bergères-les-Vertus, Blanzac, Brie-Comte-Robert, Bulles, Castiglione, Chamblon, Champigny, Châtillon, Conflans, Courboin, Crécy, Crosnes, Étampes, Ferrières, Folleville, Fontainebleau, Franconville, Gallardon, Genoa, Gentilly, Gournay, Grignan, Grigny, Herblay, Issy, Italy, Joigny, La Chapelle, La Fère, Le Mesnil, Liancourt, Lithuania, Mâcon, Mauron, Metz, Montmirail, Montmorency, Montreuil-sous-Bois, Muret, Neufchâtel, Paillart, Paris***: ***Quinze-Vingts Hospital, Saint-Barthélemy, Saint-Benoît, Saint-Étienne-du-Mont, Saint Germain-l'Auxerrois, Saint-Gervais, Saint-Jacques-de-la-Boucherie, Saint-Jacques-du-Haut-Pas, Saint-Jean-en-Grève, Saint-Laurent, Saint-Leu, Saint-Marceau, Saint-Médéric (Saint-Merry), Saint-Nicolas-du-Chardonnet, Saint-Paul, Saint-Roc, Saint-Sauveur, Saint-Sulpice, Raconi, Rethel, Richelieu, Saint-Cloud, Saint-Germain-en-Laye, Saint-Gilles, Saint-Vallier, Sedan, Verneuil, Villeneuve-Saint-Georges, Villepreux, Villiers-le-Sec, Vincennes*** *(Bois de)*, Charities on Mme de Gondi's estates, XIIIa, 63; Charity of Mlle **Dufay** and Mlle **Guérin**: see these entries.

Special types of Charities: Charities of men: see ***Folleville***; mixed Charities, IV, 76. See also ***Courboin, Joigny, Mâcon, Montreuil-sous-Bois***; Charity of Hôtel-Dieu of Paris: see **Ladies of Charity**; Charities at hospitals: see ***Angers, Quinze-Vingts***; Charity of the Court, XIIIb, 441–42; Charity with workrooms, XIIIb, 79–84; Charities owning sheep, XIIIb, 49, 85; other mentions, I, 154, 588.

Congregation of the Mission:

Chronological order of principal events:

1617: Sermon in Folleville (January 25): see ***Folleville***; Saint Vincent recounts origin of the Congregation, XI, 163–64;

1624: Saint Vincent named Principal of Collège des Bons-Enfants.

1625: Foundation contract of Congregation of the Mission, XII, 376; XIIIa, 213; work of God; no one dreamed of it, XI, 31; XII, 6–7; Saint Vincent takes up residence at Collège des Bons-Enfants, XIIIa, 75; beginnings, VII, 336; XII, 7.

1626: Approval of Company by Archbishop of Paris, XII, 376; XIIIa, 218; union of Bons-Enfants to Congregation of the Mission, XIIIa, 219; Act of Association of first four Missionaries (September 4), XIIIa, 222; this same day, Saint Vincent puts his temporal affairs in order, XIIIa, 75; pilgrimage of Missionaries to Montmartre, XII, 335.

1627: Reception into Company of first coadjutor Brother; modification of foundation contract, XIIIa, 224; approval of Company by King, XII, 376; XIIIa, 226, 258; Archbishop unites Collège des Bons-Enfants to Company, XIIIa, 230; taking possession of Collège, XIIIa, 234; King approves union of Collège, XII, 376; XIIIa, 236, 258; introduction of private vows, XII, 308; first petition to Pope Urban VIII for approval of Mission, XIIIa, 228; minutes of *Propaganda Fide* concerning petition, XIIIa, 229. *Propaganda* asks Nuncio to France for information on Mission, XIIIa, 234; Nuncio's reply to *Propaganda*, XIIIa, 238; approval of Mission by *Propaganda*, XIIIa, 239.

1628: Archbishop grants permission to give missions in his diocese and to establish Confraternities, XIIIa, 241; Saint Vincent petitions Urban VIII to authorize Congregation of the Mission, I, 38; obtains letters of recommendation from Nuncio for Prefect of *Propaganda Fide*, XIIIa, 242; and Secretary of *Propaganda*, XIIIa, 244; from King for Pope and French Ambassador to Rome, XIIIa, 243–44; Saint's new petition to Urban VIII for same purpose, I, 47; new letter of Nuncio for Prefect of *Propaganda*, XIIIa, 245; memorandum and opinion of rapporteur, XIIIa, 247; *Propaganda* rejects Saint Vincent's petition, XIIIa, 249.

1630: King orders Parlement to confirm Letters Patent of May 1627, XIIIa, 252, 258; Pastors of Paris opposed to ratification, XIIIa, 253, 258.

1631: Adrien Le Bon offers Saint-Lazare Priory to Saint Vincent, who hesitates to accept it: see ***Saint-Lazare***; Parlement confirms Letters Patent (April 4), XII, 376; XIIIa, 258; Fr. du Coudray is sent to Rome to negotiate approval of Company, I, 111; Saint Vincent lists five points essential in approval, I, 113; beginning of retreats for ordinands at Bons-Enfants.

1632: Saint Vincent asks Urban VIII to approve Congregation of the Mission, I, 140; contract of union of Saint-Lazare

Priory to Company, XIIIa, 263, 281, 284–85, 289, 472, 476–77; Archbishop of Paris approves contract of union, XIIIa, 275, 286, 290, 294, 472, 485; King does likewise, XIIIa, 280, 284, 289–90, 294, 473, 477–78, 485; consent of merchants and magistrates of Paris (March 24), VII, 502; XIIIa, 284, 289, 472, 477, 485; Parlement will review agreement and Letters Patent for registration (August 21); orders registration of Letters Patent (September 7), I, 540; IV, 297; VIII, 434; XIIIa, 284, 289, 290, 294, 472, 477–78, 486; but demands that Saint Vincent obtain new Letters from King and from Archbishop of Paris, VII, 327, 502; XIIIa, 284, 472; declaration of Adrien Le Bon on contract of January 7, 1632, XIIIa, 283, 294; entrance of Priests of the Mission into new Motherhouse, XIIIa, 271, 477.

1632–34: Saint Vincent's proceedings in Rome to obtain from Holy See confirmation of union of Saint-Lazare to the Mission, I, 148–49, 242–44, 245, 265; opposition to union, I, 149, 151, 267.

1633: Bull of Erection of Company, I, 141; XII, 376; XIIIa, 296, 314–15, 321, 395, 403, 407, 419; XIIIb, 230; King again approves union of Saint-Lazare Priory to Congregation of the Mission, XIIIa, 293, 486; Parlement registers King's Letters Patent (March 21), VII, 503; XII, 374–75; XIIIa, 473, 478, 486; *Chambre des Comptes* and *Cour des Aides* register them, (October 11), VII, 503; XIIIa, 473, 477–78, 486; official notification given to monks of Saint-Lazare of Letters of Union (April 26), XIIIa, 478.

1634: Fr. Authier, who has already united his Community to that of Paul Motta, proposes to include Congregation of the Mission in one common union; Saint Vincent has difficulty with that, I, 221–22; receives communication regarding Bull of Erection of Company; has certain words deleted that he finds disrespectful to Pastors, I, 223, 247.

1635: Foundation of house in Toul; confirmation of union of Saint-Lazare to Congregation of the Mission by Urban VIII, whose Bull is not dispatched (March 15), VII, 503–04; XIIIa, 414, 473, 479, 486.

1636: Missions with army, I, 338; beginning of seminary ministry.

1637: Opening of Internal Seminary; of house in La Rose near Agen.

1638: Opening of houses in Richelieu, Luçon, and Troyes.

1639: List of houses founded before July 14, I, 556; Missionary's life at home and on missions, I, 552–56; foundation of Alet house; death of Fr. de la Salle.

1640: Foundation of Annecy house.

1641: Death of Fr. de Sergis and Fr. Lebreton; foundation of Crécy house; Company receives permission to open house in Rome, XIIIa, 313; Archbishop of Paris approves vows taken in Company, XIIIa, 315, 420.

1642: Acceptance by King of Bull *Salvatoris Nostri*, XIIIa, 321; registration by Parlement of Letters Patent on behalf of Congregation of the Mission, XII, 375; Fr. Authier renews attempts to unite Company of Blessed Sacrament to Congregation of the Mission; first assembly of Superiors; Saint Vincent offers resignation, which is refused, XIIIa, 329; Superior General is given Assistants and Admonitor, XIIIa, 331; burse from Richelieu for instruction of twelve seminarians at Collège des Bons-Enfants; death of Fr. Pillé; establishment of house in Rome.

1643: Opening of houses in Marseilles, Cahors, and Sedan.

1644: Superior General of Mission named Chaplain General of Galleys by King, XIIIa, 337; opening of houses in Saintes and Montmirail; request to withdraw from lease of coach lines, XII, 377.

1645: Opening of houses in Le Mans, Saint-Méen, and Genoa; beginning of mission in Tunis; boys living at Collège des Bons-Enfants transfer to Saint-Charles Minor Seminary; Collège des Bons-Enfants becomes major seminary for priests.

1646: Saint Vincent sends Missionaries to Algiers and Ireland; to avoid competition with Recollects, recalls Missionary waiting in Marseilles to go to Morocco to found mission in Salé; Fr. Portail begins visitation of houses of Company, continues until 1649.

1647: Plan for new mission in Persia; Jean Le Vacher is sent to Tunis.

1648: Saint Vincent accepts Madagascar mission, where he sends Frs. Nacquart and Gondrée; death of Julien Guérin in Tunis; opening of houses in Tréguier and Agen; Mission of Arabia proposed to Saint Vincent.

1649: Fronde damages Saint-Lazare and several houses of Company; Saint Vincent makes visitation of houses in Brittany, Anjou, and Maine; death of Frs. du Coudray and Gondrée, XIIIa, 358.

1650: Foundation of Périgueux house; Saint Vincent sends to Champagne and Picardy seven priests and six Brothers to assist these two provinces ravaged by armies, plague, and famine; death of Fr. Nacquart.

1651: Closing of Périgueux house; second assembly of Superiors in Paris; Rules received and approved; question of vows examined, XIIIa, 368–73, 374–97, 420; Lambert aux Couteaux leaves for Poland with priest, two seminarians, and Brother, XIIIa, 398.

1652: Martyrdom in Ireland of Thady Lee, seminarian of the Mission; opening of Notre-Dame-de-Lorm house; assistance to Palaiseau, XIIIa, 400; several Missionaries, sent to aid distressed population of environs of Étampes, fall ill and die; mission of Niolo; Community of Orvieto speaks of uniting with Congregation of the Mission; project does not succeed.

1653: Death of Fr. Lambert; Fr. Ozenne succeeds him as head of Mission in Poland; death of Jean Guérin in Annecy.

1654: Opening of houses in Turin and Agde; death of Pierre du Chesne; missions given during Lent through Easter, V, 99.

1655: Death of Frs. Louis Thibault, Mousnier, Le Gros; King of France orders French Missionaries residing in Rome to leave; Alexander VII approves union of Saint-Lazare Priory, XIIIa, 409, 473, 479; approves, by Brief *Ex Commissa Nobis*, vows taken in Company, XIIIa, 417; Brief officially accepted by Saint-Lazare house, then (1655–56) by other houses; discourse of Saint Vincent on "little method," XI, 237–60.

1656: Mission of Lebanon offered to Saint Vincent; he accepts; plan comes to nought; Saint Vincent feels Company is not making good progress, XII, 424; mention of conference.

1657: Plague in Genoa carries off six Priests of the Mission and one Brother; death of Fr. Bourdaise.

1658: Coventual table of Saint-Méen Abbey united to Company, XIIIa, 423, 425; Common Rules of Congregation of the Mission, XIIIa, 430–71; distribution of Common Rules at Saint-Lazare, XII, 1; opening of Meaux house; death of Fr. Ozenne; Community in Naples considers union with Congregation of the Mission, VII, 360–61.

1659: Foundation of houses in Montpellier and Narbonne; sentence of fulmination (July 21) for union of Saint-Lazare Priory to the Mission, XIIIa, 472, 487; Brief *Alias nos* of Alexander VII on vow of poverty, XIIIa, 480–82; Saint Vincent names Fr. Alméras, Vicar-General, who will be responsible for heading Company after his death until election of successor, XIIIa, 483; in sealed note, to be opened and read before future General Assembly, declares Frs. Alméras and Berthe most worthy to succeed him, XIIIa, 484.

1660: Death of Fr. Portail; King again approves union of Saint-Lazare Priory to Congregation of the Mission, XIIIa, 485; death of Saint Louise (March 15); direction of shrine of

Notre-Dame-de-Bétharram offered to Saint Vincent, who does not accept it; death of Saint Vincent.

Vocation of Missionary: Conference, XI, 1; mention of other conferences, XII, 408, 416; excellence of vocation, I, 245; XI, 1; XII, 385; in what it consists, I, 40–45, 47–53, 141–44, 553; XII, 66–82; aimed at reconciling souls with God, and people with one another, XI, 5; comparison with vocation of Carthusian, III, 172–73, 204, 344; Missionary is both Carthusian and Apostle, XII, 384; conformity with vocation of Jesus, XI, 98, 121; XII, 299; angelic life, union with God's Will, XII, 389; temptations of sickness, XII, 393; most beautiful of benefices, XII, 325, 327; places one in state of perfection, XII, 300; Missionary will have same reward as religious, XII, 305; importance of persevering in vocation, XI, 98; we must esteem and love it, VII, 356; XI, 92; example of Fr. Pillé, II, 370.

Saint Vincent encourages Missionaries tempted against vocation, III, 97–99; V, 93, 110, 539, 613; VII, 308; belittles Congregation to aspirant, XII, 395; letter of encouragement to Brother threatening to leave if not changed from house, VI, 142; to another who felt urged to leave in order to be freed of temptations against purity, IV, 566; to be steward in Bishop's residence, III, 450, 475, 503; to teach and assist poor persons, IV, 440.

Writes to priests who, as excuse for leaving Company, allege poor health, III, 97, 127; VII, 387; or scandal they claimed they were giving, VI, 193; or invalidity of vows, taken, they said, without requisite intention, VII, 332; or desire to go to assist parents, II, 610, 687; or to become Carthusian, III, 172, 180, 204, 342; or Capuchin, IV, 569; or Augustinian, VI, 508; Priest of the Mission planning to enter Benedictines, VII, 141; saint congratulates Missionaries who overcame temptation to leave, III, 452, 503; V, 256.

Name, nature, direction, and organization: Saint Vincent sees inconveniences when other Communities take title of Missionaries or of Priests of the Mission, II, 466; III, 352; IV, 61, 293–96, 355; VI, 135, 371, 516–20; wants his houses, even seminaries, to be called houses of the Mission, II, 355; Missionaries not religious, but part of secular clergy, II, 142, 396; III, 247–48, 372; IV, 556; V, 319, 463, 499, 529, 546; VI, 605; VII, 59, 129, 236, 501; IX, 93; XI, 209; XII, 224, 303, 305; XIIIa, 316, 403–06, 418, 481.

In what they depend on Superior General, and in what they depend on Bishops: what Saint Vincent requests, I, 44; what Urban VIII grants, XIIIa, 298–99; Missionaries depend on Bishops for all functions that concern neighbor, I, 297, 553;

II, 155, 214, 288, 396, 637; III, 152–53, 382; V, 88, 459–60; VIII, 435–36; XII, 350–51; XIIIa, 299, 302, 314, 407; also for visitation and correction, I, 298; in what circumstances, for last instance, II, 155–56; on Superior General, for placement of subjects, VIII, 539; for domestic discipline, I, 298, 553; II, 156, 214; XII, 351; discipline and direction, XIIIa, 298–99; internal governance, VIII, 435–36; spiritual and internal direction, III, 153; that is, in all that is not function vis-à-vis neighbor, XIIIa, 299, 314, 407.

Privilege of exemption never contested by Bishops, XIIIa, 407; Alexander VII renews it, decreeing Missionaries exempt from dependence on Ordinary in everything, except what regards external ministries, XIIIa, 418; Saint Vincent declares he has contributed nothing to explanation given in Pope's Brief, V, 459–60; XII, 351; which exempts Missionaries from jurisdiction of Ordinary with regard to lifestyle, VII, 96–97; maintenance, living expenses, I, 298; expenses of the mission, I, 581.

Fundamental Rules of Company, I, 112–13; other mention, I, 273; list of houses founded under Saint Vincent, with Superiors and précis of history of each house, VIII, 604–19: see also **Assemblies**, **Assistants** (local), **Assistants of Superior General**, **Constitutions**, **Coadjutor Brothers**, **Provinces**, **Rules**, **Seminarians**, **Superiors**, **Superior General**, **Vows**, etc.

Ministries: Saint Vincent prefers they not be established in a town than to see them there through human influence, II, 260; enumeration of ministries, I, 297, 553; II, 173; III, 273; IV, 71, 106; XII, 67, 71–82, 84, 98, 202; and where they serve, IV, 72; instruction of poor in rural areas, XII, 71–74: see also **Missions**, **Foreign Missions**; mention of conference on Company's ministry to priests, XII, 426; formation of clergy, IV, 49; XI, 6, 7; XII, 74–76; by means of **Seminaries**, **Retreats for ordinands**, and **Clerical conferences**: see these words; retreats for everyone: see also **Retreats**; direction of Daughters of Charity: see **Daughters of Charity**; spiritual assistance to the military, I, 334, 343; XIIIa, 307; prison chaplains, XIIIa, 216; in hospices and hospitals: see also ***Hospitals***.

Saint Vincent does not want Missionaries to preach or hear confessions in episcopal cities or in towns in which they are established, I, 120, 519, 525, 555; II, 90, 310, 408, 621–22, 660; IV, 313, 368, 392, 398, 472, 557; V, 85, 373, 456, 604; VI, 111, 257, 277, 351, 497, 521, 557, 577, 634; VII, 91–92, 102, 108, 188, 230, 540; VIII, 250; XI, 301; XII, 4; XIIIa, 197, 214, 216, 226, 298; to hear confessions of nuns or to direct them, I, 323; III, 71, 87; IV, 287, 579; V, 86, 602; VII, 214–15; VIII,

365; to preach in convents, II, 622; VIII, 365; to bc in charge of parishes or to have collèges: see also **Pastors**, ***Collèges***; association with laywomen or nuns, VII, 432; their reputation, I, 33; Bishop of Geneva praises them, II, 226; requested for Poland, IV, 63.

Spirit of the Congregation: To put on spirit of Jesus Christ, XII, 84, 92–97; simplicity, humility, gentleness, mortification, and zeal for souls are like faculties of soul of Company, XII, 243–53; their opposites, XII, 254–63; God finishes work begun, XII, 388.

Not to entice anyone to join Congregation, VIII, 342; XI, 146–47, 377; XII, 256–57; Saint Vincent fears expansion of Company, I, 304; for twenty years, dared not pray for this, V, 468–69; should seek its greatness in lowliness, II, 265; asks God to send good vocations to Company, XI, 294; asks prayers for this, VII, 559, 626; through intercession of Saint Joseph: see **Joseph** (Saint); not to publish any writings in order to make Company known to outsiders, VI, 35, 198–99, 604; accept new establishments only if proposed by Bishops, III, 538, 612; V, 165, 351, 436; VI, 331, 634; VII, 400, 531, 558, 568, 581; VIII, 12, 326, 330; XI, 377; establishment taken from another Community can be accepted if offered by secular or spiritual authorities, VI, 30; not to multiply small establishments, IV, 466.

Endure intrigues against Company, IV, 387, 392–93; and calumny: see **Calumny**; not to be troubled if new Congregations are founded, IV, 346–47, 359–60, 392–93; if other Congregations are doing same ministries, VII, 484; VIII, 215, 366; and succeed better, VI, 420; esteem other Communities more than our own, II, 308–09; XI, 104; XII, 167; never speak disparagingly of them, III, 175; have humility that embraces Company to which we belong: see **Humility**; Company will grow only by shame and lack of success, III, 171; will last as long as charity is preserved, XI, 90; Company will subsist by humility, XII, 396; will not perish by poverty, XII, 399–400.

Admissions and departures: I, 304; IV, 168; vow to enter religious Community does not prevent admission into Company, VI, 605; VII, 59; qualities required for admission, VI, 175; VII, 251; make less account of fine appearance than of good will, VI, 208; admission of priest who makes up for unassuming manner and limited learning by a certain ability, common sense, and best of wills, VII, 540.

To be refused: married persons, even if wife enters Daughters of Charity, VII, 217–18; epileptics, VII, 306, 377; hunchbacks, deformed persons, VII, 511; those who, having no desire to enter, are presented by parents or friends, VIII, 550; beware of accepting postulants coming from another Community, III, 368; VI, 305; VII, 584; VIII, 172; Saint Vincent hesitates to accept lame man and son of mother in need, II, 312; recommends thorough examination before accepting converted Turk, VII, 391; is more particular than in past, especially regarding young people, among whom few give selves properly to God, IV, 164; does not agree that, for fear of displeasing Bishop, we stop accepting postulants from his diocese, V, 629; Company must not admit in one country postulants coming from another, VII, 542; test postulant before sending him to seminary, VI, 588; VII, 120; send necessary information to Superiors concerned, VI, 162, 175; VII, 120; documents to be furnished, VI, 176, 305; VII, 120, 241; inform postulants of what will be required of them, IV, 266; VI, 176; VII, 339; what they should bring, VI, 82, 176, 547–48; VII, 364; they may not return home once they have left to follow Our Lord, III, 521; have them examined before admission, VI, 176.

Some Missionaries leave Company, II, 321, 541; III, 371; IV, 140, 556; spiritual sloth and vanity are cause for leaving, XI, 89; sorrow and resignation of Saint Vincent at news of departures, II, 321, 326, 355; III, 215, 371; V, 428; VIII, 87; XIIIb, 297–98; allows priest to return to family, VII, 368; consents to departure of Brother asking that Company take care of elderly father, VII, 225; refuses dispensation from vows to priest who left without good reason; sets up conditions for readmission, VII, 383; as general rule, allow anyone to leave who wants to go, XIIIb, 283.

Before dismissing someone, wait as long as there is hope for correction, IV, 42; Saint Vincent does not judge it opportune to speak in Rules of dismissal of incorrigibles, V, 321; firmness in cutting corrupt members from body of Congregation, III, 372, 511; VII, 394, 442–43; Communities had better rid themselves of those who give bad example, II, 355–56, 361, 420–22; VI, 81; VII, 177; XIIIb, 298; dismissal of seminarians who left house without permission, II, 541; dismissal for lack of knowledge and intelligence, II, 360; dismissal of those who follow their own desires contrary to will of Superior in important matters, IV, 103; of those who do as they please, III, 511; purging of seminary, II, 541.

Those who leave owe nothing to Company, VI, 74; Company owes them nothing except what they brought with them when entering and what they need to return home, III, 373; IV, 551; VII, 367, 603; do not give hospitality in Community houses to those who have left, V, 112, 114, 128;

avoid all communication with them, V, 112–13, 128, 418, 565; VI, 318; VII, 324, 367, 394; Saint Vincent refuses parish to Missionary who had left, V, 433; determined not to readmit men who have left, III, 584; consents to accepting seminarian who had left, on condition that he begin his Internal Seminary anew, VII, 518.

Customs, privileges, various topics: feast days on which some small, special item is added to meal, VII, 450, 491; wearing rosary on belt, III, 376; V, 619; do not say "our Messieurs," but rather "the priests," XI, 324, 345; Saint Vincent will call them brothers, XII, 18; keep front door of house closed, II, 622; do not show outsiders Bull of Erection of Company, VI, 63; do not visit Daughters of Charity except in passing, and if necessary, I, 221; IV, 287.

Brief to read certain forbidden books, VII, 123; Saint Vincent asks Rome for privilege of giving dimissorial letters, VIII, 39; of having men receive Orders *ad titulum mensae communis*, VII, 543; VIII, 38; this last privilege granted him on behalf of Missionaries expelled from their own countries because of religion, VIII, 57; considers asking Rome permission for all Superiors to bless priestly vestments, IV, 448; Priests of Christian Doctrine request communication of privileges Congregation of the Mission enjoys, VII, 484; refused, VII, 541; plenary indulgence at point of death, XI, 193; liturgical obligations to which Missionaries are subject on feast day of patron of parish in which they live, V, 87.

Coat of arms of Company, V, 380; common faults, I, 83; Company composed mainly of humble people, XI, 31, 120, 143; XII, 91; except for two or three, one of whom is Brother, no one has brought any property to Company, XIIIb, 374.

Congregations - See **Religious Communities**.

Conrard (M.), physician of Queen of Poland - Kindness to Missionaries, V, 264; travels to France, V, 366, 377–78; returns to Poland, V, 450; other mention, V, 338.

Consolations - Harbingers of future crosses, III, 234; do not get discouraged if deprived of them, IX, 374–75, 498, 500–01; God ordinarily gives them to beginners in spiritual life, IX, 498, 500–01.

Constance (Mlle) - II, 196.

Constancy - Do not abandon what has been decided after consultation, and remain at peace, XII, 283–84; do not be too quick to change something once it has been established, XIIIa, 377.

Constans (François), Chancellor of Consul of Algiers - Sorry state of his affairs, VI, 189; mention of letter from M. Constans, VI,

353; hostile behavior toward Jean Barreau, Consul, V, 391–93, 406; VII, 556; other mentions, III, 220; V, 326–28, 354, 405, 406; VIII, 4.

Constantin (François), Priest of the Mission - Biographical data; priestly ordination, III, 296.

Constantin (Fr.), Canon of Luçon - VIII, 412.

Constantinople, city in Turkey; today, Istanbul - III, 47; IV, 147; V, 267; XI, 200, 288. See **La Haye-Vantelay** (M. de).

Constitutions - See **Rules**, **Superior General**.

Consultors - See **Councils** (Domestic).

Consumption - Persons with consumption not treated by Confraternities of Charity, X, 273.

Contarello [**Cointerel**] (Mathieu), Cardinal - See **Cointerel**.

Contarmon (M. de) - Saint Vincent asks favor, V, 139.

Conte (Claude) - Member of Charity of Courboin, XIIIb, 93.

Contemplative Life - More perfect than active life, but less than active and contemplative life together, III, 173, 344; Church has enough solitaries, III, 204.

Contempt - Humble self at being despised, accept and rejoice in this; humility prompts us to love contempt, IX, 69; Apostles gloried in it, IX, 69; example of Jesus, XII, 165, 171; XIIIb, 341; people disdain weak authority, II, 403; those who seek vainglory, I, 525; some tell troubles to outsiders, II, 588: see **Humiliations**, **Humility**.

Conti (Anna Maria Martinozzi, Princesse de), Mazarin's niece, wife of Armand de Bourbon - VIII, 62.

Conti (Armand de Bourbon), Prince - Biographical data, II, 144; VII, 315; VIII, 62; piety, XII, 348–49; fidelity to prayer, VIII, 442; XII, 348–49; asks Saint Vincent for Missionaries for Languedoc, VIII, 531; XIIIa, 199; present at obsequies of Saint Vincent, XIIIa, 208; other mentions, II, 171; VII, 315; VIII, 62.

Contradictions - Mention of conference, XII, 430; they divide hearts, XII, 218; esteem and respect for those who contradict us, VIII, 262–63; beautiful opportunities for acquiring virtue and winning hearts, XII, 364; how to make good use of them, XII, 364; other mention, I, 227.

Controversy [**Apologetics**] - Better to combat heresy by establishing truths of faith than by attacking error, I, 458; love is needed to convert someone, I, 276; be peaceful, humble and patient in debates, I, 58, 420; do not challenge ministers from pulpit, I, 276; controversies previously spoken of in Sedan instead of practices of piety, II, 468; prepare for debates and controversy: master abridged Bécan, I, 57; practicing controversy at Saint-Lazare, I, 289, 420; II, 241, 664, 669; VIII, 259; professors come to Saint-Lazare to teach art of controversy, I, 420; IV, 528; refusal of M. Péan's offer to teach it, VIII, 469; Saint Vincent permits confreres to go to philosophy and theology discussions outside house, IV, 545.

Conversations - Reference to conferences, XII, 419, 428, 434, 436; faults committed, IX, 557; X, 353; topics of conversation, I, 504; X, 361; avoid conversing with worldly people, X, 119; good to converse with one other, XIIIb, 281; Daughters of Charity must not stop to talk in streets, text of Rule of Daughters of Charity, X, 362; never speak ill of one another, XI, 110–11. See also **Affability**, **Calumny**, **Cordiality**, **Slander**.

Conversions - Saint Vincent advises Jean Barreau never to write or speak about them or support those contrary to laws of country, III, 47; conversion of heretics and sinners results from absolute mercy and omnipotence of God, VII, 583.

Coquebert (M.), Presiding Judge in Reims - VII, 524.

Coquebert (Philippe), Prior of Montmirail - VII, 334.

Coqueret (Jean), Doctor of Collège de Navarre - Biographical data, I, 190; II, 100; III, 247; VII, 161; XI, 142; esteem for Saint Vincent, XIIIa, 210; saint calls him "my good friend," IV, 98; judges him man of good counsel, I, 190; consults him on vows, III, 247; about Jansenism, III, 322; recommends that Michel Le Gras lodge with him, I, 547; Fr. Coqueret named Superior of Carmelites, II, 100; initiated retreat exercises, XI, 142; virtues, VII, 161.

Coquery (Amable), slave in Tunis - VII, 232, 250, 520–21.

Corbe (Louise), Daughter of Charity - XIIIb, 228.

Corbie, commune in Somme - Siege of town, I, 330; XII, 401.

Cordelet (M.) - Passenger on ship taking Fr. Étienne to Madagascar, VIII, 557, 561–62, 588; piety, VIII, 581, 587; tormented by Satan, VIII, 587.

Cordeliers [Franciscans] - King withdraws monastery of nuns from their direction: see ***Saint-Eutrope***; Cordeliers destined for Madagascar, V, 280; Cordeliers of Paris, V, 103; of Hungary, II, 457; other mentions, IV, 413; VIII, 528; XI, 262; XII, 295.

Cordes (Denis de), administrator of Quinze-Vingts Hospital in Paris - Biographical data, I, 258; II, 53; solicitude for Charity established at hospital, I, 258; Saint Vincent writes him about Fréneville farm, I, 480; has recourse to his counsel, I, 418, 584; contacts of M. de Cordes with Saint Vincent, I, 409, 410, 537; II, 189; one of executors of Commander de Sillery's will, II, 134; other mention, II, 53.

Cordiality - Conference, X, 390–96; definition, X, 390–92; must be accompanied by respect, IX, 115; X, 393–96; avoid excess, X, 392, 395; Saint Vincent recommends it, IX, 523; XIIIb, 281; Saint Louise plans to speak to Sisters about it, II, 292.

Cordon (Jacques de), Commander of Geneva - Biographical data, II, 90; benefactor of Annecy Missionaries, II, 90, 320, 324.

Corinth, city in Greece - Jean-François-Paul de Gondi was its Titular Archbishop, XIIIb, 131, 140.

Cork, town in Ireland - Bishop: see Robert **Barry**.

Corman (Nicolas), Brother of the Mission - Biographical data, I, 447; stops by Richelieu en route to Gascony, I, 447, 453.

Cornaire (Guillaume), Priest of the Mission - Biographical data, III, 381; IV, 36; VII, 409; in Le Mans, III, 381; Saint Vincent encourages him to remain as hospital chaplain in Le Mans despite monotony and difficulties, IV, 36–37, 90–92; relieved of ministry at request of administrators, IV, 172; conducts mission, VII, 409.

Cornaro (Federico), Cardinal - Member of Congregation of *Propaganda Fide*, XIIIa, 239.

Cornelius, personage in New Testament - III, 559.

Cornet (Nicolas), Grand Master of Navarre - Biographical data; Saint Vincent consults him on vows, III, 247; on Jansenism, III, 322; action against Jansenism, III, 74; VI, 291.

Cornette - See **Headdress**.

Cornier (Charles), Priest of the Mission - Biographical data, VIII, 69; stationed in Marseilles, VIII, 69, 348; health, VIII, 161–62; trials, VIII, 266; possibility of helping with mission in Vins, VIII, 320; dispensed from vow, VIII, 537; in Marseilles, VIII, 136–37; considered for Languedoc, VIII, 360; His niece, a Daughter of Charity, is sent to Narbonne, VIII, 137–138.

Cornuel (Claude), Presiding Judge of *Chambre des Comptes* - Legacy for benefit of galley convicts, I, 533; II, 26.

Cornuel (Guillaume), Priest of the Mission - Biographical data, IV, 474; V, 75–76; VII, 301; VIII, 54; Saint Vincent writes to him in Montmirail, VII, 622; Superior at Bons-Enfants, IV, 474, 573; V, 75; VIII, 604; needed elsewhere, V, 99; teacher at Bons-Enfants, V, 148; in Montmirail, VII, 301, 334; Superior,

VIII, 612; health, VII, 613; considered for post of Director of Notre-Dame de Bétharram Shrine, VII, 623; VIII, 54, 84; assigned to Troyes, VIII, 196–97; in Troyes, VIII, 219.

Corpus Christi - Mention of conference, XII, 411. See also ***Aix***.

Corradi (Giacomo), Cardinal - Kindness to Missionaries in Rome, V, 490; to Congregation of the Mission, VII, 38, 344; other mentions, VII, 284, 595; VIII, 23.

Corrections - To be given gently, rarely, and opportunely, V, 167; VI, 406–08; XII, 155; gently, IX, 452; Saint Vincent corrects with a smile, XII, 393; Jesus spent thirty years on earth before reproving, IX, 205; example of Saint Louise, X, 583; other mention, I, 590: see **Admonitions**, **Gentleness**.

Correlier (Thibaut), of Mâcon - XIIIb, 74.

Correspondence - Text of Rule of Daughters of Charity, X, 325; write only if necessary, V, 336; XIIIb, 316; drawbacks of correspondence between houses of Mission, XI, 111–12; but confreres are encouraged to write about matters of piety, XI, 112; don't encourage anyone to write from place where mission has been given, except in certain specific cases, XI, 94; XII, 344; avoid sentimental expressions, XII, 344; write nothing of affairs of State or world news, II, 362; write and receive letters only with permission of, and under control of, Superior, I, 555; IV, 577; V, 583; IX, 394, 512; X, 35, 325; XIIIb, 126, 129, 137, 316; letters to or from Superior General excepted, II, 363, 412, 499–500, 542, 622; V, 583; VII, 339, 611; VIII, 43, 44, 151; IX, 394; X, 326; XIIb, 129; do not write to outsiders about difficulties, II, 588; Saint Vincent reprimands Superior for withholding his letter to Missionary, VI, 197; Superiors should preserve important letters, VIII, 467–68; admonitors should write from time to time to Superior General, VII, 611; Saint Vincent proposes Fr. de la Salle as model in correspondence with women, XI, 162; recommends to Superior that he write every month, IV, 578; asks Fr. Codoing to send him confreres' letters to others, II, 319; Frs. Blatiron and Jolly write weekly, VI, 99; he suggests that Consul of Algiers write in code, III, 47; seal of Superior General, VII, 339; correspondence of Saint Vincent, I, *xxv-xlviii*.

Corse (Fr.), in Algiers - III, 223.

Corsica, island - Character of inhabitants, IV, 404–05, 439; missions in Corsica, IV, 305–06, 406–08, 417, 438; 439: see ***Niolo***; Saint Vincent sends report of mission there to houses of Company, IV, 477; plan for Missionaries' house, VII, 558, 568, 580, 593, 596; VIII, 38, 156, 548; other mention, VII, 624.

Corsi (M.), Consultor for *Propaganda Fide* - XIIIa, 250.

Cosin (M.) - I, 479.

Cospéan (Philippe), Bishop of Aire, then Nantes, then Lisieux - Biographical data, II, 435; III, 196; assists dying Louis XIII, II, 435; member of Council of Conscience, II, 583; praise for devotion of people of Toulouse, III, 196.

Cossacks - General's act of disloyalty, IV, 518; invasion of Poland, V, 235, 535; XI, 274; progress of King of Poland's armies against them, V, 335; submission, VI, 645; King led army against them, VIII, 146; new uprising, VIII, 508.

Cothereau (Claude), monk of old Saint-Lazare - XIIIa, 263.

Cotte (Nicolas), slave in Algiers - Ransomed, V, 407.

Cotti (M.), doctor - I, 188.

Couche, foundling home in Paris - I, 401, 423, 483, 497; XIIIb, 386, 401–03, 441.

Couderon (Fr.), priest of Dieppe - Accidental drowning, VI, 12.

Coudres, Saint-Martin Priory, in Eure - Creation of annuity, V, 549; proposal for union of priory to Mission, VII, 344–45.

Couillaud (Louis), tax farmer of archdeaconry of Aizenay - Signed receipt for sale of Luçon house of the Mission, XIIIa, 320–21.

Coullaré (Bénigne and Toussanine) - Members of Charity of Paillart, XIIIb, 48.

Coulommiers, town in Seine-et-Marne - III, 252; VI, 541.

Coulon (M.), squire of Maréchal de la Meilleraye - VIII, 241, 563.

Council for Ecclesiastical Affairs - See **Council of Conscience**.

Council of Conscience [**Council for Ecclesiastical Affairs**] - Members of Council; decision concerning benefices, II, 583; concerning Jansenism, III, 319; role in upholding Pope's orders, III, 323; Saint Vincent named member, II, 447, 450; rumor of his dismissal, II, 551; would like to be relieved of post, III, 71, 87; XII, 397; rarely goes to the Court and only when summoned, IV, 33; no longer member, IV, 475, 524; member for ten years, VII, 219; involved only with ecclesiastical questions or those relative to poor persons, II, 495; used influence for Bishop of Valence, III, 231; promises to remind members of Saint-Vincent de Rueil Abbey, IV, 245–46; influence with Queen, XIIIa, 150–52; Mazarin, in notebooks, proposes Council of Conscience be postponed for a time, XIIIa, 154; letters saint wrote as member of Council, II, 479, 480, 508–09, 575; III, 161, 176, 391, 617–18; IV, 174, 245, 308, 343; XIIIa, 147; letters received under same title, II, 561–62, 586, 605; III, 315, 382, 385. See also letters of Alain de Solminihac.

Council of Trent - See **Trent**.

Councils (Domestic) - Consultors named by Superior General or by Visitor, II, 542, 673; have only consultative voice, II, 336, 402–03; V, 348, 592; IX, 238; if they disagree, Superior decides, IV, 54; must not talk about what transpires at council, IV, 261–62; XIIIb, 241, 329–30; Superior should take advice of Consultors, II, 637, 673; IV, 41; of Consultors alone, not of other confreres in house, V, 348, 592; VII, 492; never present for discussion what is contrary to Rules or customs, V, 347; in important affairs, Consultors are asked for opinion and called to sign proceedings, VII, 492; domestic councils in houses of Daughters of Charity, IX, 238; XIIIb, 257–59; if Sister Servant disagrees with Councillors, it is well for her to consult Major Superiors, IX, 239.

Councils (General) of Superiors of Daughters of Charity - Minutes of proceedings, XIIIb, 240–377; usefulness of councils; Our Lord presides over them, XIIIb, 240–41; frequency, XIIIb, 259; never give opinion before turning to God, XIIIb, 271; Saint Vincent sometimes summons older Sisters, XIIIb, 359; qualities necessary in a Councillor, XIIIb, 305; do not bring closed mind to council, XIIIb, 240; Council sometimes held in Saint-Lazare parlor, XIIIb, 305, 307, 313, 318, 323, 330–31, 338, 344, 348, 353, 363; presider proposes business, XIIIb, 241; Sister on right questioned first, XIIIb, 308; manner of giving opinion, XIIIb, 241, 312–13, 361, 363; simply, XIIIb, 240; without human respect or spirit of contradiction, XIIIb, 307; do not try to be considered clever, XIIIb, 272; do not argue or impose opinion, XIIIb, 242; brevity, XIIIa, 384–85; confidentiality, XIIIb, 241, 329; Saint Vincent explains how to treat matters presented at Council, XIIIb, 271–72.

Counsel [**Advice**] - To Sisters going to Richelieu, I, 504; to a distinguished person, XIIIa, 160; Saint Vincent took advice of holy theologians, II, 396; III, 247; of Assistants, VI, 77; of older priests, XI, 373; XII, 234; of Brothers, in what concerned their duties, IV, 41; VI, 77; gave advice, when deliberating with Assistants, without trying to impose it, XII, 259; counselors: see **Charton**, **Coqueret**, **Cordes**, **Cornet**, **Deffita**, **Duval** (André), **Lhoste**, **Péreyret**, **Saveuses**; consult others in important matters, IV, 41; X, 406; XI, 314; do not seek advice of too many persons, XIIIb, 315; after seeking counsel and prayerful consideration, once mind is made up, do not worry about consequences, XIIIa, 377; in serious matters, local Superior should have recourse to Superior General: see **Superiors**; persons from whom Daughters of Charity should seek counsel are, according to circumstances, Superiors, companions, confessor, IX, 392–93; ordinarily, seek advice only from those who have grace to direct, IX, 459–60, 501.

Couplier (M.), of Nantes - VII, 60, 617.

Cour des Monnaies - Consideration of giving Michel Le Gras position there, III, 512, 518–20, 522.

Courboin, village in Aisne - Establishment of Charity, I, 177; XIIIb, 92; approval, XIIIb, 91–92; regulations, XIIIb, 85–91.

Courcelles, village, today in Levallois-Perret, near Paris - I, 476.

Courcilly (M. de), bookseller in Lyons - II, 118.

Courdilier (Fiacre), Pastor of Saint-Thibault in Joigny - XIIIb, 65.

Court - Saint Vincent goes to the Court only when summoned, IV, 33.

Courtin (M.) - I, 536; V, 54.

Courtonne (M.), secretary of Bishop of Soissons - XIIIb, 31.

Cous (Antoine de), Bishop of Condom - III, 230.

Couserans, region of Ariège - Vacant See, III, 241.

Cousin (Claude), monk of old Saint-Lazare - I, 135, 252; II, 534; XIIIa, 263, 268.

Coustart (Jean), notary in Paris - XIIIa, 283, 286, 294, 478.

Coustel (Jean), notary for Archdiocese of Rouen - XIIIa, 26.

Cousturier (M.), lawyer in Parlement - Urges Saint Vincent to appeal decision by which he lost Orsigny farm; saint refuses, VII, 422.

Coutances, town in La Manche - Coaches, III, 529; other mention, XIIIa, 73.

Coutieu (Robert), Brother of the Mission - Sent to Genoa, XIIIa, 359.

Cow - Saint Vincent takes measures for foundlings until Louise gets another wet nurse, goat, and cow, I, 497; Fr. Delville urged to sell that of Fontaine-Essarts to avoid getting female help to care for it, IV, 313.

Cozes, town in Charente-Maritime - Huguenot synod, VIII, 31.

Cracow - See ***Krakow***.

Cramoisant (Laurent), slave in Algiers - VI, 302, 328; VII, 196.

Cramoisy (M.) - VI, 178, 439, 537.

Craon, town in Mayenne - Mission given, VI, 410.

Créag (Msgr.), in Rome - VIII, 23.

Crécy, town in Seine-et-Marne - Small parish vacant near Crécy, IV, 507; mission given, XI, 162; convent of nuns, IV, 579; XI, 162; Confraternity of Charity, VI, 20; Missionaries:

foundation, II, 313; XII, 371; letters from Saint Vincent, II, 311, 363, 422; III, 211, 249; IV, 279, 579; V, 19. See also **Lhuillier** (Dominique); garden taken from Mission, XI, 188; ministries, XIIIa, 422; mission, III, 250; assistance to poor persons, III, 409; retreats for ordinands, II, 311; hospitality to man given to drink, VII, 630; list of Superiors, history of house, VIII, 609; personnel, VI, 145: see **Asseline**, **Boudet, Chiroye**, **Delville**, **Du Chesne** (Pierre), **Gallais**, **Gesseaume** (Claude), **Gilles, Grimal**, **Le Gentil**, **Le Rogueux**, **Le Soudier** (Jacques), **Lhuillier** (Dominique), **Nicolas** (Bro.), **Serre**.

Funding of establishment is uncertain, II, 358–59; difficulties created by founder; lawsuit: see **Lorthon** (Pierre); Saint Vincent recalls all Missionaries except Fr. Lhuillier, XIIIa, 422; Lhuillier forbidden by Pastor to hear confessions of sick; endures, through obedience, state of forced inaction, VII, 369; hope for quick reestablishment of personnel and ministries, VIII, 174, 363; poverty of establishment, VII, 16–17; donations, VIII, 174, 501–02; other mentions, II, 338, 554, 664; IV, 507; VI, 458; VIII, 486; XIIIa, 329.

Creil, locality in Oise - Woman locked up there at wish of Mme de Liancourt, I, 285; other mentions, XII, 377, 379.

Creil (Jean de), seigneur de Gournay - I, 247.

Crespières, village in Yvelines - Élisabeth Martin makes visitation of house of Daughters of Charity in area, II, 667; missioning of Sister, III, 300.

Crespin (Pierre), Augustinian, slave in Algiers - V, 355.

Cresté (Marie), Daughter of Charity - XIIIb, 227.

Créteil, town near Paris - VIII, 535.

Cretenet (Jacques), surgeon, founder of Missionaries of Saint-Joseph - VI, 330.

Cretté (Perrine), Daughter of Charity - Signs attestation after reading Common and Particular Rules reviewed and arranged in order by Fr. Alméras, XIIIb, 206.

Croisilles (M. de) - See **Descroizilles**.

Croissy, town in Yvelines - Mission, I, 82.

Croisy (M. de) - V, 589.

Cromwell (Oliver), Lord Protector of English Commonwealth - Emissaries imprison Francis White [François Le Blanc], V, 368; Cromwell takes children and two-thirds of property from Irish Catholics, VI, 500; orders incarceration and punishment of all Catholic priests, VI, 546; action extends to Flanders, XII, 35.

Croppet (Jacques), attorney in Parlement - XIIIa, 24, 25.

Crosnes, village in Essonne - Confraternity of Charity, I, 164.

Cross - Four parts of Cross represent virtues proper to Daughters of Charity, X, 418, 426; Saint Vincent tells Fr. Portail they will sell their crosses to assist him, III, 466.

Crowley [**Cruoly**] (Donat), Priest of the Mission - Biographical data, III, 285; IV, 375; V, 76; VI, 35; VII, 153; VIII, 371; letters Saint Vincent writes him in Le Mans, V, 420, 461, 574, 599; VI, 35, 64, 103, 116, 123, 149, 161, 170, 179, 276, 378, 421, 474; mention of letter from Saint Vincent, III, 285; mention of letters to Saint Vincent, V, 420, 574, 599; VI, 123, 149, 276, 474; Crowley assists people of devastated provinces, IV, 375; in Rethel, IV, 410; proposed for Poland, IV, 383, 411; professor at Saint-Lazare, IV, 528; V, 76; Superior in Le Mans, VI, 583; VIII, 613; called to Paris, VI, 422, 474; assigned to Genoa, VI, 521, 525; VII, 153, 231; professor at Saint-Lazare, XII, 236; sent to Richelieu, VIII, 371. See also ***Le Mans***.

Cruchette (Canon), in Tarbes - Saint Vincent writes him about Bétharram Shrine, VII, 459; Canon writes to Bro. Ducournau on same subject, VIII, 602.

Crucifix - Missionaries must always have crucifix, XI, 340; in troubles, go to foot of crucifix, IX, 393, 398; "library" of Saint Thomas, IX, 28.

Cruoly, Donat - See **Crowley**.

Cruseau (Messrs de), in Bordeaux - II, 57.

Cuissot (Gilbert), Priest of the Mission - Biographical data, I, 379; II, 78; III, 28; IV, 189–90; V, 205; VI, 459–60; VII, 12; VIII, 36; X, 467; Superior in Luçon, VIII, 607; letters Saint Vincent writes him in Le Mans, III, 28, 97; in Cahors, IV, 283; VII, 337; Cuissot's account of virtues of Saint Vincent, XIIIa, 210–12; character, III, 259; mention of letters to Saint Vincent, IV, 283; VII, 338; out giving missions, I, 379–80, 455, 467, 470; in charge of ordinands at Saint-Lazare, I, 516; in Luçon, II, 78–80, 95; proposed as Superior in La Rose, II, 79; Superior, VIII, 607; named for La Rose, II, 112, 140; Superior at Bons-Enfants, II, 531, 541; VIII, 604; in Le Mans, II, 676; recalled to Paris, III, 104; at Saint-Lazare, Assistant to Saint Vincent, III, 238; health, III, 104, 120, 133, 134; Superior in Cahors, III, 259, 522, 525; IV, 189–90, 558–59, 598; V, 205; VI, 476–77; VII, 206, 514; VIII, 36, 467, 610; X, 467; Alain de Solminihac thinks highly of him, III, 461.

At 1651 General Assembly, IV, 233; XIIIa, 369, 372, 374, 383, 397; opinion on vows, XIIIa, 380–81; Saint Vincent takes Cuissot to visit several notable people, XIIIa, 210–11; makes confession to Fr. Cuissot, XIIIa, 212; return to Cahors in 1653, IV, 520; Saint Vincent requests from Rome, on behalf of Fr. Cuissot, appointment to Gignac parish, VI, 606, 637; Priory of Bussière-Badil resigned in favor of Fr. Cuissot; he in turn resigns it, VII, 239; difficulties and settlement of Gignac affair, VII, 337; resignation of parish in his favor, VIII, 135; resigns Chavagnac parish, VII, 285; sent to Montauban to negotiate transfer of diocesan seminary, IV, 520; visits Notre-Dame de Lorm house, VII, 373; prefers not to direct Daughters of Charity in Cahors any longer, VIII, 270–71. See also ***Cahors***.

Cuissot (Jean), Priest of the Mission, nephew of preceding - Biographical data, III, 30; at Internal Seminary of Saint-Lazare, II, 360; named for La Rose, III, 83; sent to Saintes, III, 104.

Cuissy (Abbé de) - See **Amour** (Isidore).

Cum Occasione - Constitution censuring Five Propositions, IV, 394, 430, 580–85, 592–94, 598–601; V, 645; VI, 100, 152.

Cumenon (M. de) - II, 27.

Cuny [**Cugny**] (Marie), Daughter of Charity - XIIIb, 227; sent to Calais, X, 440.

Curiosity - Dangers, XI, 90; curiosity of sight, hearing, touch, X, 304; XII, 176; for knowledge, XI, 24; plague of spiritual life, XI, 24, 90; mention of conferences, XII, 406, 416.

Cursing (**Swearing**) - Practical means to correct habit of swearing, IX, 219–20.

Customs - Never prescribe things contrary to God's prohibitions, V, 348; Saint Vincent encourages Fr. Ozenne in Poland to conform to all customs of Company, V, 350; tells Fr. Crowley not to introduce any new practices unless told to do so, VI, 277.

Cuveron (Maximilien-François), seminarian of the Mission - Biographical data, VI, 175; VII, 364; entrance into Saint-Lazare, VI, 175; praise for him, VII, 364–65.

Cyprian (Saint), Bishop of Carthage - Feast, II, 132; cited, XII, 300.

Cyprus (island) - VI, 248.

Cyril of Alexandria (Saint) - Catechism, XIIIa, 33.

Cyroy (Fr.) - See **Chiroye** (Jacques).

Czartoryski (Florian-Kazimierz), Bishop of Poznań (Posen) - Esteem for Missionaries, V, 105, 128, 175; his Officialis, V, 51, 193; works to unite Holy Cross parish to Mission, V, 187, 193, 196, 201, 263; other mention, IV, 398.

Czestochowa, village in Poland - Visit of King and Queen, VI, 298.

D

Daffis (Jean), Bishop of Lombez - Opponent of Jansenist teaching, IV, 160.

Daigrand (Thomas) - Nephew whom Vincent remembers in his will, XIIIa, 100.

Dairymaid - Brings milk supply to Saint Louise, I, 360.

Daisne (Chrétien), Priest of the Mission - Biographical data, VI, 624; VII, 365; VIII, 411; letter Saint Vincent writes him in Sedan, VII, 368; mention of letter to Vincent, VII, 394; destitution of father, VI, 624; vocation doubtful, VII, 366–67; Saint Vincent permits him to leave Company to assist father; reprimands him for seeking lapsed benefice, VII, 368–69; must renounce benefice or leave, VII, 394, 442–44; after leaving, Fr. Daisne offers his services to Pastor of Saint-Jean-en-Grève in Paris, VII, 513; Saint Vincent tells Pastor he does not know Fr. Daisne very well, VII, 528; Fr. Bourdet complains that Fr. Daisne is forcibly stealing benefice from him, VIII, 411.

Dalbel (Louise), Daughter of Charity - XIIIb, 227.

Dalencé (M.), Saint Vincent's physician - VII, 453.

D'Allesau (M.), judge of Court of Appeals - Statements presented before him regarding claims on Nom-de-Jésus Hospice, II, 684.

Dalmagne (Jeanne), Daughter of Charity - Biographical data, II, 346; IX, 144; conference on virtues, IX, 144–61; maid in Saint-Germain-en-Laye, IX, 155–56, 158; at Carmel, IX, 146, 149, 156; entrance into Daughters of Charity, IX, 146, 149, 156; at Saint-Nicolas-du-Chardonnet, IX, 146; in Nanteuil, IX, 152–54; journey to Paris, II, 346; return to Nanteuil, IX, 150; falls ill there, II, 423; IX, 148, 160; in Paris, IX, 156–59, 160–61.

Dalton (Philippe), Priest of the Mission - Biographical data; Saint Vincent authorizes vows, VII, 347–48.

Damascus, town in Syria - Saint Paul's escape through window, XII, 196.

Damé (Marie), Daughter of Charity - XIIIb, 228.

Damiani (Giovanni), Brother of the Mission - Biographical data, VI, 430; VII, 18; in Genoa, ill with plague, VI, 430, 432, 435,

436, 438, 440, 442, 445; death, VI, 504, 506, 528, 530, 535, 537; VII, 15, 18.

Damiens (Gabriel), Priest of the Mission - Biographical data, II, 531; IV, 221; teacher at Bons-Enfants, II, 531, 540, 585; IV, 221; removed from Bons-Enfants for speaking about Jansenism, IV, 353; sent to Rome, XIIIa, 359–60.

Dammarie-les-Lys, village in Seine-et-Marne - II, 539.

Dammartin, town in Seine-et-Marne - Visitation, IV, 403; other mention, V, 466.

Dampierre (Marie de) - Sister of Louise and Philippe-Emmanuel de Gondi, IV, 550.

Dan (Pierre), author of *Histoire de Barbarie* - I, 5.

Dandilly (M.) - II, 341.

Daniel (Léonard), Prior of La Chapelle - Biographical data, VIII, 509; questions Saint Vincent regarding his vows, VIII, 509.

Dankow, town in Poland - VI, 646.

Danti (Baron), [possibly **Baron de Renty**] - Frequent visitor to Saint-Lazare, II, 97.

Danzig, town in Prussia, now ***Gdansk***, part of Poland - V, 152; VIII, 508.

Dardane (François), prisoner on *Saint-Dominique* - VIII, 250.

Darnaudin (Pierre), notary - I, 10.

Darthois (Françoise) - Member of Charity of Montmirail, XIIIb, 32.

Dartiguelongue (M.), Registrar for Bishop of Dax - XIIIa, 4, 5, 7.

Dassonval (Jean), seminarian of the Mission - Biographical data, V, 38; health, V, 38, 48, 82; death, praise for him, V, 188–89.

Datary (Cardinal) - Opposes union of benefices, II, 295; Assembly of French Bishops addresses letter to him, III, 525; insists that confreres accept traveling expenses from him when working in his diocese, V, 490; Assistant of Saint-Jean-en-Grève thinks dispensation for incestuous persons should go through Datary, VII, 360.

Dathan, Biblical personage - His children, X, 40; grumbling against Moses, punishment, X, 193, 348–50; XIIIb, 351.

Datineau (M.) - Saint Vincent refers Ozenne to him in England, XII, 370.

Daudignier (Fulgence), Carthusian - Recommends new convert to Saint Vincent, VIII, 489.

Daughters of Charity - Chronological table of events:

1631–32: Saint Vincent sends country women to assist Ladies of Charity of Paris with lowly, laborious tasks. See also **Ladies of Charity**.

1633: Saint Vincent entrusts three or four women to Saint Louise in her home, II, 600; III, 60; IX, 66, 166, 193–94, 358, 472–73; X, 82; XIIIb, 120, 139–40, 142, 145, 225, 231; death of Marguerite Naseau: see **Naseau**.

1634: Sisters requested by Ladies for Hôtel-Dieu: see also **Ladies of Charity**; twelve Sisters on July 31, IX, *ix*, 2; first extant conference of Saint Vincent; order of day, IX, 1–13.

1636: Foundation of Liancourt: see also ***Liancourt***; Motherhouse transferred to La Chapelle.

1638: Beginning of ministry to Foundlings; foundations in Richelieu, Saint-Germain-en-Laye.

1639: Foundation in Angers.

1640: Sisters extend Foundlings ministry to all children at La Couche; ministry to prisoners in Paris and in Nanteuil-le-Haudoin; Sisters ask Saint Vincent's permission for private vows, IX, 22.

1641: Motherhouse transferred to Saint-Laurent parish; foundation in Sedan; Saint Vincent gives Regulations to Sisters in Angers, XIIIb, 108; time of rising changed from five o'clock to four, IX, 42.

1642: March 25: Saint Louise and four Sisters make perpetual vows: see also **Vows**; beam in Motherhouse assembly room breaks; God's protection, IX, 196; foundations in Issy and Fontenay-aux-Roses.

1643: Saint Vincent preaches eulogy at death of exemplary Sister, XI, 118.

1644: Death of Jeanne Dalmagne.

1645: Foundations in Crespières, Fontainebleau, Le Mans, Nantes, Maule, Saint-Denis, Serqueux; Regulations for Sisters; petition to Archbishop of Paris for approval of Company, II, 599–604; state of Company, II, 600–02.

1646: Sister saved from danger from collapse of house, IX, 190–91, 195; June 28: first Council meeting, XIIIb, 240; second petition to Archbishop of Paris for approval of Company, III, 59–62; Prelate establishes Company as Confraternity distinct from Ladies of Charity; approves Regulations, XIIIb, 131–38; draft of Letters Patent for approval of Daughters of Charity, XIIIb, 139–41; Saint Vincent announces news to Sisters, reads Regulations to them, has them promise fidelity, IX, 255–60; state of

Company, III, 60–61; Saint Vincent's recommendations to Sisters in Angers at time of Fr. Portail's visitation, XIIIb, 127.

1647: Petition of Queen Anne of Austria to Pope with view to obtaining that Company be placed under dependence of Saint Vincent and successors, XIIIb, 141–42; Saint Vincent names first Directress for newcomers, XIIIb, 294; foundlings transferred to Bicêtre; foundations in Chantilly, Chars, Montreuil-sur-Mer, Fréneville; request for Sisters come from all sides, III, 212.

1648: Death of Élisabeth Turgis; foundation in Valpuiseaux.

1649: Saint Vincent visits Sisters in Fréneville, Angers, Nantes, Richelieu.

1650: Negotiations with M. Méliand, Attorney General, to obtain legal approval of Company, IV, 6; foundation in Hennebont; Sisters requested for Poland and Madagascar.

1651: Fruitless search for original of 1646 Act of Approval of Company by Archbishop of Paris, IV, 276–77; XIIIb, 145–46, 232; foundation in Montmirail; Sisters assist poor persons in Saint-Étienne-à-Arnes and Saint-Souplet.

1652: Great charitable activities of Sisters in Paris, IV, 396, 400; several die, IV, 416; foundations in Brienne, Warsaw, Varize; Sisters in Étampes take in orphans from devastated villages; Sister dies there, victim of charity: see ***Étampes***.

1653: Sisters nurse wounded soldiers in Châlons-sur-Marne; given charge of poor persons of Nom-de-Jésus; purchase of Motherhouse from the Congregation of the Mission, XIIIb, 234.

1654: Foundations in Bernay, Châteaudun, La Roche-Guyon.

1655: Foundations of Petites-Maisons in Paris and in Saint-Marie-du-Mont; Approval of Company by Archbishop of Paris, XIIIb, 144–47, 232–33, 237; Regulations he approves, XIIIb, 133–38; Saint Vincent reads these two documents to Sisters, X, 83; Act of Establishment and naming of Officers, XIIIb, 225–28, 323; Saint Vincent begins explanation of Common Rules, X, 86.

1656: Sisters requested for various places, X, 158–59, 180; for Saint-Malo, Cahors, Agde, Pézenas, Toulouse, Angers, hospital for mentally ill, V, 628–29, 637; VI, 139; go to La Fère on Queen's orders to nurse wounded soldiers; foundations in Arras and Cahors; Council sees usefulness of opening seminary for Sisters in rural area, XIIIb, 338–39, 343.

1657: King approves Company by Letters Patent, XIIIb, 230–37; Sisters requested for General Hospital; election of Officers, X, 210.

1658: Parlement registers Letters Patent of King, XIIIb, 236–37; Sisters requested for Le Havre, Calais, Cahors, and elsewhere, VII, 224; XII, 19–20; go to Calais to nurse wounded soldiers; two die; the others fall ill; many Sisters volunteer to take their place; foundations in Ussel and Metz; death of Barbe Angiboust.

1659: Foundations in Narbonne, Cahors Hospital, Vaux; Saint Vincent sends Rome documents needed to obtain approval of Company, VIII, 160.

1660: Death of Fr. Portail, Director; replaced by Fr. Dehorgny; death of Saint Louise; conferences on her virtues; Marguerite Chétif named Superioress; election of Officers, X, 591; installation of Superioress, September 15, XIIIa, 196; foundation in Belle-Isle-en-Mer; death of Saint Vincent.

First Daughters of Charity: Why they should be holy, IX, 12, 15; XIIIb, 328; three signs of true Daughter of Charity, X, 370; beautiful examples of **Barbe Angiboust**, **Marie-Joseph**, **Andrée**, **Marguerite Moreau**, **Marguerite Lauraine**: see these entries; their modesty in streets, X, 28; they go to visit the sick with basket on back, IX, 68, 75, 247; carrying soup pot, II, 600; III, 60; IX, 247, 274, 370, 382; X, 174; none ever refused to go where sent, IX, 408; X, 98; expenses up to January, 1643, IX, 73; simple condition of first Sisters, V, 267; IX, 14, 89, 103, 106, 114, 247, 399, 465, 473, 529; X, 209, 275, 282–83, 288, 364, 408, 463; XII, 19; XIIIb, 346; a few well-born, IX, 137, 139, 140, 247, 399; X, 84; many do not know how to read, II, 180; IX, 27, 35, 172, 282, 335; X, 408, 437, 456, 461, 463, 575; taught to read and write, I, 239, 305; IX, 6, 36, 174; to sew, I, 239; to teach catechism. See also **Catechism**.

Postulants: II, 25, 67, 125, 127; III, 212, 432–33, 457; IV, 166; V, 621, 628, 632; VI, 211; VII, 64, 224; VIII, 390, 392; sick Sisters: I, 328, 560; II, 577; IV, 257, 416; X, 111; plague, I, 348; climate of Paris unhealthy for Sisters from Angers, II, 151; from Lorraine, II, 26; deceased Sisters, I, 241, 329, 561; IV, 276, 416; XI, 118, 130; Sisters who give bad example, I, 320, 484, 560; some take what belongs to poor, II, 107; Sisters who leave, I, 352; III, 215, 472; IV, 276; V, 4; are dismissed, I, 560; XIIIb, 245–47, 283, 292–94, 296–97, 330–31, 341, 343, 353–55, 360–63, 364–65; young woman is dismissed, III, 457.

Vocation: Conferences on vocation of Daughter of Charity, IX, 13, 16–23, 190–201, 272–284, 353–65; excellence of vocation, III, 181–83; IX, 34, 97, 353–61; X, 94, 272; God Himself is Founder of Company, IV, 257; IX, 47, 92–93, 165–67, 192–96, 247, 273, 357–60, 472–73, 536–37; X, 73; and Author of Rules, IX, 166–67, 247; X, 89, 180; God blesses it, IX, 537–39; protects it, IV, 257; IX, 11, 190–91, 195–97; each

Sister receives vocation personally from God, IX, 32, 114, 138, 195, 246–47, 273, 279, 281, 360; God thought of it from all eternity, IX, 191; no vocation more beautiful in Church, IX, 32, 114, 138, 360, 458, 538; X, 92–95; nowhere is salvation easier, IX, 369; first Company of women in secular dress, IX, 165; not cloistered, IV, 6; first to assist sick in homes, IX, 14, 194, 458, 467; X, 442; no other Company has such diversity of ministries, IX, 467–68; X, 92–94, 102–04, 118; nothing more noble or more lofty than its purpose: leave everything to assist poor, in imitation of Jesus Christ, VII, 397; VIII, 186; IX, 13–14, 17–20, 51–53, 199, 457; X, 94, 100, 102, 104, 116, 179–80: see also **Poor**; Sisters free from worries of family and world, X, 546; find well-being, delight, honor in Company, X, 89, 546–47; receive hundredfold of goods they leave behind, X, 546; beautiful words of Mme Goussault: see **Goussault**; of Duchesse de Ventadour, X, 16; of Jeanne Dalmagne, IX, 159; of great servant of God, IX, 167; world cherishes and honors Daughters of Charity, IX, 98, 140; X, 73, 89, 366; sought on all sides, III, 212; XIIIb, 370; God has great plans for them, IX, 166; X, 263, 366, 437; loves them like apple of his eye, IX, 196; angels count their steps, IX, 365; X, 4; ministries demonstrate holiness of Catholic religion, X, 448.

Duty to love Company: IX, 353–65; X, 287, 300–01; to esteem it, IX, 35, 76–77, 97, 197, 458, 540–41; to persevere in it, IX, 272–84, 541; first Sisters' love of vocation, IX, 359; means God uses to call them, IX, 279; temptations against vocation, III, 182; IX, 274, 278–80, 282, 355, 361–65, 397–98, 502, 504, 516, 539–44; XIIIb, 283; encouragement for Sister tempted to leave, VI, 212; causes of growing cold in vocation, IX, 362; usual cause of loss of vocation: failure to observe Rules and customs, IX, 397–98, and attachment to self-will, IX, 516; prayer for perseverance, IX, 284; become even stronger by example of those who leave, IX, 378–79; do not go to members of religious Orders for spiritual direction, IX, 459, 503–04; X, 316; XIIIb, 281; do not associate with nuns, IX, 459–60; Sisters who persevere have happy death, X, 94; wretched state of those who leave, IX, 35, 76, 273, 275, 279–80, 407; remorse, IX, 281, 396, 407; X, 575; XIIIb, 370; they fall into oblivion, IX, 273.

Motherhouses: Rue de Versailles, Paris, I, 213; Saint Louise had "little horse" there, I, 261; search for another house, I, 308, 310; Saint Vincent prefers that new residence not be near Saint-Lazare, I, 308, 316; Motherhouse in La Chapelle, I, 310–12, 314, 317; Saint Vincent plans to buy house for Sisters, II, 147–48; new search, II, 150, 166, 176–77, 189, 194, 209; purchase of house, II, 210–11; breaking of beam, collapse of ceiling, II, 289–90, 577; IX, 63; repairs, II, 292–93; XIIIb,

342; major donation allows Sisters to purchase Motherhouse, XIIIb, 120–23; workmen in house, X, 344; construction of building, XIIIb, 374; water pipes, VIII, 3, 98; parlor, II, 656; III, 256; XIIIb, 251; chapel, VI, 512; X, 482; financial difficulties, IV, 167.

Fighting near Motherhouse; fear of Sisters, IV, 379–80; XII, 362; letter of Motherhouse Sisters to Saint Vincent, III, 214; proposed Rule for house Sisters, IX, 18; order of day, XIIIb, 124–25; reading at table, VI, 641; Sisters go to confession to parish priests, IV, 380; to Missionaries of Saint-Lazare, III, 185; X, 485; monthly, VIII, 279; Friday conference, II, 292, 593; IX, 292; XIIIb, 291–92, 300–02; Saint Louise asks Saint Vincent if roast may be served on Easter, VI, 281; occupations of Motherhouse Sisters, II, 601; III, 60–61; foundlings, II, 291–92; retreat ministry, I, 372–74; II, 184, 186–87, 188, 205, 217; V, 641; VI, 341; VII, 279, 492, 641; visits to sick poor of parish, XIIIb, 254–56; Motherhouse should serve as model for other houses; resources of Motherhouse come in part from surplus from other houses, II, 640; IX, 43, 74, 257, 388; X, 168, 254–55, 290, 551; XIIIb, 126, 137, 374; Saint Vincent recommends that Sisters in Paris and environs come each month to Motherhouse for communication and confession, VIII, 279; IX, 11, 101, 177; X, 285, 508, 554, 588; XIIIb, 126, 137; and annually for retreat, XIIIb, 138; dispositions for making retreat, II, 302; nuns, house guests, VI, 512.

Sisters' ministries: IX, 36, 466–67; X, 102–05, 118; XIIIb, 145; corporal and spiritual assistance of sick poor, IX, 18–19, 40–41, 49–55, 97, 199–200, 386, 432, 466; X, 107, 267–74, 382, 535–40, 545; XIIIb, 123, 125, 133, 135–36; not only in hospitals, but also at home, IX, 194, 467; X, 92, 118; text of Rule, X, 267, 272–73, 535, 537–39, 545; excluded from Sisters' ministry: persons who are not poor, VI, 46, 49; VII, 64, 80, 469; IX, 399; pregnant women and those with venereal diseases, X, 547; dropsy, pulmonary diseases, and epilepsy, X, 273; in exceptional circumstances, Saint Vincent permits Sisters to care for those not truly poor, I, 340; III, 16; X, 209; Sisters make patients' beds, II, 600; III, 60; VIII, 171; X, 548; XIIIb, 112, 145; give enemas, II, 600; III, 60; XIIIb, 112; perform lowliest functions, XIIIb, 144; live at expense of the Confraternity, II, 600; Saint Vincent permits night duty, II, 600; III, 60; then prohibits it, X, 547–48; service of sick must be preferred to devotional exercises and Rule, VI, 52, 514; VII, 66, 473; IX, 5, 29, 102, 171, 173, 252, 257, 339, 544; X, 3, 76, 164, 183, 435, 445, 478, 549; XIIIb, 127, 138; Sisters must regard sick persons as lords and masters, IX, 97; X, 215, 268; see Jesus Christ in them, X, 101, 268, 545; have nothing in view but God, X, 541; avoid indiscreet zeal, X, 539; or anything contrary to obedience, X, 272–74; virtues Sisters must practice when with patients, X, 267–68, 270, 545–46; XIIIb, 135; need for well-trained Sisters, II, 176–77; Sisters requested for Poland, IV, 63. See also **Illness**, **Poor**.

Saint Vincent wants Sisters to learn how to teach school, I, 426; IX, 6, 36; allows them to go to Ursulines for preparation, I, 427; Sisters teach school, IX, 381, 392, 435–36; X, 261, 456, 557; XIIIb, 268; for little girls, IX, 36, 174, 176, 432; for poor children only, IX, 467; X, 118; why boys are excluded, XIIIb, 285–88; refuse to take boys sent to them to be punished, IV, 455; Particular Rules for school Sisters, X, 526, 554–55; Sisters teach catechism and Christian morality, IX, 467; XI, 173; even to adults, XIIIb, 365; schools in Paris, II, 600; III, 60; in Chars, XIIIb, 356, 358; in Fontenay-aux-Roses, II, 392; in La Chapelle, II, 186; in Maule, X, 470; in Nanterre, IX, 435; in Nanteuil-le-Haudoin, II, 110; in Narbonne, VIII, 379; in Richelieu, I, 596; in Saint-Germain-en-Laye, I, 495; in Saint-Fargeau, VII, 64; at Saint-Laurent, near Paris, I, 502; II, 601; III, 61; in Sedan, II, 181; in Serqueux, V, 220; in Warsaw, V, 377, 389; difficulties in serving in hospitals, IV, 440–41.

Assistance for poor persons in ravaged, ruined countryside: see ***Étampes, Saint-Étienne-à-Arnes***; for poor refugees in Paris, IV, 396, 399, 401; taking boarders is contrary to custom of Company, VII, 65; XIIIb, 348, 372; Council decides that boarders may no longer be accepted, XIIIb, 288–92; exception is made; unpleasantness follows; better to have kept Rule, XIIIb, 303–04; Saint Vincent is hesitant about admission of boarders in Cahors house, VIII, 2; permits Sisters to wash church linens, XIIIb, 376–77; handwork, X, 525; Sisters are called by God to carry out ministries everywhere, X, 105.

Hospitals: public hospitals: see ***Angers, Bernay, Châteaudun, Hôtel-Dieu de Paris, Nantes, Saint-Denis***; military hospitals: see ***Calais, Châlons-sur-Marne, La Fère, Montmédy, Rethel, Sainte-Menehould, Sedan, Warsaw***; hospital for convicts: see **Galley Convicts**; children's hospitals: see ***Foundlings***; for elderly: see ***Nom-de-Jésus Hospice***; for charity cases: see ***General Hospital***; for mentally ill: see ***Petites-Maisons***; orphanages: see ***Cahors, Étampes, Bicêtre***.

Conference on Preservation of the Company, IX, 536–48; nature, direction, organization of Company: beautiful name of Daughters of Charity, X, 368, 379; XIIIb, 126, 137; signifies Daughters of God, III, 181; IX, 13, 23, 44, 342, 412; X, 103, 105, 521; people gave them this name, IX, 44; X, 379; also known as "Servants of the Poor of the Charity," IX, 256; XIIIb, 142, 146, 232–33, 236; name should keep them humble, XIIIb, 127, 138; Saint Vincent calls them women wearing poor headdress, I, 503; IX, 17; prefers, out of humility, to call them "Sisters" rather than "my daughters"; invites Saint Louise to do same, II, 164.

Company is confraternity, II, 602–03; III, 62; IX, 256; X, 83; XIIIb, 120, 123, 132–33, 142, 146, 225, 228, 230–32, 236–38; composed of unmarried young women and widows, IX, 256; X, 95; XIIIb, 120, 123, 134, 145–46, 225, 230–31; term "confraternity" is repugnant to some Sisters, V, 413; VII, 456; Saint Vincent has never admitted married women, VII, 218; recruits should always come from modest condition, IX, 473; X, 288; XIIIb, 372–73; Daughters of Charity are not nuns because not cloistered, V, 413; VII, 64; VIII, 277; IX, 432, 520; X, 522, 527, 530; XIIIb, 251; notes on their manner of living sent to Fr. Portail, II, 664; women of parish, VIII, 277; X, 530–32.

Archbishop of Paris declares Daughters of Charity dependent on him; delegates powers of Superior to Saint Vincent, XIIIb, 133; Saint Louise is upset by this dependence and limited delegation, III, 132; Queen Anne of Austria petitions him to name, in perpetuity, priests of Congregation of the Mission as Superiors General of Daughters of Charity, XIIIb, 141–42; Saint Louise expresses this desire, III, 255–56; IV, 225; Saint Vincent does same, V, 229–30; while maintaining Company in dependence on Archbishops of Paris, Cardinal de Retz delegates power of Superior to Saint Vincent and, after him, to Superiors General of the Mission, XIIIb, 146; Saint Vincent takes title of Director of Daughters of Charity, designates Saint Louise as "Directress," II, 2, 9, 11; Superioress depends in all things on Superior General of the Mission for government of Company, X, 95; Directors of Company, XIIIb, 124, 134: see **Portail**, **Dehorgny**; spiritual direction of Daughters of Charity belongs to Priests of the Mission, VIII, 270, 276–79; XII, 76–77; XIIIa, 389.

Saint Vincent long wondered whether it was better to take Superioress of Daughters of Charity from among Ladies, or from Daughters; why he chose second solution, V, 229; X, 580; office and duties of Superioress of Company, X, 95, 592–93; XIIIb, 123, 134, 323; Saint Vincent names Marguerite Chétif to succeed Saint Louise, X, 594; her election, XIIIa, 196, 201; **Officers**: see this word; Sister Servants: see also **Superiors**; Saint Vincent thinks Sisters should be changed frequently, V, 246, 260–61; XIIIb, 356; never to send a Sister alone to distant mission, II, 179.

Seminary (novitiate): I, 327; Saint Vincent suggests opening seminary of Daughters of Charity in rural area, XIIIb, 338–39, 343; importance of duty of Directress; choice of

Julienne Loret, XIIIb, 294–95; Directress must be woman of prayer and teach new arrivals to make prayer well, IV, 53; XIIIb, 302.

Qualities of postulants: V, 628; VI, 211–12; VII, 224; XIIIb, 293, 334, 370; theoretically, servants are not refused, II, 166; III, 316; V, 589, 621, 633; VII, 65; IX, 155, 358; XII, 35; nor, in certain cases, nuns who have left their Community, I, 305, 307; V, 10–11; IX, 144; XIIIb, 311–12; members of Third Order, I, 224; women who had been foundlings, XIIIb, 353; widows with young children are to be refused, I, 224; married women, VII, 218; epileptics, XIIIb, 269–70; infirm and the sick, XIIIb, 317–18, 348–49; nuns who were long in Community, XIIIb, 311; no dowry asked of postulants, simply money for first dress, X, 288; XIIIb, 372.

Saint Louise wants King to prevent Sisters from returning to world, VI, 286; those becoming infirm while working in Company are not to be sent away, XIIIb, 365; purging Company of unsuitable Sisters is necessary, VIII, 350–51; X, 206–09, 211, 245–47, 297, 349–52; thank God for purging Company, III, 473; departures should not be surprising, IX, 46; praise God for this, III, 215.

Sources of revenue for Company: X, 552; XIIIb, 374; Saint Vincent says Mass for Company on twenty-fifth of each month, VIII, 235–36; reflections of Saint Louise on Company, IV, 224–25, 276.

Perfection of Daughters of Charity: every Company has particular spirit, IX, 361, 457–58; X, 101–02; Daughters of Charity must not envy nuns of other Communities, nor be influenced by them, IX, 458–59; virtues especially suitable to them: virtues of young country women, IX, 66–77, 473; charity, humility, simplicity, IX, 465–78; X, 286; humility, charity, obedience, patience, X, 415, 418–32; charity, humility, imitation of Jesus Christ, X, 105–06; humility, obedience, detachment from creatures, modesty, X, 530–32; Daughters of Charity obliged to greater perfection than nuns, X, 116–18, 529; even though their state is lower, X, 77; in state of perfection, IX, 13; no other practice than penance and mortification, IX, 139; advice Saint Vincent proposes Saint Louise give to Sisters, I, 223; qualities necessary for Sisters sent to new establishments, IX, 204; XIIIb, 313–18; Saint Louise proposes document to Vincent concerning spiritual means for consolidating Company, VIII, 167.

How Sister Servants should act with Sister companions and vice-versa: see **Superiors**; Sister companions among themselves: see also **Charity**; older with younger and visa-versa, IX, 45, 181; X, 24, 38, 40, 64, 73, 94, 228, 298; XIIIb,

350; duties of sick Sisters; duties toward sick Sisters: see also **Illness**; contacts of Sisters with Superiors in Paris: see also **Communication**, **Confession**, **Correspondence**; with clergy, IX, 241–42; X, 553; XIIIb, 125, 135, 280, 376–77; with confessors: see also **Confession**; with Missionaries, IV, 287; with physicians, IX, 96; X, 277–78: see also **Physicians (Doctors)**; with outsiders, X, 343–47; XIIIb, 126, 137; with important people, IX, 72; XIIIb, 278, 280, 303–04; with Ladies of Confraternities, IX, 198, 242, 527, 543; X, 277; Sisters owe edification to Ladies, X, 260, 450–51; obedience and respect, IX, 7, 96, 242, 258, 426; X, 255, 312, 550; XIIIb, 125, 135; letters shown to Sister Servant before opening them, IX, 512; X, 325; nothing asked, nothing refused, X, 241; more necessary to obey Superior than Ladies, IX, 62; some Ladies are difficult to please, XIIIb, 260.

Daughters of the Cross - Foundress asks Saint Vincent to help troubled Community, II, 253, 334–35; habit, X, 299; Sisters teach catechism successfully, XIIIb, 300, 366; other mentions, IV, 6; X, 466, 499: see also **Villeneuve** (Mme de).

Daughters of Inner Life of Mary - VIII, 473–74.

Daughters of Palais Royal - See **Hospitallers**.

Daughters of Providence - Purpose of Community, I, 161; II, 312; night vigils before Blessed Sacrament, IV, 500; indebted to Saint Vincent, I, 161; after death of Mlle de Pollalion, he calls meeting of wealthy Ladies to sustain Institute, VI, 549–52; other mention, XIIIb, 441.

Dauphiné, province of France - I, 419, 527; II, 272, 516; V, 369.

Daurat (Barthélemy), Rector of Soubirous - Episcopal synod of Cahors; appointed to committee to open seminary in Cahors, XIIIa, 309.

Dauteuil (Marthe), Daughter of Charity - Biographical data, III, 116; V, 4–5; stationed in Saint-Leu parish, assigned to Nantes, III, 116; V, 5, 33; IX, 430; at Saint-Paul parish, III, 117; sent to Nantes, IX, 430; but goes to Hennebont, V, 5, 33; mentioned at Council, XIIIb, 249.

Dauzenat (M.), chaplain of Duchesse d'Aiguillon, then Finance Minister of Cardinal Richelieu - Contacts with Saint Vincent, I, 436; XIIIa, 106; other mention, I, 434.

Daveroult (Pierre), Priest of the Mission - Biographical data, V, 61; VI, 444; VII, 2; VIII, 150; letters Saint Vincent writes him in Saintes, VII, 2; in Lisbon, VII, 615; mention of letters to Saint Vincent, VII, 2, 615; sent to Châlons, V, 61; in Saintes, V, 494, 625; VI, 444; VII, 2; ready to embark from Nantes for Madagascar, VII, 102, 104, 108; VIII, 157; ship captured, VIII, 183; disembarked in Portugal, VII, 239; Saint Vincent congratulates him; tells him he can return to Paris, VII, 616–17; in Saintes again, VIII, 150; sent to Madagascar, VIII, 554; leaves Paris, VIII, 185, 207, 555; at La Rochelle, attempting to embark, VIII, 219, 225, 229, 231, 241, 247, 249, 252, 256, 561–62; in harbor of Santa Cruz, VIII, 565; at Cape Verde, VIII, 290, 567; at Cape of Good Hope, VIII, 573, 585–86, 588; teaches philosophy to passenger, VIII, 580, 584; health, VIII, 582–84; on retreat, VIII, 587; preparations for departure for Netherlands, VIII, 588; return to France, VIII, 592–93. See also ***Madagascar***.

David (Antoine), in Argenteuil - XIIIb, 107.

David (Bro.) - In Bar in 1640, II, 76.

David (Jean), Priest of the Mission - Biographical data, IV, 425; XII, 413; name added to list of possible Missionaries to Madagascar, IV, 93; death in Étampes, IV, 425–26, 428, 429, 431, 452; mention of conference on his virtues, XII, 413.

David (Mlle), sister of Jean David - Saint Vincent announces brother's death, IV, 431; death of Mlle David; legacy for Sedan house, IV, 602.

David (Toussainte), Daughter of Charity - Biographical data, III, 396; VI, 339; letter to Saint Vincent, VI, 339; in Fréneville, III, 396; signs Act of Establishment, XIIIb, 227.

David, King of Judea - Biographical data, I, 314; VI, 623; IX, 6, 40, 253, 305, 481; X, 189; XI, *xvii*; XII, 45, 340, 395; XIIIa, 168, 469; XIIIb, 336–37; God raised him from lowly station, XI, 118–19; hermits and saints imitated him in morning prayer and meditation, III, 532; mention of what he said, X, 461; citations from Psalms, VIII, 375; IX, 360; X, 325, 472–73; XI, 179; XII, 33, 49, 197, 327; XIIIb, 356; mention of Book of Psalms, XI, 186.

Dax, town in Landes - Cathedral, VI, 106; Bishop: see Jacques **Desclaux**, Jean-Jacques **Dusault**; diocese in which Saint Vincent was born, XIIIa, 1–7, 10, 23, 25, 26, 45, 47, 71, 73, 76, 80, 96, 145, 214, 219, 228–30, 234–36, 238–40, 247, 250, 289, 297; other mentions, I, 10–15, 332; II, 57; IV, 467; VIII, 159; XI, *xviii*; XIIIa, 99, 100.

Death - Glory of dying, arms in hand, VIII, 293; XI, 366; Mary, model of resignation at death of loved ones, I, 328; death of person close to Company, XI, 89; VII, 437; how to mourn death of loved ones, I, 126, 328; Saint Vincent prepares Brother for death, XI, 129; informing Superior General when confrere dies, VIII, 469: see also **Deceased**.

De Bay - See **Baius**.

Deceased - Reasons for recalling virtues of deceased, I, 587; X, 512–13, 569; several low Masses more useful for deceased than one solemn service, VI, 544–45; prayers for deceased, II, 565, 569–70; III, 443; IV, 499; V, 226, 233, 237, 289, 330, 472; VI, 171–72, 177, 530, 535–36, 544–45; VII, 140, 234, 235–36, 515–16, 538, 541, 552–53, 566–67, 575, 583, 588, 591–92; VIII, 242, 244, 246, 254–55, 275, 288, 294, 312, 315, 322, 359, 371, 375, 393, 395–96, 403, 422, 563; XI, 342; conferences in local communities on deceased confreres, III, 32; conferences on confreres, XI, 351, 376–78; XII, 413, 414, 416, 427–30, 432–33, 436–38; on Saint Louise de Marillac, X, 569–82, 582–90; on deceased Sisters, IX, 64–66, 144–61, 433–49; X, 511–23, 541–44, 569–70; praise for deceased Sisters, IX, 361, 369, 460, 496, 537; X, 94, 109, 180–81, 270, 341, 388, 434, 569, 586.

Dedroit (M.), abbot of Mouzon; mention of note from Saint Vincent, V, 185.

Deffita (M.), lawyer at Parlement of Paris - Residence on rue de la Harpe in Paris, VIII, 203; taken as arbitrator by Mother Bollain, III, 529; one of Saint Vincent's advisors, V, 53; VII, 423; other mention, II, 478.

Deheaume (Pierre), Priest of the Mission - Biographical data, V, 456; VI, 3; VII, 412; en route for Turin, receives orders to stay in Lyons, V, 456–58; sent to Turin, V, 467–68, 477; in Turin, V, 481, 485, 502; unsatisfactory, V, 598, 611; change requested and decided, VI, 3, 31; assigned to Annecy, VI, 57, 72; leaves for Annecy, VI, 86; disagrees on union of Saint-Sépulcre with Annecy Seminary, VII, 411–12.

Dehères (M.), Intendant General for Justice in Touraine - Saint Vincent requests service of him, II, 661.

Deheuze (Clément), priest - Left destitute in Paris, XIIIa, 144.

Dehorgny (Jean), Priest of the Mission - Biographical data, I, 39; II, 10; III, 2; IV, 123; V, 1; VI, 158; VII, 28; VIII, 22; IX, 37; XI, 153; praise for him, II, 69; spirit of poverty, XI, 153; letters Saint Vincent writes him at Saint-Lazare, I, 476; in Rome, II, 491, 530, 540, 581, 582, 619; III, 39, 64, 110, 163, 187, 191, 318, 358; IV, 345, 359, 368, 391, 465, 586; in Genoa, IV, 132; in Richelieu, VIII, 151, 158, 165, 253; in Cahors, VIII, 270; letters to Saint Vincent, II, 72, 73; IV, 123; VIII, 164, 170; reference to letters from Saint Vincent, III, 2, 7, 150, 190, 193; mention of letters to Vincent, VIII, 158, 253; signs letter to Urban VIII asking approval of Congregation of the Mission, I, 39, 45, 47, 53; owes vocation as Missionary to Fr. du Coudray, II, 69; contacts with Saint Louise, I, 86, 121, 189, 502, 508, 548; II,

10; with Daughters of Charity, II, 49, 197, 206, 342; admonitor to Saint Vincent, IX, 37; Director of Internal Seminary, I, 422; in Toul, I, 438; in Paris, I, 476, 516, 583; health, I, 584, 588; Commander of Saint-Esprit in Toul, II, 40, 156, 477; III, 366–67; Fr. Jolly fills post in his place, V, 29, 153; Saint Vincent plans to send him to Lorraine for visitations, II, 69; in Saint-Mihiel, II, 72; in Bar-le-Duc, II, 73; returns to Paris, II, 82, 93; professor at Saint-Lazare, II, 97; in Richelieu, II, 112; at Saint-Lazare, II, 147, 218, 249, 419; has just made visitation of Alet, II, 211; and Annecy, II, 203, 214; Saint Vincent tells Superior in Luçon Fr. Dehorgny will make visitation there, II, 279; Superior at Bons-Enfants, II, 343.

At 1642 General Assembly, II, 343; XIIIa, 323, 396; on commission to examine Rules, II, 344; XIIIa, 326, 396; Second Assistant to Superior General, II, 344; XIIIa, 331; announcement of departure for visitation in Rome, II, 426; in Rome, II, 438, 460, 491; in Paris, II, 502, 505; Saint Vincent plans to send him to Rome again for visitation, II, 502, 507; journey to Rome, VIII, 22; in Rome again, II, 518, 523, 552–53, 652; III, 2, 7, 14, 26, 48, 58, 66, 150–51, 154, 247; giving mission near Rome, II, 530; named Superior of Rome house, II, 531, 537; VIII, 609; Saint Vincent reproaches him for disobedience, II, 619; works on Rules for Company, III, 83, 238; saint relieves him of office of Superior, III, 193; at his request, III, 374; writes him two letters to show poison of Jansenist doctrines, III, 318, 358; changed from Rome, III, 613; in Castiglione, IV, 123; in Genoa, IV, 132; expected in Paris; departure from Genoa, IV, 207, 214, 220; visit of cousin to Saint Lazare, IV, 133; member of 1651 General Assembly, XIIIa, 369, 372, 374, 383–84, 397; opinion on vows, XIIIa, 378, 383.

Superior in Rome, IV, 296, 371; VIII, 609; recalled to Paris, V, 48; at Saint-Lazare, V, 66–67; Superior at Bons-Enfants, V, 99, 148; VI, 158, 178, 570; VII, 28; VIII, 604; XI, 327; no longer able to preach, VI, 498; Saint Vincent considers sending him to Genoa, VI, 630; sent to Annecy to rectify blunders of Superior, VII, 97; wants to be relieved of parish of which he is titular, VII, 374; about to leave for visitations, VIII, 51, 64, 76; visitations in Le Mans, Richelieu, Saint-Méen, Tréguier, Nantes, Luçon, Saintes, Agen, La Rose, Cahors, VIII, 129–31, 150–51, 158, 164–65, 170, 172, 217, 221–22, 241, 253, 270, 285, 305, 561; goes to La Rochelle to see Missionaries going to Madagascar, VIII, 561; consulted by Saint Vincent, V, 146, 157; VII, 528; VIII, 422; chosen to succeed Fr. Portail as Director of Daughters of Charity, VIII, 352; Director of Sisters, VIII, 459, 495; X, 595; XIIIa, 193, 196; administers Last Sacraments to Saint Vincent, XIIIa, 203; assists him on death bed, XIIIa, 204, 205; after death of saint, XIIIa, 206;

letter of Fr. Cuissot to Fr. Dehorgny, XIIIa, 210; other mentions, IV, 347; V, 273, 314, 360; VIII, 428, 527, 599; XIIIa, 260, 262, 286. See also ***Rome***.

Dejan (Marguerite, Dame), wife of Nicolas Pichard - XIIIa, 317–320.

De Justificatione - Decree of Council of Trent, excerpt, III, 325–326.

Delabarre (Jean-François), Prior of Montmirail - Biographical data, I, 470; II, 545; other mentions, I, 475; II, 545.

Delacroix [**La Croix**] (Jeanne), Daughter of Charity, sister of Renée - Biographical data, III, 291; V, 220; VIII, 323; X, 218; in praise of her, XIIIb, 306; proposed for Saint-Laurent, III, 291; Sister Servant in Serqueux, V, 220; named Assistant to Saint Louise in 1651, XIIIb, 306; in 1657, X, 218; present at Council of Company, XIIIb, 307–08, 359; Saint Vincent writes to her in Châteaudun, where she is Sister Servant, to tell her of death of Saint Louise, VIII, 312; to inform her of money received for her, VIII, 323; to recall her to Paris, VIII, 362; mention of letter to Saint Vincent, V, 220.

Delacroix [**La Croix**] (Renée), Daughter of Charity, sister of preceding - Biographical data, V, 432; VI, 417; Saint Louise asks permission for her to make vows, VI, 417; Administrators of Nantes Hospital want to dismiss her, XIIIb, 328; recalled to Paris, V, 432.

Delaferté (Emmeric-Marc), Bishop of Le Mans - Sanctioned contract Congregation of the Mission, VIII, 613.

Delaforcade (M.), merchant in Lyons - Used by Saint Vincent and Missionaries to send money, letters, and packages, V, 121, 245, 272, 275, 638; VI, 99, 120, 258, 447, 496; VII, 49,104, 190, 211–12, 233, 242, 291, 312, 518, 521; VIII, 23, 58, 448, 475, 531; other mentions, V, 275, 457; VI, 391, 639.

De la fréquente Communion - Jansenist publication by Antoine Arnauld, III, 73, 321, 358, 359, 363–64; Bishop signed it without reading it, IV, 567.

De la grâce victorieuse - Jansenist publication to be condemned by Rome, IV, 584–85.

Delahaie (Fr.) - III, 473.

Delahaye (M.), Dean of Noyon - VIII, 123.

Delahaye (M.) - VIII, 499.

Delahodde (Fr.), chaplain at château de Chantilly - Contacts with Saint Vincent, V, 243; VII, 279; with Saint Louise, III, 470; V, 242, 332, 438.

Delaistre (Jean), Prior in Montmirail - XIIIb, 32.

Delaître (Cécile), Daughter of Charity - Conference on virtues; served poor in Saint-Laurent parish in Paris, IX, 438–39.

Delamare (Mlle) - I, 182.

Delapesse (Jean-Antoine), seminarian of the Mission - Biographical data, VIII, 422; in Le Mans; vows, VIII, 422.

Delaplace (Jean-Baptiste), Doctor of Sorbonne, Commendatory Abbot of Val-Richer - Biographical data, III, 334; dedicates *Exercices spirituels dans tous les temps de l'année* (*Spiritual Exercises According to the Liturgical Year*) to Saint Vincent, III, 334.

Delartigue (Grégoire), husband of Marie De Paul - Remembered in deed of gift and will of Saint Vincent, XIIIa, 76, 77, 99.

Delattre (Guillaume), Priest of the Mission - Biographical data, II, 322; III, 32; IV, 38; letters Saint Vincent writes him in Cahors, II, 631, 636, 645; III, 123; in Agen, III, 498, 567; reference to letter from Delattre to Saint Vincent, II, 645; entrance into Saint-Lazare, II, 322; prayerful and regular; less suited for external affairs; III, 267; Superior in Cahors, II, 636, 645; VIII, 610; in La Rose, III, 125; VIII, 606; Saint Vincent reproaches him for not acting with full confidence and submission to Alain de Solminihac, II, 632–33, 646–47; for not asking advice sufficiently, II, 636–38; for excessive practices of penance, III, 123–24; illness, II, 646; Solminihac asks that he be changed, III, 32, 84; question of putting him in charge of La Rose house, III, 81, 89; of Marseilles house, III, 267; no longer in Cahors, III, 340, 342; Superior in Agen, III, 372, 498; VIII, 616; influenced too much by malcontents, III, 498–99; advised not to take on too much, III, 499; falsely accused of impugning Jesuits, III, 567; business matter is settled out of court, XIIIa, 390; death; praise for him, IV, 38. See also ***Agen, Cahors***.

Delaunay (Christophe), Brother of the Mission - Biographical data, VI, 112; VII, 102; VIII, 183; XI, 337; praise for him, XI, 347; first departure for Madagascar, VI, 112, 124, 128; shipwreck, VI, 149–50, 159; VIII, 183; XI, 337, 340, 342, 347; volunteers to go again, XI, 374; in Le Mans, VII, 102; sails again, VII, 102, 104, 107; ship captured by Spaniards, VIII, 183; XII, 33; in Saintes, VII, 239, 257–58, 323; XII, 34; promised to Superior of Le Mans house, VII, 331; called to Paris, VII, 371.

Delbène (M.), father of Fr. Étienne - VIII, 179.

Deleau (Alexis), convict in Toulon - VII, 238.

Delespiney (Gabriel), Priest of the Mission - Biographical data, III, 449; IV, 15; VI, 27; VIII, 69; XI, 207; letters Saint Vincent writes him in Toul, III, 449; IV, 15, 19, 157, 222; in Marseilles, VIII, 135, 149, 161, 173, 215, 232, 236, 242, 248, 261, 265, 275, 286, 298, 308, 339, 348; reference to letters to Saint Vincent, VIII, 135, 242, 248–49, 261, 265, 275, 286, 298, 402; and from Saint Vincent, VIII, 360; Superior in Toul, VIII, 606; Director of Internal Seminary at Saint-Lazare, VI, 27; XI, 207, 272, 295; sent to Marseilles, VIII, 69, 319; replaced as Superior by Fr. Get, VIII, 273, 299, 303, 315; goes with Jacques Beaure to open mission in Vins, VIII, 320; other missions, VIII, 372, 376; Saint Vincent sends money for La Rue, captive in Algiers, VIII, 444–45; remains in Marseilles, VIII, 315–16, 356–57, 402, 537; Superior in Marseilles, VIII, 289, 328, 610; advises Saint Vincent on personnel, VIII, 360; discouraged, VIII, 339, 348; illness, VIII, 135, 161; suggested for Narbonne, XIIIa, 198; other mention, VIII, 321. See also ***Marseilles***.

Delestoile (Jean-Baptiste), Priest of the Mission - Biographical data, I, 542; II, 76; assists poor of Lorraine, I, 541–42.

Delêtre (M.) - IV, 464.

Délivrande (***Notre-Dame***), shrine in Calvados - Offered to Congregation of the Mission, VI, 377.

Delom (M.) - II, 451.

Delon (M.), lawyer in Joigny - XIIIb, 66.

Delorme (M.) - II, 182, 252.

Delorme (Pie), Brother of the Mission - Biographical data, V, 263; requested for Poland, V, 263; Saint Vincent leaves him with Superior of Troyes house, who claims he is indispensable, V, 367.

Deleuze (M.), Bailiff of Montmirail - IV, 513.

Delville (Guillaume), Priest of the Mission - Biographical data, II, 544; III, 76; IV, 312; V, 209; VI, 79; VII, 80; X, 183; XII, 432; letters Saint Vincent writes him in Montmirail, II, 544, 547, 553, 604; III, 76; in Fontaine-Essarts (Montmirail), II, 673; in Coulommiers, III, 249; in Montmirail, IV, 312, 326; in Arras, VI, 79, 102, 161, 174, 198, 211, 307, 340, 423, 546, 588, 609, 634; VII, 80; mention of letters to Saint Vincent, III, 76; VI, 424, 546, 588, 609.

Superior in Montmirail, VIII, 612; Superior in Crécy, VIII, 609; out giving missions, V, 209; in Arras, VI, 131, 419; success of missions, VI, 79; must give missions gratis, III, 250–51; Saint Vincent admonishes him for signing leases without consulting him, IV, 326; and for having précis of Institute published, VI, 198; Delville recruits vocations for Sisters and Missionaries, but not always with sufficient discernment, VI, 80, 161–62, 547–48, 588; solicitous for Charity and Sisters in Arras, VI, 114, 156, 162, 211–13, 307, 340, 589; VII, 80; X, 183; offers parish to Company, VI, 634; death, VII, 174, 176; mention of conference on his virtues, XII, 432. See also ***Crécy, Montmirail***.

Demasé [**Matsé**], René - Lawyer for Marthe Goupil, XII, 377–381.

Demeaulx (Aimé), Canon in Mâcon - XIIIb, 78.

Demeaulx (M.), Lieutenant for Criminal Affairs in Mâcon - XIIIb, 73, 78.

Demia (Charles) - Report of Saint Vincent's stay in Châtillon, XIIIa, 49, 57.

Demonchy (Nicolas), Priest of the Mission - Biographical data, IV, 321; V, 236; VI, 366; VII, 77; VIII, 11; X, 453; letters Saint Vincent writes to him in Toul, V, 236; VI, 366, 427; VII, 321; letters from Toul to Saint Vincent, V, 553, 618; mention of other letters to Vincent, VII, 321; Director of ordinands at Saint-Lazare, IV, 321, 341; Superior in Toul, VI, 533–34; VIII, 606; out giving missions, V, 553, 618; at Saint-Lazare on return from journey to Touraine, VI, 591; sent to Metz to prepare mission to be given by priests of Tuesday Conferences, VII, 77; contacts with Bossuet, VII, 85, 100; aids start of Metz mission, VII, 103; sent to Metz to help Daughters of Charity get established there, X, 453; called to Paris, VII, 321, 359; at Saint Vincent's deathbed, XIIIa, 205; other mentions, VIII, 11, 492; XIIIa, 206. See also ***Toul***.

Demoras [**Dumoras**] (Bertrande), mother of Saint Vincent - I, 15–17; XIIIa, 1.

Demortier (Raymond), Priest of the Mission - Biographical data, VI, 300; VII, 235; VIII, 87; assigned to Turin, VI, 308; in Turin, VI, 329, 351, 510; VII, 270; VIII, 87, 231; dimissorial letters, VII, 235; health, VII, 378; VIII, 110, 118, 535; Archbishop of Turin refuses to ordain him, VIII, 87.

Demousol (Nicolas), from Fulda in Prussia (Germany) - Seeks admission into Congregation of the Mission, VIII, 522.

Demurard (M.), seigneur de Saint-Julien - Saint Vincent asks him to forgive son, VII, 618.

Demyon (M.), brother-in-law of Marquis de Fabert - Saint Vincent sends him Lives of the Saints, IV, 165, 189; will look for an ivory crucifix for him, V, 156.

Denaups (Louis), Canon in Mâcon - XIIIb, 78.

Denaups (Noël), Archdeacon in Mâcon - XIIIb, 78.

Deniac (Marguerite), Superior of Daughters of Notre-Dame in Richelieu - Saint Vincent apologizes for being unable to assign Missionary to direct nuns, IV, 287.

Denis (Saint) - Dispositions necessary to receive Communion, III, 363; feast day, V, 451; office of Saint Denis, X, 472.

Denise (Bertrand), tenant of Philippe-Emmanuel de Gondi in Villepreux - I, 473.

Denmark - *Propaganda Fide* plans to ask Saint Vincent to send Missionaries to this country, V, 71; overrun by Protestantism, XI, 279, 318.

Denoual (Anne), Daughter of Charity - Biographical data, VIII, 166; X, 533; sent to Narbonne, VIII, 187; X, 533; XIIIb, 237; arrival, VIII, 166; Saint Vincent encourages her, VIII, 380; she asks to make vows, VIII, 470; signs attestation after reading Common and Particular Rules reviewed and arranged in order by Fr. Alméras, XIIIb, 206.

Denyse, Daughter of Charity - Raises objections at being placed in home of Duchesse d'Aiguillon, I, 322 - Named for Charity of Saint-Étienne-du-Mont, I, 451; other mentions, II, 425; IV, 24; V, 356.

Depagadoy (M.), secretary of Bishop of Tarbes - XIIIa, 2, 3.

Depaul (Bernard), brother of Vincent de Paul, in Pouy - I, 16, 291–92; XIIIa, 76, 99, 100.

Depaul (François), nephew of Saint Vincent - I, 16.

Depaul (Gayon, also known as Dominique or Menion), brother of Vincent and Bernard de Paul - I, 16, 291; XIIIa, 76, 77, 99, 100.

Depaul (Jean), father of Vincent - XIIIa, 1.

Depaul (Marie), sister of Vincent, Bernard, and Gayon de Paul, wife of Grégoire - I, 16; XIIIa, 76, 77, 99, 100.

Depaul (Marie), another sister of preceding - I, 16; XIIIa, 76, 77.

Depaul (Vincent), Saint - See **Vincent de Paul** (Saint).

Dephilmain [**Philmain**] (François), Priest of the Mission - Biographical data; in Sedan, II, 468, 541.

Derbaux (Sister), Visitandine - VI, 426.

Desagie (Pierre), Municipal Magistrate in Mâcon - XIIIb, 73, 76, 77.

De Sales (Francis), Saint - See **Francis de Sales** (Saint)

Des Anglois (Jean), convict in Toulon - VI, 102.

Desartes (Gabriel), Prior of Charity Hospital in Paris - XIIIa, 21–22.

Desbordes (M.), Vicomte de Soude, Comptroller - Biographical data, VII, 267; praise for him, XIIIa, 191; executor of Commander de Sillery's will, II, 134; Saint Vincent writes of loss of lawsuit relative to Orsigny farm, VII, 267; decision not to appeal verdict, VII, 422; regrets being unable to allow Lady to enter Visitation monastery, VIII, 153–54; opposed to M. Desbordes' assuming expense of feeding Missionaries giving mission, I, 421; contacts with Saint Louise, III, 519, 523; administrator of Quinze-Vingts Hospital, VIII, 424–25; other mention, IV, 422.

Desbordes (Mlle), Treasurer of Charity of Saint-Leu - I, 371, 384.

Desboys (Pierre), lawyer in Macon - XIIIb, 74, 76, 77.

Desbrosses (M.), of Marseilles - V, 192, 227, 245.

Deschamps (Adrien), settler in Madagascar - VI, 243.

Deschamps (Edme), Priest of the Mission - Biographical data, IV, 150; XII, 414; on list of possible Missionaries to Madagascar, IV, 93; in devastated regions; sends news to Saint Vincent, IV, 150; mention of a letter from Saint Vincent, IV, 150; in Étampes, IV, 426, 428; illness, death, eulogy, IV, 494–95; mention of conference on his virtues, XII, 414.

Des Chapelles (René), priest in Le Mans - V, 422.

Desclaux (Jacques), Bishop of Dax - Praise for him, II, 566; letters from Saint Vincent, III, 243; IV, 202; V, 97; VI, 105; lawsuit against his Canons, III, 243; desire to have Missionaries' house in diocese, III, 244; intention of removing Community of nuns from jurisdiction of Regulars, IV, 202–03; Saint Vincent dissuades him from going to Paris, V, 97; goes there later, V, 98; asks Rome for privilege of *Annates* to recover cost of building cathedral, VI, 106; attitude regarding Jansenism, IV, 179, 202; takes interest in relatives of Saint Vincent, XI, 298; other mention, IV, 467.

Desclaux (Pierre), confessor of Cardinal Richelieu and brother of preceding - I, 346; XIIIa, 124.

Descortils [**Descourtils**] (Adrien), monk of old Saint-Lazare - I, 135; XIIIa, 263.

Descroizilles (Jean), Priest of the Mission - Biographical data; sent to Le Mans, VI, 124; VII, 371; VIII, 226; in Le Mans; incapable of teaching higher classes, VI, 151; insists on return to Paris; very eager to study; Saint Vincent prefers that he remain in Le Mans, VI, 422, 560–61, 584; VII, 371, 495, 535; steps taken to obtain dimissorial, VIII, 226.

Descroizilles (Fr.) - Saint Vincent requests parish for him, VIII, 492.

Desdames (Guillaume), Priest of the Mission - Biographical data, IV, 16–17; V, 50; VI, 3–4; VII, 9; VIII, 88; XI, 323; letters from Saint Vincent, VI, 318, 336, 347, 566; VII, 82, 172, 274, 415, 474, 480, 490, 506, 531, 553, 579, 625; VIII, 88, 98, 145, 193, 229, 250, 267, 279, 300, 314, 325, 353, 367, 394, 508; mention of other letters, V, 51, 110; VI, 267, 271, 346, 576; VIII, 163; Saint Vincent mentions forwarding letter to him, VIII, 420; mention of letters to Saint Vincent, IV, 16; V, 49–50, 238, 491, 609; VI, 55, 347, 360; VII, 172, 361, 415, 474, 480, 506, 529–31, 553. 579, 625; VIII, 88, 98, 105, 145, 193, 229, 251–52, 267, 279, 314, 353, 394, 508; XI, 357–58; XII, 61; concern of Saint Vincent that Fr. Desdames is not receiving his letters, VIII, 280.

In Toul, IV, 15; sent to Warsaw, IV, 251; XIIIa, 398; parish confided to him in Poland, IV, 289; assists plague-stricken, IV, 493; administers Last Sacraments to Fr. Lambert, IV, 538; Superior in Warsaw, VIII, 617; in Grodno, IV, 572; knowledge of Polish, V, 81, 118, 402; XII, 25; in Warsaw, IV, 292, 329; V, 84, 100, 106, 114, 142, 196, 313, 335, 352, 388, 474, 479, 491, 535, 574; VI, 3–6, 35, 55, 362, 464, 526, 539, 556, 620; VII, 9, 68, 90, 92, 108, 128, 155, 264; XI, *xxx*; about to begin missions, V, 201; out giving missions, V, 214, 229, 234, 238; named Consultor, V, 348; Saint Vincent allows him to live in Sokólka, if Queen so desires, V, 362; danger faced from famine, plague, capture of Warsaw by Swedes, VI, 91, 109, 112, 124, 128, 140, 347, 352, 393, 421, 447, 451, 453, 470, 472, 489, 492, 502; XI, *xxx*, 308, 323, 329, 333, 357, 364–65, 368; XII, 61; calumniated before Bishop of Poznań [Posen], VI, 298; health, VI, 4, 5, 34, 38, 41, 42, 43, 55, 144, 157, 159, 384; VIII, 252, 267; XI, 346; his brother, VI, 348; praise for him, VII, 361; XI, 368; Superior of Mission in Poland on death of Fr. Ozenne, VII, 275; VIII, 617; named to succeed Fr. Ozenne as Pastor of Holy Cross, VII, 277; enthusiasm for missions, VII, 474; journey to Krakow, VII, 481, 490, 531; Director of Daughters of Charity in Poland, VII, 275; XIIIb, 239; requests special headdress for them, XIIIb, 366; other mention, VII, 300. See also ***Poland, Warsaw***.

Des Essarts (Marie) - Member of Charity of Montmirail, XIIIb, 32.

Des Essarts (Mme) - Biographical data, IV, 327; looks after affairs of Poland in France, IV, 327, 397, 411, 612, 613; V, 108, 183, 356, 572; VI, 33, 91, 94, 98, 297, 556.

Desfodtq (M.), seminarian of the Mission - Unsuitable for Company, VI, 588.

Desfriches (François), Brother of the Mission - Biographical data; death, XI, 122.

Desgordes (Mme) - Requests tutor for son; accepts M. Le Noir, III, 75.

Desgordes (M.), son of Mme Desgordes - Saint Vincent sends him name of tutor, III, 75.

Des Hugonières (Philibert), of Châtillon-les-Dombes - XIIIb, 4, 21.

Desire - Every intense desire comes from the devil, VII, 434; even if desire seems good, it does not follow that it is from God, I, 111.

Des Isles (Nicolas), author of an *Apologie* - Aptitudes for debate, XII, 240.

Des Jardins (Georges), Priest of the Mission - Biographical data, IV, 493; V, 556; VI, 366; VII, 1; VIII, 137; letters Saint Vincent writes him in Toul, V, 556; VI, 532, 591; VII, 1, 51; in Narbonne, VIII, 365; mention of letter to Saint Vincent, VII, 1; sets out for Narbonne, VIII, 137; in Étampes, IV, 493; Superior in Toul, VI, 366, 427; VIII, 606; health, V, 556; Superior in Narbonne, VIII, 137, 144, 170; Saint Louise receives news of him there, VIII, 167; in Narbonne, VIII, 381, 470–71, 522, 619; Saint Vincent tells Fr. Get to write to him, VIII, 387. See also ***Toul, Narbonne***.

Des Jonchères (Coupperie), priest in Nantes - Question of naming him confessor of Daughters of Charity at Nantes Hospital, III, 9, 18, 21, 22; XIIIb, 261; accepts this ministry, III, 27; contacts with Sisters, III, 178, 184, 185, 216–17; letters in which he is mentioned, III, 167; IV, 298; would like Saint Vincent to stay at his house while in Nantes, III, 423; Saint Vincent consults him, III, 427; des Jonchères offers Daughters of Charity establishment in Vannes diocese, III, 428.

Des Jonchères (M.), Judge of presidial court of Nantes, brother of preceding - III, 427.

Des Jonchères (Mlle), sister of preceding - Praise for her, III, 9–10; other mention, III, 21.

Des Jonchères (Mme), mother of preceding - Fr. Lambert is lodged in her house, III, 217.

Desjours (Laurent) - Member of Charity of Joigny, XIIIb, 66.

Deslauriers (M.) - See **Chanoine** (Clément).

Deslions (Jacques), seminarian of the Mission - Biographical data, V, 605–06; VI, 579; VII, 46; *extra tempora* for ordination requested of Rome, VI, 579; VII, 46; all going well for him, V, 605.

Des Lions [Deslyons] (Jean), Dean of Senlis - Biographical data, II, 203; IV, 145; VI, 44; letters from Saint Vincent, II, 203; VI, 59, 132, 152, 167, 290; reference to letter sent to Rome, VI, 168; draft of letter to Pope, V, 645; considered for bishopric of Babylon, IV, 145, 148; Jansenist leanings; steps taken by Bishop of Pamiers to lead him back to right path, VI, 43–44; measures taken by Saint Vincent, VI, 61, 132, 152, 168, 290–95; other mentions, VI, 61, 62.

Deslions (Mlle), of Arras - Gives hospitality to Fr. Delville, VI, 549, 589, 610; other mention, VII, 364.

Desloriers (M.), convict in Toulon - VIII, 513.

Desmares (Toussaint-Guy-Joseph), Priest of the Oratory - Deputy sent to Rome by Jansenists to support cause, IV, 581, 594.

Demarest (Marguerite) - Member of Charity of Paillart, XIIIb, 48.

Desmarets [Desmaretz] (Jean), seigneur of Saint-Sorlin - Biographical data, V, 365; VI, 259; VII, 3; VIII, 243; Intendant of house of Duc de Richelieu; contacts with Saint Vincent, V, 365; VI, 259, 595, 627; VII, 4, 81, 93; VIII, 243; other mention, VII, 3.

Desmarets [Desmaretz] (Messrs), sons of Jean Desmarets - In army; Saint Vincent sends Fr. Cabel to see them, VI, 595; VII, 3.

Desmay (Jacques), Dean of Chapter of Écouis - XIIIa, 26–30.

Desmoulins (Fr.), Priest of the Oratory - Relates how Saint Vincent established Charity of Mâcon, XIIIb, 70, 71.

Desmoulins (M.), settler in Madagascar - V, 285, 306.

Desnotz (Jean), notary in Paris - XIIIa, 263, 271, 281, 284, 289, 476.

Des Noyelles (Philippe), Priest of the Mission - Biographical data; in Saintes, II, 659; III, 11–12; does not get along with Superior; lives disordered life; considered for Richelieu, III, 12; for Saint-Méen, III, 12, 31; sent to La Rose, III, 57; other mention, III, 82.

Desnoyers (M.), administrator of Sainte-Reine Hospital - Regrets inability to be of service to Saint Vincent, VIII, 388.

Des Noyers (Pierre), secretary of Queen of Poland - Biographical data, IV, 63–64; in Poland, IV, 63; expected in France, V, 366, 377, 378; in France, V, 395; departure for Poland, V, 450; in Poland, V, 491; quoted, VI, 91; other mention, V, 164.

Despennes (M.), in Marseilles - VII, 392.

Despinal (Marie), Daughter of Charity - Death, II, 650; praise for her, XIIIb, 260.

Desportes (Marquis) - Difficulties of obtaining ecclesiastical pension for him, III, 391.

Despréaux (M.) - VI, 305.

Desquenoy (Antoinette) - Member of Charity of Paillart, XIIIb, 48.

Des Rochers (Mlle), of Nantes - Welcomes Saint Louise into her home, III, 9.

Des Roches-Chamian - Prior of small priory offered to Richelieu Missionaries, I, 418, 438.

Des Vergnes (M.), Officialis of Cahors - Letter from Saint Vincent, III, 473; VIII, 617; mention of letters from Alain de Solminihac, IV, 124, 141, 272–73; Solminihac is unhappy with him, IV, 505; other mentions, IV, 153, 223.

Desvignes (Jean), Municipal Magistrate in Mâcon - XIIIb, 73.

Desvignes (M.), priest - IV, 493.

Detachment - Conferences, IX, 128–43; XII, 17–23; mention of other conferences, XII, 427, 432; detachment from relatives, friends, all things, IX, 10–11; Rule of Daughters of Charity, X, 126, 552; detachment is difficult, X, 133; fruit of love of God, XII, 95; example of Saint Vincent. See also ***Orsigny*, *Saint-Lazare***; example of Comte de **Rougement**: see this word; other mention, I, 67. See also **Attachments**, **Confidence in God**, **Disinterestedness**, **Indifference**, **Poverty**.

Detraction - Vice must be banished to preserve union in Company, XII, 91. See **Scandal**.

Deucoras (M.), in Mâcon - XIIIb, 78.

Deure (M.), supplier of purgative mineral water - I, 79, 115, 139; II, 592, 626.

De Vaux (Anne), Daughter of Charity - Signs attestation after reading Common and Particular Rules reviewed and arranged in order by Fr. Alméras, XIIIb, 206; other mention, XIIIb, 228.

Devil - Before thinking something is action of devil, find out if events have natural cause, VI, 97; see also **Possession** (Diabolical); Saint Vincent urges Saint Louise to ignore devil, I, 62; demon's actions and power, III, 138–39; has only power one gives him, I, 150; his power felt in Joigny, I, 179; must be countered with humility, I, 526; his impulses disturb because of their violence, IV, 569; does all he can to keep us from meditation, IX, 29; seeks only discord and disunion, IX, 80; is pleased with disunion among us, IX, 100; the woman who resists temptation hurls him into hell, IX, 281; seduces us, making evil appear good, X, 8; would be better than us if he had graces we receive, X, 352–53; XI, 47–48; carries his own hell everywhere, X, 565; transforms self into angel of light to give inspirations seeming to come from God, XI, 91; author of vices and father of false teachings, XII, 254–55.

Devotion - See **Piety**.

Dictation - Saint Vincent does not want professors to dictate in class, II, 240, 249, 262–66, 269–72; advises them to explain familiarly an author, II, 266, 608; reprimands Nicolas Lapostre for dictating at Tréguier Seminary, VI, 64.

Didier (Claude), pharmacist in Algiers - Helps Missionary get to the sick, III, 305–08, 310.

Didolet (Christophe), seminarian of the Mission - Biographical data, VII, 352; VIII, 63; praise for him, VII, 352; sent to Agen, VII, 352, 432; in Agen, VII, 605; Saint Vincent's evaluation, VIII, 63.

Die, town in Drôme - Bishopric of Die offered to Louis de Chandenier, V, 369.

Dieppe, town in Seine-Maritime - III, 330, 540, 597–98; V, 302, 310, 405; VI, 12, 225; VIII, 185, 566–67.

Dieppe (Jean), Priest of the Mission - Biographical data, III, 389; IV, 25; sent to Algiers, III, 389, 414; death, eulogy, III, 445–47, 451–52; Superior in Algiers, VIII, 615; other mentions, IV, 25; V, 90.

Dieu (M.) - I, 450.

Dieu (Pierre), Pastor in Courboin - XIIIb, 92, 93.

Diharse (Salvat), Bishop of Tarbes - Conferred on Saint Vincent every Order except priesthood, XIIIa, 1–4, 6.

Dijon, town in Côte-d'Or - Oratory of Dijon, VII, 232, 521; other mentions, V, 408; VII, 345.

Dimissorial Letters - Opposed by Bishops, Saint Vincent hesitates to ask Rome for privilege of giving dimissorials to seminarians of Congregation, VI, 364; requests privilege, I, 518; II, 191; III, 611; VIII, 39.

Dinet (Gaspard), Bishop of Mâcon - XIIIb, 67, 69–70, 75.

Dinet (Jacques), Jesuit - Biographical data, II, 427; IV, 178; Louis XIII tells him to ask Saint Vincent for list of priests worthy of episcopate, II, 427; Fr. Dinet assists dying Louis XIII, II, 435–36; Saint Vincent asks again for copies of supplication to Pope of French episcopate opposed to Jansenism, IV, 178; confessor of Louis XIV after death of Fr. Charles Paulin, IV, 563; other mention, XIIIa, 339.

Dinet (Jean), Canon of Mâcon - XIIIb, 78.

Dinet (Louis), Bishop of Mâcon, nephew of Gaspard Dinet - Biographical data, IV, 84; resigns bishopric in favor of Louis de Chandenier, IV, 84, 95; approves Charity of Mâcon, XIIIb, 69, 71, 77.

Direction (Spiritual) - See **Communication**, **Confession**.

Discipline - Saint Vincent has dozen disciplines bought, I, 148; allows Saint Louise this act of penance, I, 80; allows his priests as well, III, 123–24; forbids it for Daughters of Charity who have not asked permission, IX, 514; X, 136; use of discipline among Carmelites, Dominican nuns, X, 80; and Visitandines, X, 80, 318; Saint Francis de Sales, Charles V of Spain used discipline, X, 319.

Discretion - See **Secrecy**, **Confidentiality**.

Disinterestedness - Saint Vincent thinks Daughters of Charity should not ask lady for money owed, XIIIb, 303. See also **Temporal Goods**, **Detachment**, **Missions**, **Indifference**.

Detraction - See **Scandal**.

Dissay, village in Vienne - Bishop of Poitiers has country house there; gives hospitality to Saint-Cyran, I, 392, 394; XIIIa, 124, 133.

Dissimulation - See **Secrecy**.

Distractions in Prayer - Holiest persons have them, IX, 172.

Distrust of self - Source of confidence in God, III, 143.

Divine Office - Conference, XII, 264–77; text of Rule of Missionaries, XII, 264; praising God is principal act of religion, XII, 265–66; imitates angels in heaven, XII, 267; one verse capable of sanctifying soul, XII, 266; example of priests of Tuesday Conferences, V, 196; XII, 269, 348; of Canons of Notre-Dame, XII, 273; of Fr. Pillé, II, 369; of many lay people, V, 196; reciting Roman Breviary, XII, 268; in common, even when giving missions, XII, 268, 270; with attention, care, devotion, XII, 267–70, 272; pretexts alleged for being dispensed from reciting it in common, XII, 272–75; in several houses, Missionaries must recite Office in choir, with chant, V, 195; XII, 270; obligation for all houses to solemnize feast of patron of parish, with octave and commemoration in Office, V, 87; Daughters of Charity assist at Offices of parish church, X, 530, 531. See also ***Saint-Lazare***.

Divisions - Mention of conference, XII, 436.

Dizes (M.) - Preparatory retreat for entrance into Internal Seminary, VI, 615.

Doctorate - Saint Vincent does not have doctorate, I, 10; dismisses from Company Missionary who received doctorate without permission, V, 397.

Doctors - See **Physicians**.

Documents - Saint Vincent tells Superior of Genoa house that official Community documents are to be signed by Superior, not by Procurator, VII, 439.

Doignon (M.) - I, 316.

Doinel (Geneviève), Daughter of Charity - Biographical data, IV, 116; sent to Hennebont, IV, 116; IX, 430; unwell, II, 654; IV, 180; in Hennebont, XIIIb, 309; in Paris, XIIIb, 227; deposition at process of beatification of Saint Vincent, III, 263.

Dol, town in Ille-et-Vilaine - VII, 252.

Dolce (Jean), Bishop of Bayonne - Bishop of Dax promises to sign petition against Jansenism, IV, 179; Saint Vincent awaits signature, IV, 202; services rendered Missionaries by Prelate on their way to Bayonne, VII, 258, 287, 616; other mention, X, 317.

Dolivet (Julien), Priest of the Mission - Biographical data, VII, 45; VIII, 36; in Agde; health, VII, 172; Fr. Get offers to take him with him to rest in Marseilles, VII, 197–98; at request of Saint Vincent, VII, 190; in Marseilles, VII, 207–08, 223; in Agde; fervor and regularity, VIII, 36; sent to Narbonne to give missions, VIII, 137, 144.

Domestics - See **Servants**.

Domfront-en-Champagne, village in Sarthe - Confraternity of Charity, VII, 622.

Dominic (Saint) - Worked for conversion of Albigensians, I, 526; XI, 273; God inspired him with Rosary, X, 498; devil appears to him, X, 490; other mention, IX, 194.

Dominican Friars - Teach people to pray Rosary, X, 498; dissension among branches of Dominicans of Congregation of Saint-Louis in France, II, 561; III, 383, 386; object to authorizing in parishes union of Confraternity of Rosary and Confraternity of Charity, I, 288; II, 28; assist devastated regions around Paris during Fronde, IV, 520; Dominican martyred by Turks, XIIIb, 264–65; reformed convent in Paris, II, 517, 519; convent in Cahors, II, 616, 681; Dominicans in Poland, V, 362; in Persia, II, 459; other mentions, I, 175; XI, 195; XII, 303. See also **Turco** (Fr.).

Dominican Nuns - See **Saint Thomas Aquinas**.

Donchery, town near Sedan - Fr. Berthe returns to parents' home there, III, 115; Saint Vincent prevents town government from being given to Huguenot, IV, 195; other mention, VIII, 304.

Donjon [**Donion**] (Marie), Daughter of Charity - Biographical data, X, 596; proposed as Officer, X, 596.

Donyon (M.) - VII, 536.

Doorkeepers, of Saint Lazare - Brother doorkeepers, I, 478; bound to confidentiality; how to welcome visitors, XI, 188–89.

Dordrecht, town in Holland - VIII, 596.

Doreau (Anne-Gabrielle), Visitation nun in Nevers - Writes to Saint Vincent about ransom of slave, VIII, 502.

Dorgon (Richard), Canon of Verdun - Letter to Saint Vincent, I, 152; dedication of *Le Bon Laboureur* to Saint Vincent, I, 152–54; asks saint to edit second edition, I, 154.

Doronce (M.), assistant to Officialis of Cahors - IV, 273.

Dorotheus (Saint) - Made known temptations to Superior, XII, 291, 294.

Douai, town in Nord - VI, 114.

Douay (M. de), Licentiate in theology - Proposed as Principal for philosophers of Collège de Navarre; Saint Vincent recommends him, II, 649.

Doublard (Fr. de la Bouverie), priest in Angers - Contacts with Saint Vincent, VI, 409, 412, 526, 553; VII, 406.

Doublard (Pierre), merchant, "Father of the Poor" in Angers - XIIIb, 116, 118, 119.

Doudin (Henri), of Mâcon - XIIIb, 74.

Douelle [**Duelska**] (Françoise), Daughter of Charity - Biographical data, VII, 175; VIII, 280; arrival in Warsaw, IV, 519; acts as bond between two companions, IV, 541; letter from the three Sisters to Saint Vincent, IV, 575; Saint Louise considers her less open and less stable than Madeleine Drugeon, V, 214; separated from two companions because of disunion, VII, 175; Saint Vincent advises separation again, VII, 416; advises sending her back to France, VII, 626; Queen puts her to work serving poor, VIII, 280; other mention, XIIIb, 228.

Doujat (Catherine), wife of Jean Doujat - Letter from Saint Vincent, V, 7.

Doujat (Jean), Councillor at Parlement of Paris - Saint Vincent recommends business to him, V, 7.

Dourdan, town in Essonne - Saint Vincent plans to go to place near there, I, 378.

Doutrelet (Michel), seminarian of the Mission - Biographical data, III, 371; sent to Rome, XIIIa, 359–60; does not wish to renew vows, III, 372; behavior leaves room for improvement, III, 510–11; other mention, III, 373.

Douxlieux (Étienne), slave in Algiers - V, 35, 325, 355.

Dover, town in England - V, 27, 48, 50.

Dowley [du Loeus] (James), Irish priest - Biographical data, V, 158; letter from Saint Vincent, V, 158; steps taken to establish house in Spain, VII, 292, 400; steps to have priest enter Congregation of the Mission, VII, 327; letters regarding Spain, VII, 343, 391, 433; question of becoming Bishop in Ireland, VII, 345.

Doziet (Arnault), guarantor of Saint Vincent's financial status - XIIIa, 9, 11, 14.

Drago (Antoine), Priest of the Mission - Biographical data; Saint Vincent explains vow of poverty, IV, 542.

Dreux, town in Eure-et-Loir - Coaches, III, 529; mission given by priests of Tuesday Conferences, VIII, 366, 367.

Drogo (M.), in Poland - IV, 289.

Dropsy (Edema) - Cure for this condition, I, 508.

Drouard (Bertrand), Intendant for Duchesse d'Aiguillon - Biographical data, V, 17; VI, 550; suggestion concerning chaplains for Hôtel-Dieu, I, 349; trip to Aiguillon, III, 125; present at meeting held after death of Mlle de Pollalion about means of supporting Daughters of Providence, VI, 550; other mentions, III, 254, 606; IV, 167; V, 17.

Droue (Remi), galley convict in Toulon - VIII, 528.

Drouin (Jean), Seneschal of Richelieu - VIII, 306.

Drugeon (Madeleine), Daughter of Charity - Arrival in Warsaw, IV, 519; VI, 298; does not get along with companion, IV, 541; letter to Saint Vincent on state of ministries, IV, 575; Saint Louise has greater confidence in her frankness and stability than in those of Françoise Douelle, V, 214; good schoolteacher, V, 389; Saint Vincent does not want Françoise to associate with her, VII, 416; puts Marguerite Moreau under her guidance, IX, 464; other mentions, VI, 298; XIIIb, 228.

Drugeon (Sébastien), Brother of the Mission - Biographical data, III, 26.

Drunkenness - See **Intoxication**.

Dubarat (Victor), Pastor of Saint-Martin in Pau - Author of *Bétharram et le Mont-Valérien*, VII, 459.

Dubazzione (M.) - VIII, 491.

Dubignon (M.) - VIII, 538.

Dubois (Augustin), of Courboin - XIIIb, 93.

Dubois (Denis) - Member of Charity of Courboin, XIIIb, 93.

Dubois (Denis), convict in Toulon - VI, 593, 617; VII, 54, 123, 174; VIII, 321, 373.

Dubois (E.) - Member of Charity of Courboin, XIIIb, 93.

Dubois (Jean), merchant of Argenteuil - XIIIb, 107.

Dubois (Jeanne), superioress of Charity of Courboin - XIIIb, 93.

Dubois (Laurence), Daughter of Charity - XIIIb, 228.

Dubois (Sulpice), Daughter of Charity - XIIIb, 228.

Duborné (M.) - XIIIa, 211.

Dubouchart (M.) - VIII, 537.

Du Boulet-Brular (Mme) - VIII, 395.

Dubourdieu (Jean-Armand), Brother of the Mission - Biographical data, VII, 186; in Cahors, IV, 284; at Saint-Lazare; praise for him; Saint Vincent thinks of offering him consulate of Algiers, VII, 186; enshrouds body of Saint Vincent, XIIIa, 207.

Du Bourg (Moïse), Jesuit - Biographical data, VI, 563; VII, 4; book against Jansenism, VI, 563, 612; VII, 4.

Du Broc du Nozet (Edmond or Aimé), Abbot of Aumale - II, 419.

Dubuc (Louis), Priest of the Mission - Biographical data; with his family, III, 98.

Dubrus (Chevalier) - Ransomed from Algiers, VIII, 319.

Ducasse (Jacques), Master of the Mint of Navarre and Béarn - XIIIa, 21.

Ducasse (Pierre), priest - Biographical data, IV, 334; VI, 323; gives reason to hope he will help Fr. Bajoue in one of his missions, IV, 334; requests mission sermons from Saint Vincent, VI, 324; Saint Vincent doubts desire to be Missionary, IV, 544–45; legacy for Congregation of the Mission, VI, 324.

Du Chastel (Pierre), Priest of the Mission - Biographical data; Saint Vincent asks Lambert aux Couteaux to give him hospitality, II, 529; death, III, 270; other mention, II, 541.

Duchemin (Placide-Louis), Benedictine - Named Bishop of Babylon, VIII, 192.

Duchesne (Bernard), Doctor of Sorbonne - Helps Saint Vincent give first retreat for ordinands of Beauvais, I, 57.

Du Chesne (Jean), Brother of the Mission - Biographical data, V, 260; sent to Rome, XIIIa, 359–60; death, V, 260, 262.

Duchesne (Jérôme), Archdeacon of Beauvais and Doctor of Sorbonne - Biographical data, I, 57; II, 203; XI, 29; gives mission in Montmirail with Saint Vincent, XI, 29; helps Saint Vincent give first retreat for ordinands of Beauvais, I, 57; not sure Liancourt is ready for Confraternity of Charity, I, 287; contacts with Fr. des Lions, Archdeacon of Senlis, II, 203; goes to Rome to defend *De la fréquente communion* by Arnauld, III, 73; other mentions, I, 70, 287.

Du Chesne (Pierre), Priest of the Mission - Biographical data, I, 422; II, 258; III, 103; IV, 335; V, 11; VIII, 114; letters Saint Vincent writes him in Sancey, I, 521–22, 530; in Joigny, I, 545; in Claye, II, 258; in Crécy, II, 311, 363, 422; in Marseilles, V, 11; reference to letter to Saint Vincent, I, 545; praise for him, III, 259; V, 147, 216, 374.

In Montmirail, I, 441–42; sent to Troyes to preach retreat for ordinands, I, 545; Superior in Crécy, VIII, 609; at 1642 Assembly, II, 343; XIIIa, 323; assigned to Ireland, III, 137; VIII, 615; giving mission with Bishop of Tréguier, III, 195; illness, III, 274; at Saint-Lazare, III, 393–94, 401; requested as Superior in Marseilles, III, 393, 429; at 1651 Assembly, XIIIa, 369, 372, 374, 384, 387, 396–97; opinion about vows, XIIIa, 379; Superior at Bons-Enfants, IV, 335, 468–69; VIII, 604; leaves for visitations in Brittany, IV, 477; visitation in Le Mans, IV, 477; assigned to Richelieu as Superior, IV, 520; Saint Vincent plans to send him to visit Missionaries in Barbary, V, 11, 147; Superior in Marseilles, V, 11, 38; VIII, 610.

Superior in Agde, V, 101, 136, 147, 170; VIII, 114, 618; health, V, 184, 190, 216, 219, 222; permission to rest in Marseilles, V, 199, 212; death, V, 226, 232–33, 237, 374; prayers for his soul requested, V, 226, 233, 237; other mentions, I, 465; II, 537; IV, 400; V, 134, 162, 200, 376.

Duchesne (René), slave in Algiers, then Brother of the Mission - Biographical data, III, 223; V, 325; VII, 81; XI, 180; slave, III, 223, 311; sent from Agde to Marseilles, VII, 81, 115; Saint Vincent considers him for confidential mission to Algiers, VII, 179, 186; in Montpellier, VIII, 289; other mentions, V, 325, 354, 405; XI, 192.

Du Coudray (François), Priest of the Mission - Biographical data, I, 28; II, 45; III, 31, 80; letters Saint Vincent sends him in Paris, I, 56; in Rome, I, 111, 112, 119, 120, 140, 148, 164, 175, 203, 221, 242, 263; in Toul, II, 68, 74; Superior in La Rose,

VIII, 606; in Troyes, VIII, 607; III, 85; letters to Saint Vincent from Marseilles, II, 437, 439; knowledge of Hebrew, I, 242, 244; III, 108; quarrels with brother, I, 176; arrival in Rome to negotiate approval of Congregation, I, 111; presents petition to Congregation of Bishops and Regulars for approval of Congregation of the Mission, I, 140; Saint Vincent urges him to return to Paris to work on missions, I, 245, 265, 279; du Coudray imagines Saint Vincent biased against him, I, 264; in Paris, I, 334, 387–88; sent to Liancourt, I, 428; goes to negotiate opening of Troyes house, I, 415–16; Superior in Toul, I, 528; II, 45, 82; VIII, 605; in La Rose; Fr. Dehorgny owes vocation as Missionary to him, II, 69; illness, II, 119; recalled to Paris, II, 168; in Paris, II, 189, 287, 305; XIIIa, 335, 337; at 1642 General Assembly, II, 344; XIIIa, 323, 326, 331; named member of commission to prepare Rules and Constitutions, XIIIa, 326; question of sending him to Barbary to ransom slaves and give mission, II, 355; about to depart for Marseilles, II, 394; missions to galley convicts; conversions, II, 437, 439; priests of Fr. Authier desire union with Congregation of the Mission, II, 465; ill, returns to Paris; again requested for Marseilles; prepares to return there, II, 466.

Superior in La Rose, III, 31–32, 56, 63; Superior in Troyes, VIII, 607; goes to Aiguillon, III, 125; Saint Vincent counsels Fr. Portail, going to make visitation in La Rose, to be gentle and humble with Fr. du Coudray, II, 675; unorthodox opinions, III, 80, 89, 108; Saint Vincent plans to send him to Richelieu, III, 80, 89, 108; considers dismissing him from Company, III, 108; in Richelieu, III, 109, 114, 145, 285, 297; death, III, 409, 414; other mentions, I, 38, 87; XIIIa, 222–23, 235.

Du Coudray (Mlle) - Contacts with Saint Vincent and Saint Louise, I, 170, 284.

Ducournau (Bertrand), Brother of the Mission - Biographical data, I, *xxvi*; III, 8; IV, 277; V, 41; VI, 156; VII, 87; VIII, 94; XI, *xix*; letters from Saint Vincent, V, 395; from Canon Cruchette, VIII, 602; letters to Saint Vincent, IV, 455; to Saint Louise, V, 643, 646; VI, 652; VII, 640–41; to Canon de Saint-Martin, VIII, 599; Saint Vincent chooses him as secretary, I, *xii*; Ducournau's work to preserve originals of saint's captivity letters, I, 1; VIII, 599–601; entreaties to Missionaries to preserve conferences of Saint Vincent, XI, *xxvii-xxxii*; forgets to show letter to saint, IV, 308; allowed to add personal postscript to saint's letter, IV, 556; informs Saint Louise about saint's health, III, 8; acts as intermediary between Saint Vincent and Saint Louise, III, 179; V, 41; VII, 87, 158; absent from Saint-Lazare, VIII, 102; health, V, 179, 183, 184, 206, 219, 222, 251, 258; VIII, 157, 207, 211; assists dying saint, XIIIa, 204; other mentions, IV, 277; V, 272; VI, 372, 561; VII, 545; XIIIa, 211, 399; XIIIb, 230.

Du Creux, widow of Captain who is slave in Algiers - V, 328, 354, 392; VI, 189.

Duel - Comte de Rougemont's passion for duels: see his name; Saint Vincent dissuades Philippe-Emmanuel de Gondi from fighting duel: see **Gondi** (Philippe de); frequency of dueling around 1650; league against dueling; request for Brief from Pope, V, 616–18.

Duelska - See **Douelle**.

Dufaur (M.) - Saint Vincent gives news of him to M. de Forges, VIII, 61–62.

Du Faux (Mother), Visitandine - VIII, 443.

Du Fay (Isabelle) - Biographical data, I, 24; XI, 119; letters from Saint Vincent, I, 24, 30, 107, 123, 147, 167, 171, 191, 204, 226, 259; praise for her, XI, 119, 383; her charity, I, 27–28, 30–31, 204; member of Charity of Hotel-Dieu, I, 260; of another Charity, I, 31, 64; contacts with Saint Vincent, I, 35–36, 55, 69, 77, 89, 169; with Saint Louise, I, 26, 28, 33, 72, 132; infirmity, IX, 475; XI, 119, 383; health, I, 33, 122–23, 126, 128, 261–62; other mentions, I, 36, 71, 97, 117.

Dufestel (Claude), Brother of the Mission - Biographical data, VII, 347.

Dufestel (François), Pastor of Le Havre - V, 379.

Dufestel (François), Priest of the Mission - Biographical data, I, 464; II, 93; III, 2; letters Saint Vincent writes him in Sancey, I, 464; in Annecy, II, 246, 320, 324, 331, 354, 413; reference to letter to Saint Vincent, I, 464; Superior in Troyes, I, 531, 571, 578; II, 136, 167–68; VIII, 607; God blesses him there, II, 245, 249; health, I, 521–23, 528, 530; at Saint-Lazare seminary for renewal, II, 93–94, 118–19; assigned to Annecy, II, 239–40; Superior in Annecy, II, 245, 248, 252, 255; VIII, 608; relieved of office at his request, II, 331, 335–36; Consultor for new Superior, II, 402–03; Superior in Cahors, II, 429, 451–52, 489; VIII, 610; assigned to Agen, II, 462; Superior in Marseilles, II, 532; VIII, 610; pulmonary condition obliges him to leave city, II, 582; leaves Company, II, 669; reason for departure, III, 2; other mentions, II, 511; III, 82.

Du Fontpidoux (Alexandre), attorney at Presidial Court - Attempt to get Bishop of Périgueux to take him for Vicar-General, II, 680.

Du Fossé (M.) - *Mémoires*, XIIIa, 110.

Dufour (Antoine), Priest of the Mission - Biographical data, II, 530; Superior at Bons-Enfants, VIII, 604.

Dufour (Claude), Priest of the Mission - Biographical data, II, 531; III, 11; IV, 108; V, 73; VI, 12; VII, 17; XI, 371; letters of Saint Vincent to Fr. Dufour in Saintes, II, 659; III, 57, 172, 180, 204, 342, 480; in Sedan, IV, 108, 118, 134, 264, 363, 435; Superior in La Rose, VIII, 606; teacher at Bons-Enfants; unsuccessful; removed, II, 531, 540; in Montmirail, II, 548; thinks he has vocation for Carthusians; Saint Vincent dissuades him, III, 172, 180, 204, 342–45; IV, 108, 363; Superior in Saintes, II, 659; VIII, 612; deep recollection grates on confreres, III, 12, 31; Saint Vincent decides not to send him to Cahors, so as not to mortify Bishop of Saintes, III, 81; in Sedan, IV, 122, 134, 195, 522; unhappy with Superior, IV, 264, 435–36; wants to make pilgrimage to Notre-Dame de Liesse, IV, 364–65; Saint Vincent dissuades him from publishing book, IV, 436; Director of Internal Seminary at Saint-Lazare, IV, 602; out giving missions, V, 156.

Volunteers to go to assist slaves and prisoners; Saint Vincent counsels patience, III, 481; Dufour named for Madagascar, IV, 93, 108–10, 118, 134–35, 363, 522, 525; V, 425, 431; awaited in Madagascar, V, 299; voyage to Madagascar, V, 637; VI, 12–16, 19, 21, 224–31; letter to Saint Vincent from Madagascar, VI, 12; in Madagascar and Île Sainte-Marie, VI, 18, 231–42, 252–53; XIIIa, 362; death, VI, 19, 214–17, 237–40, 447, 451, 453, 455, 460, 463–64, 469, 471, 475, 478, 481, 488, 567, 583, 586, 590; VII, 15, 17; VIII, 180, 553–54; XI, 371, 378; XIIIa, 186; mention of conference on his virtues, XII, 429; other mention, V, 73. See also ***Madagascar***.

Du Four (Perrette), first wet-nurse of Louis XIV - Biographical data, V, 644; contacts with Saint Louise, V, 644; on behalf of Queen, asks for Daughters of Charity to assist wounded soldiers and patients of La Fère Hospital, X, 160; present in La Fère for arrival of Sisters, X, 165; continues to take interest in hospital, VI, 156.

Du Fresne (Charles), sieur de Villeneuve - Biographical data, I, 21; II, 15; III, 276; VI, 191; VII, 457; Saint Vincent writes from Châtillon about his arrival in Paris, I, 21; upcoming journey to Villepreux, I, 79; Saint Vincent thinks du Fresne is at Court, I, 122; contacts with saint, II, 15, 544; III, 276; contacts with Sr. Louise Ganset, VI, 191; VII, 457; generosity toward relatives of Saint Vincent, IV, 515; other mention, VI, 318.

Du Fresne (Mlle), sister of Charles du Fresne - Journey to Villepreux, I, 77, 79; to Montmirail, I, 122.

Dufresne (Denis), Brother of the Mission - Biographical data, III, 314.

Dufresner (M.), of Nantes - VIII, 398.

Duggan [Duiguin] (Dermot), Priest of the Mission - Biographical data, III, 93; IV, 99; VI, 184; VII, 14; XI, 177; departure for Ireland, III, 93; return to France, III, 478; assigned to Hebrides, IV, 99; in Hebrides, IV, 478; VI, 184; XI, 177, 261; report to *Propaganda Fide*, IV, 478; gives news of mission, IV, 121, 495–97; V, 121–23; death, VI, 583, 587, 589–90, 592, 594, 596, 602, 607, 611, 613, 616, 621; VII, 14, 15, 19, 45, 328; XI, 383.

Du Halier (M.) - II, 55.

Duhamel (Henri), Pastor of Saint-Merry in Paris - Biographical data; attitude toward Jansenism, IV, 593.

Duhamel (Jean), Priest of the Mission - Biographical data, II, 33; sent to Annecy at foundation of house, II, 18; Saint Jane Frances' opinion of him, II, 33; opinion of Mme Goussault, II, 115, 117; vacillating in vocation, II, 33, 114–15, 117; departure from Company, II, 160; excerpt from his will, XIIIa, 333.

Du Houssay (François Malier), Bishop of Troyes - Offers Troyes Missionaries Barbuise parish and revenues, V, 142; Saint Vincent is opposed, V, 312; contacts with saint, VI, 151; asks for dispensation, VII, 508, 543; other mention, VI, 394.

Duiguin - See **Duggan**.

Dujardin (M.) - Contacts with M. Barreau, V, 35, 326.

Du Lorier (Mme) - VI, 201.

Dulys (Pierre), Prior of Notre-Dame des Trois-Épis, in Alsace - Biographical data, VII, 335; VIII, 11; attempts to obtain Missionaries for priory, VII, 335; VIII, 11; two nephews, VIII, 12.

Du Marche (François), Pastor in Serqueux - III, 369, 370.

Du Maretz (Jean) - II, 209.

Du Maretz (Mme), wife of preceding - Sale of house in Paris, II, 209.

Dumas (Jean-Aimé), Priest of the Mission - Biographical data, VIII, 218.

Dumecq (Mme), Lady of Charity - I, 230.

Du Mée (Mlle), Lady of Charity - Visits foundlings in country, II, 330, 337; other mentions, I, 410, 547; II, 225, 247.

Dumesnil (Jacques), seminarian of the Mission - Biographical data; death, III, 414.

Dumesnil (M.), priest, in Bayonne - II, 7.

Dumont (Joseph), priest of Lyons - XIIIa, 45.

Du Mur (Jean), inhabitant of Clichy - XIIIa, 24.

Dunkirk, town in Nord - Siege of Dunkirk, VII, 185.

Dunois (Charles d'Orléans, Comte de) - VIII, 498.

Dunots (Humbert), Priest of the Mission - Biographical data, III, 2; influenced by Fr. Codoing, III, 3; death; conference in Rome on life and virtues, III, 481–87.

Du Noyé (Gillette), mother of Jean Martin - II, 652.

Dupart (Abbess), daughter of Mme Fouquet - Requests and receives permission to enter Visitation monasteries of Paris, VIII, 432, 542, 551.

Du Perron (Jacques), Cardinal-Bishop of Angoulême - Missions in diocese, I, 431; II, 417; proposes to Saint Vincent to establish Missionaries there, II, 475, 488; praise of Saint Francis de Sales, XI, 54; other mention, I, 488.

Du Perron (Jean Davy), Archbishop of Sens - Approves Charity of Joigny, XIIIb, 25, 27, 63–65.

Duperroy (Nicolas), Priest of the Mission - Biographical data, V, 3; VI, 4; VII, 9; VIII, 90; XI, 323; letters Saint Vincent writes him in Poland, VI, 41, 333, 360, 428, 568; VIII, 163; on eve of leaving for Poland with Fr. Ozenne, V, 3; journey to Poland, V, 38, 49: see also **Ozenne**; in Poland, V, 83, 142, 168, 363, 574, 609; VI, 4, 5, 91, 109, 112, 271, 319, 489, 539, 555, 576; VII, 9, 68, 92, 125, 128, 264, 275, 361, 416, 474–75, 532, 553, 625, 639; VIII, 90, 99, 146, 193, 251, 281, 301, 314, 354, 395, 508; ordination, V, 114; progress in learning Polish, V, 118, 229, 313; XII, 25; obedience and stability, V, 143; missions, V, 201, 234; stays in Warsaw despite entrance of Swedes into city, V, 474, 479, 535; risks dangers there, VI, 124, 140; XI, 308, 329, 357; XII, 61; Swedes mistreat him and take his possessions, VI, 91, 128, 144–45, 157, 159; XI, 323, 333; in Opole with Fr. Ozenne, VI, 326; illness, VI, 333, 337, 345, 347, 352, 360, 362, 384, 393; plans trip to France, VI, 421, 464, 472, 489; new illness, VI, 428, 447, 451, 453, 470, 472, 489, 492, 502; XI, 362, 364; in Krakow; health improves, VI, 555–56, 566; in Warsaw, VI, 620–21; health is good, VII, 90, 155; VIII, 325; prepares to leave for Krakow, VII, 173; recovery, VIII, 193. See also ***Poland, Warsaw***.

Duperroy (Victor), Priest of the Mission, brother of preceding - Biographical data, VI, 42; VII, 125; Saint Vincent gives news of brother, VI, 42; in Montmirail, VI, 312; returns to family, VI, 334; desires to come back to Congregation; saint is prepared to accept him, VII, 125, 639.

Du Plessis (Christophe), Baron de Montbard, King's Councillor - Biographical data, IV, 596; V, 17; VI, 550; opens warehouses during Fronde to benefit starving, IV, 519; member of meeting regarding Daughters of Providence after death of Foundress, VI, 550.

Duplessis (Mme) - VI, 426; VIII, 520.

Du Plessis-Praslin (César de Choiseul, Comte), Peer and Maréchal de France - Founder of Jolly Priory, VIII, 192.

Dupont (Claude), prisoner in Toulon - VI, 320.

Dupont (Louis), Priest of the Mission - Biographical data, III, 236; IV, 23; V, 553; VI, 63; VII, 42; VIII, 76; letters Saint Vincent writes him in Tréguier, V, 553, 582, 604; VI, 63, 197, 381, 586, 614; VII, 42, 119, 192, 399, 428, 565; VIII, 76, 131, 168, 221, 318; in Le Mans; recalled to Paris, III, 236; at Saint-Lazare, IV, 23; Superior in Toul, VIII, 606; Superior in Tréguier, VIII, 616; despondency, VI, 63; Saint Vincent reprimands him for withholding his letter to confrere, VI, 197; health, VI, 381; two benefices offered him; Saint Vincent does not permit him to accept, VII, 192; professor, VII, 278.

Du Pont-Courlay (Marie-Marthe), grand-niece of Cardinal Richelieu - Retreat at Saint Louise's house, II, 647.

Dupont-Fournier (M.) - See **Fournier** (M.).

Duport (M.) - Saint Vincent suggests low Masses rather than solemn service for deceased son, VI, 544.

Duport (Nicolas), Priest of the Mission, son of preceding - Biographical data, IV, 121; V, 272; VI, 25; VIII, 8; XI, 379; letters Saint Vincent writes him in Genoa, VI, 375, 394; proposed for Madagascar, IV, 93; entrusted with direction of retreat for ordinands at Saint-Lazare, IV, 121; praise for him, IV, 305; in Genoa, IV, 418; V, 275, 321, 497; VI, 25; knows enough Italian to give mission, IV, 305; gives mission to men building Missionaries' house, IV, 427; thoughts concerning vows, V, 314–15; esteemed by Cardinal Durazzo, VI, 545; plague epidemic puts life in danger, VI, 375, 395; volunteers to care for plague-stricken, VI, 396, 402; catches plague, VI, 474, 477, 480, 482, 485, 487–88, 491, 501; death, VI, 504, 506–07, 509, 528, 530, 535, 537, 567, 583, 586; VII, 18; XI, 379, 381; mention of conference on his virtues, VI, 604; XII, 429.

Duporzo (M.) - VIII, 342.

Dupré (M.), Canon of Écouis - XIIIa, 29, 30.

Du Pred (M.) - II, 538.

Du Puget (Étienne), Bishop of Marseilles - Contacts with Priests of the Mission, III, 260, 272, 394, 413, 446; VII, 49; VIII, 69; plans to erect seminary and entrust it to Congregation of the Mission, VII, 70, 74, 81, 116; wishes to resign, VII, 174;

entrusts formation of diocesan priests to Missionaries, VIII, 69; request for papers and meditations, VIII, 262.

Dupuich (Antoine), Brother of the Mission - Biographical data, IV, 284; VI, 476; considered for Cahors, IV, 284; for Richelieu, VI, 476.

Dupuich (François), Priest of the Mission - Biographical data, VI, 300; VII, 139; VIII, 72; sent from Troyes to Annecy, VI, 300; named Superior of Troyes house, VII, 140; Superior in Troyes, VII, 233–34, 348, 508, 544, 588; VIII, 72, 322, 428, 607.

Dupuich (M.) - VII, 364.

Dupuis (Étiennette), Daughter of Charity - Biographical data, VIII, 164; proposed for Nantes, XIIIb, 335; about to leave for Angers, VII, 381–82; VIII, 164; other mention, XIIIb, 227.

Dupuis (M.), seminarian of the Mission - In Cahors, II, 634.

Dupuis (Michel), Priest of the Mission - Biographical data, I, 575; II, 76; Saint Vincent requests dimissorial for him, I, 575; sent to Bar-le-Duc, II, 76; in Saint-Mihiel; Saint Vincent recalls him to Paris, II, 243.

Dupuy (Pierre), author of work on rights of Gallican Church - III, 591.

Dupuys (Jean), notary in Paris - XIIIa, 217–18, 220, 222, 225, 258.

Duquesne (Abraham), Admiral - Plunder of Flemish ships, VIII, 566.

Durand (Antoine), Priest of the Mission - Biographical data, V, 161; VI, 77; VII, 35; VIII, 4; XI, 310; letters Saint Vincent writes him in Agde, VI, 77, 314, 344; VII, 35, 171, 197, 610; VIII, 35, 113; professor at Saint-Charles Seminary; assigned to Poland, V, 161; in Warsaw, V, 176, 377; ordination, V, 187; first Mass, V, 218; diligence in studying Polish, V, 229, 313; health, V, 384, 411; return to France, V, 474, 475, 479; Superior in Agde, V, 555; advice of Saint Vincent for good leadership of house, VI, 77; XI, 310; Superior in Agde, VI, 120, 599, 620; VII, 81, 115, 316; VIII, 18, 112–13, 144, 161, 212, 618; Saint Vincent thanks Fr. Get for helping Fr. Durand, VIII, 260; prepares opening of Montpellier seminary, VII, 554; Saint Vincent asks him to replace Fr. Get temporarily in Montpellier, VIII, 4, 18; to welcome ailing Bro. Jean Le Moyne, VIII, 369; Fr. Durand prepares opening of Narbonne house, VIII, 112, 114; does not wish to return to Poland, VI, 620.

Durazzo (Stefano), Cardinal-Archbishop of Genoa - Biographical data, II, 595; III, 1; IV, 75; V, 136; VI, 26; VII, 229; VIII, 21; letters from Saint Vincent, IV, 253; VIII, 138, 384; letters to Saint Vincent, II, 595; VIII, 544; words of praise, III, 1, 157,

367; VI, 26, 118; zeal, III, 85, 191; VII, 540; emotion on children's First Communion day, III, 130; happy to have Priests of the Mission in diocese, II, 595; makes annual retreat with them, III, 501; contacts with Saint Vincent, VII, 569; with Missionaries, III, 152; IV, 79, 565, 574; V, 136, 237, 253–54, 314, 321, 397, 459, 476, 493, 500, 534; VI, 26, 118, 432, 630, 640; VII, 389, 413, 439, 559, 581, 592–93, 604, 624; kindness toward them, III, 66; V, 204, 485; VII, 229, 561; VIII, 335, 548; esteem for Fr. Duport, whom he wished to have as confessor, VI, 545; gratitude of Saint Vincent for kindness, IV, 226, 237, 253, 255; VII, 260, 328, 374–75, 558, 585; VIII, 21, 101, 116, 138, 154, 173, 359, 384; Saint Vincent awaits Cardinal's portrait, V, 206; thinks he overworks Missionaries, III, 58, 101; Cardinal gives them necessary rest after each mission, III, 122; has house built for them, IV, 427; Missionaries at his disposal during plague, VI, 113, 178, 373, 375, 381, 396; urges that other Missionaries be sent, VI, 630, 640; called to Rome by Pope, VII, 500, 628–29; departure, VII, 635; helps Missionaries in Rome buy palace of Cardinal di Bagno, VIII, 134, 138, 147, 154, 173, 211; urges Saint Vincent to take care of self, VIII, 545.

Durazzo (Marchese di), Resident Ambassador of Republic of Genoa in France; nephew of Cardinal - Saint Vincent explains why he cannot reside at Saint-Lazare, VII, 375; welcomes visit to Saint-Lazare, VII, 569; praise for Marchese, VII, 569; VIII, 77.

Durazzo (Msgr.) - Masses for his intention, VI, 630.

Du Rivau (Jacques de Beauvat, sieur), nephew of Cardinal Richelieu - Saint Vincent recommends that Richelieu Missionaries not get involved in temporal matters, except on advice of M. du Rivau, IV, 10, 11, 69, 70; other mention, III, 412.

Du Rivaux (M.), Governor-General for French in Madagascar - Gives Fr. Bourdaise news of confreres, VI, 237; godfather of Malagasy man, VI, 249; other mentions, VI, 243; VIII, 589.

Du Rosier (M.), galley convict in Toulon - VIII, 138.

Durot (Nicolas), Priest of the Mission - Biographical data, I, 282; II, 103; praise for him, I, 525; opinion of Charities of Beauvais, I, 282; giving missions in Romans, I, 405; assigned to Richelieu, I, 419; in Richelieu, I, 440, 452, 500; in Toulouse, I, 518, 525–27, 529; Saint Vincent recommends submission and return to spirit he had at Saint-Lazare, I, 597; death of mother, I, 529; leaves Toulouse diocese, where he had ministered well, II, 103; at Saint-Lazare, II, 118; in Richelieu, II, 128; Saint Vincent does not want him to have contact with Daughters in

Richelieu, II, 128; sent from Luçon to Richelieu, II, 353; illness, II, 541.

Du Rotoir (M.), in Beauvais - Gives hospitality to Saint Louise, I, 94; other mention, I, 93.

Durtal, town in Maine-et-Loire - Saint Vincent falls into Loire near Durtal, III, 419.

Du Ruisseau (M.), of Fontenay-aux-Roses - Contacts with Daughters of Charity, II, 285, 287.

Du Sault (Baron) - IV, 379.

Dusault (Jean-Jacques), Bishop of Dax - Authenticates copy of Saint Vincent's ordination letters, I, 13; at latter's request, I, 14; Vicar-General signs Saint Vincent's dimissorial letters for diaconate and priesthood, XIIIa, 5, 6.

Du Sault (M.), son of Baron and Baroness - IV, 379.

Du Sault (Mme), wife of Baron - Lady of Charity, III, 262; contacts with Saint Vincent, III, 422; saint apologizes for being unable to render immediately service requested, IV, 379.

Du Saussay (André), Bishop of Toul - Biographical data, I, 581; IV, 34; VIII, 14; author of French martyrology, I, 581; asked by Archbishop of Paris to accompany Saint Vincent on visit to Duchesse d'Aiguillon in Rueil, II, 48; misunderstanding with one of his Vicars-General, IV, 34; opposed to departure of Visitandines for Poland, IV, 253; M. Molé praises him, VIII, 196; *mandamus* regarding Jubilee, XI, 301; Officialis of Paris, IV, 398; in Toul, VIII, 14.

Dusin (Dominique), Pastor of Pouy, uncle of Saint Vincent - Letter from Saint Vincent, I, 14.

Du Soyecourt (Françoise-Antoinette), Visitandine - Biographical data; Saint Vincent permits her to spend time in Chaillot monastery, VI, 426.

Du Tartre (Marguerite) - V, 116.

Du Tillet (M.), chief Court Clerk for Parlement of Paris - XIIIa, 259, 477; XIIIb, 237.

Dutour (M.), Vicar-General of Soissons - Letter from Saint Vincent, VII, 219; other mention, VII, 301.

Duval (André), Doctor of Sorbonne - Biographical data, I, 113; II, 256; III, 247; IV, 322; XI, 21; praise for him, XI, 140, 191; counselor of Saint Vincent, I, 113, 151, 396; III, 247; IV, 322; XIIIa, 274; and of M. Alix, I, 190; words recalled by saint, II, 256; XI, 21, 140, 191; XII, 87, 306; other mention.

Duval (Armand), of Toulon, slave in Algiers - Money received for him, VIII, 331.

Duval (Jean) [**Bernard de Saint-Thérèse**], Discalced Carmelite, Bishop of Babylon - Biographical data, II, 65; arrival in diocese, II, 457: see also ***Babylon***.

Duval (M.), Canon in Tréguier - Biographical data; Saint Vincent informs him of approval of foundation of Guingamp Ursulines; thanks him for kindness to Tréguier Missionaries, V, 58.

Duval (Noël), of Le Mans - V, 599; VI, 64, 124, 151; VII, 339; VIII, 228.

Duverger de Hauranne, Abbé de Saint-Cyran - See **Saint-Cyran**.

Duvergier (M.) - III, 455.

Du Vigean (Anne de Neubourg, Marquise) - Biographical data, II, 126; IV, 507; VIII, 52; children; death of eldest son, II, 126; share in coach service, IV, 506; health, VIII, 52.

Du Vigean (Marthe), daughter of Marquise - Biographical data, VIII, 506; writes to Saint Vincent about dispute among Carmelites, VIII, 506.

Dwyer [**O'Dwyer**] (Edmund), Bishop of Limerick - Biographical data; Saint Vincent informs him of departure of eight Missionaries for Ireland, III, 90; Prelate thanks saint for good done by Missionaries in diocese, III, 353, 416; death, V, 159.

Dyé, village in Yonne - Priory of Dyé offered to Congregation of the Mission, II, 470.

E

Easter - Mention of conferences, XII, 410, 426, 431; serving roast on Easter, VI, 281.

East Indies [**Company of the Indies**] - Historical note, III, 279; Saint Vincent is asked for Missionaries for East Indies, II, 522; IV, 109; disposed to give them, II, 523, 552; Company always maintained priests in Madagascar, III, 553; secured cooperation of Missionaries, XI, 372–73; Fr. Nacquart writes to administrators of Company, III, 571; rivalry between Company and that founded by Maréchal de la Meilleraye, VII, 38, 61, 572; proposed union, VII, 60; attempt at settlement, VIII, 205; XI, 294; Maréchal unhappy that Saint Vincent sends Missionaries with Company of Indies; saint apologizes, offers explanation, VII, 61; questions M. de Flacourt about intentions of Company, VIII, 96; writes to Maréchal that he promised directors of Company of Indies to send two priests on their ship, VIII, 179; unable give them anyone, VIII, 199; tells Fr. Étienne of decision, VIII, 201, 205; requests latter to have no communication in Madagascar with representatives of Company, VIII, 201; returning Missionaries pay respects to Company, VIII, 594; other mention, III, 593. See also **La Meilleraye**, ***Madagascar***.

Ebran (M.), convict - VIII, 485.

Ecclesiastical Censures - Power of imposing censures used rarely, II, 6.

Ecclesiastical Affairs - See **Council of Conscience**.

Ecclesiastics - See **Bishops**, **Clergy of France**, **Ordinands**, **Pastors**, **Priests**, **Seminarians**, **Tuesday Conferences**.

Eclipse - See **Astronomy**.

Écouis, village in Eure - Saint Vincent, Canon and Treasurer of collegial church, takes possession of benefice, XIIIa, 26–28; takes customary oath, invites new associates to dinner, XIIIa, 28; Chapter complains that he fails in duty of residence; asks for explanation, XIIIa, 29–30.

Écrouves, village in Meurthe-et-Moselle - V, 236; VI, 533.

Edinburgh, town in Scotland - Fr. White [Le Blanc] transferred to prison here, V, 389.

Eigg, island in Hebrides - Apostolic ministry of Fr. Duggan [Duiguin], IV, 496; V, 121–22.

Egypt - Flight of Our Lord into Egypt, VI, 130; X, 197, 457; XII, 165; XIIIb, 406; Mary's prompt obedience in going there, IX, 59; ancient monasteries, XII, 339; swarms of locusts there and in Madagascar, III, 550; ravages of locusts, VI, 248; God blessed midwives who protected male children, XIIIb, 406; other mention, XI, 372.

Elbène (Barthélemy d'), Bishop of Agen - Has foundation assigned to Congregation of the Mission, IV, 50–51; contacts with Agen and La Rose Missionaries, V, 86–87, 444; VIII, 606; entrusted direction of seminary to Congregation of the Mission, VIII, 617; negligent in providing for needs of seminary and in strengthening foundation, VI, 368–69, 441–42, 562; VII, 5, 350; VIIII, 17, 222–23; mention of letter from Fr. Menestrier, VI, 472; Saint Vincent proposes delegating confrere to serve him, VII, 604: see ***Agen***.

Elect - Small number, XII, 107; XIIIb, 435; parable of wise and foolish virgins applied to Communities, X, 491–92; XI, 388.

Elections - Elections among Daughters of Charity: see **Officers**; in Confraternity of Charity, XIIIb, 5, 17, 23, 29, 33, 43, 49, 55, 58–59, 80, 86, 90, 99, 102.

Elijah (prophet) - IX, 262; his zeal, XII, 130.

Élisabeth, Daughter of Charity - See **Hellot** (Élisabeth), **Martin** (Élisabeth).

Elisha, prophet - Endowed with two-fold spirit, IX, 262.

El Kala, port in Algeria, formerly ***La Calle*** - V, 133.

Elk's Foot - Sent to Duchesse d'Aiguillon, IV, 354, 373, 411; used to cure epilepsy, IV, 354.

Ember Days - I, 600; VII, 612; VIII, 254, 361; XIIIa, 1, 2, 4, 6, 8; XIIIb, 385, 444–45, 447.

Emery (M.) - VIII, 540.

Emery (Michel Particelli, sieur d'), Comptroller of Finances - Biographical data, III, 585; other mention, V, 503.

Emfrie (Pierre), Priest of the Mission - Biographical data, VI, 534.

Emmanuel (Bro.), Brother of the Mission - Probably epileptic, VII, 306.

Enar (M.), priest of Saint-Nicolas du Chardonnet - XIIIa, 144.

Enfermés, hospice for mentally ill in Paris - I, 285; IV, 24; VII, 476.

England - Persecution by Cromwell: see **Cromwell**; martyrdom of holy priest, II, 211–12; country at war with King, XI, 114; Parliament grants freedom to confreres and Visitation nuns detained in Dover, V, 27; priests for England must go in disguise, XII, 207; other mentions, III, 303; VI, 124, 500; IX, 233; XI, 177, 190, 272, 279, 318; XII, 35, 370. See also ***Dover***.

English - English consul in Tunis tries to interfere with French Consul, V, 89–90, 265–266, 267–68; Jean LeVacher is at peace with him, XI, 334; heroic courage of English slaves in Barbary, II, 653; III, 335–36; XI, 180–81; English have cut off communication with Catholics in Hebrides, VI, 429; prevent visits to them, VI, 570; persecute Catholics, especially priests, VI, 593- 94, 603, 607, 611, 614, 621; XI, 166; spreading rumor regarding Madagascar, VIII, 96; English ship arrives at Table Bay, VIII, 586; two others join return trip, VIII, 593; other mentions, IV, 461; V, 89.

Ennery (Jean) - See **McEnery** (John).

Entretiens des ordinands - See **Conferences to Ordinands**.

Envy - Conferences, IX, 548–60; XI, 87–88; mention of another conference, XII, 420; danger of this vice, IX, 363, 557–59; XI, 87–88; causes and occasions of envy, IX, 550–52; X, 373; XI, 87; often found in Communities, especially small ones, V, 583; means for not yielding to it, IX, 550–51, 555–59; X, 374–75; XI, 87–88; leads to loss of vocation, IX, 550–52; 554–55;

appearing in Paris with regard to work of confreres in Rome, II, 319; Saint Vincent asks Missionaries to meditate once a month on this vice, along with pride and sloth, XI, 178.

Épinac - See ***Évignac***.

Epilepsy - Epileptics not accepted into Company of Daughters of Charity, XIIIb, 270; isolate them from rest of local community, VII, 306; Bro. Emmanuel probably epileptic, VII, 306; remedy against epilepsy, IV, 354; Saint Vincent advises dismissing Brother with epilepsy, VII, 377; persons with this condition are not treated by Confraternities of Charity, X, 273.

Épinay-sur-Seine, town in Seine-Saint-Denis - Mission given, VIII, 534.

Époisses, village in Côte-d'Or - Monastery of Order of Grandmont, IV, 308.

Errata - See **Appendix 2**.

Esau, biblical personage - Sells birthright for mess of pottage, X, 266; other mention, I, 314; XIIIa, 170–71.

Esbran (Fr.), priest, prisoner in Toulon - VI, 342, 617; VII, 150, 250.

Escart (Pierre), Priest of the Mission - Biographical data, I, 568; II, 32; III, 397; IV, 390; VII, 498; Saint Jane Frances calls him a saint, II, 32; harsh character, II, 84, 86, 88, 157–59; departure for Annecy, II, 18; in Annecy, II, 118, 249; letters Saint Vincent writes him there, II, 83, 120, 157, 401; refuses him permission for family visit, II, 114, 121; named Consultor, II, 336, 402; at Saint-Lazare, III, 397; departure for Richelieu, III, 408, 409; in Richelieu; mental illness, IV, 390; VII, 511; commits murder, VII, 512; death, VII, 498, 512; other mention, III, 400, 406.

Eschaux (Bertrand d'), Archbishop of Tours - II, 80.

Esmartins (M. d'), in Rome - V, 206.

Esne (Claude de Pouilly, Marquise d') - See **Pransac** (Marquise d').

Espinette (Grégoire), master pastrycook and citizen of Paris - Witness to Saint Vincent's will, XIIIa, 101.

Essarts, Village in Marne - Mission given, II, 298.

Estaing (Joachim d'), Bishop of Clermont - II, 560.

Estaing (Louis d'), Bishop of Clermont - Proposed journey to Cahors, IV, 141; intervenes in union of Saint-Pourçain Priory to Congregation of the Mission, VII, 313, 319–20, 360, 517.

Estates - Meeting, II, 362, 558; IV, 343, 461; Estates General, IV, 475–76.

Este (Rinaldo d'), Cardinal - Biographical data, IV, 61; Saint Vincent thanks him for kindness, IV, 107; response of Cardinal, IV, 123.

Estival-en-Charnie, in Sarthe - Abbey of Benedictine nuns, I, 339.

Esther - Biblical personage, XIIIb, 420, 426.

Estournel (Blanche d'), Abbess of Biaches - III, 513.

Estrades (Jean d'), Bishop of Condom - Biographical data, IV, 101; named Bishop of Périgueux, II, 679–81; III, 229; Bishop of Condom, III, 256; contacts with Alain de Solminihac, III, 256, 346–47; wishes to retain Bro. Rivet as steward; Saint Vincent opposes this, III, 450, 452, 475–76, 503; Alain de Solminihac hopes Estrades will sign Bishops' petition to Pope against Jansenism, IV, 101.

Estrées (Anne Habert de Montmaur), Lady of Nanteuil, wife of Maréchal de France - Biographical data; contacts with Sister Nicole Georgette, VII, 477.

Estrées (François Annibal, Duc d'), Maréchal de France, Ambassador to Rome - II, 38; Saint Vincent objects to Gonesse property being assigned to him, XIIIa, 341–43.

Étampes, town in Essonne - Miseries of Fronde in Étampes, IV, 400–02, 425–26; IX, 468; Daughters of Charity give relief to sick poor of Étampes, IV, 416, 419, 426; direct orphanage, supported by alms of Ladies of Charity: see also **Jeanne-Françoise** (Sister); Saint Vincent advises Saint Louise to write to Assembly about needs of Sister and orphans in Étampes, V, 646; Sister dies: see **Marie-Joseph** (Sister); Missionaries devote themselves to service of poor persons of Étampes, IV, 425, 428, 520; several fall ill, IV, 425–26, 450, 452, 473–74, 477, 494; and die: see **David** (Jean), **Deschamps** (Edme); Mme Goussault stays there en route to Angers, I, 192; Saint Vincent leaves sheep from Orsigny in walled village nearby, III, 413; other mentions, I, 480; II, 538; VIII, 556.

Ethiopia - VI, 248.

Étienne (Nicolas), Priest of the Mission - Biographical data, V, 536; VII, 570; VIII, 20–21; XII, 330; letters from Saint Vincent, V, 536; VIII, 200, 205; to Saint Vincent, VIII, 239, 290, 552; offers property to the Mission, V, 537; infirmity, VII, 570–71, 599; dispensation for ordination, VIII, 20; ordination, VII, 570, 599; VIII, 20, 95, 103; named for Madagascar, VII, 571; VIII, 96, 103, 160, 169, 179; proposed to *Propaganda Fide* for this mission, VIII, 147; disposes of property before departure,

XII, 330, 334; mention of letters to Saint Vincent, VIII, 200, 205, 239; voyage bound for Madagascar; return, VIII, 157, 185–86, 200–01, 205, 207, 219, 225, 229, 231, 239, 246–49, 251, 255–56, 290, 552–97. See ***Madagascar***.

Étiennette, Daughter of Charity - See **Dupuis** (Étiennette).

Étiolles, village in Essonne - Former Missionary becomes Pastor there, I, 527; distress of Étiolles in 1652, IV, 473–74.

Étival, Monastery of Benedictine Nuns - Mention of letter to Claire Nau, Abbess at time of Fronde, IV, 586.

Étréchy, village in Essonne - Journey of Mme Goussault to Étréchy, I, 192; distress of Étréchy in 1652, IV, 428.

Eu (Louis d'), Priest of the Mission - Biographical data, V, 411; VI, 420; VII, 41; VIII, 129–30; departure for Rome, V, 411; in Rome, VI, 636; VII, 436, 517, 543; knowledge of remedies for certain illnesses; Saint Vincent permits him to use them, VI, 420; VII, 41; saint disapproves of proposals about Pastors of Champfleur and Notre-Dame-des-Champs in Le Mans diocese, VII, 494; VIII, 130, 227; Saint Vincent asks Fr. Jolly to lend Fr. Eu to Genoa house for a time, VII, 596.

Eucharist - See **Communion**, **Mass**.

Eudes (John) Saint, Founder of Congregation of Jesus and Mary - Biographical data, V, 625; VIII, 366; Saint Vincent praises him, V, 625; fruits of mission given in Paris, VIII, 366, 367; talk of proposing spiritual direction of Quinze-Vingts to Missionaries of Fr. Eudes; Fr. Desbordes fights plan, VIII, 424; other mentions, XIIIa, 199, 386.

Eudo de Kerlivio (Louis), Vicar-General of Vannes - Biographical data, IV, 115–16; VIII, 217; letter to Saint Vincent, IV, 115; kindness to Daughters of Charity in Hennebont, IV, 116, 180, 238, 243; other mentions, IV, 262; VIII, 217.

Europe - Church diminished in large part of it, XI, 279; diversity of languages, XII, 24; other mention, XIIIa, 394.

Evangelical Counsels - Some are precepts for those who have vowed them, XII, 102; see also individual virtues.

Eve, mother of human race - Temptation, X, 14, 359; why God was angry with her, according to Ombiasses of Madagascar, III, 557; XIIIb, 381, 418.

Éveillard (Jacques), Priest of the Mission - Biographical data, V, 127; VI, 158; VII, 516; XII, 1; at Saint-Charles Seminary, V, 377; named for Poland, V, 127; in Warsaw, V, 402; obtains *extra tempora* for ordination, V, 176; ordination, V, 187, 201; first Mass, V, 218; progress in Polish, V, 229, 313; return to

France, V, 474–75, 479; giving a mission, V, 588; professor of philosophy at Saint-Lazare, VI, 158; water therapy at Bourbon-l'Archambault, VI, 423–24, 435, 440, 443, 445; Queen of Poland talks of recalling him, VI, 525–26; health does not permit return to Poland, VI, 620; collects notes on Saint Vincent's conference of May 17, 1658, on observance of Rules XII, 1; other mentions, VII, 516, 542.

Évignac [***Épinac***], parish - V, 628.

Évreux, town in Eure - Le Mareschal, Promoter of Justice for Évreux diocese, VIII, 418; Canon of diocese, VIII, 417; missions given in diocese, XI, 1.

Ex Commissa Nobis - Brief approving vows of Congregation of the Mission, V, 459, 463; XIIIa, 417–19, 419–21, 481; promulgation and acceptance of Brief, V, 467, 490, 501, 506; VII, 180; assistance of Fr. Hilarion Rancati in obtaining it, VIII, 142–43.

Examen (**Examination of Conscience**) - Mention of conferences, XII, 420, 425, 428; when, why, and how Daughters of Charity make it, IX, 6, 36; X, 485–86; XIIIb, 124–25; and the confreres, I, 203–04.

Example - Mention of conferences, XII, 421, 431; instruct priests by example, II, 637; efficacy of good example, IX, 21, 233–34; XI, 202, 348; correction by good example more efficacious than punishment, II, 6; Saint-Lazare must be example to other houses of Company, XI, 196; likewise, Motherhouse of Daughters of Charity: see **Daughters of Charity**; older owe example to new, VII, 181, 322–23, 465; IX, 45; X, 24, 38, 40, 64, 73, 94, 228, 299; XI, 73; XIIIb, 352; good example of deceased is incitement to virtue, I, 587; X, 511–13, 569. See also **Scandal**.

Excommunication - Saint Vincent's thoughts on it with regard to poverty, II, 37; against proprietors, II, 155.

Exercises (Spiritual) - Fidelity to them, II, 146; to miss one is to fail in all, IX, 61.

Exorcism - Permission of Bishop required to perform exorcism, II, 80; Saint Vincent thinks Mlle d'Atri should be exorcised secretly, I, 461; approves of Superior of Saintes house not having exorcised Benedictines of Cognac, VII, 138.

Extra Tempora - I, 539; V, 127, 176–77; VI, 349, 419, 429, 459, 579; VII, 46, 235, 571, 594; VIII, 7, 39, 58, 160.

Extreme Unction - Oils for it to be taken to Madagascar, III, 282; administered to Alexandre Véronne and the Prior's servant, I, 580; Barbe Angiboust, III, 378; Nicolas Gondrée, III, 438,

560; Elisabeth Jousteau, IV, 416; slave boy in Sidi-Regeppe, IV, 435; Mathurin de Belleville in Sierra Leone, VI, 15; dying Frenchman in Madagascar, VI, 243; René Alméras (the younger), VI, 528, 530, 533, 535, 538, 548, 562; captain at Table Bay, VIII, 583; Francis de Sales, XIIIa, 83; Saint Vincent, XIIIa, 203; two brothers are at point of receiving it, I, 583; Toussaint Bourdaise risks dying without it as did Charles Nacquart, VI, 253; Sisters must see that poor near death receive it, X, 537.

F

Faberolle (President) - I, 417.

Fabert (Abraham de) - Biographical data, II, 483; IV, 31; V, 198; VI, 147; VIII, 224; in praise of him, IV, 121–22; Saint Vincent's respect for him, IV, 165, 188–89; VI, 147; contacts with Sedan Missionaries, II, 483; IV, 31, 195–96, 344, 470, 577; V, 207, 237; VI, 147, 390, 531, 595; VII, 3, 216–17, 605; VIII, 224; member of anti-dueling league, V, 617; Saint Vincent does not want Pastor of Sedan to ask Fabert to take action against Huguenots, II, 494, 496; VII, 3; informs Fabert of Missionary's state of mind, VII, 586; difficulty in dealing tactfully with his zeal, IV, 264; mention of letters from Saint Vincent, V, 198; VII, 605; Saint Vincent sends his respects, V, 247.

Fabert (Marquise de) - II, 483; V, 247, 606; VI, 147, 390, 531.

Fabre (Augustin), author of *l'Histoire de Marseille* - VII, 238.

Fabre (M.), merchant in Marseilles - Debts and flight, VII, 238.

Faculties - Saint Vincent requests faculties from Pope for Missionaries, I, 45, 53; given by Nuncio to Missionaries going to Madagascar, III, 282.

Faith - Conference, XI, 25–26; mention of another conference, XII, 421; Saint Vincent fears falling into heresy, XI, 30; theologian's temptation against faith, XI, 26–27; conversion of heretic, XI, 28–30; insights of faith win hearts better than arguments, XI, 25–26; faith of simple is ordinarily more lively, XII, 142; never allow thought against faith to penetrate the mind, XI, 105; zeal for preserving Company from new opinions: see also **Codoing**, **Dehorgny**, **Du Coudray**; sends Cardinal Grimaldi refutation of heresy of two heads of Church, III, 73; condemnation of heresy, III, 320: see also **Church**, **Jansenism**; spirit of faith; faith of Saint Francis de Sales, XIIIa, 81–82; conference on spirit of faith, XI, 26; mention of another conference, XII, 438. See also **Poor**.

Fajemot - House in Cahors; acquisition by Cahors Seminary, II, 632, 636.

Falconieri (Lelio), in Rome - XIIIa, 313.

Falguières, small town in Tarn-et-Garonne - VI, 357; VII, 166.

Falibowski (M.) - Efforts to establish Missionaries in Krakow, VII, 9, 11, 107, 156, 175, 264.

Fallart (Hugues) - See **Foillard**.

Familiarity - To be avoided, XI, 92. See also **Cordiality**, **Respect**.

Fanchon (Françoise), Daughter of Charity - Biographical data, III, 469; V, 444–45; VII, 298–99; IX, 460; asks to take vows, III, 469; wishes to renew vows, V, 444–45; VII, 298–99; questioned during two conferences, IX, 460; X, 494; other mention, XIIIb, 227.

Fanshere, small town in Madagascar - Journey of Fr. Gondrée in area, III, 434, 560; of Fr. Nacquart, III, 555, 561, 563; of M. de Flacourt, III, 560; possibility of making settlement there, III, 573, 593; other mentions, III, 561, 653.

Fanson (Jean), captive in Algiers - Saint Vincent arranges for him to get money, VIII, 387.

Fardeau (Jacques), notary at Châtelet - XIIIa, 42, 43.

Fargis (Charles d'Angennes de), seminarian of the Mission - Biographical data, III, 389; VII, 217; by way of exception, had been allowed to live at Saint-Lazare, VII, 217–18; admitted into Congregation, VII, 306; death, III, 389–92.

Farmers-General, syndicate of tax collectors - Saint Vincent advises Fr. Gilbert Cuissot to seek help through it, III, 29.

Farnese (Girolomo), Secretary of Congregation of Regulars, later Cardinal - Biographical data, IV, 46; Fr. Vitet complains about him, IV, 46–47, 68, 73.

Fasting - Mention of conference, XII, 431; secretiveness banished only by fasting and prayer, X, 57; fasting by Carmelites, X, 80; priests and Brothers fast for peace for nine years XII, 412; fasting a problem in Madagascar, III, 578–79; condition for gaining Jubilee, IX, 41; Rule of Daughters of Charity, X, 505.

Fate Bene Fratelli, convent in Rome - Renegade converted by Saint Vincent enters to do penance, I, 9; mention of Order, XIIIa, 20.

Faults - Conference on concealing and excusing faults of Sisters, IX, 221–37; mention of another conference, XII, 407; conference on duty of informing Superiors, X, 334–42; on making allowance for failings of others, XI, 68–69; on informing

Superiors of serious faults and temptations of neighbor, XII, 289–97; text of Rule of Daughters of Charity on informing Superiors, X, 334, 339; Rule of Congregation of the Mission, XII, 289–90; mention of another conference on informing Superior of others' faults, XII, 405; of willingness to have faults made known to Superiors, XII, 405; all should agree to have them reported to Superior and to confess them at Chapter, I, 555; Superiors should ask to be admonished of faults, VII, 610–11; Sisters should accept that their faults be made known to Superiors, IX, 89; never mention faults of others in public, XI, 92; faults will serve to correct others and prevent them from falling into them, XII, 241; even saints have faults, IX, 214–15; XI, 354; faults of Saints Peter and Paul, IX, 214–15; of Saint Paula, XI, 354; physical defects may affect mental outlook, VI, 162; means of recognizing one's faults, XI, 101; God makes use of them for our good, XI, 119, 353; love shame or embarrassment coming from our faults, XI, 383.

Faure (Charles), Superior General of Augustinians of France - Biographical data, I, 224; II, 105–06; XII, 360; letters from Saint Vincent, I, 225; II, 509; letter to Saint Vincent, XII, 360; saint has little influence on him, I, 224; recommends young man to him, I, 225; informs him that resignation of title and possession of Sainte-Geneviève made by Cardinal de La Rochefoucauld in favor of Augustinians of France has been accepted by Court, II, 509; reform of Sainte-Geneviève Abbey, VI, 122.

Faure (Fr.), Dominican - III, 525.

Faussard (M.) - Saint Vincent allows Superior of Le Mans Seminary to hire Faussard as servant, VII, 533.

Fautier (Mme), in Angers - VI, 409, 412.

Favier (M.), Lieutenant-General of bailiwick of Toul - Efforts to have Trois-Épis Shrine entrusted to Congregation of the Mission; Saint Vincent thanks him, VIII, 11–12; mention of letter to Saint Vincent, VIII, 11.

Favre [Faver] (Marie-Jacqueline), Visitandine - Biographical data, I, 120; XII, 354; Superior of Second Monastery in Paris, I, 107, 120; wrote life of Mother Anne-Catherine de Beaumont-Carra, III, 196.

Fayet (Nicolas), brother of Mme Goussault - Executor of her will - XIIIb, 391–95.

Fear of God - "Grille" of Daughters of Charity, X, 530; without this fear we are in a state of neglect, XII, 115; Saint Vincent reproaches Saint Louise for her apprehension, I, 150, 158.

Félix (Abbé), in Marseilles - VII, 488.

Félix (Jean), servant, in Rome - VI, 579; VII, 46.

Felix (Saint) - Saint Adaucte wants to be his companion in martyrdom, XI, 374–75.

Fénelon (Marquis de la Mothe) - See **La Mothe-Fénelon**.

Férault (Madeleine) - Seeks dispensation, VIII, 199.

Ferdinand-Charles, Prince, Bishop of Wrocław [Breslau] - Contacts with Missionaries in Poland, V, 255; illness, V, 366; death, V, 394.

Ferentilli (Msgr. di), Roman Prelate - Competency and devotedness, IV, 137; why Mazarin does not seem to appreciate his services, III, 477–78; Saint Vincent questions proposals made to Fr. Alméras, III, 491; mention of letter to Saint Vincent, V, 203; saint speaks highly of Ferentilli to Ambassador of Portugal, V, 203; other mention, V, 176.

Féret (Hippolyte), Pastor of Saint-Nicolas-du-Chardonnet, Vicar-General of Paris - Biographical data, II, 142; III, 72; IV, 64; V, 579; VI, 44; VII, 41; VIII, 465; XII, 56; Saint Vincent "lends" him to Bishop Pavillon of Alet, who makes him Vicar-General, III, 100; Pavillon insists on retaining him, II, 614; announces approaching return to Paris, III, 100; goes to take possession of Saint-Nicolas parish in Paris, III, 71–72; Saint Vincent proposes him as Coadjutor of Bishop of Babylon, III, 165; draws him back from new opinions to which Pavillon had won him over, III, 329; tells him Ladies of Charity gave 300 livres to Bishop of Boulogne, VII, 41, 42; Fr. Féret sees number of Communions decreasing in parish, III, 321; aids parts of Paris diocese ravaged by passage of armies, IV, 511; participates, with Saint Vincent, in conference on Jansenism, VI, 44; ways to oppose Jansenism, VI, 152; contacts with Saint Vincent, IV, 464; VIII, 465, 547; XII, 56, 125; other mentions, IV, 64, 319; V, 579; VII, 548, 641; VIII, 501, 507.

Féris (M.), benefactor of Marseilles Missionaries - Ransom of his son, slave in Algiers, V, 392.

Ferns, town in Ireland - Bishop: see Nicolas **French**.

Féron (Anne) - Member of Charity of Argenteuil, XIIIb, 107.

Féron (Blaise), Archdeacon of Chartres - See **Le Féron**.

Férot (Claude), Priest of the Mission - Biographical data, IV, 428; V, 177; VI, 611; VII, 512; VIII, 158; goes to assist suffering in environs of Étampes, IV, 428–29; in Agde, V, 177; sent from La Rose to Luçon, VI, 611; in Richelieu, VII, 512; recalled to Paris, VIII, 158.

Ferrand (M.), Councillor at Parlement - XIIIa, 352–53, 355.

Ferrara - Town in northern Italy, where confreres stay, I, 264, 540.

Ferrat (M.), Bailiff in Vertus - Contacts with Saint Vincent, I, 116, 118, 132–33.

Ferraud (M.) - Member of Charity of Joigny, XIIIb, 66.

Ferré (Clémence), Daughter of Charity - Biographical data, VII, 192; in Angers, I, 603; II, 12; XIIIb, 118; recalled from Chars, VI, 651; has requisite qualities to be Sister Servant, VII, 192; other mention, XIIIb, 228.

Ferrer (Vincent), Saint - see **Vincent Ferrer**.

Ferreri (Giuseppe) - Successor to Montorio as Vice-Legate of Avignon, I, 9.

Ferreux, village in Aube - Missions, I, 28.

Ferrier (Jean), Jesuit - Biographical data; study on probabilism, VII, 547.

Ferrier (Fr.), priest - Biographical data, III, 294.

Ferrier (M. du) - Opens, with Fr. Olier, seminary at Vaugirard, then at Saint-Sulpice, II, 308.

Ferrier (René), Vice-Postulator of cause of Saint Francis de Sales in Paris - XIIIa, 81.

Ferrières-Gâtinais, town in Loiret - Birthplace of Jean Pillé, II, 364; Pastors, II, 365–68; VIII, 526; Charity of Ferrières, II, 367; XIIIb, 5.

Feuillants [Cistercians] - Division within Order, II, 518; gift of Louis Callon, III, 37; other mention, XIIIa, 60.

Fevers (Double, Tertian, Quartan) - I, 573, 580; V, 300–01, 360; VII, 282, 286.

Fevron (Antonin), chaplain of Saint-Pierre Church in Mâcon - XIIIb, 73–74, 76, 78.

Feydeau (Mathieu), Curate at Saint-Merry - Editor of *Catéchisme de la grâce*, IV, 185.

Feydin (François), Priest of the Mission - Biographical data, V, 425; VIII, 102; mention of letters to Saint Vincent, VIII, 102; named for Madagascar, V, 425; VIII, 160; proposed to *Propaganda Fide* for this mission, V, 431; Saint Vincent tells him of approaching departure, VIII, 102; journey to Madagascar; return, VIII, 157, 185, 202, 207, 219, 225, 229, 231, 247, 249, 252, 256, 554–55, 561–62, 567, 571, 574, 581, 585, 587–88, 592–93; health, VIII, 568. See also ***Madagascar***.

Fez, kingdom in Africa - IV, 302, 331.

Fiacre (Bro.) - V, 451.

Fichet (François), Brother of the Mission - Biographical data, VII, 494.

Fidelity to God - Conference, IX, 490–505; reasons for being faithful to God, IX, 490–91, 393, 493–500; in what fidelity consists, IX, 492–93, 500–02; means for remaining faithful, IX, 493–94, 502–05; fidelity of those called accomplishes Our Lord's work, III, 66–67; everyone will be edified by fidelity to observance of Rules, III, 251; will draw down God's grace, IV, 169; the lives of thousands depend on fidelity of Daughters of Charity, IX, 9; fidelity to Rules and customs assures spiritual progress, XI, 346; Our Lord finishes work begun, XII, 388.

Fiesque (Marie de) - See **Bréauté**.

Fieubet (Claude Ardier, Dame) - I, 347.

Fieulaine, village in Aisne - See **Paix** (**Notre-Dame de**).

Figeard (M.), physician - I, 196.

Filles-Dieu, convent - Debts, XIIIb, 325; other mention, II, 591.

Fîmes (Marie de), Daughter of Charity - VI, 417; XIIIb, 228.

Fiquelmont (René-Louis de), Abbot of Mouzon - Cedes Sedan parish to Priests of the Mission; conditions, II, 468, 524–25; VIII, 611; contacts with Sedan Missionaries, IV, 333; in Saint-Méen, IV, 522, 577; donates 400 livres for establishment of Confraternity of Blessed Sacrament in Sedan church, IV, 602; Saint Vincent recommends to him Daughters of Charity in Mouzon, V, 185; death, V, 211.

Fiquet (François), slave in Algiers - Became a Turk (Muslim), V, 353.

Flacourt (Étienne de), French Governor of Madagascar - Biographical data, III, 279; V, 286; VI, 245; VIII, 95; XI, 269; mention of letter to Saint Vincent, VIII, 95; dedication of book to Saint Vincent, XIIIa, 185; orders M. de Bloye to accompany Frs. Nacquart and Gondrée to Madagascar, III, 289; goes to Madagascar, III, 280, 283–84, 289, 333, 543–44; in Madagascar, III, 434, 542, 554–56, 560, 570–71, 582, 594–96; V, 286, 288, 306, 307; upsets Fr. Nacquart by injustices and methods, III, 570–72, 579–83, 582, 593–95; returns to France accompanied by four young natives, VI, 245; XI, 269; praises Fr. Nacquart, V, 286; Saint Vincent asks for information, VIII, 96.

Flacourt (Marie Sublet, Dame de) - Biographical data; asks favor of Saint Vincent, VIII, 418.

Flahan (Fr.), Priest of the Mission - Biographical data; on mission in Poissy, I, 229; dismissed from Company, I, 278.

Flamen (Gilles), priest of Amiens diocese - Witness to power of attorney to take possession of Bons-Enfants, XIIIa, 72.

Flamignon (Fr.), religious of old Saint-Lazare - IV, 307.

Flanders, Region of Belgium - IV, 279, 461; V, 89, 407; VI, 480; VIII, 220, 431, 565–66, 594, 596; IX, 213; XII, 35; Daughter of Charity from Flanders, IV, 383.

Flandin-Maillet (Antoine) - Biographical data, IX, 332–33; eloquence, IX, 333; graciously accepts illness and other trials, IX, 377; XI, 61; XII, 29.

Fléau (M.), clerk in Fontenay-le-Comte - Examined sale document for house of Congregation of the Mission in Luçon, XIIIa, 320.

Fleury (Antoine), Priest of the Mission - Biographical data, VII, 22; VIII, 51; on mission in Bruyères, VII, 22; in Saintes, VII, 426; VIII, 415; trials, VII, 181, 322; Saint Vincent writes to encourage him, VII, 355; mention of letter to Saint Vincent, VII, 426; permits him to take vows, VIII, 51; too concerned about family, VII, 357; VIII, 254.

Fleury (M. de) - Dispute with Missionaries in Toul, I, 558; II, 68, 74; death, II, 113.

Fleury (François de), Chaplain of Queen of Poland, nephew of preceding - Biographical data, I, 438; IV, 62–63; V, 50–51; VI, 5; VII, 264; XI, 333; Jansenist leanings, IV, 353; Saint Vincent informs him of next departure of Missionaries for Poland, IV, 63; mention of letters from Saint Vincent, V, 51, 580; of letters to Saint Vincent, IV, 371, 538; relationship with saint, IV, 319, 329, 371; V, 340, 580; XI, 333; with Missionaries in Poland, V, 105, 143, 263, 323–24; kindness to them, IV, 289; V, 50, 51, 70, 181, 192, 196–97, 202, 218–19, 255, 257, 338, 351, 366; VI, 182; Saint Vincent advises them to consult him, VII, 264, 275–76; Fleury accepts direction of Visitandines of Warsaw, V, 238; death, VII, 415; other mentions, V, 162, 377, 419; VI, 5.

Fleury (Henri Clausse de), Bishop of Châlons; Saint Vincent recommends Saint Louise to be submissive to him, I, 118, 124–25, 131.

Flightiness - Danger of flightiness, XIIIb, 129; no steadfastness in resolutions of frivolous spirit, XIIIb, 362.

Flogni (M. de) - V, 370.

Floods [**Inundations**] - See **Paris**.

Florence, town in Italy - Grand-Duke of Florence: see ***Tuscany***; other mention, III, 537.

Florent (Jean-Baptiste), Priest of the Mission - Biographical data, V, 20; VIII, 225; in Sedan, V, 591; VIII, 225.

Flous (M.) - II, 555.

Foillard (Hugues), Lieutenant-General in Mâcon - XIIIb, 69, 71, 73, 77.

Foix, town - François-Étienne de Caulet, Abbot of Foix: see **Caulet**; reform of Abbey, I, 210; II, 512; letter of Saint Vincent to Governor of fiefdom, III, 95.

Folleville, village in Somme - Mission given by Saint Vincent, IX, 49; XI, 2, 162; XII, 7, 73; origin of Congregation of the Mission, XI, 162–64; regulations for Charity of women, XIIIb, 40; for Charity of men, XIIIb, 48.

Fondimare (Pierre de), Priest of the Mission - "Has his heart in the corruption of flesh and blood," III, 204; departure from Company, III, 371, 373.

Fonsomme (M. de) - VI, 503.

Fontaine [**Fonteines**] (Louise-Eugénie de), nun in First Monastery of Visitation in Paris - Biographical data, II, 202; III, 70; IV, 433; V, 557; VI, 426; VII, 602; VIII, 426; letters from Saint Vincent, II, 242; III, 70; VII, 602; letters to Saint Vincent, VIII, 426, 430, 489, 504, 529, 533; reference to letter to Saint Vincent, IV, 433; words of praise for her, II, 202; asks for heart of Saint Jane Frances for her monastery; does not get it, II, 239, 250; other mentions, II, 464; V, 557; VI, 426; VIII, 476.

Fontaine (M.), in Paris - I, 208.

Fontaine, village in Marne - Mission in area, VII, 165.

Fontaine-Essarts, hamlet in Courbeteaux (Marne) - Establishment of Missionaries, II, 259, 273–74, 674; III, 78; VI, 89, 457, 616; VII, 220, 301; Missionaries' farm in Montmirail, II, 554; IV, 313; VIII, 612; other mention, VII, 613.

Fontainebleau, town in Seine-et-Marne - Journeys of Saint Vincent to Fontainebleau, II, 533, 535–36, 674; III, 62, 68; mission, II, 534, 536, 538–39; Confraternity of Charity, II, 533; Sister sent to visit patient there, III, 379; other mentions, III, 50; IV, 303; XIIIa, 348; Daughters of Charity in Fontainebleau; two Sisters sent at request of Queen, III, 21; need of assistance, VI, 652: see also **Angiboust** (Barbe), **Marguerite** (Sister).

Fontaines (Pasquier de), Priest of the Mission - Biographical data, VI, 419; VII, 101–02; VIII, 183; ordination, VI, 419, 429; sent to Madagascar, VII, 102, 104, 108; captured; returns to Paris by way of Spain, VII, 239, 257, 265, 282–83, 286–87, 616; VIII, 183; health, VII, 282, 284, 286; proposed for departure from Dieppe, VIII, 185; new embarkation from La Rochelle, VIII, 219, 225, 229, 231, 247, 249, 252, 256, 554–55; journey to Madagascar; returns to Paris, VIII, 561–62, 571, 574, 584, 587–88, 596. See also ***Madagascar***.

Fontenay-aux-Roses, town near Paris - Praise for Daughters of Charity, II, 218; problem concerning Sister Anne, II, 285–87, 291; Sister Perrette sent to Fontenay, II, 327, 328; Sister Henriette indispensable for school, II, 392; other mentions, III, 177; V, 439.

Fontenay-le-Comte, town in Vendée - VII, 637; XIIIa, 317, 320, 321.

Fontenay-Mareuil (François du Val, Marquis de) - Biographical data, II, 54; III, 375; member of Charity of Lorraine nobility, II, 54, 55; French Ambassador to Rome, II, 245, 255, 280, 297, 498; III, 375.

Fonteneil (Jean de), Vicar-General of Bordeaux - Biographical data, I, 268; II, 56; III, 56–57; VI, 323–24; VII, 258; VIII, 510; letters from Saint Vincent, I, 268, 291, 412, 481; II, 56; III, 56; VII, 354; Saint Vincent sends packet of mission documents to Canon Ducasse at Fonteneil's home, VI, 323–24; services rendered to Missionaries and Daughters of Charity, I, 269, 291, 412, 482, 487; II, 57; III, 56; VII, 258, 354; to relatives of Saint Vincent, I, 291, 481; his Congregation, II, 56–57; VIII, 510; other mention, IV, 469.

Fonteyne - See **La Fonteyne**.

Forbearance [**Mutual Support**] - Conferences, X, 383–90; XII, 30–33; mention of other conferences, XII, 430, 432; Saint Vincent notes that forbearance is practiced in Company, XII, 32; exhortations on practice of this virtue, IV, 233, 242, 265; V, 142; everyone needs support, IV, 233, 442; V, 143; VIII, 169; IX, 45, 63, 99, 431, 461; X, 385, 388, 451, 424; XII, 30, 31; especially Missionaries, to evangelize poor persons, XII, 248–49; and Superiors to govern: see also **Superiors**; bearing with ourselves, X, 386; advantages of forbearance, IX, 229–31; mutual support recommended by Rule of Daughters of Charity, X, 383; example and recommendation of Our Lord, II, 463; X, 163–64, 383, 452; XII, 30; mutual support would make Company paradise on earth, X, 384; lack of forbearance would lead Company to ruin, IX, 225–26; forbearance springs from charity, I, 597; IX, 221–22; mutual support in all things, X, 163; XII, 30; bear with complaints, X, 3; forbearance sometimes difficult, even among friends; example of two abbés, XII, 31–32; means of bearing with self, IX, 403–04; one of these is humility, X, 425; which makes us believe we are at fault rather than others, IX, 411–12; bear in mind that we ourselves need to be tolerated, IX, 63; ask pardon when we fail in forbearance: see also **Reconciliation**; prayer that

Company may have virtue of mutual support, IX, 236–37; forbearance brings recognition of faults better than reproofs, III, 480; means for changing another's heart, V, 605; needed to instill trust in those in our care and win them over to God, VII, 609; a little forbearance arranges everything, IX, 61; Sisters owe it to one another, IX, 88; needed to live in union and to avoid complaints, IX, 99; necessary sign of Daughters of Charity, IX, 461–62; example of Barbe Angiboust, X, 520.

Forbin (Bailiff de), Lieutenant-General of Galleys - II, 252, 339.

Foreign Missions Society - Petition to Pope for priests to be sent to Tonkin and Cochinchina with title of Bishops *in partibus*, IV, 595; petition to *Propaganda Fide* for same purpose, V, 15; several priests volunteer for Tonkin and Cochinchina; one makes retreat at Saint-Lazare, VI, 553; journey to Rome; Pope praises zeal, XI, 375; François Pallu receives hospitality in Missionaries' house in Rome, VI, 605; Saint Vincent does not think they intend to form Congregation, VI, 553, 630; other mentions, II, 522, 641.

Foresight - Excessive foresight is harmful to those who rely more on their own efforts than on Divine Providence, IV, 346.

Forest (Mme), Lady of Charity - Praise for her, I, 212; contacts with Daughters of Charity, I, 233, 235, 563; with Saint Vincent, I, 104; II, 194.

Forest (René), Brother of the Mission - Biographical data, IV, 109; V, 71; just back from Madagascar; ready to return there, IV, 109; about to set sail, V, 71, 76, 82; voyage, V, 281, 283; in Madagascar, V, 307.

Forêt (Anne) - XIIIa, 354.

Forêt-le-Roi, priory - I, 131.

Forez (Congregation of Priests) - See **Missionaries of Forez**.

Forges (M. de), equerry of Princesse de Conti - Saint Vincent writes him about M. Dufaur, VIII, 61.

Forges-les-Eaux, town in Seine-Maritime - Where Saint Vincent went over several years for his health, I, 54; thermal baths did not help fever, I, 573; Fr. Cogley in Forges, VI, 368, 390, 404; nuns near Forges, III, 370; Daughters of Charity in Forges, IV, 455.

Forne (Jean-Baptiste), administrator of Hôtel-Dieu - Contacts with Saint Vincent, V, 400; letter from Saint Vincent, V, 503.

Forne (M.), in Amiens - VI, 481.

Fors (Marquis de), son of Mme du Vigean - Death, II, 126.

Fort Dauphin, in Madagascar - III, 434, 567, 592, 598; V, 276, 288, 292, 298, 305, 307, 507; VI, 12, 18, 214, 216, 222, 230, 235.

Fortet, collège in Paris - II, 540.

Fortia (Anne de la Barre, Dame), Lady of Charity - I, 260, 371; II, 485.

Fortin (Blaise), priest of Coutances Diocese - Witness to taking possession of Bons-Enfants, XIIIa, 73.

Fortitude - Mention of conference, XII, 421; fortitude of Saint Francis de Sales, XIIIa, 87–88.

Fossano, town in Piedmont - Saint Vincent tells Fr. Martin to give mission in this episcopal town only on formal orders, VI, 351, 602, 639; mission in Fossano, VII, 213; other mentions, VII, 230; VIII, 87.

Fosse (*Quai de la*), in Nantes - VIII, 557.

Fouache (M.), seminarian - Departure from Company, II, 321.

Foucauld (M.) - I, 450.

Fouchet (Marie), nurse of sick poor for Charity of Joigny - XIIIb, 28.

Fouillet (Nicole), Daughter of Charity - XIIIb, 228.

Fouins (Barbe), Daughter of Charity - XIIIb, 227.

Foulé (M.), Superintendent of Finance in Provence - Steps taken concerning hospital for prisoners in Marseilles, VI, 261, 265, 279, 301, 304, 392.

Foundations - Do not seek foundations; leave to Providence, III, 197; IV, 144; VI, 610: see also **Congregation of the Mission**; what is necessary for foundation of Missionaries' house, VII, 223; accept foundations only in perpetuity, VII, 607; making small foundations is necessary for beginning Community, IV, 466; preferable that revenue of foundation be in securities, given variations in cost of living, I, 384; Saint Vincent advises Fr. Blatiron not to accept foundation in Genoa, V, 136; 1651 Assembly stresses need to fulfill conditions of foundations, XIIIa, 373; virtues necessary for Sisters sent to new foundations, IX, 203; XIIIb, 314; kindness to those they replace, XIIIb, 279; God blesses humble beginnings, II, 351; V, 219, 477–78, 485, 493; do not accept missions without financial backing, to detriment of endowed missions, I, 403; Fr. Nacquart asks about accepting foundation for maintenance in Madagascar, III, 287–88; Saint Vincent is obliged to refuse foundation for lack of personnel, V, 39–40; question about celebration of foundation Masses, VIII, 226; other mention, XII, 270.

Founders - Saint Vincent judges it natural that founders in need receive revenue, or even capital, from their foundation, III, 37–38; recognition, respect, and deference owed founders, XIIIb, 276; respect their intentions, IV, 70; give reports from time to time of activities in mission funded by them, XIIIb, 280; their rights are limited, XIIIb, 343, 375; Superioress must never complain of Sister in presence of founders, XIIIb, 277. See also **Callon**, **Gondi** (P. E.), **Gondi (**Mme de**)**, **Le Bon**.

Foundlings - La Couche before 1638, XIIIb, 397, 415, 421, 430; Ladies of Charity adopt children and entrust them to Daughters of Charity (1638); beginnings of ministry, I, 401, 407, 410, 415, 423; purchase of goat, I, 411, 423, 457; XIIIb, 140; report of Saints Vincent and Louise on ministry with foundlings, I, 408, 426; plan of M. and Mlle Hardy for organization of work, I, 410, 423; meetings of Ladies for Foundlings ministry, I, 450, 562; union of ministry of Foundlings with that of Hôtel-Dieu, I, 537; XIIIb, 400; presence of soldiers creates uneasiness; steps to disperse them, I, 431–36; question of transferring foundlings elsewhere, I, 437; painting given for foundlings, I, 446; Rule for Sisters serving them, IX, 17; Canons of Notre-Dame insist that Ladies assume total care of children at La Couche, XIIIb, 430; Saint Vincent urges Ladies to accept; tells them how ministry could function, XIIIb, 397–401; Ladies accept on January 12, 1640, II, 8; conditions of acceptance, XIIIb, 401–02; begin ministry on March 30, XIIIb, 402–03; Saint Vincent recommends ministry to Ladies at their meetings, XIIIb, 402, 405, 413, 415, 419–21, 423–26, 430; Ladies threaten to withdraw if all authority over ministry is removed from them, II, 108; Serquemanant affair, II, 485–87; lawsuit against mother of foundling, II, 137, 139; fighting near Foundling Home; fright of children and nurses, IV, 378; need for housing, III, 431.

Sister Anne will leave Fontenay-aux-Roses for Foundlings when Saint Louise is there, II, 291–92; foundlings housed in faubourg Saint-Victor, rue des Boulangers, I, 532; XIIIb, 403; in La Chapelle, Sisters' Motherhouse, II, 293; XIIIb, 403; discussion of transfer to new Motherhouse of Sisters, rue du Faubourg-Saint-Denis, II, 292–93; children in Saint-Laurent parish, III, 179, 201, 507; at Bicêtre, III, 212, 400; IV, 177; Ladies should not take in more babies, III, 585; search for housing, I, 435; IV, 177, 378; children at Treize-Maisons, IV, 170, 382; V, 139; X, 487, 490; site and origin of Treize-Maisons, X, 487; XIIIa, 340–41; plan to transfer weaned children to Enfermés, IV, 24; taking in children, I, 483, 532; II, 47; IV, 158; foundlings accepted only on order of commissioner, VI, 317; seigneurs obliged to feed abandoned children, VI, 317.

Formation of foundlings, IX, 113; administrator of Hôtel-Dieu claims to be in charge of Foundlings as well, III, 228; Ladies see to spiritual, temporal needs, III, 228; numbers at different periods, II, 166; IX, 112; XIIIb, 403, 425, 430; baptisms, I, 483; IX, 112; deaths, I, 446, 472; III, 266; XIIIb, 338, 403, 407; little boy's unusual death, XIIIb, 338; older girls placed in service, V, 215; question of placing young girl in religious Order, XIIIb, 336; Saint Vincent wonders if girls could not provide good vocations for Daughters of Charity, XIIIb, 353; Queen of Poland asks same, IX, 463; ministry is in Our Lord's hands, III, 520.

Wet-nurses, I, 415, 423, 437, 483, 497; II, 166, 178–79, 293; III, 228, 469, 504–05, 517, 519; IV, 5; VII, 114; XIIIb, 403; visit to children placed with wet-nurses, II, 328, 330, 337, 655; X, 520; XIIIb, 248, 403; invitations to visit foundlings, XIIIb, 388; organization of ministry, I, 425, 434, 593; XIIIb, 399–401; financial state, IV, 194; XIIIb, 399, 407, 430; alms for work, II, 299, 300; III, 254; foundlings have too much bread, II, 292; in dire need, XIIIb, 421, 423; visits of Saint Vincent to foundlings, I, 436, 596; II, 130–32; visit of Saint Louise, II, 474; foundlings capable of working requested for Madagascar, X, 96; Missionaries are chaplains for foundlings, XI, 65, 184; VIII, 279; XII, 78–79; dying Saint Vincent blesses foundlings, XIIIa, 205; foundlings at Hôtel-Dieu: see also ***Hôtel-Dieu***; foundlings at Bicêtre: see ***Bicêtre***; other mentions, II, 164; VIII, 234; XIIIb, 279, 413, 439, 441, 443. See also **Ladies of Charity**.

Daughters of Charity with foundlings: Saint Vincent wants ministry of Foundlings to depend on Superioress of Daughters of Charity, I, 425, 434, 593; Sisters responsible for their feeding and education, XIIIb, 447; maneuvers of Mme Pelletier, I, 429; increase in number of Sisters serving them, II, 598; Saint Vincent tells Saint Louise she is officer of Charity of Foundlings, and among most important, II, 635; Foundling Home serves as Jubilee station, V, 580; conference to Sisters on ministry of Foundlings, IX, 104–05, 115; Rule for Sisters with foundlings, II, 130, 131; fidelity to four o'clock rising, X, 477–78; virgins and mothers, X, 92–93, 95; obligation of not giving scandal to children, X, 39; Saint Vincent considers odious the rumor that Sisters placed with foundlings are unsuitable elsewhere, X, 39, 195; children call Sisters "aunts," X, 39; question of relieving Sisters of weaned infants, II, 152; Sisters ministering at Foundlings in 1645–46, II, 601; III, 61; increase in number of Sisters in near future, II, 598; personnel: see **Lauraine** (Claude), **Matrilomeau** (Marie), **Poisson** (Geneviève); other mentions, I, 574, 601; II, 300, 629; V, 579; VI, 287; IX, 52, 521, 522; X, 100, 102, 104, 118, 295,

370, 464–65, 557, 562–63, 564; XIIIb, 136, 205–06, 266, 268, 286.

Fountain of Youth - What prayer is for the soul, IX, 328.

Fouquesolle (Mme de) - Biographical data, V, 627; letter from Saint Vincent, V, 627.

Fouquet (Anne-Madeleine), Visitandine, daughter of Mme Fouquet (Marie de Maupeou) - III, 87.

Fouquet (Catherine), widow of Comte de Vertus - Biographical data; message sent in care of Abbé de Vaux, II, 223–24.

Fouquet (Élisabeth-Angélique), Visitandine, daughter of Mme Fouquet (Marie de Maupeou) - VIII, 505, 517.

Fouquet (François), Vicomte de Vaux - Biographical data, I, 471; illness, I, 471; cured of dropsy, I, 508; death, II, 53; burial, V, 558–62.

Fouquet (François), son of Mme Fouquet (Marie de Maupeou); member of Tuesday Conferences - Biographical data, I, 413; II, 4; III, 230; V, 226; VI, 78; VII, 485–86; VIII, 5; XI, 327–28; letters from Saint Vincent, VIII, 108, 144, 383, 478; letters to Saint Vincent, VIII, 538; in praise of him, II, 4–5; contacts with Saint Vincent, I, 492; mention of letter to Saint Vincent, VIII, 383; named Bishop of Bayonne, I, 413; advice of Saint Vincent, II, 4–7, 52–53; report of Prelate concerning seminary, II, 311; nephew of Bishop of Condom would like to succeed him; Saint Vincent judges him unworthy, III, 230; other mentions, I, 466–67; II, 193; Bishop of Agde: contacts with Missionaries there, V, 226; VI, 78; brought Congregation of the Mission to Agde for new foundation, VIII, 618: see also ***Agde***; Fouquet sends to Saint-Lazare, for retreat and instruction, priests preparing to teach school, XII, 138–39; other mention, VII, 485; Archbishop of Narbonne: Saint Vincent recommends moderation in zeal, VIII, 108; Prelate requests Missionaries, VIII, 108, 144, 348, 373, 383, 478–79, 619; Saint Vincent sends some, VIII, 144, 360, 537, 619; sends observations on plan for union of Narbonne Seminary to Congregation of the Mission, VIII, 538–39; Archbishop informs Saint Vincent that the Bishop of Montpellier no longer wishes to support his seminary, VIII, 272–74; Fouquet presses Saint Vincent to consent to union of Maiour parish to seminary, VIII, 478; saint's thoughts on this, XIIIa, 197; Fouquet asks for Daughters of Charity, VIII, 137; XIIIb, 370; Sisters sent to Narbonne, VIII, 144; X, 533; XIIIb, 237; on his orders, Françoise Carcireux is instructed on teaching youth, VIII, 379; X, 587; other mentions, VIII, 5, 387, 471, 521.

Fouquet (Jean) - Inquiries about M. Senant's return, VIII, 532–33.

Fouquet (Louis), Bishop of Agde, son of Mme Fouquet (Marie de Maupeou) - Saint Vincent is sending him Missioner, VIII, 59–60; awaits Prelate's reply, VIII, 72; asks for new foundation contract for Agde Seminary, VIII, 114; other mention, VIII, 260.

Fouquet (Louise-Agnès), Visitandine, daughter of Mme Fouquet (Marie de Maupeou) - III, 87.

Fouquet (Madeleine-Augustine), Visitandine, daughter of Mme Fouquet (Marie de Maupeou) - Biographical data, III, 87; other mention, III, 86.

Fouquet (Marie de Maupeou, Dame), wife of Vicomte de Vaux - Biographical data, III, 87; IV, 216; V, 344; VI, 202–03; VII, 199; VIII, 26–27; XI, 328; her charities, VI, 414; VIII, 459; services she renders Saint Vincent and his ministries as Lady of Charity or mother of Attorney General, VII, 199, 337, 403, 410, 438, 455, 467; VIII, 26–27, 29, 421; contacts with Saint Vincent, V, 365, 486, 560; VIII, 26, 59, 125, 387, 540, 543, 551; XI, 328; XIIIb, 342; Ladies of Charity meet in her home, VI, 202–03; her daughter, Mme **Dupart**: see this name; other mentions, IV, 216; V, 344, 438, 560; VI, 609.

Fouquet (Marie-Thérèse), Visitandine, daughter of Mme Fouquet (Marie de Maupeou) - Superior of Visitation of Toulouse, III, 87; VIII, 144.

Fouquet (Nicolas), Attorney General and Superintendent of Finances, son of Mme Fouquet (Marie de Maupeou) - Biographical data, II, 429; IV, 158; V, 337; VI, 207; VII, 289; VIII, 125; arbitrator in dispute, II, 429; Saint Louise speaks of sending Sister to consult him, IV, 158; Saint Vincent seeks his patronage, V, 486; review of clauses of proposed contract with Superior of First Monastery of Visitation concerning her burial place, V, 557–62; intervention concerning house for galley convicts in Paris, V, 337, 343–44; concerning chaplains' wages and hospital for galley convicts in Marseilles, VI, 207, 260, 266; VII, 289, 403, 467; donation to this hospital, VII, 438, 455, 458, 467, 488, 520, 538, 556; requests Daughters of Charity for Vaux-le-Vicomte, VIII, 125; other mentions, VIII, 421, 517; XIIIb, 145.

Fourché (Fr.), Jesuit - Helps Saint Vincent with mission in Folleville, XI, 4.

Fourché (J.), administrator of Nantes Hospital - II, 645.

Fouré (Jeanne), Daughter of Charity - Biographical data, III, 396; in Fréneville, III, 396, 400.

Fournier (François), Priest of the Mission, son of M. Fournier-Dupont - Biographical data, III, 463–64; IV, 539–40; V, 30; VII, 478; VIII, 1; letters Saint Vincent writes him in Agen, III,

463; IV, 545; V, 30, 85; in Cahors, VIII, 1; mention of letters to Saint Vincent, V, 31, 85; VIII, 1, 2; his praises; ordination, III, 611; in Agen, III, 611; IV, 539, 588; Saint Vincent permits him to go to debates on philosophy and theology, IV, 545; in Cahors, V, 590; VII, 478; VIII, 519; his cousin, VIII, 116; Saint Vincent asks him to help Fr. Cuissot with direction of Daughters of Charity in Cahors, VIII, 270, 271.

Fournier (J.), administrator of Nantes Hospital - II, 645.

Fournier (Jacques), called Larivière, galley convict in Toulon - VIII, 266, 337, 361, 402, 528.

Fournier (Louis), Captain from Île de Ré, slave in Algiers - V, 141, 145–46, 326.

Fournier (M.), physician, in Château-Thierry - I, 456.

Fournier (Mme) - Member of Charity of Montmirail, XIIIb, 33.

Fournier (Pierre), Jesuit - Biographical data; letter to Saint Vincent, II, 404.

Fournier-Dupont (M.), lawyer in Laval - Thinks he is called to priesthood; Saint Vincent disabuses him, VII, 478; letter to Saint Vincent, VIII, 518, 520; other mention, IV, 539–40.

"Fourteen" Ladies of Charity - Responsible, in turn, every three months, for spiritual assistance of patients, XIIIb, 379–83, 413, 445; Regulations for the "Fourteen Ladies," XIIIb, 382–83; 444–45; Saint Vincent wonders if seven would not be sufficient, XIIIb, 388; applauds their zeal, I, 450; XIIIb, 408, 413, 438, 444–45; meeting of "the Fourteen," II, 317.

Fracioti (Agostino), titular Archbishop of Trabzon - Saint Vincent has received documents from him, III, 274; letter delivered to him, V, 176; death, XIIIa, 196.

Framez (Charles de), Canon of Écouis - XIIIa, 26, 30.

France - State of Church in seventeenth-century France: see also **Clergy**; danger of Church being lost there, XI, 318; miseries caused by Fronde, X, 17; XI, 190: see also **Fronde**; prayers for peace, XII, 412; French move too quickly in business affairs, II, 267; missions, IV, 441; V, 573; Russian Tsar is about to send ambassador, V, 143; Missionaries have authority to establish Confraternities of Charity, X, 82; XIIIb, 225; embroiled affairs between France and England, XI, 177; prayers for peace, XI, 189; number of heretics, XI, 279; Jean Le Vacher in Tunis at peace with French merchants, XI, 334; uniformity of Church in France with Rome, XII, 211; faith preserved through catechism, XIIIa, 34; ministry of Congregation of the Mission throughout the country, XIIIa, 186, 208; other mentions, I, 249; VII, 629; VIII, 539.

Frances of Rome (Saint) - Saw her Guardian Angel, II, 380.

Franchiscou (M.), slave in Algiers - V, 354, 404.

Francière (M. de), administrator of Hôtel-Dieu of Saint-Denis - Illness; Saint Louise fears Daughters of Charity may be dismissed from hospital after his death, V, 332–33; he promises to protect them, V, 484; rumored that he is inclined to dismiss them, V, 643.

Francillon (François), Brother of the Mission - Biographical data, II, 639; III, 300; catches plague in Tunis; recovers, III, 349; nurses Superior while ill himself, III, 350.

Franconville - Visit of Confraternity of Charity, XII, 356.

Francis of Paola (Saint) - II, 565; XI, 167.

Francis Xavier (Saint) - Exactness in observing Rules and customs of his Society, I, 525; zeal, XIIIa, 186; did not see all results of it in his lifetime, V, 463; did not visit parents before leaving for Indies, II, 122; Saint Vincent proposes him as model to Fr. de Sergis, I, 342, 345; to Fr. Nacquart, III, 279–80, 283; Madagascar Missionaries' devotion to him, III, 539, 543, 566, 572, 576, 578; V, 297; VIII, 555, 568, 572, 577, 592; devotion of Fr. de Sergis, I, 544.

Franciscans [**Cordeliers**] - Love for poverty, IX, 387; X, 242; no other subject of prayer than the Passion, IX, 28; X, 457; have always needed reform, X, 84; lack nothing, X, 242; division among Franciscans in France, IV, 484, 488; VIII, 514; expelled from Marseilles, VIII, 328, 528; Third Order, XIIIa, 404; regrettable conduct of Franciscans who direct nuns of Longchamp, IV, 485–86, 489–90; Saint Vincent asks that Longchamp Abbey be removed from their jurisdiction, IV, 485, 487, 491; Franciscans of Niolo, IV, 407; of Agde, VII, 171–72; death of Franciscan in Tunisia, V, 132; vows, XII, 303–04. See also **Ange de Clavasio** (Fr.), **Bonaventure** (Saint), **Cordeliers**, **Francis of Assisi** (Saint); other mentions, IV, 413; X, 288; XI, 262; XII, 295.

Francisco (Carlo), Priest of the Mission - Genoa, VIII, 156.

Francisco (Marc), slave in Algiers - V, 326, 327.

Francis de Sales (Saint) - Biographical data, I, 55; II, 6; V, 23; VII, 215; VIII, 39; IX, 12; XI, 21; love of God, XI, 207; XIIIa, 83; piety, IX, 175, 265; XIIIa, 91; method of prayer, I, 389, 553; IV, 385; X, 471; XI, 234; XIIIa, 89; gentleness, I, 271, 375; IX, 127; X, 318; XI, 54, 57; XII, 393; XIIIa, 82, 89; condescension, I, 55; goodness, I, 586; III, 490; love of neighbor, III, 175; XIIIa, 84–86, 89, 90, 92, 93; devotion to children, IX, 330; XIIIa, 90; spirit of humility, I, 184; preached simply, XI, 255; wills body to medical science, XII, 241; prudence, XIIIa, 86–87; justice, XIIIa, 87; fortitude, XIIIa, 87–88; temperance, chastity, humility, XIIIa, 88; patience, XIIIa, 88–89; mortification, X, 318–19; sufferings, II, 6; thoughts on self-love, IX, 136.

Relationship with Saint Vincent, III, 490; IV, 588; VII, 600–601; X, 106, 286, 301, 255; XII, 343; XIIIa, 81; esteem for Saint Vincent, XIIIa, 210; they converse about Visitation Order, VII, 601; persuades Saint Vincent to become Superior of Visitation of Paris, IV, 288, 316; V, 602–03; VII, 215; XI, 160; XII, 343; Saint Vincent's devotedness to him, II, 84; VIII, 308; portrait of Saint Francis at Saint-Lazare, XI, 350; Saint Vincent's vision of soul of Saint Francis, II, 241; XIIIa, 139; Saint-Cyran thought highly of Saint Francis, XIIIa, 108.

Features of life of Saint Francis, III, 302–03; V, 478; XII, 241; disappointed heir irritated at Saint Vincent because of legacy made to Visitation convent, XIIIa, 89–90; journey of Saint Francis to Paris, V, 478; sees General of Galleys, I, 344; respect for important persons, XI, 21; original plan for foundation of Visitation, X, 83; recommends condescension to Visitandines, X, 389; and to change nothing under pretext of any advantage whatsoever, II, 515; joy and contentment at being reprimanded, IX, 178; they should esteem all other Communities greater than theirs but love theirs more than others, X, 286–87, 301; he forbids anything in rooms besides picture and book, X, 289; forbids communicating with one another without permission, X, 346–47; gave as Rule to ask and to refuse nothing, X, 224; wants Sister elected to office to accept it, XI, 128; wants Sisters of one house to be concerned about Sisters of another and, if need be, apprise Superior in Annecy of abuses, X, 266; wants Superiors to seek advice from councillors, and from them alone, concerning house matters, V, 348; Sisters tell troubles to Superior; should she fail to reassure them, then turn to someone outside; disastrous effects of this Rule, X, 361–62; too quick to draw up Rule of Visitation, III, 272; allowed Sisters to accept a few boarders, XIIIb, 290.

Writings: Visitandines have written down his conferences, XI, *xxxi*; XIIIa, 82; *Treatise on the Love of God,* I, 80, 169–70, 513; XIIIa, 84, 169; XIIIb, 282, 442; *Introduction to a Devout Life*, I, 158, 389; III, 543; IX, 12, 37, 42; 460; XII, 2; XIIIa, 93, 94; XIIIb, 19, 442; XIIIa, 130; other quotes from writings, I, 396; II, 401, 638; IX, 86, 215, 373, 374, 519; X, 223–24, 309, 397, 550; XI, 375; XII, 31, 210; XIIIa, 169; XIIIb, 282.

Death, XIIIa, 83; miracles, XIIIa, 78–79, 94–95, 212; conversions, I, 185; process of beatification, III, 226; VI, 542; VII, 517, 572–73, 598; VIII, 39; deposition of Saint Vincent at informative process in Paris, XIIIa, 80–96; Visitandines ask

Saint Vincent for postulatory letter; text and sending of letter, VII, 599–602, 606–07; chapel in church of First Monastery of Visitation in Paris to be dedicated to Saint Francis, V, 557, 559–62; life of Saint Francis by **Maupas du Tour**: see this name; given the difficulties raised about book, Visitandines are advised to stop temporarily steps in view of beatification, VI, 542; other mentions, I, 362, 368, 564; II, 134, 161, 284; III, 72, 88; V, 23, 387, 603; VI, 405; IX, 374; XII, 359; XIIIa, 170, 212; XIIIb, 275, 436.

Francis of Assisi (Saint) - Love for poverty, XI, 226; considered church in convent too beautiful; had it demolished, X, 239; on death bed, removed nightshirt in order to die naked, I, 583; humility, IX, 256; preached by his modesty, IX, 21; X, 305; prayed with arms extended, XII, 261; used only Passion of Our Lord for mental prayer, IX, 172; X, 457; devil's prediction concerning Order, IX, 518; X, 84, 288; XIIIb, 373; preferred destruction to degradation of Order, XIIIb, 344; Rule, II, 119; gave vote to lay Brothers in election of Guardians, III, 319; it was said that Order would not survive him, IX, 48; valued fact that uniformity of dress was observed among his men, X, 254; his Third Rule, XIIIa, 404–05; his feast, V, 445; VII, 299; XIIIb, 47; Saint Vincent corrects confrere who thought he had made vow to Saint Francis, IV, 569; Saint Francis did not found Daughters of Charity, IX, 359.

François, Brother of the Mission, in Montmirail - IV, 326.

François, Brother of the Mission, in Rome - II, 297, 306.

François, Brother of the Mission, in Annecy - II, 88; IV, 533.

François (M.), painter - Saint Vincent asks for news of nephew, VIII, 422.

François (Marguerite), Daughter of Charity - Among first Sisters sent to Angers, XIIIb, 116, 118.

François (Michel) - V, 200.

François (Pierre), Priest of the Mission - Biographical data, V, 377; VI, 482; VII, 319; departure for Rome, V, 377; in Rome, VI, 482; illness, VII, 319, 329.

Françoise, Daughter of Charity, in Paris - VI, 576.

Françoise, Daughter of Charity - See **Carcireux** (Françoise).

Françoise, Daughter of Charity - See **Fanchon** (Françoise).

Françoise, Daughter of Charity - See **Manceau**, (Françoise).

Françoise, Daughter of Charity - Sent to Calais, X, 440; XII, 36.

Françoise-Claire, Daughter of Charity, in Varize - V, 43.

Françoise-Paule, Daughter of Charity - See **Noret** (Françoise).

Franconville, commune in Val-d'Oise - Saint Louise's report on visit to Confraternity, XII, 356.

Frange (Jacques), galley convict in Toulon - VI, 207, 273, 276, 355.

Franqueville (M. de) - Saint Vincent reproves Jeanne Lepeintre for going to nurse gentleman, VI, 45–49.

Frascati, town in Italy - Saint Vincent encourages Fr. Jolly to go there to rest, VII, 240, 585, 595; VIII, 78.

Fréjus, town in Var - Bishop: see Louis d'**Anglure**; mission given, III, 429.

Fremin (François), captive in Algeria - Saint Vincent has money given to him, VIII, 387.

Frémiot (André), Bishop of Bourges, brother of Saint Jane Frances de Chantal - Biographical data; consulted about Visitor for Visitation Order, I, 563.

Frémon [**Frémont**] (Charles), reformer of Order of Grandmont - Biographical data; Saint Vincent supports reform, IV, 308–09.

Fremyn (M.), Presiding Judge of Parlement of Metz - Contacts with Saint Vincent, VI, 592; with Daughters of Charity sent to Metz, X, 453; mention of letter from Saint Vincent, VIII, 491; saint hopes to find house in Metz suitable for Missionaries, VIII, 14; prefers not to say anything to Fremyn, VIII, 16; M. Fremyn complains about Fr. Caset, VIII, 492.

French - Move very quickly in business, II, 267; Ambassador to Poland trying to thwart King of Sweden, VI, 83; French confreres not disposed to learn Italian, VI, 451; Frenchmen going to Rome for studies might appeal to King to avoid follow-up of their commitments, VI, 619; other nationalities would find it hard to submit to French, VI, 619; difficulty getting along with Italians, VII, 542; abandoned fort in Madagascar, VIII, 589; pay consular duties to Consul of France in Tunis, V, 89.

French (Nicolas), Bishop of Ferns, Ireland - In San Sebastián, VII, 257.

Fréneville, hamlet in commune of Valpuiseaux (Essonne) - Gift of two farms to Saint Vincent by Marquise de Herse, I, 290, 349; journeys here and sojourns of saint, I, 290, 349, 364, 465, 473–74, 476, 595; II, 528–30, 532, 534, 536–37; III, 210, 369, 392, 395, 397, 399, 400, 402, 405–06, 408, 412; other mentions, I, 357, 463, 480; III, 114.

Fresné (M. de) - VIII, 296.

Fricourt (Jean de), seminarian of the Mission - Biographical data, VII, 138; VIII, 125; in Saintes, VII, 138; Saint Vincent writes to encourage him; mention of letter to Saint Vincent, VIII, 125; very attached to family, VIII, 254; asks for saint's prayers, VIII, 415.

Friendships (Exclusive) - Conference, X, 396–402; Rule of Daughters of Charity, X, 396; love of inclination is animal love, X, 397; avoid exclusive friendships like plague, XI, 94; XIIIa, 101; dangerous, XIIIb, 126, 137.

Froger (Georges), Pastor of Saint-Nicolas-du-Chardonnet in Paris - Biographical data, I, 114; II, 68; other mentions, I, 534; II, 68, 197; XIIIb, 101.

Froment (Antoine), Priest of the Mission - Biographical data, VI, 459; VIII, 73; needs *extra tempore*, VI, 459; in Troyes, VIII, 73.

Fromentin, François, slave - M. Barreau fails to learn what became of him, V, 325, 355.

Fronde - Historical data, III, 461; IV, 111; V, 449; mention of conferences on miseries of Fronde, XII, 410, 411, 412; troubles of August 1648, III, 356; of January 1649, III, 393; Saint Vincent goes to the Court; intercedes with Queen, III, 393; pillage of Saint-Lazare, III, 394; of Orsigny farm, III, 397, 409; distress in Paris, III, 403–04; evacuation of Bons-Enfants and Saint-Lazare, III, 409, 413; Rueil Conference, III, 410–12; mustering of troops around Paris, III, 418; desecration committed by soldiers, III, 471, 478; IV, 445; anxiety in Paris regarding Mazarin's return to France; Saint Vincent thinks of sending to Le Mans part of personnel of Saint-Lazare, IV, 307; losses of Company, IV, 328–29; skirmishes in Saint-Denis (May 1652); concern of wet-nurses for foundlings, IV, 377–78; fear grips Paris, IV, 379–80; city fills with refugees, IV, 386; great misery; poor people of countryside pour into Paris; organization of assistance, self-sacrifice of Missionaries, Daughters of Charity, and other Communities, IV, 306–07, 328–29, 371–72, 380, 382, 386–87, 389, 392, 395–96, 399–400, 401–02, 421, 424, 425–26, 441, 450, 453–54, 473–74, 493, 510–11, 519–20; V, 94–95, 148; Saint Vincent provides assistance to Palaiseau, XIIIa, 400; missions for poor persons in various churches in Paris, IV, 392, 398–99; reliquary of Saint Genevieve solemnly carried in procession through streets of Paris, IV, 395, 399; mention of conference given at Saint-Lazare on this topic, XII, 412; retreat of Duc de Lorraine, IV, 395, 399; troubles of June 25, 1652, IV, 460.

Passage of two armies near Saint-Lazare, IV, 409, 411; measures to preserve Saint-Lazare and Saint-Charles Seminary from pillage, IV, 409, 411–12; Saint-Charles Seminary pillaged; seminarians disband, IV, 409, 411, 468; massacres of

July 4, 1652, IV, 412, 460; uneasiness at Second Monastery of Visitation, IV, 403; plundering by soldiers in environs of Paris; Saint Vincent asks Queen to intervene, IV, 421; high death rate in Paris, IV, 450; clergy of Paris urge King to return to capital, IV, 459; steps taken by Saint Vincent for restoration of peace and return of King, IV, 414, 459; Court reenters Paris, IV, 463, 494; penance at Saint-Lazare for cessation of troubles, XII, 412; Saint Vincent explains situation to Holy Father, IV, 445; Fronde in Bordeaux: see ***Bordeaux***; other mention, III, 406. See also ***Champagne, Étampes, Paris***, **Relations**, ***Saint -Charles, Saint-Lazare***.

Fronteau (Jean), monk of Sainte-Geneviève - Biographical data, IV, 240.

Frontevaux (Mme de) - IV, 373.

Frugality - Serve good bread and vary food sometimes, I, 378; frugality in Le Mans is excessive and has harmful effect on health, III, 501.

Fugolles (Gabriel), Brother of the Mission - Biographical data, VIII, 306.

Fulco de Chanac, Bishop of Paris - I, 243.

Fulda, town in Prussia - VIII, 523.

Fumaire Salée, small town in Tunisia - V, 89.

Fuvée (Jean), Canon of Écouis - XIIIa, 26.

G

Gabaa or Gabaon, town in Palestine - Attacks of Israelites, VI, 252.

Gabarret (Gabrielle) - See **Cabaret** (Gabrielle).

Gabat (Jacques), convict - VIII, 376.

Gabrielle (Mother) - See **Condren** (Gabrielle de).

Gaillard, territory in Savoy - Evangelized by Francis de Sales, XIIIa, 81.

Galicia, province of Spain - VII, 239, 265.

Galiot (M.) - Voyage to Madagascar, III, 280, 290.

Gallais (Guillaume), Priest of the Mission - Biographical data, II, 468; III, 25; IV, 341; V, 40; Superior in Sedan VIII, 611; gives Saint Vincent news of ministries of Sedan Missionaries, II, 468; Saint Vincent advises never to dispute with heretics, II, 441; and not to get involved in secular matters, II, 493–97;

Marquis de Fabert praises Gallais, II, 483; recalled from Sedan, II, 541; in Paris, II, 528, 536; asked to go to Fontainebleau to announce mission, II, 538; Superior in Le Mans, II, 643; III, 29, 97; VIII, 613; in Crécy, VIII, 609; letter Saint Vincent sent to him in Le Mans, II, 588; oversees use of gardens, III, 237; success of mission in Saint-Méen, III, 25, 26; in Picardy, III, 215; named for Marseilles, III, 273; gives conferences to ordinands at Saint-Lazare, IV, 341; Pastor of Touquin-en-Brie, V, 40; wrong done to Pastor of Nanteuil-le-Haudouin, V, 43.

Gallardon, village in Eure-et-Loir - Confraternity of Charity, XIIIb, 5.

Gallemant (Jacques), Pastor in Aumale - Biographical data, I, 400; II, 365; Pastor of Notre-Dame-des-Vertus, II, 365.

Gallemant (Jean), Brother of the Mission - Biographical data, I, 467.

Galley Convicts [**Galley Slaves**] - Saint Vincent named Chaplain General of Galleys, XIIIa, 58; title bestowed on his successors as Superiors General of the Mission, XIIIa, 337; jurisdiction of Chaplain General of Galleys, XIIIa, 347; spiritual assistance to galley convicts among ministries of Priests of the Mission, VIII, 277; XI, 192; XIIIa, 216, 225; Claude Dufour feels called to minister to them, III, 481; galley convicts in Paris: bequest of Claude Cornuel for ministry with galley convicts, I, 533; II, 26; among works of Ladies of Hôtel-Dieu, II, 222; V, 589; XIIIb, 413, 415, 439, 441, 443; Lady working with galley convicts, II, 218; approaching departure of convicts, II, 291; Saint Vincent laments their suffering, VII, 523.

Ministry confided to Daughters of Charity, II, 35; XIIIb, 140; Rules for Sisters with galley convicts, II, 131; IX, 18; XIIIa, *xv*; XIIIb, 221–25; number of Sisters involved, II, 291, 601; III, 61; beauty of vocation of Sisters ministering to galley convicts, X, 103; scandal, V, 337, 344; not enough bread; Sisters procure bread by begging; solution proposed by Duchesse d'Aiguillon rejected by Saint Louise, IV, 417; other mentions, II, 188, 197; IX, 206, 521; X, 93, 100, 103, 118, 465, 469, 490, 557; XIIIb, 136, 206, 266. See also **Angiboust** (Barbe), **Gesseaume** (Henriette), **Guyon** (Marguerite), **Jeanne** (Sister), **Luce** (Jeanne), **Nicole** (Sister).

Convicts in Marseilles: missions on galleys, II, 407, 437; III, 265, 271; VI, 301; VII, 134; galleys leave Marseilles because of plague, III, 465, 481; question of sending them back there, VI, 186; VIII, 273; Saint Vincent acts as banker for convicts, VI, 102, 187, 195, 207, 261, 273, 276, 278, 302, 305, 320, 322, 333, 338, 342–43, 354–55, 359–60, 372, 384, 418, 487, 524, 593, 599, 617, 627, 638; VII, 30, 34, 49–50, 54, 70, 101,

123, 134, 144, 150, 154, 174, 179, 187, 208, 222, 237–38, 245, 250, 254, 269, 274, 282, 289, 392–93, 456, 457–58, 486, 489, 539, 557; VIII, 244, 250, 266, 299, 309, 319, 321, 327–28, 330–31, 337, 360–61, 369, 373, 376–377, 387, 401–02, 445, 462, 485, 513, 528; advises Superior of Marseilles house not to wear short cassock when visiting galleys, II, 500–01; King grants power to entrust to Superior of Missionaries in Marseilles his authority regarding galley convicts there, XIIIa, 338, 347.

Beginnings of hospital for convicts, II, 574–75; principal supporters, II, 510–11, 575; III, 467; administrators, VI, 207, 259, 261, 616, 627; VII, 49, 54, 70, 168, 467; VIII, 232, 243, 249: see also **La Coste** (Simiane de); Provost Bausset responsible for receiving their accounts, VII, 81, 93, 101, 109; Saint Vincent advises Fr. Get to present his accounts, VII, 109; VIII, 376; retracts advice, VII, 121; Regulations concerning hospital, III, 271, 272; Regulations for Missionaries ministering to galley convicts, XIIIa, 348; Superior of Missionaries has right to assist at administrators' meetings, XIIIa, 366; King's subsidy for hospital; difficulties, complaints, VI, 99, 207, 260–61, 265, 301, 304, 328, 383, 392, 431; VII, 109, 263, 289, 302, 392, 467, 485, 488, 538; VIII, 232, 265, 299, 421, 462; alms for hospital, VII, 410; gift of Superintendent of Finances: see **Fouquet** (Nicolas); Saint Vincent doubts they will decide to transfer to Marseilles Hospital galley convicts fallen ill in Toulon, V, 244; wants hospital chaplaincy entrusted to secular priests, under supervision of Priest of the Mission, III, 273, 295; appeals to diocesan priests at Bons-Enfants, III, 273; one accepts and leaves for Marseilles, XIIIa, 360; advises Fr. Get to entrust chaplaincy to secular priest until Missionary is sent, V, 146; chaplains' ministry, XIIIa, 366; duties, XIIIa, 348–350; number, XIIIa, 366; housing, V, 259; XIIIa, 366; Saint Vincent thinks time has not come to ask them to live common life, VIII, 299; rights of Superior of Marseilles house in their regard, III, 295, 299; XIIIa, 347–48; wages, VI, 99, 207, 260–61, 265, 279–80, 301, 304, 320, 326, 328, 332, 359, 383, 392; VII, 101, 109, 121, 123, 134, 144, 149–50, 154, 488; VIII, 265–66, 513, 376, 421, 462, 485; XIIIa, 367; Fr. Get seeks information about them and the hospital, VIII, 387; they threaten to leave if not paid, VI, 99, 260–61; to retain them, Fr. Get pays them from house money, VI, 119; mention of letter they wrote to Saint Vincent, VI, 274, 279; galley convicts of Tunis, IV, 368, 434.

Individual galley ships: *l'Allemagne*, VI, 320; *La Bailliebault*, VI, 342, 617; VII, 150, 403; *La Capitaine*, VI, 278, 360; VII, 54, 123, 174, 282, 539; VIII, 250, 266, 276, 299, 321, 402; *La Ducale*, VII, 456, 486; *La Fiesque*, VI, 342; VIII, 331; *La Garde-Côte,* VI, 301; *La Grimaldi*, VII, 539;

La Manse, VI, 261, 360; VII, 254; VIII, 266; *La Mazarine*, VI, 276; VII, 50; *La Mercares*, VII, 134; *La Mercoeur*, VII, 254; *La Montolieu*, VI, 524; VIII, 373; *La Morgue*, VI, 384; *La Princesse*, VI, 302, 524; VII, 392; VIII, 373; *La Princesse de Morgue*, VI, 333; VII, 392, 458; *Le Prince de Morgue,* VI, 261*;* *La Reine*, VI, 187, 302, 333, 342–43, 524; VII, 70, 154, 208, 238; VIII, 360*;* *La Richelieu*, VI, 187; VII, 123, 274; VIII, 244; *La Royale*, VI, 338; *La Saint-Dominique,* VI, 305; VIII, 250, 337, 361, 369, 402; *La Saint-Louis*, VIII, 376; *La Saint-Philippe*, VI, 320, 372; VII, 557; *La Ternes*, VI, 207, 273, 276; VII, 274; other mention of galley ships, III, 311.

Gallienne (Jean), from Saint-Valéry - Slave in Algiers, V, 325, 354; ransomed, VI, 8.

Gallois (M.), son of Philippe Gallois - Wants to enter Congregation of Sainte-Geneviève, I, 225.

Gallois (Philippe), notary in Paris - I, 224.

Gallot (Thomas), ecclesiastical notary for Paris diocese - Will send power of attorney to one of M. de Saint-Aignan's men, II, 399; XIIIa, 22, 24, 56, 57, 71–72, 72–73, 219.

Galtieri (Msgr.) - Awaiting successor to obtain Brief Fr. Jolly is expecting in Rome, VIII, 79.

Gamaches (Charles de), Superior of Carmelites of France - Biographical data, VIII, 474; attitude in Carmelites affair, VIII, 70, 474.

Gamaches**,** parish in Rouen (Eure) - XIIIa, 25.

Gambart (Adrien), priest of Tuesday Conference - Biographical data, IV, 348; V, 495; VIII, 189; Saint Vincent sends him Fr. Lambert's letter, IV, 348; wants to meet with him at conference, V, 495; assigns him for two ceremonies at Visitation, VIII, 189.

Gambia, country in West Africa - No priests there, III, 331.

Gannes, village in Oise - Saint Vincent hears confession of peasant, XI, 2, 3; saint's letter to Lieutenant of Gannes, I, 218.

Ganset (Louise), Daughter of Charity - Biographical data, VII, 457; X, 522; assigned to Richelieu, I, 493, 499, 500, 502, 503, 592; Saint Vincent considers her for Saint-Laurent, I, 494; in Richelieu, I, 596; II, 3, 10, 128, 208; X, 522; at Motherhouse, II, 301, 424; suggested for Maule, VI, 191–92; other mentions, VII, 457; XIIIb, 227.

Garanita (Father), in Rome - I, 585.

Garat (Jean), monk of Chancelade - Vicar-General of Bishop of Cahors, II, 632, 637; IV, 141, 272, 505, 523–24; mention of letter to Saint Vincent, IV, 523; saint persuades him to accept Chancelade Abbey, IV, 524; Alain de Solminihac presses for dispatch of Bulls, V, 590; Abbot of Chancelade, VII, 318, 407; secretary for Cahors Synod (April 1638), XIIIa, 310.

Garbuzat (M.), merchant in Lyons - Thank-you letter to Saint Vincent, VIII, 541; other mentions, VI, 258, 278.

Gardeau (Julien), "Father of the Poor" in Angers - XIIIb, 116, 118–19.

Garden of Olives - Jesus in Garden of Olives, X, 224; XI, 195–96; XII, 50, 134.

Gardon (M.), prisoner in Toulon - VII, 557.

Garibal (M. de), Intendant of Auvergne - V, 398.

Garnier (Madeleine), Daughter of Charity - XIIIb, 227.

Garonne, river in southwest France and northern Spain - Used for travel to Bordeaux, I, 430; Saint Vincent calls it a lovely river, VII, 282.

Garron Brothers (Jacques, Philibert, René, Jean) of Châtillon, sons of Jacques Garron - Conversion, XIIIa, 52; charities, XIIIa, 52–53, 55.

Garron (Jacques), officer in company of Duc de Montpensier - Sorrow at seeing all his children converted by Saint Vincent, XIIIa, 52.

Garron (Jacques) - Huguenot, XIIIa, 50; other mentions, XIIIa, 55, 57. See also **Garron Brothers**.

Garron (Jean), son of Jacques, a Huguenot - Biographical data, VI, 75; letter to Saint Vincent, VI, 75; abjuration of heresy, VI, 76; seeks Saint Vincent's advice concerning his son's vocation, VI, 76: see also **Garron Brothers**.

Garson (Fr.), former Assistant in Chars - Disagreement with Pastor, XIIIb, 356.

Gascony, province - Language spoken, VI, 145; missionaries of Fr. de Fonteneil are to give missions in Gascony, VIII, 510; revolt in Gascony in time of Saint Louis, XI, 273; Gascons considered less simple than Picards, V, 200; Missionaries receive God's help in ministry there, I, 440, 442; Fr. Grenu is in Gascony, I, 447; as is M. Brin, V, 159; Fr. Labadie causes great harm there, IV, 185; Fr. Le Gros falls ill while making visitation, V, 454; Saint Vincent is Gascon, XIIIa, 76, 96; other mentions, I, 520; V, 120; VI, 124, 504, 505, 600; XII, 318.

Gassendi [**Cassandieux**] (Pierre), priest, astronomer - Biographical data, V, 182. See also **Astronomy**.

Gasteaud (Jacques), Doctor of Theology - Creditor of Saint Vincent, XIIIa, 24–25.

Gastines (M. de) - Contacts with Jean Barreau, V, 326; VII, 634.

Gauche (M.) - Signed Act of Establishment of Daughters of Charity at Saint-Jean Hospital in Angers, XIIIb, 119.

Gaucher (M.) - IV, 510.

Gaudin (M.), Doctor of Sorbonne - Death of his brother in Madagascar, V, 527.

Gaudoin (Marie), Daughter of Charity - Biographical data, XIIIb, 340; other mention, XIIIb, 228.

Gaudoin (Melchior), Brother of the Mission - Biographical data, VIII, 414; Saint Vincent permits him to take vows, VIII, 414, 422.

Gaulène, village in Tarn - Saint-Nicolas-de-Gaulène parish, I, 557.

Gault (Jean-Baptiste), Bishop of Marseilles - Biographical data, death, II, 437; opening of Marseilles Hospital for galley convicts, II, 510–11.

Gaulteri (Ortensio), priest in Algiers - III, 220.

Gaultier (Étienne), slave in Algiers - VIII, 532.

Gaultier (Jacques), merchant in Marseilles - VII, 317.

Gaultier (M.) - Member of Charity of Joigny, XIIIb, 66.

Gaultray (M.), secretary of Cardinal de Retz, XIIIb, 147.

Gaumont (M. de), lawyer in Parlement - Saint Vincent asks him to come to Saint-Lazare, VII, 417.

Gautier [Gontier] (Aubin), Brother of the Mission - Biographical data, V, 414–15; VI, 89; VIII, 43; considered for Poland, V, 414; in Turin, VI, 89, 565; cook, V, 501; VIII, 44; takes vows, VI, 256; Saint Vincent replies to his letter, VIII, 43.

Gautier (Christophe), Brother of the Mission - Biographical data, VIII, 463; mention of letter to Saint Vincent from Richelieu about health of Fr. Alméras, VIII, 463–64; care for Joseph Bayn in Paris, VIII, 480.

Gautier (Denis), Priest of the Mission - Biographical data, II, 79; III, 143; IV, 30; letters from Saint Vincent to Fr. Gautier in Richelieu, II, 604, 605; III, 144, 284, 296, 349, 408; in Saintes, IV, 30; from Fr. Gautier, Superior in Richelieu, to Saint Vincent, III, 304; Fr. Nacquart asks for his prayers, III, 331; Superior in Richelieu, II, 666, 669; III, 143, 286, 415–16, 431, 515; VIII, 607; his niece Daughter of Charity, XIIIa, 193.

Gautier (Geneviève), Daughter of Charity, niece of Denis Gautier - Obstinacy, XIIIa, 193; other mention, XIIIb, 227.

Gautier (M.) of Troyes - V, 584.

Gautier (M.) - III, 236.

Gavanto (Bartolomeo), author of liturgical books - V, 297.

Gavelin (M.) - VIII, 283.

Gavi, town in Piedmont - Mission given, V, 135.

Gayon - See **Depaul** (Gayon).

Gazet (Bernard), Brother of the Mission - Biographical data, III, 522.

Gdansk - See ***Danzig***.

Géard (Fr.), Penitentiary in Rome - VI, 637.

Gedoyn (Nicolas), priest of Tuesday Conferences - Biographical data, VII, 315; VIII, 511; words of praise for him, VII, 315; prepares to give mission in Épinay, VIII, 534.

Geger (M.) - II, 545.

Gémozac, town in Charente-Maritime - Mission given, III, 172.

General Hospital of Paris [***Renfermés***] - Ladies of Charity obtain from Queen house and enclosure of Salpêtrière to create General Hospital for beggars of capital; interruption of work, V, 53; Ladies hesitate to give up this work, VI, 126; Priests of the Mission and Daughters of Charity requested for hospital, VI, 257–58, 264; XI, 332; Saint Vincent refuses, VI, 268–69, 274–75; XIIIa, 195–96; seeks employee for hospital, as requested, VI, 398; beggars leave Paris so as not to be confined in General Hospital, VI, 317; director of hospital chaplains, VIII, 148; other mentions, VIII, 521; XII, 200.

Generosity - Saint Vincent prays for this virtue through intercession of Saint Martin, XI, 332.

Geneset (Jean), Brother of the Mission - Biographical data, III, 408; IV, 469; death, IV, 469, 473.

Geneva, city in Switzerland - Saint Vincent hopes to be able to go there, II, 69; conversions brought about by Saint Francis de Sales, XIIIa, 87–88; Bishops: see Jean d'Aranthon d'**Alex**, Saint **Francis de Sales**, Juste **Guérin**, Charles-Auguste de **Sales**; other mentions, II, 66, 91, 349; III, 3; IV, 535; XIIIa, 81, 87, 413.

Diocese: Mention of Missionaries being sent there, I, 578, 582; contract, II, 18; great fruits produced, II, 66; foundation for Congregation, II, 144; Saint Vincent permits missions in episcopal cities, II, 310; two Commanders of Knights of Malta named for diocese, II, 414; other references, III, 68; VIII, 608; XIIIa, 323.

Genevieve (Saint) - Historical information, X, 200; model for Daughters of Charity, IX, 67, 71–72, 75, 77; hospital Sisters take her as one of their patrons, XIIIb, 194; patroness of Mme Goussault, XIIIb, 390; mortifications, X, 200; reliquary carried in procession through Paris. See also **Fronde**; other mentions, XIIIb, 114, 420, 426.

Geneviève, Daughter of Charity - Illness, II, 535.

Geneviève, Daughter of Charity at Hôtel-Dieu of Paris - See **Poisson** (Geneviève).

Geneviève, Daughter of Charity - Stationed in Le Mans, II, 642.

Geneviève, Daughter of Charity - See **Caillou**.

Geneviève, Daughter of Charity - See **Doinel**.

Geneviève, Daughter of Charity - Asks to take vows, V, 466.

Gennes (Anne de), Daughter of Charity - Conference on her virtues, IX, 433–35.

Genoa, town in Italy - Association of priests formed, take name of Missionaries; objections of Fr. Blatiron, III, 352; Confraternity of Charity, IV, 76; visit of Charity, XII, 356; plague in Genoa, IV, 450; VI, 40, 68, 72, 83, 85, 92, 99, 120, 127, 160, 169, 172, 177, 182–83, 337, 346, 348, 349, 352, 361, 362–63, 373, 375, 380, 383, 386, 391, 392, 394–95, 396, 400, 411, 421, 423, 424, 430, 432, 434, 436, 437, 438, 440, 442, 444, 447, 451–52, 453, 454, 460, 463, 464, 469, 471, 474, 477, 480, 485, 486–87, 488, 491, 494, 497, 501, 504, 505, 506, 520, 525, 528, 530, 535, 537, 567, 586; VII, 15, 18, 91, 103, 108, 129; X, 191; XI, 333, 345, 346, 357, 367–70, 379–81; disastrous tornado, III, 368; Magdalens' Convent, VII, 611; Genoese and Piedmontese do not get along, VI, 262; Archbishop of Genoa, see **Durazzo** (Stefano); slaves from Genoa in Barbary, V, 326; Republic takes up arms against enemies of Christendom, VI, 84; other mentions, V, 133, 145, 407.

Genoa Missionaries: Ministry of Fr. Codoing in Genoa diocese; arrival of first Missionaries, II, 595; Confessions and reconciliations during mission, II, 664–665. Establishment of Company, III, 65; foundation contract, III, 4, 122, 150; letters from Saint Vincent to Genoa Missionaries, III, 459; IV, 35, 132, 440, 542, 557; V, 448, 630; VI, 375, 394; VIII, 9, 40; see also **Blatiron**, **Duport** (Nicolas), **Lamirois**, **Martin** (Jean), **Pesnelle** (Jacques), **Rivet** (Jacques), **Walsh** [**Valois**] (Patrick); priests with Jean Martin interested in entering Congregation,

III, 49; Saint Vincent prepares to send more confreres, V, 205; Missionaries live in rented house, III, 480; search for another house, IV, 228, 229, 231; Archbishop has house built for them, IV, 256, 427; they cannot offer personnel to Turin, V, 534; confreres ask Saint Vincent's help and prayers, XI, 265.

Missions, III, 25, 137, 150–51, 258, 388; IV, 291, 320, 427; V, 67, 109, 254, 476; VII, 375, 388, 467, 557, 611; VIII, 80, 92, 185, 211, 216: see also **Blatiron**; regulations for missions, XIIIa, 387–88; public penance during missions, IV, 35.

Internal Seminary, IV, 163; V, 109, 376, 497, 564, 574; VI, 262, 451; VII, 152, 231, 234, 307, 339, 371, 374, 496, 540, 581, 603; VIII, 24, 56, 100, 120–21, 216, 302; scholasticate, VII, 351, 406, 412; VIII, 25, 92–93, 120, 302, 458; seminary, III, 137, 141, 150, 154, 159, 367; VI, 57; VII, 374, 559; VIII, 156; retreats for priests and laymen, III, 85, 367; IV, 565; V, 531; VII, 374, 592; retreats for ordinands, IV, 574; VII, 231, 611, 624; conferences for clergy [Tuesday Conferences], III, 157; IV, 229; VII, 413; confreres' retreats, VII, 362.

Visitation of house by Fr. Portail, III, 102, 137, 154, 171, 190, 238, 258; by Fr. Dehorgny, IV, 123, 132; by Fr. Berthe, V, 584, 594, 598; VII, 242, 291, 307, 316, 325, 363, 375, 377, 378–79, 388, 414; God is blessing house and Missionaries, III, 192; IV, 291.

Self-sacrifice of Missionaries during plague, VI, 53, 67, 83, 85, 113, 156, 375, 396–97, 402–03; illness of Fr. **Giudice** (**Le Juge**): see this name; death of Frs. **Arimondo**, **Blatiron**, **Boccone**, **Duport**, **McEnery**, **Tratebas**, **Vincent**, and Bro. **Damiani**: see these names; no news from Genoa, VI, 527; solemn service at Saint-Lazare for Genoa Missionaries, victims of plague, VI, 545; great losses suffered there, VI, 590; news of those spared by plague, VI, 541, 557–58, 563, 564; Saint Vincent still worries about them, VI, 552; grieved at no longer receiving letters, VI, 592, 594; happy when letters reach him, VI, 605, 619, 639; may need to open new house, VI, 451; sending replacements, VI, 521, 525, 557, 559, 570, 579–80, 583, 600, 640; VII, 59, 69, 75, 104, 153, 210, 230, 234, 242; their assistance to confreres in Algiers, VI, 154.

Devotion of Genoa Missionaries to Saint Joseph, V, 109, 149, 468; VII, 581; Saint Vincent orders suspension of retreats one day a month, III, 376; prohibits Superior from rendering accounts to Archbishop, IV, 75, 408–09, 427; benefactors of mission, IV, 117, 408, 427; VI, 84; VII, 560: see **Brignole** (Maria Emanuele), **Brignole** (Rodolfo Maria), **Durazzo** (Stefano), **Monchia** (Giovanni Cristofero di), **Spinola**.

Visitation of house by Fr. Jolly, VII, 153; shameful conduct of some Missionaries, IV, 79–80, 103, 255, 306, 439, 442, 526,

529; VIII, 400; XIIIa, 392; Missionary gets doctorate without permission, V, 397; sick Missionary, IV, 102; shortage of personnel, VI, 52; VII, 497; changes of Missionaries, III, 66, 313, 368, 429; Saint Vincent asks Superior of Rome house to send priest to Genoa, III, 2, 150, 154, 190, 200; Missionaries named for Genoa: see **Huguier**, **Arthur** [**Water**] (Nicolas); list of Superiors and history of house, VIII, 614; personnel: see **Arimondo** [**Alimondo**], **Baliano**, **Blatiron**, **Boccone**, **Brunet** (Jean), **Bruno**, **Caron**, **Chardon**, **Coutieu**, **Damiani** (Bro.), **Dehorgny**, **Drago**, **Drugeon**, **Duport** (Nicolas), **Emmanuel** (Bro.), **McEnery** [**Ennery**], **Francisco**, **Goret**, **Greco**, **Huguier**, **Lagrange**, **Lamirois**, **Lavanino** (Bro.), **Le Blanc** (François) [**White**, Francis], **Giudice** [**Le Juge**], **Le Gentil** (Bro. Claude), **Le Mercier**, **Martin** (Jean), **Martinis**, **Minvielle**, **Morando**, **Nodo**, **Pesnelle** (Jacques), **Philippe** (M.), **Pinon**, **Richard** (François), **Rivet** (Jacques), **Robert** (Bro.), **Sappia** (M.), **Simon** (René), **Stelle**, **Thiébault**, **Tratebas**, **Valois**, Patrice [**Walsh**, Patrick], **Vincent** (François); other mention, VI, 565.

Missionaries passing through Genoa, III, 218; V, 271, 272, 274, 275; ships from Genoa dock frequently in Tunis, III, 58; other mentions, III, 68; V, 89, 535; VI, 196, 289, 475, 565; VIII, 176, 319, 548; XII, 61; XIIIa, 208.

Genoud (Pierre), priest, in Châtillon-les-Dombes - XIIIa, 48, 57.

Gentil (Mathurin), Priest of the Mission - Biographical data, II, 533; III, 134; IV, 59; V, 24; mention of letters to Saint Vincent, V, 24; letters Saint Vincent sends him in Le Mans, III, 236, 314, 380, 492, 501, 568, 607, 610; IV, 59, 274, 300, 563; V, 24; at Saint-Lazare, II, 533; III, 134; on mission in Villejuif, III, 139; Treasurer in Le Mans, III, 318, 612; Saint Vincent objects to excessive frugality, III, 501; too independent vis-à-vis Superior, III, 568; IV, 274, 300; V, 24–25; health, III, 493; IV, 423.

Gentilly, town near Paris - Seminary for missionaries, IV, 296; Confraternity of Charity, I, 28; other mention, III, 213.

Gentleness [**Meekness**] - Conferences, IX, 206–21; XI, 53, 54, 55; XII, 151–60; mention of another conference, XII, 418; text from Rule of Missionaries, XII, 153; motives for practicing gentleness, IX, 211–13; especially necessary for Missionaries, XII, 248–49; for Daughters of Charity, IX, 206–07; XIIIb, 370; for Superiors: see also **Superiors**; gentleness in missions, I, 526; IV, 58, 439; in preaching, I, 526; in debates, XI, 54; in admonitions: see also **Corrections**; with heretics, I, 58; IV, 58; with the poor: see also **Poor**; with slaves, IV, 127; with galley convicts, IV, 58; sick minds have greater need of gentleness than others, I, 332; gentleness wins hearts, VII, 241; other mentions, I, 304; II, 87.

Gentleness, not subtlety in arguments, converts heretics, XI, 54; rancor only makes people bitter, I, 526; Saint Vincent used harsh words only three times in his life and always regretted it, XI, 56; example and teaching of Jesus, IX, 211–12; XII, 153–54, 159–60; example of Saint **Francis de Sales**, of **Commander de Sillery**: see these names; in what gentleness consists, IX, 207–208; XI, 53; relationship between gentleness and humility, XII, 152; mix "a dash of vinegar" with it occasionally, I, 383; III, 184; IV, 391; avoid insipid meekness, IV, 571; acts of gentleness, XII, 154–59; faults contrary to gentleness, IX, 209; XII, 259; means to acquire and practice it, IX, 209–10, 213–14; XI, 55–56; cure for some illnesses, I, 523; gentleness of Fr. Nouelly, III, 223; highly recommended by Our Lord, III, 463; Saint Vincent recommends practice to Company, IV, 58; easier to bring someone around by gentleness and patience, than by being uncompromising, V, 63; a virtue that can accomplish anything in Madagascar, V, 309; means for changing another's heart, V, 605. See also **Affability**, **Condescension**, **Cordiality**, **Support**.

Genuflexion - In one's room, II, 153; before Blessed Sacrament, XI, 195–97.

Geoffroy (Yves), Priest of the Mission - Biographical data, VII, 239; dispensation requested from Rome, VII, 239, 284.

Georges II Rakoczi - See **György Rákóczi II**.

Georget (M.) - Contacts with Saint Louise, IV, 215, 217.

Georget [**Georgette**] (Nicole), Daughter of Charity - Biographical data, VII, 477; in Nanteuil-le-Haudouin; difficulties with Pastor, VII, 477, 641–42; other mention, XIIIb, 227.

Gérard (D. E.), Vicar-General of Paris - XIIIb, 107.

Gérard (Fr.), chaplain of Saint-Pierre de Mézières - IV, 602–03.

Germain (Fr.), Priest of the Mission - Left Congregation, VIII, 296.

Germain (Richard), Priest of the Mission - Biographical data, II, 27; his praises, II, 251, 304; sent to Rome, II, 251, 304; in Rome, II, 296, 304, 363; recalled to Paris, II, 426.

Germaine, schoolmistress in Villepreux - Biographical data, I, 87; accompanies Saint Louise in Champagne, I, 126, 130, 132; contacts with Saint Louise, I, 305, 397; with Saint Vincent, I, 95, 129, 160; willingly accepts going to Villeneuve-Saint-Georges to teach, I, 163; other mentions, I, 87, 96, 122, 167.

Germans - Dearth of German-speaking confreres, VI, 534; VII, 335; church built for them in Poland, IV, 382; widow drove them from France, XIIIb, 420; other mentions, II, 652; V, 89, 388.

Germany - I, 294; III, 362, 411; IV, 383; V, 127, 424; VIII, 522; XI, 188, 189, 279, 318; uniformity of Church in Germany with Rome, XII, 211.

Germon (Madeleine) - Member of Charity of Montmirail, XIIIb, 34.

Gerson (Jean), Chancellor of University of Paris - Saint Vincent recommends that Saint Louise read his writings, I, 158.

Gesse (Catherine de), Daughter of Charity - Biographical data, very ill, II, 577; Saint Louise asks permission for her to take vows, III, 301; other mention, XIIIb, 227.

Gesseaume (Claude), Brother of the Mission - Brother of Henriette, Daughter of Charity, I, 601; biographical data, IV, 243; VI, 357; VII, 354; VIII, 174; in Crécy, IV, 243; VI, 357; VII, 354, 370; journey to Paris, return to Crécy, VIII, 174; **Gesseaume** (Françoise), Daughter of Charity, niece of Claude and Henriette Gesseaume - XIIIb, 227.

Gesseaume (Henriette), Daughter of Charity, sister of Claude, aunt of Françoise - Biographical data, I, 320; II, 51; III, 216–17; IV, 242; V, 57; VII, 247; X, 440–41; XII, 35; letters Saint Vincent writes her in Nantes, IV, 242, 263; V, 57; aunt of Perrette Chefdeville, II, 51; at Hôtel-Dieu of Paris; asks permission to visit family; would find refusal hard to bear, I, 381, 388; suggested for Saint-Germain-en-Laye, I, 495, 496, 537; with family; Saint Vincent will not send her back to Saint-Germain, I, 600–01; retreat at Motherhouse, II, 204–05; assigned to Sedan, II, 204, 290–91; Attorney General forbids her to leave, II, 291; at Saint-Sulpice, II, 302–03; perpetual vows, V, 356; needed in Fontenay-aux-Roses, II, 392; proposed for Saint-Gervais, II, 558; recalled from Saint-Germain for Nantes, XIIIb, 256–57; too close to chaplain in Nantes, III, 216–17; faults; Saint Vincent proposes recalling her, III, 427; thinks they should wait a little longer, III, 603; sent to Hennebont as Sister Servant, IV, 242, 262; Saint Vincent leaves her free to stay in Nantes, IV, 263; XIIIb, 328; accepts change to Hennebont, IV, 298; Saint Vincent asks her to be submissive to new Sister Servant and united with companions, V, 57; in Nantes, V, 332; XIIIb, 328; recalled to Paris, V, 432; XIIIb, 320; difficult to replace her in Nantes pharmacy, V, 533; volunteers to nurse soldiers in Calais, VII, 247; X, 469; XII, 35–36; Saint Vincent's advice before her departure for Calais, X, 440, 444; named Sister Servant in Calais, X, 445;

with galley convicts in Paris, X, 469; other mentions, I, 384, 398; II, 328; XIIIb, 227.

Get (Firmin), Priest of the Mission - Biographical data, II, 535; III, 259; V, 106; VI, 10; VII, 6; VIII, 3–4; letters Saint Vincent writes him in Marseilles, V, 106, 121, 140 (2), 145, 162, 169, 190, 199, 212, 216, 226, 244, 247, 259, 333, 367, 379, 387, 398, 408 (2), 412, 415, 423, 432, 441, 455, 506, 529, 530, 547, 554; VI, 35, 54, 64, 71, 84, 99, 119, 165, 173, 183, 185, 195, 200, 206, 258, 260, 264, 272, 275, 278, 288, 301, 304, 314, 320, 321, 327, 332, 338, 342, 352, 354, 359, 369, 383, 391, 417, 431, 446, 465, 485, 523, 592, 598, 616, 627, 637; VII, 6, 29, 34, 49, 54, 56, 69, 73, 80, 93, 101, 109, 114, 121, 132, 144, 148, 149, 154, 160, 167, 174, 178, 184, 190, 194, 207, 212, 221, 226, 232, 237, 244, 249, 253, 262, 269, 273, 281, 288, 302, 316, 317, 325, 392, 437, 455, 457, 467, 485, 487, 519, 538, 554, 556; in Montpellier, VII, 607, 630; VIII, 3, 18, 68, 91, 117, 212, 259, 267, 272, 288; in Marseilles, VIII, 303, 315, 319, 326, 330, 336, 356, 359, 368, 372, 376, 386, 396, 401, 420, 444, 461, 485, 513, 527, 536; mention of letter from Saint Vincent, VII, 213.

Mention of letters from Fr. Get to Saint Vincent, V, 162, 190, 212, 247; VI, 119, 185, 195, 207, 259, 260, 272, 279, 289, 301, 321, 338, 342, 370, 391, 446, 485, 598, 627; VII, 6, 30, 49, 55, 69, 80, 93, 101, 110, 114, 116, 121, 132, 148, 167, 174, 178, 184, 212, 221, 249, 254, 269, 270, 282, 302, 438, 456, 458, 467, 487, 538, 556, 607; VIII, 3, 18, 68, 259, 289, 303, 315, 320, 326, 330, 336, 368, 372, 376, 420, 444, 485, 527, 536.

Assigned to Marseilles, III, 259; named Assistant, III, 273; Superior, V, 190; VIII, 610; begs to be relieved of office, V, 199; VI, 260, 264, 627–28; offers to nurse sick Missionaries of Agde in his house; thanked by Saint Vincent, V, 244, 248; VII, 198; contacts Barreau about sending money to Algiers, V, 325; Barreau has not received money, V, 354; working to get Barreau indemnified by Mercedarians, VI, 10; saint encourages him, VI, 264–65; praises him, III, 259, 273; VI, 628; VII, 554; reprimands him for lack of sincerity, V, 199–200; for taking money without explicit orders, VI, 186; is reminded of this, VI, 195; M. Barreau loses his temper with him, VII, 122; Fr. Get advises selling consulates of Algiers and Tunis, VI, 338; advises abandoning Barbary mission, VII, 133; journeys to Toulon, VI, 359; VII, 184, 212, 263; VII, 148; health, II, 537; V, 169; VI, 466, 523, 599, 616, 638; VII, 194; VIII, 117, 316, 397, 402, 421, 445; eye trouble, VI, 628; VII, 144, 207, 282, 289, 302, 316; VIII, 259, 360, 368, 376; Saint Vincent says his eyes are precious to Company and necessary for his duty, VIII, 372; recommends change of air, VII, 282; but would rather he stay in Marseilles if health permits, VII, 289, 302.

Sent to Montpellier, VII, 554; Superior in Montpellier, VIII, 275, 619; XIIIa, 471; journey to Marseilles, VIII, 4, 18, 37, 68, 287; placed again in Marseilles, VIII, 273, 289, 299, 303, 310; named Superior, VIII, 315, 320, 610; Saint Vincent asks him to send money to either Jean Barreau or Philippe Le Vacher, VIII, 328, 330, 336; for man named La Rue in Algiers, VIII, 444–45; Saint Vincent refers to missions Fr. Get is giving, VI, 185; VIII, 338, 356, 359; asks for list of missions he has given, VIII, 396; trials he and his house experience, VIII, 386; holds money from collections, VIII, 32; away giving mission, VII, 403; other mention, I, *xxv*; II, 535; V, 596; VIII, 266, 339. See also ***Marseilles, Montpellier***.

Get (Nicolas), Priest of the Mission, brother of preceding - Biographical data, VI, 628; VII, 57; VIII, 91–92; destined for Poland, VIII, 528; studies philosophy, VI, 628; does very well, VII, 555; VIII, 91; sent to Poland, VIII, 535, 537; Saint Vincent praises him, VIII, 538; other mentions, VII, 57; VIII, 386.

Gève - Pastor, II, 205.

Ghosts - Repeated underground noises in Missionaries' house in Saintes; Saint Vincent recommends caution, VI, 96–97.

Gicquel (Jean), Priest of the Mission - Biographical data, III, 508; IV, 306; V, 421; VI, 124; VII, 252; VIII, 79; XII, 11; at distribution of Common Rules, XII, 11; letters Saint Vincent sends him in Le Mans, III, 508; IV, 306, 324, 423; sends him elsewhere, VIII, 157; Superior in Le Mans, IV, 564; VIII, 613; named for mission in Madagascar, V, 425; in Paris, V, 421; VI, 124; VIII, 490; Sub-Assistant at Saint-Lazare, XII, 98; sees to proclamation of Bull for Saint-Pourçain, VII, 252, 321, 507; VIII, 79; his brother, VIII, 157; lists conferences at Saint-Lazare 1650–60, XII, 405; journal of last days of Saint Vincent, XIIIa, 191–208; at Saint Vincent's deathbed, XIIIa, 195, 203–06; after death of Saint Vincent, XIIIa, 206.

Gien (Messrs de) - III, 506.

Gignac, village in Lot - Saint Vincent asks that vacant office of archpriest of Gignac be obtained in names of Frs. Cuissot and Grimal; proceedings in Rome, VI, 606, 637; VII, 12; VIII, 135; Alain de Solminihac asks Saint Vincent to press for decision on Gignac affair, VII, 117; M. Laisné de la Marguerie consents to Fr. Cuissot becoming Titular there, VII, 337.

Gigot (Denis), Priest of the Mission - Biographical data, III, 236; V, 115; VI, 496; recalled from Le Mans, III, 236; requested for Poland, V, 115, 118; not judged suitable for Poland, V, 141; sent from Troyes to Turin, VI, 496.

Gilioli (Giovanni), Priest of the Mission - Biographical data, I, 246; Fr. du Coudray is asked to bring him to Paris, I, 246, 265, 279; in Ferrara, I, 540.

Gilles (Bro.), Franciscan - Conversation with Saint Bonaventure, XII, 88.

Gilles (Jean-Baptiste), Priest of the Mission - Biographical data, II, 322; III, 165; IV, 279–80; XII, 413; words of praise for him, II, 360; IV, 469, 473; enters Internal Seminary of Saint-Lazare, II, 322, 355, 360; at Saint-Lazare, II, 433; in Cahors, II, 489; professor at Saint-Lazare, II, 541; attends lectures at Collège des Bons-Enfants, II, 585; Saint Vincent thinks of him for bishopric of Babylon, III, 165; too zealous against Jansenism, III, 327; removed from Saint-Lazare for this reason, IV, 353; Superior in Crécy, IV, 279, 292, 353; VIII, 609; Saint Vincent recommends practice of poverty, IV, 280; member of 1651 General Assembly, XIIIa, 369, 372, 374, 397; opinion about vows in Company, XIIIa, 378, 381; advice on other questions, XIIIa, 383–84, 387; death, IV, 451,452, 469, 473, 499; mention of conference on his virtues, XII, 413; other mention, IV, 545.

Gillette, Daughter of Charity - See **Joly** (Gillette).

Gillot (M.), merchant - Saint Louise asks Saint Vincent to intercede with him to have woman placed in hospital, XII, 366.

Gillot (Pétronille), Daughter of Charity - Saint Louise asks permission for her to take vows, VIII, 104; other mention, XIIIb, 228.

Gimart (Nicolas), Pastor in Le Havre - V, 227, 379.

Gimat (Louise-Madeleine), Visitandine - Spends some days in Third Monastery of Visitation in Paris, VIII, 431, 443; Superior of Second Monastery shows dissatisfaction at this, VIII, 436.

Ginetti (Marzio), Cardinal - Biographical data, II, 438; VII, 543; other mention, VII, 543; XIIIa, 306.

Gionges (Mlle) - Mother of Sister Gabrielle **Cabaret**: see this name.

Gionges, village in Marne - Birthplace of Sister Cabaret, daughter of Seigneur, IV, 311; VIII, 235.

Girard (Louis), priest - Vicar of Saint Vincent in Châtillon-les-Dombes, XIIIa, 51, 54, 56; then, his successor, XIIIa, 57; XIIIb, 22.

Girard (M.), notary - III, 151.

Girard (M.) - VIII, 192.

Girard (Sarra) - Member of Charity of Châtillon, XIIIb, 22.

Girardin (Marie) - Benefactress of Troyes Missionaries; Saint Vincent thanks her, VIII, 322.

Giraud (M.) - VIII, 506–07.

Giraudon (M.), merchant in Marseilles - VII, 232, 249–50, 253.

Girodon (Antoine), Doctor of Theology - IV, 528.

Giroud (Michel), seminarian of the Mission - Sent to Rome, XIIIa, 359–60.

Giroust (Julien), bailiff in Joigny - Member of Charity of Joigny, XIIIb, 28, 65, 66.

Gisors, town in Eure - Priory, IV, 508; Ursulines, IX, 87.

Giudice (Girolamo) [**Lejuge** (Jérôme)], Priest of the Mission - Biographical data, VI, 53; VII, 91; VIII, 9; XI, 379; letter from Saint Vincent, VIII, 9; mention of letter from Saint Vincent, VII, 593; in Genoa, VI, 541, 605, 630; VII, 103, 210, 496; Assistant, VIII, 100; volunteers to minister to plague-stricken, VI, 53, 85; ill with plague, VI, 474, 477, 480, 482, 485, 487, 488, 491, 501, 504, 506–07; cured, VI, 520, 527, 528, 538; XI, 379; puts self at risk again, VII, 91; name put forward for new house in Corsica, VII, 580; independence, VII, 260, 593, 595–96; assigned to Rome, VII, 593–94, 595; VIII, 10, 25–26, 38, 79, 100, 156; health, VIII, 10, 79, 81, 92; Fr. Pesnelle offers to give mission with him in Giudice's region, VIII, 79, 80, 92.

Glanderon (Pierre de), Canon of Saint-Denis - XIIIa, 232.

Glatens, village in Tarn-et-Garonne - Fr. Bajoue refuses parish in Glatens, IV, 589.

Glengarry, district of Scotland - Evangelized by Fr. Duggan, V, 121.

Glengarry (M. de) - Conversion of his father, IV, 495.

Glétain (Marie-Catherine de), Visitandine - Biographical data, V, 209–10; VI, 298; letter from Saint Vincent, V, 209; Superior of Warsaw Monastery, V, 83, 348, 580; VI, 326, 346, 393; health, VI, 298.

Glogau, town in Silesia (Poland) - Court retreats there during invasion of Poland, V, 474, 535; VI, 297; Fr. Ozenne likewise, VI, 299, 303, 307.

Glossa [***Glossa Ordinaria***], compilation of annotations on Scripture texts - Cited by Saint Vincent, XIIIa, 404.

Glou (Mme de) - Contacts with Saint Vincent, VII, 597; her will, VIII, 245, 258.

Gluttony - Mention of conference, XII, 420; source of many vices, IX, 363; XII, 341; vice of Communities, XI, 298; feelings of gluttony, II, 152; often a mortal sin, V, 346: see also **Meals**, **Moderation**.

Goa, city in India - Plan to establish Missionaries in Goa, II, 522; Jesuits in Goa, III, 555; VI, 244–45; other mentions, II, 523; IV, 370.

Goat - Idea of feeding foundlings on goat's milk, III, 469; possibility of buying goat, I, 411, 423, 497, 537.

Gobelin (Balthazar), Treasurer of Bureau of Finances - XIIIa, 21.

Gobellin (M.) - XIIIa, 477.

Gobert (Évrard), Priest of the Mission - Biographical data, II, 675; III, 146; in Sedan, II, 468; vows deferred, II, 675; health, III, 146.

Goblet (Thomas), Priest of the Mission - Biographical data, IV, 474; V, 76; sent to Étampes, IV, 474; cares for sick in Bâville, IV, 494; Superior of Saint-Charles Seminary, IV, 573; V, 76, 148; VIII, 614.

God - Beauty of God, XIIIa, 160; benevolence of God; God bears all from souls He loves, XI, 348; goodness of God, XI, 388; XII, 386, 389; seeking kingdom of God, XII, 110- 126; glory of God: seek glory of God everywhere and above all things, XII, 116–17, 122–23, 124; XIIIb, 271; justice of God, XII, 114–15; if we seek God's glory, God will help and reward us, II, 296; III, 44–45; VII, 496; prefer God's glory before interests of Community, III, 44; XIIIb, 271–72; God's praises: first act of religion is to praise God, XII, 265–66; to praise God is to imitate what angels do in heaven, XII, 267; God's Name: respect we owe to it, XI, 113; God's perfections: knowing them leads us to esteem and love Him, XI, 39; God's prescience: I, 7; X, 495; holiness of God: XI, 39; service of God: XI, 39; love of God, XII, 214–16; mention of conference on love of God, XII, 421; on presence of God, XIII, 428.

Godeau (Antoine), Bishop of Grasse - Biographical data, I, 413; VI, 100; named Bishop, I, 413; contacts with Saint Vincent, I, 492; writings, V, 297; VI, 100; VIII, 556.

Godeau (Timothée), slave in Algiers - V, 405.

Godefroy (Claude) - Member of Charity of Folleville, Paillart, and Sérévillers, XIIIb, 48.

Godefroy (M.), bailiff at Saint-Lazare - IV, 158.

Godescalc, Benedictine scholar - Biographical data, III, 324.

Goirar (Jeanne), Daughter of Charity - XIIIb, 227.

Goliath, Biblical personage - Mentioned in Common Rules of Congregation of the Mission, XIIIa, 469.

Gomard (Denis), from Châtillon-les-Dombes - XIIIb, 21.

Gomard (Florence), daughter of Denis Gomard - Member of Charity of Châtillon, XIIIb, 21.

Gomer (Mme) - II, 545.

Gomorrah, town in Palestine - XI, 342.

Gonain (Marie), Daughter of Charity - Readmission to Company is considered, XIIIb, 262–66.

Gondi (Catherine de), Duchesse de Beaupréau, wife of Pierre, Duc de Retz - Biographical data, I, 219.

Gondi (Françoise-Marguerite de Silly, Dame de), Baroness of Montmirail, wife of Philippe-Emmanuel - Biographical data, I, 19; II, 15; IX, 7; XI, 3; efforts to bring Saint Vincent back to Paris from Châtillon, I, 19–20; finds his absences difficult, IX, 393; his deference in obeying her, IX, 7; X, 311; XIIIb, 277; she advises Gannes peasant to make general confession, IX, 49; persuades Saint Vincent to evangelize inhabitants of her estates in Picardy, XI, 3–4, 162–63; XII, 7; endowment for Congregation of the Mission, I, 41; XIIIa, 213, 217, 218, 219, 222, 224, 226, 228, 229, 230, 236, 238, 240, 242, 244, 245, 247, 250, 251, 252, 254, 258, 297; for Bons Enfants, VIII, 605; Saint Vincent calls her "foundress" of the Mission, III, 390; XI, 110; foundress and member of Charity of Joigny, XIIIb, 25, 27, 28; of Montmirail, XIIIb, 30–33; of Folleville, XIIIb, 47–48; of Courbain, XIIIb, 91–93; praise for her, I, 219; XII, 30; her charity, XI, 110; XII, 30; her simplicity, XII, 144; her impatience, IX, 452; her carriage, II, 15; her rosary, I, 575; last will and testament (February 25, 1619), XIIIa, 59; other mentions I, 40, 47, 48, 52, 344; XIIIa, 30.

Gondi (Henri de), Bishop of Paris, first Cardinal de Retz - Biographical data, II, 362; named Adrien Le Bon Prior of Saint-Lazare, I, 249, 540; XIIIa, 277, 279, 288, 410; Saint Vincent sings praises of parishioners of Clichy to him, IX, 507; other mentions, I, 20; II, 362.

Gondi (Jean-François de), Archbishop of Paris, brother of Henri de Gondi - Biographical data, I, 102–03; IV, 253; VIII, 33; makes visitation of Church in Clichy, XIIIa, 74; names Saint Vincent principal of Bons-Enfants, I, 22; XIIIa, 230; puts it at disposal of nascent Congregation, VIII, 604; approves foundation contract of Mission, XIIIa, 218, 222, 239, 258, 298, 298; *Propaganda Fide* suggests that Archbishop of Paris become protector of Congregation of the Mission, XIIIa, 240; unites Bons-Enfants to Congregation of the Mission, XIIIa, 219–21, 230–34, 235; grants Saint Vincent, personally and for his priests, faculty to hear confessions, preach, and erect

Charities in Paris archdiocese, XIIIa, 241; XIIIb, 94, 95; gives him full authority over Congregation of the Mission, I, 50; receives and approves request for establishment of Charity in Argenteuil, XIIIb, 103–107; called to give Rome opinion for authorization of the Mission, I, 164; bestows Saint-Lazare Priory on Mission, I, 256; VII, 327, 502–04; VIII, 605; XII, 375; XIIIa, 120, 275–80, 281, 282, 284, 286, 294, 298, 411, 412, 414–15, 477, 480, 486; has right to do so, I, 254, 257; XIIIa, 277, 288, 290–291, 293; dispenses saint from rendering accounts, I, 255, IV, 409, 427; VIII, 539; XIIIa, 278, 292, 413. Saint Vincent is exempted from obligation of annual report to him, II, 507; IV, 75; revocation of prerogative given in Rules to Archbishop, II, 523; approves vows of Mission, V, 317, 319; XIIIa, 315, 394, 420; his approval of Rules is to be sought, XIIIa, 371, 395–397, 403; approval granted, V, 321; VIII, 33; XIIIa, 403; XIIIb, 144, 230; Archbishop tells ordinands to make retreat at Saint-Lazare before each Order, I, 181; goes to Saint-Lazare to see ordinands, I, 471; urged to unite Bruyères-le-Châtel Priory to Mission, III, 234; instructions for missions, VII, 323–24; wants Le Féret for Saint-Nicolas-du-Chardonnet, III, 165; approves confessors for Jubilee Year 1641, IX, 41; saint gives him visitation report of monastery, IX, 46.

Saint Vincent tells Saint Louise to propose Rules for Charity of Montreuil to Sisters, in name of Archbishop and Pastor, I, 102; tries to inform Archbishop of everything concerning Daughters, II, 598; approves Company of Daughters of Charity and its Statutes, X, 83; XIIIb, 120, 139, 142, 146, 225; at request of Saint Vincent, II, 599–604; III, 59–62; names saint Director for life, XIIIb, 142; Saint Vincent informs Daughters of Papal Bull announcing 1653 Jubilee and Archbishop's accompanying instruction, IX, 487–88.

Appoints Saint Vincent Superior of Visitation Nuns of Paris, XIIIa, 96; authorizes him to make visitation of monastery in faubourg Saint-Jacques in Paris, XIIIa, 79; maintains him as Superior of Visitation convents in Paris, IV, 288; opposes departure of Visitandines for Warsaw, IV, 253, 382, 397; sends Saint Vincent with mission to Duchesse d'Aiguillon, II, 48; orders him to visit convent of nuns, I, 501; tells him to send confreres to Pébrac, Arles, and Cahors, I, 332; saint goes to see him in Pontoise, XIIIa, 211; at Saint Victor Abbey, I, 241; cooling in relationship, IV, 398; XIIIa, 211; approves Constitutions of the Hospitaller Nuns of Charity of Our Lady for his archdiocese, XIIIa, 102–03; nephew is named Coadjutor, II, 442; takes Jean Martin's brother with him to Toulouse, II, 652; helps those made destitute by Fronde, IV, 503; death, V, 115; other mentions, I, 256; II, 242; IV, 594; V, 148; XI, 160; XIIIa, 105.

Gondi (Jean-François-Paul de, **Retz**), Archbishop of Paris, Cardinal de Retz, son of Philippe-Emmanuel - Biographical data, II, 442–43; III, 11; IV, 463–64; V, 86–87; VI, 24; VII, 326; VIII, 33; X, 83; XI, 160–61; Saint Louise considers asking him to take her son into his service, II, 443; foe of Mazarin, IV, 463–64; urges King to return to Paris, IV, 459; in prison, IV, 515, 551; takes possession of archdiocese of Paris, V, 115; receives hospitality of Missionaries in Rome; Mazarin's anger, V, 264, 270, 274, 334, 338, 369; VI, 24; XI, 165; in exile, XI, 161; Saint Vincent does not know his whereabouts, VII, 326; VIII, 34; obliges saint to keep title of Superior of Visitation in Paris, V, 86; XI, 160; approves Rules of Mission, III, 11, 84; VIII, 33; and of changes to them, VI, 459; approves Rules of Daughters of Charity, X, 83, 192; XIIIb, 131–33, 133–38, 144–47, 225, 232, 233, 237; and Company's erection as Confraternity, VIII, 160; Saint Vincent asks for new approval of Rules of Mission, VIII, 33; writes to express gratitude to him before dying, VII, 452–53; other mentions, II, 619; VII, 327, 375; XI, 301; XIIIa, 189, 224.

Gondi (Jeanne de), Prioress of Poissy Abbey, aunt of Henri and Jean-François de Gondi - I, 25.

Gondi (Louise de), Prioress of Poissy Abbey, niece of preceding - Biographical data, IV, 550; disputes concerning her election, I, 25; health, IV, 550.

Gondi (Philippe-Emmanuel de), General of Galleys of France, then priest of Oratory, brother of preceding - Biographical data, I, 18; II, 443; IV, 550; VI, 316; VII, 220; VIII, 34; X, 311; XII, 179; named executor of wife's will, XIIIa, 65; letters from Saint Vincent, I, 18; IV, 550; VI, 316; VII, 452; letter to Saint Vincent, I, 21; mention of letter to Saint Vincent, VI, 316; Comte de Joigny: see also ***Joigny***; Seigneur de Villepreux, VI, 317; Marquis des Îles d'Or, XIIIa, 213, 218, 219, 230; patron of Gamaches church, XIIIa, 25; patron of collegial church of Écouis, XIIIa, 26–27, 28, 30; plans to fight duel; Saint Vincent dissuades him, XI, 22–23; efforts to bring Saint Vincent back to Paris from Châtillon, I, 18–21; XIIIa, 55; sends Saint Vincent to give mission to galley convicts in Bordeaux, XII, 179; has him named Chaplain General of Galleys, accepts his oath, XIIIa, 58; awaits saint in Montmirail, I, 63; takes interest in spread of Confraternities of Charity and their good operation on his lands, I, 94, 116–18, 121, 125, 126, 128, 131–33; what he did for Charity of Joigny, I, 516; XIIIb, 55, 63, 65, 66.

Saint Vincent keeps certain things from him so as not to turn him aside from vocation, I, 165; goes to console him when Cardinal de Retz is imprisoned, IV, 515; expresses gratitude, VII, 452; and submission, X, 311; XIIIb, 277; M. de

Gondi's endowment for Congregation of the Mission, I, 40–41, 44, 47–48, 52, 141; VII, 306; XIIIa, 213, 217, 218, 219, 222, 226, 228, 229, 230, 236, 239, 240, 242, 244, 245, 247, 250, 252, 258, 297; modification of aforesaid contract, XIIIa, 224–225; stands surety at time of transfer of Saint-Lazare Priory to Mission, I, 251; XIIIa, 266, 269, 285; benefactor of Montmirail Missionaries, IV, 513; VII, 220; does not wish transfer of confreres to Troyes diocese, II, 548; missions on his lands in Picardy, I, 218; age and health, VIII, 132; charity, VIII, 364; spirit of poverty, X, 241; relationship with Saint Francis de Sales, I, 344; distrust and hostility of Mazarin, XIIIa, 154; other mentions, I, 128, 433, 465, 473, 474; II, 545; IX, 49; XI, 162; XII, 7, 30, 144; XIIIa, 61.

Gondi (Pierre de), Duc de Retz, brother of Cardinal de Retz - Biographical data, I, 219; II, 547; VI, 88; VIII, 612; co-patron of Écouis church, XIIIa, 30; signs modification of foundation contract of Congregation of the Mission, XIIIa, 224–225; plans to unite La Chaussée Hospital to Missionaries' house in Montmirail, II, 547; other mentions, VI, 88; XIIIb, 392.

Gondrée (Mme) - III, 597.

Gondrée (Nicolas), Priest of the Mission, son of preceding - Biographical data; in Saintes, II, 658; III, 283; IV, 89; V, 288–89; VIII, 181; XI, 263; assigned to Madagascar, III, 278, 282–83, 284–85, 286, 288; VIII, 616; XI, 340; XIIIa, 361; goes to meet Fr. Nacquart in Richelieu, III, 283, 284, 539; travel authorization for Madagascar, XIIIa, 358; before departure, writes to Saint Vincent from Tours, III, 289; voyage, III, 539, 542–43; arrival in Madagascar, III, 542; suffering from trip to Madagascar, III, 560; named Missionary Apostolic, IV, 92, 337; in Madagascar, VIII, 552; illness and death, III, 434–43, 560; IV, 89, 90, 93; words of praise for him, XI, 263, 373; XII, 198; question of exhuming his body, V, 288–89; other mentions, III, 581; V, 306; VIII, 181; XI, 270; XIIIa, 186. See also ***Madagascar***.

Gondrin (Louis-Henri de Pardaillan de), Archbishop of Sens - Involved in affair of Carmelites, VIII, 407, 411, 516.

Gonesse, town in Val-d'Oise - Mission here, I, 294; income from castellany for work of Foundlings, II, 299; XIIIb, 326; for house of Daughters of Charity, XIIIb, 231; Congregation of the Mission objects to sale of property to Maréchal d'Estrees, XIIIa, 341, 342; other mention, I, 477.

Goneste (Fr.), priest - Retreat at Saint-Lazare, VIII, 512.

Gonod (Jean), from Châtillon-les-Dombes - XIIIb, 22.

Gontier (Aubin) - See **Gautier**.

Gontier (M.), Councillor at Parlement - Arbitrator for Saint Vincent's petition before Parlement, II, 685, 687, 691; XIIIa, 210, 351, 353–55.

Gonzague (Louise-Marie de), Queen of Poland - Biographical data, IV, 63; V, 27; VI, 6; VII, 10; VIII, 88–89; IX, 409; XI, 317; letters from Saint Vincent, IV, 251, 456; V, 186, 562; VII, 299; VIII, 105; letters to Saint Vincent, IV, 273, 472; V, 164; mention of letters from Saint Vincent, IV, 329, 411; V, 164, 335, 340, 366; XII, 370; of letters to Saint Vincent, IV, 411, 538; V, 151, 186, 187, 214, 366; VI, 447, 451, 502; XI, 368; her departure for Poland, X, 283; confinement of Queen, IV, 63; pregnancy, IV, 274, 316; birth of Prince, IV, 320, 411; child's death, IV, 348; health, IV, 518; steps for succession to throne, VI, 95, 98, 296–97; setbacks and successes of her armies, V, 562; VIII, 193; XI, 333; return to Warsaw, VI, 55; charity toward plague-stricken, IV, 502, 514; toward poor persons, IV, 538; VIII, 106, 229; misunderstanding about her gift to the poor of Paris, IV, 436–37, 612–13; request for help to Assembly of Clergy of France, V, 563; VI, 644; its response, VI, 647.

Attachment to Mlle de Villers, V, 164, 214; charity to Bro. Casimir's mother, IV, 353; concern for Sisters coming to Poland, IV, 354; contacts with Saint Vincent, V, 189, 257, 340, 411; VI, 447, 451, 453, 492, 502; XI, 368; with Saint Louise, VIII, 167; saint expresses esteem and gratitude to her, IV, 456; V, 187; VIII, 105; desire to have Visitandines in kingdom, IV, 274; V, 48; opposition of Archbishop of Paris, IV, 253, 382, 410; pleased at their arrival, V, 174; she asks for Missionaries, XIIIa, 398; Daughters of Charity, and Visitation Nuns, VIII, 617; IX, 409, 455; XIIIa, 199, 398; XIIIb, 239; Saint Vincent notifies her of their departure, IV, 251; Missionaries well treated in Vilnius because of her, IV, 327; Queen's plans for them, IV, 274, 472; V, 47, 162, 164; wants to set up foundation, V, 128; wants another establishment in Krakow, V, 351–52; esteem for Fr. Desdames, XI, 368; dissatisfaction with Fr. Ozenne, V, 165; objects to Fr. Guillot going to Sweden, V, 323; orders money to be given to Daughters and Brothers traveling to Poland, V, 335; Saint Vincent thanks her for notifying him of Fr. Ozenne's death, VII, 300; she recommends that Fr. Desdames succeed Ozenne as Superior of Mission and Pastor of Holy Cross, VII, 300; kindness to Missionaries in Poland, IV, 456, 472; V, 104, 117, 128, 142, 161, 164, 168, 181, 186, 201, 228, 249, 256, 257, 263, 564, 580; VI, 6, 326, 333, 464, 470, 472, 489, 492; VIII, 88, 90, 98, 105, 118, 145, 163; XI, 324.

Asks for Daughters of Charity, IV, 252; wants more of them, V, 164, 187; her plans for them, V, 214; kindness to Sisters, V, 215; VIII, 106; entrusts to them assistance to wounded soldiers, X, 263; stays entire day in Sisters' house, X, 576, 588; wants Sister to stay with her for service of poor, IX, 463, 502, 538, 541; X, 536, 547; XIIIb, 366–70; wants Sisters to have greater confidence in Mlle de Villers, V, 164; complains that one of them is too coarse and sharp, V, 164; little dog destined for Queen is kept at Sisters' Motherhouse in Paris, V, 364, 378; Queen has placed the first vocation with the Sisters, V, 419; other mentions, III, 113, 153, 196–97; V, 621; VI, 525; VII, 10. See also ***Poland, Warsaw***.

Gonzalez (Luís), Jesuit Provincial of Portugal - II, 356.

Good Hope, cape - Mentioned in reports of Missionaries going from France to Madagascar, III, 541; V, 284; VI, 18, 230, 232; VIII, 291, 552, 569, 570; sojourn of Fr. Étienne and companions, VIII, 573–89; description of land, products, inhabitants, VIII, 589–92; animals and birds, VIII, 584; departure of Fr. Étienne, VIII, 592.

Good Purposes - II, 155, 590; II, 104, 155; XIIIa, 316.

Goret (Jean-Pascal), Brother of the Mission - Biographical data, II, 312; III, 4; IV, 286; V, 242; XII, 54; sent to Rome, II, 339, 343; in Genoa; Saint Vincent recalls him to Paris, III, 4, 7, 27; awaited in Paris, III, 102; in Saint-Méen; not satisfactory, III, 457; in ravaged regions; becomes ill there, IV, 286–87; at Saint-Lazare, coachman, V, 344; other mentions, V, 242; XII, 54.

Gorin, Abbé de Saint-Amour - See **Saint-Amour**.

Gorlidot (François), Priest of the Mission - Biographical data, IV, 172; VI, 422; VII, 204; VIII, 73; in Le Mans, IV, 172; VI, 422, 584; recalled to Paris, VII, 204, 340; health, VII, 204, 515, 583–84; his aunt, VIII, 73.

Gorlidot (Pierre), notary in Montmirail - XIIIb, 34.

Gospel Teachings [**Maxims**] - Maxims of Saint Vincent, XII, 383–403; conferences, X, 112; XII, 98–110; mention in another conference, XII, 410; definition of Gospel maxims, X, 112; XII, 99–101; principal teachings, X, 121–26; XII, 101–03; type and scope of their obligation, XII, 101–02; opposed to worldly ways of acting, XI, 41; comparison with those of world, XII, 102–04; XIIIa, 163; they detach us from triple concupiscence, XII, 244; Jesus is author of Gospel maxims, X, 112; XII, 243, 254; He put them into practice, XII, 107–08, 244; holy and useful, XII, 106, 243–46; infallible, XII, 104; steadfast, XII, 99, 106; means of becoming established in maxims, XII, 108–09; greater regard for them, I, 558; necessity of following maxims of Jesus Christ, XIIIa, 192–93.

Gossip - Text of Rule of Daughters of Charity concerning gossip, X, 351; conference, X, 351–54; on concealing and excusing faults of Sisters, IX, 221–37; mention of other conferences, XII, 407, 409, 421, 426, 433, 435; Saint Vincent urges avoiding gossip, III, 175; IX, 15, 557; X, 351, 587; XI, 110; XII, 91; never speak ill of other houses of Company, XI, 110; nor of other Communities, XII, 167; wants Daughters of Charity to say nothing of their disagreements to their confessors, IX, 226; do not listen to gossiper, IX, 223–26; kneel down, IX, 225, 231; X, 354; admonish her, leave if she continues, X, 353; to correct ourselves of this fault, consider that we are worse than others, X, 352–53; XII, 92. See also **Scandal**.

Gothereau (Claude), monk of old Saint-Lazare - I, 135.

Goths - XI, 279.

Gouault (Mme), in Paris - II, 196.

Gouault (Sébastien), citizen of Troyes - Missionaries go to live in his house in Sancey, I, 444; letter from Saint Vincent, I, 530; kindness toward Missionaries, II, 168.

Goubert (Pierre), prisoner in Toulon - VI, 342; VII, 70.

Gouin (Françoise), Daughter of Charity - XIIIb, 228.

Gouion (Fr.), priest of Lyons, slave in Tripoli - V, 132.

Goupil (Françoise), Daughter of Charity - XIIIb, 228.

Goupil (Marthe) - Request to withdraw from lease concerning coach lines, XII, 377–78, 379–81.

Gourdon, town in Lot - III, 525.

Gournay (Charles-Chrétien de), Bishop of Toul - Entrusts Saint-Esprit house in Toul to Missionaries, II, 476; Saint Vincent apologizes for being unable to see him for a few days, I, 272; or to furnish priest to hear confessions of Dominican nuns in Toul, I, 323; other mentions, II, 69; VIII, 606.

Gournay-sur-Aronde, village in Oise - Visit of Confraternity of Charity, I, 188, 284, 288, 319; Jean de Creil, seigneur de Gournay, I, 247.

Gourrant (Fr.), Priest of the Mission - Biographical data; in Richelieu, I, 419, 452, 452; knows how to sing, I, 419; illness, I, 442.

Goussault (Mme), President of Ladies of Charity of Hôtel-Dieu of Paris - Biographical data, I, 161; II, 2; IX, 58; letters from Saint Vincent, I, 260, 338, 379, 494, 511; letter to Saint Vincent, I, 191; mention of note to her, I, 152, 313, 366; contacts with Saint Vincent, I, 161, 199, 221, 231, 263, 299, 315, 330, 391, 433, 434,

436, 450, 457, 472, 533, 534, 547, 569; with Saint Louise, I, 167, 205, 379, 392, 401, 434, 472, 492, 559, 560, 561; family, I, 357, 512; property in Bourgneuf, II, 2; her confessor, I, 311; her carriage, I, 450, 494; personal rule of life, IX, 168–69; love of silence, IX, 174; journey from Paris to Angers, I, 191–96; other journeys, I, 170, 285, 318, 328, 339–40, 341, 537; retreats at Saint Louise's house, I, 372, 373, 446; visit of Charities outside Paris, I, 161, 163, 272, 320, 494, 495; XIIIb, 393.

Named President of Ladies of Hôtel-Dieu, I, 231; meeting of Ladies in her home, I, 230, 426, 450; does not take title of Superior of Ladies of Hôtel-Dieu, but that of "servant," IX, 58; involvement with Hôtel-Dieu, I, 234, 299, 349, 495–96; with foundlings, I, 434; prepares postulants for Company of Daughters of Charity, I, 174, 320, 458, 486; consulted about qualities or admission of several young women, I, 167, 213, 218, 301, 305, 427, 560; looks for housing for Sisters, I, 235–36, 308, 310, 313; wants them to take charge of sick in Angers Hospital, I, 469; XIIIb, 117; hopes for future of Company of Daughters of Charity, IX, 168, 432, 462, 477–78; X, 94, 118, 463, 531, 532; opinion of Fr. Duhamel, II, 115, 117; Saint Vincent asks her to restore harmony in Estival Abbey, I, 339; begs her not to allow Fr. Cuissot to be unfaithful to rule of gratuity of missions, I, 379; illnesses, I, 386, 389, 391, 398, 408, 425, 457, 552, 569; death, I, 569, 586; XIIIb, 405; her will, XIIIb, 390–96; other mentions, I, 302, 371, 383, 469.

Goussault (Marie-Marthe), daughter of Mme Goussault - See **Lotin** (Marie-Marthe).

Grace - Opinion of Baius on grace, III, 323; each person receives sufficient graces from God and can accept or refuse them as he/she wills, III, 325–26; grace has its small beginnings and its progress, III, 157; XIIIa, 164–72; difference between lights of understanding and those of grace, XI, 77; God apportions grace according to individual needs, XI, 102; extent of prohibition of Clement VIII and Paul V on discussions concerning grace, III, 326; grace is wanting to those who are unfaithful to grace, VI, 194; conversion of souls is work of grace, I, 367; fear that God will withdraw grace, XII, 386; "Grace has its moments," II, 499.

Grainville (Eustache-Michel de), Priest of the Mission, son of M. Grainville - Biographical data; at Internal Seminary in Richelieu, VII, 204.

Grainville (M.) - VII, 204.

Gramberti (Francesco), secretary for Giovanni Battista Altieri - XIIIa, 314.

Granada (Luís de), Dominican - Biographical data, I, 198; V, 293; writings, I, 198; V, 293, 297; XIIIa, 112; *Memorial*, I, 373; IV, 206; catechism, III, 281; V, 296; *La Guide des pécheurs* [*The Sinner's Guide*], II, 580; IV, 206.

Grand-Caire [***Cairo***], city in Egypt - Bishop, VIII, 430.

Grandchamp, village in Sarthe - Good example of Mme Pavillon, IX, 5.

Grand-Champ (François), colonist in Madagascar - Interpreter for Missionaries, III, 554; massacred by natives, VI, 221.

Grand-Longueron (Le), hamlet in commune of Champlay (Yonne) - Mission given, III, 609.

Grandin (Martin), Superior of Carmelite nuns of France - Biographical data, VI, 60; VIII, 474; Jean des Lions writes to him, VI, 60; M. Séguier suggests that Fr. Grandin write to Jean des Lions, VI, 62; Grandin does not agree with Rome's decisions concerning visitation of Carmelite convents, VIII, 70, 474; other mentions, VI, 60; VIII, 496.

Grandmont (Order) - See **Barny**, **Frémont**.

Grandnom (Remi de), Intendant of Mme Goussault - Accompanies Mme Goussault to Angers, I, 191; other mentions, I, 433, 594; II, 15; XIIIb, 394.

Grandpré (Antoine-François de Joyeuse, Comte de), in Richelieu - I, 500; IV, 10.

Grandrye (Pierre), notary in Paris - XIIIa, 11, 16, 18, 19, 20.

Grand Turk [**Sultan Mehemet IV**] - I, 4, 7; treaty with Henry IV, IV, 147; Saint Vincent seeks influence to get him to grant Husson declaration concerning consular duties, V, 89; Turks from Algiers come to Tunis for his service, bringing women and little children for sale, V, 131; Jean Le Vacher seeks letters from him, through Vincent's intercession, to show local authorities, V, 133; Husson's problems with Dey for lack of letters from Sultan, V, 267–68; may be angry with Chevalier Paul's undertaking, VII, 226; King requests ambassador to register complaints with Grand Turk, VII, 227; imprisonment of French Ambassador to Constantinople, VII, 273, 281, 304; grants King of France fort between Tunis and Algiers, XII, 61.

Grangier (Paul), citizen of Mâcon - XIIIb, 74.

Granil (M.), administrator of Nantes Hospital - IV, 77.

Grasse, town in Alpes-Maritimes - See Antoine **Godeau**, Bishop of Grasse.

Grassin (M.) - Member of Charity of Joigny, XIIIb, 66.

Grassins (***Collège des***) - Mention of its principal, XIIIa, 144; money bequeathed to him for it by Mme Goussault, XIIIb, 396

Gratitude - Need to express it, II, 150; ingratitude is crime of crimes, III, 42; gratitude of Saint Vincent toward benefactors: see also **Benefactors**; toward priest who had saved his life, V, 543; other mentions, I, 177, 292, 603.

Gravel (malady) - Remedy, I, 6; VI, 613.

Greco (Vincenzo), Priest of the Mission - Biographical data, V, 157; VI, 110; in Rome, V, 157; sent from Genoa to Turin, VI, 110, 127, 137, 141.

Greece - III, 40; V, 89; VII, 341; mention of Greek Archbishop's visit to Saintes, VIII, 51.

Greeting - Mark of courtesy among first Christians, IX, 126; practice of greeting one other at Saint-Lazare, IX, 121, 126; recommended to Daughters of Charity, IX, 121–22, 126, 216–17.

Grégoire (M.), brother-in-law of Saint Vincent - Sale of small farm, XIIIa, 76, 77.

Gregory of Tours - Response to Pope who reacted to his deformity, XI, 118–19.

Gregory the Great (Saint) - Strictness of early Church regarding those who improperly reserved something for self, X, 178; monk found with money, XI, 156; XIIIb, 315; Judas, XI, 224; Gregory calls himself "disciple of universal Church," XIIIa, 128; moral reflections on Job, XIIIa, 163.

Gregory XIII (Pope) - Condemnation of Baius, III, 320; IV, 607; XIIIa, 166; denouncing serious faults of another to Superior is not against Gospel teachings, XII, 295; declares that simple vows of Jesuits make religious of those who take them, XIIIa, 405.

Gregory XV (Pope) - For twenty years, Jesuits petitioned for consolidation under this Pope, V, 400.

Gremy (Mme), in Le Mans - III, 236.

Greneda (M.) - Visitor to Saint-Lazare, IV, 66.

Grenoble, diocese - Bishop: see Pierre **Scarron**.

Grenu (Daniel), Priest of the Mission - Biographical data, I, 178; on mission with Fr. Belin, I, 269; military chaplain, I, 342, 343, 345, 351; in Gascony, I, 440, 442, 447; recalled to Paris, I, 482; other mention, I, 404.

Gressier (Jeanne), Daughter of Charity - Biographical data, V, 452; VII, 189; VIII, 235; elected Officer in 1658, VII, 188;

named Bursar, XIIIb, 226; desires to take vows, VIII, 235; Assistant to Saint Louise, VIII, 323, 352; Saint Vincent asks her to govern Company until Saint Louise's successor is chosen, VIII, 312; other mentions, V, 452; XIIIb, 227, 344.

Griet (Barthélemy Donnadieu de), Bishop of Comminges - Did more by suffering than by action, II, 6; Abbé de Saint-Cyran's great respect for him, XIIIa, 108.

Grignan, town in Drôme - Fr. Delespiney establishes Charity there, VIII, 161.

Grigny, village in Essonne - Young woman from Grigny, I, 235; Saint Vincent invites Saint Louise to go there, I, 318, 319, 472; Mme Goussault in Grigny, I, 320, 537; Saint Vincent hopes to go there, I, 350; goes to Grigny, I, 537.

Grille (Nicolas de), Bishop of Uzès - Contributes to condemnation of Pierre Dupuy's book on liberties of Gallican Church, III, 591.

Grimal (François), Priest of the Mission - Biographical data, II, 239; III, 82; IV, 50; VI, 21; VII, 12; question of missioning him to Annecy house, II, 239, 240; considered for Cahors, III, 82, 92; Superior in Sedan, II, 541; VIII, 611; Superior in Crécy, VI, 21; VIII, 609; sent to Agen at time of foundation, IV, 50, 51; Superior in Agen, VIII, 616; at 1651 General Assembly, XIIIa, 369, 372, 374, 397; opinion on vows taken in Congregation, XIIIa, 377, 381; at Saint-Lazare, IV, 341, 354; Second Assistant of Saint Vincent, IV, 469; saint thinks of attributing to him, nominally, benefice of Gignac, VI, 637; VII, 12; Superior in Montmirail, VIII, 612; visits dying Saint Vincent, XIIIa, 204; assists at Assembly called to verify choice of Vicar-General, XIIIa, 206; other mention, II, 536.

Grimaldi (Gerolamo), Cardinal - Biographical data, II, 305; III, 73; Nuncio in France, II, 305, 343, 349, 438, 457; Saint Vincent sends Fr. Codoing letters from him, II, 343, 349; questions Saint Vincent concerning worthiness of François Perrochel to be Bishop of Boulogne, XIIIa, 145; imminent return to Rome, II, 469, 472; Saint Vincent calls him to witness that Congregation of the Mission is resisting new opinions, II, 500; addresses to Grimaldi writings in which doctrine of Two Heads is refuted, III, 73–75; he makes suggestion to Saint Vincent which the latter rejects, III, 478.

Grimancourt (Jean de la Roche-Lambert, Seigneur de), King's steward - Executor of will of Marquise de Vins; promises to pay for her foundation, VIII, 485, 513, 536, 538; Saint Vincent feels he is delaying proceedings, VIII, 513.

Grimard [Grimaud] (M.) - VII, 350.

Grizard (Madeleine) - Member of Charity of Montmirail, XIIIb, 34.

Grodno, town in Poland - Muscovites recapture it, VIII, 280.

Grolet - Mme Goussault remembers Charity there in her will, XIIIb, 394.

Groni (M. de) - Queen of Sweden sends letters conferring appointment to bishopric, IV, 63.

Grosbois (Abbot of) - See **La Font** (Jean de).

Groslay, village in Val-d'Oise - I, 340.

Grosley, village in Eure - I, 340.

Grosmoulu (Vincent), Canon of Écouis - XIIIa, 26, 29, 30.

Grosse-Sauve (Saint-Nicolas Priory) - Power of attorney for taking possession of priory in name of Saint Vincent, XIIIa, 66.

Grougnault (Pierre de), Pastor of Mamers - VII, 535.

Groyn (M.), notary - XIIIb, 395, 396.

Guay (Toinette) - Member of Charity of Châtillon, XIIIb, 21.

Guébriant (Jean-Baptiste de Budes, Comte de), Maréchal de France - III, 39.

Guébriant (Renée du Bec-Crespin, Comtesse de), wife of preceding - Biographical data, III, 39; becomes ill near Genoa; Fr. Blatiron goes to see her, III, 39, 48, 58, 66.

Gueffier (Étienne), Agent of France in Rome - Biographical data, IV, 68; VI, 387; renders service to Alain de Solminihac in Rome, IV, 68–69; praise for him, VI, 526; other mentions, VI, 387, 482, 553; VII, 635.

Guelton (M.), Governor of Fort Dauphin - Moves Fort Dauphin away from village of natives, VI, 235; returns to Fort Dauphin with army, booty, and hostages, VI, 249–50; contacts with Madagascar Missionaries, VI, 232, 233; sets out again for Madagascar in 1659, VIII, 558, 560, 566, 573, 575, 588, 589.

Guénegaud du Plessis (Henri de), Secretary of State - Biographical data, II, 607; IV, 303; contacts with Saint Vincent, IV, 303; other mention, XIIIa, 340.

Guerche, forest near Le Mans.

Guergret (Mme) - Member of Charity of Saint-Sauveur; makes retreat in Saint Louise's home, V, 641.

Guérin (Anne-Marguerite), Visitandine - Biographical data, II, 200; IV, 318; VIII, 47; letters from Saint Vincent, IV, 318; VIII, 47; letters to Saint Vincent, VIII, 431, 443, 484, 498, 542, 551; reference to letters from Saint Vincent, II, 228, 242, 535;

reference to letter to Saint Vincent, VIII, 47; Saint Vincent receives letter from Saint Jane Frances through her, II, 200; Superiors of Paris monasteries urge Saint Vincent to order Sister Anne-Marguerite to attend meeting, IV, 318–19; establishment of Third Monastery of Visitation in Paris; saint recommends that she be content with modest house, VIII, 47–50; grants her permission to go out to prepare new house, VIII, 188.

Guérin (Gilles), Councillor of the King - Contract of Priests of the Mission and Saint Louise with Guérin (August 26, 1631), XIIIa, 259.

Guérin (Jacques), Procurator General of Augustinians in Rome - Biographical data, IV, 47; defends interests of his Congregation against Abbot of Chancelade, IV, 47, 67, 68, 73, 76, 78, 96, 136.

Guérin (Jean) [**the Elder**], Priest of the Mission - Biographical data, II, 248; IV, 532; sent to Annecy, II, 248; named Superior, II, 331, 335, 354; Superior in Annecy, II, 344, 609; VIII, 608; letters Saint Vincent sends him in Annecy, II, 335, 402, 413; assigned to Marseilles, II, 582; death, IV, 532–36, 537, 544, 558.

Guérin (Jean) [**the Younger**], Priest of the Mission - Biographical data, II, 28; illness in Lorraine, II, 119; in Paris, II, 300–01.

Guérin (Julien), Priest of the Mission - Biographical data, II, 222; III, 18; contact with Daughter of Charity, II, 222–23; in Saintes, II, 409, 519–20; arrival in Tunis; accepts lodging in house of French Consul, whose chaplain he becomes, II, 639; V, 90; in Tunis, III, 26, 58, 107, 192; Superior in Tunis, VIII, 615; letters to Saint Vincent from Tunis, II, 638, 653; III, 18, 148, 176, 199, 205, 224, 227, 300; sad state of slaves, II, 639, 653; III, 148; ransom of slaves, II, 638; III, 205, 224; mission to slaves of Bizerte, III, 199; conversion of Dey's son, II, 677; conversion of slaves, II, 653; piety of slaves, III, 176; constancy of slaves in their faith, II, 638–39; III, 224; martyrdom of Portuguese slave, III, 18–19; plague in Tunis, III, 300; death and eulogy, III, 349–51. See also **Tunis**.

Guérin (Juste), Clerk Regular of Saint-Paul, Bishop of Geneva - Biographical data, I, 564; II, 31; letters to Saint Vincent, II, 66, 225, 521; Vice-Postulator for beatification process of Saint Francis de Sales, XIIIa, 80; contacts with Saint Vincent, II, 118, 238, 246, 320, 324; with Annecy Missionaries, II, 89, 171, 249–50, 252; kindness toward them, II, 31, 61, 521; opinion on Extraordinary Visitors for Visitation Order, I, 567; other mentions, II, 33, 174, 214, 255.

Guérin (M.), secretary of Louis de Chandenier - VI, 38; VIII, 303.

Guérin (Fr.), confessor of Sisters at Saint-Gervais - II, 626.

Guérin (Mme) - Gives Ladies of Charity of Villeneuve-Saint-Georges advice of which Saint Vincent does not approve, I, 318.

Guérin (Mathurine), Daughter of Charity - Biographical data, III, 421; V, 177; VIII, 167; letters from Saint Vincent; Sister Servant in La Fère, VIII, 232, 297, 328, 340, 349; family, III, 421; postulant, III, 336; in Paris, V, 177; named Treasurer, XIIIb, 226; records conferences of Saint Vincent, IX, *xvi*; makes copies for distribution, IX, *xviii, xx*; records council minutes, XIIIb, 312, 318, 323, 330, 331, 338, 341, 342, 344, 348, 353, 356; recalled to Paris to found establishment in Belle-Isle, VIII, 167, 340, 349; letter to Saint Vincent from Belle-Isle, VIII, 459; Sister Servant in Belle-Isle; difficulties, VIII, 459–61; "Rules of Alméras" drawn up at her request, XIIIb, 147; other mention, XIIIb, 227.

Guérin (Mlle), in Paris - Biographical data, IV, 299; contacts with Saint Vincent, I, 31; IV, 299; with Saint Louise, I, 123, 283; in charge of one of Charities, I, 65; Saint Vincent thinks of inviting her to join Ladies of Hôtel-Dieu, I, 231; death of her children, IV, 299.

Guermeau (M.), administrator of Châteaudun Hospital - Writes to Saint Vincent about hospital, VI, 575.

Guerraut (M.), banker in Malta - VII, 523.

Guerre (Alexandre de) - His slanders, VII, 522.

Guerrier (Mme), Lady of Charity of Saint-Barthélemy in Paris - VIII, 465.

Guesdon (François), Priest of the Mission - Biographical data; IV, 324; V, 25; Saint Vincent forbids him to dictate to students, IV, 324; in Le Mans; recalled to Paris, V, 25.

Guespier (Antoine), Dominican - Biographical data, VII, 78; mission in Metz causes cancellation of invitation to preach Lenten sermons in Metz; compensation, VII, 78, 126, 384.

Guespreyre (M. de) - Saint Vincent explains conditions for young man recommended by him to be received at Saint-Lazare, VII, 500.

Guibert (M.) - IV, 424.

Guichenon (M. and Mme), inhabitants of Châtillon - XIIIa, 50; wife asks to be Nurse of Poor of Charity of Châtillon, XIIIb, 21.

Guidance of God - God has ordered everything as it suits Him, VI, 1; humbles and raises up, V, 450; guidance is mysterious and hidden from us, XI, 337–38, 367; sometimes hides from us success of our work, V, 463; only in heaven will we know His plan, XI, 276; unchanging in His plans, XI, 339; likes to use weak means to better show His action, II, 433; strengthens Church by destruction of all that sustains it, XI, 367–68, 372.

Guidi (Giovanni Francesco), Nuncio in France - Writes to Cardinal Ludovisi to recommend Congregation of the Mission to him, XIIIa, 242, 245, 246–47.

Guidoly [**Guidotti**] (Louis de), Sieur d'Ouessey - Member of Charity of Joigny, XIIIb, 65, 66.

Guignard (André), Principal of Collège de Navarre - Deposition concerning Saint-Lazare Priory, VII, 504.

Guillard (M.), seminarian of the Mission - In Lorraine, I, 539, 542.

Guillaume (Anne) - VIII, 309.

Guillaume (Edme), slave in Algiers, son of preceding - VI, 187, 189; VIII, 309, 319; ransomed; return to Paris, VIII, 327.

Guillemare (Jean), slave in Algiers - V, 353, 407.

Guillemin (Marin), inhabitant of Montmirail - XIIIb, 34.

Guillemin (Toussanine) - Member of Charity of Folleville, XIIIb, 48.

Guillemine (Sister) - See **Chesneau** (Guillemine).

Guilloire (M.) - II, 196; V, 427.

Guillon (M.) - IV, 143.

Guillon (Philibert), inhabitant of Châtillon - XIIIb, 21.

Guillot (Nicolas), Priest of the Mission - Biographical data, IV, 292; V, 6; VI, 311; VII, 68; permission to leave for Poland, XIIIa, 398; departure, IV, 251; in Warsaw, IV, 292, 329; V, 6, 26, 49, 70, 75, 83, 93; letters Saint Vincent writes him in Poland, IV, 571; ministers to plague-stricken, IV, 493, 518; writes poorly, V, 27; tells parents he will return soon; Saint Vincent criticizes him for this plan, V, 84, 93; sprains ankle, V, 114; departure for France; Saint Vincent's sorrow at return, V, 117, 126; arrival in Paris, V, 136, 148, 175; Saint Vincent is disposed to send him back to Poland, V, 141; Fr. Guillot requests this, V, 161–62; back in Poland, V, 179; in Montmirail, VI, 311, 457, 535, 615.

Correspondence with Sweden, V, 165; contacts with French Ambassador in Sweden, V, 180; desires to go there to minister to Catholics, V, 213, 249, 323; Saint Vincent approves plan, V, 352; project abandoned, V, 323; question of sending him to Krakow, V, 255; named Consultor, V, 348; Saint Vincent consoled by improved disposition, V, 402; arrival of Fr. Guillot in Paris, V, 479; ill with pleurisy; recovery, V, 481, 492, 535; in Paris, V, 588; Superior in Montmirail, VII, 68; VIII, 612; willing to return to Poland, VI, 621; Saint Vincent hesitates, VI, 621; VII, 481; professor at Saint-Lazare, XII, 57.

Guillotin (M.), in Étampes - I, 480.

Guillou (J.) - Member of Charity of Courboin, XIIIb, 93.

Guillou (M.) - II, 526.

Guimps, village in Charente - V, 124.

Guinea, country in West Africa - Disastrous effects of climate, VI, 13, 225; other mention, VI, 228.

Guingamp, town in Côtes-du-Nord - Ursulines, V, 58.

Guise, town in Aisne - Distress and charities in Guise and environs, IV, 94, 138, 142; VI, 561, 580.

Guise (Henriette-Catherine, Duchesse de Joyeuse and de Guise) - Biographical data, II, 559.

Gurlet (Claude), Priest of the Mission - Biographical data; assigned to Le Mans, III, 236; IV, 532; death in Annecy, IV, 532, 538, 544, 558; mention of conference on his virtues, XII, 416.

Gutinot (N.) - Member of Charity of Courboin - XIIIb, 93.

Guy, Brother of the Mission - Death, IV, 320.

Guy (M.) - Volunteers to give missions with Le Mans Missionaries, VIII, 130.

Guyard (Louis de), Vicar-General of Paris, former Principal of Collège des Bons-Enfants - Resigns title of Principal on condition of annual pension, XIIIa, 72, 219, 221, 232; other mention, I, 72.

Guyenne, province - Ravages of Fronde in this province, V, 97; revolt at time of Albigensians, XI, 273; other mentions, VI, 548; VIII, 222; XIIIa, 21.

Guyon (Marguerite), Daughter of Charity - Praise for her; placed in ministry to galley convicts, XIIIb, 266–67.

György Rákóczi II [**Georges II Rakoczy**], Prince of Transylvania - Defeated by King of Poland, VII, 83.

H

Haarlem, town in Netherlands - VIII, 596.

Habakkuk (Prophet) - Carried by angel to Daniel in lion's den, XII, 7.

Habert (Germain), Abbot of Cérisy - Biographical data, III, 292; drafted letter to Pope requesting condemnation of Five Propositions, IV, 607.

Habert (Isaac), Theologian of Paris, then Bishop of Vabres - Fights doctrine of Two Heads, III, 73; defends *Apologie des casuistes*, VII, 547.

Habit - See **Attire**.

Hacedette (Sister), Visitandine - Entrance into novitiate, VIII, 533.

Hagar, mother of Ishmael, biblical personage - III, 277; IX, 105.

Hague, town in Netherlands - VIII, 596.

Hainaut, province in Belgium - Nicolas Étienne stops there on way back from failed trip to Madagascar, VIII, 597.

Haineuve (Fr.), Jesuit - Consulted by Saint Vincent, XII, 332.

Haistrau (M.), merchant in Montfort - VII, 274.

Hal [***Halle***] (***Notre-Dame de***), Marian shrine near Brussels - VIII, 597.

Hallier (François), Doctor of Sorbonne, Bishop of Cavaillon - Biographical data, IV, 394; VI, 364; letters from Saint Vincent, IV, 394, 413, 514; to Saint Vincent, IV, 583, 600, 604; goes to Rome to combat Jansenism, IV, 581; Saint Vincent wishes him success, IV, 394, 413; congratulates him for good results, IV, 514; monetary assistance, IV, 430; Hallier sends copy of Bull *Cum Occasione*, IV, 581; provides information on condemnation and attitude of Jansenists, IV, 583–85, 600–01, 604; leaves Rome to go to Palestrina, VI, 364–65, 373.

Halluin, commune in Tourcoing (Nord) - II, 110.

Ham, town in Somme - Wretchedness and charities, IV, 94; V, 331; VI, 388, 414, 438, 467–68, 490; XIIIb, 428.

Hamburg, town in Germany - Ancient monastery in ruins, XI, 188; other mentions, V, 48, 50, 67, 161, 174; VI, 55; VIII, 146.

Hameau (André), Pastor of Saint-Paul in Paris - I, 377.

Hamelincourt, village in Pas-de-Calais - Father of missionary writes Saint Vincent from there, VIII, 446.

Hammamet, town in Tunisia - V, 119.

Hanis (Urbain), convict in Toulon - Saint Vincent received money for him, VIII, 513.

Hanivel (Marie d') - See **Trinité** (Mother).

Hanotel (Fr.), Vicar-General of Arras - Saint Vincent seeks dispensation from irregularity for priest, V, 605.

Hanseatic Towns - Several fall to Protestantism, XI, 318.

Haran (Nicole), Daughter of Charity - Biographical data, IV, 215; V, 615; VI, 107–08; VII, 66; VIII, 186; displeases two people, IV, 215–16; advice from Saint Vincent before her departure for Montmirail, IX, 430; Sister Servant in Nantes, V, 615; VII, 66, 493; VIII, 258; XIIIb, 336; letters Saint Vincent sends her in Nantes, VI, 107, 269; VII, 66, 472; VIII, 186, 217, 317; receives from her, VIII, 399; mention of letters she sent him, VI, 269; VII, 66, 472; asks to go to Madagascar, VI, 269; signs attestation after reading of Common and Particular Rules reviewed and arranged in order by Fr. Alméras, XIIIb, 206; other mention, XIIIb, 228.

Harcourt (Henri de Lorraine, Comte de), Viceroy in Catalonia - Letter from Michel Le Tellier, Secretary of State, about Saint Vincent's influence in Council of Conscience, XIIIa, 150–51; Cardinal Mazarin tells Comte that Saint Vincent has greater influence with Queen than he does, XIIIa, 151–52.

Hardemont (Anne), Daughter of Charity - Biographical data, II, 130; IV, 22; V, 33; VI, 582; VII, 157; VIII, 493; IX, 206; letters Saint Vincent writes her in Montreuil, IV, 22; in Hennebont, IV, 180, 238; in Nantes, IV, 262; in Mouzon, V, 185; in Ussel, VII, 246, 396, 447, 469; mention of other letters he wrote to her, VII, 446, 254; mention of letters she wrote to him, V, 185; VII, 246, 447, 469; at Motherhouse, II, 130; at Saint-Paul, II, 484, 527; recalled, II, 655; present at Council, XIIIb, 247–48; named to visit Sisters at Saint-Jacques and Saint-Gervais, IX, 205–06; advice from Saint Vincent before her departure for Montreuil-sur-Mer, XIIIb, 271–74, 276–82; recalled, IV, 22; visits Barbe Angiboust, ill in Fontainebleau, III, 379; advice from Saint Vincent before her departure for Hennebont, IX, 430; Sister Servant in Hennebont, IV, 116; XIIIb, 309; missioned to Nantes, IV, 242; recalled, V, 33, 57; Saint Vincent considers her for Angers, IV, 258; advice from Saint Vincent before her departure for Sedan, X, 1; Sister Servant in Sedan, X, 6; raises objections about going to thermal baths at Bourbon-l'Archambault, V, 416; sent to Petites-Maisons, V, 427–28; recalled to Motherhouse, VI, 582; missioned to Ussel as Sister Servant, VII, 157; advice from Saint Vincent before her departure, X, 381; unhappy in Ussel; Saint Vincent encourages her, VII, 246, 254–55, 396, 447, 470; wants to be sent to Cahors, VII, 248, 256; annoyed with Saint Louise, VII, 247, 255–56; recalled from Ussel, VIII, 493–95; other mentions, II, 207; V, 381; XIIIb, 227.

Hardy (Mlle) - Saint Vincent does not approve of her plan concerning Foundlings, I, 423.

Hardy (Roch-Sébastien) of Nancy, slave in Algiers - VI, 418; VII, 196, 228.

Hardy (Sébastien) - Saint Vincent complains of being too pressured by him about ministry to Foundlings, I, 410.

Harel (Jean), Superior General of Congregation of Saint-Maur - IV, 197.

Harque (Commander) - Words of praise for him, II, 143.

Hartigan [**Artagan**] (Fr.), Irish Jesuit - V, 158–59.

Hastiness - Complaints about Saint Vincent's slowness, II, 236; he declares that delay never did him any harm, II, 236, 237; VII, 304; hasty transactions never succeed, I, 424; II, 236–37; IV, 128; works of God are done gradually, II, 257, 514; make haste slowly, II, 310; V, 400; haste creates inconveniences, II, 517; he who is hasty falls back, II, 521; do not be hasty in business matters, II, 545; do not be eager to blunt point of nature, V, 537; acting in haste is to act contrary to Providence, IV, 346; grace has small beginnings and progress, III, 157; things that must last longest take the longest to develop, VII, 235; defer giving regulations as long as possible, III, 272; Our Savior waited before giving regulations, VII, 164: see **Counsel**.

Hastier (Claude), colonist of Madagascar - Gives help to Missionaries, III, 554.

Hauranne (Duverger de) - See **Saint-Cyran** (Abbé de).

Hautefort (Mme de) - See **Schomberg** (Mme de).

Hauterive (Antoinette de Ranse, Demoiselle d') - Saint Vincent does favor for her, thanks her for kindness to La Rose Missionaries, VIII, 220.

Hauterive, town in Lot-et-Garonne - VIII, 220.

Hauteville (François de or d'), Priest of the Mission - Becomes ill in Reims, VII, 402; Superior in Montmirail, VIII, 612; other mention, XIIIa, 194.

Hay - Saint Vincent advises confrere not to cut hay in wet weather, I, 473.

Hayneufve (Julian), Rector of Jesuit Collège - Appointed one of Visitors of principal convent of Dominicans in Paris, XIIIa, 137.

Hazart (Laurent), Brother of the Mission - Biographical data, V, 437; other mention, V, 437.

Headdress, of Daughters of Charity - First headdress; history of cornette, II, 206–07; simplicity of headdress, I, 503; IX, 248, 529; X, 299; Saint Vincent allows, in certain cases, cornette of white linen, II, 675; recommends uniformity, VII, 64; IX, 400; XIIIb, 125, 136; even in places where coiffe may seem strange, VI, 129–31; X, 283; forbids use of veil, II, 206, 675; IX, 545; X, 15, 282; keep hair covered, XIIIb, 251–254; ignore those who want change, IX, 140; X, 83–84; singularity in manner of wearing coiffe, II, 198, 206, 292, 675; X, 253; Queen of Poland proposes special coiffe for Sisters, XIIIb, 366, 368–69, 370; see **Attire**.

Health - Passion for good health, XII, 183: see **Illness**, **Mortification**, **Physicians**, **Remedies**.

Hébrard (Christophe), Abbot of la Garde-Dieu, nephew of Hébrard de Saint-Sulpice - Requests annuity on small Cayran farm; Saint Vincent refuses, IV, 283.

Hébrard de Saint-Sulpice (Claude-Antoine), Archdeacon of Cahors - Opposed to Jansenism, III, 345; Episcopal Synod of Cahors discusses need for seminary, XIIIa, 309; gift of small Cayran farm to Cahors Seminary, III, 461; IV, 283–84, 480; appointed to Cahors Seminary, XIIIa, 309.

Hebrides, islands of Scotland - Lifestyle of inhabitants, IV, 496–97; sending of Missionaries to islands, IV, 373, 478; VIII, 615; their reports, IV, 495–97, 517; V, 121–23; VI, 199; ministries, successes, and sufferings, IV, 495–97; V, 121–22, 149, 316, 369, 622, 627; VI, 272, 429; VII, 328–29; XI, 168; extraordinary events, V, 122–23; Saint Vincent has no news of them, IV, 373; V, 77, 622, 624, 627; VI, 112, 257, 348, 429, 570; need for personnel, IV, 497; Fr. Brin accepts mission of going to visit them but is unable: see **Brin**; faculties for priests in Hebrides, VII, 45; other mentions, VI, 112; XI, 62, 162, 180, 184, 294. See also **Clanronald**, **Duggan** [**Duiguin**], **White** [**Le Blanc**] (Francis), **MacDonald**; ***Barra, Canna, Eigg, Skye, Uist***; other mentions, XI, 62, 162, 180, 184, 294; XIIIa, 186.

Hedwig of Holstein-Gottorp, Queen of Sweden - Visit to Paris, VII, 127.

Heiltz-le-Maurupt, town in Marne - Mission given, VII, 118.

Heliopolis - Titular Bishop: see François **Pallu**.

Hellot (Élisabeth), Daughter of Charity - Biographical data, III, 28; IV, 22; IX, *xv*; secretary and assistant to Saint Louise, III, 16; records conferences of Saint Vincent, III, 28; IX, *xv-xvi*, 201, 206, 221, 237, 243, 260, 272, 284, 295, 320, 337, 344, 353,

365, 401, 415; draws up Council minutes, XIIIb, 240, 251, 262, 271, 276, 285, 295; needs to understand benefits of submitting to one another, III, 264; death, IX, 401; choice of replacement, XIIIb, 305; other mention, III, 401.

Hémet (François), Brother of the Mission - Biographical data, VII, 56; XII, 430; death, VII, 56, 58, 68, 75; mention of conference on his virtues, XII, 430.

Henault (Jeanne-Christine), Daughter of Charity - Biographical data, VI, 136; Saint Louise asks permission for her to renew vows, VI, 136; other mention, XIIIb, 228.

Hennebert (François), Brother of the Mission - Biographical data; his brother, VII, 330.

Hennebont, town in Morbihan - Letters of Saint Vincent to Daughters of Charity in Hennebont: see **Hardemont**; Louis Eudo, founder and benefactor of establishment of Sisters: see **Eudo**; sending of two Sisters to Hennebont, IV, 116; IX, 430; need for third companion, XIIIb, 309; Saint Vincent promises one; illness of Geneviève Doinel, IV, 180; health of Sister Barbe, IV, 238; question of replacing Anne Hardemont with Henriette Gesseaume, as Sister Servant, IV, 242, 263, 298; arrival in Paris of two Sisters from Hennebont, VIII, 168; other mention, V, 33. See also **Doinel**, **Gesseaume** (Henriette).

Hennequin (Jérôme), Bishop of Soissons - Approves Charity of Montmirail, XIIIb, 30, 31, 32.

Hennequin (Renée Potier, Dame) - II, 399.

Hennin (Hugues), Priest of the Mission - Biographical data, IV, 510; VIII, 306; considered for Lagny, IV, 510; Saint Vincent plans to write to him, VIII, 306.

Henri (M.), of La Rochelle - III, 290.

Henri (M.) - I, 479.

Henriette (Mme) - II, 292.

Henriette, Daughter of Charity - See **Gesseaume** (Henriette).

Henriette-Marie of France, wife of Charles I of England - Bishop of Angoulême with her in England, I, 431.

Henry II, King of England - Punished by Pope for murder of Saint Thomas Becket, IX, 305.

Henry III, King of England - Assists brother-in-law, Comte de la Marche, XI, 272–73.

Henry III, King of France - Siege of Paris; King is assassinated, IV, 461.

Henry IV, King of France - Biographical data, XII, 282–83; two conversions; Clement VIII regrets having absolved him of heresy, V, 316–17; XII, 282–84; XIIIa, 377; treaty of 1604 with Sultan, IV, 147; opening of collège of La Flèche, VIII, 519; other mention, III, 387.

Hérault (Lucien), Trinitarian - Biographical data, III, 222.

Herbin (Guillaume), notary in Paris - XIIIa, 75.

Herblay, town in Seine-et-Oise - Birthplace of Jeanne Dalmagne, IX, 144; visit of Charity, XII, 356.

Herbron (François), Priest of the Mission - Biographical data, V, 577; VI, 108; VII, 331; VIII, 183; XI, 333; mention of letters to Saint Vincent, VII, 494; XI, 374; Saint Vincent asks *Propaganda Fide* for usual powers for him for Madagascar mission, V, 577; departure for Nantes, VI, 108, 112, 124, 128; shipwrecked, VI, 149–50; VIII, 183, 554; XI, 333, 336–38, 342; in Le Mans, VII, 331, 494, 592; Saint Vincent informs him of delay of ships leaving for Madagascar, VII, 526: see ***Madagascar***.

Hercules, (Fr.), General of Fathers of Christian Doctrine - Death, VII, 541.

Heresies - Leave bad impression in places where they have been sown, VII, 356; scarcity of priestly vocations in those areas, XII, 59–60: see **Jansenism**; Labadie author of new heresies, IV, 457; in Sedan, II, 148; loss of many kingdoms to heresies of Luther and Calvin, III, 40–41; heresy of Two Heads, III, 320, IV, 156, 185, 213, 608; success of Missionaries in eradicating heresy in Montauban diocese, XIIIa, 282, 289; other mentions, I, 45, 53, 405.

Heretics - Conversion of heretics by Saint Vincent, I, 58; IV, 58; XI, 28; XIIIa, 53; other conversions, II, 298, 437; III, 172, 304; XIIIb, 388, 402; set forth Catholic doctrine without arguing controversial points; example is more effective, I, 458; II, 441–42; do not challenge ministers from pulpit, I, 276; to animate souls with spirit of Gospel is most effective means of converting heretics, II, 494–95; kindness, humility, and patience are also most efficacious means to convert them, I, 58, 420; heretics continue to be edified in Sedan, II, 468; excellence of Catholicism and importance of episcopacy, IV, 420; relapse of converted heretic, VI, 147; it is divine grace that converts, VII, 583; heretics more zealous and better distributors of alms than Catholics, VIII, 596; Sisters going to Metz are to make known holiness of Catholic religion to them, X, 448; almost 200 converted at Hôtel-Dieu, XIIIb, 388; very difficult to correct sins of intellect, XI, 354–55; Saint Vincent's zeal in safeguarding faith of Catholics in danger of falling into heresy, V, 72, 155, 269; Fr. Lumsden living among heretics in Scotland, V, 149. See also ***Algiers, Cévennes,*** **Huguenots**, ***La Rochelle, Loisy-en-Brie, Madagascar, Montauban, Richelieu, Saintes, Saint-Quentin, Sedan***, **Solminihac,** ***Velopole***; other mentions, I, 45, 53, 404, 539; II, 61.

Hermite - I, 160.

Hermit - Saint Vincent recommends hermit to Bishop of Beauvais, IV, 586.

Herod Antipas, Tetrarch of Galilee - Sends Jesus to Pilate, VI, 130; other mention, IX, 18.

Herod the Great, King of Judea - Wants to kill Infant Jesus, VII, 202; X, 69; XI, 330; XIIIb, 399, 406; massacre of Holy Innocents, X, 25; XIIIb, 397.

Héron (Jean), Mathurin - Redemption of slaves, VIII, 309.

Herse (Mme de), Lady of Charity - Biographical data, I, 291; II, 268; III, 253; IV, 419; V, 578; VI, 66; VII, 51; XII, 368; gives Saint Vincent farm near Fréneville, I, 290; contacts with Saint Vincent, I, 349, 386, 446, 468; II, 516; her charities, I, 532; IV, 511, 519; VI, 591; VII, 51; XII, 368; assists establishment of Missionaries in Rome, II, 267–68, 272–73; called to meeting at Saint Louise's home, II, 328; Saint Vincent suggests meeting of Ladies of Charity at her home, VI, 202; Mme de Herse at meetings of Ladies, III, 253–54, 266, 519, 520.

Consulted about sending Daughters of Charity to Montreuil-sur-Mer, II, 293; asks for them for Saint-André in Paris, IV, 419; concerned about churches Sisters from Saint-Martin and Saint-Médard could visit to earn Jubilee, V, 579; wants Saint Vincent and Saint Louise to visit Charity of Saint-Médard to settle trouble there, VI, 66; foundress of establishment of Sisters in Chars, VI, 650; XIIIb, 357; Saint Louise tells her she is going to withdraw Sisters from Chars, VI, 651; writes to Superior in Toul, VII, 52; other mentions, I, 472, 561, 563.

Hersé [***Hercé***], town in Mayenne - I, 358.

Hervé (Fabien) - Apostolic notary of archdiocesan Court of Paris, XIIIa, 102.

Hervy (Antoine), seminarian of the Mission - Biographical data; death, IV, 499; XII, 414; mention of conference on his virtues, XII, 414.

Heudebert (Pierre), benefice holder in Paris - Witness to Act of Union of Collège des Bons-Enfants to Congregation of the Mission, XIIIa, 221, 233.

Heurtel (François) - See **Hurtel**.

Hiernaut (J.) - Member of Charity of Courboin, XIIIb, 93.

Hilarion, Abbot of Santa Croce in Gerusalemme, Rome - See **Rancati**.

Hinx, hamlet near Dax - Saint Vincent thinks his letter to Fr. Brin may reach him in Hinx, IV, 467.

Hippocrates, wise physician of antiquity - Maxim, IV, 139.

Hirbec (Claude), prisoner in Toulon - VIII, 528.

Hirigoyen (Johannès de), slave in Algiers - VII, 196, 213: see **Basque Slaves**.

Hobier (M.) - Biographical data, I, 516.

Hodicq (Claude Philippeaux, Dame de) - Saint Vincent recommends matter to her, II, 98.

Holden (Henry), chaplain of Michel de Marillac - Biographical data, I, 300; contacts with Saint Vincent, I, 300, 390; with Saint Louise, I, 300, 314.

Holiness [**Perfection**, **Sanctity**] - Mention of conference, XII, 436; in what it consists, XII, 68–71, 244.

Holland - See ***Netherlands***.

Hollandre (Fr.), Pastor of Saint-Sauveur in Paris - Contacts with Saint Vincent, I, 114.

Holofernes, general of Nebuchadnezzar - Defeated and decapitated by Judith, X, 58; XIIIb, 420.

Holy Cross (Feast) - Mention of Ember Days after this feast, XIIIa, 4, 8.

Holy Cross, parish in Warsaw - Proceedings for union of Holy Cross to Congregation of the Mission, V, 50, 84, 105, 128, 175, 179, 181, 183, 187, 196, 201, 213, 239, 249, 263, 333–34; Pastor resigns in favor of Missionaries, V, 99; mission in Holy Cross parish, V, 105; former Pastor, V, 70, 168, 389; VIII, 88; request for indulgences for Holy Cross, V, 378; death of Lady who gave Missionaries patronage of Holy Cross, V, 419; Swedes pillage house, XI, 323; after death of Fr. Ozenne, Saint Vincent suggests that Bishop of Poznań name Fr. Desdames Pastor of Holy Cross, VII, 276, 277, 300; taking possession of parish; Fr. Desdames fears Bishop may remove him, VII, 475; donations from King and Queen, VII, 625; ravages of plague in parish, XII, 61; other mentions, VI, 5, 91; VII, 481, 532; VIII, 301, 395, 509; XI, 333.

Holy Innocents - Feast, VIII, 503, 586.

Holy Land - Louis IX left his kingdom to win back Holy Land, XI, 272; first place God deprived of Church, XI, 318–19.

Holy Orders - Michel Le Gras not old enough for this sacrament, I, 138; danger of receiving it without a vocation, I, 506; necessary to preach Word of God, IV, 440; title necessary for ordination, VIII, 38; members of Tuesday Conferences seek to remain in dispositions they had upon reception of this sacrament, XIIIa, 140; epilepsy is irregularity for reception of Holy Orders, XIIIb, 269–70.

Holy Scripture - Conference at Saint-Lazare, VIII, 259. See **Appendix II** for biblical references used in this series.

Holy See - Infallible with regard to approval of religious Orders, II, 256; knows difficulties of Orders having similar names and purposes, II, 307.

Holy Spirit - Mention of conference, XII, 427; indwelling of Spirit, XII, 93–96; how Spirit governs Church, XII, 112; works through those in whom Spirit resides, VI, 413; how Spirit formed Body of Our Lord in womb of Virgin Mary, XIIIa, 36, 40; resides in Church, XII, 387; see also **Pentecost**.

Holy Spirit House [Saint-Esprit], in Toul - Given to Missionaries, II, 476–78; VIII, 606; opposition of Grand Master, II, 477; transfer of Commander's residence to Congregation of the Mission, VI, 427.

Holy Stairs - Devotion of Pope Clement VIII, IX, 250.

Holy Water - Efficacious power, X, 480.

Holy Week - Mention of conferences on sanctifying Holy Week, XII, 410, 420, 426, 431, 434.

Honfleur, town in Calvados - VII, 208.

Honorius, Emperor of West - XIIIa, 33.

Hope - Mention of conference, XII, 421; in what virtue of hope consists, X, 403; practice of this virtue by Fr. Pillé, II, 383; hope of Saint Francis de Sales, XIIIa, 82–83. See also **Confidence in God**.

Hopille (Fr. d'), Vicar-General of Agen - Explains *Pontificale* to ordinands at Saint-Lazare, I, 516; Saint Vincent sends remedy for stones, VI, 613; death, XII, 33; other mentions, I, 404, 431.

Hôpital Général - See ***General Hospital***.

Horcholle (Fr.), Pastor of Neufchâtel-en-Bray - Saint Vincent discourages him from coming to Paris to be named graduate of abbey, IV, 1; urged several times by Fr. Horcholle to use influence to help him obtain parish, saint replies that pastorate may not be vacant, IV, 40; that he has no influence with patron of parish, IV, 74; that he is willing to send him Bulls if Fr. Horcholle is graduate of Saint-Ouen Abbey, VI, 309–10.

Horses - Saint Vincent forbids Missionaries to have horses, except where necessary; apologizes for having one himself, IV, 280; V, 422, 461–62; sometimes suggests they use one, I, 177, 287, 428; encourages Saint Louise to use one, I, 164; she has one, I, 261; VIII, 128; Saint Vincent's use of horse, I, 3; IV, 281; he offers one with carriage to Saint Louise, IV, 259; gift of two horses by Duchesse d'Aiguillon, III, 431; saint uses carriage because he can no longer use horse, V, 480–81; Bro. Parre told to get one whenever needed, VII, 562; Monvoisin told to provide one for Fr. Cornuel, VIII, 196; other mentions, I, 108.

Hospital Sisters of Mercy of Jesus - Serving in Canada, V, 54.

Hospital Sisters of Sainte-Marthe - Teach young girls in Sedan; receive paying boarders, VIII, 13.

Hospitaller Monks of Italy - Vow formula, IX, 22.

Hospitaller Nuns of Saint Augustine, called Daughters of Mercy - Came from Dieppe to Vannes, XIIIb, 319.

Hospitaller Nuns of Saint Joseph - Founded in La Flèche, XIIIb, 319.

Hospitaller Nuns of the Charity of Our Lady [***Hospitalières de la Charité Notre-Dame***] - History, X, 93; XIIIa, 102; hospital of Place Royale in Paris, I, 479; X, 93; how these hospital nuns differ from Daughters of Charity because of works, IX, 458, 467; X, 102; certification and approval of Constitutions, XIIIa, 102–03; other mentions, II, 59; VIII, 561; X, 466, 534.

Hospitalité de Nuit - Shelter in Mâcon for transient poor people, XIIIb, 69.

Hospitals - Saint Vincent's advice to hospital chaplain, IV, 36–37, 91; spiritual service of poor in hospitals is proper for Missionaries, XII, 77–79; but is secondary ministry, III, 273; hospital Sisters must obey "Fathers of the Poor," IX, 520; Sister in charge of linen should have key, X, 5; service of poor in hospitals is hard work, IV, 440–41; Daughters serving in hospitals of Angers, Nantes, Richelieu, Saint-Germain-en-Laye, Hôtel-Dieu of Saint-Denis-en-France, III, 61. See also **Daughters of Charity** (hospitals).

Hossard (M.) - Quarrels of M. Hossard with Le Mans Seminary, III, 492.

Hôtel de Montgommery - Residence sought by Congregation of the Mission in Metz, VIII, 16–17, 525.

Hôtel de Ville, in Paris, seat of government - IV, 214, 412; VIII, 98; mentioned in contract for uniting Saint-Lazare to Congregation of the Mission, XIIIa, 266.

Hôtel-Dieu of Boulogne - Mentioned in letter of Saint Vincent to Bishop, III, 105.

Hôtel-Dieu of Châteaudun - Death of Barbe Angiboust, X, 511.

Hôtel-Dieu of Paris - Historical note, IX, 8; X, 72–73; joint proprietor, with Saint Vincent, of customs dues of Angers, II, 662; administrators deal with temporal matters; Chapter of Paris, or delegate, has care of spiritual, III, 295; takes part of revenues from *aides* of Angers and Melun, V, 486; number of sheets needed each day, XIIIb, 388; home visits to sick poor relieve Hôtel-Dieu of number of sick equal to two-thirds of those it hospitalizes, X, 72–73; Legate Ward for contagious illnesses, I, 450; XIIIb, 403; contagion at Hôtel-Dieu, I, 299, 355, 363, 481, 496; XIIIb, 387; difficulty, I, 260; unemployed woman from Lorraine staying at Hôtel-Dieu, III, 158; foundlings at Hôtel-Dieu, I, 352, 483, 497; Saint Louis serves sick poor of Hôtel-Dieu, IX, 97; visits patients and approaches most diseased patient, X, 450; visit of Saint Vincent, XII, 35–36; many well-born people of both sexes visit, instruct, and exhort, IV, 92; mission at Hôtel-Dieu, VII, 535–36, 545, 573; legacy of Commander Sillery, II, 136; of Mme de Gondi, XIIIa, 65; other mention, VII, 156. See also **Augustinians**; **Ladies of Charity** of Hôtel-Dieu; chaplains of Hôtel-Dieu hear confessions of patients entering hospital, XIIIb, 388–89; Saint Vincent gets priest to accept post of chaplain, XIIIa, 179; chaplains are doing well, XIIIb, 402; collection officer of Hôtel-Dieu, III, 254.

Daughters of Charity at Hôtel-Dieu - I, 320; number and duties, II, 601; III, 60; Saint Louise works with them, I, 299, 317, 357; IX, 8; Saint Vincent reproaches her for going too often to Hôtel-Dieu, I, 290; asks her to spend two or three days there because things are going badly, I, 450; Sisters sell jelly; profits help poor, X, 255–56; interruption of visits to Hôtel-Dieu; Sisters resume ministry, I, 327, 363; their house, I, 235, 363; their confessor, VIII, 204; Saint Vincent goes to see them, I, 323; sick Daughter, I, 299; XIIIb, 317; Rules for Sisters of Hôtel-Dieu, II, 131; IX, 17; XIIIb, 206–209; possibility of Sisters making Jubilee there, V, 579; X, 192; Sisters prepare refreshments for Ladies at Hôtel-Dieu; perform their tasks in case of contagion, XIIIb, 447; other mentions, I, 347, 349, 390, 409, 437, 449, 481, 498; II, 609; VII, 641; IX, 539; XII, 362; XIIIb, 206. See also **Gesseaume** (Henriette), **Jacqueline** (Sister), **Joly** (Marie), **Poisson** (Geneviève).

Houdan, town in Yvelines - I, 455.

Houlie (Jean), Brother of the Mission, brother-in-law of Jean Bécu - Possible reference in letter to Saint Louise, I, 390.

Houmain (Fr.) - Begins, with Fr. Olier, seminary at Vaugirard and then at Saint-Sulpice, II, 308.

Hour of retiring, for Daughters of Charity - IX, 3, 42; go to bed modestly, IX, 7.

Houses of Congregation of the Mission - List, VIII, 604–19; do not allow anyone to live there and do as he pleases, VII, 306; customary not to change anything or make important decisions without advice of General or Visitor, VIII, 53; country house, II, 657.

Hubert (Bro.) - See **Bécu** (Hubert).

Hubrot (Charles), inhabitant of Montmirail - XIIIb, 34.

Hudicourt (Charles-François), seminarian of the Mission, son of Jean Hudicourt - Biographical data, VIII, 446.

Hudicourt (Jean), mason in Hamelincourt - Joy at seeing son happy in Congregation of the Mission, VIII, 446.

Hugand (Claude), Magistrate in Mâcon - XIIIb, 73.

Huguenots - Historical note, I, 404–05; II, 345; V, 8; XI, 15; Antoine Lucas capable of edifying them, II, 345; in temporal matters, Huguenot may be right against Catholic, II, 494; Saint Vincent seeks ways to have raised in Catholic faith children of Huguenot mother and of father converted to Catholicism, V, 155; Huguenot directed to him to be converted, II, 498; five Huguenots abjure heresy during mission preached by Jean-Jacques Olier, I, 367; thirty or forty others abjure to Bishop of Mende, II, 449; do not get embroiled in disputes between Catholics and Huguenots, II, 494; saint agrees that Bishop must be informed of minister's behavior disapproved of by edicts, II, 312–13; their conversion, III, 437; IV, 528; V, 331; VI, 252; XIIIb, 384; Bull condemning Jansenism saves France from falling into Calvinism again, IV, 582; saint recommends that Brother surgeon use same devotion in caring for Catholics and Huguenots, VIII, 208–09; death, in Huguenot's home, of Catholic woman refused assistance of priest; Bossuet's protest, VII, 85–86, 100; validity of baptism given by Huguenots of Poitou, VIII, 31, 134; synods, VIII, 52; XII, 239–40; Synod of Cozes, VIII, 31; Huguenots of Saint-Céré, II, 503–04; marriage with Catholics, IV, 194; Labadie becomes Huguenot in Montauban, IV, 185, 457; question of giving them alms for devastated provinces, IV, 188; Saint Vincent does not want to send Daughters to Warsaw in company of Huguenot, V, 182;

French in Madagascar act like Huguenots, III, 578; desire to see them leave Madagascar, VI, 252; some attended Easter services on ship to Madagascar, but none was converted, VIII, 572; many poor people in Amsterdam become Huguenots to receive food and clothing, VIII, 595; retreatant at Saint-Lazare is new convert from this religion, XI, 15; conversion of slave in Barbary, XI, 180–81; how they preach, using Calvin's method, XI, 267–68; they use catechism to destroy faith, XIIIa, 34; leading inhabitants of Châtillon were Huguenots, XIIIa, 50; as are many people in Loisy-en-Brie, I, 25; in Verneuil, I, 29; in Cévennes, I, 245; in Richelieu, I, 404; in Metz, X, 448; in Sedan, XIIIa, 339; other mentions, I, 193; VI, 631; VIII, 570, 573. See also **Heretics**.

Huguier (Benjamin-Joseph), Priest of the Mission - Biographical data, III, 389; IV, 291; V, 91; VI, 36; VII, 30; VIII, 32; family, VI, 36; business acumen, V, 91; sent to Tunis as French Consul, III, 389, 394, 414; from Tunis informs Saint Vincent of death of Fr. Dieppe, III, 445; freed from chain gang for large sum of money, IV, 291, 506; summoned to Paris, IV, 372; sent to Genoa, V, 170; to Agde, V, 190; question of sending him to Toulon instead of Agde, V, 190.

Serving galley convicts in Toulon: V, 199, 259, 412, 554–55; VI, 102, 187, 195, 207, 261, 273, 276, 278, 302, 304–05, 320–21, 333, 338, 342–43, 354–55, 360, 372, 384, 418, 487, 524, 593, 599; VII, 245; VIII, 513; in Marseilles, VI, 617; in Toulon, VI, 186–87, 627, 638; VII, 30, 34, 49, 50, 54, 70, 101, 123, 149–50, 154, 174, 179, 185, 187, 208, 486; Missionary from Marseilles comes to help him with added work during Jubilee, VI, 201, 207; letter of encouragement from Saint Vincent, VII, 158; question of sending him to Algiers to put M. Barreau's affairs in order; plan abandoned, VII, 179, 185–86, 190, 194, 196, 207, 212, 221–23, 227–28, 232, 234, 237, 249–50, 253–54, 263, 273, 281; VIII, 32, 327; in Marseilles or in Toulon, VII, 250, 283, 289, 393; in Toulon again, VII, 438, 456, 458, 486, 489, 539, 557; VIII, 138, 244, 250, 276, 299, 310, 321, 331, 360, 369, 373, 377, 387, 397, 402, 445, 462, 485, 528, 538; mention of letters Saint Vincent wrote to him in Toulon, V, 554; VI, 276, 278, 372, 638; VII, 186; VIII, 513; mention of letter to Saint Vincent, VIII, 310; reference to letter Saint Vincent was going to write him, VIII, 337.

Huiot (Jeanne), Daughter of Charity - XIIIb, 227.

Huitmille (Philippe), Priest of the Mission - Biographical data, IV, 533; VII, 72; in Annecy, IV, 533.

Human Respect - Conference, XI, 52; do not dwell on what people may say, XIIIb, 327, 350–52; never do anything out of human respect, II, 315; trample it underfoot, IV, 480; Saint

Vincent admonishes Fr. Cogley, IV, 471; Barbe Angiboust had no human respect, X, 515–16.

Humbert (Lord) - XIIIa, 27.

Humières (Isabelle Phelippeaux, Marquise d') - Wants Saint Vincent to hear her confession, II, 286–87.

Humiliations - Conference, XI, 50; we must love and desire them, I, 94, 275; V, 230–31; VII, 343; XI, 46, 50; XIIIb, 341; true means of becoming humble, XII, 150; example of Jesus, I, 183–84, 275; XI, 50; XIIIb, 341; Saint Vincent humbles self in speech, II, 87–88, 113, 236–37, 266, 278, 480, 566, 638; III, 568; IV, 178; V, 178–79, 340–41, 581; VII, 92, 137; VIII, 169; IX, 221, 312; X, 2, 352, 388; XI, *xvii*, 196, 236, 250, 267, 281, 303, 326, 345, 352, 354, 365; XII, 19, 29, 31, 46, 82, 124, 154–56, 160, 176, 194, 206, 220, 235, 238, 242, 252, 269, 272, 296–97, 312, 329, 341, 351, 394, 395, 396, 397; XIIIa, 179; speaks of his sins, of "abominations" of his life, I, 500; II, 193, 230, 232, 245, 287, 314, 345, 455, 620; III, 18, 121, 296; IV, 173; V, 180, 370, 635; VIII, 383; IX, 306, 464; X, 184, 213, 492; XI, 45, 108; XII, 111, 287, 296–97; calls self big scoundrel, XIIIa, 211; "fourth form student," XII, 114, 238, 394; repeats that he tended pigs, II, 5, 193; IV, 219; VIII, 159, 383; IX, 14; X, 547; XII, 19, 220, 242, 318, 395; humble origins, II, 5; IV, 219; V, 398; VIII, 159; IX, 67, 529; X, 275; XII, 351; urges continual state of interior humiliation, III, 47.

Asks pardon on his knees, IX, 452; X, 164; XI, 326; asks forgiveness of confrere, whom he thinks he has reprimanded too strongly, IX, 218; humbles self for having spoken to several Missionaries in self-satisfied way, X, 376; spoke sharply to Brother, IX, 451–52; XII, 154–55; public accusation of act of self-satisfaction, XI, 306–07; likes to show ignorance during conferences, XI, 156; XII, 14, 157, 194; how he accepts threat of dismissal of Nantes Sisters, IV, 19; speaks humbly of Congregations he founded, I, 567; IV, 392–93; V, 42; VII, 92; IX, 14, 529; X, 2, 408; XI, 2, 8, 46, 104, 280; XII, 19–20, 35, 395; calls them wretched, I, 399; V, 596; a beggary, VI, 38; calls those who belong to them poor beggars, VIII, 254; X, 2; XIIIb, 281.

Humility - Conferences, IX, 528–35; XI, 44–46, 46, 47–48, 48, 49, 50, 104, 178–79, 293–94, 350–51; XII, 161–173; mention of another conference, XII, 422; Rule of Missionaries, XII, 161; exhortation to humility, XI, 49, 50, 349; in what it consists, V, 609; XII, 166–67, 247; especially necessary for Daughters of Charity, IX, 529–30; X, 418, 422–24; for Missionaries, XI, 46; XII, 168–69, 248; during missions, XII, 247–48; in seminaries, IV, 570–71; in ministry to ordinands, XII, 168; Congregation will subsist by humility, XII, 396; connection between humility and charity, X, 425–26; truth and humility go well together, I, 140.

Humility brings grace with it, IX, 530; prepares way for all other virtues, X, 106; XII, 172; excellent means for acquiring, preserving chastity, XI, 162; mutual support, XII, 32; fruitful humility, XII, 385; source of charity, XI, 1; of peace and union in local communities, IX, 555; XII, 32–33, 91; way of winning hearts, VIII, 202; best means of acquiring and maintaining union and charity with God and neighbor, XI, 137–38; foundation of generosity, XI, 332; foundation on which Jesus Christ established execution of His plans, III, 279; V, 166; X, 161; necessary for submission of judgment, XI, 355; God raises up humble and casts down proud, IX, 530; XII, 164, 166; fills up souls empty of self, XI, 281; sister of gentleness, XII, 152; spirit of humility is antidote to pride, VII, 510; is virtue opposed to pride, IX, 365.

Example of Jesus, I, 183, 184, 332, 518; II, 87; V, 630; IX, 529; XI, 124–25, 312–13, 350, 388; XII, 161, 164, 166; of Fr. Olier, XI, 350; of Fr. Pillé, II, 373–74; of Francis de Sales, V, 478; XIIIa, 88; of Saint Louise, X, 577–78, 583; of country women, IX, 68–69; of Saint Vincent: complains that admonitor does not admonish him, IX, 293; asks God that he be always disposed to choose worst, I, 514; confesses he would not have become priest had he known what priesthood was, V, 569; always gave first place to priest from Bons-Enfants when giving missions with him, X, 184.

Art of acquiring humility is to humble self, IX, 534; XIIIb, 341; Saint Vincent asks Missionaries to meditate once a month on this virtue, XI, 178–79; marks of humility, IX, 474–76; XI, 44–45; everyone finds this virtue beautiful in speculation, XI, 44; XII, 162–63; but difficult in practice, XII, 162–63; seek neither esteem nor honors, I, 487, 518, 524–26; II, 315, 351; V, 493; VII, 116, 348–49, 531; IX, 240, 328, 520; X, 114, 120, 133–34; XI, 124–28, 179, 313–14, 387–88; XII, 20–21, 257–59; XIIIb, 339; attribute success to God, I, 57–58, 183; X, 541; XI, 313; think that, of ourselves, we spoil everything and are capable of nothing, X, 184; be humbled by defects and sins, II, 153; XI, 2, 44, 353; love contempt, VII, 305, 483; X, 124, 540–41; XI, 382; XII, 166, 171, 227; XIIIb, 336–37, 340, 341; to despise self is reasonable, XI, 47; XII, 169–71; consider self lower than everyone, even the devil, IX, 240, 301; X, 125, 195, 352–53, 444; XI, 104; be humble not only about self, but also about Community, II, 265; V, 39, 42, 537; X, 162; XI, 48, 104, 143, 293, 383, 387; XII, 167, 168, 228; virtue necessary for Sisters being sent to the country, IX, 430; prayers to ask for humility, IX, 535; XII, 173, 394. See also **Humiliations**, **Pride**, **Vanity**.

Hungary - II, 457; XII, 59.

Huntley, castle in Scotland - Marquis of Huntley, V, 368.

Huot (Jeanne), Daughter of Charity - Entered before Act of Establishment, XIIIb, 228.

Hurons - XII, 24.

Hurpy (Pierre), Priest of the Mission - Biographical data, VII, 72; with Jacques Tholard in Marcoussis, VII, 72.

Hurtel [**Heurtel**] (François), Priest of the Mission - Biographical data; death, II, 168; IV, 29; Superior of Saint-Charles Seminary, VIII, 614.

Husson (Martin), lawyer in Parlement - Biographical data, IV, 549; V, 38; VI, 121; VII, 105; VIII, 218–19; XI, 276–77; letters from Saint Vincent, IV, 549; VII, 105; to Saint Vincent, V, 118, 265; VI, 321, 333; VIII, 447, 531; mention of letter from Saint Vincent, V, 150; recommended to Duchesse d'Aiguillon, IV, 560; family, IV, 561, 597; VI, 343, 354; praise for him, IV, 560–62, 596–97; named French Consul in Tunis; Saint Vincent explains choice, IV, 549; recommended to Duchesse d'Aiguillon when preparing to leave for Tunis, IV, 549, 561; Saint Vincent prepares gifts for Dey and Pasha of Tunis, IV, 561–62; arrival in Tunis, V, 38; rule of life given by Saint Vincent, XIIIa, 401; in Tunis, V, 91, 130, 248; VI, 259; XI, 276–77, 291, 334; demands liberation of French slaves captured contrary to conventions, V, 133–34; refuses to have cotton sailcloth brought from France; displeasure of Dey, V, 333, 385, 412; XI, 302–03; difficulty in claiming consular rights, V, 89; which English Consul usurps, V, 265–66, 267–69; merchants have no record of his passports, V, 133; they are displeased with him, V, 268; discouraged, ready to cede post of Consul to another, V, 266; decree of King's Privy Council confirms him in rights and privileges of office, VI, 120–21, 165; text of decree, VI, 643; sent back to France by Dey, VI, 314, 327, 346, 348, 350, 352, 361, 363, 371; XI, 392; arrives in Marseilles and falls ill, VI, 320, 322, 332–33, 338, 343, 352–54, 359, 370; Saint Vincent summons him to Paris, VI, 321–22, 328; en route to Paris, VI, 383, 391; in Paris, VI, 392, 394; in Montmirail, VIII, 447, 531; other mention, VI, 371, VIII, 218.

Hyacinth, Saint - V, 175, 377.

I

Idleness - Mother of all vices, I, 398; often a stumbling block, VII, 506; never be idle, IX, 6, 175–76, 384–85.

Ignatius (Saint and Martyr) - IV, 91; XI, 303.

Ignatius of Loyola (Saint) - Love of chastity, XI, 197–98; greater glory of God was unique goal of his actions, XII, 123; remains, after him, unique goal of actions of his sons, XIIIb, 368; introduced practice of admonitions among his men, XI, 86; forbade them to have benefices, XII, 325; ordinance concerning Communion, III, 362; made only short draft of Rules, III, 272; multiplied establishments despite insufficient personnel, III, 163; sent novices to army, X, 446; expelled twelve Jesuits at one time, II, 355–56; chapel in his name, V, 561; feast day, XI, 197; other mentions, I, 153; XI, 49; XIIIa, 186.

Igou (M. d') - XIIIa, 122.

Ikombo, village in Madagascar - VI, 248.

Île de Ré, island in Atlantic Ocean - V, 141, 145, 146, 326; Priory of Saint-Étienne d'Ars, XIIIa, 42. See also **Fournier** (Louis), **Lanson** (François).

Îles d'Or - See **Gondi** (Philippe-Emmanuel de).

Illness [**Infirmities**] - Conferences, XI, 60–62; XII, 26–29; on care of sick, IX, 49–51, 51–55; X, 267–279; XII, 413; text of Particular Rules of DCs, X, 535–40, 545–51; beware of temptations of sickness, XII, 393; mention of other conferences, XII, 414, 424, 432; it is God who sends illness, I, 123; XI, 61; XII, 26, 29; sickness is divine state, I, 145; nowhere can we better know a person than in state of illness, XI, 60; recitation of Divine Office is adjusted to possibilities, XII, 273; patient sick persons are pleasing to God, XI, 364; sick in Community are blessing for house, XII, 26; for Company, VII, 193; XI, 61; XII, 26; are not a burden, IX, 434; avoid pampering self when ill, X, 274–76, 301–02; XII, 393; example of Bro. Antoine, of Fr. Pillé, and of Fr. Senaux, XII, 28–29; visits to sick, IV, 131; caring for sick on ship to Madagascar, VIII, 572; reasons Daughters of Charity have for visiting and caring for sick poor, IX, 49–53; XIIIb, 254–56; when traveling, visit them in stopping places, XIIIb, 273; what to do when visiting sick persons, V, 349; IX, 53–55, 176; do not allow them to lack anything, VI, 393; VII, 425; if necessary, sell chalices to have wherewithal to care for them, I, 521; XII, 334; how the Company cares for the sick, VII, 387; those who have never been ill are less suitable for consoling and assisting them, XI, 18; do not allow sick to return to work until cured, VII, 425.

Saint Vincent compassionates with sufferings of sick Missionaries, II, 623; III, 460; many colds, VI, 267, 271; VII, 90, 211; care and concern for sick men of Company, I, 521, 523, 530; visits sick in Saint-Lazare infirmary, II, 237; Missionaries should be cared for where they minister, IV, 261; VI, 196; VII, 294; in theory, no objection to Missionary's working for physical healing of sick when he knows effective remedy, VI, 420; VII, 41; extraordinary size of cyst, IV, 103.

Health problems of Daughters of Charity, VI, 307; care of sick Sisters, X, 274–77, 301–02, 548; duties of sick Sisters, X, 276–77, 548–49; it is charity to visit sick Sisters of other houses, X, 331; illness is never motive for dismissal, XIIIb, 365: see **Confraternity of Charity**, **Ladies of Charity**, **Daughters of Charity**, **Physicians**, **Remedies**, **Suffering**.

Illusions - Conference, XII, 277–88; Rule of Missionaries, XII, 277; importance of not falling into illusions and of getting rid of them, XII, 278–80; those in Community more exposed to them than others, XII, 279; what is understood by illusion, XII, 280–81; devil's ability to create illusions, XII, 281–82; signs for discerning them, XII, 284–85; means to avoid falling into them, XI, 91; XII, 286–87; illusions are contagious, XII, 288; illusion of Clement VIII: see **Clement VIII**.

Imaphalles, region in Madagascar - French military expedition to Imaphalles, V, 507, 514, 519.

Imard (Louise) - Member of Charity of Argenteuil, XIIIb, 107.

Imitation of Jesus Christ - Saint Vincent attributes this work to Thomas à Kempis, I, 373; recommends its reading, I, 373, 513; VI, 146; Fr. Mousnier takes copies to Madagascar, V, 298; readings taken from it on voyage, III, 543; Saint Vincent interprets excerpt from it, XIIIa, 161.

Immaculate Conception - Devotion of Fr. Pillé, II, 380; feast, VIII, 240, 558–59; XIIIb, 20–21; Office, VIII, 559.

Imoro, village in Madagascar - Illness and baptism of chief, VI, 222; presence of French army, VI, 242.

Incarnation - Necessity of this mystery, III, 281; knowledge of it needed for salvation, XI, 172–73, 344; XII, 72; Mary's joy in this mystery, IX, 323; praise preceded sacrifice in Incarnation, XII, 265–66; Congregation of the Mission is bound to honor it, XIIIa, 454–55.

Inchiquin [***Insiguin***] (Murrough O'Brien, Earl of), slave in Algiers - Biographical data, VIII, 337, 387, 397, 401, 420, 467.

In Coena Domini, papal letter - Statement of ecclesiastical censure against heresies, schisms, sacrilege, piracy, forgery, and other crimes; faculty to absolve from cases reserved to Pope, I, 45, 53; V, 385, 548, 571; XIIIa, 310; faculty granted to Congregation of the Mission, V, 573.

Incurables - Should not be admitted to Charity, I, 258–59; hospital for them in Rome, II, 499.

Incurables, hospital in Paris - Historical note, I, 371; no vacancies, VII, 443; hospital for incurable diseases only, X, 273.

Indies - Voyages there, III, 284; V, 78; Dutch seek to become masters of Indies, IV, 444; meeting about Indies, IV, 562; uniformity of Church in Indies with Rome, XII, 211; people do not have customs to console sorrowful, XII, 222; Church spreading there, XIIIa, 108; Saint Vincent sends Nacquart and Gondrée there, XIIIa, 358. See also II, 105, 229; IV, 118, 135; V, 277, 316, 362; VI, 104, 244; VIII, 171, 586, 590; XI, 121, 162, 180, 184, 262, 264, 270, 294, 357, 364, 375; XIIIa, 37, 487; XIIIb, 368.

Index (Congregation of the) - Decrees regarding Jansenism, VI, 153.

Indifference [**Availability**, **Openness to God's Will**] - Conferences, IX, 201–04, 401–15; X, 126–45, 219–32, 556–60, 561–69; XI, 70–71; XII, 44–47, 187–200; mention of other conferences, XII, 408, 433; sign of spirit of true Daughter of Charity, IX, 474; Rule of Daughters of Charity, X, 126, 219; of Missionaries, XII, 187; reasons to be available, X, 126–28, 556–59, 561, 563; XII, 187–88, 193–94; indifference brings peace and happiness, IV, 339; V, 410; VII, 434–35, 589; X, 222, 562–63; makes us like angels, IV, 339; X, 222–23; Jubilee cannot be gained without indifference, X, 193; example of Jesus, X, 223, 560–61, 564; XII, 192, 195; of Abraham and Isaac, XII, 196; of Apostles, IX, 401; X, 127, 223; XII, 195–96; of Saint Peter's mother-in-law, of Saint Francis de Sales, X, 223–24; of Comte de Rougemont, XII, 190–91; of soldiers, IX, 202; of parishioners who follow Pastor in procession, IX, 202; of Missionaries; in thirty years only one refused to go where assigned, XI, 212; Sisters listening to Saint Vincent are ready to go wherever sent, X, 96; Saint Louise praises their docility, X, 98; Saint Vincent recommends indifference to Saint Louise, I, 77, 212, 241; urges her to encourage it in young women and Sisters, I, 217, 223.

In what indifference consists, X, 220–21, 562; XII, 188; ask for nothing, refuse nothing, VI, 331; X, 219–31, 240, 415; XII, 46; indifference with regard to places, IV, 437; VI, 565; VII, 448, 483, 589; IX, 36; X, 105, 406, 411; to persons, II, 401; IX, 198; X, 410, 552; availability for ministry, III, 508, 510; V, 409; VII, 525, 577; X, 564–68; XII, 44–47; regarding confessors, IX, 443; X, 412, 552; and housing, VIII, 271–72;

in all things, V, 593, 630; VI, 143; VII, 636; IX, 10–11, 102, 111; X, 465; XI, 93; be docile to God's Will, implant it deeply in our hearts, XI, 70; prayer to ask for this virtue, X, 568; other mention, I, 151. See also **Attachments**, **Availability**, **Detachment**, **Mortification**.

Individuality - See **Singularity**.

Indochina - See Cochin China.

Indulgences - Request for indulgences for missions and Charities, I, 246; V, 548; for Jouy, I, 541; for Richelieu, II, 172; for La Rose, II, 352; for Congregation, V, 204; for Poland, V, 435; for Fr. Delville, VI, 419; for mission in Sillery, VI, 581; for some people in Laon, VI, 636–637; for Pastor in Aire Diocese, VII, 37; for Pastor near Notre-Dame de la Rose, VII, 361; for ordinands, VII, 498; for general confession and Forty Hours' devotion, I, 45; XIIIa, 306; 1640 petition for indulgences for reserved sins, XIIIa, 310; for unspecified faculties, XIIIa, 311; plenary indulgence for places where missions are given, V, 571, 573; Saint Vincent sends authenticated copies of Brief to houses, V, 573, 638; VI, 82; VII, 180; sends Fr. Delville Brief for indulgence requested, VI, 423; opposition of certain Bishops, VI, 63–64; plenary indulgence for Daughters of Charity at point of death, III, 316–17; for Missionaries, XI, 193; report of Fr. Lebreton to obtain indulgences for Congregation of the Mission, I, 585; could be used to spread devotion, III, 288; Brief on indulgence for those who make retreat in Company, VII, 296.

Inebriation - See **Intoxication**.

Infirmities - See **Illness, Sufferings**.

Ingoli (Francesco), Secretary of *Propaganda Fide* - Contacts with Saint Vincent or his representative in Rome, II, 35, 43, 64, 174, 287, 466; III, 247–48; Saint Vincent writes him about mission in Persia, III, 168; Nuncio in Paris recommends Congregation of the Mission, seeking approval from Rome, XIIIa, 244, 246; consulted for approval of house of the Mission in Rome, XIIIa, 313; writes again, asking for articles that would ease rejection of request, XIIIa, 251; other mentions, II, 457, 462; III, 40; XIIIa, 379.

Ingrin (M.) - V, 17.

Injuries - Endure them patiently, II, 424; III, 520; example of Our Savior, X, 150; of Saint Vincent, I, 165, 66; of Saint Jane Frances, II, 248.

Innocent III, Pope - Prohibits solemn vows, except for those in four mendicant Orders or those who follow their Rules, XII, 303; XIIIa, 380–81.

Innocent VIII, Pope - Would canonize anyone faithful to keeping Rules of Order or Community, IX, 9, 250, 368; X, 233, 285, 294, 329, 340, 434, 476, 541; XI, 73. ***Nota:*** Saint Vincent erroneously attributed this idea to Pope Clement VIII, not Innocent VIII.

Innocent X, Pope - Saint Vincent explains to him functions and ministries of Mission, IV, 71, 105; sad state of France, IV, 445; Saint Vincent asks him to create Bishops *in partibus* in Tonkin and Cochinchina, IV, 595; settlement with Louis XIV, II, 679–80; calls Congregation of the Mission to work in Persia, III, 187; receives petition on behalf of Abbess of Longchamp, IV, 484; letter French episcopate sends to denounce Five Propositions of Jansenius, IV, 607; condemns heresy of Two Heads, III, 75, 320; Jansenism, IV, 580–81, 597, 600–01; V, 645; VI, 100–02, 152–53; illness, V, 204; asks Missionaries in Rome to grant hospitality to Cardinal de Retz, V, 274; favors granted to Missionaries and faithful who attend missions, V, 548; said to dislike religious state, III, 372; does not favor increase in number of religious Orders, IV, 73; refuses to approve vows taken in Congregation of the Mission, XIIIa, 379; does not send Bulls of Urban VIII relative to union of Saint-Lazare to Mission, VII, 503; XIIIa, 473, 486; Anne of Austria entreats him to make Superior General of Congregation of the Mission, and his successors, perpetual Directors of Daughters of Charity, XIIIb, 141–42; other mentions, II, 154; IX, 487.

Innocents - See **Herod the Great**, **Holy Innocents**.

Inquisition (Congregation) - IV, 184, 430; VI, 101, 132.

Insensitivity - For things of God and neighbor, XII, 260, 412.

Inspirations - Conference, XII, 277–88; mention of conference, XII, 407; impulse that inclines us to good, X, 7; God speaks to heart, XI, 90; desire for good things does not always come from God, I, 111; signs to discern true inspirations from illusions; in what they consist, XI, 90; have recourse to spiritual director to dispel illusions, XI, 91; God's inspirations are gentle and peaceful, IV, 569. See also **Illusions**.

Instructions - Conference on their good use, IX, 305–20.

Insults - Bear them patiently, II, 424; III, 520; example of Our Lord, X, 150; of Saint Vincent, I, 165–66; of Saint Jane Frances de Chantal, II, 248.

Intemperance - See **Gluttony**.

Interior Life - Mention of conference on spiritual man, XII, 436; in what interior life consists, X, 574; reign of Jesus Christ in us, XII, 110–14; enter into interior life by practice of modesty, X, 586; necessary for Seminary Directors, VI, 71; for

Daughters of Charity, X, 586; love solitude of our room, X, 588; through recollection, Our Lord speaks heart to heart with us, V, 362; Saint Vincent encourages Fr. Get to incline boarders in Montpellier to it, VIII, 3.

Intoxication [**Drunkenness**] - Degrading vice, XII, 37, 39–40; seen even in houses of priests, XI, 8; and of Missionaries, IV, 295; XI, 105; XII, 39–40.

Introduction to the Devout Life - Saint Vincent recommends it to Saint Louise during her retreat, I, 158, 375; advises first Sisters to use it in meditation, IX, 12, 42; cites it in conference to Sisters, IX, 460; comments on its value, XII, 2; mentions it in deposition at process of beatification of Francis de Sales, XIIIa, 93–94; Saint-Cyran cites it in his interrogation, XIIIa, 130; Saint Vincent suggests it for devotional reading to women of Charity in Châtillon, XIIIb, 19; copies to be taken to Madagascar, III, 282; readings from it, III, 543; V, 138; IX, 37; XIIIb, 442; other mention, I, 389.

Inundations [**Floods**] - See ***Paris***.

Ireland - Letters written by saint to Ireland, III, 90–91; IV, 17; Holy See requests Missionaries for Ireland, II, 557, 633; III, 91, 93; pressured by Irish Bishops for Missionaries, III, 93; Saint Vincent asks Cardinal Richelieu for aid to Ireland, XI, 114; exhortation to Missionaries going to Ireland, XI, 137; departure of Missionaries, III, 90, 93, 103, 107, 115, 120, 137; ministries, III, 192, 194; IV, 107, 515; XIIIa, 186; humility of Ireland's Bishops, III, 188; mission in Limerick, IV, 18; success of Cromwell's armies, III, 194, 274; persecution and plague, IV, 18–19, 291, 341; VI, 500; XII, 35; progress of heresy, XI, 279, 318; XII, 35; return of several Missionaries to France, III, 478; murder of Thady Lee, seminarian of the Mission, IV, 342; siege and capture of Limerick: see ***Limerick***; return of other Missionaries to France: see **Barry** (Edmund), **Brin**; Fr. Brin entrusted with visiting Missionaries in Ireland: see **Brin**; Saint Vincent is urged to send two French secular priests to Ireland to report on state of Catholic religion; negotiations; abandonment of project, VI, 460–61, 498–500, 605, 618; VII, 12; wants to be able to use Irish priests outside Ireland, VII, 346, 420–21, 495; Irishman wants to enter Congregation of the Mission, VIII, 257; he does so, VIII, 341.

Irish refugee Bishops and priests in France, VII, 525; Irish refugees in Troyes, V, 82; VII, 348–49; compassion for Irish refugees, XII, 391–92; aid sent by Saint Vincent to Bishop of Cork, retired in France: see **Barry** (Robert); some Irish with Dutch fleet that arrived in Table Bay, VIII, 588; other mentions, IV, 373, 468; VI, 126, 478; XI, 190; XIIIa, 394.

Superiors of the mission and its history, VIII, 615. See also **Arthur**, **Barry** (Edmund), **Barry** (Robert), **Bourdet** (Jean), **Brin**, **Butler** (Peter), ***Cashel***, **Cogley** [Coglée] (Gerard, Laurence, Mark), **Dalton**, **Dowley**, **Duchesne**, **Duggan** [Duiguin], **Dwyer**, **Kirwan**, **White** [Le Blanc, François], **White** [Le Blanc, Georges], **Le Vacher** (Philippe), ***Limerick***, **O'Brien**, **Patriarche**, **Plunket**, **Walsh** [Valois].

Iroquois - IV, 366; XII, 24.

Isaac, Patriarch - His sacrifice: see **Abraham**; his obedience, XII, 196; other mention, I, 314, 551; XII, 197.

Isabelle (Sister) - See **Martin** (Élisabeth).

Isaiah, prophet - Cited, XII, 131, 157.

Ishmael, son of Abraham and Hagar - I, 314.

Isidore the Farmer (Saint) - God did his work while he was hearing Mass, XI, 285.

Islam - See **Mohammedanism**.

Isle-Bouchard, town in Indre-et-Loire - Ursuline Convent, V, 602.

Ispahan, town in Persia (Iran) - II, 459, 522.

Israelites - Rose early to gather manna, III, 532; campaign against town of Gabaa, VI, 252. Built Lord's temple with stones in one hand and sword in other, IX, 525; wanted Moses, not God, to speak to them, XII, 166.

Issoudun, town in Indre - Place of exile for Philippe and Antoine Bausset, VIII, 429.

Issy, town near Paris - Question of sending Henriette Gesseaume there; Saint Louise thinks she is needed elsewhere, II, 392; Saint Louise considers closing Sisters' house, II, 400; Sisters no longer there; former Daughter of Charity plans to continue service of poor, dressed as Daughter, V, 44–45; other mentions, II, 635; III, 116, 177, 232: see also **Jeanne** (Sister).

Italians - Reserved, slow to decide; temporize, II, 295; not inclined to hard work, V, 465; French find it difficult to adapt to this, VI, 262; VII, 542; Italians have problem with vows and religious state, XIIIa, 377–78, 381–82; very cautious people, distrustful of those who act too quickly, II, 267; other mentions, V, 89; VII, 594; XIIIa, 350.

Italy - Confraternities of Charity, IV, 76; VI, 26, 197; VII, 271; XIIIb, 225; bandits of Italy: see **Bandits**; other mentions, IV, 335; V, 72, 149; VI, 39, 124, 134, 373; VII, 249, 429; missions, IV, 441; V, 573; plague, VI, 40; Missionaries going there, VII, 271, 289, 291, 304, 316; VIII, 539, 601; XI, 189; XII, 125, 318,

332; XIIIa, 34, 186; XIIIb, 225, 429. See also ***Genoa***, ***Rome***, ***Turin***, etc.

Itaperina, roadstead in Madagascar - V, 285–86, 305.

Itinéraire des Clercs [***Itinerarium***] - Inspires Saint Vincent in writing to Saint Louise, I, 65; Missionaries traveling to Madagascar prayed it frequently, VI, 226; VIII, 556, 572, 597.

J

Jacob (Gérard), Mayor of Bar-le-Duc - II, 76.

Jacob (M.) - VI, 374, 593.

Jacob, Patriarch - I, 314; II, 448; IX, 373; XIIIa, 274.

Jacobins - See **Dominicans**.

Jacqueline, Daughter of Charity - Saint Vincent allows her to go to brother's wedding, I, 233; considered for Hôtel-Dieu, I, 235; niece wants to enter Daughters of Charity, I, 433; Jacqueline is slapped, I, 449; question of placing her at Saint-Jacques, I, 502; leaves Saint-Leu; Saint Louise wonders if she should try her at Saint-Jacques or at Motherhouse, II, 591; bad-tempered; Saint Vincent puts forth question of dismissal, XIIIb, 242–45; other mention, I, 436.

Jacquette, Daughter of Charity - Asks Fr. Portail's permission to take vows, VII, 408.

Jacquette, Daughter of Charity - Proposed for Nantes, XIIIb, 284; recalled, XIIIb, 312.

Jacquette, Daughter of Charity - Proposed for Chantilly, III, 298.

Jacquier (M.) - Refuses to pay two sols for each allowance of bread King gives to the poor, VI, 547, 589, 609.

Jacquinet (Jean), *Procureur Fiscal* of Joigny - XIIIb, 28, 65, 66.

Jacquinot (M.), Jesuit Provincial - Mentioned in Saint-Cyran's interrogation, XIIIa, 134.

Jaillard (M.), cousin of Fr. Jolly - VI, 401, 542; VIII, 86, 198.

Jamain (Martin), seminarian of the Mission - Biographical data, II, 535; death and virtues, II, 563–65; other mention, II, 535.

Jamen (M.) - VII, 232, 249–50, 253.

James the Greater (Saint), Apostle - Jesus gathers Peter, James, and John on Mount of Olives and Tabor, XIIIb, 386; pilgrimage to Compostela, XIIIa, 311.

James (Saint), Apostle - Cited, X, 11, 324; XI, 134.

Jamin (Gary), Brother of the Mission - Biographical data; sent from Richelieu to Saintes, IV, 38.

Jan Casimir, Cardinal, Prince, then King of Poland - Biographical data, III, 244; VI, 3; VII, 69; VIII, 89; X, 111; armies are blessed, VI, 3; progress, VI, 6; continuing war with Sweden, VIII, 193; wife requests priests for Poland, XIIIa, 398; numerous other references in volume V.

Jane Frances Frémiot de Chantal (Saint) - Biographical data, I, 31; II, 31; III, 432; V, 478; VIII, 542; IX, 26; XI, 103; letters from Saint Vincent, I, 552, 566; II, 57, 99, 114, 199; to Saint Vincent, I, 31, 120, 185, 306, 361, 563, 565; II, 31, 33, 61, 62, 67, 161; XII, 353–54; reference to letter from Saint Jane Frances to Saint Vincent, I, 236; journeys to Paris, I, 32, 302; II, 214, 223, 228; interior trials, I, 32; II, 67; XI, 103; XIIIa, 138; suffering caused by Visitandine, II, 248, 424; by her son, III, 432; IV, 257; Saint Vincent frees her from sorrow, I, 35; manner of making meditation, IX, 26, 335; X, 462; on retreat, I, 32; relationship with Saint Francis de Sales, V, 478–79; X, 106, 266; XIIIa, 93; how she composed Directory of Visitation, III, 272–73; does not wish Visitation Monasteries to be visited by others than their Superiors, despite Saint Vincent's advice to contrary, I, 564–65; II, 33–34, 58, 62, 99, 115, 118, 161; Extraordinary Visitors for Visitation Order, I, 236; recommendations to Visitandines, III, 454–55; VIII, 542; X, 346, 361–62; urges Saint Vincent to accept direction of Visitation of Paris, XI, 160; he explains Missionaries' Rule of life, I, 552–57; generosity to Annecy Missionaries, I, 565–66; II, 57–58, 61, 90, 114–15; VIII, 609; contacts with them, II, 31, 60, 90, 116, 120, 157–58, 200, 214; with Saint Vincent, II, 121; XIIIa, 137; Extraordinary Visitor, I, 563–65; II, 33, 62, 161; death, II, 238; Saint Vincent thinks there should be funeral oration, II, 242; she wills her heart to First Monastery of Paris, II, 239, 683; refusal to give it, II, 250; Saint Vincent's vision of her soul, II, 241; XIIIa, 137; other mentions, I, 368; II, 88, 117, 284; III, 303, 453; XII, 359; XIIIa, 395.

Janissaries, select corps of Turkish soldiers - Julien Guérin did not take them as attendants, III, 199.

Janin (M.), President - I, 540.

Janot (Nicolas) - Dispute with Noël Bonhomme, XIIIa, 352–55.

Jansenism - Errors, refutation: see **Arnauld** (Antoine), **Grace**, **Jansenius**, **Saint-Cyran**; Jansenism related to Calvinism, IV, 185, 186; Saint Vincent gives reasons for declaring against Jansenism, III, 319–23; refutes contrary reasons, III, 323–28; why Jansenism should be condemned by Pope, IV, 156, 182–87, 209–13; Jansenism undermines teachings on confession and frequent Communion, XI, 138–39; Discalced Carmelites and Jesuits require theology professors to teach former opinions and refute new opinions; Augustinians of Sainte-Geneviève order teachers to uphold teaching of Saint Augustine, III, 328; development of Jansenism, III, 164, 188; Rome believes most French Bishops are tainted with this error, IV, 101; petition of French Bishops asking Pope to condemn Five Propositions of Jansenius, IV, 607–08; Bishops' measures to obtain signatures for petition; Saint Vincent writes to some Bishops to this effect, IV, 156; to Bishops of Alet and Pamiers, IV, 179; to Bishop of Luçon, IV, 182; second letter to Bishops of Alet and Pamiers, IV, 209; signature of Bishops of Cahors, Sarlat, Périgueux, IV, 160; and Dax, IV, 179, 202; Saint Vincent awaits signature of Bishop of Bayonne, IV, 179, 202; Alain de Solminihac hopes Bishop of Lombez will get Bishops of Alet and Pamiers to sign, and Archbishop of Bordeaux through Bishop of Maillezais, IV, 160–61; Solminihac himself will sign, IV, 101; unsure of thinking of Bishop of Saintes, IV, 161; Bishop of La Rochelle signs only conditionally, IV, 179; Saint Vincent asks Fr. Dinet for more copies of petition; has given out all he had, IV, 178–79; number of signatories of petition, IV, 157, 183; slanderous libel against petition, IV, 160; Labadie was Jansenist before becoming Huguenot, IV, 185; eleven Bishops address counter-petition to Pope, IV, 179.

Relations with Jansenists, XII, 387; Period of calm; party circulates *Letter from a Bishop to a Priest*, IV, 395; Lambert replies to Queen of Poland regarding Jansenism, IV, 352–53; Frs. **Hallier**, **Lagault**, and **Joysel** sent to Rome to request condemnation of Five Propositions: see these names; Saint Vincent's reaction, XI, 150; other theologians make same journey to prevent condemnation; fruitless efforts, IV, 580–82, 594; meetings of Cardinals and theologians to study question, IV, 581, 582; steps taken with Pope to get him to wait before making decision, IV, 580; Saint Vincent writes Rome that Bull will be well received; asks for certain precautions, IV, 430; keeps Bishop of Cahors informed of progress of affair, IV, 498, 540; composition and publication of Bull of condemnation, IV, 581–82, 592, 597–99; sending of Bull to France and Poland; Fr. Hallier sends copy to Saint Vincent, IV, 581; who announces news to Community, XI, 149; theologians sent to Rome by party promise submission to Pope, IV, 583; do not submit, IV, 600; how to deal with them after condemnation of Five Propositions, IV, 604; rumor in Rome of approaching condemnation of several Jansenist books, IV, 584–85; Jansenist distinction of fact and right, IV, 583; General Assembly of French clergy repudiates it, VI, 100–01; Alexander VII condemns it, VI, 132, 152, 290; how Bull of condemnation is received in Paris, IV, 592–94; Saint Vincent sends copy to Bishop of Cahors, IV, 594; latter's joy, IV, 598; discussion at Sorbonne of new opinions, IV, 219; VI, 291; condemnation of Antoine Arnauld by Sorbonne, V, 587; VI, 101, 291; XI, 292–93; Saint Vincent, consulted on whether theologian who did not subscribe to censure of Sorbonne or condemnation by Rome may receive absolution, responds affirmatively, V, 587; miracles of Crown of Thorns at Port-Royal, VI, 291; attitude of Council of Conscience regarding new opinions, III, 319, 323; punishment of religious who had advanced in thesis proposition savoring of Jansenism, III, 617; zeal of Saint Vincent for propagation of faith in infidel lands, lest it disappear in France because of Jansenism, among other things, III, 40.

Meetings of theologians at Saint-Lazare and Orsigny regarding new opinions, III, 322; VI, 43–44; despite resistance of Jansenists, Saint Vincent has theologian of good party named to Sorbonne, III, 45–46, 49; brings back Fr. Féret, whom Pavillon had won over to his ideas, III, 329; Jansenists being pressured by Court, V, 590; when accused in Rome of allowing new opinions to be introduced into Company, Saint Vincent responds that, on contrary, he did utmost to banish them, II, 500; refuses to accept at Saint-Lazare postulants suspected of espousing new opinions, VI, 548; writes to discourage Fr. Dehorgny from these teachings, III, 318, 358; urges confreres not to speak either for or against new opinions; removes Fr. Gilles from teaching, for violating prohibition, III, 327; IV, 353; forbids Superior to allow in his house certain pamphlets and leaflets discussing new opinions, VII, 441–42; objects to book from printery of Port-Royal because all books from this printing house are dangerous, VI, 100.

Vigilance of Saint Vincent to safeguard Daughters of Charity against Jansenism: see ***Auteuil***, ***Chars***; advice to friend who seeks accord with Jansenists, XIIIa, 185; account of conversation with priest favorable to Jansenists, XIIIa, 188; writes to Fr. Des Lions, Dean of Senlis, to obtain act of submission to pontifical decisions on new opinions, VI, 290; zeal against Jansenism sets Jansenist seigneur against him, IV, 74; Jansenism in Beauvais, V, 107; Cahors, III, 345–48; Chars, III, 298; IV, 516; XIIIb, 310, 311, 356–57, 359; Saintes, IV, 161; Toulouse, IV, 248; some of its adherents are punished, IV, 601.

Jansenists are becoming bolder, VII, 548, 550; partisans or friends of Jansenism; see following names: **Arnauld** (M. Angélique), **Arnauld** (Antoine), **Barcos**, **Fleury** (François de), **Jansenius**, **Liancourt** (M. and Mme), **Saint-Cyran**, **Seguin** (Mme), **Séguenot**; adversaries: **Chigi** (Cardinal), **Condé** (Prince de), **Daffis**, **Olier**, **Raconis**, **Solminihac**; letter from

J. de Brevedent with thoughts on the heresy, VIII, 404–409; other mentions, VII, 546–47, 549. See also ***Port-Royal***.

Jansenius [Jansen] (Cornelius), Bishop of Ypres - Biographical data, II, 550; XI, 149; studied Saint Augustine in depth, III, 323; before dying, submitted his work to Rome, IV, 608; errors are those of Baïus [De Bay], III, 320, 323; XIIIa, 166; Arnauld defends them, XIIIa, 155; reappear in book *De la fréquente communion,* III, 321; opinion of Henri II, Prince de Condé, II, 550; of Abbot of Saint-Germain, VIII, 405; Nuncio requests list of his errors, II, 551; his doctrine and opinions taught at university in Cahors, III, 345; at University of Toulouse, III, 591; apologies for Jansenius, III, 168; IV, 584; propositions extracted from writings by Bishops of France, IV, 607–08; condemned by Popes in sense in which Jansenius taught them, IV, 583, 600; V, 587; VI, 101, 290; XI, 149; XIIIa, 185; condemnation by Sorbonne, XI, 292; some approve him without reading his books, IV, 567; Saint Vincent quotes from his *Commentary on the Gospels*, VI, 292; other mentions, III, 326, 347.

Janus (M.) - II, 674.

Japan - Jean Guérin's willingness to go there with Jesuits, IV, 535; ministry of Jesuits, XII, 25; Japanese King received Francis Xavier, VIII, 577; other mentions, XI, 121, 264.

Jaudoin (Claire), Daughter of Charity - XIIIb, 228; signs attestation after reading of Common and Particular Rules reviewed and arranged in order by Fr. Alméras, XIIIb, 205.

Jayat, village in Ain - XIIIa, 51.

Jealousy - See **Envy**.

Jean (Bro.) - See **Damiani** (Giovanni).

Jean (Young Jean) - I, 478.

Jean, servant in Luçon - Saint Vincent advises his dismissal, IV, 3.

Jean - Young boy in household of Fr. Bourdaise in Madagascar, VI, 243.

Jean-Baptiste (M.) - See **Taone** (Giovanni Battista).

Jeandé (Claude), Priest of the Mission - Biographical data, IV, 577; VI, 358; in Sedan, IV, 577; at Notre-Dame-de-Lorm; finds regional dialect difficult to understand, VI, 358; Saint Vincent suggests he go to Cahors, VI, 477.

Jean de Montmirail (Bl.) - Example of humility, IX, 233–34.

Jean de Sainte-Marie (Fr.), Superior of Dominican Convent of Holy Annunciation in Paris - Allegedly wrote book turning subjects aside from obedience, II, 561–62.

Jeanne - Member of Charity of Montmirail, XIIIb, 32.

Jeanne (Mother), Carmelite, in Pontoise - Opinion concerning dispute among Carmelites, VIII, 406.

Jeanne, Daughter of Charity, at Saint-Benoît - Brings postulants to Saint Louise, I, 296; other mention, XIIIb, 227.

Jeanne, Daughter of Charity, in Châlons - X, 5.

Jeanne, Daughter of Charity, in Issy - Letter to Saint Louise, II, 390; Saint Louise wonders if she should be sent back to Issy, II, 400.

Jeanne, Daughter of Charity from Loudun, in Angers - Deliberation about her dismissal, XIIIb, 283–84; tries virtue of companions, III, 416; Saint Louise suggests giving her another try in Richelieu, III, 421; some improvement, III, 424.

Jeanne, Daughter of Charity, at Motherhouse - IX, 255, 490.

Jeanne, Daughter of Charity, at Saint-Martin - Behavior, VI, 66; aged and infirm, IX, 488.

Jeanne, Daughter of Charity, at Saint-Paul - Sister Trumeau is preferred to her as Sister Servant, XIIIb, 302.

Jeanne, Daughter of Charity - Suggested for Hôtel-Dieu, I, 235; to nurse M. Lhoste, I, 340; at Saint-Laurent; bad-tempered, I, 449; sent to La Chapelle, I, 450; question of dismissing her for striking companion, I, 560; Saint Vincent dismisses her, I, 563.

Jeanne, Daughter of Charity - Sent to Calais, X, 440; XII, 36.

Jeanne, Daughter of Charity, with galley convicts - Unsatisfactory, II, 197.

Jeanne (the Younger), Daughter of Charity - See **Lepeintre**.

Jeanne-Baptiste, Daughter of Charity - Biographical data, IV, 215; VII, 272; recalled from Saint-Jean-en-Grève to be sent to Montmirail, IV, 215–18; Saint Vincent's advice before she leaves, IX, 430; departure, VII, 272; signs Act of Establishment, XIIIb, 227.

Jeanne-Christine, Daughter of Charity - See **Prévost** (Jeanne-Christine).

Jeanne-Françoise, Daughter of Charity - Biographical data, V, 18; letters Saint Vincent writes her at Étampes orphanage, V, 18, 21, 69, 74, 116, 160; on mission at Saint-Étienne-à-Arnes, IV, 168; mention of letters to Saint Vincent, V, 18, 74, 116.

Jeanne-Marie, Daughter of Charity - Sent to Sedan, X, 1: see **Boule**.

Jeannesson (Jeanne) - Marriage to Jean de Montholon, I, 266–67, 273–74.

Jegat (Bertrand), Priest of the Mission - Biographical data, II, 93; III, 13; in Richelieu; health, II, 92–93, 95; in La Rose; drowned in Lot River, III, 13, 26, 32.

Jehosaphat, valley in Palestine - IV, 565.

Jehot (M.) - IV, 33.

Jephtah, one of Judges of Israel - Kills daughter in fidelity to vow, XI, 156.

Jeremiah, prophet - Questions son of Rechab, XII, 119; was only a child, when God intended to make use of him, I, 589.

Jericho, town in Palestine - II, 290.

Jerome - Baptized son of Dian Machiore in Madagascar, V, 520.

Jerome (Saint) - Asks Bishop to admonish Saint Paula, XI, 354; sorrow at death of Paula, III, 223; his rendition of Ps. 65:2, XI, 199; took "sort of vow of poverty" in imitation of first Christians, XI, 211–12; flogged, XII, 283; would have written life of first Daughters of Charity, had they lived in his time, IX, 361; X, 341, 409; cited, V, 263; IX, 492.

Jerome Emiliani (Saint) - Biographical data, IV, 140.

Jerusalem, city in Palestine - Jesus in Jerusalem, IX, 321, 326; XII, 182; not necessary to make pilgrimage to Jerusalem to become saint, X, 233; excluded from first news of Christ's birth, II, 343; his weeping over city was example of suffering for us, XI, 89; his pilgrimage there, XIIIa, 310–11.

Jesse (Catherine), Daughter of Charity - Signs attestation after reading of Common and Particular Rules reviewed and arranged in order by Fr. Alméras, XIIIb, 206.

Jesuits - Founded to lead apostolic life, IX, 17; Saint Vincent's esteem for Institute, III, 567–68; XI, 121; its characteristic, IX, 457; wants Missionaries to learn from their example, XI, 49, 121; their maxim: new Superior should leave things as predecessors left them, III, 607; XIIIb, 368; nature of their vows, V, 321; VI, 631; XIIIa, 378–82, 394, 405; are religious even though Rule is not that of four Mendicant Orders, III, 248; V, 319; long wait before approval by Rome, V, 400; Paul IV makes them wear cowl, abandoned after his death, III, 382, 448–49; Jesuits accepted many establishments in beginning; unable to place sufficient number of men in them, III, 163; under direction of inexperienced Superiors, III, 191; Saint Ignatius sent novices to armies, X, 446; dismisses several Jesuits, II, 355–56.

Saint Vincent asks for help in Folleville, XI, 4, 163; XII, 7; in Châtillon-les-Dombes, XIIIa, 54; offers them endowment Mme de Gondi later proposed for Institute of the Mission; they cannot accept, XI, 164; Jesuits aid devastated population in environs of Paris during Fronde, IV, 520; participation in battle against Jansenism, III, 328; VI, 548, 589; XIIIa, 123; hostility of Jansenists toward Jesuits, III, 322–23; IV, 581–82; of Abbé de Saint-Cyran, XIIIa, 109, 134; had use of Saint-Cyran's abbey, XIIIa, 123; violent campaign instigated against them by publication of *l'Apologie des casuistes*, VII, 546–50, 627–28; atrocious persecution, XII, 48; mention of Jesuits in Mazarin's diaries, XIIIa, 154.

Success of Jesuit at Saint-Nicolas-du-Chardonnet, I, 69; Jesuit abandons Court in order to evangelize poor, XI, 123; story of Jesuit who died in Indies in odor of sanctity, II, 229; Jesuits who leave Society are in danger of going astray in Paris, III, 180; Jesuit *Relations*, XII, 24; establish Children of Mary in towns, VI, 605; offer advice on vows of Congregation of the Mission, V, 464; love of chastity, XI, 160, 197–98; receive visitors in church, not in parlor, XI, 161; simplicity in preaching merits success, V, 630; Superiors visit classes, VII, 444; method of teaching, II, 266, 272; fraternal correction, IX, 234; XII, 295; admonitions in refectory, XIIIb, 291; penances given to delinquent read aloud in refectory, XII, 55; punishment for entering rooms of others, XII, 332–33; novitiate is set apart, XII, 276; bedrooms have only latch, XII, 322, 332; those studying are dispensed from Office in choir, XII, 274; outsiders rarely invited to dinner, and always for special reason, XI, 299; have superintendent or inspector in each house, XII, 42, 55; usually send postulants to their provinces, VII, 542; regulations for travel given in writing to those making journey, XIIIb, 273; permission required to consult physician, X, 278; correspondence passes, open, through hands of Superior, X, 326; usually free to choose intentions for Masses, VI, 31–32; little respect for anyone who does not obey physician, X, 315; Rule recommends that they write each other often, V, 336; XI, 111; also write to General about helpful matters, which he may choose to share with provinces, XI, 112; but, because of abuses, correspondence now reduced to necessary, V, 336; Missionaries learn language of countries they are going to evangelize, V, 229, 362; XII, 60; no help given to those who leave, III, 373; do not become Bishops, II, 458; Superior General does not visit houses, II, 552; lay Brothers everywhere wear same habit, XI, 153; difficulties overcome to be established in Paris, III, 613; Jesuits of rue Saint-Antoine in Paris, XI, 189; of Saint-Louis in Paris, II, 436; V, 561; XIIIa, 60; in novitiate and at collège, XIIIa, 60; Michel Le Gras studies at collège de Clermont, I, 99; De Flacourt compares the work of Saint Vincent and Congregation of the Mission to Saints Ignatius, Xavier, and Jesuits, XIIIa, 186.

Jesuits in Agen, III, 567–68; in Amiens, XI, 4, 163; XII, 7; in Amsterdam, VIII, 587; in Antwerp, VIII, 596; in Bar-le-Duc, II, 29, 42; in Charleville, IV, 471; in Pera (Beyoglu), Constantinople, III, 47; in Scotland, V, 370; XI, 166, 176; in Genoa, VI, 346, 348, 361; VIII, 25, 92, 120; in India, VI, 104; XI, 270; in La Rochelle, VIII, 561; in Madagascar, VI, 244; in Montauban, VIII, 257–58; in Poland, V, 350, 362; in Rome, II, 171; IV, 393; XIIIa, 192; in Saint-Mihiel, II, 243; in Rouen, VIII, 407; in Japan, XII, 25; at 1651 Assembly, comparisons made with Jesuits in certain matters, XIIIa, 383, 385, 387, 389, 391; other mentions, I, 153, 246; II, 224, 295, 470; IV, 295, 535; V, 258; VI, 76, 252, 305, 500, 525; VII, 137; VIII, 23, 63, 578; XI, 116, 354; XII, 257; XIIIa, 62, 63, 394. See also **Binet**, **Charlet**, **Dinet**, **du Bourg**, **Jacquinot**, **Hayneufve**, **Sanchez**, **Vasquez**, etc.

Jesus Christ - Synopsis of his life, XI, 330–31; love of Jesus: conferences, IX, 365–79; XI, 32–33, 34–36; reasons to love Christ, XI, 34–35; in what this love consists, XI, 35; must be effective, XI, 32–33; advantages, XI, 35–36; means of acquiring it, XI, 36; how Daughters of Charity should love Jesus, IX, 466–67; Heart of Jesus, I, 30, 56, 111, 185, 550; III, 190; V, 20, 102, 192; VI, 201, 543; XI, 264; XII, 165, 216; union of hearts in that of Jesus, I, 25, 30, 62, 163, 172, 213; V, 65, 192.

Spirit of Jesus, I, 518; XII, 93–94; meaning of clothing self in it, XII, 92–93; to guide souls it is necessary to clothe self in this spirit, XI, 311; spirit of Jesus acts gently and sweetly, IV, 553; Saint Vincent drew Rules of Mission from spirit of Jesus Christ, VII, 164.

Imitation of Christ: obedient even to death, IX, 59; model for all our actions, I, 276, 524; XI, 201; honor hidden life of Our Lord, II, 315; He preferred apostolic life to solitude, III, 344; before acting, ask how Christ would act, XI, 43, 312–13; principal aim of Missionaries is imitation of Jesus Christ, XII, 66–68, 98; duty of Daughters of Charity to conform their lives to His, XIIIb, 126, 137; Christ is model for all virtues: see name of each virtue.

Teachings (maxims) of Jesus Christ: conferences, X, 112, 121–25; XII, 98–110; Rule of Missionaries, XII, 99; of Daughters of Charity, X, 112; in what these maxims consist, XII, 98–110; motives for following them, X, 103, 112; XII, 243–45; how they differ from those of world: see **Maxims of World**; all Christians must follow them, but especially Daughters of Charity, X, 113; Jesus Christ is their author, XII,

243; He observed them first, X, 112; XII, 244; His refuge in Will of His Father, I, 551; they are holy, XII, 244; steadfast, XII, 99, 104–05; infallible, XII, 104; advantageous, XII, 105, 244–46; direction and scope of their obligations, XII, 101–02; how they detach us from three concupiscences, XII, 244; means of being well grounded in these teachings, XII, 108–09; principal teachings, X, 121–22; XII, 101–03; for Missionaries, XII, 246.

Name of Jesus: Litanies of the Name of Jesus, I, 192, 581; XIIIb, 15; Confraternity of Holy Name of Jesus, Nom-de-Jésus Hospice: see ***Nom-de-Jésus***; Passion of Jesus Christ, XII, 159–60; place ourselves in wounds of Our Lord, II, 119; Jesus Christ died for all, III, 324; made it His duty to form twelve good priests, His Apostles, XI, 7; His family, I, 206; at moment of temptation, VIII, 516; feast of Name of Jesus, I, 414; patron of Confraternities of Charity, XIIIb, 7.

Jésus-Marie (Antoine de), Benedictine, Bishop of Miliapur - II, 523.

Jeure-Millet, Ambassador to Rome - VII, 378.

Jews - Pay consular duties to Consul of France, V, 89; resent Barreau, V, 327; many remained cold and hardened in spite of words and miracles of Jesus, VI, 166; many lived in Metz, VII, 77; Barreau may have misled them about Greek merchant, VII, 133; passport for Jewish merchant from Tunis, VII, 168; one sent to Fr. Pesnelle for conversion, VIII, 111; Sisters going to Metz are to make known to them holiness of Catholic religion, X, 448; no customs to console sorrowful, XII, 222–23; given life by Esther, XIIIb, 420.

Joachim (Saint) - Mme de Gondi implores his help, XIIIa, 59.

Joan of Arc (Saint) - What she did for France, XIIIb, 426.

Joanna of Chuza (Saint), wife of Herod's Procurator - Serves poor under direction of Blessed Virgin and Apostles, IX, 18; Saint Vincent recommends that Ladies of Charity have devotion to her, XIIIb, 437; other mention, X, 439; XIIIb, 194.

Jobe (Jacques), slave in Algiers - VII, 208.

Jaudoin [**Jodoine**] (Claire), Daughter of Charity - XIIIb, 228.

Job, Patriarch - Cited, VII, 203; IX, 45, 475, 502, 524; X, 423; XI, 134; XII, 48; XIIIb, 398; trials, IX, 45, 61; XI, 134; patience in trials, II, 379; III, 398; IX, 274, 406–7; XII, 48; God allowed devil to afflict him, XII, 228; God afflicted him to prove his love and fidelity, IX, 39; excerpts from Gregory the Great's moral reflections on Job, XIIIa, 163; other mention, XIIIa, 128.

John the Almsgiver [**Jean l'Aumônier**] (Saint), Archbishop of Alexandria - Avenges affront against nephew, X, 372.

John the Baptist (Saint) - Renders homage to Jesus at Visitation, XIIIa, 40; preferred apostolic life to solitude, III, 344; principal practice was penance, XII, 130; gives witness to Jesus Christ, XII, 222; Church honors him as martyr, XI, 167; taught disciples to pray, II, 158; feast day, VIII, 59, 468; XIIIa, 9, 13, 266; poorly fed and clothed in desert, IX, 129; like a foundling in desert, XIIIb, 406; precursor of the Lord, XIIIa, 69–70; other mentions, IX, 51, 156; X, 266; XIIIa, 160.

John Berchmans (Saint), Jesuit - Saint Vincent considers him a saint, X, 79.

John Chrysostom (Saint) - Opinion on small number of priests saved, VII, 479; on efficaciousness of humility, XI, 5; says God prefers barking of dogs to praises of man who doesn't pray properly, XII, 267; gave sparkle to things when repeating something important, XII, 347.

John the Evangelist (Saint) - Patron of Angers hospital, XIIIb, 114; delights in recommending fraternal charity, IX, 123; X, 354, 379–80; XI, 90; cited, IX, 342; X, 385; XI, 67, 90, 176, 184, 315; XIIIa, 167, 391; XIIIb, 345; speaks of three vices reigning in world, XII, 17–18; cited by Council of Trent, III, 325; Saint Vincent suggests that Peter was concerned for John, XI, 90; Jesus gathers Peter, James, and John on Mount of Olives and on Mount Tabor, XIIIb, 386; patron of Mme Goussault, XIIIb, 390; other mentions, III, 324; XIIIa, 39.

John of God (Saint) - XIIIa, 20.

Joigny, town in Yonne - Philippe-Emmanuel de Gondi, Comte de Joigny and his wife the Comtesse, XIIIa, 31, 58, 213, 218–19, 222, 224, 226, 228–30, 234, 236, 238–40, 242, 244–47, 250–52, 258, 297; XIIIb, 63, 65; Mme de Gondi, Comtesse de Joigny, XIIIb, 30–32, 47–48, 91; missions given in Joigny, I, 35, 177–79, 526, 528; III, 609; IV, 30; V, 438, 475; Confraternity of Charity, I, 286, 516–17; IV, 76; XIIIb, 23, 85; establishment and Rule for women's Charity, XIIIb, 23; for mixed Charity, XIIIb, 54; Joigny Hospital, VIII, 365; parishes: Saint-André, Saint-Antoine, Saint-Jean, Saint-Thibault, XIIIb, 65, 66; Saint Vincent seriously ill there, I, 546; other mentions, I, 161, 545.

Jolly (Edme), Priest of the Mission - Biographical data, IV, 234; V, 29; VI, 23; VII, 11–12; VIII, 7; XI, 329; letters from Saint Vincent to Fr. Jolly in Rome, V, 459, 463, 489, 498, 505, 567, 595, 616, 619, 633, 642; VI, 27, 43, 68, 90, 105, 115, 133, 174, 196, 208, 295, 305, 318, 349, 363, 373, 385, 400, 411, 419, 429, 450, 459, 481, 494, 509, 524, 541, 552, 579, 593, 603, 618, 629,

635; VII, 11, 25, 37, 45, 55, 59, 95, 162, 223, 229, 238, 246, 252, 261, 267, 284, 292, 318, 326, 343, 359, 390, 400, 406, 411, 420, 433, 484, 497, 507, 516, 529, 541, 560, 569, 585, 594, 598–99, 606, 628, 635; VIII, 7, 20, 37, 57, 70, 77, 85, 101, 109, 116, 133, 147, 154, 160, 171, 173, 175, 197, 208, 213, 259, 262, 285, 302, 326, 335, 346, 359, 366, 441, 548; from Fr. Jolly to Saint Vincent, IV, 234; V, 433, 467, 472, 480, 496, 640; VI, 90, 132, 363, 373, 411, 419, 429, 450, 459, 481–483, 509, 524, 525, 541, 552, 603, 604, 618, 629, 635; VII, 37, 38, 45, 252, 284, 326, 343, 359, 390, 400, 406, 411, 433, 497, 507, 516, 529, 541, 560, 569, 585, 594, 598; VIII, 20, 37, 70, 77, 109, 133, 147, 154, 173, 197, and ones Saint Vincent did not receive, VI, 483; mention of letters Saint Vincent wrote him, IV, 234–235; V, 145; VII, 624; usually writes to Saint Vincent every week, VI, 99; mention of letters he wrote to Fr. Portail, VI, 349, 385; to his brother and cousin, VI, 366; VIII, 198; his nieces, VI, 542.

Sent to Rome as seminarian, XIIIa, 359–60; VII, 351; VIII, 209, 284, 311, 321, 338, 345, 349, 358; reference to letter to Saint Vincent, VI, 132; VII, 585.

Saint Vincent's esteem for Fr. Jolly, V, 460, 489, 610; VI, 401; VII, 47, 265, 326, 585; Master at Saint-Esprit in Toul, V, 29, 30, 153; free to keep or resign that benefice, V, 30; first stay in Rome, IV, 93, 234; recalled from Rome; arrives in Genoa, V, 136; then in Marseilles, V, 145; finally in Paris, V, 153, 176; Director of Internal Seminary at Saint-Lazare, V, 376; prepares to return to Rome, V, 369–70; en route for Rome, V, 376–77, 384, 423; in Rome, Superior and Procurator General to Holy See, V, 459, 476, 550, 573, 590; VI, 23, 87, 99, 101, 105, 168, 169, 172, 182, 205, 256, 282, 299, 409–10, 432, 434, 436, 485, 486, 488, 496–97, 520, 557, 559; VII, 81, 107, 152–53, 230, 235, 512, 518, 550, 583, 593–94, 602, 624–25; VIII, 118, 138, 142, 143, 210, 213, 239, 360, 537, 544, 609; XI, 329; XII, 59; XIIIa, 191; Saint Vincent asks him to send confrere to Turin, VI, 308.

Pope obliges all ordinands of Rome to make ordination retreat in Fr. Jolly's house: see ***Rome***; examines Common Rules of Mission with view to proposing changes: see **Rules**; Saint Vincent thanks him for services rendered to Company, V, 460; VII, 594; VIII, 37, 57, 134; recommends that he moderate his work, V, 506; not to risk contagion, V, 634; VI, 67–68, 134–35; to take care of self, VI, 459, 482, 495; VIII, 20, 101, 109; to return to Paris if air of Rome is bad for him, VI, 450; saint expresses concern about his health, VI, 494; promises to recall him before following summer, VI, 603; advises him to spend summer in Palestrina or Frascati, VII, 508, 585, 595, 598, 629; VIII, 78, 86; health, VI, 28, 449, 450, 459, 482, 496, 509, 604; VIII, 78, 101; Duchess proposes that he defend P. Le

Vacher, V, 482; humbles self, V, 433, 496; submits resignation as Superior, V, 472; sends Louis de Chandenier Bulls conferring abbey on Claude de Chandenier, V, 497; ready to take risk to serve plague-stricken, V, 640; Saint Vincent considers him for Lebanon mission, VI, 28; principal matters negotiated by him at Court of Rome: approval of vows of Congregation of the Mission: see **Vows**; authentic interpretation of vow of poverty: see **Poverty**; union to Congregation of the Mission of priories of ***Saint-Lazare, Saint-Pourçain, Coudres***, and ***Bussière-Badil***: see these words; union of conventual table of Saint-Méen Abbey to Saint-Méen Seminary: see ***Saint-Méen***; acquisition of residence for Rome Missionaries: see ***Rome***; approval of Company of Daughters of Charity: see **Daughters of Charity**; permission to put priests in charge of Barbary consulates: see ***Algiers***; settlement of problems delaying beatification of Saint Francis de Sales: see **Maupas du Tour**; carrying out foundation of Duchesse d'Aiguillon in Loreto: see **Aiguillon** (Duchesse d'); see also ***Rome***; other mentions, I, *xxv*; V, 435; VIII, 80; IX, *xviii*.

Jolly (Martin), slave in Algiers - V, 325, 354; VII, 290.

Jolly, priory - Death of Prior; choice of successor, VIII, 192, 210.

Jolly (Sister), Benedictine - Gives Saint Vincent reasons for leaving convent, VIII, 416.

Joly (Gillette), Daughter of Charity, sister of Marie Joly - II, 24; in Sedan, V, 222; question of recalling her, II, 291; V, 261; other mention, XIIIb, 227.

Joly (M.) - VIII, 472.

Joly (Marie), Daughter of Charity, sister of Gillette Joly - Biographical data, I, 174; II, 16; V, 207; IX, 8; in praise of her, I, 211; one of first Sisters in Company, X, 519; mention of letter Saint Vincent wrote her, V, 208; at Saint-Sauveur, IX, 8; at Hôtel-Dieu, I, 299–300, 320; at Saint-Paul, I, 378, 388; proposed for Saint-Germain-l'Auxerrois, I, 388; at Saint-Germain-l'Auxerrois, I, 600; II, 24; despite large number of patients, finds time to do laundry for others in order to earn a little money, II, 179–80; assigned to Sedan, II, 169, 175–80; in Sedan, II, 194, 204, 205–06, 233, 247; recalled to Paris, V, 207, 222; reason for recall, V, 260–61; flees Motherhouse; returns same day, V, 223–25; determined not to return to Sedan, V, 237, 240; in great demand there, V, 246, 250, 260–61; deliberation on her dismissal, XIIIb, 349–52; signs attestation after reading of the Common and Particular Rules reviewed and arranged in order by Fr. Alméras, XIIIb, 205; other mentions, XIIIb, 227, 318, 354.

Jonah, prophet - Saint Louise asks if she is Jonah, who should be removed from Company, III, 507; allusion to him during confreres' voyage to Madagascar, III, 540; swallowed by whale, IX, 408–409; X, 416.

Jonathan, biblical personage - David weeps for him, XI, *xvii.*

Joseph, Brother of the Mission - At Saint-Méen, III, 457.

Joseph (Fr.) [François Le Clerc du Tremblay], *"l'Eminence grise,"* confidant of Cardinals Richelieu and Mazarin - Jesuits disapprove of him, VI, 548, 589.

Joseph (Saint) - Devotion of Saint Vincent, I, 155–56; V, 68; XI, 198; XIIIa, 160; XIIIb, 114; of Mme Goussault, XIIIb, 390; one of the patrons of hospital Sisters, XIIIb, 194; prayers of Genoa Missionaries for vocations; Saint Vincent imitates them, V, 109, 149, 468; VII, 581; model for work, IX, 380–81; acts of his life, VII, 202; XI, 330; his obedience, IX, 59; Jesus was submissive to him, IX, 7, 14, 181, 427; X, 72, 228, 230, 461; XII, 345–46; XII, 345–46; conformity of his affections, desires, and actions to those of Jesus, X, 439; XII, 177; Jesus had to earn his living along with Joseph, IX, 137, 343; Mme de Gondi implores his help, XIIIa, 59; other mentions, VIII, 568; IX, 122; X, 102.

Joseph, Patriarch - I, 343; II, 448; V, 487; VI, 216.

Joseph Calasanctius [**Calasanz**] (Saint), Founder of Poor Clerks Regular of the Mother of God of Pious Schools (Piarists) - IX, 553.

Joshua, leader of Hebrews - V, 506.

Josse (Jean), Prior of Montmirail - Biographical data, I, 121.

Jouailly (M.), nephew of Lambert aux Couteaux - Account of visit with Saint Vincent, IV, 340.

Jouchet (Pierre), Canon of Mâcon - XIIIb, 78.

Jouet (M.) - Signatory of Act of Establishment of Daughters of Charity at Saint-Jean Hospital in Angers, XIIIb, 119.

Jouhaud (Jean), Abbot of Prières - See ***Prières***.

Jourdain (Hector), Brother of the Mission - Biographical data, I, 42.

Jourdain (Jean), Brother of the Mission - Biographical data, I, 42; II, 178–79; VI, 274; XI, 351; steward in house of Marquise de Maignelay, where he met Saint Vincent; enters Congregation, XI, 352; at Saint-Lazare, I, 473; II, 178, 537; XI, 352; hastiness and cordiality, XI, 352; illness, II, 178; VI, 274; death, VI, 306, 309, 312; XI, 351; conference on his virtues, XI, 351–56;

mention of another conference, XII, 427; other mentions, I, 188; XIIIa, 235.

Jourdaneau (J.), secretary of Bishop of Périgueux - XIIIa, 8.

Journeys - Mention of conference on proper behavior while traveling, XII, 422; wishes for good journey, I, 65, 175; Saint Vincent recommends that Sisters sent to province observe customary order during journey, be reserved, and not get involved in conversations, I, 504; X, 4, 165, 445, 453, 467; stop to visit Blessed Sacrament and sick, to instruct children and poor people; not to sit at innkeeper's table in hostels, but keep to themselves, XIIIb, 273; declares, in 1651, that nothing bad occurred during Sisters' journeys, XIIIb, 310; what Missionaries should do while traveling, XI, 85; disadvantages of useless journeys, VI, 434.

Jousse (Claude-Espérance), Superior of Orléans Visitation - Biographical data, I, 370.

Jousteau (Élisabeth), Daughter of Charity - IV, 16; XIIIb, 228.

Joustel (Louis), Brother of the Mission - Biographical data, VI, 566.

Jouy, village in Île-de-France - I, 541.

Joyeuse (Fr. Ange de), Capuchin - Biographical data; wore Capuchin habit, X, 254.

Joyeuse (François, Duc de), Cardinal - Biographical data, II, 393; V, 564; seminary he opened in Rouen, II, 393; V, 565.

Joysel (François), Doctor of Sorbonne - One of group of theologians sent to Rome to obtain condemnation of Jansenism, IV, 394, 581, 601.

Joyeux (Dom), Prior of Carthusians - Appointed one of Visitors of principal convent of Dominican Monks in Paris, XIIIa, 136–37.

Jubilee - Conferences, IX, 38–43, 479–90; X, 186–96; mention of another conference, XII, 422; explanation of Jubilee, IX, 38–39, 480–81; X, 186–87; grace of Jubilee, IX, 39; benefits, IX, 39, 481–84; X, 187–191; means of gaining it, IX, 40–41, 487–89; X, 191–93; obstacles to benefitting from Jubilee, X, 193–96; crew sailing for Madagascar makes Jubilee, III, 330; Jubilee of 1636, I, 341; Jubilee of 1641, II, 217–18, 222, 225; IX, 38–43; Jubilee of 1645, II, 564; Jubilee of 1648, III, 316, 317; for peace, III, 540; Jubilee of 1650, IV, 5; Jubilee of 1653, IV, 560–61; Jubilee of 1655–56, V, 411, 573, 575–76, 579–80, 584, 595, 605, 630; VI, 169–70, 172, 195, 201, 207; X, 186–196; XI, 301; in Tunis, XI, 291.

Judas, Apostle - Received great graces, I, 183; began well but ended badly, II, 146; IX, 114, 492; X, 246–48; believed to have worked miracles, XI, 307; bad Communion, IX, 185–86, 261, 264; murmurs against Jesus, X, 97–98, 246–47, 349 -50; who did not send him away, IV, 42; temptation, IX, 267; X, 250, 359–60; thievery, X, 173; betrayed Jesus, IX, 207; ruined by envy, IX, 549; and avarice, IX, 362, 450, 546; X, 134–35, 247; XI, 224–25; XIIIb, 315; perfidy, IX, 280; X, 411–12, 425, 427, 576, 590; XII, 159; XIIIb, 354; better had he not been born, X, 426; unhappy state, X, 174; XI, 312; election of his successor, X, 217, 580, 595; XII, 45; XIIIb, 360, 386; Christ suffered because of him, I, 314.

Judith, Jewish biblical heroine - Defeated Holofernes, XIIIb, 420; decapitated him, X, 58; other mention, XIIIb, 426.

Judith, Daughter of Charity - Left Company, V, 40, 43.

Juif (François), surgeon - Operates on sick doctor, XII, 293.

Juilliot (M.), secretary to Bishop of Saintes - XIIIa, 104.

Julian the Apostate, Roman Emperor - XIIIa, 32.

Julienne, Daughter of Charity - See **Loret** (Julienne).

Jullie [**Julles**] (Pierre), Brother of the Mission - Biographical data, VI, 142; in Agen, VI, 142, 145.

Justice - Mention of conference, XII, 421; God's justice: commutative and distributive justice, XII, 114–16; XII, 400; Beatitude, XII, 418; justice before charity, II, 68; mention of act of justice, V, 34; not improper for Congregation of the Mission to demand it for slaves, V, 398; allow for God's justice, XII, 400; justice of Francis de Sales, XIIIa, 87; justice is established by God, XIIIa, 190; must be accompanied by mercy, I, 449; Intendant of Justice orders distribution of King's funds to aid religious, II, 93.

Justinian I, Eastern Emperor - XII, 237.

K

Kafirs, white inhabitants of Madagascar - Introduced superstitious ceremonies and observances there, III, 545.

Karkadiou (M.), ship's captain - Piety, VIII, 572, 584–85.

Kempis (Thomas à) - See **Thomas à Kempis**.

Khmelnitsky (Bogdan) - Hetman of the Ukranian Cossacks who attacked Sweden, VI, 128.

Killala, town in Ireland - Bishop: see Francis **Kirwan**.

Kindness - Fr. Nouelly's kindness, III, 223; Saint Vincent recommends practice to Company, IV, 58.

Kingdom of God - Conference on seeking kingdom, XII, 110–26; what the kingdom is, XII, 112–13; we must seek it in ourselves, XII, 111; before all else, and not worry about the rest, XII, 112, 117; how to make God reign in us, XII, 122–23.

Kings - Rule by Divine Right, VI, 30; God allows great disturbances to show Kings they depend on Him, V, 449–50; in kingdom through which Saint Vincent passed, King is never spoken of, out of respect, X, 358; advice on manner of receiving King, IV, 44–46; VI, 367, 390, 534; VIII, 343; Kings represent sovereign power of God on earth, XI, 70.

Kirwan (Francis), Bishop of Killala, Ireland - Refugee in France, V, 422.

Kiss - Allowed in reconciliation: on cheek, never on lips, X, 306; XIIIb, 129, 154; kiss floor as penance, IX, 29, 220, 292, 301, 470; X, 583; XIIIb, 163, 179; Saint Louise kissed feet of Sisters, X, 583; confreres kiss Rules distributed by Saint Vincent, XII, 11; he kisses floor at end of conference, XII, 33.

Klesl (Melchior), Cardinal - Member of Congregation of *Propaganda Fide*, XIIIa, 229.

Knowledge [**Learning**] - Saint Vincent encourages confreres to work at acquisition of knowledge, but to have greater appreciation for acquisition of virtue, XI, 115, 120; XII, 57–58, 117, 141; gratitude for those who favor advancement of knowledge and virtue in priestly state, VIII, 66; humble scholars are treasures of Company, XI, 115; lack of knowledge does not prevent acceptance of postulant, if he has necessary qualities, V, 497; average knowledge suffices, VIII, 40; Company should consider itself blessed that members are of humble condition and have little learning, XI, 120; not the most learned who bear most fruit, IV, 131; VII, 534; study in moderation, VIII, 40; XI, 116; XII, 57, 142; with indifference, XII, 197; to carry out ministry well and not to gratify ambition or curiosity, XI, 116; XII, 57, 164; dangers of learning, XI, 115–16; without good life, learning is sterile, XII, 74; working at virtue is best study, IV, 131; kindness converts better than forceful arguments, XI, 54; knowledge is useless for prayer, IX, 174. See also **Controversy**, **Philosophy**, **Theology**.

Knoydart, area in Scotland - Evangelized by Fr. Duggan, V, 121–22.

Korah, biblical personage - Murmurs against Moses; punishment, X, 348–50; XIIIb, 351; his children, X, 40.

Koran - III, 546.

Kotolambo, demons of Madagascar - VI, 245.

Krakow [***Cracow***], city in Poland - Bishop: see Andrzej **Trzebicki**; plague in Krakow; Queen of Poland has two Missionaries distribute alms, IV, 411, 502, 539; Daughters of Charity go to Krakow to serve poor persons, IX, 463; arrival of Fr. Ozenne, V, 434; siege of Krakow, VI, 464; Fr. Ozenne assists wounded, VI, 470, 472, 489, 492, 502; Daughters of Charity do likewise, VI, 470, 472; Queen is thinking of establishing confreres in Krakow, VI, 526; King and Queen make solemn entrance into Krakow; arrival of Fr. Duperroy and Visitandines, VI, 555, 568; plan for house of Missionaries there, V, 255, 351; VI, 621; VII, 9, 11, 107, 175, 275, 530–31; XII, 25; Fr. Ozenne goes there for this purpose, VII, 156, 173, 264; also Fr. Desdames, VII, 481, 490, 531; Daughters of Charity may have to travel to Krakow by way of Vienna, VIII, 146.

L

Labadie (Jean), apostate priest - Biographical data, IV, 185; dangerous nature of his teaching, IV, 185; Saint Vincent asks Queen to prevent his preaching, IV, 457.

La Barde (Denis de), Bishop of Saint-Brieuc - VII, 487.

La Barre (Pierre de), Seneschal of Richelieu - Biographical data, V, 7; other mention, IV, 10.

Labat (Fr.), Dominican - III, 383, 387.

Labat (Jean), Brother of the Mission - Biographical data, V, 599.

La Bataillère (M. de), administrator of Le Mans Hospital - VII, 372, 410, 532; VIII, 227.

Labatut (Hugues de), Bishop of Comminges - Biographical data, II, 143.

Labbé (Étiennette) - Member of Charity of Montmirail, XIIIb, 34.

Labbé (François), Priest of the Mission - Biographical data, IV, 494.

La Bécherelle (Mme de) - Funded mission in Beuvardes, II, 546; VII, 220.

La Bédoyère (Huchet de), Attorney General for Parlement of Rennes - III, 83.

Labeille (Philippe), Brother of the Mission - Biographical data, VIII, 341.

La Beraudière (François de), Bishop of Périgueux - Biographical data, II, 430.

La Bernardière (M. de) - Failure of arrangement involving his brother, V, 372.

Labiche (Jeanne), Daughter of Charity - XIIIb, 228.

Labidière (Mme de) - Promises money for Masses, VIII, 27.

Labille [**Labitte**] (Antoinette), Daughter of Charity - XIIIb, 227.

Labilon (Marguerite), Supervisor of Furnishings of Charity of Argenteuil - XIIIb, 107.

La Bistrade (Jacques de), Seigneur des Marets and Master of Appeals - I, 233.

La Bistrade (M. de) - II, 207.

La Bistrade (Mlle de) - I, 233, 354.

Laboue (Julienne), Daughter of Charity - Signs attestation after reading of Common and Particular Rules reviewed and arranged in order by Fr. Alméras, XIIIb, 206.

La Bourlerie (M. de), assistant tutor of young Louis XIV - III, 487–88.

La Bouverie [***Les Bouveries***], locality near Angers - Saint Vincent has correspondence sent to priest residing there, VI, 409, 412.

La Brière (Nicolas de), Priest of the Mission - Biographical data, VII, 127; VIII, 196; at Bons-Enfants, VII, 127; in Montmirail, VII, 334; VIII, 196; at Bons-Enfants again, VIII, 219; assigned to Poland, VIII, 528; leaves for Poland, VIII, 535, 537–38; other mention, XIIIa, 200.

La Bruyère, village in Oise - Confraternity of Charity, I, 295.

La Carisière (Mlle) in Nantes - Contacts with Saint Louise, III, 9, 178.

La Champignière, town in France - Birthplace of Clémence Ferré, Daughter of Charity, XIIIb, 118.

La Chapelle, village near Paris - Mission given, I, 542; II, 406; Confraternity of Charity, I, 377, 424, 447; suggests that Saint Louise visit in view of finding new house there, I, 312, 313; Motherhouse of Daughters of Charity, I, 310, 363, 450, 494, 505, 509, 574, 596, 599–600, 603; II, 131; X, 581; Saint Vincent hopes to go there, I, 385, 468, 491, 550; II, 185, 207, 215, 224; Saint Louise asks Saint Vincent to go, II, 195; asks what time Sisters should go, II, 223; or if they should go, II, 225; Saint Vincent goes there, I, 330, 409, 533; Saint Louise thinks there might be house near property there, III, 179; see also **Daughters of Charity**; other mentions, I, 334, 473, 476, 551; II, 138, 139, 147; III, 401; IV, 382, 421; XIIIb, 297.

La Chapelle-Orly, village in Oise - I, 338.

La Chassaigne (Mlle de) - Founding member of Charity of Châtillon-les-Dombes, XIIIb, 4.

Lachau (Robert), Jesuit, Rector of Collège de Montferrand in Clermont-Ferrand - Questions on instruction of ordinands; Saint Vincent's response, XIIIa, 312–13.

La Chaussée - See ***Chaussée***.

La Cloche (M. de), Lieutenant-Commander - VIII, 584.

La Contour (François de Moussy, sieur de), King's assistant in Metz - VII, 78, 85, 86, 113.

La Coste (Gaspard de Simiane de), administrator of prison hospital in Marseilles - Biographical data, II, 510; III, 295–96; joy that Missionaries are chaplains at prison hospital, II, 510–11; gives Saint Vincent news of hospital, II, 574–75; Saint Vincent writes him that service of hospital "is not in accord" with duties of Missionaries, III, 295; contacts with Missionaries in Marseilles, III, 429; XIIIa, 366; death, III, 465–68.

La Couche - Historical data, XIIIb, 386. See also **Foundlings**.

La Cour (Jean de), resident of Dax - Saint Vincent buys back from his heirs some family property, XIIIa, 99.

La Couture, parish in Le Mans - I, 91; III, 236.

La Croix (Jeanne de) - See **Delacroix** (Jeanne de).

La Croix (Mme de), in Beauvais - I, 93.

La Dauversière (Jérôme Le Royer de), founder of Hospitaller Nuns of Saint-Joseph of La Flèche - XIIIb, 319.

Ladies of Charity - Foundation of Charity of Hôtel-Dieu in 1634; first meeting, I, 230–31; number of Ladies in July 1634; works, request for indulgence from Rome, I, 246–47; number of Ladies in 1656, VI, 58; at beginning and in 1657, XIIIb, 430; talks of Saint Vincent to Ladies, XIIIb, 378–89; 397–440; Saint Louise gives advice, III, 261–62; letter of Saint Vincent to Ladies, III, 402; recommends that they personally visit sick, XIIIb, 378–79, 408, 411; enumerates reasons for being exact in attending meetings, XIIIb, 383–85, 386–87, 407; seeks to revive their languishing charity, XIIIb, 411–20; they serve poor there as Saint Louis once did, XI, 274; meetings of Ladies, I, 230, 234, 238, 336, 407, 450, 562; II, 8, 50, 75, 163–64, 169, 179, 187, 247, 260–61; III, 149, 155, 253–54, 262, 268, 403–05, 431, 472, 506, 507–08, 519, 610; IV, 53, 201, 342, 391, 511, 561, 577; V, 74, 215, 241, 365, 394, 589; VI, 20, 202, 203, 388, 397, 414, 422, 437, 454, 467, 479, 490, 503, 531, 543, 561, 580, 596, 608, 626, 632; VII, 13, 33, 42, 276, 380, 395, 402, 421, 492, 535–36, 545, 562, 573, 587–88, 597, 614; VIII, 13, 27, 32, 46, 52, 60, 71, 82–83, 107, 123, 239, 382, 384, 389, 391, 398, 409;

IX, 537; X, 255; XI, 171, 198, 306; XII, 368; meetings of officers, I, 260, 426, 470, 602; II, 147, 209, 233, 539; III, 253; IV, 415; meetings with three widows, II, 328; at meetings, Saint Vincent questions Ladies on fidelity to Regulations, X, 454; beam breaks in ceiling on morning meeting should have been held, IX, 196–97; report on state of works, XIIIb, 426–40; general Regulations of Ladies, XIIIb, 443–47; Regulations of "Fourteen Ladies," XIIIb, 382–83; see also **"Fourteen" Ladies of Charity**.

Gift of Queen of France, III, 404, XII, 391; of Queen of Poland; misunderstanding about gift, IV, 436–37; of Mme Goussault in her will, XIIIb, 393; collections, II, 261; fewer donations, VII, 348–49; Mme Goussault wants president to be called "servant," IX, 58; election of Ladies, III, 256; Saint Vincent writes to Mazarin that Ladies are prepared to receive Court triumphantly on its return to Paris, IV, 459–60; recommends to Ladies interests of Louis de Chandenier, involved in lawsuit, VIII, 302–03; Saint Vincent always went to Notre-Dame on Saturday of Ember Days for Mass with Ladies, I, 600; XIIIb, 385; writes summary of their meetings, to be sent to Rome, VII, 252–53, 361; Ladies aided by Daughters of Charity: see **Daughters of Charity**; Ladies reproach Saint Vincent for allowing Saint Louise to travel, III, 17; he tells Saint Louise she will have many disputes on part of Ladies, II, 248; she complains of their negligence and of measures they are taking: see ***Bicêtre***; Ladies distrust Daughters of Charity and treat them very harshly, VIII, 263; Ladies are impressed that Daughters earn money for poor by selling homemade jelly, X, 255–56.

Difficulties with Ladies in parishes; their complaints; assistance of Daughters of Charity, I, 283; II, 151, 558; III, 298; Ladies outside of Paris, I, 467, 500; Fr. Olier asks Saint Vincent to come to encourage his Ladies of Charity, II, 475; God is blessing works of those in parishes of Paris, III, 417; Saint Vincent assures them of his prayer, III, 424; their prayers for King and Queen of Poland, IV, 456; two sorts of Ladies in Paris, VI, 57–58; Sisters are to honor and respect them, IX, 7; originally, Daughters were not independent from Ladies, IX, 255; Saint Vincent instructs Ladies to receive Communion in thanksgiving for Pope's election, XI, 171; Ladies read about missionary work in Scotland, XI, 261; they are established in Angers, XIIIb, 269; devout women who followed Our Lord are models for Ladies, XIIIb, 436; dying Saint Vincent blesses them, XIIIa, 205; other mention, I, 510.

Ministry at Hôtel-Dieu: beginnings, I, 230–31; Ladies instruct patients and prepare them for general confession, I, 234, 246; III, 424–25; "Fourteen Ladies" responsible, in turn, every three months, for spiritual assistance of patients, XIIIb, 379–83, 413, 445; meeting of "Fourteen Ladies," II, 317; Saint Vincent congratulates them for zeal, XIIIb, 402, 438; wonders if seven would not be sufficient, XIIIb, 388; Lady said to have died of illness contracted at Hôtel-Dieu, I, 355; devout young women are sought to render same service for those with contagious diseases so Ladies would not be at risk, I, 450; Ladies distribute light meal to sick each day, I, 246; XIIIb, 402–03, 432, 439, 445; only to sickest, XIIIb, 389; no light meal for about twenty days because of plague, I, 496; XIIIb, 387; light meal resumed, I, 498; meal more abundant in beginning, XIIIb, 387; expenses incurred, XIIIb, 427; zeal of Ladies slackens; some miss turn for distribution, III, 262; others distribute food in a hurry, or say light meal serves no purpose, XIIIb, 389; Saint Louise fears it will be discontinued, III, 505; Ladies ask for help of four Daughters of Charity, I, 231; then, they think they can manage without them, I, 232; employ Daughters there, II, 601; III, 60; Daughters help them with light meal, III, 158; XIIIb, 140; Ladies maintain group of chaplains at Hôtel-Dieu, I, 311, 349; XIIIa, 179; XIIIb, 413; fruitful results of Ladies' visits, XIIIb, 384, 388–89, 402–03; plague prevents Ladies from going to Hôtel-Dieu, I, 299; they resume visits, I, 426; Saint Vincent recommends that Ladies not reprove nuns and chaplains but inform officers instead, XIIIb, 389, 411; other mention, III, 403; interest in coach lines, VI, 125–26. See also ***Hôtel-Dieu***; Saint Vincent consults Ladies about Charity of Arras, VI, 156.

Ministry with foundlings: Canons of Notre-Dame and others pressure Ladies to take over work of La Couche, I, 410, 423; XIIIb, 421, 430; they decide to attempt it with a few children whom Daughters of Charity will raise (1638), I, 407; XIIIb, 421; Saint Vincent approves project, I, 410–11, 423; difficulties, I, 432, 436; ministry of Foundlings joined to that of Hôtel-Dieu, I, 537; XIIIb, 400–01; Saint Vincent invites Ladies to extend work by taking in all children of La Couche, XIIIb, 397–401; conditions under which they assume responsibility for foundlings, II, 107–08; XIIIb, 401–02; they accept proposal that very day, II, 8; put into execution on March 30, XIIIb, 403; he persuades them to visit children, XIIIb, 387–88, 404; to continue to support ministry, XI, *xvii*; XIIIb, 405–07, 413, 415, 420–23, 423–24; meeting to consider case of unnatural mother of foundling, II, 137, 139; matters concerning foundlings, II, 292, 444, 655; III, 212, 213, 228–29, 420; saint plans to discuss with them care of little boy, V, 261, 269; money spent for ministry, XIIIb, 430; Mlle du Mée visits children, II, 225, 330, 337; special meetings of Ladies for work of Foundlings, I, 562; IV, 193; Saint Louise complains that

Ladies do not give sufficient support to work, III, 505, 507; questioning rights of Ladies regarding administration of work, II, 108; endowment, II, 486–87. See also ***Bicêtre***, **Foundlings**.

Work for devastated provinces: Assistance sent by Ladies to Lorraine: see ***Lorraine***; to Champagne and Picardy: see ***Champagne***; to Étampes: see ***Étampes***; in Paris diocese, IV, 519; town magistrates of Rethel express gratitude for services received, IV, 231; Ladies appreciate service of Fr. Berthe in Picardy and Champagne, VI, 28; monthly trips to devastated provinces, VI, 624; Ladies no longer send much help, VI, 58, 624; VII, 348–49; Saint Vincent praises aid to provinces devastated by war, XI, 64.

Other ministries: visits and instruction of convicts, V, 589; XIIIb, 413, 415, 441, 443; General Hospital: see ***General Hospital***; propagation of faith in infidel countries or among heretics, XIIIb, 439; possibility of providing for young woman converted from heresy, VI, 148; Saint Vincent has recourse to Ladies to help Consul of Algiers pay debts, VI, 479; tries to interest them in expedition of Chevalier Paul against Algiers, VIII, 32; explains why Ladies are unable to donate money for Canada, IV, 365–66; Saint Vincent asks Saint Louise's opinion about letter written to Ladies, III, 400; other mentions, III, 23, 418; VIII, 278, 457, 540.

See also **Aiguillon** (Duchesse d'), **Bailleul** (Mme de), **Beaufort** (Mme de), **Bragelogne** (Mme de), **Brienne** (Mme de), **Condé** (Princesse de), **Dufay** (Mlle), **Dumecq** (Mme), **Du Mée** (Mlle), **Du Sault** (Mme), **Fieubet** (Mme), **Fortia** (Mme), **Fouquet** (Mme), **Goussault** (Mme), **Guérin** (Mlle), **Herse** (Mme de), **Labidière** (Mme de), **Lamoignon** (Mlle de), **Lamoignon** (Mme de), **Laurent** (Mlle), **Ligin** (Mme de), **Mirepoix** (Baronne de), **Mussot** (Mme), **Nemours** (Mme de), **Pollalion** (Mlle), **Romilly** (Mme), **Sainctot** (Mme de), **Saint-Mandé** (Mme de), **Saunier** (Mme), **Schomberg** (Mme de), **Séguier** (Madeleine), **Souscarrière** (Mme), **Talon** (Mme), **Traversay** (Mme), **Ventadour** (Mme de), **Verthamon** (Mme de), **Villesabin** (Mme de), **Viole** (Mlle).

Ladvocat [**Lavocat**] (François), Canon of Paris - Biographical data, I, 498; tries to settle dispute relating to Foundlings, II, 485–87; other mention, XIIIa, 181.

Lafargue (M. de) - VII, 161, 196, 213, 521.

La Faye (Georges de), Canon of Écouis - XIIIa, 26, 29, 30.

La Faye (Thomas de Meschatin), Vicar-General of Lyons - Approves Charity of Châtillon, XIIIb, 19–20, 21; other mentions, XIIIa, 45, 47.

La Fère, town in Aisne - Distress and aid, IV, 94; news from there about Court in Sedan, VI, 390; Confraternity of Charity, VII, 614; choice of Daughters of Charity for hospital, X, 160–61; XI, 327; Saint Vincent's advice before their departure, X, 161–66; words of praise for them X, 233–34; journey, VI, 66; poverty of hospital, VI, 156; replacement of Marie-Marthe Trumeau, Sister Servant, VII, 191–92; victim of calumny, VIII, 233; Mathurine Guérin named Sister Servant, VIII, 167; letters from Saint Vincent to Mathurine Guérin: see **Guérin** (Mathurine); Mathurine recalled to Paris, VIII, 340, 349.

La Ferrière (Chevalier de), ship's captain - Dey of Tunis tries to make Jean Le Vacher pay what La Ferrière owes him (the Dey), V, 408; XI, 303; other mention, V, 244.

La Ferrière-Sorin (M.), administrator of Nantes Hospital - Asks for two Daughters of Charity, IV, 77.

La Ferté (Henri II, Baron de), Maréchal de France - Presence of his army near Montmédy, VIII, 15.

La Ferté (Scipion-Marc, seigneur de) - Friend of Alain de Solminihac, II, 429.

La Ferté-Bernard, town in Sarthe - VII, 542.

La Flèche, town in Sarthe - Slave, native of this town, III, 223; Visitation Monastery, V, 10–11; collège, VIII, 519; Hospitaller Nuns of Saint Joseph, XIIIb, 319.

Lafon (Jean-Jacques), Pastor of Sainte-Geneviève in Senlis - II, 281.

Lafons (Fr.), priest of Roule - II, 651, 654.

La Font (Jean de), Abbot of Grosbois [Grobosc] - Decision on controversy between Abbots of Sainte-Geneviève and Chancelade, III, 586–88, 590; IV, 47, 67, 124, 141, 223.

La Font (M. de), Lieutenant-General of Saint-Quentin - Thanks Saint Vincent for assistance to poor of town and environs, V, 378.

La Fonteyne (Antoine de), magistrate of Mâcon - XIIIb, 73, 76, 77.

La Forêt-le-Roi (commune) - Saint Vincent addresses letter to M. Colletot there, I, 131.

La Forest des Royers (M. de), Admiral - Words of praise for him, V, 279, 281, 300; voyage to Madagascar, V, 281, 302, 304–05; in Madagascar, V, 300–01, 306–07, 508, 510–11, 514, 519; death, V, 527; other mention, V, 310.

Lafortune, slave in Algiers - VIII, 331, 337.

La Fosse (Jacques de), Priest of the Mission - Biographical data, IV, 428; V, 210; VI, 119; VII, 50; VIII, 276–77; XI, *xiv-xv*; letters from Saint, VII, 308; VIII, 276; XI, *xiv-xv*; mention of letters to Saint Vincent, VI, 592, 599; VII, 50; parents adopt Julienne Loret, III, 263; his character; dissented slightly from some truths that were disputed and settled, VI, 122; poems, IV, 176, 428, 474; in Étampes, IV, 428; falls ill, brought back to Paris on litter, IV, 450, 452; Saint Vincent questions him during conference, XI, *xiv-xv*, 156; cannot place him in Sedan, V, 210; sent to Marseilles, VI, 120, 122; in Marseilles, VI, 119, 183, 195, 301, 486, 523–24, 592, 599, 617; VII, 50, 55; assigned to Troyes, VII, 150, 158, 168; departure for Troyes, VII, 178; travel expenses, VII, 233; arrival in Troyes, VII, 197; does not renew vows after Brief; tempted to leave Company; Saint Vincent encourages him, VII, 308–09; explains why Missionaries are engaged in direction of Daughters of Charity, but not of nuns, VIII, 276–79.

La Fosse, town in France - Departure of confreres going to La Rochelle, VIII, 55.

Lagault (Jérôme), Doctor of Sorbonne - Biographical data, IV, 394; sent to Rome to obtain condemnation of Five Propositions; Saint Vincent encourages him and gives him news, IV, 394, 413; Lagault informs Saint Vincent of condemnation of Jansenists, IV, 580–82; Saint Vincent tells him that money awaits him in Paris, IV, 430; benefice to be offered to him, IV, 601; letter to Saint Vincent after condemnation of Five Propositions, IV, 604.

Lagault (Mme) - I, 302.

Lage (Anne de), Superior of Poitiers Visitation - Contacts with Abbé de Saint-Cyran, XIIIa, 107, 122, 124, 131, 133–34.

La Gève - Relative of Pastor is on retreat at Motherhouse of Daughters of Charity, II, 205.

Lagny, town in Seine-et-Marne - Distress and charities, IV, 510; sale of salt to support missionaries in Crécy, VIII, 609; other mention, XII, 371.

La Gouvernelle (M.), Lieutenant of Duc de Mercoeur's guardsmen - People of Marseilles revolt against him, VIII, 310.

La Grange (Mme de) - Ill in Fréneville, I, 475.

La Grange (Pierre Pons de), Pastor of Saint-Jacques-du-Haut-Pas - Biographical data, II, 641.

Lagrange (Robert de), seminarian of the Mission - Biographical data, VII, 612; VIII, 156; in Genoa, VII, 612; VIII, 156.

La Gravelle, village in Mayenne - VIII, 519.

La Guerche - Woods owned by Le Mans house, IV, 198; V, 576; VI, 124, 151, 277. See also ***Le Mans***.

La Guibourgère (Jacques-Raoul de), Bishop of Saintes, Maillezais, and La Rochelle - Biographical data, II, 55; III, 20; IV, 160–61; V, 146; VI, 597; VII, 617; VIII, 241; XII, 59; letters from Saint Vincent, IV, 420; VI, 597; to Saint Vincent, II, 298, 299, 439, 557; mention of another letter from Saint Vincent, VI, 598; entrusts Saintes Seminary to Priests of the Mission, II, 173, 257; VIII, 612; transfer to See of La Rochelle, III, 20; Alain de Solminihac thinks he will sign petition against Jansenism without difficulty, IV, 160–61; Bishop puts condition on his signature, IV, 179; contacts with Saint Vincent, II, 55, 417, 519, 660; XII, 59; kindness to Missionaries, II, 299, 439; III, 539; IV, 386; VIII, 561; approves Constitutions of Hospitaller Nuns of the Charity of Our Lady, XIIIa, 103–04; other mentions, II, 409, 659; III, 81; V, 146; VII, 617; VIII, 241.

La Haye (G. M. de), Visitandine - VIII, 451.

La Haye-Aubert (M. de) - III, 478.

La Haye-Vantelay (M. de), Ambassador of France to Constantinople - Saint Vincent asks him to obtain declaration from Grand Turk safeguarding consular rights of M. Husson, V, 88; King directs him to see to preservation of these rights, VI, 644; to protest avanias (insults) against M. Barreau, VII, 227; imprisoned, VII, 273, 281, 304; his son, VI, 480; VII, 281, 304.

La Hodde [**La Hogue**] (M. de) - See **Delahodde** (M.).

Laigneau (M.), in Le Mans - V, 599.

Laisné [**Lainé**] (Guillaume), called **Lamontagne**, prisoner in Toulon - VIII, 266, 299, 369, 397, 528.

Laisné (Fr.), Cistercian, son of Élie Laisné de la Marguerie - Given responsibility of establishing reform of Val-des-Choux, IV, 246.

Laisné (Louis), brother of preceding - Attorney General for Parlement of Dijon, IV, 246; Intendant of Burgundy and friend of Saint Vincent, IV, 591; Presiding Judge of Parlement of Dijon, VI, 37; consents to union of Cahors Seminary to archpriestly benefice of Gignac, VII, 337–38; other mention, III, 162.

Laisné (Nicolas), seminarian of the Mission - Biographical data, III, 131; unsatisfactory, III, 236.

Laisné [**Lainé**] (Pierre), known as **de Rosier**, prisoner in Toulon - VIII, 276, 445, 528.

Laisné (Pierre), Priest of the Mission - Biographical data, III, 131; V, 360–61; VII, 44; in Saint-Méen, V, 360; Saint Vincent replies to his letter, VII, 44.

Laisné de la Marguerie (Élie) - Biographical data, I, 389; II, 37; III, 162; IV, 149; V, 46; VI, 606; foundation for missions to be given every five years in villages of Angoumois, I, 430–31; implementation of foundation, I, 430–31; IV, 149; V, 124–25; contacts with Saint Vincent, I, 445; IV, 592; retreat at Saint-Lazare, I, 389; ordained a priest, II, 37; arbitrator between Alain de Solminihac and unionized priests of Cahors diocese, IV, 270, 272, 504–05, 563; death leaves vacant office of Archpriest of Gignac, VI, 606; other mentions, III, 162; V, 17, 46.

Laisné de la Marguerie (Louis), brother of Fr. Laisné, Cistercian - Attorney General for Parlement of Dijon, IV, 246; Intendant of Burgundy and friend of Saint Vincent, IV, 591; Presiding Judge of Parlement of Dijon, VI, 37; consents to union of Cahors seminary to office of Archpriest of Gignac, VII, 337, 338; other mention, III, 162.

Lajus (Dominique de), slave in Tunis - VI, 258–59, 273; VII, 190, 212, 233, 521.

Lalande (Bertrand de), Lieutenant General of Presidial Court of Dax - I, 11.

La Lane (Noël de), Abbot of Valcroissant - Sent to Rome by Jansenists to prevent condemnation, IV, 581, 594.

Lallemant (Charles), Jesuit - Biographical data, VIII, 269; Saint Vincent asks him to continue to assist Visitation nun in Paris, VIII, 269–70.

Lallemant (Jérôme), Jesuit - Biographical data, I, 104, 193.

La Loire (Antoine de), attorney in Parlement - XIIIa, 11, 14.

Lalutumière (Abbé de) - His seminary, VI, 526.

La Maignère (Pierre de), mason in Dax - XIIIa, 76.

La Manière (Jacques de), seminarian of the Mission - Biographical data, V, 207; in Sedan, V, 207, 210–11.

La Marche (Comte de) - Revolt against Saint Louis, XI, 272–73.

Lamare (Mme de), of Paris - VII, 313.

La Mare (Savinien de), in Joigny - XIIIb, 65–66.

La Marguerie, village in Charente - Missions, I, 430; V, 124.

Lambert (Jacques), slave in Algiers - V, 36; VI, 188.

Lambert (Jacques), prisoner in Paris - Asks Saint Vincent's help in recovering freedom, VIII, 545.

Lambert (M.) - VII, 288.

Lambert (Marie), lady-in waiting of Queen Anne of Austria - Biographical data, III, 276–77.

Lambert aux Couteaux - See **Aux Couteaux**.

Lambin (M.), banker at Court of Rome - V, 29, 272, 275; health, VI, 509; Saint Vincent sends him packet in Sedan, VIII, 178; death, VIII, 304.

Lambo (Pierre), indigenous child in Madagascar - VI, 222.

La Meilleraye (Abbé de), administrator of Nantes Hospital - Letter Saint Vincent plans to send him about Sisters at hospital, V, 532–33.

La Meilleraye (Charles de la Porte, Duc de), Governor of Brittany - Biographical data, II, 362; V, 279; VI, 245; VII, 37; VIII, 96; XI, 294; his chaplain: see **Annemont** (Fr. d'); his squire: see **Coulon** (M.); will hold meeting of Estates, II, 362; sends soldiers to evict Benedictines from Saint-Méen Abbey, III, 33; sends ships to Madagascar, welcomes Missionaries there; Missionaries' contacts with him, V, 279–81, 286, 299, 301, 419; VI, 245, 270; desire to populate Mascarene Island, V, 299; quarrels with Company of Indies, VII, 38, 572; talk of agreement with them, XI, 294; dissatisfied that Saint Vincent offers him only one Missionary for voyage to Madagascar, XI, 324; proposes Madagascar mission to Capuchins, thinking that Saint Vincent prefers Company of Indies, VII, 37, 57; saint clears up misunderstanding and is prepared to give him several Missionaries, VII, 60–61; Duke accepts, VII, 73; delays departure of ships for Madagascar, VII, 526; Saint Vincent wonders if Duke will accept his Missionaries, VII, 572; VIII, 96; Duke accepts; saint thanks him, VIII, 178; at Duke's request, Saint Vincent promises not to send priests on ships of Company of Indies, VIII, 199–200, 201; tentative agreement between Duke and Company of Indies, VIII, 205–06; approaching departure for Madagascar of Duke's ship, VIII, 225; contacts between Duke and Fr. Étienne, VIII, 241, 291, 555–56, 565; Duke orders captains to make no important decisions during voyage without consulting Fr. Étienne, VIII, 564, 574; they obey, VIII, 576–77; illness, VIII, 178–79; other mentions, VIII, 256, 580, 583, 586, 589; XI, 370.

La Mère (Jeanne), Daughter of Charity - XIIIb, 228.

Lamet (Gabriel de), seigneur de Condun - Former Abbot of Saint-Léonard-de-Chaumes, XIIIa, 12.

Lamirois (Léonard), Brother of the Mission - Biographical data; cook in Genoa; Saint Vincent encourages him, IV, 349;

enlightens him regarding doubt, IV, 531; in Lagny, IV, 511; mention of two letters to Saint Vincent, IV, 531.

Lamoignon (Guillaume de), Chief Justice, brother of Madeleine de Lamoignon - Biographical data, I, 384; IV, 377; V, 504; VII, 60; VIII, 205; Saint Vincent counts on his protection, IV, 377; kindness towards sick Missionaries in Étampes, IV, 474, 495; intervention in disagreement between Chandenier brothers, V, 504–05; between Company of Indies and Duc de la Meilleraye, VII, 60, 61; VIII, 205; named Chief Justice, VII, 298; speech in Parlement, VII, 404; his children, VIII, 472; words of praise for him, VII, 178; contacts with Saint Vincent, VII, 178, 187; other mentions, IV, 378, 381.

Lamoignon (Madeleine de), daughter of Marie des Landes - Biographical data, II, 247; III, 149; IV, 5; VI, 609; VII, 33; Lady of Charity, II, 247, 655; III, 149, 155, 177, 254, 262, 417, 506; IV, 5; VI, 103; brings Daughters of Charity to Saint-Denis Hospital, III, 419; concern for foundlings, IV, 378, 380; contacts with Saint Louise, III, 262; IV, 5; Saint Vincent gives her bracelets and rings from Fr. Lambert in Poland, IV, 354; Saint Vincent thanks her and asks for continued support, IV, 377; spells out intentions of Queen of Poland regarding donation, IV, 436; congratulates her on brother's nomination as Chief Justice, VII, 298; Archbishop of Paris explains why he refused to allow Visitandines, requested by Queen of Poland, to leave, IV, 382; letter from Mother Marie-Angélique Arnauld concerning Queen of Poland's gift, IV, 612–13; Saint Vincent asks Superior of Second Visitation Monastery in Paris to allow Madeleine de Lamoignon to visit her sister, Sister Marie-Elisabeth, there, VII, 33; other mentions, IV, 419; V, 496; VI, 609; VII, 158, 410.

Lamoignon (Madeleine Potier de), wife of Guillaume de Lamoignon - Biographical data, VIII, 428; asks permission to visit Sister Marie-Élisabeth in Visitation convent, VII, 33; XII, 367; letter she addresses to Saint Vincent concerning aid to Picardy, XII, 367; asks Saint Vincent for Daughters of Charity for Charity of Auteuil, VIII, 428–29; thanks him for granting request, VIII, 465; especially since she heard he was hesitating, VIII, 501.

Lamoignon (Marie des Landes de) - Biographical data, II, 208; III, 149; IV, 4; Lady of Charity, II, 444, 630; III, 155, 417, 420, 422, 506; IV, 53; XIIIb, 413; meeting of Ladies in her home, II, 485; III, 268; IV, 53; contacts with Saint Vincent, III, 404; with Saint Louise, II, 399, 410; III, 424; IV, 4; other mentions, II, 485; XIIIb, 243–44.

Lamoignon (Marie-Élisabeth de), Visitandine, sister of Madeleine de Lamoignon - Death, VII, 33.

Lamontagne [**Lin**] - See **Laisné** (Guillaume).

La Mortat, town in France - VI, 89.

La Mothe-Fénelon (Antoine de Salignac, Marquis de) - Biographical data, V, 17; founder of league against dueling, V, 616–17.

La Mothe-Fénelon (Louis de Salignac de), Bishop of Sarlat - Coadjutor named without his consent, I, 414.

La Motte - Property near Luçon which Fr. Chiroye wants to purchase, III, 526–27.

Lamotte-Couplier (M. de), in Nantes - VI, 270.

La Moussardière (M. de) - VIII, 496.

Lamran (M. de), ship's lieutenant - Wounded, VI, 15, 230.

La Mucette (Claude), Daughter of Charity - XIIIb, 228.

Lamy (Antoine), auditor at *Chambre des Comptes* - Foundation of mission, I, 28; administrator of Quinze-Vingts Hospital, I, 258.

Lamy (Catherine Vigor), wife of preceding - Foundation of mission, I, 28; desires to make retreat with Saint Louise, I, 372; contacts with Saint Vincent, II, 129; concern about staffing of Charity at Saint-Germain-l'Auxerrois, I, 365; president of Charity of Gentilly, I, 28.

Lancelot (Claude), fellow student of Michel Le Gras - I, 37.

Lancre (Martin de), prisoner in Toulon - VI, 261, 302, 333, 384, 524; VII, 134, 254, 486.

Lancry de Bains - See **Bains**.

Lancy (Mlle de), in Laon - VI, 414.

Landas (M.) - Recommended by Fr. Olier, II, 560.

Landes - Area in southwestern France from which Saint Vincent came, IX, 70; XIIIa, 100.

Landrecies, town in Nord - IV, 104.

Laneplan (M. de) - Member of Estates of Béarn, VII, 460, 623.

La Neufville-Roy - Saint Louise visited Confraternity of Charity there, I, 188.

Lange (Martin de), French Consul in Tunis - Concern about Jean Le Vacher's illness, III, 300; death, III, 395.

Langeais, town in Indre-et-Loire - I, 194.

Langlois (Louis), Priest of the Mission - Biographical data, V, 494; VI, 430; XII, 138; in Saintes, V, 494, 625; rights to inheritance contested; Saint Vincent summons him to Paris, VI, 430, 446, 448–49; in Paris, VI, 505, 563; entrusts him with retreatants, XII, 138–39.

Langlois (M.) - Arrangements regarding coaches, V, 54.

Langlois (M.) - VI, 215.

Langlois (M.) - VII, 524.

Langres, town in Haute-Marne - Bishop: see Sébastien **Zamet**; priories in Langres diocese, II, 105, 143, 399; XIIIa, 66–67.

Languages - Missionaries in Italy must speak Italian, V, 534; VII, 568; Missionaries sent to foreign countries should study local language, V, 229, 334, 361–62; XII, 24–26, 60; young people have more aptitude for languages than older men, V, 128; Saint Vincent encourages confreres in Poland to learn Polish, V, 389; they are making progress, V, 402; men in Turin, destined for Genoa, are making progress, VII, 104; sadness when confrere does not work sufficiently at this, V, 534; VI, 308; example of Saint Vincent Ferrer, II, 232; of Saint Vincent himself for Picardy, II, 237; IV, 340; and Bresse, XIIIa, 54; example of Bro. Demortier, VI, 351; of Fr. Nacquart, III, 331, 554, 561, 576, 583, 596; XII, 60; of Fr. Mousnier, V, 283; of Fr. Bourdaise, V, 525; of Fr. Dufour, VI, 240; Daughters should learn low Breton for Hennebont mission, XIIIb, 309; difficulty in Rome house, II, 232; older man will have more difficulty, II, 304; Missionaries stranded at Table Bay do not know language for converting people, VIII, 587; after coming of Holy Spirit, Apostles spoke new languages, IX, 322.

Languedoc, province - Revolt at time of Albigensians, XI, 273; Estates of Languedoc, II, 558, 605, 613–14; V, 241, 617; VI, 190; violence and sacrileges of soldiers in Languedoc regiment, III, 383; *gabelles* (salt taxes) of Languedoc, VI, 99; endowment to permit Priests of the Mission to be established in jurisdiction of Parlement of Languedoc, IV, 144; plague, V, 28; Governor's request for Missionaries to preach missions there, VIII, 531; other mentions, I, 587; III, 340; V, 101, 147; VII, 549; VIII, 360; XI, 302; XII, 318.

Lanier, Jean - See **Lasnier**.

Lanier (Laurent), Mayor of Angers - II, 662; XIIIb, 118–19.

Lannes, village in Landes - II, 566.

Lannoy (Comte Charles de), Governor of Montreuil-sur-Mer - Asks for Daughters of Charity for Montreuil Hospital, II, 293; Saint Vincent tells Sisters how to act with Count, XIIIb, 274, 276–83; who is "extremely frank and open," XIIIb, 276.

La Noue (M. de) - Contacts with Louis Rivet, VIII, 128, 150.

La Noue (Messrs de) - Contacts with Daughter of Charity, I, 484.

La Noue (P. de) - Member of Charity of Courboin, XIIIb, 93.

Lanson (François de), Prior of Saint-Étienne-d'Ars on Île-de-Ré - Saint Vincent resigns Saint-Léonard-de-Chaumes Abbey in his favor, XIIIa, 42–44.

Laon, town in Aisne - Misery and charities in Laon diocese, IV, 112, 138, 482–83; V, 61, 64, 79, 99, 123, 137; VI, 412, 414, 490, 503, 531, 543, 561, 580; VII, 421–22, 535, 544, 545, 596–97; VIII, 389, 391; XIIIb, 428; Pastor of Laon: see **Mignot** (M); Saint Vincent tells Bro. Parre to return there, VIII, 149; other mention, VI, 637.

La Paix (Antonin de) - Martyrdom, III, 18–19.

La Pause (Jean de Plantavit de), Bishop of Lodève - Resignation of bishopric in favor of François de Bosquet, II, 605, 617–18.

La Pérouse (Prior of), nephew of d'Aranthon d'Alex - Biographical data, VII, 209; VIII, 487; makes seminary at Saint-Sulpice, VII, 398; letters to Saint Vincent, VIII, 487, 490, 492.

La Perrine, abbey in Le Mans diocese - III, 71.

La Pesse (Jean-Antoine de) - See **Delapesse**.

La Pesse (M. de), Director of Accounts for Chambéry - His son, V, 604; Fr. Martin, Superior in Turin, offers hospitality in his house, VI, 522.

Laplatte (Abbé) - Manuscript history of Mâcon, XIIIb, 67.

La Pompe (Mme de) - Contacts with Saint Vincent, II, 233.

La Porte (Commander), uncle of Cardinal Richelieu - I, 200.

La Porte (Mme de) - Member of Charity of Saint-Gervais, II, 558; XIIIb, 304.

La Porte (M.) - Attorney for M. Bonhomme, in Saint Vincent's petition to Parlement against him to obtain property of Nom-de-Jésus Hospice, II, 691.

Lapostre (Nicolas), Priest of the Mission - Biographical data, VI, 64; XI, 154; questioned at Saint-Lazare during conference, XI, 154; Saint Vincent reprimands him for dictating to students at Tréguier Seminary, VI, 64; recalled to Paris, VI, 586; sick in Tréguier, VI, 614.

La Proutière (Mme de) - VII, 279–80.

La Queue-en-Brie, village in Seine-et-Marne - See **Parmentier** (M.).

La Queue-les-Yvelines [***Gallius-la-Queue***], village in Yvelines - birthplace of Bro. Jean Jourdain, XI, 351.

La Quin (M. de) - I, 453.

Larcher (Antoinette), Daughter of Charity - Biographical data, III, 216; sent to Nantes, III, 8; XIIIb, 249; left for Paris, III, 216.

La Réole, town in Gironde - Dominican priests of La Réole, III, 386.

Largentier (M.) - Delegated by Queen to work with Saint Vincent for union of Saint-Corneille de Compiègne Abbey to that of Val-de-Grâce, IV, 244–45; writes to Saint Vincent, IV, 244.

Larivière, prisoner in Toulon. See **Fournier**, Jacques - VIII, 402.

La Rivière (Louis Barbier, Abbé de) - Biographical data, III, 411.

Larmuyre (Jean) - Writes to Saint Vincent about inheritance of cousin of late Canon of Luçon, VIII, 411.

La Roche (M. de), Councillor at Parlement of Bordeaux - IV, 271.

La Roche (Fr. de), priest, son of preceding - Saint Vincent recommends him to Queen, IV, 271; willing to help Saintes Missionaries, V, 124.

La Roche-Guyon, town in Val-d'Oise - Duc de Liancourt, seigneur of Roche-Guyon, I, 385; III, 370; IV, 299; other mention, V, 381.

La Roche-Saint-André (M. de), ship's captain - Kindness to Missionaries sent to Madagascar, VI, 215, 241.

La Rochefoucauld (François de), Cardinal - Biographical data, I, 209; II, 105; III, 586; IV, 65; VI, 93; IX, 143; contacts with Saint Vincent, II, 552; resigns title and income from Sainte-Geneviève Abbey, II, 509–10; ordinances, III, 586–88; great services rendered to Church, IV, 85; VII, 376; exact and mortified life, IX, 143, 168; goes to confession frequently, X, 99; uncle of the Abbés de Chandenier, IV, 65; VI, 93; VII, 376; VIII, 354; other mention, II, 509.

La Rochefoucauld (François, Duc de) - Biographical data, VIII, 150; Saint Vincent refuses benefice for his son, II, 551; member of household works with Fr. Louis Rivet, VIII, 150.

La Rochefoucauld (Louis de), Abbot of Vertueil, Bishop of Lectoure, son of preceding - Question of naming him for Episcopal See of Périgueux, II, 680; Saint Vincent opposes nomination, III, 256–57.

La Rochelle, town in Charente-Maritime - Transfer of episcopal see from Maillezais to La Rochelle, III, 20, 34; Bishop: see Jacques-Raoul de **La Guibourgère**; ignorance of Catholics of La Rochelle at beginning of seventeenth century, XIIIa, 34; Saint Vincent in La Rochelle, XII, 209; XIIIa, 34; port of embarkation for Missionaries sent to Madagascar, III, 283–84,

290, 330, 434, 539, 570; VI, 12, 16, 224; VIII, 202, 219, 221, 225, 229, 231, 239–40, 246–47, 248–49; 251–53, 256, 290, 557–64; other mentions, IV, 468; VII, 617; XIIIa, 12, 14, 24, 103–04, 242–43, 245–46, 247, 248, 251.

La Rochemaillet (Michel de), Councillor at *Cour des Monnaies* - Relinquished office to brother, III, 585.

La Rochemaillet (René-Michel de), brother of preceding - relinquishes to Michel Le Gras office of Councillor at *Cour des Monnaies*, III, 512–13, 585.

La Rocheposay (Henri-Louis Chastaignier de), Bishop of Poitiers - Contacts with Abbé de Saint-Cyran, I, 394, 396; XIIIa, 107, 122, 124, 133; with Richelieu Missionaries, I, 438; IV, 39, 69; with Saint Vincent, IV, 114.

Laroque (Mother de), Prioress of Pouget Monastery - Election, III, 239; waiting for King's patent, III, 257; Saint Vincent cannot obtain perpetual confirmation, III, 341.

La Roquette (Bernard de), slave in Algiers - VII, 196.

La Roquette (Jean de), slave in Algiers - VII, 196.

La Rose (M. de), secretary of Cardinal Richelieu - III, 352; V, 342.

La Rose, Marian Shrine in Sainte-Livrade (Lot-et-Garonne) - Duchesse d'Aiguillon provides initial foundation there for four Missionaries, I, 589; provides second one to increase number to seven, II, 318–19; letters from Saint Vincent to La Rose Missionaries, III, 85, 503; IV, 543; V, 444, 584, 608; VI, 180; VIII, 115; mention of letters received from one of them, V, 608; Bro. Jacques Rivet asked to go there, III, 451, 452, 475, 477; benefactors of Missionaries: see **Aiguillon** (Duchesse d'), **Hauterive** (Mlle d'); Missionaries exposed to dangers from public unrest, IV, 279, 372; from plague, V, 28; they hear confessions of pilgrims, IV, 313; income of house, VI, 181; visitations by Fr. Lambert aux Couteaux, II, 69, 78, 467; by Fr. Portail, II, 642, 675–76; III, 11, 32, 62, 64, 68, 80, 89, 92, 102–03, 109, 114–16, 124, 137; by Fr. Berthe, VI, 504–05; by Fr. Dehorgny, VIII, 254; Saint Vincent wants to visit house, III, 431; presence of Fr. Alméras in house, III, 68–69; shortage of personnel, III, 13, 451; IV, 545; VIII, 254; Saint Vincent augments personnel, I, 582; establishment has enough Brothers, VII, 514; change of Brothers gives rise to quarrels, III, 522; **Fr. Jegat** is drowned; Frs. **Du Coudray** and **Boucher** scandalize people by their unorthodox opinions: see these names; disorder, II, 78; good results of 1658 retreat, VII, 431; women should not be allowed in house and garden, VIII, 254; Fr. Bauduy receives permission to go to La Rose to regain health, V, 441–42; question of sending there

Frs. **Bourdet** (Jean), III, 84; **Brisjonc**, **Delattre**, **des Noyelles**, **Le Soudier** (Samson), III, 83; **Testacy**, III, 92; and **Michel**: see these names; assignments and changes, I, 589, V, 442; list of Superiors and history of house, VIII, 606; Missionaries who belonged to La Rose house: see **Bajoue**, **Bécu** (Benoît), **Boucher** (Léonard), **Boussordec**, **Brin**, **Brunet**, **Chrétien**, **Codoing**, **Cuissot** (Gilbert), **Delattre**, **du Coudray**, **Dufour** (Claude), **Férot**, **Jegat**, **Lesseignet**, **Rivet** (Jacques), **Savinier**, **Soufliers** (François); other mentions, II, 57, 79, 352; III, 56, 83, 115, 498; IV, 540, 588; V, 607; VI, 442, 606; VII, 361; VIII, 387; XIIIa, 323, 329.

Larroque (Pierre de), Pastor in Pouy - III, 244.

La Rue, captive in Algiers - Mother inquires about money she sent for him, VIII, 444–45.

La Ruelle (Marie), Daughter of Charity - XIIIb, 227; signs attestation after reading of Common and Particular Rules reviewed and arranged in order by Fr. Alméras, XIIIb, 206.

La Salle (Jean de), Priest of the Mission - Biographical data, I, 30; II, 371; XI, 107; letters from Saint Vincent, I, 133, 478; letter to Saint Vincent, I, 271; mention of letter to Saint Vincent, I, 478; giving mission in Mesnil, I, 133; in southeast, I, 268, 271, 279, 291, 306; in Saint-Germain-en-Laye, I, 411, 414, 422–23; goes to Liancourt, I, 285–87; prepares Regulations for Charity there, I, 358; at Saint-Lazare, I, 38, 88, 178, 285, 472, 478, 485, 516; XIIIa, 210, 222–23, 235; health: sciatica, I, 287; Director of Internal Seminary, II, 371; XI, 107; in charge of ordinands, I, 377, 515; XI, 146; Saint Vincent proposes him as model in correspondence with women, XI, 161–62; XII, 344; death, I, 580, 583, 586–87; words of praise for him, XII, 238–39; other mentions, I, 38, 45, 47, 53, 162, 506; XI, 122; XIIIa, 235, 259, 262.

La Saulssaye (Mme de) - Member of Charity of Montmirail, XIIIb, 32.

Lascaris (Paul), Grand Master of Order of Knights of Malta - Biographical data; thanks Saint Vincent for good done by Missionaries in parishes dependent on Great Priory, I, 380.

Lasnier [**Lanier**] (Jean), Brother of the Mission - Biographical data, V, 414; assigned to Poland, V, 414; assigned to Saint-Lazare pharmacy, V, 534; enshrouds body of Saint Vincent, XIIIa, 207.

Lasserre (M.), of Lisbon - Lent money to Pierre Daveroult, VII, 617.

Lateran Council - Decision relative to religious Orders, XIIIa, 380; to permanent union of benefices, I, 257; XIIIa, 415, 429.

La Terrade (Olivier de la Trau, sieur de), Superior General in France of Order of Saint-Esprit - Biographical data, II, 156; other mentions, II, 171, 477.

La Thane (Jean de), Master of Paris Mint - XIIIa, 11, 15, 21.

La Thiérache, region of Picardy - Shortage of bread there, IV, 218.

Latin - Missionaries to Poland know it, so can begin forming seminarians, IV, 251; difficult for people of Madagascar to pronounce, V, 311; not useful for young people to begin studying it if they have no way of making progress, V, 591.

La Touche-Frélon (M. de), Attorney General and Councillor at Parlement of Rennes - Expels Missionaries from Saint-Méen Seminary, III, 83.

La Tour d'Auvergne - See **Auvergne**.

La Tournelle, Paris prison - Mentioned in letter from Jacques Lambert to Saint Vincent, VIII, 545.

La Tousche (M.), farmer - Worked plot near house of Congregation of the Mission in Luçon, XIIIa, 318.

Latre (Charles de), priest - VIII, 378.

Laubardemont (M. de) - Questions Saint Vincent about Abbé de Saint-Cyran, XIIIa, 107; other mention, XIIIa, 124.

Laubespine (Charles de), Keeper of the Seals - Biographical data, IV, 61.

Laudin (Denis), Priest of the Mission - Biographical data, IV, 137; VI, 515; VII, 76; VIII, 129; letters Saint Vincent sends him in Le Mans, VI, 515, 560, 583; VII, 76, 141, 204, 225, 241, 294–95, 330, 338, 370, 409, 440, 465, 494, 532, 591, 621, 637; VIII, 129, 226, 371, 421; mention of letters to Saint Vincent, VI, 560; VII, 331, 370, 440, 532, 591, 637; VIII, 129–130, 421; saint asks him to admit Melchior Gaudoin to vows, VIII, 414; sent to Périgueux, IV, 137; recalled to Paris, IV, 174, 175; named Superior in Le Mans, VI, 515; in Le Mans, VIII, 159, 613; Prior of ***Bussière-Badil***: see this word; health, VII, 533. See also ***Le Mans***.

Laudin (Gabriel), Priest of the Mission - Biographical data, VI, 210; VII, 141; proposed for Madagascar, VI, 210; sent to Toul to help with ordination retreats, VI, 457; assigned to Tréguier, VI, 585, 586, 614; mention of letter Saint Vincent wrote to him there, VI, 614; plans to enter Benedictines, VII, 141.

Laudoy (M.), Comte de Seguin - See **Seguin**.

Laumonion (M.) - II, 616.

Launier (Adrien), slave in Algiers - V, 405.

Launois (Évrard) - Makes retreat at Saint-Lazare, VI, 588.

Laur (M.) - In Agde, VIII, 115.

Lauraine (Claude), Daughter of Charity - Retreat at Motherhouse, II, 205; XIIIb, 228; signs attestation after reading of Common and Particular Rules reviewed and arranged in order by Fr. Alméras, XIIIb, 206.

Lauraine (Marguerite), Daughter of Charity, at Saint-Laurent - Retreat at Motherhouse, II, 205; looked at crucifix of rosary instead of watching Saint-Laurent fair, IX, 31–32.

Laurence (Yves), Priest of the Mission - Biographical data, VI, 521; VII, 211; VIII, 221; assigned to Turin, VI, 521, 525; leaves for Turin, VI, 578–79; vows, VII, 211, 242; in Turin, VIII, 221, 231.

Laurent (Bro.) - See **Hazart** (Laurent).

Laurent (Claude), Daughter of Charity - XIIIb, 228.

Laurent (Daniel), of Rousset, Archdeacon of Mâcon - XIIIb, 78.

Laurent (M.), magistrate of Joigny - XIIIb, 65.

Laurent (Mme), Lady of Charity - Going to see Saint Louise, I, 115; health, I, 121, 126; other mention, I, 116.

Laurent (Mlle) - I, 300, 302.

Lauzun [***l'Ausun***], village in Lot-et-Garonne - XI, 246.

Lavagna, town in Italy - Mission given, III, 385.

Laziness - See **Sloth**.

Laval, town in Mayenne - Missionary from this place, III, 611; Fr. Lucas suggests seeking Laval Priory, which Saint Vincent opposes, III, 612; other mentions, VII, 478; VIII, 518–19.

Laval (Jacques), slave in Algiers - V, 36.

Lavalle (Marguerite), Daughter of Charity - XIIIb, 228.

Laval-Boisdauphin (Marie Séguier, Marquise de) - Biographical data, VII, 16; VIII, 153; benefactress of Crécy Missionaries, VII, 16; contacts with them, VIII, 153, 363.

Laval-Montigny (François de), Grand-Archdeacon of Évreux - IV, 596.

La Vallette (Bernard de Nogaret de), Duc d'Épernon -His violent attacks against Bishops of Bazas and Condom, III, 347–48.

La Valette (François de), Bishop of Vabres - Biographical data, II, 555.

La Valette (Jean de), brother of preceding - See ***Beaulieu*** (Abbot of).

La Valette (Jean-Louis de Nogaret de), Duc d'Épernon - Conjectured that he offered Saint Vincent bishopric, I, 2.

La Valette (Louis de Nogaret de), Cardinal-Archbishop of Toulouse - Biographical data; Saint-Cyran claims Cardinal scoffed at accusations against him, I, 394; Richelieu has Masses said for repose of soul, I, 583.

La Valette (Louis de Nogaret), Bishop of Mirepoix, brother of preceding - Nicolas Pavillon recommends him to Saint Vincent, II, 594.

Lavanino (Giovanni), Brother of the Mission - Biographical data, VII, 559.

Lavardin (Philibert de Beaumanoir de), Bishop of Le Mans - Biographical data, III, 488; V, 420; VII, 205; VIII, 226; Alain de Solminihac entreats Saint Vincent to oppose Lavardin's elevation to bishopric, III, 348; saint advises Lavardin to register oath of fidelity with *Chambre des Comptes*, III, 488; difference of opinion with this Prelate about tax on his chapels, III, 569; Fr. Crowley [Cruoly] offers to give retreat to his ordinands, V, 420; Lavardin prohibits Le Mans Missionaries from giving missions during Advent and Lent, VI, 151; sends them to give missions in certain parishes of diocese, VIII, 226, 519; wants to be accompanied by one of them on pastoral visits, VII, 205; Saint Vincent seeks from him, through confreres, dimissorial letters for two seminarians, III, 611.

Lavau (M. de) - IV, 30.

Lavaur, town in Tarn - Bishop: Charles-François d'Abra de **Raconis**: see this name.

La Verdure - Mentioned in letter to Saint Louise regarding Sister who had worked with convicts there, V, 337

Lavergne (Jean), convict in Toulon - VIII, 513.

La Vie (Thibaut de), Chief Justice of Parlement of Pau - Would like Saint Vincent to accept Bétharram shrine for his Congregation, VIII, 432, 602.

Lavieuville (Charles-François de), Bishop of Rennes - VI, 37.

La Vigne, port in France - Ship for Madagascar stranded near there, VIII, 557.

La Ville-aux-Clercs (M. de) - See **Brienne**, Henri-Auguste de Loménie, Comte de.

La Villette, section of Brussels - VIII, 597.

La Villette, former village; today, section of Paris - I, 365; II, 24, 150–51; IV, 421.

Lavocat (François) - Involved in dispute concerning foundlings, II, 485–88.

La Vrillière (Louis Phélypeaux, seigneur de) - Mention of letter for Étienne Gueffier, France's agent in Rome, VI, 553.

Lawrence (Saint), Deacon - Martyrdom, IX, 483; Saint Vincent prays for spirit of Saint Lawrence for Missionaries, XI, 214.

Lawsuits - See **Legal Proceedings**.

Laxity - Mention of conference, XII, 432; growing slack in one thing can easily lead to another, IX, 243; consequences of growing slack, XI, 14; difficult for Community to recover from laxity, XI, 182.

Laymann (Paul), German Jesuit - Writings, V, 298, 319.

Lazarus (Saint) - Loved by Jesus, who wept for him, I, 126, 328; III, 442; XII, 221; comparison of retreatants of Saint-Lazare with Lazarus leaving tomb, XI, 13; Missionaries must be like resurrected Lazarus and not carcasses of Lazarus, patron of Saint-Lazare house, XI, 14; feast day, I, 211.

Lazarus - Parable of Lazarus and rich man, XI, 117, 297.

Laziness - See **Sloth**.

Leah, wife of Jacob - X, 304.

Leaving the House - Conference, XI, 325–26; mention of conferences on trips into town, XII, 424, 437; Rule of Missionaries, I, 555; of Daughters of Charity, X, 327, 362, 504; XIIIb, 126, 137; do not be gadabouts, X, 363; XIIIb, 314; do not go out without permission; say where you are going, X, 78, 327; XIIIb, 126, 137; pray before going out and on return, X, 504–05; before Blessed Sacrament, if it is in house, XI, 326; never go out alone, III, 456, 462; V, 349; Superiors should not give companion requested of them, XI, 325; go only to place where you are sent, IX, 177; do not linger with men; practice modesty of eyes when outside, XI, 325: see also **Modesty** in dress; in contacts, XI, 325; on returning, present self to Superior, IX, 177–78; X, 327; XIIIb, 126, 137.

Lebanon - Fr. Berthe proposed for mission of [Mount] Lebanon, VI, 22–23, 27–28; visiting Bishop from Lebanon, VII, 274; mention of letter to Saint Vincent, VIII, 113; Fr. Sylvestre, Capuchin, seeks funds for Lebanon mission; Saint Vincent's opinion of plans, VII, 341; other mention, VIII, 583.

Lebas (Toussaint), Priest of the Mission - Biographical data, V, 166; VIII, 36; XI, 174; in Agde, V, 166, 199, 555; letters Saint Vincent writes him in Agde, V, 166; VIII, 112; serious illness, V, 376, XI, 174; virtuous and regular, VIII, 36; XI, 174; sent to

Narbonne, VIII, 137, 144; Saint Louise receives news of him there, VIII, 167.

Le Beauclerc (M.), secretary to Louis XIII - XIIIa, 237.

Le Bègue (Fr.), Priest of Fr. Authier's Congregation of Blessed Sacrament - Contacts with Saint Vincent, II, 438; Superior of Senlis Seminary, II, 281, 506; in Marseilles, VIII, 136.

Lebel (M.) - Contacts with Saint Vincent and Fr. Get, V, 192, 227, 245, 248.

Leberon (Charles-Jacques de Gélas de), Bishop of Valence - Saint Vincent intervenes on his behalf at Council of Conscience, III, 231, 240; other mention, I, 406.

Le Blanc (Charles), Priest of the Mission - Biographical data, IV, 424; V, 421; VII, 101; VIII, 158; in Le Mans, III, 97; IV, 424; recalled to Saint-Lazare, V, 421; mention of letter from Saint Vincent, V, 422; on verge of embarking for Madagascar, VII, 101, 104, 108; shipwreck and return, VII, 239, 257, 284, 616; captured by Spaniards, VIII, 183; in Le Mans again, VII, 534, 621; unable to go to Madagascar, VIII, 158, 179.

Leblanc (Denis), Vicar-General of Paris - II, 243; XIIIa, 231.

Le Blanc (François) - See **White** (Francis).

Le Blanc (Georges) - See **White** (George).

Le Boeuf (Éloi), Brother of the Mission - Biographical data; death, XI, 104.

Leboeuf (Guillaume), Pastor of Saint-Jean in Joigny - XIIIb, 65.

Leboeuf (Jean) - Member of Charity of Joigny, XIIIb, 66.

Leboeuf (M.), auditor - Member of Charity of Joigny, XIIIb, 66.

Le Boindre (Renée) - See **Le Vayer** (Renée).

Le Bon (Adrien), Prior of Saint-Lazare - Biographical data, I, 134; II, 49; IV, 176; VII, 502; XI, 17; the only Prior who, to preserve his title, requested letters of appointment from Rome, I, 244, 540; resignation of priory in favor of Saint Vincent, I, 134–37, 248–54; V, 536; VII, 502; VIII, 434, 605; XII, 375; XIIIa, 263–75, 276–80, 283–86, 288–90, 294, 410–12, 472, 476–78; often regretted handing over priory, XIIIb, 279; gift of Rougemont farm, I, 250; gratitude and esteem of Saint Vincent, V, 168; XI, 142; saint prostrates self at feet of Prior whenever he sees him dissatisfied, XIIIb, 279; criticizes Brother who failed in respect for Prior, XI, 96; Prior considers going to live in Liancourt, I, 321; requests title of bailiff of Saint-Lazare for nephew, I, 379; Saint Vincent asks Guillaume Delville to welcome Prior in Montmirail, II, 604; asks Denis Gautier to welcome Prior in Richelieu, II, 605; death; discourse of Saint Vincent on this occasion, XI, 141–42; signed, with Saint Vincent, deed for place at Saint-Laurent fair, XIIIa, 305–06; circular letter announcing death, IV, 176; epitaph, IV, 176; XIIIa, 373; other mentions, I, 473, 477–78, 497, 580; II, 49, 534, 537–38; III, 537; IV, 1; XI, 17.

Le Bon Laboureur - Dedication to Saint Vincent, I, 152.

Le Boucher (Fr.), Vicar-General of Moutiers-Saint-Jean Abbey - Letter to Saint Vincent, II, 497.

Le Boucher (Nicolas), notary in Paris - XIIIa, 217–18, 220, 222, 225, 258.

Le Bourg (M.), ship's captain - III, 594, 597–99.

Lebourgais (Jacques), Priest of the Mission - Biographical data, III, 380.

Le Bourget, in Seine-Saint-Denis, near Paris - Correspondence regarding lease and Adrien Le Bon, I, 473, 478.

Le Bouthillier (Victor) - Coadjutor of Archbishop of Tours, II, 95; Archbishop of Tours, III, 296.

Le Boysne (Léonard), Priest of the Mission - Biographical data, II, 326; III, 458; V, 360; VI, 510–11; VII, 40; in Luçon, II, 326; in Saint-Méen, III, 458; V, 360; Prior of Saint-Nicolas-de-Champvent, VI, 510–11, 629; VII, 40; health, V, 360–61; VII, 44.

Le Bret (Dom), Benedictine - Contacts with Saint Vincent, I, 263–64.

Le Bret (Jacques), Auditor of Rota in Rome, then Bishop of Toul, cousin of Dom Le Bret, Benedictine - Biographical data, I, 149; II, 41; kindness to Missionaries, I, 149; II, 43, 44; contacts with Saint Vincent, II, 105, 231; VIII, 305, 341; Saint Vincent sees to Le Bret's business matter, II, 65, 145, 467; question of naming him Bishop of Toul, II, 491–92; other mentions, I, 263.

Le Bret (Jeanne) - Member of Charity of Joigny, XIIIb, 48.

Le Bret (Julien), seigneur de Flacourt, State Councillor - I, 540.

Le Bret (Fr.), Pastor in Pompierre - Mention of letter from Saint Vincent, and his reply, VIII, 492.

Lebreton (Louis), Priest of the Mission - Biographical data, I, 538; II, 17; letters Saint Vincent sends him in Rome, I, 538, 581, 590; II, 17, 35, 43, 63, 104, 141, 154, 170; in Rome, Procurator General to Holy See, VIII, 609–10; Saint Vincent asks him to obtain from Holy See plenary indulgence for faithful, XIIIa, 310; giving missions, II, 170; worked with Italian priest, II,

306; ministering to shepherds of Roman countryside, II, 155; negotiates approval of vows and authorization of house in Rome: see also **Vows**, ***Rome***; negotiates other business, II, 280; God's blessing on him, II, 214–15; death, II, 231–32, 262, 269; Saint Vincent recommends that his successor follow his example, II, 236, 278; other mentions, II, 114, 117, 288, 306; VIII, 608; XIIIa, 313–14, 379.

Le Breton (Fr.), priest of Tuesday Conferences - Giving missions in Montmirail, I, 467–68, 470–71, 476; very fervent, I, 467; Vicar-General of Bayonne, II, 7; Vicar-General of Agde, VII, 35.

Lebrun (Guillaume), Brother of the Mission - Biographical data, V, 600.

Le Camus (M.) - II, 222.

Le Camus (M.) - VII, 337–38.

Le Cat (M.) - Kindness to Agen Missionaries, VI, 562; VII, 432.

Le Cercieux (Toussaint), prisoner in Toulon - VI, 638; VII, 274.

Le Clerc (François), Canon in Écouis - XIIIa, 26, 29, 30.

Le Clerc (Gabrielle), wife of Michel Le Gras - Marriage, III, 513, 537; disagreement with cousins, VII, 279.

Le Clerc (M.), Director of Collège of Beauvais - Ordinands lodge at Collège during vacation period, I, 57.

Leclerc (Pierre), Brother of the Mission - Biographical data, VI, 68; in Agen; would like change of mission; Saint Vincent dissuades him, VI, 68, 143; mention of letters to Saint Vincent, VI, 68, 142, 146.

Le Cocq (Jean), seigneur de Courbeville - Delegated by Parlement for Rueil conference, III, 411.

Le Coigneux (Jacques), judge - Delegated by Parlement for Rueil conference, III, 411.

Le Contre [**Le Coutre**] (Michelle), Daughter of Charity - XIIIb, 228.

Le Coust (Grégoire), priest of Coutances diocese - Saint Vincent's Assistant in parish of Clichy, XIIIa, 74.

Lectoure, town in Gers - Louis de la Rochefoucauld, Bishop: see **La Rochefoucauld**.

Lee [**Lye**] (Thady), seminarian of the Mission - Biographical data; martyrdom, IV, 342.

Lefébure (Marie), Servant of Poor in Charity of Montmirail - XIIIb, 34.

Lefebvre (Augustin), Priest of the Mission - Coming to Paris, II, 529; Superior in Toul, VIII, 605.

Lefebvre (Claude), known as **Lanal**, convict in Marseilles - VIII, 376.

Lefebvre (Louis), slave in Tunis - VII, 222.

Lefebvre de Caumartin (Louis), Councillor at Parlement - Delegated by Parlement for Rueil conference, III, 411.

Le Féron (Blaise), Archdeacon of Chartres and Vicar-General - Biographical data, XI, 29; XIIIa, 70; power of attorney to take possession of Bons-Enfants, XIIIa, 70; presents to Pope Urban VIII, on behalf of Saint Vincent, first petition for approval of Congregation of the Mission (1627), XIIIa, 228–29; gives mission in Montmirail with Saint Vincent, XI, 29.

Le Feron (M.), uncle of Nicolas Étienne - Saint Vincent's reaction to offer of Saint-Martin Priory, V, 536–37.

Le Féron (M) - Presents opposition of Pastors of Paris to approval of Congregation of the Mission, XIIIa, 257.

Lefèvre (M.) - Attorney of Alain de Solminihac at Great Council, III, 589, 591.

Le Fèvre (Mlle) - Enjoys catechism lesson of Mme Goussault, I, 195.

Le Flond (Mlle) - In Arras, VI, 131.

Legal Proceedings (Lawsuits) - Settle differences amicably rather than by lawsuit, I, 214, 339, 489; II, 509–10; III, 42, 69; V, 408, 412, 415, 599–600, 612; VI, 36, 585; VII, 439; VIII, 227; XII, 105; XIIIa, 390; Saint Vincent reproaches Bishop for his many lawsuits, II, 479; Our Lord disapproved of lawsuits, II, 480; saint prefers to give up endowments rather than take benefactors to court, VI, 88; XII, 200; Jesus and Saint Paul had only one lawsuit and lost it, along with their life, III, 42; sometimes necessary to maintain lawsuits, III, 69; V, 408, 416; protection against lawsuits, IV, 425; precautions to take before beginning proceedings in a lawsuit, VII, 97, 99; Saint Vincent advises demanding justice from those withholding money owed to slaves, V, 398; debtors who refuse to pay their debts, VII, 99; those who refuse to pay tithes, VI, 398, 445; those who, without legal intervention, would be covered by statute of limitations, VI, 161; lawsuits cause mental strain and could be harmful to vocation, V, 545; Saint Vincent intervenes in some lawsuits, I, 540; V, 7; VI, 399, 597; VIII, 302; refuses to intervene in others, III, 611; VIII, 213; is apprehensive about lawsuits and lawyers, VII, 392; justice even in loss of lawsuits, VIII, 175; lawsuits Fr. Codoing has with transport services, II, 517; lawsuit of Fr. Louis Langlois, VI, 563; lawsuits concerning ***Annecy, Crécy, Marseilles, Orsigny, Saint-Lazare, Saint-Léonard de Chaumes Abbey, Saint-Méen, Toul***: see these words; other mention, I, 558.

Légat, ward in Hôtel-Dieu for contagious diseases - Saint Vincent has heard that Saint Louise knows of young women willing to serve there, I, 450.

Le Gauffre (Thomas), Master of Accounts - Makes ordination retreat at Saint-Lazare, II, 37.

Le Gay (Marie-Catherine), Visitandine - Asks Saint Vincent for prayers, VIII, 437.

Legay (Pierre), ecclesiastical notary - XIIIa, 234–35.

Legendre (Renault), Priest of the Mission - Biographical data, V, 66; VI, 579; VII, 509; in Rome, V, 66, 546; VI, 605; VII, 509, 543; Saint Vincent writes to him in Rome, V, 322; Fr. Legendre leaves Rome with French confreres on orders from King of France, V, 271, 274–75; after having put papers of house in safe place, V, 273; sent to Genoa, VI, 579; his brother, V, 277–78; VII, 509.

Le Gentil (Claude), Brother of the Mission - Biographical data, III, 368; V, 137; VIII, 274; goes to thermal baths in Moulins; promised to Superior in Genoa, III, 368; en route for Genoa, III, 388–89; detained in Marseilles by Fr. Portail, III, 429; recalled to Paris, V, 137; in Marseilles; health, V, 259, 380, 387; arrives in Paris from Crécy, VIII, 274.

Leghorn [***Livorno***], town in Italy - Ships coming from Leghorn, V, 133; VII, 347; merchants, V, 326; other mentions, V, 328, 390, 407; VI, 361, 371, 384, 413, 650; VII, 179, 361; VIII, 586.

Leglay (Claude) - Shoemaker with gift of converting heretics, XII, 240.

Le Gouverneur (Guillaume), Pastor in Saint-Malo - VII, 519.

Legouz [**Legouts**] (Jacques), Priest of the Mission, son of Mme Legouz - Biographical data, VI, 73; VII, 347; VIII, 85; leaves Marseilles for Rome, VII, 347; arrival in Rome, VII, 401; in Rome, VII, 436; health, VII, 543; VIII, 85; disposition, VII, 508; VIII, 85.

Legouz (Mme) - Saint Vincent sings praises of her son; nothing will be asked for his maintenance, VI, 73.

Legouz [**Legoux**] (René), Priest of the Mission; brother of Jacques Legouz - Biographical data, VIII, 85; in danger of death, VIII, 421, 423; other mention, VII, 347.

Legrand (Guillaume), slave in Tunis - VII, 208.

Le Grand (M.) - Proposed for Saint-Lazare Seminary by Fr. Delville, VI, 548.

Le Gras (Antoine), secretary of Queen Marie de Medicis - Husband of Saint Louise de Marillac, XIIIa, 260; XIIIb, 116, 139, 145, 225, 231; date of death, IV, 298; Saint Vincent promises to pray for repose of his soul, I, 181; services rendered to Geneviève d'Attichy, III, 518; other mention, I, 337.

Le Gras (Colombe), Daughter of Charity - Signs attestation after reading of Common and Particular Rules reviewed and arranged in order by Fr. Alméras, XIIIb, 206.

Le Gras (Marguerite), Daughter of Charity - Signs attestation after reading of Common and Particular Rules reviewed and arranged in order by Fr. Alméras, XIIIb, 206.

Le Gras (M.) - Owner of property abutting Saint-Lazare, XIIIa, 341.

Le Gras (Michel), son of Saint Louise de Marillac - Biographical data, I, 26; II, 13; IV, 257; VII, 490; X, 570; contacts with Saint Vincent, I, 173, 603; VII, 279; lazy disposition, III, 512; enters Saint-Nicolas-du-Chardonnet Seminary, I, 26; unhappy there, I, 33, 34; Saint Vincent thinks he should stay in seminary, I, 37; teachers are content with him, I, 70; leaves seminary to enter Jesuit collège as a boarder and wearing cassock, I, 99, 103, 104, 105–06; Saint Vincent wants him to write thank-you note to Fr. Bourdoise, I, 109; gives Saint Louise news of Michel's health, I, 54, 76, 79, 88, 103, 121, 125, 129, 351, 366, 451, 452, 601; Michel speaks with elderly Jesuit, I, 282; when Michel is not at Jesuit collège, Saint Vincent houses him at Bons-Enfants, I, 86, 109, 116, 132, 262, 316, 320, 388, 390, 398; or at Saint-Lazare, I, 293, 320, 359, 371; has him purged, I, 121, 126–27, 293, 320; and bled, I, 127, 129, 293; gets permission for him to eat meat during Lent, I, 145; Michel about to be promoted to third year, I, 121; mother wants him to take Holy Orders, I, 138; Saint Vincent agrees he should remain in seminary because "priestly state is better for him," I, 197, 301; Michel decides to study theology, I, 349; Saint Vincent agrees he should be ordained, I, 427–28; Michel hesitations about vocation, I, 314, 505–06; makes retreat; reflects on vocation, I, 312; presents thesis in philosophy, I, 355–56; Saint Vincent advises that Michel not leave Paris, I, 363; even to study at university in province, I, 341; finds him more disposed to priestly state, I, 385; question of sending him to live with his uncle, Bishop of Riez; he is not studying; has made no decision, I, 398; apprehensive about priesthood, I, 433; declares that, if he took Orders, it would be only to please his mother, I, 506; studies at Sorbonne; persevering in vocation, I, 509;

seems to be of another spirit, has taken good resolutions, I, 493, 511; received without title at Saint-Nicolas, I, 534; agrees to take examination at Saint-Nicolas, I, 573.

Saint Vincent proposes to lodge him with M. Rebours or M. Coqueret, I, 547; could be part of mission, II, 151; question of finding him work in Linas or Normandy, II, 425; Mme Pelletier suggests serving Coadjutor of Paris as almoner or under another title, II, 442–43; mother does not know his whereabouts, II, 549, 626, 627–28; difficult proceedings in Rome in view of obtaining dispensation, II, 586; relationship with young lady and marriage plan; their "capture," II, 593, 634; III, 36; misdemeanor in Missionaries' house, II, 630.

Falls ill; refuses hospitality of Saint-Lazare offered by Saint Vincent; agrees to be guest of his doctor; Saint Vincent sends two Sisters to nurse him, III, 16; almost cured, III, 18; completely cured, III, 27; mother hopes illness will benefit his soul, III, 23; stays out all night, III, 36; disappears without saying where he is going, III, 119; matter for which Saint Louise desires Saint Vincent's consent, III, 167; news of affair is leaking out, III, 179; Saint Louise suggests he could attend meeting at Duchesse d'Aiguillon's house, III, 384; bailiff at Saint-Lazare, III, 432, 444, 472, 585; IV, 257, 259; V, 451; proceedings in view of marriage, III, 432, 471, 472, 502–03, 513; in view of buying office at Mint, III, 444, 512, 518–19, 520, 522, 585; marriage, daughter, III, 537; serious illness; two Sisters go to nurse him, IV, 25, 257, 258, 259; deafness; death, V, 451; Other mentions, I, 69, 94, 101, 160, 170, 305, 310, 311, 336–37, 375, 498, 548–49, 596; II, 13, 16, 47, 128; VII, 490.

Le Gras, (Mlle) - See **Louise de Marillac** (Saint).

Le Gras (Simon), Bishop of Soissons - Biographical data, III, 76; VII, 220; upcoming journey to Paris, I, 177; ministries of Missionaries in his diocese, I, 421, 467, 470; VII, 220; Saint Vincent tells Fr. Delville to go to receive Bishop's orders and blessing, II, 547; his part in having Missionaries remain in Montmirail, II, 548; mention of letter to Saint Vincent, II, 553; wants Missionaries in Montmirail, III, 76; negotiations with Saint Vincent about union of Saint-Corneille de Compiègne Abbey to Val-de-Grâce, IV, 243; not in favor of union, IV, 245; Saint Vincent writes him about Abbess of Biaches, III, 513.

Le Gros (Jean-Baptiste), Priest of the Mission - Biographical data, III, 396; IV, 321; V, 75; at Saint-Lazare, III, 396; Superior at Saint-Charles, IV, 541; VIII, 614; at 1651 General Assembly, XIIIa, 369, 374, 397; opinion about vows, XIIIa, 380, 383; at Saint-Lazare, IV, 321; escapes massacre at Hôtel de Ville [City Hall], IV, 412; titular Consul for France in Tunis, IV,

561; Superior in Richelieu, V, 75, 196; VIII, 607; on round of visitations, V, 454; death, V, 471; other mentions, V, 474, 476, 502, 585, 602.

Le Gros (Jeanne), in Vesles - VI, 503.

Le Gros (Pierre), prisoner in Toulon - VII, 150, 539; VIII, 250.

Le Havre, town in Seine-Maritime - Natives of Le Havre enslaved in Tunis, V, 227, 248, 325, 353, 379, 393, 398, 407; VI, 302, 315, 327, 328; VII, 134, 195–96, 208, 222, 228, 237, 469; presence of Duchesse d'Aiguillon, VII, 222, 245; VIII, 32; Duchess wants to found house of Daughters of Charity there, XII, 19–20; ships anchored in port, V, 174; Pastor: see **Bourdon**, Michel; other mentions, VII, 617; X, 411.

Le Huby (Étienne), freed slave - VII, 519.

Leiden, town in Netherlands - Fr. Étienne passes through when returning to France, VIII, 596.

Le Jarriel (M.), banker - I, 148–49.

Le Jay (Nicolas), Baron de Tilly, Chief Justice of Parlement of Paris - Biographical data, II, 351.

Le Jeune (J.) - Member of Charity of Courboin, XIIIb, 93.

Lejeune (Jean), Brother of the Mission - Biographical data, IV, 168.

Lejeune (Jean-François), seminarian of the Mission - Biographical data, VI, 547; Saint Vincent is pleased with him, VI, 547.

Le Joine (Marie), Daughter of Charity - Signs attestation after reading of Common and Particular Rules reviewed and arranged in order by Fr. Alméras, XIIIb, 205–06.

Le Joint (Marguerite), Daughter of Charity - See **Le Soin** (Marguerite).

Lejuge (Barbe) - Member of Charity of Montmirail, XIIIb, 32, 33.

Lejuge (Jérôme) - See **Giudice**.

Le Juge (Thomas), priest of Saint-Nicolas - Biographical data, I, 103.

Leleu (Fr.), Priest of the Mission - Giving mission in Poissy, I, 229; in Amiens, I, 490.

Le Lièvre (Anne), Daughter of Charity - XIIIb, 228.

Le Lièvre (Fr.), Archdeacon of Toul - IV, 16.

Le Loup (Guillaume), slave in Algiers - VI, 8.

Le Magasin charitable - Printed organizational plan for distribution to needy in Paris, IV, 519.

Lemaire (M.), banker in Paris - IV, 73.

Le Maistre (Marie) - See **Belot**, Mme.

Le Maistre (Nicolas), Doctor of Sorbonne - Biographical data, III, 45; Saint Vincent asks Mazarin for chair of theology at Sorbonne for him, III, 45–46; Mazarin responds favorably to request, III, 49.

Le Mans, town in Sarthe - Bishops: Emmeric-Marc **Delaferté**, Philibert de Beaumanoir de **Lavardin**, see these names; movement of troops in Le Mans; uneasiness of population, IV, 324; letter of Saint Vincent to Superior of Le Mans Visitation, II, 578; Saint Louise is asked to pass through Le Mans en route from Nantes, III, 23; Saint Vincent writes to Visitation Nun in First Paris Monastery, sending her to Le Mans, XII, 372; XIIIa, 183; other mentions, I, 236; II, 13; XIIIa, 72.

Daughters of Charity from Le Mans: II, 328; IX, 435–36; postulants from Le Mans, I, 426; V, 621; dismissal of Daughter of Charity born in Le Mans, XIIIb, 292; Daughters of Charity sought for Le Mans Hospital, II, 624, 628–29; departure of Sisters for Le Mans, II, 640, 641; IX, 201; difficulties, II, 650; return of Sisters to Paris, II, 655; other mentions, III, 290; VIII, 323.

Letters of Saint Vincent to Le Mans Missionaries, II, 588; IV, 36, 90; V, 621; VII, 332, 387, 526; VIII, 414: see also **Bienvenu** (Étienne), **Cornaire**, **Crowley [Cruoly]**, **Gentil**, **Gicquel**, **Herbron**, **Laudin** (Denis), **Lucas** (Antoine).

Foundation of Le Mans house; Fr. Gallais takes possession, II, 579, 585; verification of Letters Patent of King by Parlement, III, 492; Procurators of house: see **Gentil**, **Molony**; Saint Vincent admonishes Treasurer for economizing too much, III, 501; gives him helpful advice on temporal matters, IV, 59–60, 274–75; admonishes him for building too much and without permission, IV, 275, 300; Superior is forbidden to have a horse, V, 461; asks that customary dinner may be given on Corpus Christi to Lieutenant-General and officers who accompany him, III, 314; Confreres leaving for Ireland meet others in Le Mans, also going there, III, 93; dispute over woods owned by house, IV, 198; V, 576; VI, 124, 151, 277; over land, VII, 338–39; over meadows, V, 421, 599; over gardens and houses, III, 237; over fishponds, III, 380; chapels are dependent on it, III, 381, 569; IV, 425; repurchase of Valobron, III, 236; complaints and disputes of administrators, tenants, and others regarding temporal matters, III, 237, 380–81, 492, 611, 612; IV, 198, 425; V, 600; VI, 35–36, 64–65, 161, 179, 584–85; VII, 76, 371–72, 410, 532, 591, 621; VIII, 226–28; poverty of establishment, III, 115; IV, 60; debts, III, 607; of which Saint-Lazare pays part, IV, 275; VI, 378; VII, 77; large pension owed to Abbé Lucas; settlement of two-thirds of pension, VI, 378; tax imposed by Bishop on chapels of the Mission, III, 569, 607.

Saint Vincent speaks of sending some of Saint-Lazare personnel driven from Paris by troubles of Fronde, IV, 307; passage of troops in Le Mans; Saint Vincent urges Superior to remain at his post and to put precious articles in safe place, IV, 324–25; missions: III, 314, 608; IV, 424; V, 574–75; VI, 123, 180; VII, 204, 440, 533; VIII, 226, 519; Bishop prohibits giving missions during Advent and Lent, VI, 151; outside priests help Missionaries during missions, VII, 340, 535; VIII, 130; seminary accepts only young boys, III, 372.

Minor and major seminaries, III, 493; VI, 116, 560; ceremonies are taught there, III, 509; chant, V, 421; VI, 277; Saint Vincent forbids teacher to dictate in class, IV, 324; incompetence of some professors, VI, 179; seminarians, III, 236; IV, 98, 101; VII, 241; VIII, 422; number, III, 175; VI, 179; discontent, VII, 591; cost of room and board, IV, 59–60; VI, 36; ordinands, III, 493, 607; Bishop would like them to take everyone free of charge, V, 420–21; retreatants, VII, 339; hospital chaplaincy, IV, 172: see **Cornaire**; letter to hospital administrators telling of change of chaplains, IV, 172; Bishop has Missionaries accompany him on pastoral tours, VII, 205.

Visitation of house by Fr. Portail, II, 621, 623, 631, 641; by Saint Vincent, III, 393, 405, 408–09, 412, 415; by Fr. Lambert, IV, 275; by Fr. du Chesne, IV, 469, 477; by Fr. Alméras, V, 24–25; by Fr. Berthe, V, 501; VI, 378, 382; by Fr. Dehorgny, VIII, 129, 130–31, 159, 165; proposed visitation, VII, 591; dearth of personnel, VI, 583; VII, 331, 340, 371–72, 409, 440; VIII, 159, 165; Missionaries' retreats, VI, 123, 150; departure of Brother, VI, 65, 103; sending of Brother to Le Mans, VII, 465; two Brothers who do not intend to persevere may not remain in house as servants, VII, 225; servants, VI, 150; VII, 533; scandal over changing of pictures, V, 24–25; passage of Missionary through Le Mans, VIII, 371; Missionaries from Le Mans, III, 479; mention of Missionary who refused to go there, VII, 177; other mention, XII, 64.

List of Superiors and history of house, VIII, 613; Missionaries in Le Mans house: see **Alain**, **Bienvenu**, **Brin**, **Charpentier**, **Cornaire**, **Crowley** [**Cruoly**], **Cuissot** (Gilbert), **Delauney**, **Descroizilles**, **Duggan** [**Duiguin**], **Dupont** (Louis), **Fichet**, **Gallais**, **Gaudoin**, **Gentil**, **Gicquel**, **Gigot**, **Gorlidot**, **Guesdon**, **Gurlet**, **Herbron**, **Labat**, **Laisné** (Nicolas), **La Pesse** (Bro. de), **Laudin** (Denis), **Le Blanc** (Charles), **Le Rogueux**, **Le Roy** [**Roy**](Bro. Jean), **Le Vacher**

(Philippe), **Lucas** (Antoine), **Molony**, **Nicolas** (Bro.), **Noizeau**, **Olivier**, **Picardat**, **Pintart**, **Proust**, **Rivet** (François), **Taillié**, **Thibault** (Nicolas), **Turpin**, **White** [**Le Blanc**](George).

Le Mareschal (Fr.), Canon - Recommends to Saint Vincent young man wishing to make retreat at Saint-Lazare, VIII, 417.

Le Marinel (Martin), Pastor of Montreuil-sous-Bois - Biographical data, I, 100; contacts with Saint Vincent, I, 102, 105.

Lemasson (M.), royal notary - XII, 379.

Le Masson (Marie-Angelique), Visitation Nun - Health, II, 202.

Le Mercier (Jean), seminarian of the Mission - Sent to Rome, VII, 347; arrival in Rome, VII, 401; regrets not being able to study theology there, VII, 351; sent to Genoa to pursue theology studies, VII, 406; departure for Genoa delayed, VII, 412; threatens to leave if not given means of studying theology, VII, 434; leaves, then asks to be readmitted; allowed with provisos, VII, 517, 518; Saint Vincent informs him of these, VII, 518; enters internal seminary of Richelieu, VII, 598; other mention, VII, 529.

Lemerer (Gilles), Priest of the Mission - Biographical data, VII, 399; VIII, 137; admitted as priest into Congregation, VII, 399; in Agde, VIII, 137, 170.

Lemeret (Jeanne), Daughter of Charity - Assigned to Poland, V, 414; other mention, XIIIb, 227.

Le Mesnil-sur-Oger, village in Marne - Saint Louise visits Charity of Mesnil on advice of Saint Vincent, I, 116, 118, 125, 132; mission of Mesnil; death of Missionary during mission, I, 313; other mentions, I, 73, 74, 129, 421, 423.

Lemoine - Collège in Paris, adjoining Bons-Enfants - I, 166, 465.

Le Monastier - See ***Monestier***.

Lemoyne (Jean), Brother of the Mission - Biographical data, V, 380; VIII, 112; sent from Marseilles to Agde, V, 380; Saint Vincent does not want him to go to confession outside house, VIII, 112–13; permission to return to Agde, VIII, 369; Saint Vincent looks for house for him, VIII, 387.

Le Moyne (Jean), seminarian of the Mission - Biographical data; entrance into Saint-Lazare, VI, 527.

Le Nariel (André), Apostolic Notary in Paris - XIIIa, 26.

Lendormie (Claude) - Member of Charity of Folleville, XIIIb, 48.

Lenfant (Georges), Paris notary, Sieur de la Patrière - Legal right to pension from Saint-Léonard de Chaumes Abbey, XIIIa, 17–20.

Lenfantin (Radegonde), Daughter of Charity - Biographical data, VI, 79; VII, 199; VIII, 352; X, 181; sent to Arras, VI, 79; advice of Saint Vincent before departure, X, 181; travel authorization, XIIIb, 229; arrival in Arras, VI, 102–03; in Arras, VI, 115, 131, 214, 547, 589; VII, 199, 365; VIII, 352; leaves house without informing anyone, VIII, 546; other mention, XIIIb, 228.

Le Noir (Jacques), Priest of the Mission - Biographical data, II, 529; Fr. Lambert is asked to send him back to Paris, II, 541.

Le Noir (Fr.), priest in Paris - Recommended by Saint Vincent as tutor, III, 75.

Lent - Mention of conferences, XII, 410, 416, 419, 422; Lenten practices in Poland differ from those in Rome, V, 349; problems of keeping the Lenten fast in Madagascar, V, 296; its observance on ship bound for Madagascar, VIII, 570–71.

Lenti (Marcello), Cardinal - Biographical data, II, 232; kindness toward Congregation of the Mission in general and Rome house in particular, II, 232, 240, 351, 394, 405, 415, 418, 505–06; pastoral change in his diocese, II, 434; other mention, II, 426.

Leo I (Saint), Pope - Cited, III, 324.

Léon (Fr.), Carmelite - In Rome, II, 583.

Léonard (Bro.) - See **Lamirois** (Léonard).

Léonard (M.), administrator of Nantes Hospital - II, 645.

Leonessa, town in Italy - Mission, VIII, 38, 147.

Le Page (Renaud), prisoner in Toulon - VI, 187, 343; VII, 149, 250, 486; VIII, 250.

Lepanto [today ***Návpaktos***], town in Greece - Victory of Don Juan of Austria over Turks, VI, 71.

Lepeintre (Jeanne), Daughter of Charity - Biographical data, I, 485; II, 188; III, 23; IV, 171; V, 8; VI, 44–45; VII, 476; VIII, 502; IX, 520; XII, 363; letters Saint Vincent writes to her in Saint-Germain-en-Laye, II, 230; in Nantes, III, 602; IV, 171, 281; V, 8; XII, 363; in Châteaudun, VI, 44; mention of letters to Saint Vincent, V, 9; VI, 45, 47; Ladies at Saint-Sulpice insist on keeping her, I, 450; Duchesse d'Aiguillon asks for her change, I, 557; accompanies Saint Louise to Angers, I, 596; for health reasons, wears headdress different from other Sisters, II, 198, 206, 210, 292; proposed for Saint-Germain-en-Laye, II, 188; for Fontenay, II, 292; leaves Saint-Germain in Paris without permission, II, 327; proposed to visit foundlings entrusted to wet-nurses, II, 337; sent to Le Mans, II, 642; return from Le Mans, II, 655; replaces Saint Louise when she is absent from Motherhouse, III, 16, 23; question of sending her to Nantes, III, 178; responsible for visiting Sisters in Nantes and Angers, XIIIb, 272–73, 283–84; visitation of Nantes house, III, 185; preparing to leave for Nantes, III, 208; Sister Servant in Nantes, III, 217, 254; IX, 520; XII, 363; congestion, III, 215; character, III, 427; offers resignation, which Saint Vincent refuses, III, 602–03; removal from Nantes judged beneficial by some, IV, 298; recalled to Paris, V, 57; XIIIb, 312; proposed for Poland, V, 215; Sister Servant in Châteaudun, V, 240; XIIIb, 317; Saint Vincent reproves her for leaving Châteaudun without permission to nurse M. de Franqueville, VI, 45–47, 48–49; Saint Louise suggests withdrawing her from Châteaudun, VI, 325; in Paris, VI, 380; VII, 476; Sister Servant in Saint-Fargeau, VIII, 502; other mention, XIIIb, 227.

Le Pelletier (Claude), Minister of State - Biographical data; Saint Vincent tells him there is vacancy at Nom-de-Jésus Hospice for woman recommended by him, VIII, 344.

Lepers - See ***Saint-Lazare***.

Lepine (M.), slave in Algiers - III, 223.

Le Pouget, monastery near Castelnau-de-Montratier (Lot) - Alain de Solminihac plans to go there by order of Queen, II, 489; election of new Prioress: see **Laroque** (Mother de).

Leprestre (D.) - Writes to Saint Vincent about rift among Carmelites, VIII, 496.

Le Prévost (Charles), King's Councillor - XIIIb, 237.

Leprosy - Physical condition not cured at Saint-Lazare, but spiritual leprosy is, XI, 13; number of patients decreased, XIIIa, 263–64, 280–81.

Lepruvost (M.), delegate for clergy of Artois - Plans to see Saint Vincent, VIII, 378.

Le Puy, town in Haute-Loire - Bishop: Henri de **Maupas du Tour**, see this name; other mention, III, 383.

Lequeux (Jean), Brother of the Mission - Biographical data, II, 538; IV, 250; absent from Paris, IV, 250.

Lerida, diocese in Spain - Nomination of Bishop by King of Spain, XIIIa, 151–52.

Le **Rogueux** [**Leroqueux**] (François), Brother of the Mission - Biographical data; assigned to Le Mans, II, 676; will not be sent to Genoa, III, 4.

Le Rond (Toussaint), slave in Algiers - V, 36, 119, 147.

Le Roseau (Françoise), Daughter of Charity - See **Roseau**.

Le Roule, village near Paris - I, 122; II, 651.

Le Roux (Frédéric), chaplain for collegial church of Écouis - XIIIa, 30.

Le Roux (Jean) - Predecessor of Saint Vincent as Canon of Écouis, XIIIa, 27.

Le Roux (M.), tax collector for Duc de Retz - XIIIa, 30.

Le Roux (M.), in Nantes - VIII, 596.

Le Roux (M.) - Saint Vincent thanks Mme. Goussault for welcoming him, I, 379.

Le Roux (Mme) - Contacts with Mme Goussault, I, 379; in Grigny, I, 537; retreat at Saint Louise's home, II, 187, 188–89.

Leroy (Antoinette), Daughter of Charity - XIIIb, 228.

Le Roy (Françoise-Angélique), Visitandine - Travel authorization to go to Le Mans to assume leadership role, XII, 372; XIIIa, 183.

Le Roy (Jean), Priest of the Mission - Biographical data, recalled to Paris, II, 541.

Le Roy (M.), in Paris - Young man for whom Saint Vincent requests dispensation from Rome, VIII, 198–99.

Le Roy (M.), chief clerk of M. Le Tellier - IV, 81; V, 96.

Le Roy (M.), administrator of work of Foundlings - II, 108, 137; III, 228–29.

Le Roy (M.) - VI, 608.

Le Roy (Mme) - Biographical data; Saint Vincent sends regards, IV, 82.

Le Roy (Marie-Agnès), Visitandine, sister-in-law of Mme Le Roy - Biographical data, I, 361; III, 86; IV, 80–81; V, 14; VII, 418; VIII, 188; letters from Saint Vincent, IV, 80, 403; V, 14; VII, 418; VIII, 188, 195; mention of another letter from Saint Vincent, IV, 80; letters to Saint Vincent, VIII, 436, 471, 511; Superior of Second Monastery of Paris, I, 361, 368; VIII, 441, 443, 466; in Mons; Saint Vincent urges her to return to Paris, IV, 81; organizes sending of Visitandines to Warsaw; difficulties, IV, 354; V, 14–15; uneasy because of disturbances in Paris; Saint Vincent reassures her, IV, 403; advice regarding dowry of candidates, VII, 418–20; involved with furnishing house purchased for Third Monastery in Paris, VIII, 188, 498; other mention, IV, 319.

Le Roy (Pierre), monk of Saint-Victor, brother of chief clerk of M. Le Tellier - Biographical data, V, 96–97; Saint Vincent advises monks of Mont-Saint-Éloy Abbey to ask for Le Roy as Abbot, V, 96–97.

Lesage (Jacques), Priest of the Mission - Biographical data, II, 235; III, 82–83; IV, 25; Saint Vincent asks Bishop of Mende to lend money for Lesage's clothing, II, 235; in Sedan, II, 468; question of sending him to Algiers, III, 82; departure, III, 271; devotion to slaves in North Africa, III, 304–08; Superior in Algiers, VIII, 615; illness, death, obsequies, III, 304, 308–11; Saint Vincent announces death, III, 349; other mentions, III, 389; IV, 25; V, 90.

Le Sargy (M.), in Tunis - V, 118.

Les Baronies [***Baronnies***] ***of Luçon*** - Property discussed in foundation contract for Luçon house, XIIIa, 319, 321.

Lescar - Bishop: Jean du Haut de **Salies**, see this name.

Lescar (M.), converted heretic - I, 539.

Lescellier (Jacques), monk of Saint-Lazare - I, 135; XIIIa, 263.

Leschassier (François), Sulpician - Delivers letter to Saint Vincent, VI, 60; saint consoles Sulpicians on death of Jean-Jacques Olier, XIIIa, 184.

Lescot (Jacques), Bishop of Chartres - Biographical data, II, 507; III, 186; IV, 159; thanks Saint Vincent for missions given in his diocese by Priests of the Mission, II, 507; III, 186; Missionary delegated to settle differences between Sainte-Geneviève Abbey and Chancelade, IV, 68, 159–60, 162–63; Saint Vincent testifies before him regarding Abbé de Saint-Cyran, XIIIa, 104–05, 107, 110.

Lescot (Vincent), Brother of the Mission - Biographical data, IV, 3.

Lescuyer (Pierre), seminarian of the Mission - Biographical data; dismissed from Company, II, 321.

Lesguier (M.) - III, 585.

Le Soin [**Le Joint**] (Marguerite), Daughter of Charity - Assigned to Saint-Denis, III, 419; other mention, XIIIb, 227.

Le Soin (Marie), Daughter of Charity - XIIIb, 227.

Le Soudier (Jacques), Priest of the Mission - Biographical data, II, 96; III, 32; IV, 232; V, 19; VIII, 145; XII, 368; letters Saint Vincent writes to him in Saint-Quentin, IV, 232; in Crécy, IV, 579; V, 19; in Montmirail, V, 437; ordination, II, 191; has left Paris for Salé (Morocco), III, 32, 40; in Marseilles, III, 82, 92, 466; in devastated regions of Picardy, IV, 232, 450, 452; XII, 368; Superior in Crécy, IV, 579; V, 19; VIII, 609; Superior in Montmirail, VIII, 612; ill at Saint-Lazare, VIII, 145, 148, 151, 157, 159, 161, 169, 301; XII, 374; getting better, VIII, 219, 221, 225.

Le Soudier (Samson), Priest of the Mission - Biographical data, II, 96; III, 12; letters Saint Vincent sends him in Luçon, II, 96, 191; in Luçon, II, 140; in Saintes; does not get along with Superior, III, 12, 31, 57; available to Fr. Portail for placement, III, 82; considered for La Rose, III, 83.

Le Sourd (M.), physician - I, 213.

Lespiney (Gabriel de) - See **Delespiney**.

Lesquielle, village in Aisne - Wretchedness and charity, IV, 104.

Les Roches, priory - Michel Le Masle, Prior, biographical data, I, 418.

Lesseignet (Claude), Brother of the Mission - Biographical data, VI, 180.

Lessius [**Leys**] (Léonard), Jesuit theologian - Thoughts on nature of religious state, V, 318.

Lestang (François de), from Paris, slave in Algiers - Money sent to be given him a little at a time, VIII, 328, 337.

Lestang (Jean de), Priest of the Mission - Biographical data; reproved for urging man to enter Congregation of the Mission, VIII, 342.

Lestang (Mme), cousin of Gabrielle Le Clerc, wife of Michel Le Gras - VII, 279–80.

Lestang (Marie Delpech de) - Foundress of Community and orphanage, XIIIb, 441.

Lestocq (Guillaume de), Pastor of Saint-Laurent in Paris - Biographical data, I, 134; III, 298; IV, 541; steps taken to have Saint-Lazare Priory given to Congregation of the Mission and accepted by Saint Vincent, XIIIa, 271–75; Saint Vincent explains his difficulties with this, I, 134–37; contacts with Daughters of Charity of his parish, I, 449; other mentions, II, 425; III, 298, 400; IV, 541.

Lestradie (M.) - Nephew leaves Saint-Charles Seminary, VIII, 50.

Lesueur (André), prisoner in Toulon - VI, 302, 333, 487; VII, 179, 456, 486.

Le Tellier (Michel), Minister of State - Biographical data, II, 648; IV, 81; V, 96; consulted by Mazarin, III, 393; contacts with Saint Vincent, IV, 81; Saint Vincent's influence in Council of Conscience, XIIIa, 150–51; Le Tellier's praise of this, V, 96.

Letter of Authorization - See **Obedience**.

Le Tonnelier (Étienne), Pastor of Saint-Eustache in Paris; Syndic for Pastors in Paris - Raises, in their name, objections to approval of Congregation of the Mission, XIIIa, 253, 258; presents needs of Picards, XII, 367.

Le Tort (Jeanne-Françoise), Superior of Angers Visitation - Saint Vincent fears he will not be able to give Angers Monastery one of Sisters she desires to succeed her, VI, 163.

Leuville-sur-Orge, village in Seine-et-Oise - IV, 512.

Le Vacher (Jean), Priest of the Mission, brother of Philippe - Biographical data, III, 252; IV, 367; V, 38; VI, 54; VII, 7; VIII, 90; XI, 151; letters from Saint Vincent, III, 253; IV, 523, 596; VII, 521; to Saint Vincent, III, 335, 354; IV, 367, 434, 552, 590; V, 130, 132, 267; mention of letters from Saint Vincent, VI, 275; VII, 101, 524; VIII, 331; mention of letters Saint Vincent received from him, VI, 523; VII, 521; XI, 167, 393.

Sick in Marseilles, receives order from Saint Vincent to sail for Tunis, III, 252, 253; ill of plague in Tunis; his cure, III, 300, 349–50; rule of life, appointed director of the Mission, XIIIa, 401; in Tunis, III, 393, 445; V, 265, 393; VI, 208, 346, 348, 353, 371, 466–67, 523, 570; VII, 101, 103, 244–45, 250, 253, 303, 318; VIII, 90, 376; XI, 334; Superior in Tunis, VIII, 615; Vicar Apostolic, IV, 88; in La Cantara, V, 118; proceedings in Rome to renew his faculties, VI, 526, 636; VII, 29; strength, zeal, and courage amid trials and fatigue, XI, 151, 261, 277; XII, 250; expelled from Tunis by Bey for refusing to have sailcloth sent from France, XI, 291, 302; joy of slaves in Tunis at his return, XI, 291; new expulsion for preventing Christians from becoming Turks; retires to Bizerte; ministry in Bizerte; return to Tunis, XI, 276–77; wants bolt of cloth to thank Bey for authorizing his return, V, 455, 506; new avania (insult) provoked by refusal to pay debts of Chevalier de la Ferrière, V, 408; XI, 303.

Report of Jean Le Vacher, V, 157; Saint Vincent has it read in Saint-Lazare refectory, V, 624; Le Vacher asks that something be done for M. Husson, whose consular rights are not being respected, V, 133–34, 267–68; interim Consul after death of Fr. de Lange, IV, 372; V, 90; until arrival of M. Husson, IV, 596; and after his departure, VI, 327, 386, 447, 461; XI, 386, 392; Saint Vincent asks *Propaganda Fide* to authorize M. Le Vacher as acting Consul, VI, 386, 401, 461, 629, 636; *Propaganda* refuses; Saint Vincent asks if refusal constitutes prohibition, VII, 39, 46; Le Vacher's steadfastness in consular duties, XI, 386.

Ministry among slaves, III, 354; IV, 367–68, 434–35; V, 119, 130–32; XI, 192, 276, 393–95; debt to merchant in Marseilles, IV, 506; at his request, Bey exempts priests and monks who are slaves from galleys and other work, V, 131; obtains release of Frenchmen captured at sea, IV, 523; ransoms slaves, IV, 523, 552, 590; V, 119, 147; VI, 273, 275; VII, 522; recounts heroism of two boys, III, 335.

Money sent him for Missionaries and slaves, V, 191, 216, 227, 248; VI, 54, 259, 273, 275, 279, 289, 304, 320, 322; VII, 7, 103, 124, 134, 144–45, 148, 154, 190, 196, 212, 232, 250, 458, 463, 468, 519, 520, 522–24, 539, 555, 556, 557; VIII, 331, 337, 357, 514; sends money to brother in Algiers, VI, 466; told not to allow Barreau to draw any bills of exchange on him, VI, 486; Saint Vincent's surprise that he taxed French ships to pay off debts of private individual, III, 394–95; drew up bill of exchange on Fr. Get's account, despite formal prohibition, VI, 599; incurred debt by excessive spending, VII, 522; Le Vacher borrows money to send to M. Barreau, VII, 7–8, 93, 103; Saint Vincent admonishes him, VII, 122–23; Le Vacher advises Saint Vincent to withdraw Missionaries from Barbary until King of France has punished Turks for avanias, VII, 303; loses his mother, XI, 392; deprivations, V, 133–34, 248; VI, 629; interior trials, VII, 524; Duc de Mercoeur lodges complaint against him, VIII, 527; other mentions, VII, 168; VIII, 218, 358, 531, 537. See also ***Tunis***.

Le Vacher (Mme) - III, 519; see also Catherine **Butefer**.

Le Vacher (Philippe), Priest of the Mission, brother of Jean - Biographical data, III, 93; IV, 25; V, 34; VI, 8; VII, 28; VIII, 4; XI, 261; letters Saint Vincent sends him in Algiers, IV, 126, 360; in Marseilles, VII, 402, 410; VIII, 32; mention of other letters from Saint Vincent, V, 145, 146; VI, 154, 208, 275, 418; VII, 437; VIII, 331; mention of letters to Saint Vincent, V, 482; VI, 185, 200; VII, 325, 410, 438, 459; VIII, 135; Louis XIV writes to Pasha on Le Vacher's behalf, V, 644; in Le Mans; assigned to Ireland, III, 93, 103; sick in Ireland, III, 274; in Marseilles, IV, 25, 88; proposed to *Propaganda Fide* for Algiers; request for faculties, IV, 25–26, 88; *Propaganda* grants faculties of Missionary Apostolic and title of Vicar Apostolic; Saint Vincent hesitates sending him, IV, 88; arrival in Algiers, IV, 291; Saint Vincent spells out line of conduct for him, IV, 126–29, 360–61; in Algiers, V, 149, 325–28, 530; VI, 154–55, 183, 200,208, 279, 353, 371, 384; Superior in Algiers, VIII, 615; ministry among slaves, V, 339, 355, 363; VII, 208; ransom of slaves, V, 141, 145, 146; VI, 8, 273, 275, 289, 304; VIII, 377; zeal, IV, 372; VI, 346, 348; XI, 261, 277–78, 386; XII, 250; strives to reform enslaved priests and monks, V, 35; VI, 9; Saint Vincent wants Le Vacher and Barreau to consult one another, V, 34–35; deprivation, V, 248; health, V, 355, 407; calumniated by apostate, V, 482; in Leghorn (Livorno), VI, 413; in Marseilles, VI, 418, 421; awaited in Paris, VI, 421, 431, 441; in Paris, VI, 446, 455, 466, 470, 472, 478, 486, 489, 492, 613, 628; VII, 28, 57, 70, 94, 103, 133, 186, 195; XI, 395; takes up collections to pay M. Barreau's debts but nets little, VI,

480, 485, 570, 629; VII, 34, 49, 55, 74, 90–91, 106, 115; VIII, 326–27; loses his mother, XI, 392.

Saint Vincent would like to put him in charge of Consulate of Algiers; proceedings with *Propaganda Fide*, VI, 401, 461, 629, 636; refusal of *Propaganda*, VII, 39; saint requests from Rome renewal of his faculties, VI, 526, 636; VII, 29; about to depart for Marseilles, VII, 186, 194, 207, 221, 228; en route to Marseilles, VII, 232–33; in Marseilles; waits for favorable occasion to reenter Algiers with money collected, VII, 244, 245, 250, 253, 263, 269, 281, 289–290, 303, 325, 402–03, 410, 456, 458, 463, 488, 519–520, 522, 554–56, 609, 632–33; VIII, 4, 18, 68, 69; interim Superior in Marseilles, VII, 282–83, 554; VIII, 18; about to embark for Algiers, VIII, 135, 138; report on money he took to Algiers, VIII, 319; groundless anxiety, VIII, 149; received partial payment in 1659, VIII, 309–10; is requested to clarify situation with regard to money sent, VIII, 321; presence at martyrdom of Borguñy, XI, 290; other mentions, V, 391; VII, 228, 557; VIII, 328, 358, 397: see also ***Algiers***.

Levant - Ladies of Charity work for Levant missions, V, 394; M. de **la Haye-Vantelay**, French Ambassador to Levant: see this name; other mentions, V, 405; VII, 226; IX, 173; XII, 125.

Levasseur (David), Brother of the Mission - Biographical data, II, 30; III, 104; in Bar-le-Duc, II, 30, 76; in Saintes, III, 104.

Levasseur (M.), notary - XII, 380.

Levasseur (Martin), Priest of the Mission - Biographical data, III, 481; V, 66–67; VIII, 22; in Genoa, V, 136; sent to Cahors, V, 212, 227; arrival in Cahors, V, 247; requests ordination papers, VIII, 22.

Levasseur (Richard), monk of Saint-Lazare - I, 135; XIIIa, 263.

Le Vayer (M.), in Le Mans - VII, 533.

Le Vayer (Renée Le Boindre), widow - Explains to Saint Vincent situation vis-à-vis confessor; asks him for line of conduct, VIII, 332.

Le Vazeux (Achille), Priest of the Mission - Biographical data, III, 481–82; IV, 293; V, 252–53; VI, 330; VII, 40; letters Saint Vincent writes him in Rome, IV, 293, 346, 355, 387; in Annecy, VI, 330; petitions *Propaganda Fide* to impede multiplication of Congregations having same ministries, IV, 610; opposed to approval of Congregation of Missionaries for Indies; Saint Vincent admonishes him for this, IV, 293–94, 345, 346–47, 355–56, 359, 368; deems vows made in Congregation null, and even "mortal sin to make and to renew them," IV, 345; hasty, touchy character, IV, 345, 360, 368, 387–88; recalled from Rome, IV, 521.

Superior in Annecy, V, 252, 261; VI, 404; VII, 190; VIII, 608; negotiates foundation for Turin establishment, V, 252, 373; Saint Vincent tells him why Company has no house in Lyons, VI, 330; sent to Turin to help Fr. Martin with missions, VI, 521, 523, 525, 552, 557; Fr. Le Vazeux cannot carry out this plan, VI, 578; through hastiness, causes failure of project to unite benefice to Company, VII, 40, 406: see ***Saint-Sépulcre***; quarrels with lawyer in Annecy, VII, 91, 95–97; recalled from Annecy, VII, 270; leaves Company, XIIIa, 202; other mention, VII, 79.

Lévêque (M.), agent of Queen of Poland in Paris - Complains that packets sent to or from Poland are too large, V, 336; contacts with Saint Vincent, XI, 274; Saint Vincent will pay postage for letters, VI, 556; other mention, V, 356.

Lévesque (M.), physician in Paris - XIIIb, 96.

Lévesque (Nicolas), Vicar-General of Beauvais - I, 93.

Levies (Anne), Daughter of Charity - XIIIb, 228.

Le Vigan, commune in Lot - Chapter of Vigan, IV, 506; XIIIa, 309.

Levy (Jean), in Châtillon - XIIIb, 22.

Leyo (Alexis), prisoner in Toulon - VII, 154.

L'Hay, town near Paris - Dispensation requested of Rome for some inhabitants of L'Hay, II, 105, 142.

Lhermitte (Anne) - Member of Charity of Montmirail, XIIIb, 32.

L'Hospital (Paul Hurault de), Archbishop of Aix - Leases Saint-Léonard de Chaumes Abbey to Saint Vincent, XIIIa, 8–11; resigns Saint-Léonard de Chaumes Abbey to Saint Vincent, XIIIa, 12–16; legal difficulty concerning transfer of Abbey, XIIIa, 17–19.

Lhoste (Jean-Marie), administrator of various hospitals in Paris - Biographical data, I, 340; assures Saint Vincent that his rights over Orsigny farm are indisputable, VII, 422–23.

Lhoste (Mme) - Correspondence between Saints Vincent and Louise about room for her, II, 194, 218, 292.

Lhuillier (Dominique), Priest of the Mission - Biographical data, V, 231; VI, 20; VII, 16; VIII, 152; XII, 371; Superior (without title) in Crécy, VIII, 609; letters Saint Vincent writes him in Crécy, V, 231; VI, 20, 356; VII, 16, 369, 461, 630; VIII, 152, 174, 274, 294, 363, 486; XII, 371; mention of letters to Saint Vincent, VI, 20, 356; VII, 461; VIII, 152, 363; contacts with M. and Mme de Lorthon, V, 231; VI, 20; VIII, 153; with Pastor of Crécy, VI, 356; with Bishop of Meaux, VI, 458; lives alone and is in no condition to give missions, VII, 16, 369; falls ill; Saint Vincent suggests he come to Paris for health care, VII, 461–62. See also ***Crécy***.

Lhuillier (Hélène-Angélique), Visitandine - Biographical data, I, 55–56; II, 99; III, 70; V, 345; XII, 353–54; letters from Saint Vincent, I, 236; II, 463; XII, 359; mention of letter to saint, I, 236; Saint Vincent reports on recent visitation of Saint-Denis Visitation, II, 463; Superior of First Monastery of Paris, I, 55; II, 115; III, 70; XII, 353; contacts with Saint Vincent, I, 56; II, 132; III, 360; Saint Vincent plans to go see her at Saint-Denis, III, 303; Jansenists seek to win her to their party, III, 360; health, I, 326; II, 202, 464; III, 70, 303; very ill, V, 345; other mention, I, 367.

Liancourt, town in Oise - Saint Vincent speaks of going to Liancourt, I, 280; journeys and sojourns of Saint Louise there, I, 282, 284–88, 319; II, 329, 337; III, 357, 470, 472; Saint Vincent suggests she go there for change of air, III, 369; she asks to be excused, III, 370; mission in Liancourt under direction of Bishop of Beauvais, I, 283; establishment of Charity of Liancourt; Saint Vincent fears ministry may suffer from poor organization, I, 286–87; Liancourt may not be ready for Charity, I, 287; preparation of regulations for Charity, I, 295, 340, 354, 358; Sister Geneviève sent to Liancourt, I, 353; Sister Élisabeth Martin recalled from there to be placed in Nantes, XIIIb, 248–49; Daughters of Charity from Liancourt, I, 330, 383; II, 198, 301; III, 419; Mme de Liancourt asks Saint Vincent to find chaplains for Liancourt, I, 381; Adrien Le Bon volunteers, I, 321; Saint Vincent sends Mme de Liancourt to Fr. Bourdoise, I, 384–85; other mentions, I, 296, 428; VII, 563.

Liancourt (Jeanne de Schomberg, Duchesse de), wife of Roger, Duc de Liancourt - Biographical data, I, 285; II, 162–63; V, 344; VI, 549; IX, 174; XI, 355; contacts with Saint Vincent, I, 320–21, 505, 511; IV, 299; IX, 174; with Saint Louise, I, 286, 409, 502; II, 162–63, 478; IV, 299; V, 344; she invites Saint Louise to Liancourt, I, 319; to visit Charities in Liancourt and environs, II, 329–30, 337; retreats at Saint Louise's house, I, 372; II, 656; has woman in Creil locked up, I, 285; health, I, 493; Saint Vincent invites her to aid Daughters of Providence, VI, 549, 552; attachment to Jansenist party: see also **Liancourt** (Duc de); offers house for Charity of Liancourt, I, 295; death of son, III, 36; Mazarin's thoughts on her, XIIIa, 155; other mentions, I, 330, 488; VII, 372. See also ***Liancourt*** (town).

Liancourt (Roger, Duc de) - Contacts with Saint Vincent, I, 341; II, 255, 297; IV, 299; V, 344; with Saint Louise, I, 488; IV, 299; member of Charity of Lorraine, II, 54, 285, 406; member of league against dueling, V, 617; Saint Vincent hopes Bull *Cum*

Occasione will detach Duke and wife from Jansenist party, IV, 593; VI, 152, 168, 293; saint's hope is dashed, VI, 293; XI, 355; death of their son, III, 36; other mentions, I, 319; II, 338; VI, 179, 549, 552; VII, 372.

Liard, small coin - I, 439.

Libeauchamp (M.) - VIII, 223.

Libya - Monks of Libyan desert, XII, 339.

Lièbe (François-Ignace), Priest of the Mission - Biographical data, IV, 559; V, 471–72; VI, 62; VII, 324; letter from Saint Vincent, VII, 382; mention of letters to Vincent, VII, 382; Superior at Bons-Enfants, VIII, 604; sent from Richelieu to Montech, IV, 559; Superior in Montauban, V, 471; VIII, 618; Saint Vincent writes him at Notre-Dame-de-Lorm, where he has just transferred seminary from Montech, VI, 62; sent to Richelieu, VI, 358, 380; in Saintes, VI, 444; behavior gives bad example, VII, 177; leaves Company and lives in Richelieu, VII, 324; desire to go to Luçon to work in missions, VII, 382–83; Saint Vincent refuses to dispense him from vows, VII, 383, 451.

Liesse (***Notre-Dame de***), village in Aisne - Saint Vincent refuses Fr. Dufour permission for pilgrimage to Notre-Dame de Liesse, IV, 364–65; and to a Daughter of Charity, I, 356; grants it to Fr. Jolly, V, 640; pilgrimages to Notre-Dame de Liesse, VI, 559; VII, 545; VIII, 245; other mention, VI, 415.

Ligin (Mme de), Lady of Charity - Health, I, 340; death, I, 355.

Lignières-la-Doucelle, village in Mayenne - VII, 494.

Ligny (Dominique de), Bishop of Meaux - VII, 369; VIII, 363, 486.

Ligny (Mlle de) - II, 337.

Lillers, town in Pas-de-Calais - Fr. Dufestel, Dean of Saint-Omer-de-Lillers, II, 669; III, 3.

Lillesson (Jean) - Member of Charity of Courboin, XIIIb, 93.

Limerick, town in Ireland - Bishops: see Richard **Arthur**, Edmund **Dwyer** [**O'Dwyer**]; mission given, III, 416–17; IV, 18; ravages of plague, IV, 18–19; siege of town by Cromwell's troops; poverty, IV, 344; seige and slaughter in Limerick, IV, 291, 341–42; confreres preached in diocese 1646–52, VIII, 615.

Limoges, town in Haute-Vienne - VIII, 412, 511.

Limouron, hamlet in Villamblain (Loiret) - Journey of Saint Vincent to Limouron, I, 477–78; Fr. Barreau, Prior of Limouron, XIIIa, 271; transfer of priory to Adrien Le Bon, XIIIa, 266; other mention, I, 479.

Limousin, province - Missions of the priests of Fr. de Fonteneil, VIII, 510; people live on bread made from chestnuts, IX, 70; other mentions, I, 304; IV, 125; VII, 447.

Lin [**Lamontagne**] - See **Laisné** (Guillaume).

Linas, village in Essonne - II, 425.

Linens - Sent to Bro. Parre for distribution, VIII, 382, 384; conditions under which Daughters of Charity may accept care of church linens, XIIIb, 376–77.

Linet [**Livet**] (Jean), secretary of Archbishop of Lyons - XIIIa, 47; XIIIb, 20.

Lingendes (Jean de), Bishop of Sarlat and Mâcon - At Saint-Lazare, II, 322; efforts to become King's tutor, II, 429.

Lion, gulf - I, 3.

Lion, village in Loiret - Fr. Portail passes through, I, 275.

Lionne (Catherine-Agnès de), Visitandine - Authorization to go to Abbeville Monastery as Superior, XIIIa, 157; Superior of Abbeville Monastery, VI, 163; sent to Amiens as Superior, XIIIa, 189.

Lionne (Hugues de), Minister of State - Biographical data, III, 249; V, 270; VIII, 466; contacts with Saint Vincent, III, 249; notifies Fr. Berthe of order for French confreres and him to leave Rome, V, 270, 272, 273–74; requests and obtains permission for daughters Élisabeth and Madeleine, students at Visitation convent, to leave it to see entrance of King and Queen into Paris, VIII, 466, 471.

Lionne (Marie-Marguerite de), sister of Catherine-Agnès - Superior of Amiens Visitation, IV, 82.

Lions - Gift from Jean Barreau, Consul in Algiers, VIII, 261–62, 276.

Lisbon, city in Portugal - II, 522; VII, 211, 213, 216, 615–16; VIII, 503.

Lisieux, town in Calvados - Bishop: see Philippe **Cospéan**; coaches, III, 529.

Lisieux, collège in Paris - Fr. Gilles, professor here before entering Saint-Lazare, II, 355, 360.

Lisle-Marivault (Fr. de), Doctor of Theology - Drowned in Seine, IV, 297.

Lissardy (Adamé de), slave in Algiers - VII, 196, 213.

List of Establishments and Superiors - VIII, 604–19.

Litanies - Litany of Holy Name of Jesus is part of Missionaries' morning prayers, I, 581–82; this litany or that of Blessed Virgin is sung at meetings of Charity of Châtillon, XIIIb, 15; Saint Vincent encourages Sisters to say Litany of Virgin in evening and that of Jesus in morning, when traveling, X, 445; other mention, I, 194.

Lithuania - Queen of Poland requests Missionaries, IV, 274; and Sisters, V, 335; possibility of visit by King and Queen of Poland, IV, 518; plan for Charity in Lithuania, V, 335.

Liverdi (Abbé de), nephew of Bishop Liverdi - Makes retreat at Saint-Lazare, VII, 278.

Liverdi (Balthazar Grangier de), Bishop of Tréguier - Letters from Saint Vincent, IV, 313; VI, 138; VII, 278; mention of letters to him, VI, 382, 587; letters to Saint Vincent, III, 270, 616; VIII, 456; participates in ministries of Missionaries, III, 104, 270; VIII, 616; requests Missionary for month or two to help him "apply self to his episcopal duties," III, 195; reports to Saint Vincent on fruits of mission given by Priests of the Mission; thanks him for it, III, 616; plans to entrust direction of seminary to Priests of the Mission, IV, 357, 359; contacts with Saint Vincent, IV, 547; VII, 43; leaves Paris to return to Tréguier, V, 581, 582; asks Missionaries to preach, by exception, in Tréguier, V, 604; desires Daughters of Charity for three hospitals, XI, 327; Saint Vincent apologizes for not being able to send them, VI, 139; for recalling professor from Tréguier Seminary, VII, 278; writes Liverdi that Rule of Missionaries prohibits their hearing confessions of outsiders in places where they live, IV, 313; Liverdi denies Missionaries use of Brief giving them right to absolve from cases reserved to Holy Father, VI, 63–64; zeal for his diocese, VII, 399; health, VII, 428; Saint Vincent's esteem for him, VII, 566; increases revenues of seminary by union of chapels, VIII, 168; agrees that seminary Superior may accept donation, VIII, 222; asks Saint Vincent to take back Missionary who left Company, VIII, 456; unfavorable to vows of Missionaries, XIIIa, 377; esteem for Congregation of the Mission, XIIIa, 383.

Livet (Jean) - See **Linet** (Jean).

Livorno - See ***Leghorn***.

Livry, town in Seine-Saint-Denis - Rougemont farm in vicinity of Livry, II, 589; IV, 422, 423; Pastor in Livry, XIIIa, 479.

L'Obligeois (M.) - V, 427, 484.

Lodève, town in Hérault - Bishops: see François de **Bosquet**, Jean de Plantavit de **La Pause**; other mentions, IV, 308–09.

Loger (M.), attorney for Saint-Lazare at Parlement - II, 687; advice from Saint Vincent, XIIIa, 190.

Loire, river of France - V, 277; XIIIa, 13; XIIIb, 310.

Loisel (Pierre), Pastor of Saint-Jean-en-Grève in Paris - Biographical data, IV, 217; VII, 513; asks Saint Vincent for information about Fr. Daisne, VII, 513; saint's reply, VII, 528.

Loisy-en-Brie, village in Marne - Mission given, I, 24, 25; visit of Saint Louise to Charity of Loisy, I, 116, 118; many Protestants there, I, 25.

Lombard (Peter), known as Master of the Sentences - Biographical data, IX, 281; his work, I, 289; IX, 281.

Lombardy - Region of Italy, VII, 400; XI, 341.

Lombet, (M.) - Man in Lyons to whom Saint Vincent could address letters for Fr. Berthe, V, 272, 275.

Lombez, town in Gers - Bishop: see Jean **Daffis**.

Loménie (Henri-Auguste de) - See **Brienne** (Comte de).

London, city in England - Fr. Brin stopped there en route to Scotland and Hebrides, V, 620, 622, 624, 627; VI, 39, 499.

Longchamp, abbey near Paris - Division among nuns; Saint Vincent suggests that Queen have recourse to Pope to introduce reform there, IV, 271; saint's report to Cardinal Barberini on disorders of abbey, of which he has just made visitation, IV, 483–92.

Longueil (René de), Marquis de Maisons - Biographical data; delegated by Parlement for Rueil conference, III, 411.

Longueville (Anne-Geneviève de Bourbon, Duchesse de), second wife of Henri II, Duc de Longueville - Biographical data, II, 611; VIII, 407; needs wet-nurse for son, II, 611; her children, V, 382; VI, 95; VIII, 498; has them brought to Saint Vincent for blessing, VIII, 498; her chaplain: see **Aubert** (M.); defender of Jansenists, VIII, 407; wants to pay expenses of mission; Saint Vincent is opposed, III, 250–51; other mention, XIIIb, 304.

Longueville (Henri II, Duc de) - Steps taken by him and wife for son's marriage to niece of Queen of Poland, VI, 95, 98; Saint Vincent seeks help from him for Queen, VI, 296.

Longueville (Louise de Bourbon, Duchesse de) - Biographical data, I, 285; Jean de la Salle visits woman Duchess had locked up in Creil, I, 285; warned against Abbé de Saint-Cyran, she acknowledges she was mistaken, I, 394; XIIIa, 124–25.

Longueville (Marie d'Orléans, demoiselle de), daughter of Henri II, Duc de Longueville, and of Louise de Bourbon; wife of

Duc de Nemours - Biographical data, I, 460; IV, 82; boarder at Visitation, IV, 82; Lady of Charity, XIIIb, 440.

Lorain (Vincent) - Member of Charity of Courboin, XIIIb, 93.

Lord of Charity - Saint Louise asks Saint Vincent if he has this picture in one of his books, III, 255; pictures, VI, 111.

Loret (Julienne), Daughter of Charity - Biographical data, III, 263–64; IV, 53; V, 215; VIII, 235–36; IX, *xvi*; records conferences of Saint Vincent, IX, *xv-xvi*, 430, 440; Officer of Company; words of praise for her, III, 16; named Directress of newcomers; recites Community prayers, XIIIb, 294–95; Saint Vincent wants her formed in mental prayer so as to teach newcomers, IV, 53; recommends that she teach them to pray well, XIIIb, 302; present at Councils of Company, XIIIb, 305, 312, 344; sent to Chars, XIIIb, 311; Sister Servant in Chars, IV, 203, 516; suggested for Angers, IV, 258; traveling makes her ill, V, 215; Sister Servant in Fontenay, V, 426; renews perpetual vows, VIII, 235; named Assistant, VIII, 312; X, 595–96; XIIIb, 226; other mentions, III, 401, 469–70; IV, 159; V, 484; XIIIb, 227, 332.

Loreto [***Loretto***] (***Our Lady of***) - Journey to Loreto of Jansenist theologians on mission to Rome, IV, 583; of French Missionaries expelled from Rome by King of France, V, 271, 274; endowment by Duchesse d'Aiguillon; proceedings and difficulties: see **Aiguillon** (Duchesse d'); dedication of chapel in Paris, XIIIa, 61; XIIIb, 296.

Lorfebvre (M) - Admitted to Internal Seminary in Richelieu, VIII, 341.

Lorm (***Notre-Dame de***), in village of Castelferrus, Tarn-et-Garonne - Letters from Saint Vincent to Missionaries there, IV, 557, 587; VI, 62: see also **Barry** (Edmund); union of Notre-Dame-de-Lorm chapel and Saint-Aignan parish to Congregation of the Mission, under name of Fr. Bajoue, IV, 374, 383, 466; Bajoue wants to resign these benefices; Saint Vincent urges him not to hurry, IV, 558, 588; taking possession of chapel, VI, 590; question of uniting Bajoue's benefices to Company, VII, 373; Saint Vincent recommends leasing benefices of Brial and Falguières, VI, 357–58; VII, 166–67; disagreement and settlement with clergy of Castelferrus, VI, 476; VII, 430; attempt to set fire to Missionaries' house, VII, 505.

Transfer of Montech Seminary to Lorm, VI, 62–63; VIII, 618; payment of room and board for seminarians, VIII, 257; hope for increase in number of seminarians, VI, 477; VII, 167, 373; plan to transfer seminary to Montauban, VI, 476–77; VII,

167, 373, 430, 505; visitation by Fr. Berthe, VI, 475, 477, 590; by Fr. Dehorgny, VIII, 172; by Fr. Cuissot, VII, 373; mission given near Lorm by Jesuits, VIII, 258; Saint Vincent permits Fr. Get to go there to rest, VII, 282, 289; list of Superiors and history of mission, VIII, 618; personnel: see **Admirault** (Claude), **Bajoue**, **Barry** (Edmund), **Dupuich** (Antoine), **Jeandé**, **Lesseignet**, **Lièbe**, **Lucas** (Jacques), **Thieulin**, **Treffort**; other mentions, V, 184, 233; VII, 5; VIII, 387.

Lorme (M. de), physician in Paris - VII, 427.

Lorraine (Charles, Duc de) - Leads army to gates of Paris, makes peace, withdraws, IV, 395, 399; ally of Spain, IV, 462.

Lorraine (Charles-Louis de), Abbot of Chailli - Proposed for bishopric of Condom; opposition of Saint Vincent, III, 249.

Lorraine, province - Character of inhabitants, X, 448; misery in Lorraine, I, 541; II, 74, 93; IV, 133, 279; IX, 70; X, 17; XII, 401; people take refuge in Paris, I, 532, 542, 582; III, 202; assistance furnished poor by Missionaries, I, 539, 541, 582; II, 42, 45, 48, 68, 74–75, 82, 93, 119, 144, 173, 246; VIII, 278; X, 17; Ladies of Charity of Lorraine, II, 25, 68, 75, 260–61, 414; XIIIb, 407; assistance to nobles, II, 54, 82, 173, 260–61, 285, 406, 533; Queen Anne of Austria, II, 533; Benedictines, II, 307; postulants from Lorraine, I, 508, 573; II, 25–26, 125, 127; Daughters of Charity from Lorraine, II, 286; VII, 192; XIIIb, 118; other mentions, I, 323; II, 55, 69, 82, 189; VI, 495; IX, 195; XII, 15. See also ***Bar-le-Duc***, **Liancourt** (Duc de), ***Lunéville, Metz, Nancy, Pont-à-Mousson,*** **Regnard** (Mathieu), ***Saint-Mihiel***, ***Saint-Nicolas***, ***Toul***, ***Verdun***.

Lorthon (M. de) the younger - Complains about Missionaries, VI, 20.

Lorthon (Mme de), wife of Pierre de Lorthon - Saint Vincent urges Fr. Lhuillier to show her a letter, V, 231; to obey her, VI, 20; hopes she will find usual hour for Mass acceptable, VIII, 153; she gives Fr. Lhuillier reason to hope that Crécy house will soon be able to maintain personnel and ministries once again, VIII, 174.

Lorthon (Pierre de), King's secretary - Founder of Missionaries' house in Crécy, V, 19; VIII, 153, 487; Saint Vincent recommends Lorthon's nephew to Superior of Crécy house, V, 19, 20; Lorthon does not keep promises to Missionaries, leading to lawsuit with Bishop of Meaux, VII, 16; XII, 200; XIIIa, 422; Prelate seeks information on arrears owed by M. de Lorthon, VII, 369–70; Saint Vincent hopes Lorthon will find usual hour for Mass acceptable, VIII, 153; Lorthon raises objections about sending Missionaries to Crécy, VIII, 363, 487; other mention, VI, 20.

Lot, Abraham's nephew - God orders him to leave Sodom, XI, 342; wife looks back during flight, XIIIa, 378.

Lot, river near Cahors - Alain de Solminihac mentions it in letter to Saint Vincent, IV, 509.

Lotin (Marie-Marthe Goussault), wife of Nicolas Lotin - Preparations for marriage, I, 357, 512; retreat at Saint Louise's home, II, 187–88; other mentions, I, 594; XIIIb, 391–93.

Lotin (Nicolas), Seigneur de Martilly, son-in-law of Mme Goussault - Biographical data, I, 512; named in Mme Goussault's will honorary guardian for her children who are minors, XIIIb, 391–92.

Loudun, town in Indre-et-Loire - Jeanne of Loudun: see Jeanne (Sister); possessed nuns, I, 592; II, 456; X, 298; Loudun record offices, I, 438; II, 358; coaches, I, 418; other mentions, I, 452, 458; VII, 511.

Louis, weighted coin - Saint Vincent asks to borrow money in this form from Saint Louise, II, 50.

Louis VII, King of France and Duc d'Aquitaine - Gave use of Gonesse property to Saint-Lazare Priory, XIIIa, 342–43.

Louis IX (Saint), King of France - Conquers self by expedition to Holy Land, I, 111; peacefulness on his return, I, 132; Saint Vincent praises him, XI, 272–73; visits sick poor of Hôtel-Dieu, IX, 97; X, 450; XI, 274; Saint Louise's patron saint, VIII, 105; feast day, VIII, 105, XIIIb, 104; one of patrons of the Daughters of Charity in hospitals, XIIIb, 194; other mentions, IV, 485, 488; IX, 12; XIIIb, 114, 455.

Louis XIII, King of France - Has mission given at Court, I, 442; hoping to renew episcopate through Saint Vincent, XI, 120; established Missionaries in Crécy, VIII, 609; Dauphin refuses to look at him, IX, 267; legacy for Saint Vincent for foundation in Sedan: see *Sedan*; King's esteem for Congregation of the Mission, XI, 120; takes revenues of Congregation of the Mission, II, 359; in Versailles, II, 400; asks Saint Vincent to send him list of those qualified to be Bishops, II, 427; income on his estate, II, 430; handled business of violence to property in Montmirail, II, 545; illness and death, II, 430–31, 435–36; IX, 91, 94; X, 276; XII, 183; gave his heart to Jesuits, II, 436; suppressed deplorable practices during Corpus Christi Procession in Aix, II, 576; contributed to support of Daughters of Charity, III, 61; XIIIb, 325–26; granted letters patent for union of Saint-Lazare to Congregation of the Mission, VII, 502; XIIIa, 412; granted letters patent for transfer of Bons-Enfants to Congregation, VIII, 604–05. Other mentions, I, 254, 411, 540; III, 387; VIII, 518; XIIIa, 15–16, 58, 147, 226–

27, 236–37, 243–44, 252–53, 258, 280, 289, 293, 295, 321, 473, 477–78, 485; XIIIb, 72, 225.

Louis XIV, King of France - Chancellor's respect for young Louis XIV, IX, 107; Saint Vincent will see M. Chavigny for King's letter for Rome, II, 438; King will make reduction on grain tax, II, 444; Solminihac's presence in Cahors Diocese is useful to King, II, 451; lays claim to revenue from coach lines, II, 465; Duc de Bellegarde wants King to return coaches of France to him, II, 469; King authorizes Congregation of the Mission to build enclosure around Saint-Lazare, II, 589, 607; revenue given to support Daughters of Charity, II, 601–02; brother of Jean d'Estrades in Holland on King's business, II, 679; settlement between King and Pope, II, 679–80; King has written to Solminihac about Capuchin Provincial, III, 162; people want King to oblige them to attend Mass, III, 172; Solminihac wants him to order Governor of Valence not to interfere in office of Bishop, III, 240; King decides to write to Pope about problem of Jansenism, IV, 184; also writes about reform of Order of Grandmont, IV, 308; refuses to look at his father, IX, 267; makes Stations for Jubilee on foot, IX, 488; passes through Richelieu, IV, 44; journey through Normandy, Guyenne, and Burgundy, IV, 147; reinstating his authority could bring peace, IV, 414; recommends protection of Congregation of the Mission to French Ambassador to Vatican, V, 54; coronation in Reims, V, 145, 176; orders French confreres in Rome to leave and return to France, V, 270–72, 273–74, 334, 338–39, 369; prohibition on transporting contraband material into Barbary, V, 412; letter to Pasha of Algiers requesting protection for M. Barreau and Fr. Philippe Le Vacher, V, 644; seeks redress from Great Lord against King of Tunis, VI, 346, 348; VII, 226–27; grants safe-conduct for confreres serving in Picardy and Champagne, XIIIa, 367–68; going to Sedan, VI, 367; letters and ordinances concerning consular rights of M. Husson, VI, 372, 384, 643, 649, 650; prefers not to send another Consul, VI, 401; letters to Chevalier Paul about proposed expedition to Algiers, VII, 174, 187; King has not yet registered displeasure with Algiers for its treatment of Consul, VII, 234, 250, 253; journey to Lyons, VII, 320; peace treaty with Duke of Savoy, VIII, 68; goes to Bordeaux to conclude peace with Spain, VIII, 77; possible gift of two lions from Consul in Algiers, VIII, 261–62; in Marseilles, VIII, 273; rumor he has prepared ships to rescue captives, VIII, 316; illness, XII, 433; may grant clemency on occasion of his marriage, VIII, 429; entrance into Paris after marriage, VIII, 466, 481; confirms union of Saint-Lazare to Congregation of the Mission in March 1660, XII, 382; draft of letters patent for approval of Daughters of Charity, XIIIb, 139; letters patent approving

Company of Daughters of Charity, XIIIb, 230. Other mentions, III, 558; IV, 461, 585; XIIIa, 147–48, 338, 339–40, 346, 347, 348, 425, 485, 488; XIIIb, 72, 235, 236.

Louise, Daughter of Charity - See **Boucher** (Louise), **Ganset** (Louise).

Louise, Daughter of Charity at Saint-Jacques-de-la-Boucherie - Very ill, III, 316, 317; Saint Vincent refers to conference on her virtues, IX, 350.

Louise, Daughter of Charity at Motherhouse - Saint Louise asks permission for her to take vows, VIII, 105.

Louise de Marillac (Saint Louise de, Mlle Le Gras) - Biographical data, I, 23; II, 1; III, 7–8; IV, 4; V, 10; VI, 34; VII, 23; VIII, 97; IX, *xi*; XII, 358; letters of Saint Vincent to Saint Louise, I, 23, 27, 28, 30, 34, 35, 37, 46, 54, 59, 60 (2), 61 (2), 62, 63 (2), 64, 67, 68, 69, 70, 71, 72, 75, 76, 78, 80, 81, 84, 85, 87, 88, 90, 91, 95, 96, 99, 100, 101, 102, 104, 105, 106, 108, 110, 114, 115, 116, 118, 121, 124, 126, 127, 129, 131, 137, 139, 145 (2), 146, 147, 150, 155 (2), 156, 157, 158, 159, 160, 162, 163, 167, 168, 169 (2), 170, 172, 173 (2), 174, 175, 180, 182, 186, 187, 196, 199, 200, 201, 205, 211, 212, 213, 215, 216, 218, 220, 223, 230, 232 (2), 234, 235, 237, 238, 239, 240, 241, 258, 261 (2), 262, 263, 270, 271, 280 (2), 281, 283, 284, 286, 287, 290, 293 (2), 299, 300, 301, 303, 305, 306, 307, 308 (2), 309, 310, 311, 312, 314, 316, 317, 319, 326, 327, 328, 329, 330, 333, 337, 339, 341, 347, 348, 349, 351, 352, 353, 354, 355, 357, 358, 363, 364, 366, 370, 372 (2), 373, 374, 376, 377, 381, 382, 383, 384, 385, 386, 387, 390, 391, 397, 400, 401, 407, 408, 410, 423, 425, 426, 427, 432, 433, 434, 435, 437, 445, 446, 449, 450, 451, 457, 468, 469, 471, 483, 484, 485, 491, 493, 495, 496, 497, 498, 499, 501, 503, 505, 507 (2), 509, 510, 511, 513, 531, 532, 533, 534, 537, 547, 548, 549, 550, 551, 557, 559, 560, 561, 562, 569, 572, 573, 574, 575, 576 (3), 579 (2), 588, 591, 593, 595, 599, 602; II, 1, 8, 10, 12, 14, 23, 25, 35, 47, 48, 49, 50, 67, 77, 106, 125, 126, 127, 128, 129, 131, 139, 147, 150, 163, 164, 165, 166, 169, 175, 177, 178, 180, 181, 182, 184, 185, 186, 187, 189, 190, 194, 196, 197 (2) 198, 205, 206, 207, 209, 210, 215, 216 (2), 217, 224, 226, 233, 244, 247, 259, 260, 287, 289, 290, 300, 302, 317, 323, 327, 328, 329 (2), 337, 338, 341, 423, 425, 482, 484, 539, 571, 597, 627, 634, 640, 654; III, 7, 15, 21, 27, 118, 149, 177, 201, 202 (3), 210, 212, 215, 234, 290, 302, 317, 356, 369, 379, 380, 395, 399, 406, 415, 417, 419, 423, 424, 425, 430, 433, 444, 472, 520, 537, 608, 610; IV, 19, 23, 52, 177, 192, 217, 256, 258, 259, 381, 516, 564; V, 45, 64, 134, 186, 243, 337, 343, 400, 427, 532, 569; VI, 155, 340, 456, 511, 582, 640; VII, 280, 382, 427, 436, 453, 477; VIII, 124, 166, XII, 358.

Letters of Saint Louise to Saint Vincent, I, 26, 33, 78, 294, 336, 359, 414, 429, 431, 481, 484, 488; II, 107, 137, 162, 179,

183, 194, 204, 212, 222, 225, 285, 290, 299, 301, 346, 390, 392, 399, 410, 411, 442, 444, 474, 478, 484, 485, 487, 512, 526, 549, 557, 573, 576, 578, 590, 591, 592, 596, 598, 609, 626, 629, 635, 639, 647, 650 (2), 654, 655, 667; III, 8, 22, 35, 116, 117, 119, 132, 155, 158, 167, 177, 178, 201, 208, 210, 213, 228, 231, 233, 253, 254, 255, 261, 263, 265, 277, 297, 300, 302, 311, 316, 370, 378, 384, 422, 469 (2), 470, 502, 504, 506, 507, 512, 517, 518, 522, 585; IV, 4, 115, 158, 170, 193, 203, 206, 215, 224, 276, 298, 379, 416, 419, 458, 530, 536, 541; V, 32, 40, 42, 44, 177, 214, 223, 240, 242, 332, 345, 356, 381, 413, 416, 426, 438, 444, 451, 460, 465, 470, 483, 555, 568, 578, 589, 641; VI, 65, 70, 136, 191, 201, 209, 280, 286, 287, 313, 325, 341, 379, 417, 511, 576; VII, 87 (2), 113, 130, 157, 188, 191, 272, 279, 286, 298, 381, 407, 426, 432, 445, 456, 464, 476, 489, 492, 597; VIII, 97, 104, 127, 167, 187, 190, 204, 214, 234 (2), 244, 258, 263, XII, 362, 366.

Letter of Saint Louise to Mme de Herse, VI, 650; to Fr. Pouvot, VI, 651; to Sister Nicole Georgette, VII, 641; from Bro. Ducournau, V, 643, 646; VI, 652; VII, 640, 641; contact with Mme Goussault, I, 379.

Chronology of Saint Louise's life:

1591: Birth, II, 204; V, 178; patron saint, III, 233; VIII, 105.
1595: Second marriage of father, Louis de Marillac, widower of Marie de la Rozière, to Antoinette Le Camus.
1601: Birth of half-sister, Innocente, baptized December 28.
1604: Death of father.
1613: Marriage to Antoine Le Gras, I, 67; birth of son, Michel.
1618 or **1619**: Saint Francis de Sales visits in her illness.
1623: Husband's serious illness; makes vow to remain widow if he dies, renews vow annually, II, 573–74; III, 233, 234; violent temptation against faith; freed from it on June 4, Pentecost Sunday, through intercession of Saint Francis de Sales; God helps her see future vocation; indicates priest destined to be her Director, II, 573–74.
1624 or **1625**: Places self under direction of Saint Vincent, I, 80; IV, 225; VIII, 236; X, 575; death of Antoine Le Gras.
1626: Moves from rue Courteau-Villain to rue Saint-Victor, near Collège des Bons-Enfants, where Saint Vincent lives, I, 128; he writes first extant letter of their correspondence, I, 23.
1627: Address on rue Saint-Victor, I, 29.
Between 1626–29: Desires to consecrate self to service of poor, I, 46; Saint Vincent asks her to await patiently manifestation of God's Will, I, 24; ponders it enough for both of them, I, 54; engages her in works of charity, I, 26, 35, 37.
Between 1627–33: choice of young woman as her servant, I, 27, 106, 139.

1629: Saint Vincent sends her to visit Charity of Montmirail with his good wishes and advice, I, 64–65.
Around 1630: Gives candlesticks to Visitandines of Paris, I, 175.
1630: Visits Charities: Saint-Cloud, I, 67; Villepreux, Sannois, Franconville, Herblay, Conflans, I, 75; XII, 355–56, where she instructs children, I, 75; Saint Vincent recommends that she do nothing except in obedience to Bishops and Pastors, I, 75; foundress and superior of Charity of Saint-Nicolas-du-Chardonnet in Paris, I, 69–70, 71, 72; visits poor of parish, I, 156; Saint Vincent directs to her young country women working in Charities of Paris, I, 68; sends her to visit Charities in Beauvais diocese and nearby, I, 85–86; visits Charities of Montmirail, I, 89; of Beauvais, I, 91–94; wants to honor adorable hidden life of Our Lord; Saint Vincent advises her to remain in present state until God advances her to another, I, 71, 82.
1631: Visit of Charity of Montreuil, I, 99–107; her poverty, I, 109; wishes to become servant of poor young women; Saint Vincent asks her to wait until Our Lord manifests His Will, I, 111; contract of Priests of the Mission and Saint Louise with Gilles Guérin, XIIIa, 259; visit of Charities of Montmirail, Mesnil, and environs, I, 116, 119, 121–132; change of lodging, I, 127, 132; upset on learning of false promise of marriage attributed to her, I, 138.
1632: Retreat, I, 158; changes lodgings, I, 158, 160–61; visits Charity of Villeneuve-Saint-Georges, I, 162–64; concern for galley convicts of Paris, I, 168; visits Charity of Asnières, I, 173; and others, even in Soissons diocese, I, 180; asked to draw up regulations, I, 174.
1633: Saint Vincent tells her that Our Lord wishes to make use of her for something that concerns His glory, I, 186; visit of Charities of Verneuil, Pont-Sainte-Maxence, Gournay, La Neufville-Roy, Bulles, I, 188; Saint Vincent's mind is not enlightened enough before God concerning a difficulty, I, 200; together with her, he founds Company of Daughters of Charity; makes her Superioress; her address: rue de Versailles, I, 213. See also **Daughters of Charity**.
1634: Saint Vincent founds Confraternity of Ladies of Hôtel-Dieu.
1635: Visit of Charities: Beauvais, I, 281; Bulles, I, 284; Liancourt, I, 282, 284–87; Saint Vincent asks Theologian of Beauvais to deliver letters to Saint Louise in Liancourt, I, 284.
1636: Transfer of Motherhouse of Daughters of Charity to La Chapelle; Saint Vincent invites her to visit Charities of Grigny and Villeneuve-Saint-Georges, I, 318–19; visit of Charity of Gournay, I, 319.

1638: Beginning of ministry of Foundlings, I, 407; Saint Vincent asks her to assemble Ladies of Charity in Saint-Germain-en-Laye, I, 494, 495.
1639: Journey to Angers with Sisters named for Hôtel-Dieu, I, 593 ff.
1640: Beginning of ministry with galley convicts, II, 35; Saint Louise signs contract for Sisters' services at Angers hospital, XIIIb, 116; caring for foundlings at Motherhouse, XIIIb, 403.
1641: Saint Vincent buys house, rue du faubourg Saint-Denis, opposite Saint-Lazare, for Daughters of Charity, II, 210–11.
1642: Sisters leave Motherhouse in La Chapelle for rue du faubourg Saint-Denis; March 25, Saint Louise makes perpetual vows with four other Sisters; visits Charities of Liancourt and environs, II, 329, 337.
1644: Request for permission for pilgrimage to Chartres, II, 526; Saint Vincent approves, II, 529.
1645: Saint Vincent tells Archbishop of Saint Louise's part in forming Daughters, II, 600.
1646: Journey to Nantes with Sisters who are to serve in hospital; II, 675; III, 7–8; proposes topics for Saint Vincent's conferences to Daughters of Charity, XII, 362.
1648: Reply to Fr. Codoing regarding young women from Moncontour and Saint-Méen who want to become Daughters of Charity, III, 336.
1649: Journey to Liancourt, III, 472–73.
1650: Marriage of Michel Le Gras.
1651: Birth of granddaughter Louise-Renée, III, 537.
1652: Serious illness, IV, 335; Saint Vincent contacts her about plans regarding Poland, IV, 349; she will have three Sisters ready to go to there, IV, 354; soup for the poor is prepared and distributed from her home, IV, 400; sends Sisters in Valpuiseaux medications for the sick, IV, 401; does not have enough Sisters to care for sick and poor in Paris, IV, 401.
1653: Opening of Nom-de-Jésus Hospice, IV, 530.
1654: Saint Vincent dissuades her from attending relative's first Mass, V, 186.
1655: Saint Vincent appoints her Superioress for life (August 8), XIIIb, 226; she signs Act of Establishment, XIIIb, 227.
1656: Serious illness, V, 610; designates Marguerite Chétif as choice of replacement after her death, X, 594.
1660: Swelling under left arm, accompanied by fever; receives Last Sacraments, VIII, 281; death, VIII, 312; X, 569.

Works: service as Lady of Charity, XIIIb, 385; records conferences of Saint Vincent, IX, *xv*, 1, 13, 16, 23, 30, 38, 49, 51, 55, 66, 78, 92, 104, 115, 128, 162, 171, 179; X, 381, 533; guards them jealously, IX, *xvi*; records Council minutes,

XIIIb, 304, 359; trains country girls to assist sick poor, III, 60; praise for her administration as Superioress of Daughters of Charity, IX, 351; X, 95, 552; XIIIb, 226, 325, 374; ministry for **Hôtel-Dieu**, **Foundlings**, **Nom-de-Jésus Hospice**, **Daughters of Charity**: see these words.

Words and writings: Seal used for letters, III, 261; pious writing in form of conversation with woman, VII, 88.

Her role in development of Rules of Daughters of Charity, XIIIa, *xv*. Thoughts on following: fidelity to Rules, IX, 169; preparation for Communion, IX, 269–71; good use of admonitions, IX, 294–95, 454; notable faults of some Sisters, IX, 297–98; benefit to be drawn from conferences, IX, 310; prayer, IX, 324; spirit of world, IX, 345, 346; love of vocation, IX, 355, 356; obedience, IX, 428; X, 74–75; confession, IX, 446; indifference, IX, 402–03; Jubilee, IX, 489; fidelity to God, IX, 493; most common reason for loss of vocation, IX, 516; preservation of Company of Daughters of Charity, IX, 544–45; envy, IX, 558–59; temptations, X, 18–20; sin of scandal, X, 43–44; mortification, X, 51; secretiveness, X, 60–61; poverty, XIIIb, 342; life and virtues of Sisters: Jeanne Dalmagne, IX, 158; Anne de Gennes, IX, 435; Marie Lullen, IX, 437; Marguerite Bossu, IX, 437–38; Cécile Delaître, IX, 438–39.

Other interventions in conferences of Saint Vincent, IX, 91, 260, 399, 470, 528, 544, 547; X, 495, 520, 522, 537, 563; during Councils of Community, XIIIb, 243–45, 247–48, 249–250, 252–253, 254, 255–56, 258–59, 260, 261–62, 263, 265–70, 272–77, 278–81, 283, 285, 287, 288–94, 296–97, 299–304, 306, 309–10, 310–12, 316–17, 320–22, 325, 328–29, 332–33, 335–40, 341–42, 339–42, 348–49, 355, 362–63, 364–65, 368, 369–73, 374–75.

Virtues, faults, state of soul: Conferences on her virtues, X, 569–82, 582–90. Saint Vincent saw in her only small speck of imperfection, no mortal sin, X, 575, 578; proposed her to Daughters of Charity as beautiful portrait to gaze at and imitate, X, 577, 582, 585–86; wishes her spirit for Jeanne Lepeintre, XIIIb, 283; declares her a saint, X, 589, 590; in heaven, X, 589, 597; with great influence before God, X, 576.

Interior spirit, X, 570–71, 574–75, 583–84; purity, X, 575; humility, X, 570, 577–78, 583–84; humbles self, II, 195, 392, 577, 626; IV, 224, 276; IX, 292, 325, 528; asks that Sister be appointed to admonish her of faults, IX, 292, 297; tenders resignation as Superioress; Saint Vincent does not accept, IX, 256.

Love for Sisters, X, 583–84; especially for sick, X, 570; for poor persons, X, 570, 578, 584, 585; gentleness, X, 577–79; forbearance, X, 578–79; treated all Sisters alike, X, 574;

resignation in suffering, X, 570, 579, 584; prudence, X, 571–72; love of poverty, X, 572–74, 579; modesty, X, 585–86; discretion, XIIIb, 329; Saint Vincent permits her to use discipline three times a week, I, 80; to wear penitential belt of little silver rosettes, I, 97; asks Saint Vincent's permission to fast and abstain, III, 233.

Great love of family, X, 570; fear of predestination, III, 201; scruples, I, 263, 301–02; interior trials, I, 92,101, 108, 150; interior abandonment, I, 157; thoughts against faith, I, 150; sadness and temptations, IV, 564; thoughts of discouragement, V, 426, 427–28; thoughts of death, II, 593; apprehensions, I, 150, 158; II, 651; IV, 206; exaggeration, II, 482; hastiness, X, 574; Saint Vincent reproaches her for her little faith, II, 177, 294; spirit of envy and weakness, V, 45; loath to be elected Superioress by Sisters, V, 413.

Devotions: Received Communion three times a week before foundation of Daughters of Charity, I, 97; Saint Vincent admonishes her for not going to Communion because of interior trial, I, 108; permits her to receive Communion, I, 46, 65, 356; V, 344; approves her not going out because of health, I, 233; abstains from Communion because of uneasy conscience, II, 513; asks to receive Communion every day of novena to Holy Spirit, III, 201; asks, in another year, to abstain from communicating during the same period, III, 312; novena to Blessed Mother, V, 451; devotion at Communion, I, 67; X, 584.

Confession, I, 46, 341, 375, 549; IV, 206; weeps while confessing, X, 575; annual confession, I, 303.

Retreats, I, 46, 158, 182, 270, 341, 374, 549; II, 198; IV, 564; V, 240; Saint Vincent gives permission to hear Mass daily during retreat, I, 513.

Devotion to Blessed Virgin, I, 81; II, 526, 626; V, 451; VII, 408; VIII, 215; XIIIb, 296; explains chaplet she prays, II, 630; Saint Vincent advises her not to say certain prayers to Blessed Virgin any longer, IV, 203; allows one of them only during son's illness, planning to make decision later, IV, 259.

Devotion to thirty-three acts of holy humanity, I, 80; to words "God is Who is," IV, 206; to "God is my God," III, 233.

Spiritual direction: Saint Vincent begins to direct her in 1624–25, I, 80; IV, 225; VIII, 236; X, 575; attachment to him, I, 80; suffers from his absences, I, 24, 26, 33; Saint Vincent recommends *Imitation of Christ* and *Treatise on the Love of God*, I, 513; encourages her to adore God's good pleasure, I, 550; expresses need to be guided a little severely, II, 651; Saint Vincent tells her he will remind her of her faults, I, 409; and she should be disposed to take advice, I, 151; tells her to prepare for a good scolding, I, 158; wants her to go to God through love, not fear, because God is love, I, 81; tells her how to make up for negative things she said about doctor, I, 199; how to act in success and in humiliations, I, 94; prepares her for suffering, III, 234; consoles her in sufferings and afflictions, I, 138, 145, 155, 550–51; sustains her in temptations, I, 62; recommends mixing a dash of vinegar with gentleness of spirit, I, 383; that she honor inactivity and unknown condition of Son of God, I, 54, 156; that she not try to run ahead of Providence, I, 59, 60; Providence cannot be hurried or delayed, I, 557; recommends conformity to God's Will, I, 36, 54, 61, 71, 82, 109, 126; fidelity to Our Lord, I, 28; submission, I, 24; tranquility, I, 29, 109, 111, 318; indifference, I, 212; trust, I, 84; II, 185, 627–28; sincerity, I, 263; simplicity, I, 28, 302; avoidance of singularity, I, 376, 409; humility, I, 28; peace and tranquility, I, 318; moderation of zeal, I, 92; cheerfulness, I, 36, 69, 145, 189, 200, 309, 313, 315, 351, 356, 374, 377, 492, 551, 573; II, 16, 303; that she not overburden herself with devotions, I, 375; that she exercise her authority, I, 377; love her poverty, I, 561; expresses fear of offending God by not receiving Communion, II, 512–13; mention of her writing to Fr. Lambert, III, 217.

Rapport with Saint Vincent: he borrows money from her, I, 310; II, 50; calls her "my daughter," "my dear daughter" in early letters, I, 54–56, 59, 60, 61, 62, 63, 107; avoids tender expressions in correspondence, I, 374; goes to La Chapelle, where she lives, without seeing her, I, 330; goes to see her only if she sends for him, I, 574, 576.

Tells her to take care of herself because she is needed by poor people, I, 307; because she is no longer like a private individual, I, 216; tells her to eat meat during Lent, I, 145; to eat more, I, 284, 353–54, 356; to leave for country when she is better, I, 293, 398; not to go out so as not to get sick, I, 389; to eat eggs, I, 400; she asks Saint Vincent's permission to fast the last two days of Lent 1657, VI, 280; solicitude of Saint Vincent for her health, I, 200, 319, 340, 341, 355, 510, 531, 548, 559, 602; III, 399, 433.

Her concern for Saint Vincent's health, II, 485, 627; V, 470–71, 483–84; VII, 477; VIII, 264; sends or recommends remedies, I, 61, 202, 588; II, 576; III, 369, 370; IV, 170; V, 470–71; VI, 155, 512; VII, 426, 427, 432–33, 453; VIII, 245; sends gifts, I, 155, 220; title she gives him in letters, III, 502; contacts with son Michel: excessive anxiety regarding him, I, 34, 37, 63, 67, 69, 314, 507–08, 547, 577; II, 627; III, 432; Saint Vincent tells her "Our Lord did well not to choose you for His mother," I, 109; "I have never seen a mother so much a mother as you," I, 576; troubles and worry son gives her, I, 63, 509; II, 628, 651; III, 23; Saint Vincent tells her Michel is doing well,

I, 160, 366, 433; advice concerning letter to Michel, I, 513; to atone for his faults, she commissions picture of Blessed Virgin for chapel at Saint-Lazare, paid for from sale of rings, II, 626, 629–30; is inspired to surrender him to God, III, 22; wonders if he has large cross in his room, II, 577; attributes his bad conduct to faults of parents, I, 314; other mentions, I, 301, 338, 502, 511. See also **Le Gras** (Michel).

Health: Saint Vincent recommends that she take care of self, I, 61, 67, 116, 169, 172, 215, 224, 238, 284, 334, 389, 410, 469, 511, 557; II, 16, 303; III, 399, 433; inquires about her health, I, 169, 217; she is often ill, I, 61, 146, 280, 356, 386; II, 210, 624; IV, 419; IX, 492; XIIIb, 301; has cold, I, 202; fever, I, 213, 410; II, 317; V, 239, 569; VI, 271, 425; VII, 200; IX, 492; at beginning of stay in La Chapelle, better than in Paris, I, 410; falls ill there; Saint Vincent asks her to leave if air is bad for her, I, 551; ill in Angers, I, 602, 604; new illness, II, 1, 8, 11, 15; recovering, II, 16; well again, IV, 236, 239; very serious illness; improves, IV, 335; in good health, IV, 402, 568; in fairly good health, V, 10, 62, 69, 74, 116; VII, 67, 257, 473; feeling better, V, 432; fever, V, 461; VI, 108, 115; well again, V, 580; recovering from serious illness, V, 610, 616; cured, V, 622, 623; falls out of bed; almost recovered, VI, 140, 213; in fairly good health, VII, 67, 365; not completely well, VIII, 187; Lenten diet, VI, 210; purgings, I, 213; Saint Vincent suggests purging to relieve headache, I, 574; bloodletting, I, 488; II, 488; VII, 130–31; tea every day, V, 471, 556; therapeutic water, I, 563; Saint Vincent encourages her to take the waters, II, 329; he said in 1647 she was "as if dead" for ten years, III, 257; IX, 256; and in 1657, for twenty years, X, 301; health did not allow her to lead common life, IX, 135; X, 301, 579; XIIIb, 301, 324; or dress like other Sisters, II, 198–99; had to eat food different from Community, X, 579; last illness, VIII, 280, 288, 294, 297, 300; X, 585; death, VIII, 312, 315, 317, 322, 324, 351, 394; other mentions, I, 330, 507.

Miscellanea: Why she is called "Mademoiselle," I, 23–24; understands Latin, I, 76; gives pictures to young women, I, 71; to Saint Vincent, I, 81–82; to Saint-Lazare, II, 626, 630; painting for Foundling Home, I, 446; Saint Vincent regrets that Fr. Dehorgny left without giving her money, I, 508; named in Mme Goussault's will, XIIIb, 392–93, 396; Saint Vincent asks for topics for following day's conference, I, 575; she receives report from meeting of Ladies, II, 25; Saint Vincent sends her woman seeking work as chambermaid, II, 338; honor received in Nantes humbles her, III, 23; speaks well of M. Cornier's niece, a Daughter of Charity, VIII, 137–38; relationship with Marguerite Naseau, IX, 65; reference to her role as Superioress, X, 529, 548, 553, 559, 562, 566, 592, 593; other mentions, I, *xxv, xxvi*; II, 81, 109–11, 613, 642, 644; XIIIb, 118, 122, 205, 225, 231, 395.

Louise Michel, Daughter of Charity in Nantes - Biographical data, V, 33; sent to Nantes, IX, 430; recalled, V, 33, 57.

Louise-Christine, Daughter of Charity - See **Rideau**.

Louistre (Jean), Priest of the Mission - Biographical data, II, 28; XI, 256; giving mission in Saint-Prix, II, 28; mission at Court, XI, 256; departure from Company, II, 321.

Louistre (Robert), Brother of the Mission - Biographical data, I, 474; II, 55; at Saint-Lazare, I, 474; II, 55; arranges place on Châteaudun coaches for Saint Louise, I, 593.

Lourdelot (Jean), Pastor in Châtillon - Resigns parish, XIIIa, 44–47.

Louvain, town in Belgium - Baïus [De Bay], Doctor and Dean of University of Louvain, XIIIa, 166.

Louvel (Abraham), priest of Le Mans diocese - III, 290.

Louvet (Antoine), Pastor of Saint-André in Joigny - XIIIb, 65–66.

Louvetel (Guy), seminarian of the Mission - Biographical data, VIII, 295; dimissorial letters, VIII, 295–96.

Louviers, town in Eure - Possessed nuns of Louviers, II, 456.

Louvre, royal palace in Paris - IX, 315; XIIIa, 343; silence observed in palace, XI, 201; printing office of Louvre, V, 157.

Love of God - Conferences, IX, 365–79; XI, 32–33, 34–36; mention of another conference, XII, 421; what love of God is, IX, 17; affective and effective love, IX, 373–74, 466–68, 470–71; reasons to love God, IX, 365–73; not straining to attract God to self, XI, 207–08; example of Francis de Sales, XIIIa, 83–84; vocation of Missionary is to make God loved; so he himself must love God, XII, 215–16; love must inspire all our actions, IX, 18; love creatures only for God and according to God, II, 122; means to acquire and preserve love of God in us, IX, 18, 370, 376–78; effects of this love, X, 286; external signs of this love, IX, 366–70; one can love God wholeheartedly without feeling sweetness of this love, IX, 373; avoid excess in making acts of love of God, XI, 203–04; without balance in this, bodily health will suffer effects, laxity will be consequence, XI, 204–07.

Loyac (Jean de), chaplain of Duchesse d'Aiguillon - Biographical data, I, 322.

Lucas (Antoine), Priest of the Mission - Biographical data, I, 39; II, 27; III, 92; IV, 97–98; V, 101; letters from Saint Vincent, I,

279, 421; in Montmirail, I, 441; in Joigny, I, 515; in Saint-Prix, II, 27; in Varize, II, 347; in Le Mans, III, 612; IV, 97; mention of letter from Saint Vincent, I, 546; mention of letter to Saint Vincent, V, 261; difficult disposition, II, 211; talent as controversialist, I, 277; Fr. Olier asks for him to convert heretic, II, 345; Saint Vincent upbraids him for treating heretics with contempt, I, 279; esteemed by Fr. de Condren, II, 346; in Paris, I, 58; XIIIa, 235, 286; giving mission at Berry-au-Bac, where he falls ill, I, 95; giving missions with Fr. Portail, I, 110, 275, 279; Saint Vincent urges him to rest in Montmirail before going back to work, I, 421, 441; in Montmirail, I, 441–42, 467; giving missions in Joigny, I, 515; sent to Sancey, I, 530; Jacques Chiroye sent to Joigny to care for Fr. Lucas, I, 545; needs to be bled more, I, 546; in Saint-Prix, II, 27; in Alet, II, 114, 211, 221; after returning to Saint-Lazare, goes to give missions, II, 309; at 1642 Assembly, II, 343; XIIIa, 323, 331, 396; giving mission in Varize, II, 347; at Saint-Lazare, III, 92; XIIIb, 279; in Richelieu, III, 145; Superior in Le Mans, III, 314, 568, 611–12; IV, 172, 564; V, 101; VIII, 613; missions, III, 314, 608; at 1651 Assembly, XIIIa, 369, 372, 374, 397; account of Assembly, XIIIa, 374; opinion on vows, XIIIa, 383; in Sedan, V, 198, 209, 223, 237, 250, 261; other mentions, I, 39, 41, 45, 47, 53, 456; XIIIa, 344.

Lucas (Jacques), Priest of the Mission - Biographical data, II, 675; IV, 95; V, 625; VII, 373; vows delayed, II, 675; named Superior in Luçon, IV, 95–96; Superior in Luçon, IV, 119, 149; VIII, 607; act of disobedience, IV, 149; in Saintes, V, 625; health, V, 625–26; in Notre-Dame-de-Lorm, VI, 476–77; VII, 373, 431.

Lucas (M.), Priest of the Mission - See **Arimondo** (Luca).

Lucas (M.) - VII, 394.

Lucas (Martin), Provost of collegial church of Notre-Dame-de-Coëffort in Le Mans - Benefactor of Le Mans Missionaries, to whom he gave this church and rights on Hôtel-Dieu in return for pension, III, 29; IV, 275; VIII, 613; two-thirds of which he proposes to cancel by payment, VI, 378–79; other mention, IV, 424.

Luce (Jeanne), Daughter of Charity - With galley convicts, X, 517; other mention, XIIIb, 227.

Lucé, village in France - II, 226.

Lucerna, town in Piedmont - Good results of mission given in neighboring locality, V, 638; Fr. Martin scheduled for mission in Lucerna, VI, 2.

Lucien (Fr.) - See **Hérault** (Lucien).

Lucifer, archangel who became devil - Descent into hell caused by disunion, IX, 81, 85; envy and pride, IX, 558.

Luçon, town in Vendée - Theologian and Pastor of Luçon, II, 144; Bishop: see Pierre de **Nivelle**; letters of Saint Vincent to Luçon Missionary, II, 96, 191; see **Chiroye**, **Le Soudier** (Samson); foundation contract for Richelieu house imposes obligation of giving missions in Luçon diocese, I, 514; XIIIa, 317; foundation of house, I, 514; II, 79; VIII, 607; foundation contract, XIIIa, 317; Saint Vincent thanks Fr. Codoing for agreeing to go there, I, 514; Masses said regularly for intention of foundation's donors, VIII, 607; repairs and furnishing of house, II, 95, 353; mission in Luçon, II, 275, 310, 397, 405; postulant from Luçon, VIII, 306; Missionaries leave, but return at end of 1646 at request of Bishop and Chapter, III, 144–45; foundation of Claude Thouvant, III, 145, 147; Fr. Chiroye receives orders to go there to await personnel being prepared for him, III, 145–47; Saint Vincent cautions him about costly plan, III, 526–27; refuses priory Fr. Pignay, Dean of Luçon, wishes to unite to Luçon house, V, 100, 120; Fr. Pignay's foundation, VII, 182–83; missions, III, 490; V, 101; VI, 611; ordinands, II, 353–54; V, 100; visitation of Luçon house by Fr. Dehorgny, II, 279; by Fr. Lambert, III, 217; by Saint Vincent, III, 409, 425, 428; by Fr. Lambert, IV, 149; by Fr. Berthe, VI, 505, 536–37; by Fr. Dehorgny, VIII, 222, 241, 253, 561.

List of Superiors and history of house, VIII, 607; personnel: see **Bonaflos**, **Boussordec**, **Chiroye**, **Cuissot** (Gilbert), **Delaunay**, **Durot**, **Férot**, **Le Boysne**, **Le Soudier** (Samson), **Lucas** (Jacques), **Rivet** (François); other mentions, I, 403, 419, 556; VIII, 412; XIIIa, 323, 329. See also ***Chasnais***, **Constantin**, **Pignay**.

Lucy (Saint) - Feast: December 13, XIIIa, 1, 2, 6.

Ludes, village in Marne - Mission given, VII, 178.

Ludovisi (Ludovico), Cardinal - Member of Congregation of *Propaganda Fide*, XIIIa, 229; reply of Nuncio to *Propaganda Fide*, XIIIa, 238–39; Nuncio recommends to him Congregation of the Mission, which is requesting approval in Rome, XIIIa, 242, 245; present at meeting of Cardinals who rejected petition of Saint Vincent, XIIIa, 250.

Ludovisi (Niccolò), Cardinal - See **Albergati-Ludovisi** (Niccolò).

Luke (Saint) - Cited, XII, 12, 317, 318, 319; XIIIa, 119; feast day, XI, 321; other mention, XIIIb, 437.

Lukewarmness - See **Tepidity**.

Lullen (Marie), Daughter of Charity - In Le Mans, IX, 435–36; in Nanterre, IX, 435–36; sent to Montreuil-sur-Mer, XIIIb,

273–74; love for little children, IX, 435–36; for poor, IX, 435; humility and other virtues, IX, 436–37; conference on her virtues, IX, 435–37.

Lumague (André), banker in Lyons - Biographical data, I, 539; contacts with Saint Vincent, I, 539; II, 245, 248, 250, 252, 255.

Lumague (Jean-André), seigneur de Villers-sous-Saint-Leu - Biographical data; Saint Vincent accompanies him to Villers, I, 235; in Tivoli, where wife died, XI, 341.

Lumague (Marie de) - See **Pollalion** [**Poulallion**].

Lumsden (Thomas), Priest of the Mission - Biographical data, IV, 373; V, 129; VI, 184; XI, 166; mention of letter to Saint Vincent, XI, 176; proposed to *Propaganda Fide* for Scotland, IV, 373, 478; ministers in Scotland amid persecutions, V, 129–30, 148–49; VI, 184, 545; XI, 166, 177, 261.

Lunéville, town in Meurthe-et-Moselle - Aldermen thank Saint Vincent for aid to inhabitants, II, 289.

Lunis (Mlle) - III, 520.

Luther (Martin) - Heresy, II, 46; III, 40; IV, 209, 213; XI, 30; XIIIa, 164; Saint Vincent refers to him as heretical priest, XII, 76; other mention, III, 362.

Lutherans - Opposed to King of Poland, XI, 274; esteem for Clement VIII, XI, 317–18.

Luxembourg, palace in Paris - VIII, 473.

Luynes (Louis-Charles d'Albert, Duc de) - Won over to Jansenism, VI, 651; XIIIb, 310–11.

Luzarches, town in Val-d'Oise - Mission given, I, 275; Fr. de Sergis passes through with troops for whom he is chaplain, I, 334, 338.

Luserna San Giovanni, abbey - VIII, 272.

Luzarches (M. de) - I, 149; II, 426.

Lyons, town in Rhône - Bishops: see Denis de **Marquemont**, Alphonse-Louis Duplessis de **Richelieu**, Camille de Neufville de **Villeroy**; Saint Vincent would be happy to see Missionaries established in Lyons; waits for God to manifest His Will, V, 42, 412; proposal made to him; accepts in principle, V, 194; rejects conditions imposed, V, 429–30; VI, 331; journey of Missionaries to Lyons, II, 160, 262, 426; V, 456–58; VI, 88, 127, 137, 262, 300; VII, 151, 291, 316, 586, 59; on Fr. Alméras's route from Cahors to Annecy, III, 125.

Congregations established, or on point of being established, in Lyons: see **Missionaries of Forez**, **Missionaries of Lyons**, **Saint-Joseph** (Congregation); Visitation, V, 272,

275; King's journey to Lyons, VII, 320; question of meeting here of King with Court of Savoy, VII, 320, 378; Council of Lyons, XIIIa, 380; Lyons coaches, III, 273, 389; V, 170; VI, 120, 578, 593; VII, 81, 228, 499; VIII, 23; money left there for Annecy, II, 245; merchant from Lyons, II, 450; bookseller, see **Courcilly**, (M. de) II, 118; other merchants: see **Delaforcade**, **Lumague**, **Mascarini**, **Turmeau**. Other mentions, I, 404; II, 118; III, 446; IV, 27, 294; V, 132, 245, 550; VI, 383, 391, 517, 637; VII, 57, 416, 420, 518; VIII, 448, 532, 542; IX, 192; XII, 190; XIIIa, 44, 45, 46, 49, 50, 56; XIIIb, 8, 19, 20.

M

Mac Donald, laird of part of islands of Uist and Skye - Fr. Duggan [Duiguin] plans to evangelize his lands, V, 121.

Macé (Jean-Baptiste), priest of Saint-Sulpice, I, 177.

Macé (M.) - Member of Charity of Argenteuil, XIIIb, 107.

Macé (René), priest of Saint-Sulpice, I, 177.

Mac Fimine, laird of part of Isle of Skye - Fr. Duggan [Duiguin] plans to evangelize his lands, V, 122.

Macheret, hamlet in Saint-Just-Sauvage (Marne) - Monastery of Order of Grandmont, IV, 309.

Machiavelli (Nicolò) - Author of works on Roman Index, XIIIa, 364.

Machicore (Andian or Dian), son-in-law of King Ramach of Madagascar - Baptized by Jesuit, VI, 244; it was believed he could change weather at will, III, 564–65; allowed son to be baptized, V, 287; predicted that French would soon be expelled from island, V, 287; taken prisoner; lived on good terms with Fr. Bourdaise, V, 519–20; one of his sons taken hostage, V, 526; his mother requests Baptism before dying, VI, 223.

Machicores, region in Madagascar - VI, 221.

Machon (Louis), Canon in Toul - Dedicated *Ten Meditations* to Saint Vincent, XIIIa, 148.

Mac Leod, laird of part of Isle of Skye - Fr. Duggan [Duiguin] plans to evangelize his lands, V, 122.

Mâcon, town in Saône-et-Loire - Confraternity of Charity; difficulties and successes, I, 281; report of Abbé Laplatte on beginning of Macon Charity, XIIIb, 67; from town archives, XIIIb, 73; from report of capitular deliberations, XIIIb, 78; night shelter for poor transients, XIIIb, 69; Bishops: see Gaspard **Dinet**, Louis **Dinet**, Jean de **Lingendes**; value of diocese, IV,

85; Saint-Nizier Church, XIIIb, 68, 69, 72, 77; Saint-Pierre Church, XIIIb, 74, 76, 78; Saint-Vincent Church, XIIIb, 75; other mention, XIIIb, 79.

Macqueville (Charles de), Bishop of Soissons - Approves Charity of Courboin, XIIIb, 91–93.

Madagascar - *Geographical elements*: various pieces of information, III, 279–80, 544–45; part of East Indies, IV, 72; XI, 162, 180, 184, 270, 357, 364; regions of Madagascar: see ***Amboule*** (valley), ***Anossi*** (region), ***Antavares, Machicores, Mahafalles, Manamboules, Mandrare, Matatanes***; small towns of Madagascar: see ***Fanshere, Ikombo, Imoro, Tolagnaro***.

Products of country: agricultural, III, 545; V, 311–12; animals, III, 545; price of cows, III, 578; precious stones, XII, 301; competency of goldsmiths, V, 522–23.

Inhabitants: foreigners: Portuguese and Dutch, III, 553; French colony: see below; indigenous races, III, 544, 545; natives are charitable and gentle, V, 308; strongly inclined to sexual indulgence, III, 551, 573; V, 300, 517–18; VI, 236, 249; very abstemious, V, 308; government and administration, III, 544; tyranny of masters, III, 551–52; V, 309; chiefs of Madagascar: see ***Boulle, Machicore, Madamboro, Mananghe, Masse, Panola, Ramach, Ramassy, Ramouse, Sero***; slaves, III, 551; V, 309; VI, 244; forest thieves, III, 544; V, 519.

Languages: III, 576; V, 309–10, 525; XIIIa, 187; dictionary of Malagasy language by M. de Flacourt; dedication to Saint Vincent, XIIIa, 185.

Hardships: ravages caused by grasshoppers, III, 550; VI, 219, 248; food shortage two or three months a year, V, 522; famine, V, 523; VI, 243; illnesses among foreigners caused by climate and food, V, 300–01; many deaths, III, 575; especially among youngest and most robust, III, 577; ravages of dysentery among natives, VI, 247.

Customs: food, III, 545, 574; V, 308–09; clothing, V, 309; dances, V, 309, 524–25; punishment for thieves, III, 551; for adulterous women, V, 517; marriage, III, 551–52; VI, 244, 253; fate of infants born during night of Saturday and Sunday, III, 552; certain roots produce milk for old women; grandmothers nurse grandchildren, V, 308; how mothers treat children, V, 308; names given to children, III, 552; remedies, V, 308; funerals, III, 552–53.

Religion: beliefs, III, 545–46, 553, 557; V, 525–26; demons, VI, 245; soothsayers, VI, 245–46; priests, III, 546, 558, 563; V, 525–27; VI, 247; superstitions, III, 547, 564; VI, 246–47; idols or *olis*, III, 549–50, 565; V, 526; VI, 246; exorcisms, III, 549; practices borrowed from Mohammedanism, III, 545–46;

circumcision, III, 546; V, 519; feasts, III, 547–48; fasts, III, 546–47; cult of dead, V, 519.

French in Madagascar: navigation companies: see **East Indies** (Company), **La Meilleraye** (Duc de); governors in Madagascar: see **Flacourt** (Étienne de), **Pronis** (M. de), **Du Rivaux** (M.); how Frenchmen are recruited for Madagascar, III, 577; dissolute life of some, III, 572, 579; V, 300, 517; bloody clashes between French and natives, III, 571, 578; V, 287; French casualties, III, 575–76; V, 287; natives set fire to Fort Dauphin, V, 287–88; ill-fated journey of French to Imaphalles, V, 507–08, 510, 519; French take and keep hostages, V, 520; two buildings in Fort Dauphin catch fire, V, 507; burning of Fort Dauphin, V, 509; reconstruction of Fort Dauphin and church, V, 509–10; death of M. de Pronis, Governor, V, 520–21; assassination of M. de la Forest, V, 527; revolt against French, VI, 220–21; return of French expedition from interior, VI, 249; marriage of French with native women, V, 508, 517; VI, 219; native children in France, III, 560; V, 419, 425; VI, 221; VII, 91, 102, 104, 107, 259; XI, 269.

Madagascar mission: evangelization before 1648; sojourn of two priests in 1615, III, 555–56; VI, 244; of Fr. de Bellebarbe, secular priest: see **Bellebarbe**; religious state of island in 1648, III, 553–56; letter of Saint Vincent to Missionary, V, 566; qualifications for Missionary destined for Madagascar, III, 576–78; V, 299; things needed by mission, III, 574–75; V, 290–98, 523; *Propaganda Fide* reserves Madagascar mission to Discalced Carmelites, III, 278; XIIIa, 361; Nuncio offers it to Saint Vincent, III, 278; XI, 373; XIIIa, 361; travel authorization for Frs. Nacquart and Gondrée, XIIIa, 359; advice to Fr. Nacquart, III, 278–84; Fr. Nacquart thanks him; asks for information, III, 286–88; *Propaganda Fide* grants two Missionaries powers of Missionaries Apostolic, IV, 92; mention of this privilege, IV, 337; *Propaganda* erects Madagascar mission, names Fr. Nacquart Prefect, XIIIa, 361; mention of this appointment, IV, 92, 337; V, 551; VIII, 281–82; Fr. Gondrée writes from Tours to tell Saint Vincent secular priest wishes to be part of voyage, III, 289; from Richelieu to La Rochelle, III, 539; from La Rochelle to Saint Vincent Island off Cape Verde, III, 330–31, 539–40; on Saint Vincent Island; Portuguese Christians, III, 330, 540; Fr. Nacquart writes to Saint Vincent from Cape Verde, III, 330; from Saint Vincent Island to Cape of Good Hope, III, 540–41; stop at Saldanha Bay, III, 541–42; from Cape of Good Hope to Madagascar, III, 542; occupations of Missionaries aboard ship, III, 542–44; arrival in Madagascar after voyage of six and a half months, III, 542.

Death of Fr. Gondrée: see **Gondrée**; Fr. Nacquart tells Saint Vincent of death, III, 434; report of Fr. Nacquart, III, 538; Saint Vincent distributes copies, IV, 89, 109, 517; other letters of Fr. Nacquart, III, 570, 592, 598.

Ministries, XI, 192; ministry of Missionaries among indigenous people, III, 554–66; among French, III, 554, 556, 572–73, 576–77, 581; conversion of heretics, III, 554; IV, 93, VI, 240; baptisms, III, 555, 560, 562, 563, 566, 597; IV, 93; V, 286, 290; XI, 270; XIIIa, 186–87; laying foundation stone of church, III, 566; V, 288; plan for school in Fanshere, III, 573; picture catechism, III, 563, 565; V, 516; difficulties of Fr. Nacquart with M. de Flacourt, Governor, III, 570–72, 580, 593; plan for journey to France, III, 595–96; death, IV, 518; V, 285, 306; mention of death, V, 512, 525; VI, 216, 253; VIII, 181, 552.

Saint Vincent proposes to *Propaganda Fide* sending of new Missionaries, IV, 93; list of proposed Missionaries, IV, 93; Fr. Dufour and Bro. Forest are among them, IV, 109, 118; faculties granted to Missionaries by Holy Office, IV, 93; XIIIa, 362–65; Saint Vincent looks forward to departure of ship, IV, 109, 321, 329; requests *Propaganda Fide*, through Nuncio, authority to choose four Missionaries destined for Madagascar, to grant them usual powers, and to name one of them Prefect of Mission, in case Fr. Nacquart has died, IV, 338; embarkation postponed, IV, 354, 363, 518; Saint Vincent informs Prefect of *Propaganda Fide*, IV, 369, 443; upcoming departure, IV, 522; V, 71, 73, 76; Saint Vincent proposes to *Propaganda Fide* names of Frs. Dufour and Mousnier, IV, 525; tells Cardinal Barberini of imminent departure of two priests, with agreement of Nuncio; will send names to Rome, V, 78; requests from *Propaganda Fide*, for Fr. Bourdaise, powers of Missionary Apostolic, and for Fr. Mousnier those of Prefect of Mission, V, 551; mention of conference on "Journey and Mission of Madagascar," XII, 419.

Frs. Mousnier and Bourdaise, and Bro. Forest have left Paris, V, 82; from Paris to Nantes, V, 276–78; from Nantes to Saint-Nazaire, V, 280–81; from Saint Nazaire to Madagascar with stops at Cape Verde and Cape of Good Hope, V, 281–85, 302–05; arrival in Madagascar, V, 285, 305–07; letters of Fr. Mousnier, V, 276, 292; of Fr. Bourdaise, V, 298, 302, 507; Saint Vincent mentions them, XI, 213; ministry of Missionaries among indigenous people, V, 290, 310–12, 515–20, 523–24, 527; VI, 217–19, 220–24, 242–45, 246–51; among French, V, 300, 517; VI, 220; conversion of heretics, V, 525; VI, 252; baptisms, V, 299, 311, 515, 516, 518, 522–23, 528; VI, 223, 244, 248, 250; religious marriages, V, 299, 517; VI, 219, 249;

number of neophytes, VI, 233; gifts, V, 300; Fr. Bourdaise gives remedies to sick, V, 290, 518; VI, 223, 246–47, 248; church fire, V, 508–09; transformation of hut into chapel, V, 509; reconstruction of church, VI, 234, 236; plan for hospital and boarding school, X, 96; death of Fr. Mousnier, V, 510–14; mention of death, V, 637; VI, 21–22, 38, 216; VIII, 181, 552–53.

Missionaries appeal to priests in France for help, III, 572, 576, 581, 599; V, 290–91, 299; VI, 215, 224, 251, 252; to Brothers, III, 574, 581; V, 290, 299; VI, 215; to Daughters of Charity, III, 573; V, 278–79, 300; IX, 409; X, 82, 96; request for foundlings, V, 278, 279; X, 96; Daughters of Charity volunteer for Madagascar, V, 278; VI, 269; VII, 88, 473.

Next departure of Missionaries, V, 419, 424; Saint Vincent requests usual powers from *Propaganda Fide* for Frs. Dufour, Prévost, and Feydin, V, 430–31; advice to Missionaries about to embark, V, 440–41; Duc de la Meilleraye agrees that Saint Vincent send Missionaries on ships of Company of Indies, XI, 294; another sailing envisioned, V, 577; four ships leave La Rochelle for Madagascar with three Priests of the Mission and one secular priest, VI, 12, 224; secular priest is drowned, VI, 12–13, 225; XI, 370–71; occupations of Missionaries at sea, VI, 14–15, 226–29; illness and death of Fr. de Belleville, VI, 15–18, 227–30; conversion of heretic, VI, 19, 231; creation of confraternity for conversion of inhabitants of Madagascar, VI, 231; preaching of Fr. Dufour, VI, 240; VIII, 553; arrival in Madagascar, VI, 231–34; feast of Blessed Sacrament, VI, 234; letter of Fr. Dufour, VI, 12; Fr. Dufour leaves for Île Sainte-Marie, VI, 235; VIII, 554; dies there, VI, 237–39; VIII, 254; Fr. Prévost likewise dies there, VI, 241; Fr. Bourdaise informs Saint Vincent of death of three confreres, VI, 214; saint mentions this loss, VI, 436; adds long report about island and ministry, VI, 216; arrival in Nantes of ship with these two letters, VI, 440, 443, 445, 447, 451–452, 453, 469, 471, 475, 481, 488–489, 492, 501; XI, 367, 370; Saint Vincent tells confreres of death of Fr. Dufour and companions: see **Dufour** (Claude); distributes copies of Fr. Bourdaise's report, VI, 35, 38, 460, 463, 478, 589, 604; VII, 29, 37, 84, 180; is asked to have them printed but refuses, VI, 35, 199, 604; death of Fr. Bourdaise; Saint Vincent writes to him, VIII, 180.

Saint Vincent asks *Propaganda Fide* for usual powers for Frs. Herbron and Boussordec, destined for Madagascar, V, 576–77; Duc de la Meilleraye complains that Saint Vincent designates only one priest for him, XI, 324; Frs. Boussordec, Herbron, and Bro. Delaunay embark at Nantes, VI, 112, 124, 128, 140; shipwrecked in Loire, VI, 149–50, 159; XI, 333–34, 336–38, 340; shipwreck does not discourage Missionaries, ready to depart again, XI, 374.

Saint Vincent asks *Propaganda Fide* for usual powers for Frs. Laudin and Arnoul, named for Madagascar, VI, 210; counts on departure of ship, VI, 270, 272, 495, 525, 570, 583; VII, 29, 61, 67, 68, 73, 75, 91; rumor that Duc de la Meilleraye, convinced Saint Vincent prefers former Company of Indies to his, is appealing to Capuchins, VII, 37, 57; Saint Vincent writes to apologize and explain himself, VII, 60–61.

Preparations for sending more Missionaries, VII, 84; Frs. Le Blanc (Charles), de Fontaines, Arnoul, Daveroult, and Bro. Delaunay leave for Nantes, VII, 101–02, 104, 107, 112; embarkation, VII, 125, 128; storm; ship takes refuge at Lisbon, then returns to sea without Fr. Daveroult; Spanish seize it and take passengers to Spain, VII, 211, 213, 215, 216; letter of Saint Vincent to Frs. Arnoul and de Fontaines; tells of Fr. Le Blanc's return to Paris, VII, 257; journey to Saintes of Bro. Delaunay and two native boys VII, 257, 258–59; Frs. de Fontaines and Arnoul return to Paris, VII, 283, 616; Saint Vincent urges Fr. Daveroult, who remained in Lisbon, to return to Paris; indicates how to do it, VII, 616.

New departure planned; Saint Vincent is disposed to send two or three priests, VII, 473, 496; voyage deferred, VII, 526, 530, 541; Saint Vincent considers Frs. Herbron and Turpin, VII, 526–27; proposes latter to *Propaganda Fide*, VII, 576; preparations for departure, VIII, 90, 96, 115, 145, 160, 169, 185, 186; Saint Vincent asks from *Propaganda Fide* usual powers for Fr. Étienne, VIII, 147; title of Prefect of Mission for Fr. Bourdaise, or, in case of his demise, for one chosen by Nuncio, VIII, 282; announces intention of sending three priests and Brother on Duc de la Meilleraye's ship, and two priests on vessel of Company of Indies, VIII, 179; informs Fr. Bourdaise that he is sending him four priests and a Brother, VIII, 182; promises Duke, who demands this, not to send anyone on latter vessel, VIII, 200; gives notice of this decision to Fr. Étienne and to Director of Company of Indies, VIII, 201; gift of Fr. Étienne to Madagascar mission, XII, 330; advice of Saint Vincent to Bro. Patte, VIII, 208–09.

Journey from Paris to Nantes, VIII, 555–56; in Nantes, VIII, 556–57; Frs. Daveroult, Feydin, and de Fontaines go from Nantes to La Rochelle by land; Fr. Étienne and Bro. Patte by sea, VIII, 557; former wait at La Rochelle for other two, VIII, 219, 221, 225, 229, 231; whose vessel is shipwrecked, VIII, 240, 246, 251, 255–56, 558–61; and who, disembarking at Saint-Jean-de-Luz, go to La Rochelle from there, VIII, 240, 561; at La Rochelle and on board ship in roadstead, VIII, 561–64, 241, 247, 249, 252, 256; in Canary Islands, VIII, 564; from Canaries to Cape Verde, VIII, 565; at Cape Verde, VIII, 566; from Cape Verde to Cape of Good Hope, VIII, 568–69; occupations of Missionaries during voyage, VIII, 570–73; sojourn of ten to twelve months at Cape of Good Hope, VIII, 573–92; from Cape of Good Hope to Amsterdam, VIII, 592–94; from Amsterdam to Paris, VIII, 594–97; report of voyage by Fr. Étienne, VIII, 552; Saint Vincent recommends Madagascar Missionaries to prayers of confreres, XI, 214, 391; praises their zeal, XI, 192; XII, 198; admirable perseverance, XI, 368, 372; XII, 48; what this mission cost him, VI, 179; VII, 60; list of Superiors and history of mission, VIII, 616; other mentions, III, 372; IV, 107, 431; V, 148, 566; VI, 348, 455, 565; XI, 62, 294; XIIIa, 208. See also ***East Indies***, **La Meilleraye** (Maréchal de).

Madamboro (Andrian), brother of King of Madagascar - III, 564.

Madame Royale [**Marie-Christine of France**], Duchess Regent - Biographical data, VI, 495; M. Tevenot, her physician, V, 253; Jean Martin has found favor with her, V, 635; she wants him to give mission near Turin, VI, 495, 497, 510, 521, 525, 581–82; VII, 583; XI, 380; is pleased with results, VII, 89; Fr. Le Vazeux asked to help with mission, VI, 525; she sends troops to Bra, VI, 639; distressed at disunion in Bra, VII, 89; priests in Turin open mission in Bra, XI, 380; joy at its success, VII, 118–19; efforts to establish Congregation of the Mission in house of Sant'Antonio Fathers in Piedmont, VIII, 101–102; mission given on her lands in Cherasco, VII, 583; VIII, 29; funds establishment in Piedmont, VIII, 101–02; other mentions, VI, 3; VIII, 618.

Madeleine, monastery - See ***Sainte-Madeleine***.

Madeleine, Daughter of Charity - Death, V, 44.

Madeleine, Daughter of Charity - VI, 380.

Madeleine, Daughter of Charity - Rather strong passions, I, 239.

Madrid, old section in suburbs of Paris - I, 400.

Maecenas, Roman chevalier, patron of Virgil and Horace - I, 6.

Magalotti (Cardinal Lorenzo) - Member of Congregation of *Propaganda Fide*, XIIIa, 229, 239.

Magdalen (Saint) - See **Mary Magdalen** (Saint).

Magdalens (Congregation) - Some take vows; others do not, V, 320–21; other mention, VII, 272.

Mage (Collège) - II, 555.

Magi - Expressed gratitude at birth of Jesus, XIIIa, 40.

Magnac (Antoine de Salignac, Marquis de) - Biographical data, IV, 125; VII, 548; founder of Magnac Seminary, IV, 125; asks

Alain de Solminihac for priest, IV, 125; confidence he inspires in this Prelate, VII, 548, 550, 628.

Magnac-Laval, village in Haute-Vienne - Seminary established here, IV, 125.

Maguelonne, collège in Toulouse - III, 197.

Mahafalles, region of Madagascar - VI, 221, 249.

Maheut (Nicolas), Sub-Prior of monks at Saint-Lazare - lodging at Saint-Lazare, XIIIa, 268; his brother, IV, 314; death from plague, I, 186; other mentions, I, 135; XIIIa, 263.

Maignelay (Claude-Marguerite de Gondi, Marquise de) - Biographical data, II, 109; III, 276; IV, 6–7; VI, 550–51; XI, 160; letters from Saint Vincent, III, 276; to Saint Vincent, II, 109, 111, 125; Bro. Jourdain, her equerry and majordomo, I, 42; XI, 352; mistrusts Mazarin, XIIIa, 155; contacts with Saint Vincent, II, 125, 126–27, 218; IV, 23; requests Daughters of Charity for Charity of Nanteuil-le-Haudouin, II, 110, 111; does not insist; has found good servant girl, II, 125; interest in Nanterre schools, II, 206; in Daughters of Charity of Saint-Roch parish in Paris, IV, 7; attempts to get Saint Vincent to resume direction of Paris Visitandines, III, 276; XI, 160; benefactor of Daughters of Providence, VI, 550–51.

Maillard [**Maillart**] (Antoine), Priest of the Mission - Biographical data, III, 286; IV, 40; VI, 40; VII, 297; VIII, 125; desires to go to Madagascar, III, 286, 597; proposed to *Propaganda Fide*, IV, 93; praise for him, IV, 40; Procurator in Richelieu, III, 287; IV, 40; Procurator at Saint-Lazare, III, 286; IV, 321; VI, 40, 409–10, 412, 553; VII, 297, 317; VIII, 125, 174, 218, 295, 414; with dying Saint Vincent, XIIIa, 203, 205; at death of saint, XIIIa, 206.

Maillard (Fr.), chaplain at Hôtel-Dieu of Angers - IV, 568.

Maillet (Mlle) - Journey through Touraine, VI, 591; dissatisfaction with Superior of Toul Missionaries, VIII, 492.

Maillezais (Diocese) - Transfer of Episcopal See to La Rochelle, III, 20; Bishops: see Henri de **Béthune**, Jacques-Raoul de **La Guibourgère**.

Maillotins - Revolt, IV, 461.

Mailly (Mlle) - VI, 503.

Maine (Province) - III, 26; VI, 277.

Mainz (Council) - Condemns those who deny universality of redemption, III, 324.

Maiour, parish in Narbonne - VIII, 478.

Maisonneuve (M. de) - IV, 8.

Maisons, village near Paris - I, 68; XIIIb, 206.

Majorca - V, 339; VI, 10; XI, 288.

Maladrerie - Farm belonging to house of Montmirail Missionaries, II, 547.

Malagasy - Language of Madagascar being learned by Frs. Nacquart and Gondrée, III, 331; also studied by Fr. Mousnier on voyage to Madagascar, V, 283; Fr. Mousnier gives instructions on how to prepare to learn it, V, 292; Fr. Bourdaise learns it, V, 305; description of language, V, 309–10; Saint Vincent encourages those setting out for Madagascar to study language, V, 441.

Malassis (Michel), priest in Rouen - XIIIa, 26.

Maldachini (Francesco), Cardinal - Offers house to Missionaries in Rome, VII, 629.

Maldonia - Prince of Maldonia, VI, 110.

Malemaison (M. de) - VI, 585.

Malgouvernés Abbey - XIIIa, 53.

Malier (François), Bishop of Troyes - His part in uniting La Chaussée Priory to Congregation of the Mission, VIII, 612.

Malines, town in Belgium - Nicolas Étienne visits there on return from aborted journey to Madagascar, VIII, 596.

Mallet (Jean), Canon of Écouis - XIIIa, 26, 29, 30.

Malleville (M.), prisoner in Toulon - VI, 372.

Malta (Island) - V, 127; VI, 466; VII, 523; monk relegated there for favoring Jansenism, IV, 601; other mentions, V, 89, 132; VI, 466; VII, 523.

Malta (Knights) - Visits made by Missionaries in parishes dependent on Grand Priory, I, 380, 454, 528; generosity of Commander de Sillery in favor of Order, II, 135–36; victory of Knights of Malta over Turks, VI, 71; Knights of Malta, slaves in Tunis, VII, 101; two Commanders of Malta for Geneva diocese, II, 414; other mentions, II, 134; V, 405; XI, 303; XIIIa, 394. See also **Lascaris** (Paul).

Mamers, town in Sarthe - VII, 535.

Mammedie - See ***Hammamet***.

Manafiafy, roadstead of harbor in Madagascar - V, 285.

Manamboule (King) - Fr. Bourdaise takes two of his young sons to raise, VI, 236.

Manamboules, region in Madagascar - VI, 221, 236, 242.

Mananghe (Andrian or Dian), a King of Madagascar - V, 528; VI, 221.

Mance (Mlle) - Return from Canada, VII, 448.

Manceau (Françoise), Daughter of Charity, niece of Nicolas and Simon - Biographical data, VII, 191; XII, 34; in La Fère, VII, 191; sent to Calais, VII, 200; X, 440; dies in Calais, X, 440; XII, 34.

Manceau (Nicolas), Priest of the Mission, brother of Simon - Biographical data, IV, 208; other mention, XII, 34.

Manceau (Simon), Priest of the Mission, brother of Nicolas - Biographical data, III, 296; IV, 168; ordained priest in Richelieu, III, 296; death, IV, 208.

Manchon (M.) - Mission in faubourg Saint-Germain, XIIIa, 199.

Mancini (Francesco Maria), Cardinal - Biographical data, VIII, 349.

Mancini (Laure), niece of Mazarin - V, 58.

Mandrare, region of Madagascar - VI, 221.

Manessier (Nicolas), Jansenist theologian - Sent to Rome by Jansenists, IV, 581, 594.

Manferet (Pierre), in Langres - Saint Vincent tells him to take possession in his own name of Saint-Nicolas-de-Grosse-Sauve Priory, XIIIa, 67.

Mangabais [**Mangabe**], small island near Madagascar - V, 280.

Mansard (Marc), prisoner in Toulon - VI, 278, 360, 599, 617; VII, 123, 282.

Mantes, town in Yvelines - I, 474.

Marans, town in Charente-Maritimes - I, 6.

Marbais (M.), surveyor of Saint-Lazare - VI, 354.

Marbais (Antoine), prisoner in Toulon, son of M. Marbais - VI, 276, 370; VII, 50, 282.

Marbe (Fr.) - Preached at Saint-Jacques, recommending needs of Picards, XII, 367.

Marbeuf (Claude de), Chief Justice of Rennes Parlement - Saint Vincent recommends Fr. de Beaumont, imprisoned for Saint-Méen affair, III, 52.

Marca (Pierre de), Bishop of Couserans, then Archbishop of Toulouse - Biographical data, VII, 547; attitude in dispute on probabilism, VII, 547, 549; requests Daughters of Charity for diocese, X, 317, 364; influence in nomination of Bishops in Catalonia, XIIIa, 150; other mention, III, 241.

Marceille (Nicolas), Priest of the Mission - Biographical data, I, 472; Procurator at Saint-Lazare, I, 472, 478–79, 480, 520; other mention, I, 304.

Marcellus (Saint), Pope - Legend has it that Emperor Maxentius obliged him to work as a stable hand, XI, 18.

Marchais, village in Aisne - Mission given there, XI, 29; Jean Bécu is there, I, 466, 468.

Marchand (M.), banker in Rome - Contacts with Saint Vincent and with Superior of Missionaries in Rome, I, 148, 176, 244, 539, 586, 591; II, 17–18, 64, 172, 359, 431; Saint Vincent tells Fr. Codoing to borrow money from him, II, 296; saint repays money Fr. Codoing borrowed from Marchand, II, 395; reference to letter he wrote to Saint Vincent, II, 426; asks Fr. Codoing if he can do anything with his help to resolve Saint-Yves affair, II, 433; his agent in Lyons, II, 450.

Marchand (M.) - At Cape of Good Hope, VIII, 586.

Marchand (M.) - Disagreement with Superior of Le Mans Missionaries, V, 600.

Marchant (Jacques), author of *Hortus Pastorum* - V, 297; XIIIa, 152.

Marchant (M.) - Member of Charity of Joigny, XIIIb, 66.

Marchefroy, village in Eure-et-Loir - Mission given there, VIII, 258.

Marchenoir, town in Loir-et-Cher - Mission given there, 348.

Marches, region of Central Italy - Mission given there, VI, 636.

Marcheville (Comte de), French Ambassador to Turkey - Asks for Missionaries, I, 246.

Marcheville (M. de) - Gives half of house in Paris to Abbé de Saint-Cyran, XIIIa, 122.

Marciac, town in Gers - Dominicans, III, 386.

Marcillac (Sylvestre de Cruzy de), Bishop of Mende - Letter from Saint Vincent, II, 234; thank-you to Saint Vincent, II, 298, 449; requests Missionaries to give missions in diocese, II, 417; other mention, I, 304.

Marcoussis, town in Essonne - Mission given there, I, 71.

Marcq (Pierre de), Vicar-General of Sens - Approval of Charity of Joigny, XIIIb, 63, 64, 65.

Maréchal (Andrée), Daughter of Charity - V, 43; XIIIb, 227, 336; signs attestation after reading of Common and Particular Rules reviewed and arranged in order by Fr. Alméras, XIIIb, 206.

Marescotti (Count), Canon of Saint-Peter's in Rome - VIII, 349.

Maretz (Mme) - See **Du Maretz**.

Margaret (Saint), Queen of Scotland - Given as patroness by Saint Vincent to Sisters in Angers, XIIIb, 114; and in other hospitals, XIIIb, 194.

Margarit (Dom Josep) - Influence regarding appointment of Ordinary for diocese of Solsona, Spain, XIIIa, 151.

Marguerin (Gilles), slave in Algiers - VI, 328; VII, 196.

Marguerite (Bl.), sister of Saint Louis - Foundress of Longchamp Monastery, IV, 485.

Marguerite, Daughter of Charity - Replaced in Richelieu, II, 675.

Marguerite, Daughter of Charity, in Valpuiseaux - III, 583.

Marguerite, Daughter of Charity, at Saint-Paul - I, 233, 283, 411, 533; II, 148; IX, 8.

Marguerite, Daughter of Charity - XIIIb, 228.

Marguerite, Daughter of Charity - Returned from Fontainebleau, left without saying a word, III, 214.

Marguerite, Daughter of Charity - Dismissed from Company, XIIIb, 297.

Marguerite, Daughter of Charity - Replaced at Saint-Jacques, I, 503.

Marguerite, Daughter of Charity - V, 410.

Marguerite, Daughter of Charity - See **Chétif** (Marguerite).

Marguerite, Daughter of Charity, in Poland - See **Moreau** (Marguerite).

Marguerite, Daughter of Charity, from Saché - See **Turenne** (Marguerite de).

Marguerite-Dorothée, Visitandine - Illness, VIII, 489; improved, VIII, 505; fear she may lose an eye, VIII, 530.

Marguerite Bourgeois [**Bourgeoys**] (Saint), nun of Congregation of Notre-Dame - Return to France from Canada, VII, 448.

Marguerite de Valois, repudiated wife of Henry IV - Saint Vincent, chaplain, XIIIa, 10, 12, 15, 16, 18–19, 20; temptation of one of her chaplains, XI, 26.

Marguerite du Saint-Sacrement, Carmelite - VIII, 406.

Maria Teresa, Infanta of Spain - Marriage to Louis XIV, VIII, 77; entrance into Paris after marriage, VIII, 466, 484, 489, 531.

Mariage (M.), slave in Tétouan - V, 191, 212; VII, 93.

Mariana (Fr.), Jesuit, in Madagascar - VI, 244.

Marie, Daughter of Charity - IV, 159.

Marie, Daughter of Charity - Asks to renew vows, V, 466.

Marie, Daughter of Charity, at Saint-Paul - See **Joly** (Marie).

Marie, Daughter of Charity, at Hôtel-Dieu - VII, 464.

Marie, Daughter of Charity, at Saint-Laurent - Father wants her to come home, I, 412; she displeases Ladies, who request her recall, II, 151.

Marie, Daughter of Charity, at Saint-Sauveur - I, 318.

Marie, Daughter of Charity, at Saint-Sulpice - I, 435; II, 187.

Marie, Daughter of Charity, changed from Foundlings, I, 601 - See **Matrilomeau** (Marie).

Marie, Daughter of Charity, in Nantes - See **Trumeau** (Marie-Marthe).

Marie, Daughter of Charity, in Nanteuil - VII, 642.

Marie, Daughter of Charity, from Fîmes - VI, 417; XIIIb, 228.

Marie, from Joigny - I, 517.

Marie, Daughter of Charity, from Péronne - I, 354.

Marie, from Valence - See **Tessonnière**.

Marie, Daughter of Charity, from Tours - See **Thilouse**.

Marie, daughter of indigenous man - Baptized at Cape of Good Hope, VIII, 587.

Marie - Saint Vincent tells Saint Louise that Marie will follow her instructions, I, 211.

Marie, Daughter of Charity - Saint Vincent would approve of her staying in Liancourt, but Saint Louise needs her, I, 286.

Marie - Sent to Saint Louise by Mme Goussault, I, 301.

Marie - Saint Vincent is consoled by Saint Louise's charity toward her, I, 377.

Marie, Daughter of Charity - Mlle de la Bistrade and Mme Forest express concern that she is bearing all the burden because her companion has health problems, I, 233.

Marie de l'Incarnation - See **Acarie**.

Marie-Denyse [**Denise**], Daughter of Charity - Raises objections at being placed in house of Duchesse d'Aiguillon, I, 322; named for Charity of Saint-Étienne-du-Mont, I, 451; other mentions, II, 425; IV, 24; V, 356.

Marie-Joseph, Daughter of Charity - Death in Étampes, IV, 474; V, 646; X, 409.

Marie-Madeleine, Daughter of Charity - Saint Vincent writes to her in Valpuiseaux, IV, 235, 249.

Marie-Madeleine de Jésus, Carmelite - See **Bains** (Lancry de).

Marie-Marthe, Daughter of Charity - See **Trumeau** (Marie-Marthe).

Marie-Monique, Daughter of Charity - Saint Vincent consents to Saint Louise reproving her, II, 50.

Marigny (Pierre de Roucherolles, Baron de) - See **Roucherolles** (Pierre de).

Marillac (Catherine de Médicis, Mme de), wife of Maréchal de Marillac - Illness, I, 122; death, I, 126.

Marillac (Jeanne Potier, Mme de), wife of Michel de Marillac, son of Marie de Creil and René de Marillac - Pregnancy, I, 505; contacts with Saint Louise, II, 183; III, 316, 518, 610; VII, 286, 299; absent from Paris, VI, 66.

Marillac (Louis de), Maréchal de France, brother of Valence de Marillac - Biographical data; Saint Vincent consoles Saint Louise after condemnation of Maréchal, I, 156–57; other mentions, I, 122, 150, 155.

Marillac (Louis de), father of Saint Louise; step-brother of Louis de Marillac, Maréchal de France - I, 23, 156.

Marillac (Mlle Le Gras, Saint Louise de,) - See **Louise de Marillac** (Saint).

Marillac (Marie de Creil, Mme de), wife of René de Marillac - Contacts with Saint Louise, I, 284, 387, 505; II, 183; III, 518, 610; VI, 65–66; VII, 299.

Marillac (Michel de), Keeper of Seals, brother of Saint Louise's father, Louis, and of Maréchal Louis de Marillac - Biographical data, XI, 233; Saint Louise stayed in his home, I, 337; man of prayer, XI, 233; imprisonment in Châteaudun, I, 150; other mention, I, 155.

Marillac (Michel de), son of René de Marillac, Councillor at Parlement - Biographical data, I, 409; contacts with Saint Louise, I, 505; III, 512, 519; VII, 286; marriage plans, I, 387; ill, VI, 65; other mentions, I, 150; V, 503.

Marillac (René de), cousin of Saint Louise, son of Michel de Marillac, Keeper of Seals - I, 284, 387.

Marillac (René de), son of Michel de Marillac and Jeanne Potier - I, 505.

Marillac (Valence de), step-sister of Saint Louise's father - See **Attichy** (Mlle d').

Marin (Bro.) - See **Baucher** (Marin).

Marin (M.) - Father of two daughters, one in Paris Visitation, other wishes to enter, VIII, 520.

Marin (Mlle) - Desires to enter Visitation, VIII, 504, 520.

Mariquot (Claude) - Member of Charity of Courboin, XIIIb, 93.

Maris (Thomas) - Witness to request for withdrawal from lease, XII, 378.

Mark (Saint), Evangelist - Cited, XI, 237; XII, 49, 317, 318, 319; feast day, XI, 351; XIIIb, 338.

Marle, town in Aisne - Destitution and charity, IV, 138; XIIIb, 428.

Marmiesse (Bernard Coignet, Abbot of) - Intervention in disagreement between Bishop of Cahors and unionized priests of diocese, IV, 270, 505.

Marmoutiers, abbey in Indre-et-Loire - II, 666; IV, 508.

Maro (M.), native of Madagascar - VI, 249.

Maronite - Saint Vincent invites Fr. Du Coudray to bring Maronite with him from Rome, I, 242, 246.

Marot (M.) - Member of Charity of Joigny, XIIIb, 66.

Marquemont (Denis de), Archbishop of Lyons - Approves Charity of Châtillon, XIIIa, 55; XIIIb, 19, 20; has Visitandines cloistered, despite original intent of Saint Francis de Sales, X, 83; other mentions, XIIIa, 44, 45, 47.

Marqueth (M.), former attorney of King in Laon - IV, 483.

Marriage - Outline of meditations for woman preparing to marry, II, 184–85; impediments, II, 44–45; clauses in Michel Le Gras' marriage contract, III, 512; marriage between Catholics and Huguenots, IV, 194.

Marrin (Fr.), Dominican - III, 386.

Marseilles, city in Bouches-du-Rhône - Saint Vincent pursues debtor to Marseilles, I, 3; galleys: see **Galley Convicts**; plague, III, 465–68, 481; VI, 99; Marseilles comes to aid of plague-ravaged Genoa, VI, 383; assists poor, VII, 115; revolts against royal authority, VII, 238, 245, 250, 468; VIII, 310, 429;

refuses subsidies for Chevalier Paul for expedition against Algiers, VII, 185, 190; rumors of ships being equipped, VIII, 340.

Bishops: see Jean-Baptiste **Gault**, Étienne **Du Puget**; Consuls, VI, 354, 371, 649; Lieutenant of Admiralty: see Antoine de **Valbelle**; Assistant Seneschal: see Antoine de **Bausset**; Provost: see Pierre de **Bausset**; Trade Commission, V, 265, 268; merchants, III, 46; V, 333, 380–81, 405; VI, 466; VII, 133, 249: see also **Picquet** (Thomas), **Rimbaud**, **Roman**; King has people notified of rights and privileges of Consul of France in Tunis, VI, 120–21; unhappiness with tax Jean Le Vacher levies on ships entering Tunis harbor, III, 394–95; merchants displeased that M. Husson prevents entrance of certain merchandise into Barbary, V, 333, 385, 412; XI, 291, 302; bankrupt merchant of Marseilles flees Algiers, VI, 346, 348, 350; VII, 238; commercial relations with Barbary, V, 133–34, 353, 404; refuge for penitent girls, VIII, 250; mission in Marseilles, II, 398; VI, 201.

Slaves from Marseilles in Barbary, III, 224; V, 404. See also **La Coste**; house of Congregation of the Blessed Sacrament, VIII, 136; mediation of Archbishop of Arles in pacification of Marseilles, III, 161. Other mentions, II, 45; III, 7; V, 170, 200, 227, 393, 554–55; VI, 124, 256, 480, 487; VII, 631; VIII, 291, 307, 368, 369, 441; XII, 61; XIIIa, 346.

Marseilles Missionaries: letters from Saint Vincent, II, 500; III, 252; IV, 301; V, 11; VII, 158, 402, 410; VIII, 32: see **Delespiney**, **Get** (Firmin); letters saint receives from them, III, 170; money sent to Fr. Codoing for trip to Marseilles, II, 252.

Foundation of Marseilles house, II, 466, 567; XIIIa, 335; Duchesse d'Aiguillon takes steps at Court to help pay for buildings, V, 145; loan from administrators of hospital for galley convicts, V, 163, 170, 199–200; income for hospital, VI, 99; resolutions concerning establishment of Mission, XIIIa, 365; Saint Vincent reprimands Fr. Get for lack of candor in borrowing and for spending more than he said for buildings; orders him to halt construction, V, 199–200; makes him ask creditors for delay, promises him to pay them a little at a time, V, 212; coat of arms of Mission affixed above door of new building, V, 380; construction continues, V, 259; VII, 144.

Difficulties with neighbors, V, 106, 408, 412, 415; VI, 264, 273; garden leased, V, 146, 163; VIII, 287; means proposed for irrigating garden, VII, 227, 556; Fr. Delespiney is told not to purchase house overlooking garden, VIII, 243; Saint Vincent objects to women entering enclosure, VIII, 286–87; possession of garden is disputed with Missionaries, VIII, 299; question of house and garden is in God's hands, VIII, 328.

Revenues from coaches, VII, 539; M. Féris, benefactor, V, 392; gift of Marquise de Vins: see **Vins** (Marquise); lawsuit against Missionaries to contest gift made to "Priests of the Mission" of Marseilles, VI, 517.

Importance of ministries, III, 258–60; VIII, 273; XII, 125; dealings with hospital administrators, III, 259–60; saint tells Fr. Get to turn over care of sick to another priest, V, 146.

Missions, VI, 185, 261, 276, 279; VII, 302, 392, 403, 437, 485, 519, 556; VIII, 173, 262, 316, 320, 338, 357, 372, 376, 401; retreats for ordinands, V, 145; VII, 49; VIII, 237; spiritual retreats, V, 432; ministry to galley convicts: see **Galley Convicts**.

Plan for seminary, III, 258, 272; Saint Vincent advises dismissing seminarians not paying sufficient fee, III, 394, 413; seminary grows in grace and in numbers, VI, 265; Saint-Victor novices accepted, VI, 99, 120, 122; XIIIa, 408; are taught breviary and ceremonies, XI, 348; Saint Vincent inquires about state of seminary, VI, 432, 446; receives good news, VI, 486; dismissal of Saint-Victor novices, VII, 149–50; XIIIa, 409; Saint Vincent asks that they no longer be accepted, VII, 161; happy to be free of them, VII, 178; not a diocesan seminary, VII, 70, 161; XIIIa, 408; plan for diocesan seminary, VII, 70, 74, 81, 116; passage of Frs. Alméras and Portail, III, 64, 68–69, 154; of Fr. Le Soudier (Jacques), III, 82; of Fr. Nouelly and Jean Barreau, III, 221; of M. Legouz (Jacques), VII, 347; of Fr. Le Vacher (Jean), III, 252–53.

Superior of Marseilles house acts as intermediary between Saint Vincent and slaves and Missionaries in Barbary, V, 11, 121, 140, 145, 162–63, 170, 190–91, 200, 216–17, 227–28, 245, 247–48, 259, 325, 353, 379–81, 392, 398, 407, 408, 455, 482, 506, 530; VI, 8, 54, 183–84, 185, 187, 189, 200–01, 207, 258–59, 273, 275, 278–79, 288–89, 302, 304, 314–15, 320–21, 321–22, 327–28, 354, 359–60, 384, 391–92, 418, 431, 446, 466–67, 486–87, 523, 599; VII, 6–7, 30, 93, 103, 114, 123, 134, 144–45, 148–49, 154, 161, 168, 179, 190–91, 195–97, 208, 212–13, 221–22, 228–29, 232–33, 237–38, 245, 250, 269, 273–74, 288, 458, 463, 468–69, 519–20, 522–24, 539, 609; VIII, 4, 18, 162, 273, 309, 356–57, 360, 537; XII, 125–26; total from collections for Philippe Le Vacher is kept in Marseilles, VII, 187, 194, 207, 212, 263, 283, 325; VIII, 4, 18, 32, 68; various concerns relative to Barbary, V, 367, 412; VI, 10, 121, 165, 384, 447, 628; VII, 94–95, 145, 185, 226, 317–18.

Fr. Alméras unable to make visitation of Marseilles house: see **Alméras** (René the younger); Saint Vincent suggests that Fr. Codoing make visitation in Marseilles and Annecy, II, 531–532; Saint Vincent considers going himself, III, 413;

prevented, III, 429; Fr. Portail makes visitation, III, 102, 103, 137, 154, 238, 258, 267, 271; remains in Marseilles to negotiate with administrators of hospital for galley convicts concerning spiritual services for latter, III, 271, 272, 295, 299, 394, 428, 465; Fr. Berthe makes visitation, V, 574; VI, 593, 600, 638; VII, 6, 24, 30; during plague, Fr. Tratebas' family welcomes Fr. Portail and other Missionaries into their home, VIII, 161; dearth of personnel, VIII, 262.

List of Superiors and history of house, VIII, 610; Personnel of the house: see **Admirault** (Claude), **Asseline**, **Bauduy**, **Beaure**, **Brisjonc**, **Brunet**, **Champion** (Louis), **Chrétien**, **Cogley** [Coglée] (Mark), **Cornier**, **Delespiney**, **Dolivet**, **Du Chesne** (Pierre), **Duchesne** (René), **Du Coudray** (François), **Dufestel** (François), **Get** (Firmin), **Huguier**, **La Fosse**, **Le Gentil**, **Lemoyne**, **Le Soudier** (Jacques), **Le Vacher** (Philippe), **Mugnier**, **Parisy**, **Portail**, **Sicquard**. Missionaries assigned to Marseilles, II, 502; changes, VI, 338, 446; VII, 608; disorders, VI, 185, 207, 279; Missionaries traveling to Marseilles: see **Berthe**, **Le Vacher** (Philippe), **Portail**; M. Husson lives with Marseilles Missionaries: see **Husson**.

Marsollier (Messrs.) - VII, 423.

Marteau (Fr.), Pastor of Sorbon (Ardennes) - VII, 574.

Martha (Saint) - Grumbles against her sister, II, 84; Jesus reproaches her too great solicitude, IV, 346; union of roles of Martha and Mary, VI, 145; VIII, 585; XI, 33; Martha served poor persons for love of God, IX, 18; model for coadjutor Brothers, I, 143; VI, 167; XII, 83, 84, 93, 98; XIIIa, 299, 432, 446; Saint Vincent's devotion to her, X, 439; Saint Louise's devotion, III, 159; other mention, I, 552.

Marthe (Ignace-Joseph de), Priest of the Mission - Biographical data, VII, 571; VIII, 7; Saint Vincent asks Rome for dispensation for age, and *extra tempora* so he can be ordained and sent to Madagascar, VII, 571; VIII, 7; in praise of him, VIII, 99, 100; assigned to Poland, VIII, 99–100, 528, 535, 537, 538.

Marthe, Daughter of Charity, at Saint-Leu, Saint-Paul, Saint-Jacques-de-la-Boucherie; considered for Nantes, XIIIb, 249; see **Dauteuil**.

Marthe, woman with Saint Louise - I, 80.

Marthe de Jésus, Carmelite - See **Du Vigean** (Marthe).

Martin - Accompanied Philippe Le Vacher to Marseilles, VII, 269.

Martin (Élisabeth [Isabelle]), Daughter of Charity - Biographical data, I, 320; II, 16; III, 178; IX, 148; health, I, 320, 355; II, 16, 81; XII, 363; proposed for Saint-Paul, I, 376; permission to go to Argenteuil, I, 469; in Paris, I, 502; sent to Angers Hospital, II, 12; XIIIb, 116, 118; Sister Servant in Angers, II, 81; Sister Servant in Richelieu, II, 208; desired in Angers, II, 224; goes to Nanteuil to see ailing Jeanne Dalmagne, II, 423–24; IX, 148, 160; in Liancourt, XIIIb, 248; Saint Louise sends her to visit Sisters in Saint-Germain-en-Laye, Maule, and Crespières, II, 667; Sister Servant in Nantes, III, 8; XIIIb, 248–49, 256–57, 260; sick, III, 178; personality, III, 183; judged necessary to recall her, III, 208; sent to Richelieu, III, 216; death, III, 415; other mentions, I, 468; II, 223.

Martin (Isaac), servant of Agde Missionaries - VIII, 112.

Martin (Jean the elder), Priest of the Mission - Biographical data, II, 251; III, 3; IV, 207; V, 184; VI, 1; VII, 24; VIII, 29–30; XI, 245; letters Saint Vincent writes to him in Genoa, II, 620, 649, 651; III, 38, 48, 58, 66, 106, 135, 140, 154, 155, 156, 159, 166, 170, 190, 194, 200, 203, 207, 301, 312, 313, 332; IV, 207, 214, 220, 221, 226, 228, 231, 237, 239, 246, 255, 304, 438; in Sedan, V, 198, 206, 210, 222, 224, 237, 240, 245, 250, 260; in Lyons, V, 456, 458; in Turin, V, 467, 477, 481, 485, 500, 529, 534, 543, 583, 594, 597, 610, 623, 635, 641; VI, 1, 29, 40, 56, 72, 86, 89, 92, 110, 127, 137, 141, 157, 169, 171, 204, 256, 262, 282, 299, 307, 329, 351, 433, 484, 520, 556, 577, 600, 638; VII, 24, 58, 74, 103, 111, 142, 147, 152, 210, 230, 234, 241, 270, 283, 290, 312, 377, 414, 454, 582; VIII, 42, 65, 86, 110, 118, 230, 237, 246, 271, 355, 385, 402, 482, 535; letters from Fr. Martin in Turin to Saint Vincent, V, 586, 638; VI, 196, 335, 415, 581; VII, 89, 118, 136, 213, 483; VIII, 29; mention of letters to Saint Vincent, IV, 220, 226; V, 207, 222, 240, 245, 250, 260, 477, 485, 500, 534, 594; VI, 29, 56, 72, 86, 110, 127, 137, 157, 169, 171, 256, 262, 282, 307, 329, 433, 435, 496, 556, 577, 600, 601, 638; VII, 24, 58, 74, 103, 234, 241, 271, 284, 312, 377, 414, 582; VIII, 86, 110, 118, 237, 246, 271, 355, 385, 402, 482, 535; XI, 369; mention of note from Saint Vincent about some persons who abjured heresy, V, 241.

Praise for him, II, 251; VII, 581; marks of affection from Saint Vincent, III, 140, 155, 186, 194, 200; IV, 214; VIII, 43; mother, II, 652; III, 49, 187; brother, II, 419, 652; III, 187, 301; IV, 207, 214, 232, 247, 304, 438; V, 529, 535, 543; VII, 152, 230.

Sent to Rome, II, 251; in Rome, II, 297; assigned to Barcelona, II, 498; in Genoa, II, 619, 625; III, 3, 26, 27, 41, 102, 108, 122, 258, 460; in charge of seminary, III, 106, 135, 137, 140, 150, 166; missions in ***Quarto al Mare*** and ***Niolo***: see these words; health, III, 301, 312; Saint Vincent encourages him to trust in God, III, 207; fears too great zeal may be harmful to his health, II, 625, 652; III, 58, 150; tells Fr. Blatiron to keep him in Genoa, IV, 492.

Recalled to France, named for Sedan house, V, 184, 193; in Sedan, V, 198, 552; Superior in Sedan, VIII, 611; recalled from Sedan, V, 262; in Paris; questioned during two conferences, XI, 245–46, 266.

Leaves Paris for Lyons in order to go to Turin, V, 456; Superior in Turin, V, 468; VI, 68, 141, 363–64, 429, 510, 525, 552, 604; VII, 146, 594; VIII, 58, 618; informs Saint Vincent of ravages of plague in Genoa, VI, 169, 172, 469, 471; XI, 369–70; missions, V, 500, 594, 610, 623, 635; VI, 2, 72, 111, 128, 137, 160, 169, 205, 308, 329, 435–36, 495, 639; VII, 24, 142, 152, 230, 414, 454, 483; VIII, 42, 65, 237, 385: see ***Pianezza, Scalenghe, Lucerna, Villafranca, Racconigi*** (***Raconi***), ***Castelnuovo, Savigliano, Bra, Cavallermaggiore, Chieri, Fossano, Cherasco, Bene Vagienna, Mondovi***; hears confessions of Visitandines occasionally at request of Archbishop, VI, 522; regains freedom, VI, 602; refuses to be their ordinary confessor, VII, 313; Saint Vincent encourages him not to expose himself to contagion, VI, 68; entirely disposed to risk serving plague-stricken if disease enters Genoa, VI, 72; charity to Genoa house afflicted with plague, VI, 525; confreres are discouraged, VII, 146, 147, 231, 290, 312, 378; thinks he is cause, offers to resign as Superior, VI, 600; rumor that he is seriously ill, VII, 147; health, VIII, 157, 206–07, 210, 230, 237, 246, 271, 355, 402, 483; Saint Vincent urges cook to prepare chicken broth for him, VIII, 44.

Saint Vincent recommends humility, V, 477–79, 485, 486, 594, 635; VI, 329; VII, 143, 231; gentleness, V, 544; VII, 290, 312; moderation in work, V, 529, 583, 598, 611; VI, 160, 172, 257, 263, 282, 308, 497; VII, 146, 147; VIII, 42, 67, 385; other mentions, I, *xxv*; II, 409; V, 493. See also ***Turin***.

Martin (Jean the younger), Priest of the Mission - Biographical data; Saint Vincent invites him to come to Paris to discern vocation, II, 409; VIII, 128; benefice, VIII, 128, 150.

Martin (Saint), Bishop of Tours - Feast day, VIII, 481; XI, 331; XIIIa, 267; XIIIb, 18; gives half his cloak to poor man, XI, 331; XII, 63; goes through villages to instruct poor people, XI, 332; shuns honors, XII, 326; one of patrons of Châtillon, XIIIb, 3; of church in Buenens, XIIIb, 18; sermon of Saint Francis de Sales, V, 478; other mention, XI, 335.

Martin (Simon), Minim - Dedicates French translation of *Sinner's Guide* to Saint Vincent, II, 580; his works, V, 297.

Martin, in Villepreux - I, 219.

Martineau (Samuel), Bishop of Bazas - Contacts with Alain de Solminihac, III, 346; exposed to violence of Duc d'Épernon, III, 347, 348; takes steps against heretic Labadie, IV, 457;

Bishop of Cahors hopes he will sign Bishops' petition to Pope against Jansenism, IV, 101.

Martinion (Martin), Jesuit - VIII, 587.

Martinis (Girolamo di), Priest of the Mission - Biographical data, V, 275; VI, 87; VII, 230; XI, 174; in Rome, V, 275; health, V, 376; XI, 174; agrees to be enclosed in college of *Propaganda Fide* where case of plague has been found, VI, 133, 157; XI, 330; assigned to Turin, VI, 87, 205, 256, 282; his praises, VI, 256–57; remains in Rome, VI, 299, 374; suggested anew for Turin, VI, 579, 619; allowed to renew vows, VI, 631; in Turin, VII, 230; assigned to Genoa, VII, 234, 242; departure postponed, VII, 243.

Martinot - Name scratched out in letter to Saint Louise, I, 505.

Martisans de Celhay, Basque slave - VII, 161, 179.

Martyrdom - Different kinds of martyrs, XI, 167–68; martyrdom of charity, X, 442; XI, 374; blood of martyrs, seed of Christians, IV, 257; VI, 239; X, 443; XI, 339, 366, 368; all Missionaries should desire martyrdom, XI, 334–35, 357, XII, 123; those are martyrs who endure willingly difficulties of consecrated life, IX, 214; as is anyone who gives his/her life for God, IX, 361; martyred Popes, X, 442; XI, 18, 335, 338, 368; example of woman in Tunis, II, 639. See also **Borguñy**, **Lee**.

Mary, Mother of Jesus - Jesus was submissive to her, IX, 7, 14, 181, 427; X, 72, 461; XIIIa, 443; what Jesus was for her, IX, 5, 14; X, 228, 461; XII, 177, 345–46; what she was for Jesus, VII, 202; IX, 5, 318; XII, 177; her merits, IX, 483–86; Immaculate Virgin, IV, 566; XIIIa, 40; purity, X, 384; virginity, XII, 338; XIIIa, 36; XIIIb, 417; great grace and modesty, XII, 16; Annunciation, X, 458, 498; XII, 265–66; XIIIb, 417; Visitation, II, 279; IX, 204; X, 498.

Model of love of God, IX, 18; of acquiescence to God's Will, I, 328; VII, 437; of humility, X, 317, 431, 432; of perseverance, XIIIb, 417; of love of solitude, IX, 268; of modesty, IX, 72; of work, I, 369; IX, 380–81; of submission, IX, 59; X, 417; of tact in manner of making visits, IX, 204; duty to invoke her, X, 367, 402, 473; XII, 110; XIIIb, 340; respect to be shown to her name, XI, 113; Saint Vincent establishes in Charities devotion to Mary, XIIIb, 3, 45, 48–49, 51, 54, 61, 84, 90, 99, 103; recourse to her for conversions, III, 172; for safety during travel, III, 540–41.

Recommends Marian devotion to Daughters of Charity, I, 504; IX, 175; they fast on eve of her feasts, X, 505; exhorts Sisters to act, in contacts with women, as they would with

Mary, X, 504; Mary is their patroness, VII, 408; X, 85, 500; XIIIb, 114; their model, X, 92; Saint Vincent's devotion to Blessed Virgin, I, 6, 62, 81, 350; X, 311; encourages others to such devotion, II, 140; devotion of Fr. Étienne, VIII, 240, 558, 559, 567, 579, 588; of Fr. Pillé, II, 380; of court clerk, XI, 144; confreres should have special devotion to her, XIIIa, 456; mention of Blessed Virgin in closing of Saint Vincent's letters, I, 28, 30, 35, 56, 59, 60, etc.; blessing of candles on feast of Purification, VIII, 570; devotional practices: see **Angelus**, **Rosary**, **Litanies**; other mention, I, 67.

Mary (Saint), one of women who followed Jesus - IX, 18.

Mary of Egypt (Saint) - X, 508.

Mary Magdalen (Saint) - Feast day, I, 241; XIIIa, 305; kneels at feet of Jesus as a sinner, X, 58–59; XII, 291; grumbling of Judas, X, 98, 246–47, 349; Mary mourns dead Lazarus, XII, 221; listens to Jesus, IX, 4–5; Jesus prefers her idleness to less discreet zeal of Martha, II, 85; provided, along with other devout women, for Jesus and Apostles, IX, 343, 386; served poor persons for love of God, IX, 18; Magdalen at tomb of Jesus, X, 510; sojourn in Provence, VI, 260; IX, 482; Saint Vincent's devotion to her, I, 241; X, 439; devotion of Saint Louise, III, 159; of Mme de Gondi, XIIIa, 59; Saint Vincent encourages Saint Louise to honor solitude of Our Lord, as she did, I, 513; good Missionary should unite offices of Martha and Mary, XI, 33; as Bro. Patte did, VIII, 585; not always possible, VI, 145; crucifix with her figure at foot used by Missionaries on Table Bay, VIII, 576; other mentions, I, 121, 369; II, 84; XIIIb, 390.

Mascarene Islands - Talk of sending colonists, V, 279, 299; priests requested for islands, V, 299; VII, 60.

Mascarini (M.), banker in Lyons - II, 250, 255.

Mass [Eucharist] - Mention of conferences on celebration of Eucharist, XII, 412, 416, 426; center of devotion, IX, 5; differences in celebration of Eucharist in first half of seventeenth century, XII, 211–12; celebrated same way throughout the world, IX, 173; Saint Vincent recommends that priests say Mass daily, XI, 85; XIIIa, 80, 140, 159, 299; Masses served by clerics, XII, 390; asks grace for two young priests never to say Mass through routine, III, 296; recommends daily Mass for Daughters of Charity, IX, 5; except for reasons of charity: see **Rules**; how to celebrate Mass, XI, 83; how to hear it, IX, 5.

Saint Vincent wants his priests to have free intentions, V, 429; VI, 31; customary not to receive Mass stipends, XII, 313, 314; receive no stipends during missions for Masses said for intention of faithful, V, 266; poverty justifies exceptions, III,

394; Saint-Lazare house rarely receives Mass stipends, VII, 2; destitution of period makes Mass stipends rare, II, 92; Saint Vincent permits Fr. Lebreton to receive stipends, on condition that he give them to poor persons, I, 539; asks Lebreton's opinion on this matter, II, 63; Mass stipends are not for relatives, IV, 322; Mass stipends for retreatants, II, 250; Saint Vincent instructs Bro. Parre to draw money for poor priests to say Masses for intention of benefactors, VI, 561, 580; saint asks two confreres in Turin to help with Mass obligations of those in Genoa, VII, 104; question raised about celebration of foundation Masses, VIII, 226; Saint Vincent leaves vestments and sacristy to find person who had shown him antipathy, XIIIa, 210; asks to be remembered at *Nobis quoque peccatoribus*, III, 296.

Massac (M. de) - VI, 366.

Massari (Dionigi), Secretary of *Propaganda Fide* - Saint Vincent congratulates him on promotion to post of Secretary, III, 500; affairs submitted to him by saint, IV, 61, 296, 554, 605; signature on decree of *Propaganda Fide*, impeding multiplication of Congregations having same works in France, IV, 611; Saint Vincent informs him of death of Archbishop of Myra, V, 103; risks catching plague, VI, 134.

Masse (Andrian or Dian), son or nephew of Dian Mananghe - Praise for him, V, 528; death, VI, 221.

Massé (Étiennette), Daughter of Charity - XIIIb, 228.

Massé (Fr.), priest - I, 177, 311.

Massiot (Guillaume de), Vicar-General of Dax - XIIIa, 3–7.

Masson (Paul), Pastor of Val-Saint-Germain - Biographical data, XIIIa, 173; deposition at beatification process of Saint Vincent, XIIIa, 173.

Masson (M.) - Wants to enter Saint-Lazare, VI, 548.

Masson (M.) - VIII, 524.

Master, name given to Canon-administrator of Hôtel-Dieu - Saint Vincent finds it inadvisable for him to speak to him, I, 234.

Matatanes, region in Madagascar - III, 544, 576, 578, 583.

Mathias (Saint) - Election as Apostle, IX, 280; XII, 45; XIIIb, 386; feast day, I, 189; VIII, 290, 567, 587.

Mathieu (Bro.) - See **Régnard** (Mathieu).

Mathieu (Fr.), Prior of Reformed Jacobins of Saint-Honoré Convent in Paris - Appointed one of Visitors of principal convent of Dominican monks in Paris, XIIIa, 137.

Mathoud (Étienne), Presiding Judge of Election - Founder of Charity Hospital of Mâcon, XIIIb, 73.

Mathoud (Philibert), Procurator for bailiwick of Mâcon - XIIIb, 74, 77.

Mathurin Fathers [Trinitarians] - Historical note, II, 394; III, 47; V, 91; crisis in Order, II, 421; sending money to Jean Barreau, III, 47; give hope for more, III, 126; stopped ransoming ten years ago, V, 91; preparing ransom in 1655, V, 353; vow to take place of slaves tempted to apostatize, XI, 385; other mentions, VIII, 316, 328.

Mathurine, Daughter of Charity - Departure from Company, III, 472.

Mathurine, Daughter of Charity, in Richelieu - Saint Louise asks permission for her to renew vows, VI, 136.

Mathurine (Sister) - See **Guérin** (Mathurine).

Matrilomeau (Marie), Daughter of Charity - Sent to Angers, II, 12; other mention, I, 601.

Mattei (Signori) - Their mansion in Rome, VII, 328, 406, 413.

Matthew (Saint), Apostle and Evangelist - Mentioned, XI, 227; cited, XI, 243; XII, 12, 101, 106, 108, 119, 317–19; XIIIa, 33, 119.

Maubuisson, hamlet in Saint-Ouen-l'Aumône (Val-d'Oise) - Journey of Saint Vincent here, I, 88; Abbess of Maubuisson, XIIIa, 125.

Manferet (Pierre), of Langres - Saint Vincent charges him to take possession, in his name, of Saint-Nicolas-de-Grosse-Sauve Priory, XIIIa, 67.

Mauge [Mauger] (Jacques), prisoner in Toulon - VI, 321; VII, 250; VIII, 250.

Maule, village in Yvelines - Élisabeth Martin appointed to make visitation of house of Daughters of Charity, II, 667; Sisters sent to Maule, III, 300; VI, 191; Sisters from Maule at Motherhouse, II, 635; X, 470; Sister native to environs of Maule, V, 466; VII, 465; Jean Fouquet writes from Maule to Saint Vincent, VIII, 532; mission near Maule, XI, 157; other mention, VIII, 548.

Mauléon (Joannès de), Basque slave in Algiers - V, 36, 147.

Mauljean (Edme), Vicar-General of Sens - Grants Saint Vincent's request for power to absolve from reserved cases in Sens diocese, I, 17, 18.

Mauny (Count of) - Saint Vincent comments on Michel Le Gras' relationship with him, I, 549.

Maupas du Tour (Henri de), Bishop of Le Puy - Biographical data, II, 296; III, 226; IV, 258; VII, 38; VIII, 507; preaches funeral oration in Paris for Saint Jane Frances de Chantal, II, 248; named Bishop of Le Puy; Saint Vincent urges sending Bulls to him, II, 296, 297; asks Fr. Codoing to handle matter for him in Rome, II, 319; rumor of plan to go to Rome for beatification of Francis de Sales, III, 226; complaint in Rome about his biography of Francis de Sales; measures taken by Saint Vincent to avoid consequences of denunciation, VI, 542, 635; VII, 38, 319, 517, 572; writes to Saint Vincent about events in his diocese, III, 382; opinion on disagreements among Carmelites, VIII, 507; visit to Saint Vincent, IV, 258; to Fr. Olier, II, 446; contacts with Nicolas Pavillon, II, 618; preaches funeral oration for Saint Vincent, XIIIa, 209; other mentions, II, 297, 307; V, 17; VII, 411, 507.

Maupeou (Jean de), Bishop of Chalon - Visit to Saint Vincent, VII, 321; retreat at Saint-Lazare, VII, 405; consecrated in Saint-Lazare Church, VIII, 339, 344; Saint Vincent apologizes for not admitting to Congregation young man he presented, VIII, 550.

Maupeou (Madeleine-Élisabeth de), Visitandine - Biographical data, III, 355; V, 557; VI, 425; VIII, 410; letters from Saint Vincent, III, 355; V, 557; VI, 425; to Saint Vincent, VIII, 505, 516; mention of another letter from Saint Vincent, V, 557; desired for monasteries in Compiègne and Bayonne, III, 355–56; Saint Vincent asks her to observe terms of earlier contract regarding bodies entombed in church of First Monastery of Paris, V, 557–62; journey to Melun, VIII, 410, 430, 505, 517, 551; return to First Monastery of Paris by way of Port-Royal and Madeleine convent, VIII, 529.

Maupeou (Marie de), sister of Madeleine-Élisabeth - See **Fouquet** (Mme).

Maure (Anne Doni d'Attichy, Comtesse de) - Contacts with Saint Louise, I, 336; II, 549; III, 168, 179; family, I, 86; concern for Marie-Angélique d'Atri, I, 462–63; other mention, I, 410.

Maure (Louis de Rochechouart, Comte de) - Biographical data, I, 460; concern for Marie-Angélique d'Atri, I, 460, 461–62; Saint Louise asks help for son Michel, III, 518; contacts with Saint Vincent, III, 357; other mention, I, 336.

Maurice, Byzantine Emperor - XII, 276.

Maurice (D.), Provincial of Barnabites; appointed one of Visitors of principal convent of Dominican Monks in Paris, XIIIa, 136.

Maurice, Daughter of Charity, at Saint-Sulpice - Returns to family, II, 187.

Maurice (Fr.), Discalced Carmelite - Fr. Olier wary of his contacts, III, 292–93.

Maurice, Greek Emperor - XII, 276.

Maurice (Jean), chaplain of Saint-Antoine Hospital in Joigny - XIIIb, 27–28, 66.

Maurice (Joseph), priest in Lyons - XIIIa, 45.

Maurisse (Fr.) - Offers two priories in Saintes to Saint Vincent, IV, 388; Saint Vincent's response, IV, 474; saint advises Saintes Missionaries not to accept Fr. Maurisse as boarder, VI, 315–16.

Mauron, town in Morbihan - Mission, VII, 131.

Mauroy (M. de) - Saint Vincent apologizes for being unable to accept spiritual ministry to poor persons of General Hospital, VI, 274, 275.

Maury, of Montmirail - XIIIb, 34.

Maxentius, Roman Emperor - Saint Catherine of Alexandria rebukes him for persecuting Christians, X, 495–96.

Maxims of Gospel - See **Gospel Teachings**.

Maxims of Saint Vincent - XII, 383–403; under respective headings.

Maxims of the World - Conferences on spirit of world, IX, 337, 344; in what it consists, IX, 346, 347–51; differs from spirit of Jesus, XIIIa, 163; conference on maxims of Jesus Christ and those of the world, X, 112–26; pleasures, riches, honors of world, XII, 95–96; reasons to avoid spirit of world, IV, 57; IX, 337–43, 344–45; Jesus hates world, X, 121; those who mingle with worldly-minded become worldly, IX, 542; X, 120; world promises satisfactions but gives only troubles, V, 539; earthly things are uncertain and perishable, VI, 439; Saint Vincent cautions Missionary not to discuss affairs of state verbally or in writing, II, 362; signs of worldly spirit in Daughter of Charity, IX, 348–52; how to preserve self from it, IX, 337–40, 343–44, 346–47, 353; maxims of world, X, 113–16, 118–21; XII, 102–03; not all are bad; how to discern good from bad, XII, 103; XIIIa, 163; latter must be despised, X, 115–16; Jesus hated them, XI, 124; devil is their author, XII, 254; they are deceptive, XII, 104–05; contrary to spirit of Daughters of Charity, X, 113.

Maytie (Arnaud-François de), Bishop of Oloron - Consecration in Saint-Lazare Church, VIII, 339, 344; staying at Saint-Lazare, VIII, 462; reference to conference on his consecration, XII, 437.

Mazarin (Jules) [**Mazarini** (Giulio)] Cardinal and Prime Minister - Biographical data, II, 64; III, 20; IV, 45; V, 172; VI, 391; VII, 94–95; VIII, 265; XI, 20; silence in his residence, XI, 201; letter of Mazarin to Comte d'Harcourt, XIIIa, 151; letters from Saint Vincent: on nomination of head of school of philosophy at Collège de Navarre, II, 648–49; transfer of episcopal See of Maillezais to La Rochelle, III, 20; choice of Fr. Le Maistre as theology professor at Sorbonne, III, 45; choice of Louis de Chandenier as Bishop of Mâcon, IV, 84; Saint Vincent's efforts to bring about peace, IV, 414; tries to convince Mazarin to return Court to Paris, IV, 459–64; mention of letter from Saint Vincent, III, 494.

Letters of Mazarin to Saint Vincent: Queen has bestowed bishopric of Bayeux on Édouard Molé, II, 615; and approves transfer of See of Maillezais to La Rochelle, III, 34; Mazarin accepts Fr. Le Maistre for vacant chair of theology at Sorbonne, III, 49; assures him that Abbé de Chailli has qualities of good Bishop, III, 249; thanks him for good advice, III, 494; replies about bishopric of Mâcon, IV, 95; his sister, X, 209; XI, 171; his niece Laure Mancini, V, 58; health, II, 533; excerpts from notebooks, XIIIa, 154–55.

Hostile to Jansenism, III, 319; IV, 592; Saint Vincent obtains letters of recommendation from him, II, 254, 257, 419, 438; Mazarin agrees to Cardinal de la Rochefoucauld's resignation of Sainte-Geneviève Abbey, II, 509–10; helps Master of Dominicans to restore union in Order, III, 387; Mazarin's alleged marriage to Anne of Austria, III, 356; Saint Vincent promises to speak to him about bishopric of Babylon, III, 169; recommends that he leave France, III, 393; Cardinal at Rueil conference, III, 411; accompanies Court to Richelieu, IV, 45; re-entry into France, IV, 307; journey to Reims for King's consecration; besieged in Stenay by troops of Maréchal de Fabert, V, 176; in Toul, VI, 534; in Marseilles, VIII, 273; letters to Chevalier Paul about proposed expedition to Algiers, VII, 174, 187; negotiations about Bishop of Sarlat becoming Coadjutor of Cahors, IV, 475, 563; V, 172; contacts with Saint Vincent, II, 619, 681; III, 231; V, 368–69; VII, 94; VIII, 429; other mentions, II, 551, 679; III, 105, 244, 352, 391, 478; IV, 585; VI, 391; X, 3; XIIIa, 151.

Mazessat (Marie) - Member of Charity of Paillart, XIIIb, 48.

Mazure (Guillaume), Pastor of Saint-Paul in Paris; uncle of Nicolas Mazure - I, 377.

Mazure (Nicolas), nephew of Guillaume, whom he replaced as Pastor of Saint-Paul in Paris - Biographical data, I, 376–77; relationship with Daughters of Charity in parish, I, 376, 533;

Fr. Gilles cites him regarding vows, XIIIa, 382; other mention, II, 133.

McEnery [**Ennery**] (John), Priest of the Mission - Biographical data, III, 388; IV, 355; V, 48; VI, 57; VII, 18; XI, 381; his praises, VI, 469, 471; departure for Genoa, III, 388–89; theology professor, director of students at Saint-Lazare, IV, 355; not gentle enough for Corsica, IV, 439; proposed for Scotland, IV, 478; in Troyes, V, 48, 82; in Turin, V, 477, 493; considered for Genoa, VI, 57; in devastated regions, VI, 58; sent from Turin to Genoa, V, 623; VI, 86, 92, 127; dies of plague, VI, 430, 432, 435, 436, 438, 440, 442, 445, 453, 454, 464, 469, 471, 474, 477, 480, 485, 486, 488, 491, 501, 504, 505, 528, 530, 535, 537, 567, 583, 586; VII, 15, 18; XI, 381; mention of letter from Saint Vincent, V, 624; mention of conference on his virtues, XII, 428.

Meals - Mention of conferences, XII, 425; consider self unworthy of food God provides, X, 106; be faithful everywhere to Motherhouse customs regarding meals, I, 438; V, 350; X, 290, 326; breakfast, V, 384; decline invitations from outsiders, I, 539; IV, 195, 470; V, 334, 347, 384, 536; VII, 394; XI, 95; do not invite outsiders to Community meals without permission, X, 257–67; XI, 95, 101, 298–99.

Conduct during meals, XII, 40, 415, 420, 423, 426; mention of conferences, XII, 415, 420, 423, 426; meal times for Missionaries, I, 554; Saint Vincent corrects abuse regarding meals of confreres returning from mission, VII, 593; XI, 296–97; use of portions, I, 438, 554; meat other than beef or mutton not usually eaten at Saint-Lazare, X, 327; something extra served on certain feasts, VII, 450, 491; food should be healthful and sufficient, I, 378; III, 501; XI, 299; eating too much and too often is harmful to health, XII, 41–42; do not discuss what has been eaten, XI, 93.

Saint Louise asks Saint Vincent if Sisters may be served roast on Easter, VI, 281; Sisters should take meals in private while traveling, XIIIb, 273; Saint Vincent praises them for frugality, X, 573.

Wine does not help digestion, XII, 41; abuse of wine, XII, 37–40, 41–43; Saint Vincent reduces individual serving of wine at Saint-Lazare, XII, 41; reduces it in 1659 because of frost on vines, XII, 233–34; recommends diluting it well with water, XI, 105, 297; XII, 42–43; example of Alain de Solminihac, XII, 342; of Turks, X, 290; Daughters of Charity do not drink wine, I, 358; X, 290; or beer, VI, 162; reading at table: see **Reading**, **Banquets**, **Gluttony**, **Mortification**, **Moderation**. Necessity of offering reception for Governor of Table Bay, VIII, 576–77.

Meaux, town in Seine-et-Marne - Bishops: see Dominique de **Ligny**, Dominique **Séguier**; Visitandines of Meaux, III, 453; ministries of confreres in diocese from their house in Crécy, VIII, 609; first attempt at establishment of Missionaries in Meaux, VI, 458; seminary personnel, VII, 354; Superior and history of house, VIII, 619; other mentions, VII, 462; VIII, 502; XIIIa, 323, 396, 422.

Meaux-Boisboudran (Guillaume de), Grand Prior of Order of Malta in France - II, 143.

Mede (Thomas), Irish priest - IV, 240.

Medici (Ferdinando de'), Grand Duke of Tuscany - VI, 361, 372, 650.

Medici (Marie de [Maria de' Medici]), mother of Louis XIII - III, 476; Antoine Le Gras was her secretary, XIIIa, 260; XIIIb, 116, 139, 145, 205, 225, 231; other mentions, VIII, 405; XIIIa, 16.

Meditation - Conferences, IX, 23, 30, 320; X, 456–59, 459–64, 470–75; XI, 75–83, 232–36, 358–61; mention of other conferences, XII, 408, 428, 435; text of Rules of Daughters of Charity, X, 459, 482; Saint Vincent recommends fidelity to meditation, IX, 25, 28–29, 30, 43, 172; even on days of rest, VIII, 442; or if prevented from making it at regular time, X, 470–71, 484; make it at home, as far as possible, IX, 36; he changes Sisters' hour of rising to allow time to make meditation, IX, 42; questions Sisters from various houses on fidelity to meditation, X, 468–70, 484; in case of necessity, prefer service to Mass and meditation: see **Rules**; fidelity to meditation depends on faithfulness to rising, III, 532.

All good things come through prayer, XI, 361; excellence of prayer and confidence in God, XII, 390; dispositions for meditation, XII, 390; person of prayer is capable of anything; an impregnable rampart, XI, 76; prayer is for soul what soul is for body, IX, 327; X, 459, 470; what dew is for plant, IX, 316; air, X, 484; food, IX, 316, 321–22, 327; we draw needed strength from it, IX, 321, 328; center of devotion, IX, 3, 25; God abandons person who abandons prayer, X, 471; prayer unites us with God, IX, 321; by it He enlightens intellect, inflames will, and spurs us on to do good, IX, 330; X, 483; in it, we see our faults, as in a mirror, and what God desires of us, IX, 327; in meditation we preach to ourselves, XI, 76; persons of prayer will have their reward, IX, 326; dispositions to be brought to meditation, XI, 75; impossible for Missionary to persevere in vocation without prayer, III, 532; same for Daughter of Charity, IX, 321, 327; X, 470; prayer is primer for preachers, VII, 171; reservoir from which Superiors draw what has to be done, XI, 311; of prayer shown by prayer of Moses, IX, 329; teaching of Jesus, IX, 325; example of Jesus, IX, 321, 326; of angels and saints, IX, 322; of Michel de Marillac, XI, 233; of a peasant, XI, 262; of Saint Francis de Sales, XIIIa, 89; in what meditation consists, IX, 328; definition of mental and vocal prayer, IX, 328–30.

Safeguarding uniformity in manner of making meditation, X, 298–99; method of Saint Francis de Sales, I, 553; IV, 385; IX, 42, 175; X, 460–61, 471–75; XI, 234–35; of Saint Jane Frances de Chantal, IX, 26, 335; X, 463; of judge, IX, 25; of Brother of the Mission, XI, 186; for persons who do not know how to read, IX, 27–28, 172; X, 456–58, 461; or are subject to headaches, IV, 384; VIII, 55, 63; or suffer spiritual dryness, IX, 42.

Meditation requires preparation, XI, 358; mortification is condition for making meditation well, IX, 336; X, 225; XI, 81; read points of meditation previous evening, IX, 335; make meditation with respect, confidence, and humility, X, 106; how to place ourselves in presence of God: see **God** (Presence); invoke divine aid, X, 473; how to understand points of meditation, IX, 335–36; X, 474; XII, 58.

Consider aim of meditation, XI, 321; avoid spirit of curiosity, XI, 233; and too great mental strain, XI, 76, 82, 361; do not toy with seeking reasons or making beautiful reflections; meditation is not literary work, IX, 26; XI, 77, 232–33, 361; ask God often to enlighten and inspire us, XI, 77; use understanding only to energize will, XI, 83, 234, 360; books and knowledge do not help to make meditation, IX, 27, 174; as easy for simple persons to make it as for learned, and they often do it better, IX, 3–4, 330–34; X, 457, 461–62; teaching of Saints Thomas and Bonaventure, IX, 27–28; example of Bro. Antoine, IX, 332–33; of Bro. de l'Enfant-Jésus, X, 463; of Carmelite, X, 462; of Brothers of the Mission, IX, 175, 331; strive more for acts of affection than for understanding, XI, 175–76, 234–35; do not try to picture in meditation what is not so in its nature, XI, 82, 361; vary method according to whether subject is Mystery or virtue, XI, 80, 360.

Not to be content with good thoughts, but apply them to self, XI, 81; enter into details of one's faults, XI, 272; meditation must aim at practice, IX, 25; resolution is principal part of meditation, IX, 28; XI, 79; take practical resolutions, II, 217; X, 460, 484; XI, 79, 235, 360; take care to remember them, IX, 4; they should apply preferably to actions of day, IX, 30; not to be discouraged at failure in this, XI, 79–80; offer resolutions to God, X, 460; XI, 361; thank God for graces received in meditation, X, 460; XI, 235, 361; time of thanksgiving must equal that of petition, XII, 399; teach meditation to retreatants, XI, 148; those who have made meditation well can be distinguished from others, IX, 334; not to be surprised by dryness and distractions, IX, 172, 333–34; Saint Teresa suffered them for twenty years, IX, 42, 333; distaste and dryness are trials from God, XI, 82; drowsiness, another enemy of meditation; causes and remedy, IX, 29; sighing and its causes, XI, 100.

Topics of meditation given by Saint Vincent to Daughters of Charity, IX, 11–12; recommends that Directress teach new arrivals how to make meditation well, IV, 53; XIIIb, 302; afternoon and evening meditation, X, 469–70, 484, 488; never cease to be in prayerful state, IX, 325, 332. Other mention, I, 197–98.

Meekness - See **Gentleness**.

Meglat (Jean), prisoner in Toulon - VI, 261, 360; VII, 254.

Melancholy - Strange disposition, I, 239; sadness and melancholy at change of mission, X, 136; attachments result in sadness and melancholy, X, 140; pride gives rise to melancholy and sadness, X, 424.

Melchisedech, King of Salem - Foundling, XIIIb, 398, 406.

Méliand (Blaise), Attorney [Procurator] General - Contacts regarding galley convicts, II, 222; foundlings, III, 232; IV, 23; approval of Company of Daughters of Charity, IV, 6; forbids Sister Henriette Gesseaume to leave, II, 291; secretary mislays Letters of Approval of Company of Daughters of Charity, XIIIb, 145, 232; other mentions, III, 228, 492.

Mellini [**Millini**](Giovanni Garzia), Cardinal - XIIIa, 249.

Melun, town in Seine-et-Marne - Ursulines, VIII, 410–11, 430, 505, 516–17, 519; taxes from Melun, I, 552; V, 486, 503–04; VIII, 395, 608; travel there by water, III, 379, 380; other mentions, II, 539; VI, 118, 579; VIII, 551.

Melun (Ernestine de Ligne-Aremberg, Dame de) - In Beuvardes, II, 546; money owed Montmirail Missionaries, VII, 551; leaves Second Monastery of Visitation in Paris to see entrance of King and Queen into Paris, VIII, 484.

Melun (Guillaume de), Prince of Épinoy - In Beuvardes, II, 546.

Memphis, city in Egypt - IV, 269.

Ménage (Catherine), Daughter of Charity - Her praises, VII, 472; other mention, V, 614.

Ménage (Françoise), Daughter of Charity, sister of preceding - Biographical data, V, 614; VI, 514; VII, 471; sent to Nantes, IX, 430; letters Saint Vincent writes her in Nantes, V, 614; VI,

514; VII, 471; mention of letter she wrote to him, V, 614; other mention, XIIIb, 228.

Ménage (Madeleine), Daughter of Charity, sister of preceding - Biographical data, VI, 417; X, 218; Saint Louise asks permission for her to renew vows, VI, 417; praise for her, VII, 472; elected Bursar of Company, X, 218; present at Councils of Company, XIIIb, 359; other mentions, V, 614; XIIIb, 227.

Ménage (Marguerite), Daughter of Charity, sister of preceding - Biographical data, VII, 200; sent to Calais for sick and wounded soldiers, VII, 200; X, 440; death, XII, 34; other mentions, VII, 472; XIIIb, 227.

Menand (Robert), seminarian of the Mission - Biographical data, VI, 138; in Tréguier, VI, 138, 614.

Ménard (M.), physician - V, 223.

Ménard (Marguerite), Daughter of Charity - Biographical data, IV, 517; judged worthy to be Assistant, but not named because of short time in Company, XIIIb, 305–06; in Chars, IV, 517.

Menardeau (Claude), Councillor at Parlement - Delegate to Rueil conference, III, 411.

Mende, town in Lozère - Bishop: see Sylvestre de Cruzy de **Marcillac**; other mention, I, 278.

Menessier (Marguerite), Daughter of Charity - XIIIb, 228.

Menestrier (Edme), Priest of the Mission - Biographical data, IV, 537; V, 31; VI, 145; VII, 4; VIII, 17–18; letters Saint Vincent writes him in Agen, IV, 537; VI, 368, 441, 471, 504, 562, 612; VII, 4, 349, 352, 431, 514, 604; VIII, 17, 52, 63, 116, 222; mention of letters received from him, VI, 441, 472, 562, 563; VII, 349, 604, 605; VIII, 17, 52, 116, 222.

Health, V, 31; his uncle, VII, 605; Superior of Agen Seminary, VIII, 616; directs it to satisfaction of Saint Vincent, VI, 613; returns from thermal baths, VII, 349; wants to get rid of Brother; receives order to keep him, VII, 514–15; resigns Saint-Pourçain Priory, VI, 401–02; VIII, 116; other mention, V, 86: see ***Agen***.

Menochius (Giovanni Stefano), Italian Jesuit - mention of synopsis of his Scripture Commentaries, III, 483, 486.

Menoiste (Antoine), Procurator of Charity of Folleville - XIIIb, 48.

Menthon (M. de), Savoyard nobleman in Annecy - Money Saint Vincent sent him, II, 120, 203.

Mercaddé (Jean), ship owner - XIIIb, 21.

Mercier (Fr.), priest, in Paris - Desires to be member of Tuesday Conference, VIII, 204.

Mercier (Pierre), from Talmont (France), slave in Algiers - V, 405.

Mercoeur (Duc de), Governor of Provence - Negotiates with rebels of Marseilles, VII, 250; complains about Jean Le Vacher, VIII, 527.

Mercoeur (Françoise de Lorraine, Duchesse de) - Recommends slave in Algiers to Saint Vincent, V, 354.

Mercuès, village in Lot - Missionaries visit Alain de Solminihac there, II, 429; letters of Solminihac from this place, II, 428, 450, 489, 512; III, 162, 239, 256, 340, 341, 445, 461, 463, 516, 524, 586; IV, 26, 101, 124, 141, 152, 159, 163, 189, 247, 270, 272, 310, 475, 480, 498, 503, 508, 540, 562, 598; V, 173; VII, 546; willing to give conditional absolution in chapel, IV, 504; letters of Nicolas Sevin from there, VIII, 466, 603.

Mercy - Justice accompanied by mercy, I, 449; conference on spirit of compassion and of mercy, XI, 308; mention of another conference, XII, 418; distinctive feature of God, XI, 308, 328; we should be continually grateful for God's mercy, II, 146; God's mercy accompanies work of missions with His blessings, II, 256; teach people to hope in God's mercy, IV, 91; immensity of God's mercy, II, 383; graces in ministry are result of God's pure mercy, not of our wretched prayers, III, 274–75; purging Company of Daughters of Charity is act of mercy, III, 472; God never abandons even a wicked man who hopes for His mercy, IV, 317; God's increased mercy is on penitents who observe exactly decisions of Church, V, 322.

Mercy [**Mercedarians**] (Order) - Historical information, VI, 89–10; VII, 38; VIII, 287; XI, 63; vow taken by Mercedarians, XI, 385; dissension among Fathers of Mercy, III, 47–48; VI, 481; Jean Barreau stands security for them with Turks; unable to pay and is put in prison, III, 218; in vain does Saint Vincent urge Fathers of Mercy to pay their debts, III, 47–48; steps to have them indemnify Jean Barreau for insult to which he was subjected because of one of their priests, Fr. Sérapion, VI, 10, 302, 315, 354; VII, 468; VIII, 309–310, 326–27: see **Sérapion**; Saint Vincent will contact Provincial to free Consul in Algiers from avania, VI, 200; Spanish Mercedarians mistreated in Algiers; Father of Mercy expected in Algiers for ransom of slaves, V, 390–91; service rendered by Saint Vincent to Provincial of Mercedarians, VI, 365, 450, 482–83, 510, 526, 553, 619; VII, 38, 344; ransom of slaves, V, 391; other mentions, II, 394; III, 126; IV, 86; VII, 437; VIII, 316, 319; XIIIa, 60: see **Brugière** (Sébastien).

Marland (Marie) - Has gardens and stables near confreres' house in Luçon, XIIIa, 318.

Merlet (M.) - Will make decision regarding health of Fr. Alméras, III, 69.

Merlin (Gilbert), treasurer of Charity of Courboin - XIIIb, 93.

Mesgrigny (Louis de), Abbot of Quincy - See ***Quincy***.

Mesgrigny (Nicolas de), Advocate General at tax court - Ordained a priest, II, 38.

Meslin (Edme), priest in Joigny - XIIIb, 66.

Mesmes (Henri de), President *à mortier* - Delegate to Rueil conference, III, 411.

Mesnard (Mme), Anne Le Roux - Saint Vincent hopes for her prayers, I, 340.

Mesnil - Death of confrere during mission there, I, 313.

Mesnin (M. de) - VIII, 218.

Mesplède (Louis), Dominican - Teaches Jansenistic opinions, III, 345.

Mespuits, village in Essonne - Farm given to Saint Vincent by Mme de Herse, I, 290; agreement with farmer, II, 536, 538; gift of Saint Vincent to church, II, 539; other mentions, I, 478; III, 407.

Messier (Louis), Archdeacon of Beauvais - Helps Saint Vincent with retreat to ordinands of Beauvais, I, 57; other mentions I, 303, 317; II, 433.

Messier (M.), brother of Louis Messier - Biographical data; present at Saint-Lazare for theological debates of students, II, 433; other mention, I, 57.

Mestay (Mme) - II, 261.

Métayer (Michelle), Daughter of Charity - XIIIb, 228.

Métezeau (Fr.), Oratorian - Recommends Saint Vincent to M. Beynier of Châtillon, XIIIa, 50–51.

Methods of preaching, teaching, debating - See **Controversy**, **Preaching**, **Seminaries**.

Metz, town in Moselle - Character of inhabitants, X, 448; assistance for poor of Metz, I, 542, 582; II, 42, 93, 228; aldermen express gratitude to Saint Vincent, II, 149; he informs Superioress of Metz Visitation of coming delivery of money, II, 227; Parlement registers union of Saint-Esprit Commandery with Congregation of the Mission, II, 477; mission in Metz, VI, 639; VII, 62–63, 77–78, 85, 91, 100, 102, 108, 111, 112, 116,

128, 136, 137, 169–70, 384, 385, 404; X, 451; XII, 3, 15; town-house of la Haute-Pierre, VII, 78; of Montgommery, VIII, 16, 17, 525; plans for opening Missionaries' house, VIII, 14, 16, 449, 455, 525; Daughters of Charity named for Metz foundation, VII, 192, 200, 257; X, 447; Saint Vincent's advice to them on eve of departure, X, 447–53; they have not yet sent news of themselves, VII, 299; other mentions, VII, 148; X, 411, 524; XIIIa, 283, 289, 294.

Meuporense, town in Poland - King plans to open minor seminary there, V, 164.

Meurisse (Louise) - Member of Charity of Folleville, XIIIb, 48.

Meusnier (Jean), Brother of the Mission - Biographical data, V, 114; Saint Vincent considers sending him to Poland, V, 114–15, 127.

Meynard (M.) - I, 147.

Meyster (Étienne), Priest of the Mission - Biographical data, I, 278–79.

Mézières, town in Ardennes - IV, 602.

Michael (Saint) - Saint Vincent speaks of him on his feast day, X, 86, 98; defeated fallen angels in battle, XII, 282; Mme de Gondi implores his help, XIIIa, 59.

Michaud (M.), notary of Archdiocese of Lyons - XIIIa, 45.

Michaud (Fr.), Rector of Hôtel-Dieu of Châtillon - XIIIa, 57.

Michel (Guillaume), Priest of the Mission - Biographical data, III, 13–14; VI, 368; VII, 4; VIII, 177; put at disposal of Fr. Portail for placement, III, 82; sent to Sedan, VI, 368; in Sedan, VI, 403, 529, 595; VIII, 4; assists sick and wounded soldiers in Montmédy, VI, 489; is asked to counsel sons of Jean Desmarets, VI, 595; VII, 4; leaves to put mother's affairs in order, VIII, 177.

Michel (Louise), Daughter of Charity - Sent to Nantes, IX, 430; recalled from Nantes, V, 57.

Michel (Philippe), merchant in Limoges - VIII, 412.

Michel du Saint-Esprit (Fr.), Carmelite - Result of inquiry made about him by Saint Vincent, IV, 269.

Michelangelo, artist - IX, 418.

Michelangelo, young man from Savigliano - Has arrived in Paris, VI, 522; does not have vocation, VI, 558; enters seminary, VI, 602.

Michelle - At Saint-Nicolas-du-Chardonnet, I, 231; IX, 8.

Micquel (Madeleine), Daughter of Charity - Sent to Nantes, IX, 517; XIIIb, 312.

Midot (Jean), Vicar-General of Toul - Biographical data, I, 417; II, 68; IV, 32; kindness to Toul Missionaries, I, 417; II, 68; III, 449, 450; IV, 33; Saint Vincent writes to him, IV, 32.

Mignot (Fr.), Pastor in Laon - VI, 413, 552.

Mikhailovich (Alexis), Grand Duke of Moscow - Son is offered succession to throne of Poland, VI, 296–97.

Milan, town in Italy - II, 506; IV, 521; VI, 205, 257; VII, 239; VIII, 120, 176, 191, 210; confrere requests to be treated there instead of in Genoa, IV, 102.

Millenarianism - Heresy that arose in early days of Church, XII, 317.

Milleret (Jeanne), Daughter of Charity - Signs attestation after reading of Common and Particular Rules reviewed and arranged in order by Fr. Alméras, XIIIb, 206.

Millini - See **Mellini**.

Milly, village in Île de France - I, 441.

Miloir (François), Priest of the Mission - Biographical data, I, 177.

Minerva, convent of Santa Maria sopra Minerva in Rome - III, 316.

Minims - Historical data, II, 581; recite Divine Office *media voce*, XII, 270; Minims of Trinità dei Monti in Rome, VII, 635; of Chaillot in Paris, VIII, 501; other mention, I, 194.

Minor Orders - Saint Vincent does not advise them for Saint Louise's son, I, 138; Michel Le Gras says he will take them to please his mother, I, 506; Bishop Solminihac wants his men who were taking them to assist at ordinations, III, 240; Saint Vincent's reception of Minor Orders, XIIIa, 2.

Minvielle (Jean), Brother of the Mission - Biographical data, VIII, 56.

Miracles - Supposed miracles of Port-Royal, VI, 391–92; miracles worked through intercession of Saint Francis de Sales, XIIIa, 78–79, 94, 212.

Miremont, small town in Somme - VIII, 123.

Mirepoix - Bishops: see Louis de Lévy de **Ventadour**, Louis de Nogaret de **La Vallette**.

Mirepoix (Armand Dupeyré, Marquis de), Governor of Comté de Foix - Biographical data; Saint Vincent recommends interests of Bishop of Pamiers, III, 95.

Mirepoix (Catherine Caulet, Baronne de), sister-in-law of Marquise de Mirepoix - Biographical data, VII, 206; lawsuit with sister-in-law; Saint Vincent recommends case to Bishop of La Rochelle, VI, 597; contacts with Saint Vincent, VII, 206; with Saint Louise, VII, 382; retreat at Saint Louise's house; requests admission to Ladies of Hôtel-Dieu, VII, 492; other mention, XIIIb, 366.

Mirepoix (Louise de Roquelaure, Marquise de), wife of Alexandre de Levi, Marquis de Mirepoix - VI, 585.

Miriam, sister of Moses - X, 348–49; XIIIb, 351.

Miron (Judge) - VIII, 533.

Mirsane (Gabriel), surgeon of La Flèche, slave in Algiers - III, 223.

Misericorde - Sister placed there, X, 182.

Missanath - Superstitious banquet and gathering in Madagascar, III, 547, 558.

Missergent, locality - Saint Vincent wills house, woods, and land to one of his sisters, XIIIa, 99, 100.

Mission (Congregation) - See **Congregation of the Mission**.

Missionaries of Forez - Proposal of house in Lyons, VI, 330, 420.

Missionaries of Indies - Saint Vincent disagrees with members of M. de Ventadour's Community taking name of Missionaries; asks Fr. Le Vazeux to oppose it at *Propaganda Fide*, IV, 293–96; Fr. Le Vazeux goes beyond his intentions, IV, 610; and obtains from *Propaganda* decree that jeopardizes existence of new Congregation, IV, 611; Saint Vincent reprimands Fr. Le Vazeux, IV, 345, 346–47, 355, 359, 392; apologizes to M. de Ventadour, while showing him inconveniences of same name, IV, 355, 359; opening of seminary in Gentilly, IV, 296; departure for America; accident on Seine, IV, 297; Saint Vincent believes missionaries sent to Indies by M. de Ventadour have no legitimate mission, IV, 371: see **Ventadour** (Henri de Lévis de).

Missionaries of Lyons - Saint Vincent asks that they not take name of Priests of the Mission, VI, 516–20.

Missionaries of Blessed Sacrament - See **Blessed Sacrament** (Missionaries).

Missionaries of the Clergy (Congregation) - Founded by Jean de Fonteneil, I, 268; Saint Vincent writes to him, I, 268; II, 56–57.

Missions - Mention of conferences, XII, 419, 429; missions are principal ministry of Congregation of the Mission, IV, 48,

49, 391; XI, 121; XIIIa, 214, 225, 228; missions are among most important and most necessary of benefits, IV, 285; Saint Vincent refuses to give them up for ministry of seminaries exclusively, II, 256; wants each house, even seminaries, to assign at least two priests to give missions, II, 506; IV, 49; V, 254; accepts Bétharram Shrine on condition that priests will give missions, VII, 459–60; contributing to missions while remaining at home, XII, 416.

Priests of Company accept help of outside priests to give missions, I, 154, 177; III, 249–50; IV, 79–80; VII, 47, 117, 335–36, 340, 535; XIIIa, 387; Jean-Jacques Olier reports on missions, I, 324, 366; missions are given gratuitously, I, 298, 421; III, 250–51, 275; VI, 170, 179–80; VII, 450; XII, 95, 307, 313, 314; XIIIa, 214, 226, 236, 253, 258–59, 276; honoraria for Masses said for intention of faithful are not accepted during missions, V, 266; if Bishops offer to cover travel expenses, Missionaries should refuse, unless ordered to accept, V, 490; under same conditions, they refuse what might be offered for expenses of non-Vincentian priests associated with mission, VI, 636; and what may be accepted from benefactors or from those who do not live where mission is given, I, 133; what is offered as alms, VI, 170; VII, 450.

Saint Vincent permits missions in episcopal cities, II, 310, 397, 405; his reservations, II, 90, 405; considers this forbidden, unless Bishop demands otherwise, II, 90; IV, 369, 392; V, 604; VI, 257, 351, 639; VII, 102, 108; XII, 4; or where episcopal towns are small, numerous, and in need, as in Piedmont, VII, 271; or where inhabitants of countryside have taken refuge in towns, IV, 392, 398; no confrere is to give missions to nuns, unless Bishop orders it, IV, 52; XI, 161; encourages missions in less important places, II, 350–51; missions succeed better in rural areas than in towns, III, 609.

How first missions were given, II, 91; VI, 577; use of cots, II, 91; sermons and catechetical talks, VI, 400; XI, 95; XII, 237–38; XIIIa, 370, 388; book of sermons and catechetical talks, VII, 271; XII, 238; length of sermons, XIIIa, 370–71, 388; public penances, IV, 35; confessions, children's Communion, processions, setting up Charities, manner of dealing with heretics, contacts with Pastor: see **Confessions**, **Communion** (First), **Processions**, **Confraternity of Charity**, **Heretics**, **Pastors**; practice of settling differences, VII, 424.

Bear with difficulties encountered during missions, I, 226; be faithful to observance of Rules, III, 250; XI, 93; to order of day, I, 554; taking meals together, XI, 93; faults to be avoided during missions, I, 179; indulgences granted during missions, V, 571, 573; Saint Vincent asks superiors to keep record of all missions given, VIII, 346–47; Saint Vincent asks Fr. Firmin Get for list of missions he has given, VIII, 396, 401, 420; continue mission until everyone has fulfilled obligations, I, 555; II, 170; VII, 71; how returning Missionaries are welcomed at Saint-Lazare, VII, 593; IX, 127; XI, 114, 297; days of rest during mission, I, 515; rest between missions, III, 58; XIIIa, 217; month of vacation, I, 555; VIII, 39, 59; XIIIa, 370, 383; activities of Missionaries during this time, VIII, 89, 91, 93; XII, 235; XIIIa, 217; 1651 Assembly decides that no age limit be put on those giving missions, but young priests should not be given this work right away, XIIIa, 369; members of 1651 Assembly approve inviting members of Tuesday Conferences to join them in missions, XIIIa, 370; see also **Cases of conscience**, **Controversy**.

Unless necessary, say nothing to Bishops of faults noted in parish, VI, 420; accounts of what is done on missions, IV, 587; VIII, 468; XI, 112; instructions for missions in Archdiocese of Paris, VII, 324; not to worry if mission doesn't succeed as desired, III, 206; good to return from time to time to places where mission has been given, III, 332; plenary indulgences and faculty to absolve from reserved cases: see **Reserved Cases**, **Indulgences**.

Particular missions: see ***Annecy, Ay, Bene Vagienna, Bra, Breda, Bruyères, Castelnouvo, Cavallermaggiore, Ceranesi, Cévennes, Charmes-la-Côte, Cherasco, Claye, Fontaine, Fossano, Gavi, Gémozac, Guingamp, Joigny, Lavagna, Limerick, Lucerna, Luçon, Ludes, Mauron, Mondovi, Niolo, Pianezza, Plessala, Pleurtuit, Quarto al Mare, Raconi (Racconigi), Saché, Saint-Cyr-les-Colons, Saint-Ilpize, Savigliano, Scalenghe, Sisteron, Vetralla, Villafranca Piemonte, Vins, etc.***

Missions, Foreign - Zeal of Saint Vincent for foreign missions, III, 40, 164, 278–85; ready to leave for Indies, XI, 357; willing to send priests wherever Holy See wishes, II, 288; not elsewhere, IV, 371; wonders if it is more perfect to represent to Superior desire to go to infidel countries than to be silent but ready to go if Superiors wish, XII, 46; recommendations to Missionaries leaving for distant lands, XI, 64; *Propaganda* will assure Congregation's service to distant lands, II, 457; perhaps God plans to transfer Church outside of Europe, III, 40–41, 164, 187–88; V, 425; XI, 279, 318–20; vocation of Missionary is to go everywhere, XI, 264, 357; XII, 79, 197, 215; praise for missionary work, XI, 65; to devote self to salvation of unbelievers is kind of martyrdom, XI, 374; even simply showing unbelievers beauty of Catholic religion would be good result, VII, 133; example of seniors, XII, 198; example of Spanish Jesuit who returned from Indies, then went back, II, 229.

Virtues needed for those sent to infidel countries, III, 279, 281; V, 462; XII, 197–98; need for Missionaries to study language of country: see **Languages**; use pictures to instruct indigenous peoples: see **Pictures**; reasoning drawn from nature and customs, III, 280–81; thank God for good done by Company in foreign missions, XI, 262.

Missions entrusted to Company: see ***Barbary, Madagascar***; missions proposed to Company: see ***Arabia, Canada, East Indies, Lebanon, Morocco, Persia, Salé***; *Propaganda Fide* Seminary for foreign missions: see ***Propaganda*** (Seminary).

Missions-Étrangères - See **Foreign Missions Society**.

Mobavec (Guillaume), slave in Algiers - III, 223.

Mockeries - Do not ridicule others, X, 118–19.

Moderation [**Sobriety**] - Conference on moderation in eating and drinking, XII, 37–43; on moderation and silence at meals, XI, 105; mention of conferences, XII, 423, 426, 433; moderation of country women, of peasants in Limousin, Gascony, and other places, of nuns of Lorraine, of Virgin and Jesus, IX, 69–71; of **Alain de Solminihac**: see this name; text of Rule of Daughters of Charity, X, 326; moderation necessary for them, IX, 70; excess in drinking and eating, obstacle to vocation, IX, 363; frugality is soul of Company, XIIIb, 290; example of moderation, V, 34. See also **Gluttony**, **Mortification**, **Meals**.

Modesty - Mention of conferences, XII, 407, 410, 411, 415, 426; text of Rule of Daughters of Charity, X, 305; virtue necessary for Daughters of Charity, IX, 72; X, 305–07, 585; XIIIb, 346; modesty is their veil, X, 530, 532; different ways of observing modesty, X, 586; in dress, IX, 72; XI, 325; XIIIb, 251; headdress, XIIIb, 251–54; recreations, X, 305, 306; in streets, IX, 31–32, 98; X, 48, 200, 304–05, 323, 338, 363, 451, 530, 532; XI, 325–26; 360–61; XIIIb, 126, 137; avoid dallying with outsiders in streets or homes, X, 362, 531; XIIIb, 126, 137; example of Saint Francis of Assisi, IX, 21; X, 305; of village girls, IX, 71; of deceased Sisters, X, 586; of Visitandines, X, 106–07; of coadjutor Brother, IX, 72; failures in modesty, IX, 552–53; X, 323, 363, 586–90.

Moger (Jacques), convict in Toulon - VI, 187.

Mogilev [***Mohilev***], town in Poland - Re-capture by armies of King of Poland, V, 335.

Mohammed, Founder of Islam - I, 12; III, 544, 557; V, 339.

Mohammedanism [**Islam**] - II, 458; III, 331, 544–46, 557; V, 91, 339; VIII, 566; religion of people of Senegal Islands, Cape Verde Islands, and Gambia, III, 331.

Moidart, district in Scotland - Evangelized by Fr. Duggan [Duiguin], V, 121.

Moiset (M.), from La Fère - Married man who wants to become Missionary; Saint Vincent dissuades him, VII, 217.

Moisson (Nicolas), King's lawyer in Mâcon - XIIIb, 73, 74, 77.

Moissonnier (Jean-Baptiste), Priest of the Mission - I, *xxxi.*

Molard (Jean), from Mâcon - XIIIb, 74.

Moldavia [***Moldova***], republic in Eastern Europe - Wages war on Poland, VI, 645; state of Catholic religion in Moldavia, XII, 59; other mention, VII, 390.

Molé (Édouard), son of Mathieu Molé - Biographical data; appointed Bishop of Bayeux diocese; Saint Vincent's opposition, II, 615.

Molé (Mathieu), Attorney General, then Chief Justice and Keeper of Seals - Biographical data, I, 114; II, 128; III, 411; IV, 44; VI, 499; VIII, 195; IX, 168; contacts with Saint Vincent, I, 114–115, 134, 401, 578; II, 128, 619; III, 492; IV, 44; VIII, 195; requests Bayeux diocese for son Édouard, II, 615; steps taken with him concerning Foundlings, II, 151, 486–87; III, 505; to obtain publication and validation in Parlement for Bull *Cum Occasione,* IV, 583; delegated by Parlement for Rueil Conference, III, 411; Saint Vincent gives account of two proposals, IV, 184; VIII, 195; XIIIa, 377; other mentions, VI, 499; XIIIa 128.

Molina (Antonio de), Carthusian - III, 363.

Molina (Carlos) - Author of books on Index, XIIIa, 364.

Molina (Luis), Jesuit theologian - Biographical data, III, 324.

Mollin (Jean), Priest of the Mission - Biographical data, II, 539.

Molony (Thady), Priest of the Mission - Biographical data, IV, 305; V, 375; VI, 474; VII, 370; ill at Saint-Lazare, IV, 418; in Le Mans, V, 575; VI, 474, 515; office of Procurator does not please him, VII, 370; mention of letter from Saint Vincent, VII, 370; mention of letters to Saint Vincent, VI, 474; VII, 409; considers entering Carthusians, VII, 409; Saint Vincent recommends that Superior send him to give missions, VII, 409, 440; serious fault, VII, 440, 441; Saint Vincent requests that he resume office of Procurator, VII, 494; put in charge of boarders, VII, 534; no longer willing to be Procurator, VII, 591.

Monaco - Marriage of Prince's daughter to son of Marchese di Pianezza, VIII, 177.

Monboisin (M. de) - VIII, 505.

Monceaux (M. de), King's Councillor - Saint Vincent objects to donation of Gonesse property, XIIIa, 341–42.

Monchia (Giovanni Cristoforo di), Priest of Genoa - Biographical data, IV, 266; VI, 83; VII, 377; benefactor of Missionaries in this town; Saint Vincent thanks him, IV, 266–67; confidence Fr. Blatiron shows him, V, 136; dies of plague, VI, 83, 84; compromise concerning inheritance, VII, 439; other mentions, VII, 377, 389.

Moncontour, town in Côtes-du-Nord - Young women from Moncontour request admission to Daughters of Charity, III, 336.

Mondion (Jacques de), Pastor in Saché - Letters to Sisters, II, 216; contacts with Saint Louise, II, 423; Saint Louise fears offending him by sending home young woman he had enter Daughters of Charity, XIIIb, 268–69: see ***Saché***.

Mondovì, town in Italy - VII, 483.

Monestier, town in Haute-Loire, today ***Le Monastier*** - Disorders in Benedictine abbey, III, 382.

Money - Question between Saint Vincent and Saint Louise, I, 548; Saint Louise has money only in French currency, II, 138; money given to Congregation cannot be diverted in favor of relatives, IV, 322–23; should not be given to confreres passing through, except in certain circumstances, VII, 99; obligation to manage money well, X, 245–56; Sisters must not keep money of the poor, X, 529; management and safeguarding of it, X, 549; confreres do not carry money; one man is designated to do so, XI, 322; money not needed to live in Madagascar, III, 282.

Mongeny (Jeanne-Marguerite de), Visitandine - Biographical data, VI, 164.

Mongert [**Monget**] (Madeleine), Daughter of Charity - Biographical data, III, 168; XIIIb, 118; sent to Angers, II, 12; XIIIb, 118; health, III, 168.

Monica (Saint) - Grace received by Louise de Marillac on feast of Saint Monica, VI, 313.

Mongie (Sieur de la) - Has gardens and stables near Luçon house of confreres, XIIIa, 318.

Monique (Marie), Daughter of Charity - II, 50.

Monluc (Mother de), Abbess of Saint-Jacques - Recommends priest to Saint Vincent, VIII, 423.

Monopotapa, kingdom at Cape of Good Hope - VIII, 591.

Monnellet (M.) - Money given him for confreres in Annecy, II, 214.

Mons, town in Belgium - Mons Visitation, IV, 83; VIII, 436; Canonesses of Sainte-Vautrude, VIII, 597.

Monstier (M.) - Willing to grant water rights to Firmin Get in Marseilles, VII, 227.

Monstrel, town - Former name of Montreuil, III, 369.

Mont-de-Marsan, town in Landes - IV, 334.

Mont-Dieu, village in Ardennes - Carthusian Monastery, III, 204.

Montal (Fr.) - IV, 27.

Montauban, town in Tarn-et-Garonne - Bishops: see Anne de **Murviel**, Pierre de **Bertier**; transferring seminary there is considered, VI, 476–77; VII, 167, 430, 505; transfer takes place, VIII, 618; XIIIa, 198; Jesuit collège, VIII, 257; Labadie's stay in Montauban, IV, 185, 457; healthful state of town, IV, 467; V, 28; heretics in diocese converted during missions, I, 249; XIIIa, 282, 289, 411; list of Superiors and history of mission, VIII, 618; other mentions, III, 163; IV, 466, 520–21, 558–59; V, 454, 471, 502; VI, 180, 358; VII, 282; VIII, 306.

Montbard (Christophe du Plessis, Baron de) - See **Du Plessis** (Christophe).

Montchal (Charles de), Archbishop of Toulouse - Biographical data, I, 430; II, 103; III, 196; IV, 143; letters from Saint Vincent, I, 492; II, 455, 554; IV, 143; references to other letters, I, 431, 487; Montchal thanks saint for missions given in Toulouse diocese, II, 103; brother's illness, II, 556; desire to entrust seminary to Priests of the Mission, III, 538; Saint Vincent does not ask that they be established in Toulouse or in diocese so as not to anticipate call of Providence, III, 538; IV, 144; death, IV, 248; other mentions, I, 519, 527, 543; II, 512, 652; III, 187, 196–97; VI, 517.

Montchal (M. de), brother of Charles de Montchal - III, 538; IV, 143.

Montdésir (Mlle de) - Works with Sisters and poor people of Issy, II, 400; V, 44.

Montdidier, town in Somme - I, 213.

Monte Citorio - Permanent residence of Missionaries in Rome, VIII, 610.

Montebas (Vicomte de) - Member of association against dueling, V, 617.

Montech, town in Tarn-et-Garonne - Diocesan seminary transferred there, IV, 520; Jean d'Agan, Pastor of Montech: see **Agan** (Jean d'); Priests of the Mission ministering in seminary, IV, 559; Fr. Le Gros dies there, V, 471; seminary transferred from Montech to Notre-Dame de Lorm, VI, 62–63; seminary transferred from Montech [*sic*] to Montauban, XIIIa, 198: see ***Montauban***.

Monteil (François-Adhémar de), Archbishop of Arles - Saint Vincent writes his thoughts on establishment of reform in Saint-Césaire Abbey, III, 161, 176; action of Prelate for pacification of Marseilles, III, 161; writes to Saint Vincent to obtain ransom of members of his diocese enslaved in Algiers, V, 147; saint promises to help in this, V, 150.

Monteil (Jacques-Adhémar de), Bishop of Saint-Paul-Trois-Châteaux - IV, 203.

Montelon [**Monthelon**](M. de) - III, 587–89; XIIIa, 119.

Montereil - See **Montreuil** (Jean de).

Montevit (Germain de), Priest of the Mission - Biographical data, II, 29; death, II, 29, 42.

Montfaucon, today part of Paris - Corpses of criminals exposed here, XII, 31.

Montferrand (Collège) - Jesuits worked with ordinands there, XIIIa, 312.

Montfort (Canon de), in Annecy - VIII, 488.

Montfort, village in Maine-et-Loire - VII, 274.

Montfort-le-Routrou, town in Sarthe - Mission given there, VI, 123, 179.

Montgeron, village in Essonne - Mission given there, III, 134–35.

Monthelon (M. de), friend of Saint Vincent - Mentioned in interrogation of Saint-Cyran, XIIIa, 119.

Montheron (M. de) - In Rome, II, 457, 492, 583; III, 165.

Montholon (Guy-François de) - Biographical data, I, 266; letters from Saint Vincent, I, 266, 273; conflict with brother, I, 266–67; brother escapes from Saint-Lazare, I, 273.

Montholon (Jean) - Secret marriage to Jeanne Jeannesson, I, 266–67; incarcerated at Saint-Lazare; Saint Vincent fears he might escape, I, 267; he escapes, I, 273–74.

Monthoux (Fr. de) - Decides not to accompany Visitandines going to Poland, V, 82; letter to Queen of Poland, V, 174.

Monthuis (Pierre) of Montreuil, prisoner in Toulon - VI, 524.

Montigny (Mlle de) - VI, 513.

Montigny (Fr. de) - Name given to Jean Bécu in Nancy, I, 589.

Montigny-Seruyent (M.) - Writes to ask Saint Vincent to intervene in favor of Fr. Eudes, VIII, 424.

Montlhéry, village in Essonne - Missions given there, II, 151; VII, 71; other mention, XIIIb, 206.

Montmagny (Charles Huault de), Governor of Canada - III, 596.

Montmartre, section of Paris - Nuns of Montmartre Abbey, III, 477; Prioress, III, 370; girl raised in abbey, VIII, 520; pilgrimage to Montmartre, X, 136; pilgrimage of first Missionaries to Montmartre, XII, 335.

Montmaur [**Montmort**] (Henri-Louis-Habert, seigneur de), Master of Requests - Good will toward Rome Missionaries, II, 267, 272–73; contact with Saint Vincent, II, 511; letter of M. de la Coste to M. de Montmaur, II, 574; brother-in-law of Mme d'Argensolles, III, 513–14.

Montmédy, town in Meuse - Siege of Montmédy, XII, 46; assistance given to sick and wounded soldiers by Daughters of Charity, X, 381; by Missionaries, VI, 489; other mention, VIII, 15.

Montmirail (Bl. Jean de) - How he came to clean his shoes, IX, 233–34.

Montmirail, town in Marne - Air is thin, VII, 623; and good, VI, 311, 334; Mme de Gondi, Baronne de Montmirail, XIIIa, 62, 63, 65, 213, 218, 219, 222, 224, 230, 236; Saint Vincent gives mission in area; converts heretic, XI, 29–30; uprising of populace against garrison, IV, 561; birthplace of M. Husson, IV, 549; Saint Vincent introduces him to Duchesse d'Aiguillon, IV, 560; Husson writes from this town, VIII, 447; journey of Adrien Le Bon to Montmirail, II, 604; money sent to nuns of Montmirail, VI, 542; young woman from this place is judged too childish to take habit of Daughter of Charity, XIIIb, 362; Missionaries in transit in Montmirail, I, 179, 180, 421, 422, 442, 456; II, 259, 273; mission given in Montmirail by Jean Bécu, I, 446–47, 470–71, 464–76; illusion of tree trunk turned to stone, XII, 280–81.

Petition for establishment of Charity in villages of barony, XIIIb, 92–93; beginning of Charity of Montmirail (1618), I, 456; XIIIb, 31–32; approval, XIIIb, 31; Rules, XIIIb, 29, 35; elections and receptions, XIIIb, 33–34; Saint Louise visits Charity, I, 63, 64, 88–89, 116–23; mixed Charity established; unsuccessful, IV, 76; other mentions, I, 90, 94, 176–77; VII, 284; Montmirail Missionaries: letters from Saint Vincent, IV, 512; V, 49, 437; VII, 622: see **Bayart**, **Champion**, **Delville**, **Guillot**, **Monvoisin**; Missionaries from Montmirail visiting Saint-Lazare, II, 664.

Saint Vincent advises Superior to take possession of house before leasing out farms dependent on it, II, 544; Bishop of Soissons approves establishment, II, 554; III, 76–77; inhabitants of Montmirail try to keep Missionaries there, II, 548; benefactors of house, II, 546, 554; IV, 513; VI, 89; VII, 220, 301, 551; great ordeal; on this occasion Saint Vincent sends Fr. Codoing to Montmirail, II, 674; two priests from there sent to Crécy, III, 250; poverty of house, VII, 17, 220; only two priests at end of 1657, VI, 615; losses suffered force reduction of personnel to one or two priests, VII, 220; complaints of Duc de Noirmoutiers, VI, 88; of inhabitants, VII, 219, 551.

Priory, hospital, and farm of La Chaussée: see ***Chaussée***; Saint-Jean-Baptiste Chapel, VI, 88; La Maladrerie and its farm, II, 547; VII, 220; farm in Fontaine-Essarts, II, 554; IV, 313; in Chamblon, II, 545; in Vieux-Moulin, II, 554; VI, 312; VIII, 218; difficulties of administration of farms, IV, 326; V, 437; presence of women on farms, IV, 312; tenant farmers do not pay, IV, 326; or they request delay or reduction in payment, VI, 311–12; VIII, 6.

Missions, I, 441; II, 546; III, 77; V, 438; VI, 535, 615; VII, 301, 334; VIII, 53, 219; Simon Le Gras, Bishop of Soissons, does not easily authorize missions in diocese, VII, 220; retreats, II, 546; Missionaries help confreres in Toul with retreats for ordinands, VI, 457, 535; assist poor of area, III, 409; Saint Vincent praises M. Bayart for bringing wounded soldiers to Hôtel-Dieu, IV, 513; alms given to Hôtel-Dieu, II, 545; Saint Vincent advises Missionaries to give asylum to refugees, despite fear of pilfering, V, 49; visitation of house by Fr. Berthe, VII, 613; VIII, 54, 84.

List of Superiors and history of house, VIII, 612; personnel: see **Arthur** (Nicolas), **Bayart**, **Champion** (Louis), **Cornuel** (Guillaume), **Delville**, **Dumas**, **Duperroy** (Victor), **François** (Bro.), **Grimal**, **Guillot** (Nicolas), **Hauteville** (François de), **Hazart**, **La Brière**, **Le Soudier** (Jacques), **Monvoisin** (Jean), **Pinson**, **Roze**; priests being sent to Montmirail or Fontaine-Essarts, VI, 89.

Daughters of Charity in Montmirail: departure of Sisters Jeanne-Baptiste and Nicole Haran for Montmirail, IX, 430; plan of Sister Nicole from Montmirail to go to Issy to serve poor, V, 44; M. Champion requests that there be at least two Sisters in house, V, 65; Jeanne-Christine Prévost accompanies two Sisters for hospital, V, 208, 222, 225; the two Sisters ministering in hospital are satisfactory, VII, 220; other mentions, IV, 215, 513.

Montmorency, town in Val-d'Oise - Saint Vincent plans to go there to establish Charity, I, 280; house for illegitimate girls, I, 424; mission in Montmorency valley, II, 91; other mention, II, 178.

Montois [**Montou or Monthoux**] (Fr. de), Director who was to accompany Visitation Nuns to Poland - Contacts with Saint Vincent, XII, 371.

Montolieu (Chevalier Jean-Baptiste de) - Philippe Le Vacher plans to visit him, VII, 94; in court with Rappiot, VII, 288.

Montorio (Pietro Francesco), Vice-legate of Avignon - Biographical data, I, 9; receives abjuration from renegade with whom Saint Vincent fled from Tunis, takes saint to Rome, learns secrets of alchemy from him, I, 9, 12; promises to help him get ahead, I, 13; other mention, VIII, 601.

Montpellier, town in Hérault - People inclined to be undisciplined by nature, VII, 608; proposal for house of Daughters of Charity, VII, 256; epidemic, VIII, 69; Bishop: see **Bosquet** (François de); Missionaries in Montpellier: at request of Bishop, Saint Vincent sends Fr. Get to Montpellier to take over direction of seminary, VII, 554–55; regrets having accepted it too quickly, VII, 607, 631; letters to Fr. Get, Superior of house: see **Get** (Firmin); advises Fr. Get about formation of seminarians, VII, 607–09; VIII, 3–5; Fr. Durand replaces Fr. Get during latter's journey to Marseilles, VIII, 18, 37; Missionaries receive insufficient salary from Bishop, VII, 631; Saint Vincent promises a Brother, VII, 608; personnel: see **Duchesne** (René), **Get** (Firmin), **Parisy**.

Archbishop of Narbonne informs Saint Vincent that Bishop of Montpellier intends to close his seminary, VIII, 267, 272–73; seminary drags on; Saint Vincent thinks confreres should withdraw, VIII, 273–74, 289; Fr. Delespiney thinks of visiting Fr. Get there, VIII, 275; return of Fr. Get to Marseilles, VIII, 299, 303, 315, 320; XIIIa, 471; Montpellier is on Fr. Alméras's route from Cahors to Annecy, III, 125; Superior of house and its history, VIII, 619; other mention, VIII, 319.

Montpensier (Anne-Marie-Louise d'Orléans, Duchesse de), granddaughter of Henri de Bourbon, Duc de Montpensier - Biographical data, III, 317; V, 443; VI, 280–81; VII, 65; Saint Vincent indicates to Pastor of Richelieu how he ought to pay his respects to her, V, 443; asks for Daughters of Charity for Saint-Fargeau Hospital, VI, 280–81; VII, 64; other mentions, III, 317; VII, 65, 640.

Montpensier (Henri de Bourbon, Duc de) - XIIIa, 52.

Montpezat, village in Lot-et-Garonne - Mission given there, I, 430.

Montreuil [**Montereil**] (Jean de), secretary for King's Ambassador in Rome - Biographical data, II, 245; about to depart for Rome, II, 245, 251, 258; in Rome, II, 280.

Montreuil-sous-Bois, town near Paris - Saint Vincent goes there, I, 96; foundation and rule of Confraternity of Charity (1627), XIIIb, 94; visit of Charity by Saint Louise, I, 99–106; by Mlle de Pollalion, I, 282; people of Montreuil are given to mockery, I, 102; other mention, I, 272.

Montreuil-sur-Mer, town in Pas-de-Calais - Comte de Lannoy entrusts to Daughters of Charity ministry for bashful poor and orphans, XIIIb, 271; Saint Vincent tells Anne Hardemont, chosen for foundation, how to act during journey and, once there, with founder, young women caring for orphans, and Marie Lullen, companion, XIIIb, 273–83; June 26, 1647, two Sisters leave Paris without receiving blessing of Saint Vincent, absent at time, III, 208, 210; Saint Vincent recalls them to Paris, IV, 22; other mentions VI, 524; XIIIb, 140, 249.

Montrouge (Jacques), Bishop of Saint-Flour - IV, 28; VII, 194.

Montry (Robert de), Paris merchant - Began work of Madeleine for young women of loose morals wishing to change their lives, I, 187; X, 124.

Mont-Saint-Eloy Abbey - Saint Vincent advises monks to ask for Pierre Le Roy as Abbot, V, 95.

Montserrat - Priests of Santa Maria de Montserrat Monastery are not religious, although they take three vows, XIIIa, 405.

Monvoisin (François), Priest of the Mission - Biographical data, VIII, 100; assigned to Poland, VIII, 99; Saint Vincent asks Officialis of Arras for dimissorial letter for Monvoisin's ordination, VIII, 122.

Monvoisin (Jean), Priest of the Mission - Biographical data, VI, 457; VII, 300; VIII, 6; Superior in Montmirail, VIII, 612; letters Saint Vincent writes him there, VII, 300, 334, 551, 613; VIII, 6, 53, 84, 196, 218; mention of letters to Saint Vincent, VII, 301, 334, 551, 613; VIII, 6, 84, 197, 218; sent from Montmirail to Toul for ordinands' retreat, VI, 457; mission in Sézanne, VI, 535, 615; in Beuvardes, VII, 301, 334; in Vendeuvre, VII, 334: see ***Montmirail***.

Moors - Have custom of giving away their children in return for something else, VI, 243.

Morainvilliers, village in Yvelines - Inhabitants not very religious; establishment of Daughters of Charity considered, VI, 339.

Morals - Loose morals: see **Casuists**.

Moran (Mme) - I, 398.

Morancy (Élisabeth), Daughter of Charity - XIIIb, 228.

Morand (M.), of Lyons - II, 262, 269.

Morando (Antonio), Priest of the Mission - Biographical data, IV, 247; V, 275; VII, 543; in Genoa, IV, 247, 492; giving mission in Tivoli diocese, V, 275; and other places, VII, 543.

Morangis (Antoine Barillon de) - Biographical data, III, 48; IV, 397; M. de Vertamont wished to discuss with him question raised in Mende, II, 235; commissioned by King to investigate disorder among Mercedarians, III, 47–48; other mentions, III, 163; IV, 397; V, 17.

Morangis, village in Essonne - Foundation of Saint-Eutrope, II, 172.

Morar [***Moray***], district in Scotland - Evangelized by Fr. Duggan [Duiguin], V, 121, 122; by Fr. Lumsden, VI, 546.

Moras (Antonin de), chaplain of Saint-Pierre Church in Mâcon - XIIIb, 73–74, 76.

Moras (Bertrande de), mother of Saint Vincent - See **Demoras**.

Mordec, village in Ille-et-Vilaine - V, 597.

Moreau (Charlotte), Daughter of Charity - Biographical data, VI, 325; in Châteaudun, VI, 325, 424–25; other mention, XIIIb, 228.

Moreau (Étienne), Bishop of Arras - Abbot of Saint-Josse, VI, 82, 609; other mentions, VI, 79; X, 182; XIIIb, 229.

Moreau (Jean), *Procureur Fiscal* of Clichy - XIIIa, 24.

Moreau (Marguerite), Daughter of Charity - Biographical data, V, 120–21; VI, 55–56; VIII, 315; IX, 455; in Angers, V, 215; departure for Poland, IX, 455; arrival in Warsaw, IV, 519; writes to Saint Vincent about difficulties experienced by Sisters, IV, 575; reference to letter to Saint Vincent, V, 491; refuses invitation of Queen of Poland to remain at Court near her; edification of Saint Vincent, IX, 463, 502, 538, 541; Queen's proposal for foundlings; Sister Moreau's response, IX, 463; Fr. Lambert places her under direction of Sister Drugeon, IX, 464; Saint Vincent asks her to keep an eye on young people of her house, V, 120; Fr. Ozenne would like another Sister Servant, V, 238; she suspects Saint Vincent of withholding her letters to Saint Louise, V, 338; set in her ways, V, 362; health, V, 388, 395; Queen is satisfied with her, VI, 55; again asks her to remain near her to minister to poor, X, 536; XIIIb, 366; Saint Vincent consults Saint Louise and her Councillors about this, XIIIb, 366–69; in Warsaw, V, 215, 491; VI, 385, 393; VIII, 315; other mentions, VI, 326; XIIIb, 228.

Moreau (Nicolas), prisoner in Toulon - VII, 123.

Moreau, widow in Montmirail - VI, 311; VIII, 6.

Morel (Claude), Doctor of Sorbonne - Biographical data, I, 177; other mention, III, 74.

Morel (M.), notary - XIIIa, 66.

Morel (Philibert), Canon of Mâcon - XIIIb, 78.

Morennes (Claude de), monk of Saint-Lazare - I, 135, 371; XIIIa, 27.

Morice (Fr.), Barnabite - Advises Jeanne Dalmagne to enter Daughters of Charity, IX, 156; esteem for her, IX, 158, 161.

Morin (Jean), priest - Acting on behalf of Saint Vincent, named Canon of Écouis, notifies Chapter of nomination and takes possession of canonry, XIIIa, 26, 27.

Morin (M.), captain of regiment which includes men from Clichy - People are clamoring for their sons and Saint Vincent is writing to him about it, I, 335.

Morlaix (Joseph de), Capuchin - Willing to send men to accompany Fr. Mousnier to Madagascar, V, 280.

Morocco - See **Recollects**, ***Salé***.

Mortagne-sur-Gironde, village in Charente-Maritime - Mission given there, I, 183.

Mortemar [Mortemart] (Diane de Grand-Seigne, Marquise de) - Biographical data; asks Saint Vincent for tutor for son, II, 650; he sends temporary one, II, 654; she withdraws daughter, boarder at Motherhouse of Daughters of Charity, without paying expenses, XIIIb, 303.

Mortemar [Mortemart] (Gabrielle de), daughter of above, wife of Marquis de Thiange - XIIIb, 303.

Mortification - Conferences, X, 44, 318; XI, 59; XII, 173; mention of another conference, XII, 434; text of Rule of Missionaries, XII, 173–74; of Daughters of Charity, X, 318, 324; Saint Vincent reminds Sisters of very great fault of putting fragrance on their linen, IX, 21; mortification especially necessary for Missionaries, XI, 103; XII, 249–50; Missionary without mortification is only carcass of Missionary, XI, 365; be very mortified, XI, 93; persevere in mortification; ways of mortifying self, XII, 400.

No one is exempt from mortification, X, 201, 203, 228–30; nature tends toward evil; mortification is indispensable for practice of virtue, X, 45–48, 198–99; of indifference, X, 225; necessary to make meditation well, IX, 336; XI, 81; to avoid complaining, X, 152; to do God's Will, XII, 136; example of vine-dresser, XII, 184–85; those who do not mortify themselves do not avoid suffering, X, 151–53; whoever flees Cross finds more weighty problems, XI, 59; mortification brings happiness to those who love God, X, 229, 325; equanimity, X, 229–30; gives greater consolation than when natural inclinations are followed, X, 125, 325; difficult only in beginning, IX, 141; X, 203, 227; XII, 185; easier to renounce pleasure than to love suffering, IV, 55; more we give in to nature, more it demands, XI, 59; sensuality worms its way into everything, XI, 59–60; to renounce self is to establish Jesus in us, XII, 184; degree of mortification measures degree of virtue, XI, 59; mortification acquired by repeated acts; be content to lead others to it step by step, V, 443.

Example of Jesus, IX, 129, 134; X, 199, 320; XII, 185–86; teaching of Jesus, IX, 136; XII, 173–86; lesson of Saint Paul, X, 320; of Princesse de Condé, X, 320; of Fr. Pillé, II, 378; of monk to whom vinegar was repugnant, X, 17; of Carmelites and Sisters of Saint Thomas [Dominicans], X, 49, 80.

Necessary to mortify self interiorly and exteriorly, I, 223; X, 324; XI, 59; mortification of senses, IX, 20–22; X, 17, 48–49, 123, 124, 199–201, 226, 323, 573; XII, 176, 233–34, 260: see **Meals**; of tongue, X, 324; of passions, X, 44–48, 49–50, 201–03, 229, 321–23; XII, 184–85; of comforts, X, 3; XI, 191; XII, 18, 260; of will, II, 257, 278; IX, 248; X, 3, 124, 152, 203, 226, 323; XII, 176; of memory, X, 124, 203, 226–27; XII, 181; of knowledge, X, 123; XII, 260; of understanding, X, 123, 203, 226, 323; of judgment, V, 436; X, 323; XII, 175–76; renunciation of relatives: see **Relatives**; of concern for health, XII, 183; of old man, XII, 184; bodily austerities: see **Discipline**, **Fasting**; love of suffering: see **Sufferings**.

Ministries of Daughters of Charity do not allow many penances; for ordinary mortifications, permission of Superior needed; for extraordinary ones, that of Director, IX, 513, 515; X, 80, 318; interior and exterior mortifications appropriate for them, X, 47–48; means of mortifying self, X, 49–52; mortification is also daughter of charity, XII, 364. See also **Attachments**, **Detachment**, **Penance**, **Sufferings**.

Moscoso y Sandoval (Balthazar), Archbishop of Toledo - proceedings for foundation of Missionaries' house in his diocese, VI, 364; VII, 400, 433; his chaplain expresses desire to enter Congregation of the Mission, VII, 327.

Moses, leader and lawgiver of Hebrews - His law, II, 158; III, 557; V, 428; IX, 252, 258–59; XII, 9–10, 107; XIIIb, 360; those who observed it performed miracles, XII, 107; his teaching, XI, 312; his prayer, V, 505, 572; IX, 328–29; XI, 194; his marvels, V, 489; his rod, XI, 30, 48; punishment of those who murmur against him, X, 193, 348–49; XIIIb, 351; cited, XIIIa, 468; other mentions, VI, 216, 248; IX, 514; X, 329; XI, 191, 372; XII, 80, 166; XIIIb, 398, 406, 416.

Motelet (Jean), notary in Paris - XIIIa, 11, 16, 18, 19, 20, 66, 67.

Motta (Paul) - Biographical data; founder of Community considering union with that of Fr. Authier and with Mission, I, 221–22.

Motte-Haudancourt (Henri de la), Bishop of Rennes - Contacts with Saint Vincent, III, 111.

Moucaut (M. de) - IV, 457.

Mouchy (Charles de), Governor and Lieutenant-General in Lorraine and Barrois - II, 76.

Moufel (C.), notary - XII, 378, 380, 381.

Moufle (M.) - VII, 126.

Moulan (M.) - I, 342.

Moulard (Charles) - XIIIa, 346.

Moulin (Claude-Félicine), wife of Seigneur des Essarts - Biographical data, IV, 327.

Moulins, town in Allier - Saint Vincent has Fr. Alméras, who is ill, taken there, VI, 540, 554, 570, 571; Bro. Claude takes thermal baths there, III, 368; V, 137.

Mount Lebanon - Fr. Berthe proposed and chosen for mission of Mount Lebanon, VI, 23, 28; Capuchin takes up collection to purchase administration of Mount Lebanon, VII, 341.

Mousnier (Jean-François), Priest of the Mission - Biographical data, IV, 525; V, 71; VI, 21; VIII, 181; XI, 213; Saint Vincent proposes him to *Propaganda Fide* for Madagascar, IV, 93, 525; customary faculties, XIIIa, 362; departure, V, 71, 76, 82; journey, V, 148, 276–85, 302–05; arrival in Madagascar, V, 285, 305–07; Nuncio promises to send his name to Rome, V, 175–76; Saint Vincent reminds *Propaganda Fide* that Fr. Mousnier had received faculties of Missionary Apostolic, V, 431, 551; letters Fr. Mousnier writes Saint Vincent from Madagascar, V, 276, 292; Superior in Madagascar, V, 299, 300, 306, 307, 441; VIII, 616; X, 96; XI, 213, 263; XIIIa, 186; journey to Imaphalles, V, 507–08; Saint Vincent recommends him to prayers of Company, XI, 214; illness and death, V, 510–13, 637; VI, 21, 38, 216–17; VIII, 181, 552–53; virtues, V, 513–14; other mention, VI, 492. See also ***Madagascar***.

Moussinot (Claude), Apostolic Notary of archdiocesan court of Paris - XIIIa, 102.

Moustier-Ventadour, village in Corrèze - Ruins of château of Ventadour, XI, 348.

Mouthaudry (François de), Canon of Mâcon - XIIIb, 78.

Moutiers-Saint-Jean, town in Côte-d'Or - Letter sent from this town to Saint Vincent, VIII, 132; Moutiers-Saint-Jean Abbey: see **Chandenier** (Claude de), **Le Boucher** (M.).

Mouton (Jacques), Priest of the Mission - In Montmirail, I, 442; falls ill, I, 455, 456; brought back to Paris; recovers, I, 471; on mission in Joigny, I, 515; returns to Paris, I, 526.

Mouzon (Abbot of) - See **Fiquelmont** (René-Louis de).

Mouzon, village in Ardennes - Daughters of Charity assist poor there, V, 185.

Mozzolino (Silvestro), Dominican, author of theological compendium - XIIIa, 404.

Mugnier (Jean-Jacques), Priest of the Mission - Biographical data, V, 64; VI, 77; VII, 243; accepted into Internal Seminary, II, 360; mention of letter to Saint Vincent, VI, 602; stationed in Marseilles, XIIIa, 359; in Picardy, V, 64; sent to Agde, V, 184; question of sending him to Toulon instead of to Agde, V, 190–91; should leave for Agde as soon as Fr. Huguier arrives in Toulon, V, 199; in Agde, V, 212, 226, 244, 248, 380; Superior, VIII, 618; Saint Vincent tells him to leave Agde along with confreres, V, 399; has left Agde, VI, 77; proposed for Turin, VI, 87; remains in Marseilles, VI, 89, 186; in Toulon, VI, 207; supposed to give mission in Nans, VI, 273; considered for Annecy, VI, 321–22, 332; in Annecy; lent to Turin, VI, 578; in Turin, VI, 602; VII, 243.

Mulger (Philiberte) - Member of Charity of Châtillon, XIIIb, 4, 21.

Murcantius - Mention of his *Instructions*, III, 483.

Muret, town in Haute-Garonne - Mission, Confraternity of Charity, ecclesiastical conferences, I, 527.

Murmuring [**Complaints**] - Mention of conferences, XII, 409, 426; text of Rule of Daughters of Charity, X, 347; Saint Vincent advises against murmuring, IX, 63, 99; X, 96–98, 147, 193, 195, 236; XI, 110–11; especially to outsiders, II, 588, 633; X, 164, 165; never complain about Superiors, IX, 46–47; X, 36; XI, 94; or companions, IX, 14–15.

Grumbling is serious fault, X, 347; one of seven sins God abhors, IX, 291; X, 193, 348; worse than homicide, IX, 33, 46; X, 97, 150; murmuring is sin of Adam, XI, 97; murmuring of Judas, X, 97, 246, 349; always accompanied by scandal, IX, 277; X, 24, 348; harm it causes, IX, 540; how God punishes it, X, 349–50; how He chastised Miriam, sister of Moses, also Korah, Dathan, and Abiram, X, 348–49; Judas, X, 349; obstacle to union, IX, 15; may cause temptation against vocation,

X, 15; tends to ruin of Company, X, 17. See also **Sufferings**, **Superiors**, **Union**.

Murot (M.) Member of Charity of Joigny, XIIIb, 66.

Murviel (Anne de), Bishop of Montauban - Good effects of missions in his diocese, II, 473; clashes with Coadjutor, II, 555–56; XIIIa, 147.

Muscovites - At war with Poland, V, 128–29, 187, 195, 218, 239, 335; XI, 274, 317; cessation of hostilities, VI, 645; new invasion of Poland, VIII, 280, 314; Tsar has no designs on Poland, V, 143.

Muset (Claude), Daughter of Charity - Biographical data, VII, 200; sent to Calais, VII, 200; X, 440; devoted to nursing soldiers despite epidemic, XII, 34.

Muslims - Inhabitants of Cape Verde, VIII, 566.

Musnier (Mlle) - I, 497.

Mussot (Mme), Lady of Charity - Ill, I, 299; getting better, I, 302; contacts with Saint Vincent, I, 320–21; with Saint Louise, I, 382, 383, 384; opinion of Mlle Laurent, I, 303.

Musy (Fr. de), Priest of the Mission - Biographical data, V, 481–82; VI, 57; VII, 59; mention of letters from Saint Vincent, VI, 169, 282; entrance into Saint-Lazare, V, 481; assigned to Turin, V, 534, 636; VI, 57, 72, 86, 88, 89, 110; praise for him, VI, 92, 128; en route for Turin, VI, 127; in Turin, VI, 137, 141, 160, 255, 557; Saint Vincent fears he does not exert self much, VI, 169; unsettled in vocation; wants to make home visit, VI, 282, 434, 484, 495–96, 510; departure, VII, 59.

Mutual Assistance - Encouraged by Saint Vincent, V, 625.

Mutual Support - See **Forbearance**

Mutuality - XIIIb, 281.

Myra (Archbishop of) - See Antoine-François de **Saint-Félix**.

Mysteries of Trinity and Incarnation - Saint Thomas and Saint Augustine state that explicit knowledge of these is necessary means for salvation, I, 119; X, 271; XI, 172, 343–44; XII, 72; opposing opinions of other Doctors, XI, 344; XII, 72; ignorance of country people about these Mysteries, I, 141; teaching Mysteries is duty for Daughters of Charity, X, 271; and for Missionaries, XI, 172–74, 343–45; XII, 71–73.

N

Nacquart (Charles), Priest of the Mission - Biographical data, III, 77; IV, 89–90; V, 71; VI, 216; VIII, 181; XI, 263; letters of Saint Vincent to Fr. Nacquart in Richelieu, III, 278; to Saint Vincent from Richelieu, III, 286; from Cape Verde, III, 330; from Madagascar, III, 434, 538, 570, 592, 598.

Journey to Madagascar, III, 278, 284, 286; XI, 340, 373; virtues needed for mission, III, 279; travel authorization; *Propaganda* grants faculties of Missionary Apostolic; named Prefect of Mission; journey and arrival in Madagascar; prepares Fr. Gondrée for death: see also ***Madagascar***; praise, VIII, 552; XI, 263, 373; XII, 198; learns native language, III, 331, 554, 561, 596; XII, 60; in Madagascar; Superior, IV, 89, 321, 517; V, 71, 148, 301, 311, 517, 518, 521; VIII, 616; XIIIa, 186; ministry on island; reports, death, see ***Madagascar***; other mentions, III, 77; V, 282, 284–86, 291, 300, 306; VI, 216; VIII, 281.

Name of Jesus - See ***Nom-de-Jésus***.

Nancy, town in Meurthe-et-Moselle - Assistance for poor persons by Priests and Brothers of the Mission, I, 541–42, 582, 589; II, 42, 74, 93; Saint Vincent regarded in Nancy as refuge of afflicted poor, II, 404; **M. de Fontenay**, former Governor of Nancy; **Roch-Sébastien Hardy** from Nancy, enslaved in Algiers: see these names; other mentions, I, 600; VI, 418; XIIIb, 118.

Nans (M. de) - IV, 447.

Nans, village in Var - Mission given, VI, 273.

Nanterre, town near Paris - Journey of Saint Vincent to Nanterre, II, 206; Marie Lullen had charge of children there, IX, 435; pastor praises her, IX, 436; Sister from Nanterre, I, 401, 433.

Nantes, town in Loire-Atlantique - Bishop: see Philippe **Cospéan**, Gabriel de Beauvau de **Rivarennes**; Duchesse d'Aiguillon asks for Sisters, I, 600; port of embarkation for Missionaries sent to Madagascar, V, 71, 82, 277–78, 280, 419, 424; VI, 112, 124, 149, 159; VII, 38, 67, 75, 102, 107, 104, 111, 112; VIII, 115, 150, 157–58, 169, 200, 205, 208, 221, 239, 246, 248, 251, 255, 555–57, 560–61; XI, 334, 336, 374; and to Ireland, III, 103, 137; ship lost on river there, VIII, 183; arrival of ships from Madagascar, V, 637; VI, 21, 440, 443, 445, 447, 451, 453; XI, 270, 367, 370; exiled Irish clergy arrive there, V, 422; Sainte-Croix parish, VII, 473; Visitandines of Nantes, III, 9, 18, 22, 35; V, 10; other mentions, III, 438, 560; IV, 468; VI, 278, 514, 587; VII, 617; VIII, 186, 574, 596; XIIIb, 248; young man in Nantes Seminary, XI, 370.

Daughters of Charity of Nantes: administrators of hospital ask for Daughters of Charity, II, 644, 654; VIII, 317; XIIIb, 318; selection of personnel for Nantes Hospital; Élisabeth Martin named Sister Servant, XIIIb, 248–49, 257; Saint Louise reminds Saint Vincent to reply to administrators, II, 650; her dealings with them, III, 16, 23, 35; V, 32; Fr. Lambert's dealings with them, III, 217; conference to Sisters sent there, IX, 517–21; Saint Vincent sends Saint Louise to Nantes with six Sisters, II, 675; journey; names of Sisters, III, 8, 9; arrival in Nantes; Sisters receive royal welcome, III, 9; Saint Vincent lacks news, III, 15; letters Saint Louise writes from Nantes, III, 8, 22, 35; confessor for Sisters there, III, 17–18; difficulty detaining Saint Louise in Nantes, III, 35; two more Sisters needed, III, 36; postulants from Nantes, VIII, 398, 399.

Letters of Saint Vincent to Sisters in Nantes, III, 181; V, 4: see **Gesseaume** (Henriette), **Haran**, **Hardemont**, **Lepeintre**, **Ménage** (Françoise), **Trumeau**; from Sisters to Saint Vincent, VIII, 399.

Serious situation there, III, 168; division and discord, IX, 518; Saint Louise thinks Sisters should be changed; asks Saint Vincent to encourage Sisters and warn them of certain disorders, III, 178; letter of Saint Vincent, III, 181; departure of two Sisters for Nantes, III, 208; visitation of house by Fr. Lambert; division among Sisters; misunderstanding with confessor; three Sisters leave hospital, among them Élisabeth Martin, Sister Servant, III, 216; Jeanne Lepeintre, appointed to make visitation of Nantes, replaces Élisabeth Martin: see **Lepeintre**; Saint Vincent hopes to send confessor, XII, 363; two Sisters chosen for Nantes, XIIIb, 284.

Saint Vincent plans to visit Sisters in Nantes, III, 418, 421, 423, 424; Saint Louise asks him to do so, III, 422; Saint Vincent in Nantes; Sisters falsely accused; shortcomings of Sisters; Sisters to be changed; eight Sisters are necessary, III, 425–28, 431; visitation recommendations, XIIIb, 143; Saint Vincent requests that their community room be private, III, 604.

Sisters' living space too restricted, III, 602; boys entering kitchen; Sisters are spied on; sick Sister, III, 604–05; attitude of Bishop of Nantes toward Sisters, III, 426, 604; IV, 77; XIIIb, 320; death of two Sisters; M. la Ferrière-Sorin asks that they be replaced, IV, 77; three Sisters sent to Nantes, V, 57; Saint Vincent advises them, IX, 430; calm follows storm, IV, 171; calm continues, IV, 281.

Sister leaves Company; Saint Vincent writes to console Sisters, V, 4; division among Sisters, V, 9, 57–58; too much communication with outsiders, V, 57.

Visitation by Fr. Alméras, V, 9; XIIIb, 322; Marie-Marthe Trumeau and two other Sisters sent to replace Jeanne Lepeintre and two companions, recalled to Paris, V, 43, 57; IX, 517; XIIIb, 312; recall of Sisters discussed in Council, XIIIb, 318–23; Sisters at hospital have never been able to please administrators, XIIIb, 320; complaints of administrators, XIIIb, 320–21; Saint Vincent recalls Marie-Marthe Trumeau and two others to Paris, V, 432; Saint Louise awaits them, V, 452; administrators want only six Sisters instead of eight, XIIIb, 328.

Letter of Saint Vincent to Abbé de la Meilleraye, who was asking for good pharmacist to replace Henriette Gesseaume, V, 532–33; XIIIb, 330, 335; Nicole Haran replaces Marie-Marthe Trumeau; choice of another Sister for Nantes; Sisters live in peace, XIIIb, 336.

Fr. Berthe's visitation of house, VI, 504, 505; Sisters are overburdened, VII, 66; only six Sisters for more than a hundred patients; Saint Vincent gives hope for relief and speaks of naming Assistant, VII, 472–73; Saint Louise reminds him of this plan, VII, 493; prepares to send help, VIII, 187; Nicole Haran begs for help, VIII, 258–59, 317; Fr. Mousnier visits them en route to Madagascar, V, 278.

Visitation by Fr. Dehorgny, VIII, 217; aide of Sisters at hospital goes to Motherhouse to become Daughter of Charity; Sister Servant requests Sister to replace aide, VIII, 399.

Confessors of Sisters: Frs. **des Jonchères**, **Cheneau**, **Truchart**: see these names; Sister Servants: **Martin** (Élisabeth), **Lepeintre**, **Trumeau**, **Haran**: see these names; other Sisters in Nantes: **Bagard**, **Baucher**, **Brigitte**, **Carré** (Claude), **Dauteuil**, **Delacroix** (Renée), **Gesseaume** (Henriette), **Hardemont**, **Jacquette**, **Larcher** (Marie), **Marie** from Tours, **Ménage** (Francoise), **Michel** (Louise), **Miquel** (Madeleine), **Noret** (Marguerite), **Perrette** from Sedan, **Renée**, **Thilouse**, **Vaux** (Anne de): see these names; other mentions, III, 61, 114; XI, 328; XIIIb, 140, 142, 231, 263, 296.

Nanteuil-le-Haudouin, town in Oise - Marquise de Maignelay asks Saint Vincent for two Daughters of Charity: one for school, other for Charity, II, 109–11, 218; God has sent good servant for Charity; no need to send Sisters; II, 125, 126; Jeanne Dalmagne in Nanteuil: see **Dalmagne**; not advisable to send here Sister from Paris, II, 423; Pastor of Nanteuil displeased with Sisters, IV, 298; and with Pastor of Touquin-en-Brie, who enticed to his parish one of Nanteuil Sisters, V, 40, 43; Nicole Georgette at variance with Pastor, whose virtue Saint Louise praises, VII, 477, 642; other mentions, II, 198; III, 232.

Nantouillet (Louise d'Aguesseau, Marquise de) - Asks what is needed to ransom her son, slave in Algiers, VIII, 337, 401.

Naples, kingdom in Italy - Diocese there given to Augustinian for defending Catholic truth, IV, 601; confreres working in bandit country in mountains, XII, 249.

Naples, town in Italy - VII, 83, 360.

Napoli di Romania - See ***Nauplia***.

Napollon (Jean and Louis), bankers in Marseilles - V, 140, 145, 227; VI, 187, 273, 302, 315; VII, 7, 34, 123–24, 186–87, 195, 222, 228, 410, 455, 458; VIII, 309, 336, 356, 420.

Narbonne, town in Aude - Character of inhabitants, X, 534; Archbishops: see Claude de **Rebé**, François **Fouquet**; M. Beauregard named general agent for clergy of province, II, 572.

Narbonne Missionaries: Saint Vincent promises two priests to Archbishop of Narbonne for seminary, VIII, 108–09; departure of Frs. Lebas, Dolivet for Narbonne, with Fr. des Jardins as Superior, VIII, 144, 170; Saint Louise receives news of them, VIII, 167; Archbishop requests added personnel, VIII, 273, 348, 373, 383, 478; delay in sending men, VIII, 387; Saint Vincent sends Frs. Delespiney and Parisy, XIIIa, 197–98; clauses proposed in foundation contract are contrary to customs of Company, VIII, 538; XIIIa, 197–98; union of Maiour parish to seminary, VIII, 478; after opposing union, Saint Vincent accepts it, XIIIa, 198; Prince de Conti requests Missionaries for diocese, XIIIa, 199; Archbishop proposes to give seminary cottage near water, VIII, 479; letter of Saint Vincent to Fr. des Jardins, Superior, VIII, 365; Superior of house (Georges des Jardins) and its history, VIII, 619; other mentions, VIII, 5, 112, 118.

Daughters of Charity in Narbonne: Archbishop of Narbonne asks for Daughters of Charity, VIII, 125, 137; XIIIb, 370; sending of Sisters Carcireux, Denoual, and Chesse, VIII, 137, 144, 145, 160, 187; travel authorization, XIIIb, 237; advice received before departure, X, 533; arrival, VIII, 166; Sister Carcireux sent to Alet diocese for instruction in teaching youth, VIII, 379; X, 587; Sisters find it difficult to live separated, VIII, 380–81; difficulties, VIII, 470–71; praise for Sisters, X, 571, 587.

Nardeux (M.), member of Charity of Joigny - XIIIb, 66.

Naseau (Marguerite) - Biographical data, I, 68; IX, 64; life, IX, 64, 166, 193, 358, 472; schoolmistress in Suresnes, I, 68; sent from Saint-Sauveur to Villepreux, I, 128; IX, 358; serving in Saint-Nicolas-du-Chardonnet parish, IX, 194; illness and death, I, 186, 187, 241; IX, 194; X, 82; conference after her death, IX, 64.

Nathan, Jewish prophet - IX, 305, 481; X, 189.

Nathanael, biblical personage - V, 405.

Naudé (Marguerite), member of Charity of Courboin - XIIIb, 93.

Naudé (N.), member of Charity of Courboin - XIIIb, 93.

Naudé (Nicolas), member of Charity of Courboin - XIIIb, 93.

Naudé (Pierre), member of Charity of Courboin - XIIIb, 93.

Naulot (Jean) - Has garden and stables near Luçon house of confreres, XIIIa, 318.

Nauplia [***Navplion***], town in Greece - VI, 278; VIII, 377, 397.

Navailles (Philippe de Montault-Bénac, Duc de) - Biographical data, VI, 547; illness, VI, 547; brought to Saint-Lazare, VI, 588.

Navain (Marie), Daughter of Charity - XIIIb, 228.

Navarre, collège in Paris - II, 648; XIIIa, 200.

Navarre (Regiment) - Plunder and violence in Rethel, IV, 204–05.

Navarre, region in France - Parlement, VII, 460, 623; Jacques Ducasse, Extraordinary Master of Mint in Navarre and Béarn, XIIIa, 21; Louis XIII, King of Navarre, XIIIa, 226, 236, 252, 275, 277, 280, 286, 289, 321; Louis XIV, King of Navarre, XIIIa, 339, 346, 347, 425; XIIIb, 139, 230.

Navarro [**Navarrus**] (Martín), Spanish canonist - Teaching on vows of religion, XIIIa, 404–05; not to be followed in everything, XIIIa, 382.

Nazareth, town in Palestine - Residence of Holy Family, II, 122; VII, 202; X, 461; Jesus did not go to visit relatives in Nazareth, II, 122; returned there once, was not well received, V, 541, 546; VII, 53.

Nebuchadnezzar, King of Chaldea - Punished by God, XIIIa, 170.

Nègre, cape on northern coast of Tunisia - V, 89.

Négriau (M.) - Appointed administrator of hospital for galley convicts in Marseilles by Duc de Richelieu, VIII, 243.

Nelz (Jean de), seminarian of the Mission - Biographical data, IV, 493–94.

Nemours (Charles-Amédée de Savoie, Duc de) - Biographical data, II, 90.

Nemours (Henri de Savoie, Duc de), Archbishop of Reims, brother of Charles-Amédée - Biographical data, IV, 201; presides at meetings of Ladies of Charity, IV, 201, 391–92; asks Pope to establish Bishops *in partibus* for Tonkin and Cochin-China, IV, 595–96; same request to *Propaganda*, V, 17.

Nemours (Marie d'Orléans, Duchesse de) - See **Longueville**.

Neruet (Pierre) - Witness of Saint Vincent's will, XIIIa, 100–01.

Nesmond (Anne de Lamoignon, Mme de), wife of François-Théodore - Biographical data, II, 399; III, 17; V, 242; request for Sisters for Saint-Denis Hospital, II, 399; Lady of Charity, III, 17; other mentions, II, 445; IV, 464; V, 242.

Nesmond (François de), Bishop of Bayeux, son of François-Théodore and Anne de Lamoignon - Calls Priests of the Mission to Notre-Dame-de-la-Délivrande, VI, 377; other mention, II, 445.

Nesmond (François-Théodore de), Presiding Judge - Biographical data, II, 444; III, 411; delegate to Rueil conference, III, 411; discussion with Saint Vincent on manner justice is rendered, XIIIa, 194.

***Netherlands* [*Holland*]** - V, 143; VII, 526; VIII, 576, 577, 578–79, 582, 587–94, 596; IX, 213; XI, 279, 318; brother of Jean d'Estrades has gone there for the King, II, 679.

Neufchâteau, town in Vosges - Carmelites of Neufchâteau, VI, 591; VII, 51–52.

Neufchâtel-en-Bray, town in Seine-Maritime - Mme Goussault has been there, I, 340; Regulations of Charity of Neufchâtel, XIIIb, 5–8; Fr. Horcholle, Pastor: see **Horcholle**.

Neufchèze (M. de) - Convert from Huguenot religion; reportedly sent money for slave in Algiers, V, 405.

Neufville (Ferdinand de Neufville de Villeroy), Coadjutor, then Bishop, of Saint-Malo, then Bishop of Chartres - Biographical data, III, 65; IV, 40; VI, 365; VII, 561; kindness to Saint-Méen Missionaries, III, 65, 110, 141–42; some confreres find fault with how he is handling matters, III, 115; his authority regarding confreres' house, VI, 149; contacts with Saint Vincent, IV, 40, 477; VI, 365; esteem for Louis Thibault, V, 330, 369, 376; requests Daughters of Charity for Saint-Malo, V, 628–29; Saint Vincent sends report to Rome on behalf of Prelate, VII, 561; other mentions, III, 51, 423; V, 360; XIIIa, 427.

Neufville (Louise de Malval, demoiselle de) - Foundress of boarding school in Sedan, V, 445–47; Saint Vincent recommends her work to Ladies of Charity, VIII, 13.

Neuilly-Saint-Front, town in Aisne - VII, 551.

Neulhy [*Neuilly-le-Réal*], near Saint-Pourçain-sur-Sioule (Allier) - VI, 93.

Nevelet (Fr.), Archdeacon of Troyes - Death, I, 412.

Nevers, town in Nièvre - Visitandines, II, 243; VIII, 502–04; other mention, II, 313.

Newfoundland, large island off east coast of Canada - V, 281.

New Testament - Reading in French forbidden to Brothers of the Mission, except for few older ones, VII, 222; Missionaries read it on board ship to Madagascar, VIII, 572; Saint Vincent recommends to his priests daily reading of chapter of New Testament, XI, 102; XII, 108.

New Year - Pictures and maxims for year, VII, 446; mention of conferences on faults of past year and obligation of spending new year well, XII, 406, 410, 415, 421, 425, 436; best wishes, I, 408; IV, 517; V, 251, 256, 500; VI, 173, 177; VII, 54, 58; VIII, 242, 244, 246, 248, 250, 253, 255.

Nibas, village in Somme - VII, 10.

Nice, town in Alpes-Maritimes - I, 7; V, 145.

Nicolas (Saint) - Feast day, VIII, 239–40, 557; other mentions, XIIIa, 10, 16.

Nicolas III, Pope - Approved Third Rule of Saint Francis, XIIIa, 404–05.

Nicolaïtes - See **Saint-Nicolas** (Community).

Nicolas, Brother of the Mission - Sent from Crécy to Le Mans, II, 676; III, 4; has office of treasurer, without having charge of money, III, 318; at Saint-Lazare, VI, 312.

Nicole (Sister) - Saint Vincent writes to Saint Louise about her, I, 382.

Nicole (Georgette or Georget), Daughter of Charity - Does not get along with Pastor in Nanteuil, VII, 641.

Nicole, Daughter of Charity - Will no longer be Sister Servant of Sisters ministering to galley convicts, XIIIb, 266–67.

Nicole, Daughter of Charity - Many health problems, I, 233; aged, I, 234; is better, I, 235; unsatisfactory, I, 357; at Saint-Sauveur, I, 388; changed from that house, I, 496; showing greater good will, I, 537.

Nicole, Daughter of Charity from Montmirail - Intends to leave Company without giving up habit, V, 44.

Nicporynt, town in Poland - V, 396.

Nieuil-sur-l'Autize, village in Vendée - Saint-Augustin Abbey, III, 352.

Nîmes, town in France - On Fr. Alméras' route from Cahors to Annecy, III, 125.

Nineveh, capital of Assyria - God sends prophet Jonah there, IX, 408–09; X, 416.

Niolo, valley in Corsica - Description, IV, 404–08; inhabitants; religious and moral situation, IV, 404–08; mission, IV, 404–05; Saint Vincent sends to all houses report on this mission, IV, 438, 477.

Nivelle (Fr.) - Saint Vincent makes inquiries about his qualifications to be Pastor, VI, 536–37.

Nivelle (Pierre), Bishop of Luçon - Praise of him, III, 490; XI, 260; satisfaction with ministries carried out by Missionaries in his diocese, II, 275; asks for them for Luçon, III, 145; Saint Vincent finds that Superior of Luçon house takes refuge too easily behind wishes of Bishop, III, 527; IV, 149; recommends that he do nothing contrary to his intentions, IV, 2; V, 469–70; steps taken with Prelate regarding resignation of parish, VI, 178, 439, 536; reimbursement of money owed him, VI, 439, 537; Saint Vincent strongly urges him to sign petition to Pope in view of obtaining condemnation of Jansenism, IV, 182–87; wants Fr. Chiroye to hand over parish to Bishop, V, 409; mention of letter of saint to Prelate, VI, 610; illness, XI, 260; mandated and funded daily Mass there, VIII, 607; other mentions, II, 353; XIIIa, 319.

Noah, Hebrew patriarch - Construction of ark, III, 188; IX, 547; XI, 339; allows self to be taken by surprise by wine; conduct of his children, IX, 47; only a few saved in his ark, XII, 197.

Noailles (Charles de), Bishop of Rodez - III, 294.

Nobility - Audacity and insolence regarding Church, II, 446; they call for confrere when they are sick, II, 545.

Nobles (Jean de), Archdeacon of Mâcon - XIIIb, 78.

Noblet (M.), pharmacist in Paris - VI, 343, 353.

Nodo (Sébastien or Bastien), Brother of the Mission - Biographical data, I, 453; II, 93; III, 7; IV, 440; ill in Richelieu, I, 453; II, 93, 95; Saint Vincent tells Fr. Portail Nodo is coming to Paris, II, 529; sent to Genoa, III, 7, 26, 39; in Genoa, III, 66, 136, 151, 187; IV, 440, 492; desires to go to Barbary, III, 335; Saint Vincent writes to encourage him and to dissuade him from illusions, IV, 440; mention of letter from Saint Vincent, III, 136; temptation persists, IV, 492.

Noëlle, Daughter of Charity - Saint Louise asks permission for her to take vows, VIII, 187.

Nogent, town in France - Candidate to Daughters of Charity from there, I, 409, 427; Mme de Brou in charge of Charity there, I, 485; benefice acquired by simony, II, 398.

Nogent-sur-Seine, town in Aube - Birthplace of Félix Begat, slave in Tunis, VI, 322; VII, 196; mission given here, VI, 393.

Noirmoutiers (Louis de la Trémouille, Duc de) - Biographical data, VI, 88; Saint Vincent apologizes for unintentionally displeasing him, VI, 88; his children, VII, 613; other mentions, VIII, 447–48, 531.

Noirmoutiers (Renée-Julie Aubérie, Duchesse de), wife of preceding - VIII, 416.

Noizeau (Edme), Brother of the Mission - Biographical data, V, 574; disobedient, V, 601.

Nom-de-Jésus [***Name of Jesus***], hospice in Paris - Historical data, IV, 530; V, 139; VII, 32; VIII, 73; IX, 521; XI, 184; lawsuit to take possession of building, II, 684, 690; XIIIa, 351–56, 356–57; beginnings of ministry, IV, 530, 541; poor do not go out, V, 156; Saint Vincent teaches them catechism, XIIIa, 173; Priests of the Mission are chaplains there, VIII, 279; XI, 184; XII, 77, 79; Daughters of Charity serve poor of hospice, V, 139, 357; VII, 32; IX, 521–22; X, 100, 103–04, 295, 557; residents of hospice, V, 427, 589; VIII, 73, 344, 521; dying Saint Vincent blesses residents, XIIIa, 205; other mentions, VII, 272; VIII, 502; XIIIa, 210.

Norais (Élisabeth Merault, Demoiselle), wife of Jacques Norais - Illness, III, 398: see **Norais** (Jacques).

Norais (Jacques), King's secretary - Gift of farm to Saint Vincent, II, 538; on condition of large pension, VII, 423; saint consoles him and his wife on losses suffered from pillage of Orsigny house, III, 397.

Norais (M.), son of Jacques and Élisabeth Norais - Lawsuit against Saint Vincent regarding Orsigny farm, to which he lays claim; saint refuses to appeal decision against him, VII, 422, 423.

Noret (Françoise-Paule), Daughter of Charity - Biographical data, II, 198; VII, 189; family business, II, 301, 303; placed at Saint-Denis Hospital, III, 419; journey to Nantes in company of Saint Louise, III, 8; chosen as Saint Louise's Assistant, VII, 188; deeply involved with business affair, XIIIb, 306; other mentions, II, 198; XIIIb, 227.

Noret (Marguerite), Daughter of Charity - Sent to Nantes, III, 8; XIIIb, 259.

Noret (Mlle) - Mentioned in letter from Saint Louise to Saint Vincent, VII, 88.

Normandy (Province) - Missions in Normandy, V, 610; VI, 31; letter to nobleman in Normandy, V, 39; Missionary from Normandy, III, 13; Sisters from Normandy, II, 222, 328; XIIIb, 292–93; noblemen from Normandy, VIII, 337; King makes trip there, IV, 147; Normans are considered less straightforward than Picards, V, 200; other mentions, I, 320; II, 330, 425; III, 529; IV, 461; VI, 229; VIII, 229, 366, 367; XI, 374; XII, 28.

Norway - XI, 318.

Notre-Dame - Chapel in Courboin, XIIIb, 93.

Notre-Dame - See ***Ardilliers, Buglose, Lugan***, etc.

Notre-Dame-de-la-Rose - See ***La Rose***.

Notre-Dame de Paris - Dean acts as agent regarding differences between Sainte-Geneviève Abbey and Chancelade, IV, 67–68; irreverence and indecencies committed in this church, IV, 328; clergy visit Priests of the Mission, III, 303; saint's Masses at Notre-Dame, I, 600; II, 414; III, 206; Chapter of Notre-Dame, V, 115; possibility of Sisters making Jubilee there, V, 579; X, 192; Sisters may not go there for devotion without permission, X, 136–37; Divine Office is sung in choir, XII, 270; Canons are faithful to this, XII, 273; Canons provide spiritual care for sick of Hôtel-Dieu, III, 295; pressure Ladies to take on work of Foundlings, XIIIb, 430; other mentions, I, 236; II, 130; XI, 352; XIIIb, 421.

Notre-Dame de Pitié, chapel in Paillart - XIIIb, 47.

Notre-Dame des Champs, in commune of Saint-Jean-d'Assé (Sarthe) - VIII, 130.

Notre-Dame (Sisters of) - In Richelieu, IV, 287; V, 602; VII, 466; in Saintes, VII, 214; Saint Vincent asks Fr. Lucas if girls go to their school in Joigny, I, 517.

Nouelly (Boniface), Priest of the Mission - Biographical data, II, 532; III, 6; IV, 25; sent from Annecy to Rome, II, 532; sent to Algiers, III, 6; advice received before departure, XIIIa, 344; arrival, II, 677; in Algiers, III, 25, 50, 94, 218; Superior in Algiers, VIII, 615; difference of opinion with Jean Barreau; Saint Vincent's advice, III, 50–51; appointed Vicar-General to Archbishop of Carthage, III, 64–65; letter Saint Vincent writes him in Algiers, III, 50, 126; illness, death, and burial, III, 218–24, 242; other mentions, III, 304–05, 308–09; IV, 25; V, 90; VIII, 615.

Nouery - Dean of Nouery, VI, 331.

Noulleau (Jean-Baptiste), theologian for Saint-Brieuc diocese - Condemnation of blasphemy, XIIIa, 344.

Nourquier (M.), Canon of Écouis - XIIIa, 29, 30.

Nouveau (M. de) - IV, 307.

Novitiate - See **Seminary**, **Internal**.

Novy, village in Ardennes - VI, 596, 625, 632.

Noyers - Notre-Dame Abbey, III, 151.

Noyers (François Sublet, Seigneur des), Secretary of State - Biographical data; contacts with Michel de Marillac, I, 336–37; II, 150; Mazarin's judgment of him, XIIIa, 154; other mentions, II, 221, 400, 430.

Noyon, town in Oise - Letter of priests of Tuesday Conferences of Noyon to Saint Vincent, II, 440, 441; Henri de **Baradat**, Bishop; **Bourdin**, Vicar-General; **Delahaye**, Dean: see these names; Archdeacon writes Saint Vincent story of statue of Our Lady, VIII, 94; aid to people of diocese, V, 99.

Nuncios in Paris - See **Bagno** (Giovanni Francesco di), **Bagno** (Nicolò di), **Bichi** (Alessandro), **Grimaldi**, **Piccolomini**, **Scotti**.

Nuptials - Saint Vincent permits Daughter of Charity to attend brother's wedding, I, 233; regrets it, I, 388.

O

O (Louise-Marie Séguier, Marquise d') - XIIIb, 310.

Obedience - Community exercise to be held three times a week, IV, 578.

Obedience (letter of authorization) - Given by Saint Vincent to Missionaries going to Madagascar, III, 282; to two Sisters going to La Fère, X, 160; Missionary must show *celebret* to Superior of house in which he is placed, IV, 146, 551; letters of authorization to travel, VIII, 417, 517, 529; XIIIa, 157, 189, 358, 359, 398; XIIIb, 228, 237, 238.

Obedience (virtue) - Conferences, IX, 55–64, 415–30; X, 62–75, 307; XI, 70; XII, 345; reference to other conferences, XII, 409, 413, 417, 420; text of Rules of Missionaries, XII, 345–46; of Daughters of Charity, X, 308, 315; in what obedience consists, IX, 422; X, 426; XII, 349–50; why obey, IX, 59, 424–25, 427–28; X, 74; Community not possible without obedience, IX, 419–20, 422; X, 63; XII, 349; no union without obedience; no order, without union, X, 308–09, 314; whoever enters

Community makes commitment to obey, X, 64–65; to disobey is sin, XII, 348; to obey Superiors is to obey God; to disobey them is to disobey God, X, 68–69, 309–10, 427–28; XII, 349–50; whoever obeys has spirit of Holy Spirit; whoever disobeys has spirit of devil, X, 65–66, 310–11; obedience makes indifferent acts good, X, 66, 273; doubles merit of good acts, I, 507; IX, 418–19, 423–24; X, 66, 273, 310; best actions not meritorious without this virtue, X, 67–68, 273; one act of submission worth more than many good works, I, 75; so much work can be done through sheer obedience, III, 200; obedience better than assistance at Mass, V, 569; one enters Company to do whatever obedience ordains and not to live according to one's own will, IV, 326.

Beauty of obedience, IX, 421, 426; X, 313; always accompanied by many other virtues, IX, 508; particularly necessary for Daughters of Charity, I, 223; IX, 56, 416–18; X, 418, 422, 426–28; by it, they can give greater glory to God than nuns, IX, 424; enclosure of obedience is their cloister, IX, 178; seniority does not dispense from obedience, IX, 420; X, 73; do not obey if what is commanded is sinful, against Rule, or against intention of higher authority, IX, 58, 62, 423, 426.

Example of Jesus, IX, 56; X, 65, 69; XII, 347, 351–52, 432; of Fr. Pillé, II, 374; of soldiers, II, 619; IX, 422; of Councillor at Parlement, XIIIb 282; of inhabitants of Clichy, IX, 507; of Saint Vincent, as chaplain to Gondis, X, 311; of country women, IX, 75–76; of animals, IX, 111; of Abraham, XII, 178; beautiful words of Saint Francis de Sales, XIIIb, 282; necessary to obey: Providence, IX, 56, 59, 62; Pope, IX, 56; XII, 350; Bishops, I, 501, 543–44, 590; III, 152–53; IX, 56; XII, 350–51; Pastors, IX, 56; X, 312, 315; XII, 351; Superiors, I, 590–91; IX, 56, 58, 60–61, 101, 417, 419; X, 311, 553–54; XII, 351; Rules: see **Rules**; Director, IX, 56–57; confessor, IX, 56–58; X, 412; civil authorities, III, 429; XI, 70; XII, 398; Ladies of Charity, IX, 56, 426; X, 273, 312, 315, 540; physicians, III, 301; IX, 96, 176, 420; X, 273, 312, 315, 539–40; administrators, I, 600; equals and inferiors: see also **Condescension**; vow of obedience to Superior General obliges one to obey individual Superiors, V, 85.

How to obey: IX, 56, 57, 76, 425, 428; X, 314; promptly, IX, 57, 59; X, 314; exactly, X, 57, 70, 314; willingly, IX, 6, 59; X, 70; cheerfully, with discernment, IX, 57, 59; totally, X, 69; with perseverance, X, 71; without objecting, VII, 64; neither murmuring nor criticizing, IX, 291, 525; X, 347; solely to please God, IX, 59; X, 71; with submission of judgment, IX, 60; X, 70, 310, 313–14; follow intention of Superior, X, 70; accept all sorts of ministries: see also **Indifference**; ask permissions: see **Permissions**; means of acquiring obedience,

IX, 425, 427, 429; X, 71–72, 74–75; reprimands disobedient Missionaries, I, 544; II, 619; disobedience of Daughters of Charity, X, 550; XIIIb, 375; prayers to ask for obedience, IX, 516; X, 317–18; other mentions, I, 554; II, 37. See also **Punctuality**.

Obidos (Comte d') - Gives hospitality to Fr. Daveroult; ready to facilitate his return to France, VII, 615–16; mention of letter to Saint Vincent, VII, 615; thanks from Saint Vincent, VII, 617.

O'Brien (Dermot), Priest of the Mission - Biographical data, III, 93; sent to Ireland, III, 93, 103; other mention, IV, 479.

Obriot (M.) - II, 312.

Observance - Of daily exercises, I, 504; of Rule, I, 518.

Obstinacy (Stubbornness) - Spirit of the devil, IX, 531–32.

Octobre (M.), concierge of Château de Montmirail - I, 442, 456, 467, 476.

Oderico (Nicolò), Brother of the Mission - Biographical data; delay in vows, V, 619; VI, 174; has given little satisfaction during internal seminary in Rome, V, 619; desires to assist plague-stricken, VI, 174; ill with dropsy, VI, 174, 196; intends to leave Company, VI, 483, 526.

Officers of Company of Daughters of Charity - Conference on election of officers, X, 210–19; names, number, function, XIIIb, 123–24, 134–35, 323–24, 326; duties, X, 214; XIIIb, 325–28; importance of office, X, 210–14, 591–92; XIIIb, 327; reasons for changing Officers often, XIIIb, 306; Council of Officers, V, 452; draft of Rules concerning them, IV, 459; times for elections, X, 210; qualifications of Sisters proposed as Officers, X, 215–16, 592–94; XIIIb, 305–06; what must be done before election, X, 580–81, 589; manner of conducting election, X, 216–17; Sisters leaving office accuse themselves of faults, X, 218–19, 596; confidentiality regarding what is said and done in elections, X, 216, 589, 597; term of office, X, 596; proposals for election of Superioress and continuation of other Officers, VII, 188–89; in Saint Louise's absence, Saint Vincent summons Officers regarding Michel Le Gras' illness, III, 18.

Officers of Confraternity of Charity - Honor and obedience due them, I, 504.

Officers of Congregation of the Mission - Represent Our Lord; principal Officers sometimes should take precedence, V, 608.

Officers of Ladies of Charity - Election and responsibilities, XIIIb, 443–45.

Official Documents - See **Acts**.

Oisey - Prior of Oisey, XIIIb, 63.

Ogier (M.) - Attorney and notary in Paris, XIIIa, 66, 67.

Oléron (***Île d'***), in Charente-Maritime - VIII, 291, 563.

Olier (Jean-Jacques), Founder of Saint-Sulpice Community - Biographical data, I, 208; II, 308; III, 292; IV, 28; V, 93–94; VIII, 400; XI, 350; letter from Saint Vincent, IV, 314; letters to Saint Vincent, I, 324, 366; II, 345, 446, 474, 560; III, 292; XII, 357; member of Tuesday Conferences, I, 324; priestly ordination, IV, 175; takes part in preaching exercises at Saint-Lazare, XII, 237; in composing *Conferences for Ordinands,* XII, 236; reform of Pébrac Abbey, I, 208–09; visits Abbey, I, 278; regrets not having taken part in mission, I, 277; reports on mission he gave in Saint-Ilpize, I, 324; others, I, 366; Sébastien Zamet offers him bishopric of Langres; discussions on this subject, I, 277–78; XIIIa, 122; speaks to Saint Vincent about Abbé de Saint-Cyran, XIIIa, 105; hostile to Jansenism, III, 292; esteem for Fr. Boudet, I, 500; for Fr. Lucas, II, 345; Saint Vincent asks various services of him, I, 332; IV, 314; XIIIa, 210; Pierre Scarron seeks Saint Vincent's support in getting Olier named Coadjutor in Grenoble, V, 93–94.

Fr. Olier becomes Pastor of Saint-Sulpice; Vaugirard Seminary he founded is transferred to Saint-Sulpice parish, II, 308; first companions, I, 209, 278; II, 308; IV, 175; wants "of the Mission" to be part of name of his Community, IV, 62; author of book on seminaries, IV, 190; founder of Community of *L'Intérieur de Marie*, VIII, 400, 473, 476; his niece: see **Aubrai** (Mlle d'); death, VI, 285, 295; Saint Vincent consoles priests of Saint-Sulpice, XIIIa, 184; saint's advice sought in selection of successor, VI, 285; reference to conference on Olier's virtues, XI, 350; other mentions, IV, 28, 125.

Oliva (Treaty of) - VIII, 193, 280, 301, 314, 353, 394.

Olivier (Henri), of Mâcon - XIIIb, 74.

Olivier (Fr.), Priest of the Mission - Faults, V, 600; Superior in Le Mans asks for someone to replace him in teaching chant, VI, 277.

Ollainville, village in Essonne - Saint Louise asks Saint Vincent's permission to go there, VII, 286–87; return, VII, 299.

Oloron, town in Basses-Pyrénées - Bishop: see Arnaud-François de **Maytie**.

Ombiasses - Masters of ceremonies, customs, superstitions of Madagascar, III, 546, 548–52, 557, 562–65, 576, 582; V, 515, 525, 526; VI, 220, 247; are all surgeons, V, 299; de Flacourt learned fundamentals of the language from them, III, 544–45; V, 519.

Ombilambo, wandering people of Madagascar - III, 544–45; V, 519.

Openness to God's Will - See **Indifference**, **Availability**, **Will of God**.

Opole, town in Poland - Residence of Frs. Ozenne and Duperroy in 1657, VI, 318–19, 326, 334, 346, 384, 393–94, 428.

Orange - Prince of Orange, VIII, 596.

Orange (Second Council) - Teaching on grace, III, 325; on universality of redemption, XIIIa, 168; condemnation of Semipelagians, XIIIa, 166.

Oratories - Saint Vincent advises Fr. Ozenne to have oratory in house for examen and praying Office, V, 350.

Oratory (Priests of) [**Oratorians**] - Praise, XI, 121; their moderation, XII, 41; opinion of Fr. Gilles concerning them, XIIIa, 382; they have Rule, IX, 93; no vows, XIIIa, 376; no parlor, XI, 161; may inherit, V, 499; give nothing to those who leave, III, 373; union with Fr. Romillion's priests, II, 459–60, 465; union of Oratory with Saint-Nicolas de Grosse-Sauve Priory, XIIIa, 67; fear that Fr. Bérulle's death might lead to downfall of Oratory, IX, 47–48; Oratorians refute Saint-Cyran's teaching, I, 394; XIIIa, 123; Jansenist tendencies of several Oratorians, III, 292–93; XIIIb, 358; false preaching of another, III, 592; Saint Vincent refuses postulant wishing to leave Oratory of Saint Philip Neri, VII, 584.

Oratorians work at Roman Court to prevent approval of Congregation of the Mission, I, 164; II, 460; approval of vows of Congregation of the Mission, V, 399; Saint Vincent fears Oratorians' opposition to Fr. Codoing's efforts regarding Saint-Yves affair, II, 415, 467, 470, 472; Oratorians in Rome send confreres in Paris reports of activities of Superior of Missionaries, II, 171; Pavillon goes to Oratory for greater tranquility, II, 613.

Establishments: Aubervilliers or Notre-Dame-des-Vertus, I, 27, 124; VII, 345; Isle d'Aix, VIII, 562; Dijon, VII, 232, 520, 521; Fossano, VII, 214; Genoa, VIII, 120; La Rochelle, VIII, 561; Lyons, XIIIa, 45, 50; Mâcon Seminary, XIIIa, 45, 50; Marseilles, VI, 201; Bourbon, VIII, 413; Paris, I, 124; IV, 328; XIIIa, 60, 201, 224; XIIIb, 358; Pézenas, II, 613; Rome, III, 613; VI, 134; XI, 266; Rouen, VIII, 407; Tours, VIII, 413, 438–39; other mentions, VII, 420; XIIIa, 62, 63. See also **Bence**, **Bérulle**, **Borja**, **Bourgoing**, **Condren**, **Desmoulins**, **Gondi** (Philippe-Emmanuel de), **Séguenot**.

Orbais-l'Abbaye, village in Marne - Saint Vincent doubts union of Orbais Abbey to Mission is possible, VII, 219.

Order of Day - Saint Vincent explains practice of Company to Saint Jane Frances de Chantal, I, 554; schedule for meeting with Sisters, II, 131–32.

Ordinands - Number at Saint-Lazare in June 1638, I, 471; they will be at Bons-Enfants, and Michel le Gras' room is needed for them, I, 513; blessings on them at Saint-Lazare in May 1639, I, 543; Saint Vincent tells Saint Louise he will accept a certain person among the ordinands, II, 23; how to work with them in Rome, II, 142, 232; ministry with them in jeopardy there, II, 240; difficult in Crécy to serve them lunch, II, 311; Fr. Codoing changes manner of dealing with them, II, 349; Saint Vincent is happy about news of ordinands in Rome, II, 434; Fr. Codoing gets funding in Rome to prepare ordinands, II, 472; Duchesse d'Aiguillon sponsors ministry in Rome, II, 542; ministry with ordinands in Rome, III, 493; large number, IV, 256; VI, 257; VII, 36; left satisfied, V, 99.

Ordinands (retreats) - References in conferences to ministry to ordinands, XII, 383, 422, 430, 434, 436; one of ministries of Mission, I, 297, 553; IV, 71, 106; V, 374; XII, 235–36; XIIIa, 119–20; no funds available for it, II, 358; ministry came about imperceptibly, without anyone thinking of it, XI, 142–43; XII, 8; origin: see also ***Beauvais***; excellence and usefulness, XI, 7–10, 137–38, 143; XII, 13–17; dispositions necessary for those directing ordinands, XI, 281–82; good results of retreats, II, 37; accept nothing from ordinands, if this can be done easily, V, 490; VII, 269; Saint Vincent encourages Fr. Codoing in ministry with them, II, 449; questions posed on their instruction, XIII, 312–13; humility necessary to direct ordinands, XI, 138; outline of conference to ordinands, XIIIa, 158–60; *Conferences to Ordinands* [*Entretiens*], XII, 236–37; Saint Vincent reprimands Superior for going to country during ordinands' retreat, VII, 293; retreats in several dioceses, VIII, 366; in Luçon, II, 353–54; Reims, II, 440; ***Annecy***, ***Beauvais***, ***Genoa***, ***Richelieu***, ***Rome***, at ***Bons-Enfants***, ***Saint-Lazare***: see these words; other mentions, I, 181–82, 377, 403; II, 103; V, 442. See also **Retreats**.

Orgeval (M. d') - VI, 387.

Orient - Franciscan missions, XI, 262.

Origen, Church Father - Biographical data, XI, 24; words of Origen, XI, 24; taught catechism, XIIIa, 32.

Origny-Sainte-Benoîte, village in Aisne - I, 180.

Orkneys - Islands in Scotland evangelized by Fr. Lumsden, VI, 546.

Orléans (Catherine-Angélique d'), Abbess of Saint-Pierre de Reims - Biographical data, IV, 82.

Orléans, town in Loiret - Mme Goussault passes through, I, 193; as does Saint Louise, III, 15; and Saint Vincent, III, 408, 412; journey of Jeanne Lepeintre to Orléans, VI, 45, 46, 48, 49; Visitandines, I, 370, 595; III, 15; coaches, I, 603; II, 318; VI, 125; X, 467; XIIIb, 310; other mentions, I, 402, 404, 593–94; II, 160; III, 244, 290; IV, 113; V, 277; VI, 262; X, 182.

Orléans (Gaston, Duc d') - Biographical data, III, 411; negotiations for annulment of marriage to Marguerite de Lorraine, I, 265; at Rueil Conference, III, 411; contacts with Saint Vincent, IV, 414; confessors, I, 164; II, 416; desire to see Court return to Paris, IV, 460, 463; other mention, I, 428; V, 617.

Orléans (Marie d'), Duchesse de Nemours - See **Longueville** (Marie d'Orléans, demoiselle de).

Orléans (M.) de - Signs deed of Bishop Poncher of Paris in 1518, XIIIa, 479.

Orléans (Philippe d') - Biographical data, IV, 303; title of *Monsieur*, IV, 44, 303.

Ornano (Henri-François-Alphonse d'), chief equerry of Gaston d'Orléans - IV, 414.

Orosius (Paul) - Teaches that everyone has sufficient grace to be saved, XIIIa, 168.

Orphan Girls - See **Lestang** (Marie Delepech de).

Orsay, commune in Essonne - Mission given, III, 135.

Orsigny, farm in Saclay (Essonne) - Historical note; gift of farm to Saint Vincent, II, 538; III, 4; IV, 312; V, 365; VI, 43; Saint Vincent at Orsigny, II, 538; III, 4, 64, 66, 181, 186, 358, 408, 412, 413; IV, 510, 511; V, 365; VI, 43; VIII, 119–20; XII, 47; pillage of farm, III, 397, 405, 408–09, 412, 413; dismissal of female employee, IV, 312; farm helps Saint-Lazare house subsist, IV, 329; heirs of donor enter claim for possession of farm; win lawsuit, VII, 266, 267, 293; sentiments of Saint Vincent on this occasion, VII, 265–66; XII, 47–51, 105; refuses to appeal, VII, 422–25; other mention, VI, 633. See also **Norais** (Jacques).

Orthez, town in Pyrénées-Atlantique - III, 243.

Orthodox (Greek) - Opposed to King of Poland, XI, 274.

Orvieto, town in Italy - Priests there show interest in Congregation of the Mission, IV, 465–66.

Osny, village in Val-d'-Oise - I, 476.

Ostend, town in Belgium - Ship from there captured French vessel heading for Madagascar, XII, 24.

Ostia, town in Italy - Missions, II, 231, 405; Ostia Seminary, II, 505; Vicar-General of Ostia, II, 426.

Ouessey [**Ouessay**] (Louis de Guidoly or Guidotti, sieur d') - XIIIb, 65–66.

Our Lady of Loretto, in the Marches - Parish considered as residence for confreres in Rome, II, 36, 44.

Our Lady of the Rotunda - Kindness of Canon to confreres in Rome, II, 35, 44.

Outsiders - Conferences on relations with outsiders, X, 342–47, 362–64; text of Rule of Daughters of Charity, X, 342, 362; Sisters will not tell temptations to outsiders, X, 365.

Ouvre-Logues, reef off coast of Brazil - Confreres pass through en route to Madagascar, VIII, 568–69.

Ozena - Disease Saint Vincent compares with sin infecting the soul.

Ozenne (Charles), Priest of the Mission - Biographical data, II, 167; IV, 290; V, 3; VI, 5; VII, 8–9; XI, 323; letters Saint Vincent writes him in Troyes, II, 167; in Dover, V, 37, 47, 52; XII, 370; in Warsaw, V, 81, 98, 104, 108, 113, 117, 126, 141, 151, 161, 167, 173, 179, 181, 183, 187, 192, 195, 201, 213, 218, 228, 234, 238, 248, 251, 255, 257, 263, 267, 312, 323, 330, 333, 337, 346, 361, 366, 374, 383, 388, 394, 396, 402, 411, 418, 424; in Krakow, V, 434, 449, 453; at Court of Queen of Poland, V, 491, 572, 579, 588, 609, 621; VI, 5, 33, 55, 90, 109, 140, 464; in Glogau, VI, 182, 209, 266, 271, 297, 303, 306; Opole, VI, 326, 345, 362, 384, 393; Warsaw, VI, 539, 555, 569, 576, 620; VII, 8, 36, 67, 83, 90, 107, 124, 127, 155, 175, 180, 263; mention of letters to Saint Vincent, V, 27, 37, 47, 52, 81, 104, 117, 151, 173, 187, 218, 234, 251, 312, 323, 334, 346, 374, 383, 396, 418, 424, 434, 491, 572, 588, 609, 621; VI, 5, 33, 91, 109, 182, 209, 266, 297, 303, 306, 319, 345, 362, 384, 393, 464, 555, 620; VII, 8, 36, 83, 84, 90, 107, 124, 127, 155, 175, 263; XI, 323; mention of letters from Saint Vincent, V, 418; Saint Vincent writes to him every week, V, 188; later, does not do so, VII, 67; forwards to Ozenne letter from his brother, VI, 299; mention of letter from Saint Louise, VI, 306; correspondence with Edme Jolly, V, 527.

Superior in Troyes, II, 541; IV, 497; VIII, 607; maintains union among confreres, V, 192; assigned to Poland, IV, 573; departure, V, 3, 15; English capture ship, V, 15; in Dover, V, 27,

50; arrives in Hamburg, V, 67; Saint Vincent does not know if he is in Warsaw, V, 70, 75, 77; arrival in Warsaw, V, 81, 83; retreat, V, 99; mission at Holy Cross, V, 105; in Warsaw, V, 153, 215; Superior in Warsaw, VIII, 617; Queen of Poland unhappy with him, V, 165; Saint Vincent suggests that he not offer his services to the collège, but concentrate on rural missions and seminary, V, 219; conversions, V, 338; war obliges him to leave Warsaw; follows Court to Krakow, V, 434; then into Silesia, V, 474, 479, 535; gives news of confreres in Poland, V, 632; XI, 323; in Glogau, VI, 183, 319; in Opole, VI, 326, 334, 336–37, 347, 361, 428; in camp on outskirts of Krakow, VI, 464, 470, 472, 489, 492, 502, 569; return to Warsaw imminent, VI, 526, 566; Saint Vincent tells him to spare nothing in Fr. Duperroy's care, VI, 568; in Warsaw, VI, 620; VII, 8; journey to Krakow, VII, 156, 173, 264; speaks a little Polish, XII, 25; health, IV, 290; V, 579; VI, 307; VII, 265; death and eulogy, VII, 274, 276, 282, 283, 285, 297, 300, 304; reference to conference on his virtues, XII, 433; other mention, I, xxv. See also ***Poland***.

Ozenne (Jacques), Brother of the Mission - Biographical data, VII, 84.

Ozenne (Laurent), Priest of the Mission - Biographical data; nephew of Charles Ozenne, VI, 272; VII, 84; finds repetition of prayer difficult, VI, 272; VII, 84.

P

Pagne - Clothing worn by inhabitants of Madagascar, III, 545.

Paillart, village in Oise - Women's Charity: regulations, establishment, and approval, XIIIb, 40, 47–48; men's Charity: regulations and approval, XIIIb, 48, 53.

Paillet (M.) - II, 685; XIIIa, 354.

Paillole, house in Pouy - I, 16.

Paimboeuf, town in Loire-Atlantique - VI, 150, 159; VIII, 558.

Pain d'Avoine (Catherine), Daughter of Charity - XIIIb, 228.

Paisant (Étienne), notary in Paris - II, 211; XII, 377, 378, 380; XIIIa, 263, 271, 281, 283, 284, 286, 289, 294, 355, 422, 476, 478.

Paix (***Notre-Dame de la***), in Fieulaine (Aisne) - Historical note, VII, 614; VIII, 28; sick find comfort in chapel there, VIII, 94; at request of Bishop of Noyon, Bro. Parre assures good order in devotions of people, VIII, 28, 46, 60, 82, 83, 93–94, 107, 149; Saint Vincent, deputed to seek priest for this shrine, asks if Prelate had not already found one, VIII, 60, 71; letter from M. d'Abancour regarding Fr. Ameline's lawsuit against Huguenots, VIII, 457; letter from Fr. Ameline concerning lawsuit against Huguenots, VIII, 539–40.

Pajot (Charles), Jesuit - Biographical note, V, 292; classical works, V, 292, 297.

Palaiseau, commune in Essonne - Misery and plague; Saint Vincent sends Missionaries there with Sisters; several fall ill, IV, 415, 426, 450; safe-conduct for Missionaries sent to this place, XIIIa, 400.

Palestine - VI, 248.

Palestrina, town in Italy - François Hallier goes there for protection from plague and hot weather, VI, 373–74; Saint Vincent advises Fr. Jolly to accept small church and lodging, VII, 508; to go there or to Frascati during hot weather, VII, 585, 595, 598; VIII, 78, 86.

Palletan (locality) - Estate of Mme de Gondi, XIIIa, 63.

Pallu (François), Canon of Tours, then titular Bishop of Heliopolis, Egypt - Biographical data, VI, 605; VII, 572; prepared to leave for mission to Far East, IV, 596; receives hospitality of Missionaries in Rome, VI, 605; Saint Vincent does not think he wants to establish Congregation, VI, 630; M. Pallu writes to Company of Indies concerning journey to Indies, VII, 572; other mention, VIII, 595.

Palluau (Gilbert de Clérembault de), Bishop of Poitiers - Coolness toward Richelieu Missionaries, VII, 511; satisfied with retreat for ordinands given by Missionaries, VIII, 329; Duchesse d'Aiguillon obtains from him letter for Alain de Solminihac, VIII, 51–52.

Palotta (Giovanni Battista), Cardinal - Biographical data, IV, 46.

Pamiers, town in Ariège - Bishop: see François-Étienne de **Caulet**.

Pamphili (Camillo Astalli), Cardinal - Biographical data; Saint Vincent congratulates him on promotion to cardinalate; asks his protection, IV, 106; signs decree of *Propaganda Fide* impeding multiplication of Congregations having same ministries in France, IV, 611.

Pangois (Fr.), priest of collegiate church of Coëffort - IV, 425; VIII, 130.

Pannier (M.), merchant in Saint-Quentin - V, 60.

Panola [**Panole**] (Andrian or Dian), King of region of Anossi in Madagascar - His children's interest in instruction, III, 561; ambushes against French, V, 519, 527.

Pantin, commune near Paris - XIIIa, 479.

Paon (Jeanne), Daughter of Charity - XIIIb, 227.

Papillon (Marie), Daughter of Charity - Biographical data, X, 447; sent to Metz, X, 447; other mention, XIIIb, 228.

Paquinot (Georges), Brother of the Mission - Biographical data, VI, 578; sent to Turin, VI, 578, 579.

Para (Canon) - Officialis of Luçon, VIII, 254.

Parable of wise and foolish virgins - IX, 41; X, 491–93.

Paracelsus, doctor and alchemist - I, 5.

Paradis (Jean), Pastor of La Chapelle - I, 425.

Paradise - Having one will with God is foretaste of paradise, I, 61; being united in perfect charity is paradise, IX, 125; being gentle and respectful will make house a paradise, IX, 212; Company will be like paradise if it observes law of love, X, 380; being patient, friendly, gracious creates paradise, X, 384; paradise is love, union, and charity, XI, 67.

Parcollet (Claude), Daughter of Charity - XIIIb, 228.

Pardon - Custom of kneeling to ask forgiveness, VII, 260: see **Reconciliation**.

Parfait (Fr. de), Canon of Notre-Dame in Paris - XII, 273.

Paris (André de), galley convict - Saint Vincent receives money for him, VIII, 360.

Paris - City saved from famine by Saint Genevieve, XIIIb, 420; punished by Charles VI; rose up against him; besieged by Henri III, avenged by King's assassination, IV, 461; benefice of Saint-Lazare belongs to city; its conferral rests with Bishop, I, 243; placed in hands of Canons Regular of Saint Augustine in 1517, I, 244, 248; plague in city: 1631–33: I, 114–15, 122, 124, 126, 128, 186, 187–88; in 1635–36: I, 299, 315, 316, 348, 350; Spanish threaten Paris; fright of inhabitants, I, 331; influence of Jansenist ideas seen in Paris in noticeable diminution in number of Communions, III, 321, 358; false rumors of disorder in city, VI, 7; Fronde in Paris: see also **Fronde**; floods of 1658, VII, 107, 110, 111, 114.

Bishops: see **Fulco de Chanac**, Étienne de **Poncher**, Henri de **Gondi**, Jean-François de **Gondi**, Jean-François-Paul de **Gondi**; Chapter of Paris, VI, 493; XII, 273; XIIIb, 430; natives of Paris, IV, 426; VIII, 229, 235.

Auteuil, Bons-Enfants (Collège), ***Boulangers*** (rue des); ***Chaillot***, ***Charité*** (Hospital), ***Foundlings*** (Hospice), ***Enfermés*** (Hospice), ***Fortet*** (Collège), ***Hôtel-Dieu***, ***Hôtel de***

Ville, ***Incurables*** (Hospital), ***Lisieux*** (Collège), ***Luxembourg*** (Palace), ***Nom-de-Jesus*** (Hospice), ***Notre-Dame*** (Church), ***Quinze-Vingts*** (Hospital), ***Saint Barthélemy*** (Parish), ***Saint-Benoît*** (Parish), ***Saint-Lazare, Saint-Louis*** (Hospital), ***Salpetrière, Sorbonne, Val-de-Grâce***, etc.: see also these words; ***Bourget*** (chaussée du), III, 337, 338; ***Cordiers*** (rue des), XIIIa, 42; ***Coutellerie*** (rue de la), XIIIa, 16; ***Courteau-Villain*** (rue), I, 127; ***Épernon*** (rue de l'), VI, 98; ***Grève*** (place de), IV, 380; ***Harpe*** (rue de la), VIII, 203; ***Maçons*** (rue des), VIII, 502; ***Mauvaises-Paroles*** (rue des), V, 36; ***Monnaye*** (rue de la), XIIIa, 15; ***Pavée*** (rue), XIIIa, 75; ***Petits-Champs*** (rue des), XIIIa, 42; ***Pitié*** (Hospital), ***Pont-Neuf*** (bridge), VI, 202; ***Quincampoix*** (rue), XIIIa, 15; ***Quinze-Vingts*** (Hospital), ***Roule*** (Le), I, 122; ***Saint-André-des-Arts*** (rue), VI, 98; ***Saint-Antoine*** (faubourg): see also ***Saint-Antoine*** (Porte), III, 337; ***Saint-Denis*** (chaussée), II, 607; ***Saint-Denis*** (faubourg), IV, 400; ***Saint-Germain-des-Prés*** (faubourg), II, 233; XI, 255; XIIIa, 20, 199; **Saint-Jacques** (faubourg): see also **Capuchins**, **Oratory**, **Visitation**; ***Saint-Martin*** (faubourg), II, 176, 589; ***Saint-Maur*** (chemin de), III, 337–38; ***Saint-Victor*** (Porte), I, 22; XIIIa, 75, 97, 222, 263; ***Saint-Victor*** (rue), I, 29, 128; XIIIa, 75; ***Seine*** (rue de), XIIIa, 16, 20, 24; ***Vallée-de-Fécamp*** (rue de la), III, 337; ***Versailles*** (rue de), I, 213, etc.; other mentions, X, 15; XIIIa, 329; XIIIb, 225.

Paris (M.) - VI, 401, 542.

Parishes - Saint Vincent ponders whether Missionaries should accept parishes, II, 393: disadvantages, II, 281, 656; IV, 589; V, 236, 409, 436; VI, 355, 634; VII, 188, 268, 374: see also **Daisne** (Chrétien); Saint Vincent refuses parish in Senlis, II, 281; in Angoulême, V, 436; in Arras, VI, 634–35; in Poitiers, VII, 188; refuses house for Missionaries in Rome because parish is attached, V, 465; union of parishes can be easily effected, II, 434; conditions for union of parish to Company, V, 196, 202, 538–39; thinks union of parish is useful where Company has direction of seminary, VII, 268; but this is contrary to Rules of Institute, XIIIa, 197; Company burdened with two parishes in Toul, V, 236; obliged to celebrate feast of patron saint of parish, even if not its Pastor, V, 87; parishes are hindrance to more universal good of missions and seminaries, V, 193; ministry of parish Sisters, XII, 362; Rules for parish Sisters, II, 131; IX, 18; X, 527, 535, 537, 545.

Parisis - Tax placed on fees posted on price lists and notices, V, 503.

Parisos (M.) - I, 539.

Parisot (M.) - II, 457.

Parisy (Antoine), Priest of the Mission - Biographical data, VI, 119; VII, 151; VIII, 19; sent to Marseilles, VI, 119; in Marseilles, VI, 279, 446, 523; VII, 151; act of disobedience; absolution, VI, 186, 342, 383, 386; mutilation of document, VI, 186; health, VII, 168; proposed for Toulon, VII, 207, 221, 228; in Toulon, VII, 237, 245, 250, 254, 274, 282, 289, 403; in Marseilles, VII, 438; named for Montpellier, VII, 554; health, VIII, 19; in Montpellier, VII, 632; VIII, 69, 92, 267, 289; XIIIa, 471; Saint Vincent's concern for his health, VIII, 330; in Marseilles again, VIII, 303, 348; requested for Agde, VIII, 212, 260; missioned to Narbonne, VIII, 348, 360, 373, 387, 478, 537; XIIIa, 198; Saint Vincent agrees to his ordination to priesthood, XIIIa, 198.

Parlement - Definition, I, 136; V, 46; VIII, 134; IX, 25; XI, 5; XIIIa, 11; its decree recorded Letters Patent confirming contract of union of Saint-Lazare, I, 540; office for nephew of Commander Sillery, II, 136; approval of Missionaries in Annecy region by Chambéry Parlement, II, 321; lawsuit after death of Cardinal Richelieu referred to Parlement, II, 457; letter from Saint Vincent, II, 589; petitions of Saint Vincent, II, 684, 690; decree expelling Missionaries from Saint-Méen, III, 12, 33, 43; de Beaumont imprisoned at Parlement of Rennes, III, 51; Paris Parlement in fear of rebels, IV, 412; deprives Church of property whenever it can, VII, 423; brief on poverty goes before it prior to distribution, VIII, 134; example given in some chambers of high reputation, XI, 201–02; registration in Paris Parlement of union of Saint-Lazare to Congregation of the Mission, XII, 374; of Letters Patent on behalf of Congregation of the Mission, XII, 375; XIIIa, 258.

Parlor - Precautions for Missionaries when in parlor with women, XI, 161; XII, 19, 341; XIIIa, 389; decision to have parlor without grille in Motherhouse of Daughters of Charity, III, 256; XIIIb, 249–51.

Parmentier (Fr.), Pastor of La Queue-en-Brie - Esteem for Fr. Pillé, II, 381.

Parmentier (Noël), Priest of the Mission - Biographical data, VI, 162.

Parre (Jean), Brother of the Mission - Biographical data, III, 429; V, 59; VI, 388; VII, 13; VIII, 26; XI, 306; letters of Saint Vincent to Bro. Parre in Saint-Quentin, V, 59; VI, 414, 422, 490, 502; VII, 614; VIII, 26, 46, 60, 71, 82, 93, 107, 123, 149, 157, 190, 445, 453, XII, 374; in Ham, VI, 388, 397, 437, 454, 467; in Laon, VI, 531, 543; VII, 421, 535, 587, 596; in Reims, VI, 561, 572, 580, 596; VII, 395, 401, 573; VIII, 382, 384, 389, 398, 409; in Rethel, VI, 573, 608, 625, 632; VII, 13, 33, 379,

544, 562; VIII, 391; Saint Vincent mentions sending letters to various places to ensure that Parre receives necessary news, VIII, 391; reference to letter written on July 12, 1660, VIII, 392; letter of Bro. Parre to Saint Vincent from Saint-Quentin, VII, 135; mention of letters to Saint Vincent, V, 60; VI, 437, 454, 467, 490, 531, 561, 580, 597, 632; VII, 13, 33, 395, 402, 421, 535, 544, 573, 614; VIII, 26, 46, 60, 82, 382, 389, 398, 409.

Studies needs of poor people and clergy of Champagne and Picardy, sends information to Saint Vincent and Ladies of Charity of Paris, receives from them aid which he distributes to needy, V, 60, 99; VI, 388, 397, 414, 422, 437–38, 454, 467–68, 490, 502–03, 531, 543, 561, 572–73, 580, 596, 608, 625–26, 632; VII, 13, 380, 395, 402, 407, 421, 535, 544, 562, 573–74, 588, 597, 614; VIII, 26, 46, 60, 71, 82, 94, 107, 123, 278, 382, 384, 389, 391, 398, 410, 445, 453; X, 191; XI, 306–07; XIIIb, 433; Bro. Parre in Saint-Quentin, VI, 437, 467, 531, 543; VII, 421; VIII, 382, 384, 390, 391, 457; initiates Confraternity of Charity in Rethel, VII, 573; in Reims and Saint-Quentin, XI, 306; at request of Bishop of Noyon, assures good order in devotion of people of Notre-Dame-de-Paix, VIII, 26, 46, 60, 82–83, 93–94, 149.

Trials, VIII, 82; sends Saint Vincent news of Sisters in La Fère, VIII, 232; awaited in Paris, VIII, 52; invited to come for retreat, VIII, 83; postpones trip until later, VIII, 93, 107; health, VII, 562, 587, 597; VIII, 382; nephew welcomed at Saint-Lazare, VII, 562; visit of brother-in-law, VII, 545; other mentions, I, xxvi; III, 429; VIII, 541.

Parriel (Pierre), Chancellor of University of Cahors - III, 346–47.

Parrot (Fr.), monk of Chancelade - One of two deputies sent to Paris by Alain de Solminihac for approval of Augustinians of Chancelade; sent to lodge at Bons-Enfants, III, 163; met Saint Vincent in Richelieu, III, 461; not as skillful in business as companion Fr. Vitet, III, 589; Saint Vincent welcomes him at Saint-Lazare for retreat, IV, 124; arrival in Paris, IV, 135; must be present for election of new abbot, IV, 160; Alain de Solminihac displeased with him, IV, 248; does not want him and Fr. Vitet informed of steps he has taken at Court to have Nicolas Sevin as Coadjutor, IV, 223–24.

Parthenay, town in Deux-Sèvres - IV, 166.

Pascal (Bro.) - See **Goret** (Jean-Pascal).

Pascon (M.) - VI, 650.

Pasha, high-ranking official in Turkey and North Africa - Imprisons Bro. Jean Barreau in Algiers, III, 218; releases him, IV, 147; French consul's dealings with him, V, 89–90; Saint Vincent asks Bro. Jean Barreau to get passport from him for confrere coming to Barbary to make visitation, V, 147; slave owner makes him tremble, V, 326; puts Spanish Mercedarians under duress, V, 390; holds men from Marseilles for ransom, V, 391; new Pasha arrives in Algiers, V, 404; Louis XIV asks his protection for M. Barreau and Fr. Philippe Le Vacher, V, 644; former Pasha is reinstated, VI, 10; mistreatment of M. Barreau, VII, 91; considering sending someone to negotiate with him release of M. Barreau, VII, 185; his apparent authorization releasing M. Barreau from Rappiot's debts, VII, 221; Pashas in various kingdoms oppress Christians, VII, 341; King is due to reply to him, VII, 458; his part in apostasy and martyrdom of Bro. Borguñy, XI, 288–89.

Pasquier (Balthazar), Brother of the Mission - Biographical data, V, 501.

Pasquier (M.) - Offers house and chapel to Saint Vincent for foundation of Missionaries; saint informs Bishop of Agen of proposal, IV, 50; thanks M. Pasquier; awaiting approval of Prelate, IV, 51.

Pasquier (Pierre), chaplain in Clichy - XIIIa, 74.

Pasquier (young man) - I, 473.

Passelaigue (Jean de), Bishop of Belley - II, 354–55.

Passion of Christ - Mention of conferences, XII, 421, 434; excellent subject of prayer for Daughters of Charity who do not know how to read, IX, 27, 28, 172; X, 456; its merits form part of treasure of Church, IX, 39; devotion of Fr. Pillé to Passion, II, 380; wounds of Jesus, II, 119; VIII, 516; His gentleness is apparent in Passion, XII, 159–60.

Passions - See **Mortification**; people in South more prone to passion, XI, 200.

Pastors - Good Missionary does everything Pastor does and more, XII, 325; Pastors who desire to make retreat in houses of the Mission are most welcome, II, 546; before and after each mission, Missionaries seek blessing of Pastor, II, 226; VI, 374; do nothing during mission without his consent, II, 226; V, 88; XII, 351; show Pastors great honor and respect, XI, 95; Saint Vincent causes removal of words offensive to Pastors in Bull of Approval of Congregation, I, 222–23; they occasionally invite outside preachers to church, IV, 56; Superior General has authority to change Pastors in parishes confided to Congregation as often as deemed necessary, V, 202; Missionaries go to receive blessing of Pastors, VII, 389; on arrival, Daughters of Charity go to receive blessing of Pastor; all owe him obedience and respect, X, 312, 315; XIIIb, 125, 135; Saint Vincent has Saint Louise apologize to Pastor, I, 75.

Pastour (M.) - Receives hospitality in Missionaries' house in Marseilles, VII, 194; mention of letter to Fr. Get, VII, 270.

Patience - Conference, XI, 56; virtue of perfect, X, 147; softens hearts, III, 376; V, 626; difficulties pass, III, 382; compassion toward others, XI, 56; example of Jesus, III, 376; V, 605, 626; VII, 146; XI, 56; of Fr. Pillé, II, 375; of Saint Francis de Sales, XIIIa, 88–89; one of the virtues that can accomplish anything in Madagascar, V, 309; virtue necessary for Missionaries, VII, 146; for Daughters of Charity, X, 428; for Superiors: see also **Superiors**; patience in trials, XII, 402; after mentioning concerns to competent persons, adore God's guidance; practice patience, IX, 393: see also **Forbearance**; calm responses to provocation, XII, 402; patience in physical sufferings, XII, 402; easier to convince someone by gentleness and patience, than by being too uncompromising, V, 63; other mentions, I, 58, 123, 332, 441–442, 523, 577.

Patissier (Catherine) - Member of Charity of Châtillon, XIIIb, 21.

Patrebé (Fr.), Jesuit, in Madagascar - Forced to leave after evangelizing, VI, 244–45.

Patriarche (Salomon), Brother of the Mission - Biographical data, III, 93; IV, 261; sent to Ireland, III, 93, 103; recalled because of mental illness; sent to Saint-Méen, III, 478; illness continues; Superior of Saint-Méen would like to be rid of him, IV, 261.

Patrocle (Guillaume), Brother of the Mission - Biographical data, IV, 418; XII, 413; death and eulogy, IV, 418, 426–27; mention of conference on his virtues given at Saint-Lazare, XII, 413.

Patte (Philippe), Brother of the Mission - Biographical data, VII, 482; VIII, 157; faithful to God and Company, VII, 482; capable surgeon, VIII, 157, 179, 225, 229, 584; sent to Madagascar, VIII, 157, 185, 207, 208, 219, 225, 229, 231, 240, 554; Saint Vincent advises him to avoid all discussion with Huguenots while at sea and to give example of Christian virtues, VIII, 209; from Paris to Nantes, VIII, 555–57; in Nantes, VIII, 557; from Nantes to La Rochelle, VIII, 557–58, 561; shipwreck, VIII, 246–47, 248–49, 251, 255–56; in La Rochelle, VIII, 561, 563–64; at sea, VIII, 570–73; at Cape of Good Hope, VIII, 574, 580, 584–85, 587–88; other mention, VII, 482. See also ***Madagascar***.

Patto (M.) - VIII, 368.

Pau, town in Pyrénées-Atlantiques - VIII, 432, 602.

Paul (Chevalier) - Biographical data, VII, 94; VIII, 32; plans expedition against Algiers, VII, 94; Saint Vincent considers self fortunate to bear his name; met him at Mazarin's residence, VII, 94; encourages proposed expedition, VII, 145, 154, 174,

179, 184, 187, 207, 212, 226, 233; continues to hope it will take place, VII, 263; prepared to give large sum to make it happen, VIII, 32, 310, 316; Chevalier Paul outside Algiers, VIII, 527, 538.

Paul (M.) - Recommends priest who wants to make retreat at Saint-Lazare, VIII, 477.

Paul (Saint), Apostle - Biography by Godeau, VIII, 556; features of his life, I, 184, 405; II, 22, 146; IV, 54; V, 473; IX, 18, 214, 283, 386–87, 492, 498; X, 10–11, 144, 223, 574; XI, 3, 44, 311; XII, 30, 105, 120, 195–96, 221; XIIIa, 462; XIIIb, 351, 431; virtues, III, 279; X, 223; XI, 305, 312; XII, 205, 221, 291; teachings, III, 324; IV, 317; VII, 442; VIII, 587; IX, 165, 188, 237, 282, 285–286, 342, 348; X, 350; XII, 222; XIIIa, 38,39; disagreement with Saint Peter, IV, 233; VII, 442; IX, 10, 178; with Saint Barnabas, IV, 233; VII, 442; cited, IX, 390, 498, 513, 549; X, 10, 49–50, 70, 89, 138, 175, 295, 305, 306, 316, 317, 319, 320, 404, 452; other mentions: I, 133, 166, 184; II, 19, 493; III, 42, 345, 364, 403, 476, 497, 558; V, 609; VII, 202, 448, 619; VIII, 40, 577; IX, 3, 136, 185, 247, 263, 264, 337, 359, 386, 482; X, 10, 50, 70, 89, 175, 295, 305, 306, 316, 317, 319, 320, 404, 452, 487, 505, 538, 585; XI, 3, 4, 19, 55, 144, 182, 205, 227, 315, 385; XII, 24, 50, 80, 89, 94, 95, 137, 154, 162, 165, 184, 195–96, 203, 213, 219–21, 281; XIIIa, 109, 118, 167, 172; XIIIb, 381, 398, 417, 420; writings on Two Heads Peter and Paul, III, 73–75; feast of his conversion, XI, 162; Mme de Gondi invokes his assistance, XIIIa, 59; other mention, X, 49.

Paula (Saint) - Unhappy with reprimand from Saint Jérôme, XI, 354; he mourns her death, III, 223.

Paulati (M.) - Favors authorizing Missionaries' establishment in Rome, XIIIa, 313.

Paulin (Charles), Jesuit, King's confessor - Biographical data, IV, 46; V, 171; Alain de Solminihac writes to him, IV, 475, 498; Fr. Paulin supports request of Bishop of Cahors regarding Bishop of Sarlat, whom Solminihac wants as Coadjutor, V, 171; death, IV, 563.

Paul IV, Pope - Obliges Jesuits to wear cowl, III, 382, 448.

Paul V, Pope - Forbids discussion on "matters of grace," III, 326; grants Clichy parish to Saint Vincent, XIIIa, 23; other mention, I, 13.

Paussin (Fr.), priest - Sent to Marseilles for spiritual assistance to galley convicts, XIIIa, 360.

Pauzo (M.), notary in Paris - XIIIa, 341.

Pavia, town in Italy - Bishop: Francesco Billi [Bigli], VI, 639; siege of Pavia, V, 604.

Pavillon (Mme) - Her praise, IX, 5.

Pavillon (Mlle) - I, 286.

Pavillon (Nicolas), Bishop of Alet - Biographical data, I, 159; II, 94; III, 100; IV, 64; VI, 190; VII, 499; VIII, 283; IX, 555; XI, 235; letters from Saint Vincent, III, 260; IV, 64, 209; VI, 190; letters to Saint Vincent, II, 219, 340, 543, 558, 572, 586, 594, 605, 613, 617; III, 100, 268; IV, 119, 267, 325; words of praise for him, II, 146; III, 105, 260; IV, 65.

Retreat at Saint-Lazare, I, 159; takes part in preaching exercises there, XI, 235, 265; XII, 237; in composing *Entretiens des ordinands*, XII, 236; Saint Vincent uses his method of repetition in speaking to the confreres, XII, 315; mission in Joigny, I, 177–78, 515–16, 528; at Saint-Germain-l'Auxerrois, I, 365; at Saint-Germain-en-Laye, I, 442, 448; XI, 256; in Grigny, I, 472; Saint Vincent involves him in Charities, I, 162; speaks to him about Michel Le Gras, I, 427–28; named Bishop of Alet, I, 413; goes to his diocese with Fr. Blatiron, I, 580; VIII, 608; Saint Vincent promises to visit him in Alet, I, 520, 526, 544; Bishop recommends needs of diocese to Saint Vincent, II, 220; Archbishop of Narbonne, II, 558–59; M. de Beauregard, II, 572; Bishop of Mirepoix, II, 594; plan of Bishop of Lodève to cede his episcopal See to M. du Bosquet, II, 605, 613, 617; M. de Ciron, IV, 119; sends him report on certain abuses, II, 587.

Opens seminary in Alet; entrusts it to Priests of the Mission, II, 221, 256; sadness at recall of Missionaries, II, 340; inaugurates retreats for priests, visits his diocese, II, 543; complete renewal of diocese, III, 157.

Contacts with Saint Vincent, I, 492; II, 339; saint asks him to take M. de Benjamin as boarder for a time, III, 260; refuses, III, 268; cooling in friendship, IV, 213; XIIIa, 211; Pavillon supports giving two priories to Congregation of the Mission, IV, 388; Saint Vincent offers Pavillon hospitality at Saint-Lazare, VI, 190; contacts with Michel Le Gras, I, 452; with **Hippolyte Féret**, **Claude and Louis de Chandenier**, **Claude de Rueil**, **Brandon de Bassancourt**, **François-Étienne de Caulet**: see these names; Brunet delights in his conversation, III, 496; Solminihac hopes Pavillon will sign petition of episcopate to Pope against Jansenism, IV, 102, 160; Pavillon does not respond to letter of invitation for this, IV, 179; Saint Vincent persists, IV, 209; Pavillon refuses, IV, 268; censures, along with several Bishops, *Apologie des casuistes*, VII, 499; Solminihac wishes him to explain censure by declaration, VII, 548; other mentions, II, 94; VIII, 283. See also **Alet**.

Payon (Jeanne) - Gift to Antoine Maillard, VII, 297.

Peace - Kingdom of God is peace in Spirit, who will reign in you if your heart is at peace, I, 111; peace is worth more than all worldly possessions; God rewards it even in this life, III, 611–12; if we bring about peace in others, should we not also preserve it among ourselves, III, 612–13; peace does not preclude suffering, IV, 171; human condition never the same; sometimes at peace, sometimes persecuted, IV, 281–82; confidence that God will soon give peace, IV, 329; God dwells only in peaceful place, IV, 395; difficult to succeed in any duty without peace of mind, V, 410; charity demands sowing peace where it does not exist, V, 602; according to world, peace and health are treasures of life; also two sources of good, VI, 188; trust in God is basis of all good leadership and peace and enrichment of soul, VII, 612; respect and gentleness foster peace; where there is peace, God abides, IX, 207; God dwells only in place of peace, IX, 395; pray for peace, that God will reunite hearts of Christian Princes, XI, 189; God's Spirit is spirit of peace, gentle inspiration, XII, 285; peace is goal of war, XIIIa, 307.

Péan (François), author of works on controversy - Offers to give conferences at Saint-Lazare on controversy; Saint Vincent refuses, VIII, 469.

Pébrac, village in Haute-Loire - Fr. Portail in Pébrac, I, 331. See also **Olier**; other mentions, I, 208–10, 366–37.

Pecoul (M.) - I, 489.

Pelagius, heresiarch - Teachings about gaining salvation, XIIIa, 165; opinions went against need of interior grace for salvation, XIIIa, 166.

Peleüs (Fr.), chaplain of Pierre Séguier - I, 344.

Pelletier (Catherine Vialart, Mme), Daughter of Charity - Biographical data, I, 352; II, 442; suggested for Hôtel-Dieu, I, 352; with foundlings, I, 426, 429, 436; wants to keep her belongings, I, 425; Saint Vincent does not have great faith in her submissiveness; her difficulties, I, 426; other mentions, I, 378, 412, 447, 488, 495.

Pelletier (Nicolas) - Biographical data, II, 486; plans to stop paying for foundlings he was supporting; steps taken by Ladies of Charity, II, 486–87, 488.

Pellieux (Claudine) - Member of Charity of Valpuiseaux, IV, 235.

Penance - Mention of conferences, XII, 431, 437; penance necessary for everyone, even priests, X, 319; XI, 117; impose penances on self for faults, IX, 219–20, 244; for those who suffer, XII, 401; permission of Superior necessary for extraordinary penances: see also **Mortification**; spirit of penance of

Daughter of Charity, XI, 118; penitential practices permitted by Saint Vincent for Saint Louise, I, 80; penances for priest unable to make repetition of prayer, XII, 63–65; for student, for fighting, XII, 54; for disobedient seminarian: see also **Boucher** (Philippe-Ignace); for unruliness, VII, 225; for disobedient Brother, V, 601; for one who lacked sobriety, XI, 181; authorizes public penances during missions, IV, 35; errors of Antoine Arnauld on public penance, III, 322, 358–66; in giving penances, confessor must abide by rules of Council of Trent, V, 322; Assembly of 1651 considers establishing penances for certain faults, XIIIa, 371. See also **Discipline**, **Fasting**.

Penitentiary - Does not think cases of conscience submitted by de Sergis are permissible, I, 527; has his eye on seminarians educated by Congregation of the Mission, II, 271; Saint Vincent asks Fr. Codoing to request dispensation from him, II, 280–81; indicates errors in writings of Arnauld, III, 322; his opinion and solution to strange nocturnal noises in Saintes, VI, 96–97; sends money for distribution to poor, VI, 596, 625; saint requests Fr. Jolly to get dispensations from him, VI, 631; VIII, 199; and to see that letter is delivered safely to him, VI, 637.

Pennier (Denis), Priest of the Mission - Biographical data, IV, 167; V, 80; in Richelieu, IV, 637; Superior in Tréguier, V, 80; VIII, 616.

Penot (M.), Registrar in Joigny - XIIIb, 66.

Pentecost - Saint Louise's special devotion, III, 311; period for election of Officers of Daughters of Charity, VII, 597; X, 210; mention of conferences, XII, 408, 411, 421, 423; other mentions, XII, 25–26; XIIIa, 29, 30.

Pepin (M.) - M. Pepin and coaches, III, 529; IV, 506–07; V, 54; VI, 125.

Pera, district in Constantinople - III, 47.

Percheron (Michelle), Daughter of Charity - Signs attestation after reading of Common and Particular Rules reviewed and arranged in order by Fr. Alméras, XIIIb, 206.

Perceval (Étienne), of Mâcon - XIIIb, 74.

Perceval (Guillaume), Priest of the Mission - Biographical data, I, 530; II, 93; enters Internal Seminary for renewal, II, 93–94; leaves, II, 119; dismissed from Company, II, 541, 620; other mention, I, 304.

Perdreau (René), Brother of the Mission - Biographical data, I, 522; other mention, I, 531.

Perdu (Jacques), Priest of the Mission - Biographical data, I, 226; II, 112; III, 98; giving missions in Poissy, I, 226; in Richelieu, I, 404, 417, 420, 421, 437, 442; II, 112, 142, 353; death, II, 528; III, 98.

Péréfixe (Hardouin de Beaumont de), King's tutor, Bishop of Rodez, then Archbishop of Paris - Biographical data, IV, 45; other mention, III, 293.

Péreyret (Jacques), Grand Master of Collège de Navarre - Biographical data, III, 247; Saint Vincent consults him, III, 247, 322.

Perfection [Holiness] - Conference on obligation to strive for holiness, X, 197–210; mention of another conference, XII, 417; first goal Saint Vincent gives Congregation, XII, 67–68; whoever does not advance on path to holiness falls back, II, 146; X, 198; example of Jesus, X, 197; teaching of Jesus, XII, 68; holiness does not consist in ecstasies, XI, 285; nor in multiplication of acts, X, 284; consists in doing all actions well, II, 146; XII, 69–71; even smallest, X, 205–06; done in conformity with Will of God, XI, 285–87; XII, 126–27; self-renunciation necessary for this, X, 199–201, 575; different states of perfection, XII, 300; obstacles to holiness, X, 204.

Péricard (François de), Bishop of Angoulême - V, 436.

Périgord (region) - Ravages caused by armies, V, 97.

Périgueux, town in Dordogne - Great desolation in Périgueux diocese, II, 429, 680–81; III, 230, 240, 257, 293–94; Alain de Solminihac presses for nomination of Bishop; asks for Philibert de Brandon, II, 430; renewed insistence, III, 240, 256–57, 294; Abbot of Vertueil desires See of Périgueux, II, 680–81; Solminihac exhorts new Bishop to go to his diocese, III, 229–30; Saint Vincent opposes this choice, III, 256; Bishops: see François de **Bourdeille**, Philibert de **Brandon**, Jean d'**Estrades**.

Périgueux Missionaries: Saint Vincent ready to give Philibert de Brandon as many Missionaries as he requests for his seminary, III, 474; Prelate asks for two priests; Saint Vincent proposes two others for missions, IV, 48–49; hopes to open seminary shortly, IV, 89; Solminihac urges sending Missionaries to Périgueux, even if only three to begin, IV, 102; Charles Bayart and Denis Laudin, Priests of the Mission, have left for this town, IV, 137; Bishop of Cahors sends Bishop of Périgueux copy of establishment of Missionaries in Cahors and Letters Patent of King, IV, 142; Fr. de Bassancourt, Vicar-General, prefers that seminary be directed by their own priests; Solminihac would like to prevent departure of Missionaries but fails, IV, 189–91; Saint Vincent recalls them, IV, 174–75;

Superior of house and its history, VIII, 617; debt owed late Bishop by Saint-Lazare, IV, 430.

Permissions - Conference on practice of doing nothing without permission, IX, 505–17; to ask permission is to give merit to act of obedience, IX, 506–07; this edifies others, IX, 508; do not fear wearying Superiors, IX, 514; times when permission must be asked, IX, 508, 509–14; do not extort permissions, IX, 514; do not ask or give general permissions, IX, 514; if refused, do not grumble and say you will never ask for anything again, XI, 93; means of growing strong in this practice, IX, 515.

Pernambuco [***Fernambuco***], town in Brazil - II, 105.

Pernes (Louis de), Baron de Rochefort - Buys consent of Abbess on behalf of young nun, II, 516.

Péronne, town in Somme - VIII, 597.

Perquisites - Saint Vincent is seeking priests to accept these from Mother de la Trinité, I, 399.

Perra (Gui) - XIIIb, 21.

Perra (Jeanne), daughter of Gui Perra - Member of Charity of Châtillon, XIIIb, 4, 21.

Perraud (Hugues), Priest of the Mission - Biographical data, III, 83; IV, 265; V, 135; VI, 423; VII, 27; VIII, 129; XII, 436; proposed for Saintes, III, 83; in Saintes, III, 104; letters Saint Vincent writes him in Richelieu, III, 458; IV, 265; in Bourbon, VI, 539; in Moulins, VI, 571; his sister, V, 135; at Saint-Lazare, V, 344; Saint Vincent hopes thermal baths will do him good, III, 458; encourages him, IV, 265; at thermal baths of Bourbon, VI, 423, 424, 435, 440, 443, 445, 523, 524, 527, 538, 539; in Moulins, where he has taken Fr. Alméras, who is ill, VI, 571; mention of letters to Saint Vincent, VI, 538, 539; health, VI, 639; VII, 27, 73, 75, 84; last illness, VIII, 129, 145, 148, 149, 151, 157, 159, 169, 207, 219, 221, 225, 229; XII, 374; death, VIII, 242, 244, 246, 251, 254, 255, 275, 563; mention of conference on his virtues, given at Saint-Lazare, XII, 436.

Perrette, Daughter of Charity, in Valpuiseaux - III, 583.

Perrette, Daughter of Charity, mother of Carthusian - Death, IV, 416.

Perrette, Daughter of Charity, from Sedan - Named for Nantes, XIIIb, 249; placed in Angers, III, 8; is unsatisfactory, III, 17, 22, 209; departure from Company, III, 214.

Perrette, Daughter of Charity - See **Chefdeville**.

Perrier (M.), in Mâcon - XIIIb, 77.

Perrin (Nicolas), Brother of the Mission - Biographical data, IV, 529; death, IV, 543, 558.

Perrin (Nicolas), Brother of the Mission - Biographical data; death; words of praise for him, VII, 588.

Perrine, Daughter of Charity - See **Bouhery** (Perrine).

Perrine (Sister), Daughter of Charity - Native of Saché, II, 215.

Perrine (Sister), Daughter of Charity - Asks to make vows, V, 466.

Perriquet (Fr.), Vicar-General of Bayonne - Saint Vincent urges him to remain in Bayonne, II, 192–93; other mentions, II, 7; VII, 154.

Perrochel (François), Bishop of Boulogne - Biographical data, I, 277; II, 219; III, 104–05; V, 107; VII, 41; XI, 255; in praise of him, III, 104–06; letters from Saint Vincent, III, 104; V, 107; his Officialis, V, 108; mention of another letter, II, 534; mention of letters from Bishop, VII, 41; participates in preaching exercises at Saint-Lazare, XI, 265; XII, 237; in composing *Entretiens des Ordinands*, XII, 236; giving missions in Joigny, I, 515, 526, 528; in Saint-Germain parish in Paris, XI, 255; Saint Vincent's deposition concerning Perrochel's worthiness to be Bishop of Boulogne, XIIIa, 145; Perrochel declines bishopric of Boulogne because he cannot pay what Rome asks of him, II, 492; consecrated Bishop of Boulogne, XIIIa, 147; health, II, 548; takes up collection for poor of diocese, VII, 41–42; other mentions, I, 277, 278; II, 219.

Perrot (Robert), notary in Montmirail - XIIIb, 34.

Persecution - Conference on fortitude in persecution, XI, 66; persecution is effect of God's goodness, XII, 226; God allows friends to suffer persecution, XII, 226–27; permits it to test innocents, XII, 227; to punish sinful for faults, XII, 228; a purge, XII, 228–29; a Company not persecuted is close to ruin, XII, 229; suffer patiently and in silence, XII, 230–32; minor persecutions prepare for greater ones, XII, 232; persecution of Daughters in Nantes, 425–27; of Christians in Barbary, IV, 590–91; God would not permit persecution if it made those persecuted useless for His service, XII, 232; well received, it turns into good, IV, 393; bloodletting needed, XII, 232; example of Saint Vincent, V, 399; consider self happy when persecuted for sake of justice, XII, 227–29.

Perseverance - Crown of heaven promised to those who persevere, V, 613; IX, 496; and to those alone, II, 146; IX, 492, 500; Judas began well but ended badly, II, 146; IX, 492; no perfection without perseverance, II, 146; practice of humility, simplicity, and exact observance of Rule is true sign of perseverance, III,

339; Saint Vincent urges Ladies of Charity to persevere in good works, XIIIb, 411–20. See also **God**.

Persia - See ***Babylon***.

Persy (Marie de) - Denied habit of Daughter of Charity, XIIIb, 330–31.

Peru - Won over to faith by catechism, XIIIa, 34.

Pescheloche (Renée), Daughter of Charity - Biographical data, VI, 379; Saint Louise asks permission for her to make vows, VI, 379; other mention, XIIIb, 227.

Pesnelle (Jacques), Priest of the Mission - Biographical data, V, 271; VI, 299; VII, 251; VIII, 24; letters from Saint Vincent to him in Rome, V, 545; VI, 448; in Genoa, VII, 251, 259, 305, 342, 362, 374, 388, 413, 438, 491, 495, 539, 557, 567, 580, 592, 603, 611, 624; VIII, 24, 55, 80, 92, 100, 111, 119, 155, 175, 185, 211, 216, 400, 442, 458; letters to Saint Vincent, VII, 467; VIII, 453, 480; mention of letters to Saint Vincent, VI, 448; VII, 305, 362, 388, 413, 438, 495, 500, 539, 557, 567, 580, 592, 603, 611, 624; VIII, 24, 55, 80, 111, 119, 155, 185, 216; sent to Rome, XIIIa, 359–60; in Rome, V, 271, 273, 274; VI, 374; in Loretto, V, 274–275; named for Turin, VI, 299, 308; named for Genoa, VI, 630; Superior in Genoa, VII, 371, 500, 595, 596; VIII, 41, 79, 100, 101, 118, 231, 549, 614; giving missions in Ceranesi, VII, 438; mission to Penitents, VII, 611; anxieties, VI, 449; excessive sadness at lack of success, VII, 389; words of praise for him, VI, 299, 308.

Death of father; Saint Vincent dissuades him from traveling to France to receive inheritance, V, 545; brothers dispute his share, VI, 448–49; seem better disposed to accept his claims; receives visit from one of them in Genoa, VII, 362; affair placed in hands of mediator, VII, 495; Saint Vincent wishes to be kept informed of discussions, VII, 540; correspondence between saint and brothers of Fr. Pesnelle, VIII, 56, 111, 121, 185, 211, 453, 480; brothers are disposed to sharing, VIII, 156; arrangement proposed, VIII, 216; consents to sign document they request of him, VIII, 454, 481; secret marriage of his sister, VIII, 453; other mentions, I, *xxvi*; V, 498–99.

Peter (Saint), Apostle - Cited, VII, 442; X, 159; XI, 58; XII, 92; Jesus calls him Satan, IV, 56; XII, 65, 155, 218; denial and repentance, IV, 42; IX, 214, 253; X, 590; XII, 30, 219; XIIIb, 354; Arnauld's opinion of Peter's denial, V, 646; imperfections, X, 574; his authority in Church, III, 73–75, 256; IX, 484; X, 127; punishes Ananias and Sapphira, X, 167–68, 170; XI, 211; XIIIb, 351; difference of opinion with Saint Paul, IV, 233; VII, 442; IX, 10, 178; features of his life, VI, 165–66; IX,

56; X, 217, 422; XI, 90; XII, 157, 195, 300; XIIIb, 353, 386, 438; his trade, III, 597; cure of mother-in-law, X, 224; feast of Chair of Saint Peter in Rome, VIII, 564; Order of Saint Peter, XII, 304, 306; Mme de Gondi implores his help, XIIIa, 59; other mentions, I, 111-12, 184; XI, 69, 144, 198; XII, 154, 162; XIIIa, 141.

Petit (Jean), slave in Algiers - III, 223.

Petit (Fr.), Pastor of Saint-Fargeau - Writes to Saint Vincent about legacy, VIII, 501.

Petit (Marie), Daughter of Charity - Biographical data, VIII, 235; Saint Louise asks permission for her to take vows, VIII, 235; other mention, XIIIb, 228.

Petit (Messrs) - VI, 350.

Petit Saint-Lazare - See ***Saint-Charles Seminary***.

Petites-Maisons, hospice in Paris - Historical note, II, 405; V, 400; VI, 583; VII, 199; missions at this hospital, II, 405; places reserved long in advance, VII, 199; XIIIb, 245; patients quarrel constantly, XIIIb, 245; question of putting there Daughter of Charity unsuitable for Company, XIIIb, 243–45; administrators plead for Daughters of Charity, X, 93; beginning of ministry; Anne Hardemont named Sister Servant, V, 427; Cécile Angiboust proposed to replace her, VI, 583; Sisters are as faithful to prayer as they can be, X, 469; other mentions, X, 100, 103; XIIIb, 206: see also **Beguin** (M.).

Petizon, King's lawyer in Sedan - Contacts with Saint Vincent, V, 261, 269; with Sedan Missionaries, IV, 195.

Pétronille, Daughter of Charity - see **Gillot**.

Peyraux family - IV, 174.

Peyresse (Fr.), chaplain at Bétharram - VIII, 602.

Pézenas, town in Hérault - Presence of Nicolas Pavillon, II, 606, 613, 617; Bishop of Agde wants Daughters of Charity there, V, 629.

Pharaoh, King of Egypt at time of Moses - Daughter adopts infant Moses, XIIIb, 398, 406; miracles of Moses in his presence, V, 489; punished by God, XIIIa, 170.

Pharisees - Envy caused them to seek to take life of Our Lord, IX, 549; Apostles instructed not to speak to them, X, 345.

Phelipeau (Jacques), clerk of Registrar of Angers - XIIIb, 118.

Phelippeaux - See **Pontchartrain**.

Phénix (Sister), Daughter of Charity - Judged suitable to be Assistant of Company, XIIIb, 305, 306.

Philip (Saint), Apostle - Feast day; request made to Jesus, IX, 311.

Philip Neri (Saint) - XI, 266–67: see also **Oratory**.

Philippe, Brother of the Mission - Accompanies Fr. Portail on mission, I, 279; in Cévennes; zeal, I, 289; cannot return to Paris because of approach of Spaniards, I, 331; other mention, I, 332.

Philippe (Fr.), Priest of the Mission - Biographical data, VIII, 25; in Genoa, VIII, 25, 120, 156.

Philippe (M.) - See **Navailles**.

Philippe, Daughter of Charity - See **Bailly** (Philippe).

Philippe-Auguste - King; granted Saint-Lazare Priory revenue rights, XIIIa, 343.

Philistines, ancient people of Asia - God permits them to carry off Ark of the Covenant, XI, 319; illusion to their defeat by David, XIIIa, 469.

Philosophy - Very helpful when used properly, XII, 57–58.

Physicians [Doctors] - Must be obeyed, III, 301; IX, 96, 97, 176, 420; X, 273, 312–13, 315, 539–40; too eager to please; concerned only with physical health, VI, 628; said to kill more patients than they cure, IV, 259; doctor who prescribes according to his skill/conscience is free in God's sight even if results are not what he intends, VII, 483.

Pianezza, town in Piedmont - Mission given, V, 534.

Pianezza (Filippo Emanuele Filiberto Giacinto di Simiane, Marchese di), Prime Minister of Piedmont - Biographical data, V, 252; VI, 2–3; VII, 89; VIII, 66; letters from Saint Vincent, V, 373, 455; VII, 243; mention of other letters, V, 457, 458, 611; VI, 72; mention of letters to Saint Vincent, V, 534; VI, 72; words of praise for him, V, 476, 500; VI, 30, 601; plans to fund Missionaries' house in Turin, V, 252–53; VIII, 618; Saint Vincent's observations on proposal for foundation contract, V, 373; announces sending of four Missionaries, reminding him that they may not minister in towns, V, 455–56; new foundation for Turin house requires fifth Missionary, V, 611; VI, 2–3, 31, 57, 86; sending of fifth Missionary deferred, VI, 72, 256; kindness toward Missionaries; gratitude of Saint Vincent, V, 476, 477, 481, 636; VI, 32, 137, 204, 282, 308, 329, 436, 520, 557–58, 639; VII, 143, 231, 235, 243, 271, 378, 582; VIII, 66, 110, 238, 482–83; saint recommends Missionaries obey him in all things and accept his advice, VI, 262, 484, 521, 601, 602, 639; satisfaction with results of mission in Bra, VII, 89; in Pianezza, V, 534; Saint Vincent fears he might oblige Missionaries to minister in towns, V, 456; VI, 111, 497; to assist nuns, V, 456; to hear confessions of nuns, VII, 313; people of Savigliano turn to him to have confreres remain among them, VI, 416; pilgrimage to Santa Maria di Savona, VIII, 231; health, VI, 577, 600–01; visit of Chandenier brothers, VIII, 176–77; son is to marry daughter of Prince of Monaco, VIII, 177; other mentions, V, 476; VI, 141; VII, 147. See also ***Turin***.

Picard, secretary to Bishop of Amiens - XIIIb, 47.

Picardat (Edme), Brother of the Mission - Biographical data, I, 531; V, 574; VIII, 428; assigned to Troyes house; refuses to go; Saint Vincent insists, V, 575; refuses again, V, 601; begs Saint Vincent to take him back into Company, VIII, 428.

Picardy (Province) - Character of Picards, V, 200, 212; invasion by Spaniards, I, 331; home of Lambert aux Couteaux, II, 237; other Missionaries from there, VII, 108; Labadie causes great harm there, IV, 185, 457; Saint Vincent hopes to send Missionaries to Picardy soon, IV, 89; misery and aid: see also ***Champagne***; other mentions, I, 218, 376, 561; V, 98; VI, 163, 389; VIII, 518, 537; XIIIa, 62, 63, 379.

Picariaux (Collège) - VIII, 330.

Picaut (Catherine) - Son is slave in Tunis, V, 393.

Piccolomini (Celio), Nuncio in Paris - Biographical data, VII, 13; VIII, 191; contacts with Saint Vincent, VI, 553, 618–19; VII, 484, 530, 541; relations not as cordial as with preceding Nuncio, VII, 13; present at funeral of Saint Vincent, XIIIa, 208; other mentions, VII, 548; VIII, 191, 411.

Picpus Monks - Give aid to poor of Paris diocese during Fronde, IV, 520.

Picpus, former village, part of Paris today - III, 337.

Picquet (François), Consul of France for Aleppo and Tripoli - Mistreated by Turks, VII, 274; Bishop of Babylon, VIII, 192.

Picquet (Thomas), Governor of Bastion of France in Barbary - See also ***Bastion***.

Pictures - Church teaching on images of saints, XI, 30; good means of making meditation, for those who do not know how to read, IX, 28, 335; X, 462; useful for teaching Mysteries, III, 282; Madagascar Missionaries make good use of them, III, 563, 565; V, 516; Saint Vincent sends picture to M. de Saint-Martin, I, 332; promises to send others to Fr. Gilles, IV, 280; picture from Charity, II, 14; picture of Lord of Charity, III, 255; VI, 111; pictures depicting presence of God, VII, 574; Saint Louise sends New Year's pictures for Saint Vincent's blessing before distribution, VII, 446; painting destined for altar dedicated to Blessed Virgin, II, 626, 629–30.

Piedmont - II, 40; V, 165, 594, 610; VI, 141, 196, 405, 429, 435, 451, 495, 522, 566; VII, 119, 211, 285; VIII, 619; XI, 369, 380: see also ***Turin***.

Pierre (Claire-Madeleine de), Visitandine - Biographical data, I, 594; Superioress of Angers monastery, II, 16; in Tours, II, 626.

Pierre (Fr.), Carmelite, slave in Algiers - III, 223.

Pierron (Nicolas), Priest of the Mission - Biographical data, VII, 354.

Piètre (M.) - VIII, 98.

Piety - Do not sacrifice exercises of piety for work, XI, 284; if necessary, sacrifice them to practice of charity: see also **Rules**; piety of Fr. Pillé, II, 379–80; some seminarians come to seminary to learn it, II, 263–64; needed in seminary, II, 266; its attraction in seminary, II, 270–71; introducing it into minds of those who will be part of court, II, 581. See also **Consolations**, **Spiritual Dryness**.

Pignay (Nicolas), priest, Doctor of Sorbonne - Biographical data, IV, 539; V, 100; VI, 316; VII, 182; VIII, 462; gift of two priories to Agen Seminary, IV, 539; V, 125; new dignities, V, 100–01; Dean of Luçon, VI, 316; offer of small priory to Luçon mission; Saint Vincent recommends that it be refused, V, 120, 125; hospitality in Missionaries' house, VI, 316; VIII, 462; foundation in favor of Luçon house, VII, 182–83.

Pignerol, town in northwestern Italy - Vicar General mentioned in letter to Fr. Codoing, II, 472.

Pilate, Governor of Judea - VI, 130; IX, 56, 278, 290, 533.

Pilgrimages - Virtue of Daughter of Charity does not consist in making pilgrimages, I, 356; Saint Vincent asks Fr. Jolly to have pilgrimage to seven churches made in Rome, VI, 554; not customary for Superiors to allow confreres to go on pilgrimages, VII, 151.

Pillé (E.), Pastor of Ferrières, brother of Jean Pillé - Recommends his vicar to Saint Vincent, VIII, 526.

Pillé (Jean), Priest of the Mission - Biographical data, I, 270; II, 339; XII, 28; regret at having been Pastor, XII, 327; ill at Bons-Enfants, I, 270; Superior, I, 316, 376; VIII, 604; frees Saint Vincent of difficulty, XIIIa, 377; Saint Vincent plans to ask him for notes on Jacques Gallemant, whose vicar Fr. Pillé had been, I, 400; his virtue, death, eulogy, II, 339, 363–89; XII, 28; other mention, XIIIa, 286.

Pimpernelle (M.), physician in Paris - IV, 170.

Pingré (Pierre), Bishop of Toulon - Praise for him; about to leave Paris for Toulon, VII, 488; Saint Vincent asks him to take care of his health, VIII, 392.

Pinon (M.) - Saint Vincent explains to him that vow of poverty in Congregation does not prevent possessing and receiving revenues, VII, 129; M. Pinon writes of intention to set up lifelong annuity for his son, VIII, 439.

Pinon (Pierre), Priest of the Mission, son of preceding - Biographical data, VI, 120; VII, 129; VIII, 24; XI, 379; words of praise for him, VII, 129; sent to Genoa, VI, 120, 289, 301, 305; in Genoa, VII, 594; escapes ravages of plague, VII, 129; XI, 379; named Director of Internal Seminary in Genoa, VIII, 24, 56, 100, 121; other mention, VIII, 439.

Pinson (Denis), Brother of the Mission - Biographical data, VII, 552; in Montmirail, VII, 552, 613; mental instability, departure, VIII, 53.

Pinson (François), seminarian of the Mission - Sent to Rome, XIIIa, 359–60.

Pintart (Guillaume), Brother of the Mission - Biographical data, VII, 367; has copies of paintings sent from Sedan to Le Mans, VII, 367, 372, 393; has always seemed a little vain, VII, 591.

Pious Schools (Clerks Regular of Mother of God, **or Piarists**) - IX, 553.

Pique (Fr.), Pastor of Saint-Josse in Paris - Ready to leave for Far East missions, IV, 596.

Pirot (Georges), Jesuit - Author of *Apologie des casuistes*, VII, 499.

Pisa, town in Italy - Jewish convert comes from there to Genoa, IV, 565.

Piscot (M.) - I, 335.

Pise (Antoine de), Judge of elections in Mâcon - XIIIb, 74, 76.

Pise (François de), Cantor of Mâcon - XIIIb, 78.

Pitié, hospital in Paris - Steps to have person admitted to la Pitié, III, 303; XII, 366; poor administration, VI, 126.

Pius V, Pope - Condemnation of Baius, III, 320; IV, 607; XIIIa, 166.

Place Royale (Daughters of) - See **Hospitaller Nuns of the Charity of Our Lady**.

Plasencia, city in Spain - Bishop: see Luís Crespi de **Borja**; nobleman from Plasencia diocese, VIII, 311.

Placide (Fr.), Benedictine - V, 273, 275.

Plague - Extent to which one should risk danger while visiting and assisting plague-stricken; advice to Bishop of Cahors, IV, 500–01; to Superiors of Genoa and Rome houses, V, 634; VI, 68, 133, 134–35, 156; plague at Hôtel-Dieu, XIIIb, 387; high death rate from plague in 1656, X, 191; plague in ***Agen, Algiers, Angers, Cahors, Genoa, Italy, Krakow, Languedoc, Marseilles, Milan, Montauban, Paris, Saint-Lazare, Hôtel-Dieu, Richelieu, Rome, Tunis, Vilnius, Warsaw***: see these words; other mentions, I, 130–31; XIIIa, 55.

Plainevaux (M.) - Opposes Congregation of the Mission on benefice of Saint-Esprit in Toul, III, 366.

Plancain (Madeleine), Abbess of Longchamp - IV, 484.

Planchamp (Jean-Jacques), Priest of the Mission - Biographical data, V, 457; VI, 32; VII, 145; VIII, 45; blindness, V, 457; cousin of Fr. Musy, V, 481; VI, 92; sent to Turin, V, 457, 458; in Turin, V, 502; VI, 510; letters from Saint Vincent, VI, 32, 254; VII, 145; VIII, 45; mention of letters to Vincent, VI, 32; VII, 146; VIII, 45; brother intends to enter Saint-Lazare, VI, 92; vows, VI, 254, 256, 329; anxiety about parents, VIII, 45; leaves Turin and Company, VIII, 87.

Planchois (M.) - Pension owed him by Le Mans Missionaries, III, 608, 610–11.

Plancoët (***Notre-Dame de***) in Côtes-du-Nord - Saint Vincent regrets that Fr. Bourdet, Superior in Saint-Méen, has accepted chapel of Plancoët, II, 656–57, 663; request for Missionaries, III, 6; question of withdrawing them, III, 141.

Plassac, village in Charente-Maritime - I, 486–87.

Platel (Fr.) - Plans to resign benefice in favor of Fr. Jolly, V, 30; other mention, IV, 33.

Plenevaux (M.) - III, 449; IV, 16.

Plessal, commune in Côtes-du-Nord - Mission in this place, VII, 486.

Plessis, commune in France - XII, 377, 379.

Pleurtuit, town in Ille-et-Vilaine - Mission, VI, 302.

Pliny the Younger - Cited, V, 470.

Ploesquellec (Guillaume de), Priest of the Mission - Biographical data; in Rome, II, 296; good preacher, II, 304; not yet taken vows, II, 352.

Plouvier (Adrienne), Daughter of Charity - Sent to Cahors, VII, 365; X, 464.

Plunket (Luke), Priest of the Mission - Biographical data, VI, 364; VII, 46; Saint Vincent receives dimissorial letter from Rome, VI, 364; requests *Extra tempore* for ordination, VI, 579; withdraws request, VII, 46; Fr. Plunket is sent to Tréguier, VI, 585, 586, 614; mention of letter from Saint Vincent, VI, 614; sent to Saint-Méen, VII, 278; for ordination, needs dimissorial letter left in Tréguier, VII, 399, 429; repugnance for teaching chant and ceremonies; Saint Vincent tells him to obey, VII, 524–26, 577.

Pluyette Foundation - History, I, 66; XIIIa, 220–21, 232.

Pluyette (G.) - Letters concerning Pluyette scholars, I, 66, 73, 74, 88, 90, 520, 602; requests money from Pluyette Foundation for nephews, I, 66; sum due Principal of Senlis, I, 73; further questions about division of money among nephews, I, 74; report on Mathieu Pluyette, I, 88; who is studying in Senlis, I, 91; request for money G. Pluyette claims is owed him, I, 520; money due Étienne Pluyette, I, 602.

Pluyette (Jean), priest, Principal of Collège des Bons-Enfants - I, 66; XIIIa, 220–21, 232; other mention, VIII, 604.

Pluyette (Nicolas), cleric of Paris diocese - XIIIa, 73.

Pluyette Scholars - Mathieu, nephew of G. Pluyette, I, 66, 73, 74, 88, 90, 91; cousin Denis, I, 66, 74, 90, 91; cousin Étienne, I, 90, 91, 520, 602; Pierre, XIIIa, 73.

Poirier (Mme) - Member of Charity of Arras; informs Saint Vincent of departure of Radegonde Lenfantin, VIII, 546.

Poisson (Charlotte), Daughter of Charity - Ill at Motherhouse, III, 158.

Poisson (Geneviève), Daughter of Charity - Biographical data, I, 351; II, 484; III, 158; IV, 158; IX, 490; at Hôtel-Dieu, I, 352, 353, 358; III, 158; recuperating at Motherhouse, II, 484; Sister Servant at Foundlings, III, 213, 229, 232, 263, 399; IV, 158, 380, 381; questioned at conference, IX, 490; elected Treasurer, X, 218; signs Act of Establishment, XIIIb, 227; present at meetings of April 13, 1651, XIIIb, 227, 304–07; and February 29, (*sic*) 1658, XIIIb, 359.

Poissy, town in Yvelines - Mission, I, 226–29; Prioresses of Saint-Louis Abbey: see also **Gondi** (Jeanne de), **Gondi** (Louise de); Saint Louise is raised in abbey, I, 25; other mentions, I, 124; IV, 548; X, 160; XIIIb, 118.

Poitiers, town in Vienne - Bishops: see Henri-Louis Chastaignier de **La Rocheposay**, Gilbert de Clérembault de **Palluau**; Visitation Monastery: see also **Lage** (Anne de); Daughters of Calvary, XIIIa, 132; ordinands there, II, 417; Bishop commissions Missionary to visit part of Archdeaconry, IV, 69; Missionaries in Richelieu will give retreats to priests and preach missions in diocese, VIII, 607; other mentions, I, 403, 420, 556; II, 2, 142; III, 150; IV, 559; V, 627; VI, 510; VII, 188, 511; VIII, 226, 329; XII, 377, 379; XIIIa, 109, 124, 133; XIIIb, 142.

Poitou - Missions in Poitou, II, 191; III, 304; aspirants to Daughters of Charity from Poitou, III, 27; examination of validity of baptism conferred by Huguenot ministers in Poitou, VIII, 21, 31, 134; René Duchesne from Poitou, III, 223; other mentions, I, 27, 403, 453, 458; IV, 602; V, 76, 98; XII, 318.

Poland - Polish are won over more easily by cordiality than by strictness, V, 167; ravages of heresy in Poland, V, 562; XI, 279, 318; ignorance, sin, and many heresies have established their throne there, IV, 573; uniformity with Rome of Church in Poland, XII, 211; ministry of Missionaries in Poland, XIIIa, 186.

1645: Departure for Poland of new Queen, Louise-Marie de Gonzague: see **Gonzague**.

1650: Confinement of Queen; Saint Vincent hopes to make establishment in Poland in spring of 1651, IV, 89.

1651: Authorization for Missionaries to travel to Poland, XIIIa, 398; arrival of Frs. Lambert, Desdames, Guillot, Zelazewski, and Bro. Posny, IV, 251.

1652: Birth and death of infant Prince; King and Queen set up foundation for Missionaries, IV, 352; are benevolent toward Company, IV, 372; arrival of first Daughters of Charity, XIIIb, 313; plague in Warsaw and Krakow, IV, 493, 502, 513, 518; IX, 464; XII, 61.

1653: Fr. Lambert dies of plague; Cossack rebellion, IV, 518; XII, 416; Court prepares return to Warsaw, which it had fled because of plague, IV, 571; Fr. Ozenne is awaited there, V, 37, 50, 52.

1654: Return of Fr. Guillot to France; arrival in Poland of Fr. Ozenne, successor of Fr. Lambert; and of Frs. Durand, Éveillard, Simon, Bro. Duperroy, and first group of Visitandines; Saint Vincent prepares to send more Missionaries, V, 105, 114–15, 117–18, 126–28, 141, 148, 151, 161; is also sending book and perhaps Sisters, V, 151; will try to send two Brothers with Sisters, V, 235, 239; Muscovites' entrance into territories of Polish royalty, V, 128–29; Fr. Guillot returns to Poland; revolt of Cossacks united in Moscow to wage war against Poland; advance of their armies, V, 195, 235, 239; parish entrusted to Missionaries.

1655: Saint Vincent will try to send two Brothers, V, 263–64; looking for appropriate Daughters to send, V, 267; hopes to send two Brothers with the Daughters, V, 324, 330; is sending two Brothers, V, 367; King of Poland retakes Mogilev, V, 335; King and Queen about to leave on journey, V, 351; Muscovites and Cossacks advance and threaten Warsaw, V, 418, 424, 434, 454; XI, 180, 189–90, 274, 275, 276; invasion by King of Sweden, XI, 279; Court takes refuge in Krakow, X, 111; Fr. Ozenne is with Court, V, 434; from Krakow they go to Silesia, V, 474, 479, 535; Frs. Durand, Éveillard, Simon, and Guillot return to France, V, 474, 475, 479; Swedes, masters of Warsaw, V, 479; Tartars and Cossacks join King of Poland against Swedes, V, 535; Fr. Zelazewski leaves Company.

1656: Saint Vincent seeks resources and defenders for Poland, V, 563, 572, 609; steps taken for succession to throne, VI, 95, 98, 296; prayers and penance of Assembly of Clergy of France for Poland; success of army, V, 562–63; King of Poland enters Galicia; consecration of kingdom to Blessed Virgin, V, 572; siege of Warsaw by King of Poland, VI, 3, 6, 55; battle is imminent, VI, 83; rumors of bad news about Poland, VI, 90, 91, 94, 109; Swedes retake Warsaw, mistreat Fr. Duperroy, ransack Missionaries' house, VI, 91, 112, 124, 128, 144, 157, 159; XI, 317, 318, 323, 333; sad situation of Poland, XI, 317, 320; Swedes abandon city in order to defend Sweden against Muscovites, VI, 128, 144; news is better, VI, 140.

1656–57: Plague and famine in Warsaw, VI, 140, 144, 157, 159, 182, 347; X, 191.

1657: Polish Court in Glogau (Silesia) with Fr. Ozenne, VI, 182; in Opole with Frs. Ozenne and Duperroy, VI, 326; Queen of Poland seeks assistance from Assembly of Clergy of France, VI, 644; Assembly declares itself powerless, VI, 647; Fr. Ozenne writes that Swedes are in Warsaw or have been through it, VI, 319; Swedes approach Warsaw, VI, 352, 385; besiege city, X, 263; enter, then abandon, it, VI, 393, 421, 447, 451, 453, 470, 472, 489, 492, 502; Fr. Ozenne and Daughters of Charity assist soldiers wounded at siege of Warsaw, X, 263; Polish Court encamps just outside Krakow, VI, 464; Fr. Ozenne ministers to sick and wounded of siege of Krakow, VI, 502; Krakow surrenders to Polish armies; King and Queen make their entrance, accompanied by Frs. Ozenne and Duperroy, VI, 555; success of Polish armies, VI, 464, 502, 555, 566; hope for return to Warsaw soon, VI, 566; entrance of King and Queen into Warsaw; Frs. Ozenne and Duperroy find Fr. Desdames there, VI, 620; damages suffered during war by houses belonging to Mission, VII, 9; King of Poland imposes conditions on Prince of Transylvania; siege of Riga, VII, 83; flu epidemic; Court expected in Warsaw in two weeks, VII, 90; Saint Vincent awaits instructions about sending men to new establishment, XII, 25; will soon send priest and brother, VII, 264–65.

1658: Meeting of Diet; Court is out of Warsaw, VII, 107; prospect of new battles, VII, 155; death of Fr. Ozenne; Fr. Desdames replaces him as Superior; plague in Warsaw, VII, 474; XII, 61.

1659: Saint Vincent hopes to send Missionaries when peace is restored and plague is no more, VII, 475, 481; to respond to request to give missions, VII, 491; Poland against Jansenists, VII, 549; foresees sending new Missionaries, VII, 579; VIII, 106, 118, 194, 229; return of Court to Warsaw, VII, 480; success of Polish army, VIII, 193; new invasion of Muscovites; preparation of peace treaty with Sweden, VIII, 280, 300–01.

1660: Plans to send Missionaries, VIII, 301; three other Daughters of Charity are sent, XIIIb, 238; Treaty of Oliva, VIII, 193, 252, 353; other mentions, XI, 364, 366; XIIIa, 208; See also **Cossacks**, ***Krakow***, **Gonzague** (Louise-Marie de), ***Lithuania***, **Muscovites**, ***Oliva***, ***Warsaw***, etc.

Pollalion [**Poulallion**] (Marie de Lumague, demoiselle de), Foundress of Daughters of Providence - Biographical data, I, 161; II, 109; III, 265–66; IV, 499–500; VI, 549; XI, 341; family, XI, 341; Lady of Charity, I, 230, 260; XIIIb, 383, 385; visits Charities, I, 161, 258; recruits young women for Saint Louise, I, 237; Saint Vincent asks Saint Louise to spend a week in Grigny; Mlle de Pollalion could visit her Sisters occasionally, I, 318; contacts with Saint Vincent, I, 161, 221, 261, 451, 533; II, 312; with Saint Louise, I, 163, 167, 282, 285, 288, 551; III, 265; with Marquise de Maignelay, II, 109–10; asks Saint Vincent's permission to spend night before Blessed Sacrament from time to time, IV, 500; death, VI, 54–50; other mentions, I, 285, 305, 385; II, 260; XII, 40; XIIIb, 441. See also **Providence** (Daughters).

Polucci [**Paolucci**] (Francesco), Msgr. - V, 595.

Pomerania, region of Europe - Filled with soldiers, VIII, 146.

Pommier (Jean), Canon of Mâcon - XIIIb, 78.

Pompierre, village in Vosges - VIII, 492.

Pomps - Renounce worldly pomps, III, 189; XII, 181.

Poncher (Étienne de), Bishop of Paris - Entrusts administration of Saint-Lazare Priory to monks of Saint-Victor, I, 243, 248; XIIIa, 410, 479.

Ponchin (Abel), Priest of the Mission - Biographical data, V, 127; illness, V, 179; death, V, 181.

Pont-à-Mousson, town in Meurthe-et-Moselle - Misery and assistance, II, 93; letter of Town Magistrates expressing thanks and asking for help, II, 165.

Pont-Carré (Mme de) - Abbé de Saint-Cyran accuses her of forming cabal against him, XIIIa, 123.

Pont-de-Vie [***Pontdevie***], house of Missionaries in Luçon - VIII, 607; XIIIa, 318–21.

Pont-Saint-Esprit, near Uzès in Gard - On Fr. Alméras' route from Cahors to Annecy, III, 125.

Pont-Saint-Pierre, village in Eure - XIIIa, 29.

Pont-Sainte-Maxence, town in Oise - Confraternity of Charity, I, 188; passage of troops, I, 338, 343.

Pontanus (Fr. Antoine) - I, 12, 14.

Pontchartrain (Claude-Phelippeaux de), daughter of Paul, wife of Pierre de Hodicq - II, 98.

Pontchartrain (Françoise-Élisabeth Phelippeaux de), Superior of Paris Visitation, sister of Claude-Phelippeaux de Pontchartrain - Biographical data; Saint Vincent announces visit on Sister's profession day, II, 70–71; goes to Saint-Denis to ask favor of Superior, II, 98; saint refuses a request she makes of him because he is not "spiritual father" of Sisters of Saint-Denis, and because of his occupations and infirmities, II, 282, 284.

Pontchartrain (Paul Phelippeaux, sieur de), Secretary of State - II, 98; XIIIa, 58.

Pontie (M.) - IV, 505.

Pontifical, liturgical book - Explained during retreats at Saint-Lazare, I, 516; III, 204; VI, 100.

Pontoise, town in Val-d'Oise - Journeys of Saint Vincent to Pontoise, I, 129, 205, 317, 377, 450, 561; II, 463; XIIIa, 211; of Mme Goussault, I, 318; clerical conference of Pontoise, II, 283; other mentions, I, 116, 438, 476; III, 121; V, 30; VIII, 406.

Ponts-de-Cé, town in Maine-et-Loire - Customs dues, II, 81, 359.

Pontus (Toinette Guay), widow - Member of Charity of Châtillon, XIIIb, 21.

Poor - Mention of conferences to Missionaries on spiritual assistance to poor, XII, 423, 425, 426; conference to Daughters on assistance to poor, IX, 190–201; serving poor persons is great and honorable, IX, 97, 256; X, 546; Jesus served poor persons, IX, 50, 467; they represent Jesus, IX, 199; X, 268, 545; XI, 26; their great sufferings; true religion is found among them,

XI, 190; God rewards royally those who serve persons who are poor, IX, 199; even in this world, IX, 74; X, 545–47; and in next world, III, 384; poor intercede for benefactors from heights of heaven, IX, 200; faith is their great possession, IX, 74; Saint Vincent considers self blessed that God wishes to use Company of Missionaries for evangelization of poor, V, 66; XI, 329; XII, 71–72, 75–76, 77; example of Daughters of Charity who preferred service of poor to that of nobles: see also **Angiboust** (Barbe), **Moreau** (Marguerite); regret of Daughter of Charity who took too much pleasure in serving poor persons, IX, 537; see God in poor persons, IX, 5; XI, 26; be their visible Guardian Angels, father, and mother, IX, 5; serve them in God and for God, IX, 197; with joy, courage, fidelity, love, IX, 466; with humility, gentleness, forbearance, patience, respect, X, 545; XII, 248; love them, XI, 349; honor them, IX, 22; in case of necessity, prefer their service to prayer, IX, 29; catechize them, XI, 342–45; peaceful death for friends of poor, XII, 391; compassion for Irish refugees, XII, 391–92: see also **Charity**, **Confraternities of Charity**, **Ladies of Charity**, **Daughters of Charity**, **Illness**.

Poor Clares - Poor Clares of Pouget in Castelnau-de-Montratier, II, 489–90; of Cahors, II, 490, 632.

Pope - Dignity of Sovereign Pontiff, XII, 350; right to our allegiance, IX, 56; XII, 350; consult him in doubts about doctrine, IV, 156, 183, 209–13; VI, 293; infallible in confirmation of religious Orders and canonization of saints, XII, 306; he alone has power to send every priest throughout the world, II, 64–65, 288; III, 164, 169, 187; XI, 373; Bull, *In coena Domini,* not yet received in France, V, 571; Popes obliged by persecuting Emperors to care for animals, XI, 18; martyred Popes, X, 442; XI, 18, 335, 338, 368; other mention, I, 591.

Porcher (Nicolas), Officialis of Paris - Fulmination of Bull uniting Saint-Lazare Priory to Mission, VII, 252, 327; XIIIa, 486–87; petition of Saint Vincent for union, VII, 502; verdict of fulmination, XIIIa, 472–80; formalities, VII, 504.

Porchod (Jacques), from Châtillon-les-Dombes - XIIIb, 22.

Porchon (Étienne), witness to Saint Vincent's will - XIIIa, 100, 101.

Porphyry - In charge of troops of Maximus, won over by Catherine of Alexandria, X, 496.

Port-Louis, Morbihan - Port of embarkation for Madagascar, VII, 91; VIII, 186, 221, 558.

Port-Royal - Disastrous influence of Port-Royal, IV, 517; VI, 121; dangers of books from its shop, VI, 100; supposed miracles at Port-Royal, VI, 291, 292; Marie-Angélique d'Atri at Port-Royal, I, 460, 461–62; Mme de Pont-Carré at Port-Royal, XIIIa, 123; time will reveal its errors, XII, 365; Saint Louise wants to visit there, III, 518; relationship of Saint-Cyran with nuns of Port-Royal, XIIIa, 125.

Port-Sainte-Marie, town in Lot-et-Garonne - Dominicans, III, 386.

Portail (Antoine), Priest of the Mission - Biographical data, I, 38; III, 10; IV, 23; V, 332; VI, 70; VII, 26; VIII, 105; IX, *x*; XI, *xv*; letters Saint Vincent writes to him in Croissy, I, 82; in the Cévennes, I, 110, 289, 304; in Montmirail, I, 176; in another place, I, 275; in Pébrac, I, 331, 338; in Fréneville, I, 463; in..., II, 217; in Paris, II, 528, 532, 534, 536, 537; in Le Mans, II, 621, 623, 631, 641; in Richelieu, II, 663, 665, 668, 674; III, 10; in Saintes, III, 30; in La Rose, III, 62, 80, 89, 92, 109, 114; in Cahors, III, 102, 124, 133, 137; in Rome, III, 204, 237, 246; in Genoa, III, 258; in Marseilles, III, 271, 272, 295, 299, 376, 393, 412, 428, 464; in Toul, V, 440; mention of letter Saint Vincent wrote him in Annecy, III, 466; reference to letter from Fr. du Chesne to Fr. Portail, II, 422; Saint Vincent wants him present when changes are made to Rules, II, 670; letter to confrere he wrote for Saint Vincent, II, 687; mention of letter to Saint Vincent, III, 68; dispositions regarding Fr. du Coudray, III, 89; soon to leave for Rome, III, 115.

Saint Vincent's esteem for Fr. Portail, XI, 250, 253, 254, 257, 265, 326; XII, 11, 41; niece of Fr. Portail, VIII, 362; he knew Mme de Gondi, XI, 110; XIIIa, 64; Bro. Antoine, XII, 29; Fr. Pillé, XII, 28; pastor of nearby La Rochelle, died a holy man, XII, 209–10; no thought of foundation of Mission, XI, 31; XII, 6–8; nor of Daughters of Charity, IX, 93, 472, 473, 536; fear of preaching, I, 83; writes to Sister Marie Joly for Saint Vincent, II, 247; takes up residence in Bons-Enfants with Saint Vincent, XII, 7.

Power of attorney to take possession of Collège des Bons-Enfants (March 2, 1624), XIIIa, 70; takes possession of Bons-Enfants in name of Saint Vincent (March 6, 1624), XIIIa, 72; signs Act of Association with Saint Vincent and first companions (September 4, 1626), XIIIa, 222–23; takes possession of Bons-Enfants in name of Congregation of the Mission (July 15, 1627), XIIIa, 234; gives missions in Croissy, I, 82; in the Cévennes, I, 110, 289, 304; in Montmirail, I, 177; in Pébrac, I, 331, 338; resting at Fréneville farm, I, 463; in Paris, I, 478, 559; II, 28, 289, 293, 520; represents Saint Vincent in Paris, II, 307; suggests topic for conference to Sisters, II, 444–45; saint asks him to write to confreres regarding freedom of correspondence with Superior General, II, 542; after week off, will continue visitation Fr. Lambert was making, II, 585; negotiates entrance of Daughters of Charity into Le Mans Hospital, II, 628; sends Sisters back from there, II, 655; see also ***Le Mans***; requested for visitation of Cahors, III, 83; visits houses in ***Le Mans***, ***Richelieu***, ***Saint-Méen***, ***Saintes***, ***La Rose***, ***Cahors***, ***Marseilles***, ***Rome***, ***Genoa***, and Daughters of Charity in ***Angers***: see these names; on return to France, again visits Marseilles; discusses with hospital administrators spiritual ministry for galley convicts; plague forces him to leave house; welcomed by family of confrere, Fr. Tratebas: see also ***Marseilles***; Alain de Solminihac requests of Saint Vincent, through Fr. Portail, another man for his seminary, III, 153; arranges instruction of heretic who wants to convert, III, 445–46; visits again houses in ***Annecy***, ***Bons-Enfants***, and ***Toul***: see these names.

Member of 1642 General Assembly, II, 343; XIIIa, 323, 327, 396; and of commission to prepare Rules of Company, II, 344; XIIIa, 326, 397; member of 1651 General Assembly, II, 343; XIIIa, 369, 372–73, 374, 383–84, 396–97; opinion concerning vows in Company, XIIIa, 379, 383; requests dispensation from Fr. Codoing in Rome, II, 397; mention of letter from Fr. Codoing, II, 505; works on Rules, VI, 366, 594; correspondence with Fr. Jolly regarding Rules, VI, 349, 385, 387, 412; suggests topic to Saint Vincent for conference to confreres, XI, 158; speaks at conferences, XI, 178; XII, 14, 157; collected what was said at conferences; devised method for sermons and catechism, XII, 237–38.

First Assistant of Saint Vincent, II, 344; IV, 469; XI, 86; XIIIa, 331, 483, 484; saint shares news with him, II, 535, 536; Director of Daughters of Charity since 1640, IX, 398; speaks to several Sisters about making retreat, II, 302, 303; Saint Louise intends to write to him, II, 630; zeal for sanctification of Sisters, X, 569; assists at conferences of Saint Vincent to Sisters, IX, 436, 438, 445, 449, 451, 453, 544; X, 485, 518; presides at some, IX, 49, 395, 448–49; assists at Sisters' Council meetings, IV, 193; X, 593; XIIIb, 240, 318, 322, 331, 334, 338–39, 345, 347, 348, 350, 359, 362, 364, 372–73; consulted for Sisters' vows, V, 357; VI, 70; VII, 298, 408, 465; VIII, 105, 235; mentioned in relation to his office as Director of Sisters, IV, 23, 159; V, 332, 401, 461; VI, 136; VII, 158, 254, 445, 457; VIII, 352; IX, 160, 453, 464, 496, 501, 504–05, 526, 557; X, 12, 18, 25, 27, 30, 37, 54, 55, 131, 136, 139, 151, 171, 192, 212, 222, 226, 242, 261, 333, 354, 361, 379, 414, 514, 518–19, 529, 553, 566, 581, 597; XIIIb, 314; went twenty years without seeing his mother, II, 689.

Health, I, 270, 516; III, 300; V, 588; VI, 213, 594, 639; VII, 26–27, 73, 75; VIII, 280–81; speaks Italian, but is too elderly to preach, VI, 498; difficulty speaking, XII, 241; death, VIII, 288, 294, 297, 300, 312; X, 569; Saint Vincent eulogizes him, VIII, 288, 294, 300; his virtues, X, 580–81; mention of conference given at Saint-Lazare on his virtues, XII, 437; other mentions, I, *xxxvi*, 24, 38, 45, 47, 53; III, 318; IV, 510, 576, 589; V, 344; VII, 253, 528; VIII, 208, 599; XI, 236; XII, 264, 311; XIIIa, 259, 262, 335, 337, 365–66, 367; XIIIb, 97, 122, 131, 238.

Portier (M.) - III, 471.

Portnal (Mme de) - Feels better, thanks to purgative or mineral water Saint Vincent recommends to Saint Louise, I, 139.

Porto, town in Italy - II, 170; VI, 636.

Portugal - Saint Vincent sees Portuguese Ambassador to Paris on behalf of Nuncio, V, 46, 68; delivers to him letter from Msgr. di Ferentilli, V, 203; Ambassador organizes papers of Archbishop of Myra, who died in Paris, V, 103; Fr. Daveroult in Portugal, VII, 239; charity of several Queens of Portugal, X, 451; Portuguese Christians on Cape Verde, VIII, 290, 567; traders, VIII, 566; Portuguese language necessary in Indies, VIII, 592; other mentions, II, 523; V, 328; VI, 104, 525; VIII, 577, 587–89, 593.

Posny (Jacques), Brother of the Mission - Biographical data, IV, 329–30; V, 51; sent to Warsaw, IV, 251; XIIIa, 398; in Warsaw, IV, 329, 571; V, 51; ill in Poland, IV, 354; assists plague-stricken, IV, 493; Fr. Ozenne proposes to send him back to France, V, 105; his fault, V, 234–35; repentance, V, 263.

Possession (Diabolical) - Possessed nuns of Louviers, II, 456; of Cognac, VII, 138; of Chinon, II, 80, 95, 112; of Loudun, I, 592; II, 456; X, 298; presumed possession of Marie-Angélique d'Atri, I, 459–63: see **Exorcism**.

Postulants - See **Daughters of Charity**, **Congregation of the Mission**.

Potier (Augustin), Bishop of Beauvais - Biographical data, I, 56; II, 51; Prelate does not stand on ceremony, I, 93; member of Council of Conscience, II, 583; establishes in Beauvais, with help of Saint Vincent, retreats for ordinands of his diocese, I, 56; Charities, I, 91; interest for Charities in diocese, I, 282, 286, 288; Saint Vincent asks Saint Louise to speak to him about setting up Charity, I, 282; saint tries to persuade Bishops near Paris to send seminarians to Saint-Lazare for ordination retreat, I, 531; has mission given in diocese, I, 58; gives one himself, I, 283; saint proposes him to Rome as judge in affair, II, 319; contacts with Saint Vincent, I, 317, 492, 531; II, 51, 399, 429, 463; III, 379; esteem for Fr. de la Salle, XII,

238; Mazarin's opinion of him, XIIIa, 154; other mentions, I, 385, 387; II, 183, 319, 446, 492.

Potier (Jeanne), niece of Augustin Potier - See **Marillac** (Jeanne Potier, dame de).

Potrincourt (Mlle de) - Ill, I, 150.

Pouget (Monastery) - Alain de Solminihac entrusted with visitation there, II, 489–90. See also **Laroque** (Mother de), Prioress.

Pouilly (Claude) - See **Pransac** (Claude).

Poulain (Louis), clerk in Dax - Witness to Saint Vincent's will, XIIIa, 100, 101.

Poulet (Marie), Daughter of Charity - Biographical data, VII, 200; X, 440; sent to Calais to nurse sick and wounded soldiers; falls ill, VII, 200; X, 440; XII, 34; praises Barbe Angiboust, X, 519, 522; other mention, XIIIb, 228.

Poupet (M.) - XIIIa, 478.

Pourié (Charles) - Member of Charity of Courboin, XIIIb, 93.

Pourrade (M. de) - Elected Administrator of hospital for galley convicts in Marseilles, VIII, 243, 249.

Poussard (Anne), Duchesse de Richelieu - See **Richelieu** (Anne Poussard).

Poussay (M.) - VII, 524.

Pousset (M.) - In Le Mans, III, 29, 611.

Pouvot (Fr.), Pastor of Chars - See ***Chars***.

Pouy [***Poy***], village in Landes, today Saint-Vincent-de-Paul - Birthplace of Saint Vincent, I, 15; II, 82–83; XIIIa, 1, 10; his family in Pouy, I, 15; XIIIa, 7, 99; stipend in parish of Pouy, III, 245; Mme de Ventadour, Marquise de Pouy, II, 82; Fr. Brin in Pouy, IV, 467; shrine of Notre-Dame-de-Buglose in Pouy: see also ***Buglose***.

Poverty - Conferences, X, 166–81, 232–45, 245–56; XI, 71, 72, 152–59, 209–13, 217–32; XII, 307, 314, 328; mention of other conferences, XII, 420, 427, 432; text of Rule for Missionaries, XII, 307, 315, 319–23; conversation with confrere regarding poverty, XI, 72; explanation of Rule of Missionaries, XII, 314–27; 328–35; of Daughters of Charity, X, 166–81, 245, 256.

Before Jesus, virtue of poverty was unknown, XI, 227; first Christians lived in community of goods, XI, 211; XII, 313, 319; punishment of Ananias and Sapphira for withholding part of property, X, 167–68; XI, 211; in early Church, necessary to renounce possessions in order to become priest, XI,

210; under Pope Telesphorus, every priest had to have benefice; from that time everything began to decline, XII, 324.

Material goods are only a means; not to be sought for sake of having them, XI, 212, 223; riches are source of all kinds of evil, XI, 221–24; poverty makes us think of God, XI, 72; those who renounce all are moved naturally to love God, XII, 309, 317; spirit of poverty is vital principle of God; contrary spirit is spirit of damnation, X, 244; XI, 212; reward promised for voluntary poverty, IX, 73; God rewards here below those who leave all for love of Him, XII, 317–18.

Every member of Community is obliged to practice poverty by promise made to Superiors on entrance, X, 169–70, 235; XI, 217–19; by vow later made to God, XI, 156–57, 219–20; XII, 308; motives for observing vow of poverty, XI, 220; poverty is crux of Communities, XI, 209, 213, 217; Congregation will not perish through poverty, XII, 391; foundation of Congregation of the Mission, XI, 71; of Company of Daughters of Charity, X, 174, 178–79, 594; XIIIb, 345–46; good Missionary is detached from goods of world, XI, 321; Congregation of the Mission will be ruined sooner by riches than by poverty, II, 517, 519; XI, 72, 297; undesirable to admit rich persons into Company of Daughters of Charity, XIIIb, 373; impossible to persevere in vocation without poverty, X, 177, 248; XI, 225, 230; punishments inflicted in ancient communities for failures in poverty, X, 178–79; XI, 156.

Example of Jesus, III, 115; VIII, 175; IX, 71; XI, 210, 226, 228, 322; XII, 307–08, 315–16; teaching of Jesus, XI, 227; XII, 315–19; example of Apostles, XII, 17; punishment of Judas, X, 173, 246–48; XI, 224–25; Saint Francis of Assisi orders demolition of church he deems too beautiful, X, 239; called poverty his "lady," XI, 226; example of Saint Vincent, XI, 158–59; of Saint Louise, X, 573, 579; of Fr. de Gondi, X, 241; of Fr. Pillé, II, 376; of country women, IX, 72, 74–75; of Saint-Lazare community, X, 241; increasing with public calamities, IV, 328.

Nature of poverty, XI, 227–28; XII, 309–10; do not keep money on you, XI, 322; do not aspire to benefices or other ecclesiastical dignities: see also **Benefices**; among Missionaries and Daughters of Charity, objects, such as clothing, books, pictures, belong to Community; use only with permission of Superior, X, 166, 168; XII, 333; do not keep, use, give, receive, take, borrow, request, or purchase anything without permission, IX, 100–01, 505–17; X, 170, 551; XII, 321; do not use, without permission, what is for use of another member of Community; accept what serves for personal use of another only if Superior desires it, X, 232, 234–37; XII, 321; be prepared to surrender all at slightest sign from Superior, XII, 321; do nothing that smacks of ownership, XII, 321.

In theory, ask for nothing for personal needs; refuse nothing of what is given on Superior's order, X, 238, 240–41; XI, 154; accept worst if it is given, XII, 322; be content with what is necessary, X, 167; if someone forgets to give what is indispensable, request it of person responsible for inquiring into individual needs, X, 231, 237, 242; XI, 154; XII, 320; inform Superior if that person does not do duty properly, X, 242–43.

Live poorly, X, 194, 551; XII, 322; have nothing superfluous or uncommon, XI, 154, 155, 159; XII, 322; even with permission of Superior, who may not give this permission, XII, 333–34; take care of goods of poor and of Community, II, 623, 624; III, 527; IV, 280; X, 245–56, 549; XI, 25; XIIIb, 325; do not appropriate goods to self, II, 107; IX, 362, 390, 444; X, 38, 134, 173–75, 178–79, 236, 249–52, 256, 289, 529; XIIIb, 315–16; do not lock room; keep nothing locked up, except for money or important papers, XII, 322, 331–33; do not take books from one house to another without permission, VII, 293; XII, 322–23; personal papers may be taken, XII, 322; refuse gifts the poor may wish to offer, X, 545; houses of Daughters of Charity must give surplus to Motherhouse: see also **Daughters of Charity**; obligation for Missionaries, on returning from journey, to hand in money to Superior, XI, 155, 157.

Practice poverty in food and drink, VI, 162; IX, 69–71, 247, 363; X, 152, 290, 326; XIIIb, 282; in clothing, IX, 248, 556; X, 152, 239–41, 252–54; XII, 18; in buildings and furnishings, II, 427, 623; VIII, 49; X, 239–40; XIIIb, 342; in books, VII, 293; XI, 154–55, 229; XII, 321–22, 333; in church vestments, II, 310; in everything, IX, 248; X, 124, 194, 289, 551; duties of Sisters who manage goods of poor, X, 255; dangers in money management, X, 165, 248.

Faults against poverty, X, 171, 249–51; XI, 152–55, 157–58; XII, 22–23; explanation of practices that seem contrary to vow of poverty, XII, 312–14; means of acquiring spirit of poverty, XI, 229–31; XII, 323–24; trust in times of poverty, XII, 388.

Simple, hardworking Daughters of Charity are burden to no one, IX, 387; desirable to serve poor at expense of Sisters, IX, 388; world praises their disinterestedness, XIIIb, 373; they require nothing from postulants, X, 288; except what is necessary for first habit, XIIIb, 372; Saint Vincent prefers that Sisters not give their goods to family during their lifetime, XIIIb, 364.

Questions raised at 1651 Assembly regarding Missionaries' obligations concerning vow of poverty, XIIIa, 390–91; steps taken in Rome to obtain authentic explanation of vow of poverty, VI, 459, 482; VII, 401, 635; Saint Vincent rejoices that this question is settled, VIII, 37, 57, 71, 133; text of Brief *Alias Nos*, XIIIa, 480–82; reading of Brief to Saint-Lazare community; Saint Vincent's commentary, XII, 311–12; copy of Brief sent to each house, VIII, 134; saint awaits opinion of Fr. Jolly regarding explanation of conditions of vow, VI, 419.

Missionary may retain ownership of immovable goods and simple benefices and right to acquire them, but may not dispose of them without permission, IV, 14, 542; V, 547; VI, 430; VII, 129; XI, 153, 209–10, 322; XII, 311–12, 329–30; XIIIa, 481; revenue to be used in good works or to assist relatives in need, VI, 255; VII, 311; XI, 322; XII, 311–12, 329–30; Missionary who leaves Company has right to use and ownership of his goods and benefices, IV, 14; XI, 210; XII, 312; XIIIa, 390; vow of poverty does not exclude inheritance from parents, IV, 14; V, 499, 545; XIIIa, 390; question is brought before Parlement, VI, 446, 448, 449; Parlement does not recognize validity of gift to his Community made by member of Community, IV, 14; reasons why, VII, 339–40; Saint Vincent refuses to ratify foundation contract giving Missionary right to use certain goods during his lifetime, VII, 183; poverty of spirit: mention of conference, XII, 417; other mentions, I, 137, 554; II, 37.

Poyanne (Jean-Henri-Gabriel de Baylens, Marquis de) - Biographical data, III, 243; IV, 515; Saint Vincent thanks him for service to relative, IV, 515.

Poznań, town in Poland - Officialis of Poznań, V, 51; VII, 92; Palatine of Poznań joins with Swedes against Poland, XI, 274; pillage of Poznań by Swedes, XI, 276; Bishops: see Florian-Kazimierz **Czartoryski**, Albert **Tholibowski**; Bishop is getting parish for Missionaries there, VII, 107; wants Congregation to serve in diocese, VII, 625.

Pra (Anne-Françoise de) - Biographical data, V, 83.

Praise - Avoid praising person in his presence, XI, 93, 94, 108; praise only virtue, not natural talents, X, 119–20; pay no attention to praise, XI, 179, 388; priest's praise for zeal of Missionaries, I, 33.

Pransac (Alexandre de Redon, Marquis de), husband of Claude de Pouilly, VIII, 419.

Pransac (Claude de Pouilly, Marquise d'Esne) - Asks Saint Vincent to keep son in Saint-Lazare prison, VIII, 419.

Prat (André), Consul of France in Salé - Requests Missionaries for Salé; Saint Vincent thanks him, apologizes for not sending any; Recollect got there ahead of them, III, 78.

Prat (Henri), Consul of France in Salé, son of preceding - III, 79; IV, 331; V, 191.

Prayer - Missionary's weapon, XI, 281; means of obtaining graces and virtues, IX, 10, 142, 231, 251, 317, 343; X, 57, 71, 580; XI, 99, 110, 208–09, 229; XII, 47, 122, 135, 262, 286; XIIIb, 420; its excellence; dispositions for meditation, XII, 390; prayer for humility, XII, 394; time of thanksgiving must equal that of petition, XII, 399; example of Jesus, XI, 195; pray for one another, especially at Mass and Communion, XI, 68; prayer is natural to soul; example of little children, IX, 330; two kinds of prayer: mental and vocal, IX, 329–30; manner of praying in common among Daughters of Charity, X, 482; Saint Vincent gives example of meditative prayer, XI, 321–22; ejaculatory prayers (aspirations), like darts of love, IX, 32; X, 268; Saint Vincent recommends them to Daughters of Charity, IX, 332; X, 268, 538; prayers of Saint Vincent, III, 241, 258; IX, 22–23, 92, 103, 236, 243, 252–53, 265–66, 271–72, 284, 336, 464, 469–70, 516–17, 535, 548; X, 42, 52, 85–86, 209–10, 217, 230–31, 266–67, 270–71, 306–07, 317–18, 354–55, 366–67, 380, 402, 417, 432, 439, 459, 464, 555, 568; XI, 208–09, 216, 232, 257, 278–79, 281, 284, 309; XII, 10, 12, 95–96, 113–14, 124, 149, 150, 173, 212, 217–18, 224–25, 232, 252, 259, 263, 296–97, 306, 324, 334–35, 352; XIIIb, 251, 440; prayer for humility, XII, 394. See also **Angelus**, **Rosary**, **Meditation**.

Prayer (Mental) - See **Meditation**.

Prayer (Repetition) - See **Repetition of Prayer**.

Preaching - Conferences, XI, 237–60, 265–69; mention of other conferences, XII, 421, 436; purpose of preaching is to draw souls to heaven, XIIIa, 31; three kinds of preaching, XIIIa, 31; "little method" comes from God, XI, 238; in what it consists, XI, 249; parts, XI, 239–40; vary points, depending on topic, XI, 254; efficacy, XI, 238–42, 244–48, 255–57; ineffectiveness of other methods, XI, 251, 254, 259; preacher who does not use "little method" endangers his salvation, XI, 247–48; need of preaching in seminaries, II, 266, 271; prayer of Saint Vincent to obtain fidelity of Missionaries to "little method," XI, 257; preach simply, II, 264; V, 568; VII, 231; VIII, 173, 237; XI, 10, 41, 237, 250, 314; XII, 20–22, 145, 181–83, 209, 251; to obtain conversion of souls and not esteem of others, I, 183, 276; VIII, 173, 236–37; XI, 10, 77, 115, 388; XII, 20–22, 163, 181–83; example of Jesus, I, 184; VI, 399; XI, 242–44, 258; XII, 21, 209; of Apostles, VIII, 237; XI, 237, 244; XII, 21; of Saint Vincent Ferrer, XI, 259; of Saint Francis de Sales, V, 478; XI, 255; of Saint Philip Neri and Oratorians, XI, 266–67; of pastor in La Rochelle, XII, 209; of Nicolas Sevin, V, 573,

576; XII, 21; of Jesuits, V, 630; of Fr. de Musy, VI, 127; Saint Vincent kneels at feet of priest to beg him to preach simply, V, 573; XII, 21; in praise of simple preaching, XII, 385.

Use familiar comparisons, XI, 314; have natural delivery; example of actors, VI, 399; citing profane author serves as stepping stone to Gospel, XI, 41; go into detail, XI, 10; when one has choice of two thoughts, sacrifice better to God and prefer other, XII, 182, 209; strive to be moderate in order to be uniform, XII, 209–10; avoid speaking too long, VI, 623; avoid harsh words, I, 526; be circumspect in explaining sixth Commandment, I, 439, 448, 453; use prudence and charity so no listener feels offended or sees self personally in preacher's words, VI, 344; be humble and respectful with heretics; do not challenge ministers from pulpit, I, 276, 420; do not glory in success, XI, 388; join example to preaching to make it efficacious, XI, 252; prayer is great book for preachers, VII, 171.

Saint Vincent reproaches self for not having formed young Missionaries in preaching, IV, 121; Superiors must form confreres in preaching and have them minister outside house, IV, 527; preaching exercises at Saint-Lazare, I, 289; VIII, 90, 91, 93; XI, 236, 265; XII, 235, 237, 240–42; XIIIa, 373; care taken by Huguenot ministers to be formed in preaching according to Calvin's method, XII, 239; Saint Vincent considers having Fr. Codoing's sermons copied or printed for Company only, I, 527; manuscript collection of preaching and catechism methods for use in Company, VII, 271; XII, 238; Saint Vincent recommends that Missionaries never preach to priests or monks, VI, 34; sermon preached twice daily in refectory at Saint-Lazare, VI, 83–84. See also **Congregation of the Mission**, **Vincent de Paul**.

Préau (Philibert), of Mâcon - XIIIb, 74.

Préchonnet (Anne-Thérèse de), Visitandine - II, 228.

Précy-sur-Oise, commune in Picardy - XII, 377–78, 379.

Predestination - No infallible signs, only very probable ones, IV, 316–17; conformity with Son of God is sign of predestination for Daughters of Charity, I, 353; Saint Louise's fear, III, 201.

Premonstratensians - Saint Vincent writes to Vicar-General of Reformed Premonstratensians of Verdun about Abbot of Cuissy, IV, 330; Canon desires Mont-Saint-Éloi Abbey, V, 96.

Préraux (M.), gentleman from Poitiers - Saint Vincent recommends him to Lady, V, 627.

Presence of God - Mention of conference, XII, 428; doing God's Will is preferable to remaining in God's presence, XI, 287; placing self in God's presence during prayer, IX, 4; XI, 234;

and, from time to time, outside of prayer, IX, 6; how to place self in God's presence, IX, 28, 31; X, 471–73; XI, 359; example of person distracted from presence of God only three times in a day, XII, 136.

Pressigny, village in Indre-et-Loire - Mission given, VII, 204.

Prévost (Bernard), Seigneur of Saint-Cyr - Thanks Saint Vincent for mission given in Saint-Cyr, II, 274–75.

Prévost (François), Brother of the Mission - Biographical data, V, 447; assists dying Saint Vincent, XIIIa, 204.

Prévost (Jeanne-Christine), Daughter of Charity - Biographical data, III, 298; V, 208; VI, 379; VII, 367; X, 233; praise for her, V, 208; proposed for Chars, III, 298; sent to Sedan, V, 208; en route for Sedan, V, 222, 223, 225, 241, 246; in Sedan, V, 269; Saint Louise asks permission for her to renew vows, VI, 379; assists sick poor of Stenay by order of Queen, VI, 403, 530; X, 233; elected Assistant but is needed in Sedan; Saint Vincent names another in her place, X, 595–96; other mentions, VII, 367; XIIIb, 227.

Prévost (Fr.) - Biographical data; ill in Paris, II, 348; learned and astute businessman, II, 355; accepted into Internal Seminary, II, 360; praise for him, II, 360; other mention, II, 348.

Prévost (Marie), Daughter of Charity - Biographical data, VIII, 235; Saint Louise asks permission for her to renew vows, VIII, 235.

Prévost (Marie de Moncy, dame), wife of Bernard Prévost - Thanks Saint Vincent for mission in Saint-Cyr, II, 275.

Prévost (Nicolas), Priest of the Mission - Biographical data, V, 207; VI, 13; VII, 17; VIII, 181; XI, 371; assigned to Madagascar, V, 431; journey to Madagascar, VI, 13, 15, 227, 228, 230; ship anchors at Sainte-Marie, near Madagascar, where he disembarks, VI, 19, 232; on Île Sainte-Marie, VI, 234, 235, 237; death, VI, 214, 215, 217, 241, 447, 452, 453, 455, 460, 463, 464, 469, 471, 475, 478, 481, 488, 491, 501, 528, 530, 535, 537, 567, 583, 586; VII, 17; VIII, 180, 553, 554; XI, 372; his nephew, VII, 366; ministry in Madagascar, XIIIa, 186; mention of conference at Saint-Lazare on his virtues, XII, 429. See also ***Madagascar***.

Pride - Conferences, IX, 528–35; XI, 178–79; mention of another conference, XII, 420; Saint Vincent asks Missionaries to meditate once a month on pride, envy, and sloth, XI, 178–79; warns confrere against complacency, I, 183; pride spoils any good we do; leads to damnation, IX, 530; God resists proud and punishes haughty, permitting her to fall into serious sin, IX, 530, 534; source of impurity, X, 304; of vanity, disobedience, ambition, singularity, obstinacy, IX, 531–33; of envy and aversion, X, 374; of division in communities, XII, 91–92; of all sins, IX, 530, 534; vice of all vices, I, 409; contrary to spirit of Daughters of Charity, IX, 362; they have nothing of which they might be proud, IX, 529; two kinds of pride, IX, 529–30; pride hides under appearance of good, IX, 532–33; means of combating it, IX, 532–35; not to follow opinion of others is pride, X, 296; vice of people of Cahors, X, 465; difficult for proud spirits to survive in Company, II, 326; source of disorders, VII, 160. See also **Humility**, **Vanity**.

Prières (Abbey) - Testimony of Dom Jouhaud, Abbot, regarding Abbé de Saint-Cyran, XIIIa, 105; cabal of Abbot, I, 394; XIIIa, 123, 134.

Priests - Grandeur of priesthood, XI, 6, 7, 191, 194; 278; XII, 86, 89; priest should be more perfect than religious as such, II, 5; among priests, desire for temporal goods is greater than among laymen, XII, 304; Church has no greater enemies than bad priests, V, 350; duty of priests to procure mercy and be merciful to criminals, VII, 443; they are principal cause for disorders in Church, VII, 479; XI, 279–80; XII, 76; according to early Fathers, few priests will be saved, VII, 479; treasure of Church, VII, 43; obligation of doing penance, XI, 117, 191; should be intercessors for people before God, XI, 194; Saint Vincent would not have become priest had he known what priesthood was, V, 569; VII, 480; letters to priests, IV, 316; V, 221, 543; priests will have great reason to fear God's judgments, V, 570; first priests renounced property, XI, 210; XII, 304; origin of patrimonial title; how much was required in 1655, XI, 211; Jesuits do not admit Indians to Orders, XI, 270; respect owed to priests by Daughters of Charity, X, 315; by Brothers: see also **Coadjutor Brothers**, **Clergy of France**, **Retreats**, **Seminaries** (Diocesan), **Vocation**.

Prisons - Visits to prisoners by members of Charities, XIIIb, 30, 43, 410, 439; mission to prisoners, I, 418; other mentions, I, 479; XI, 184. See also **Galley Convicts**, **Algiers**.

Processions - During missions, I, 439, 448, 453; III, 130; V, 532; XI, 95; processions for peace in Paris in 1652, IV, 395, 399; scandalous processions in Aix, II, 576; Sunday procession in parishes, IX, 202; Rogation Day procession, III, 303; VI, 317.

Procurator - Superior entrusts him with house money, V, 531; has key to strongbox, VI, 475–76; receives daily reports from Brothers; makes monthly report to Superior, IV, 80; does not have Superior's permission to authorize important work, III, 568; IV, 274, 300; reprimand of Procurator who provokes complaints by excessive frugality, III, 501; Procurator appointed by General or Visitor to handle business affairs under Superior, VII, 492.

Prodigal Son - Saint Vincent's commentary to Daughters of Charity, IX, 550–51.

Profanations - By soldiers during Fronde, III, 471; IV, 445.

Prometheus, figure in Greek mythology - Example of those unprepared to receive Holy Communion, XIIIa, 41.

Pronetti (M.), seminarian of the Mission - Biographical data, VII, 104; Saint Vincent requests his identification documents from Superior of Turin house, VII, 104; Pronetti gives cause for concern about solidity of vocation, VII, 235; departure from Company, VII, 379; other mentions, VII, 111, 231.

Pronis (M. de), Governor of Madagascar - Relieved of functions; replaced by M. de Flacourt, III, 279; returns to Madagascar, V, 281, 285; again becomes Governor, V, 300; in Madagascar, V, 507, 508, 510–11, 515, 516, 517, 525; illness and death, V, 520–21; other mention, V, 527.

Propaganda (College) - Depends on priests of *Propaganda Fide*, IV, 356; wish that seminaries of Missionaries of the Indies be connected with it, IV, 359; Alexander VII confides spiritual direction of college to Congregation of the Mission, V, 606; VIII, 610; plague has victim there; Fr. de Martinis, spiritual director, agrees to be enclosed there, VI, 133, 157; XI, 329–30; Fr. Jolly gives spiritual conferences, VI, 115; VII, 390; preaches retreats, VIII, 197; XII, 59.

Propaganda [***Propaganda Fide***], Congregation of Propagation of the Faith - Letters from Saint Vincent, III, 333; IV, 24, 92, 301, 336, 337, 478, 525; V, 15, 430, 551, 576; VI, 210; VII, 576; VIII, 146, 281; to Prefect: see also **Barberini** (Antonio); to Secretaries: see **Ingoli**, **Massari**, **Alberici**; letters from Prefect of *Propaganda*, II, 556; V, 55; minutes of session regarding approval of Congregation of the Mission, XIIIa, 229; response of Nuncio in France to request for information on this matter, XIIIa, 238; minutes of session approving request, XIIIa, 239; Nuncio asked to transmit news of approval to Saint Vincent, XIIIa, 240; report to *Propaganda* on petition of Saint Vincent, XIIIa, 247; decision of *Propaganda* on petition, XIIIa, 249; letter to Nuncio announcing decision, XIIIa, 250; letter from Nuncio to Msgr Ingoli in support of Missionaries, XIIIa, 251; letter to Nuncio confirming decision, XIIIa, 252; petition of Fr. Le Vazeux to *Propaganda* to impede multiplication of Congregations having same ministries, IV, 610; decree in response, IV, 611; letters from Prefect of *Propaganda* to Saint Vincent, II, 556; V, 55; possibility of its protection for the Mission, II, 288; Jean Le Vacher appointed Vicar-Apostolic in Tunis; *Propaganda* agrees to do same for his brother in Algiers, IV, 88; Missionaries require its approval and faculties granted by it, IV, 371; Ambassador of Portugal orders papers of Archbishop of Myra to be forwarded to it, V, 103; Saint Vincent obtains faculties for confreres in Scotland, VII, 329; problem with Irish students having to promise to return to Ireland under direction of *Propaganda*, VII, 330, 346, 420–21; other mentions, I, 538; XIIIa, 379. See also ***Algiers, Arabia, Babylon, Canada,*** **Congregation of the Mission**, ***Denmark, Egypt, Hebrides, Ireland, Madagascar, Mont-Lebanon, Salé, Scotland, Sweden, Tonkin, Tunis.***

Propaganda (Seminary) - Question of opening seminary at College of *Propaganda*, VI, 541, 630–31; Saint Vincent prefers direction to be offered to others rather than to Missionaries, VI, 541; informed that *Propaganda* would like his priests; foresees certain organizational difficulties, VI, 554; *Propaganda* decides not to entrust seminary either to Company or to French; Nuncio asks Saint Vincent to look for priests in Paris disposed to be part of this seminary, VI, 618; he thinks it will be easy to find some for Rome, but few will agree to go to foreign missions, VI, 618–19; VIII, 441–42; seminary is about to be opened, VII, 285; Fr. Jolly gives hospitality to priest who is to minister in seminary, VII, 361; *Propaganda* seems disposed to having Fr. Jolly and confreres minister in seminary, VII, 436; VIII, 441; other mention, VI, 636.

Propagation of Faith (Daughters of) - Foundation of Institute in Sedan, V, 445–47.

Propagation of Faith (Work) - Historic note, V, 73.

Property - Saint Vincent unable to accept property offered by priest, V, 221; no special attention given to those who bring property to Company, VII, 339; property should be given to Company before entering, VII, 339–40; VIII, 228.

Prosper (Saint) - Letter of Saint Prosper "translated and adapted" by Jansenists, IV, 395; teaches that everyone can be saved, XIIIa, 168.

Prost (Benoîte) - Member of Charity of Châtillon, daughter of Ennemond Prost, XIIIb, 4, 21.

Prou (Charlotte), Daughter of Charity - XIIIb, 228.

Proust (Jean), Brother of the Mission - Biographical data, V, 99; VI, 616; VII, 1; VIII, 226; former Procurator at Bishop's residence in Fontenay, VII, 637; distributes aid in Picardy and Champagne, V, 99; sent to Toul, VI, 616; recalled to Saint-Lazare, VII, 1; stationed in Le Mans, VII, 637; in Le Mans, VIII, 324; Saint Vincent allows him to sell house in order to assist parents, VIII, 226; frequently uses keys to treasury in Le Mans, VIII, 422.

Provence - Missionaries of Fr. Authier's Congregation from there, I, 221; II, 309; VIII, 136; Fr. du Coudray ready to return there, II, 466; other mentions, I, 587; V, 145; VI, 184, 260–61; VII, 537, 540, 552, 553, 566, 575, 583, 591; VIII, 266; XI, 273, 302; XIIIa, 346.

Providence - Conference on Trust in Divine Providence, X, 403–17; text of Rule of Daughters of Charity, X, 403; do not try to get ahead of it, but follow it, I, 59, 284, 557; II, 154, 237, 462, 499, 502, 514, 521; III, 192, 197, 200; IV, 39, 128; V, 165, 187, 400; VI, 12; VII, 16, 292, 560; VIII, 175, 298, 482; its actions and attributes, I, 314, 343; II, 121, 131, 183, 192, 213, 226, 250, 340, 466, 489, 627; III, 259, 603; IV, 104, 284, 519; VI, 133, 207, 647; VII, 39, 275; VIII, 66; IX, 4, 10, 11; XII, 68; calls Missionaries to new assignments, I, 342, 525; II, 232, 239, 245, 338–39, 364, 394–95, 490- 91; V, 38, 566, 610; VI, 331, 335; VII, 159, 631; provides new candidates for Daughters of Charity, I, 216; II, 127, 423; III, 36; care of Foundlings, II, 330; III, 254; IX, 104; XIIIb, 421, 425; guides both Companies, I, 407, 585; II, 18, 113, 170–171, 598; III, 10, 140, 247, 255; IV, 144, 277; V, 205, 329, 467, 468, 619, 641; VIII, 208, 278, 330; IX, 2, 47; X, 105, 447; XI, 17; XIIIb, 338; trust God's Providence for necessities of life, I, 346; II, 82, 86, 517; IV, 362; IX, 73–74, 362, 536; X, 239, 242; XII, 367; need to be submissive to it, I, 121, 126, 138, 211, 382, 401, 509, 604; II, 33, 62, 69; III, 173, 368, 371, 398, 449; IV, 360, 381, 388; VI, 362, 493, 540; VII, 31, 211, 213; VIII, 280, 299, 369; IX, 75; XI, 208; great hidden treasures in it, I, 59; orders all for the best, II, 19; III, 159–160; IV, 466; VIII, 452; God's protection of Missionaries, I, 346; II, 663, 669; VI, 10; VIII, 569, 583; of Daughters of Charity, II, 290; IX, 65, 191, 195–97. See also **Lumague**; Daughters of Charity are daughters of Providence, IX, 62; what God uses to give being to something, He also uses to preserve it, VIII, 277; ask God's Providence to provide, II, 306; Saint Louise desires strength and love to recognize guidance of Providence, III, 10; Providence must call us and we must follow it, III, 53; we belong to God and His Providence, IV, 16; it provides for needs of God's creatures, II, 48; IV, 350; conniving is sin against Providence, IV, 387; we are not children of Providence if we are not indifferent, V, 633–34; God's Providence is honored by preparing remedies against foreseen ills, VII, 326; with time, Providence takes care of our hopes and concerns, VII, 378; God's special Providence is obvious in lack of success, VII, 490; Providence has upset plans many times; do not set hopes on anything, VII, 527; God afflicts in one way, but God's goodness consoles in another, VII, 545; may give cause for concern to those He loves, VIII, 118; prolongs life of those Providence uses in extraordinary works, VIII, 178; example of

Saint Vincent, IV, 61; XI, 71; of Rechab, XII, 118–19; entrust affair to Providence, IV, 345; beware of relying more on our own efforts than on Providence, IV, 346; Providence will ordain for the best what concerns Sant'Antonio Abbey and palace near Turin confreres, VIII, 110; Superiors, as instruments of Providence, should see to needs of those in their charge, XII, 120; Providence considers purpose and indicates means to attain it, XIIIa, 39–40; other mentions, I, 245, 290, 350, 543, 565; II, 66, 118. See also **Congregation of the Mission**.

Providence (Daughters) - See **Daughters of Providence**.

Provinces - Grouping of establishments of Mission into provinces, XIIIa, 329.

Prudence - Conferences, XI, 41, 42–43; XII, 139–50; mention of another conference, XII, 421; effects of prudence; example of Jesus and Samaritan woman, XI, 41; in what prudence consists, XII, 145; supernatural prudence, XI, 42, 43; XII, 140, 145–46; human prudence, XI, 42, 43; XII, 146, 255–57; contrary to simplicity, XII, 255; some rely more on their own efforts than on Providence IV, 346; simplicity and supernatural prudence go well together, XII, 141; inseparable, XI, 42; XII, 141, 146, 148–49; alliance of supernatural prudence and simplicity apparent in Jesus, XII, 148–49; in priests of Tuesday Conferences, XII, 149; prudence of Saint Louise, X, 571–72; of Fr. Nouelly, III, 222; of Saint Francis de Sales, XIIIa, 86–87.

Human means are useless in divine matters, II, 433; III, 192–93; have recourse to human needs as if God were not supposed to help, and to divine means as if we had no human means, IV, 362; permissible to use all licit, reasonable, and appropriate means to achieve good end, IV, 479; human prudence and divine wisdom, XII, 390, 399; other mention, I, 310. See also **Hastiness**.

Prudentius (Saint), Bishop of Troyes - XIIIa, 166.

Prudhomme (M.) - III, 236.

Prussia - Swedes forced there from Poland, VI, 645.

Psalms - Seven Penitential Psalms recited during Lent, VIII, 571; should be chanted devoutly, XI, 282.

Puget (Gasparde) - Member of Charity of Châtillon, XIIIb, 11, 21, 22.

Pullen (Nicolas), Priest in Montmirail - XIIIb, 32, 34.

Punctuality [**Exactness**] - Mention of conferences, XII, 408, 415, 435; recommended by Saint Vincent, XI, 97; efforts to incite Company to this, IV, 321.

Punishments - See **Penance**.

Puppy - Motherhouse Sisters care for little dog for Queen of Poland, V, 239, 364.

Purgatory - Fire of purgatory is greater and fiercer than we can imagine, IX, 482; other mentions, I, 598; IX, 17, 39, 54, 481, 484, 486, 487. See also **Deceased**.

Purity - Breaking off attachments is important commitment to purity, X, 529; in praise of purity, XII, 401; mention of conference, XII, 418. See also **Chastity**.

Purity of Intention - Conference, IX, 284–88; mention of another conference, XII, 423; act in all things in God and for God, not from human respect, IV, 471, 480; IX, 197; best means of having purity of intention is to do always Will of God, XII, 128; makes all actions equal, XI, 172; other mention, XI, 440.

Puy (Diocese) - Bishop: see Henri de **Maupas du Tour**.

Puy (Town) - Ministry of Tuesday Conferences there, XII, 357.

Puylaroque, village in Tarn-et-Garonne - VII, 117.

Puy-l'Évêque, town in Lot - III, 525.

Pyrenees - Fr. Blatiron was familiar with these mountains, IV, 404; Notre-Dame-de-Bétharram is situated at their foot, VII, 623; Treaty of the Pyrenees, IV, 462; VII, 545, 579; VIII, 27, 300.

Q

Quarré (M.) - Died of plague in Rome, VI, 182.

Quarré (Charles), notary in Paris - II, 540.

Quartan Fever - I, 500; II, 153; III, 120, 133, 134; VII, 496; VIII, 191, 206–207, 210, 214, 237, 246, 271, 402; XIIIa, 165.

Quartier (M.), physician in Paris - I, 129.

Quarto al Mare, town near Genoa - Mission given, III, 190.

Quatre-Vaux, hamlet in commune of Rigny-Saint-Martin (Meuse) - VI, 532.

Québec, Canada - See **Vironceau de Saint-Joseph**.

Quimperlé (Abbey of Sainte-Croix de) - XIIIa, 224.

Quincy - Louis de Mesgrigny, Abbot, opposed to contract of union of Saint-Lazare Priory to Congregation of the Mission, I, 149; XIIIa, 284, 477.

Quinville (Marie), Daughter of Charity - XIIIb, 228.

Quinze-Vingts, hospital in Paris - Historic note, I, 258; II, 53–54; VIII, 366; courtyard too small to accommodate crowds at mission given by Fr. Eudes and his priests, VIII, 366, 367; Confraternity of Charity of Quinze-Vingts, I, 258; confiding spiritual direction of hospital to priests of Fr. Eudes is discussed, VIII, 424–25.

Quiqueboeuf - Bailiff of Council of State in Brittany, III, 110.

Quirinal, Apostolic Palace in Rome - XIIIa, 239, 249.

R

Rabel (Pierre), secretary of Bishop of Dax - I, 10.

Rabobe - Malagasy Ombiasse; claimed to have caused Fr. Nacquart's death, V, 525.

Racconigi [***Raconi***], town in Piedmont - Mission, VI, 196, 204; Charity established, VI, 197.

Rachel, wife of Jacob - XIIIa, 274.

Raconis (Charles-François d'Abra de), Bishop of Lavaur - Biographical data; zeal against Jansenism, II, 550–51; combats heresy of Two Heads and Arnauld's book on frequent Communion, III, 73.

Raggio (Baliano), priest, brother of M. Raggio - Benefactor of Genoa house, V, 208, 354; other mention, VI, 188.

Raggio (M.), of Genoa - Slave in Algiers, V, 354; ransomed, VI, 188.

Raggio (the Younger) - Assumes cassock at Saint-Lazare, V, 208; other mentions, V, 238, 241.

Railleard (Marie), Daughter of Charity - XIIIb, 228.

Rainssant (Fr.), Pastor in Ham - Thanks Saint Vincent for good done in parish through alms distributed by Missionary, V, 331.

Rainssant (Jeanne Le Gros), in Vesles - Indigence; Saint Vincent gets assistance for her, VI, 503, 572.

Raisin (M.) - III, 130.

Rakoczi - See **György Rákóczi II.**

Rallu (Jacques), notary in Paris - XIIIa, 422.

Ramach (Andian or Dian), one of Kings of Madagascar - His youth, III, 555; VI, 244; relapses into superstition, III, 556; promises to live as good Christian as soon as there are priests and church in his village, III, 434; IV, 93; Baptism and cure of grandson, III, 561–62; contacts with Fr. Nacquart, III, 558,

562–63, 573; who attempts in vain to lead him back to Catholic religion, III, 582; captured by Spanish Captain, VI, 244.

Ramanore, village chief in Madagascar - Asks Fr. Nacquart for healing, III, 558–59, 561.

Ramassy (Andian or Dian), one of Kings of Madagascar, father of Andian (Dian) Ramach; VI, 244.

Rambert (M.) - VII, 273, 302.

Rameville (M. de), Brigadier General in King's army - Saint Vincent asks him for protection for farm, IV, 422.

Ramini - White inhabitants of Madagascar consider him their ancestor, III, 544.

Ramouse (Andian or Dian), one of leaders in Madagascar - Contacts with Fr. Bourdaise, VI, 249.

Rancati (Hilarion, né Bartolomeo), Abbot of Santa Croce in Gerusalemme - Biographical data, V, 567; VI, 430; VII, 48; VIII, 86; consulted by Fr. Jolly, V, 567; VI, 430; VII, 543; kindness toward Congregation of the Mission; gratitude of Saint Vincent, VI, 482; VIII, 86, 134, 141, 142–43; other mention, VII, 48.

Randon (Jehan), Sieur de Compen - Witness to transactions regarding withdrawal from lease, XII, 378, 379.

Rangouze (Sieur de) - Praises Saint Vincent, XIIIa, 156.

Rantigny, village in Oise - Charity of Liancourt assists sick in Rantigny, I, 295.

Rapaccioli (Francesco Angelo), Cardinal - Has mission given in Terni, IV, 392; death, VI, 350; solemn service at Saint-Lazare for repose of his soul, VI, 350, 373.

Raportebled (Madeleine), Daughter of Charity - Biographical data, V, 357; VIII, 17; X, 447; Saint Louise asks permission for her to take perpetual vows, V, 357; missioned to Poland, V, 414; at Saint-Denis Hospital, V, 643; considered for Nantes, XIIIb, 335–36; Sent to Metz as Sister Servant; Saint Vincent gives advice to her and companions before departure, X, 447; in Metz, VIII, 17; other mention, XIIIb, 227.

Rappiot (M.), merchant in Marseilles - Bankruptcy; consequences for Jean Barreau, VI, 346, 348, 350, 353, 360, 361; VII, 91, 94–95; seizure of Rappiot's merchandise by Fr. Get, VI, 359, 370; by two letters, one to Consuls of Marseilles, other to Grand Duc of Tuscany, King requests seizure of Rappiot's merchandise, VI, 372, 384; text of these letters, VI, 649–50; Philippe Le Vacher goes to Livorno (Leghorn) to try to do something about Rappiot's effects, VI, 413; Turks send man to Marseilles to seize merchandise, VI, 418; action of Fr. Get to compensate M. Barreau for wrong M. Rappiot did him, VII, 94, 168; Saint Vincent considers sending Missionary to Algiers to settle Rappiot's debts, VII, 185; not to pay them, VII, 179; hesitates to send money to M. Barreau and to slaves for fear Rappiot's creditors might seize it, VII, 195, 197, 303, 463; Fr. Get tells Saint Vincent that M. Barreau has been released from Rappiot's debts by Turks, VII, 212; in new letter, is not so positive, VII, 221; Consuls of Marseilles deal with Rappiot, VII, 288.

Rasgibel, mountain near ruins of Utica - V, 131.

Rash Judgment - Serious fault, II, 158; IX, 215; if affair has a hundred facets, always look at best side, IX, 215; other mentions, I, 309; II, 39.

Rasine (Fr.), priest of Luçon - Saint Vincent does not think Fr. Chiroye should resign parish for Rasine's benefit, V, 469–70.

Rassary (Fr.), priest - Guest of Saintes Missionaries; collaborator in ministry of missions, VI, 316; Saint Vincent recommends that Fr. Rivet welcome him again in his house, VII, 72.

Rastignac (Comte de) - Lawsuit with Alain de Solminihac, III, 231.

Rat (Marie), Daughter of Charity - XIIIb, 228.

Ratier (Fr.), confessor of Daughters of Charity in Angers - XIIIb, 284.

Ratsihomankena, soothsayer in Madagascar - VI, 245–46.

Ravelon (Jean Coquebert de), Knight of Malta - Letters sent to Saint Vincent, VII, 523; other mention, VII, 524.

Ré (***Île de***) - Saint-Étienne-d'Ars Priory, XIIIa, 42: see also **Fournier** (Louis).

Reading - Daughters of Charity learn to read, II, 601; III, 61; X, 491; Saint Vincent recommends this, IX, 6, 36, 174; how to read in public, XI, 135–36; avoid reading through curiosity, XI, 24; Saint Vincent recommends practice of spiritual reading to Charity of Châtillon, XIIIb, 19; to Daughters of Charity, IX, 95; XIIIb, 125, 136; his preferred books: see **Francis de Sales**, **Gerson**, **Granada**, **New Testament**, **Thomas à Kempis**; reading at table customary in Missionaries' houses, I, 554; not to be omitted, XI, 93, 94; listen to it, XI, 105; what is read at Saint-Lazare, II, 229; V, 624; XII, 10, 239; policy of not reading works on disputed topics, VIII, 100.

Rebardeau (Fr.) - Consulted by Saint Vincent, I, 527.

Rebé (Claude de), Archbishop of Narbonne - Revenues from diocese; tax Archbishop must pay, II, 221; business with Duchesse de Guise, II, 558–59; witness to resignation of Bishop of Lodève, II, 617; death, VII, 499; other mentions, VI, 649; IX, 555.

Rebours (Hilarion), Carthusian, cousin of Saint Louise - Biographical data, I, 547, 548.

Réchab, biblical personage - For three centuries, descendants refused to drink wine, in imitation of him, IX, 112, 546; XI, 202; XII, 6, 118–19.

Rechau (Baron de) - Help given to Missionaries during Plessala mission, VII, 487.

Recollection - Mention of conference, XII, 437; efforts to incite Company to practice, IV, 321; other mention, I, 227. See also **Interior Life**.

Recollects [**Reformed Franciscans**] - Lay Brothers have no vote for Guardian, III, 319; all wear same habit, VI, 129; assist poor persons in environs of Paris during troubles of Fronde, IV, 520; ministry in Ferrières when Fr. Pillé was Pastor, II, 365–66; Recollects of Paris, III, 179; XIIIa, 60; request permission of Rome to resume former mission in Morocco, IV, 332; news that one of them was destined for Salé (Morocco) deters Saint Vincent from sending Missionaries there, III, 79, 82, 92–93.

Reconciliation - Conferences, IX, 179; X, 375–80; Rule of Daughters of Charity, X, 375; reasons for asking pardon, VII, 259–60; IX, 20, 87, 89, 179, 218; X, 372, 375–78; nothing wins hearts like this practice, XIIIb, 279; example of Saint Vincent, IX, 180; X, 376; XI, 236, 326; XII, 155; of Daughter of Charity, IX, 87; of Ursulines of Gisors, IX, 87; of Turks, X, 377; kneel to ask pardon, IX, 37, 87, 179; X, 376; XII, 91; ask pardon as soon as one sees displeasure has been given, IX, 179–80; before going to bed, IX, 99; XIIIb, 138; before confessing or saying Mass, X, 376; sometimes prudent to defer asking pardon, IX, 88.

What a Sister should do whose forgiveness is asked, X, 378; serious fault to withhold forgiveness, IX, 218–19; how Sister should act toward companion who refuses to forgive her, IX, 88, 180, 218; to reconcile two Sisters, do not take sides, but excuse both, IX, 85–86; exercise of reconciliation two or three times a week among Daughters of Charity, IX, 180; reconciliation of faithful with Pastor, XI, 4–5; during missions given by confreres, VII, 486–87; XI, 93, 95.

Recreation - Mention of conference, XII, 407; Saint Vincent recommends that Sisters in Nantes take daily recreation together,

III, 604; thinks lay Brothers do not need recreation, XI, 332; changes recreations into conversations, IV, 321; topics for conversation, III, 456; XIIIb, 281; converse seriously, usefully, pleasantly, IV, 528; cheerfully and respectfully, XI, 92; with modesty and reserve, X, 306, 486; example of professors of Sorbonne, XI, 201; Saint Vincent almost always goes to recreation, IV, 528; other mentions, I, 555; XIIIa, 387.

Recules (Fr. de), monk of Chancelade - Goes to Paris on business for Order, II, 451.

Red Sea - Proposed voyage of Bourdaise, V, 508, 514.

Redoys (Fr.), chaplain of Bishop of Luçon - VI, 178.

Refuge, shelter in Paris for refugee girls - I, 532; IV, 420.

Régimont (M.), Captain of *Armand* - VI, 15, 227.

Regnard (Louis), slave in Tunis, son of Nicolas Regnard - V, 393.

Regnard (Mathieu), Brother of the Mission - Biographical data, I, 456; II, 42; III, 410; IV, 381; V, 99; VII, 112–13; IX, 70; letter to Saint Vincent, II, 391; cited, IX, 70–71; donates property to Company, VII, 339; sent to Montmirail, I, 456; charity, journeys to Lorraine, I, 582; II, 42, 45, 68, 74–75, 82, 144, 173, 391; X, 17; in Champagne, V, 99; gets supplies to Foundlings during Fronde, III, 410; IV, 381; journey to Metz, VII, 112.

Regnard (Nicolas), jeweler in Paris - V, 393.

Regnault (Nicolas), Priest of the Mission - Biographical data, IV, 522; V, 207; retreat, V, 207; in Sedan, IV, 522, 577–78; V, 237, 246; recalled to Paris, V, 207, 246.

Regnier (Jacques), Priest of the Mission - Biographical data, I, 45, 228; other mention, XIIIa, 235.

Regnier (M.) - VIII, 223.

Regnier (Mme) - Member of Charity of Joigny, XIIIb, 28.

Regnoust (M.), Director of priests at General Hospital - VIII, 148.

Regularity - Conference, XI, 75; observance among seminarians, II, 265. Daughters in Nantes are careless in observance, III, 427; regularity and good order should be primary aims of house, IV, 3; lack of this would soon ruin Company, IX, 173; other mention, I, 135–36.

Regulars (Congregation) - Decree with regard to Dominicans, III, 387.

Rehoboam, son of Solomon, King of Israel - I, 314.

Reims [***Rheims***], town in Marne - Ordination retreats, II, 440; seminary, II, 506; Archbishops: see Léonor d'Estampes de

Valençay; Henri de Savoie, Duc de **Nemours**; Confraternity of Charity, V, 591; XI, 306–07; Hospital Sisters of Sainte-Marthe, V, 102; anointing and coronation of King, V, 145, 176; Jean Parre in Reims, VI, 503, 561–62, 572, 573, 580–81, 596–97; VII, 395, 402, 535, 574, 597; VIII, 382, 384, 389, 391, 398, 409; misery and charity, V, 99, 386; VIII, 203; XIIIb, 428; missions, VII, 166; Fr. Berthe pretends to be ill there, III, 115; other mentions, IV, 362; V, 26, 208, 222, 225; VI, 596, 632; VII, 402, 444, 524, 537; VIII, 29, 506; X, 5; XIIIb, 142, 308.

Relations, name give to annual Jesuit report from Canada missions - XII, 24.

Relations, name given to accounts of ministry activity of confreres in devastated areas - Historical note, V, 79; VII, 348–49; VI, 58; excerpts, IV, 138, 142, 151–52, 187, 218, 260, 301, 474; V, 79–80, 94–95, 102, 123; VII, 348. See also **Reports** (Ministry accounts).

Relatives - Priests do well who take mother into their house to care for her, X, 290; permissible to leave Community to care for parents in need, II, 611; V, 542; XII, 177–78; Saint Vincent tries to retain Missionaries tempted to return home, II, 610; V, 539, 613; advises allowing Brother, who wanted to assist aged father, to leave, if father cannot be taken into house of Company, VII, 225–26.

Detachment from relatives, XII, 23, 327; meaning of "to hate one's relatives," XII, 177; visits to relatives are dangerous, II, 121, 610; III, 521; IV, 351, 603; V, 541, 545–46, 613; VII, 52–53; example of Jesus, II, 121; IV, 351; V, 541, 545–46; VII, 53; of Saint Vincent, XII, 179–80; of Fr. Alméras, V, 347; visits have led to loss of several vocations, XII, 179; Saint Vincent does not consider sister's religious profession valid reason for going home, IV, 351; nor First Mass of relative, V, 186; nor desire to see if father is in need, IV, 591, 603; nor fear of losing inheritance, V, 499, 545; Missionary may assist relatives with revenue from inheritance, VII, 311; with money from sale of landed estate, VIII, 226; not with Mass stipends or what reverts by law to Congregation, IV, 322; decides that postulant enter Daughters of Charity without saying good-bye to parents, XIIIb, 249.

Relaxation - Saint Vincent encourages Saint Louise to get as much rest as possible, I, 145; good to have some relaxation, X, 306.

Relics - Of true Cross, I, 518, 520; conference on respect for relics of saints, XI, 40.

Religious - Reflections on Community life, XIIIa, 161; letters from religious to Saint Vincent, II, 482, 497; religious are in state of holiness to be acquired, XII, 300; religious state more perfect than secular state, XIIIa, 191; Rome does not favor formation of new religious bodies, III, 372; IV, 555; French episcopate likewise, III, 247; aversion at Saint-Lazare for religious state, II, 37; good number of religious leave monasteries to go to preach Gospel to unbelievers, IV, 364; others would leave, if they could, III, 205; composure of monks and nuns on death of relatives, I, 328–29; formerly, young women called to service of God were wealthy and of gentle birth, IX, 74; all houses of nuns in Paris are in debt, XIIIb, 325; need to choose good Superioress, XIIIa, 162; abominations committed in monastery of nuns, II, 280; non-observance of Rules leads to irregularity in monasteries. See also **Rules**.

Saint Vincent is Superior of several Communities, X, 507; promotes monastic reform, IV, 286, 330; V, 382; endeavors to have rule of enclosure respected: see also **Visitation**; services rendered to monks, V, 142, 386–87, 415; discourages monks from thought of leaving their Order to be more perfectly united to Jesus or to transfer to another Order, IV, 130; V, 313; or to be Bishops, IV, 20; recommends choice of Abbot, V, 95–97; tries to have election of another annulled, III, 618; sends monk to monastery of nuns to communicate Queen's orders to Prioress, II, 508; makes appointment for nun in Paris, II, 414; asks Abbess to receive nun into her monastery, IV, 129; visits houses of nuns, I, 501; IX, 46; X, 455; XI, 44: see also ***Longchamp***; advises Vicar-General to be indulgent toward monks Bishop wished to censure, II, 5–6; recommendations to Pastor in Sedan on conduct with Capuchins in parish, IV, 362; V, 155–56, 552; endeavors to avoid friction with members of another Community, II, 534: see also ***Salé***; glad that Communities are growing; recommends that confreres not oppose them, IV, 148; VI, 135; VII, 484.

Contacts of Missionaries and Daughters of Charity with monks and nuns, VII, 171–72: see also **Daughters of Charity**, **Congregation of the Mission**, **Missions**, **Retreats**, **Augustinians**, **Capuchins**, etc.

Religious Communities - Advantages of Community life, IX, 2; dispositions of those wishing to live in Community, XIIIa, 161; laxity often comes from leniency of Superiors, II, 403; holiest Communities are well tested, IV, 442; VII, 290; God humbles them to raise them up again, III, 385; many Communities in Paris ruined by having magnificent buildings constructed, VIII, 49; goods of houses often squandered in this, XI, 25; Saint Vincent applies to Communities parable of wise and foolish virgins, X, 491–92; XI, 388–89; interests of God surpass those of Communities, XIIIb, 272; Church forbids institution of new Orders, unless they profess one of four approved Rules, III, 248; Saint Vincent does not think God wants several Communities with similar ministries in same kingdom, V, 42: see also **Congregation of the Mission**.

Remedies - Saint Vincent sees no problem with Missionaries giving remedies to help poor sick people: see also **Eu** (Louis d'); saint takes remedies for erysipelas, V, 474; milk diet, VII, 515, 530, 584; VIII, 85; change of air, II, 95; VI, 628; VII, 294; XI, 61; XII, 27–28; seasons for spa, II, 95, 519; III, 368, 458; IV, 267; VIII, 129: see ***Bourbon-l'Archambault, Forges-les-Eaux***; see also **Scrofula**, **Gravel**, **Dropsy** (edema); Saint Louise sends or recommends remedies, I, 61, 202, 588; II, 576; III, 369, 370; IV, 170; V, 470–71; VI, 155, 512; VII, 426, 427, 432–33, 453; VIII, 245.

Remi (Saint), Bishop of Reims - Feast day, XIIIa, 266–67.

Remus, founder of Rome - Foundling, XIIIb, 398, 406.

Renar (François), priest - Biographical data, I, 165; II, 41; on mission, I, 165, 177–78, 228–29, 403, 515, 526, 528; seriously ill, II, 41; other mentions, I, 309, 560.

Renard (Jean), from Mâcon - XIIIb, 74.

Renault (Marie-Euphrosine), Visitandine - VIII, 427.

René, Brother of the Mission, in Sancey, Troyes diocese - I, 466, 522, 531.

Renée, Daughter of Charity - VIII, 97.

Renée, Daughter of Charity - Saint Louise displeased with her, III, 470; leaves Company, III, 472.

Renée, Daughter of Charity at Motherhouse - Saint Louise asks permission for her to make retreat, III, 117, 118.

Renée, Daughter of Charity in Nantes, at Saint-Barthélemy - See **Delacroix** (Renée).

Renée, Daughter of Charity from Angers - Saint Louise asks permission for her to renew vows, VII, 87.

Renée, Daughter of Charity, native of Saché, II, 215.

Renegades - Saint Vincent was purchased by renegade in Barbary, I, 7–9; woman rescued from renegade, II, 638; Spanish renegade, victim of plague in Algiers, III, 306; conversions, V, 401–02.

Renel (Jacques de), Priest of the Mission - Biographical data, I, 178.

Renewal - Mention of conference, XII, 437.

Renfermés - See ***General Hospital of Paris***.

Rennes, town in Ille-et-Vilaine - II, 666, 668; V, 360; VI, 74, 365, 597; XIIIb, 319; Parlement of Rennes, III, 53, 83, 110; postulants, VI, 75; coach line, XII, 377, 379; Bishops: see Henri de la **Motte-Haudancourt**, Charles-François de **Lavieuville**.

Renou (M.), Registrar of Presidial See of Angers - Signs Act of Establishment of Daughters of Charity in Angers Hospital, XIIIb, 119.

Renouard (M.) - I, 160.

Renouard (M.), slave in Algiers, son of Nicolas Renouard - VI, 237, 469.

Renouard (Nicolas), slave in Algiers - VII, 134, 196, 237, 469.

Renty (Élisabeth de Balzac, Baroness), wife of Gaston de Renty - Letter from Saint Vincent, V, 178; from Baroness to saint, VIII, 500.

Renty (Gaston de) - Biographical data, II, 258–59; member of association for assistance to Lorraine nobility, II, 54; other mentions, II, 97; V, 53.

Renunciation - See **Attachments**, **Detachment**, **Indifference**, **Mortification**.

Repetition of Prayer - Historical data, XI, *xiii*; mention of conference, XII, 405; usefulness, IX, 4; good means to enkindle devotion, XII, 234; XIIIb, 301; was not customary before Saint Vincent, XII, 8, 234; introduced in other Communities, XII, 8; in seminaries, XII, 235; Repetition as practiced at Saint-Lazare, XI, *xx-xxii*; two or three times a week, IX, 331; should be made very simply, IX, 4; without searching for good thoughts or beautiful words, XI, 78; Saint Vincent is edified by Brothers' Repetition, IX, 175, 331; X, 60, 225–26; XIIIb, 301; admonitions given during Repetition: see also **Admonitions**; some disapproved of his correcting priests in presence of Brothers, XIIIa, 392–93; confreres should hold Repetition for ordinands, II, 318; not held often on board ship to Madagascar, VIII, 572; other mention, II, 245.

Reports (ministry accounts) - Custom of giving Missionaries edifying accounts of missions, IV, 587; XI, 112; Saint Vincent sends houses reports from Madagascar Missionaries, IV, 89, 109, 517; VI, 460, 463, 478, 604; VII, 29, 37, 84; account of Niolo mission, IV, 438, 477; report from Jean Le Vacher, V, 624; Saint Vincent resists pressure to have reports published, VI, 35, 199, 604; and usually anything that might inspire outsiders with esteem of Missionaries, VI, 199; would rather this be made known by good works than by printed word, II, 310–

11; ***Relations***: periodic reports about devastated countryside, IV, 474: see also ***Champagne***; other mention, VII, 512.

Reports (Information) - Mention of conference on not giving information to individuals, XII, 416; Saint Vincent not influenced by tales, IV, 300. See also **Admonitions**.

Reproaches - Listen humbly to them, III, 339.

Reputation - Too good a reputation is very harmful, I, 567; V, 485; good reputation of those who have been in seminaries, II, 271; Daughter of Charity who speaks ill of her sister, kills her, IX, 228–29.

Reserved Cases - Not all Bishops have given Missionaries faculties to absolve from reserved cases; some have granted this with restrictions, V, 88; Saint Vincent asks Rome for faculty for Missionaries to absolve from cases reserved to Pope, V, 548; explanation of Brief that grants it to him, V, 571, 603; sends authenticated copies of it to houses, V, 573, 638; some Bishops refuse to recognize these faculties, VI, 64; others add restrictions to them, V, 626; other mention, VI, 581.

Resignation - See **Sufferings**.

Resolutions - See **Prayer**.

Respect - Conferences, IX, 115–28, 206–21; X, 390–96; mention of other conferences, XII, 409, 428; respect Superiors, IX, 100, 116, 124; XI, 92; Pastors and Vicars, XI, 95; peers, IX, 100, 116, 122, 124; XI, 92; doctors' orders, IX, 176; reasons for mutual respect, IX, 206–07; God is in neighbor, IX, 117; Sisters are spouses of Christ, IX, 118, 208; X, 393; all have been redeemed by Christ's Blood, X, 394; serve same Master, IX, 100; have Guardian Angel, X, 394.

Example of God, IX, 116; of Three Persons of Blessed Trinity, IX, 118, 119, 122, 128; of angels, IX, 115; of Saint Francis de Sales, IX, 127–28; teaching of Jesus, IX, 207, 211; of Saint Paul, IX, 124; X, 394; of Saint John the Apostle, IX, 123.

In what mutual respect consists, IX, 207–08; X, 393; cordiality and respect go together, IX, 115; X, 394–96; cordial respect preserves union, IX, 119, 120, 125–26, 212–13; means to have mutual respect, IX, 209–10, 213–21; faults against respect, IX, 209; mutual respect causes us to have good opinion of one another, IX, 122, 213–15; to take everything in good part, IX, 123; to be gracious in condescending, IX, 216; with smiling countenance, IX, 127, 215; yield to others, IX, 217; greet one other, IX, 121, 124, 216–17; simply, IX, 126; as at Saint-Lazare, IX, 121, 126–27; avoid being ceremonious in external expressions of respect, IX, 217; not all Daughters of Charity show cordial respect, IX, 116.

Responsibilities - Conference on responsibilities and positions of authority, XI, 124–28.

Rest - Custom in Congregation of the Mission, I, 458, 555; II, 27, 30; III, 58; Saint Vincent accedes to Cardinal Richelieu's desire that Missionaries take day of rest weekly during mission, I, 458.

Restal (M. de) - III, 204, 371.

Restitution - Duty of confessors toward those who must make restitution, IV, 531; XIIIa, 370, 386; case of restitution, IV, 531; VI, 606–07.

Retaux - Young woman from Retaux, I, 311.

Rethel, town in Ardennes - Disastrous situation of town; Town Magistrates ask Saint Vincent's help, IV, 199, 204, 230, 323; V, 12; of Ladies of Charity, XIIIb, 448, 449; Ladies are too overwhelmed by demands to add to usual charity, IV, 201; no new funds for Rethel allocated by Ladies, VII, 13; three hundred livres for Rethel allocated by Ladies, VII, 33; Ladies will try to send Jean Parre vestments and money for wheat; praise for him, VII, 380; Lieutenant-General thanks Saint Vincent for help, IV, 236–37; Confraternity of Charity, VII, 573; Ladies assist poor of Rethel and environs, XIIIb, 428; as do Brothers of the Mission, IV, 236–37, 410; Bro. Parre distributes alms of Ladies, VI, 414, 490, 503, 573, 580, 608, 626, 632; VII, 544; VIII, 391; Saint Vincent tells him he can return there, VIII, 149; slave in Algiers from area, V, 36; Ladies of Charity hold solemn memorial service for Saint Vincent, XIIIa, 209; other mentions, VII, 166; VIII, 27, 389.

Retreats - *Retreat ministry*: XI, 12–14, 14–15, 15, 16, 142–48; mention of conferences to retreatants, XII, 412, 424, 426, 434, 437; nature of spiritual retreat, XIIIa, 161; usefulness, XI, 85, 142; good results, II, 288; XI, 16, 214–15; number of retreatants at Bons-Enfants, I, 516; at Saint-Lazare, II, 28; VIII, 462; XI, 12; Fr. Codoing changes way of dealing with them, II, 349; ordinands accommodated at Bons-Enfants and Saint-Lazare, VIII, 605; do not encourage them to join Congregation, XI, 146–47, 377–78; trust in Providence regarding retreat expenses, XII, 385; one of ministries of Company, XI, 12–16, 214–16; established by God Himself, XI, 142; thank God for this grace, XI, 14; strive not to be unworthy of it or to disregard it, XI, 12–14, 215–16; how this ministry began; Fr. Coqueret's idea, XI, 142–43; reasons for this ministry, XI, 142–43; means for accomplishing it, XI, 143–46; means for guiding retreatants, XI, 148; accept retreatants whenever they present themselves, XI, 97; even priests sent to receive correction; inconveniences may be represented if they arise, III, 382; watch out for those who, under guise of retreat, are looking for security, free room and board, VII, 391; conduct of those in charge of retreatants, XI, 145–48; take nothing from retreatants, if house is not inconvenienced, V, 490; indulgence for those who make retreat in houses of Company, VII, 296; Saint Vincent recommends retreatants to prayers of Community, XI, 15, 85, 214; retreats of Ladies at Motherhouse of Daughters of Charity: see **Daughters of Charity**.

Retreats for Missionaries: mention of conferences, XII, 414, 417, 420, 421, 424, 429, 433; XIIIa, 200; make annual retreat, I, 555; two men at a time, if more cannot do so each time, VI, 530; without interruption, VII, 296; in one's house, even Superiors, VI, 123; never in religious houses, IV, 103; do not go out during retreat, III, 71; effective remedy for moving forward, VII, 431; monthly retreat has drawbacks; Saint Vincent wonders whether it should be continued at Saint-Lazare, III, 376; congratulates Superior who has established it in his house, VIII, 81; dissuades Superior from making short retreat every Friday, V, 469; advises retreat for Missionary tempted against vocation, IV, 359; retreat recommendations, XI, 92–93, 94–95; other mentions, I, 118, 331; VI, 111, 122.

Retreats for Daughters of Charity: text of Rule, X, 508, 523; Saint Vincent recommends fidelity to annual retreat as far as service allows, IV, 239; VI, 514; IX, 11, 176; Sisters far from Paris make it where they are; others come to Motherhouse, VII, 366; X, 523.

Saint Vincent's retreats: Besides annual retreat, he sometimes made another at Pentecost, I, 158; IV, 214; and even a third, II, 396; retreats in ***Soissons*** and ***Valprofonde***: see these words. See also **Vincent de Paul**.

Other retreats: Retreats for **Ordinands**, for Saint **Louise**, for **Visitation Nuns**: see these words.

Retz - See **Gondi** (Jean-François-Paul).

Reuben, biblical personage - Fr. Bourdaise wishes he could imitate him and conceal bad news from Saint Vincent, V, 507.

Revenue - Of Saint Louise, I, 559; of certain dioceses, II, 221.

Rey (Hugues), priest in Châtillon - XIIIa, 48; XIIIb, 21.

Rey (Marie), nurse for poor of Châtillon - XIIIb, 10, 22.

Rhébé (M. de), Provost of Saint-Pierre in Mâcon - XIIIb, 69, 71.

Rheims - See ***Reims***.

Rhodes (Alexandre), Jesuit - Return from Far East, IV, 595.

Rhodes (Catherine Pot de), Prioress of Saint-Pardoux Monastery - Wants niece Gasparde as Assistant, II, 489, 508.

Rhodes (Gasparde Pot de), niece of preceding - Named Assistant of Saint-Pardoux Monastery, II, 508–09.

Rhodes (M. de) - II, 509.

Ribadeneyra (Pedro de), Jesuit - His *Lives of Saints*, V, 297.

Ribemont, town in Aisne - Misery and charity, IV, 94.

Ribier (Fr.), Prior of Bruyères-le-Châtel - Suggests uniting Priory to Congregation of the Mission, III, 234.

Ribier (Abbé) - Favor requested by him of Rome, VII, 509, 512; Saint Vincent receives Brief for him; sends it to him, VII, 594, 599.

Ribot (Pierre) - Slave in Algiers, V, 328, 407; VI, 8, 189; ransomed, VI, 327; arrival in Paris; "plague disappeared from Algiers when he left," VI, 343.

Ricanetti, town in Italy - Missions in diocese, V, 274.

Ricard (M.) - Participates in preaching exercises at Saint-Lazare, XI, 265.

Ricard (Raoul), attorney at presidial court of Beauvais - His praise, I, 93.

Richard, convict on *Fiesque* - Money for him, VIII, 331.

Richard (François), Priest of the Mission - Biographical data, III, 26; IV, 120–21; V, 493; VI, 25; VII, 148; mention of letters Saint Vincent wrote to him in Turin, VI, 484; in Rome; missioned to Genoa house, III, 26, 39, 41, 48, 58; left for new post, III, 65, 66; in Genoa, III, 122, 137, 151, 187; IV, 120; requested by Superior in Turin for mission, V, 493; refused so as not to displease Cardinal of Genoa, V, 534; tempted to return to France, V, 623; placed in Turin, V, 623, 637; VI, 25; in Turin, VI, 56, 72; tempted to return to family, VI, 282, 434, 484; goes home, VI, 495, 496, 510; Saint Vincent does not know what became of him, VII, 148.

Richard (Mme) - I, 156.

Richelieu (Alphonse-Louis du Plessis de), Archbishop of Lyons, brother of Cardinal - Sent to Rome to obtain annulment of marriage of Gaston d'Orléans to Marguerite de Lorraine, I, 265; misunderstanding sets him against Saint Vincent and Missionaries, IV, 295; VI, 518.

Richelieu (Anne Poussard, Duchesse de), wife of Duc de Richelieu - Asks Richelieu Missionaries to help Sisters of Notre-Dame in spiritual distress, V, 601–02; other mention, VIII, 306.

Richelieu (Armand du Plessis, Cardinal de) - Biographical data, I, 346–47; II, 44; VI, 510; XI, 114; silence in his residence,

XI, 201; dealings with Saint Vincent, I, 453, 458; II, 144, 145, 154, 160, 172; XI, 114; XIIIa, 107, 318; promises to support, in Rome, after death of reigning Pope, Saint Vincent's request concerning Congregation of the Mission, II, 44, 154–55; establishes fund to educate twelve seminarians at Collège des Bons-Enfants, II, 257, 585; VII, 605; benefactor of Richelieu Charity, I, 448, 453, 458, 500; founder and benefactor of Missionaries in Richelieu, I, 402, 438; II, 13, 150, 275, 294; IV, 8; VIII, 607; and in Luçon, VIII, 607; benefactor of Rome Missionaries, II, 170, 457; VII, 610; and of Luçon, I, 514; II, 275, 353; XIIIa, 319; gives Saint-Nicolas-de-Champvent Priory to Congregation, VI, 510; gives proceeds from sale of record offices of Loudun, but dies before signing act of donation, II, 358; legacy of 60,000 livres to same house, II, 406, 426; large debts of estate and claims of heirs greatly diminish amount, II, 462.

Reform of religious Communities, I, 351; Cardinal Richelieu and Abbé de Saint-Cyran, XIIIa, 104, 106, 124; Priory of Langres diocese dependent on one of Richelieu's abbeys, II, 143–44, 171, 280; his confessor, I, 346; his niece: see **Aiguillon** (Duchesse d'); illness and death, II, 305, 358, 362; Marseilles house to offer daily Mass for repose of his soul, VIII, 610; XIIIa, 336; other mentions, I, 510, 583; II, 65, 100, 220, 255, 306, 430; VI, 324; VIII, 405.

Richelieu (Armand-Jean du Plessis, Duc de), brother of Emmanuel, Comte de Richelieu - Biographical data, III, 267; VI, 207; VII, 3; VIII, 243; Saint Vincent advises Superior of Richelieu Missionaries not to meddle in his affairs, III, 515; naval victory, III, 267; acts of administration as General of Galleys of France, VI, 207, 259, 261, 592, 617, 627; VII, 49, 54, 70, 80, 93–94, 101, 109, 168, 438; VIII, 243, 249; XIIIa, 337; coolness with Duchesse d'Aiguillon, VI, 479; his intendant: see also **Desmarets**; at spa of Bourbon-l'Archambault, VII, 289; other mentions, VII, 3, 121.

Richelieu (Emmanuel-Joseph Vignerod, Comte de), grand-nephew of Cardinal - Biographical data, VI, 372; Abbot of Saint-Ouen of Rouen and Marmoutiers, Prior of Saint-Martin-des-Champs in Paris, IV, 197.

Richelieu (town) - Situated in region of many heretics, I, 404; piety of inhabitants; hardy people, living in peace, I, 516; Saint Vincent's visit, XII, 396; King's journey to Richelieu, IV, 44; VIII, 343, 385–86, 414; saint sends Fr. Alméras there for the occasion, VIII, 385, 413–14, 421, 423; church, I, 452, 539; II, 172; collège, I, 418–19; VIII, 330; Daughters of Notre-Dame, III, 456; IV, 287; V, 602; VII, 466; plague epidemic, I, 591, 596; II, 3; Duchy of Richelieu, I, 419, 439; Daughter of Charity from Richelieu, II, 165; V, 466; VI, 136; X, 522; postulants, II, 107, 112, 127; III, 431–32, 433, 444, 606; VII, 224.

Richelieu Missionaries: letters from Saint Vincent, I, 589; II, 78; III, 142, 146, 212, 278, 284, 458; IV, 11, 389; VIII, 102: see also **Beaumont** (Pierre de), **Codoing**, **Gautier** (Denis), **Lambert aux Couteaux**; from Missionaries to Saint Vincent, II, 294; III, 286, 304; mention of letter from saint, III, 102.

Foundation contract, I, 403–04, 418; II, 79; approval of contract by Bishop of Poitiers, I, 438; benefactors: see **Aiguillon** (Duchesse d'), **Richelieu** (Armand Duplessis, Cardinal de); Frs. Lambert aux Couteaux and Perdu in Richelieu, I, 402, 404, 417, 437; Saint Vincent also sends Frs. Codoing, I, 402; Durot, I, 405; Buissot, Benoît, Bécu, and Gourrant, I, 419; construction of buildings for Congregation of the Mission, I, 418, 438; Fr. Lambert furnishes house, I, 420, 438, 452; disposition of Superior while awaiting union of Richelieu parish to Mission, I, 439–40; revenues of house, I, 418, 438, 452; temporal affairs, I, 420; III, 144, 515, 606; IV, 8, 11, 39–40, 321; VIII, 306, 347; union of Saint-Nicolas de ***Champvent*** Priory, of priory of M. des **Roches-Chamian**; fief of ***Bois-Bouchard***; mill and small farm of ***Tuet***; ***Saint-Cassien*** seigneury: see these words.

Richelieu parish, I, 418; II, 282; III, 573; IV, 313; V, 196; parochial practices, I, 439; III, 515; Saint Vincent advises Pastor to be more careful to see that parishioners settle quarrels amicably, VI, 468–69.

Mission to prisoners in Richelieu, I, 418; mission in Richelieu, I, 439, 447–48, 452, 458; in Verteuil, VIII, 305; other missions, III, 145, 304; conversion of heretics, III, 304; Archbishop of Tours complains that Richelieu Missionary preached in favor of so-called possessed persons, II, 80–81, 95; diocesan seminary, III, 144; IV, 39; Internal Seminary, IV, 477, 520; V, 75, 376, 443, 574; VI, 262, 468; VII, 27, 204, 518; VIII, 257, 306, 341; retreats, IV, 173; VI, 637; VII, 509; retreats for ordinands, II, 208, 294; IV, 166; VIII, 307, 329; chaplaincy of Champigny: see also ***Champigny-sur-Veude***.

Richelieu Missionary, commissioned by Bishop of Poitiers, visits part of archdeaconry, IV, 69; contacts of Missionaries with Sisters of Notre-Dame, III, 456; Saint Vincent permits Missionaries to assist them in times of extraordinary need, but not as a rule, IV, 287–88; V, 602–03; VII, 466; Daughters of Charity in Richelieu dissatisfied with direction of Fr. de Beaumont, VI, 51; who is too abrupt with them, VII, 178; contacts between Missionaries and Sisters, II, 128; VI, 51; VII, 466.

Journeys of Saint Vincent to Richelieu for canonical visitation, I, 515, 519, 591, 594, 597; II, 69, 170, 208, 297, 304, 528, 530; III, 428, 430–33, 444, 456, 461; canonical visitation by Fr. Portail, II, 664, 665, 668, 674; III, 10, 30; by Fr. Berthe, V, 474; VI, 382; VII, 512; by Fr. Dehorgny, VIII, 51, 129, 131, 150, 158, 165, 170; Saint Vincent suggests that Fr. Alméras go there from La Rose, if he is not well, III, 93–94; Community retreats, II, 604; IV, 85; how Divine Office is recited there, V, 195; VIII, 570; XII, 268, 270, 271.

Two Richelieu Missionaries volunteer for foreign missions, III, 278, 286–87; Internal Seminary of Saint-Lazare transferred to Richelieu during Fronde, III, 408, 413, 462; XI, 174; difficulties of Fr. Codoing: see **Codoing**; instructions Saint Vincent gives on occasion of King's passing through Richelieu, IV, 44–46; of Mlle d'Orléans' passing through Champigny, V, 443; renewal of vows, V, 502; Bishop of Poitiers set against Missionaries, VII, 511.

Personnel on February 21, 1638, I, 442; insufficiency of personnel, IV, 167; VIII, 165; assignments and changes, I, 500; III, 12; VI, 476, 587; VII, 323; VIII, 169, 306–07; disedifying Missionary, IV, 167; list of Superiors and history of house, VIII, 607: see also **Admirault** (Claude), **Beaumont**, **Bécu** (Benoît), **Bélart**, **Blatiron**, **Boussordec**, **Buissot**, **Chiroye**, **Codoing**, **Colée**, **Constantin**, **Crowley** [**Cruoly**], **Cuissot** (Gilbert), **Dehorgny**, **Delaunay**, **Du Chesne**, (Pierre), **Du Coudray**, **Durot**, **Escart**, **Ferot**, **Feydin**, **Gautier** (Denis), **Gazet**, **Geneset**, **Gobert**, **Gourrant**, **Grainville**, **Jamin**, **Jegat**, **Labeille**, **Lambert Aux Couteaux**, **Lebas**, **Le Gros**, **Lejeune** (Jean), **Le Mercier**, **Lestang** (Jean de), **Lièbe**, **Lorfebvre**, **Lucas** (Jacques), **Maillard**, **Manceau** (Simon), **Manceau** (Nicolas), **Nacquart**, **Nodo**, **Pennier**, **Perraud**, **Rivet** (François), **Rivet** (Jacques), **Rivet** (Louis), **Robin** (Jacques), **Servin**, **Tholard**, **Tumy**.

Missionaries passing through Richelieu: see **Alméras** (René the Younger), **Barry** (Edmund), **Corman**, **Gondrée**; Adrien Le Bon given hospitality, II, 605; other mentions, I, 453; II, 82, 93, 417; III, 147, 415, 490; VI, 584; VII, 241; VIII, 134, 439, 440; XI, 111; XIIIa, 329.

Fr. Lambert, Superior, asks for Daughters of Charity for sick, I, 402; Saint Vincent keeps Charity of Richelieu in mind, I, 411, 439, 448, 464, 469, 516; speaks of it to Cardinal Richelieu, I, 453; who requests its establishment and promises annual support until collections can procure what is necessary, I, 458; large number of sick hastens departure of Sisters, I, 493; Barbe Angiboust and Louise Ganset are sent there, I, 499–505; Saint Vincent praises them, I, 516; disagreement develops between them, I, 592; ministries interrupted by plague, I, 596; II, 3; joy of Sister at soon seeing Saint Louise, who has to go to Angers, I, 592, 596; at invitation of Saint Vincent, they prepare to meet Saint Louise, II, 3, 10, 24, 26; Saint regrets that there won't be more of them soon in Richelieu, II, 130; serving in hospital there, II, 601; attire of Daughters there, II, 675; financial difficulties, IV, 167; the two Sisters don't get along, VI, 50–52; Sister Cécile Angiboust sent to rest in Richelieu, VI, 455, 456; illness of two Sisters; service of sick suffers from this, VIII, 164, 170–71; other mention, I, 594.

Daughters of Charity in Richelieu, II, 2–3; see also **Angiboust** (Barbe), **Bouhery** (Perrine de), **Carcireux** (Françoise), **Dupuis** (Étiennette), **Ganset**, **Georgette** [**Georget**], **Jeanne** from Loudun, **Martin** (Élisabeth), **Royer** (Charlotte), **Thilouse** (Marie) from Tours, **Turgis** (Élisabeth); letters from Saint Vincent, VI, 50; VIII, 312; assignments and changes, III, 415; VIII, 341.

Other mentions, I, 81, 164, 190, 208, 439, 655; II, 51; III, 61, 427; X, 524; XIIIb, 140.

Richer (Philippe), notary in Paris - XIIIa, 42, 43, 333, 334, 477.

Richevillain (Antoinette), Daughter of Charity - XIIIb, 228; signs attestation after reading of Common and Particular Rules arranged in order by Fr. Alméras, XIIIb, 206.

Ricouard (Gué de Bagnols, dame) - Gift for mission of Persia, II, 457.

Rideau (Louise-Christine), Daughter of Charity - Biographical data, X, 595; elected Treasurer, VIII, 312; X, 595, 596; native of Saché, II, 215, 216; other mention, XIIIb, 227.

Rien (M. de) - Illness at Saint-Lazare, I, 516.

Riga, town in Latvia - Siege of Riga, VII, 83.

Rigault (Mlle) - Saint Vincent tells Jeanne-Françoise to entrust orphanage in Étampes to her, V, 18, 21.

Rigaut (Jean), prisoner in Toulon - VI, 305, 342.

Righini (Cesare), Bishop of Sarsina - V, 157.

Rigny-Saint-Martin, village in La Meuse - VI, 532.

Rimbaud (M.), merchant in Marseilles - Sending of letters of exchange, VII, 232, 249–50, 253.

Ringworm - Common ailment in Lorraine, II, 74; Sisters find it also in Poland, IV, 575.

Riollant (M.), physician in Paris - IV, 258.

Riou (Fr.), Priest of the Mission - III, 82.

Riquet (Madeleine), Daughter of Charity - XIIIb, 228.

Rising - Mention of conferences to Missionaries about four o'clock rising, III, 530; XII, 431; Saint Vincent sends circular requesting fidelity to this Rule, III, 530; reiterates recommendation in several conferences, IX, 94, 364; X, 454–55–56, 477, 479–82; reasons for four o'clock rising, III, 531–33; grace of prayer depends on fidelity to rising, III, 532; example of Saint Vincent, IX, 24; for whom four o'clock rising was difficult, XII, 82; example of Cardinal de La Rochefoucauld and of Chief Justice, IX, 168; habit facilitates exactitude in rising, IX, 24; those who rise on time are better disposed than others, IX, 303; other mention, I, 554.

Reasons exempting one from rising with community, III, 534; IX, 24, 303; examination of objections of health, fatigue, custom, etc., III, 533–35; means of being faithful to this practice, III, 535–36; IX, 298; the bell: an annoying agitator, XI, 221; practice at Saint-Lazare for preventing relaxation on this point of Rule, X, 477–78; laxity among Missionaries, III, 530; six o'clock rising once a week, III, 534; in early years Sisters rose at five o'clock, IX, 3, 24, 25, 30, 35; rising is fixed at four o'clock in 1641, IX, 42; instructions on rising, X, 479–82.

Rivalry - Often found in Communities, chiefly in small ones, V, 582–83.

Rivanaigre (Pierre), seminarian of the Mission - Biographical data, II, 642.

Rivarennes (Gabriel de Beauvau de), Bishop of Nantes - Suspicious of Daughters of Charity in Nantes, III, 426; other mentions, III, 604; IV, 77; V, 32, 43; IX, 520; XIIIb, 320.

Rivet (François), Priest of the Mission,- Biographical data, III, 453; V, 137; VII, 32; VIII, 51; in Saintes, III, 453; V, 137; VI, 537; in Saint-Méen; requests sub-diaconate, V, 361; in Luçon; assigned to Richelieu, VI, 537–38; arrival in Richelieu, VI, 611; in Le Mans; recalled to Paris, VII, 204; at Saint-Charles Seminary, VIII, 51; other mention, VII, 32.

Rivet (Jacques), Brother of the Mission, brother of François and Louis - Biographical data, II, 538; III, 450; V, 80; VI, 376; VII, 31; XI, 380; letters Saint Vincent writes him in Condom, III, 450, 452, 475; in La Rose, III, 503; in Tréguier, V, 80; in Genoa, VII, 31; mention of letters to Saint Vincent, III, 503; VII, 31; Bishop of Condom would like to keep him as major-domo, III, 450; Saint Vincent urges him to leave Condom for La Rose, III, 451, 452, 475, 477; or Agen, III, 475, 477; or Richelieu, III, 477; in La Rose, III, 503; in Tréguier; recalled to Paris, V, 80; sent to Genoa, V, 137; ill, VI, 376, 396; escapes ravages of plague, VI, 506; XI, 380; other mention, IV, 386.

Rivet (Louis), Priest of the Mission, brother of François and Jacques - Biographical data, III, 142; IV, 386; V, 68; VI, 96; VII, 32; VIII, 30–31; letters Saint Vincent writes him in Richelieu, III, 142; in Saintes, III, 381, 509, 599; V, 68, 416, 422, 425, 494, 538, 565, 585, 587, 612, 625; VI, 96, 268, 315, 355, 398, 443, 491, 505, 563; VII, 72, 99, 105, 137, 181, 214, 236, 240, 258, 322, 450, 574; VIII, 30, 50, 128, 150, 324, 343; mention of letters to Saint Vincent, V, 625; VI, 444, 563; VII, 137, 322, 574; VIII, 30, 50, 128, 150; death of father, IV, 386; acting Superior in Richelieu during Superior's absence, III, 143; in Saintes, III, 343, 452; IV, 473; V, 137; named Superior, V, 585–86; Superior in Saintes, VII, 357; VIII, 241, 612; Saint Vincent admonishes him for lack of charity toward Brother and Madagascar native, VII, 258–59; health, VII, 425, 450; VIII, 31, 129, 150; other mentions, I, *xxvi*; VII, 32. See also ***Saintes***.

Rivet (M.) - Death, IV, 386.

Rivet (Sister), Daughter of Charity, widowed mother of François, Jacques, and Louis Rivet - At Nom-de-Jésus Hospice, VII, 31–32; other mentions, V, 81, 137; VI, 445.

Rivière (Abbé de la) - His chapels in Le Mans, III, 381; see also **Barbier** (Louis).

Roandries, leaders in Madagascar - III, 548, 552, 554–56, 562; V, 311, 510, 511, 516, 528; VI, 221.

Roanne, town in Loire - I, 404; VI, 262.

Robert, Brother of the Mission - Desire to be monk, III, 390.

Robert, (Étienne), notary and tax collector - Signed sale of house to Missionaries in Luçon, XIIIa, 320.

Robert Bellarmine (Saint), Jesuit Cardinal Archbishop of Capua - How he prepared Bishop for death, XI, 126; Saint Louise wonders if his catechism is too scholarly for Sisters, XIIIb, 299; praise for his catechism, XIIIb, 300; Saint Louise wants it explained to Sisters, XIIIb, 301.

Robiche (Louis), Priest of the Mission - Biographical data; praise for his virtues, II, 567–70.

Robidé (Marie), Daughter of Charity - XIIIb, 227.

Robin (Jacques), Brother of the Mission - Biographical data, III, 522; VII, 514; Superior of Agen house would like to get rid of him, VII, 514.

Robin (Philippe), Dean of Saint-Frambourg - II, 204.

Robineau (Louis), Brother of the Mission - Biographical data; Saint Vincent's secretary, I, *xxvi*; IV, 424; V, 245; VI, 564; VII,

137; VIII, 448; XI, 86; business that fell to him as secretary, V, 245; VI, 564, 585, 616; VII, 137, 440, 575; VIII, 448; manuscript work on saint's virtues, III, 356–57; VII, 266; informs saint of loss of lawsuit concerning Orsigny farm, VII, 266; records conferences of Saint Vincent, XI, 86, 150, 159, 171; other mentions, XII, 391, 393.

Robineau (M.) - Recommends to Saint Vincent priest wanting to make retreat at Saint-Lazare, VIII, 477.

Robiolis (Tommaso), Priest of the Mission - Biographical data, VII, 542.

Robodet (Marie), Daughter of Charity - Signs attestation after reading Common and Particular Rules reviewed and arranged in order by Fr. Alméras, XIIIb, 206.

Rocamadour, town in Lot - Alain de Solminihac wants to restore devotion to Virgin there, IV, 27.

Roch (Saint) - Feast day, IX, 30, 34; Mass in his honor, III, 308; his charity, IX, 30, 34, 38.

Roche (M.) - II, 571.

Roche (Nicolas), Priest of the Mission - Biographical data, I, 178.

Rochechouart (François de) - See **Chandenier** (François de).

Rochechouart (Louis-Victor) - See **Vivonne**.

Rochefoucauld - See **La Rochefoucauld**.

Rochepot (Françoise-Marguerite de la) - See **Gondi** (Françoise-Marguerite de Silly).

Rochepot (M. and Mme de), parents of Mme de Gondi - She makes provision in her will for payment of their debts, XIIIa, 62.

Rochereau (Laurent) - Chaplain of the Debonds Chapel, XIIIa, 318–19.

Roches-Chamian (Michel le Masle, Prior) - Biographical data, I, 418; other mention, I, 438.

Rocqueville (M. de) - V, 326.

Rodez, town in Aveyron - Bishops: see Charles de **Noailles**, Hardouin de **Péréfixe**; conduct of diocesan clergy after death of Charles de Noailles, III, 293–94.

Rodriguez (Alphonsus), Jesuit - Writings read in Saint-Lazare refectory, XII, 10.

Rogation Days - Explanation, practice of Canons of Notre-Dame, XI, 40.

Roger (Jean), Apostolic Notary - XIIIa, 480.

Roger (Marie), Daughter of Charity - XIIIb, 228.

Roggenbach (Johann Konrad), Bishop of Basel - VII, 336.

Rogue (Pierre), Brother of the Mission - Biographical data; shepherd, II, 80; departure from Company, II, 194.

Rohan (Henri Chabot, Duc de), Governor of Anjou - Sides with Princes during Fronde, IV, 320.

Roland (M.) - Makes retreat before entering Saint-Lazare Seminary, VI, 615.

Rolando (Giovanni Antonio) - Biographical data, VIII, 216.

Romagna, ancient province of Italy - Moral and religious state of inhabitants, V, 138.

Romainville, town near Paris - Mission, XIIIa, 479.

Roman (M.), merchant in Marseilles - VII, 161, 179, 190, 194, 196, 208, 213, 233.

Roman Ritual - Saint Vincent advises Missionaries to take copies to Madagascar, III, 280; sends two to them, III, 282.

Romanesque (M.) - IV, 449.

Romans, town in Drôme - I, 402.

Rome, city in Italy - Character of Romans, II, 295, 350; great prudence required to succeed in negotiations with Roman Court, II, 267, 295; and to know how to take one's time, III, 193, 459, 613; XIIIa, 377; to say that, in Rome, presentable men are needed, is to speak as a Roman, III, 491.

Unhealthful climate, II, 63, 231, 262, 269; VIII, 20, 86, 302; very hot, III, 345; VII, 595; plague epidemic, V, 634, 640; VI, 29, 39, 40, 68, 72, 83, 87, 99, 132, 133–35, 157, 160, 169, 172, 183, 205, 257, 349, 362, 373, 380, 386, 402, 411, 526–27, 541, 552; X, 191; XI, 346; Pope prohibits all kinds of assemblies, even solemn Masses, VI, 106; case of plague at *Propaganda*; closure of establishment: see also ***Propaganda*** (College).

First stay of Saint Vincent in Rome, IX, 250, 368; X, 294, 476; XII, 282; second visit, I, 9, 12–15; VIII, 601; his remembrance of Holy City, I, 112; desire to return there third time, II, 361, 470; IV, 105; Fr. Codoing urges him to establish headquarters of Superior General in Rome; Saint Vincent sees disadvantages, II, 361, 434, 453, 461, 470.

Journey of Chandenier brothers to Rome: see **Chandenier** (Claude de); French Minims of Rome, VII, 635; sermons in church of Oratory in Rome, XI, 266–67; Cardinal Durazzo in Rome: see also **Durazzo** (Stefano); other mentions, V, 180,

193, 584; VI, 121, 289, 358, 374, 387, 409, 412, 420, 485, 557, 579, 593, 604, 605; VII, 512; VIII, 131, 169, 170, 191, 192, 197, 515, 544, 545; XII, 61; XIIIb, 329, 406.

Missionaries in Rome: letters from Saint Vincent, II, 17; III, 344, 479; V, 154, 322, 545; VI, 192; VII, 482, 518: see also **Alméras** (René the Younger), **Berthe**, **Codoing**, **Dehorgny**, **Du Coudray**, **Jolly** (Edme), **Lebreton**, **Le Vazeux**, **Portail**; letters of Rome Missionaries to Saint Vincent: published letters: see **Berthe**, **Jolly** (Edme); letters mentioned, VI, 439, 453, 504, 505, 558, 563, 564; VIII, 31, 239; XI, 375, 379.

Rome is one of most important houses of Company, VIII, 273; Fr. Lebreton, Superior, obtains faculties for confession, I, 538; Saint Vincent advises him to accept small chapel outside Vatican rather than parish, I, 538; Vice-Gerent allows Missionaries to minister in Rome and to perform duties for poor persons and priests, II, 63, 214, 232; XIIIa, 313; Saint Vincent wants house to be called house of the Mission and chapel to have title of Most Holy Trinity, II, 63; VIII, 610; advises Fr. Lebreton to rent or buy small house, II, 18, 141; to buy hospice, II, 44, 155; search for house, II, 36, 40, 43–44, 170, 426, 427; Saint Vincent refuses those offered: Santa Maria della Rotonda, II, 35, 44, 45; Our Lady of Loreto, II, 36, 44; Cardinal Bichi's palace, II, 36; small church of Saint-Jean, II, 36; chapel offered by Cardinal di Bagno, II, 170; Saint-Yves Church, II, 295, 305, 306, 309, 362, 397, 415–16, 419, 433, 462, 467, 470; method of sending money to Fr. Codoing, II, 245; rent for house, II, 304–05; Oratorians oppose conferring Saint-Yves-des-Bretons parish on Missionaries, II, 305, 306, 309, 472; Fr. Codoing, Superior, chooses house and residence, receives money from Saint Vincent, II, 430, 432, 438, 449, 464, 469; obtains power of attorney to buy house, II, 552, 582; God is blessing mission there, II, 327; V, 610; Saint Vincent makes proposal concerning the work, II, 359; Codoing's proposal for minor seminary, II, 552; Fr. Portail or Fr. Alméras is considered for visitation there, II, 624; III, 68–69; Rome pressures Saint Vincent to send Missionaries to Ireland, II, 633; Fr. Dehorgny chooses small place for his lodging, III, 65.

Fr. Alméras, Superior, continues search, III, 459; discouraged, III, 613; resigned, IV, 52; adds personal money to sum at his disposal for purchase; Saint Vincent persuades him to shift burden of search to someone else, IV, 134; decides to purchase house where Missionaries are living, V, 66; prevented, V, 153; refuses house of Irish, V, 157; and San Giovanni Mercatelli, V, 465; Fr. Jolly, Superior, undertakes new search, V, 619; has eye on house Pope wants to use for good work, V, 633; Cardinal di Bagno suggests helping Missionaries find housing in Saint

John Lateran palace; Fr. Jolly declines, VII, 40, 47; decree of Congregation for Apostolic Visitation to provide Priests of the Mission housing in Rome, VII, 246; Saint Vincent prepared to accept on approval Saint-Nicolas house, VII, 268; another lodging under consideration, VII, 292; Saint Vincent happy to see Missionaries poorly lodged, VII, 328, 343, 406, 560; little hope of suitable house if not purchased; lack of funds makes this difficult, VII, 343; Missionaries still have no house of their own, VII, 378; Matteis' town house offered Fr. Jolly, VII, 406, 413; Cardinal Maldachini offers house, which Saint Vincent refuses, VII, 629; Cardinal Durazzo seeks house for them, VIII, 109; purchase of Cardinal di Bagno's residence in Monte Citorio, VIII, 117, 134, 139, 147, 154, 173, 194, 211, 482; Pope prefers that Missionaries do not have church, VIII, 175–76.

Saint Vincent hesitates to allow Missionaries in Rome to dress as Italians do, II, 306–07; tells them to wear surplice when hearing confessions, IV, 598; Rome Missionaries calumniated: accused of doing nothing, II, 491; suggestion made to Saint Vincent for instruction of children who may later be called on to work at Roman Court, II, 581; Cardinal de Retz given shelter in Missionaries' house; displeasure of Mazarin, who orders expulsion of French Missionaries in Rome, V, 270–76, 334, 338–39, 369; XI, 165; Mazarin retracts prohibition, V, 363, 369; Saint Vincent recommends establishing or continuing custom of wearing rosary on belt, V, 619.

Line of conduct outlined by Saint Vincent for Fr. Jolly for assistance to plague-stricken, V, 634; Missionaries await orders to serve them, V, 640; VI, 172, 182–83; Fr. de Martinis enclosed in college of *Propaganda*, where plague has broken out: see also **Martinis**; penances of Missionaries to bring about cessation of scourge, V, 640; works of house, VII, 319.

Confessions for poor, prisoners, and country people, I, 538; spiritual assistance for incurables, II, 395, 405; missions to shepherds, II, 155, 343, 350–51, 395, 405; XIIIa, 314; missions in Porto diocese, II, 170; in Spoleto diocese, IV, 52; in Terni, IV, 392; in Apennines, V, 137; in Vetralla, V, 487–89; in Breda, V, 531; at Saint John Lateran, V, 595; in Leonessa, VIII, 38, 147; in other places, I, 581; II, 356; IV, 291, 320, 371, 391; V, 109, 154, 476, 505, 546; VI, 618; VII, 360, 401, 508, 561; in Roman countryside in winter, III, 345.

Retreats, II, 304, 306, 349, 491; V, 490; VII, 39, 391; retreats for ordinands, II, 232, 304, 318, 327, 349, 358, 395, 406, 438, 449, 491, 542; V, 490; VII, 261, 268, 360; VIII, 198, 209, 284, 311, 321, 358, 361; XIIIa, 191; donation of Duchesse d'Aiguillon for this ministry, II, 305, 318, 406, 449, 542; Saint

Vincent thinks house is too poor to give retreats gratuitously, VII, 269; Pope decides that ordinands of Rome prepare for ordination by retreat at house of Priests of the Mission, VIII, 208, 209, 238, 254, 345, 563; exempts no one, VIII, 349; measure incites jealousy, VIII, 285, 345; XIIIa, 192; Jesuits want to conduct ordination retreats, VIII, 368.

Queen of France promises 1,000 écus for Rome Seminary, II, 498; plan for Internal Seminary, II, 498–99, 502; Internal Seminary established by Fr. Jolly, VI, 451, 525, 604; VII, 39–40, 55, 434, 516, 542; VIII, 101, 302; Saint Vincent advises that no one of French descent be accepted there, VII, 542; Pope sends eight confreres to visit suffragan dioceses of Rome, VIII, 361; major seminary, II, 395, 398, 415, 502, 505–06; spiritual direction of College of *Propaganda*: see also ***Propaganda*** (College); opening of seminary for foreign missions at College of *Propaganda*, direction by Priests of the Mission discussed: see also ***Propaganda*** (Seminary).

Protector of Rome Missionaries: see **Durazzo** (Stefano); benefactors: see **Aiguillon** (Duchesse d'), **Bagno** (Nicolò di), **Brignole** (Maria-Emanuele), **Herse** (Mme de), **Montmaur** (M. de); revenue of house, II, 342, 406, 491, 514; Saint Vincent takes from revenue 3,000 livres owed to Saint-Lazare house, II, 542; visitation by Fr. Portail, III, 14, 68, 115, 133, 137, 171, 190, 193, 203, 204, 237, 246; by Fr. Berthe, VII, 435–36, 439; VIII, 99.

Assignments and changes, I, 538, 582–83; II, 18, 40, 114, 117, 142, 215, 306, 502; III, 271; V, 205, 623; VI, 496, 570; VII, 153, 580; XIIIa, 359–60; list of Superiors and history of house, VIII, 609–10; Rome Missionaries: see **Alméras** (René the Younger), **Baliano**, **Bauduy**, **Berthe**, **Blatiron**, **Blondel**, **Boulier**, **Brunet**, **Champion** (René), **Chardon**, **Codoing**, **Damiens**, **Dehorgny**, **Doutrelet**, **Duchesne** (Jean), **Du Coudray**, **Eu** (Louis d'), **François** (Pierre), **Germain**, **Giroud**, **Giudice** [**Lejuge**], **Greco**, **Jolly** (Edme), **Lebreton**, **Legendre** (Renault), **Legouz** (Jacques), **Le Mercier**, **Levasseur** (Martin), **Martin** (Jean), **Martinis**, **Morando**, **Oderico**, **Pesnelle** (Jacques), **Pinson**, **Ploesquellec**, **Taone**; other mentions, I, 567; VI, 196; XII, 318; XIIIa, 208, 327, 329; XIIIb, 147.

Rome Gazette - Saint Vincent mentions information gleaned from *Gazette*, III, 73, 74.

Rome (M.) - V, 206, 492.

Romillion [**Romaillon**] (Jean-Baptiste), Cofounder of Priests of Christian Doctrine - Biographical data; parts company with César de Bus, II, 459; VII, 484; his houses unite with Oratory despite him, II, 465; other mention, VII, 484.

Romillon (Fr.), chaplain at Champigny-sur-Veude Hospital - Complaints against him, III, 412; Duchesse d'Aiguillon acquiesces to his leaving, III, 605; withdraws consent, IV, 10, 12; praise for Fr. Romillon, IV, 69.

Romilly (Michel), Knight of Malta, slave in Tunis - Mother sends him money, VII, 144, 148, 250, 520, 522, 539.

Romilly (Louise Goulas, dame de) - Biographical data, II, 444; III, 471; V, 394; called to meeting at Saint Louise's home, II, 328; Lady of Charity, V, 394; concern for foundlings, II, 444, 485–88; III, 213, 229; for Michel Le Gras, III, 471, 472; letter to Saint Louise, III, 506; children: see **Romilly** (Chevalier de) and **Flacourt** (Marie de).

Romulus, founder of Rome - Foundling, XIIIb, 398, 406.

Rondet (M.) - I, 542.

Room and Board - Room and board for students, I, 106, 135; for ordinands in Paris, II, 89; for seminarians at Bons-Enfants, II, 658; III, 235; at Saint-Charles, VIII, 51; in Richelieu, III, 144; in Le Mans, IV, 59–60, 98; in Cahors, III, 153, 244; IV, 504–05; at Notre-Dame-de-Lorm, VIII, 257.

Roquépine (Charles de Bouzet, Abbé de), Queen's chaplain - VIII, 52.

Roquet - See **Taquet**.

Roquette (M.), agent of Comte de Brienne - Saint Vincent requests of him passport to Poland, V, 414.

Rosary [**Chaplet**] - Origin, X, 498; excellence, IX, 175; Saint Francis de Sales recited it every day, IX, 175; may substitute for meditation, IX, 175; Missionaries carry it on their belt, III, 376; V, 619; Daughters of Charity do same, IX, 31; it is their breviary, X, 499; they pray it every day, X, 445; and when traveling, I, 504; text of Rule of Sisters, X, 497; how to recite it, IX, 95; X, 498–99; Saint Vincent prays it with residents of Nom-de-Jésus, XIIIa, 173; recommends it to members of Charities, XIIIb, 25, 45, 105, 111, 112; prayer beads of Turks, X, 498; Saint Vincent inquires about twelve-bead chaplet attached to painting of Virgin sent him by Saint Louise, II, 629, 630.

Rosary (Confraternity) - Union of Confraternities of Charity and of Rosary in parishes; Dominicans opposed to this, I, 288; II, 28; Confraternity of Rosary in Ferrières, II, 366; in Sedan, III, 526.

Rose (Anne), Daughter of Charity - XIIIb, 205, 227.

Rose, Nicolas - See **Roze**.

Roseau [**Le Roseau**] (Françoise), Daughter of Charity - XIIIb, 227.

Roses (Jeanne) - Member of Charity of Courboin, XIIIb, 93.

Rosier [**Laisné**] (Pierre) - See **Laisné**.

Rospigliosi (Giulio), Papal Secretary of State - Biographical data, VI, 132; Saint Vincent receives answer to petition, VI, 132.

Ross, region of Scotland - Evangelized by Fr. Lumsden, VI, 546.

Rossat (Simon), of Mâcon - XIIIb, 74.

Rosta (Fr.) - See **A Rosta**.

Roté (Michel), Canon of Troyes - Contacts with Saint Vincent, I, 413.

Roton (Fr.), chaplain of Commander de Sillery - Upcoming trip to Annecy, II, 58, 60.

Rotterdam, town in Netherlands - VIII, 574, 596.

Roucelin (M.) - Member of Charity of Joigny, XIIIb, 66.

Roucherolles (Pierre de), Baron de Pont-Saint-Pierre - Protests that Canons of Écouis are unfaithful to residency requirement, XIIIa, 29.

Rouen, town in Seine-Maritime - Seminary of Cardinal de Joyeuse, I, 208; II, 172, 393, 506; V, 565; Parlement, VI, 449; VII, 424; port of embarkation for Hamburg, V, 128, 161, 403, 419; VI, 55; VIII, 535, 537; XIIIa, 199; coaches, II, 430, 432, 449, 457, 552; III, 529; V, 54; VI, 125; VII, 610; XIIIb, 231, 325; Saint-Ouen parish, IV, 197; VI, 310; natives of Rouen, or living there, III, 331, 540; V, 282, 380; VII, 540; VIII, 185, 481; Archbishops: see François, Duc de **Joyeuse**; François de Harlay de **Champvallon**; missions in diocese, VI, 124; Visitation Monastery, XII, 359; Jansenist-leaning Carmelites upset area Catholics, VIII, 407; other mentions, II, 62; V, 302; VI, 310; VII, 93; VIII, 499; XIIIa, 25–26; XIIIb, 142.

Rougemont (Comte de) - Model of detachment, X, 142–43; XI, 103; XII, 190–91; conversion and charities; dies a Capuchin, XIIIa, 55.

Rougemont, farm in Sevran - Historical information, V, 365; VIII, 119–20; by contract of union of Saint-Lazare Priory to Congregation of the Mission, Adrien Le Bon granted Rougemont farm, dependency of priory, I, 250; XIIIa, 265, 285, 290; donates it to Saint Vincent on February 11, 1645, I, 250; saint asks Parlement for authorization to cut trees in forest of farm, II, 589; counts on produce of Rougemont and Orsigny farms to provision Saint-Lazare, IV, 329; place of rest for him and tired confreres, V, 365; XIIIa, 200; other mention, IV, 422.

Rouillac (Louis de Goth, Marquis de), Ambassador of France to Portugal - II, 523.

Roujon (M.) - III, 381.

Roule, parish in Paris - Priest from there is tutor for Marquise de Mortemart's son, II, 651.

Rousse (Jean), Pastor of Saint-Roch - Biographical data, IV, 7; V, 427; sends Daughters of Charity away from parish, IV, 7; fear he might do it again, V, 427–28.

Rousseau (Mme) - I, 121.

Rousseau (Marie-Renée), Visitandine - III, 15.

Roussel (Jacques), Rector of Jesuits of Bar-le-Duc - Biographical data, II, 29; informs Saint Vincent of death of M. de Montevit, II, 29, 42; charity toward Missionaries sent to Bar-le-Duc, II, 76.

Roussel (Fr.), Priest of the Mission - Ill, II, 347–48.

Rousselot (Nicole), Daughter of Charity - Signs attestation after reading Common and Particular Rules reviewed and arranged in order by Fr. Alméras, XIIIb, 206.

Roux (Arnaut), lawyer at Council - XIIIa, 342, 343.

Rouy, locality in Brittany - Fr. Codoing is there, III, 76.

Rouyer (Blaise), brother of Gérard - XIIIa, 73.

Rouyer (Gérard), porter at Bons-Enfants - XIIIa, 73.

Roy (Jean), Brother of the Mission - Biographical data, V, 601; VI, 565; difficulty with Fr. Crowley, V, 601; leaves Congregation second time, VI, 565.

Roy (M.) - Writes from Lyons to Saint Vincent about ransom of slave, VIII, 532.

Roye, town in Somme - Journey of Fr. Étienne to Roye, VIII, 597; other mention, I, 345.

Royer (Charlotte), Daughter of Charity - Biographical data, III, 431; VI, 50; VIII, 164; in Richelieu, III, 430; letters Saint Vincent wrote her in Richelieu, VI, 50; VIII, 312; doesn't get along with companion, dissatisfied with Director, VI, 51–52; Saint Vincent tells her to nurse sick in place outside parish, VI, 52; illness prevents her from working, VIII, 164, 170; other mention, XIIIb, 227.

Royer (Nicolas and Ponce), Priests of the Mission - Biographical data, III, 77; mission in Montmirail, III, 77; Saint Vincent sends greetings, III, 78.

Roze [**Rose**] (Nicolas), Priest of the Mission - Biographical data, II, 339; V, 82; VII, 364; VIII, 446; about to leave for Marseilles, II, 339; reference to letter to Saint Vincent, II, 673; Superior in Troyes, V, 82; VIII, 607; Titular of Barbuise parish, V, 82, 312; at Saint-Lazare, VII, 364; VIII, 446.

Roze [**Rose**] (Fr.), priest in Poland - V, 264, 335, 338.

Rozée (M.), merchant in Rouen - One of directors of French Company of Sénégal, III, 331, 540; Fr. Mousnier writes to him, V, 282; contact with Saint Vincent, V, 282.

Rozière (M. de) - II, 181.

Rubrics - See **Ceremonies**, **Mass**.

Rueil [***Ruel***], town in Hauts-de-Seine - Journeys of Saint Vincent to Rueil, I, 453, 480; II, 48, 139, 145, 509; Duchesse d'Aiguillon in Rueil, II, 48; III, 201; V, 60; negotiations for peace, III, 411, 430; Saint-Vincent Abbey in Rueil, IV, 246; château of Rueil, I, 403; other mentions, I, 401, 441, 447.

Rueil (Claude de), Bishop of Angers - Claude de Rueil and Sisters of hospital, II, 223, 224; Pavillon expects him in Alet, II, 341; recommends to Saint Vincent affair involving this Prelate, II, 543; other mention, I, 194.

Rufin (M.) - Physician of Visitation nuns in Paris, VIII, 489.

Rufin [**Ruffin**] (M.), merchant of Paris - III, 280, 290.

Rufisque, roadstead in Senegal - V, 282; VIII, 566.

Ruhaut (Marguerite), Daughter of Charity - Sent to Metz, X, 447.

Rules - Observance of Rules: Conferences to Daughters of Charity, IX, 162–70, 171–78, 243–60; X, 76–78, 79–86, 86–91, 433–39; to Congregation of the Mission, XI, 72; XII, 1; mention of other conferences, XII, 417, 432, 434, 435, 436; good order of Communities depends on observance of Rules, VII, 501; text of Rule of Daughters of Charity on observance, X, 433; every Community needs Rule, III, 343; IX, 24, 93; exactness to Rule, I, 178; II, 622; IX, 56, 61, 423.

Importance of observance, III, 250; reasons for observing Rules and Regulations, IX, 8–9, 34, 93–94, 248–51; XI, 72–73; Rules are taken from Gospels, IX, 248–49; X, 79; XII, 3, 109; come from God, VII, 164; IX, 93, 247–48; X, 79, 86, 89–90, 180, 219–20, 433; XI, 72; XII, 6–9; expression of God's Will, IX, 251; X, 86–87, 437; guide to God, like a ship to port, VII, 165; IX, 167–68; X, 89, 220, 307–08, 340–42; XI, 73; keep us safe from spirit of world, IX, 338; sanctify, X, 233, 284–85, 342–43, 366, 433–34; XI, 346; XII, 2–3; Clement VIII ready to canonize any religious faithful to Rule: see also **Clement VIII** and **Innocent VIII**; channels by which God sends graces to individuals and Company, IX, 259; X, 293, 340; by practice of Rules, we earn merit and make satisfaction, IX, 250; pleases God, X, 327–28; makes one happy, X, 232; difficult for one who does not observe Rules to persevere in vocation, IX, 34, 249, 283; XI, 73; all goes well where Rule is followed; Communities that neglect Rules fall into ruin, IX, 9, 167, 543–44; X, 87–88, 366, 410; XI, 348, 390; XIIIb, 344; Sisters who don't keep Rules are like Foolish Virgins, or even worse, X, 493, 495; observance of Rules maintains uniformity, IX, 93, 173; X, 213, 285, 287, 292; XII, 211; other mention, II, 86.

Rules are not burden; like wings are for birds to fly, X, 79, 80, 81; nothing is easier than to observe them, IX, 94, 103; X, 79, 88–89; above all, for those accustomed to doing so, X, 438; example of Cardinal de La Rochefoucauld, IX, 168; of Mme Goussault and Mathieu Molé, IX, 168; Superiors must observe Rules and see that they are observed: see also **Superiors**; important to choose as Superiors those who are examples of regularity, XI, 75; to violate Rule is not sin in itself, IX, 249; can be sin, by reason of circumstances, if one violates at same time Commandment of God or of Church, or commitments of vows, or in scandal or contempt for Rule, II, 153; X, 35, 42, 80–81, 88, 90–91; XII, 274–75, 348; how to observe Rules, XI, 73; means for fidelity, IX, 10–11, 251–55; X, 81–82; XI, 74–75; love them, XI, 92; esteem them, X, 350; read them, IX, 544; X, 82, 433; XI, 74; be attached to them and exact, XI, 94; Daughters of Charity must read them every month, IX, 102, 544; X, 525; read some article every day, X, 437; if with others at time for exercise, excuse self and leave, IX, 31, 43, 98; XI, 97; do not follow order contrary to Rules, IX, 58, 127; X, 184, 315; urgent service of poor takes precedence over Rule, VI, 52, 514; VII, 66, 473; IX, 5, 29, 35, 102, 171, 173, 252, 257, 339, 544; X, 3, 76, 164, 183, 434–35, 445, 478, 549; XIIIb, 127, 138; prayer of Saint Vincent for grace to observe Rules well, X, 380.

Rules of Congregation of the Mission: inserted into foundation contract, XIIIa, 215–17; five fundamental Rules of Mission, I, 112–13; old Rules, III, 287; VI, 541, 615; Saint Vincent regrets that Rules are not yet drawn up, I, 273; preparation for Rules, II, 155, 396, 540; III, 11, 83–84, 238, 371; 1642 General Assembly studies Rules; forms commission to recast them, II, 344; XIIIa, 326, 396; Saint Vincent presses for approval of Rules by Holy See, II, 470, 523; III, 373; 1651 General Assembly re-examines them, XIIIa, 368–71, 394–95; document presented for approval of Archbishop of Paris, XIIIa, 395; after archiepiscopal approval, Saint Vincent has qualms about making modifications, V, 321; Frs. Alméras and

Portail visit houses to see if Rule is observed, III, 64; first edition (1655) contains printing errors; copies not distributed, V, 335; printing errors, XII, 127; revision, V, 600; VI, 349, 366, 385, 387, 524, 594; steps taken with Archdiocese, VI, 459; text of Rules and comparison with Codex Sarzana, XIIIa, xv, 430–71; distribution of Rules at Saint-Lazare; Saint Vincent's discourse, XII, 1–12; why he did not urge publication, III, 272; VII, 163–65; XII, 5–7; preface, VII, 163; not customary to insert into Rules of Community Bulls which authorize them, VII, 367; nor to speak of vows there, XII, 298; nor to mention all minor practices of Company, VIII, 81; Rule does not allow Missionaries to be involved in care of nuns, III, 71, 87; nor to absolve persons from heresy, VII, 367.

Rules sent to houses, VII, 179, 180, 182, 271, 289, 291, 296, 312, 323, 331, 373, 401; with circular signed by Fr. Alméras, VII, 296, 401; copy sent to Apostolic Commissary, VII, 497; Rules not to be given to outsiders, VII, 180; Saint Vincent asks Cardinal de Retz for new approval because of minor corrections, VIII, 33; explanation of Common Rules, XII, 66–137, 139–232, 243–63, 277–352. Conferences, XII, 66–82, 83–97, 98–110, 110–26, 126–37, 139–50, 151–60, 161–73, 173–86, 187–200, 201–12, 213–25, 225–32, 243–53, 253–63, 277–88, 289–97, 297–306, 307–14, 314–24, 324–27, 328–35, 336–45, 345–52; allusion to Chapter 9, §2, VIII, 588; Rules for duties, II, 523, 540; III, 83; see also **Assistants**, **Assemblies**, **Superiors**, **Vicars-General**; regulations for confreres acting as military chaplains, XIIIa, 307–09; for Marseilles Missionaries ministering to galley convicts, XIIIa, 348–50; for Missionaries in Tunis, XIIIa, 401–02; and in Algiers, XIIIa, 344–45.

Rules for Daughters of Charity: 1634 order of day, IX, 2–7; Sisters do not have written Rule, IX, 1, 92, 111, 169; preparation of Rules, I, 223, 318; II, 131; Regulations of 1640: first written Rule, I, 594; IX, 17; first article, IX, 18; second article, IX, 19; rising and prayer, IX, 24–25, 35; learning to read, examen, spiritual reading, IX, 36–37; explanation of Rules, IX, 94–103; text of 1645 Rules, XIIIb, 123; revisions, III, 11; 1646 Rules; text, approval by Archbishop of Paris, XIIIb, 131; explanation of Rule, IX, 256–60; Saint Louise would like copy and for Rules to be read from time to time to Company, III, 179; asks that way of life be drafted in writing, sent to individual houses, and read monthly at Motherhouse to assembled Sisters, IV, 224; her observations on outline of Rules, IV, 459; Sisters do not have special directory, IV, 572; text of 1655 Rule, XIIIb, 133ff.; approval by Archbishop of Paris, XIIIb, 144; explanation of Common Rules by Saint Vincent, XIIIb, 147–69; sent to Edme Jolly in Rome to seek their approval, VIII, 160.

Preparation of Common Rules; not yet ready to be shown, VI, 75; why Saint Vincent has taken so long to put Rules in writing, XIIIb, 324; origin of term Common Rules, X, 100; conferences on articles of Common Rules, X, 86–99, 100–11, 112–26, 126–45, 146–59, 166–81, 219–31, 232–45, 245–56, 257–67, 267–79, 280–92, 293–307, 307–18, 318–29, 330–42, 342–55, 355–67, 368–80, 383–90, 390–402, 403–17, 418–32, 433–39; explanation of Common Rules, X, 86–159, 166–81, 219–380, 383–439; of order of day, X, 479–91, 497–511, 523–26; of Rules for Sisters in parishes, X, 454–64, 479–87, 488–91, 497–500, 501–11, 523–26, 527–32, 535–36, 537–41, 545–55; mention of Rules for Sisters who teach school, X, 555; Rules are not to be changed, IX, 544–47; X, 83–84, 288; nor communicated to outsiders, IV, 224; Saint Vincent hesitates having them printed, X, 437, 499, 526; publication by Fr. Alméras, XIIIa, xv.

Particular Rules, II, 131; IX, 17, 94; X, 91–92; Rules for Sisters at Angers Hospital, I, 600; XIIIb, 108; Rules and specific advice for particular ministries, XIIIb, 169–225: parishes, 169; school teachers, 177; in villages, 182; in hospitals, 185, 189, 206; advice to hospital Sisters, 195–206; with Foundlings, 209, 216; with galley convicts, XIIIa, xv; XIIIb, 221.

Rules for Charities: for parish Charities, XIIIb, I, 67, 79–107; Ladies of Hôtel-Dieu, XIIIb, 443; Ladies at Court, XIIIb, 441.

Rumelin (Michel Thépaut, sieur de), Canon Theologian of Tréguier - Biographical data, III, 447; V, 581; VII, 43; VIII, 75; Saint Vincent thanks him for kindnesses, III, 447; V, 581; VIII, 75, 284; founder of Tréguier Seminary, V, 581; VIII, 75, 76; VIII, 616; problems with conditions of foundation, V, 581; other mention, VII, 43.

Rus - See **Vas**.

Ruyter (M. de), Dutch admiral - VIII, 593.

Ry, village in Seine-Maritime - VI, 310.

Ryan (Fabian), Irish Dominican - III, 315.

Rymon (François de), Lieutenant in *élection* of Mâcon - XIIIb, 74.

S

Sables d'Olonne, town in Vendée - III, 205.

Sablonceaux, village in Charente-Maritime - Reform of abbey, I, 208–09; abbey placed under direction of Abbot of Chancelade, III, 225; mention of letter from Prior to Alain de Solminihac, IV, 161.

Sablonnière (M.) - Impoverished gentleman, VIII, 123.

Saché, village in Indre-et-Loire - Daughters of Charity native to Saché, II, 215: see **Turenne** (Marguerite de); Pastor: see **Mondion** (Fr. de); mission, III, 269.

Sachetti (Giulio), Cardinal - Biographical data, VII, 327; mention of letter to Mme de Chastelain, VII, 327; other mention, VII, 391.

Saclay, village in Essonne - See ***Orsigny***.

Sacraments - Mention of conference on administration of Sacraments, XII, 436; at Saint-Lazare, practice in administering sacraments, VIII, 90, 91, 93; XII, 234–42; consequences of receiving them in bad dispositions, III, 470; Missionaries unable to administer Sacraments to Portuguese on Saint-Vincent Island because of language difficulties, III, 540; those on ship held conferences on Sacraments, VIII, 572; preparation for their administration given at Saint-Nicolas-du-Chardonnet, X, 502; see also **Communion**, **Confession**.

Sainctot (Marie Dalibray, dame), Lady of Charity - Biographical data, I, 230.

Saint-Aignan (Paul Chevalier, Canon de) - Biographical data, II, 156; III, 314; VIII, 549; attempts to reform Saint-Eutrope Monastery: see ***Saint-Eutrope***; offers Saint Vincent priory to help defray expenses of retreats for ordinands; offers him another, II, 280; union of two priories to Congregation of the Mission rejected, II, 295; resigns Dyé Priory in favor of Congregation of the Mission, II, 399; Saint Vincent invites him to resign priory in favor of Missionary, II, 462; proceedings in Rome for union to Company of priory offered by Fr. de Saint-Aignan, II, 470, 523; Fr. d'Authier desires it, II, 465–66; other mentions, III, 314; VIII, 549.

Saint-Aignan, village in Tarn-et-Garonne - Fr. Bajoue, incumbent of parish, would like to resign it; Saint Vincent tells him to wait, IV, 558; Fr. Edmund Barry takes possession of this parish, VI, 358, 380, 590.

Saint-Alban (Comte de) - Saint Francis de Sales helps settle disagreement between Count and heretic, XIIIa, 91.

Saint-Albin (Jeanne de), Daughter of Charity - Biographical data, III, 425; V, 461; tempted to leave Company, V, 461; other mention, XIIIb, 227, 284.

Saint-Amand, parish in Toul - Entrusted temporarily to Missionaries, III, 65.

Saint-Amour (Louis Gorin, Abbé de) - One of delegates sent to Rome by Jansenists to prevent condemnation of Five Propositions of Jansenius, IV, 581, 594; gives his version of condemnation, IV, 583.

Saint-André, church in Châtillon - XIIIa, 44, 46, 47, 48, 57; XIIIb, 21.

Saint-André, parish in Joigny - XIIIb, 65, 66.

Saint-André-des-Arts, parish in Paris - Ladies ask for two Daughters of Charity, IV, 416, 419; other mentions, X, 259; XIIIb, 206.

Saint-Angel (M. de) - I, 278.

Saint-Antoine Hospital (chapel of), in Joigny - XIIIb, 65.

Saint-Armand (M. de) - In debt to Troyes Missionaries, II, 168.

Saint-Astier - Gabriel de la Baume de Foursat (Abbot of), his praise, IV, 162.

Saint Augustine (Canons Regular) - Saint Vincent dissuades confrere from entering Augustinians, VI, 508; gratitude confreres should have toward them, XI, 142; scandal given by Augustinians of Paris, XII, 53; split in Order by foundation of Congregation of Chancelade: see **Chancelade** (Augustinians of Reform); abbeys of Order: see ***Saint-Girard, Sainte-Geneviève;*** priories: see ***Saint-Lazare, Saint-Nicolas de Grosse-Sauve***; Hôtel-Dieu de Saint-Denis should be turned over to them, V, 333; Saint-Lazare entrusted to them in 1513, VIII, 434, 605; XIIIa, 410; other mentions, I, 243–44, 248; XIIIa, 394.

Saint-Barthélemy, parish in Cahors - Union of parish to Cahors Seminary, II, 632; Saint Vincent admonishes Superior of seminary for having abandoned service of parish during Lent and while Pastor was sick, II, 632, 636; other mentions, IV, 27, 480; VII, 338.

Saint-Barthélemy, parish in Paris - Establishment of Charity, XIIIb, 139; Ladies of Charity: see **Brou** (Mlle), **Guerrier** (Mme); Daughters of Charity in parish: see **Gesse** (Catherine de), **Delacroix** (Renée); other mentions, I, 261; VIII, 204.

Saint-Barthélemy, seminary in Cahors diocese - Curate taken by Bishop of Sarlat, IV, 27.

Saint-Benedict, church in Poland - Question of establishing Missionaries there, IV, 372.

Saint Benedict (Order) - See **Benedictines**.

Saint-Benoît (Jeanne de), Daughter of Charity - Entered before Act of Establishment in August 1655, XIIIb, 227.

Saint-Benoît, parish in Paris - Confraternity of Charity, I, 95; IX, 166; Daughters of Charity caring for poor: see **Jeanne** (Sister); only Sister there in 1634, IX, 8; Saint Vincent wants Sister Nicole to go to Saint-Benoît or elsewhere, I, 357; apologizes for being unable to hear confession of woman from Saint-Benoît, I, 376; other mention, XIIIb, 206.

Saint-Bertrand-de-Comminges, in Haute-Garonne - Bishop: see Barthélemy Donnadieu de **Griet**.

Saint Bibiana, church in Rome - Saint Vincent mentions it to Fr. Louis Lebreton, II, 36.

Saint-Bonaventure (César de), Carmelite - Biographical data; Saint Vincent writes regarding person recommended by him, IV, 453; mention of letter to Saint Vincent, IV, 453.

Saint-Briant, commune - VII, 487.

Saint-Brieuc - Bishop: see Denis de **La Barde**.

Saint-Caprais-de-Lerm, village in Lot-et-Garonne - Praise for Pastor, VII, 514.

Saint-Cassien, seigneury near Loudun - IV, 8.

Saint-Céré, village in Lot - II, 503.

Saint-Césaire, abbey in Bouches-du-Rhône - Steps taken by Saint Vincent for its reform, III, 161, 176.

Saint-Chamond (Melchior Mitte de Miolans, Marquis de), Ambassador of France in Rome - Contacts with Saint Vincent, II, 467, 469, 472; other mentions, I, 428; II, 498.

Saint-Charles, seminary in Paris - Historical information; IV, 292; V, 126; VI, 158; VII, 28; beginnings of seminary, II, 257, 585; site, III, 6; Saint Vincent changes name from Petit Saint-Lazare to Saint-Charles Seminary, IV, 292; seminary doing well, IV, 335; soldiers pillage it, IV, 409, 411; guards posted to avoid more looting, IV, 411–12; seminarians sent away because of danger, IV, 468; return, IV, 573; seminary gradually reestablished, V, 76; number of students increases, VI, 158; VII, 28; seminary is full, VI, 257; number of seminarians, III, 6, 175; V, 76; late vocations, VI, 107; cost of room and board, VIII, 51; some of its students, III, 113; V, 377; VII, 619; VIII, 50; acceptance of Brief *Ex Commissa Nobis*, V, 501.

List of Superiors and history of house, VIII, 614; Missionaries serving at Saint-Charles: see **Alméras** (René the Younger), **Codoing**, **Durand**, **Éveillard**, **Goblet**, **Hurtel** [**Heurtel**], **Lambert Aux Couteaux**, **Le Gros** (Jean-Baptiste), **Simon** (René), **Talec** (Nicolas); other mentions, III, 372, 409; IV, 342; V, 20, 51.

Saint-Christophe, island in Cape Verde archipelago - III, 540, 594.

Saint-Christophe, parish in Paris - Disagreement between Pastors of Saint-Christophe and Saint-Laurent, III, 298.

Saint-Cloud, town in Hauts-de-Seine - Visit of Charity by Saint Louise, I, 67–68, 69, 75; Daughters of Charity native to Saint-Cloud, II, 342; III, 506, 517; Saint Vincent considers mission there, I, 87.

Saint-Côme [***Saint-Cosme***], parish in Paris - II, 197; VIII, 204, 234; XIIIb, 206.

Saint-Corneille, abbey - Union with Val-de-Grâce, IV, 243.

Saint-Crispin-le-Grand, abbey - François Perrochel restores religious there to original discipline of Rule, XIIIa, 146.

Saint-Cyr-les-Colons, village in Yonne - Seigneur of Saint-Cyr and wife thank Saint Vincent for mission, II, 274, 275.

Saint-Cyran (Jean Duverger de Hauranne, Abbé de) - Biographical data, I, 392–93; III, 319–20; VIII, 404; XI, 320; XIIIa, 104; residences in Paris, XIIIa, 105, 122; nephew: see **Barcos**; illness contracted at bedside of Mme d'Andilly, I, 392–93; XIIIa, 112; esteem of Duchesse de Longueville, XIIIa, 124–25; contacts with Anne de Lage: see **Lage**; his *Théologie familière,* IV, 585; direction of nuns of Port-Royal, XIIIa, 125; his opinion of Church, III, 359; VIII, 404–05, 409; XI, 320; XIIIa, 135–36; of Council of Trent, IV, 184; XIIIa, 108, 134–36; of attrition and contrition, XIIIa, 132; of need for delay of absolution from mortal sins, III, 360; XIIIa, 105, 108–09, 125, 132; of vows, XIIIa, 109, 131; of Jesuits, III, 322; XIIIa, 109, 134.

Relationship with Saint Vincent, begun around 1624, XIIIa, 105; frequent contacts for fifteen years, XIIIa, 105; fewer contacts after 1632, XIIIa, 110, 120; Abbé de Saint-Cyran asks Saint Vincent for hospitality at Bons-Enfants, XIIIa, 122; helps him win lawsuit over possession of Saint-Lazare, XIIIa, 106, 119, 120, 127–28; offers him Bonneville Priory, XIIIa, 119; saint sometimes went to eat at abbé's home, XIIIa, 110; uses Saint-Cyran's influence with Bishop of Poitiers for foundation of Visitation monastery, XIIIa, 107; never called him teacher, XIIIa, 107, 130; did not prohibit his priests from visiting him, XIIIa, 106; visit of saint to Saint-Cyran in 1637;

details of interview; letter of abbé to saint following visit, I, 392; XIIIa, 105–07, 111–34; Saint Vincent gives horse to abbé, I, 392; XIIIa, 116; Saint-Cyran's opinion of Saint Vincent, XIIIa, 113–14, 120; Saint Vincent's opinion of Saint-Cyran, III, 361; XIIIa, 105; Saint-Cyran accused of grave errors by Sébastien Zamet and others, I, 394; XIIIa, 121–24; his interrogation, XIIIa, 110–36; Saint Vincent's deposition, XIIIa, 104–10; abbé promoted ideas of Jansenism, XIIIa, 166; death, II, 489; other mentions, III, 362, XIIIa, 171.

Saint-Denis, town near Paris - Saint Vincent in Saint-Denis, II, 71, 98, 463; III, 303, 380; IV, 414, 422; VI, 327; VII, 204; Battle of Saint-Denis, IV, 377, 382; Fr. Portail in Saint-Denis, VI, 385; Saint Vincent proposes that Saint Louise go there or elsewhere for fresh air, III, 369; she agrees, III, 370; he suggests she go alone, V, 643; Daughters of Charity or postulants from Saint-Denis, III, 232; XIIIb, 317; Court in Saint-Denis (1652), IV, 414; Abbé de Saint-Denis: Henri de Maupas du Tour; Saint-Denis plain, IV, 421; other mentions, I, 312; V, 372; VI, 281; XIIIa, 232, 341.

Daughters of Charity of Saint-Denis: Historical observation, III, 419; question of entrusting care of patients in hospital to Daughters of Charity, II, 399; plan is carried out, II, 599, 601; M. de Francière, administrator of hospital, and Daughters of Charity: see **Francière** (M. de); death at Motherhouse of Sister returned from Saint-Denis, III, 444; Sisters who ministered in Saint-Denis: **Angiboust** (Barbe), **Le Soin** (Marguerite), **Noret** (Françoise), **Raportebled**, **Turgis**, **Vallin**: see these names; other mentions, II, 635; III, 61; XIIIb, 140, 231.

Visitation Monastery: Saint Vincent goes to monastery, II, 98; VI, 327; to make visitation, II, 463; III, 380; to see Hélène-Angélique Lhuillier, who is ill, III, 303; Directress there is able to bear her cross, XII, 365; profession of Marie de Chaumont, II, 70–71; apologizes to Superior for being unable to render to Visitandines service they request of him because he is infirm, overburdened with business, and is not their "spiritual father," except for those in Paris house, II, 282, 284; tells Superior he is resigning as Superior of Paris monasteries, VIII, 314; troubles of Fronde force nuns to find refuge for six months among Sisters of First Monastery of Paris, IV, 403: see **Pontchartrain** (Françoise-Élisabeth Phelippeaux de); other mention, II, 463; saint informs Fr. de la Salle about butcher staying at Saint-Lazare en route to fair, I, 479.

Saint-Denis, faubourg - Site of Saint-Lazare, I, 248; XII, 377; XIIIa, 410; Congregation of the Mission is established there, I, 556; refugee girls housed there, IV, 393; soup for poor is distributed there, IV, 400.

Saint-Dyé-sur-Loire, village in Loir-et-Cher - Mme Goussault passes through, I, 193; also Saint Vincent, II, 533; saint writes to Fr. Portail from there, II, 533, 535.

Saint-Espir (Abbé de) - VII, 126.

Saint-Esprit (Michel du) - Carmelite in foreign missions, IV, 269.

Saint-Esprit, military Order - I, 40; see also Holy Spirit House, ***Toul***.

Saint-Étienne, church in Montmirail - Establishment of Confraternity of Charity, XIIIb, 31.

Saint-Étienne, town in Dauphiné - See **Thévenin** (M.).

Saint-Étienne-à-Arnes, village in Ardennes - Defeat of Turenne nearby; Priests of the Mission sent there; they bury bodies, IV, 150; Saint Vincent encourages Daughters of Charity assisting poor, IV, 168; discussion to see if Sisters should be sent to help Sister Chesneau, alone there, XIIIb, 307–09.

Saint-Étienne-d'Ars, priory on Île de Ré - Saint Vincent resigns title to Saint-Leonard-de-Chaumes Abbey to its prior.

Saint-Étienne-du-Mont, parish in Paris - Foundation of Charity, I, 359; XIIIb, 139; Mme de Beaufort, President: see **Beaufort** (Mme de); meeting of Ladies of Charity, I, 450; Saint Vincent has no confidence in this Charity, I, 451; infringements of churchwardens on rights of Ladies, II, 293; Daughters of Charity serving in Charity of Saint-Étienne, I, 451; II, 176, 177, 328, 600; III, 60; IV, 216; other mentions, XIIIa, 42; XIIIb, 206.

Saint-Étienne-la-Cigogne, village in Deux-Sèvres - Canon of Poitiers offers parish to Congregation of the Mission, VII, 188.

Saint-Eustache, parish in Paris - Charity established, I, 96; servants of poor leave it; Saint Louise's thoughts on request for Daughters of Charity, VII, 476; Étienne Le Tonnelier, Pastor: see **Le Tonnelier**; recommends needs of Picards, XII, 367; General of the Galleys and Mme de Gondi reside in parish, XIIIa, 61, 66, 224; other mentions, VII, 88; XIIIa, 42, 258.

Saint-Eutrope, convent in Paris diocese - Disorders among nuns, II, 280, 296; steps taken in Rome by Fr. de Saint-Aignan to have monastery withdrawn from direction of Franciscans, II, 105, 172, 280, 296, 319.

Saint-Fargeau, town in Yonne - Duchesse de Montpensier requests Daughters of Charity for hospital, VI, 280–81; Sisters open school and take in boarders; Saint Vincent advises Sister Servant to get rid of boarders, VII, 65; Duchess desires third Sister, VII, 640; Jeanne Lepeintre, Sister Servant in Saint-

Fargeau, VIII, 502; several young women from Saint-Fargeau apply to Daughters of Charity, VII, 64; legacy to Crécy house from Dean of Saint-Fargeau, uncle of Fr. Petit, VIII, 363–64, 501.

Saint-Félix (Antoine-François de), Archbishop of Myra - Biographical data, V, 103; death, funeral services, V, 103–04.

Saint-Fiacre - Br. Servin travels there, VIII, 486.

Saint-Floran (Abbé de), Councillor at Parlement - Member of Tuesday Conferences, II, 265.

Saint-Florent-lez-Saumur, village, today part of Saumur - Abbot of Saint-Florent, III, 235.

Saint-Flour, town in Cantal - Bishops: see Charles de **Noailles**, Jacques de **Montrouge**; two Sisters from Saint-Flour on retreat at Motherhouse of Daughters of Charity, VI, 341; other mention, VII, 327.

Saint-Frambourg, commune, today, part of Villers-Saint-Frambourg - See **Robin** (Philippe).

Saint-François, monastery - Question of placing it under direction of Archbishop of Paris, II, 105.

Saint François-de-Paule, church in Tours - Mme Goussault receives Communion there, I, 194.

Saint-Germain, faubourg - Archbishop of Myra buried there, V, 103.

Saint-Germain-des-Prés, abbey in Paris - Henri de Bourbon, Abbot: see **Bourbon** (Henri de); question of appointing Officialis to act as agent with regard to differences between Saint-Geneviève Abbey and Chancelade, IV, 68; other mention, III, 383.

Saint-Germain-en-Laye, town in Yvelines - Mission given in Saint-Germain, I, 411, 421, 422, 441, 448; XI, 255; death of Louis XIII: see **Louis XIII**; Court in Saint-Germain, III, 393; XIIIa, 137; Sister Jeanne Dalmagne, servant in Saint-Germain: see **Dalmagne**; journeys Saint Vincent made there, I, 493; II, 435; III, 369, 393, 408; XII, 212.

Establishment of Charity, I, 411; composition, I, 495; President: see **Chaumont** (Mme de); Saint Vincent wants Saint Louise to go to Saint-Germain to organize Charity, I, 411, 494, 495; asks her who is being sent there, II, 327; tells her whom to send, II, 328; other mentions, II, 399–400, 463; III, 410, 514; VI, 192; X, 533; XIIIa, 237, 295.

Daughters of Charity in Saint-Germain: Ladies ask Saint Vincent for Sister, I, 411; arrival of two Sisters, I, 423;

Élisabeth Martin sent for visitation, II, 667; Sisters usually faithful to prayer, X, 484; Sister from Saint-Germain on retreat at Motherhouse, III, 232; sick Sister, V, 426; convalescing, V, 427; Mlle d'Anse intends to speak to Queen about needs of Saint-Germain Sisters, VI, 652. Sisters serving in Saint-Germain: see **Angiboust** (Barbe), **Chefdeville** (Perrette), **Gesseaume** (Henriette), **Lepeintre**; other mentions, I, 439, 485, 537, 600–01; II, 187, 188, 601; III, 61, 444; IX, 155; XIIIb, 118, 140.

Saint-Germain-l'Auxerrois, parish in Paris - Pastor asks for Daughters of Charity, I, 364; Charity established, (1637), I, 365; XIIIb, 139; Marie Joly sent there; is withdrawn and assigned to Sedan: see **Joly** (Marie); Ladies request as replacement Sister who knows how to nurse sick and prepare remedies, II, 175; choice of replacement, II, 177, 178; Sisters faithful to meditation, X, 468; failure to rise at four o'clock because they work late in evening, X, 477; Sisters of Saint-Germain, II, 138, 600; III, 60; VIII, 190; other mentions, I, 267; II, 205; III, 378; X, 259; XII, 379; XIIIa, 15, 209; XIIIb, 206.

Saint-Gervais, parish in Paris - Establishment of Charity, XIIIb, 139; Daughters requested for Charity, II, 558; Sisters complain of being considered employees, II, 590; Sister Anne Hardemont named to visit Sisters, IX, 205–06; Sisters at Saint-Gervais, II, 600; III, 60: see **Gesse** (Catherine de); confessor: see **Guérin** (Fr.); Pastor: see **Talon** (Charles-François); parish is mentioned in Mme Goussault's will, XIIIb, 391, 393, 395; other mention, II, 175.

Saint-Gilles, village - Mission, IV, 113.

Saint-Girard, monastery in Limoges - Under direction of Abbot of Chancelade, III, 225.

Saint-Hippolyte, parish in Paris - Daughters of Charity serve there, XIIIb, 206.

Saint-Ilpize, parish in Paris - Daughters of Charity minister there, XIIIb, 206.

Saint-Ilpize, village in Haute-Loire - Mission given by Fr. Olier, I, 324–25.

Saint-Jacques Abbey - See **Monluc** (Mme de).

Saint-Jacques, faubourg - Malagasy boy at boarding school there, VI, 221; Visitation Monastery, XI, 171.

Saint-Jacques (M. de) - Recently deceased in Le Mans, III, 237.

Saint Jacques, parish - Preaching for needs of Picards, XII, 367.

Saint-Jacques (M. de) - Appointed administrator of hospital for galley convicts in Marseilles by Duc de Richelieu, VIII, 243.

Saint-Jacques-de-la-Boucherie, parish in Paris - Sister Anne Hardemont named to visit Sisters in parish, IX, 205; assignments and changes, I, 357, 411, 502; Sisters who ministered in parish: see **Louise** (Sister), **Dauteuil**, (Marthe); other mentions, II, 188; XIIIb, 206.

Saint-Jacques-de-l'Hôpital, hospital in Paris - X, 521.

Saint-Jacques-du-Haut-Pas, parish in Paris - Establishment of Charity, II, 641, 644; illness of Sister, IV, 416; Sister assigned here second time, VI, 513; other mention, I, 124; XIIIb, 205.

Saint-Jaume, seigneurie - Fief in which Luçon house of the Mission was situated, XIIIa, 320.

Saint-Jean, church in Lyons - XIIIa, 47.

Saint-Jean (Counts de), in Lyons - They give rectorship of Châtillon to Saint Vincent, XIIIa, 49; and, after him, to Louis Girard, XIIIa, 56.

Saint-Jean, hospital in Angers - Establishment of Daughters of Charity, XIIIb, 108–19.

Saint-Jean (Mother de), religious of Montmartre Abbey - III, 477.

Saint-Jean (Nicolas de), chaplain of Queen Anne of Austria - Retreat at Saint-Lazare, VI, 148; exchange of letters with Saint Vincent, VI, 390, 403; looks after Daughters of Charity sent to La Fère, VI, 66; X, 165; on behalf of Queen, requests them for Calais, XII, 20; accompanies Court to Sedan, VI, 368, 534; speaks to Queen about mission in Metz, VII, 136; Saint Vincent asks Superior of Marseilles house to give Saint-Jean hospitality, VIII, 298; other mentions, V, 644; VII, 126; VIII, 262, 276, 343.

Saint-Jean, parish in Arras - See ***Arras***.

Saint-Jean, parish in Joigny - XIIIb, 65.

Saint-Jean, parish in La Rochelle - Missionaries bound for Madagascar minister there, VIII, 561.

Saint-Jean, parish in Paris - XIIIa, 17–19.

Saint-Jean-Baptiste, hospital in Faubourg Saint-Germain-des-Prés-lez-Paris - Saint Vincent makes donation, XIIIa, 20–22.

Saint-Jean-d'Assé, village in Sarthe - VIII, 130.

Saint-Jean-de-Jerusalem (Order) - Noël Brulart de Sillery, priest of this Order, funds missions in Geneva diocese, VIII, 608–09.

Saint-Jean-de-Luz, town in Pyrénées-Atlantiques - Slaves from this town, VII, 196, 213; ship carrying Fr. Étienne, driven by storm onto coast of Spain, anchors in port, VIII, 239–40, 247, 249, 251, 256, 560–61, 564.

Saint-Jean-de-Maurienne, diocese - Bishop: see Paul Millet de **Châles**.

Saint-Jean-des-Bois, monastery in Oise - III, 513.

Saint-Jean-des-Vignes, monastery - XIIIb, 92.

Saint-Jean-en-Grève, parish in Paris - Problems involving Daughters of Charity, IV, 215, 217–18; Saint Vincent notifies Assistant Pastor of dispensation in process in Rome, VII, 360; letter to Saint Vincent from Pastor regarding Fr. Daisne, VII, 513; saint's response, VII, 528; other mentions, VIII, 98; XIIIb, 206.

Saint-Jeoire, town in Haute-Savoie - Prior proposes uniting parish to Congregation of the Mission, VIII, 67.

Saint John before the Latin Gate, church in Rome - Saint Vincent's response to Fr. Lebreton, II, 36.

Saint John Lateran (Chapter) - Canon makes retreat at Missionaries' house in Rome, VIII, 349.

Saint John Lateran Palace - Cardinal di Bagno offers to use influence to lodge Rome Missionaries there, VII, 40, 47.

Saint John Lateran, parish in Rome - Mission requested for parish, V, 595.

Saint-Joseph (Congregation) - See **Cretenet** (Jacques).

Saint-Joseph (Mother de), of Montmartre Abbey - III, 477.

Saint-Josse Abbey - See **Moreau** (Étienne).

Saint-Josse, parish in Paris - Pastors of Saint-Josse: see **Abelly**, **Pique**.

Saint-Julien - See ***Sancey***.

Saint-Julien, church - Site of Saint Vincent's ordination in Château-l'Évêque, XIIIa, 7.

Saint-Jure (Jean-Baptiste de), Jesuit - Contacts with Saint Vincent, IX, 89.

Saint-Just (Abbé de), Vicar-General of Lyons - Saint Vincent points out drawbacks of several Communities having same or similar names, VI, 516.

Saint-Laurent Island - Name formerly given to Madagascar, III, 278, 331, 544; IV, 72, 92, 107, 109, 337; V, 305, 431, 551, 577; VI, 210; VII, 58; VIII, 146, 282, 552, 562, 573, 586, 616; XIIIa, 358, 361.

Saint-Laurent, parish, today, within Paris - Establishment of Charity, I, 283, 296; **Guillaume de Lestocq**, Pastor: see this name; problems with another parish, III, 298; transfer of Sisters' Motherhouse to Saint-Laurent parish: see **Daughters**

of Charity; interment of Saint Louise's body in Saint-Laurent Church, VIII, 312; Daughters of Charity entrusted with poor and schools of parish, I, 318, 391, 502: see Sisters **Delaître**, **Jeanne**, **Lauraine** (Marguerite), **Marie**; after Council deliberation, Saint Vincent decides that two Sisters from Motherhouse will visit sick parishioners several times a week after dinner, XIIIb, 254–56; Saint-Laurent fair, III, 369; IX, 32; contract for place at fair, XIIIa, 305; other mentions, I, 134, 312, 483, 494; IV, 380; V, 344; VIII, 198; X, 472.

Saint-Lazare, priory - *Chronological order of events*: house was founded to take in lepers, XI, 13; XIIIa, 410; with time, it took name of priory, I, 248; XIIIa, 410; formerly administered by secular priests appointed by Bishop of Paris, I, 243; XIIIa, 478–79; priory always depended, in both spiritual and temporal matters, on Bishop of Paris, who never renounced rights, I, 149, 244, 248, 540; XIIIa, 277–78, 290–91, 478–79.

Between 1342–49: Fulco de Chanac, Bishop of Paris, removes administration of priory from secular priests, gives it to other priests, I, 243.

Between 1513 -17: Poncher, Bishop of Paris, entrusts administration of priory to Reformed Canons Regular of Saint-Augustine, I, 243, 248; VIII, 605; XIIIa, 410, 479.

1611: Henri de Gondi, Bishop of Paris, names Adrien Le Bon Prior, I, 248, 540; XIIIa, 277.

Around 1620: Although not required, Adrien Le Bon gets letter of appointment from Court of Rome for office of Prior, in order to be more sure of retaining position, I, 244.

1630–31: Measures taken by Adrien Le Bon and Guillaume de Lestocq, Pastor of Saint-Laurent, to get Saint Vincent to accept union of priory to Congregation of the Mission, I, 134–37, 248–49; V, 536; VIII, 434; XIIIa, 271–74.

1631: Petition of monks of Saint-Victor against union (December 17), I, 151; VII, 502.

1632: Contract of union of Saint-Lazare Priory to Congregation of the Mission (January 7), XIIIa, 263–71, 281, 285, 289, 476: see also **Le Bon**; at times Adrien Le Bon regrets having ceded priory to Saint Vincent, XIIIb, 279; monks of Saint-Lazare grant power of attorney in their name to carry out all formalities of union (January 7–8), XIIIa, 476; Archbishop of Paris approves contract of union (January 8), XIIIa, 275–80, 289–90, 294, 477–78, 485; Letters Patent by which King approves union (January), XIIIa, 280–83; consent of merchants and magistrates of Paris (March 24), VII, 502; XIIIa, 284, 289, 472, 477, 485; petition of monks of Saint-Victor to Parlement to prevent registration of letters of union (May 13), I, 151; XIIIa, 472; Pastors of Paris register complaint, I, 149; XIIIa, 472; Fr. Pillé encourages Saint Vincent in midst of lawsuit, II, 382; XIIIa, 377; services Saint-Cyran renders him on this occasion: see **Saint-Cyran**; Parlement declares that, not withstanding opposition, it will review agreement and Letters Patent for registration (August 21); orders registration of Letters Patent (September 7), I, 540; IV, 297; VIII, 434; XIIIa, 284, 289–90, 294, 477, 478, 485; but requires Saint Vincent to obtain new letters from King and Archbishop of Paris, I, 151; VII, 327, 502; XIIIa, 284, 472; declaration by which Adrien Le Bon renews Act of January 7, 1632, but without requesting union in Court of Rome (December 29), XIIIa, 283–86, 294; letters by which Archbishop of Paris approves new act of union (December 31), XIIIa, 286–93, 294, 472, 486; reserving to self all spiritual and temporal jurisdiction and authority concerning priory, XIIIa, 278; Saint Vincent dispensed from obligation of making annual report to Archbishop, II, 507; IV, 75, 409, 427; XIIIa, 292.

1632 or **1633**: Nicolas Maheut, sub-Prior of Saint-Lazare, dies of plague, I, 186.

1632–34: Saint Vincent's proceedings in Rome to obtain confirmation of union of Saint-Lazare to the Mission, I, 148, 242–44, 245; opposition to union of Saint-Lazare to Mission, I, 149, 151, 267.

1633: Letters Patent of King in favor of union (January), XII, 374; XIIIa, 293–95, 473, 478, 486; registration by Parlement (March 21), VII, 503; XII, 374–75; XIIIa, 473, 478, 486; report of notification of letters of union given to monks at Saint-Lazare (April 26), XIIIa, 478; contract for place at fair (May 1633), XIIIa, 305–06; registration by *Chambre des Comptes* (October 11), VII, 503; XIIIa, 473, 477–78, 486.

1634: *Cour des Aides* does likewise (January 9), VII, 503; XIIIa, 473, 477–78, 486; petition to Pope Urban VIII to confirm letters of union, I, 248; XIIIa, 409.

1635: Confirmation of union by Urban VIII, whose Bulls are not expedited (March 15), VII, 503–04; XIIIa, 409, 414, 473, 479, 486.

1636: Saint-Lazare transformed into camp at approach of Spanish army, arms distributed to soldiers; Saint Vincent prepares to evacuate house (August 15), I, 331; case of plague at Saint-Lazare (October), I, 348, 350.

1637: Epidemic of dysentery (August), I, 380.

1639: Consecration of Pavillon, Bishop of Alet, in Saint-Lazare church (August 22), I, 413–14.

1640: Canonical visitation of house (August-September), II, 113, 118, 127, 129.

1641: Canonical visitation by Fr. Lambert, II, 237.

1642: Superiors' meeting at Saint-Lazare (October), XIIIa, 322.

1644: All is going so well that Saint-Lazare seems like little paradise (February), II, 492; all is going well, II, 535.

1644–46: Saint-Lazare receives no help because of its perceived wealth, II, 514, 624.

1645: Erection of seminary (Petit Saint-Lazare or Saint-Charles) at end of Saint-Lazare enclosure on rue du Faubourg-Saint-Denis; construction of building for ordinands on site of small infirmary, II, 585; Saint Vincent later calls it "new building," XI, 336; property surrounded by walls, II, 586, 589, 607.

1649: Six hundred soldiers, billeted at Saint-Lazare, pillage house (January), III, 394, 405; XII, 48; personnel of Saint-Lazare reduced to be able to assist more than 2,000 poor; seminary transferred to Richelieu; only seven or eight priests, 18 or 19 students, and a few Brothers remain (February), III, 409, 413; penury of house because of troubles, III, 394, 499.

1651: Superiors' meeting (July) at Saint-Lazare, XIIIa, 374.

1652: Poverty into which troubles have thrown house, IV, 19, 328–29, 334, 371–72, 450, 452, 454; Saint Vincent speaks of sending part of seminary to Le Mans to relieve Saint-Lazare (January), IV, 307; poor refugee priests in Paris receive hospitality at Saint-Lazare (June), IV, 399; uneasiness at passage of armies along length of enclosure (July), IV, 409, 411; need for armed protection, IV, 411–12.

1653: City of Paris intends to pasture, in Saint-Lazare enclosure, animals destined to feed inhabitants (April), IV, 548.

1655: Alexander VII approves union of Saint-Lazare Priory to Congregation of the Mission; text of Bull (April 18), XIIIa, 409–16, 473, 479; Brief *Ex Commissa Nobis* by which Alexander VII approves vows made in Congregation of the Mission, XIIIa, 417–19, 420; assembled members of Saint-Lazare house accept Brief (October 22), XIIIa, 419–21.

1656: Renewal of vows (January 25) after *Ex Commissa Nobis,* V, 501.

1658: Augustinians of Sainte-Geneviève Abbey have not withdrawn claims to Saint-Lazare; await death of Saint Vincent to act, VII, 261–62, 326; Saint Vincent urges Rome to expedite Bulls of union (August-September), VII, 261, 284, 292; receives them (October), VII, 318; loss of Orsigny farm, VII, 265–66, 422–25.

1658–59: Prepares fulmination of Bulls, VII, 318, 326, 360, 508.

1659: Attestations from Pastors that Priests of the Mission from Saint-Lazare have given missions in parishes of Paris diocese, XIIIa, 479; request to obtain fulmination (April 8), XIIIa, 473–74; ecclesiastical court of Paris orders enquiry *de commodo et incommodo* (April 23), XIIIa, 474; ecclesiastical court posts public notices informing all who might claim rights or interest in fulmination (April 30), XIIIa, 474; report of public notices (May 2); new ordinance of ecclesiastical court to summon by similar public notices those claiming rights (May 10); report of execution of ordinance (May 12); Officialis decides to go to Saint-Lazare to draw up report of state of premises and to hear witnesses (May 21); report of subpoena of witnesses (May or June); Officialis goes to Saint-Lazare, hears five witnesses, and draws up report of state of premises (June 27), XIIIa, 475; Officialis orders all documents to be sent to ecclesiastical court to be ordered as thought proper (June 28), XIIIa, 475; decision of fulmination (July 21), XIIIa, 472, 487; Saint Vincent takes possession of Saint-Lazare (August 7), VIII, 78; program aims at making all priests qualified for both missions and seminaries, VIII, 90, 91, 93; XII, 234–35.

1660: Consecration of Bishop of Oloron (April 11) and Bishop of Chalon (May 9) in Saint-Lazare church, VIII, 339, 344.

Seigneury, property, dependencies, revenues; jurisdiction of bailiff, I, 379: see **Le Gras** (Michel); justice, II, 151; IV, 158; feudal dues, II, 151; church, XIIIa, 373; Saint-Lazare church exempt from tax on chapels, III, 569; Saint Vincent requests and obtains that it not be numbered among stations of Jubilee (1656), XI, 301; burials, II, 388; in church of Saint-Lazare, III, 39: see **Le Bon**; new building, XI, 336; small infirmary, II, 585; Saint-Luc Infirmary, XIIIa, 207; masons work continually to repair buildings, VIII, 49; garden, VIII, 81; XI, 228; enclosure of grounds, II, 586, 589, 607; VIII, 119; wall, XI, 228; mills, I, 355; parlor, XII, 19; room to lock up offenders, VII, 225; XII, 54; main building, XI, 236; XII, 242; needy state of house, III, 115; property rentals, II, 341; country house, VIII, 119; Rougemont farm: see ***Rougemont***.

Donations (1640), II, 119, 144: See **Sillery** (Noël Brulart de); attraction of stay at Saint-Lazare, VI, 532; XI, 228–29; repayment of debts, II, 147–48; its poverty, II, 542, 624; IV, 19, 328–29, 334, 371–72, 450, 454; V, 170, 217; VI, 624, 634; VII, 242; many expenses, takes in little, VI, 486; obligation for individual houses to help Motherhouse, VI, 181; Saint-Lazare owes money to Richelieu house, IV, 321.

Monks of old Saint-Lazare: those who signed contract of union of priory to Congregation of the Mission, XIIIa, 263; Bull of union guarantees payment of pensions, VII, 359;

XIIIa, 265–69, 285, 290: see also **Cousin** (Claude), **Le Bon**, **Flamignon**, **Maheut**, **Morennes**; community: fidelity of Brothers to particular examen, X, 485; Brother doorkeepers, I, 478.

Some entries into Internal Seminary, I, 304; number of seminarians, I, 528; II, 360, 541; III, 108; V, 75; VI, 257, 620; VII, 27; number increases, II, 144; VI, 162, 612–13; seminary begins to fill up, V, 241; rather full, V, 574; full, VI, 162, 265; gift of Commander de Sillery to Saint-Lazare for Internal Seminary, II, 144; seminarians form association to encourage devotion to Blessed Virgin, III, 438; examination of seminarians by Superior General and Assistants, XIIIa, 372; seminarians no longer permitted to go into town, good results of prohibition, V, 349–50; seminarian's time prolonged six months because of disobedience: see **Boucher** (Philippe-Ignace); directors of Internal Seminary: see **Alméras** (René the younger), **Dehorgny**, **Delespiney**, **Dufour** (Claude), **Jolly** (Edme), **La Salle** (Jean de).

Advice of Saint Vincent to students, XI, 23–24, 115–17; XII, 57–58; directors of students, IV, 355, 528; XIIIa, 372; professors: see **Crowley** [**Cruoly**], **Damiens**, **Dufour**, **McEnery** [**Ennery**], **Éveillard**, **Gilles**, **Guillot**, **La Brière**, **Marthe**, **Watebled** (Pierre); number of students, I, 528; II, 433; IV, 528; V, 76; VI, 267, 277, 620; VII, 555; VIII, 38, 92; they go to Bons-Enfants for theology (1639), I, 528; theology taught at Saint-Lazare (1642), II, 360; author explained without dictating to students, II, 240–41, 269–70; textbooks: see **Bécan**, **Binsfeld**; examinations, XIIIa, 372; theological debates, II, 251, 433; training in preaching, XIIIa, 373; decision that students no longer communicate with older confreres, XIIIa, 372; on class days, recreation taken in garden, not in enclosure, XI, 187; outings and vacations, VIII, 119; quarrel among students, XII, 53–54; death of student: see **Jamain**; five new priests (March 1651), IV, 168; 35 priests at Saint-Lazare (March 1652), IV, 329; patients in infirmary, II, 237; IV, 425, 429, 473, 477; VIII, 118–19, 129, 189, 395, 397, 462; only one student is ill, V, 610; Missionaries worn out from work of missions, VI, 382.

Exercises and customs: order of day, I, 554; Archbishop of Paris requires recitation of Divine Office, XIIIa, 278, 291; at Saint-Lazare, not very faithful to Office in common, XII, 269–71, 287, 348; recited poorly, XII, 264, 269; Saint Vincent does not agree to having confreres wear amice and domino in Saint-Lazare church, I, 136; but accepts chanting Solemn Mass and Vespers on Sundays and feast days, I, 137; XII, 264, 270; hour for High Mass on Sundays, XIIIa, 372; poverty of vestments, II, 310.

Repetition of Prayer, Conferences, Meals, Reading at table: see these words; list of conferences given at Saint-Lazare 1650–60, XII, 405–38; outsiders go into refectory on their own, as if invited, XI, 101; recreations, V, 384; Councils, XII, 120; Saint Vincent sometimes consults senior confreres, XII, 234; training sessions in **Preaching**, **Catechism**, **Controversy**, **Cases of Conscience**, Moral **Theology**, Administration of **Sacraments**, conferences on **Holy Scripture**: see these words; Community retreats, I, 216, 289, 304, 331, 587; II, 337; V, 447; VII, 304; in several groups, III, 246; X, 509; canonical visitations, II, 113, 118, 127, 129, 237.

Missionaries at Saint-Lazare wear rosary on belt, III, 376; bell is rung to announce arrival of visitor, IV, 221; someone makes rounds to ask each one what is needed, X, 231, 242; XI, 155; XII, 320; practices of courtesy and mutual respect customary at Saint-Lazare, IX, 121, 126; prevailing practice to assure fidelity to prayer, X, 477–78; current affairs not discussed, II, 45; reserve with which topics are discussed, III, 327; IV, 352–53.

Ministries: missions - V, 109, 363, 584, 588, 595, 598, 610, 627; VI, 277, 382; VII, 73, 74, 84, 92, 125, 148, 481; VIII, 230.

Retreat ministry: retreatants, I, 159, 204, 214, 293; II, 28, 482; VIII, 61, 124, 488, 490, 496, 512, 522, 549; XI, 146, 200; XII, 138, 256–57; XIIIa, 195; mention of conference, XII, 437; see also **Machon**, **Pavillon**; retreatants received free of charge, XI, 13; good food must be provided for boarders, XII, 386; Claude de Chandenier offers Saint-Pourçain Priory to Saint Vincent to help with retreat expenses, VII, 314; advice for retreat directors, XII, 138–39; XI, 142–48; large number of retreatants at Saint-Lazare, XI, 12, 214; coming from farthest part of Champagne, XI, 16; Bishops, Chief Justice, Doctor come for retreat, I, 159; XI, 200; soldiers, XI, 12, 15; many priests, XI, 13; Community members and others discerning vocation, XI, 13, 15; young Lutheran girl, in footman's attire, comes to make retreat, I, 294; good results of retreats, II, 288; XI, 13, 15, 214–15; XIIIa, 149; cordiality of Saint-Lazare house contributed to edification and sometimes to conversion, IX, 121; dedication to Saint Vincent of *Ten Meditations* of retreatant at Saint-Lazare, XIIIa, 148.

Retreats for ordinands: Archbishop of Paris requires all ordinands to make preparatory retreat at Saint-Lazare, I, 181, 255, 516; XIIIa, 278–79, 291–92, 298, 413; not only those of his diocese, but, in general, all those of kingdom who receive Orders in Paris, II, 36; no exception for those with degrees, I, 516; extends this to clerics who present themselves for Minor Orders, III, 235; Bishop of Beauvais endeavors to have Bishops close to Paris send ordinands to Saint-Lazare, I, 531; ordinations at Saint-Lazare, III, 137; IV, 320; number and length of ordination retreats annually; average number of retreatants, VII, 314; VIII, 124; exceptionally, none for June 1656, V, 622, 623, 627; work with ordinands at beginning and end of Lent 1654, V, 110.

Mention of certain retreats, I, 235, 237, 293, 498; IV, 256, 292, 341; V, 148, 363, 573, 575, 584, 588, 592, 594; VI, 277, 389; VII, 27, 36, 125, 128, 148, 481, 498, 599; VIII, 124, 221, 230, 536; **Noël Brulart de Sillery** makes ordination retreat: see **Sillery** (Noël); among ordinands are Bachelors, Licentiates, and Doctors, I, 516; XI, 9; XII, 22; priories offered to Saint Vincent; revenues will help defray expenses of retreats for ordinands: see ***Bruyères-le-Chatel***, **Saint-Aignan** (M. de), ***Saint-Pourçain***; Archbishop of Paris comes to see ordinands, I, 471.

Preachers for ordinands, IV, 320, 341; V, 573, 575–76; VII, 27, 125: see **Bossuet**, **Caulet** (François-Étienne de), **Sevin**; directors, IV, 121, 341, 573; V, 588; XI, 143, 146; Saint Vincent obtains Brief of indulgences for ordinands, VII, 498; good results of these retreats, I, 203–04; edification of Carthusian during retreat, III, 204; Saint Vincent entreats community to give good example, XI, 9; Missionaries' humble, simple way of acting edifies ordinands, XII, 168.

Canon de Mareschal asks Saint Vincent to welcome ordinand for retreat, VIII, 417; Saint informs Chapter of Paris of seminarian on retreat, whom he believes should not be called to Orders, VI, 494; see **Ordinands**.

Leprosarium: no lepers at Saint-Lazare in 1632, XIIIa, 264; none for long time, I, 249; XIIIa, 410–11; lepers at Saint-Lazare, I, 273.

House of detention: brother of M. Barreau enclosed at Saint-Lazare, V, 149; Saint Vincent refuses mother's request to incarcerate son on retreat at Saint-Lazare, XIIIa, 195; Marquise d'Esne requests that son be locked up at Saint-Lazare, VIII, 419; escapc of detainee, I, 273; Saint Vincent obtains release of M. Demurard's son, unjustly detained, VII, 619; Parisian magistrate praises good order reigning in house, XI, 17; Saint Vincent recommends ministry to incarcerated, XI, 16–19; XII, 78; complains that boarders are not fed well enough, XI, 299–300; other mention, I, 479.

Asylum for mentally ill: two or three patients in 1632; this, more than anything else, made Saint Vincent stay at Saint-Lazare, XI, 17; **Tuesday Conferences**, conferences for **Ladies of Charity** of **Hôtel-Dieu**: see these words.

Miscellanea: Rumor circulating about Saint-Lazare, I,

464; petition for compensation for land unlawfully seized, III, 337–38; hospitality for outsiders who came for retreat, but only for eight days, V, 31, 597; VII, 375–76; VIII, 61, 124; exceptions: see **Chandenier** (Claude and Louis de), **Vincy** (M. de); servants, IV, 499; fidelity to particular examen, X, 485; meetings of Pastors at Saint-Lazare, I, 201, 214; of Doctors assembled to discuss current questions: see also **Jansenism**; Motherhouse must serve as model for other houses, XI, 196; Superior of house and its history, VIII, 605; other mentions, I, *xxx,* 243, 308, 452; X, 559, 581; XIIIa, 110.

Saint-Léonard, town in Haute-Vienne - VIII, 411.

Saint-Léonard de Chaumes [***Chaulmes***], abbey in Vérines (Charente-Maritime) - Saint Vincent assumes lease of abbey, XIIIa, 8; Act of Resignation of abbey by Archbishop of Aix in favor of Saint Vincent, XIIIa, 12–16; legal problem concerning transfer of abbey (May 28, 1611), XIIIa, 17–20; Saint Vincent, Abbot of Saint-Léonard, XIIIa, 20, 24; Act of Resignation of abbey by Saint Vincent in favor of François de Lanson, XIIIa, 42–44; other mention, I, 15.

Saint-Leu, parish in Paris - Saint Vincent plans to give companion to Sister Barbe to help with large number of patients, I, 371; Daughters of Charity serve sick of parish, I, 407; II, 600; III, 60; IX, 206: see Sisters **Barbe**, **Jacqueline**, **Marthe** (**Dauteuil**); establishment of Charity, XIIIb, 139; Mlle Desbordes, treasurer of Charity: see **Desbordes** (Mlle); other mentions, II, 48; XIIIb, 206.

Saint-Leu d'Essérent, village in Oise - I, 282, 338.

Saint-Livrade-sur-Lot, town in Lot-et-Garonne - presence of Benoît Bécu at nearby Notre-Dame-de-la-Rose, II, 57.

Saint-Louis (Congregation), branch of Dominicans in France - See **Dominicans**.

Saint-Louis, hospital in Paris - Filled with plague-stricken, I, 114–15; priest from Saint-Nicolas is taken there, I, 128; Saint Vincent worries about sick Sister there, I, 348; she survives, I, 349; Marguerite Naseau dies there, IX, 64, 66, 194, 473; X, 82; other mentions, I, 188, 241.

Saint-Louis (Jesuits), in Paris - See **Jesuits**.

Saint-Louis, parish in Paris - IV, 334; XIIIb, 206.

Saint-Louis-des-Français (Community), in Rome - Six Oratorians are part of it, III, 613–14; Saint Vincent fears offending Community by requesting Saint-Yves Church for Rome Missionaries, II, 296, 416, 472; proposal that priests and revenue of Saint-Yves Church, transferred to Saint-Louis,

XIIIa, 332; be transferred to Congregation of the Mission, XIIIa, 332–33.

Saint-Luc (M. de) - Person suggested to discuss dangers of Huguenots in Montauban, IV, 457–58; sent with army to Montauban to repress advances of Huguenots, VIII, 257.

Saint-Lyé, village in Aube - Mission postponed, I, 521.

Saint-Malo, town in Ille-et-Vilaine - Bishops: see Achille de Harlay de **Sancy**, Ferdinand de **Neufville**; Pastor: see Guillaume **Le Gouverneur**; Saint-Malo Seminary: see ***Saint-Méen***; Daughters of Charity requested for hospital, IV, 298; V, 628; VI, 75; slaves from Saint-Malo, V, 327, 404; VII, 519; merchants of Saint-Malo, VIII, 290, 565; other mentions, XIIIa, 369, 397, 424. See also ***Plancoët*** (Notre-Dame de).

Saint-Mamès (Chapter), in Langres - Proceedings against Oratorians regarding Saint-Nicolas de Grosse-Sauve Priory, XIIIa, 67.

Saint-Mandé (Jérôme de l'Arche, Seigneur de) - III, 253.

Saint-Mandé (Mlle de), Lady of Charity - III, 262.

Saint-Mandé (Marie de Fortia, Mme de), Lady of Charity, wife of Jérôme de Saint-Mandé - Support for ministry of Foundlings, III, 253–54; IV, 193–94.

Saint-Marc - Prior, VIII, 197, 218.

Saint-Marceau [***Saint-Marcel***], faubourg in Paris - Confraternity of Charity, V, 243; possible house there for foundlings, IV, 177; other mention, I, 427; IV, 177.

Saint-Marcel, hospital in Paris - Took in plague-stricken, I, 115.

Saint-Martin, abbey in Pontoise - Saint Vincent visits Archbishop of Paris there, XIIIa, 211.

Saint-Martin, church in Montmirail - XIIIa, 63.

Saint-Martin (César de and Louis de) - Executors of Saint Vincent's will, XIIIa, 99–100.

Saint-Martin (Jean de), Councillor at Presidial Court of Dax, brother of Canon de Saint-Martin - Contacts with Saint Vincent, I, 15–16; in Paris, I, 58; saint sends him small picture, I, 332; asks help to provide for needs of his family, I, 84–85; XIIIa, 76; two letters from Saint Vincent concerning captivity in Tunis found among papers, I, 1; VIII, 313; other mentions, I, 412; IV, 467, 469.

Saint-Martin (Fr. de), Canon of Dax - Biographical data, V, 569; VIII, 313; XI, 298; correspondence with Saint Vincent concerning captivity letters, I, 1; VIII, 313; Bro. Ducournau writes him on same subject, VIII, 599; in Paris, I, 85; assists Saint Vincent's family, IV, 515; V, 569; XI, 298.

Saint-Martin (Fr. de), Chaplain of King of Poland - VI, 5.

Saint-Martin (M. de) - Lays claim to Archdeaconry of Alet, II, 221.

Saint-Martin, parish in Buenens - XIIIa, 44, 46, 47–48, 57.

Saint-Martin, parish in Paris - Daughters of Charity serving poor of parish, V, 579; VI, 66: see **Jeanne** (Sister).

Saint-Martin, priory in Dreux - Offered to Saint Vincent, V, 536–37.

Saint-Martin, priory in Ham - VI, 438.

Saint-Martin, roadstead near La Rochelle - Departure of ships, VI, 12, 15, 224.

Saint-Martin d'Agès (M. de), son of Jean de Saint-Martin, Councillor - Discovers among father's papers two letters in which Saint Vincent writes of captivity in Tunis, I, 1; VIII, 313; in Paris, XIIIa, 76.

Saint Mary Major, Basilica in Rome - Papal Briefs issued from there, XIIIa, 419, 482.

Saint-Maur (Benedictines of) - Bishop of Saint-Malo asked General of Benedictines to put reformed monks into Saint-Méen Abbey, but he lacked subjects, III, 54; question of naming General to act as agent with regard to differences between Sainte-Geneviève Abbey and Chancelade, IV, 68; Saint Vincent writes to Superior General about Saint-Ouen affair, IV, 197; Benedictines raise opposition to union of conventual table of Saint-Méen Abbey: see ***Saint-Méen***; Reformed Benedictines of Brittany and Lorraine are ordered to unite with Saint-Maur, II, 307; Saint Vincent writes to Fr. Jolly about difficulties in this affair, VII, 162; other mention, III, 383.

Saint-Maur-les-Fossés, town near Paris - Fr. de Mesgrigny goes there with Fr. Brandon, II, 38.

Saint-Maurice, island in Indian Ocean, today Mauritius - IV, 444.

Saint-Médard, parish in Paris - Daughters of Charity minister there, V, 579; other mention, XIIIb, 206.

Saint-Méen, town in Ille-et-Vilaine - Postulants, III, 336; Abbot of Mouzon in Saint-Méen, IV, 522, 577; Priests of the Mission ministering in Saint-Méen: letters of saint to Missionaries, II, 621; IV, 356; V, 613; VII, 44, 524, 577: see **Bourdet** (Jean), **Codoing**, **Thibault** (Louis), **Serre**, **Plunket**; of Saint-Méen

Missionaries to Saint Vincent: see **Serre**; mention of letter from Missionary to Saint Vincent, V, 613.

Foundation of Saint-Méen Seminary, under direction of Priests of Mission, with conventual revenue of Benedictine abbey, II, 621; III, 51, 111; Benedictines raise opposition, II, 621; Parlement of Rennes sides with them, III, 111; Saint Vincent prefers to lose it than to go to court, II, 621; in face of entreaties of Bishop of Saint-Malo, and so as not to reveal his motive, he asks his priests not to abandon abbey, III, 33; approves of and justifies rights of Bishop of Saint-Malo, III, 42–44, 52–55, 111–13; VII, 162; misunderstanding by S. Ropartz, III, 115; Priests of the Mission expelled from abbey by Parlement of Rennes; proceedings to reestablish them; King's Council sets aside decision of Parlement and reinstates Missionaries, III, 12–13, 25, 26, 33, 43, 51; Bishop interdicts Saint-Méen Church; forbids people from entering, under penalty of excommunication, as long as Benedictines stay there, III, 33; Saint Vincent writes to Fr. Bourdet, Superior of seminary, to remain at his post; Fr. Bourdet goes off, leaving Fr. de Beaumont there alone, III, 42; abbey invaded by order of Parlement of Rennes; Fr. de Beaumont seized and put into prison in leg irons; Saint Vincent asks Chief Justice of Parlement of Rennes for his release, III, 53; release of Fr. de Beaumont, III, 53, 56, 65; Missionaries reinstated in abbey by King's officers, III, 83, 94, 110.

Proceedings in Rome to obtain union of conventual revenues of abbey to seminary, III, 110–13; VI, 365, 451; VII, 635; approval of union, VII, 219; text of Bulls, XIIIa, 423–29; Procurator General of Benedictines opposes sending them, VII, 162; Saint Vincent has Bulls; plans to send them to Dol, VII, 252; proclamation of Bulls, VII, 411.

Strained relations between Bishop of Saint-Malo and Missionaries, III, 115; Saint Vincent reprimands Louis Serre, Superior, for having promised six months' hospitality in seminary to former Rector of Mordec, V, 597; order for Divine Office, XII, 268; Missionaries have obligation of reciting Office in choir and of chanting High Mass several times a week, in addition to Sundays and feast days, XII, 270; missions: V, 109, 628; VI, 302; VII, 131, 486; seminary is for "young boys," III, 372; chant and ceremonies taught there, VII, 524, 578; number of seminarians, III, 175; VII, 44; Missionaries hear confessions in their church because of pilgrims, IV, 313.

Fr. Bourdet, Superior, agrees to serve at Notre-Dame de Plancoët chapel; Saint Vincent reprimands him for this, II, 656; serving this chapel impedes ministries; Saint Vincent urges Fr. Codoing to continue both missions and seminary, enlisting, when needed, help of priests from outside, III, 141; plan for Internal Seminary for postulants from Brittany, VII, 120; canonical visitation by Fr. Portail, II, 663, 666, 668; III, 84; by Saint Vincent, III, 409, 418, 419, 424; by Fr. Berthe, V, 502; VI, 382; by Fr. Dehorgny, VIII, 131.

Sick Missionaries, IV, 320, 372; assignments and changes, III, 457; VI, 527–28; list of Superiors and history of house, VIII, 613; Saint-Méen Missionaries: see **Beaumont**, **Bourdet** (Jean), **Bureau** (**Beaure**), **Caset** (Michel), **Codoing**, **Goret**, **Guy** (Bro.), **Joseph** (Bro.), **Laisné** (Pierre), **Le Boysne**, **Patriarche**, **Plunket**, **Rivet** (François), **Serre**, **Servin**, **Thibault** (Louis), **Turbot**, **White** [**Le Blanc**] (George); other mention, II, 664.

Saint-Merri [***Saint-Médéric***], parish in Paris - Fr. Duhamel, Pastor, IV, 593; establishment of Charity, XIIIb, 139; establishment of Daughters of Charity, II, 600; III, 60; other mentions, I, 267; XIIIa, 8, 16; XIIIb, 206.

Saint-Mesmes (Marquis de) - Member of association against dueling, V, 617.

Saint-Michel (Order) - Philippe-Emmanuel de Gondi was knight of this Order, I, 40.

Saint-Michel, section of Toulouse - Fr. De Sergis was being asked to give examination there, I, 518.

Saint-Mihiel, town in Meuse - Terrible misery; distribution of aid by Missionaries, II, 30, 46, 72–73, 93, 243–44; gratitude of authorities, II, 408; journey of Fr. Lambert to Saint-Mihiel, II, 324.

Saint-Nazaire, town in Loire-Atlantique - Madagascar Missionaries pass through Saint-Nazaire, V, 280–81; VI, 149–50, 159–60; VIII, 240, 558; XI, 336–37.

Saint-Nicaise, abbey in Reims - VIII, 29.

Saint-Nicolas, abbey in Angers - Abbé de Saint-Cyran establishes reform there, XIIIa, 131.

Saint-Nicolas, chapel in Montmirail - Establishment of Charity there, XIIIb, 32.

Saint-Nicolas, house in Rome - Lodging Missionaries there is discussed, VII, 268–69.

Saint-Nicolas, village in Lorraine - Birthplace of Marguerite François, XIIIb, 118.

Saint-Nicolas Community [**Nicolaïtes**] - Founded by Fr. Bourdoise, XI, 185; members do not take vows, XIIIa, 376; priest of Saint-Nicolas hospitalized with plague, I, 128; letter from Saint Vincent to Community, I, 535; Ambassador of

Turkey requests Priests of the Mission or of Saint-Nicolas, I, 246; aid to destitute in environs of Paris during Fronde, IV, 473, 520; boarders of Community, I, 472, 535; II, 174–75; inherit furnishings of Archbishop of Trabzon, XIIIa, 196; have large number of holy functions, V, 221; staff elementary schools, XII, 138; direct seminary, XII, 234; practical formation given, VII, 268; X, 502; XIIIa, 201; Saint Vincent's esteem for this Community, II, 175; V, 221; XI, 185–86; XIIIa, 201; Michel Le Gras in Saint-Nicolas Seminary: see **Le Gras** (Michel); other mentions, I, 178, 536, 549, 573; XIIIb, 392.

Saint-Nicolas-de-Champvant - See ***Champvant***.

Saint-Nicolas de Grosse-Sauve, priory in Langres diocese - Power of Attorney for Saint Vincent to take possession, XIIIa, 66.

Saint-Nicolas-des-Champs, parish in Paris - Fr. Pillé, non-beneficed priest at Saint-Nicolas-des-Champs, II, 365; Daughters of Charity here faithful to hour of rising, X, 477; other mentions, I, 64; XIIIa, 15.

Saint-Nicolas-du-Chardonnet, parish in Paris - Pastors: see **Féret**, **Froger**; assistance to galley convicts given by parish, I, 168; 1,500 parishioners did not make Easter duty in 1648, III, 321; mission for refugees, IV, 399; seminary, XIIIa, 201.

Confraternity of Charity, I, 69, 72, 85–86, 95–96, 175, 188, 235, 286, 533; IX, 166; XIIIb, 139; Regulations, I, 96, 114, 281; Marguerite Naseau served in Charity, IX, 194, 473; text of Regulations, XIIIb, 99–102; Saint Vincent thinks of entrusting ministry with convicts to this Charity, I, 168; Daughters of Charity at Saint-Nicolas, I, 320; II, 600; III, 60; IV, 159; IX, 8: see **Angiboust** (Barbe), **Dalmagne**; their "room," I, 327, 337, 348, 386; Saint Vincent advises avoiding renting house that previously served as Motherhouse of Sisters, I, 340; Sisters are punctual for time of rising, X, 477; other mentions, I, 115, 242, 300, 534; VI, 547; XIIIa, 76, 144.

Saint-Nizier, church in Mâcon - XIIIb, 68, 69, 72, 77.

Saint-Nom-de-Jésus (Confraternity) - Union of two Confraternities of Saint-Nom-de-Jésus and of Charity of Montreuil-sous-Bois, I, 102; XIIIb, 94.

Saint-Nom-la-Bretèche, village in Yvelines - Saint Vincent invites Fr. Belin to catechize and hear confessions there, I, 269–70.

Sant'Onofrio - See Cardinal **Barberini** (Antonio).

Saint-Ouen, abbey in Rouen - Saint Vincent, named Vicar-General of Comte de Richelieu, Abbot of Saint-Ouen, during detention of latter, IV, 197; in this capacity, he presents Pastors for parishes which depend on abbey, VI, 310.

Saint-Ouen-l'Aumône, town in Val-d'Oise - See **Alix** (Michel).

Saint-Pandelon, hamlet in Landes - Fr. Brin in Saint-Pandelon, IV, 467.

Saint-Pardoux-la-Chapelle, town in Dordogne - Saint-Pardoux Abbey, II, 489, 508.

Saint-Paul (Anne de Caumont, Comtesse de) - Edifying death, XI, 108.

Saint-Paul (Charles de Paris, Comte de) Abbot, son of Duchesse de Longueville - Biographical data, V, 382.

Saint-Paul (Congregation of Clerks Regular) - See **Guérin** (Juste).

Saint-Paul (Fr. de), Augustinian - Saint Vincent asks Abbot of Sainte-Geneviève to welcome him in monastery for a month, III, 487–88.

Saint-Paul, parish in Gascony - Saint Vincent had property in this area, XIIIa, 76, 99.

Saint-Paul, parish in Paris - Pastors: see **Hameau** (André), **Mazure** (Guillaume), **Mazure** (Nicolas); large parish, with many sick; Ladies are negligent, I, 283; establishment of Charity, XIIIb, 139; condition of Charity, XIIIb, 247; other mention, I, 233; establishment of Daughters of Charity, II, 600; III, 60; Sisters have great deal of work, X, 469; XIIIb, 247–48; faithful to meditation, X, 468; rise at four o'clock, X, 477; Saint Vincent asks Saint Louise to visit them, I, 312; situation at Saint-Paul, I, 376, 378; Saint Louise can expect nothing but trouble and difficulty with Sisters at Saint-Paul, I, 401; Pastor wants them totally dependent on him, I, 533; great number of poor and sick served by Sisters during Fronde, IV, 400, 401; Saint Vincent agrees to their taking into their house Fr. Perraud's sister to teach her how to write, V, 135; change of personnel, II, 655; XIIIb, 302; Daughters of Charity who minister in parish: see Sisters **Chesneau**, **Dauteuil** (Marthe), **Hardemont**, **Jeanne**, **Marguerite**, **Marie**, **Martin** (Élisabeth), **Trumeau**; other mentions, I, 388, 411; III, 471; IX, 8.

Saint-Paul-Trois-Châteaux, town in Drôme - Bishop: see Jacques-Adhémar de **Monteil**.

Saint Peter's [***Saint-Pierre***], Church in Rome - Edict issued from there, XIIIa, 23; Bulls issued from there: Bull of Erection of Congregation of the Mission, XIIIa, 304; Bull confirming union of Saint-Lazare Priory to Congregation of the Mission, XIIIa, 416, 486; Bull uniting Saint-Méen Abbey to seminary, XIIIa, 429; Chapter, VII, 629; Canon, VIII, 349.

Saint-Pierre, church in Mâcon - XIIIb, 74, 76, 78.

Saint-Pierre-de-Bouguenais, commune in Loire-Atlantique - M. Étienne hears Mass there, VIII, 557.

Saint-Pierre-de-Mézières - See Fr. **Gérard**, chaplain.

Saint-Pierre-de-Montmagneris, priory - Union with Agen Seminary, IV, 539.

Saint-Pourçain-sur-Sioule, town in Allier - Resignation of abbey by Louis de Chandenier, in favor of Congregation of the Mission, V, 368; he is asked to present successor to recently deceased lieutenant of judge of Saint-Pourçain, V, 596; Saint Vincent sends to Claude de Chandenier models of annuities for Saint-Pourçain Priory, V, 549; bailiffs, VI, 93; Saint Vincent inquires about judge's request, VI, 93–94.

Louis de Chandenier offers priory to Saint-Lazare to help defray expenses of retreats for ordinands, VII, 314; Edme Menestier, titular incumbent of priory, VI, 401–02; VIII, 116; taking possession, VI, 38; steps taken in Rome for union of priory to Congregation of the Mission, VI, 402, 482, 494, 629; VII, 38, 48; Bull of union, VII, 48, 239, 318; Bishop of Clermont requests, in return for acquiescence, commitment of continual, permanent mission in diocese; Saint Vincent proposes instead mission in Saint-Pourçain every five years, VII, 314; fulmination of Bull, VII, 252, 313, 517; saint fears necessary formalities were not fulfilled in fulmination, VII, 319–20, 321, 360; thanks Fr. Jolly for information received on this point, VII, 628; steps taken in view of new fulmination, VIII, 78–79, 116.

Saint-Preuil, village in Charente - Union of Saint-Preuil parish to Saintes Seminary, IV, 559–60; V, 101; VIII, 612; a Pastor asks to exchange his parish with that of Saint-Preuil; Saint Vincent refuses, V, 538–39; agrees that Superior of Saintes Seminary should not allow anything to be lost from his rights on benefice of Saint-Preuil, VI, 398.

Saint-Prix, village in Seine-et-Oise - Mission, II, 27–29.

Saint-Quentin, town in Aisne - Wretched situation of inhabitants, IV, 111, 260, 301; V, 378–79; X, 190–91; assistance of Ladies of Charity for poor, VI, 454, 502–03; XII, 368; XIIIb, 428; by Missionaries: see **Le Soudier** (Jacques), **Parre**; Lieutenant-General of Saint-Quentin thanks Saint Vincent for charity, V, 378; Confraternity of Charity, XI, 306; enclosing poor of Saint-Quentin is discussed, VI, 503; sermons of heretics (Huguenots), VIII, 457, 540; mail coach, VIII, 453; other mentions, V, 60; VIII, 94, 350.

Saint-Remy, church in Amiens - Saint Vincent sends letter to Jean Bécu in care of organist-chaplain of Notre-Dame, residing near there, I, 490.

Saint-Remy (François de), Archdeacon of Langres - Advises his brother Pierre to dedicate thesis in philosophy to Saint Vincent; saint dissuades him, IV, 219; saint responds to one of his letters, II, 313; thanks him for sending pamphlet, IV, 241.

Saint-Remy (Pierre de), brother of François - Biographical data, IV, 219; proposal for dedicatory letter to Saint Vincent; saint seeks lodgings for him in Paris, IV, 219; thanks him for sending thesis in philosophy, IV, 241.

Saint-Roch, church in Warsaw - Giving this benefice to Warsaw Missionaries is discussed, VII, 264, 474.

Saint-Roch, parish in Paris - Pastors: see **Coignet**, **Rousse**; Saint Vincent still unable to give any Daughters of Charity to Pastor, II, 209; Pastor sends Sisters away, IV, 7; fear of new dismissal, V, 427–28; Confraternity of Charity, IV, 217; behavior of Sister, VII, 279, 280, 286; other mentions, IV, 216; VIII, 512; XIIIb, 206.

Saint-Sauveur, church in Melun - Privileged altar, VII, 45.

Saint-Sauveur, parish in Paris - Confraternity of Charity, I, 95–96, 114, 138, 317; V, 641; IX, 193; XIIIb, 139; established in 1630, IX, 8, 65; first in Paris, IX, 166, 193, 472; Regulations, I, 281, 296; XIIIb, 95, 97; Saint Louise studies Regulations, I, 294–95; Marguerite Naseau placed at service of Ladies: see **Naseau**; Daughters of Charity of Saint-Sauveur, II, 600; III, 60; rebellion of Sisters, I, 534: see Sisters **Jeanne**, **Marie**, **Nicole**; other mention, I, 128; IX, 194; XIIIa, 71, 75; XIIIb, 206.

Saint-Sauveur-Saint-Médard, parish in Clichy-en-Garenne - XIIIa, 23, 24.

Saint-Sauveur-sur-École, village in Seine-et-Marne - VI, 579.

Saint-Sépulcre, priory in Annecy - Steps taken for union of priory to Annecy Seminary; Saint Vincent thinks Fr. Le Vazeux has moved too quickly, VI, 331–32; difficulties, VII, 40; Saint Vincent asks to abandon negotiations begun in Court of Rome, VII, 406, 411; Prior's resignation is "null and void," VII, 498.

Saint-Séverin, parish in Paris - VIII, 502; XIIIb, 206.

Saint-Simon (Louise de Crussol, Marquise de) - III, 357.

Saint-Souplet, village in Marne - Defeat of Turenne nearby; Missionaries bury bodies, IV, 150; have grain brought in to feed poor, IV, 264; Daughters of Charity serve poor there, IV, 169.

Saint-Sulpice (Community) - Steps taken in Rome for approval of priests of Saint-Sulpice, VI, 420; Saint Vincent has no objection to their forming Congregation, but does not approve taking name of Mission, VI, 135; members do not take vows, XIIIa, 376; aim to establish seminaries, usually in large cities, V, 221; their praise, V, 221; VI, 197; Saint Vincent denies that they intend to establish themselves in Lyons, VI, 330; address of Saint Vincent to Sulpicians on death of their Founder, XIIIa, 184.

Saint-Sulpice, parish in Paris - Pastors: see **Olier**; at Easter time 1648, Communions were 3,000 fewer than usual, III, 321; passion for dueling rages in parish, V, 616; oath taken in Saint-Sulpice Church by anti-dueling league, V, 617; Confraternity of Charity, I, 105, 109; XIIIb, 139; composed of "good Princesses and great Ladies," IX, 97; meeting of Ladies, II, 475; Ladies are fond of Sister Jeanne, I, 450–51.

Daughters of Charity at Saint-Sulpice, I, 535; II, 600; III, 60; Barbe Angiboust entrusted with visiting them, I, 320; Sisters badly treated, II, 188; gentlemen meddling in Charity hold them in contempt and suspicion, II, 286, 291; make them take remedies to sick who are not of Charity, II, 291; confusion of Sisters, II, 302; their number, II, 327; IV, 420; very busy, X, 469; Saint Louise complains that Pastor wants refugee girls to help Sisters, IV, 420; missioning of Sisters, II, 327, 328; sick Sisters, II, 300, 327; IV, 416, 420; not very faithful to meditation because of large number of patients, X, 469; Sisters at Saint-Sulpice: see Sisters **Anne**, **Catherine**, **Gesseaume** (Henriette), **Lepeintre**, **Maurice**; other mentions, I, 109, 559; XIIIa, 9, 49; XIIIb, 206.

Saint-Sulpice (Seminary) - Beginnings, II, 308; established by Fr. Olier, VI, 295; Sulpicians strive to enlighten minds of students, XIIIa, 201; renewal of clerical promises, XII, 335; guests at seminary subject to house rules, VIII, 62; students: see ***La Pérouse*** (Prior of), **Bausset** (M.); retreat of M. Demurard's son, VII, 619; documents preserved in seminary archives, I, 324, 577; II, 345, 446, 474, 560, 606; III, 233, 234, 292; XIIIb, 411; other mention, XII, 234.

Saint-Thibault, parish in Joigny - Pastor is witness to establishment of Charity, XIIIb, 65.

Saint-Thomas (Marchese di) - See **San Tommaso**.

Saint Thomas Aquinas (Sisters of) [**Dominicans**] - Saint Vincent thinks it contrary to aims of Company for confreres to hear confessions of Dominican nuns, I, 323; directed by Fr. de Blampignon, VII, 126; austerities, X, 80, 88–89; aim of Institute is to chant praises of God and to serve neighbor when they can, X, 92; Mlle d'Atri in Dominican convent, I, 462; other mention, X, 287.

Saint-Thomas-du-Louvre (Deanery) - Bossuet is there, VIII, 525.

Saint-Valéry, commune - Home of Jean Gallienne, V, 325, 354.

Saint-Vallier, commune in Drôme - Confraternity of Charity, XIIIb, 5.

Saint Victor - Foundling Home, I, 532.

Saint-Victor, abbey in Marseilles - Novices live with Marseilles Missionaries: see ***Marseilles***; other mentions, XIIIa, 366, 479.

Saint-Victor, abbey in Paris - Abbey gives complete independence to houses of Order, which until then were united to it, I, 149; XIIIa, 264, 479; Saint Vincent meets with Archbishop of Paris there, I, 241.

Saint-Victor (Canons Regular) - Claims on Saint-Lazare Priory: see ***Saint-Lazare***.

Saint-Victor-de-Buthon, village in Eure-et-Loir - Commander de Sillery invites Pastor to become monk of Knights of Malta, I, 454–55.

Saint-Vincent, church in Mâcon, XIIIb, 75.

Saint-Vincent, abbey in Rueil - Saint Vincent promises to speak to Queen about abbey, IV, 246.

Saint-Vincent Island, at Cape Verde - Stay of Fr. Nacquart on island; finds Portuguese Catholics there, III, 330, 540.

Saint-Vivien, parish near La Rochelle (Charente-Maritime) - On leaving Congregation, Fr. Vageot obtains letters of appointment to Saint-Vivien, V, 426.

Saint-Yaguen, village in Landes - III, 245.

Saint-Yves-des-Bretons, parish in Rome - Historical note, II, 295; steps taken to confer parish on Rome Missionaries; Oratorians oppose it: see ***Rome***; report on this church, XIIIa, 332.

Sainte-Baume, in commune of Plan d'Aups (Var) - Mission nearby, VI, 260–61; pilgrimage of Saint Vincent, IX, 482.

Sainte-Beuve (M. de), bailiff - XIIIa, 478.

Sainte-Chapelle, in Paris - VIII, 29.

Sainte-Colombe, abbey in Saint-Denis (Yonne) - Disagreement of Abbot with Fr. Get, VI, 264, 273, 279; other mention, V, 201.

Sainte-Croix, parish in Nantes - Assistant is kind to Sister Nicole Haran, VII, 473.

Sainte-Croix - Benefice in Lyons, XIIIa, 49.

Sainte-Croix (Fr. Bonaventure de), slave in Algiers - Ransomed; in Genoa, VIII, 319.

Sainte-Croix (Marcel) - See **Santacroce**.

Sainte-Croix, parish in Warsaw - See ***Holy Cross***.

Sainte-Geneviève (Canons Regular) - Reform of Congregation, VI, 122; Canons are seigneurs of Auteuil, VIII, 465; Saint Vincent writes to Rome on behalf of Order, II, 105–06; steps taken by him so Queen might agree to resignation by Cardinal de La Rochefoucauld of title and possession of Saint-Geneviève Abbey in favor of Canons Regular, II, 509; XII, 360; Rule among them to uphold opinions of Saint Augustine, III, 328; opposition to establishment of Congregation of Chancelade, II, 429; III, 83, 163, 340, 341, 586–92; IV, 136, 162, 247–48, 272; VII, 318; claims to Saint-Lazare Priory, IV, 297; VII, 261, 326; retreatants sent to Saint-Lazare, XI, 377: see also **Blanchart**, **Faure**, **La Rochefoucauld** (Cardinal).

Saint-Geneviève (Congregation of France) - See **Sconin**, Antoine.

Sainte-Geneviève, library in Paris - I, xxxii; XII, 236.

Sainte-Geneviève Nuns, in Angers - II, 223, 224.

Saint Helena Island - VIII, 592–93.

Sainte-Livrade, town in Lot-et-Garonne - II, 57.

Sainte-Marie, island near Madagascar - Language, climate, population; colony of France, III, 556, 582–83; cruelty of mothers, III, 552; ships make frequent journey from Madagascar to Île Sainte-Marie, V, 280; Frs. **de Bellebarbe**, **Dufour,** and **Prévost** on island: see these names; desire to make settlement there, VI, 230.

Sainte-Marie (Congregation) - See **Visitation Nuns**.

Sainte-Marie-de-Bellecour, commune - II, 245.

Sainte-Marie-du-Mont, town in Manche - House of Daughters of Charity, VII, 87; X, 524.

Sainte-Marie-Madeleine, monastery in Paris - Historical note, I, 187; II, 200; X, 124–25; troubles and unrest of Visitation nuns there, II, 200–02; Saint Vincent at Madeleine, I, 187, 234, 260; X, 124; for canonical visitation, I, 272; XIIIa, 101; to hold chapter, I, 310; to ask Superior to receive penitent in monastery, III, 302–03; Saint Louise asks Saint Vincent about speaking to priest there, II, 593; chapel built on model of chapel in Loreto, XIIIb, 296; drawbacks of having two categories of penitents, V, 320–21; Saint Vincent fears that new Father Superior may be given too much authority, III, 528–29; Mother Superiors of monastery: see **Alorge**, **Bollain**, **Turpin** (Marie-Euphrosine);

other mentions, I, 367, 369; VII, 272; VIII, 292–93; X, 190; XIIIb, 392, 441. See also **Maupeou** (Madeleine).

Sainte-Marie-Madeleine-de Limouron, Benedictine priory - XIIIa, 266.

Sainte-Marthe (Hospital Sisters) - House in Reims, V, 102; proposed foundation in Sedan, VIII, 13.

Sainte-Marthe (M. de) - I, 418.

Sainte-Menehould, town in Marne - Daughters of Charity nurse wounded soldiers during siege, V, 65; X, 519.

Sainte-Radegonde, chapel near Châteaudun (Eure-et-Loir) - IV, 307.

Sainte-Reine, commune in Haute-Saône - VIII, 388.

Sainte-Vautrude (Canonesses of) - VIII, 597.

Saintes, town in Charente-Maritime - Bishops: see Jacques-Raoul de **La Guibourgère**, Louis de **Bassompierre**; clerical conferences, II, 660; Fronde in Saintes, IV, 278, 291, 320, 334; possible sojourn of King, VIII, 343; governor: see **Pernes** (Louis de); heresy has dried up priestly vocations in Saintes diocese and left bad impression among Catholics, VII, 356; missions, II, 360; abbey: see ***Saint-Léonard-de-Chaumes***; Saintes Missionaries: letters from Saint Vincent, II, 658, 659; III, 600, 614; IV, 30, 131, 278, 591; V, 425, 452; VI, 564; VII, 2, 355, 425; VIII, 64, 125: see **Daveroult**, **Dufour** (Claude), **Gautier** (Denis), **Fleury** (Antoine), **Rivet** (Louis), **Thibault** (Louis), **Vageot**, **Watebled** (Pierre); Bishop has Missionaries come to Saintes to rest, II, 299.

Fr. Blatiron assigned to Saintes, II, 359–60, 395; great poverty of house, II, 519; Saint-Preuil Priory united to establishment: see ***Saint-Preuil***; priory offered by Fr. Maurisse, IV, 388; Fr. Louis Rivet takes possession of Fr. Martin's benefice, VIII, 128, 150; dispute with Chevalier d'Albret about tithes: see **Albret** (Chevalier d'); debtors of establishment are not paying, VII, 99; Saint Vincent encourages Superior to remain in house despite troubles of Fronde, IV, 278; instructs him on manner of welcoming King, if he visits seminary, VIII, 343.

Missions, III, 172; V, 494, 625; VII, 575; VIII, 324; expectations of Canons concerning missions to be given in parishes dependent on Chapter, VI, 268; auxiliaries of Saintes Missionaries in missions, VI, 316; VIII, 150; seminary, II, 257, 659; III, 172; V, 452–53, 494; VI, 506; VII, 2, 72, 426; number of seminarians, V, 626; VI, 444; XII, 60; teaching of chant, VII, 138; Saint Vincent recommends that priests sent by Vicars-General be accepted into seminary, III, 381–82; Act of Establishment could be used as model for Lorm, IV, 559–60.

Retreat for ordinands, III, 172; Saint Vincent does not want Superior to take boarders in house, VI, 315–16; exception for M. Rassary: see **Rassary**; and for another priest, VII, 105.

Servants, V, 626; VI, 97; underground noises in house terrify Superior; Saint Vincent tries to reassure him, VI, 96; Superior leaves Company; Saint Vincent explains how to act with regard to him: see **Vageot**; canonical visitation by Fr. Portail, III, 11, 30–31, 57; by Fr. Lambert, III, 218; by Fr..., V, 422–23; by Fr. Berthe, VI, 444, 504, 505, 537, 563; by Fr. Dehorgny, VIII, 51, 129, 150, 222, 254; retreats of Missionaries, VII, 323; VIII, 127; stay in Saintes of Bro. Christophe Delaunay and two natives from Madagascar, VII, 239, 258–59, 323; of Fr. Étienne, VIII, 564; only one coadjutor Brother in house, VI, 145.

List of Superiors and history of house, VIII, 612; Saintes Missionaries: see **Baucher**, **Bisson**, **Bréant**, **Cuissot** (Jean), **Daveroult**, **Des Noyelles**, **Du Chesne** (Jean), **Dufour** (Claude), **Fleury** (Antoine), **Fricourt** (Jean de), **Gautier** (Denis), **Gondrée**, **Guérin** (Julien), **Jamin**, **Langlois** (Louis), **Le Soudier** (Samson), **Levasseur** (David), **Lièbe**, **Perraud**, **Rivet** (Louis), **Testacy**, **Thibault** (Louis), **Vageot**, **Watebled** (Pierre); other mentions, VIII, 134; XIIIa, 323, 329.

Saintonge, province - Confraternity of Charity, I, 487; abbey ruined during troubles of Fronde, IV, 343; other mentions, I, 543, 545; V, 98.

Saints - Saints are saints because they have made good use of temptations, X, 10; respect due their name, XI, 113; and their relics, XI, 40; they see in God all good works of faithful; comparison with mirrors, XI, 363; have won victory by patience in difficulties and perseverance in holy works, V, 613; All Saints' Day has more abundant grace because number of intercessors is greater, XI, 382.

Saldanha, bay at Cape of Good Hope - Ship carrying Fr. Nacquart to Madagascar stops there, III, 541; Fr. Mousnier, V, 285; ship carrying Fr. Étienne passes near bay, VIII, 569; King of Saldanha, VIII, 591.

Salé, town in Morocco - Consul of France in Salé asks for Missionaries, II, 678; Saint Vincent agrees, III, 6; chooses Jacques Le Soudier, who sets out, III, 32, 40; Recollect priest arrives ahead of him; Saint Vincent detains Fr. Le Soudier in Marseilles, III, 79, 82, 92–93; at new request from Consul of France, Saint Vincent asks *Propaganda* to allow him to send Missionaries to Salé; *Propaganda* gives consent, IV, 301–02, 331–32; learning that Recollects have taken measures to send priests to Salé, Saint Vincent renounces plan, IV, 331–32; Consuls of France in Salé: see **Prat** (André), **Prat** (Henri).

Sales (Charles-Auguste de), Bishop of Geneva - Biographical data, V, 82; VII, 96; entrance into Geneva, IV, 534; assists at funeral of Fr. Guérin, Superior of Annecy Missionaries, IV, 536; esteem for Fr. Guérin, IV, 534, 537; for Annecy Missionaries, V, 82; sides against Missionaries in ongoing lawsuit between Fr. Le Vazeux and Annecy lawyer, VII, 96–97; in Saint-Sépulcre affair, VII, 411–12; evil-minded person antagonizes him against Missionaries, VII, 517; letter of Saint Vincent, VII, 536; Bishop agrees to adjudicate dispute involving Missionaries in diocese, VII, 536.

Sales (Comte de) - Present at funeral of Superior of Annecy Missionaries, IV, 536.

Saliboski (M. de), in Warsaw - V, 70.

Salies (Jean du Haut de), Bishop of Lescar - Desires Missionaries for Notre-Dame de Bétharram, VII, 460, 623; VIII, 54; letter to Saint Vincent; saint's response does not reach him, VIII, 432–33; mention of new letter from Bishop, VIII, 602; Saint Vincent apologizes; explains conditions for accepting Notre-Dame de Bétharram, VIII, 432ff.

Salles (Robert), priest - His death leaves parish of Gamaches deanery in Rouen diocese available for Saint Vincent, XIIIa, 25.

Sallo (Jacques de), sieur de Beauregard - Attorney for Saint Vincent in Luçon, XIIIa, 318–19.

Sallo (Mme de) - Contacts with Saint Vincent, VI, 611.

Salmon (M.) - IV, 551.

Salome, biblical personage who ministered to poor persons under guidance of Mary and Apostles, IX, 18.

Salpêtrière, hospital in Paris - Renovated as shelter for beggars of Paris, V, 53; Saint Louise asks Saint Vincent's permission to accompany two Sisters there, VI, 380.

Saluce (M. de) - Settlement with Superior of Montmirail, VIII, 218.

Saluces - See ***Saluzzo***.

Saluzzo, town in Piedmont - Saint Vincent allows mission to be given, even though it is episcopal town, VII, 271.

Salvation - Difficult to be saved in place where God does not wish us, V, 540; working for our salvation our first obligation, XII, 68; excellence of vocation of those who devote themselves to salvation of souls, I, 369.

Salvatoris Nostri, Bull of Erection of Congregation of the Mission - Text of Bull, XIIIa, 296–304, 321; not to be shown to outsiders, VI, 63; authentic copy sent to Poland, IV, 383, 398; prohibits parochial work in cities or episcopal towns, IV, 313–14; VI, 111; gives Congregation Blessed Trinity as patron, XI, 172; royal approval of Bull, XIIIa, 321–22; other mentions, I, 140–41, 223, 247, 264, 420, 519; II, 18; III, 247; IV, 360, 368, 395; VI, 519; XIIIa, 315, 403, 407, 417, 419, 454, 456; XIIIb, 120, 139, 141, 144.

Salve Regina - Saint Vincent sang this hymn for renegade's wife in Barbary, I, 8.

Salviati (Collège) - Admission of Rector to Internal Seminary in Rome, VI, 451, 525; VII, 55.

Samson, biblical personage - His strength, IX, 527.

Samuel, Judge of Israel - Prompt obedience, III, 531; reproved Saul for rashness, XII, 86.

San Giovanni Mercatelli, parish in Rome - Decision not to accept house, V, 465.

San Salvatore, abbey near Rome - II, 530; considered for place of rest for Rome Missionaries, III, 65; Fr. Portail urged to leave there, III, 237; Cardinal Francesco Barberini supported Missionaries there, IV, 43.

San Sebastián, town in Spain - VII, 257; VIII, 560.

Sancey, village near Troyes; now Saint-Julien (Aube) - Missionaries reside for two years in house leased by Sébastien Gouault, I, 444, 530; Fr. François Dufestel in Sancey; Saint Vincent tells him to await time of ordinands to give retreat there, I, 464; Bishop of Troyes finances house for missions in his diocese and retreats for Pastors and ordinands, VIII, 608; other mention, I, 523.

Sanchez (Thomas), Jesuit theologian - XIIIa, 404.

Sanctity - See **Holiness**.

Sancy (Achille de Harlay de), Bishop of Saint-Malo - Abbot of Saint-Méen, III, 43, 54; takes conventual table of Saint-Méen Abbey from Benedictines; establishes seminary under direction of Priests of the Mission, III, 26, 51, 53, 54–55; VIII, 613; XIIIa, 424–29; Benedictines' dislike for him, III, 52; intervention in lawsuit that ensues, III, 25, 33, 43, 65; mention of letter Sébastien Zamet writes Sancy about Abbé de Saint-Cyran, III, 362; see also ***Saint-Méen***.

Sandrois (Pierre), son of Andian Mananghe, one of Kings of Madagascar - VI, 222.

Sanguin (Nicolas), Bishop of Senlis - Saint Vincent requests dimissorial letter for seminarian of the Mission, I, 574; objects to being given best parish in diocese, II, 281; proposes Sanguin to Rome as judge in affair, II, 319; Alain de Solminihac accepts him as arbitrator in quarrel with priests, IV, 270.

Sanguinet (Joseph), Pastor of Saint-Yaguen (Landes) - III, 245.

Sanguinet (M.), of Bordeaux - Letter to Saint Vincent, VIII, 524; mention of letter from Saint Vincent, VIII, 524.

Sannois - Saint Louise's report of visit to Confraternity, XII, 355.

Sansterre (Messrs de) - III, 383.

Santacroce (Marcello di) [**Sainte-Croix** (Marcel)], Cardinal - Biographical data, V, 378; VI, 553; VII, 39; Cardinal Protector of Poland, V, 378; kindness toward Congregation of the Mission, VI, 553; contacts with Fr. Jolly, VII, 39, 570.

Sant'Antonio, abbey in Piedmont - Steps taken for union of abbey to Congregation of the Mission, which had seminary there; opposition of Superior General of Sant'Antonio, VI, 557; VII, 290, 378, 454, 508, 582, 629; VIII, 66, 68, 101, 110, 231.

Santa Cruz, harbor near island of Tenerife - Layover of ship carrying Fr. Étienne, VIII, 564–65.

Santé, hospital in Paris - I, 114, 188.

Santeuil (M. de), in Sedan - Saint Vincent does not want Missionaries to dine at his home, nor with other outsiders, IV, 470; Santeuil displeased at recall of Marie Joly, V, 260.

Santeuil (Mlle de) - Displeased at recall of Marie Joly, whose return she requests, V, 246, 250, 260–61; Saint Vincent tells her he cannot send third Daughter of Charity to Sedan, VII, 23.

Santiago de Compostela, town in Spain - Frs. de Fontaines and Arnoul are patients in hospital there, VII, 239, 257.

San Tommaso (Marchese di), first Secretary of State for Savoy - Efforts toward union of Sant'Antonio Abbey to Mission, VII, 378; VIII, 231.

Sapphira, wife of Ananias - Saint Peter punishes both for holding back part of property, X, 167–68, 173; XI, 211; XIIIb, 351.

Sappia (Giacomo), Priest of the Mission - Biographical data, VIII, 10; named consultor to Superior of Genoa house, VIII, 100.

Saraureda (Andrea da Souza da) - Name given at Baptism to Andian Ramach, VI, 244.

Sarlat, town in Dordogne - Bishops: see Louis de Salignac de **Lamothe-Fénelon**, Nicolas **Sevin**; Jean de **Lingendes**; Fr. Barreau named coadjutor of Bishop of Sarlat, I, 414; Officialis receives Brief regarding dispute between Sainte-Geneviève Abbey and Chancelade, IV, 68; diocese needs Sevin as Bishop, V, 172; Chavagnac parish, in Sarlat diocese: see ***Chavagnac***; other mention, III, 163.

Sarrasin (Pierre), member of Charity of Courboin - XIIIb, 93.

Sarsement (Gabriel), clerk of Archbishop of Sens - XIIIb, 64, 65.

Sartrouville, commune in Yvelines - I, 130.

Sarvoisy (Mme) - I, 212.

Sarzana (Codex), early draft of Common Rules or Constitutions of Congregation of the Mission - Historical information, XIIIa, *xv,* 430; cited in comparison with Common Rules of 1658, XIIIa, 430–71.

Satan - Saint Vincent declares Satan has great empire in Richelieu, I, 405; Our Lord uses this harsh word with his followers, III, 184.

Saujon (Anne Campet de) - Biographical data, VIII, 473; writes to Saint Vincent about Daughters of Blessed Virgin, VIII, 473; saint's response, VIII, 476.

Saujon, town in Charente-Maritime - Mission, V, 625.

Saul, first King of Hebrews - Looking for she-ass, found kingdom, I, 111; reproved by God for performing function of sacrificer, X, 67; XI, 312; XII, 8; other mention, XIIIa, 469.

Saulger, Nicolas - Secretary to Louis XIII, XIIIa, 322.

Saulieu (M. de) - VIII, 504.

Saulnier (Nicolas), notary in Paris - XIIIa, 77, 223.

Saumur, town in Maine-et-Loire - Journey of Saint Louise to Saumur, I, 402, 595–96, 599; of Élisabeth Turgis and other Sisters, III, 216: see ***Ardilliers*** (*Notre-Dame*); other mentions, I, 194–95, 402, 404.

Saunier (Mme) - Wishes to become Lady of Charity, I, 238.

Saurat, commune in Ariège - Home of slave Jean Castres, VIII, 162.

Saussay - See **Du Saussay** (André).

Sausson (M.), notary in Marseilles - XIIIa, 346.

Sauvage (Jean), slave in Algiers - V, 36.

Sauvage (René), Priest of the Mission - Biographical data; Saint Vincent invites him to give missions, II, 608.

Sauvageon (Guillaume), Vicar of Châtillon-les-Dombes - Invests Saint Vincent with rectorship of Châtillon, XIIIa, 47–48.

Savary (Nicolas), slave in Algiers - VI, 8.

Savary (Pierre), Priest of the Mission - Biographical data, I, 466, 522; in Sancey, I, 465, 522, 523, 531.

Saveuses (Charles de), priest, Councillor at Parlement - Biographical data, IV, 114; VIII, 28–29; Saint Vincent consults him, IV, 114; requests of Duchesse d'Aiguillon Gisors Priory for him, IV, 508; directs attention to Avançon church in total ruin, VIII, 29; M. de Saveuses believes that decision dispossessing Saint Vincent of Orsigny farm is unjust, VII, 423.

Savigliano, town in Piedmont - Mission, VI, 329, 335, 351, 415, 433, 496; Fr. Martin speaks of opening house there, VI, 433–34; Marchese di Pianezza proposes to transfer Turin Missionaries to this place, VI, 484, 496, 498, 521, 557–58, 577; plan fails because of Rule prohibiting Missionaries from preaching and hearing confessions in towns, VII, 230; young man from Savigliano at Saint-Lazare, VI, 522, 558–59, 578.

Savinier (Annet), Priest of the Mission - Biographical data, I, 278; II, 78; entrance into Saint-Lazare, I, 278, 304; mission in Duchy of Aiguillon, I, 442; in La Rose, I, 589; at Saint-Lazare, II, 78–79, 95, 118; short renewal in Internal Seminary, II, 93; in Mende, II, 235.

Savoie-Nemours (Henri de) - See **Nemours**.

Savona, town in Italy - Shrine of Santa Maria di Savona, VIII, 120, 231; other mentions, VI, 469, 471.

Savone (Fr.), Jesuit - I, 247.

Savoy - Missionaries authorized to establish Charities, X, 82; XIIIb, 225; difficulty with establishment of confreres, VI, 517; Court of Savoy, VII, 210, 378; other mentions, IV, 294, 390, 404; V, 252, 534, 603; VI, 57, 72, 87, 141, 256, 283, 405, 600; VII, 28, 243, 284, 496, 586; VIII, 68, 354, 491; XIIIa, 81, 208; collèges founded by Savoyards in Avignon, VI, 517.

Savry [**Auvry**], Claude, Provincial of Mercedarians - VIII, 309.

Sazay (M.), honorary Lieutenant-General of La Rochelle - VI, 598.

Scalenghe, town in Piedmont - Mission, V, 586, 597–98.

Scandal - Conferences, X, 20–30, 31–44; in what it consists, X, 26–27; distinction between scandal received and scandal given, X, 25–27, 28, 33; often as much harm done to listeners as to those who give scandal, III, 499; X, 26; source of division, poison of Communities, XII, 91; to destroy good reputation is murder, IX, 228; harm it causes Daughters of Charity, IX, 225; example of Saint Vincent, III, 499; of Mme de Gondi, XI, 110; reasons to avoid it, X, 20–22, 23–26, 27–30, 43; malice of scandal, III, 499; X, 31, 38; God censures those who give scandal, X, 23, 27, 31–32, 38–39; work of devil, X, 32, 37, 39; nothing more evil in Communities, XIIIb, 313; means to avoid giving scandal, X, 49–51, 54; do not be scandalized by anything, X, 41; prayer of Saint Vincent to ask God that Daughters of Charity do not give scandal, X, 42; Daughters of Charity more exposed to this sin than cloistered nuns, X, 20; how Daughters of Charity can scandalize, X, 33–40, 41–42, 43–44; never speak ill of other Communities, XII, 167; other mentions, I, 228, 560; mention of other conferences, XII, 407, 409, 421, 426, 433, 435; see also **Gossip**.

Scapular of Mount Carmel (Confraternity) - VI, 605.

Scarron (Jean), Provost of Merchants in Paris - Saint Vincent asks him to have concession from King registered, II, 606.

Scarron (Pierre), Bishop of Grenoble - Asks Saint Vincent to intercede with Queen Regent to have Jean-Jacques Olier named Coadjutor, V, 93–94.

Scholasticism - See **Theology**.

Schomberg (Anne de la Guiche, Duchesse de) - Lady of Charity, III, 508; contacts with Sisters in Nanteuil, IV, 298.

Schomberg (Marie de Hautefort, Duchesse de), daughter-in-law of Anne de la Guiche - Biographical data; Mazarin distrusts her, XIIIa, 155.

Schomberg (Maréchal Henri de), husband of Anne de la Guiche - IV, 298.

Scientia Media - III, 324: see **God**.

Scio [*Chios*], Island in Aegean Sea - Saint Vincent worries about captive who might be detained there, VIII, 377.

Scoliège (Anne), Daughter of Charity - In Fontainebleau, III, 22.

Sconin (Antoine), Superior General of Sainte-Geneviève - Biographical data; Saint Vincent recommends Irish priest to him, IV, 240.

Scotland - Saint Vincent offers *Propaganda* Missionaries for Scotland, IV, 478; ministry of Missionaries in Scotland, IV, 495–97; V, 77, 121–23, 129–30, 149; VI, 545–46; persecution, V, 369, 389, 627; XI, 166, 176–177, 275; XII, 35; Fr. Brin, sent to Scotland to visit Missionaries, returns without having seen them: see **Brin**; Saint Vincent has no news of them, V, 627, 112, 570; Cardinal di Bagno invites Saint Vincent to choose two priests to visit missions of Scotland and Ireland, VI, 460–61, 605, 618; VII, 12; saint writes him on this subject, VI, 498; Superior of the mission and its history, VIII, 615; other mentions, V, 72, 622; XI, 190, 279, 294, 318; XIIIa, 186: see **Duggan** [**Duiguin**], ***Hebrides***, **White** [**Le Blanc**] (Francis), **Lumsden**.

Scots College, in Paris - XI, 260.

Scotti (Renuccio), Nuncio to Paris - Contacts with Saint Vincent, II, 64, 104, 141; XIIIa, 311.

Scotus (John Duns), Franciscan theologian - XIIIa, 112.

Scrofula - "The King's Evil," illness cured by touch of Kings of France and seventh child of same family, V, 289; VI, 633; victim of scrofula in Nanteuil, IX, 152.

Scruples - Saint Vincent tells Fr. de Fonteneil not to have scruples, I, 482; see also **Tholard** (Jacques).

Scuola Pia [**Scolopi or Piarists**] - Order of Poor Clerks Regular of Mother of God of Pious Schools, IX, 553–54.

Scupoli (Lorenzo), author of *Combat Spirituel* [*Spiritual Combat*] - Cited, IV, 55.

Scurvy - Contracted by confreres on voyage to Madagascar, III, 541; VI, 234.

Seal - I, *xxvii*; V, 380; confreres should seal letters to Superior General with Community seal provided by local Superior, VIII, 152.

Sébastien (Fr.) - See **Brugière** (Sébastien).

Secrecy [**Confidentiality**] - Soul of affairs, XIIIb, 241; Superior does not have right to know secrets, V, 606; God's affairs, divulged to outsiders, cease to be God's affairs, X, 589, 597; text of Rule of Daughters of Charity, 383; violation of confidentiality in grave matter is mortal sin, X, 365; cases where secrecy is imposed on Daughters of Charity, X, 364–65; keep quiet about business within Company, X, 580–81, 597; Saint Vincent replies with discretion, XII, 399; discretion about what is done or said in **Chapter**, **Council**, **Confession**, **Election of officers**: see these words.

Secretiveness - Conference, X, 52–62; detrimental spirit, X, 52–56, 60–61; signs to recognize it, X, 56–57; means to rid self of it, X, 57–59.

Sedan, town in Ardennes - Heresy in Sedan; conversion of Duc and Duchesse de Bouillon, II, 148; siege of Sedan, XIIIb, 350; grumbling of inhabitants about prayer for King, IV, 31; Court in Sedan, V, 184; VI, 147, 367, 390, 487; M. de Fabert, Governor: see **Fabert**; obstacles to erection of Sedan diocese, IV, 602; former Pastor, IV, 196; work of Mlle de Neufville for instruction of young girls, V, 445; VIII, 13; natives of Sedan,

I, 313; IV, 24; IX, 195; coach, III, 214, 215; children of M. Desmarets, VI, 595; VII, 3; Confraternity of Charity, VII, 367; other mention, VI, 14; Sedan Missionaries: letters from Saint Vincent: see **Cabel**, **Cogley** [**Coglée**] (Mark), **Daisne**, **Dufour** (Claude), **Gallais**.

Foundation of King Louis XIII for missions in Sedan, II, 435–36, 462, 524–25; VII, 3; XIIIa, 339–41; mission, II, 431, 462; transfer of parish to Priests of the Mission by Abbot of Mouzon, II, 468; conversions, II, 483; discussions with Archbishop of Reims about establishment of Missionaries, II, 524–25; contract for establishment, II, 468, 524–25; arrival of Priests of the Mission; spiritual state of town when they took over parish, II, 468; purchase of country house and garden, XI, 188.

Saint Vincent's instructions to parish priests concerning manner of acting with Governor, IV, 31–32, 57, 195, 470, 577; VII, 605; VIII, 224; with heretics, II, 441, 493–97; with townspeople, II, 442; with Capuchins, IV, 118, 194, 362; V, 155, 552; with priest Fr. Cogley [Coglée] was planning to forbid to preach, IV, 333, 344; recommends to Fr. Gallais not to get involved in secular affairs, II, 493–97.

Rule of not ministering in town does not apply to Sedan Missionaries because of parish, IV, 313; obligation to say Office in choir, V, 195; disagreement with churchwardens about Confraternity of Rosary, III, 526; Confraternity of Blessed Sacrament, IV, 522, 602; Fr. Cogley leases tithes to Huguenots, IV, 435; would like to revoke consent to exempt Huguenot townsman from tithes, IV, 333; ***Balan***, annexed from Sedan: see this word; abjurations, V, 155; maintaining schools, V, 207, 210–11, 237, 445, 591; VI, 403; VII, 444; assistance for poor, II, 660; IV, 117, 165, 188, 483, 521, 577, 602; V, 26, 46, 246, 269, 446; VIII, 203, 304; XIIIb, 428; legacy for Sedan house, IV, 602–03; meeting of church administrators, VII, 443; Saint Vincent recommends that Superior consult Governor's wife for any charity to be done, V, 606; asks confreres to offer help to sons of M. Desmarets, VII, 3; to pay taxes, IV, 118, 189; informs Jean Martin that office of Bailiff should be left to Governor, V, 261; relapse of converted heretic, VI, 147; Missionary from Sedan sent to Stenay on Queen's order, VI, 403.

Question of sending René Alméras to Sedan for canonical visitation, III, 67–68; canonical visitations by Fr. Berthe, IV, 164–65, 188–89; VI, 625; VII, 366, 606, 613; VIII, 15; Missionaries' retreats, VI, 530; VII, 296; sick Missionaries, IV, 164; V, 26, 46; VI, 622; faults of some, III, 98; V, 417; VII, 151, 216; insufficient personnel, IV, 122, 164–65; VI, 530;

VIII, 165, 305; kindness of M. de Séraucourt, VIII, 12; list of Superiors and history of house, VIII, 611; Sedan Missionaries: see **Alain**, **Bayart**, **Berthe**, **Cabel**, **Cogley** [**Coglée**] (Mark), **Daisne**, **de Philmain**, **Dufour** (Claude), **Firmin**, **Florent**, **Gallais**, **Get** (Firmin), **Gobert**, **Grimal**, **Jeandé**, **La Manière**, **Lesage**, **Lucas** (Antoine), **Martin** (Jean), **Michel**, **Pintart**, **Prévost**, **Regnault**, **Sevant**, **Sirven**; other mentions, II, 663, 664; IV, 578.

Daughters of Charity: Native of Sedan, see **Perrette**; requested for Sedan, II, 148, 151, 169; choice of Marie Joly: see **Joly** (Marie); choice of companion, II, 179–80; sent by coach, II, 182; question of sending Henriette Gesseaume, II, 290; recall of **Marie Joly**, sending of **Jeanne-Christine Prévost**: see these names; advice of Saint Vincent to Sisters sent to Sedan, on order of Queen, to care for sick, wounded soldiers, X, 1; Queen requests that Sister from Sedan go to aid soldiers in Stenay; Jeanne-Christine Prévost is chosen, VI, 403; X, 233; Fr. Mark Cogley [Coglée] does not want them separated, IV, 189; Superior of Congregation of the Mission is asked to receive vows of two Sisters, VI, 379; illness of Sister, VI, 529–30; Saint Louise cannot send third Sister, VII, 23; Sister Jeanne-Christine not released from Sedan to become Officer, X, 596.

Sisters on mission in Sedan: see **Boule**, **Cabry**, **Hardemont**, **Jeanne-Marie**, **Joly** (Gillette), **Joly** (Marie), **Pescheloche**, **Prévost** (Jeanne-Christine), **Thibault** (Anne); other mentions, II, 599, 601; XIIIb, 309.

Séguenot (Claude), Oratorian - Biographical data, III, 293; VIII, 413; Fr. Olier considers him dangerous because of Jansenist opinions, III, 293; welcomes Fr. Alméras at Oratory in Tours, assists him in illness, VIII, 413; response to thanks of Saint Vincent, VIII, 438.

Séguier (Dominique), Bishop of Meaux - Biographical data, VI, 60; VII, 16; appointed Visitor of principal convent of Dominican monks in Paris, XIIIa, 136–37; contacts with Saint Vincent, II, 130, 259, 311; proposed to Rome as judge in Saint-Eutrope affair, II, 319; assists dying Louis XIII, II, 435; what he did for Crécy Missionaries, II, 312–13, 554; IV, 250; VI, 356; supports cause of Missionaries in legal action taken by Pierre de Lorthon, VII, 16; XII, 200; faults for which he reserves right to penalize Crécy Missionaries, II, 155–56; desire for seminary, II, 173; opens one in Meaux, VI, 458; VIII, 619; discussions with Saint Vincent about qualifications of Jean des Lions [Deslyons] for episcopacy, VI, 60; illness and death, XII, 199, 200; other mentions, III, 251; VI, 61; XIIIa, 422.

Séguier (Louis), Baron de Saint-Brisson, Councillor of King, cousin of Chancellor - XIIIa, 263.

Séguier (Fr.), Canon Theologian of Paris - Letter to Saint Vincent, VI, 61; other mention, VI, 60.

Séguier (Madeleine Fabri, Dame), wife of Pierre Séguier - Biographical data, I, 221; II, 247; III, 213; VI, 286; contacts with Saint Vincent, I, 221, 239, 312, 533; with Saint Louise, I, 356; II, 291–92, 482; III, 444, 610; VI, 286; with Mme Goussault, I, 569; with Fr. Olier, III, 292; services asked of Chancellor through her, II, 247; III, 292; Saint Vincent does not dare to present requests she would have trouble communicating to her husband, I, 231; she makes donation for Charity of Daughters, I, 272; for Charity of Saint-Laurent, I, 283; will be present at meeting of Ladies of Hôtel-Dieu, I, 336; solicitude for ministry of Foundlings, I, 432, 434, 537; III, 213; for Mlle de Pollalion's Community, VI, 550; Saint Vincent plans to talk to her about ministry to galley convicts, I, 533; other mentions, I, 412; II, 429.

Séguier (Pierre), Keeper of Seals, then Chancellor - Biographical data, I, 334; II, 108; III, 319; IV, 61; V, 171; VI, 420; asks Saint Vincent for Missionaries to accompany army, I, 334; Saint Vincent tells Fr. de Sergis how to act with regard to Keeper of Seals, I, 343–45; contacts with Saint Vincent, I, 505; II, 182, 234, 509–10; III, 492, 516, 525; with Ladies of Charity concerning ministry of Foundlings, I, 432; II, 108, 444; has to go to Rueil conference, III, 411; involved in nomination of Nicolas Sevin as Coadjutor of Cahors, III, 516, 525; V, 171; against Jansenism, III, 319, 617; IV, 583; Fr. Olier would like him to prevent Fr. Séguenot from coming to Paris, III, 292–93; Saint Vincent mentions drawbacks of two Congregations having same name; Séguier shares opinion, IV, 61, 295; VI, 518; Fr. Séguier opposed to having Bull approving Fr. Authier's Institute authorized by King, IV, 295; does not think he can refuse to put seal on Letters Patent of King in favor of Missionaries of Forez because this Congregation is strongly protected, VI, 420; recalled to Court, IV, 192; Solminihac seeks to have him confirm decree against Huguenots, II, 503–04; advises Saint Vincent on dismissal of confrere, II, 619–20; respect for young Louis XIV, IX, 107; other mentions, I, 221, 418; II, 247.

Seguin (Laudoy, Comte de), slave in Algiers - VIII, 503.

Seguin (Mme) - Favorable to Jansenists, III, 292–93.

Seine - Overflow, VII, 107, 110–12.

Seissez (Emmanuel), Intendant of Portuguese Ambassador in France - VII, 615.

Self-love - We are too soft on ourselves, IX, 136; XI, 60; gentle persons do not have self-love, XII, 259, 318; makes us too sensitive, unable to bear rebukes, XI, 306; better to yield to another's opinion than to remain attached to our own: see **Condescension**; mortification of judgment: see **Mortification**; other mention, I, 179.

Self-will - Anatomy of human will, IV, 55; no mortification more difficult than that of self-will, V, 443; renouncing self-will leads to perfection, IX, 519; God rejects actions inspired by self-will alone, X, 67; XII, 130; what Saint Bernard says about it, XI, 306.

Seminaries (Diocesan) - Regulations of Council of Trent concerning seminaries are to be respected as coming from Holy Spirit, II, 505; Saint Vincent prefers seminaries for priests or seminarians in Sacred Orders to minor seminaries; results of minor seminaries are poor, scanty, long in coming, II, 171–73, 214, 505, 520; V, 564–65; recommends that Superior of Cahors accept only young men who have worn cassock and have decided to give themselves to Church, IV, 284; seminarians must follow determination of local Bishop with regard to Easter duty, V, 87; seminarians should remain considerable length of time in seminary in order to be solidly formed in virtue, III, 244; they are treasure of Church, VII, 44; those in Rome should pay room and board, VII, 269; seminaries are almost only way to reform priestly state, IV, 252; VI, 442, 444; their direction should be entrusted to Communities, IV, 190–91.

Importance of furnishing seminaries with persons having requisite qualities, II, 489; donations no longer used by religious Orders for formation of seminarians should be used for seminaries, III, 43–44, 111–12; directors and seminarians are dependent on Superior or his replacement, VI, 408; obligation of seminary Superior to render account to Bishop or to Chapter has regrettable consequences, II, 507.

Principal aims of Congregation of the Mission: missions and seminaries, III, 273; XII, 74; seminary ministry as important as that of missions, V, 494; Missionary who wishes to dedicate self to missions to exclusion of seminaries is only half Missionary, VII, 577; vow of devoting life to salvation of poor country people does not impede ministering in seminaries, V, 87–88; XII, 75; Saint Vincent refuses to abandon missions in order to retain only ministry of seminaries, II, 256; accepts no seminary unless there will be at least two priests for missions, II, 506; exception for Cahors seminary, IV, 49; houses of Company that maintain seminary must call themselves, as others, houses of the Mission, II, 355; preparation at Saint-Lazare for seminary ministry, XII, 234–36.

Foundation of seminary at ***Bons-Enfants*** (around 1636); transformation into ecclesiastical seminary (1645); opening of seminaries in ***Annecy*** and ***Alet*** (1641): see these words; seminaries directed by Priests of Mission in April 1647, III, 175; minor seminaries under their direction in 1648, III, 372; Paris seminaries, XII, 234; XIIIa, 200–01; number of seminaries increasing, VIII, 366, 368; situation in Richelieu, IV, 39; no ministry more lofty than that of seminary director, III, 136; VI, 413–14; seminary directors give good Pastors to Church, more than if they themselves ministered as Pastors, II, 394; III, 464; accept this ministry, if invited, XII, 75.

Principal mission of Directors is to form seminarians to solid piety and devotion, IV, 570; VII, 608; VIII, 3; using prayers, reprimands, conferences, good example for their formation, IV, 570; must be devout and spiritual, IV, 570; VI, 71; VIII, 3; mistrustful of self and trusting in God, III, 464; gentle and humble, VI, 406–08; firm but not severe; gentle but not soft, IV, 571.

Subjects taught in seminary, II, 265; IV, 570; XII, 235; seminarians will not lack knowledge if they have virtue, nor virtue if devoted to prayer, VIII, 3; teach not sciences but their application, II, 214; example of Saint-Nicolas Seminary in Paris, X, 502; involve more advanced students in missions, IV, 49; union of parish to seminary to permit seminarians' training in parochial functions is useful, VII, 268; but contrary to Rules of Institute, XIIIa, 197; no dictations in class, II, 240, 249, 262–66, 269–72; IV, 324; VI, 64; VII, 307; VIII, 120, 458; avoid even dictating notes, VIII, 120; follow manual; explain it, have it recited and resolve difficulties, II, 240: see **Theology**.

Seminary, Internal [**Novitiate**] - Necessary in Congregation of the Mission, III, 211; VI, 321; seminarian is not there to examine vocation but to strengthen it, VI, 175; length of seminary, I, 555; II, 97; VII, 308, 497; rule of separation, I, 555; in Internal Seminary, Superior can easily appoint companion for those who leave house, III, 462; Saint Vincent thinks study during seminary could be obstacle to validity of vows, VII, 497; permits two men, at end of seminary, to study philosophy, VIII, 458; advice to those leaving to begin further studies, XI, 23; seminarians must have certificate and money to clothe themselves for first time, VI, 547–48; number at Saint-Lazare in December 1657, VII, 10; sending seminarians on mission, II, 395; seminary purged; thirty remain, II, 541; growing in number and virtue, II, 144; qualities of director, V, 443; caution seminarians against mental strain in prayer, VIII, 56; Internal Seminaries in ***Genoa, Rome, Richelieu, Saint-Lazare***: see these words; seminary for priestly renewal, II, 93, 119, 360, 584; III, 297; other mention, XIIIa, 371.

Seminary [**Novitiate**] **of Daughters of Charity** - Saint Vincent recommends that Saint Louise form beginners in solid virtue, I, 223; in mental prayer, IV, 53; XIIIb, 302; occupations and number of Sisters in seminary, II, 601; III, 61; Daughters of Charity enter seminary to be formed for their duties, XIIIb, 124, 135; Saint Louise entrusts care of beginners to **Julienne Loret**, Assistant (1647): see this name; organization of seminary, XIIIb, 294–95; seminary planned for province, XIIIb, 342–43; perhaps in Ussel, X, 381.

Semi-Pelagians - Their thinking on necessity of interior grace for every action, IV, 608; agreed with Saint Augustine concerning grace, XIIIa, 165–166

Semusse (M.) - Death, I, 414.

Senant (M.) - Needed in Maule to settle family affair, VIII, 532–33, 548.

Senaux (Nicolas), Priest of the Mission - Biographical data, III, 98; V, 188; VII, 134; XII, 28; stays four months with family for health reasons, III, 98; in Troyes, V, 188; death; his praises, VII, 134, 138, 140, 142, 143, 165; XII, 28.

Sené (M. de), slave in Algiers - V, 35.

Sené (Nicolas), seminarian of the Mission - Biographical data, IV, 510; XII, 371; Saint Vincent sends instructions to Lagny, where he assists poor, IV, 510; must return to Paris, XII, 371.

Seneca (Lucius Annaeus), Greek philosopher - Cited, IV, 55; examined self daily on how he spent day, X, 486.

Senecey (Marie-Catherine de la Rochefoucauld, Baronne de) - Biographical data, III, 293; VI, 550; contacts with Alain de Solminihac, III, 293, 294; member of assembly to discuss Daughters of Providence after death of Mlle de Pollalion, VI, 550; Mazarin's opinion of her, XIIIa, 155.

Senegal, in Africa - Fr. Nacquart requests priests for this country, III, 331, 540.

Senlis (collège) - Correspondence from G. Pluyette regarding nephew Mathieu, I, 66, 73, 88, 91.

Senlis, town in Oise - Twenty Missionaries requested by Chancellor, I, 334; coach, I, 188, 353; establishment of Fr. Authier's Congregation, II, 281, 309, 506; home town of **Jeanne Gressier**, VIII, 235; **Des Lions** [**Deslyons**], Dean of Senlis; **Sanguin**, Bishop: see these names; other mentions, I, 319; VIII, 597.

Sens, town in Yonne - Saint Vincent requests and obtains power to absolve reserved cases in Sens diocese, I, 17; Archbishops: see Octave de Saint-Lary de **Bellegarde**, Jean Davy **Duperron**, Louis-Henri de Pardaillan de **Gondrin**; priests from Sens diocese, V, 46; VI, 210; VII, 529, 569; Fr. Pillé, native of Sens diocese, II, 364; other mentions, V, 438; VI, 579; XIIIa, 228; XIIIb, 64, 142.

Senson (Jean), slave in Algiers - VII, 228.

Sensuality - Conference, XI, 59–60; mention of another conference, XII, 423. See also **Mortification**, **Meals**; other mention, I, 179.

Sententiarum Libri IV - Work of Peter Lombard, suggested by Saint Vincent to Fr. Portail for reading by younger confreres, I, 289.

Sephora, wife of Moses - Led and judged people of God, XIIIb, 420.

Serain, commune in Aisne - Saint Louise passes through, I, 180.

Sérapion (Fr.), Mercedarian monk - Arrival and sojourn in Algiers, V, 405–06; avania (affront) against M. Barreau, VI, 9–10; steps taken with Mercedarians for compensation to M. Barreau, VI, 10, 200, 302, 315, 354, 481, 482–83; VII, 468; VIII, 309–10, 326–27.

Séraucourt (M. de) - Letter from Saint Vincent, VIII, 12; saint suggests he be asked to help with distribution of charitable donations, IV, 482–83, 602; V, 26; serves as intermediary between Jean Parre and Saint Vincent, VIII, 409; mail for Parre sent via him in Reims, VI, 544, 562, 597; VII, 380, 402, 574; confreres arriving for mission in Sillery are to call on him, VI, 581.

Sercelles (M. de) - IV, 507.

Sérévillers, village in Oise - Women's Charity: regulations, establishment, approval, XIIIb, 40–48; men's Charity: regulations, approval, XIIIb, 48–53.

Sergent (M.) - Contacts with Saint Vincent, VI, 182; VII, 10; awaited in Paris, VI, 555.

Sergis (Robert de), Priest of the Mission - Biographical data, I, 79; II, 103; XI, 122; letters Saint Vincent writes him in Luzarches, I, 334; with the army, I, 342; in Roye, I, 343; in Amiens, I, 346, 350; in Aiguillon or Toulouse, I, 429; in Angoulême, I, 486; in Toulouse, I, 518, 524, 543; shortcomings, I, 208, 486–87, 519, 524; in Joigny for mission, I, 178, 179; in southwest, I, 183, 207–08; army chaplain, I, 334, 343–47, 350; ministry in Duchy of Aiguillon, I, 404, 440, 442; in Montpezat, I, 430; in

La Marguerite, I, 430; awaited in Toulouse by Archbishop, I, 442; visits Charities in Saintonge and in Bordeaux diocese, I, 487; urged to leave for Toulouse, I, 500; mission in Vernon and Muret, I, 526–27; Saint Vincent reproves him for not renting house in Toulouse to begin retreats for ordinands, as requested, I, 543–44; good results of labors in Toulouse diocese, II, 103; contacts with Michel Le Gras, I, 79, 312, 314; in Paris, II, 118; death, II, 167, 173; other mentions, I, 224, 482, 597; XI, 122.

Sergriffio (Fr.) - Nuncio thanks Msgr. Ingoli for favors done for Fr. Sergriffio, XIIIa, 251.

Serisé (Mlle), in Montmirail - VII, 334.

Sermons - Saint Vincent wants Missionaries to be reminded frequently of his advice on this matter, I, 439; tells first Sisters to give preference to his conferences over sermons, IX, *ix-x,* 62; book of sermons, VII, 271.

Sero (Andian), in Madagascar - III, 561.

Serquemanant (Mlle) - Disagreement with Ladies of Charity concerning foundlings, II, 485–87.

Serqueux, village in Seine-Maritime - Pastor, III, 369, 370; Daughters of Charity established here, III, 211, 369, 506: see **Delacroix** (Jeanne); discussion on admission to Daughters of Charity of two young women from Serqueux, XIIIb, 371–73.

Serre (Louis), Priest of the Mission - Biographical data, III, 211; IV, 66; V, 329; VI, 149; VII, 44; VIII, 342; letters of Saint Vincent to Fr. Serre in Crécy, III, 211; in Saint-Méen, III, 527; V, 329, 597, 628; VI, 149, 288, 500, 527; letters to Saint Vincent from Saint-Méen, V, 358; VI, 302; VII, 131, 486; mention of letter to Saint Vincent, VI, 500; Superior in Saint-Méen, III, 457; IV, 66; V, 376, 614; VII, 44, 45, 498, 544; in Crécy, VIII, 609; Superior of seminary, VIII, 613; Saint Vincent reprimands him for having taken boarder in Saint-Méen house, V, 597; for having allowed ladies to enter house, VI, 149; mission in Évignac, V, 628; in Pleurtuit, VI, 302; in Mauron, VII, 131; in Plessala, VII, 486; other mention, VIII, 342.

Servants - How chaplain should treat servants, I, 344; Saint Vincent advises Fr. Chiroye in Luçon to dismiss servant and keep Brother, IV, 3; *ancilla* (servant), origin of title of Sister Servant, IX, 58; Daughters of Charity are servants of poor, IX, 71; title of Company is *Sisters of the Charity, Servants of the Sick Poor*; to say Servants of the Poor is the same as saying Servants of Jesus Christ, IX, 256; poor are your masters, and you are their servants, IX, 556; servants of poor, although unworthy of name, X, 25; Rules make you good Christian women, good servants of God, and good Daughters of Charity, X, 433–34; when ill, it is unreasonable that servants be better treated than their masters, X, 551.

Serville, village in Eure-et-Loir - Birthplace of Barbe Angiboust, X, 511; and sister Cécile-Agnès, XIIIb, 118.

Servin (Guillaume), from Amiens, slave in Algiers - Biographical data, VIII, 307; XI, 180; ransom, V, 217, 247, 325; Jean Barreau praises him, V, 405; coadjutor Brother at Saint-Lazare, V, 405; XI, 180, 192; in Richelieu; tries Superior's patience, VIII, 307, 341; passes through Crecy, VIII, 486.

Sessa (Jean), printer in Venice - V, 296.

Sesty (Augustin), slave in Algiers - Problems ransoming him, V, 327, 355, 392.

Sevant (Jean), Priest of the Mission - Biographical data, VI, 529; VII, 4; in Sedan, VI, 529, 595; VII, 4, 366; is asked to counsel sons of Jean Desmarets, VI, 595; VII, 4.

Severus (Alexander), Roman Emperor - XIIIa, 32.

Sévigné (Françoise-Marguerite de), daughter of Mme de Sévigné - Boarder at Paris Visitation; mother requests that she be allowed to leave convent to see entrance of King and Queen into capital, VIII, 471–72.

Sévigné (Marie de Rabutin, Marquise de), mother of preceding - Requests permission for daughter to leave Visitation convent to see entrance of King and Queen into capital, VIII, 471–72.

Sevin (François), Capuchin - J. de Brevedent mentions something Vincent said to Fr. Sevin about Saint-Cyran, VIII, 404.

Sevin (M.), brother of Nicolas Sevin - Contacts with Saint Vincent, IV, 223, 343, 481, 540.

Sevin (Marie Véron, demoiselle) - Biographical data, I, 103; looks for house for Saint Louise, I, 127, 132, 138–39; contacts with Saint Vincent, I, 129.

Sevin (Nicolas), Bishop of Sarlat - Letters from Saint Vincent, IV, 342; VIII, 547; to Saint Vincent, VIII, 466; letter from Bishop to René Almeras, VIII, 603; nomination for Sarlat diocese, III, 240, 256; steps taken by Alain de Solminihac to have him as Coadjutor with right of succession, IV, 223, 475, 481, 498, 609; V, 171–73; Saint Vincent's deposition for appointment of Sevin to Cahors, XIIIa, 181–82; preserves town of Sarlat under authority of King during troubles of Fronde, IV, 336, 343; opposition to Jansenism, IV, 101, 160, 594; esteem for Congregation of the Mission, IV, 447; contacts with Alain de Solminihac, IV, 563; with Saint Vincent, VII, 498; "steals" two priests from Cahors diocese, IV, 27; retreat preacher for ordinands at Saint-Lazare; simplicity of his talks, V, 573, 576, 594; XII, 21; in Paris, V, 629; VII, 550; VIII, 189; resignation from Sarlat diocese, VII, 376; requests Daughters of Charity for small hospital in Cahors, XII, 20; sends pills to ailing Saint Vincent, VIII, 467; other mentions, IV, 540; VII, 206, 285, 569; XII, 239, 335.

Sevran, town in Seine-Saint-Denis - Mission, IV, 560, 561, 564. See also ***Rougemont*** (farm).

Sézanne, town in Marne - Mission, VI, 507, 535, 570, 615; Our Lady of Sézanne Abbey, VII, 201.

Sfax, town in Tunisia - V, 89.

Sforza (Federico), Cardinal - XIIIa, 361.

Sheep - Saint Vincent attempts to take flock from Orsigny to Richelieu, III, 408–09; had originally intended to leave them and two horses in Fréneville, III, 412–13.

Shepherds - Care of shepherds in Rome, II, 155; XIIIa, 314; Saint Vincent wants Fr. Codoing to give them mission, II, 343, 350–51; is consoled by his work with them, II, 395; praises God for blessing work, II, 405.

Short cassock - Saint Vincent forbids wearing it on galleys, II, 500–01.

Sibert [Libert] (Nicolas) - Property owner in Faubourg Saint-Martin, XIIIa, 305.

Sibour (Françoise-Marie), Visitandine - Writes from Compiègne to Saint Vincent about convent there, VIII, 450; writes from First Monastery of Paris to tell him of her return, VIII, 530.

Sibyls - Their gift of prophecy, VI, 245.

Sicily - Baptism of Dey's son from Tunis, II, 677; other mention, V, 89.

Sickness - See **Illness**.

Sicoex (Claude) Brother of the Mission - Biographical data; returns to family, VI, 386.

Sicquard (Louis), Brother of the Mission - Biographical data, V, 259; VII, 81; VIII, 68; in Marseilles, VII, 81, 222; VIII, 68.

Sidi-Regeppe, small town in Tunisia - IV, 435.

Siena - Fr. Lebreton is advised to assume mission expenses of priest from there, I, 581; saint would be happy to see latter united in spirit to Lebreton, I, 585.

Sierra Leone, cape on west coast of Africa - Ship detained going from France to Madagascar; incidents between French and natives, VI, 15, 230; stop permits Fr. Dufour to see Fr. de Belleville, dangerously ill, VI, 15, 228.

Sign of the Cross - Practice among first Christians, X, 505; XIIIa, 175; Saint Vincent teaches Sign of Cross to poor people of Nom-de-Jésus, XIIIa, 174–75.

Sigongne (Mme) - Wants to become Daughter of Charity, II, 526.

Silence - Conferences, XI, 84, 199–203; XII, 52–56; mention of other conferences, XII, 406, 409, 419, 424, 427, 433, 438; silence especially necessary for Communities, XI, 84; XII, 54; serious consequences of lack of silence in Community, XII, 53–54; rather than submit to conditions jeopardizing Rule of silence, Saint Vincent would have preferred to renounce Saint-Lazare Priory, I, 135.

Silence is praise to God, X, 77; XI, 113, 199; XII, 52; in silence we can hear God speaking to our hearts, IX, 98; an indispensable means for interior recollection, IX, 268; not to waste time, XII, 52; example of Jesus, XI, 201; of ordinands, XI, 200; of two Dominicans, XI, 84; of Mme Goussault, IX, 174; how silence is kept at Court, among nobles, and at Sorbonne, XI, 200–01; how police in Constantinople treat noisy persons, XI, 200; Rule of silence demands that everything be done without noise, XI, 113, 199; that one know how to speak opportunely, XI, 84; in low voice, IX, 217; times and places of silence, I, 555; IX, 6–7, 98, 174, 257; X, 490–91; XI, 105; XII, 54–55; failures in silence at Saint-Lazare, XI, 199–200; XII, 56; means to observe it, XI, 84; XII, 55; efforts to incite Company to it, IV, 321.

Silesia, province of Poland - See ***Glogau***.

Sillery (Nicolas Brulart, Marquis de), Chancellor of France - Gentleness, XII, 158; other mention, XIIIa, 16.

Sillery (Noël Brulart, Commander de), brother of Nicolas de Sillery - Biographical data, I, 97; II, 58; V, 558; XI, 234; letters from Saint Vincent, I, 489; II, 101; to Saint Vincent, I, 97; his praises, XII, 151; mention of letter from Saint Vincent, I, 97; converted by Saint Francis de Sales, I, 185; contacts with Saint Vincent, I, 492; XI, 234; Saint Vincent was his director, I, 97; Sillery desires to change his life, I, 98; ordination to priesthood, I, 235; goes to Troyes as Saint Vincent's companion, I, 552; aided by Missionaries for visit of parishes dependent on Great Priory of Malta, I, 380, 454–55, 528; contacts with Visitandines, I, 367, 369, 563, 565; II, 61, 115, 118; benefactor of Saint-Lazare, II, 119, 136, 148, 662; of Troyes, I, 415, 444, 528, 553, 570–71, 578; II, 101–02, 168; VIII, 608; of Annecy, I, 552–53, 565–68, 582; II, 58–59, 61, 66, 89–90,

144; of Temple, I, 424; funds mission in Brie-Comte-Robert, I, 465; illness, death, and praise, II, 132–35, 144, 160, 226; VIII, 608–09; his tomb, V, 558–62; his will, II, 144; saint asks Lord to glorify his soul, II, 414; other mentions, I, 464, 465, 515; II, 33, 34, 138, 143; XIIIa, 377.

Sillery, village in Marne - Mission, VI, 572, 573, 580, 596, 626; repair of church, VI, 632.

Silli-en-Gouffern, village in Orne - Mission given, VIII, 226.

Silvestro - See **Mozzolino**.

Simeon (Saint) - XIIIb, 431.

Simon (Jacques), captive - Saint Vincent tells Fr. Delespiney he has received money for Jacques Simon, VIII, 266.

Simon (M.), of Marseilles - V, 405.

Simon (Nicolas) - XIIIa, 354.

Simon (René), Priest of the Mission - Biographical data, V, 127; VI, 120; VII, 307; VIII, 24; XI, 379; professor of humanities at Saint-Charles Seminary; considered for Poland, V, 127; ordination to priesthood, V, 176, 187; first Mass, V, 218; studies Polish language, V, 229, 313; return to France, V, 474, 475, 479; in charge of ordinands at Saint-Lazare, V, 588; sent to Genoa, VI, 120, 289, 301, 304; escapes plague epidemic, VI, 504, 506, 507, 520, 527, 528, 538, 541; XI, 379; Saint Vincent has not heard from him since the plague in Genoa, VI, 552; in Genoa, VI, 403, 605, 630; VIII, 231, 549; Queen talks of recalling him to Poland, VI, 525–26; cannot leave Genoa to return to Poland, VI, 620; Saint Vincent reprimands him for adding something to author being explained, VII, 307; director of Internal Seminary of Genoa, VIII, 24; named house Assistant, VIII, 100; Saint Vincent recommends that he be relieved of direction of Internal Seminary and of some classes, VIII, 120–21; reprimands Superior who allowed him to give notes in class, VIII, 458; other mention, VII, 361: see ***Genoa, Poland, Warsaw***.

Simon of Cyrene - I, 153; IV, 91.

Simonnet (M.), Lieutenant-General in Rethel - Thanks Saint Vincent for alms distributed to poor people devastated by passage of army, IV, 236.

Simonnet (Messrs), bankers in Paris - V, 145, 227; VI, 187, 273, 315, 321, 627, 638; VII, 7, 103, 123, 149, 174, 186, 191, 195, 221, 228, 249, 302, 316, 410, 455, 458; VIII, 309, 331, 336, 420.

Simony - Providing for material needs of monks at Saint-Lazare cannot be considered simony, I, 136; request for dispensation for minor act, II, 397–98; question of simony in transfer of bishopric of Lodève, II, 617–18.

Simplicity - Conferences, XI, 40; XII, 139–50; mention of another conference, XII, 407; Saint Vincent calls simplicity his gospel, IX, 476; text of Rule for Missionaries, XII, 139–40; virtue necessary for Missionaries, XII, 246–47; for Daughters of Charity, X, 286; very rare, even in cloister, XII, 246; found in most Daughters of Charity, X, 78; God loves to communicate with simple, IX, 308, 315, 330–31; XII, 140, 141; more lively faith found among them, XII, 142; he who proceeds simply, proceeds with assurance, XI, 40; virtue loved and esteemed by all, XII, 142, 152; God is simplicity personified, XI, 40; XII, 143; virtue recommended by Jesus, XII, 139–41, 167–69; Jesus is simplicity personified, XII, 150; simplicity of Fr. Pillé, II, 377; of Mme de Gondi, XII, 144; of village girls, IX, 68; Saint Vincent loves it more than all other virtues, I, 265; in what it consists, X, 286; XII, 139, 143–44, 246; not to be mistaken for foolishness, XII, 142; simplicity and straightforwardness are part of spirit of Jesus, XI, 41; give calm responses to irate remarks, XII, 402; related to prudence: see **Prudence**.

Acts: XII, 144–45, 246; means: consider others in Jesus and Blessed Virgin, XI, 23; simple persons say things as they are, I, 140; IX, 476; X, 78, 119; make self known to Superiors, X, 52–62; don't seek esteem of others, IV, 471, 479; do nothing on the sly or use ambiguous language, V, 470; avoid refined language or fashionable words, IX, 349; never do good in one place to be esteemed in another, II, 351; simplicity in preaching, XII, 385; Saint Vincent's rule of simplicity, XII, 398: see also **Preaching**; marks of simplicity, IX, 476; simplicity with shrewd and crafty persons; XII, 398; other mentions, I, 263, 310; II, 84.

Sincerity - Saint Vincent reprimands Fr. Get for failing in this virtue natural to Picards, V, 200, 212; other mentions, I, 263, 310; II, 84.

Singlin (Nicolas) - Biographical data, IV, 593; recommends submission to Bull condemning Jansenism, IV, 593; took no steps to suggest to Saint Vincent that he say nothing against Saint-Cyran, XIIIa, 107.

Singularity [**Individuality**] - Mention of conference, XII, 409; in what it consists, X, 11–12, 285; shun singularity, daughter of pride, IX, 176, 532; X, 11–12, 296; and source of division in Communities, XII, 206; difficult to keep Sisters from being harmed by it, X, 253; apparent singularity, XII, 207; Daughter of Charity would be individualistic by living according to teachings of another Community, X, 286–87; 299–301. See also **Uniformity**; other mention, I, 409.

Sinigaglia [***Senigallia***], town in Italy - Mission, VI, 636; diocese of Cardinal Nicolò de Bagno, VII, 46.

Sins - Sins enter into order of predestination, XI, 353; their effects, IX, 39; avoid sin, even venial, more than devil, X, 99; XIIIb, 136; sins of intellect are most dangerous; can almost never be corrected, XI, 354; state of mortal sin does not prevent one from hearing Mass, X, 376; love shame that comes from our faults, XI, 383: see **Confession**; seven capital sins, IX, 291.

Sion, town in Switzerland - Capuchins of Sion, II, 122.

Sirauldin (Valentin), townsman of Mâcon - XIIIb, 74, 76, 77.

Sirmond (Jacques), Jesuit - Biographical data, I, 496.

Sirven (Pierre), Brother of the Mission - Biographical data, IV, 577; VI, 622; VII, 393; VIII, 393; in Sedan, IV, 577, 603; Bishop of Montauban asks to send him on mission to Belval Abbey, V, 224, 237; illness, VI, 622; health improves, VII, 393; death, words of praise, VIII, 393, 394, 396, 402, 422.

Sisteron, town in Alpes-de-Haute-Provence - Mission, VII, 392, 485.

Sister Servants - See **Superiors**.

Skyddie (John), Priest of the Mission - Biographical data, II, 343; leaves for Rome, II, 343; death, III, 90.

Skye, island in Hebrides - Evangelized by Fr. Duggan [Duiguin], V, 121–22.

Slander - See **Gossip**, **Scandal**.

Slaves - On Saint-Vincent Island, III, 330; need for funds to ransom them, IV, 552; commitment of Congregation of the Mission to Christian slaves in Barbary; no slaves in Catholic religion, VI, 220; see also ***Algiers, Tunis***.

Sloth [**Laziness, Idleness**] - Conferences, XII, 88, 89; mention of another conference, XII, 420; definition, X, 153; spiritual sloth, XI, 88; sin of sloth, X, 153–58; laziness is vice of priests, VIII, 126; Saint Vincent asks Missionaries to meditate once a month on this vice, along with pride and envy, XI, 178; dangers of idleness, XI, 27; causes bad thoughts, conversations, grudges, envy, jealousy, IX, 385; leads to impurity, XII, 342; obstacle to vocation, IX, 364; spiritual sloth and vanity are causes of leaving Community, XI, 89; holiness can be found in forced idleness, VII, 506; greatest of mortal sins, X, 153; See also **Work**, **Tepidity**.

Smith (Richard), Titular Bishop of Chalcedon - At Saint-Lazare, III, 193.

Smyrna - Consul is asked to help with ransom of slave, VIII, 397.

Snakes - Starving people of Lorraine reduced to eating snakes, II, 93.

Snowball - Company of Daughters of Charity began as little snowball, X, 82.

Sobriety - See **Moderation**.

Sodality - See **Children of Mary**.

Sodom, town in Palestine - XI, 342.

Soignies, town in Belgium - Fr. Étienne passes through, VIII, 597.

Soissons, town in Aisne - Saint Vincent makes retreat in Soissons at early stages of project for Mission, II, 278; mission planned for this town, II, 548, 553; in diocese, VI, 615–16; Saint Vincent thanks Vicar-General, who was suggesting union of Orbais Abbey to Congregation of the Mission, VII, 219; Bishops: see Charles de **Bourbon** [**Bourlon**], Jérôme **Hennequin**, Simon **Le Gras**, Charles de **Hacqueville** [**Macqueville**]; coaches, II, 218, 309, 359, 430, 457, 491, 517, 552; Missionaries visit poor in Soissons valley, IV, 111; Saint Vincent advises prudence to Saint Louise in ministering in Soissons diocese, I, 85; other mentions, I, 42, 49, 177; XIIIa, 228, 361; XIIIb, 92.

Sokólka, village in Poland - Queen of Poland gives Fr. Desdames pastorship of Sokólka, IV, 289; Fr. Desdames' place of residence, IV, 572; V, 28, 81; Fr. Desdames recalled to Warsaw, V, 84; Saint Vincent prefers assembling all Missionaries in Warsaw rather than having one or more in Sokólka, V, 361–62, 388; Fr. Lambert's body reposed there until 1686, IV, 538.

Soldat (Nicolas), in Mâcon - XIIIb, 74.

Soldiers - Saint Vincent provides them with chaplains and nurses: see ***Calais***, ***Châlons***, ***Krakow***, ***La Fère***, ***Sainte-Menehould***, ***Sedan***, **Sergis** (Robert de), ***Warsaw***; difficult continuing mission to them, I, 464; soldiers frighten those at Saint-Lazare during passage in July 1652, IV, 411; request for help for soldiers hospitalized in Rethel, V, 12; Mark Cogley [Coglée] assists soldiers in Sedan, V, 47; they leave sacrileges, thefts, etc. wherever they pass, V, 97; other mention, I, 411.

Solimon (Pierre), Father of Poor in Angers - XIIIb, 116, 118, 119.

Solminihac (Alain de), Bishop of Cahors - Biographical data, I, 206; II, 428; III, 32; IV, 26; V, 171; VI, 106; VII, 117; VIII, 2; X, 95–96; anxious to have Sisters, X, 95–96; XIIIb, 338; letters from Saint Vincent, I, 206; III, 224; IV, 135, 161, 198, 500,

592; to Saint Vincent, II, 428, 450, 489, 503, 512, 616, 679; III, 153, 162, 229, 239, 256, 293, 340, 341, 345, 461, 463, 516, 524, 586; IV, 26, 101, 124, 141, 152, 159, 163, 189, 222, 247, 270, 272, 310, 475, 480, 498, 503, 508, 540, 562, 598; V, 171, 590; VII, 117, 546, 627; mention of letters from Saint Vincent, III, 239; IV, 26, 159, 310, 452, 498; to the Queen, IV, 609; his health and age, IV, 154; holiness, X, 464; XII, 123; moderation, X, 200, 551; XII, 342; severity, X, 466; ready to risk life during plague in Cahors, IV, 480; Saint Vincent advises him not to endanger self, IV, 501; civil authorities prevent him, IV, 505–06; he acquiesces, IV, 509; zeal for reform of monasteries, II, 489–90: see **Le Pouget**; nomination of good Bishops, II, 429–30, 616, 679–81; III, 163, 229–30, 240, 256–57, 293–95, 342, 348; IV, 27, 249; opposition to Huguenots, II, 503; VIII, 52; XII, 239; against Jansenism, II, 489; III, 345–47; IV, 160–61, 186, 248, 498, 540, 594, 598; V, 590; VII, 546, 547, 550; against laxism, VII, 499, 546–50, 627–28; desire to be relieved of Chancelade Abbey, IV, 141, 223; Fr. Garat succeeds him, V, 590; steps taken to have Nicolas Sevin as Coadjutor: see **Sevin**; to have Congregation of Chancelade erected as distinct Congregation: see **Chancelade**.

Concern for his seminary, II, 429, 451, 452, 489, 633, 636; III, 32, 63, 81–84, 153, 162, 175, 244, 259, 340; IV, 101, 125, 252, 284, 447; VI, 634; VIII, 89; XIIIa, 309; difficulties with his clergy, III, 516, 525, 591; IV, 191, 199, 270, 272–73, 311, 503–06, 540–41, 562–63; VII, 117; visitation of diocese, II, 512; III, 241; IV, 102; attachment to cause of King; prefers to remain in diocese than to go to Paris, II, 451; in Paris, II, 616, 636.

Contacts with Saint Vincent, III, 99; IV, 452; XIIIa, 211; gives hospitality in Chancelade Abbey to two Missionaries, I, 207–08; Saint Vincent intends to send several priests to him in Cahors, I, 332; five Missionaries will work in his diocese, VIII, 611; Solminihac promises to pay debt assumed by Fr. Delattre, II, 632; money given him, III, 125; Prelate does not wish his seminarians to enter Saint-Lazare, III, 340, 341–42; urges neighboring Bishops to have Priests of Mission head their seminaries, III, 517; IV, 142: see ***Périgueux***; calls Daughters of Charity to Cahors: see ***Cahors***.

Accused of being always involved in lawsuits and retaining titular abbey along with diocese, IV, 69; lawsuits, III, 231; health, II, 512; IV, 152–54, 160, 161–62, 163, 192; VII, 546; other mentions, II, 506, 646; IV, 49, 76, 96, 283; VI, 106; VII, 206, 338, 374.

Solomon, King of Israelites - What Ombiasses of Madagascar say of him, V, 525–26; had precious stones thrown into foundation of temple of Jerusalem, IX, 12, 203; XIIIb, 317; cited, XI, *xx-viii*, 69; XIIIa, 107; other mentions, I, 314; XII, 119.

Soly (M.), bookseller - VII, 48.

Somaschi (Order) - IV, 140.

Sommerécourt, village in Haute-Marne - VIII, 491.

Sorbon, village in Ardennes - VII, 574.

Sorbonne [***University of Paris***] - How Masters of Sorbonne take recreation, XI, 201; admit to their table only Doctors or Bachelors, X, 261; XI, 299; dissatisfaction at inclusion in ordinance of Archbishop of Paris obliging all diocesan seminarians to attend retreats for ordinands at Saint-Lazare, I, 516; they go, not to be instructed, but to become better, II, 264; XII, 22; professors of Sorbonne are accustomed to dictate notes, II, 264, 266, 271; they do not seem to learn more by writing, II, 265; four Doctors advise Saint Vincent on dismissal of confrere, II, 619; two Doctors gave conferences to ordinands, V, 99; young Doctor preaches ordination retreat at Saint-Lazare, VII, 27; students of Bons-Enfants go to Sorbonne to study theology, XIIIa, 200; Saint Vincent has professor, opposed to Jansenism, named to Sorbonne, III, 45–46, 49; two Doctors go to Rome to prevent condemnation of *De la fréquente communion,* III, 73, 74; Sorbonne would not appoint anyone in favor of Jansenism, VIII, 406; division in Sorbonne regarding Jansenism, III, 320; IV, 219; condemnation of Baius [De Bay], III, 320, 323; of Jansenist thesis, III, 617; of Jansenius and Arnauld, V, 587, 645–46; VI, 101–02, 121, 291; XI, 292; of laxism, VII, 547; Doctor of Sorbonne and priests preparing to go to America, IV, 296; hesitations of Sorbonne concerning case of loan at interest, VI, 288; teaching of Sorbonne regarding usury, VII, 240; decision regarding difficulty concerning Masses, VIII, 172; relationship with Bons-Enfants, VIII, 605; XIIIa, 71, 72, 75–76, 97, 98, 219, 223, 230, 232, 234, 237, 241; other mentions, I, 509; II, 28; VII, 438, 546; VIII, 502; XI, 29; XIIIa, 26, 229, 258, 472, 487.

Sorcerers - In Montauban diocese, II, 473; superstitious practices, XII, 284.

Soret (Jean), of Clichy - XIIIa, 24.

Sorus (M.) - II, 528, 535.

Sossin (M.), notary in Marseilles - V, 163; VIII, 310.

Soubirous - Its Rector is named for Cahors Seminary, XIIIa, 309.

Soudé (Desbordes, Vicomte de) - See **Desbordes**.

Soudé, village in Marne - I, 421.

Soudier (M.) - See **Le Soudier**.

Soudin (Claude), Brother of the Mission - Biographical data; ill at Saint-Lazare, VII, 369–70.

Soudron, village in Marne - I, 118.

Soufliers (François), Priest of the Mission - Biographical data, I, 162; II, 49; at Saint-Lazare, I, 371, 441, 516; Saint Vincent commends manner of dealing with heretics, I, 420; employs him in service of Daughters of Charity, I, 376, 434; II, 49, 206; dispensation requested by Fr. Soufliers in Rome for couple who want to get married, II, 105, 142; letters from Fr. Codoing, II, 262, 270, 304; Superior in La Rose, II, 319, 344, 417; VIII, 606; sent to Cahors as Superior, II, 462; leaves Congregation, II, 541; other mention, I, 277, 441.

Soufliers (M. de), *Procureur Fiscal* of Duc de Noirmoutiers in Montmirail - VIII, 447.

Souillard (Jean), Pastor of Clichy - Pays off debt to Saint Vincent, XIIIa, 97–98.

Soulet (M.) - XIIIa, 354.

Soulières, village in Marne - I, 118.

Sourdis (Chevalier de) - Journey to Madagascar, VI, 215, 232, 241; Corpus Christi procession upon arrival, VI, 233; contacts with confreres, VI, 234.

Sourdis (François Escoubleau de), Cardinal-Archbishop of Bordeaux - Establishes conferences for priests in diocese, XI, 11.

Sourdis (Henri Escoubleau de), Archbishop of Bordeaux, brother of François de Sourdis - Contacts with Alain de Solminihac, I, 208–09; death, II, 616.

Souscarrière (Mme de), Lady of Charity - I, 495; II, 128, 317, 328, 444.

Sousse, town in Tunisia - V, 89.

Souvignes, locality - XIIIb, 390, 395.

Souville (M. de) - Member of association against dueling, V, 617.

Souvré (Jacques de) - Biographical data, VII, 344.

Souyn (M.), bailiff of Reims - Thanks Saint Vincent for relief sent to town and environs, IV, 263.

Soyront [Sérand] (Jean) - Pastor of Châtillon before Saint Vincent, XIIIa, 49.

Spada (Bernardino), Cardinal - Biographical data; thanks Saint Vincent for missions given by Rome Missionaries in Albano diocese, IV, 177; opinion on privilege requested by Saint Vincent, XIIIa, 311.

Spada (Virgilio), brother of Cardinal Spada - Contacts with Fr. Jolly, VII, 268, 343.

Spagirite Physician - Owner of Saint Vincent when latter was slave, I, 5.

Spain - Plan for Missionaries' house in Spain: see ***Barcelona, Catalonia, Toledo***; war between France and Spain, I, 330, 331, 333–34, 335; IV, 81, 462; VI, 647; peace between them, VIII, 564–65; despite great knowledge, Spanish theologians do not dictate in class, II, 240, 266, 272; IV, 324; Spanish is most common language in Algiers, III, 305; Fr. Dieppe gave Spanish lessons on journey to Marseilles, III, 445; Duchess proposes informing Spanish Nuncio of Philippe Le Vacher's innocence, and sending the latter money, V, 482; danger of Church being lost there, XI, 318; other mentions, I, 11; IV, 461; V, 89, 328; VI, 244, 409; VII, 211, 213, 217, 239, 287, 407, 579; VIII, 240, 256, 311, 338, 559, 597; XI, 189; XIIIa, 21, 34, 350; XIIIb, 429; Spanish would find it hard to submit to French, VI, 619; Spanish capture four priests en route to Madagascar in 1659, VIII, 554; arrive in Table Bay with Dutch fleet, VIII, 588; one of them dying on return trip to Holland, VIII, 593; other mentions, V, 89; XIIIa, 21, 350.

Spartans [**Spartiates**] - XI, *xxix*.

Spinola (Family) - VIII, 176.

Spinola (Giovanni Battista), Bishop of Matera - Biographical data, III, 37–67.

Spinola (M.) - VII, 307.

Spirit of Daughters of Charity - Conferences, IX, 456–64; 465–70; 470–78.

Spirit of the World - Conferences, IX, 337–44, 344–53; take care not to be carried away by it, I, 524; Company should keep at a distance from it, IV, 57; it prevents living virtue of poverty in Community, XI, 220–24; difference between spirit of world and that of Jesus Christ, XIIIa, 163.

Spiritual Dryness [**Aridity**] - Mention of conference, XII, 408; letter of Saint Vincent to student of the Mission, who complained about spiritual dryness, V, 631; don't be discouraged in midst of this trial, IX, 498, 499; honor, in trials, interior state of abandonment of Jesus and saints, I, 157; example of Jesus, IX, 499; of nobleman who became priest, IX, 499; God gives consolations at beginning, IX, 498: see also **Tepidity**.

Spiritual life - Not beginnings that count in spiritual life, but progress and end, II, 146.

Spiritual Progress - Missionaries faithful to Rule will progress spiritually, XI, 346–47.

Spoleto, town in Italy - Missions in diocese, IV, 52; V, 274; Bishop: see Lorenzo **Castruccio**.

Stability (vow) - Saint Vincent wonders if it suffices to make this vow, II, 37; wonders whether it constitutes religious state, II, 141–42; when it is made, II, 155; how it is practiced by those ministering in seminaries, V, 87–88; Archbishop of Paris approves vows, including this one, XIIIa, 316.

Stabot (Pierre) - XIIIa, 21.

Stelle [**Estelle**] (Gaspard), Priest of the Mission - Biographical data, VI, 521; VII, 153; VIII, 25; Saint Vincent assigns him to Turin house, VI, 521, 525; he leaves Paris, VI, 578, 579; Superior in Turin receives order to send him to Genoa, VII, 153, 210, 230, 234, 236; admitted to vows, VII, 375; writes to Saint Vincent, VIII, 25; saint replies that he is capable of giving missions and urges him to give up desire for further study, VIII, 40; sends money to brother, VI, 599, 627, 638.

Stenay, town in Meuse - Siege of Stenay, V, 176; Annonciades of Stenay, V, 473; Missionary and Daughter of Charity go to Stenay at request of Queen, VI, 403, 530; Fr. Annat sends publication to Pastor of Stenay, VII, 23–24; army of Maréchal de la Ferté in environs of Stenay, VIII, 15.

Stephen (Saint) - Feast day, VIII, 586; his example at time of stoning, XIIIb, 222–23.

Stock - Saint Vincent suggests that Saint Louise might increase revenue by buying stock in salt, I, 559.

Stockholm, city in Sweden - Sons of Comtesse de Brienne are ill there, V, 249.

Sturla Marina - Discernment to remain or not in this small settlement near Genoa, IV, 79.

Suarez (Francisco), Jesuit theologian - Opinion on necessary qualifications for religious state, XIIIa, 406.

Submission - Our Lord will draw glory from it, I, 75; example of Saint Vincent, I, 544; his submission to God's Will, I, 579; submission of opinion, II, 89; of judgment, II, 120–21, 152–53; III, 47; IX, 60; XI, 355; necessary for union in community, X, 309.

Sucy-en-Brie, village in Val-de-Marne - Request of four women of Sucy, I, 309; no follow up, I, 311; other mentions, I, 312; XIIIb, 118.

Sufferings [**Infirmities**] - Conferences, X, 146–59; XII, 26–29; mention of other conferences, XII, 418, 432; letters of consolation to grieving persons, III, 397; IV, 145–46; V, 197; VI, 428; VII, 201, 246, 254; VIII, 374; text of Rule of Daughters of Charity, X, 146; do not be surprised at trials, X, 150; XI, 103; everyone suffers, VII, 202, 322; X, 150, 151; crosses everywhere, IV, 130; one who flees crosses finds heavier ones, IV, 357; XI, 59; good is rarely done without suffering, IV, 361; happy those who suffer, III, 398; IV, 130, 227; VIII, 175, 233; X, 153; better to have demon in body than to be without cross, V, 197; no place better than at foot of Cross, I, 155; good unaccompanied by suffering is not perfect good, V, 15; suffering comes from God, XII, 26; God sends crosses to those He loves and who love Him, III, 120, 398; IV, 356; VI, 1; X, 146; XI, 170, 362–63; God rewards us with crosses for what we do for Him, XI, 167; when soul is tested, it is sign that God has great plans for her, X, 148–50; reason to be concerned about those God does not test, XI, 134.

Price of sufferings, I, 123; VI, 1, 428; VII, 246; XI, 167–68, 364–66; we go to heaven only by suffering, VII, 255; shortest way to holiness, IV, 222; sufferings are trial, V, 547; cross that raises us above earth, VIII, 374; fruitful, V, 547; XI, 338–39, 368; devil uses crosses to battle against us; let us use them to bring him down, I, 227; example of Jesus, IV, 282–83; VIII, 374; X, 150; XII, 27; of saints, XII, 27; of Tobit, X, 146; of Saint Jane Frances: See **Chantal**; welcome all sufferings as sent by God, X, 148; XI, 290; with resignation, without murmuring or being disheartened, I, 126; IV, 88, 103; V, 211; X, 149–50, 151–53; rejoice in them, I, 227; sorrows are found everywhere, IV, 265; VI, 63; VII, 322; endure them patiently at foot of Crucifix, IX, 393, 398; confide them to Superiors, not to others, VII, 446; IX, 15, 33, 63, 276, 398, 413, 501, 541; X, 149, 164, 355–62; with permission, seek help of prudent person, X, 361; consolations for afflicted persons, I, 126; IV, 265; V, 14–15, 197, 410; VI, 449; VII, 246, 255; VIII, 374. See also **Trials**, **Illness**, **Murmuring**, **Patience**, **Persecution**, **Spiritual Dryness**, **Temptations**.

Suffren (Jean), Jesuit - Biographical data, VI, 641.

Suivry (Mme de) - I, 262.

Sunday - How Daughters of Charity should keep it holy, X, 499, 501; problems with obligation among French in Madagascar, III, 579.

Superior General - Request to Urban VIII for permission to accept and use temporal goods, I, 44, 52; Saint Vincent's successors to be elected for one three-year term, I, 143; he should be permitted to enact statutes for progress of Congregation, I, 144; vows made to him; only he or Pope may dispense from them, I, 590–91; may be notified in case of significant failings, II, 86; decision on solemn vow of stability, II, 155; may decide all matters of domestic discipline, government, II, 156; III, 153; desirable to have residence in Rome, II, 361, 434, 461, 470; Fr. Alméras will not work toward this, IV, 52; freedom of subjects to write to him, II, 363, 499–500; option of using goods of one house for another, II, 419, 434; God's goodness gives graces to the General for the whole Company, II, 453; discipline and disagreements with members of Company revert to Superior General, II, 637; perpetuity of his service, III, 40; term of office, III, 373; internal direction belongs to Superior and Officers, III, 523–24; changes or extraordinary matters must be proposed to him, IV, 41; only he has authority to bless vestments, IV, 448; obligation to turn to him concerning anything contrary to Rules and practices, V, 592; confreres are encouraged to write to him, XI, 112; fulfilling duty of state is not a burden, XII, 392.

Superior General of the Mission: Has complete authority, XIIIa, 302–03; Saint Vincent offers resignation to 1642 General Assembly, which does not accept, XIIIa, 329; Saint Vincent offers resignation every year, IX, 240; King names Superior General of the Mission Chaplain General of Galleys of France, XIIIa, 337; circular letters to local Superiors concerning missions, VIII, 346–347; eulogizing Louis de Chandenier, VIII, 375; importance of keeping letters addressed to Superior or members of house, VIII, 467–469.

Formulation of Rules of Superior General, XIIIa, 326–28, 329–30; Saint Vincent intends to send them to Rome along with those of other offices, II, 523; Rules for election of Superior General, XIIIa, 329, 370, 385, 394–95; Rules concerning ballots by which he names Vicar-General and proposes two candidates for election of future Superior General, XIIIa, 327, 330; removing Superior General from office, XIIIa, 327; Saint Vincent is urged by Fr. Codoing to establish residence of Superior General in Rome, II, 361; saint considers this for nearly a year, II, 434; finds great difficulties in proposal, II, 453, 461, 470; asks Rome if perpetuity of Superior General can be authorized by Archbishop of Paris without recourse to Holy See, III, 40.

Duties and responsibilities, VIII, 436: Superior General must not be away long, even for visitations, II, 552; his duty, or that of Visitor, is to name Procurator and other Officers of houses, VII, 492; must be able to assign men to parishes entrusted to Company, V, 202; to send Missionaries from one house to another, VIII, 539; he alone has this authority, III, 522; entrusted with entire Company, X, 212; must be obeyed, II, 619; has his Admonitor and Assistants, named by Company, II, 673; each confrere may write to him freely: see **Correspondence**; Superior General of Daughters of Charity: see **Daughters of Charity**.

Superior General (Assistants) - See **Assistants**.

Superiors - Conference on responsibilities and positions of authority, XI, 124–28; mention of other conferences, XII, 422; Rules of local Superior, II, 669; VII, 366; do not aspire to office of Superior, II, 326; VII, 159; IX, 532, 533, 554, 557; X, 13, 125, 135, 322, 558, 565; XI, 124–28; XII, 44–47.

Choice and replacement of Superiors: Superior General keeps list of those apt for office of Superior, XIIIa, 386; no advantages to being Superior, not even to those who seek office, IV, 524; XII, 46; not young people, V, 351; nor saints, wise, or elderly as such, IX, 420, 525; XII, 44–45; XIIIb, 303; but those who add spirit of leadership and good judgment to knowledge, XII, 45; and love Rule and vocation, XIIIa, 395; good idea to try out Superior before naming him, giving him tentative direction of house, V, 585; every priest named Superior must humble self and submit, IV, 524.

Saint Vincent is requested to introduce into Company removal from office and changing of Superiors more frequently than in past, II, 331–32; good for Superiors to ask from time to time to be relieved of office, while remaining entirely indifferent, III, 602; all Superiors conform to this practice, III, 374; XI, 127; Saint praises submission of Superiors leaving office, IV, 95, 119; XI, 128; replies to Superiors who wanted to leave office, V, 469, 566; VII, 259; VIII, 202, 268; what God wills and does not will is made known through Superiors, VII, 482.

Importance and dangers of office of Superior: There is "malignancy" in being in charge, which infects soul, XI, 125; Superiors faithful to obligations have much to suffer, VII, 567, 610; faults of community are imputed to Superiors, X, 211; XI, 125, 196; laxity of community most often comes from leniency of Superior, II, 403; X, 211–13.

Rights of Superiors, limits: do nothing contrary to aim and customs of Institute; exception, VI, 78; neither change nor make innovations in important matters, except by order of Visitor or Superior General, II, 267, 272, 325, 355, 514, 515; III, 607; IV, 31–32, 39, 333; V, 592; VI, 516, 560, 623–24; VIII,

53; XIIIb, 279; only Superior can see to what is done or not done in house, V, 25; all important documents are drawn up in his name and signed by him, VII, 439; matters of importance, such as building, lawsuits, extraordinary expenses, are referred to Superior General, II, 236, 249, 350–51, 637; IV, 54, 261, 274, 300; VII, 444; XI, 314; new Superior must take care not to change everything on arrival, especially when Visitor has just been there, III, 607; entrusts house money to Procurator, V, 531; must change nothing in practices or daily schedule, VII, 367–68.

All Officers of house are subject to authority of Superior, VII, 492; office of Superior not carried out well in houses, III, 191; Superior can remove Officers he has named, but not those named by higher authority, IV, 122, 165; everything is directed by Superior and two Assistants; he has final authority, V, 347–48, 592; Superior has rights of Pastor regarding confreres; therefore, can bring them Viaticum, VII, 604; may not authorize family visits, VIII, 226; nor pilgrimages or other journeys that are not for ministry, VII, 151; rights with regard to correspondence of Missionaries: see **Correspondence**; vows are made and renewed in his presence, VIII, 56; Saint Vincent intends to request for Superiors authority to bless sacred vestments, IV, 448.

Duties of Superiors: principal duty is overall guidance of house, VII, 534; firm and unwavering with regard to goal, gentle and humble with regard to means, II, 332, 336, 402–03, 637; V, 553; VI, 623; is not obliged to follow majority opinion, II, 336, 403; must trust in God, II, 605; VI, 623; VII, 390; XI, 31; should do his duty, and remain at peace if he does not succeed as he wishes, VII, 390; seek advice, II, 605; VI, 77; IX, 419, 431: see **Councils** (Domestic); companion should relieve him of temporal matters, I, 526.

Must be concerned with both spiritual and temporal, XI, 315–16; must see that community does not lack necessities, XII, 120; that it has suitable nourishment, properly served, I, 378; spend only what is possible without going into debt, V, 447; in diocesan establishments, Superior represents temporal needs of house to Bishop; this concern must not be left to Superior General, VII, 350; Superior signs documents as delegated, not by community, but by Superior General, VII, 491–92; other mentions, I, *xxvi,* 143.

Should give example in everything; IV, 570; VII, 260; X, 214, 292; XIIIb, 275; especially regarding regularity, IV, 599; and time of rising, III, 536; watch over observance of Rules, II, 336; V, 553; VII, 260; IX, 533–34; X, 292; XI, 92; be persuaded that others would be better suited for position of Superior,

IX, 239, 240; do not make others feel weight of authority; act as an equal rather than as Superior, IV, 56, 570; VI, 77; IX, 239, 240, 419; XIIIb, 274; example of Carmelite Superior, I, 525; means of advancing in way of perfection, II, 402; be kind and patient, I, 110, 304, 332, 525; II, 402, 605; III, 376, 510; IV, 42, 181–82, 529, 557; V, 63, 323, 417, 605; VI, 105, 116; VII, 151–52, 290, 312, 567, 606, 610; VIII, 169, 202, 401; IX, 100; downfall of communities comes from cowardice of Superiors in not holding firm, II, 422.

How to act with quick-tempered, touchy, critical persons, IV, 97; be "accommodating," IV, 556; except for what is sinful or contrary to Rules, IX, 431, 533–34; even sometimes in things good in themselves, X, 387; be affable and obliging; communicate willingly, XIIIb, 281; be united with confreres and do not put wrong interpretation on what they do, VII, 79; encourage them in trials, VII, 181, 322; be respectful, IX, 239; strive for union of hearts, IV, 238–39; be firm, II, 403; IV, 42; VII, 605; XIIIb, 351; do not tolerate evil, but try to remedy it, VII, 152; admonish and correct: see **Admonitions**; other mention, II, 86.

Familiarize young Missionaries with all ministries, as part of formation, IV, 121, 527; observe and guide them, VI, 179; visit classes, VII, 444; see that older confreres give good example to young, VII, 181, 322–23; weekly visits to confreres is praiseworthy, II, 325; be absent from house as infrequently as possible, VIII, 56; make retreat in house, VI, 123; do not multiply retreats, V, 469; hold "obedience" on regular days, IV, 578; ask to be reminded of faults, VII, 610; remain free to officiate or to preach, or to have others do this, IV, 195; must not accept any Missionary into house if he does not have either obedience (celebret) or letter from Superior, IV, 146, 551; obey Major Superiors, XIIIb, 375; leave choice of subjects to Superior General, II, 432; do not get rid of troublesome confreres to burden other houses with them, VII, 515; do not have Bishops intervene in matters that do not concern them, III, 523–24; should not accept invitation of Pastor to board Missionaries, V, 536.

Duties of subjects toward Superiors: Do not dwell on external aspect of Superiors, nor even on virtue, but consider in them God alone, III, 615; believe that they always act for best, IV, 390; learn to understand that Superiors may see things differently from subjects, II, 453; obey without grumbling or criticism: see **Obedience**; vow of obedience made to Superior General obliges obedience to local Superiors, V, 85; pray for them, XI, 108; communicate with them, X, 52–62; with great openness of heart, X, 54, 60; confide troubles to them, IX,

398; X, 237; mention attachments to Superiors, IX, 130; respect them, IX, 239; let them speak, IX, 241; know how to yield when of different opinion, IX, 238, 239; make known temptations and notable faults of neighbor: see **Admonitions**; submission to Superiors, III, 327–28; duties and prerogatives of subjects are in reference to Superior, VII, 497.

Superior of Daughters of Charity: chosen for three years, XIIIb, 123–24, 134; Saint Vincent names Saint Louise de Marillac Superior for life, XIIIb, 226; duties of Superior, X, 95; XIIIb, 123, 134, 323; nomination of Marguerite Chétif after death of Saint Louise: see **Chétif**.

Sister Servants (local Superiors) of communities of Daughters of Charity: why they are called Sister Servants, IX, 58; in beginning, named for one month, IX, 8; distribute duties, V, 33; do not leave house without informing someone, X, 78; submit resignation at least every six months, IX, 240; when Sister Servant stands at meeting, other Sisters should do likewise, XIIIb, 262; advice to Sister Servant, II, 231; VII, 381; XII, 363.

Of nuns: Conference to Visitation nuns before election of Superior; reasons to make good choice; qualities of good Superior; means, XIIIa, 162.

Supligeau (M.), clerk of salt granary in Le Mans - V, 599.

Suresnes, town near Paris - Birthplace of Marguerite Naseau, I, 68; IX, 64–65, 472; and Barbe Toussaint, XIIIb, 118.

Survire (Nicolas), Brother of the Mission - Biographical data, V, 251–52; assists dying Saint Vincent, XIIIa, 204–05; enshrouds his body, XIIIa, 207.

Sutherland, county in Scotland - Fr. Lumsden ministers there, VI, 546.

Suzanne, Daughter of Charity - I, 340; entered before Act of Establishment, XIIIb, 228.

Susanna, woman who followed Our Lord - IX, 18.

Suze (Louis-François de la Baume de), Bishop of Viviers - Contacts with Saint Vincent, I, 304.

Suzy, village in Aisne - Birthplace of Sister Julienne Loret, IV, 516.

Swearing - See **Cursing**.

Sweden - Country won over to heresy, XI, 279, 318; *Propaganda* plans to ask Saint Vincent for Missionaries for Sweden, V, 70–71; question of sending there Fr. Guillot, who desires this, V, 165, 180, 213, 323, 352; French Ambassador to Sweden: see

Avaugour (Baron d'); war between Sweden and Poland, V, 418, 424, 454, 535; VI, 645–46; XI, 274, 279, 317; Swedes seize, pillage, and abandon Warsaw, V, 474; VI, 128, 144, 319, 421, 447, 451, 453, 470, 472, 489, 492, 502, 566; XI, 323; Poland comes to grips with King of Sweden, VI, 83; peace with Poland, VIII, 280, 314: see ***Oliva*** (Treaty), ***Poland, Warsaw***; journey of Queen of Sweden to Paris, VII, 127; other mentions, V, 89; XI, 189.

Sweerts (M.), Flemish painter - VIII, 595.

Sylvestre (Fr.), Capuchin - Saint Vincent writes him about memorandum received from him, VII, 340.

Symard (M.), magistrate - Member of Charity of Joigny, XIIIb, 65–66.

Syon (Hugues), in Mâcon - XIIIb, 74.

T

Tabarka, town in Tunisia, small port near Algerian border - V, 133; VII, 522.

Table Bay, at Cape of Good-Hope - Fr. Étienne at Table Bay, VIII, 569, 573, 592.

Tables - **Biblical References**: see **Appendix 1**; **Errata**: see **Appendix 2**; **List of Establishments and Superiors**, VIII, 604–19; **Topics treated in conferences at Saint-Lazare (1650–60)**, XII, 405–38.

Tabor (***Mount***), in Palestine - Transfiguration of Jesus, XI, 331; XII, 160; XIIIb, 386.

Tacaille (Anne and Claude), Daughters of Charity - XIIIb, 228.

Tagus, river in Spain - VIII, 503.

Talec (Nicolas), Priest of the Mission - Biographical data, IV, 546; VI, 158; mention of letters to Saint Vincent, IV, 546; in Tréguier; Saint Vincent congratulates him for having resigned possession of benefice; indicates way of freeing self from pension, IV, 546–47; Superior of Saint-Charles Seminary, VI, 158; VIII, 614; Saint Vincent allows him to rest at Rougemont, XIIIa, 200.

Talmond (Henri de la Trémoille, Prince de) - Biographical data, II, 497.

Talmont, village in France - V, 405.

Talon (Charles-François), Pastor of Saint-Gervais - I, 472; II, 558; XIIIb, 393.

Talon (Françoise Doujat, Mme), Lady of Charity, wife of Omer Talon - Biographical data, VII, 544; idea that letter from Bro. Jean Parre suggests to her at meeting of Ladies, XI, 306–07.

Talon (Omer), Advocate General for Parlement of Paris - Biographical data, II, 478.

Tanguy (Fr.), Priest of the Mission - Sent to Agde, VIII, 137; in Agde, VIII, 170.

Taone (Giovanni Battista), Priest of the Mission - Biographical data, V, 271; VI, 174; in Rome, V, 271–72, 274–75; Superior in Rome, V, 378; Saint Vincent renounces plan to place him in Turin, V, 467, 477; departure from Company, VI, 174, 318.

Taquet [**Roquet**] (Charles), seminarian of the Mission - Biographical data, VI, 175; VII, 364; entrance at Saint-Lazare, VI, 175; money sent for him, VII, 364.

Tarbes, town in Hautes-Pyrénées - Saint Vincent is ordained Subdeacon and Deacon in Tarbes, XIIIa, 4–6; Bishop: see Salvat **Diharse**; see also **Cruchette**.

Tardif (M.) - XIIIa, 107.

Tarrisse (Grégoire), Superior General of Benedictines of Saint-Maur - III, 112; IV, 197.

Tartars [**Tatars**] - Join forces against enemies of Poland, V, 535; other mentions, I, 14; VIII, 146.

Tartas, town in Landes - III, 245.

Tastet (M. de) - Sends regards to Saint Vincent, VI, 324.

Taufin (Fr.), Pastor in Troyes diocese - Guilty of simony, II, 397–98.

Tauler (Johannes), Dominican - Biographical data; edified by ulcerated poor person, X, 176.

Tavernier (Louise) - Member of Charity of Paillart, XIIIb, 48.

Tavernier (Marie), from Pontoise - V, 301.

Taverns - Danger of frequenting taverns, XI, 325; Bishop of Saintes reserves to himself suspension of priests who go to taverns, V, 626.

Taxes - Pay them without complaining, VI, 30; paid by dioceses, II, 220–21; grain tax, II, 444; postal tax in Algiers, III, 46; tax on consumer goods, III, 394; tax on French ships to Tunis, III, 394; chapel, clergy taxes, III, 569, 607; Mark Cogley [Coglée] urged to pay taxes in Sedan, IV, 118; tax on importation of firewood, V, 140; state tax in Poland, V, 193; consulate taxes in Algeria, V, 407; avoid speaking to people about taxes, VI, 2; Languedoc salt tax used as income for Marseilles hospital, VI,

99; VII, 101; Provence salt tax used as income for Marseilles hospital, VI, 260–61; VIII, 266, 376, 462, 485, 513; difficulties about salt tax in Le Mans, VI, 179; clergy tax in Le Mans, VII, 76; property tax, VIII, 462; other mention, XIIIa, 75.

Tax-farmers - Money owed to Congregation of the Mission, III, 394, 409; source of revenue in Marseilles, VII, 325; VIII, 462, 485, 513; thoughts on how to deal with them, VIII, 227–28.

Taylor (Patrick) [**Taillié** (Patrice)], seminarian of the Mission - Biographical data, VII, 495; VIII, 130; lacks dimissorial letters, VII, 495; recalled from Le Mans, VIII, 130.

Telesphorus (Saint), Pope - During his pontificate, priests were free to own personal goods, XII, 324.

Téluatz (Fr.), Priest of the Mission - II, 28.

Tely (Étienne), of Châtillon - Signs report of Charles Demia, XIIIa, 57.

Temperament - Moderated with age; we take it with us wherever we go, III, 616.

Temperance - Mention of conference, XII, 421; example of Saint Francis de Sales, XIIIa, 88. See also **Mortification**, **Moderation**.

Temple (Order) - Attempt to open seminary in Templars' house in Paris, I, 424–25; their devotion to Our Lady of Loreto, XIIIb, 296; other mention, XIIIb, 392.

Temporal Goods - Conference on attachment to temporal goods, XI, 71–72; greater desire for property among priests than among laity; God punishes them in their heirs; property held in common in primitive Church; grave consequences of division of property, XII, 304; spreading empire of Christ is better than adding to possessions, III, 527; damage to property of house is common fault in Communities, XI, 25; Community that lacks nothing is near ruin, II, 517–18; care of temporal goods is necessary; how to do it, XI, 25, 315–16; XII, 95, 112; never to detriment of spiritual, I, 463; and never ceasing to trust in Providence: see **Providence**; example of Our Lord and Apostles, XII, 119–20; Saint Vincent gives confreres advice on economy, II, 623, 624; agrees to their claiming tithes, V, 612; VI, 398, 445; to having property, usurped by seculars, restored to Church, VI, 65, 161; to consolidating their lands instead of farming them themselves, VIII, 347; except in certain cases, IV, 326: see also **Poor**, **Poverty**.

Temptations - Conferences, IX, 272–84; X, 7–20; XI, 26–27, 133–35, 169–70; mention of another conference, XII, 431; text of Rule of Daughters of Charity, X, 355; generally, all servants of God are tempted, I, 562; III, 182, 615; IV, 547; V, 473, 613; VI, 449; IX, 274, 282–83, 540; Jesus was tempted, X, 9; apostles also, IX, 283; X, 10; persons who follow natural inclinations are not tempted, nor are those who have such taste for things of God that everything is agreeable to them, IX, 282; as is often case for those beginning spiritual life, XI, 134, 169; temptation is good time to recognize spiritual mettle of soul, XI, 56; not to be tempted is bad sign, XI, 134, 170; many feel abandoned by God because they are not tempted, IX, 282–83; XI, 170; our life is nothing but temptation, III, 342; devil tempts under appearance of good, X, 14–17; to prevent good or continuation of good, IX, 274.

God permits temptation to manifest His power and glory, IX, 274; to test and sanctify us, X, 10–11, 15, 405; XI, 169; greater merit in one day of temptation than in month of tranquility, XI, 133; spiritual progress is observed in temptation, XI, 88; in what temptation consists; difference between temptation and inspiration, X, 8; temptation is evil only if we consent to it, X, 405; resist temptation as soon as we can, IX, 277; have recourse to prayer, X, 15, 18; not to be freed from it, but in order not to yield to it, XI, 134; manifest temptations to Superiors, not to others, IX, 501, 504, 541; X, 355–62; unless Superiors permit it, X, 361; Saint Vincent reassures Missionary who thought he lost his esteem by communication of temptation, IV, 356; reread retreat resolutions, IX, 282; change of place does not dispel temptations, III, 616; VI, 69; those who want to follow Christ will suffer temptation, V, 539; correction given with smile, XII, 393; beware of temptations during sickness, XII, 393.

Dispositions more or less perfect in face of temptations, XI, 134; temptation often followed by great consolations, XI, 169; temptations to which Daughters of Charity are most often exposed, X, 11–17; temptations against vocation: see also **Daughters of Charity**, **Congregation of the Mission**; against chastity: see also **Chastity**.

Tenerife, largest of Canary Islands - VIII, 564.

Tepidity [**Lukewarmness, Sloth**] - Mention of conferences, XII, 411, 415; in what tepidity or sloth consists, X, 153; spiritual sloth and vanity are causes for leaving Company, XI, 89; from it spring complaints and murmurings, X, 154; non-observance of Rules, X, 156; state of damnation, VIII, 126; God curses tepid, VIII, 126; X, 154; threatens to vomit them, X, 156–57; marks of tepidity, X, 158; XI, 88–89.

Teresa of Ávila (Saint) - Reformer of Carmel, I, 571; VIII, 406; great teacher of spiritual life, IV, 553; felt repugnance entering religious life, VI, 114; waits twenty years for God to give her gift of prayer, IX, 42, 333–34; makes vow to act always for greater glory of God, XII, 123; often asks God for good priests, XII, 16; disciplined herself with nettles, III, 485; cited, IX, 204, 269.

Ternes (Marquis de), Lieutenant-General of Galleys of France - Authority over prisoners' hospital in Marseilles, VI, 627; VII, 93.

Terni, town in Italy - Mission given, IV, 392.

Ternier, territory in Savoy - Evangelized by Saint Francis de Sales, XIIIa, 81.

Terrade (Olivier de la Trau, Sieur de la) - General of Saint-Esprit Order in France, II, 477.

Tertullian, Father of Church - His opinion on public penance, III, 359; informs us that first Christians made Sign of Cross often, X, 505.

Tessonnière (Marie) - Biographical data, I, 406; II, 281; Saint Vincent writes her about union of Fr. Authier's priests to Mission, II, 281.

Testacy (Charles), Priest of the Mission - Biographical data, II, 642; III, 81; Saint Vincent gives permission for two weeks with family, II, 642; no news of his return, II, 676; consults Fr. Portail about plan to name him Superior in Cahors, III, 81, 89; Fr. Portail is not in favor, III, 92; Fr. Testacy, Superior in Cahors, VIII, 610; Bishop of Cahors complains that Fr. Testacy worries Saint Vincent for trifles, III, 153; Bishop speaks to Fr. Testacy about not accepting two boys into seminary, III, 162; is too inexperienced, III, 163; Saint Vincent writes to Fr. Testacy for information, III, 238; Fr. Testacy is removed from Cahors at request of Bishop and sent to Saintes, III, 259; other mentions, III, 340, 408.

Tétouan, town in Morocco - See **Mariage**.

Tévenot (M.), physician of Marie-Christine of France, Duchesse de Savoy - V, 253.

Texel, island in Netherlands - Harbor, VIII, 594.

Theatines (Order) - In Genoa, VIII, 120.

Thenac, village in Charente-Maritime - Mission given, V, 124.

Thermal Baths - See **Baths**.

Theodosius I, Roman Emperor - Submits to penance Saint Ambrose imposes on him, IX, 304–05; other mention, XIIIa, 33.

Théologie Familière - Book by Saint-Cyran condemned by Rome, IV, 585.

Theology - Exercises in moral theology at Saint-Lazare, VIII, 90, 91, 93; XII, 235–36; classes at Saint-Lazare, VII, 495; Jesuits in Genoa do not teach scholastic theology, VIII, 92; Saint Vincent does not want it taught in Genoa house, VIII, 25, 93; eliminates it at Collège des Bons-Enfants because it is of little or no use, XIIIa, 200; mention of conference on moral theology, XII, 436. See also **Cases of Conscience**.

Theron (Andian or Dian), King of Madagascar - Warring against French on island, VI, 221.

Théroude (Toussaint), Priest of the Mission - Biographical data, VIII, 355; arrives at Saint-Lazare; grieves at death of Abbé Louis de Chandenier, VIII, 355.

Thevenin (Fr.), Pastor of Saint-Étienne (Loire) - Urges Saint Vincent to abandon missions in order to dedicate self exclusively to seminary ministry, II, 255–57; Fr. Codoing keeps money Saint Vincent sends for Fr. Thevenin, II, 267, 272.

Thiange (Marquis de) - XIIIb, 303.

Thibault (Anne), Daughter of Charity - Sent to Sedan, X, 1.

Thibault (Claude), Daughter of Charity - XIIIb, 228.

Thibault (Jean), Priest of the Mission - Biographical data, II, 79; in Luçon, II, 79, 140; at Saint-Lazare, II, 301; gives concern about perseverance in vocation, II, 321, 325–26.

Thibault (Louis), Priest of the Mission, son of M. and Mme Thibault - Biographical data, II, 519; III, 130–31; IV, 12; V, 109; letters Saint Vincent writes him in Saintes, II, 519, 658; in Montgeron, III, 134; in Saint-Méen, III, 456; IV, 12, 66, 260, 316, 476; Saint Vincent awaits him in Paris, II, 658; Bishop orders him to receive seminarian, II, 659; Superior in Saintes, VIII, 612; his long labors, III, 134; begins conference at Motherhouse of Daughters of Charity in place of Saint Vincent, who was delayed, IX, 337; Superior in Saintes, VIII, 612; Superior in Saint-Méen, III, 421; V, 109; VIII, 613; zeal for recruiting Daughters of Charity, III, 317, 457, 472; Saint Vincent keeps him informed of parents' dispositions; tells him gist of his response to their letter, IV, 12; success of mission, IV, 66; at 1651 General Assembly, XIIIa, 369, 372, 374, 384, 387, 397; opinion of vows taken in Company, XIIIa, 377, 381; Saint Vincent fears overwork will injure his health, III, 527; health, IV, 372; death, V, 329, 330, 369, 375–76; praises, V, 358–60.

Thibault (M. and Mme) - Saint Vincent tells them his sentiments regarding their desire to enter a Community and to give part of their property to Church or the Charity, IV, 12–15;

M. Thibault proposes foundation for missions, which Saint Vincent cannot accept, IV, 476.

Thibault (Nicolas), seminarian of the Mission - Biographical data, VI, 584; to be ordained on Christmas 1657, VI, 584.

Thibault (Pierre) - Married in Sedan, killed in Vandy, IV, 189.

Thibault (Sister), Daughter of Charity, sister of Jean Thibault - Saint Vincent does not agree that she should be dismissed, II, 329.

Thibaut (Vincent) - Property adjustment, III, 337–38.

Thiébault (François), seminarian of the Mission - Biographical data, VIII, 25; Saint Vincent cannot recall who he is, VIII, 25.

Thiérache, in Picardy - Misery provoked in region by troubles of Fronde, IV, 218.

Thiercelin (Mlle de) - II, 545.

Thierry (Jean), Brother of the Mission - Biographical data, VIII, 35; in Agde; gives no satisfaction, VIII, 35; dismissed from Company, VIII, 112.

Thierry (M.) - Opposes Congregation of the Mission regarding benefice of Saint-Esprit in Toul, III, 366.

Thiers, town in Puy-de-Dôme - House of Order of Grandmont, IV, 309.

Thieulin (René), Priest of the Mission - Biographical data, VI, 358; VII, 5; in Notre-Dame de Lorm; hesitates to hear confession because of limited knowledge of dialect, VI, 358; promised to Agen house, VII, 5; Saint Vincent writes to him, VI, 380.

Thilouse (Marie), Daughter of Charity, from Tours - Biographical data, II, 667; III, 421; causing problems, II, 667; sent to Nantes, III, 421, 422, 427.

Tholanghare [***Tolagnaro***], village in Madagascar - Location of Fort-Dauphin and home of Missionaries, III, 544, 567; V, 513; VI, 231, 236, 243; inhabitants well-disposed toward Catholic religion, V, 524; other mention, VI, 248.

Tholard (Jacques), Priest of the Mission - Biographical data, II, 19; III, 138; V, 208; VII, 20; VIII, 59; XI, 106; letters of Saint Vincent to Fr. Tholard in Annecy, II, 19, 123, 152; in Villejuif, III, 138; in Maule, V, 483; in Bruyères-le-Châtel, VII, 20; in Marcoussis, VII, 71; mention of letters to Saint Vincent from Troyes, VII, 309; VIII, 72; sister and niece, VIII, 73; XIIIb, 348–49; Saint Jane Frances de Chantal's opinion of him, II, 32; difficulty hearing women's confessions, II, 19–23, 114, 118,

123–24, 152–54; III, 139; Saint Vincent dispenses him from hearing confessions, III, 139, 250; at least "of all sorts of people," VIII, 73; in Annecy, II, 18, 402, 609; XI, 106, 107; health, II, 88; in Villejuif, III, 138; in Coulommiers, III, 250; Superior in Tréguier, III, 447; VIII, 616; giving mission near Maule, V, 208; XI, 157; not far from Paris, V, 363; in Maule, V, 483; in Bruyères-le-Châtel, VII, 20; in Marcoussis, VII, 71; in Troyes, hesitates to renew vows, VII, 310; Saint Vincent considers sending him to give missions in Agde diocese, VIII, 59, 72; in Richelieu; recalled to Paris, VIII, 307; in Paris, VIII, 341.

Tholen, town in Netherlands - Fr. Étienne passes through, VIII, 596.

Tholibowski (Albert), Bishop of Poznań - Vacancy in diocese, V, 249; given to Tholibowski, V, 249, 257; contacts with Missionaries in Poland, V, 263; VI, 298; gives parish to Missionaries in Warsaw, VII, 107; at death of Fr. Ozenne, Saint Vincent offers Bishop Fr. Desdames for Holy Cross parish, VII, 276; letter of Saint Vincent to Bishop on this topic, VII, 276, 300; fear he might take parish from Company, VII, 475; Bishop wants Company to minister in Poznań diocese, VII, 625.

Thomas (Guillaume) - Associate Canon of Church of Paris, XIIIa, 221, 233–34.

Thomas (Fr.), priest of Angoulême - Offers parish to Congregation of the Mission; Saint Vincent thanks him but declines, V, 435.

Thomas (Saint), Apostle - Apostle of Indies, VIII, 240, 560; XII, 79.

Thomas à Kempis, Augustinian - Author of *The Imitation of Christ*, I, 373; III, 483; V, 298.

Thomas Aquinas (Saint) - Writings, V, 297; crucifix was his library, IX, 28; teachings: Jesus did not take vows, XII, 299; XIIIa, 375; public vows acquire, simply by that fact, certain spiritual and divine solemnity, XIIIa, 406; to set aside one exercise of piety for another is to leave God for God, X, 556; explicit knowledge of Mysteries of Trinity and Incarnation necessary as means to salvation, I, 119; X, 271; XI, 172–73, 343–44; XII, 72; XIIIa, 174; more difficult to put up with mortifications coming from without than voluntary ones, IV, 55; God has never worked any miracles to confirm errors, VI, 291–92; more meritorious to love neighbor for love of God than to love God without practical application to neighbor, XII, 214; no one can be lost in practice of charity, XIIIb, 437; if we were not free, religion would be fruitless and pure folly, XIIIa, 171; no one can be absolved of sins without confessing them and having contrition for them, XIIIb, 357; besides absolute Commandments, some others oblige only *quoad preparationem animi*, XII, 102; other mentions, I, 584; V, 453.

Thomas Becket (Saint), Archbishop of Canterbury - Punishment of King Henry II, who had him murdered, IX, 305.

Thomas of Villanova (Saint) - Canonization, VII, 329.

Thomassin (Marie-Cécile), Visitandine - Biographical data; Saint Vincent gives permission for Fr. Lallemant to enter monastery each time there is need, VIII, 269.

Thonon, town in Haute-Savoie - Sainte-Chapelle de Thonon, VIII, 67.

Thou (M. de), French Ambassador at The Hague - VIII, 596.

Thouvant (Claude), Archdeacon of Aizenay - Benefactor of Luçon house, III, 145, 147; mission funded by him, III, 490.

Thouvenot (M.) - Contacts with Saint Vincent, VI, 522.

Thouvignon (Dominique), Commander of Saint-Esprit de Toul - resigns this benefice in favor of Charles de Gournay, Bishop of Toul, with request that he give it to Priests of the Mission, I, 417; II, 40, 476–77.

Thualt (M.), notary - XIIIb, 396.

Thuillier (M.) - XIIIa, 21.

Thulon (M.) - Member of Charity of Joigny, XIIIb, 66.

Tillon (Hélène) - Member of Charity of Châtillon, XIIIb, 22.

Time - Mention of conference on good use of time, XII, 434. See also **Work**.

Timothy (Saint) - Quote from Saint Paul's letter to Timothy, XI, 55; other mention, III, 482.

Tinien (M.) - Letter of Fr. Lucas to M. Tinien, I, 278.

Tinti (Abbé), Agent of King of France in Rome - Intervention in Chancelade affair, IV, 27, 136; in foundation of Duchesse d'Aiguillon, VIII, 7; Duchess complains about his dishonesty, VIII, 21, 39.

Tintillier (Mme) - Saint Vincent informs her of money being sent, VII, 364.

Tiron-Saint-Priest (M.) - I, 29.

Titus (Saint) - Mention, III, 482.

Tivoli, town in Lombardy - XI, 341.

Tivoli, town near Rome - Saint Vincent urges Fr. Jolly to go to rest in Tivoli or Frascati, VII, 240; Giovanni Battista Taone gives missions in diocese, V, 378.

Tizon (G.), member of Charity of Courboin - XIIIb, 93.

Tobit, biblical personage - Disconsolate at having lost his sight, V, 513; God tested his love and fidelity, IX, 39; his charity, X, 146.

Toinette (Mlle), in Clermont - I, 284.

Tolagnaro - See ***Tholanghare***.

Toledo, city in Spain - Plan to open Missionaries' house, VI, 363–64; VII, 292, 343, 391, 400, 407, 433; Archbishop: see Balthazar **Moscoso y Sandoval**; Prelate's chaplain wants to enter Congregation of the Mission, VII, 327.

Toledo [**Tolet**] (Francisco), Cardinal - Biographical data; author of *Summa casuum conscientiae absolutissima*, II, 608; reassures Clement VIII, tortured with remorse for having absolved of heresy Henry IV, who then relapsed into error, V, 317; XII, 283; XIIIa, 377.

Toniello, priest, consultor for *Propaganda* - XIIIa, 250.

Tonkin - Situation of Catholic Church in area; petition to Rome requesting nomination of Bishops *in partibus*, IV, 595; V, 15–16; fund destined to assure stipends of Bishops, IV, 605; V, 16, 78; decision of Rome awaited in Paris, V, 78; decision is favorable, VI, 605; Saint Vincent does not think missionaries destined for Tonkin and Cochin-China have another intention, VI, 553; does not think they want to form Congregation, or could, if they wanted, VI, 630: see also ***Cochin China***, **Pallu**.

Tonnerre, commune in department of Yonne - Vicar-General of Moutiers-Saint-Jean Abbey lauds work of Priests of the Mission there, II, 497.

Tonnerre (Louis de Clermont, Chevalier de), slave in Tunis, son of Comtesse de Tonnerre - VII, 145, 523; VIII, 331, 337.

Tonnerre (Marie Vignier, Comtesse de) - Sends money for son, VII, 519; reimburses Saint Vincent for loan to son, slave in Algiers, VII, 523; VIII, 331, 337.

Topics treated in conferences at Saint-Lazare (1650–60) - XII, 405–38.

Tor dei Specchi, Community in Rome - Members are not nuns, although certain take simple vows, XIIIa, 405.

Toul, town in Meurthe-et-Moselle - Bishops: see André **Du Saussay**, Charles-Chrétien de **Gournay**, Jacques **Le Bret**; Vicar-General: see **Midot**; Judges: see **Fremyn**, **Trélon**; Lieutenant-General of bailiwick of Toul: see **Favier**; charity of Duchesse d'Aiguillon toward nuns in Toul, III, 202–03; town in distress because of large number of soldiers garrisoned there, IV, 16; passing of Court through Toul, VI, 534; diocese offered to François Hallier, IV, 601; letters from Saint Vincent to Toul Missionaries, I, 323, 378, 558; II, 68, 74; III, 69: see **Caset**, **Delespiney**, **Demonchy**, **des Jardins**; letters received from them, V, 553, 618.

Foundation of establishment, I, 417; Saint Vincent reprimands Superior who does not feed confreres well, I, 378; M. Fleury sells Missionaries his share in two small houses adjoining hospital, II, 113; great regularity, union, cordiality in house, II, 492; how Missionaries got Saint-Esprit house in Toul, I, 417; II, 476–78; they reside there, II, 70, 75; possession of house contested by Order of Saint-Esprit; lawsuit, I, 417, 438, 540, 544; II, 68–69, 156; III, 366–67, 449; IV, 16; rights of Missionaries recognized by town, II, 156; Saint Vincent asks protection of magistrate of Toul, II, 476; decree of King's Council, II, 477; settlement, II, 171; affair taken to Rome, II, 40–41, 105, 477, 541; rights of Mission defended there by Fr. Midot, Vicar-General, II, 41; and by Fr. Le Bret, II, 491–92; Commanders of Saint-Esprit de Toul: see **Dehorgny**, **Jolly** (Edme); Fr. Jolly resigns Commandery in favor of Congregation of the Mission, V, 153; formalities with view to union, VI, 427; VII, 1, 51–52.

Charity toward poor, I, 542; II, 42, 45, 74, 93; missions, IV, 15; V, 618; VII, 52, 358; care of two parishes, Écrouves and Toul, impedes ministry of missions, V, 236; VI, 457, 533; retreats for ordinands, VI, 366, 427, 457, 535; saint unable to send priest, as requested, VI, 533; canonical visitation by Fr. Dehorgny, I, 438; II, 69, 82, 93; Fr. Lambert aux Couteaux, II, 324; Fr. Portail, V, 440; Fr. Berthe, VII, 613; VIII, 13, 15, 16.

List of Superiors and history of house, VIII, 605–06; Jacques Le Soudier, consulted for position of Superior, asks to be excused for health reasons, V, 19; Toul Missionaries: see **Aulent**, **Bécu** (Jean), **Boucher** (Léonard), **Bourdet** (Étienne), **Brin**, **Caset**, **Colée**, **Delespiney**, **Demonchy**, **Desdames**, **des Jardins**, **Du Coudray**, **Dupont** (Louis), **Joustel**, **Lambert aux Couteaux**, **Lefebvre** (Augustin), **Proust**; other mentions, I, 556, 582; II, 45, 113, 260; III, 65, 68; VII, 137; X, 453; XIIIa, 329.

Toulon, town in Var - Bishop: see Pierre **Pingré**; prisoners in Toulon: see **Auroy**, **Ballagny**, **Bonner**, **Chocart**, **Deleau**, **Dubois** (Denis), **Duval**, **Esbran**, **Frangé**, **Lancre** (Martin de), **Le Cercieux**, **Le Gros** (Pierre), **Le Page**, **Lesueur**, **Mansart**, **Marbais**, **Meglat**, **Moger**, **Traverse**; Missionaries who ministered to prisoners: see **Huguier**, **Mugnier**, **Parisy**; journey of Fr. Get to Toulon: see **Get** (Firmin); hospital for prisoners, V, 244; VI, 186–87; galleys for Rome in port of Toulon, II, 339;

may need to return to Marseilles, VII, 488; other mentions, V, 412; VI, 121, 201, 207; VII, 316; VIII, 545.

Toulouse, town in Haute-Garonne - Saint Vincent studies at University of Toulouse and receives diploma of Bachelor of Theology, I, 10; legacy of woman of Toulouse, I, 2; incurs debts there, I, 14; hires horse, I, 3; plans to return here, I, 520, 526; piety of inhabitants, III, 196; Parlement, I, 2; registers Act of Establishment of Cahors house, VIII, 611; Archbishops: see Pierre de **Marca**, Charles de **Montchal**; Visitation Nuns, III, 198; VIII, 144; sermons of Fathers of Christian Doctrine in Toulouse, XII, 209; mission given by so-called Missionary, VI, 517–18; Jansenism in diocese, IV, 248; supporters of probablism (laxism) in Toulouse, VII, 547, 550, 628; decree of Parlement suppressing preaching of Huguenots, II, 503–04; confreres evangelize Toulouse diocese: see **Boudet**, **Durot**, **Sergis**; brother of Jean Martin is going to Toulouse, II, 652; III, 187; Charles de Montchal wishes to establish Priests of the Mission in diocese and confide seminary to them; waits for saint to express desire, III, 538; saint prefers to wait until called, III, 538; IV, 144; on occasion of foundation given him, offers services to Archbishop, IV, 144; Jansenism and other false teachings in town, III, 591–92; decree of Parlement regarding Solminihac, IV, 124; Daughters of Charity requested, V, 629; IX, 527–28; X, 95, 317; Dominicans of Toulouse, III, 386; other mentions, III, 227; VIII, 5; XI, 85; XIIIa, 109.

Toulouse (Raymond VII, Comte de) - Revolt against authority of Saint Louis, XI, 273.

Tounère (Marie-Catherine), Visitandine from Compiègne - Mother de Fontaine asks permission for her to enter and stay for a time in First Monastery of Paris, VIII, 530.

Touquin, village in Seine-et-Marne - V, 40.

Touraine, province - VI, 591; IX, 275; XIIIb, 267.

Tournan, town in Seine-et-Marne - Mission given, VI, 356.

Tournelle, prison in Paris - VIII, 545, 546.

Tournemynes [**Tournemine**] (Paul), Chevalier de Camzillon de Chameville - Proxy for Archbishop Paul Hurault de l'Hospital in affair of Saint-Léonard de Chaume Abbey, XIIIa, 19–20.

Tourneton (Marguerite), Daughter of Charity - Departure from Company, III, 209, 211.

Tournisson (Fr.), Priest of the Mission - In Crécy, III, 318.

Tournus, town in Saône-et-Loire - Abbé de Tournus: see also **Chandenier** (Louis de), Canons of Tournus, VII, 320; passage of Court through town, VII, 321; other mentions, V, 550; VII, 404; VIII, 132.

Tours, town in Indre-et-Loire - Birthplace of Martin Jolly: see **Jolly** (Martin); Hôtel-Dieu, I, 194; Dominican Convent, VII, 384; Visitation, II, 626; sojourn in Tours by Saint Vincent, II, 529; III, 409; by Saint Louise, II, 10; III, 9; by Fr. Gondrée, III, 289; by Fr. Mousnier, V, 277; by Fr. Alméras, VIII, 413, 421, 423, 483; Daughters of Charity from area, III, 301, 421, 422; canonry in Champigny-sur-Veude promised to man from Tours, III, 605; return of Ribot, brother of Algerian slave, VI, 8; other mentions, I, 420, 499, 500, 502, 594, 596; II, 12; IV, 46; VI, 262; VIII, 371.

Touschard (M.) - Saint Vincent entrusts him with errand for Dax, I, 332.

Toussaint (Barbe), Daughter of Charity - Arrival in Angers, I, 603; II, 12; XIIIb, 118; trial to companions, III, 416; almost completely calmed down, III, 424.

Toussainte (Sister) - See **David**.

Toussainte (Sister) - See **Allou**.

Toutblanc (Louis), secretary to Duc de Retz - Legacy for Montmirail Missionaries, II, 554; VIII, 612.

Traitez des droits et libertez de l'Église gallicane - Book censured by many French Bishops, III, 591.

Trambly (Antoine), of Mâcon - XIIIb, 74.

Tranchot (M.) - His praise, II, 571.

Tranchot (Mlle) - Takes interest in Charity of Saint-Benoît, I, 96; of Villeneuve-Saint-Georges, I, 128; in Michel Le Gras, I, 138; Saint Vincent advises Saint Louise to stay at her house in Villeneuve, I, 161; other mention, II, 571.

Tranquility - Saint Vincent asks Saint Louise to honor tranquility of Our Lord, I, 171.

Transylvania - Prince of Transylvania joins enemies of Poland, VI, 645; VII, 83.

Tratebas (Antoine), Priest of the Mission - Biographical data, V, 411; VI, 411; VII, 18; VIII, 161; XI, 153; his father, VI, 617, 628; his family gives hospitality to Fr. Portail during plague epidemic in Marseilles, VIII, 161; questioned in course of conference, XI, 153; sent to Genoa, V, 411; risks life to serve plague-stricken, VI, 411, 432, 491; death, VI, 504, 506, 509, 528, 530, 535, 537, 567, 583, 586; VII, 15, 18; XI, 379, 381; mention of conference on his virtues, XII, 429.

Traversay (Anne Petau, Dame de) - Biographical data, I, 336; II, 222; III, 253; V, 282; VI, 203; VIII, 465; Lady of Charity, I, 336, 495; II, 328; VI, 203; concern for galley convicts, II, 222, 224; for foundlings, II, 328, 444, 485–88; III, 253–54; for Sisters who minister to them, II, 299, 300; contacts with Saint Vincent, I, 497; III, 303; V, 344, 357; with Saint Louise, II, 478, 598; V, 344; gift of Christmas crib to Fr. Étienne, VIII, 585; other mentions, I, 593; V, 282; VIII, 465.

Traverse (Vincent) - Prisoner in Toulon, VI, 195, 418, 599, 617; VII, 101, 179, 245, 486; VIII, 299, 361.

Trabzon [***Trébizond***] - Saint Vincent sends Archbishop letter of Cardinal Antonio Barberini, V, 176; death and succession, XIIIa, 196; see also Agostino **Fracioti**; other mention, III, 274.

Treatise on the Love of God - Book by Saint Francis de Sales, I, 513; XIIIa, 84; XIIIb, 442.

Treffort (Simon), Priest of the Mission - Biographical data, II, 633; IV, 141; VI, 477; VII, 373; in Cahors, II, 633; III, 81; IV, 141, 273, 451, 452, 480; Saint Vincent suggests he go to Lorm to give missions, VI, 477; in Notre-Dame de Lorm; needs encouragement, VII, 373.

Tréguier, town in Côtes-du-Nord - Bishop: see Balthazar Grangier de **Liverdi**; Canons: see **Duval** (Fr.), **Rumelin**; fondness of clergy of diocese for wine, VIII, 168; Bishop asks for Daughters of Charity to minister in three hospitals, XI, 327; Saint Vincent unable to accommodate him, VI, 139; union of Archdeaconry of Tréguier to Le Mans house proposed to saint; he declines, VII, 535.

Tréguier Missionaries: letters from Saint Vincent, IV, 546; V, 80, 582: see **Dupont** (Louis); talk of giving direction of Tréguier Seminary to Congregation of the Mission; revenue insufficient, II, 434; difficulties presented by foundation: see **Rumelin**; Bishop entrusts seminary to Priests of the Mission, asks them to preach, by exception, in Tréguier, increases seminary revenues by union of chapels, agrees that Superior may accept foundation, refuses Missionaries permission to use powers given them by Rome concerning absolution of cases reserved to Pope, complains to Saint Vincent about recall of seminary professor; Saint Vincent reminds him that Missionaries cannot hear, in their houses, confessions of outsiders: see **Liverdi** (Balthazar Grangier de); benefactors of seminary, VIII, 222: see **Duval** (Fr.), **Rumelin**; Saint Vincent gives Fr. Dupont permission to preach there for a week by order of Bishop, on occasion of Jubilee, V, 604–05.

Superior carries out obligations of foundation ahead of time, VIII, 76; threat of lawsuit between seminary and

Chapter, VIII, 168–69; priests formed in seminary, IV, 313; God blesses seminary, VII, 566–67; censure of professor who dictates lessons, VI, 64; missions, III, 616; canonical visitation by Saint Vincent, III, 409; by Fr. Berthe, VI, 381–82; by Fr. Dehorgny, VIII, 76, 131, 170, 221, 285; assignments, V, 535; division among Missionaries, V, 582; VIII, 318; lapse of Missionary, VII, 42; insufficiency of personnel, VI, 198, 382, 586–87; VII, 399, 429; list of Superiors and history of house, VIII, 616; Tréguier Missionaries: see **Butler** (Peter), **Dupont** (Louis), **Lapostre**, **Laudin** (Gabriel), **Menand**, **Pennier**, **Plunket**, **Rivet** (Jacques), **Talec**, **Tholard**.

Treilles (François) - XIIIa, 21.

Treilles (Girault) - XIIIa, 21.

Treize-Maisons, in Paris - See **Foundlings**.

Trélon (Cauchon, Seigneur de), Judge - Benevolence toward Troyes Missionaries, II, 69, 74; correspondence with Saint Vincent, I, 558; III, 449; one of executors of will of Commander de Sillery, his uncle, II, 134.

Tremollières (M.) - Secretary-Councillor of King, XIIIa, 148.

Trémon (M. de), Governor of Mâcon - XIIIb, 75.

Trent (Congregation of Council) - Pope consults Congregation before issuing Brief *Ex Commissa Nobis* on vows in Congregation of the Mission, XII, 306, 351; XIIIa, 417, 420, 482.

Trent (Council) - Regulations of Council of Trent to be respected as coming from Holy Spirit, II, 505; Saint Augustine should be explained by Council of Trent and not Council of Trent by Saint Augustine, III, 328; Saint-Cyran admits legitimacy and ecumenicity of Council, XIIIa, 121, 134–36; Saint Vincent has not heard him contradict it, XIIIa, 108; saint could give statutes to his Congregation, but they must not contradict decisions of Council, XIIIa, 248, 303–04, 315, 317, 396; regulations of Council recommended to Madagascar Missionaries, III, 280; collection of Canons and Decrees of Council, III, 282; V, 297; Council recommends recourse to Pope in difficulties, IV, 213; VI, 293; promotes seminaries, II, 256; XIIIa, 309–10; Saint-Méen Seminary in conformity with Trent, III, 51, 53.

Council of Trent condemns beforehand errors of Jansenism, IV, 607; teaches universality of redemption, III, 325; possibility of willfully resisting movement of grace, XIIIa, 169, 171; allows public penance for public sins, III, 362; IV, 35; asks that penance be proportionate to gravity of sin, V, 322; counsels confession of venial sins for greater purity, XIIIb, 357; ordinances regarding seminaries, II, 505; III, 53,

111; regarding accountability of seminary to Bishop, II, 507; conditions of admission to seminaries, XIIIa, 428; demands that any ecclesiastical post be given only after examination, XIIIa, 87; that religious houses not part of any Congregation be united to form one Congregation, III, 225; authorizes Society of Jesus, despite prohibition against founding new religious Orders, XIIIa, 381; wants nuns to be examined before receiving habit and profession, IV, 486, 490; to have extraordinary confessor four times a year, XIIIb, 262; forbids giving seculars permission to enter cloister, except for necessity, VI, 284; VIII, 153–54; by exception, Jesuits not obliged to follow one of the four Rules of the time, XIIIa, 381; Council regulations concerning election of Superioresses, III, 454–55; Council declares choosing worst among those presented is sinful, X, 218; Council refers to Holy See difficulties arising from its decrees, IV, 183; war prevents Pope from making decision with all conditions prescribed by Council, IV, 211; other mention, I, 43, 51; XIIIa, 102, 162; XIIIb, 387.

Trente-Trois, collège in Paris - Historical note, VIII, 203.

Trévoux, town in Ain - Confraternity of Charity established, XIIIb, 74.

Trévy (M. de) - II, 18.

Trials - Trials draw down graces of God on those who bear with them, I, 157; IV, 222, 356; IX, 184–85; example of Jesus, XI, 333; of Saint Vincent, XI, 338, 339, 367, 373–74; of Saint **Jane Frances de Chantal**: see this name; virtue recognized especially in trials, VIII, 374; great plans always pass through trials, XI, 367–68; trials found everywhere, IV, 265; VI, 63; VII, 322; to be endured patiently at foot of Cross, IX, 393, 398; make them known to Superiors, not to others, VII, 446; IX, 15, 33, 63, 276, 398, 413, 502, 503, 541; X, 149, 164, 355–67; unless Superiors cannot give help, X, 361; consolation for afflicted persons, I, 126; IV, 265; V, 14, 197, 410; VI, 449; VII, 246, 255; VIII, 374: see also **Murmuring**, **Persecution**, **Spiritual Dryness**, **Sufferings**, **Temptations**.

Trier (***Trèves***), town in Germany - VII, 537.

Trinitarians - See **Mathurin Fathers**.

Trinité (Mother de la), Superior of Troyes Carmel - Biographical data, I, 399; II, 116; letters Saint Vincent writes to her, I, 399, 415, 443, 569, 577; II, 132, 228; benefactor of Troyes Missionaries, I, 415–16, 443; II, 132; of Annecy, I, 571; inspiration, II, 116; Saint Vincent urges her not to leave Troyes, II, 229.

Trinity (Mystery) - Mention of conferences on this Mystery, XII, 411, 427, 432; explanation of Mystery, XIIIa, 175–79; conference on worship owed to Blessed Trinity; Blessed Trinity, patron of Congregation of the Mission, XI, 172; according to great Doctors, explicit knowledge of this Mystery is necessary means for salvation, I, 119; X, 271; XI, 172–73, 344; XII, 72–73; XIIIa, 174; worship of Blessed Trinity recommended to members of Charity of Châtillon, XIIIb, 18; zeal of Daughters of Charity will teach Mystery, XI, 173; Blessed Trinity, model of uniformity, X, 292; XII, 210; XIIIb, 274; of union, IV, 238; IX, 80, 81; XIIIb, 275.

Tripoli, town in Barbary - Pasha requests Missionary, V, 180; other mentions, V, 132; VIII, 162; XIIIa, 346.

Tripoli, town in Syria - VII, 274.

Tristan (Claude), member of Tuesday Conferences - Biographical data, II, 265; VII, 382; Vicar-General of Beauvais, VII, 382.

Trobois [**Trubois**] (M.) - II, 528; debt he owes Saint Lazare, II, 528, 535.

Trois-Épis (***Notre-Dame***) - Historical note, VII, 335; shrine offered to Saint Vincent for Congregation, VI, 534; VII, 335; Lieutenant-General of bailiwick of Toul presses for end to affair, VIII, 11.

Tronson (Germain), notary in Paris - XIIIa, 25.

Tronson (Mme) - Superior of Daughters of Blessed Virgin, VIII, 473.

Troyes, town in Aube - Climate considered one of best in kingdom, VII, 150; Bishops: see also René de **Breslay**, François Malier **du Houssay**; journeys and sojourns of Saint Vincent in Troyes, I, 412, 552, 557, 558, 559; Commander de Sillery in Troyes, I, 577–78; presence of two Irish regiments and numerous Irish refugees, V, 82; in great misery; Saint Vincent does not know how to help them, VII, 348; Visitation Monastery, I, 556; II, 134, 135, 168; Carmel: see **Trinité** (Mother); Daughters of Charity natives of Troyes, II, 194; XIIIb, 360- 62; other mentions, II, 147; V, 584; VI, 300; VII, 507, 529.

Troyes Missionaries: letters from Saint Vincent, I, 521, 522, 530; II, 167; IV, 350; VI, 507, 574; VII, 139, 308, 347; VIII, 72, 276; Fr. Grenu sent to Troyes, I, 404; imminent departure of Missionaries destined for new establishment, I, 444; choice of lodging, I, 443; difficulty of finding place either in town or in faubourg, I, 570; Missionaries will live in borrowed house in Sancey: see **Sancey**; benefactors of house: see **Girardin**, **Sillery** (Noël Brulart de), **Trinité** (Mother); revenues, II, 359; Saint Jane Frances de Chantal hopes that Troyes will give two priests and Brother to Annecy house, II, 61; missions, I, 521, 528; VI, 381, 393, 570; VII, 166, 334; seminary professors, VI, 507, 574; VII, 235; VIII, 219; number of seminarians, V, 82; Bishop wants to unite Barbuise parish to seminary to increase revenues; Saint Vincent refuses: see **Barbuise**; retreats for ordinands, I, 445, 531; assistance for Irish refugees, V, 82; VII, 348; for poor people, III, 409; canonical visitation by Saint Vincent, I, 552, 557, 558, 559; II, 69; by Fr. Alméras, III, 68; V, 261, 312; by Fr. Berthe, VIII, 15; illness of Missionaries, IV, 290.

List of Superiors and history of house, VIII, 607; Troyes Missionaries: see **Bourdet** (Jean), **Brin**, **Charond**, **Cornuel**, **Dalton**, **Dassonval**, **Delorme**, **du Chesne** (Pierre), **du Coudray**, **Dufestel** (François), **Dupuich** (François), **McEnery** [**Ennery**], **Froment**, **Gigot**, **la Fosse**, **Lucas** (Antoine), **Ozenne** (Charles), **Perceval**, **René** (Bro.), **Rose** (Nicolas), **Savary**, **Senaux**, **Tholard**, **Villain**; other mentions, III, 68; V, 118, 251; VI, 579.

Troyes (Claude de), notary in Paris - XIIIa, 25.

Truchart (Fr.), confessor of Daughters of Charity in Nantes - III, 604; V, 9, 57; XIIIb, 321, 328.

Truffar (Marie) - Member of Charity of Paillart, XIIIb, 48.

Truillard (M.) - Captain of cavalry of Prince of Moldavia; VI, 109; Saint Vincent forwards letters from his father, VIII, 369, 420.

Truluy (Mme), Lady of Charity - III, 213.

Trumeau (Marie-Marthe), Daughter of Charity - Biographical data, V, 57; VII, 191; VIII, 127; ill in Angers, III, 21, 35; Sister Servant at Saint-Paul, XIIIb, 302; in Nantes in same capacity, V, 57; IX, 517; XIIIb, 312; recalled to Paris, V, 432; sent to La Fère, X, 160; Sister Servant, X, 163; in La Fère, VII, 191; X, 233; calumniated, VIII, 233; sent to Cahors, VIII, 127; X, 533; other mention, XIIIb, 118, 227.

Trust in God - See **Confidence in God.**

Trzebicki (André), Bishop of Krakow - VII, 490.

Tubeuf (Jacques) - Biographical data, II, 92.

Tubeuf (Mme), daughter of Mlle Montdésir - V, 44.

Tuesday Conferences [**Priests' Conferences**] - Historical data, VII, 62; beginnings, I, 201, 202, 203; progress, I, 413; II, 264; Prelates of Assembly of Estates of Languedoc intend to have conferences in their dioceses, II, 614; Rule, VII, 230; XIIIa, 140–43; do not accept those who have been members of some other group, VII, 584; praise for their simplicity, II, 264, 270;

XII, 149–50, 247; for their piety, V, 196; XII, 269, 348; for their virtue, XI, 8; King chooses Bishops from among them, I, 413; meetings, I, 214, 238; II, 616; meetings held at Saint-Lazare moved to Bons-Enfants at beginning of 1658, VII, 405; topics discussed at meetings, I, 527; VII, 405; XI, 80, 325, 350; XII, 304; same subject discussed fourteen times, X, 559–60; those unable to attend send thoughts to meeting, X, 562; missions given by these priests, VIII, 366, 534: see ***Metz***; dying Saint Vincent blesses them, XIIIa, 205; Alet, II, 543, 614; Angoulême, II, 488, 501; Dauphiné, I, 527; Genoa, IV, 229; VII, 413; Marseilles, VII, 302; VIII, 136; Metz, VII, 92, 102, 170; Muret, I, 527; Noyon, II, 440, 441; Pontoise, II, 283; Puy, XII, 357; Saintes, II, 660; Queen's suggestion for mission to be proposed at meeting, II, 534; other mentions, II, 41, 53, 71, 219, 296, 316, 405; VI, 115; VIII, 108; XIIIa, 370, 386. See also **Abelly**, **Alix** (Michel), **Barreau** (M.), **Blampignon**, **Bossuet**, **Chandenier** (Claude de), **Chandenier** (Louis de), **Fouquet** (François), **Gedoyn**, **Godeau**, **Maupas du Tour**, **Olier**, **Pavillon** (Nicolas), **Perriquet**, **Perrochel**, **Saint-Floran**, **Tristan**.

Tuet, mill and small farm - Property of Richelieu Missionaries, IV, 8.

Tulle, town in Corrèze - Bishop: see Jean-Richard de Genoulhac de **Vaillac**; sad state of diocese, IV, 27.

Tulloue (Robert), notary in Paris - XIIIa, 21.

Tumy (Ambroise), Brother of the Mission - Biographical data, III, 408; VIII, 563; death, VIII, 563.

Tunis, town in Barbary - Saint Vincent, slave in Tunisia, I, 4–9, 12; VIII, 599–601; benefactor of Mission of Tunis: see **Aiguillon** (Duchesse d'); consulate: see **Huguier**, **Husson**, **Le Vacher** (Jean); slaves; confreres ministering to slaves: see **Guérin** (Julien), **Le Vacher** (Jean); Saint Vincent considers sending Pierre du Chesne to visit Barbary Missionaries, V, 147; seizures of Turkish corsairs, V, 133; raid on Calabria, V, 390; distraint of English against Tunis; Saint Vincent would like French to imitate this, V, 387; other mentions, V, 145, 150, 162, 393, 530; VI, 153, 613; VII, 105, 411, 437; VIII, 600; XI, 290; XII, 61: see also **Barbary**.

Turbot (Jean), Priest of the Mission - Biographical data; in Saint-Méen, III, 458.

Turco (Tommaso), Superior General of Dominicans - Letters from Saint Vincent, III, 383; letters to Saint Vincent, II, 561, 562; III, 315, 385.

Turenne (Henri de la Tour, Vicomte de), Maréchal de France - Biographical data, IV, 423; army defeated at Saint-Étienne, IV,

150; Saint Vincent asks him for soldier to guard Livry farm, IV, 423; reference to Turenne's wife, VII, 419.

Turenne (Marguerite de), Daughter of Charity - Hesitation in giving her the habit, II, 195, 198; dismissed from Company, XIIIb, 267–69.

Turet (Jeanne), Daughter of Charity - XIIIb, 228.

Turgis (Denis), notary in Paris - XIIIa, 20, 22, 59, 66.

Turgis (Élisabeth Le Goutteux), widow, Daughter of Charity - Biographical data, I, 326; II, 13; III, 216; retreat at Motherhouse, I, 326; Saint Vincent agrees to her making few months' seminary, I, 327; proposed for Hôtel-Dieu, I, 352; at Foundlings, I, 431, 468, 488, 574; Saint Louise proposes that she replace her in her absence, II, 302; Saint Vincent hesitates to send her to Angers Hospital, I, 600; in Angers, 601; II, 12; recall to Paris is considered, II, 81; arrival in Paris, II, 137, 139; Sister Servant in Richelieu, III, 8, 216; Sister Servant in Chars, III, 298; Sister Servant in Saint-Denis, III, 419; asks Saint Louise for catechism, XIIIb, 299; death, XIIIb, 295; other mentions, II, 196, 337.

Turin, town in Piedmont - Archbishop: see Giulio Cesare **Bergera**; threat of plague, VI, 40, 72, 86, 89; plague does not materialize, VI, 92, 110, 127; Visitation nuns of Turin, VI, 522, 602; VII, 312; Missionaries called to Turin by priest of Piedmont, V, 165; by Marchese di Pianezza, V, 252, 412; initial negotiations, V, 252–54, 373–74; Saint Vincent specifies what is necessary to accept foundation; departure of first Missionaries for Turin, V, 455; arrival, V, 476, 477; benefactors of establishment: see **Pianezza** (Marchese), **Belletia** (Judge); correspondence between Saint Vincent and Turin Missionaries: see **Gontier** (Aubin), **Martin** (Jean), **Planchamp**; Saint Vincent advises beginning slowly with modest mission, V, 477–79, 485.

Blessed Sacrament Church offered to them, V, 253, 636; search for housing, VI, 30, 87, 262; VII, 508; Missionaries not suitably housed, VII, 59; house remains empty nine months of year, VIII, 176; Marchese di Pianezza proposes to install them in Savigliano; difficulties of project: see also ***Savigliano***; procures housing for them, but it is inadequate, VII, 231, 243; they leave second time to live in larger rented house, and air is better, VII, 290; efforts of Marchese di Pianezza to have them given palace at disposition of Pope, VIII, 110; gentleman offers them small church, outside of Turin, with a few rooms he has had built, VIII, 237; Saint Vincent recommends that Superior rely on Providence for lodging without doing anything to anticipate it, VIII, 271, 482–83; project of uniting ***Sant'Antonio*** Abbey and Priory-parish of ***Saint-Jeoire*** to Company: see these words; missions, VIII, 246, 272: see

Martin (Jean); calumnious complaints against Missionaries taken to Parlement of Turin, VI, 1–2; Senate proposes expelling them as disturbers of the peace, VI, 29; Missionaries engaged in missions for nine months of year, VIII, 153; proposal for diocesan seminary, V, 594; VI, 138, 558, 600; VIII, 66–67, 110.

Canonical visitations by Fr. Berthe, VI, 308, 600; VII, 24, 28, 30, 49, 242, 291, 312, 378–79, 414, 436, 439; VIII, 230; number of confreres, VI, 57; not zealous enough in study of Italian, V, 534, 544; VI, 308; totally disposed to sacrifice their lives if plague enters Turin, VI, 67; postulants sent to Saint-Lazare: see **Michelangelo**, **Pronetti**; to Genoa, VI, 262; VII, 231, 234; establishment progresses slowly, VII, 231; receives temporarily Missionaries sent to reconstitute Genoa house vacated by plague, VI, 525, 557–58, 578, 579, 600, 604, 620; VII, 59, 75, 103; Saint Vincent presses for their departure for Genoa, VII, 153, 210, 230, 234, 242; retreat and renewal of vows, VII, 378.

Illness of several confreres, VII, 312; malaise, VII, 290, 312, 378; Missionaries who do not give edification, VII, 242, 312; VIII, 87; inadequacy of personnel, V, 485, 500, 534; VI, 2–3, 31, 86–87, 141, 160, 170, 205, 256, 299-300, 497, 570; VIII, 118; Saint Vincent sends Fr. Le Vazeux, Superior in Annecy, to help Fr. Martin; Fr. Le Vazeux is detained: see **Le Vazeux**; saint proposes to Fr. Martin help of priest who left Fr. d'Authier's Community, VI, 496, 559; visit of Fr. Berthe, V, 584, 594, 598; VIII, 206–07; of Louis and Claude de Chandenier, VIII, 176, 191; way of life of Turin Missionaries reminds Chandeniers of Saint-Lazare, VIII, 176.

Turin Missionaries: see **Beaure**, **Cauly**, **Deheaume**, **Demortier**, **McEnery** [**Ennery**], **Gontier** (Aubin), **Laurence**, **Martin** (Jean the Elder), **Martinis**, **Mugnier**, **Musy**, **Paquinot**, **Planchamp**, **Richard**, **Stelle**, **Taone**; confreres whose placement in Turin is considered, but not executed: see **Baliano**, **Bonnet**, **Chardon**, **Gigot**, **Greco**, **Pesnelle**; other mention, VI, 196.

Turin (M.) - VII, 10.

Turks - Definition, IV, 127; V, 35; XIII, 265b; reconcile quickly, III, 227; X, 377; they do not drink wine, X, 291; victory of Venetians over Turks, VI, 71: see also ***Algiers, Barbary, Constantinople, Tunis***.

Turmeau (M.), merchant in Lyons - VI, 92; VII, 374.

Turpin (Marie-Euphrosine), Visitandine - Biographical data, I, 267; II, 454; Saint Vincent invites her to come to Madeleine Convent in Paris, I, 267; Superior of Amiens convent; saint writes to her, II, 454.

Turpin (Pierre), Priest of the Mission - Biographical data, V, 575; VI, 276; VII, 494; VIII, 422; in Le Mans, V, 575; VI, 276; VII, 494; fine cantor, VI, 277; ordination, VI, 584; qualities and faults, VI, 584–85; wants to go to Madagascar, VII, 527; Saint Vincent proposes him to *Propaganda*, VII, 576; Procurator in Le Mans, VIII, 422.

Tuscany (Ferdinand II de Médicis, Grand Duke of) - Louis XIV writes about bankrupt Rappiot, merchant in Marseilles, VI, 372, 650; other mention, VI, 361.

Tyrry (M.) - III, 271.

Tyszkiewicz (Georges), Archbishop of Vilna (Vilnius) - Holiness, IV, 252; Fr. Lambert goes to see him, IV, 274; Saint Vincent wants details about interview, IV, 315; receives excellent details, IV, 327; kindness of Prelate toward Missionaries, IV, 353, 382.

U

Ubaldini (Roberto), Cardinal - XIIIa, 250.

Ugolini (Stefano), Secretary of Briefs for Pope Alexander VII - XIIIa, 419.

Uist, island in Scotland - Evangelized by Fr. Duggan [Duiguin], IV, 496; V, 121.

Uniformity - Conferences, X, 280–92; 295–303; XII, 201–12; mention in other conferences, XII, 409, 424; text of Rule of Missionaries, XII, 201; of Daughters of Charity, X, 280, 295, 298; uniformity fosters union, IX, 79; X, 280, 282, 284; XI, 109; XII, 206, 210; offers happiness, XII, 208; example of Holy Trinity: see **Trinity**; of Jesus, XII, 205–06; of Church, XII, 211; of nature, XII, 204; teaching of Saint Paul, X, 295; XII, 203–04; obvious exceptions: sick and infirm, X, 301–02; XII, 207; no privileges for those who have given their goods to Company, VII, 339.

Be uniform in showing knowledge, XII, 209–10; in manner of preaching, XII, 209–10; of praying, X, 299; in **Communion** and in **Attire**: see these words; in food, see also **Meals**; in name of houses, which must everywhere be called "Mission," II, 355; in everything, XII, 206; XIIIb, 125, 136; reasons for difference between attire of Brothers and that of priests, XII, 207.

In what uniformity consists, X, 280–81, 295; XII, 201–03; extremes, XII, 202–03; way to have uniformity is to practice one's Rules: see also **Rules**; come often to Motherhouse to conform self to it by learning customs well, X, 281–82; know how to be average in order to be uniform, XII, 209; uniformity is necessary in a Company, V, 384; need to conform to spirit of Motherhouse, IX, 400; prayer for uniformity, XII, 212; see also **Singularity**.

Union - Conferences, IX, 78–92; XI, 109–12, 137; Rules of Daughters of Charity, X, 368; Saint Vincent recommends that members of Charities "cherish one another as Sisters whom Jesus Christ has chosen by His love," XIIIb, 136; union necessary among members of same Company, IV, 265; V, 169; VIII, 186; IX, 10, 32, 44, 294, 431, 518, 523; X, 184; union brings about peace, V, 169; IX, 79–80; preserves one's vocation, IX, 79, 81; in union is strength, IX, 79, 293–94; success of works is compromised without it, X, 163; disunion causes scandal, IX, 82–83, 85, 212; XIIIb, 277; caused Lucifer to be damned, IX, 81, 85; God so loves union that He has given all things means of union, IX, 81–82; Holy Trinity, model of union: see **Trinity**; Jesus, model of union in Communion, IX, 81; one who is divisive is unworthy to receive Communion, IX, 81, 83; those who foment disunion in Company merit dismissal, XIIIa, 389; to preserve union, avoid innovations, II, 355; union among houses of Company, XI, 109; exhortation to Missionaries going to Ireland, XI, 137; in what union consists, IX, 19, 79; union with one another through Jesus Christ, XI, 137; union with God, I, 157.

Minor misunderstandings always exist in Communities, III, 462; especially in small ones, V, 582–83; even among Angels and Apostles, III, 462; Community's reputation suffers from lack of union, IX, 212; rude, ill-mannered people more easily lack union, IX, 89; causes of disunion, XIIIa, 388: see also **Friendships (Exclusive)**, **Aversions**, **Calumny**, **Scandal**, **Mockeries**, **Murmurings**; means to maintain or reestablish union, IX, 85–91; XI, 110–11; XII, 89–92; XIIIa, 389: see also **Charity**, **Condescension**, **Insults**, **Reconciliation**, **Support**; know how to forgive, IX, 87–88; example of porters, IX, 86; uniformity maintains union: see also **Uniformity**.

University of Paris - See ***Sorbonne***.

Urban VIII, Pope - Letters from Saint Vincent, I, 38, 47, 140, 248; XIIIa, 242, 245; petition presented on behalf of Saint Vincent, XIIIa, 228; Pope present at session of *Propaganda Fide* approving Congregation of the Mission, XIIIa, 239; letter of Louis XIII to Pope, supporting request for privileges for Company from *Propaganda*, XIIIa, 243; Pope is present at session of *Propaganda* refusing petition of Saint Vincent, XIIIa, 249–50; note of *Propaganda* on willingness of Urban VIII to give faculties for simple mission, but not for new religious Order, XIIIa, 250–51; Bull of Urban VIII for erection of Congregation of the Mission, XIIIa, 296–304; mention of Bull, I, 141; VI, 519; XI, 172; XIIIa, 314, 315, 395, 403, 407, 419, 454, 456; XIIIb, 120, 230; Bulls for union of Saint-Lazare Priory to Congregation of the Mission, XIIIa, 486: see also ***Saint-Lazare***; will allow union of parishes to seminary, II, 417; priests of Fr. Authier say he refuses them his approval, II, 466; privileges accorded by Urban VIII to Missionaries of Rome house, V, 22, 548; XIIIa, 313, 314; refuses to reserve to himself and to Superior General dispensation from vows of Missionaries, II, 154–55; XIIIa, 378; Pope approves Constitutions of Visitation nuns, XIIIa, 93; Bull against Jansenius, III, 320, 323; IV, 607; false rumor of Pope's death, II, 250; solemn service at Saint-Lazare for repose of his soul, II, 522; other mentions, I, 97, 540–41, 553, 556; II, 63, 156, 240; III, 387; VI, 542; IX, 58; XIIIa, 264; XIIIb, 139, 141, 144, 230.

Uriah, Biblical personage - Put to death by David, IX, 253.

Ursulines - Saint Vincent allows Daughters to go to Ursulines to learn instruction of youth, I, 427; hesitations on this subject, X, 499; young woman from Ursulines could teach Daughters in La Chapelle, II, 186; differences between Ursulines' schools and those of Daughters of Charity, IX, 467; X, 118; method of Ursulines, III, 232; Ursulines of ***Cahors, Gisors, Guingamp, Isle-Bouchard, Melun, Moulins***: see these words.

Ussel, town in Corrèze - Advice of Saint Vincent to Sisters Anne Hardemont and Avoie Vigneron, sent to Ussel Hospital, X, 381; letters he writes them, VII, 246, 254, 396, 446, 447, 469; receives from them, VIII, 493; other mention, VIII, 495. See also **Hardemont**, **Vigneron** (Avoie).

Usury - Case of conscience regarding lending at interest, VI, 288; solutions approved in Sorbonne regarding usury may be followed without criticizing those who think otherwise, VII, 240.

Utica, town in Tunisia - Ruins, V, 131; titular Bishop: see Pierre de **Bertier**.

Uzes, town - Bishop: see Nicolas de **Grille**.

Uzziah, biblical King - Stricken with leprosy for having touched censer, XII, 86.

V

Vabres - Bishops: see Isaac **Habert**; François de **La Valette**. See also Jean de la Valette-Cornusson, Abbé **Beaulieu**, candidate for bishopric.

Vacations - Saint Vincent's opinion on vacations for students, VIII, 119–20; vacation times for Missionaries: see **Missions**.

Vacherot (M.), physician - Biographical data, II, 337; III, 16; Michel Le Gras stays at his home during illness, III, 16, 36; doctor for Saint-Lazare, III, 69; much appreciated by Saint Vincent, IV, 258; sister's illness, III, 263; other mention, II, 634.

Vaddé - Member of Charity of Joigny, XIIIb, 66.

Vageot (Philippe), Priest of the Mission - Biographical data, III, 287; IV, 385–86; V, 123–24; letters Saint Vincent writes him in Saintes, IV, 385, 472, 591, 603; V, 123; in Richelieu, III, 287; mention of letters to Saint Vincent, IV, 385, 603; V, 124; Superior in Saintes, IV, 389; V, 262; VIII, 612; illness, IV, 472–73; wants to go home because of father's situation; Saint Vincent dissuades him, IV, 591; he complies, IV, 603; missions, V, 124; in Paris, V, 416; about to leave Company, V, 422; leaves without saying goodbye, V, 425; XI, 277; goes home, returns to Paris, seems disposed to return to Saintes, V, 538; Saint Vincent urges Saintes Missionaries to have no contact with him, V, 565.

Vagré (Guillaume), Brother of the Mission - Biographical data, VIII, 1.

Vaillac (Jean-Richard de Genoulhac de), Bishop of Tulle - Illness, IV, 27.

Vaillant (Jean), in Clichy - XIIIa, 24.

Vaius (Étienne), Titular Bishop of Cyrene, Grand Master of Order of Saint-Esprit - Opposes union of Saint-Esprit in Toul to Congregation of the Mission, II, 41, 477.

Val-de-Grâce Abbey - Historical note, II, 424; proceedings for union of Saint-Corneille de Compiègne Abbey to Val-de-Grace, IV, 243–45; Abbess: see **Compans**; priory, XIIIa, 155.

Val-de-Puiseau - See ***Valpuiseaux***.

Val-des-Choux Abbey - Question of establishing reform there, IV, 246.

Valbelle (Antoine de), Lieutenant of admiralty in Marseilles - VII, 317.

Valbelle (Mme de) - Helps with ransom of captive, VIII, 377.

Valençay (Henri d'Estampes), Bailiff of Valençay, Ambassador to Rome - Saint Vincent seeks his protection, V, 54; other mentions, IV, 271, 585.

Valençay (Léonor d'Estampes de), Bishop of Chartres, then Archbishop of Reims - Biographical data, II, 395; III, 284; responsible for Missionaries' establishment in Richelieu, III, 284; contacts with Lambert aux Couteaux about this, I, 420, 438–39, 448; Saint Vincent lends him priest as chaplain, II, 395; sends others to preach retreat for ordinands, for which Prelate thanks him, II, 440; negotiates with him foundation of Sedan house, II, 524; saint asks Fr. Lambert to write to Bishop, II, 530; Bishop designates places where missions are to be given, VIII, 611; Saint Vincent urges Superior in Richelieu house to visit him, III, 284; death, IV, 194; other mention, II, 462.

Valence, town in Drôme - Bishop: see Charles-Jacques de Gélas de **Leberon**; Governor, III, 240; Saint-Victor novices studying in this town, VI, 99–100, 120; Company of priests in Valence: see also **Blessed Sacrament** (Priests); Marie de Valence: see **Tessonnière**.

Valenciennes, town in France - Nicolas Étienne passes through on way back to Paris, VIII, 597.

Valentinian III, Roman Emperor of West - XIIIa, 33.

Vallegrand, locality - Mission preached by Saint Vincent, I, 448.

Vallin (Anne), Daughter of Charity from Angers - Biographical data, II, 16; X, 513; in Paris, VII, 464; questioned on virtues of Barbe Angiboust, her Sister Servant in Saint-Denis, X, 513; other mention, XIIIb, 227; signs attestation after reading of Common and Particular Rules reviewed and arranged in order by Fr. Alméras, XIIIb, 206.

Valobron - See ***Le Mans***.

Valognes, town in Manche - III, 529.

Valois (Patrice), Priest of the Mission - See **Walsh** (Patrick).

Valon (M. de) - Excesses of soldiers of Languedoc regiment, of which he was Commander, III, 383.

Valprofonde (Carthusian monastery) - Saint Vincent makes retreat, II, 124.

Valpuiseaux, village in Essonne - Confraternity of Charity, IV, 235; misery and illness, IV, 400–02: see also ***Fréneville***; Daughters of Charity in Valpuiseaux; letters from Saint Vincent, III, 583; IV, 235, 249, 400; plans to visit them, III, 369; sends news of them to Saint Louise, III, 396; they return to Valpuiseaux, which they had left because of troubles and misery, IV, 400; Sisters on mission in Valpuiseaux: see **Marguerite**, **Marie-Madeleine**, **Perrette**.

Valton de la Fosse (M.), former administrator of Nantes Hospital - Complains of Sisters at hospital, III, 425.

Valus (Étienne), Grand Master of Saint-Esprit Order - Opposed union of house in Toul to Congregation of the Mission, II, 477.

Vancamberg (Gaspard), from Antwerp, slave in Algiers - VI, 392; VII, 8.

Vandals - God used them to afflict Church, XI, 279.

Vandy, village in Ardennes - IV, 189.

Vanity - Do not seek to be noticed: see also **Humility**; while preserving self from vanity, take care not to fall into contrary excess, IX, 349; God sometimes punishes it by vice of impurity, X, 304; Brothers are less inclined to it, XII, 87; vanity insinuates itself even into objects of devotion, X, 289; saint fears vanity in having Fr. Bourdaise's report printed, VI, 35; thought of putting fragrance on her linen would be great fault in Sister, IX, 21; excusing rather than accusing self in confession is vanity, IX, 441–42; vanity and sloth are cause of loss of vocation, XI, 89; vanity in **Attire**, **Preaching**, etc.: see these words; other mentions, I, 179, 319.

Vannes, town in Morbihan - Question of entrusting seminary to Priests of the Mission, II, 343, 419; project abandoned, II, 434; offer of another mission in Vannes diocese, III, 428; other mentions, V, 365; VIII, 217; XIIIb, 319.

Vanuci (M. de) - II, 418.

Varize (M. et Mme de) - Their praise, II, 347–48: see also ***Varize*** (village).

Varize, village in Eure-et-Loir - Mission given, II, 347–48; Daughters of Charity in Varize; Mme de Varize accepts sending two Sisters, given for Varize, to Châteaudun, IV, 416; they teach school and care for sick; Sister is needed, V, 43; recall of Sister Claude, VIII, 362: see also **Andrée** (Sister).

Varle (Marie) - Member of Charity of Montmirail, XIIIb, 32.

Varlet (Jacques), slave in Algiers; brother is Barnabite - V, 354; VII, 195, 208.

Vas [**Rus**] (Pierre), Brother of the Mission - Biographical data, II, 676.

Vasquez (Gabriel), Jesuit theologian - Opinion on vows of religion, XIIIa, 406.

Vasse (M.) - Right to indemnity from Notre-Dame de Coëffort, III, 28.

Vassi (M. de), prisoner in Toulon - VII, 403.

Vassy, town in Haute-Marne - Mission given, VII, 117.

Vaucouleurs, town in Meuse - VI, 187.

Vaucresson, village in Hauts-de-Seine - XIIIa, 386.

Vaugin (Jean), Brother of the Mission - Biographical data; departure from Company, VIII, 403; other mention, VIII, 535.

Vaugirard (commune), annexed to Paris in 1860 - Vaugirard Seminary transferred to Saint-Sulpice, II, 308.

Vaurette, priory in Lot - Steps taken for union of priory to Cahors Seminary; opposition, II, 451, 616; income used to support establishment of Missionaries in Cahors diocese, VIII, 611.

Vaux (Anne de), Daughter of Charity - Missioned to Nantes, XIIIb, 312; advice of Saint Vincent before departure, IX, 517; signs attestation after reading of Common and Particular Rules reviewed and arranged in order by Fr. Alméras, XIIIb, 206; other mention, XIIIb, 228.

Vaux (Guy Lasnier, Abbé de), Vicar-General of Angers - Biographical data, I, 591–92; II, 23–24; III, 15; V, 64–65; VI, 512–13; VII, 493; IX, 57; Saint Vincent writes about sending Daughters of Charity to Angers Hospital, I, 591–52, 594, 600; saint instructs Saint Louise to see him on same subject, I, 599; and to ask for money if needed, I, 602; Abbé de Vaux welcomes her in his house, I, 601; Saint Vincent thanks him for kindness to Saint Louise and Sisters, I, 603; correspondence between Abbé de Vaux and Saint Vincent, III, 15, 21, 431; V, 64; VII, 595; contacts of Abbé de Vaux with Saint Louise, II, 23, 106–07, 164, 190, 223; III, 35; V, 65; VI, 512; VII, 493; with Sisters of Angers Hospital, II, 81; IX, 57; XIIIb, 262–63, 284; in Paris, II, 50; upcoming trip to Paris, III, 277; other mention, II, 535.

Vaux (Jeanne de), Daughter of Charity - Entered before Act of Establishment, XIIIb, 228.

Vaux-le-Vicomte, hamlet in commune of Maincy (Seine-et-Marne) - Choice of Daughters of Charity to be sent there, VIII, 124; Sister recalled from Vaux, VIII, 128; Attorney General urges Madeleine-Élisabeth Maupeou, Visitandine, to go there, VIII, 517.

Vaux-Renard, village in Rhône - XIIIb, 78.

Veines (M. de) - I, 435.

Velletri, town in Italy - II, 351, 505.

Velopole [*Wielopole*], town in Poland - Local lord plans to make foundation of Missionaries there, V, 152.

Velopolski [**Velopolske**] (Comte de) - Extent of his seignorial power, V, 152; wishes to open Missionaries' house in Velopole, V, 148, 152, 193, 197; steps taken for this, V, 152, 161, 174, 176; other mentions, V, 153, 213.

Vence, town in Alps-Maritimes - Bishop: see Antoine **Godeau**.

Vendeuvre-sur-Barse, town in Aube - Mission given, VII, 334.

Vendôme (César de Bourbon, Duc de) - Biographical data, V, 58; VII, 169; VIII, 316; authorizes opening of Ursuline Convent in Guingamp, V, 58; Saint Vincent's dealings with Vendôme in his position as Grand Master of Navigation and Trade, V, 412; VII, 169, 233; rumor circulated by Duke's secretary, VIII, 316.

Vendôme (Françoise de Lorraine, Duchesse de), wife of César de Vendôme - Authorizes Ursuline Convent in Guingamp, V, 58; other mention, VII, 392.

Veneranda (Saint), martyr - Saint Vincent asks for notes on her life, I, 581.

Venerandus (Saint), martyr - His life, II, 104.

Venice, town in Italy - V, 530; Ambassador residing in Rome, II, 492; success of Venetians and Order of Malta in naval battle against Turks, VI, 71; efforts to help Order of Malta against Turks, VII, 605; other mention, V, 89.

Ventadour (Anne de Levis de), Archbishop of Bourges - Accepted as arbitrator for dispute between Alain de Solminihac and unionized priests of Cahors diocese, IV, 270; his Vicar-General, VII, 550.

Ventadour (Catherine-Suzanne de Thémines de Montluc, Duchesse de), wife of Charles de Ventadour - Biographical data; legacy for foundation of Missionaries' house in Cauna, II, 144.

Ventadour (Charles de Levis de), brother of Archbishop of Bourges - II, 144–45.

Ventadour, château in Moustier-Ventadour (Corrèze) - Ruins, XI, 348.

Ventadour (François-Christophe de Levis de), Duc d'Amville, brother of Archbishop of Bourges - See **Amville**.

Ventadour (Henri de Levis de), Canon of Paris, brother of Archbishop of Bourges - Biographical data, IV, 293–94; attempts to form new Order of missionaries in France, IV, 610;

always rises at midnight to chant Matins, XII, 273; Saint Vincent laments Canon's desire for absolute authority over missions in America, IV, 296; solicited by Canon to give priests for America, Saint Vincent requests faculties for them from *Propaganda*, IV, 336; Canon does not follow through, IV, 371; other mentions, IV, 355, 359. See also **Missionaries of Indies**.

Ventadour (Louis de Levis de), Bishop of Mirepoix, brother of other Ventadours - Letter of this Prelate about *Apologie des casuistes*, VII, 549.

Ventadour (Marie de la Guiche de Saint-Gérand, Duchesse de), second wife of Charles de Ventadour - Biographical data, III, 506; V, 643; VI, 281; VII, 157; VIII, 494; X, 16; asks for Daughters of Charity, III, 506; Baroness of Pouy, VII, 428; contacts with Saint Louise, V, 643; offers Sisters roast on Easter Sunday, VI, 281; foundress of Ussel mission, VII, 157, 247, 256, 396, 447–48, 470; X, 381; Saint Vincent regrets inability to give her what she was asking; she makes retreat at Saint Louise's house, VII, 428; esteem for Daughters of Charity, X, 16; other mentions, VII, 427; VIII, 494.

Ventelet (Mme de), in Orsigny - Saint Vincent writes about pharmacist with gift of curing scrofula, VI, 633.

Verdun, town in Meuse - Saint Vincent assists poor there through Missionaries, I, 542, 582; II, 42, 93; birthplace of Bro. Martin Jamain, II, 563; monastery of Reformed Premonstratensians, IV, 330.

Verdure, village in Pas-de-Calais - Problem with Sister, V, 337.

Verissey, village in Saône-et-Loire - XIIIb, 78.

Verneuil, village in Oise - Saint Vincent establishes Charity, I, 28–29; asks Saint Louise to visit it, I, 188; lease of coaches in Verneuil, III, 529; other mention, I, 353.

Vernon, town in Eure - Saint Vincent returns foundation money to Pastor of Vernon, III, 38.

Vernon-lès-Joyeuse, village in Ardèche - Mission given, I, 526.

Véron (Anne), Daughter of Charity - XIIIb, 228.

Véron (François), celebrated controversialist - Biographical data, I, 218; IV, 528; method of disputation, I, 420; disciples, IV, 528.

Véron (M.), of Paris - I, 127.

Véron (M.), Captain of *Maréchale* - VIII, 291, 563, 570, 573, 583.

Véronne (Alexandre), Brother of the Mission - Biographical data, I, 342; II, 348; III, 158–59; IV, 260; V, 20; VI, 155; VII, 222;

VIII, 461; XI, 152; highly appreciated by Saint Vincent, I, 583; II, 535; seriously ill, I, 580, 583, 588; infirmarian at Saint-Lazare, I, 457, 475; II, 348, 378; III, 158, 370, 466; IV, 260, 510; V, 20, 535; VI, 155; VII, 453; Saint Vincent asks him to do what Fr. Grimal asks, II, 536; wanted to have him care for Joseph Bayn, VIII, 461; responsible for office of Bursar, II, 373; XI, 152; carries it out with great care, III, 318; at repetition of prayer, accuses self of breach of Rule, XI, 332; Saint Vincent asks his pardon, XII, 396; at bedside of dying Saint Vincent, XIIIa, 205; enshrouds his body, XIIIa, 207; other mentions, I, 479; II, 546; VI, 438, 456; VII, 222, 574.

Versailles - Presence of King and M. des Noyers, II, 400; other mention, XIIIb, 206.

Verteuil-sur-Charente, village in Charente - Mission given, VIII, 305.

Verthamon (François de), Councillor of State and Master of Requests - Visited by Saint Vincent, II, 234; appointed, among others, to regulate disputes in Dominican convent in Paris, XIIIa, 136–37; highly respected by Saint Vincent, VII, 178; other mentions, III, 176; IV, 244.

Verthamon (Marie Boucher d'Orsay, Dame de) - Negotiations with Ladies of Hôtel-Dieu about work of Foundlings, II, 107–08; asks Saint Louise to attend service for one of her aunts, II, 591; Lady of Charity, III, 508.

Vertueil (Abbé de) - See **La Rochefoucauld** (Louis de).

Vertus, town in Marne - I, 116.

Vertus (***Notre-Dame des***), shrine in Aubervilliers - Fr. Gallemant, Pastor, takes Fr. Pillé as Vicar, II, 365; Oratorians at Notre-Dame des Vertus, I, 27, 124; VII, 345; Frs. Dieppe and Huguier go there on pilgrimage, III, 446; as does Daughter of Charity, I, 497; Saint Vincent reminds Daughters that they may not go there without permission, X, 37, 41–42, 136.

Vervin (Mlle de) - VI, 310.

Vervins, deanery in Aisne - Alms given to poverty-stricken by Missionaries, IV, 138.

Vesles-et-Caumont, village in Aisne - VI, 503.

Vestments - Saint Vincent will ask Rome for faculties for all Superiors to bless vestments, IV, 448; devastated villages cannot celebrate Mass for want of vestments, IV, 111, 112, 151; vestments stolen, IV, 111, 151; Ladies of Charity hope to send some to Bro. Jean Parre, VII, 380; VIII, 382, 384, 390, 391, 410, 445; Saint Vincent sends vestments, VIII, 453; other mentions, I, 45, 53.

Vetralla, town in Italy - Mission given, V, 487.

Veuves, village in Loir-et-Cher - Mme Goussault passes through, I, 194.

Veylle (Claude de), in Mâcon - XIIIb, 74.

Veyrac de Paulian - See **Vins**.

Veyris (M. de) - VIII, 524.

Vézelay, commune in Yonne - Louis Fouquet has mission given, VIII, 59; Abbot of Vézelay: see **Fouquet** (Louis).

Vezon (Jean) - Lease drawn up under this name by Marthe Goupil for coach and carriage routes, XII, 377, 379.

Vialart (Félix de), Bishop of Châlons - Biographical data, II, 242; V, 62; writes to Saint Vincent about nun, II, 515; Saint Vincent finds chaplain for him, II, 395; asks him to pardon fault of Missionary, V, 64; mention of letter to Saint Vincent, V, 63; in Paris, V, 65; other mentions, II, 242; V, 62.

Vialart (Michel), late husband of Mme de Herse - I, 291.

Vias (Balthazar de), French Consul to Algiers - Biographical data, VI, 208; resigns office of Consul in favor of Fr. Lambert aux Couteaux, II, 678; XIIIa, 346.

Vicars-General - Saint Vincent recommends to his priests submission to diocesan Vicars-General, II, 637; III, 381–82; Vicars-General of the Mission: decisions of 1642 Assembly relative to Vicars-General, XIIIa, 327–28; memo indicating choice of Fr. Alméras for functions of Vicar-General, XIIIa, 483.

Videlles [*Videuille*], village in Essonne - V, 177.

Vieil-Moulin (Farm) - See ***Montmirail***.

Vieille-Brioude, commune in Haute-Loire - Fr. Olier writes from there, I, 325.

Vienna, city in Austria - V, 450; VIII, 146.

Vienne, town in Isère - III, 537.

Vieux-Moulins - Farm bequeathed to Congregation of the Mission by Louis Toutblanc, VIII, 612.

Viffort, village in Aisne - Spiritual needs of parish, I, 177.

Vigean (Anne de Neubourg, Marquise de) - Illness, VIII, 52.

Vigier (Antoine), Rector of Priests of Christian Doctrine - Inspection and certification of documents relative to Hospitaller Nuns of Notre-Dame, II, 59; XIIIa, 102, 103; approval of their Constitutions, XIIIa, 103.

Vigiti Magna, town at Cape of Good Hope - VIII, 591.

Vigne (M.), in Paris - XIIIa, 43.

Vigne, port near Nantes - VIII, 557.

Vigneron (Avoie), Daughter of Charity - Biographical data, V, 466; VI, 136; VII, 157; VIII, 493; X, 381; Saint Louise asks permission for her to renew vows, V, 466; VI, 136; sent to Ussel Hospital, VII, 157; X, 381; in Ussel, VII, 247, 397; doesn't agree with Sister Servant, VII, 447, 449; mention of letters to Saint Vincent and Fr. Portail; saint encourages her in difficulties, VII, 254; dissatisfaction with Saint Louise, VII, 256; mention of letters from Saint Vincent, VII, 397; writes sharp letter to Saint Louise; Saint Vincent reproaches her, VII, 446; tells him her distress at recall of Anne Hardemont and its effect on Ussel Hospital, VIII, 493–94; asks to make retreat and renew vows, VIII, 495; signs attestation after reading of Common and Particular Rules reviewed and arranged in order by Fr. Alméras, XIIIb, 206; other mention, XIIIb, 227.

Vigneron (Geneviève), Daughter of Charity, sister of Avoie - XIIIb, 228.

Vignier (M.), Baron de Ricey, Intendant of Justice for Lorraine - II, 477.

Vignoles (M. de), from Béarn - III, 243.

Vignon (M.), merchant in Amsterdam - VIII, 596.

Villafranca Piemonte, town in Piedmont - Mission given, VI, 172.

Village Girls - Virtues proposed for imitation by Daughters of Charity, IX, 66–77; Rule for those who live far from Motherhouse, X, 523.

Villain [**Billain**] (François), Priest of the Mission - Biographical data, VI, 507; VII, 233; proposed to *Propaganda* for Madagascar, IV, 93; in Troyes, VI, 507; mention of letters to Saint Vincent, VI, 507, 574; saint recommends submission to his Superior, VI, 574; death and praises, VII, 233, 235.

Villain (Mauricette), Daughter of Charity - XIIIb, 228.

Villarceaux (Anne Mangot, Seigneur de) - Biographical data; Saint Vincent writes about alms to be distributed in Lorraine, II, 68; relies on Villarceaux for order of distribution, II, 74, 75.

Villars (Abbé de) - VI, 649.

Villars (Mlle de) - Writes to Saint Louise, I, 69.

Ville-l'Évêque, location of Sainte-Madeleine parish, in Paris - I, 460.

Villebourg (Seigneur de) - See **Voysin**.

Villecien, village in Yonne - Saint Vincent writes to Saint Louise from there, I, 36; Pastor of Villecien: see **Maurice** (Jean).

Villecot (M.) - Contacts with Saint Vincent, II, 244.

Villefranche-de-Rouergue, town in Aveyron - Peasant revolt, II, 451.

Villegoubelin (Mme de) - Letter to Saint Louise, I, 270; gives lodging to Saint Louise on trip to Beauvais; her praises, I, 270, 283.

Villejuif, town near Paris - Mission given, III, 135, 138–39.

Villenant (M. de) - VIII, 204.

Villenant (Mlle de) - Contacts with Saint Vincent, III, 523; with Saint Louise, III, 51; with Augustinian nuns of Hôtel-Dieu, III, 262.

Villenauxe, town in Aube - VII, 46.

Villeneuve (Marie l'Huillier d'Interville, dame de), Foundress of Daughters of the Cross - Biographical data, I, 130; II, 138; IV, 6; letters to Saint Vincent, II, 253, 334; mention of letter from her, II, 414; seeks Saint Vincent's counsel in trials, II, 253, 334; contacts with Saint Louise, II, 138: see also **Daughters of the Cross**; her regulations preclude accepting upperclass boarders, XIIIb, 304; other mention, XIIIb, 300.

Villeneuve-Saint-Georges, town in Val-de-Marne - Saint Louise is invited to visit and reconstitute Charity there, I, 128, 161–62; Saint Louise in Villeneuve, I, 162; renewed invitations, I, 217, 318; Fr. Soufliers teaches catechism there, I, 162; choice of young woman to teach school, I, 170; four armies camp in area for month, IV, 495; other mentions, I, 163, 164; III, 134.

Villeneuve-sur-Lot, town in Lot-et-Garonne - Mission given, IV, 334; revolt of inhabitants, IV, 372.

Villenosse (M. de) - I, 167.

Villepreux, village in Yvelines - Confraternity of Charity, I, 75–80, 94; IX, 193; Procurator for Charity; Ladies losing enthusiasm, I, 78; school for girls, I, 87, 117, 121–22, 128, 163; abandonment of child, VI, 316–18; journeys and work of Saint Vincent in Villepreux, I, 76–77, 79, 219; III, 393; IV, 515; IX, 193; of Saint Louise, I, 75–80, 117; of Marguerite Naseau, I, 128; IX, 358; Fr. Belin in Villepreux, I, 76, 77, 79, 87, 121–22, 270; other mentions, I, 87, 357, 359, 473, 480; VI, 565; XIIIa, 65.

Villequier (Antoine de), Governor of Boulogne - Esteem for François Perrochel, III, 105.

Villeroy (Camille de Neufville de), Archbishop of Lyons - agrees to establishment of Priests of the Mission in Lyons, V, 194;

institutes Society under name of "Priests of the Mission"; Saint Vincent requests that name be changed, VI, 516–20; Duchesse d'Aiguillon will write him about putting Marseilles house under Bishop's jurisdiction, XIIIa, 366.

Villeroy (Ferdinand de Neufville de) - See **Neufville**, Ferdinand de.

Villeroy (Nicolas de Neufville, Duc de), Maréchal de France and King's tutor - Biographical data, III, 110.

Villers (Mlle de), lady-in-waiting of Queen of Poland - Biographical data, V, 164; Queen thinks Daughters of Charity do not show enough confidence and submission to Mlle de Villers, V, 164; she refuses to do something Saint Vincent asks of her, V, 165; Saint Louise fears Queen wants to make Mlle de Villers "directress" of Sisters, V, 214; letter of Saint Vincent to her in Poland, V, 631; written communication of Mlle de Villers with Saint Vincent, V, 622; VII, 176, 276; with Saint Louise, V, 239; benevolence toward Missionaries in Poland, VII, 10; on her death, Queen thinks of having Sister Marguerite Moreau replace her for distribution of alms to poor, X, 536; XIIIb, 367, 369; other mentions, V, 215, 338, 378; VI, 56; VII, 92.

Villers-sous-Saint-Leu, village in Oise - Saint Vincent goes there, I, 235; mission given, I, 237; Saint Vincent urges Saint Louise to stay at Mlle de Pollalion's home there, I, 282; Henriette Gesseaume asks to go to Villers, I, 388; birthplace of Perrette Chefdeville, XIIIb, 249.

Villesabin (Mme de), Lady of Charity - Biographical data, I, 230.

Villeseneux, village in Marne - Saint Vincent encourages Saint Louise to go there, I, 118.

Villevaude, small locality in Meaux diocese - Decision to be made as to what to do about mission there, II, 528.

Villiers-le-Bel, village in Val-d'Oise - Fr. de la Salle abashed by questions of woman whose confession he hears, XII, 239; other mention, I, 89.

Vilnius [***Vilna***], town in Lithuania - Archbishop: see Georges **Tyszkiewicz**; plague, V, 129; confreres open seminary, VIII, 617.

Vincennes (***Bois de***), near Paris - Saint Vincent goes there, I, 106; urges Saint Louise to go there, I, 217; prisoners in Château de Vincennes: Cardinal de Retz, IV, 515; V, 115; Abbé de Saint-Cyran, XIIIa, 105; other mentions, XIIIa, 61; XIIIb, 94.

Vincent (François), Priest of the Mission - Biographical data, V, 411; VI, 430; VII, 18; departure for Genoa, V, 411; in Genoa;

mention of letters to Saint Vincent, V, 448; ill with plague, VI, 430, 432, 435, 436, 438, 440, 442, 445, 453, 454, 464, 469, 471; death, VI, 474, 477, 480, 485, 486, 488, 491, 501, 504, 505, 528, 530, 535, 537, 567, 583, 586; VII, 15, 18; mention of conference on his virtues, XII, 429; other mention, VII, 551.

Vincent (Saint), martyr - I, 245; feast day, IX, 162.

Vincent de Paul (Saint) - Chronological order of events of his life:

1581: Birth (April 24); age, I, 584; II, 83, 351; III, 480; IV, 71; V, 371; VIII, 34, 104, 133, 184; X, 204, 228; XI, 137, 309, 329, 352, 365; XIIIa, 1, 3, 5, 7, 80, 104, 145, 181; birthplace, II, 82–83; III, 196; VII, 428; XIIIa, 76; name, I, 11; VII, 94; patron saint, II, 323.

1582–95: Father was poor farmer, VII, 617; VIII, 159, 600; tends father's flocks and pigs, I, 206; II, 5, 193; IV, 219; VIII, 159, 383, 600; IX, 14, 89; X, 547; XI, *xviii*; XII, 19, 220, 242, 318, 395; frugality of family meals, IX, 70; remained in countryside till age of fifteen, IX, 67; student of fourth form, XI, *xviii*; XII, 114, 238, 394; tutor in Comet family, I, 6.

1596: Receives Tonsure and Minor Orders (December 20), XIIIa, 2.

1598: Receives Subdiaconate (September 19), XIIIa, 4; and Diaconate (December 19), XIIIa, 6; loses father, I, 14.

1600: Priestly ordination (September 23), XIIIa, 7.

1600–04: First journey to Rome, I, 112; IX, 250, 368; X, 294, 476; XII, 242.

1604: Bachelor of Theology at University of Toulouse, I, 10, 14; XIIIa, 16, 26, 28, 45, 47, 58, 145; XIIIb, 20, 31, 64, 65, 92.

1605: In Toulouse; journey to Bordeaux; legacy of elderly woman from Toulouse; trip to Marseilles to make debtor pay, I, 2–3; captured by Turks on return voyage from Marseilles; sold as slave in Tunis, I, 3–5; wound received, I, 4.

1605–07: Slavery in Tunis, I, 5–9; VIII, 599–600; converts master, flees with him, lands at Aigues-Mortes on June 28, 1607, I, 7–9; VIII, 599; in Avignon (July), I, 9–10.

1607–08: Studies in Rome, I, 12.

1608: Goes to Paris, I, 15; takes up residence on rue de Seine, XIIIa, 16, 20, 24; hopes for honorable retirement and benefice, I, 13, 15.

1609: Chaplain of Queen Marguerite de Valois, XIIIa, 10, 12, 15, 16, 18–19, 20; accused of theft, XI, 305.

1610: Commendatory Abbot of Saint-Léonard de Chaumes (May 17), XIIIa, 8, 12, 18, 19, 24, 42.

Between 1609–11: Violent temptation against faith, XI, 27.

1611: Fr. Bourgoing resigns pastorate of Clichy in his favor (October 13), XIIIa, 22; gift to Charity Hospital (October 20), XIIIa, 20.

1612: Takes possession of Clichy parish (May 2), XIIIa, 22.

1613: Enters, as tutor, house of Philippe-Emmanuel de Gondi, General of Galleys, I, 344; lives in his home, rue des Petits-Champs, XIIIa, 42.

1614: Pastor and Dean of Gamaches, XIIIa, 25.

1615: Canon of Écouis (May 27), XIIIa, 26.

1616: Resigns Saint-Léonard Abbey, XIIIa, 42.

1617: Sermon in Folleville (January 25), XI, 3; leaves Paris, arrives in Châtillon-les-Dombes (around March), I, 18; XIIIa, 50; named Pastor there (July 29), XIIIa, 45; first Confraternity of Charity, founded in Châtillon (August), IX, 166; erection of Charity, XIIIb, 20–21; entreaties to have him return to Paris, I, 19–21; returns to Paris (December 24), I, 21.

1618: Submits resignation as Pastor of Châtillon (January 31), XIIIa, 57; mission in Villepreux; launches Charity there (February 23), I, 75; sets up third one in Joigny (September), XIIIb, 23; fourth in Montmirail (October 1), XIIIb, 29; where he goes again in months of November and December, XIIIb, 31–34; on return, finds in Paris Francis de Sales, who remains there until September 13, 1619; frequent conversations between two saints: see also **Francis de Sales**.

1619: Named Chaplain General of Galleys (February 8), XIIIa, 58, 338; Saint Jane Frances de Chantal arrives in Paris on April 6 and becomes Superioress of Visitation Monastery, founded by Francis de Sales on May 1: see also **Jane Frances**; included in will of Mme de Gondi, XIIIa, 64.

1620: Founds two Charities in Folleville, Paillart, and Sérévillers: one for women, other for men (October 11 and 23), XIIIb, 40, 48.

1621: Sets up mixed Charity in Joigny (May), XIIIb, 54; Mâcon (September), XIIIb, 67; mocked by townspeople, I, 281; mission in Montmirail, I, 57.

1622: Named Superior of Visitation of Paris, XIIIa, 95; establishes mixed Confraternity in Courboin (June 19), XIIIb, 85.

1623: Mission to galley convicts in Bordeaux; home visit, XII, 179–80.

Around 1623: Licentiate in Canon Law at University of Paris, XIIIa, 71, 73, 74–75, 98, 214, 219, 225, 230, 235, 236, 241, 259; XIIIb, 94.

Between 1608–25: Visits Saint Mary Magdalen grotto, near Marseilles, IX, 482.

Between 1613–24: Leaves rue des Petits-Champs with Gondis to establish himself at rue Pavée, XIIIa, 75, 217.

1624: Named Prior of Saint-Nicolas de Grosse-Sauve, XIIIa, 66; Principal of Collège des Bons-Enfants (March), I, 22; XIIIa, 71, 219, 234–35; his servant, III, 499; Fr. Portail takes possession of Bons-Enfants in Saint Vincent's name, XIII, 72.

Around 1624: Makes retreat with Carthusians of Valprofonde; delivered there from temptation suffered "in exercise of his vocation," II, 124; another retreat in Soissons to combat too natural eagerness to carry out plan for the Mission, II, 278.

1624 or 1625: Louise de Marillac places herself under his direction, I, 80.

1625: Foundation of Congregation of the Mission (April 17), XIIIa, 213; death of Mme de Gondi (June 23), I, 19; XIIIa, 226; goes to Provence to tell Philippe-Emmanuel of wife's death (June); leaves Gondi household and goes to live at Collège des Bons-Enfants (between October and December), XIIIa, 75.

Around 1626: Goes to thermal baths in Forges, as in previous years, I, 54–55.

1626: Archbishop of Paris approves Congregation of the Mission (April 24), XIIIa, 218; Act of Association of first Missionaries (September 4), XIIIa, 222; makes gift of property to siblings (September 4), XIIIa, 75; resigns as Pastor of Clichy, XIIIa, 97; mission in Loisy-en-Brie (October or November), I, 25.

1627: Sets up Charity in Montreuil (April 11), XIIIb, 94; King approves Congregation of the Mission (May), XIIIa, 226; absent from Paris for long time (June 5), I, 26; union of Collège des Bons-Enfants to Congregation of the Mission (June 8), XIIIa, 230; founds Charity in Verneuil (October 8), I, 29; giving missions near Lyons, I, 31.

1628: Giving missions in Joigny (January 17), I, 35; in Villecien (February 9), I, 36; deposition on virtues of Francis de Sales (April 17), XIIIa, 80; faculties renewed as Superior of Visitation of Paris (May 9), XIIIa, 96; proceedings initiated in Rome for approval of Congregation of the Mission (June), I, 38–45, 47–53; XIIIa, 242–52; gives retreat for ordinands in Beauvais (September 15), I, 57; converts three heretics, I, 58; mission in Beauvais diocese, I, 58.

1629: Launches Charity at Saint-Sauveur in Paris, XIIIb, 95; journey to Montmirail, where Fr. de Gondi summons him, I, 63; founds Charities in Beauvais, I, 91–92.

1630: Receives in Paris visit of nephew (August), I, 85; journey to Maubuisson, I, 88; last Will and Testament (September 7, 1630), XIIIa, 98; visits Charities of Beauvais (November), I, 91–92; Prior of Saint-Lazare offers him priory, XIIIa, 271; minor illness, I, 79.

1631: In Montreuil-sous-Bois, I, 96; short trip to countryside (April), I, 104; return from mission; beginning of retreats for ordinands at Bons-Enfants (April), I, 104; injured by kick from horse (May), I, 108.

1632: Moves to Saint-Lazare Priory, which becomes Motherhouse of Congregation of the Mission (January 8), XIIIa, 271.

1632 or **1633**: Visits Sub-Prior of Saint-Lazare, ill with plague, I, 186.

1633: Approval of Congregation of the Mission by Urban VIII (January 12), XIIIa, 296; dangerous fall from horse (April), I, 199; Tuesday Conferences (June), I, 201; retreat; foundation of Company of Daughters of Charity (November 29), I, 216.

1634: Foundation of Charity of Hôtel-Dieu (Ladies of Charity), I, 230.

Around 1634: Mission in Villers-sous-Saint-Leu, I, 237.

1635: Canonical Visitation of Madelonnettes Convent (February 12), XIIIa, 101; inspection and certification of documents relative to Hospitaller Nuns of Notre-Dame, XIIIa, 102, 103; journey to Liancourt (June), I, 280; plans to travel to Fréneville, I, 290; wants to dissuade brother from coming to Paris (August), I, 292; retreat (August), I, 289.

1636: Journey to Pontoise (May); plans to visit Ursulines in Beauvais (May), I, 317; retreat (August), I, 331; goes to Orléans, stops in Fréneville on return journey (December 30), I, 364.

1637: Journey to Pontoise and environs of Dourdan, I, 377.

1638: Beginning of work of Foundlings (January), I, 410; in Fréneville (June), I, 473, 476; journey to Limouron (June), I, 478; to Rueil, I, 486; to Saint-Germain-en-Laye (September), I, 493; to Richelieu (December), I, 515; Archbishop of Paris orders him to visit nuns' convent (September), I, 501; promises Bishop Pavillon to visit him in Alet, I, 520, 526, 544; speaks of occasion which might soon take him to Gascony, I, 520.

1639: Mission in Joigny (February), I, 526; testimony on Abbé de Saint-Cyran (April), XIIIa, 104; beginning of assistance for Lorraine (May), I, 541; journey to Troyes (July), I, 552, 558, 559; to Richelieu, I, 591, 594; stops in Fréneville on return from Richelieu, I, 595.

1640: Expansion of ministry of Foundlings; plans to go to Annecy, II, 87; Robert Lauchau's questionnaire on instructions of ordinands, with saint's response (June 4), XIIIa, 312.

1641: Appointed Visitor to Jacobins (Dominicans), XIIIa, 136; journey to Richelieu, II, 208; Archbishop of Paris approves vows taken in Congregation of the Mission (October 19), XIIIa, 315; vision of three globes (December), XIIIa, 137.

1642: Journey to Richelieu (June), II, 294, 297; to Beauvais (July), II, 303; First Assembly of Superiors (October); offers resignation, which is refused, XIIIa, 322–31; considers going to Rome house, II, 361.

1643: Assists dying Louis XIII, II, 435; deposition concerning appointment of François Perrochel as Bishop of Boulogne, XIIIa, 145; becomes member of Council of Conscience.

Around 1643: Named Vicar-General of Saint-Ouen Abbey in Rouen, IV, 197.

1644: Superior General of the Mission named perpetual Chaplain General of Galleys (January), XIIIa, 337; serious illness, II, 530; journey to Richelieu (October), II, 528; stops in Fréneville on return trip, II, 530, 532, 534.

1645: Beginning of Barbary mission.

1646: Approval by Archbishop of Paris of Institute of Daughters of Charity; retreat, III, 71, 84; beginning of mission of Ireland and Scotland.

1647: Spends a few days in Fréneville, III, 210.

1648: Mission of Madagascar; journey to Saint-Germain-en-Laye; plans to go to Fréneville, III, 369.

1649: Troubles of Fronde; leaves Paris on January 14 for Saint-Germain-en-Laye, sees Queen and Mazarin, asks latter to leave France for sake of peace; goes to Villepreux, III, 393; in Fréneville, where he stays one month, III, 392, 395, 397, 399, 402, 406, 412; in Orléans, III, 408; visitation of houses: Le Mans, III, 413; Angers, III, 417; Saint-Méen, III, 419; Nantes, III, 425; Richelieu, III, 428, 444; falls into water near Durtal; rescued by one of his priests, III, 419; returns to Paris on June 13, II, 449.

1650: Assistance to Provinces of Picardy and Champagne.

1651: Wound is painful (March), IV, 170; General Assembly; discussion chiefly about vows, XIIIa, 368–73; serious illness (August), IV, 246; account of General Assembly, XIIIa, 374–95; approval of Rules of Congregation of the Mission by General Assembly, XIIIa, 395–97; beginning of mission in Poland, XIIIa, 398.

1652: Assistance to poor people of Paris and environs: see also **Fronde**; negotiations with Mazarin and Duc d'Orléans with view to peace, IV, 414; tries to persuade Mazarin that time has come for Court to return to Paris; unwise to try to punish city, IV, 459–61; dismissed from Council of Conscience (September), IV, 475; visit of Longchamp Abbey, IV, 484, 488; on doctor's advice, goes to Orsigny for change of air, IV, 511, 512.

1653: Foundation of Nom-de-Jésus Hospice, XIIIa, 173; mission of Sevran and other places, IV, 561, 564, 576; retreat, V, 24.

1654: Goes to reestablish Charity in countryside (June), V, 153.

1655: Ill throughout month of March, V, 351; talks of going to Rougemont or Orsigny to recover health (April), V, 365; Alexander VII approves union of Saint-Lazare to Congregation of the Mission (April 18), XIIIa, 409; discourse on Little Method (August 20), XI, 237; Alexander VII approves vows taken in Congregation of the Mission (September 22), XIIIa, 417; saint renews vows, together with men of Saint-Lazare house (October 22), XIIIa, 419; bad leg immobilizes him from mid-November to January 20, 1656, V, 470, 474, 475, 479, 481, 483, 487, 492, 535, 644.

1656: Begins annual retreat on September 17, VI, 95; continues until September 24, VI, 104; cold obliges him to stay in his room (November 25), VI, 155.

1657: Receipt signed (June 4), XIIIa, 423; retreat (September-October), VI, 512, 522, 529, 531.

1658: fall from carriage puts life in danger (January), VII, 68, 73, 75, 90, 100; XIIIb, 359; indisposition keeps him in his room (June), VII, 206; annual retreat, October 25-November 4, XIIIa, 190; bad leg prevents going out, VII, 405, 417, 426.

1659: Persuaded that end is near, says good-bye by mail to Fr. de Gondi and Cardinal de Retz (January 9), VII, 452; health improves, VII, 454; confined to room (February 12), VII, 473; one leg, bothersome for nearly a year, is healed; other improves (March), VII, 477; unable to preside at conference of June 20 because of illness, 482; inflammation of eyes (June-July), VII, 637; VIII, 1, 31; condition of leg worsens (July 13), VIII, 30; retreat, VIII, 166, 169; during retreat, prepares notes for election of Vicar-General (October 7), XIIIa, 483; and of Superior General (October 9), XIIIa, 484; premonition of approaching end (October 5), VIII, 166; legs can no longer support him (December 19), VIII, 230; new infirmity affects leg (December 30), VIII, 239.

1660: Legs prevent him from going downstairs, from saying Mass, standing up, or sleeping (January 30, March 5, July

16), VIII, 269, 301, 385; loses Fr. Portail (February 14) and Saint Louise (March 15); still in pain (August 18), VIII, 452; condition of legs (September 16), XIIIa, 199; rumor spreads that condition is hopeless, VIII, 437; Cardinals write, urging him to take care of himself; Holy Father dispenses him from obligation of Divine Office, VIII, 515, 544; Last Sacraments (September 26), XIIIa, 203; death (September 27), XIIIa, 206; funeral services, XIIIa, 208.

Family: Humble origins, II, 5; IV, 219; V, 398; VIII, 159; IX, 67, 529; X, 275; father, I, 14; XII, 351; XIIIa, 1; mother, I, 10, 14, 15; XIIIa, 1, 99; uncle, I, 14; brothers and sisters, I, 13, 16, 17, 85, 291; XIIIa, 76–77; nephews, I, 16, 85, 481; IV, 322; V, 569; XIIIa, 77; letter to slandered relatives, III, 24; suffering and distress of relatives during Fronde; Marquis de Poyanne comes to aid of one of them, IV, 515; family is living on alms, XI, 298; saint refuses to intervene for relatives involved in lawsuit, V, 440; VIII, 213; asks pardon of Saint-Lazare community because relative took meals in the house for several days, XI, 300; home visit, XII, 179: see also **Depaul**.

Health: Illnesses in 1644, 1651, 1655; bad legs in 1655, 1658, 1659, 1660: see above; unable to genuflect, XI, 196; indispositions, I, 79, 121, 220, 320, 352, 478, 499; II, 169, 576, 592; III, 369; IV, 512; VII, 59, 136, 206, 639; fever, I, 61, 108, 196, 280, 306, 356, 491, 580, 588; II, 51, 147, 150, 153, 190, 424; IV, 342, 511; V, 468, 474; VII, 477; colds, II, 424; V, 644; VI, 155; congestion, II, 51; III, 610; V, 45–46; inflammation of eyes, VII, 637; VIII, 1, 31; catarrh, II, 187, 188; wound, IV, 170; sore foot, II, 586; numbness of finger, IV, 54; frequent insomnia, IX, 24; purging, I, 199, 386, 547, 573, 580, 588; II, 287; III, 424, 610; VII, 453; XIIIa, 203; mineral waters and purgatives, I, 79, 115; II, 190; IV, 258; bloodletting, I, 196, 501, 546, 547, 580; II, 169, 178; III, 424; V, 644; sweats, I, 580; II, 147; syrups, I, 588; VI, 155; tea, VII, 427; extra rest in morning, VI, 155; X, 455; always rises at 4 o'clock, except when made to sweat, IX, 24; change of air, I, 226, 280; III, 369; IV, 511, 512; V, 365; seasons for thermal baths in Forges, I, 54; obliged, in 1656, to accept room with fire and curtained bed, X, 302; body's destiny, XII, 384; refuses extra food, XII, 401; could not preside over conference, XII, 435.

Concern of Saint Louise for his health: see also **Louise de Marillac** (Saint); concern of Duchesse d'Aiguillon: see also **Aiguillon** (Duchesse d'); of Mlle du Fay, I, 72; of Alain de Solminihac, IV, 163; of Nicolas Sevin, VIII, 467; speaks simply of his health to Saint Louise, I, 573, 588; II, 147, 627; VII, 427; horse kicks him (1631), fall from horse (1633), almost drowns in river (1649), thrown under carriage (1658): see above.

Miscellanea: virtues: See **Charity**, **Humility**, etc.; ministries: see also **Confraternity of Charity**, **Ladies of Charity**, etc.; studied language of Bresse region, XIIIa, 54; of Picardy, II, 237; IV, 340; understands only a little Italian, II, 349; recollections of his missions: II, 495; IX, 254; X, 470; conversion of heretics and sinners, I, 58; IV, 58; XI, 28; XIIIa, 52–53; sermons, XIIIa, 31, 36, 38, 67; conferences to Ladies of Charity, XIIIb, 378–440; to Visitation nuns, XIIIa, 162; to ordinands, XIIIa, 158; to poor of Nom-de-Jésus, XIIIa, 173; to priests of Saint-Sulpice, XIIIa, 184; advice to individuals, XIIIa, 179, 185, 188, 190; books dedicated to him: see **Books**; tribute of M. de Rangouze, XIIIa, 156.

Vincent of Xaintes (Saint), Bishop of Dax - Saint Vincent's patron, II, 323; XIIIa, 99.

Vincente, Daughter of Charity - See **Auchy**.

Vincent Ferrer (Saint) - Biographical data, I, 152; Saint Vincent imbued with his virtues, I, 152; secondary patron, II, 323; XIIIa, 99; received from God grace to make self understood by foreigners, II, 232; strove for sanctity at thought that God would raise up zealous priests to prepare people for last judgment, XI, 6–7, 62, 104; teachings: condescension leads rapidly to state of holiness, I, 228; X, 387; XII, 175–76; preaching is useful only if done from depths of compassion, I, 526.

Vincy (Antoine Hennequin, Seigneur de) - Biographical data, I, 36; II, 129; VII, 500; brother of Mlle du Fay, XI, 119; cousin of Mme de Brou, I, 485; by exception, welcomed at Saint-Lazare, V, 31; contacts with Saint Vincent, I, 122, 191, 479; on mission, II, 423; Saint Vincent asks to borrow his carriage, II, 129, 131; received into Congregation of the Mission four hours before death, II, 584, 588; other mentions, I, 148, 449; VII, 500.

Vinot (Claude) - Member of Charity of Montmirail, XIIIb, 32.

Vins (Laurence Veyrac de Paulian, Baroness de Castelnau, Marquise de), wife of Maréchal de Vins - Biographical data, VII, 487; VIII, 135; foundation for establishment of Missionaries in Marseilles, VII, 487, 515, 537, 539, 540, 552, 553, 556, 566, 575, 583, 591; VIII, 135, 401, 513; saint tells of receiving news of foundation, XII, 125; income due Fr. Get, VIII, 396, 420, 444, 462; Saint Vincent will send Fr. Get copy of her will, VIII, 376.

Vins (Melchior Dagouz de Montauban, Seigneur de), Maréchal - VIII, 528; legacy from his widow, Laurence Veyrac de Paulian, XII, 125.

Viole (M.), Judge of Court of Inquiry for Parlement - Summoned to Rueil conference, III, 411.

Viole (Madeleine Deffita, Mlle de) - Biographical data, I, 313; II, 474; III, 155; V, 44; VI, 203; VII, 33; VIII, 27; contacts with Saint Vincent, I, 313, 447; II, 474, 485, 598; young women sent by her to live with Daughters of Charity, I, 320, 357; V, 44; Lady of Charity, VI, 203; Treasurer for Ladies of Hôtel-Dieu, VIII, 203; XIIIb, 383; part played in work of Foundlings, I, 447, 562; II, 478, 485, 635; III, 253, 297; of orphanage in Étampes, V, 74, 116; of assistance to poor in Champagne and Picardy, VI, 397, 423, 454, 503, 561, 572, 580, 596, 625–26; VII, 33, 42, 380, 396, 421, 545, 597, 614; VIII, 27, 82, 203, 304; present at meeting to find means for sustaining Daughters of Providence after death of Mlle de Pollalion, VI, 550; other mention, I, 327.

Virgins - Parable of wise and foolish virgins, X, 491–96; fate reserved for foolish virgins is, as for all nuns, cause for fear, X, 492.

Vironceau de Saint-Joseph (Catherine), Superioress of Sisters of Mercy at Hôtel-Dieu in Québec - Saint Vincent apologizes for not being able to send help, IV, 365.

Virtue - Acquired by repeated acts, V, 443; why some people are fervent and others lax, VIII, 126; virtues must be deeply imprinted on hearts, XI, 105; virtues meditated but not practiced are more harmful than profitable, VII, 378; virtue of others should serve as example, XI, 347–48; virtue always has two vices at its sides, VIII, 36, 40; XI, 206; excess is usually praiseworthy in comparison with default, VIII, 36; sometimes opposite, III, 123; lax persons easily see excess in virtue of others, VIII, 36; virtues which constitute principal spirit of Missionaries: see also **Congregation of the Mission**; and of Daughters of Charity: see **Daughters of Charity**; affability without flattery, XII, 394; condescension, XII, 398; discretion, avoiding novelties, XII, 399; humility that bears fruit, XII, 385; humble response to praise, XII, 394; Congregation will subsist by humility, XII, 396; mortification, XII, 400; patience in trials and physical sufferings, XII, 402; doing penance for those who suffer, XII, 401; divine wisdom versus human prudence, XII, 399; in praise of purity, XII, 401; rule of simplicity, XII, 398.

Visigoths - God made use of them to afflict Church, XI, 279.

Visions - Vision of three globes, II, 241; XIIIa, 137–39.

Visitation Nuns [**Visitandines**, **Sisters of Sainte-Marie**] - Directory, III, 272; praise for lifestyle and Constitutions, XIIIa, 86; spirit of Institute, IX, 457; must have greater love for their Order and Rules, X, 287; fate reserved for foolish virgins is, as for all nuns, cause for fear, X, 492; discussion of

Extraordinary Visitors for Visitation Order, I, 236, 564; Saint Vincent holds opinion contrary to that of Saint Jane Frances in question of establishing Visitors for Order, I, 361, 564; II, 33–34, 57–60, 61, 62, 99, 115, 161, 199–202; prohibits confrere in Annecy to get involved in question of Visitor, II, 333; convents present to Bishops choice of priests as Superiors, VIII, 476; what Constitutions say on this subject, VIII, 489; novitiate lasts seven years, IX, 523; directresses teach novices to pray well and to give account of prayer, X, 483; called "Sisters" and not "Daughters," II, 164; canonical visitation made every year, X, 214–15.

Before election of officers, list of suitable Sisters is drawn up, X, 595; XIIIa, 385; no one discusses election, X, 589; outgoing officers ask pardon for faults, X, 219; rendering of accounts by Superior and Bursar, X, 214–15.

Penances determined according to gravity of faults, XIIIa, 387; make retreat in groups of six, four times a year, X, 509; extraordinary confessor four times a year, X, 508; Sisters ask permission to write letters, given, unopened, to Superior, X, 325–26; Sisters warned of one fault make known another to those who admonish them, IX, 300; take discipline on Fridays, X, 80, 318; do not speak to one another without permission, X, 331; moderation at table, X, 106; Superior writes permissions they want to request of Father Superiors, X, 506.

Long-time boarders with them, who take habit, do not usually persevere, V, 565; XIIIb, 290; forbidden to take more than six in their houses, XIIIb, 290; harm caused by visits of outsiders, X, 344; Saint Vincent recommends that Daughters not be cloistered, as Visitandines were, X, 83–84; spirit of Daughters of Charity is not that of Visitandines, X, 431; Daughters held to higher virtue than Visitandines, X, 527; number of Visitation monasteries in 1628, XIIIa, 93; Saint Vincent consoles Visitandine in trials, VIII, 374; Sisters dismissed from Rouen monastery, II, 62; forcible expulsion of Visitandine who refused to leave convent, XIIIb, 341; other mentions, X, 124, 190: see also **Jane Frances** (Saint), **Francis de Sales** (Saint).

Monasteries of Paris: Saint Vincent named Superior, XIIIa, 96; at request of Saint Francis de Sales: see also **Francis de Sales**; reappointed by Archbishop of Paris in 1628, XIIIa, 96; cure of nun in Paris Visitation monastery by Francis de Sales, XIIIa, 95; Saint Vincent's responsibilities as Superior, IV, 288; X, 506; annual confessions kept for him for more than a month, I, 303; this ministry is heavy cross for him, VII, 215; strictness in permitting outsiders to enter monasteries, VI, 284; VIII, 153; outline of conference before election of Mother Superior, XIIIa, 162; Saint Vincent at Visitation, I,

259; II, 180, 244; testimonial to Saint Jane Frances of good spirit of Paris nuns, I, 556; Saint Vincent takes resolution during 1646 retreat to continue no longer as Superior, III, 71, 87; stops going to Sainte-Marie (Visitation monastery) for nearly eighteen months, despite appeals of Visitandines, III, 197–98, 276; IV, 288; V, 86; XI, 160; Cardinal de Retz, entreated by Marquise de Maignelay, obliges him to resume obligations, IV, 288; V, 86, 603; XI, 160; resigns again in 1660, VIII, 314; refugee nuns in Paris during Fronde are enclosed in monastery under direction of Visitandines, IV, 399; debts of Visitandines, XIIIb, 325; epileptic nun, VII, 306; postulant, I, 212; Visitandine sent home, VI, 310; other mention, II, 160.

First Monastery of Paris: Foundation, I, 55; benefactors: see also **Sillery** (Noël Brulart de); churches, chapels and tombs, V, 557–58; Saint Jane Frances promises heart to monastery; fruitless attempts to get it: see also **Jane Frances** (Saint); canonical visitations, I, 116; II, 60, 216; IV, 82; XIIIa, 79; collection of conferences, VI, 117; Saint Vincent plans to go to monastery, I, 199; fixes meeting of Ladies of Charity there, II, 247; leaves letters and money for Annecy, II, 120, 320; convent assists convent in Metz, II, 227–28; welcomes Sisters from Saint-Denis, Chaillot, and Dammartin during Fronde, IV, 403, 433; Sisters fear removal of Fr. Blampignon, Director; Saint Vincent reassures them, VIII, 425, 426; Nicolas Sevin presides at renewal of vows in 1658 and 1659, in place of ailing Saint Vincent, VIII, 189; permission to enter monastery, VIII, 270, 504, 530, 542; departures, VI, 426; postulants, VIII, 504, 520; boarders, VIII, 533: see **Amaury**, **Fontaine**, **Le Gay**, **Lhuillier (Hélène-Angélique)**, **Maupeou (Élisabeth de)**, **Marguerite-Dorothée**, **Sibour**.

Second Monastery of Paris: Foundation, I, 107; canonical visitations, I, 120, 357; II, 60; Saint Vincent fixes meeting there with Isabelle du Fay, I, 107; leaves letter for Annecy there, II, 320; reassures frightened Sisters during Fronde, IV, 403; proposes that Nicolas Sevin replace him at renewal of vows on November 21, 1659, VIII, 189; habit taking of young Chandenier girl, II, 71; Queen of Poland asks for Sisters of Second Monastery of Paris; departure and return of Sisters; opposition of relatives and of Archbishop: see also ***Warsaw*** (Visitation); Saint Vincent encourages Superior at this time, V, 14; permission to enter monastery, III, 477; VII, 33; VIII, 542; to leave it, VIII, 188, 471; postulants, VIII, 484, 511; boarders, IV, 82; VIII, 471, 484, 512: see **Bouvart** (Marie-Augustine), **Gimat**, **Guérin** (Anne-Marguerite), **Le Roy** (Agnès).

Third Monastery of Paris: Foundation of Amfreville couple, choice of house on rue Montorgueil; saint thinks house costs too much, VIII, 47–50; renovations and expenses,

VIII, 188, 443, 498–99, 543; permissions to enter monastery, VIII, 432, 484, 542, 551; request for Sister cook, VIII, 443; dismissal of turn Sister, VIII, 499: see also **Guérin** (Anne-Marguerite), **Gimat**.

Monasteries in other towns: ***Abbeville, Amiens, Angers, Bayonne, Chaillot, Compiègne, Dammartin, La Flèche, Le Mans, Lyons, Meaux, Melun, Metz, Mons, Nantes, Nevers, Orléans, Poitiers, Reims, Saint-Denis, Toulouse, Tours, Troyes, Turin, Warsaw***: see these words.

Visitations - Importance, II, 113, 657, 670; X, 265; goal, II, 621–23; VIII, 165; inadvisable for Superior General himself to make them, II, 552; qualities necessary for Visitor, IX, 204–05; dispositions for making visitation; example of Blessed Virgin visiting Elizabeth, II, 279; IX, 204; how to make visitation, II, 672; Visitor must see to maintaining simplicity and poverty in clothing, X, 238–40; visitation not to be prolonged, III, 124, 237; Daughters of Charity go to Visitor for confession, communication, and other spiritual help, X, 524; observe recommendations of Visitor, II, 237; Sisters named to visit houses of Daughters of Charity in Paris, IX, 205–06; visitations made by **Saint Vincent**, **Frs**. **Alméras**, **Berthe**, **Dehorgny**, **Lambert aux Couteaux**, **Le Gros**, **Portail**, **Sisters Jeanne Lepeintre** and **Élisabeth Martin**: see these names.

Visits - No useless visits, IV, 131; IX, 268; X, 36; XIIIb, 126, 137; permission required for visits, X, 327, 330–31; text of Rule of Daughters of Charity regarding visits, X, 330; customary in all Communities, X, 331; visits are usually waste of time, X, 330; avoid all visits at time of spiritual exercises, IX, 98; XIIIb, 314; make them informally, XIIIb, 274; with companion, XIIIb, 281; Daughters of Charity must not allow anyone in their rooms, not even women, X, 333: see also **Chastity**; visits to Blessed Sacrament: see **Blessed Sacrament**; visits to sick poor: see also **Illness**.

Vitelleschi (Mutius), Superior General of Jesuits - Became mentally confused, XIIIa, 385.

Viterbo, town in Italy - Bishop: see Francesco Maria **Brancaccio**; missions in diocese, V, 467, 487.

Vitet (Fr.), Augustinian of Chancelade reform - Sees Saint Vincent in Richelieu; return to Cahors, III, 461; efforts in Paris for approval of Chancelade reform; disagreement with Alain de Solminihac on how to proceed, III, 586–92; steps taken in Rome, IV, 27; gives account to Saint Vincent, IV, 46, 66, 73, 76, 78, 96; Solminihac would like Vitet to have Grosbois decision rescinded, IV, 124, 141; and get Bishop of Chartres to put Brief into effect immediately, IV, 159–60; finds Vitet's mentality "strange and disagreeable," IV, 160; accuses him of not wanting to bring business to close, IV, 248; Fr. Vitet's thinking on what is advisable in order to have success in Rome, IV, 135–36; other mention, IV, 153.

Vitkiski, benefice in Poland - Question of union with Congregation of the Mission, V, 361, 388, 402; Queen offers it to Company, VIII, 105, 163; Fr. Duperroy has church repaired, VIII, 281; Saint Vincent desires union as quickly as possible, indicates steps to take, VIII, 353.

Vitry, known as Droue - See **Droue**.

Vivien (Nicolas), Master of Accounts - Foundations, XIIIa, 373.

Viviers, town in Ardèche - Bishop: see Louis-François de la Baume de **Suze**.

Vivonne (Louis-Victor de Rochechouart, Duc de) - Biographical data, II, 651; his tutor, II, 651, 654.

Vocation - To ecclesiastical state: in what vocation consists, IX, 279; true vocation comes from God, VI, 176; VII, 479; XIIIb, 360–61; signs of vocation, VI, 175; IX, 279; XIIIb, 361; spiritual sloth and vanity are causes for leaving Congregation, XI, 89; parents should neither thwart nor force vocation of children, I, 505; VII, 619; great number of priests have no vocation, VII, 479; vocations very rare in heretical regions, VII, 356; XII, 59; Saint Vincent declares that, were he not already a priest, he would never become one, VII, 480.

Vocation to religious life: salvation can be worked out in every vocation, XIIIa, 190; God delights in testing vocations, VI, 192–93; VII, 201; those who succeed in one vocation would do poorly in another, IV, 306; if someone consults you about vocation, reply according to Gospel principles, XII, 147; Saint Vincent exhorts priests not to try to attract retreatants to Company, XI, 377; XII, 257, 395; dissuades monks and nuns from thought of leaving Community, IV, 552; VII, 202; vocations among young boarders in convents or seminaries are not solid, V, 564; XIIIb, 288; vocation of Missionary: see also **Congregation of the Mission**; vocation of Daughter of Charity: see also **Daughters of Charity**.

Voseillan (M.), from Le Mans - III, 380.

Voureq (Louis), native of Madagascar - Saint Vincent reprimands Superior of Saintes house for poor reception of Voureq, VII, 259.

Vows - Conference, XII, 297–306; on virtues that are object of vows, XII, 307–52; difference between simple and solemn vows, XII, 303; vows give everyone right to same graces and reward, XII, 305; usefulness of vows in every Community, XIIIa, 376; vows put one in state in which Jesus was, XII, 299; not everyone thinks He took vows, XII, 299; XIIIa, 375; vows are like new baptism, continual martyrdom, holocaust of self, XII, 302; contribute to state of perfection, XII, 300; true peace acquired by renouncing everything, XII, 301; reward assured to those who take vows, XII, 302–03; violation of vow is sacrilege, X, 249; renewal of vows gives renewed strength and draws new graces, IX, 278.

Vows of Missionaries: why Missionaries must take vows, III, 247, 372; IV, 139–40, 554, 556; V, 314–22; XIIIa, 315, 375–83, 393; practice of taking vows began in 1627 or 1628, V, 318, 463; XII, 308; in 1639, most Missionaries took four vows; Saint Vincent considers fifth vow, that of obedience to Bishops, I, 554; other proposals, hesitations, II, 37, 104, 116, 141–42, 155, 518; asks Rome that Missionaries may take vows of religion; Urban VIII refuses, XIIIa, 379; Archbishop of Paris approves vows (October 19, 1641), V, 318, 463–64; XIIIa, 403–06; text of approval, XIIIa, 315–17; Saint Vincent renews vows at Saint-Lazare with several confreres (February 24, 1642), V, 318; 1642 Assembly approves them, V, 316–17, 464; likewise some theologians of Paris, III, 246–47; V, 464; opposition and grumbling, III, 246; V, 399, 464–65; renewal of vows at Saint-Lazare in 1647, III, 246.

Steps taken by Saint Vincent to obtain in Rome approval of vows, III, 247, 372, 374; IV, 139; discussions on vows at 1651 Assembly of Superiors, XIIIa, 375–83, 393–94; Assembly decides to maintain vows and to request papal approval, V, 316, 318, 464–69; XIIIa, 368–69, 395; Archbishop of Paris again approves vows in 1653, V, 317; XIIIa, 403–06; Fr. Blatiron would like only priests of Company destined for principal offices to take vows; letter by which Saint Vincent tries to disabuse him, V, 314; saint renews proceedings in Rome after 1651 Assembly, IV, 554–56; V, 399; report of theologians on vows, XIIIa, 403–08; Brief by which Alexander VII approves vows, V, 458–59; text of Brief *Ex Commissa Nobis*, XIIIa, 417–19; Saint Vincent regrets that questions of vows and of exemption have been decided in same Brief, VIII, 38; acceptance of Brief and renewal of vows by Saint-Lazare house, V, 463–65, 490, 501; XIIIa, 419–21; by other houses, V, 501, 506; Saint Vincent urges those hesitating to renew vows, VII, 308, 310.

Before whom, where, how to take vows, VII, 540; VIII, 56; XIIIa, 316, 403, 406; register of those who take vows, VIII, 468; vows in Congregation of the Mission are not vows of religion: see also **Congregation of the Mission**; why no mention of vows in Common Rules, XII, 298–99; delay in vows, V, 619; VI, 27, 584: see also **Obedience**, **Poverty**.

Vows of Daughters of Charity: Sisters do not yet have vows in 1640, IX, 13; in course of conference, they express desire to make vows; Saint Vincent tells them to request this individually of Superiors, IX, 22; perpetual vows of five Sisters (March 25, 1642), V, 356; X, 511; requests for taking vows, VII, 408; VIII, 104, 214, 235; X, 138, 249; their vows are not vows of religion: see also **Daughters of Charity**; vows for first time, III, 298, 300; V, 466; VI, 379; VII, 408; VIII, 104, 187, 234, 470; renewal of vows, V, 445, 466; VI, 70, 136, 379, 417; VII, 87, 299, 408, 465, 471, 489; VIII, 214, 235; perpetual vows, VII, 408; VIII, 215, 235; IX, 432; other mentions, II, 302; IX, 503–04.

Voysin (François), Seigneur de Villebourg - Biographical data; retreat for ordinands, II, 37.

Vszinski (M.) - Saint Vincent promises to welcome him cordially at Saint-Lazare, VII, 83.

Vuarin (Roland), Pastor of Paillart - XIIIb, 48.

W

Wallachs - Join enemies of Poland, VI, 645.

Walsh (Patrick) [**Valois** (Patrice)], Priest of the Mission - Biographical data, III, 203; IV, 305; V, 379; VI, 57; goes to Genoa from Rome house, III, 203; letters Saint Vincent writes him in Genoa, IV, 417, 426; desires to go to Ireland, IV, 305; Fr. Get receives order to send Saint Vincent letters exchanged between Fr. Walsh and Irish priest, V, 380; Fr. Blatiron asks Fr. Walsh to teach philosophy, VI, 57.

Walsh (Thomas), Archbishop of Cashel, Ireland - Biographical data; thanks Saint Vincent for work of Missionaries in diocese, III, 353–54.

War - War everywhere; disastrous effects, XI, 189–90; stems from those who find fault with government, X, 357–58; peace is goal of war, XIIIa, 307.

Ward (William) - See **Webster**.

Warin [**Varin**] (Simon), Priest of the Mission - Biographical data; VII, 394.

Warsaw, city in Poland - *Missionaries*: Queen of Poland summons Missionaries to Warsaw, IV, 63; travel authorization ("Celebret") given to Frs. Lambert, Desdames, Guillot,

Zelazewski, and Posny before departure, XIIIa, 398; departure from Paris, IV, 251; arrival in Warsaw, IV, 273, 289; difficulties created by certain Community to prevent Missionaries' establishment in Poland, IV, 398; V, 84, 142, 235; letters of Saint Vincent to Missionaries in Poland: see **Desdames**, **Duperroy**, **Guillot**, **Lambert aux Couteaux**, **Ozenne** (Charles), **Zelazewski**; question of entrusting Saint Benedict Church to Missionaries, IV, 372; church built for Germans, IV, 382; Sokólka parish conferred on Fr. Desdames: see also ***Sokólka***; foundation of King and Queen, IV, 352; King and Queen buy house for Missionaries, assign to it considerable revenue, IV, 456, 571; VIII, 617; union of Holy Cross Parish to Congregation of the Mission: see also ***Holy Cross***; foundation of Comte **Velopolski**: see this name; new royal foundation, V, 396; M. Fleury obtains resignation of benefice in favor of Missionaries, V, 351; benefice given by Queen, VIII, 163; Vitkiski benefice: see also ***Vitkiski***; Queen asks for another Missionary, IV, 387.

Death of Fr. Lambert aux Couteaux, IV, 538; arrival in Warsaw of Frs. Ozenne and Duperroy, V, 81; Fr. Guillot goes to France, V, 117; returns to Warsaw, V, 179, 183; upcoming departure of Frs. Éveillard and Simon for Warsaw, V, 126–27; Fr. Berthe is sent to Poland with two Brothers, V, 414; at moment of embarcation, receives orders to return to Paris because of events in Poland, V, 419, 424; return to France of Frs. Éveillard, Simon, Durand, and Guillot, V, 474, 475, 479; displeasure of Saint Vincent, V, 564; defection of Fr. Zelazewski, V, 491; Fr. Ozenne requests return of four Missionaries to Poland; not possible to satisfy him, VI, 620; death of Fr. Ozenne, VII, 274; Saint Vincent awaits favorable occasion to send other Missionaries to Poland, VII, 36, 176, 415; VIII, 99, 163, 252, 268, 280, 354, 394, 508, 528; their departure from Paris, VIII, 535, 537; XIIIa, 199, 201; forbids Warsaw Missionaries to attend banquets, V, 334, 346–48, 592; recommends observance of Lent as in Rome, V, 349; deplores dispersion of confreres in several small, distant places, V, 361–62; critical situation of Missionaries, VI, 257; proposed house in Krakow: see also ***Krakow***.

Self-sacrifice of confreres among plague-stricken, IV, 472, 493, 502, 518, 538–39; suffering of plague-stricken, IV, 513–14; Saint Vincent would like to have Internal Seminary in Warsaw, VII, 275; mission at Holy Cross, V, 105; other missions, V, 201, 214, 228, 234, 238, 264, 335; Saint Vincent hopes Missionaries will soon begin seminary and ministry with ordinands, V, 136, 142, 179, 187; VIII, 89; Queen of Poland bestows benefice for this purpose, VIII, 88–89, 118; Saint Vincent gives Fr. Desdames permission to sell property,

VIII, 508; Bishop of Poznań is disposed to oblige ordinands to make retreat at house of Mission before reception of Orders, V, 174; invasion of Poland hinders establishment King was about to make, XI, 275; Saint Vincent concerned by lack of news of confreres in Warsaw, V, 580, 588; VI, 4, 307; thinks they have been ordered to leave, XI, 276; siege of Warsaw, VI, 3, 6, 38, 42; city is in enemy hands, VI, 109, 112, 128; sufferings of Missionaries, VI, 144, 157; XI, 308, 329.

List of Superiors and history of house, VIII, 617; Missionaries in Poland: see **Desdames**, **Duperroy** (Nicolas), **Durand** (Antoine), **Éveillard**, **Guillot**, **Lambert aux Couteaux**, **Ozenne** (Charles), **Posny**, **Simon**, **Zelazewski**; other mentions, XI, 364; XIIIa, 186: see also **Gonzague**, ***Poland***.

Daughters of Charity: Conference before departure for Poland, IX, 455–56; Queen invites them to Warsaw, IV, 63, 252, 387; IX, 455; Saint Louise has them ready to leave, IV, 354, 410; Mlle de Lamoignon does not think departure is urgent, IV, 419; arrival in Warsaw, IV, 472, 519; IX, 462; welcomed by Queen, adapting to country and learning language, IX, 462; letter from Saint Vincent, V, 120, 169; mention of other letters, V, 168, 580; letters to Saint Vincent, IV, 575; ministries, IV, 575; Queen evinces some displeasure toward Sisters, V, 164; slight misunderstandings among them, IV, 541; VII, 175, 416; Saint Vincent exhorts them to union, V, 169; Queen requests additional Sisters, V, 179; VIII, 89; saint seeks occasion to send two more, V, 181–82, 183; journey postponed until Spring 1655, V, 186; decision on housing, V, 186–87; 188; Sisters give people impression that they want to be better off, V, 229; other Sisters prepare to leave Paris, V, 330; open schools but have not begun care of sick, V, 377; Saint Vincent sends three other Sisters, V, 414; events in Poland obliges him to recall them to Paris before they leave France, V, 419, 424; Sisters assist wounded soldiers at siege of Warsaw, X, 263; at siege of Krakow, VI, 470, 472; Saint Vincent wonders about location of Sisters, VI, 621.

Council deliberation on headdress proposed by Queen, XIIIb, 366–70; Queen's sentiments regarding foundlings, response of Marguerite Moreau, IX, 463; Queen would like to keep Marguerite near her for poor, XIIIb, 366; Sister's refusal; Saint Vincent's edification, IX, 463, 502, 538, 541; new request of Queen; Council deliberation on question; agrees that Sister should accept, XIIIb, 366–70; King and Queen spend day in house of Daughters of Charity as sign of satisfaction, X, 576, 588; preparing to send more Sisters, VIII, 146, 160, 229, 508; travel authorization, XIIIb, 238; departure of three Sisters, VIII, 394, 535, 537; XIIIa, 197, 199, 201; mention of letter from Saint Louise to Fr. Ozenne and Sisters, VI, 306; prepares to send two more Sisters to Poland, VIII, 107; Queen is satisfied with their work, VIII, 253; they are well and doing good work, VIII, 280.

Sisters sent to Poland: see **Douelle**, **Drugeon**, **Moreau** (Marguerite); other mentions, V, 28, 50, 201, 238, 484, 491, 622; VI, 129, 266, 271, 346, 555; VII, 11, 92, 127, 156; IX, 555; XIIIb, 226: see also **Gonzague**, ***Poland***, **Villers** (Mlle de).

Visitation Nuns: Invited by Queen, IV, 252, 274, 348, 354; opposition of relatives and Archbishop of Paris, IV, 382, 397, 410; V, 14; departure and journey of nuns, IV, 573; V, 15, 27, 48, 52, 82, 129; XII, 370–71; in Warsaw, V, 174, 238, 251, 491, 580, 622; VI, 266, 271, 346, 555, 621; their land has been ravaged, VI, 393; death of two servants, VII, 416.

Watebled (Jean), Priest of the Mission, brother of Pierre Watebled - Biographical data, V, 76; VI, 158; VIII, 196–97; philosophy professor at Saint-Lazare, V, 76, 631; theology professor, VI, 158; *extra tempora* with view to ordination, V, 176; at thermal baths of Bourbon, VI, 423, 424, 435, 440, 443, 445; Superior at Bons-Enfants, VIII, 196, 604; XIIIa, 196, 200, 202; Coste states mistakenly that originals of two captivity letters of Saint Vincent were sent to Watebled from Dax, I, 1; VIII, 313; other mention, VIII, 226.

Watebled (Pierre), Priest of the Mission, brother of Jean Watebled - Biographical data, III, 250; IV, 30; XII, 414; given to Fr. Delville for mission, III, 250; Superior in Saintes, III, 600, 601; IV, 30; VIII, 612; not very prepossessing exteriorly, but wise and virtuous, III, 600, 601–02, 615; Saint Vincent encourages him during troubles of Fronde, IV, 278–79; gives morning conferences to ordinands at Saint-Lazare, IV, 320; Director of Brothers, IV, 355; assists destitute in environs of Villeneuve-Saint-Georges, IV, 474; Ill, IV, 493; death, IV, 495, 499; mention of conference on his virtues given at Saint-Lazare, XII, 414.

Water (James), Priest of the Mission - Biographical data, II, 633; III, 81; IV, 452; V, 205–06; recalled from Cahors to be sent to Ireland, II, 633; in Cahors, III, 525; IV, 452; V, 205–06.

Water [**Arthur**] (Nicolas) - Nephew of preceding: see **Arthur**.

Water (purgative and mineral) - Use Saint **Vincent** and Saint **Louise** made of it; see these names; water merchant: see **Deure** (M.).

Weaver - Saint Vincent asks Jean Martin in Sedan to apprentice boy to weaver, V, 241.

Webster (William), priest - Martyrdom, II, 211–12.

Wedding - Saint Vincent permits Daughter of Charity to attend brother's wedding, I, 233; later regrets it, I, 388.

Wet-nurses - Correspondence between Saint Vincent and Saint Louise about wet-nurses for babies, I, 415, 423, 437, 497; II, 47; wages, II, 166; attend to children for week, II, 178–79; may move to Motherhouse with foundlings, II, 293; Ladies have Mass said for them, III, 228; not enough nurses for children, III, 504; money for their food, III, 505; for feast days, III, 517; threaten to bring back babies, III, 519; money owed them, III, 585; commissioners want to take babies from them, IV, 24; employment as wet-nurse may keep woman from falling into sin, VII, 113–14; payment conditions for country wet-nurses, XIIIb, 403. King's wet-nurse: see **Du Four**, Perrette.

White (Francis) [**Le Blanc** (François)], Priest of the Mission - Biographical data, IV, 99; V, 368; VI, 184; VII, 328–29; XI, 166; proposed to *Propaganda* for Hebrides, IV, 99; no news from White, IV, 373; in Genoa, IV, 305; in Hebrides, VI, 184; VII, 328–29; XI, 168, 261, 263; in prison, V, 368, 369–70, 389–90; XI, 166, 176, 180; release, XI, 260, 275; return to France, XII, 33–34.

White (George) [**Le Blanc** (Georges)], Priest of the Mission - Biographical data, II, 676; III, 29; in Le Mans, II, 676; III, 29; sent to Ireland, III, 93, 103; in Saint-Méen; sent back to Paris, III, 457–58.

Wiart (Fr.), Priest of Saint-Nicolas - Biographical data, I, 104; other mention, I, 105.

Will of God - Conferences, XI, 37, 38, 282–84; XII, 126–37; excellence of conformity to God's Will, III, 207; VIII, 452; XII, 152; nothing more holy or perfect than doing God's Will, XI, 70; different ways of doing God's Will, XII, 127; active and passive submission to God's Will, XII, 134; what is needed to conform fully to God's Will, XI, 37–38; XII, 127–28; to conform our will to God's Will is to sanctify self, II, 47; XII, 129, 130–33; glorifies God, XII, 128; imitates Our Lord, XI, 282; XII, 129–30, 137; fulfills what we pray for in Our Father, XI, 282; perfect state, XI, 37; good above all other goods, VII, 267; anticipated paradise, IX, 507; true happiness, XII, 137; accepting God's Will more important than success, XII, 389; perpetual communion, I, 233; more than ecstasy; perfection of love, XI, 285; thought that such is His good pleasure consoles us in trials, XI, 89; by trials borne with resignation, God leads us to His pure love, III, 120; great peace of mind results from this submission, V, 410; VI, 493; example of Tauler: see also **Tauler**; God's Will must be done for love of God, XI, 384–85; means for doing God's Will in all things, XI, 284; XII, 135–

36; how to know His Will, XII, 133–35; Saint Vincent's peace of mind in hearing of departure of confreres, II, 321; III, 215; V, 428; mention of conferences on duty of accepting state in which God places us, XII, 424, 433; prayer of Saint Vincent to do God's Will, XII, 137; Bishop expresses God's Will, II, 250, 253; XII, 384; discerning God's Will, XII, 389; work fulfills God's Will, XII, 400; assistance in doing it, II, 195; doing will of Superiors is God's Will for us, II, 267; Saint Vincent prays that God's Will be done, VIII, 231; reasons for doing God's Will, IX, 405–07; submission to God's Will, XI, 38; union with God's Will leads to angelic life, XII, 389; other mentions, I, 131, 145, 293, 301, 398, 491, 501, 521, 550–51, 580–581, 597; II, 59–60, 100, 115, 117.

Wine - Fondness of priests of Tréguier diocese for wine, VIII, 168; Saint Louise proposes that Sisters sell wine, III, 263; not served at Motherhouse of Daughters of Charity, X, 290; Turks do not drink wine, X, 290–91; Saint Vincent encourages watering wine well, XI, 105, 160, 297; XII, 342; other mention, I, 358; see also **Meals**.

Wisdom - Infallibility of divine wisdom, XII, 390; human prudence and divine wisdom, XII, 399; wisdom of world opposed to that of Christ.

Wishes - For New Year, I, 408; IV, 517; V, 500; VI, 173, 177; VII, 54, 58, 75; VIII, 242, 246, 248, 250, 253, 255; for safe journey, I, 65, 175.

Women - Women should not depend on men for finances of Confraternity, I, 70; Bishop of Bayonne does not admit women into his house, II, 4–5; young women from Lorraine do not last in Company, II, 26; two young women from Richelieu wish to be postulants, II, 107; Saint Paul's exhortation to women, II, 184; means for woman to obtain grace of living well with her husband, II, 185; men and women working together do not agree on administrative matters; women are careful, trustworthy administrators, IV, 76; never touch girls or women, II, 572; women may not enter house without knocking, II, 622; not proper for women to be on farms of Congregation of the Mission, IV, 312–13; nor allow them to enter houses, VI, 149; VIII, 254; regulations for women in Lithuania who want to form a Charity, V, 335; postulants from Saint Méen will be welcome, V, 628; qualifications of prospective Daughters of Charity, V, 628; test young women who want to be Daughters of Charity, V, 632–33; VI, 211; candidates should not be weak or delicate young women, V, 633; be wary of communication with women, VII, 215, 295, 432; cut short conversations with women; precautions to take in parlor, XI, 161; XII, 19, 341;

confreres should not maintain correspondence with women, even consecrated, XI, 161; do not become attached to devout women, XII, 344: see also **Chastity**; priest of Tuesday Conferences asks about possibility of women serving in missions, VIII, 534; Jesus allowed women to minister to him, XI, 316, 322; to safeguard purity of Daughters of Charity, Saint Vincent prohibits night duty, care of women in labor, and those suffering from venereal disease, X, 547–48; do not get too close to women, XI, 95, 161; XII, 342–43.

Work - Conference, IX, 379–91; mention of other conference, XII, 417; some persons always need to be kept busy, II, 588; priest should have more work than he can do, XI, 191; God finishes work begun, XII, 388; Daughters of Charity should always keep busy, IX, 6, 96, 175, 387; should say little and do much, VI, 52; reasons why Sisters should work, IX, 380–81; thanks to work, no one is burden to anyone, IX, 43, 74, 387–88; idleness is cause of many faults: see **Sloth**; God commands us to work, IX, 381–83; works constantly Himself, IX, 384; example of Jesus, IX, 385–86; of Saint Paul, IX, 386–87; of ancient monks, IX, 387; of Fr. Pillé, II, 377; of ants and bees, IX, 383, 389; how Daughters of Charity can occupy themselves in free time, IX, 6, 96, 174, 380–81, 389; good works speak more favorably than ostentation, II, 310–11; are fulfillment of God's Will, XII, 400; time set aside for service of poor is not to be devoted to manual labor, IX, 43; or to exercises of piety, XI, 284; goal of work, IX, 389–90; perform all tasks well, even lowliest or least important, XII, 408; workshop for youth, XIIIb, 82–83; workers at Nom-de-Jésus: see **Nom-de-Jésus**.

Works of Mercy (Corporal and Spiritual) - Practiced by Ladies who care for foundlings, XIIIb, 405; and sick poor, XIIIb, 418, 439.

Y

Y (Fr. de), Canon in Reims - Thanks Saint Vincent for aid of Missionaries to poor of province, V, 386.

Yart (M.) - See **Wiart**.

Ypres, town in Belgium - Bishop: see Cornelius **Jansenius**.

Yvain (Jean-François), seminarian of the Mission - Biographical data, VI, 162.

Z

Zacchaeus - Gospel personage, V, 488.

Zachary [**Zechariah**] (Saint), father of Saint John the Baptist - Graces that visit of Blessed Virgin merits for him, II, 279.

Zamet (Sébastien), Bishop of Langres - Biographical data, I, 277; offers his bishopric to Fr. Olier, I, 277–78; XIIIa, 122; Founder of Institute of Blessed Sacrament, XIIIa, 114; adversary of doctrines of Saint-Cyran, I, 394; III, 362; XIIIa, 121–23, 124, 134.

Zeal - Conferences, XI, 62 (2), 120–24; mention of another conference, XII, 412; exhortations of Saint Vincent on spirit of zeal, XI, 184–85, 189–94, 260–65, 357–58, 368–69, 373–76, 390–92; XII, 250–52; what zeal is, XII, 250; flame of love, XII, 250; faults opposed to zeal, XII, 260–61; Church needs industrious workers, XI, 33; shameful for priest to aspire to die in his bed, I, 276; Christ, model of zeal, XI, 1, 62; XII, 215; lack of zeal in priests strengthens heretics in errors, XI, 28; effects of cooling of zeal in Communities, XI, 183; appeal of Fr. Olier to priests whom Paris "detains," I, 325.

True zeal not disheartened by adversity and lack of success, XI, 373; knows no obstacle, XI, 193; God rewards equally zeal that produces fruit and that which, because of circumstances, may not go beyond good desires, V, 154; Saint Vincent would consider self blessed to die near bush in course of mission, V, 204; envied persons giving missions in Cévennes, I, 245; or evangelizing islanders of Madagascar, III, 284.

If Congregation of the Mission did not promote glory of God, better it did not exist, XI, 2; hope that those who enter it do so with desire of martyrdom, XI, 334; and ready to go anywhere, XI, 264, 357; XII, 46–47, 215; and to suffer anything, XI, 357; XII, 46; confrere without zeal is carcass of Missionary, XI, 14; fainthearted who would speak of abandoning ministries of Company should be considered antichrists and false brothers, XI, 184; XII, 79–82; example of Missionaries in ***Barbary***, ***Ireland***, ***Hebrides***, ***Madagascar***, ***Poland***, ***Genoa***, ***Turin***: see these words; of Missionaries in France, XI, 1; appeal from Madagascar Missionaries to lazy priests, III, 566–67; VI, 223–24; example of Daughters of Charity should animate Missionaries; example of four Sisters sent to Calais, XII, 34; example of Francis de Sales, XIIIa, 90, 92–94.

Avoid indiscreet zeal, I, 79; X, 539; indiscreet zeal of Martha, II, 85; with young people, zeal often goes to excess, II, 84; excessive zeal, II, 159; unite zeal with prudence, I, 290;

devil incites us to do more than we can, and we end up unable to do anything, I, 92; no harsh zeal, II, 84, 157; Saint Vincent recommends moderation in zeal of **Frs. Blatiron**, **Martin** (Jean the Elder), **Thibault** (Louis): see these names; advises Barbary Missionaries not to seek conversion of Turks and renegades if this would jeopardize ministry, IV, 127–28; begin on small scale, V, 219; other mentions, I, 119, 406. See also **Charity**, **Foreign Missions**.

Zebedee, Gospel personage - Jesus does not give Zebedee's sons place mother requests for them, I, 506; IX, 10.

Zeeland [***Zealand***], province in Netherlands - Departure of ship for Zeeland, VIII, 588, 593.

Zelazewski (Stanislaw-Kazimierz), Priest of the Mission - Biographical data, III, 113; IV, 292; V, 51; at Saint-Charles, III, 113; permission to travel to Warsaw, XIIIa, 398; departure for Warsaw, IV, 251; in Warsaw, IV, 292, 329, 354; studies theology, IV, 353; assists plague-stricken, IV, 493; in Sokólka, IV, 572; V, 28, 51, 81; vacillating in vocation, IV, 349, 383; V, 114, 117, 126, 175, 181, 313, 335, 338, 377; wants to leave Poland, V, 105; Saint Vincent encourages him to persevere, V, 110; his mother, IV, 353; V, 111–12, 338, 377; mention of letters from Saint Vincent, V, 114, 181; health, V, 111; would like to remain with Missionaries without being member of Company, V, 112, 114, 128; departure, V, 117, 126; Saint Vincent hopes he will return, V, 141; returns, but continues to give concern about perseverance, V, 162; on mission, V, 201, 234; Saint Vincent recommends to support him, V, 167, 258, 264; asks Fr. Ozenne to dismiss him, V, 434–35; his complaints and bad turns, V, 491.

APPENDIXES

1. - BIBLICAL REFERENCES

An attempt has been made to include most of the scriptural references used by Saint Vincent. Some listed here are indirect biblical allusions, although not noted in the text. The references are taken from the New American Bible (NAB), except those taken from the Douai-Reims Bible (D-RB).

GENESIS
2:7 – XII, 183
3:1-24 – XII, 278
3:5 – XII, 278
3:19 – IX, 382
8:21 – III, 496
9:20-26 – IX, 47
12:1 – XII, 178
13:9 – III, 186
16 – IX, 105
18:27 – IV, 446
18:30 – IV, 446
19:1-29 – XI, 342
22:1-18 – XII, 196
22:1-19 – XI, 339; XII, 118
22:1-24 – XI, 156
29:17 (D-RB) –X, 304
38:8 – XIIIa, 184
39:6-21 – III, 18
47:11-12 –V, 487
49:10 (D-RB) – IV, 83

EXODUS
2:5 – XIIIb, 398
4:1-9 – III, 286
4:13 – VI, 251
4:16 – XI, 194
8:15 – V, 489; XI, 208; XIIIa, 274
16:16-30 – II, 73
17:9-12 – XI, 191, 194
17:11-12 – V, 572
17:11-13 – V, 506
20:5 – X, 345
20:5-6 – IX, 497
24:12 – V, 428
25:40 – XIIIa, 184
32:9-10 – IX, 329
32:10 – II, 421

NUMBERS
12 – X, 348
12:9-15 – XIIIb, 351
13:32 – VIII, 554
14:30 – XI, 372
15:32-36 – XIIIb, 351
16 – X, 348; XIIIb, 351
17:25 – X, 193
22:28 – II, 5
26:10-11 – X, 40

DEUTERONOMY
7:6 – IX, 195
28 – IX, 259
28:6 – X, 329
32:10 – VIII, 103

JUDGES
11:1-40 – XI, 156
20:9-10 – VI, 252

1 SAMUEL
2:6 – VI, 91, 252
3:2-9 – III, 531
5:1 – XI, 319
13:2-15 – X, 67
15:26 – XI, 312
17:45 – XIIIa, 307

2 SAMUEL
6:7 – VI, 167
12 – X, 189
12:1-15 – IX, 305
12:13 – IX, 253; XIIIb, 357
12:13-14 – IX, 481

1 KINGS
12:12-14 – XIIIb, 315
17:7-24 – XI, 144
19:7 – II, 83
19:11 – XI, 91; XII, 285
19:11-13 – II, 86-87

2 KINGS
2:9 – IX, 262

2 CHRONICLES
3:6 – XIIIb, 317

2 PARALIPOMENON
34:2 – III, 174

TOBIT
2 – X, 146

JUDITH
13:1-10 – X, 58; XIIIb, 420

ESTHER
4:14 – II, 316

JOB
1:8 – IX, 407
1:1 – 2:13 – III, 398
1:21 – VIII, 175; XII, 48
1:22 – II, 379
5:17-18 – VIII, 182
7:1 (D-RB) – VII, 203
7:20 (D-RB) – IX, 45; XI, 134
8:2 – VIII, 37
9:28 – IX, 475; X, 423
10:1-2 – VIII, 36
11:2-3 – VIII, 37
14:2 – V, 316; XI, 103
15:12-13 – VIII, 37
19:21 – XI, 336
29:12 – XIIIb, 398, 411
32:1 – VIII, 36
42:7-9 – VIII, 37

PSALMS
1:3 – V, 497
6:2 – XII, 156
8:3 – IX, 108; XIIIb, 397
10:17 – XII, 14
11:7 – XII, 114
15:5 (D-RB) – XI, 210
16:5 – XII, 327, 335
17:8 – VIII, 103
19:5 – XII, 75
22:7 – XII, 394
22:26 – XIIIa, 375
24:21 (D-RB) – III, 571
25:21 – III, 571
26:8 – II, 369
27:10 – XII, 327
31:24-25 – VII, 462
33:6 (D-RB) – III, 281
33:9 – XI, 143

33:19 (D-RB) – III, 437
34:6 – III, 281
34:9 – X, 325
34:15 – I, 214, 558
34:19 – III, 437
34:39 – VIII, 288
37:25 – XIIIb, 414
39:10 – XII, 49, 230
40:2 (D-RB) – III, 223
40:18 – VII, 510
41:2 – III, 223; XIIIb, 412, 414
41:3 – XIIIb, 414
45:3 – X, 113
50 (D-RB) – III, 123; IX, 6
50:14 (D-RB) – VIII, 375
50:14 – XIIIa, 376
50:16 – XI, 113
50:23 – XII, 266
51 – III, 123; IX, 6
51:4 – XIIIb, 356
51:14 – V, 85
56:8 (D-RB) – IX, 268
62:2 (D-RB) – III, 436
65:2 – XI, 113, 199; XII, 52
66:13-14 – XII, 299
69:4 (D-RB) and (NAB) – XIIIa, 274
69:21 – VI, 85; XI, 308
72:11-12 – XIIIb, 397
72:12 – XIIIb, 398
73:22 – X, 561; XII, 192, 248, 310
73:22-23 – XI, 179
73:23 – XII, 192
73:23-24 – XI, 371; XII, 193
75:12 (D-RB) – III, 97
76:12 – III, 97
77:11 – XI, 208
78:70-71 – IX, 360
80:5 – XII, 129
83:8 (D-RB) – II, 146
83:11 (D-RB) – XII, 327
84:8 – II, 146
84:11 – XIIIa, 94
90:15 (D-RB) – III, 437
90:17 – VIII, 352
91:1 – XI, 32; XII, 121
91:15 – III, 437; X, 545; XIIIb, 404
95:7 – XII, 275
95:7-8 (D-RB) – X, 430
98:4 (D-RB) – II, 646
99:4 – II, 646
100:3 – XI, 119
104:35 (D-RB) – III, 550
105:35 – III, 550
112:2-3 – XIIIb, 405
112:5 – XIIIb, 405, 410, 412, 414, 419
112:5 (D-RB) – XIIIb, 415
113:5 (D-RB) – III, 366
115:5 – III, 366
115:15 (D-RB) – III, 148
116:15 – III, 148
118:23 – VIII, 209
118:46 (D-RB) – III, 565
118:125 (D-RB) – III, 281
119:5 (D-RB) – XII, 384
119:46 – III, 565
119:63 – XII, 85
119:71 – II, 375; XI, 69
119:125 – III, 281
121:1 (D-RB) – II, 385
122:1 (D-RB) – X, 213
122:1 – II, 385
123:1 – X, 213

124:5 (D-RB) – XI, 218
125:5 – V, 257; XI, 122, 218
134:16 (D-RB) – III, 366
135:16 – III, 366
137:4 – III, 440
139:7 – XI, 98
145:15-16 – XII, 388
147:16 – III, 565

PROVERBS

3:32 (D-RB) – II, 377; XI, 24; XII, 21, 141
6:6 – IX, 383
6:16 – X, 193
6:16-19 – IX, 291; X, 348
8:31 (D-RB) – X, 588
10:9 – XI, 24, 40
14:13 – I, 276
14:30 – IX, 559
16:1 – VII, 526
19:17 – XIIIb, 422
20:10 – XIIIa, 126
21:28 – V, 80
23:26 – XI, 132
24:16 – IX, 159; X, 319, 351; XI, 69, 285
26:11 – V, 405
28:27 – XIIIb, 405, 411, 412, 414, 422
31:10 (D-RB) – I, 76

ECCLESIASTES

3:1 – II, 416
3:1ff – VIII, 405
3:3 – XIIIa, 107, 136
15:17 (D-RB) – XIIIa, 172
21:29 (D-RB) – III, 496
31:10 (D-RB) – XIIIa, 172

SONG OF SONGS

1:3 – XI, 148
2:15 – VI, 252
3:4 – III, 440
4:9 – XI, 205
8:6 – VI, 157

WISDOM

4:13 – IV, 428; V, 359
11:20 – IV, 196

SIRACH

3:25 – V, 347
3:29 – XIIIb, 404
4:7 – XI, 58
5:5 – XIIIb, 356
17:12 – X, 265; XI, 304
18:23 – XI, 358
19:1 – X, 206
19:9 – XI, 69
21:2 – X, 304
21:26 – III, 496
31:10 – XIIIa, 376
35:17 – IX, 32
38:1 – IX, 97
41:1 – XIIIa, 83
45:1 – IV, 538

ISAIAH

1:3 – XI, 191
1:11-15 – XI, 319
5:4 – II, 367
6:8 – VI, 253
7:15 – XII, 157
14:13-14 – XII, 90
38:17 – IX, 45
49:15 – V, 441
53:3 – V, 111
53:11 – XIIIb, 355

58 – XII, 131
58:7 – XIIIb, 414
59:1 – IV, 446
61:1ff – XI, 98
65:2 – XIIIa, 168
66:2 – III, 484

JEREMIAH
1:6 – I, 589; II, 140
1:14 – XI, 280
6:14 – XI, 126
12:11 – III, 240
14:9 – XI, 359
35:1-10 – IX, 546
35:1-19 – XII, 118-119
35 – IX, 112; XI, 202; XII, 6
48:10 – VIII, 126; X, 154; XIIIb, 410

LAMENTATIONS
1:12 – XII, 160
4:4 – II, 369; III, 566

BARUCH
6:2 – XI, 390

EZEKIEL
3:18 (D-RB) – VI, 224
33:3 – XI, 386
33:14-15 – IX, 40

DANIEL
1:1-21 – X, 275
12:3 – XI, 345
14:31-39 – XII, 7

HOSEA
2:16 – IX, 174; XI, 84

AMOS
3:6 – XII, 134, 227

JONAH
1-4 – IX, 409; X, 416

ZECHARIAH
13:7 – V, 287

MALACHI
2:7 – VI, 69
4:2 – VII, 358

MATTHEW
Conference 197 (XII, 98-110) contains numerous references to Chapters 5-7 of Matthew. These are not delineated below.
3:9 – V, 216; VIII, 103; XI, 254
3:21 (D-RB) – VIII, 74
4:1-11 – X, 10
4:4 – X, 201, 229
4:17 – XII, 102
4:18-22 – VIII, 40
5:3 – VII, 344; XI, 102, 243, 382; XII, 101, 181, 254, 309, 315
5:3-12 – X, 122
5:5 – III, 498; VII, 255; XI, 102
5:7 – XIIIb, 412, 414
5:8 – III, 486
5:9 – VII, 533
5:10 – III, 44; IV, 88, 130, 301, 393; V, 35, 547; VI, 154, 623; VII, 480; XII, 228, 229
5:10-11 – VIII, 233, 287
5:13 – XI, 315;
5:16 – XIIIb, 404
5:17 – XIIIb, 360
5:23-24 – IX, 83, 179; X, 375; XIIIa, 210
5:27-28 – X, 205
5:39 – VI, 130

5:40 – I, 558; IV, 20; V, 483; XII, 51
5:41 – X, 386; XI, 88
5:44 – IV, 150; XII, 225
5:48 – XII, 68
6:1-4 – VII, 115
6:9 – IX, 333
6:9-14 – X, 498
6:10 – XI, 282
6:20 – VIII, 229
6:21 – X, 139
6:23 – VII, 496
6:24 – I, 519; II, 494; VII, 201, 556
6:26-29 – XII, 119
6:33 – I, 215; II, 690; VII, 121, 171, 424; VIII, 175, 482; X, 251; XI, 65; XII, 110, 151; XIIIb, 373
7:3-5 – X, 352
7:7 – X, 220
7:9 – VIII, 393, 395, 403, 422
7:13 – IV, 358; V, 113
7:13-14 – XI, 243
7:15 – X, 345; XI, 224
7:19 – XIIIb, 246
7:21-23 – XII, 131
7:22 – VI, 292
7:22-23 – IX, 41
7:26 – XIIIb, 362
8:5-9 – I, 297
8:9 –VIII, 435; X, 221; XI, 165
8:14-15 – X, 224
8:20 – V, 465; VI, 87; VII, 21, 328, 343; VIII, 49, 272, 482; IX, 342; XI, 210, 231; XIIIb, 342
8:21-22 – IV, 350, 591; V, 542, 546; VII, 52
8:22 – XII, 178
8:25 – X, 360
8:34 – VII, 21
9:29-31 – IV, 480
9:33-34 – VIII, 401
9:37 – V, 499; XIIIa, 275, 358
9:37-38 – IV, 358, 362; V, 109; VII, 69, 304, 356, 390, 491, 626; VIII, 145, 150, 342; XI, 361
9:38 – VII, 566
10:8 – XII, 313, 314
10:16 – IV, 534; XI, 42; XII, 140
10:16-17 – X, 162
10:16-20 – XII, 123
10:17 – XII, 141
10:17-20 – XII, 141
10:22 – XIIIb, 410
10:29-30 – IV, 346
10:34 (D-RB) – XIIIa, 307
10:37 – V, 540; VII, 357; X, 127; XII, 178
10:37-38 – IX, 136
10:38 – XII, 310
10:39 (D-RB) – VIII, 560
10:40 – XIIIa, 68
11:12 – I, 289; VII, 333; VIII, 127; XI, 386, XIIIb, 162
11:25 – III, 555; IX, 315; X, 457; XII, 141
11:28-30 – X, 89
11:29 – VII, 471; XI, 50; XII, 153, 161
11:29-30 – X, 270
11:30 – VII, 203, 589
12:7 – VII, 66
13:1-9 – IX, 313
13:12 – IX, 319

13:16 – XII, 12
13:18-44 – XI, 314
13:31-32 – XI, 346
13:34 – XI, 41
13:43 (D-RB) – X, 271
13:47-48 – XI, 215
13:47-49 – VI, 81
13:55 – IX, 534; XII, 338
13:55-56 – IX, 139
13:57 – XIIIb, 109
15:13 – II, 502
15:22-28 – VII, 527
15:24 – XI, 144
16:6 – X, 345, 581
16:19 – IX, 484
16:21-23 – IV, 56; XI, 283, 286
16:23 – XII, 218
16:24 – III, 182; VII, 202; IX, 136, XII, 173
16:25 – VI, 448, 452, 454, 455, 470, 471, 475, 478, 488, 492, 501, 535, 538, 567; VII, 19
16:26 – XII, 70
17:5 – VII, 479; XI, 121
17:21 – I, 179, 227; X, 57
17:24-27 – VI, 30
18:1-11 – X, 86
18:3-6 – XIIIa, 33
18:4 – XII, 166
18:6 – X, 22, 32
18:10 – X, 22; XIIIa, 33
18:15 – XI, 304; XII, 295
18:19 – XIIIb, 383
18:20 – IX, 2, 312; XIIIb, 240, 383
18:32 – XI, 129
19:7-8 – IX, 515
19:14 – XIIIa, 33
19:21 – IV, 350, 591; V, 542, 546; IX, 73; XI, 147, 155, 227, 230, 243, 286; XII, 100, 147, 301
19:24 – XI, 243
19:27 – XII, 300
19:28 – IV, 143; XII, 303
19:29 – II, 688; VII, 357; VIII, 578; XII, 147, 317, 318
19:30 – IV, 62; XII, 166
20:1 – VII, 559
20:1-2 – V, 180
20:1-16 – V, 313
20:1-17 – V, 528
20:6-7 – III, 593
20:15 – XI, 87
20:18-19 – VIII, 293
20:20-23 – I, 506
20:26-27 – X, 327; XI, 125
20:26-28 – VII, 159
20:28 – XI, 52, 124, 313
21:5 – VII, 590
21:12-13 – IV, 391
21:16 – IX, 108
21:23 – III, 43
21:37 – XI, 90
22:12 – XI, 193
22:12-13 – X, 370
22:17-21 – VI, 30
22:17-22 – VI, 2
22:21 – XII, 149
22:24 – XIIIa, 184
22:37 – IX, 365; XI, 34
22:40 – VII, 397
23:3 – XII, 294
23:9 – VIII, 175
23:12 – V, 486; IX, 530; XII, 163

23:27 – XIIIa, 119
23:37 – XIIIa, 170
24:9 – VIII, 233
24:11 – XII, 80
24:33 – XI, 224
24:35 – XI, 43
25:1-13 – X, 491; XI, 388; XIIIa, 119
25:11-12 – X, 157
25:12 – XII, 399
25:21 – VII, 231, 271, 531, 608; VIII, 237; IX, 495; XI, 73, 346
25:23 – VII, 449, 474, 506; IX, 495
25:31-42 – XIIIb, 4
25:34 – IX, 200; XIIIb, 415
25:34-36 – XII, 77; XIIIb, 429
25:34-36, 40 – XIIIb, 9
25:40 – VIII, 322; XIIIa, 84
25:41 – XIIIb, 412
25:43-48 – VII, 115
25:44-45 – X, 268
26:8 – XII, 256
26:15 – XIIIb, 315
26:22 – X, 412, 427
26:24 – X, 426
26:25 – X, 576
26:26 – XI, 176
26:31 – V, 287
26:39 – VIII, 182, 374
26:49 – XI, 225
26:52-54 – IX, 56
27:4 – X, 248
27:21 – XI, 351, 383, 388
27:28 – VIII, 175
27:32-33 – IV, 91
27:38 – XI, 351
27:40 – XI, 88
27:46 – IX, 499; XII, 160
27:63 – XI, 383
28:18-20 – VIII, 183

MARK

1:35 – XI, 312
1:40-44 – IV, 480
3:21 – V, 150; VIII, 74 (D-RB), XI, 19; XII, 78
4:25 – IX, 319
4:41 – V, 37
6:3 – XII, 338
6:4 – VII, 53
6:46 – XI, 312
7:32-36 – IV, 480
7:37 – XI, 43; XII, 49, 148
8:33 – IV, 391; XII, 65
8:35 – XII, 183
9:29 – I, 227
10 – XII, 317, 318
10:14 – XII, 78
10:21 – IV, 350
10:29-30 – XII, 318-19
10:30 – VIII, 578
10:42-44 – VII, 151
10:45 – IV, 182
12:42-44 – V, 220
14:30-31 – VII, 146
14:34 – IV, 145
15:21 – IV, 91
15:41 – VIII, 278
16:14 – XI, 353
16:15 – XI, 237; XII, 24
16:16 – XIIIa, 32

LUKE

1:28 – XII, 265
1:38 – XIIIb, 417

1:46 – XI, 193
1:46-55 – X, 317
1:68 – XIIIa, 67
1:79 – VI, 251
2:29 – II, 521
2:34 – IV, 415; XIIIa, 193
2:51 – IX, 318; XII, 346
3:8 – VII, 251
3:16 – IV, 133
4:12-13 – VI, 193
4:16-30 – IV, 351
4:18 – VII, 356; VIII, 41; XI, 26, 122, 283; XII, 3, 79, 299
4:18-19 – XI, 98
4:23 – III, 613; IV, 280-281; XI, 252
4:24 – V, 541
4:28-29 – V, 541
4:28-30 – VII, 53
5:4-6 – VII, 358
5:12-14 – IV, 480
6:13 – VIII, 183
6:24 – III, 554; X, 167, 572
6:26 – XI, 104
6:27 – IV, 150
6:29 – VI, 130
6:36 – XIIIb, 9
7:22 – II, 155
8:3 – XI, 316
8:6 – III, 567
9:23 – III, 182; VII, 589
9:47-48 – IX, 362
9:50 – II, 425
9:51-53 – V, 483
9:58 – VII, 406, 560; VIII, 272, 482; X, 573
9:59-60 – VI, 484
9:59-62 – II, 611; VII, 483; XIIIb, 249
9:60 – II, 688; XI, 147
9:62 – II, 688; XIIIb, 410, 412, 419
10:1 – III, 565; XI, 321; 322
10:2 – V, 149, 469, 574; VI, 253; VII, 69; VIII, 145, 150
10:3 – X, 467
10:4 – X, 165
10:16 – I, 558; II, 157; III, 484-85; IX, 312, 399; X, 68, 309, 339; XII, 294, 350; XIIIb, 155
10:20 – XII, 258
10:21 – IX, 331
10:22 – XI, 77
10:23 – XII, 12
10:38-41 – VI, 145
10:41-42 – IV, 346
11:1 – IX, 333; X, 461; XI, 209
11:9 – IV, 230
11:10 – VII, 255
11:17 – X, 317
11:20 – XIIIa, 274
11:27 – XI, 388
11:27-28 – IX, 313
11:44 – XIIIa, 119
12:1 – VII, 442
12:14 – II, 495
12:15 – XII, 102
12:24 – VII, 171
12:32 – XI, 387
12:37-38 – III, 536
12:43 – III, 442
12:49 – XI, 264
12:58 – VII, 424
13:7 – XII, 384
13:24 – VII, 181, 201, 322
13:25-27 – X, 157

14:10-11 – VII, 515
14:26 – VII, 53; IX, 136; X, 127; XII, 177; XIIIb, 109
14:26-27 – IX, 136
14:29-30 – XIIIb, 412, 415, 433
14:30 – XIIIb, 419
14:33 – VIII, 375; XII, 310, 316, 331, 347
15:3-7 – IV, 314
15:4 – VII, 22
15:10 – IX, 406; X, 59
15:10 (D-RB) – XIIIb, 380
16:9 – X, 545
16:10 – VII, 525
16:19-31 – XI, 296
16:30-31 – VI, 293
17:10 – VII, 568
18:18-23 – IV, 471
18:22 – IV, 350; XI, 147
18:29-30 – XII, 319
18:32 – VIII, 233
19:1-10 – V, 488
19:10 – VII, 356
19:40 – III, 403
19:41-44 – IX, 539
21:1-4 – III, 188; V, 370
21:18-19 – IV, 87
21:19 – VII, 396
22:3-6 – XI, 225
22:15 – IX, 265
22:28 – XI, 129
22:42 – VIII, 288; XII, 310
22:61 – XIIIb, 354
23:43 – XI, 130
24:19 – III, 576
24:26 – VII, 202
24:36 – IX, 80

JOHN

1:9 – XI, 315
1:27 – IV, 133
1:48-49 – XI, 383
2:5 – I, 544, 558
2:17 – II, 366
3:29-30 – XII, 222
4:4-43 – XI, 41
4:7-38 – XI, 344
4:10 – IX, 540
4:34 – XII, 130
5:1-9 – III, 566
5:21 – VIII, 247, 249, 252, 256, 413
6:38 – VII, 202, 506; VIII, 41
6:44 – IX, 411
6:53 – XI, 132, 176
6:57 – XII, 113
6:60 – XII, 166, 248, 310
6:67 – III, 215; VI, 81; XIIIb, 436
6:68 – VII, 291
7:12 – XI, 383
7:16 – XI, 311; XII, 94, 175, 310
8:7 – XII, 149
8:12 – VIII, 41
8:29 – XII, 94, 176, 351
8:54 – XII, 124
10:27 – XI, 91
10:30 – XIIIb, 274
11:21 – VI, 223
11:36 – III, 442
11:49-52 – VI, 292
12:4-6 – XI, 225
12:13 – XIIIa, 67
12:25 – IV, 21; V, 111, 442; VI, 157
12:26 – XI, 129

13:1 – VIII, 268
13:21-26 – IV, 55
13:34 – XII, 12
13:34-35 – VIII, 186
13:35 – VIII, 169; IX, 211; X, 425; XI, 67
14:9 – IX, 311; XI, 35
14:10 – XII, 14; XIIIb, 274
14:12 – XII, 182
14:13 – IX, 325
14:15 – IX, 367
14:18 – III, 436
14:20 – XIIIb, 274
14:23 – IX, 4; XI, 34, 35
15:1-5 – XI, 314
15:5 – VIII, 41
15:8 – XI, 32
15:12 – XII, 100
15:13 – III, 310; VI, 53, 85, 171, 177; VII, 15, 19; XI, 330
15:15 – IV, 57
15:16 – V, 540; VI, 176; VII, 159; IX, 456; XIIIb, 384
15:19 – IX, 345
15:20 – IV, 88
16:2 – V, 399
16:16 – XII, 80
16:20 – I, 276; XI, 303
17:3 – XII, 72; XIIIb, 409
17:9 – X, 121
17:11 – IX, 2
17:14 – IX, 542
17:21 – XIIIb, 274
18:8 – IV, 18
18:23 – IX, 454
19:15 – X, 360
20:19-23 – VIII, 182
20:21 – XII, 75
20:23 – IX, 484
20:28 – II, 387; III, 441
21:15-17 – VI, 165-66; XII, 350
21:22 – II, 39

ACTS

1:1 – IX, 257; XII, 5 (D-RB), 315
1:15-26 – X, 217
1:15-36 – XIIIb, 386
1:16, 20 – XIIIb, 360
1:20 (D-RB) – IX, 140
1:21-26 – IX, 280; XII, 45
1:24-25 – X, 217, 580
2:1 – IX, 323
4:32 – III, 329; IV, 238, 597; V, 149; VII, 198; XI, 110, 211; XII, 204, 313, 317
4:34-35 – XI, 97
5:1-11 – XI, 211; XIIIb, 351
5:3-4, 9 – X, 168
5:41 – XII, 402
6:7 – VIII, 183
8:37 – III, 562
9:1-9 – X, 223
9:3-6 – V, 473
9:6 – XII, 195
9:16 – XII, 196
10:9-17 – XIIIb, 353
15:1-30 – XIIIb, 386
15:28 – XIIIb, 387
15:36-40 – VII, 442
16:5 – VIII, 183
16:13-15 – VIII, 279
17:4, 12, 34 – VIII, 279
19:14 – VI, 292
20:28 (D-RB) – XIIIa, 68
20:29 – XII, 80
20:33-34 – IX, 386

22 – IX, 280
22:6-11 – X, 223
26:12-18 – X, 223
39:42 – VIII, 279

ROMANS

2:24 – VI, 253
4:18 – XI, 339
6:19 – IX, 20
7:19 – XI, 170
8:6 – XII, 398
8:13 – VII, 201, 202, 448; X, 50, 175, 319; XII, 174; XIIIb, 435
8:15 – X, 404, 460
8:15-16 – XIIIa, 167
8:21 – VII, 518, 590; VIII, 10; XII, 192
8:28 – II, 85; VI, 97; VII, 266; VIII, 298
8:29 – X, 85; XI, 99
8:35 – IV, 317; XI, 63
9:16 (D-RB) – XIIIa, 172
10:2 – II, 84
10:17 – XII, 15, 24
11:33 – II, 85, 119; IV, 18; VII, 54; VIII, 175, 552
11:34 – III, 304
12:3 – VIII, 40
12:10 – IX, 100, 124; X, 394; XII, 89
12:15 – X, 452
12:16 – XI, 58
12:20 – VI, 174
12:21 – V, 235
13:8 – XII, 213; XIIIb, 412, 414
15:6 – XII, 203

1 CORINTHIANS

1:22-23 – X, 103
1:26-30 – XI, 120
1:27 – II, 433
1:31 (D-RB) – XIIIa, 172
2:1, 4 – I, 405
2:2 – V, 497; VII, 357
2:4 – XI, 244
2:9 – XI, 39
3:2 – IX, 498
3:15 – IX, 482
4:7 (D-RB) – XIIIa, 172
4:9 – XII, 50
4:13 – IX, 69
4:16 – X, 295
6:3 – XII, 303
6:12 – IV, 479
6:17 – XI, 286
7:9 – VII, 619
7:20 – XI, 92
7:29 – II, 83
8:1 – VIII, 40; X, 124; XI, 117
9:22 – IV, 97; VIII, 577; XI, 308
9:27 – X, 50; XII, 27
10:13 – VII, 203, 255
10:31 – IX, 287; X, 505; XI, 283; XII, 133
11:23-30 – IX, 263
11:27-29 – IX, 185
11:31 – X, 319
13:1-13 – XI, 385
13:4 – II, 202; III, 33; V, 15; XII, 219
13:4-7 – IX, 100, 124
14:34-35 (D-RB) – XIIIb, 381
14:38 – XIIIa, 164
14:39 – I, 166

15:9 – XI, 44
15:10 – XIIIa, 36
15:10 (D-RB) – XIIIa, 172
15:26 – XII, 262
16:22 – IX, 372

2 CORINTHIANS

1:8 – V, 234; VIII, 318
2:14 – IV, 599
3:5 – XII, 9
4:5 – VIII, 237
4:10 – III, 497; X, 320
4:17 – X, 50
5:14 – I, 546; VIII, 382; XIIIa, 167, XIIIb, 434
6:8 – III, 44; V, 230
6:15 – II, 494
7:1 – XIIIb, 356
8:9 – XI, 88; XII, 305
9:7 – XI, 74
9:9 – XIIIb, 414
11:1 – XI, 227
11:8-9 – I, 133
11:14 – XII, 281
11:29 – X, 445; XII, 221
11:31 – III, 595
12:7 – III, 287; V, 473
12:7-9 – X, 10
12:9 – II, 19, 140; VIII, 516; XI, 151
12:19 (D-RB) – XIIIa, 118

GALATIANS

2:11-14 – VII, 442
2:19-20 – VIII, 41
2:20 – VIII, 127; X, 221, 585; XII, 137, 184
3:26 – VIII, 375
3:27 – XII, 184
6:2 – VIII, 169; X, 383, 452; XII, 220
6:9 – IX, 348
6:10 – X, 261
6:14 – II, 376; XI, 16

EPHESIANS

4:1 – III, 174
4:1-2 – XI, 54
4:2 – I, 405
4:11 – IX, 513
4:26 – IX, 100, 179; X, 377
5:22-33 – II, 184
6:11 – VIII, 225

PHILIPPIANS

1:6 – VIII, 209; XII, 388; XIIIa, 83, 205
1:21 – IV, 154
1:23 – II, 134; III, 441
1:27 – II, 249; XII, 204 (D-RB)
2:2 – XII, 203, 204
2:7 – XII, 165
2:7-8 – XII, 165
2:8 – II, 374; VI, 134, 144; X, 487; XII, 299, 347; XIIIb, 10
2:8-11 – VIII, 414
2:13 (D-RB) – XIIIb, 417
3:19 – X, 116; XII, 40
4:4 – X, 306
4:4-5 – X, 305
4:13 – X, 163; XI, 76
4:17 – V, 158

COLOSSIANS

1:11 – 1, 405
2:3 – XII, 389
3:3 – XII, 385
3:9 – V, 462

3:9-10 – XII, 184
3:12 – VIII, 325

1 TIMOTHY
1:9 – XII, 199; XIIIa, 109
1:15 – VII, 356
1:17 – IV, 580
2:4 – XIIIa, 167
2:12-14 – XIIIb, 381
4:16 – XI, 252
6:10 – XI, 223
6:11-12 – III, 483
6:15 – XIIIa, 359, 399
6:20 – XII, 387

2 TIMOTHY
2:3-4 – II, 493
2:23-24 – XI, 55
3:12 – V, 539; XI, 170; XII, 226
4:2 – XI, 126

HEBREWS
1:3 – XI, 315
2:10 – VII, 461-62
2:17 – II, 448
2:18 – VIII, 268
4:14-15 – XI, 19
6:4-6 – III, 476; VI, 194; VIII, 35; XI, 182, 205; XIIIb, 419
7:3 – XIIIb, 398
7:26 – VII, 479
8:6 – VII, 479
10:33 – XII, 50
10:34 – XII, 50
10:37 – II, 134
11:6 – XIIIa, 32
12:2 – XII, 50
12:4 – III, 403; XI, 88
12:6 – XII, 47
13:17 – X, 317; XIIIa, 68

JAMES
1:2 – XI, 134; XII, 50, 232
1:2-4 – VIII, 317
1:17 – IX, 247; XII, 9
1:26 – X, 324
4:6 – IX, 530

1 PETER
2:2 – III, 484
2:9 – IV, 370
2:13 – XI, 58; XII, 92
2:21 – XI, 89
2:23 – VIII, 233
4:8 – XI, 69
5:8 – VII, 203

2 PETER
1:10 – VIII, 351
2:19 – XII, 245
2:22 – V, 405
3:9 – XIIIa, 167
3:15-16 – VII, 442

I JOHN
1:8 – X, 385
2:2 – III, 325; XIIIa, 167
2:16 (D-RB) – IX, 342; XIIIb, 345
2:16 – XII, 18
2:18 – XI, 184
3:1 – VIII, 375
3:11 – XI, 90
3:23 – VIII, 186
4:16 – IX, 44
5:19 – XII, 245

REVELATION
2:4-5 – VI, 194
3:1 – IX, 468; X, 368
3:15-16 – X, 157

3:16 – VIII, 351
3:19 – XII, 49
5:8-9 – XII, 267
12:7-9 – V, 143
12:17 – VII, 442
14:4 – XII, 402
14:13 – III, 310; XI, 33; XII, 115
17:14 – XIIIa, 359, 399
20:1-15 – XII, 317
21:1-27 – VIII, 600

2. - ERRATA

The editors have tried to ascertain the present location of the letters and documents, but, with the closing of houses and the merging of provinces, there is no guarantee that the locations indicated are correct.

VOLUME 1

P. *xxv,* § 3, l. 7 - Edmond Jolly *read* Edme Jolly

P. *liv*, n. 5 - *156a read* 156b

P. *lvii,* n. 16 - *Add, after 1983):* English translation by Louise Sullivan, D. C., *Spiritual Writings of Louise de Marillac,* 1991, New City Press, 202 Comforter Blvd, Hyde Park, NY 12538.

No. 1, p. 7, last line - Nice *read* Annecy. Saint Vincent wrote *Nicy*, an archaic form of Annecy.

No. 1, p. 9, n. 29 - Giuseppi *read* Giuseppe

No. 1, p. 10, § 1, l. 1 - stones from Turkey *read* turquoises

No. 12, p. 23, n. 1, l. 18 - Bishop *read* Msgr.

No. 16, p. 29, n. 3, l. 4 - 1613 *read* 1631

No. 26, p. 39, n. 3, l. 4 - one of his sisters became a Daughter *read* two of his sisters became Daughters

No. 26, p. 39, n. 6, l. 2 - Ausust *read* August

No. 28, p. 47 - *At top right, insert date* August 1, 1628

No. 29, p. 55, n. 4, l. 2 - -aint *read* Saint

No. 65, p. 104, n. 1 - Company *read* Society

No. 107, p. 158, citation - *Replace with* Congregation of the Mission, 29, via Fassolo, Genoa, Italy.

No. 112, p. 165, n. 4 - Guidi di Bagno *read* Guido di Bagni

No. 122, p. 174, n. 1 - *Replace n. 1 with* Date Marie Joly arrived in Paris to serve in the Confraternities of Charity.

No. 135, p. 195, § 2, l. 5 - poor of the farms *read* poor of the General Hospital (*Renfermés*)

No. 146, p. 206, citation - *Replace citation with* Archives Diocésaines, Cahors, Fonds Alain de Solminihac, liasse 1, no. 25.

No. 146, p. 208, l. 2 - religion *read* those of a religious Order

No. 146, p. 214, last line - go the *read* go to the

No. 198c, p. 281, citation, l. 2 - Company *read* Society

No. 207b, p. 300, n. 2, l. 1 - Lancaster County *read* Lancastershire

No. 207b, p. 301, l. 5 - that *read* than

No. 207b, p. 301, n. 2, l. 1 - Frankfort *read* Frankfurt

No. 224, p. 321, n. 8, ll. 1 and 2 - Wignerod *read* Vignerod

No. 224, p. 322, n. 8, l. 9 - Paris: 1882 *read* Paris: Didier, 1882

No. 229, p. 328, § 1, l. 2 - willing *read* being willing

No. 234, p. 333, n. 2, l. 14 - Augsbourg *read* Augsburg

No. 245, p. 346, heading - *Read* **TO ROBERT DE SERGIS**

No. 253a, p. 355, citation, l. 2 - Company *read* Society

No. 281, p. 394, nn. 5, 6 - Chasteigner *read* Chastaignier

No. 283, p. 398, n. 2, l. 1 - Louis-Denis *read* Louis-Doni

No. 294, p. 422, § 3, l. 4 - senimary *read* seminary

No. 295, p. 423, § 2, l. 5 - founding *read* foundling

No. 295, p. 424, l. 6 - that *read* than

No. 297, p. 426, § 2, l. 1 - Foundings *read* Foundlings

No. 298, p. 429, l. 3 - Founding *read* Foundling

No. 299, p. 431, l. 4 - able to wrok *read* able to work

No. 307, p. 441, § 1, l. 5 - Montmirail *read* to Montmirail.

No. 308, p. 444, n. 2, l. 1 - to *read* from

No. 323, p. 466, n. 3, l. 7 - Bishop of Rodez (1664)

No. 335, p. 483, citation - *Replace citation with* Archives diocésaines, Evêché d'Amiens, copy.

No. 365, p. 520, § 2, l. 10 - Gascogne *read* Gascony

No. 368, p. 525, § 1, l. 11 - Company *read* Society

No. 376, p. 538, n. 1, l. 5 - 17 *read* 19

No. 376, p. 538, n. 3 - Guidi di Bagno *read* Guido di Bagni

No. 377, p. 543, n. 1 - these two words, which seem *read* this word, which seems

No. 381a, p. 557, l. 3 - stronger girl; I could not tell you whom. *read* more capable young woman; I would not know whom else to tell you.

No. 388a, p. 564, n. 4, l. 6 - Company *read* Society

No. 390, p. 566, l. 2 - *Delete* without a date,

No. 392, p. 569, l. 2 - *Delete* always

No. 408, p. 590, last line - *missionis* read *missiones*

No. 408, p. 591, l. 3 - dismissedonly *read* dismissed only

No. 408, p. 591, l. 6 - I shall *read* well as

No. 410, p. 594, n. 6, l. 1 - the hospital of Saint John *read* Saint-Jean Hospital

No. 414, p. 600, § 2, l. 1 - Nancy *read* Nantes

VOLUME 2

P. *xiii*, no. 694 - Nov *read* Now

P. *xxii*, l. 8 - expression has *read* expression have

No. 421, p. 12, n. 1, l. 6 - Marthe Trumeau *read* Matrilomeau

No. 418, p. 6, n. 7, l. 1 - Donadieu *read* Donnadieu

No. 421, p. 12, n. 1, l. 4 - Monget *read* Mongert

No. 433, p. 35, n. 2 - *Here and henceforth in this volume, replace* Bishop *with* Msgr. *before* Ingoli.

No. 446, p. 59, n. 3, l. 1 - Temple *read* Templars

No. 453, p. 72, n. 7, l. 3 - Conty *read* Conti

No. 477, p. 124 - *Replace n. 1 to read* The retreat mentioned here as in Valprofonde is the same as the one made in Soissons, mentioned in No. 580, p. 278. Valprofonde was in the Diocese of Soissons. (Cf. *Vincentiana*, 1984, p. 547).

No. 505, p. 168, n. 8, l. 1 - *After* Hurtel *insert* (or Heurtel)

No. 519, p. 187, date - *Delete* or March

No. 530a, p. 202, n. 6, ll. 1, 3 - Fonteines *read* Fontaine

No. 537, p. 210, n. 4, l. 1 - Maretz *read* du Maretz

No. 557, p. 232, n. 2, l. 2 - Antonio, a Capuchin *read* Francesco Antonio, a Capuchin

No. 558a, p. 234, citation - *After* AA-4 *replace what follows with* This gift from Carrie Estelle Doheny was transferred to DePaul University, Chicago, in 2001.

No. 561, p. 238, citation - *Replace citation with* In 1997, the original autograph letter was in the Provincial House of the Congregation of the Mission in Beirut.

No. 569, p. 250, n. 9 - Fonteines *read* Fontaine

No. 574, p. 260, citation - *Replace with* Original autograph letter, formerly in the archives of the Province of Lille, Daughters of Charity; its present location is unknown.

No. 580, p. 276, citation - *After* Cassagnac *insert* its present location is unknown.

No. 580, p. 278, l. 15 - *Add superscript 3 after Soissons. Add note 3*: This is the same retreat mentioned in No. 477 as being made in Valprofonde. Valprofonde was in the Diocese of Soissons. (Cf. *Vincentiana*, 1984, p. 547).

No. 580, p. 278, last line, replace superscript 3 with 4. In the note, replace 3 with 4

No. 583, p. 282, n. 1 - *After* Phelippeaux *insert* de

No. 587, p. 285, l. 1 - Maître Belot *read* Madame Belot

No. 595, p. 297, l. 4 - *Insert* de *before* Liancourt

No. 600, p. 301, citation - *Replace with* The original autograph letter was formerly in the Archives of the Mission, Paris; its present location is unknown.

No. 601, p. 302, citation - *Replace with* The original autograph letter was formerly in the Archives of the Mission, Paris; its present location is unknown.

No. 603. p. 311, citation - *Replace with* The original autograph letter was purchased by DePaul University, Chicago, in January 2011.

No. 604, p. 313, citation - *Replace with* A copy of the original was formerly in the Archives of the Mission; its present location is unknown.

No. 606, p. 316, l. 5 - comformity *read* conformity

No. 610, p. 320, citation - *Replace with* St. Margaret's Convent, Whitehouse Loan, Edinburgh, Scotland; copy made from the original in Saint Vincent's handwriting. At some point, the letter was sent from Annecy to the Archbishop of Edinburgh.

No. 610, p. 321, § 2, l. 1 - Fourdim *read* Fouache; *delete* n. 5.

No. 617, p. 329, citation - *After* Rome *insert* Mundelein Collection

No. 625, p. 343, n. 9, l. 4 - *Replace* one of his sisters became a Daughter *with* two of his sisters became Daughters

No. 629, p. 349, citation - *Replace* in the public and university library of *with* Bibliothèque publique et universitaire

No. 631, p. 354, citation - *Replace with* Original autograph letter, Lauinger Library of Georgetown University, Washington, D.C., Talbot Collection.

No. 634, p. 363, citation - *Replace with* The original signed letter was formerly in the Archives of the Mission, Paris; its present location is unknown.

No. 636, p. 389, citation - *Replace with Lettres choisies de Saint Vincent de Paul*, Letter 36, formerly in the Archives of the Mission, Paris; its present location is unknown.

No. 644, p. 404, citation - *Replace the first sentence with* A copy, made from the original, was formerly in the Archives of the Mission, Paris; its present location is unknown.

No. 653, p. 414, citation - *Replace the first sentence with* A copy, made from the original, was formerly in the Archives of the Mission, Paris; its present location is unknown.

No. 654, p. 417, n. 9 - de Perron *read* du Perron

No. 654, p. 419, n. 19 - de Nozet *read* du Nozet

No. 654, p. 421, n. 26, l. 2 - *Add at end* The quote is from the Roman poet Juvenal.

No. 668, p. 443, n. 3, l. 1 - *Replace* Jean-François *with* Jean-François-Paul

No. 674, p. 453, citation - *Replace with* A copy, made from the original, was formerly in the Archives of the Mission; its present location is unknown.

No. 676, p. 455, citation - *Replace with* The original autograph letter belonged formerly to the Daughters of Charity, 33 rue Caulaincourt, Paris; its present location is unknown.

No. 679, p. 464, n. 5 - Fonteines, *read* Fontaine

No. 682, p. 469, citation - *Add after* Mission,: Rome, Mundelein Collection

No. 693, p. 482 - *Insert date at top right of letter:* [near the end of 1642]

No. 695, p. 485, n. 1, l. 1 - Lavocat *read* Ladvocat

No. 704, p. 498, citation - *Replace citation with* A copy, made from the original in 1854, was formerly in the Archives of the Mission; its present location is unknown.

No. 717, p. 515, citation - *After* l'Institut*, insert* 23, Quai de Conti,

No. 725, p. 528, citation - *Replace with* Original autograph letter, DePaul University, Chicago, acquired by Edward Udovic, C.M., in January 2008.

No. 726, p. 530, citation - *Replace with* Original autograph letter, Archives of the Mission, Paris.

No. 727b, p. 536, citation - *Replace with* Original autograph letter, formerly the property of Sisters of Charity, Mount Saint Vincent, Halifax, Nova Scotia.

The letter was lost in 1951, when Mount Saint Vincent, with all its contents, was destroyed by fire.

No. 729, p. 539, citation - *Replace with* Archives of the Daughters of Charity, Province of France-Nord, 9, rue Cler, 75007 Paris

No. 731, p. 540, citation - *Replace with* Archives of the Society of Jesus, Borgo Santo Spirito 5, 00195, Rome, Italy, original autograph letter.

No. 732, p. 543, citation - *Replace with* The original autograph letter was formerly in the Archives of the Mission, Paris; its present location is unknown.

No. 733, p. 544, citation - *Replace with* The original autograph letter was formerly in the Archives of the Mission, Paris; its present location is unknown.

No. 738, p. 554, n. 5 - Vieux-Moulins *read* Vieux-Moulin

No. 740, p. 556, citation - *Replace with* A copy of the original autograph letter, written in Italian, was formerly in the Archives of the Mission, Paris; its present location is unknown.

No. 741, p. 557, date - *Replace* March 1645 *with* 1644

No. 743, p. 558, citation - *Replace with* The original autograph letter was formerly in the Archives of the Mission, Paris; its present location is unknown.

No. 744, date - *Replace with* [1645-46]

No. 773, p. 599, citation, l. 2 - *Replace* preserved *with* formerly preserved.

No. 773, p. 599, l. 4 - *Add, at the end of the citation* Its present location is unknown.

No. 787, p. 620 - *Replace citation with* Ducournau Archives, Congregation of the Mission, Philadelphia, USA; gift of St. John's University, New York.

No. 794, date - *Replace with* [March 25, 1646]

No. 808, p. 650, citation - *Replace with* A seventeenth-century copy was formerly in the Archives of the Mission, Paris; its present location is unknown.

No. 812, p. 654, n. 2, l. 3 - the erection *read* establishment

No. 826, p. 673, heading - ESSART *read* ESSARTS

No. 826, p. 673, citation - *Replace with* The original autograph letter was formerly at the major seminary of Bernay (France); its present location is unknown.

No. 826, p. 674, Addressed, second line - *Replace both* **Essart** *with* **Essarts**

No. 826, p. 674, n. 2, l. 2 - **Essart** *read* **Essarts**

No. 827, p. 677, § 1, l. 4 - they were baptized *read* he was baptized

Index, p. 695, 1st column, next to last line - *Replace with* **BARBERINI**, Francesco Antonio, Cardinal: 570

Index, p. 695, 1st column, last line - *Replace with* **BARBERINI**, Francesco, Cardinal: 660

Index, p. 696, **DALMAGNE** - *Replace* 629, 656 *with* 627

Index, p. 696, **DU COUDRAY** - *Replace* 435 *with* 434

Index, p. 697, **FONTEINES** *read* **FONTAINE**

VOLUME 3

No. 829, p. 1, citation, l. 1 - *After Rome, add*: Mundelein Collection,

No. 832, p. 14, § 1, l. 1 - wise *read* spiritual

No. 848, p. 38, citation, l. 2 - Archives of the Mission, DePaul University, Chicago (USA), original autograph letter, formerly at St. Mary's Seminary, Perryville, Missouri, transferred to DePaul in 2001.

No. 855, p. 55, l. 1 - *Delete* he did both to

No. 862, p. 64, citation, l. 1 - *Replace with* Archives of the Motherhouse of the Daughters of Charity, Paris, original signed letter.

No. 864, p. 67, citation - *Replace with* Archives of the Mission, Paris, original autograph letter, gift of the Congregation Romaine de Saint Dominique, Paris, June 19, 2003.

No. 866, p. 70, n. 1, ll. 2, 4 - Fonteines *read* Fontaine

No. 866, p. 71, n. 5, l. 1 - Fonteines *read* Fontaine

No. 866, p. 72, n. 9, penultimate line - Sainte-Agnès *read* Holy Angels

No. 868a, p. 76, citation - *Replace with* The original autograph letter was purchased at auction in Paris on November 7, 1997, by the Archivist of the Département de la Marne.

No. 868a, p. 76, n. 2 - *Replace with:* Present-day Rennes.

No. 870, p. 83, n. 18 - *Replace* younger brother *with* nephew

No. 876, p. 90, heading and n. 1, l. 2 - Dwyer *read* O'Dwyer

No. 882, p. 104, n. 7, l. 4 - *Replace* one of his sisters became a Daughter *with* two of his sisters became Daughters

No. 887, p. 112, § 1, l. 4 - Councils give *read* Council gives

No. 925, p. 168, n. 3 - niece *read* cousin

No. 926, p. 168, citation - Add at the end, photograph in the Archives of the Mission, Rome.

No. 949, p. 196, n. 1, l. 9 - Faber *read* Favre

No. 973, p. 217, § 2, l. 6 - he shows *read* they show

No. 984, p. 235, l. 11 - the the Abbot *read* the Abbot

No. 1018, p. 276, citation - *Replace with* The original autograph letter, formerly in St. Patrick's Seminary, Manly, NSW, Australia, is now in The Veech Library, Catholic Institute of Sydney, 99 Albert Road, Strathfield, NSW.

No. 1020, p. 280, n. 8 - Ruffin *read* Rufin

No. 1057a, p. 352, date - August *read* July.

No. 1064, p. 358, citation, l. 4 - *Replace the last sentence with* This letter was donated by Abel Berland to DePaul University, Chicago.

No. 1068, p. 372, n. 5 - *Replace* 2 *with* 3

No. 1089a, p. 399, citation - *Replace with* Archives of the Mission, Paris, original autograph letter, presented to the Congregation of the Mission by the Sisters of Notre-Dame de Charité.

No. 1103a, p. 433, citation - *Replace first sentence with* The original autograph letter was formerly the property of the Jesuits in Aix; its present location is unknown.

No. 1105, p. 444, citation - *Replace with* Original autograph letter, formerly at the Miséricorde in Agen, now in the Archives of the Motherhouse of the Daughters of Charity, Paris.

No. 1146, p. 494 § 2, l. 2 - Portail *read* Alméras

No. 1176, p. 535, § 1, l. 4 - persuade them to tender *read* persuade them to anything other than a tender

Index, p. 620 - FONTEINES *read* FONTAINE

Index, p. 621 - LAVARDIN, Philippe *read* LAVARDIN, Philibert

VOLUME 4

No. 1212, p. 15, citation - *Replace with* Original signed letter, Archives of the Motherhouse of the Daughters of Charity, Paris.

No. 1271 p. *viii* - Replace Antonio Barberini *with* Luigi Capponi.

No. 1221, p. 29, n. 2 - *After* Hurtel *insert* (or Heurtel)

No. 1254a, p. 76, citation - *Replace with* Diocesan Archives of Cahors, Solminihac collection, liasse 2, no. 51, extract of the original. A letter from Fr. Vitet to Saint Vincent (cf. No. 1256), dated September 5, 1650, alludes to this letter.

No. 1271, p. 99, heading - **ANTONIO BARBERINI** *read* **LUIGI CAPPONI**; delete superscript on **BARBERINI**.

No. 1271, p. 99, n. 1 - *Delete.*

No. 1367, p. 209, n. 2, l. 6 - n. 8 *read* n. 7

No. 1416, p. 266, n. 1 - Cristoforo Monchia *read* Cristoforo di Monchia

No. 1434, p. 288, n. 4 - Jean-François de Gondi, Archbishop of Paris *read* Jean-François-Paul de Gondi, Cardinal de Retz

No. 1456, p. 317 - *Add footnote* 1Cf. Rm 8:35. (NAB)

No. 1490, p. 365, citation - *Replace with* Archives du Monastère des Augustines, 32 rue Charlevoix, Quebec, Canada, original signed letter.

No. 1502, p. 383, n. 3 - *Replace* XIII, no. 81, *with* XIIIa, no. 84a.

No. 1549, p. 457, n. 2 - n. 9 *read* n. 13

No. 1564, p. 488, l. 1 - September 29 *read* September 27

No. 1572, p. 501, § 1, l. 9 - unable *read:* able

No. 1573, p. 503, citation - *Replace first sentence with* A copy of this letter was formerly in the Archives of the Diocese of Cahors, Alain de Solminihac collection, file 19, no. 13; its present location is unknown.

No. 1630, p. 583, n. 5, l. 3 - *Delete* 1630,

Index, p. 615, **BARBERINI**, Antonio Cardinal - 1271 *read* 1493

Index, p. 616 - *entry after* **CABARET**: **CAPPONI**, Luigi Cardinal: 1271

VOLUME 5

No. 1692, p. 65, n. 2, l. 4 - Loudon *read* Loudun

No. 1707, p. 88, § 1, l. 8 - cannot not be *read* cannot be

No. 1708, p. 89, l. 11 – Cape Nègre *read:* Cap Nègre

No. 1721, p. 111, § 1, penultimate line - soul *read* life

No. 1729, p. 121, § 3, l. 2 - Clanranald *read* Clanronald

No. 1788, p. 207, n. 4, ll. 3, 4 - *Delete*: , the first house not in the environs of Paris

No. 1822, p. 252, l. 3 - Marquese *read* Marchese

No. 1822, p. 253, § 1, l. 5 - His Royal Highness, *read* Her Royal Highness

No. 1834, p. 271, § 1, penultimate line - Loretto *read* Loreto

No. 1835, p. 274, last line - Loretto *read* Loreto

No. 1842, p. 319, § 1, l. 4 - *Delete* that

No. 1845, p. 326, n. 5 - secretary *read* Chancellor

No. 1853, p. 339, § 2, n. 6 - *Add at the end* He was referring to Pedro Borguñy.

No. 1893a, p. 405, n. 3 - Pt 2:22 *read* 2 Pt 2:22

No. 1908, p. 421, n. 4, l. 4 - nos.1908, 1912, *read* no. 1912

No. 2001, p. 536, n. 1, l. 8 - Manangue *read* Mananghe

No. 2053, p. 599, n. 2 - *Replace footnote to read* Noël Duval, business advisor for Donat Crowley (cf. VI, *64*).

No. 2066, p. 612, n. 1 - Moissanx *read* Miossanx

VOLUME 6

No. 2130, p. 83, n. 12 - Monchia *read* di Monchia

No. 2157, p. 124, n. 3, l. 4 - *Delete*: , vol. VI, no. 2157

No. 2229, p. 273, n. 2 - Le Vacher *read* Barreau

No. 2333, p. 413, l. 4 - Migot *read* Mignot

No. 2344, p. 426, n. 1, l. 1 - de Soyecourt *read* du Soyecourt

No. 2425, p. 567, § 2, l. 4 - Dupont *read* Duport

No. 2453, p. 607, § 2, l. 11 - Him *read* to Him

No. 2467, p. 630, n. 7 - Mario *read* Marius

No. 2471, p. 636, § 1, l. 2 - Senigaglia *read* Sinigaglia (Senigallia)

No. 2474, p. 640, § 2, l. 7 - able do *read* able to do

Appendix 1, p. 643, l. 16 - Majesty and his Council has ordained and ordains *read* Majesty, with his Council, has ordained and does ordain

Appendix 6, p. 651, § 1, l. 2 - and the for *read* and for the

Index, p. 654 - **CARPENTIER**, Auguste *read* **CARPENTIER**, Augustin

Index, p. 656 - **RICHELIEU**, Armand-Jean du *read* **RICHELIEU**, Armand du

VOLUME 7

No. 2482, p. 15, n. 2, l. 2 - Louis Duport *read* Nicolas Duport

No. 2490a, p. 33, n. 1, l. 1 - Marguerite *read:* Madeleine

No. 2515, p. 71, citation - insert at beginning: Soeurs de la Foi, 8 rue de Graeninghe, Courtrai, Belgium.

No. 2515, p. 72 - *After the postscript, add* Addressed: Monsieur Tholard, Priest of the Mission, in Marcoussis

No. 2517, p. 73, citation - *Replace with* Archives of the Mission, Toulouse, original signed letter, from the Hains Family Collection, Marseille. This is one of the letters sold at auction in Nimes October 28, 1989, by Xavier Charmoy (cf. no. 2505, citation) and purchased by J. M. Lebats, C.M.

No. 2546, p. 114, citation - *Replace with* Archives of the Mission, Toulouse, original signed letter, from the Hains Family Collection, Marseille. This is one of the letters sold at auction in Nimes October 28, 1989, by Xavier Charmoy (cf. no. 2505, citation) and purchased by J. M. Lebats, C.M.

No. 2571, p. 145, n. 4 - Clermont, *read* Clermont-Tonnerre, Knight of Malta,

No. 2580, p. 158, § 2, l. 4 - Ablet *read* Haslé

No. 2597, p. 179, § 3, l. 1 - 25 *read* 21

No. 2597, p. 179, § 3, l. 2 - 36 *read* 30

No. 2597, p. 180 - *After signature, add postscript:* We are in doubt as to whether we will send M. Huguier or Bro. Duchesne to Algiers. We shall see. Please do not speak to anyone about this, nor of M. Le Vacher's departure for Marseille, which will be soon, nor about the money either.

No. 2614, p. 208, § 2, l. 2 - Varles *read* Varlet

No. 2617, p. 212, citation - *Replace with* Archives of the Mission, Toulouse, original signed letter, from the Hains Family Collection, Marseille. This is one of the letters sold at auction in Nimes October 28, 1989, by Xavier Charmoy (cf. no. 2505, citation) and purchased by J. M. Lebats, C.M.

No. 2630, p. 232, citation - *Replace with* Archives of the Mission, Toulouse, original signed letter, from the Hains Family Collection, Marseille. This is one of the letters sold at auction in Nimes, October 28, 1989, by Xavier Charmoy (cf. no. 2505, citation) and purchased by J. M. Lebats, C.M.

No. 2662, p. 279, § 1, l. 4 - de la Prontière *read* de la Proutière

No. 2705, p. 350, § 1, ll. 1-2, 4 - Grimaud *read:* Grimard

No. 2706, p. 351, n. 1, l. 1 - 1654 *read* 1658

No. 2717, p. 369, citation - *Insert after signed letter*; , gift of Thérèse and Henri Fries.

No. 2737, p. 400, citation - *Replace citation with* Archives of the Mission, DePaul University, Chicago, original signed letter, gift of Abel Berland. The last six lines are in the saint's handwriting. The editors have included in brackets the additions Coste made from the original.

No. 2741, p. 406, § 2, l. 2 - Saint-Sépulchre *read* Saint-Sépulcre

No. 2745, p. 411, l. 10 - Saint-Sépulchre *read* Saint-Sépulcre

No. 2753, p. 425, n. 2, l. 1 - Martin *read* Marin or Martin

No. 2796a, p. 485, citation - *Replace first sentence with* Archives of the Mission, Paris, original signed letter.

No. 2796a p. 486, postscript, l. 1 - and a *read* with this

No. 2819, p. 521, § 2, l. 2 - Martissans *read* Martisans

VOLUME 8

Title page - September 1660) *read* March 1661)

Library of Congress Cataloging-in-Publication Data, l. 6 - v. 7. December 1657-June 1659 - *read* v. 8. July 1659-March 1661.

No. 2926, p. 64, heading and n. 1, l. 1 - **MARTIN** *read* **MARIN**

No. 2927, p. 67, § 1, l. 1 - Saint-Joire *read* Saint-Jeoire

No. 2942a, p. 93, citation - *Replace first sentence with* Original signed letter, purchased by the Province of Paris in 2005.

No. 2942a, p. 93, § 1, l. 2 - *After* Noyon *insert superscript and add footnote for Baradat*: Henri de Baradat, Bishop of Noyon (1626-60), had asked Jean Parre to try to mitigate the excessive display of devotion at Notre-Dame-de-la-Paix at the time of distribution.

No. 2992, p. 158, n. 1, l. 2 - three *read* two

No. 3062, p. 250, § 1, l. 3 - Mauger *read* Mauge

No. 3076b, p. 276, n. 3 - Delete the second sentence.

No. 3090, p. 298, citation - *After the first sentence, add*The original was donated to DePaul University, Chicago, in June 1954 by Justin Turner.

No. 3098, p. 309, § 2, l. 3 - Savry *read* Auvry

No. 3116a, p. 337, § 1, l. 5 - received here from *read* received here for

No. 3116a, p. 337, § 1, l. 7 - [J.] Le Vacher *read* [P.] Le Vacher

No. 3147, p. 374, n. 1 - Mk *read* Mt

No. 3243 p. 496, § 1, l. 3 - Moussardière *read* de la Moussardière

No. 3259, p. 515, heading, signature, and n. 1 - Ludovisio *read* Ludovisi

No. 3296, p. 589, § 1, l. 4 - de Rivaux *read* du Rivaux

Appendix 4, p. 612, § 1, l. 3 - René *read* Louis

Appendix 4, p. 613, last §, l. 1 - Harlay de Sancey *read* Harlay de Sancy

VOLUME 9

Conf. 5, p. 31, § 1, l. 3 - dooutside *read* do outside

Conf. 23, p. 183, § 6, l. 10 - *Replace question mark with period*

Conf. 27, p. 209, l. 1 - Two faults *read* Some faults

Conf. 41, p. 367, § 1, l. 5 - his feelings *read* her feelings

Conf. 43a, p. 409, n. 4 - Jon 1:4 *read* Jon 1-4

Conf. 43a, p. 410, § 1, l. 7 - There is *read* There are

Conf. 51, p. 470, § 2, l. 2 - Saint Appoline *read* Saint Apollonia

Conf. 52, p. 470, § 1, l. 2-3 - Daughters of Charity *read* we're going to look once again at the spirit of the Company of the Daughters of Charity to see in what it consists,

VOLUME 10

Conf. 61, p. 2, § 1, ll. 2-11 - *After* Quoi *delete italics for the rest of the paragraph.*

Conf. 73, p. 128, § 2, l. 11 - that does deserve *read* that doesn't deserve

Conf. 75, p. 163, § 1, l. 10 - made *read* make

Conf. 78, p. 193, § 3, l. 10 - Abiron *read* Abiram

Conf. 79, p. 201, l. 10 - *After* of God *add footnote* Cf. Mt 4:4. (NAB).

Conf. 87, p. 295, § 1, l. 6 - practices and maxims *read* maxims and customs

Conf. 87, p. 295, § 1, l. 7 - temporal guidance *read* temporal direction

Conf. 88, p. 308, § 2, l. 1 - let's look the *read* let's look at the

Conf. 89, p. 318, § 2, l. 10 - their need *read* his/her need

Conf. 91, p. 352, § 2, l. 13 - have a such a good *read* have such a good

Conf. 103, p. 464, l. 7 - pronounce the words *read* pronounce the words....

Conf. 115, p. 545, n. 1, l. 1 - Mlle Gras *read* Mlle Le Gras

VOLUME 11

Conf. 8, p. 11, n. 1 - Escombleaux *read:* Escoubleau

Conf. 129, p. 205, n. 2 - Sng *read* Sg

Conf. 136, p. 266, § 5, l. 5 - Capucins *read* Capuchins

Conf. 155, p. 321, § 1, l. 5 - has it principal *read* has its principal

Conf. 160, p. 337, n. 5, l. 4 - *After* wrecked *add period; delete rest of the note.*

Conf. 160, p. 339, § 1, l. 9 - one Son *read* one son

Conf. 175, p. 382, § 3, l. 5 - in our heasrts *read* in our hearts

Conf. 176, p. 386, § 3, l. 2 - After "the violent bear it away," *insert superscript 8 and add footnote 8*: Cf. Mt 11:12. (NAB)

VOLUME 12

Conf. 217, p. 311, n. 8 - on September 22, 1655, see XIIIa, 417-19 *read* on August 12, 1659, see XIIIa, Doc. 120, pp. 480-82.

Conf. 221, p. 339, § 1, l. 10 - Lybia *read* Libya

Supplement 15, p. 372, citation - *Add at the end of the citation* An earlier copy of this document was published in vol. XIIIa, Doc. 50b, p. 183.

Appendix 2, p. 420, l. 4 - Spiritual Communion *read:* Spiritual Communication

VOLUME 13A

Doc. 10, p. 21, n. 1 - Denis Tulloue *read* Robert Tulloue.

Doc. 35c, p. 147, l. 1 - Anne de Muriel *read* Anne de Murviel

Doc. 57, p. 196, n. 14 - Augustin Fracioti *read* Agostino Fracioti

Doc. 65a, p. 239, l. 1 and n. 3 - Ludovisio *read* Ludovisi

Doc. 65b, p. 239, citation, l. 4 - Ottavio Bandino *read* Ottavio Bandini

Doc. 65c, p. 240, § 3, ll. 2-3 - directive co-mes *read* directive comes

Doc. 67, p. 242, heading - Ludovisio *read* Ludovisi

Doc. 71, p. 245, heading - Ludovisio *read* Ludovisi

Doc. 71a, p. 247, l. 1 - Ludovisio *read* Ludovisi

Doc. 73c, p. 252, n. 2, l. 2 - Ludovisio *read* Ludovisi

Doc. 85a, p. 309, § 2, l. 7 - Antoine-Claude *read* Claude-Antoine

Doc. 89, p. 327, § 3, l. 2 - was completed *read* were completed

Doc. 92, p. 340, § 1, ll. 5 and 6 – removing and putt-ing *read:* removing and put-ting

Doc. 102, p. 366, n. 5 - Camille de Neufville de Villeroy *read* Alphonse-Louis du Plessis de Richelieu

Doc. 110, p. 406, § 1, l. 5 - *Add footnote for* Suarez: Francisco Suarez, Jesuit theologian.

Doc. 111, p. 409, l. 6 - to satify their senses *read* to satisfy their senses

Doc. 115, p. 422, l. 2 - Pallu *read* Rallu

Doc. 117a, p. 430, n. 1, § 2, l. 2 - William *read* Warren

Doc. 119, p. 473, l. 4 – October 18 *read* October 11

VOLUME 13B

Doc. 132a, p. 65, l. 8 - François Courtiller *read* Fiacre Courdilier

Doc. 136, p. 84, § 1, l. 8 - their death *read* death

Doc. 146a, p. 139, § 2, l. 10 - to to have *read* to have

Doc. 146a, p. 139, § 2, ll. 11-12 - Saint-Germain-de-l'Auxerrois *read* Saint-Germain-l'Auxerrois

Doc. 149, p. 147, l. 4 - December *read* January

Doc. 149a, p. 147, n. 1, last line - promugation *read* promulgation

Doc. 149a, p. 150, l. 1 - nor *read* or

Doc. 159, p. 271, § 1, l. 4 - meeeting *read* meeting

Doc. 166, p. 314, § 3, l. 9 - is is *read* is

Doc. 168, p. 323, n. 1, l. 1 - Naming *read* Appointment

Doc. 184, p. 376, § 5, l. 1 - turned our *read* turned to our

NEW CITY PRESS
of the Focolare
Hyde Park, New York

About New City Press of the Focolare

New City Press is one of more than 20 publishing houses sponsored by the Focolare, a movement founded by Chiara Lubich to help bring about the realization of Jesus' prayer: "That all may be one" (John 17:21). In view of that goal, New City Press publishes books and resources that enrich the lives of people and help all to strive toward the unity of the entire human family. We are a member of the Association of Catholic Publishers.

Saint Vincent de Paul

Books published by
New City Press of the Focolare

New City Press publishes books related to the history, life, and writings of St. Vincent de Paul, The Congregation of the Mission, and some of the most well-known followers of his spiritual life.

Please check our website www.newcitypress.com for updated titles and pricing.

Periodicals
Living City Magazine,
www.livingcitymagazine.com

Scan to
join our
mailing list for
discounts and promotions
or go to
www.newcitypress.com
and click on
"join our email list."

Saint Vincent de Paul
Correspondence, Conferences, Documents

The most complete collection of Saint Vincent de Paul's writings ever made available in English. Prepared by the Vincentian Translation Project. Fully annotated and indexed. Sr. Marie Poole, D.C. (ed.)

Correspondence

Volume 1: Letters 1-416	978-0-911782-50-9	$45.00
Volume 2: Letters 417-828	978-0-911782-79-0	$45.00
Volume 3: Letters 829-1205	978-1-56548-022-3	$45.00
Volume 4: Letters 1206-1645	978-1-56548-063-6	$45.00
Volume 5: Letters 1646-2090	978-1-56548-036-0	$45.00
Volume 6: Letters 2091-2474	978-1-56548-085-8	$45.00
Volume 7: Letters 2475-2649	978-1-56548-102-2	$45.00
Volume 8: Letters 2650 & later	978-1-56548-125-1	$45.00

Conferences

Volume 9	978-1-56548-226-5	$45.00
Volume 10	978-1-56548-251-7	$45.00
Volume 11	978-1-56548-306-4	$45.00
Volume 12	978-1-56548-337-8	$45.00

Documents

Volume 13 & 13b	978-1-56548-191-6	$69.95

Series Index

Volume 14	978-1-56548-498-6	$45.00